THE

1997

Information Please Entertainment Almanac

THE
1996
INFORMATION
PLEASE
ENTERTAINMENT
ALMANAC

A WORKING MEDIA BOOK

Robert Moses and Beth Rowen, EDITORS

EDITORIAL STAFF
Kimberly Caviness and So-Chung Shinn

DESIGNER
Eleanor Ramsay

DESIGN AND PRODUCTION STAFF
Linda Bean-Pardee, Elizabeth Murphy, Madeleine Newell and John Perry

PRODUCTION AND MANUFACTURING MANAGER
Andrew Gluck

GENERAL MANAGER
Timothy Haley

HOUGHTON MIFFLIN COMPANY
BOSTON   NEW YORK

The Information Please® Entertainment Almanac

ISBN: 0-395-740118

Printed in the United States of America
WP 10 9 8 7 6 5 4 3 2 1

Additional copies of **The 1996 Information Please Entertainment Almanac** may be ordered directly by mail from:

Customer Service Department
Houghton Mifflin Company
Burlington, MA 01803

Phone toll-free (800) 225-3362 for price and shipping information
In Massachusetts, phone (617) 272-1500

The IPEA was a few years in the making and the work of many people. We owe a great debt to two in particular: Steve Lewers and Alan Andres at Houghton Mifflin. Steve saw the opportunity the book represented and trusted us with the project, and Alan's vision supported the process. The IPEA represents many late-night and lunch-time discussions (arguments) about what it would take to create the best all-around entertainment reference available.

Many organizations and individuals were generous with their time and expertise as the IPEA developed: Steve Vana-Paxhia, Bill Trippe and Paul Evenson at INSO Corporation; Madeleine Newell for her patience and persistence; Linda Bean-Pardee for her scrupulous organization; Christine Schaefer for her research and editorial contribution; Susan Chicoski, Lori Galvin-Frost, Ann-Marie Imbornoni and Lisa Sacks for proofreading; Eric Rachlis and Michael Schulman at Archive Photos; Susan Kaplan at Billboard Publications; Ted Drozdowski at the *Boston Phoenix*; Paul Sacksman at *Musician* magazine; Karen Oertley at *Amusement Business*; C.G. O'Connor at the *Hollywood Reporter*; Evelyn Bernal at *Rolling Stone*; Richard Jameson and Gavin Smith at *Film Comment*; Gary Ink at *Publishers Weekly*; Tara Herman at *Wired*; Jack Fowler at the *National Review*; Gail Horwood at *Worth*; everyone at Matador Records; Briggs and Briggs, Cambridge, Massachusetts; Shelly Cagner at Arbitron Company; Nicole Field at PC Data; the League of American Theatres and Producers; National Public Radio; Nielsen Media Research; Gail Parenteau and the *Village Voice*.

1996 INFORMATION PLEASE ENTERTAINMENT ALMANAC

Table of Contents

Entertainment
Business

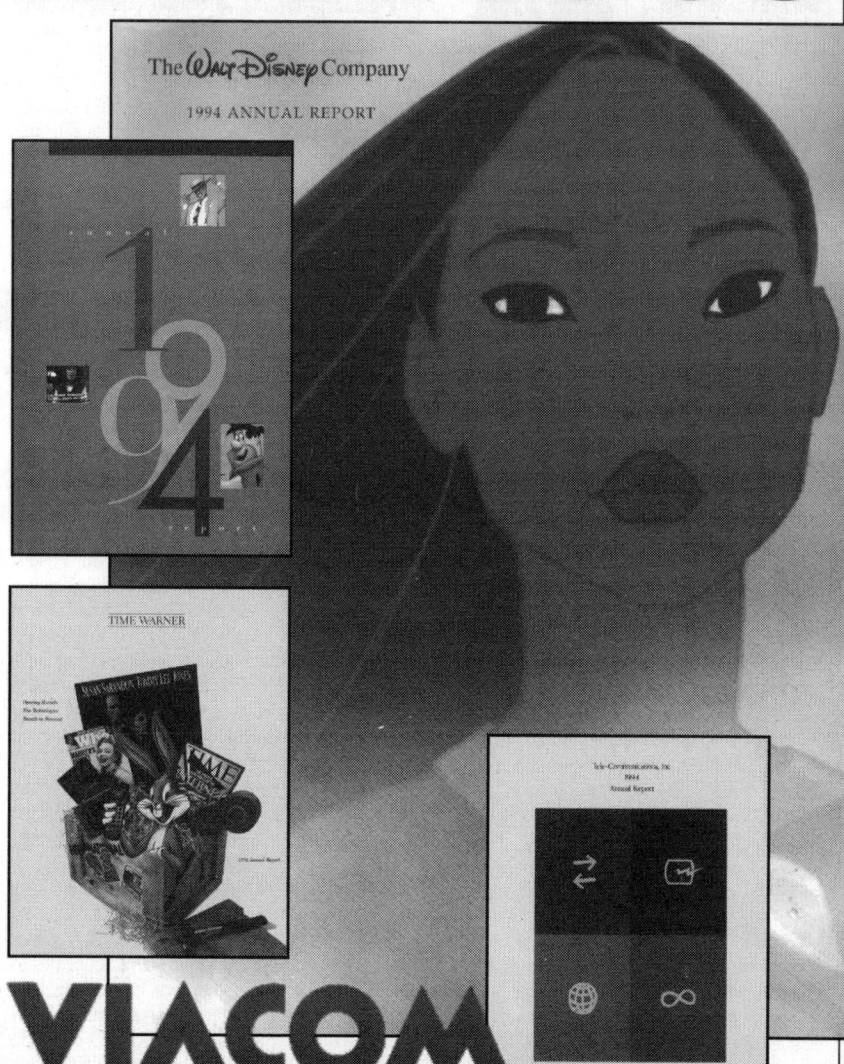

The Walt Disney Company
1994 ANNUAL REPORT

TIME WARNER

Tele-Communications, Inc.
1994
Annual Report

VIACOM

Critical Mass

■ BY ROBERT MOSES

Robert Moses is an editor of the *Information Please Entertainment Almanac* and president of Working Media, Inc.

Media analysts have stretched metaphors to seismic and intergalactic realms to convey the effects of this year's changes in the entertainment and media business. Those following the stories of Disney, Time Warner, MCA and a host of other media businesses watched an industry consolidating into massive enterprises that exert a gravitational pull on our economy and a related atomization of audiences into quark-sized units.

In the global market for entertainment product, a major media company must be enormous, selling name brands through every distribution channel. A movie, for example, can no longer be simply a movie. It must be an entertainment event that generates a soundtrack recording; a home video and a director's-cut laserdisc; a cable feature and a subsequent broadcast movie event; a novelization and a "making-of"

THE BUSINESS

book; magazine features on the stars with behind-the-scenes stories; a cable special on the "making-of" and a television series spinoff (or at least a Saturday morning cartoon show); action figures available at fast-food outlets; a CD-ROM game; and a World Wide Web site. This bundle of name-brand product requires the financial resources of an economic giant. But all of that energy and money is focused on an audience composed of individuals, individuals who exercise increasing control over what and when they choose to watch, listen, read or interact with — just as the nightly celestial display depends on the lonely hydrogen atom for its brilliant fire.

Those observing the entertainment firmament could find a swirling mass of money and entertainment properties consolidating into the brightest star in the sky following the August acquisition of ABC/Capital Cities by the Walt Disney Company. The $19 billion deal burst over the heads of surprised analysts like a supernova, creating one of the largest entertainment providers in the world. In retrospect, the move was seen as a natural: simply put, the most prestigious producer of programming combining with the most profitable program delivery system. Disney characters were projected to populate ABC's Saturday morning schedule. ABC's ownership of cable sports networks ESPN and ESPN 2 amplified Disney's interest in sports, evident in its ownership of the Mighty Ducks hockey team. Disney TV productions (such as *Home Improvement* and *Ellen*) and movies were seen as guaranteed to hold the best programming slots on ABC. Stockholders and Wall Street cheered the deal.

One week later, Disney chairman Michael Eisner again shocked the media by hiring as president his old friend Michael Ovitz, the chairman of Creative Artists Agency, the most powerful agency in Hollywood. Eyebrows were raised at the thought of two of the more autocratic executives in Hollywood working hand-in-hand. Viacom chairman Sumner Redstone commented that "Ovitz has always been his own king. Now, he's going to another kingdom where he's no longer the king but merely a royal prince." But Eisner noted, "We have the need to stimulate creative talent around the world. I can't do that all alone." Two months previously, Ovitz was embroiled in unsuccessful negotiations with new MCA owner Edgar Bronfman, Jr. to helm that entertainment conglomerate. This

Steven Spielberg, Jeffrey Katzenberg and David Geffen

time, he apparently couldn't resist the opportunity to head the largest entertainment company in the world though it cast doubt on the future of the company he had built and promised to reshuffle the deck of agents and stars throughout Hollywood. It also marks the apotheosis of the agent as the dominant force in the moviemaking process. Ovitz has long-time relations with many Hollywood creatives and has been an important deal-maker. But he has never exercised control of a media giant with interests that extend far beyond the insular world of Hollywood. That he has taken the helm of Disney's operating units indicates the critical importance of a media company's relationship with those who make the entertainment products.

The stealth Disney deal overshadowed a long-rumored acquisition that would have made headlines in any other year. Westinghouse Electric Corporation put its financial house in order and launched a $5.4 billion offer for the once-Tiffany network, CBS. Westinghouse has some experience in broadcasting, as it owns two cable networks, production and syndication operations and four television stations. Though broadcasting accounts for just 10 percent of its sales, it is Westinghouse's most profitable business. CBS owner Laurence Tisch's campaign to wring out expenses from the network, while appraising various suitors for a sale, had sapped morale and sunk the web from first to third in the 1994–1995 ratings. David Letterman cheered, though, as he now had another appliance manufacturer to torment.

John Malone

Yet another megadeal, Time Warner's proposed acquisition of Turner Broadcasting Systems, provided more speculation among observers and Wall Street as this goes to press. How would TCI's John Malone, the largest outside shareholder in Time Warner react? Would Ted Turner, who apparently has abandoned his quest for his very own television network, settle into a Number Two role? Would Time Warner's Michael Fuchs, newly ascendant, accept a role as Turner's right-hand man? Time's corporate structure is already Byzantine at best and the prospect of incorporating Turner's corporate culture — one headed by a head-strong maverick — promises business-page entertainment for months to come.

The deals also reopened the debate about how news coverage is influenced when news organizations are controlled by entertainment companies or industrial behemoths. What if CBS was investigating Westinghouse's defense contracts? Would ABC be reduced to happy, family news in the Disney mold? ABC's capitulation and apology to the tobacco companies for their nicotine-spiking story so close on the heels of its purchase by Disney confirmed these dark suspicions for many. The consternation seemed to disregard the ongoing merger of news and entertainment throughout the media. No one remained unconvinced that the evening news and proliferating network news magazines weren't governed by the same ratings imperatives as *Rosanne*. But there was serious discussion of media gigantism and the effects of consolidating 15 percent of the nation's economy into just a few hands.

The late summer flurry of activity also put in the shade the development of DreamWorks SKG, the new megastudio founded by director Steven Spielberg, former Disney executive Jeffrey Katzenberg and record label founder and movie producer David Geffen. A look at what had been the year's biggest story provides an outline of the modern media giant.

That these three men were responsible for some of the most successful movie and musical events of the last three decades already lends a Hollywood gleam to the new studio. But the alacrity with which they were able to raise capital for their dream factory provided the

Edgar Bronfman, Jr.

real fire. At this writing, DreamWorks has yet to begin production on anything, but the elements now in place point to an imposing presence in the entertainment universe. With $100 million in capital from the partners, the trio set out to increase their cash on hand. They did, with $500 million from former Microsoft co-owner Paul Allen and, reportedly, another $400 million from institutional investors including the California Public Employees retirement fund. They then secured a bank-debt facility of $1 billion to be restructured or repaid in 10 years — essentially a billion-dollar checkbook.

What to do with such a facility? DreamWorks will operate a film production unit that will release films domestically through MCA, which has been long associated with Spielberg. Cap Cities/ABC will invest in a joint venture to produce and distribute television programming, though the relationship may be less extensive after the Disney/ABC deal. Silicon Graphics will help create a digital studio, presumably to work on the animated features for which Katzenberg is well known and the special effects that drive many of Spielberg's projects. Microsoft has come aboard to help develop interactive games and films. Two record labels, DreamWorks for soundtracks and SKG for recording artists, have a marketing and distribution deal with MCA's Uni division domestically and MCA International (MCA is the current owner of Geffen Records). A publishing enterprise would round out the complete portfolio of media businesses.

DreamWorks's relationship with MCA adds luster to a company that was roiled by a change in ownership, from Matsushita Electric Industrial Company to 80 percent control by the Joseph Seagram Company. The new man in charge at MCA is Seagram scion Edgar Bronfman, Jr., who fulfilled a long-held ambition to find a place in the entertainment industry. He has for some time been a contentious stockholder at Time Warner, swinging Seagram's 15 percent stake. Bronfman calmed the waters at MCA with the consideration shown to revered industry figures Sidney Scheinberg and Lew Wasserman as he eased each of them into an emeritus role. But the public courtship of Ovitz to lead MCA and his subsequent demurral led to questions of Bronfman's experience and ability to manage

Gerald Levin

Sen. Bob Dole; inset: Snoop Doggy Dogg

Hollywood's outsized egos. His subsequent hiring of Ovitz's number two at CAA, Ron Myer, is intriguing and generally viewed as positive by the creative community. Bronfman's next hire, Doug Morris, former chairman of Warner Music made his relationship with Time Warner even more contentious.

As if Time Warner chairman Gerald Levin needed more problems. The Turner deal topped a year of turmoil for Levin. His campaign to add more cable properties to Time Warner's already vast holdings brought him even with dominant operator Tele-Communications, Inc., in number of cable households. But Wall Street's nervousness about cable portfolios kept Time Warner stock relatively depressed and shareholders restive. Then Warner Music Group, a division with nearly $4 billion in revenues and a healthy $720 million in cash flow, exploded into internecine warfare. Rumors throughout 1994 of political pressure on Robert Morgado, who had built Warner into an international presence, culminated in a succession struggle that saw Doug Morris, head of Atlantic Records, elevated to leadership of all Warner labels over respected, long-time Warner Bros. label heads. Morgado remained under fire from within, and Levin finally moved to quell the dissension from Morris partisans by firing Morgado and installing Michael Fuchs in June 1995. Fuchs now runs his former fiefdom at HBO and Time Warner's interactive business as well as Warner Music. Fuchs promptly fired Morris after determining that his defense of rap music against the perjorations of Sen. Robert Dole and moral standards crusader William Bennett jeopardized Time Warner's corporate goals. He then moved to oust the remaining Morris loyalists, including the recently installed chairman of Warner Bros. Records, Danny Goldberg and president of Warner Music U.S., Mel Lewinter. Fuchs also began negotiating to sell Time Warner's interest in Interscope Records, a major rap label.

Levin's move to bolster Time Warner's cable holdings squared with the consolidation of the cable industry into the hands of a few mega-operators. The consolidation was driven primarily by fear of programming competition from regional Bell systems and the move by cable operators into telephony with its required massive investment in equipment. The promise of rate deregulation in the telecommunications bill currently before Congress made funding such acquisitions more palatable. Due to huge up-front investments in infrastructure, the cable industry has traditionally been low on war chests though it boasts admirable cash flows and reliable banking relations. Now that most of the country is wired for cable, the industry needs another generation of financing to upgrade systems for the expected push for video-on-demand and to take the battle with the phone companies into voice and data carriage.

Most smaller systems had neither the heart for the battle nor the resources to play in what had become a war of titans and were willing to sell to the larger companies. The large operators — TCI, Time Warner, Comcast, Cox, Continental and Cablevision Systems — have adopted a strategy of clustering their systems by acquiring franchises in the same areas to

ENTERTAINMENT AND THE U.S. ECONOMY

The entertainment industry revenues listed below equaled $127.47 billion. Figures are based on 1994 statistics unless otherwise noted.

INDUSTRY	SALES
FILM	$5.4 billion in box-office receipts
TELEVISION	
NETWORK, NATIONAL SPOT AND LOCAL SPOT	$29.05 billion based on 1994 advertising revenue (network: $11.08 billion; national spot: $8.74 billion; local spot: $9.24 billion)
CABLE	$24.08 billion based on 1994's pay-per-view and premium subscription fees and advertising revenue (basic services: $15.6 billion; pay-per-view: $2.97 billion; premium: $2.58 billion; advertising revenue: $2.93 billion)
RADIO	$10.30 billion based on network, national spot and local spot advertising revenue
RECORDED MUSIC	$12.07 billion based on manufacturers recommended retail price
PUBLISHING	
BOOK	$18.70 billion based on end-user spending
MAGAZINE	$8.5 billion based on advertising revenue
PERFORMING ARTS	
THEATER	$129.53 million in ticket sales based on a survey of 231 theaters nationwide, assuming ticket sales account for 46.7% of annual earned income
OPERA	$176.7 million based on preliminary data
DANCE	No comprehensive data available

market more efficiently to consumers, sell advertising and build phone capacity. Three of those operators, TCI, Cox and Comcast, joined with long-distance carrier Sprint to develop the means to marry cable's access to the home with Sprint's long-distance network, an important step toward making cable a real player in the telephone business. Regional Bell US West, which also owns a stake in Time Warner entertainment businesses, has recently shown renewed interest in obtaining a stake in Cablevision Systems Corporation. The public had an inkling of the future in the proposed merger in 1993 of Bell Atlantic and TCI, a megamerger that foundered on the shoals of government regulations by February 1994. That the telecommunications bill looks like a sure bet indicates how different the regulatory environment has become.

The large cable operators were just one beneficiary of the telecommunications bill that passed the Senate in June and the House in August 1995 by broad majorities. The vote marked what could be the most sweeping change in the regulatory environment for communications since the Communications Act of 1934 established the public's interest in the airwaves. "It is the intention of this bill to get everybody into everyone else's business," said bill sponsor Sen. Larry Pressler (R-SD), and he may accomplish that. On the other side of the aisle, Rep. Ed Markey (D-MA), a long-time critic of media giants, said that "The consumers of America should be placed on red alert." Vice President Al Gore noted bitterly that the bill had been "sold to the highest bidder in every telecommunications industry," and it was "abhorrent to the public interest." At press time, President Clinton had threatened to veto the bill, noting, a little late, that it "promotes mergers and concentration of power." The

Sen. Larry Pressler

media industry counts enough votes to override a veto attempt.

The bill would lift rate regulation on cable systems reasoning that with the threat of the Bell systems delivering programming via phone lines, and with the advent of direct broadcast satellite delivery of programming, the cable operators no longer enjoy the monopoly they once held. Even power companies, the other outfits with wires into homes, have shown interest in providing programming or at least computerized, smart-home features to America's households. Cable and long-distance providers will be able to enter the market for local phone service.

Broadcasting companies will no longer have a cap on the number of television and radio stations that they can own, thus increasing the prospect of further consolidation of programming power. Allowing companies to own broadcast stations that provide TV for up to 50 percent of the country makes broadcasting more appealing, as can be seen in Westinghouse's purchase of beleagured CBS. At first glance, the bill would seem to favor the cable industry, giving it rate relief and allowing cable companies to compete with phone companies based on the Bells' ability to deliver programming, an ability believed by some to be as much as 10 years in the future. But what can't be forecast are the myriad of alliances, the results of investment in new technology and the creativity born of competition that the bill will yield. The competition will be confusing and messy, yes, but lively indeed.

It is no accident that the consolidation of the media takes place in an anti-regulatory environment. The promise of enormous profit makes the burden of enormous investment in technology and infrastructure salable to Wall Street. The government itself is even getting into the act, auctioning off parts of the wavelength spectrum for use in personal communications and data transmission. But the free-market warriors who have wrought this new environment are setting free the marketplace for media giants while awkwardly attempting to close the market for ideas.

HOME ENTERTAINMENT

CD-ROM

Reference	$156 million based on end-user spending
Educational Software	$522 million based on end-user spending
Video Games	$2.93 billion based on end-user spending
ON-LINE SERVICES	$1.43 billion in subscription fees of consumer-oriented services (Dialog, Lexis/Nexis, Dow Jones News Retrieval and CompuServe are not included)

VIDEO

Rentals	$9.39 billion based on 1994 consumer spending
Sales	$4.64 billion based on 1994 consumer spending

Sources: Association of American Publishers; Magazine Publishers of America; Opera America; Radio Business Report; Recording Industry Association of America; Theatre Communications Group; Variety, and Veronis Suhler and Associates, Inc.

TOP ENTERTAINMENT COMPANIES

Rank*	Company	1994 Sales (in millions)
1.	Time Warner Inc.	15,905
2.	Walt Disney Co.	10,055
3.	Sony Corp.	8,726
4.	News Corp.	8,640
5.	Viacom Inc.	7,363
6.	Capital Cities/ABC Inc.	6,379
7.	Pioneer Electronic Co.	5,128
8.	PolyGram NV.	4,943
9.	Tele-Communications Inc.	4,936
10.	MCA Inc.	4,818
11.	CBS Inc.	3,712
12.	Rank Organization PLC.	3,585
13.	Turner Broadcasting System Inc.	2,809
14.	Carlton Communications PLC	2,215
15.	Tribune Co.	2,155
16.	Comcast Corp.	1,375
17.	Grupo Televisa SA	1,288
18.	Home Shopping Network Inc.	1,126
19.	British Sky Broadcasting	860
20.	Cablevision Systems Corp.	837

* Rank as of July 6, 1995
Source: The Hollywood Reporter

Oddly, the forces of competition so loudly hailed in Congress have been deemed ineffective against the moral decay encouraged, according to its critics, by the media. From Sen. Dole's rapping of rap, to the proposal for an anti-violence chip in televisions (v-chips), to the legislation of penalties for transmission of offensive material on the Internet, Congress attempted to legislate the content on the wires if not the wires themselves. The week that Dole opened his campaign against rap music (and the vision of Dole glumly considering the lyrics of Snoop Doggy Dogg is truly delicious), *Billboard* magazine featured a front-page story that anxiously pondered the future of rap as its sales dropped and listeners fled to more melodious recordings. Dole no doubt did more to sell gangsta rap than Time Warner; any kid who read the newspaper that day must have figured that if Dole hated the stuff it must be ok. And the initiatives to install v-chips and regulate the Net betray a fundamental misunderstanding of the movement toward individual control of the media.

As market forces created larger and larger entertainment conglomerates, those companies marketed their products to narrower and narrower audiences. Just a few years ago, the public marveled at the cable companies' declaration of an impending 500-channel future, providing information and entertainment to those with even the most specialized interests. Though rate regulation halted the development of many cable networks, video on demand — a technological extension of the current pay-per-view cable option — promises to free the television viewer from the programmer's schedule entirely. And the advent of commercial use of the World Wide Web looks more and more like million-channel television — with programming done one person at a time.

This is merely the latest in the ongoing ascension of the individual as the primary audience for entertainment. For years, large media companies have taken control over smaller and smaller units of distribution. For example, there is effectively no longer a Top 40 selection of music that represents America's most popular music. The audience for recorded music is fragmented into dozens of special interests, and, until the late 1980s, each of these forms of music was typically served by independent record companies and distributors. Now those companies are owned by the major labels. Independent production companies and distributors used to serve the audience for foreign or low-budget, challenging films. Now, companies such as Miramax (owned by Disney) or New Line (owned by Turner) belong to media conglomerates. The progress of new technology and new media choices can be read as the story of the increasing primacy of individual taste over corporate programmers.

But what will this audience of individuals choose to download onto their computer/TV screens? If it's the equivalent of on-line chat rooms or the tabloid-informed talk shows — ABC's Jeff Greenfield referred to them as "a parade of dysfunctional horrors and leering hosts and audiences who were last seen crowding around the guillotine in Paris 200 years ago" — maybe the government's assertion of its rights to influence the public mind isn't misplaced. But it will be hard to make the case that government seeks to lift the public mind out of the gutter as it systematically dismantles the institutions that introduced the arts and letters to the broadest audience in history. Concurrent with and related to the freeing of the media marketplace is the debate over funding for public broadcasting. And in July, the House moved to end all funding for the arts and humanities foundations within two years.

In 1996, the megacorporations that supply information and entertainment will continue to gather mass and velocity unfettered by government regulation. And yet, all the assets that they control must continue to be focused on the smallest unit of measure in the entertainment audience — the individual. ∎

Should (TV, music and videos) have ratings so people know how much sex and violence to expect?

> **Television**
> Should: 84%
> Should not: 13%
> **Video games/Tapes**
> Should: 79%
> Should not: 17%
> **Music**
> Should: 72%
> Should not: 23%

If so, should the Government require ratings or should they be left up to each industry?

> **Television**
> Government: 39%
> Industry: 40%
> **Video games/Tapes**
> Government: 35%
> Industry: 42%
> **Music**
> Government: 33%
> Industry: 36%

Will ratings keep children from seeing or listening to inappropriate material?

> **Television**
> Will: 30%
> Will not: 63%
> **Video games/Tapes**
> Will: 32%
> Will not: 63 %
> **Music**
> Will: 22%
> Will not: 72%

Who Owns What?

A major media company can no longer content itself with a quaint concentration on making movies or publishing books. It must be a vertically integrated colossus able to market entertainment in any form. This is our guide to who controls what you watch, listen to and read. (Note that these media properties are extremely fluid. This is a snapshot taken in August 1995.)

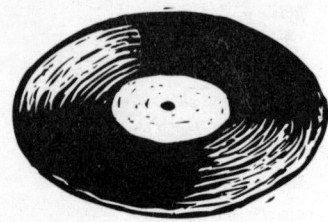

TIME WARNER INC.

Time Warner's cable and movie businesses are partially owned by US West (25.5%) and Japanese companies Hochu Corp. and Toshiba Corp. (11.2%)

MOVIES

Warner Bros., HBO Pictures, Savoy Pictures (3%)

MUSIC

WARNER BROS. RECORDS — Warner Bros., Reprise, Giant, Maverick, Qwest, Sire, Warner/Nashville, American Recordings, Slash, Tommy Boy, Luaka Bop, 4AD ATLANTIC RECORDING GROUP — Atlantic, Interscope, Time Warner Audio Books, Rhino, Select, Beggars Banquet, Big Beat, Mammoth, Matador, TAG Recordings, Celtic Heartbeat, Curb, Lava, Atlantic Nashville, Atlantic Theatre, Atlantic Classics, Mesa/Bluemoon, 143, Lava, Big Beat ELEKTRA ENTERTAINMENT — Elektra, East/West America, Asylum, Nonesuch MUSIC PUBLISHING — Warner/Chappell; Columbia House music club; investment in Music Choice cable radio; Inscape multimedia joint venture with HBO and investment in Accolade computer game company

PUBLISHING

MAGAZINES — *Time, Life, Fortune, Sports Illustrated, Money, People, Sports Illustrated for Kids, Entertainment Weekly, In Style, Southern Living, Progressive Farmer, Southern Accents, Cooking Light, Parenting, Baby Talk, Martha Stewart Living, Sunset, Health, Hippocrates, Asiaweek, President, Dancyu, Elle Japon, Who, Vibe* BOOK PUBLISHING — Little, Brown, Warner Books, Oxmoor House, Sunset Books, Time Life Books, Book-of-the-Month Club, History Book Club, Children's Book of the Month Club, Crafter's Choice book club, Quality Paperback Club, Home Style book club MULTIMEDIA — Pathfinder Web site OTHER — D.C. Comics, Turner Publishing (19.6%), magazine/direct reponse catalogs *BBC Music, Jazziz, huH*

TELEVISION

CABLE PROGRAMMING — HBO, Cinemax, HBO Pictures, Time Warner Cable, Full Service Network interactive TV test, Turner Broadcasting (19.6%), Courtroom Television (55%), Comedy Central (50%), E! Entertainment TV (49%), The Sega Channel (33%), Black Entertainment Television (15%), QVC (8%), Catalog 1 (50%) BROADCAST PROGRAMMING — Warner Bros. Television, Witt-Thomas Productions, The WB Television Network, Time TelePictures Television, Warner Bros. Distribution GAMES — 3DO (13%), Crystal Dynamics (10%), Atari (25%) HOME VIDEO — A*Vision Entertainment, Warner Home Video

BERTELSMANN AG

MUSIC

BMG Music, Arista Records, Arista/Nashville, Career Records, BMG Classics/RCA Victor, Private Music, RCA Records, Reunion Records, Imago Recording Company, Windham Hill, Zoo Entertainment

MUSIC PUBLISHING — BMG Songs, Killer Tracks, Reunion Music Group; BMG Direct music clubs

TELEVISION
Video production — Nice Man (50%)

PUBLISHING
MAGAZINES — *Parents, YM, Family Circle, McCall's, American Homestyle, Fitness, Child, Louis l'Amour's Western Magazine*
BOOK PUBLISHING — Bantam Doubleday Dell Publishing Group; Bantam Books, Doubleday, Delacorte, Dell, BDD Young Readers, Bantam Classics, Golden Apple, Loveswept, New Age Books, New Fiction, New Sciences, Peacock Press, Perigord Press, Spectra, Sweet Dreams; Doubleday book clubs
MULTIMEDIA — America Online (5%), BMG Interactive Entertainment, ION multimedia publisher (partnership), Rocket Science Games (partnership)

THE SEAGRAM COMPANY LTD.
In April, 1995 The Seagram Company acquired 80 percent of MCA, Inc.

MOVIES
Universal Pictures, Cinema International (49%), United International Pictures (33%)

MUSIC
MCA Records, Geffen Records, Uni Distribution, (510), Radioactive (joint venture), Fort Apache/MCA, MCA Publishing, MCA Concerts

PUBLISHING
BOOK PUBLISHING — The Putnam Berkley Group (Ace, Berkley Prime Crime, Coward-McCann, Diamond, Grosset & Dunlap, Grosset Books, HP Books, Jove, Perigee Books, Philomel, Platt & Munk, Price Stern Sloan, G.P. Putnam's Sons, Riverhead Books, Sandcastle, Serendipity, Jeremy P. Tarcher, Wee Sing, Wonder Books)
MULTIMEDIA — Universal Interactive, Interplay (minority holder)

TELEVISION
USA Network (50%), MCA TV, MCA Home Video, Universal Pay Television

VIACOM
MOVIES
Paramount Pictures, Cinamerica Theatres (50%), Famous Players theaters in Canada

MUSIC
RETAILING — Blockbuster Music (Sound Warehouse, Music Plus Super Club)
MUSIC PUBLISHING — Famous Music

PUBLISHING
BOOK PUBLISHING — Simon & Schuster: Simon & Schuster, Pocket Books (Archway, Folger Shakespeare Library, Golf Digest Books, Minstrel, Pocket Books, Pocket Star Books, S&S Audio, Washington Square Press, MTV Books), Scribner, Fireside, The Free Press (Lexington Books), Hudson River Editions, Rawson Associates, Charles Scribner's Sons, Simon & Schuster Children's (Alladin, Little Simon, Macmillan Books for Young Readers, Margaret McElderry Books, Rabbit Ears, Simon & Schuster Books for Young Readers), Allyn and Bacon, Educational Management Group, The New York Institute of Finance, Markt&Technik, Bureau of Business Practice, Touchstone, Nickelodeon Books; Macmillan Publishing USA: Macmillan General Reference (American Express Travel Guides, ARCO, ChekChart, Audel, Baedeker's, Betty Crocker, Burpee, Frommer's, HM Gousha, Harrap's, Horticulture, JK Lasser, Monarch, Travel Bugs, The Unofficial Guides, Webster's New World, Weight Watcher's), Macmillan Library (Charles Scribner's Sons, G.K. Hall, Macmillan Reference, Sandak, Schirmer Books, Academic Reference, Throndike Press, Twayne Publishing), Macmillan Digital, Macmillan Computer Publishing; Simon & Schuster Education Group
MAGAZINES — *Nickelodeon Magazine, Nick-At-Nite Magazine*
MULTIMEDIA — Simon & Schuster

Interactive, Viacom New Media, Viacom Interactive Services, MacMillan Digital, Computer Curriculum Corporation, StarSight (26%), Byron Preiss Multimedia (20%)

TELEVISION
CABLE OPERATIONS — Viacom cable systems
CABLE PROGRAMMING — Showtime, The Movie Channel, FLIX, MTV, VH-1, Nickelodeon, Sundance Film Channel (33%), USA Network (50%), Comedy Central (50%), Sci-Fi Channel (50%), All News Channel (50%), Showtime Satellite Networks
BROADCAST OPERATIONS — 12 TV stations and 12 radio stations;
BROADCAST PROGRAMMING — Paramount Television, Viacom Productions, Laurel Entertainment, Paramount TV Syndication, United Paramount Network
HOME VIDEO — Paramount Home Video, Republic Home Video, MTV Home Video (partnership with Sony)
RETAILING — Blockbuster Video

TELE-COMMUNICATIONS, INC.

TELEVISION
CABLE OPERATIONS — TCI Communications Inc., cable systems
CABLE PROGRAMMING — Liberty Media: Discovery Channel (49%), The Learning Channel, QVC networks, Home Shopping Networks (40%), The Family Channel (18%), Starz! (90%), Encore (90%), Court TV (33%), Black Entertainment Television (18%), E! Entertainment (10%), Prime Ticket, Request TV, Viewer's Choice, tv! Network, What On Earth interactive news source delivered to personal computers

(partnership with Reuters), MacNeil/Lehrer Productions, the International Channel, Digital Music Express cable radio (30%), Cable Health Club, Republic Pictures TV (50%), Southern Satellite Systems program distribution, Netlink satellite program distribution
NEW TECHNOLOGY — TCI Technology Ventures: Sega Channel (33%), Primestar satellite television (partnership with six cable operators), EPG (Viewer's Guide) (25%), The Microsoft Network (investment with Microsoft in interactive service), Acclaim Entertainment (investment), AND Interactive (investment), Netscape provider of on-line access (investment), Western Telecommunications provider of long-distance voice and data (investment)
OTHER — partnership with Sprint to offer long-distance service

RADIO
Prime Sports Radio

TURNER BROADCASTING SYSTEMS, INC.
Both Time Warner and Telecommunications, Inc., own a portion of TBS. At this writing, Time Warner is making an effort to acquire all of TBS.

MOVIES
Castle Rock Entertainment, New Line Cinema Corporation (includes Fine Line Features), Turner Pictures Worldwide

TELEVISION
CABLE PROGRAMMING — CNN, CNN Headline News, TBS, TNT, Turner Classic Movies, Cartoon Network, The Airport Channel, SportSouth (44%)
HOME VIDEO — Turner Home Entertainment

PUBLISHING
BOOK PUBLISHING —Turner Publishing

SONY CORPORATION

MOVIES
Columbia Pictures, TriStar Pictures, Sony Pictures Classics, Triumph Releasing, Sony Theatres, Columbia TriStar International Distribution

MUSIC
Columbia, Chaos, Epic, Epic Associated, Epic Soundtrax, Sony 550 Music, Crescent Moon, Okeh, TriStar Music, Relativity, Sony Classical, Soho Square, Sony Wonder

TELEVISION
PROGRAMMING — Columbia TriStar Television, Columbia TriStar Television Distribution
HOME VIDEO — Columbia TriStar Home Video

THE NEWS CORPORATION, LTD.

MOVIES
Twentieth Century-Fox

MUSIC
Twentieth Century-Fox Records

TELEVISION
BROADCAST PROGRAMMING: Fox Broadcasting (Fox Network)
CABLE PROGRAMMING: f/x and f/xM cable networks
HOME VIDEO: Fox Video
BROADCAST OPERATIONS: 8 US TV stations

PUBLISHING
MAGAZINES — TV Guide, Mirabella
BOOK PUBLISHING — HarperCollins (Harper Collins, Harper Perennial, Harper Children's Books, Collins San Francisco, Harper San Francisco, Harper Reference, Harper Business, Basic Books), ReganBooks, Scott, Foresman, Zondervan;
NEWSPAPERS — The New York Post
ONLINE — Delphi

THE WALT DISNEY COMPANY

In August, Walt Disney acquired ABC/Capital Cities creating — at this point — the largest media company in the world.

MOVIES
Hollywood Pictures, Touchstone Pictures, Walt Disney Pictures, Miramax Film Corp. (Disney has also become a theatrical producer with its production of *Beauty and the Beast* and ownership of a Broadway theater)

MUSIC
Hollywood Records, Walt Disney Records, Disney Music Publishing

TELEVISION
BROADCAST OPERATIONS — KCAL-TV, Los Angeles and 8 ABC television stations
BROADCAST PROGRAMMING — ABC television network, Buena Vista Television, Touchstone Television, Walt Disney Television,
PRODUCTION — DreamWorks SKG (partnership), DIC Animation City
CABLE PROGRAMMING — The Disney Channel, Arts & Entertainment Network (37.5%), ESPN (80%), ESPN 2, Lifetime (50%), The History Channel
HOME VIDEO — Buena Vista Home Video

RADIO
ABC Radio Networks, 11 AM, 10 FM radio stations; ABC Distribution

PUBLISHING
MAGAZINES — *Discover, Disney Adventures, FamilyFun, Family PC* (joint venture with Ziff-Davis), Shopping guides, Diversified publishing group, Agricultural publishing, Chilton Publications, Grupo Editorial Expansion (LA), NILS Publishing Co., *W, Women's Wear Daily, Institutional Investor,* International Medical News Group
BOOK PUBLISHING — Hyperion Press, Disney Press, Mouse Works, Miramax Books
NEWSPAPERS: *Fort Worth Star-Telegram, The Kansas City (MO) Star Newspapers* and related publications in 13 states
MULTIMEDIA — Disney Software

Wigstock

Mo

Pocahontas

Hoop Dreams

Die Hard
With a
Vengeanc

To Die For

14

ovies

Rob Roy

Batman Forever

Hugh Grant

15

Big and Bigger

■ BY MARTHA SOUTHGATE

IT ALL STARTED WITH A LITTLE-READ 1985 NOVEL, *FORREST GUMP*. Nine years later, that novel, the story of the tragedies and triumphs of a good-hearted idiot, became one of the most successful films of all time. Who'da thunk it?

Martha Southgate is a senior writer at *Premiere* magazine.

But that was the movie business in 1994 and 1995. Unexpected winners, unexpected losers and a few 500-pound gorillas that neatly crushed anybody that got in their way.

On paper, it all looked good in Tinseltown. Total box-office revenues rose 4 percent in 1994 to a record 5.26 billion, 10 separate movies earned more than $100 million each — which hasn't happened since 1990. Ticket sales topped $1.21 billion, 3 percent more than last year. Business appeared to be booming. But all was not as fabulous as it seemed. While the hits were hits of unparalleled proportions, anything less than a $60 million take nearly qualified a film as a loser. A lot of films that would have been hailed as winners in years past were now sadly welcomed as also-rans. If you couldn't hit one out of the ball park — as *The Lion King* or *Forrest Gump* — then you might as well not even step up to the plate.

MOVIES

This is, as you might expect, not the best thing in the world for innovative thinking about the art of film. It's pretty much agreed by critics that the most interesting films these days are coming from independent filmmakers and smaller distributors such as New Line and Miramax. The big boys just can't afford to take chances. So they don't. Instead we end up with *Dumb and Dumber* (which can only lead to Dumbest).

Beyond that, there seems to be a real feeling in the land that being well-meaning but not very bright makes you somehow superior. There have been reams of print spent on the current wave of anti-intellectualism that *Gump* exemplifies but the fact that it's become something of a critics' cliché doesn't mean it's not true. Audiences seem to be finding comfort in easy answers these days, and that search for simplicity extends to the local bijou as well. There's even been some talk (in a recent *New York Times* article) that the most interesting work is coming from your television screen. A good episode of *ER* makes you think that there's some truth to that.

Another thing odd about this movie year was that *Forrest Gump* wasn't completely forgotten by February when the Oscar nominations were announced. Most of the prestige product of fall fizzled or faded next to the feel-good vibes of the *Gump* juggernaut. Usually movies that are released in the summer, as *Gump* was, are just sand-covered memories by the time the nominations roll around. That's why the studios save their most high-toned movies for the end of the year — they know they're more likely to garner an Oscar nod if their films are seen close to nominating time. But there was just something about the good-hearted Gump that touched people and made the movie an enormous commercial success long beyond the summer and the holiday season. Some argue it was his very blankness, which allowed folks to see him the way they wanted to, liberal, conservative, whatever.

A number of the films that were predicted to have the biggest box-office success in 1994 instead sank smoothly beneath the surface — and some of them had stars that rarely put a foot wrong. Does anybody remember *Junior,* featuring a pregnant Arnold Schwarzenegger

Junior, The Lion King, Forrest Gump and **Dumb and Dumber**

— apparently a prospect more terrifying to audiences than *The Terminator*? Or *I.Q.* — Meg Ryan and Tim Robbins in a romance that generated winter chills at the box office? Or *Richie Rich*, starring the fast-aging, fast-cooling Macaulay Culkin as the richest boy in the world?

On the other hand, as always, there were the unexpected smashes. Like *The Santa Clause*, a slick, wisecracking film that took Tim Allen off the small screen and onto the big in a big way. Or the rise and rise of Jim Carrey, who now has three ridiculous but staggeringly successful films (*Ace Ventura, The Mask* and *Dumb and Dumber*) under his belt and provided riddles in *Batman Forever*. The fall will see the follow-up to his launching pad, *Ace Ventura: When Nature Calls,* and he will earn $20 million for *Cable Guy*. He's come a long way since he was "the white guy on *In Living Color*," his unofficial moniker for years.

Pulp Fiction

The huge success of Carrey (who was able to *turn down* $14 million for a part after *The Mask*) and the somewhat lesser success of Tim Allen points also to Hollywood's continuing search for stuff that works, and the film industry's perpetual attraction to proven talent and high concept. Carrey was known from his work on *In Living Color,* and *Ace Ventura* was not a hugely expensive movie. When it turned into one of the biggest hits of the year, the industry was stunned. But not too stunned to put Carrey back to work as fast as his little legs could carry him. Allen was more of a known quantity from his work on TV's *Home Improvement* and that made Disney more willing to take a chance on him. As it turned out, he came up aces. Expect to see many more standups (such as Ellen DeGeneres) making the leap to film in the year to come, thanks to these guys.

And then there was *Pulp Fiction.* Along with *Forrest Gump,* this movie seemed to define the zeitgeist better than any other this year. On the one hand, there was Forrest's loving, simple, feel-good steadfastness. On the other, in the dazzling *Fiction,* there was sex, drugs, violence, cynicism — and some of the most scabrously funny dialogue ever. The initial buzz was good and the film's surprise win of the Palme d'Or at Cannes was an unexpected hint of things to come. But the film's distributor, Miramax, managed to take the film out of the art-house circuit and make it a mainstream success thanks to canny marketing and a highly marketable and charming director/screenwriter in Quentin Tarantino. Not since the heyday of Spike Lee has there been a director who is so much a willing part of the selling of his film. Conveniently, Tarantino is also a talented director whose love for film comes through in every frame. Despite the critical success of *Pulp Fiction,* the film's impact on the industry as a whole has been minimal. Sure there's a little more room for quirky movies with tough guys and tough talk, but that's still not where the money is. As summer 1995 approached, "big," "boffo" and "blowing stuff up" were still the watchwords.

After the bombing in Oklahoma City, there was some talk about toning down the "blowing up" in films and television. But the huge opening of *Die Hard With a Vengeance* (approximately $21 million over Memorial Day weekend alone) quelled that discussion fast. The American fascination with exploding stuff hadn't diminished a bit, despite Oklahoma City's graphic demonstration of the horror a real explosion can wreak.

Die Hard With a Vengeance might have packed the biggest boom in the early summer but it receded as the summer brought near-record box office receipts. A reconfigured *Batman Forever* featured not only Carrey but a lighter spirit and a more kid-friendly approach thanks to its new director Joel Schumacher, taking over the series from Hollywood's quirkiest big-box-office director, Tim Burton. The result was the biggest opening since *Jurassic Park* and $100 million in 10 days. And there was also *Apollo 13,* a thinking man's thriller starring Tom Hanks, who is perhaps the most powerful and well-loved actor in Hollywood at the moment. Yes, it's about an event that a

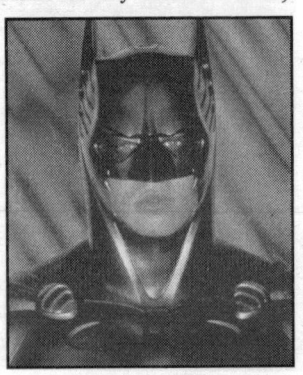

Batman Forever

significant proportion of the movie-going audience doesn't even remember, but with Ron Howard upping the tension and Hanks's natural charm, it was the most grown-up popcorn movie of the summer, and it kept on growing, fueling a summer box-office bonanza that usually relies on kiddie fare. The summer also gave us *The Bridges of Madison County*, featuring the softer side of Clint Eastwood and Meryl Streep (getting to work out her Italian accent this time) and the already successful hard-guys (Denzel Washington and Gene Hackman) in a sub flick *Crimson Tide*. Sandra Bullock's breakout charmer *While You Were Sleeping* (in which Bill Pullman gets the girl) was around through the summer, *Casper* opened with hauntingly large grosses, and the annual animated Disney extravaganza — 1995's was *Pocahontas* — needed Central Park for its premiere extravaganza, solidifying Disney's stake in New York.

Outside from Hollywood, the two summer films that had the biggest *Pulp Fiction*-style buzz after this year's Cannes Festival were Gus van Sant's *To Die For* (starring the suddenly omnipresent Nicole Kidman) and Larry Clark's frighteningly raw *Kids* (written by a 20-year-old guy named Harmony Korine who was once one of *Sassy* magazine's "Ones to Watch"). While, like *Pulp*, neither is likely to rack up big numbers at the box office, both are sure to make (or in van Sant's case, remake) their director's reputations.

Art-house buzz aside, the film that's likely to define the summer, and that may redefine the movie industry, is Kevin

The Bridges of Madison County

Costner's *Waterworld*. Okay, he didn't direct it, but he stars in it and produced it, and finished it up after director Kevin Reynolds quit after delivering his cut. It's the most expensive movie ever made. At last report, the budget was $175 million — an amount that insiders say is unlikely to be recouped. More importantly, even if it was a *Gump*- or *Lion King*-level smash, spending

47TH ANNUAL DIRECTORS GUILD OF AMERICA AWARDS

The DGA Awards, which honor directorial excellence in film and television were announced in bicoastal ceremonies at Los Angeles's Beverly Hilton and New York's Marriott Marquis on March 11, 1995. The DGA motion picture winner is considered a shoo-in for the best director Oscar. Only three times since 1949 has the DGA winner not gone on to win Oscar's helming award. Here are the film awards.

Outstanding Directorial Achievement
Robert Zemeckis, *Forrest Gump*

Outstanding Directorial Achievement in a Documentary
Steve James, *Hoop Dreams*

Lifetime Achievement
James Ivory

The 52nd Golden Globe Awards honoring excellence in film and television were presented January 21, 1995 at Los Angeles's Beverly Hilton.

MOVIES

Best Drama
Forrest Gump

Best Actor in a Drama
Tom Hanks, *Forrest Gump*

Best Actress in a Drama
Jessica Lange, *Blue Sky*

Best Supporting Actor in a Drama
Martin Landau, *Ed Wood*

Jessica Lange, Blue Sky

Best Supporting Actress in a Drama
Dianne Wiest, *Bullets Over Broadway*

Best Musical Comedy
The Lion King

Best Actor in a Musical or Comedy
Hugh Grant, *Four Weddings and a Funeral*

Best Actress in a Musical or Comedy
Jamie Lee Curtis, *True Lies*

Best Foreign Language Film
Farinelli, Belgium

Best Director
Robert Zemeckis, *Forrest Gump*

Martin Landau, Ed Wood

Best Screenplay
Quentin Tarantino, *Pulp Fiction*

Best Original Score
The Lion King

Best Original Song
"Can You Feel the Love Tonight?," *The Lion King*

nearly $200 million to get it onto the screen makes $300 million (the *Gump* gross) look like small potatoes indeed. Interestingly, and unusually, Universal made no attempt to counter the reams of bad press and nasty speculation surrounding the movie. The only person to speak up was a disgruntled writer of the film, who took out a full page ad in *Variety* to chastise the naysayers who hadn't seen a frame of the film.

A film of this size can't help but send shock waves through the industry one way or the other. If somehow, it hits, the roof

Waterworld

will be completely off in terms of what studios are willing to spend in order to sell tickets (and even before results are finally tabulated, the new Stallone vehicle *Assassins* for Christmas is said to cost $150 million). But if *Waterworld* tanks, there's bound to be a period of retrenchment and rethinking. For one thing, there will probably be some questioning of just how much power movie stars should (or can profitably be) allotted on a film. It's ironic that another Costner film provoked this discussion, because it was the success of his *Dances With Wolves* that opened the door for big-budget films directed and produced by stars. If *Waterworld* fails, it doesn't mean there will be hundreds of thoughtful little pictures with no stars, no explosions and no nasty language, but there may be a consideration of just how much money is sensible to spend in order to turn a reasonable profit. That might be a refreshing change for old Tinseltown.

The other thing that 1996 holds for Hollywood is increased scrutiny as the elections approach. Presidential hopeful Bob Dole fired the opening shot (to use an inappropriate metaphor) in early June when he took the industry to task for films such as *Natural Born Killers* and *True Romance,* which he called "nightmares of depravity" (though he didn't see either movie). "We have reached the point where our popular culture threatens to undermine our character as a nation," he thundered, although, intriguingly, he didn't go after Arnold Schwarzenegger's heavy artillery. Some, particularly in the industry, guessed that Dole didn't include the star in his attack because he's a well-known Republican. Whether it was a heartfelt cry or a bid for political capital, Dole's complaints started a firestorm of punditry and made it clear that, for better or worse, Hollywood remains a part of the political process.

So what does it all add up to? Pronouncements about the future of the movie industry are made all the time but they're hard to make accurately. Did anyone think that *Forrest Gump* would really become a cultural touchstone? Don't bet on it. But you can bet that the explosion of the entertainment industry worldwide will fuel a continued interest in movies that have the broadest possible appeal. That means more blockbusters based on proven commodities (such as *Batman Forever* and *Ace Ventura: When Nature Calls*) and the ongoing search for stars whose appeal crosses as many lines as possible (keep an eye on Sandra Bullock). The multimedia world is just beginning to touch the way films are made and distributed, and it's an influence that's sure to be felt this year. Stars will continue to be paid ludicrous amounts of money as long as they can put fannies in the seats. That's one thing about Hollywood that's not likely to change. The rest remains to be seen. As William Goldman so wisely observed about the industry he's toiled in for so long, "Nobody knows anything." They're all just looking for the next big thing. The search will continue. ∎

Natural Born Killers

The Movies of 1994–1995

These movies, listed alphabetically, opened in U.S. theaters between October 1, 1994 and August 11, 1995.

AMATEUR

Director/Writer: Hal Hartley; **Director of Photography:** Michael Spiller; **Editor:** Steve Hamilton; **Music:** Hal Hartley and Jeffrey Taylor; **Production Designer:** Steve Rosenzweig; **Producers:** Hal Hartley and Ted Hope
Sony Pictures Classics; R; 105 minutes
Release: 4/95
Cast: Isabelle Huppert, Martin Donovan, Elina Lowensohn and Damian Young

While reassessing her calling, a nun (Huppert) makes a living writing pornographic stories (though she's a virgin). She helps amnesiac former pornographer Thomas (Donovan) piece together his past, which includes turning his wife into a famous porn star.

APOLLO 13

Director: Ron Howard; **Writers:** William Broyles, Jr. and Al Reinert; **Director of Photography:** Dean Cundey; **Editors:** Mike Hill and Dan Hanley; **Music:** James Horner; **Production Designer:** Michael Corenblith; **Producer:** Brian Grazer
Universal; PG; 135 minutes
Release: 6/95
Cast: Tom Hanks, Kevin Bacon, Bill Paxton, Gary Sinise, Ed Harris, Kathleen Quinlan and Jean Speegle Howard
Based on the book *Lost Moon* by Jim Lovell and Jeffrey Kluger

In April 1970, the crew of Apollo 13, led by Jim Lovell (Hanks) left Earth for a weeklong adventure that included a walk on the moon. But things went very wrong for Lovell and his crew (Bacon and Paxton) and they nearly died in space. This 1995 summer blockbuster rocketed box office sales to a record-high five-day performance.

ARIZONA DREAM

Director: Emir Kusturica; **Writers:** Emir Kusturica and David Atkins; **Director of Photography:** Vilko Filac; **Editor:** Andrlja Zafranovic; **Music:** Goran Bregovic; **Producers:** Claudie Ossard and Richard Brick
Kit Parker Films; NR; 142 minutes
Release: 6/95 (completed in 1992)
Cast: Johnny Depp, Faye Dunaway, Jerry Lewis, Vincent Gallo and Lili Taylor

Axel Blackmar (Depp), a fish counter for the New York Department of Fish and Game, dreams of moving to Alaska but winds up a car salesman in Arizona at the request of his often pink-clad uncle (Lewis). A crazed mother (Dunaway) and her stepdaughter (Taylor) both fall for Blackmar and do not hide their rivalry.

AN AWFULLY BIG ADVENTURE

Director: Mike Newell; **Writer:** Charles Wood; **Director of Photography:** Dick Pope; **Editor:** Jon Gregory; **Music:** Richard Hartley; **Production Designer:** Mark Geraghty; **Producers:** Hilary Heath and Philip Hinchcliffe
Fine Line; R; 113 minutes
Release: 7/95
Cast: Hugh Grant, Alan Rickman, Georgina Cates, Alan Cox and Peter Firth
Based on the novel by Beryl Bainbridge

Grant and Newell team up again, but this dark, eccentric film bears no resemblance to *Four Weddings and a Funeral*. (*An Awfully Big Adventure* was made before *Four Weddings*.) The proud, bitchy Meredith Potter (Grant) runs a small-time Liverpool repertory company and hires ingénue Stella (Cates) before he sees her act. P. L. O'Hara, the company's leading man, steps in at the last minute to play Captain Hook in *Peter Pan* and is immediately taken with Stella. The experienced thespian and director get pleasure from taking physical and emotional advantage of wide-eyed company members.

BABE

Director: Chris Noonan; **Writers:** George Miller and Chris Noonan; **Director of Photography:** Andrew Lesnie; **Editors:** Marcus D'Arcy and Jay Friedkin; **Music:** Nigel Westlake; **Production Designer:** Roger Ford; **Animatronics:** Jim Henson's Creature Shop, John Cox and Robotechnology and Rhythm and Hues; **producers:** George Miller, Doug Mitchell and Bill Miller
Universal; G; 91 minutes
Release: 8/95
Cast: James Cromwell and Magda Szubanski
Voices of: Christine Cavanaugh, Miriam Margolyes, Danny Mann, Hugo Weaving, Evelyn Krape, Miriam Flynn and Roscoe Lee Browne
Based on the novel *Babe the Gallant Pig* by Dick King-Smith

Babe (voice of Cavanaugh), a homesick piglet who is awarded to Farmer Hoggett (Cromwell) at the county fair, sees his new farmmate, the sheepdog Fly (voice of Margolyes), as his surrogate mother. Babe must prove his worth to the farm else he become Christmas dinner. The crafty swine learns that he can herd sheep better than any sheep dog.

BAD BOYS
Director: Michael Bay; **Writers:** Michael Barrie, Jim Mulholland and Doug Richardson; **Director of Photography:** Howard Atherton; **Editor:** Christian Wagner; **Music:** Mark Mancina; **Production Designer:** John Vallone; **Producers:** Don Simpson and Jerry Bruckheimer
Columbia; R; 126 minutes
Release: 4/95
Cast: Martin Lawrence, Wil Smith, Téa Leoni and Tcheky Karyo

Based on the story by George Gallo
Marcus Burnett (Lawrence) and Mike Lowery (Smith), two renegade Miami cops, have four days to recover $100 million worth of stolen heroin before the FBI takes over the case.

BAD COMPANY
Director: Damian Harris; **Writer:** Ross Thomas; **Director of Photography:** Jack N. Green; **Editor:** Stuart Pappé; **Music:** Carter Burwell; **Production Designer:** Andrew McAlpine; **Producers:** Amedeo Ursini and Jeffrey Chernov
Touchstone Pictures; R; 108 minutes
Release: 1/95
Cast: Ellen Barkin, Laurence Fishburne, Frank Langella, Spalding Gray, Michael Beach, Gia Carides and David Ogden Stiers
A former CIA agent (Fishburne), newly employed by a roguish industrial espionage company, teams up with the boss's sometime girlfriend (Barkin) in a scheme to take over the company.

BALLET
Director/Producer/Editor: Frederick Wiseman; **Director of Photography:** John Davey
Zipporah Films; NR; 170 minutes
Release: 3/95
Cast: American Ballet Theatre dancers
This profile of New York's American Ballet Theatre follows the company in the spring and summer of 1992, from rehearsals in New York to performances in Athens and Copenhagen, stopping in the administrative offices for a behind-the-scenes look at dance.

BALLOT MEASURE 9
Director/Producer: Heather MacDonald; **Director of Photography:** Ellen Hansen; **Editors:** Heather MacDonald and B. B. Jorissen; **Music:** Julian Dylan Russell, Sunny McHale Skyedancer and the Family Values

Zeitgeist Films; NR; 72 minutes
Release: 6/95
Cast: Donna Red Wing, Kathleen Saadat, Scott Seibert, Jim Self, Elise Self, Cindy Patterson, Ann Sweet, Tom Potter, Lon Mabon, Bonnie Mabon, Scott Lively and Oren Camenish
This documentary examines the bitter cultural war waged in Oregon over the 1992 anti-gay ballot iniative that would have ended equal rights protection for homosexuals.

BANDIT QUEEN
Director: Shekhar Kapur; **Writer:** Mala Sen; **Director of Photography:** Ashok Mehta; **Editor:** Renu Saluja; **Music:** Nusrat Fateh Ali Khan and Roger White; **Production Designer:** Eve Mavrakis; **Producer:** Sundeep Singh Bedi
Arrow; NR; 119 minutes
Release: 7/95
Cast: Seema Biswas and Nirmal Fandey
Based on Phoolan Devi's prison diaries
In Hindi with English subtitles
This movie biography of lower-caste Phoolan Devi (Biswas) chronicles Devi's life from childhood to her leadership of a band of outlaws that robbed, kidnapped and murdered members of India's upper castes.

BAR GIRLS
Director: Marita Giovanni; **Writer:** Lauran Hoffman; **Director of Photography:** Michael Ferris; **Editor:** Carter DeHaven; **Music:** Lenny Meyers; **Producers:** Lauran Hoffman and Marita Giovanni
Orion; R; 95 minutes
Release: 4/95
Cast: Nancy Allison Wolfe, Camilla Griggs, Liza D'Agostino, CeCe Tsou, Michael Harris, Justine Slater and Paula Sorge
Based on the play by Lauren Hoffman
Eight beautiful lesbians who frequent Los Angeles's Girl Bar have no problem meeting and sharing partners. Loretta (Wolfe) and Rachel (D'Agostino) are the one couple on somewhat solid ground, but none of their friends can understand what keeps them together.

THE BASKETBALL DIARIES
Director: Scott Kalvert; **Writer:** Bryan Goluboff; **Director of Photography:** David Phillips; **Editor:** Dana Congdon; **Music:** Graeme Revell; **Production Designer:** Christopher Nowak; **Producers:** Liz Heller and John Bard Manulis
New Line; R; 102 minutes
Release: 4/95
Cast: Leonardo DiCaprio, Bruno Kirby, Lorraine Bracco, Ernie Hudson, Patrick McGaw, James Madio, Mark Wahlberg, Juliette Lewis and Jim Carroll
Based on the novel by Jim Carroll
Jim Carroll (DiCaprio) descends, along with several of his friends, from a somewhat normal 13-

year-old New York teen into a heroin addict and hustler. The movie is set in the 1990s, but Carroll's book reflects his experiences growing up in the 1950s.

BATMAN FOREVER

Director: Joel Schumacher; **Writers:** Lee Batchler, Janet Scott Batchler and Akiva Goldsman; **Director of Photography:** Stephen Goldblatt; **Editor:** Dennis Virkler; **Music:** Elliot Goldenthal; **Production Designer:** Barbara Ling; **Producers:** Tim Burton and Peter MacGregor-Scott
Warner Bros.; PG-13; 121 minutes
Release: 6/95
Cast: Val Kilmer, Tommy Lee Jones, Jim Carrey, Nicole Kidman, Chris O'Donnell, Michael Gough and Pat Hingle
Based on the characters created by Bob Kane and published by DC Comics
The Riddler (Carrey) and Two-Face (Jones) form a partnership in order to destroy the Caped Crusader (Kilmer). The Riddler has developed a machine that saps other people's intelligence as they watch television, but he doesn't have the resources to install the contraption globally. Two-Face doesn't have the gray matter to outwit Batman, but he can fund the Riddler's endeavor with thievery.

BEFORE THE RAIN

Director/Writer: Milcho Manchevski; **Director of Photography:** Manuel Teran; **Editor:** Nicolas Gaster; **Music:** Anastasia; **Production Designers:** Sharon Lamofsky and David Munns; **Producers:** Judy Counihan, Cedomir Kolar, Sam Taylor and Cat Villiers
Gramercy; NR; 116 minutes
Release: 2/95
Cast: Katrin Cartlidge, Rade Serbedzija, Gregoire Colin and Labina Mitevska
In Macedonian, Albanian and English with English subtitles

Three episodes: "Words," "Faces" and "Pictures" link together to form this haunting drama of violence, hatred and war. In "Words" a young monk (Colin) hides in his monastery a young Albanian Muslim girl. "Faces" presents an English couple (Cartlidge and Mitevska) about to end their marriage and the woman's Pulitzer Prize-winning-photographer lover (Serbedzija). In "Pictures," Aleksandar, the photographer, returns home to war-torn Macedonia where the suffering in "Words" and "Faces" takes on new meaning.

BEFORE SUNRISE

Director: Richard Linklater; **Writers:** Richard Linklater and Kim Krizan; **Director of Photography:** Lee Daniel; **Editor:** Sandra Adair; **Production Designer:** Florian Reichmann; **Producer:** Anne Walker-McBay
Castle Rock; R; 100 minutes
Release: 1/95
Cast: Ethan Hawke and Julie Delpy
A young American traveler (Hawke) and a French graduate student (Delpy) meet on the Eurail and form a conversationally intimate, 14-hour relationship in Vienna.

BELLE DE JOUR

Director: Luis Buñuel; **Writers:** Luis Buñuel and Jean Claude Carriere; **Director of Photography:** Sacha Vierny; **Editor:** Walter Spohr; **Art Director:** Robert Clavel; **Producers:** Robert and Raymond Hakim
Miramax; R;100 minutes
Release: 7/95
Cast: Catherine Deneuve, Jean Sorel, Michel Piccoli, Genevieve Page, Pierre Clementi, Francisco Rabal, Francois Fabian and Maria Latour
A rerelease of the 1967 film
In French with English subtitles
Elusive Severine (Deneuve) is outwardly passive and distant, even with her adoring husband (Serizy). Inwardly, she is beset by complex, intense sexual fantasies, which eventually draw her to afternoon prostitution in a brothel. A ruthless young gangster becomes obsessed with her and the resulting tragedy brings further fantasies. *Belle de Jour* is the most elegant of Buñuel's surreal masterpieces.

BILLY MADISON

Director: Tamra Davis; **Writers:** Tim Herlihy and Adam Sandler; **Director of Photograpy:** Victor Hamer; **Editor:** Jeffrey Wolf; **Music:** Randy Edelman; **Production Designer:** Perry Blake; **Producer:** Fitch Cady
Universal; PG-13; 99 minutes
Release: 2/95
Cast: Adam Sandler, Darren McGavin, Bridgette Wilson, Bradley Whitford, Josh Mostel, Norm MacDonald, Mark Beltzman, Larry Hankin and Theresa Merritt
Beer-drinking prankster Billy Madison (Sandler) stands to inherit his father's (McGavin) hotel empire, but there's a catch: he must pass all 12 school grades two weeks at a time or else the inheritance passes to his father's shady aide (Whitford).

BLESSING

Director/Writer: Paul Zehrer; **Director of Photography:** Stephen Kazmierski; **Editors:** Andrew Morreale and Paul Zehrer; **Music:** Joseph S. DeBeasi; **Production Designer:** Steve Rosenzweig; **Producers:** Melissa Powell and Paul Zehrer
Starr Valley Films; NR; 94 minutes
Release: 4/95
Cast: Melora Griffis, Carlin Glynn, Guy Griffis, Clovis

Siemon, Gareth Williams, Randy Sue Latimer, Tom Carey and Frank Taylor

Twenty-three-year-old Randi (Griffis) dreams of becoming a marine biologist and leaving the family dairy farm, where life is a grind and family relations are tense. Randi sees a glimmer of hope when milking machine maintenance man Lyle (Williams) drifts into town and tempts her to go west to see whales.

BORN TO BE WILD

Director: John Gray; **Writers:** John Bunzel and Paul Young; **Director of Photography:** Donald M. Morgan; **Editor:** Maryann Brandon; **Music:** Mark Snow; **Production Designer:** Roy Forge Smith; **Producers:** Robert Newmyer and Jeffrey Silver
Warner Bros.; PG; 98 minutes
Release: 4/95
Cast: Wil Horneff, Helen Shaver, John C. McGinley, Peter Boyle, Tom Wilson, Titus Welliver and Jean Marie Barnwell
Rick (Horneff), a troubled teen, establishes a friendship with Katie, a lab gorilla. When it's time for Katie to return to her no-good owner (Boyle), Rick flees with her to a hippie's home near the Canadian border, and they plot Katie's break for freedom.

THE BOYS OF ST. VINCENT

Director: John N. Smith; **Writers:** John N. Smith, Des Walsh and Sam Grana; **Director of Photography:** Pierre Letarte; **Editors:** Werner Nold and Andre Corriveau; **Music:** Neil Smolar; **Production Designer:** Real Ouellette; **Producers:** Sam Grona and Claudio Luca
NR; 210 minutes
Release: 12/94
Cast: Johnny Morina, Brian Dodd, Jonathan Lewis, Jeremy Keefe, Henry Czerny, Sebastian Spence, Phillip Dinn, Greg Thomey and Lise Roy
For 15 years, the church and police conceal the fact that a priest at a Newfoundland orphanage molested several young boys. The scandal isn't revealed until a handful of the victims have the courage to publicize the story.

BOYS ON THE SIDE

Director: Herbert Ross; **Writer:** Don Roos; **Director of Photography:** Donald E. Thorin; **Editor:** Michael R. Miller; **Music:** David Newman; **Production Designer:** Ken Adam; **Producers:** Arnon Milchan, Steven Reuther and Herbert Ross
Warner Bros.; R; 115 minutes
Release: 2/95
Cast: Whoopi Goldberg, Mary-Louise Parker, Drew Barrymore, Matthew McConaughey, Anita Gillette, James Remar, Amy Aquino, Dennis Boutsikaris and Estelle Parsons

IT'S A KIDS' MOVIE, STUPID

BY KIMBERLY CAVINESS

What Sucks and What Doesn't in Kids' Movies

Like father, like son. Hamilton "Mel" Morris, 8, likes his movies to be scary and funny. Like his dad,

Mel and Errol Morris

Errol Morris, the Cambridge, Massachusetts-based documentary maker who made the Oscar-winning *The Thin Blue Line* and *A Brief History of Time*, Mel can more readily list movies he hates than loves. Of all of his father's work, Mel's current favorite is "I Dismember Mama," the first episode of Fox's 1995 series, *Interrotron Stories With Errol Morris*. We accompanied Mel to *Batman Forever* to find out what's good and what sucks at the movies.

What Doesn't Suck

• *Batman Forever*, according to Mel, is great and the best of the trilogy. "It's not like really boring like other movies can be. And there are really many stupid parts." Stupid in this case is a good thing and high praise.

"It was really funny and it's about Batman and he kills bad guys," explains Mel. "It was better than the others because the others don't have the funny parts. Funny is important." The low part was definitely the mushy ending. "The kiss!" Mel scrunches up his face in stomach-churning protest. "No kids will like that. No, no, no, no, no, no!"

• *Dumb and Dumber*. "It's great because it's really stupid and because they do really weird things like go 3,000 miles out of their way to go to this place and do things that are unimaginably stupid."

Dumb and Dumber is a double-whammy hit with Mel because it stars his all-time favorite actor, Jim Carrey. "The other guy doesn't do that many things. Jim Carrey is weird and funnier." In fact, for our screening of *Batman Forever*, Mel soaked his head with Kool-Aid to dye his hair as red as Carrey's the Riddler, his favorite character. "The Riddler wasn't serious like everyone else. He wasn't trying to kill everyone else. He was just doing stupid things. He wanted to kill Batman but he didn't make any effort. Jim Carrey

CONTINUED ON NEXT PAGE ▶

Dumb and Dumber

is really really really really really stupid and funny."

That's it. End of Mel's movie picks for kids. Television-wise, this discriminating junior viewer recommends *The Simpsons* and *Beavis and Butt-Head*. "I like them because they're really stupid in a funny way. And disgusting."

What Sucks

Predictably, Mel's list of films kids hate is twice as long.

- He refuses on principle to see *Pocahontas*.
- He's not looking forward to *Free Willy 2*. "The first one was good, but I sort of got bored in the middle of the movie because you don't see any scary parts."
- "The worst film ever made is *Fantasia*. It's bad because there are no words and Disney made it. I don't like their animated movies. They're not near too violent. They have," he is aghast to report, "*ballerina alligators* dancing."
- Two thumbs down for *Barney Goes Camping*. "All Barney movies are bad. Barney is stupid, Barney is dumb and Barney is purple."

As far as *The Lion King*, last year's runaway top-grosser, it's neither love nor hate. "I liked that, sort of," Mel admits, even if it is Disney.

Your correspondent, Mel Morris

Three women, one a recently-dumped lesbian (Goldberg), one with AIDS (Parker) and another pregnant and fleeing an abusive relationship (Barrymore), bond while roadtripping across the country.

THE BRADY BUNCH MOVIE

Director: Betty Thomas; **Writers:** Laurice Blehwany, Rick Copp, Bonnie Turner and Terry Turner; **Director of Photography**: Mac Ahlberg; **Editor:** Peter Teschner; **Music:** Guy Moon; **Production Designer:** Steven Jordan; **Producers:** Sherwood Schwartz, Lloyd J. Schwartz and David Kirkpatrick
Paramount; PG-13; 95 minutes
Release: 2/95
Cast: Shelley Long, Gary Cole, Christopher Daniel Barnes, Christine Taylor, Paul Sutera, Jennifer Elise Cox, Jesse Lee, Olivia Hack, RuPaul, Michael McKean and Henriette Mantel

Based on the television characters created by Sherwood Schwartz

The cheesy, polyester-loving Bradys are back, living in their own 1970s microcosm surrounded by 1990s culture. They haven't changed a bit, but the times certainly have. The Brady kids don't seem to notice, or even care, that their style is completely different than their grunged-out peers.

BRAVEHEART

Director: Mel Gibson; **Writer:** Randall Wallace; **Director of Photography**: John Toll; **Editor:** Steven Rosenblum; **Music:** James Horner; **Production Designer:** Tom Sanders; **Producers:** Mel Gibson, Alan Ladd, Jr. and Bruce Davey
Paramount; R; 179 minutes
Release: 5/95
Cast: Mel Gibson, Sophie Marceau, Patrick McGoohan, Catherine McCormack and Brendan Gleeson
William Wallace (Gibson), a 13th-century proletarian, leads fellow Scots in a bloody battle for freedom from Britain's tyrannic rule. It is Wallace's stirring passion for Scottish autonomy that inspires his men to endure the violent struggle.

THE BRIDGES OF MADISON COUNTY

Director: Clint Eastwood; **Writer:** Richard LaGravenese; **Director of Photography**: Jack N. Green; **Editor:** Joel Cox; **Music:** Lennie Niehaus; **Production Designer:** Jeannine Oppewall; **Producers:** Clint Eastwood and Kathleen Kennedy
Warner Bros.; PG-13; 135 minutes
Release: 6/95
Cast: Clint Eastwood, Meryl Streep, Annie Corley, Victor Slezak and Jim Haynie

Based on the best-selling novel by Robert James Waller
Thankfully, Eastwood has managed to remove the purple prose from this celluloid version of Waller's best-selling book. *National Geographic* photographer Robert Kincaid (Eastwood) and middle-aged Italian housewife Francesca Johnson (Streep) fall madly in love and spend four amorous days together in Johnson's farmhouse while her husband and children are away at the Iowa State Fair.

THE BROTHERS McMULLEN

Director/Writer: Edward Burns; **Director of Photography:** Dick Fisher; **Editor:** Dick Fisher; **Music:** Seamus Egan; **Producers:** Edward Burns and Dick Fisher
Fox Searchlight Pictures; R; 97 minutes
Release: 8/95
Cast: Edward Burns, Mike McGlone, Jack Mulcahy, Connie Britton, Maxine Bahns, Elizabeth P. McKay and Jennifer Jostyn
The Brothers McMullen won the Grand Jury Prize at the 1995 Sundance Film Festival, placing Burns among a group of Sundance alums facing pressure from the industry to fulfill high expectations. In addition to writing, directing and producing, Burns also stars in the movie about three Long Island Irish-Catholic brothers who are involved in rocky relationships. Barry (Burns) and Patrick (McGlone) move in with their older brother Jack (Mulcahy) and his wife Molly (Britton). Jack has begun to look at other women, Barry and his girlfriend recently split and Leslie (Jostyn) has Patrick tied around her finger. The brothers, dogged by Catholic guilt, help each other work out their problems.

THE BROWNING VERSION

Director: Mike Figgis; **Writers:** Ronald Harwood and Terence Rattigan; **Director of Photography:** Jean Francois Robin; **Editor:** Herve Schneid; **Music:** Mark Isham; **Production Designer:** John Beard; **Producers:** Ridley Scott and Mimi Polk
Paramount; R; 97 minutes
Release: 10/94
Cast: Albert Finney, Greta Scacchi, Matthew Modine, Julian Sands, Ben Silverston and Michael Gambon
Based on the play by Terence Rattigan
A curmudgeonly classics teacher (Finney) comes to the conclusion that his life has been a failure. To add to his torment, his wife (Scacchi) is sleeping with one of his young colleagues (Modine).

BULLETPROOF HEART

Director: Mark Malone; **Writer:** Gordon Melbourne; **Director of Photography:** Tobias A. Schliessler; **Editor:** Robin Russell; **Music:** Graeme Coleman; **Production Designer:** Lynne Stopkewich; **Producers:** Robert Vince and William Vince
Keystone Pictures; R; 100 minutes
Release: 4/95

Cast: Anthony LaPaglia, Mimi Rogers, Matt Craven, Peter Boyle, Monika Schnarre and Joseph Maher
Based on the story by Mark Malone
Hitman Mick's (LaPaglia) latest assignment is to knock off the seductive Fiona (Rogers). Things get complicated when Mick falls for his prey, who doesn't think dying is such a bad idea.

BULLETS OVER BROADWAY

Director: Woody Allen; **Writers:** Woody Allen and Douglas McGrath; **Director of Photography:** Carlo DiPalma; **Editor:** Susan E. Morse; **Production Designer:** Santo Loquasto; **Producer:** Robert Greenhut
Miramax; PG; 85 minutes
Release: 10/94
Cast: John Cusack, Dianne Wiest, Mary-Louise Parker, Rob Reiner, Jennifer Tilly, Jim Broadbent and Chazz Palminteri

Intellectual, not-so-talented playwright David Shayne (Cusack) and hoodlum Cheech (Palminteri) collaborate to see Shayne's script through production on 1920s Broadway. Shayne's play is subjected to a grande dame leading lady (Wiest), surly backers and a talentless ingénue (Tilly).

BURNT BY THE SUN

Director: Nikita Mikhalkov; **Writers:** Nikita Mikhalkov and Roustam Ibraguimbekov; **Director of Photography:** Vilen Kaluta; **Editor:** Enzo Meniconi; **Music:** Edouard Artemiev; **Producers:** Nikita Mikhalkov and Michel Seydoux
Sony Pictures Classics; R; 134 minutes
Release: 4/95
Cast: Nikita Mikhalkov, Oleg Menchikov, Ingeborga Dapkounaite, Nadia Mikhalkov, Andre Oumansky, Viatcheslav Tikhonov, Svetlana Krioutchkova and Vladimir Llyine
In Russian with English subtitles
Set in 1936 Russia, the Kotov family, including war-hero Serguei Petrovitch (Nikita Mikhalkov), his young wife Maroussia (Dapkounaite) and their 6-year-old daughter (Nadia Mikhalkov), enjoy an idyllic Sunday in Russia's beautiful countryside. The tranquility will not last as Stalin begins his brutal rule.

BUSHWHACKED

Director: Greg Beeman; **Writers:** John Jordan, Danny Byers, Tommy Swerdlow and Michael Goldberg; **Director of Photography:** Theo Van de Sande; **Editor:** Ross Albert; **Music:** Bill Conti; **Production Designers:** Mark W. Mansbridge and Sandy Veneziano; **Producers:** Charles B. Wessler and Paul Schiff
Twentieth Century-Fox; PG-13; 90 minutes
Release: 8/95
Cast: Daniel Stern, Ari Greenberg and Janna Michaels
Based on the story by John Jordan and Danny Byers

A tough deliveryman (Stern) falsely accused of murder evades the F.B.I. by posing as a scout leader. He takes five boys and a girl on an adventure in the wilderness, and the perceptive scouts figure out their leader is not who he claims to be.

BYE BYE, LOVE
Director: Sam Weisman; **Writers:** Gary David Goldberg and Brad Hall; **Director of Photography:** Kenneth Zunder; **Editor:** Roger Bondell; **Music:** J. A. C. Redford; **Producers:** Gary David Goldberg, Brad Hall and Sam Weisman
Twentieth Century-Fox; PG-13; 107 minutes
Release: 3/95
Cast: Matthew Modine, Randy Quaid, Paul Reiser, Janeane Garofalo, Amy Brenneman, Eliza Dushku, Ed Flanders, Maria Pitillo, Ross Malinger, Johnny Whitworth, Rob Reiner and Mae Whitman
Three divorced dads (Modine, Quaid and Reiser) use humor and friendship to cope with the burden of single parenthood, ex-wives and failed plans.

CAMILLA
Director: Deepa Mehta; **Writer:** Paul Quarrington; **Director of Photography:** Guy Dufaux; **Editor:** Barry Farrell; **Music:** Daniel Lanois; **Production Designer:** Sandra Kybartas; **Producers:** Christina Jennings and Simon Relph
Miramax; PG-13; 90 minutes
Release: 12/94
Cast: Jessica Tandy, Bridget Fonda, Hume Cronyn and Graham Greene
A former concert violinist (Tandy) and a young aspiring musician (Fonda) set out on an adventurous journey to see a Canadian performance of a Brahms concerto.

CANDYMAN: FAREWELL TO THE FLESH
Director: Bill Condon; **Writers:** Rand Ravich and Mark Kruger; **Director of Photography:** Tobias Schliessler; **Editor:** Virginia Katz; **Music:** Philip Glass; **Production Designer:** Barry Robison; **Producers:** Sigurjon Sighvatsson and Gregg D. Fienberg
Gramercy; R; 94 minutes
Release: 3/95
Cast: Tony Todd, Kelly Rowan, Timothy Carhart, Veronica Cartwright, William O'Leary and Fay Hauser
Slasher Candyman (Todd), a tortured slave in a previous life and now a crusader for the repressed, reappears in New Orleans just in time for Mardi Gras and to haunt the aristocratic Tennant family.

CARMEN MIRANDA: BANANAS IS MY BUSINESS
Director/Narrator: Helena Solberg; **Director of Photography:** Tomasz Magierski; **Editors:** David Meyer and Amanda Zinoman; **Producers:** David Meyer and Helena Solberg

International Cinema Inc.; NR; 90 minutes
Release: 7/95
Interviews with: Aurora Miranda, Caribé da Rocha, Synval Silva, Estela Romero, Cesar Romero, Alice Faye and Rita Moreno
Reenactments with: Cynthia Adler, Erick Barreto and Leticia Monte
In English and Portuguese with English subtitles
This documentary examines actress Carmen Miranda's life in Hollywood and in Brazil. Fantasy sequences resurrect Miranda's days as a star, and interviews reveal that Hollywood and the government exploited her dizzy Latin image.

CASPER
Director: Brad Silberling; **Animation Director:** Eric Armstrong; **Writers:** Sherri Stoner and Deanna Oliver; **Director of Photography:** Dean Cundey; **Editor:** Michael Kahn; **Music:** James Horner; **Production Designer:** Leslie Dilley; **Producer:** Colin Wilson
Universal; PG; 95 minutes
Release: 5/95
Cast: Christina Ricci, Bill Pullman, Cathy Moriarty, Malachi Pearson and Amy Brenneman
Based on the character Casper the Friendly Ghost created by Joseph Oriolo in the story by Oriolo and Seymour Reit
Villainous mansion-owner Carrigan Crittenden (Moriarty) hires widower ghost therapist Dr.

Harvey (Pullman) to rid her haunted Whiplash mansion of its menacing visitors. Harvey and his lonely daughter Kat (Ricci) move in and Kat immediately befriends Casper (voice of Pearson).

CIRCLE OF FRIENDS
Director: Pat O'Connor; **Writer:** Andrew Davies; **Director of Photography:** Ken MacMillan; **Editor:** John Jympson; **Producers:** Frank Price, Arlene Sellers and Alex Winitsky
Savoy Pictures; PG-13; 112 minutes
Release: 3/95
Cast: Chris O'Donnell, Minnie Driver, Geraldine O'Rawe, Alan Cumming, Saffron Burrows, Aidan Gillen and Colin Firth
Based on the novel by Maeve Binchy
Three innocent colleens are determined to lose their small-town ways when they go off to university in Dublin. Benny (Driver), the plainest of the three, wins the heart of handsome jock Jack Foley (O'Donnell).

CITY UNPLUGGED
Director: Ilkka Jarvilaturi; **Writer:** Paul Kolsby; **Director of Photography:** Rein Kotov; **Editor:** Christopher Tellefsen; **Music:** Mader; **Producer:** Lasse Saarinen
Filmhaus; NR; 99 minutes
Release: 6/95

Cast: Peeter Oja, Ivo Uukkivi, Milena Gulbe, Monika Mager, Enn Klooren and Vaino Laes
In Estonian with English subtitles
A group of thieves attempts to steal newly independent Estonia's treasury ($970 million in gold) before it gets to the capital Tallinn. Their outrageous scheme involves buying up all the city's batteries and candles and pulling the plug on the power.

CLEAN, SHAVEN
Director/Writer/Producer: Lodge H. Kerrigan; **Director of Photography:** Teodoro Maniaci; **Editor:** Jay Rabinowitz; **Production Designer:** Tania Ferrier
Strand Releasing; NR; 80 minutes
Release: 4/95
Cast: Peter Greene, Molly Castelloe, Megan Owen, Robert Albert and Jennifer MacDonald
Peter Winter (Greene), a murderous schizophrenic, frantically searches for his daughter Nicole (MacDonald), whom he hasn't seen since he was institutionalized several years earlier. In unsettling scenes, Winter's schizophrenia causes him to gouge his own scalp with scissors and scrub his skin with steel wool.

CLERKS
Director/Writer: Kevin Smith; **Director of Photography:** David Klein; **Editors:** Scott Mosier and Kevin Smith; **Music:** Scott Angley; **Producers:** Scott Mosier and Kevin Smith
Miramax; R; 90 minutes
Release: 10/94
Cast: Brian O'Halloran and Jeff Anderson
Two New Jersey clerks, one in a convenience store (O'Halloran) the other in a video store (Anderson), philosophize about their going-nowhere lives and complain about their annoying customers in this day-in-the-life look at the service industry.

CLUELESS
Director/Writer: Amy Heckerling; **Director of Photography:** Bill Pope; **Editor:** Debra Chiate; **Music Supervision:** Karyn Rachtman with score by David Kitay; **Production Designer:** Mona May; **Producers:** Scott Rudin and Robert Lawrence
Paramount; PG-13; 113 minutes
Release: 7/95
Cast: Alicia Silverstone, Stacey Dash, Brittany Murphy, Paul Rudd, Dan Hedaya, Donald Faison and Elisa Donovan
The Aerosmith video regular has finally found her niche in movies. As Cher, Silverstone plays the perfect dumb-blond clotheshorse. Cher and her best friend Dionne (Dash), both named "after great singers who now do infomercials" bring their cellular phones to school so they don't miss a beat, deal with their boyfriends and take on a protégée (Murphy) who wasn't blessed at birth with their looks and locks.

OVERLOOKED MOVIES

These are the movies (with directors) released between October 1994 and August 1995 that we think deserved more attention or wider audiences than they received. If you missed them in the theater, give them a chance on video.

The Boys of St. Vincent, John N. Smith
The Browning Version, Mike Figgis
Clerks, Kevin Smith
Cobb, Ron Shelton
Federal Hill, Michael Corrente
Heavenly Creatures, Peter Jackson
The Indian in the Cupboard, Frank Oz
Ladybird, Ladybird, Ken Loach
Mrs. Parker and the Vicious Circle, Alan Rudolph
Vanya on 42nd Street, Louis Malle

MOVIES THAT SHOULD ONLY BE SEEN ON VIDEO

Some movies actually improve when reduced to the small screen ... not many, but there are some whose intimate scale (or silliness) feel more appropriate to TV.

Koyaanisqatsi
We know it's on the next page, too, but some people feel the only way to see this is with a big, fat blunt in hand. That's frowned upon in the theater.

Natural Born Killers
The cutting, the nervousness, the lurid color is all swiped from tabloid TV and it all seems even more subversive seen on the same screen as *Hard Copy*.

My Dinner With Andre
We always want this kind of repartee to enliven our dinner parties, and with the video version — even if it's just you and the pizza box — it can.

The Flintstones
It just wouldn't be the same sitting in a small seat in a crowded theater when you grew up enjoying Bedrock's finest lounging on a couch in your own livingroom.

MOVIES THAT SHOULD NEVER BE SEEN ON VIDEO

While the dawning of the home video brought with it a treasure-trove for the movie fan, it also reduced some magnificent works to mere shadows of themselves. If we had our way, our selection of such titles should be issued with a caution label: Repeated viewings may cause loss in sense of wonder.

Lawrence of Arabia
The essential wide-screen epic. Even letterbox makes all that sand look like a beach party movie.

Rebel Without a Cause
Director Nicholas Ray was a master of composition for the wide screen. Television reduces the tragedy to melodrama.

Once Upon a Time in the West
First there are the vast expanses of the Old West, but you also need the scale of those extreme close-ups of Henry Fonda's soulless eyes to know just how evil a character he truly is.

Blade Runner
Part of the appeal is losing yourself in the din and confusion of one of the most carefully realized visions of the future ever put on film. At home it's too easy to jump up and grab a beer.

2001
See *Blade Runner* (above), and the soundtrack needs to echo in the cavernous dark to convey the utter solitude of space.

Sunrise
Murnau's silent masterwork depicts turbulent emotions that read as bathos on a small screen. Also, the tipsy world of the big city is a thing of beauty and wonder whose detail can only be appreciated in large scale.

Napoleon
How on earth do you contain Abel Gance's silent triptych on a 19" screen?

Hidden Fortress
Want to see where George Lucas got the inspiration for *Star Wars?* The neglected Kurosawa epic features prison riots, swashbuckling escapes and two (non-robotic) comic rogues. When not seen on a theater's wide screen, the story seems like a comic . . . like *Star Wars*.

COBB
Director/Writer: Ron Shelton; **Director of Photography:** Russell Boyd; **Editors:** Paul Seydor and Kimberly Ray; **Music:** Elliot Goldenthal; **Production Designer:** Armin Ganz; **Producer:** David Lester
Warner Bros.; R; 130 minutes
Release: 1/95
Cast: Tommy Lee Jones, Robert Wuhl and Lolita Davidovich
Based on the biography by Al Stump
Shelton's biopic of the abusive Ty Cobb (Jones) depicts the baseball legend as an unparalleled performer and a racist in both his career and personal life.

COLONEL CHABERT
Director: Yves Angelo; **Writers:** Yves Angelo and Jean Cosmos; **Director of Photography:** Bernard Lutic; **Editor:** Thierry Derocles; **Production Designer:** Patrick Bordier; **Producer:** Jean-Louis Livi
October Films; NR; 110 minutes
Release: 12/94
Cast: Gérard Depardieu, Fanny Ardant, Fabrice Luchini, André Dussollier, Daniel Prevost, Olivier Saladin, Maxime Leroux and Eric Elmosnino
Based on the novel by Honoré De Balzac
In French with English subtitles
Colonel Chabert (Depardieu), believed to have been killed in the Napoleonic War, returns home after a 10-year absence to find his wife has remarried and taken his fortune.

CONGO
Director: Frank Marshall; **Writer:** John Patrick Shanley; **Director of Photography:** Allen Daviau; **Editor:** Anne V. Coates; **Music:** Jerry Goldsmith; **Production Designer:** J. Michael Riva; **Producers:** Kathleen Kennedy and Sam Mercer
Paramount; PG-13; 109 minutes
Release: 6/95
Cast: Dylan Walsh, Laura Linney, Ernie Hudson, Joe Don Baker, Tim Curry and Taylor Nichols
Based on the novel by Michael Crichton

A professor (Walsh) travels to the Congo to return his beloved Amy, a talking gorilla, to her natural environment. Dr. Karen Ross (Linney) and explorer Herkemer Homolka (Curry), who are pursuing treasures in King Solomon's mines, join the pair, and the group depends upon Amy's knowledge of the jungle.

COUNTRY LIFE

Director/Writer: Michael Blakemore; **Director of Photography:** Stephen Windon; **Editor:** Nicholas Beaumann; **Music:** Peter Best; **Production Designer:** Laurence Eastwood; **Producer:** Robin Dalton
Miramax; PG-13; 107 minutes
Release: 7/95
Cast: Sam Neill, Greta Scacchi, John Hargreaves; Kerry Fox, Michael Blakemore and Googie Withers
Suggested by Anton Chekov's play *Uncle Vanya*
This adaptation of Chekov's play is set in the Australian outback just after World War I with Uncle Jack (Hargreaves) and Sally (Fox) tending the family estate while Sally's father Alex (Blakemore) establishes himself as a London drama critic. Jack loves Alex's wife Deborah (Scacchi), but carries on at the estate on Alex's behalf.

THE COW

Director: Karyl Kachyna; **Writers:** Karyl Kachyna and Karel Cabradek; **Director of Photography:** Petr Hojda; **Editor:** Jan Svoboda; **Music:** Petr Hojda; **Producer:** Karel Skop
Czech Television; NR; 94 minutes
Release: 2/95
Based on the novel by Jan Prochazka
In Czech with English subtitles
Cast: Radek Holub and Alena Mikulova
Slightly retarded Adam (Holub), his wife Roza (Milulova) and their rustic neighbors dream of a better future as they live on a mountainside in eastern Europe.

CRACKING UP

Director/Editor/Producer: Matt Mitler; **Writers:** Matt Mitler and Theodore P. Lorusso; **Director of Photography:** Mark Traver; **Music:** Arthur Rosen;
Foolish Mortal Films, Inc.; NR; 90 minutes
Release: 3/95
Cast: Matt Mitler, Carolyn McDermott, Sherry Anderson, John Augustine, Kevin Brown, Kimberly Flynn, Debra Wilson, Jason Brill, Jeff Eyres, David Wells, Todd Alcott, Gail Dennison, The Poster Boys and Chuck Montgomery
Danny Gold (Mitler), a selfish, crackhead comedian, is maniacally driven to become a star. He's got the looks and the talent to succeed, but his vices have a strong hold on his life.

CRIMSON TIDE

Director: Tony Scott; **Writer:** Michael Schiffer; **Director of Photography:** Dariusz Wolski; **Editor:** Chris Lebenzon; **Music:** Hans Zimmer; **Producers:** Don Simpson and Jerry Bruckheimer
Buena Vista; R; 113 minutes
Release: 5/95
Cast: Denzel Washington, Gene Hackman, Matt Craven, George Dzundza, Viggo Mortensen, James Gandolfini, Lillo Brancato, Jr. and Rocky Carroll
Based on the story by Michael Schiffer and Richard P. Henrick

Koyaanisqatsi
Philip Glass's score for this trance-inducing epic sounds like a wheezy calliope played on an AM radio unless you've got a home theater set-up.

McCabe and Mrs. Miller
Director of photography Vilmos Zsigmond preflashed all the film stock for this Altman ode to the frontier. The colors and gradations are therefore subtle and beyond the reach of TV resolution.

Days of Heaven
Nestor Almendros photographing in low light and painting a living landscape of the prairies is simply too beautiful for TV.

L'Avventura
Too often dismissed as an exercise in aesthetic alienation, Antonioni's masterwork can't be conveyed on the confined canvas of a cathode-ray tube any more than a de Chirico could be experienced from a postage-size fine art reproduction.

Priscilla, Queen of the Desert
The sights and sounds of this road trip through glamour are too big for television. Big is better when it comes to 1994's most frivolous and fun film.

The Rocky Horror Picture Show
Seeing this camp classic without an audience of transvestites and ghouls robs it of any entertainment value whatsoever.

Apocalypse Now
The thundering movement of men and machines in Coppola's journey to the heart of darkness looks like the dance of the tin soldiers in the letterbox version.

The Sound of Music
There's something about large-scale musicals from *Top Hat,* to *Guys and Dolls,* to *South Pacific* to *The Sound of Music* that gets lost in the translation to the small screen — and it's not just the sound reproduction from that 2" speaker. Perhaps the movement on-screen, the dancing and blossoming of emotion shrinks from majestic to much ado about very little people.

MOVIES BEST SEEN AS CD-ROM GAMES

Johnny Mnemonic
Mortal Kombat

A right-wing Russian nationalist leader has seized control of a nuclear base and is threatening to bomb the United States. The United States responds by sending a fleet of submarines command-  ed by Lt. Commander Ron Hunter (Washington) and Capt. Frank Ramsey (Hackman) to defend the world against nuclear attack.

CROSS MY HEART AND HOPE TO DIE (TI KNIVER I KJERTET)

Director: Marius Holst; **Writers:** Lars Saabye Christensen and Marius Holst; **Director of Photography:** Philip Ogaard; **Editor:** Hakon Overas; **Music:** Kjetil Bjerkestrand and Magne Furuholmen; **Production Designers:** Tomas Backstrom, Anne Frilseth and Erik Gustavson; **Producer:** Petter J. Borgli
Nordic Screen Development Schibsted Film, Norsk Filmjetil Bjerkestrand; NR; 96 minutes
Release: 4/95
Cast: Martin Dahl Garfalk, Jan "Devo" Kornstad, Kjersti Holmen, Reidar Sorensen, Bjorn Sundqvist, Bjorn Floberg and Gisken Armand
In Norwegian with English subtitles
Schoolboy Otto (Garfalk), too small and shy to fit in anywhere, is taken with a mysterious stranger Frank (Kornstad), who draws him into a web of stolen cars, dead girls and ominous predictions.

CRUDE OASIS

Director/Writer/Producer/Editor: Alex Graves; **Director of Photography:** Steven Quale; **Music:** Steven Bramson; **Production Designer:** Tom Mittlestadt
Miramax; R; 80 minutes
Release: 7/95
Cast: Jennifer Taylor, Robert Peterson and Aaron Shields
Karen Webb (Taylor), involved in an unhappy, childless marriage, frequently dreams about a young man standing knee-deep in a river. Her mundane life changes dramatically when she spots the man (Shields), and becomes obsessed with learning more about him.

CRUMB

Director: Terry Zwigoff; **Director of Photography:** Maryse Alberti; **Editor:** Victor Livingston; **Producers:** Lynn O'Donnell and Terry Zwigoff
Sony Pictures Classics; R; 120 minutes
Release: 4/95
This documentary of underground cartoonist Robert Crumb reveals that his family is more twist-ed than even his day-in-the-life, sometimes erotic, sometimes racist cartoons that slam both the world and himself. Crumb's brother, Charles, rarely leaves his mother's dimly lit house and his other brother Max sits on a bed of nails and eats string.

THE CURE

Director: Peter Horton; **Writer:** Robert Kuhn; **Director of Photography:** Andrew Dintenfass; **Editor:** Anthony Sherin; **Music:** Dave Grusin; **Production Designer:** Armin Ganz; **Producers:** Mark Burg and Eric Eisner
Universal; PG-13; 95 minutes
Release: 4/95
Cast: Joseph Mazzello, Brad Renfro, Annabella Sciorra, Diana Scarwid, Bruce Davison and Nicky Katt
Two lonely outcasts Eric (Renfro) and Dexter (Mazzello) search for an AIDS cure to save Dexter's life. Their desperation prompts them to try any-thing, including eating microwaved Butterfingers and embarking on a Huck Finn-like journey down the Mississippi.

DANGEROUS MINDS

Director: John N. Smith; **Writer:** Ronald Bass; **Director of Photography:** Pierre LeTarte; **Editor:** Tom Rolf; **Music:** Wendy and Lisa; **Production Designer:** Donald Graham Burt; **Producers:** Donald Graham Burt and Jerry Bruckheimer
Buena Vista; R; 94 minutes
Release: 8/95
Cast: Michelle Pfeiffer, George Dzundza, Renoly Santiago, Bruklin Harris, Wade Dominguez and Courtney B. Vance
Based on the book *My Posse Don't Do Homework* by LouAnne Johnson
Johnson, a former Marine, wrote a memoir about her experience as a high school teacher in a New York innercity classroom. Pfeiffer doesn't look like a Marine, but she does pull off the teacher thing when she shows up for the first day of school wearing barrettes and a lace collar. She takes her job seriously and gets involved in her students' lives and tries to help them make some-thing of their less-than-hopeful lives.

DARKER SIDE OF BLACK

Director/Writer: Isaac Julien; **Directors of Photography:** Arthur Jaffa and David Scott; **Editor:** Joy Chamberlain; **Music:** Trevor Mathison; **Producer:** David Lawson
Normal Films; NR; 55 minutes
Release: 1/95
Cast: Ice Cube, Buju Banton, Chuck D., Shabba Ranks and Cornell West
This documentary explores Jamaican dancehall music, focusing on lyrics that advocate violence against homosexuals and women.

DEATH AND THE MAIDEN

Director: Roman Polanski; **Writers:** Rafael Yglesias and Ariel Dorfman; **Director of Photography:** Tonino Delli Colli; **Editor:** Herve de Luze; **Music:** Wojciech Kilár; **Production Designer:** Pierre Guffroy; **Producers:** Thom Mount and Josh Kramer
Fine Line; R; 103 minutes
Release: 12/94
Cast: Sigourney Weaver, Ben Kingsley and Stuart Wilson
Based on the play by Ariel Dorfman

Convinced her husband (Wilson) has brought home the man (Kingsley) who raped and tortured her 15 years earlier while she was a political prisoner, Pauline Escobar (Weaver) exacts her revenge.

DESTINY TURNS ON THE RADIO

Director: Jack Baran; **Writers:** Robert Ramsay and Matthew Stone; **Director of Photography:** James Carter; **Editor:** Raul Davalos; **Music:** Steve Soles; **Production Designer:** Jean-Phillippe Carp; **Producer:** Gloria Zimmerman
Savoy Pictures; R; 102 minutes
Release: 4/95
Cast: James LeGros, Dylan McDermott, Quentin Tarantino, Bobcat Goldthwait, Allen Garfield, Nancy Travis and James Belushi
Escaped felon Julian Goddard (McDermott), suffering from the heat of the Nevada desert, gladly accepts a ride from mysterious hipster Johnny Destiny (Tarantino). Goddard gets off at the Marilyn Monroe motel, owned by his former partner-in-crime Harry Thoreau (LeGros), who made off with the cash in the bank robbery that landed Goddard in jail. Goddard faces an uphill battle in trying to retrieve his share of the cash and his former girlfriend Lucille (Travis).

DIE HARD WITH A VENGEANCE

Director: John McTiernan; **Writer:** Jonathan Hensleigh; **Director of Photography:** Peter Menzies; **Editor:** John Wright; **Music:** Michael Kamen; **Producers:** John McTiernan and Michael Tadross
Twentieth Century-Fox; R; 112 minutes
Release: 5/95
Cast: Bruce Willis, Samuel L. Jackson and Jeremy Irons
Based on the original characters by Roderick Thorp
Down-and-dirty New York City cop John McLane (Willis) returns in the third *Die Hard* movie. In this

installment, a sick German terrorist (Irons) has planted chemical bombs throughout Manhattan and demands that smart-aleck McLane solve his riddles and puzzles else he detonate the bombs, one of which is ticking away in a school building.

DISCLOSURE

Director: Barry Levinson; **Writer:** Paul Attanasio; **Director of Photography:** Anthony Pierce-Roberts; **Editor:** Stu Linder; **Music:** Ennio Morricone; **Production Designer:** Neil Spisak; **Producers:** Barry Levinson and Michael Crichton
Warner Bros.; R; 128 minutes

Release: 12/94
Cast: Demi Moore, Michael Douglas, Donald Sutherland, Caroline Goodall, Dennis Miller, Roma Maffia, Dylan Baker and Nicholas Sadler
Based on the novel by Michael Crichton
An executive at a computer company is on the receiving end of unwanted sexual advances from his new boss, who is also an old girlfriend. He risks his career to prove that he is the victim of sexual harassment, not the aggressor.

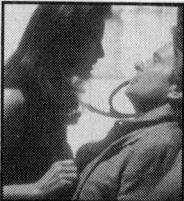

DOLORES CLAIBORNE

Director: Taylor Hackford; **Writer:** Tony Gilroy; **Director of Photography:** Gabriel Beristain; **Editor:** Mark Warner; **Music:** Danny Elfman; **Production Designer:** Bruno Rubeo; **Producers:** Taylor Hackford and Charles Mulvehill
Castle Rock; R; 131 minutes
Release: 3/95
Cast: Kathy Bates, Jennifer Jason Leigh, Judy Parfitt, Christopher Plummer, David Strathairn and Eric Bogoisan
Based on the book by Stephen King
Dolores Claiborne (Bates), a Maine housekeeper who has faced challenges and hardship all her life, is suspected of killing her boss, a wealthy elderly invalid. While the police investigate the crime and question Claiborne, she relives the details of the murder of her abusive husband and is reacquainted with her New York journalist daughter (Leigh), who has been avoiding her mother since Claiborne was accused of the murder.

DON JUAN DEMARCO

Director/Writer: Jeremy Leven; **Director of Photography:** Ralf Bode; **Editor:** Tony Gibbs; **Music:** Michael Kamen; **Production Designer:** Sharon Seymour; **Producers:** Francis Ford Coppola, Fred Fuchs and Patrick Palmer
New Line; PG-13; 97 minutes
Release: 4/95
Cast: Johnnny Depp, Marlon Brando, Faye Dunaway and Geraldine Pailhas
An institutionalized young man (Depp) with an extremely vivid imagination thinks he is the famous 17th-century lover Don Juan. Psychotherapist Jack Mickler (Brando) treats the delusional man but finds that Don Juan's charm and imagination enrich his life more than he helps his patient.

DOUBLE DRAGON

Director: James Yukich; **Writers:** Michael Davis, Peter Gould, Paul Dini and Neal Shusterman; **Director of Photography:** Gary B. Kibbe; **Editor:** Florent Retz; **Music:** Jay Ferguson; **Production Designer:** Mayne Berke; **Producers:** Ash R. Shah,

Sunil R. Shah, Alan Schecter, Jane Hamsher and Don Murphy
Gramercy; PG-13; 93 minutes
Release: 11/94
Cast: Robert Patrick, Mark Dacascos and Scott Wolf
Based on the video game *Double Dragon*.
Two brothers (Dacascos and Wolf) must protect a mega-city in southern California from the power-hungry Koga Shuko (Patrick) by keeping from him the second half of the double-dragon medallion, which is necessary to control the city.

DOUBLE HAPPINESS

Director/Writer: Mina Shum; **Director of Photography:** Peter Wunstorf; **Editor:** Alison Grace; **Music:** Shadowy Men on a Shadowy Planet; **Production Designer:** Michael Bjornson; **Producers:** Steve Hegyes and Rose Lam Waddell
Fine Line; PG-13; 87 minutes
Release: 8/95
Cast: Sandra Oh, Alannah Ong, Stephen Chang, Johnny Mah, Frances You, Callum Rennie and Claudette Carracedo
In English and Cantonese with English subtitles
Jade Li (Oh), a Chinese-Canadian woman, dreams of being an actress, but has a hard time finding work because casting directors want her to play a stereotypical Asian when she would prefer to play a Westerner. Her traditional parents think a successful future entails marrying the right man and pressure her into dating the men they choose.

D.R.O.P. SQUAD

Director: David Johnson; **Writers:** David Johnson, Butch Robinson and David Taylor; **Director of Photography:** Ken Kelsch; **Editor:** Kevin Lee; **Music:** Mike Bearden; **Production Designer:** Ina Mayhew; **Producers:** Butch Robinson, Shelby Stone and David Johnson
Gramercy; R; 86 minutes
Release: 10/94
Cast: Eriq La Salle, Vondie Curtis-Hall, Ving Rhames, Leonard Thomas, Michael Ralph, Billy Williams, Eric A. Payne, Crystal Fox and Vanessa Williams
A group of black revolutionaries kidnap and counsel other African Americans to stimulate race consciousness in the community.

DROP ZONE

Director: John Badham; **Writers:** Peter Barsocchini and John Bishop; **Director of Photography:** Roy H. Wagner; **Editor:** Frank Morriss; **Music:** Hans Zimmer; **Production Designer:** Joe Alves; **Producers:** D. J. Caruso, Wallis Nicita and Lauren Lloyd
Paramount; R; 102 minutes
Release: 12/94
Cast: Wesley Snipes, Gary Busey, Yancy Butler, Michael Jeter, Corin Nemec and Kyle Secor
Based on a story by Tony Griffin, Guy Manos and Peter Barsocchini
A U.S. marshal (Snipes) goes undercover as a stunt sky-diver to apprehend a group of airborne kidnappers.

DUMB AND DUMBER

Director: Peter Farrelly; **Writers:** Peter Farrelly, Bennett Yellin and Bobby Farrelly; **Director of Photography:** Mark Irwin; **Editor:** Christopher Greenbury; **Music:** Todd Rundgren; **Production Designer:** Sidney J. Bartholomew, Jr.; **Producers:** Charles B. Wessler, Brad Krevoy and Steve Stabler
New Line; PG-13; 106 minutes
Release: 12/94
Cast: Jim Carrey, Jeff Daniels, Lauren Holley and Teri Garr

Lloyd (Carrey) and Harry (Daniels) drive across the country to return a suitcase full of cash, which unbeknownst to them is lost ransom money.

ED WOOD

Director: Tim Burton; **Writers:** Scott Alexander, Larry Karaszewski and Ruldolph Grey; **Director of Photography:** Stefan Czapsky; **Editor:** Chris Lebenzon; **Music:** Howard Shore; **Production Designer:** Tom Duffield; **Producers:** Tim Burton and Denise DiNovi
Touchstone Pictures; R; 120 minutes
Release: 10/94
Cast: Johnny Depp, Martin Landau, Sarah Jessica Parker and Patricia Arquette
Edward D. Wood, Jr., often called the worst filmmaker in Hollywood history, was also a war hero and a cross-dresser. Burton's biopic of Wood (Depp) re-creates the making of some of Wood's films and highlights his friendship with down-and-out actor Bela Lugosi (Landau).

THE ENGLISHMAN WHO WENT UP A HILL BUT CAME DOWN A MOUNTAIN

Director/Writer: Christopher Monger; **Director of Photography:** Vernon Layton; **Editor:** David Martin; **Music:** Stephen Endelman; **Production Designer:** Charles Garrad; **Producer:** Sarah Curtis
Miramax; PG; 99 minutes
Release: 5/95
Cast: Hugh Grant, Tara FitzGerald, Colm Meaney and Ian McNeice
The residents of Wales's Ffynnon Garw take pride in their town's mountain, and go to great lengths to prevent two English cartographers (Grant and Garrad) from reducing it to hill status. Innkeeper Morgan the Goat (Meaney) masterminds the hill-enhancement effort.

EROTIQUE

Let's Talk About Sex
Director: Lizzie Borden; **Writers:** Lizzie Borden and Susie Bright; **Director of Photography:** Larry Banks; **Editor:** Richard Fields; **Music:** Andrew Belling; **Production Designer:** Jane Ann Stewart; **Producers:** Christopher Wood and Vicky Herman
Based on a story by Lizzie Borden
Cast: Wade Dominguez and Dianna Miranda

Taboo Parlor
Director/Writer: Monika Treut; **Director of Photography:** Elfi Mikesch; **Editor:** Steve Brown; **Production Designer:** Petra Korink; **Producers:** Monika Treut and Michael Sombetzki
Cast: Priscilla Barnes and Camilla Soeberg

Wonton Soup
Director: Clara Law; **Writer:** Eddie Ling-Ching Fong; **Director of Photography:** Arthur Wong; **Editor:** Jill Bilcock; **Music:** Tats Lau; **Production Designer:** Eddie Mok; **Producers:** Teddy Robin and Ling-Ching Fong
Cast: Tim Lounibos and Hayley Man
Released as one film by Odyssey Group; NR; 91 minutes
Release: 5/95
These three erotic short films each dispel the myth that only men fantasize about sex. *Let's Talk About Sex* features a woman (Miranda) who works on a telephone sex line and creates a fantasy for herself and a regular caller (Dominguez). In *Taboo Parlor* two European lesbians (Barnes and Soeberg) pick up a man and fatally punish him because of his gender. The final segment, *Wonton Soup*, occurs in Hong Kong where Adrian (Lounibos) does not feel he is Chinese enough for his girlfriend (Man). To remedy the situation, he takes a course in authentic Chinese cooking and buys a book on sexual positions.

EXIT TO EDEN

Director: Garry Marshall; **Writers:** Deborah Amelon and Bob Brunner; **Director of Photography:** Theo Van de Sande; **Editor:** David Finfer; **Music:** Patrice Doyle; **Production Designer:** Peter Jamison; **Producers:** Alexandra Rose and Garry Marshall
Savoy Pictures; R; 113 minutes
Release: 10/94
Cast: Dan Aykroyd, Dana Delany, Rosie O'Donnell and Paul Mercurio
Based on the novel by Anne Rice
Two LA cops (Aykroyd and O'Donnell) go undercover at an S&M island resort to break up an international diamond-smuggling operation.

EXOTICA

Director/Writer: Atom Egoyan; **Director of Photography:** Paul Sarossy; **Editor:** Susan Shipton; **Music:** Mychael Danna; **Producers:** Atom Egoyan and Camelia Frieberg
Miramax; R; 103 minutes
Release: 3/95
Cast: Mia Kirshner, Don McKellar, Elias Koteas, Arsinee Khanjian and Bruce Greenwood

Though mostly set in a Canadian strip joint, the film centers on relationships and secrecy. Christina (Kirshner), a stripper, is involved with club owner D.J. Eric (Koteas), but she also has a spiritual relationship with regular Francis (Greenwood). Adding comic relief to the eerie film is gay pet-shop owner Thomas (McKellar) who runs an illegal, exotic bird smuggling operation, which has piqued auditor Francis's curiousity.

FAR FROM HOME: THE ADVENTURES OF YELLOW DOG

Director/Writer: Phillip Borsos; **Director of Photography:** James Gardner; **Editor:** Sidney Wolinsky; **Music:** John Scott; **Production Designer:** Mark S. Freeborn; **Producer:** Peter O'Brian
Twentieth Century-Fox; PG; 81 minutes
Release: 1/95
Cast: Mimi Rogers, Bruce Davison, Jesse Bradford and Tom Bower
For three weeks, a boy (Bradford) and his dog Dakotah struggle for survival in the Canadian wilderness after being thrown overboard on a boat trip.

FARINELLI

Director: Gérard Corbiau; **Writers:** Gérard Corbiau, Andrée Corbiau and Marcel Beaulieu; **Director of Photography:** Walther Vanden Ende; **Editor:** Joelle Hache; **Music:** Christopher Rousset; **Production Designer:** Jon Hutman; **Producers:** Vera Belmont, Linda Gutenberg, Aldo Lado, Dominique Janne and Stéphane Thenoz
Sony Pictures Classics; R; 110 minutes
Release: 3/95
Cast: Stéfano Dionisi, Enrico Lo Verso, Elsa Zylberstein, Jeroen Krabbe and the voices of Derek Lee Ragin and Ewa Mallas Godlewska
In French and Italian with English subtitles
Admirers swooned and wept when they heard Carlo "Farinelli" Broschi (Dionisi), a renowned 18th-century castrato, perform. He especially affected women who were sexually attracted to him. His manipulative brother Riccardo (Broschi), who composed Farinelli's music, lent a hand in the bedroom with Farinelli's assignations.

FASTER, PUSSYCAT! KILL! KILL!

Director/Editor: Russ Meyer; **Writers:** Russ Meyer and Jack Moran; **Director of Photography:** Walter Schenk; **Music:** Igo Kantor; **Producers:** Russ and Eve Meyer
Strand Releasing; NR; 83 minutes
Release: 1/95
Cast: Tura Satana, Haji, Lori Williams, Susan Bernard, Stuart Lancaster, Paul Trinka, Dennis Busch, Ray Barlow and Mickey Foxx
A rerelease of the 1965 film

Ace Ventura: When Nature Calls, **director:** Steve Oedekerk; **cast:** Jim Carrey, Ian McNeice, Simon Callow, Maynard Eziashi and Bob Gunton (Warner Bros.)

American Buffalo, **director:** Michael Corrente; **cast:** Dustin Hoffman, Dennis Franz and Sean Nelson (Samuel Goldwyn)

The American President, **director:** Rob Reiner; **cast:** Michael Douglas, Annette Bening, Martin Sheen, Michael J. Fox and Richard Dreyfuss (Columbia Pictures)

Angus, **director:** Patrick Read Johnson; **cast:** Kathy Bates, George C. Scott, Charles M. Talbott and Ariana Richards (New Line Cinema)

Assassins, **director:** Richard Donner; **cast:** Sylvester Stallone, Antonio Banderas and Julianne Moore (Warner Bros.)

Before and After, **director:** Barbet Schroeder; **cast:** Meryl Streep, Liam Neeson, Eddie Furlong, Julia Weldon and Alfred Molina (Hollywood Pictures/Caravan Pictures)

Big Green, **director:** Holly Godberg Sloan; **cast:** Olivia D'Abo, Steve Guttenberg, Jay Snaders, Bug Hall and Patrick Renna (Walt Disney Pictures)

Blue in the Face, **directors:** Wayne Wang and Paul Auster; **cast:** Michael J. Fox, Jim Jarmusch, Harvey Keitel, Madonna, Lou Reed, Roseanne and Lily Tomlin (Miramax)

Bogus, **director:** Norman Jewison; **cast:** Whoopi Goldberg, Gérard Depardieu, Haley Joel Osment and Nancy Travis

Bottle Rocket, **director:** Wes Anderson; **cast:** Andrew Wilson, Owen Wilson, Luke Wilson, Bob Musgrave and Lumi Cavazos (Columbia Pictures)

Broken Arrow, **director:** John Woo; **cast:** John Travolta, Christian Slater, Samantha Mathis, Howie Long and Delroy Lindo (Twentieth Century-Fox)

Canadian Bacon, **director:** Michael Moore; **cast:** Alan Alda, John Candy, Rhea Perlman, Kevin Pollak and Rip Torn (Gramercy Pictures)

Carrington, **director:** Christopher Hampton; **cast:** Emma Thompson and Jonathon Pryce (Gramercy Pictures)

Three well-endowed strippers speeding along the desert use their impressive strength to victimize their male oppressors. *Faster, Pussycat! Kill! Kill!* is probably the most well-known, and most kinetic, of Meyer's trash masterpieces.

FEDERAL HILL
Director/Writer/Producer: Michael Corrente; **Director of Photography:** Richard Crudo; **Editor:** Kate Sanford; **Music:** Bob Held and David Bravo; **Production Designer:** Robert Schleinig; **Producers:** Michael Corrente, Libby Corrente and Richard Crudo
Trimark; R; 97 minutes
Release: 12/94
Cast: Nicholas Turturro, Anthony De Sando, Libby Langdon, Michael Raynor, Jason Andrews, and Robert Turano
The friendship between two Italian Amercians (Turturro and De Sando) from Providence, Rhode Island, falls apart when one of the men falls in love with a blue-blooded Brown University student (Langdon).

FIRST KNIGHT
Director: Jerry Zucker; **Writer:** William Nicholson; **Director of Photography:** Adam Greenberg; **Editor:** Walter Murch; **Music:** Jerry Goldsmith; **Production Designer:** John Box; **Producers:** Jerry Zucker and Hunt Lowry
Columbia; PG-13; 131 minutes
Release: 7/95
Cast: Sean Connery, Richard Gere, Julia Ormond, Ben Cross and John Gielud
Based on a story by Lorne Cameron, David Hoselton and William Nicholson
This retelling of the King Arthur legend may be weak on plot, though certainly not on beautiful people. King Arthur (Connery) needs a wife, and Guinevere of Leonesse (Ormond) is the perfect candidate. En route to her wedding, Guinevere and her party are attacked by warlord Malagant's troops. Sir Lancelot (Gere) saves the day and falls for Guinevere, who must choose between the hero Lancelot and the king.

FLUKE
Director: Carlo Carlei; **Writers:** Carlo Carlei and James Carrington; **Director of Photography:** Raffaele Mertes; **Editor:** Mark Conte; **Music:** Carlo Siliotto; **Production Designer:** Hilda Stark; **Producers:** Paul Maslansky and Lata Ryan
MGM; PG; 95 minutes
Release: 6/95
Cast: Matthew Modine, Nancy Travis, Samuel L. Jackson, Eric Stoltz and Max Pomeranc
Based on the novel by James Herbert
Fluke escapes from the dog pound and begins to remember his previous life as businessman Tom Johnson (Modine), who was killed in a car accident. The intuitive canine begins to suspect the crash may not have been an accident and Johnson's partner Jeff (Stoltz) may have

intentionally run him off the road. Fluke searches for Johnson's family to protect them from the sinister Jeff.

FORGET PARIS

Director: Billy Crystal; **Writers:** Billy Crystal, Lowell Ganz and Babaloo Mandel; **Director of Photography:** Don Burgess; **Editor:** Kent Beyda; **Music:** Marc Shaiman; **Production Designer:** Terence Marsh;
Producer: Billy Crystal
Castle Rock; PG-13; 95 minutes
Release: 5/95
Cast: Billy Crystal, Debra Winger, Joe Mantegna, Cynthia Stevenson, Richard Masur, Julie Kavner, William Hickey, John Spencer and Cathy Moriarty
Middle-agers Mickey (Crystal) and Ellen (Winger)

meet in Paris, spend a week together doing the typical tourist routine and return to Los Angeles and marry. Friends of the couple entertain each other with details of the couple's marriage, which has its problems due to conflicting schedules and personalities.

FORREST GUMP

Director: Robert Zemeckis; **Writer:** Eric Roth;
Director of Photography: Don Burgess; **Editor:** Arthur Schmidt; **Music:** Alan Silvestri; **Production Designer:** Rick Carter; **Producers:** Wendy Finerman, Steve Tisch and Steve Starkey
Paramount; PG-13; 136 minutes
Release: 7/94
Cast: Tom Hanks, Robin Wright, Gary Sinise, Mykelti Williamson, Sally Field, Michael Humphreys and Hanna Hall
Based on the novel by
Winston Groom

Forrest Gump (Hanks) is a simple man who achieves fame as a football star, a Vietnam hero and a wealthy businessman. *Gump* struck a chord in audiences who yearned for simplicity and straightforwardness. Critics saw its success as a retreat to know-nothingism.

FREE WILLY 2: THE ADVENTURE HOME

Director: Dwight Little; **Writers:** Karen Janszen, Corey Blechman and John Mattson; **Director of Photography:** Laszlo Kovacs; **Editor:** Robert Brown; **Music:** Basil Poledouris; **Production Designer:** Paul Sylbert; **Producers:** Lauren Shuler-Donner and Jennie Lew Tugend
Warner Bros.; PG; 98 minutes

Casino, **director:** Martin Scorsese; **cast:** Robert De Niro, Sharon Stone and Joe Pesci (Universal)

City Hall, **director:** Harold Becher; **cast:** Al Pacino, John Cusack, Bridget Fonda, Danny Aiello and David Paymer (Columbia Pictures)

Clockers, **director:** Spike Lee; **cast:** Harvey Keitel, John Turturro and Delroy Lindo (Universal)

Coldblooded, **director:** M. Wallace Woldodarsky; **cast:** Jason Priestly and Peter Riegert

Copycat, **director:** Jon Amiel; **cast:** Holly Hunter, Sigourney Weaver and Harry Connick, Jr.

The Crossing Guard, **director:** Sean Penn; **cast:** Jack Nicholson, David Morse, Anjelica Huston and Robin Wright (Miramax)

Cry, the Beloved Country, **director:** Darrell James Roodt; **cast:** James Earl Jones, Richard Harris and Charles Dutton

Cutthroat Island, **director:** Renny Harlin; **cast:** Geena Davis, Matthew Modine, Frank Langelia, Paul Dillon and Patrick Malahide (MGM)

A Day to Remember, **director:** James Foley; **cast:** Jerry Barone, Mary Elizabeth Mastrantonio and Al Pacino (Miramax)

Dead Man Walking, **director:** Tim Robbins; **cast:** Susan Sarandon, Sean Penn, Robert Prosky and Ray Berry

Dead Presidents, **directors:** Allen and Albert Hughes; **cast:** Larenz Tate, Keith David, Chris Tucker and Freddie Rodriguez (Hollywood Pictures)

Devil in a Blue Dress, **director:** Carl Franklin; **cast:** Denzel Washington, Tom Sizemore, Jennifer Beals and Don Cheadle (TriStar Pictures)

The Doom Generation, **director:** Gregg Araki; **cast:** Rose McGowan, James Duval and Johnathon Schaech (Samuel Goldwyn)

Dracula: Dead and Loving It, **director:** Mel Brooks; **cast:** Leslie Nielsen, Peter MacNicol, Steven Weber and Amy Yasbeck (Columbia Pictures)

Duston Checks In, **director:** Ken Kwapis; **cast:** Jason Alexander, Faye Dunaway, Rupert Everett and Eric Lloyd (Twentieth Century-Fox)

Father of the Bride 2, **director:** Charles Shyer; **cast:** Steve Martin, Diane Keaton, Kimberly Williams, Martin Short and Kieran Culkin (Touchstone Pictures)

The Fantasticks, **director:** Michael Ritchie; **cast:** Joe McIntyre, Joel Grey, Jonathan Morris and Jean Louisa Kelly (Paramount)

Feast of July, **director:** Chris Menaul; **cast:** Embeth Davidtz (Touchstone Pictures)

CONTINUED ON NEXT PAGE ▶

Four Rooms, **directors:** Allison Anders, Alexandre Rockwell, Robert Rodriguez and Quentin Tarantino; **cast:** Tim Roth, Antonio Banderas, Jennifer Beals, Madonna, Marisa Tomei and Tamlyn Tomita (Miramax)

From Dusk Till Dawn, **director:** Robert Rodriguez; **cast:** Harvey Keitel, George Clooney, Quentin Tarantino and Juliette Lewis (Miramax)

Get Shorty, **director:** Barry Sonnenfeld; **cast:** John Travolta, Gene Hackman, Rene Russo, Danny DeVito, Dennis Farina and Delroy Lindo (MGM)

Gold Diggers: Secret of Bear Mountain, **director:** Kevin Dobson; **cast:** Christina Ricci and Anna Chlumsky (Universal)

Goldeneye, **director:** Martin Campbell; **cast:** Pierce Brosnan, Sean Bean, Izabella Scorupco, Famke Janssen, Joe Don Baker and Robbie Coltrane (United Artists)

The Grass Harp, **director:** Charles Matthau; **cast:** Piper Laurie, Sissy Spacek, Walter Matthau, Edward Furlong, Nell Carter, Jack Lemmon, Mary Steenburgen, Roddy McDowall and Charles Durning

Grumpier Old Men, **director:** Howard Deutch; **cast:** Walter Matthau, Jack Lemmon, Ann-Margret, Sophia Loren, Kevin Pollack and Daryl Hannah

Halloween: The Curse of Michael Myers, **director:** Joe Chappelle; **cast:** Donald Pleasance, Mitch Ryan, Mariann Hagen, Mariah O'Brien and Paul Stephen Rudd (Miramax)

Heat, **director:** Michael Mann; **cast:** Al Pacino, Robert De Niro and Val Kiilmer

Hellraiser: Bloodline, **director:** Kevin Yagher; **cast:** Bruce Ramsay, Doug Bradley and Valentina Vargas (Miramax)

Home for the Holidays, **director:** Jodie Foster; **cast:** Holly Hunter, Robert Downey, Jr., Anne Bancroft, Dylan McDermott and Charles Durning (Paramount)

Homeward Bound: The Incredible Journey II, **director:** David R. Ellis; **cast:** Robert Hays, Kim Griest, Michael J. Fox and Sally Field (Walt Disney Pictures)

How to Make an American Quilt, **director:** Jocelyn Moorhouse; **cast:** Winona Ryder and Alfre Woodard (Universal)

The Horseman on the Roof, **director:** Jean-Paul Rappeneau; **cast:** Juliette Binoche and Olivier Martinez (Miramax)

I'm Not Rappaport, **director:** Herb Gardner; **cast:** Walter Matthau, Louis Gossett Jr., Amy Irving, Boyd Gaines and Craig T. Nelson (Gramercy Pictures)

Jack and Sarah, **director:** Tim Sullivan; **cast:** Richard Grant and Samantha Mathis (Gramercy Pictures)

Release: 7/95
Cast: Jason James Richter, August Schellenberg, Jayne Atkinson, Jon Tenney, Elizabeth Peña, Michael Madsen, Francis Capra and Mary Kate Schellhardt
A sequel to 1993's *Free Willy*
Free Willy 2 achieves something rare: it outdoes the original. Jesse (Richter), the abandoned boy from *Free Willy*, is living happily with a loving foster family and things are going great until he discovers he has a half brother Elvis (Capra), a tough eight year old from New York. Jesse's family (including new member Elvis) go on a camping trip, which includes a whale watch. Predictably, Jesse and Willy are reunited. Willy and his family are endangered when crude oil leaks into the water and catches fire. It's up to Jesse to save the whales.

FRENCH KISS

Director: Lawrence Kasdan; **Writer:** Adam Brooks; **Director of Photography:** Owen Roizman; **Editor:** Joe Hutshing; **Music:** James Newton Howard; **Production Designer:** Jon Hutman; **Producers:** Tim Bevan, Eric Fellner, Meg Ryan and Kathryn F. Galan
Twentieth Century-Fox; PG-13; 108 minutes
Release: 5/95
Cast: Meg Ryan, Kevin Kline, Timothy Hutton, Jean Reno, François Cluzet and Laurent Spielvogel
Kate (Ryan) must overcome her fear of flying if she

has any chance of winning back her fiancé (Hutton), who falls madly in love with a beautiful French woman while on a business trip in Paris. On the flight to France, Kate meets French jewel thief Luc (Kline) and once they land, they become inseparable, but not for obvious reasons.

FRIDAY

Director: Gary Gray; **Writers:** Ice Cube and D. J. Pooh; **Director of Photography:** Gerry Lively; **Editor:** John Carter; **Music:** Frank Fitzpatrick; **Production Designer:** Bruce Bellamy; **Producers:** Ice Cube and Pat Charbonnet
New Line; R; 90 minutes
Release: 4/95
Cast: Ice Cube, Paula Jai Parker, Chris Tucker, Bernie Mac, John Witherspoon, Regina King, Nia Long, Anna Maria Horsford and Faizon Love
Craig Jones (Cube), a 22-year-old Los Angeles man who recently became unemployed, spends his days with his best friend, the constantly stoned Smokey (Tucker), trying to find a way to pay off drug dealer Big Worm. Guns and drug use are commonplace in this look at LA's underclass.

FROM ONE PRISON

Director: Carol Jacobsen; **Director of Photography:** Susan Gardner; **Editors:** Carol Jacobsen and Annette Wilson; **Producer:** Carol Jacobsen

NR; 70 minutes
Release: 6/95
Women interviewed: Violet Allen, Juanita Thomas, Geraldean Gordon and Linda Hamilton
In this documentary, four severely abused women who eventually killed their male attackers tell shocking stories about their violence-filled lives before prison and the unspeakably degrading conditions of their current prison existence.

FUN
Director: Rafael Zelinsky; **Writer:** James Bosley; **Editor:** Monika Lightstone; **Music:** Marc Tschanz; **Production Designer:** Vally Mestroni; **Producer:** Rafael Zelinsky
Neo Modern; NR; 105 minutes
Release: 10/94
Based on the play by James Bosley
Cast: Alicia Witt, Renée Humphrey, William R. Moses, Leslie Hope and Ania Suli
Bonnie (Witt) and Hillary (Humphrey) in one day meet, become best friends and murder an elderly woman just for fun. In a series of interviews from jail with a prison psychiatrist and a reporter, the girls reveal they come from violent families and that abuse was partly responsible for their crime.

FUNNY BONES
Director: Peter Chelsom; **Writers:** Peter Chelsom and Peter Flannery; **Director of Photography:** Eduardo Serra; **Editor:** Martin Walsh; **Music:** John Altman; **Production Designer:** Caroline Hanania; **Producers:** Simon Fields and Peter Chelsom
Buena Vista; R; 128 minutes
Release: 3/95
Cast: Jerry Lewis, Oliver Platt, Lee Evans, Freddie Davies, George Carl, Leslie Caron, Ruta Lee, Oliver Reed and Amir Fawzi
Aspiring stand-up comic Tommy Fawkes (Platt), always overshadowed by his famous father George (Lewis), blows his big chance when his comedy act bombs in Las Vegas. Devastated, he returns to Blackpool, England, looking for the same happiness he experienced in childhood. What he finds is a long-hidden family secret that leads him to question himself and his father.

THE GLASS SHIELD
Director/Writer: Charles Burnett; **Director of Photography:** Elliot Davis; **Editor:** Curtiss Clayton; **Music:** Stephen James Taylor; **Producers:** Thomas Byrnes and Carolyn Schroeder
Miramax; PG-13; 109 minutes
Release: 6/95
Cast: Michael Boatman, Lori Petty, Ice Cube, Elliott Gould and Richard Anderson
J. J. Johnson (Boatman), a young rookie Los Angeles policeman, is disillusioned by his new position when he encounters racism and corruption on the force. He acquiesces in the scandals until he and fellow rookie Fields (Petty), who also suffers from discrimination, team up to publicize the conspiracy.

Jade, director: William Friedkin; cast: David Caruso, Chazz Palminteri, Linda Fiorentino, Michael Biehn and Richard Crenna (Paramount)

The Journey of August King, director: John Duigan; cast: Jason Patric, Thandie Newton, Larry Drake and Sam Waterston (Miramax)

Jumanji, director: Joe Johnston; cast: Robin Williams, Bonnie Hunt, Kirsten Dunst and David Alan Grier (TriStar Pictures)

The Juror, director: Brian Gibson; cast: Alec Baldwin, Demi Moore, Joseph Gordon Levitt, Anne Heche and James Gandolfini (Columbia Pictures)

Leaving Las Vegas, director: Mike Figgis; cast: Nicolas Cage, Elisabeth Shue, Julian Sands and Laurie Metcalf

Mallrats, director: Kevin Smith; cast: Shannen Doherty, Jason Lee and Stan Lee (Gramercy Pictures)

Mary Reilly, director: Stephen Frears; cast: Julia Roberts and John Malkovich (TriStar Pictures)

Mighty Aphrodite, director: Woody Allen; cast: Woody Allen, F. Murray Abraham, Claire Bloom, Helena Bonham-Carter and Olympia Dukakis (Miramax)

Mr. Holland's Opus, director: Stephen Herek; cast: Richard Dreyfuss, Glen Headly, Joseph Anderson, Jay Thomas and Olympia Dukakis (Hollywood Pictures)

Mr. Wrong, director: Nick Castle; cast: Ellen DeGeneres and Bill Pullman (Touchstone Pictures)

The Money Train, director: Joe Ruben; cast: Wesley Snipes, Woody Harrelson, Jennifer Lopez and Robert Blake (Columbia Pictures)

Moonlight and Valentino, director: David Anspaugh; cast: Elizabeth Perkins, Whoopi Goldberg, Kathleen Turner and Jon Bon Jovi (Gramercy Pictures)

National Lampoon's Senior Trip, director: Kelly Makin; cast: Matt Frewer and Tommy Chong (New Line Cinema)

Never Talk to Strangers, director: Peter Hall; cast: Rebecca De Mornay and Antonio Banderas (TriStar Pictures)

Nick of Time, director: John Badham; cast: Johnny Depp, Christopher Walken, Charles Dutton, Peter Strauss and Roma Maffia (Paramount)

Nixon, director: Oliver Stone; cast: Anthony Hopkins, James Woods and Joan Allen

Now and Then, director: Lesli Glatter; cast: Demi Moore, Melanie Griffith, Rosie O'Donnell, Rita Wilson and Christina Ricci (New Line Cinema)

CONTINUED ON NEXT PAGE ▶

Othello, **director:** Oliver Parker; **cast:** Laurence Fishburne, Kenneth Branagh and Irène Jacob

Powder, **director:** Victor Salva; **cast:** Mary Steenburgen, Jeff Goldblum, Lance Henricksen, Sean Patrick Flanery and Brandon Smith (Hollywood Pictures)

The Prophecy, **director:** Gregory Widen; **cast:** Christopher Walken, Elias Koteas, Virginia Madsen, Eric Stolz and Amanda Plummer (Miramax)

Reckless, **director:** Norman Renè; **cast:** Mia Farrow, Scott Glenn, Mary-Louise Parker, Tony Goldwyn and Stephen Dorff (Samuel Goldwyn)

Restoration, **director:** Michael Hoffman; **cast:** Robert Downey, Jr., Sam Neill, David Thewlis, Meg Ryan, Sir Ian McKellan and Hugh Grant (Miramax)

Richard III, **director:** Richard Loncraine; **cast:** Sir Ian McKellen, Annette Bening, Jim Broadbent, Robert Downey, Jr. and Nigel Hawthorne (United Artists)

The Run of the Country, **director:** Peter Yates; **cast:** Albert Finney, Matt Keeslar, Victoria Smurfit and Anthony Brophy (Columbia Pictures)

Sabrina, **director:** Sydney Pollack; **cast:** Harrison Ford, Julia Ormond, Greg Kinnear, Lauren Holley and Angie Dickinson (Paramount)

The Scarlet Letter, **director:** Roland Joffe; **cast:** Demi Moore, Robert Duvall, Gary Oldman and Joan Plowright (Hollywood Pictures)

Screamers, **director:** Christian Duguay; **cast:** Peter Weller and Roy Dupuis (Triumph)

Sense and Sensibility, **director:** Ang Lee; **cast:** Emma Thompson, Kate Winslet, Alan Rickman, Hugh Grant and Greg Wise (Columbia Pictures)

Seven, **director:** David Fincher; **cast:** Morgan Freeman, Brad Pitt and Gwyneth Paltrow (New Line Cinema)

Showgirls, **director:** Paul Verhoeven; **cast:** Elizabeth Berkley, Kyle MacLachlan, Gina Gershon, Glenn Plummer and Robert Davi (United Artists)

The Stars Fell on Henrietta, **director:** James Keach; **cast:** Robert Duvall, Aidan Quinn and Brian Dennehy

Strange Days, **director:** Kathryn Bigelow; **cast:** Ralph Fiennes, Angela Bassett, Juliette Lewis and Tom Sizemore (Twentieth Century-Fox)

Sudden Death, **director:** Peter Hyams; **cast:** John Claude van Damme (Universal)

Theodore Rex, **director:** Jonathon Betuel; **cast:** Whoopi Goldberg (New Line Cinema)

A GOOFY MOVIE

Director: Kevin Lima; **Writers:** Jymm Magon, Chris Matheson and Brian Pimental; **Editor:** Gregory Perler; **Music:** Carter Burwell; **Production Designer:** Fred Warter; **Producer:** Dan Rounds
Walt Disney; G; 76 minutes
Release: 4/95
Voices of: Bill Farmer, Jason Marsden and Wallace Shawn
Based on a story by Jymm Magon

Goofy (voice of Farmer) and his teenage son Max (voice of Marsden) experience typical problems between father and son: Max thinks his father is the ultimate square and Goofy thinks Max is becoming a troublemaker. Goofy takes Max on a road trip hoping the two can bond.

GORDY

Director: Mark Lewis; **Writer:** Leslie Stevens; **Director of Photography:** Richard Michalak; **Editor:** Lindsay Frazer; **Music:** Charles Fox; **Production Designer:** Barcie Waite; **Producer:** Sybil Robson
Miramax; G; 89 minutes
Release: 5/95
Cast: Doug Stone, Kristy Young, Michael Roescher, Deborah Hobart, Ted Manson, James Donadio, Tom Lester and Tom Key
When Gordy's family is taken from the farm to the slaughterhouse, the pig runs away in search of his kin. His wealthy adopted family makes him the mascot of their company, but his fame can't ensure his safety or that of his family.

A GREAT DAY IN HARLEM

Writers: Jean Bach, Susan Peehl and Matthew Seig; **Director of Photography:** Steve Petropoulos; **Editor:** Susan Peehl; **Music Consultation:** Johnny Mandel; **Producer:** Jean Bach
Castle Hill Productions; NR; 60 minutes
Release: 2/95
Narration by Quincy Jones; interviews with Art Kane, Dizzy Gillespie, Art Blakey, Sonny Rollins, Marian McPartland and others
A nostalgic tribute to a community of jazz greats, this documentary focuses on a 1958 photo shoot for *Esquire* magazine, in which 57 musicians from three generations of jazz posed for photographer Art Kane. Interspersed with live footage from the event are interviews, bios and plenty of music from jazz greats Thelonious Monk, Count Basie, Mary Lou Williams, Bud Freeman and many others.

HEAVEN'S A DRAG

Director: Peter Mackenzie Litten; **Writer:** Johnny Byrne; **Music:** Kiki Dee, Elton John and Acoustic Alchemy; **Producer:** Gary Fitzpatrick

First Run Features; NR; 96 minutes
Release: 6/95
Cast: Thomas Arklie, Ian Williams, Tony Slattery, Dilly Keane, Ian McKellen, Jean Boht and John Altman
It doesn't take Simon (Arklie) long to get over the AIDS death of his lover Mark (Williams); in a matter of days, he's a swinging bachelor again. Things change when Mark, now an invisible man, moves back into their apartment and brings up painful issues the pair never discussed.

HEAVENLY CREATURES

Director: Peter Jackson; **Writers:** Peter Jackson and Frances Walsh; **Director of Photography:** Alan Bollinger; **Editor:** Jamie Selkirk; **Music:** Peter Dasent; **Production Designer:** Grant Major; **Producer:** Jim Booth
Miramax; R; 99 minutes
Release: 11/94
Cast: Melanie Lynskey and Kate Winslet
Based on a true story
Set in 1950s New Zealand, two teenage girls (Lynskey and Winslet) create a fantasy world that turns deadly when they plan and execute a murder.

HEAVYWEIGHTS

Director: Steven Brill; **Writers:** Judd Apatow and Steven Brill; **Director of Photography:** Victor Hammer; **Editor:** C. Timothy O'Meara; **Music:** J. A. C. Redford; **Production Designer:** Stephen Storer; **Producers:** Joe Roth and Roger Birnbaum
Buena Vista; PG; 98 minutes
Release: 2/95
Cast: Ben Stiller, Tom McGowan, Aaron Schwartz, Anne Meara, Jerry Stiller, Shaun Weiss, Tom Hodges and Kenan Thompson
This poke at the proliferating infomercial industry has former obese child now svelte entrepeneur Tony Perkis (Ben Stiller) running a summer camp for overweight boys. Perkis plans to whip them into shape and make a before-and-after infomercial on his successful weight-loss plan.

HIDEAWAY

Director: Brett Leonard; **Writers:** Andrew Kevin Walker and Neal Jimenez; **Director of Photography:** Gale Tattersall; **Editor:** B. J. Sears; **Music:** Trevor Jones; **Production Designer:** Michael Bolton; **Producers:** Jerry Baerwitz, Agatha Hanczakowski and Gimel Everett
TriStar; R; 112 minutes
Release: 3/95
Cast: Jeff Goldblum, Christine Lahti, Alicia Silverstone, Jeremy Sisto, Alfred Molina and Rae Dawn Chong
Based on the novel by Dean R. Koontz

Things to Do in Denver When You're Dead, director: Gary Fleder; **cast:** Andy Garcia, Christopher Walken, Christopher Lloyd, Treat Williams and Gabrielle Anwar (Miramax)

Three Wishes, director: Martha Coolidge; **cast:** Patrick Swayze, Mary Elizabeth Mastrantonio and Joseph Mazzello

The Tie That Binds, director: Wesley Strick; **cast:** Daryl Hannah, Keith Carradine, Julia Devin, Vincent Spano and Moira Kelly (Hollywood Pictures/Interscope Pictures)

To Die For, director: Gus Van Sant; **cast:** Nicole Kidman, Joaquin Phoenix and Matt Dillon (Columbia Pictures)

Tom Sawyer, director: Peter Hewitt; **cast:** Jonathan Taylor Thomas, Brad Renfro, Eric Schweig, Amy Wright and Charles Rocket

Total Eclipse, director: Agnieszka Holland; **cast:** Leonardo DiCaprio, David Thewlis and Romanie Bohringer

To Wong Foo, Thanks for Everything Julie Newmar, director: Beeban Kidron; **cast:** Wesley Snipes, Patrick Swayze and John Leguizamo (Universal)

Toy Story, director: John Lasseter; voices of Tom Hanks, Tim Allen, John Morris, Annie Potts and Jim Varney (Walt Disney Pictures)

The Truth About Cats and Dogs, director: Michael Lehmann; **cast:** Uma Thurman, Janeane Garofalo and Ben Chaplin (Twentieth Century-Fox)

Twelve Monkeys, director: Terry Gilliam; **cast:** Bruce Willis, Brad Pitt and Madeleine Stowe (Universal)

Unstrung Heroes, director: Diane Keaton; **cast:** John Turturro, Michael Richards, Andie MacDowell and Nathan Watt (Hollywood Pictures)

Vampire in Brooklyn, director: Wes Craven; **cast:** Eddie Murphy, Angela Bassett, Allen Payne, Kadeem Hardison and Zakes Mokae (Paramount)

Waiting to Exhale, director: Forest Whitaker; **cast:** Whitney Houston, Angela Bassett, Loretta Devine, Lela Rochon, and Gregory Hines (Twentieth Century-Fox)

White Man's Burden, director: Desmond Nakano; **cast:** John Travolta, Harry Belafonte and Kelly Lynch

White Squall, director: Ridley Scott; **cast:** Jeff Bridges, Balthazar Getty, David Lascher, Ryan Phillippe and Scott Wolf (Hollywood Pictures) ■

Mourning the death of one daughter, Hatch Harrison (Goldblum) must protect his other daughter Regina (Silverstone) from the wicked Vassago (Sisto). Harrison died in a car crash and was brought back to life by a medical team. After the accident, he became psychically connected to Vassago and learns through telepathy Vassago's evil intentions. High-tech computer graphics enhance Harrison's "photo-surreal journeys."

HIGHER LEARNING

Director/Writer: John Singleton; **Director of Photography:** Peter Lyons Collister; **Editor:** Bruce Cannon; **Music:** Stanley Clarke; **Production Designer:** Keith Brian Burns; **Producers:** John Singleton and Paul Hall
Columbia; R; 127 minutes
Release: 1/95
Cast: Omar Epps, Kristy Swanson, Michael Rapaport, Jennifer Connelly, Ice Cube, Tyra Banks, Regina King and Laurence Fishburne

A group of students deal with issues of race and sexuality as college freshmen on a polarized campus.

HIGHLANDER: THE FINAL DIMENSION

Director: Andy Morahan; **Writer:** Paul Ohl; **Director of Photography:** Steven Chivers; **Editor:** Yves Langlois; **Music:** J. Peter Robinson; **Producers:** Claude Leger and James Daly
Miramax; PG-13; 94 minutes
Release: 1/95
Cast: Christopher Lambert, Mario Van Peebles, Deborah Unger and Mako
Third in the *Highlander* series
Kane (Van Peebles), who was buried 400 years ago by Connor MacLeod (Lambert), is unearthed when archaeologist Alex (Unger) excavates the burial ground. Kane is out to kill Connor, a feat that can only be achieved by decapitating him.

HOOP DREAMS

Director: Steve James; **Writer:** Peter Gilbert; **Director of Photography:** Peter Gilbert; **Editors:** Frederick Marx, Steve James and Bill Haugse; **Music:** Ben Sidran; **Producers:** Frederick Marx, Steve James and Peter Gilbert
Fine Line; PG-13; 171 minutes
Release: 10/94
Cast: William Gates, Arthur "Bo" Agee, Emma Gates, Sheila Gates, Curtis Gates, Willie Gates, Isaiah Thomas, Spike Lee and Earl Smith

Filmed over a period of five years, this highly-acclaimed documentary follows two African-American high-school basketball players from Chicago as they struggle to realize their NBA dreams. The omission of *Hoop Dreams* from the 1994 Oscar Best Documentary category prompted the Motion Picture Academy to revamp the nomination process for documentaries.

HOTEL SORRENTO

Director/Producer: Richard Franklin; **Writers:** Richard Franklin and Peter Fitzpatrick; **Director of Photography:** Geoff Burton; **Editor:** David Pulbrook; **Music:** Nerida Tyson Chew; **Production Designer:** Tracey Watt
Castle Hill Productions; NR; 112 minutes
Release: 5/95
Cast: Caroline Goodall, Caroline Gillmer, Tara Morice, Joan Plowright, John Hargreaves, Ben Thomas and Ray Barrett
Based on the play by Hannie Rayson
After 10 years of not seeing each other, three sisters reunite in their native Australia. Meg (Goodall), who lives in England, recently published a novel that chronicles their family history, and her siblings Pippa (Morice) and Hilary (Gilmer) can hardly suppress their anger and hurt.

HOUSEGUEST

Director: Randall Miller; **Writers:** Michael J. Di Gaetano and Lawrence Gay; **Editor:** Eric Sears; **Music:** John Debney; **Production Designer:** Paul Peters; **Producers:** Joe Roth and Roger Birnbaum
Hollywood Pictures; PG; 88 minutes
Release: 1/95
Cast: Sinbad, Phil Hartman, Kim Greist, Jefferey Jones, Stan Shaw and Ron Glass
Evading loansharks in a Philadelphia airport, Kevin Franklin (Sinbad) cons his way into a weekend stay at the home of Gary Young (Hartman), who thought he had been reuinted with an old college pal.

THE HUNTED

Director/Writer: J.F. Lawton; **Director of Photography:** Jack Conroy; **Editors:** Robert A. Ferretti and Eric Strand; **Music:** Motofumi Yamaguchi; **Producers:** John Davis and Gary W. Goldstein
Universal; R; 110 minutes
Release: 2/95
Cast: Christopher Lambert, John Lone, Joan Chen, Yoshio Harada, Yoko Shimada and Mari Natsuki
Paul Racine (Lambert) on business in Japan falls for the mysterious Kirina (Chen), and their one passionate night ends in death. A Japanese ninja cult led by Kinjo (Lone) hunts Racine because he witnessed the crime.

I AM CUBA

Director/Producer: Mikhail Kalatozov; **Writers:** Yevgeny Yevtushenko and Enrique Pineda Barnet; **Director of Photography:** Sergei Urusevsky; **Editor:** N. Glagoleva; **Music:** Carlos Fariñas
Milestone Film; NR; 141 minutes
U.S. Release: 3/95; completed in 1964

Cast: Luz Maria Collazo, José Gallardo, Sergio Corrieri, Mario González Broche, Jean Bouise, Raúl Garcia and Celia Rodríguez

In Spanish, Russian and English with English subtitles

This film depicts Cuba as an island ripe for revolution in the last days of Fulgencio Batista's reign — just before Castro's overthrow of the government. Women were forced by poverty into prostitution, farmers lost their land and leftist students and peasant workers were gunned down by hostile police.

I CAN'T SLEEP

Director: Claire Denis; **Writers:** Claire Denis and Jean-Pol Fargeau; **Director of Photography:** Agnes Godard; **Editor:** Nelly Quettier; **Production Designers:** Thierry Flammand and Arnaud De Moleron; **Producer:** Bruno Pesery

New Yorker Films; NR; 110 minutes

Release: 8/95

Cast: Katerina Golubeva, Richard Courcet, Vincent Dupont, Laurent Grevill, Beatrice Dalle and Alex Descas

In French with English subtitles

Denis takes a potentially explosive subject and understates it with an artistic, undramatic treatment. *I Can't Sleep* is based on the true story of gay couple who kill more than 20 elderly women. Daïga (Golubeva), a Polish woman who recently immigrated to France, does not understand French enough to heed the warning she hears on the radio: "Don't open your doors to strangers; the granny killer is out." She takes a job as a chambermaid in the same hotel that the murderers, Camille (Courcet) and Raphaël (Dupont), live.

I LIKE IT LIKE THAT

Director/Writer: Darnell Martin; **Director of Photography:** Alexander Gruszynski; **Editor:** Peter Frank; **Music:** Sergio George; **Production Designer:** Scott Chambliss; **Producers:** Ann Carli and Lane Janger

Columbia; R; 104 minutes

Release: 10/94

Cast: Lauren Velez, Jon Seda, Rita Moreno and Griffin Dunne

Lisette (Velez) and Chino (Seda) are a black-and-Latino couple with three young children living in a small Bronx apartment. Their passionate love holds them together through marital affairs, Chino's incarceration and financial ruin.

IMAGINARY CRIMES

Director: Anthony Drazan; **Writers:** Kristine Johnson and Davia Nelson; **Director of Photography:** John J. Campbell; **Editor:** Elizabeth King; **Music:** Stephen Endelman; **Production Designer:** Joseph T. Garrity; **Producer:** James G. Robinson

Morgan Creek Productions; PG-13; 107 minutes

Release: 10/94

Cast: Harvey Keitel, Fairuza Balk, Elisabeth Moss, Chris Penn, Seymour Cassel, Kelly Lynch, Vincent D'Onofrio and Sam Fuller

Based on the novel by Sheila Ballantyne

A widower (Keitel) with two daughters (Balk and Moss) juggles the responsibilites of raising his children and maintaining his fraudulent real-estate business. His oldest daughter assumes the role of guardian to protect her sister when she realizes their father is a fake.

IMMORTAL BELOVED

Director/Writer: Bernard Rose; **Director of Photography:** Peter Suschitzky; **Editor:** Dan Rae; **Music:** Georg Solti; **Production Designer:** Jiri Hlupy; **Producer:** Bruce Davey

Columbia; R; 203 minutes

Release: 1/95

Cast: Gary Oldman, Jeroen Krabbé, Isabella Rossellini, Johanna Ter Steege and Valeria Golino

Ludwig von Beethoven's protégé (Krabbé) searches for Beethoven's "Immortal Beloved," the secret love whose name Beethoven never revealed.

THE INCREDIBLY TRUE ADVENTURE OF TWO GIRLS IN LOVE

Director/Writer: Maria Maggenti; **Director of Photography:** Tami Reiker; **Editor:** Susan Graef; **Music:** Terry Dame; **Production Designer:** Ginger Tougas; **Producer:** Dolly Hall

Fine Line; R; 95 minutes

Release: 6/95

Cast: Laurel Holloman, Nicole Parker, Kate Stafford and Nelson Rodriguez

Randy Dean (Holloman) and Evie (Parker), girls from different economic backgrounds, meet in high school and fall in love.

INDIAN IN THE CUPBOARD

Director: Frank Oz; **Writer:** Melissa Mathison; **Director of Photography:** Russell Carpenter; **Editor:** Ian Crafford; **Music:** Randy Edelman; **Production Designer:** Leslie McDonald; **Producers:** Kathleen Kennedy, Frank Marshall and Jane Startz

Paramount; PG; 96 minutes

Release: 7/95

Cast: Hal Scardino, Litefoot, Lindsay Crouse, Richard Jenkins, Rishi Bhat, Steve Coogan and David Keith

Based on the novel by Lynne Reid Banks

For his birthday, Omri (Scardino) receives a small plastic American Indian and a cupboard. He soon discovers that the cupboard brings to life the Indian, and his adventure begins. Little Bear (Litefoot), the Indian, and Omri become best friends, and Omri must feed and shelter Little Bear and keep him a secret, which takes some creativity.

INTERVIEW WITH THE VAMPIRE

Director: Neil Jordan; **Writer:** Anne Rice; **Director of Photography:** Philippe Rousselot; **Editors:** Mick Audsley and Joke Van Wijk; **Music:** Elliot Goldenthal; **Production Designer:** Dante Ferretti; **Producers:** David Geffen and Stephen Woolley

Warner Bros.; R; 120 minutes

Release: 11/94

Cast: Tom Cruise, Brad Pitt, Kirsten Dunst, Antonio Banderas and Christian Slater
Based on the novel by Anne Rice

Vampires Lestat (Cruise), Louis (Pitt) and their adopted daughter (Dunst) travel through centuries sucking the blood of unsuspecting victims. A sumptuous setting of the popular Rice series.

IN THE MOUTH OF MADNESS
Director: John Carpenter; **Writer:** Michael De Luca; **Director of Photography:** Gary B. Kibbe; **Editor:** Edward A. Warschilka; **Music:** John Carpenter and Jim Lang; **Production Designer:** Jeff Steven Ginn; **Producer:** Sandy King
New Line; R; 95 minutes
Release: 2/95
Cast: Sam Neill, Julie Carmen, Jurgen Prochnow and Charlton Heston
Insurance investigator John Trent (Neill) searches for immensely popular horror novelist Sutter Cane (Prochnow) whose stories are so hypnotic they drive readers insane.

INTO THE DEEP
Director: Howard Hall; **Director of Photography:** Noel Archambault; **Editor:** Barbara Kerr; **Music:** Micky Erbe and Maribeth Solomon; **Supervising Sound Editor:** Peter Thillaye; **Producer:** Graeme Ferguson
IMAX Corporation; PG; 35 minutes
Release: 12/94
Narrator: Kate Nelligan
Schools of fish slither past, a lobster molts its shell and sharks, starfish and jellyfish show their true colors on an almost eight-story-high screen in this underwater documentary made with the new IMAX 3-D camera. Only a few theaters in the United States are equipped to screen IMAX films.

I.Q.
Director: Fred Schepisi; **Writers:** Andy Breckman and Michael Leeson; **Director of Photography:** Ian Baker; **Editor:** Jill Bilcock; **Music:** Jerry Goldsmith; **Production Designer:** Stuart Wurtzel; **Producers:** Carol Baum and Fred Schepisi
Paramount; PG; 96 minutes
Release: 12/94
Cast: Tim Robbins, Meg Ryan, Walter Matthau, Gene Saks and Lou Jacobi
Albert Einstein (Matthau) plots to pair his scientist niece (Ryan) with an auto mechanic (Robbins). A beguiling premise with a high-octane cast makes this a sleeper.

IS THAT ALL THERE IS
Director/Writer: Lindsay Anderson; **Director of Photography:** Jonathan Collinson; **Editor:** Nicolas Gaster; **Music:** Alan Price; **Producer:** Trevor Ingman

Yaffle Films for BBC Scotland; NR; 54 minutes
Release: 5/95
British director Anderson created this filmed self-portrait shortly before he died in 1994. By filming his daily routine, the film exemplifies the director's view that in the big picture, one human life is truly insignificant.

JEFFERSON IN PARIS
Director: James Ivory; **Writer:** Ruth Prawer Jhabvala; **Director of Photography:** Pierre L'homme; **Editors:** Andrew Marcus and Isabel Lorente; **Music:** Richard Robbins; **Production Designer:** Guy-Claude François; **Producer:** Ismail Merchant
Touchstone; PG-13; 144 minutes
Release: 3/95
Cast: Nick Nolte, Greta Scacchi, Gwyneth Paltrow, Simon Callow, Thandie Newton, Seth Gilliam and James Earl Jones
Thomas Jefferson's (Nolte) ambassadorship to Paris from 1784 to 1789 was marked by personal and political struggle. He fell in love with Maria Cosway (Scacchi) and perhaps fathered several children with his young slave Sally Hemings (Newton). The film,

loaded with historical data (both the French and American revolutions are covered) depicts Jefferson as a true Renaissance man — inventor and politican with interest in art, gardening, architecture and music.

JEFFREY
Director: Christopher Ashley; **Writer:** Paul Rudnick; **Director of Photography:** Jeffery Tufano; **Editor:** Cara Silverman; **Music:** Stephen Endelman; **Production Designer:** Michael Johnston; **Producers:** Mark Balsam, Mitchell Maxwell and Victoria Maxwell
Orion Classics; R; 92 minutes
Release: 8/95
Cast: Steven Weber, Michael T. Weiss, Patrick Stewart, Bryan Batt, Nathan Lane, Christine Baranski and Sigourney Weaver
Based on the play by Paul Rudnick
Jeffrey (Weber) is an actor who loves sex, but has decided that with AIDS around it's just not worth the trouble. His vow of celibacy is undermined when he meets Steve (Weiss), who is both irresistibly attractive and H.I.V. positive. Humor and sadness surround the new pair and their friends, all facing the difficult realities of AIDS.

THE JERKY BOYS
Director: James Melkonian; **Writers:** James Melkonian, Rich Wilkes, John Brennan and Kamal Ahmed; **Director of Photography:** Ueli Steiger; **Editor:** Dennis M. Hill; **Production Designer:** Dan Leigh; **Producers:** Roger Birnbaum and Joe Roth
Touchstone; R; 75 minutes

Release: 2/95
Cast: Johnny Brennan, Alan Arkin and Kamal
The gold-album comedy team Johnny B. and Kamal (playing themselves) made a big mistake when they took their shtick to the big screen. The telephone pranksters are up to their old tricks — annoying businesspeople with rude calls. They also get involved with the New York mob, irritating boss Lazarro (Arkin).

JOHNNY MNEMONIC

Director: Robert Longo; **Writer:** William Gibson; **Director of Photography:** Français Protat; **Editor:** Ronald Sanders; **Music:** Brad Fiedel; **Production Designer:** Nilo Rodis Jamero; **Producer:** Don Carmody
TriStar; R; 98 minutes
Release: 5/95
Based on William Gibson's short story
Cast: Keanu Reeves, Dolph Lundgren, Ice T, Dina Meyer and Henry Rollins
Johnny Mnemonic (Reeves), a 21st-century information courier, has 24 hours to get rid of data that is stored in a chip in his head, else he lose his noggin to Japanese hitmen

working for a pharmaceutical company. He faces a major obstacle: he is missing part of the access code necessary to download the information.

JUDGE DREDD

Director: Danny Cannon; **Writers:** William Wisher and Steven E. DeSouza; **Director of Photography:** Adrian Biddle; **Editors:** Alex Mackie and Harry Keramidas; **Music:** Alan Silvestri; **Production Designer:** Nigel Phelps; **Producers:** Charles M. Lippincott and Beau E. L. Marks
Buena Vista; R; 91 minutes
Release: 6/95
Cast: Sylvester Stallone, Armand Assante, Rob Schneider, Max von Sydow and Diane Lane
Based on the story by Michael DeLuca and William Wisher, which was based on the *Judge Dredd* characters owned by Fleetway Publications and created by John Wagner and Carlos Ezquerra
Set in a post-apocalyptic future, all living people dwell in lawless cities. Because crime fighting doesn't allow for legal niceties, judges also act as jury and executioner. Judge Dredd (Stallone) takes his job seriously, making no exceptions for offenders. Things change when he is framed for a murder he didn't commit and sent to a penal colony. He gets away en route, and he and Judge Hershey (Lane) team up to clear his name.

JUNIOR

Director: Ivan Reitman; **Writers:** Kevin Wade and Chris Conrad; **Director of Photography:** Adam Greenberg; **Editors:** Wendy Greene Bricmont and Sheldon Kahn; **Music:** James Newton Howard;

Production Designer: Stephen J. Lineweaver;
Producer: Ivan Reitman
Universal; PG; 110 minutes
Release: 11/94
Cast: Arnold Schwarzenegger, Danny DeVito, Emma Thompson, Frank Langella, Pamela Reed, Judy Collins, Ellen McLaughlin and Anna Gunn

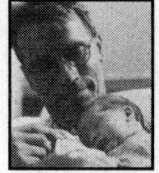

A geneticist (Schwarzenegger) injects himself with the fertility drug he developed to prove the drug's effectiveness and experiences all the symptoms associated with pregnancy.

JURY DUTY

Director: John Fortenberry; **Writers:** Neil Tolkin, Barbara Williams and Samantha Adams; **Director of Photography:** Avi Karpick; **Editor:** Stephen Semel; **Music:** David Kitay; **Production Designers:** Deborah Raymond and Dorian Vernaccio; **Producers:** Yoram Ben-Ami and Peter M. Lenkov
TriStar and Triumph Films; PG-13; 86 minutes
Release: 4/95
Based on the story by Barbara Williams and Samantha Adams
Cast: Pauly Shore, Tia Carrere, Stanley Tucci, Brian Doyle-Murray, Abe Vigoda and Shelley Winters
In an obvious rip-off of the O.J. Simpson case, Tommy (Shore) views jury duty as a $5-a-day job. He intentionally and pathetically prolongs a high-profile murder trial so he can stay sequestered in a luxury hotel room.

JUST CAUSE

Director: Arne Glimcher; **Writers:** Jeb Stuart and Peter Stone; **Director of Photography:** Lajos Koltai; **Editor:** William Anderson; **Music:** James Newton Howard; **Production Designer:** Patrizia von Brandstein; **Producers:** Lee Rich, Arne Glimcher and Steve Perry
Warner Bros.; R; 105 minutes
Release: 2/95
Based on the novel by John Katzenbach
Cast: Sean Connery, Blair Underwood, Laurence Fishburne, Ruby Dee, Kate Capshaw, Ed Harris, Kevin McCarthy and Hope Lange
Eminent Harvard law professor Paul Armstrong (Connery) returns to the courtroom after years in the classroom to save Floridian Bobby Earl Ferguson (Underwood) from the electric chair for murdering and raping an 11-year-old girl.

A KID IN KING ARTHUR'S COURT

Director: Michael Gottlieb; **Writers:** Michael Part and Robert L. Levy; **Director of Photography:** Elemer Ragalyi; **Editors:** Michael Ripps and Anita Brandt-Burgoyne; **Music:** J. A. C. Redford; **Production Designer:** Laszlo Gardonyi; **Producers:** Robert L. Levy, Peter Abrams and J.P. Guerin

Walt Disney; PG; 91 minutes
Release: 8/95
Cast: Thomas Ian Nicholas, Joss Ackland, Art Malik, Paloma Baeza and Ron Moody
An earthquake sends Calvin Fuller (Nicholas), an insecure Little Leaguer, tumbling down a crevice in the earth. He lands in King Arthur's (Ackland) Camelot and predictably falls for the king's daughter, Princess Katey (Baeza). King Arthur is under the influence of the evil Lord Belasco (Malik) and Merlin (Moody) has promised Fuller that if can break the spell he will return home.

KIDS
Director: Larry Clark; **Writer:** Harmony Korine; **Director of Photography**: Eric Alan Edwards; **Editor:** Chris Tellefson; **Music:** Louis Barlow; **Producer:** Cary Woods
Excalibur Films; NR; 95 minutes
Release: 7/95
Cast: Leo Fitzpatrick, Justin Pierce, Chloe Sevigny and Rosario Dawson
Kids dives into New York's teen culture, finding loveless sex, aimless wandering and random violence. The story and style are stark and terrifying, making *Kids* one of the most controversial movies of the year. Originally rated NC-17, considered an audience killer by movie companies, Miramax, the intended distributor of *Kids*, created the subsidiary Excalibur Films to distance the film from parent company Disney. Excalibur then released the movie unrated.

KISS OF DEATH
Director: Barbet Schroeder; **Writer:** Richard Price; **Director of Photography**: Luciano Tovoli; **Editor:** Lee Percy; **Music:** Trevor Jones; **Production Designer:** Mel Bourne; **Producers:** Barbet Schroeder and Susan Hoffman;
Twentieth Century-Fox; R; 101 minutes
Release: 4/95
Cast: David Caruso, Nicolas Cage, Samuel L. Jackson, Helen Hunt, Kathryn Erbe, Stanley Tucci, Michael Rapaport, Ving Rhames and Anne Meara
Based on the 1947 movie written by Ben Hecht and Charles Lederer
Ex-con Jimmy Kilmartin (Caruso), doing his best to stay clean, risks it all for his cousin Ronnie (Rapaport) when he helps him in a car heist. The police foil the job, which Ronnie needed to pull off to pay back brutal thug Little Junior (Cage), and Kilmartin finds himself back behind bars. Police offer Kilmartin a deal: he walks if he can deliver Little Junior.

THE K.K.K. BOUTIQUE AIN'T JUST REDNECKS
Directors/Writers/Producers: Camille Billops and James V. Hatch; **Director of Photography:** Dion Hatch; **Editor:** S. A. Burns; **Music:** George Booker and Christa Victoria
NR; 76 minutes
Release: 3/95
This guided tour through an underground area depicts racism in its many forms. Both fantasy and real-life segments present instances of hatred including a salesman modeling a white-hooded robe.

LADYBIRD, LADYBIRD
Director: Ken Loach; **Writer:** Rona Munro; **Director of Photography:** Barry Ackroyd; **Editor:** Jonathan Morris; **Music:** George Fenton; **Production Designer:** Martin Johnson; **Producer:** Sally Hibbin
Samuel Goldwyn; NR; 101 minutes
Release: 12/94
Cast: Crissy Rock, Vladimir Vega, Ray Winstone and Sandie Lavelle
Based on a true story
A British mother (Rock) of four, each from a different man, loses her children to England's social services. She struggles to build a new life with the Paraguayan poet and political exile (Vega) she meets in a bar.

LAMB
Director: Colin Gregg; **Writer:** Bernard Maclaverty; **Director of Photography:** Mike Garfath; **Editor:** Peter Delfgou; **Music:** Van Morrison; **Production Designer:** Austen Spriggs; **Producer:** Neil Zeiger
Capitol Entertainment; NR; 110 minutes
Release: 2/95
Cast: Liam Neeson, Hugh O'Conor, Ian Bannen, Ronan Wilmot and Frances Tomelty
Based on Bernard Maclaverty's novel
Brother Michael Lamb (Neeson), a teacher in a British school for troubled boys, protects the institution's biggest troublemaker Owen (O'Connor) from its sadistic headmaster (Bannen). Lamb, losing his faith, takes Owen away from the abuse, and the two become transients in seedy modern Britain.

THE LAST GOOD TIME
Director: Bob Balaban; **Writers:** Bob Balaban and John McLaughlin; **Director of Photography:** Claudia Raschke; **Editor:** Hughes Winborne; **Music:** Jonathan Tunick; **Production Designer:** Wing Lee; **Producers:** Dean Silvers and Bob Balaban
Samuel Goldwyn; NR; 95 minutes
Release: 4/95
Cast: Armin Mueller-Stahl, Olivia d'Abo, Maureen Stapleton and Lionel Stander
Based on the novel by Richard Bausch
Joseph Kopple (Mueller-Stahl), a 70-year-old man deep in debt to the IRS, has a fling with Charlotte (d'Abo), a young punk woman in her 20s. Though he still often thinks of his long-deceased wife, Kopple enjoys the companionship and social activities he and Charlotte share.

THE LAST SEDUCTION
Director: John Dahl; **Writer:** Steve Barancik; **Director of Photography:** Jeff Jur; **Editor:** Eric L. Beason; **Music:** Joseph Vitarelli; **Production Designer:** Linda Pearl; **Producer:** Jonathan Shestack
October Films; R; 110 minutes
Release: 10/94

Cast: Linda Fiorentino, Peter Berg, J.T. Walsh, Bill Nunn and Bill Pullman

Femme fatale Bridget Gregory (Fiorentino) steals drug-deal money from her husband (Pullman) and leaves town to plot her plan to get rid of him, using any device necessary — lies, divorce or murder. Because of a technicality, Fiorentino was denied a Best Actress Oscar nomination, and became a cause célèbre.

LEGENDS OF THE FALL

Director: Edward Zwick; **Writers:** Susan Shilliday and Bill Wittliff; **Director of Photography:** John Till; **Editor:** Steven Rosenblum; **Music:** James Horner; **Production Designer:** Lilly Kilvert; **Producers:** Edward Zwick, Bill Wittliff and Marshall Herskovitz
TriStar; R; 133 minutes
Release: 12/94
Cast: Brad Pitt, Anthony Hopkins, Aidan Quinn, Julia Ormond, Henry Thomas, Karina Lombard, Gordon Tootoosis, Christina Pickles, Paul Desmond and Tantoo Cardinal
Based on the novella by Jim Harrison
Set in Montana and spanning three decades, three brothers fall in love with the same woman (Ormond), who marries one (Quinn), sleeps with another (Pitt) and grieves the death of the third (Thomas).

LEONA'S SISTER GERRI

Director/Producer: Jane Gillooly; **Director of Photography:** Andrew Neumann; **Editor:** C. L. Monrose; **Music:** Caleb Sampson
Newton Television Foundation; NR; 57 minutes
Release: 3/95
On June 8, 1964 Gerri Santoro's lover attempted to perform an abortion on the six-and-a-half-month pregnant woman. Instead, he left a bloody body in a Connecticut hotel room. The picture of the victim was published in *Ms.* magazine and has become a symbol of the feminist movement, made even more famous in *Our Bodies, Ourselves.* This is the story of the real life behind a political icon.

LIE DOWN WITH DOGS

Director/Writer: Wally White; **Director of Photography:** George Mitas; **Editor:** Hart F. Faber; **Music Supervision:** Jellybean Benitez; **Producers:** Wally White and Anthony Bennett
Miramax; R; 86 minutes
Release: 8/95
Cast: Wally White, Bash Halow and Randy Becker
Tommie (White), a struggling, young, gay New Yorker, spends his summer vacation in gay hot spot Provincetown, Massachusetts. White wore many hats in this production, serving as writer, director, co-producer and star.

LITTLE GIANTS

Director: Duwayne Dunham; **Writers:** James Ferguson, Robert Shallcross and Tommy Swerdlow; **Director of Photography:** Janusz Kaminski; **Editor:** Donn Cambern; **Music:** John Debney; **Production**

Designer: Bill Kenney; **Producer:** Arne Schmidt
Warner Bros.; PG; 107 minutes
Release: 10/94
Cast: Rick Moranis, Ed O'Neill, John Madden, Shawna Waldron, Mary Ellen Trainor, Mathew McCurley, Susanna Thompson, Brian Haley, Alexa Vega, Todd Bosley and Devon Sawa
When tomboy Becky O'Shea (Waldron) is rejected from the town's peewee football team because she's a girl, she forms her own team, recruiting other kids who could not make the highly competitive squad.

LITTLE ODESSA

Director/Writer: James Gray; **Director of Photography:** Tom Richmond; **Editor:** Dorian Harris; **Music:** Dana Sano; **Production Designer:** Kevin Thompson; **Producer:** Paul Webster
Fine Line; R; 99 minutes
Release: 5/95
Cast: Tim Roth, Edward Furlong, Vanessa Redgrave and Maximilian Schell
Russian hitman Joshua Shapira (Roth), banished from his Brighton Beach neighborhood by his father and the community, returns to his old turf for a job, and learns from his delinquent brother (Furlong) that their mother (Redgrave) is dying.

A LITTLE PRINCESS

Director: Alfonso Cuarón; **Writers:** Richard LaGravenese and Elizabeth Chandler; **Director of Photography:** Emmanuel Lubezki; **Editor:** Steven Weisberg; **Music:** Patrick Doyle; **Production Designer:** Bo Welch; **Producer:** Mark Johnson
Warner Bros.; G; 100 minutes
Release: 5/95
Cast: Eleanor Bron, Liam Cunningham, Lomax Study, Liesel Matthews and Vanessa Lee Chester
Sara Crewe (Matthews), a privileged young British girl, must attend a posh New York boarding school while her widowed father fights in World War I. When she learns her father is missing and she's penniless, Sara uses her imagination to help her through the hard times.

LITTLE WOMEN

Director: Gillian Armstrong; **Writer:** Robin Swicord; **Director of Photography:** Geffrey Simpson; **Editor:** Nicholas Beauman; **Music:** Thomas Newman; **Production Designer:** Jan Roelfs; **Producer:** Denise DiNovi
Columbia; PG; 115 minutes
Release: 12/94
Cast: Winona Ryder, Susan Sarandon, Gabriel Byrne, Trini Alvarado, Samantha Mathis, Kirsten Dunst, Claire Danes and Eric Stoltz
Based on the novel by Louisa May Alcott

The four March sisters, (Ryder, Alvarado, Danes and Mathis: older Amy, Dunst: younger Amy) come of age in New England in the 1860s in a poor but loving family headed by strong matriarch, Marmie (Sarandon).

LIVING IN OBLIVION

Director/Writer: Tom DiCillo; **Director of Photography**: Frank Prinzi; **Editor**: Camilla Toniolo; **Music**: Jim Farmer; **Production Designer**: Therese Deprez; **Producers**: Michael Griffiths and Marcus Viscidi
Sony Pictures Classics; NR; 91 minutes
Release: 3/95
Cast: Steve Buscemi, James Le Gros, Catherine Keener, Dermot Mulroney, Danielle von Zernick, Peter Dinklage, Rica Martens and Tom Jarmusch
In this behind-the-scenes look at low-low-budget filmmaking, director Nick Reve (Buscemi) runs into every problem imaginable while trying to create his black-and-white film *Living in Oblivion*. His leading man, the hip, egomaniacal Chad Palomino (Le Gros), emerges as a manipulative scene-stealer; his love scenes don't work out as planned and dwarf Tito (Dinklage) can't (or won't) get his lines straight.

LOSING ISAIAH

Director: Stephen Gyllenhaal; **Writer**: Naomi Foner; **Director of Photography**: Andrzej Bartkowiak; **Editor**: Harvey Rosenstock; **Music**: Mark Isham; **Production Designer**: Jeannine C. Oppewall; **Producers**: Howard W. Koch, Jr. and Naomi Foner
Paramount; R; 108 minutes
Release: 3/95
Cast: Jessica Lange, Halle Berry, David Strathairn, Cuba Gooding, Jr., Daisy Eagan, Marc John Jefferies and Samuel L. Jackson
Based on the novel by Seth Margolis
Social worker Margaret Lewin (Lange) is immediately taken by Isaiah (Jefferies), an infant who survived after his crack-addicted mother Khalia Richards (Berry) dumped him in the trash. She convinces her family to adopt him, but years later, the cleaned-up Richards wants her son back. Unwilling to let him go that easily, Lewin and Richards face off in a bitter custody battle.

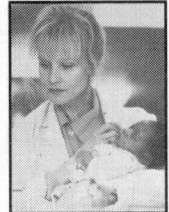

LOVE AFFAIR

Director: Glenn Gordon Caron; **Writers**: Robert Towne and Warren Beatty; **Director of Photography**: Conrad L. Hall; **Editor**: Robert C. Jones; **Music**: Ennio Morricone; **Production Designer**: Ferdinando Scarfiotti; **Producer**: Warren Beatty
Warner Bros.; PG-13; 108 minutes
Release: 10/94
Cast: Warren Beatty, Annette Bening, Katharine Hepburn and Garry Shandling
A remake of the 1957 *An Affair to Remember*, which is a remake of 1939's *Love Affair*
A man (Beatty) and a woman (Bening) meet on an airplane and fall in love. They plan to reunite on the top of the Empire State Building in three months, after they each break off their current engagements. Destiny keeps them apart until love prevails.

LOVE AND HUMAN REMAINS

Director: Denys Arcand; **Writer**: Brad Fraser; **Director of Photography**: Paul Sarossy; **Editor**: Alain Baril; **Music**: John McCarthy; **Production Designer**: François Seguin; **Producer**: Roger Frappier
Sony Pictures Classics; R; 99 minutes
Release: 6/95
Cast: Thomas Gibson, Ruth Marshall and Mia Kirshner
Based on Brad Fraser's play *Unidentified Human Remains and the True Nature of Love*
A group of Canadian twentysomething friends face uncertainty about their careers and sexuality, and the friends use and abuse these insecurities in their relationships. To complicate matters, a serial killer stalks the women.

A LOW DOWN DIRTY SHAME

Director/Writer: Keenen Ivory Wayans; **Director of Photography**: Matthew F. Leonetti; **Editor**: John F. Link; **Music**: Marcus Miller; **Production Designer**: Rob Wilson King; **Producers**: Roger Birnbaum and Joe Roth
Hollywood Pictures; R; 108 minutes
Release: 12/94
Cast: Keenen Ivory Wayans, Jada Pinkett, Charles S. Dutton, Salli Richardson, Andrew Divoff, Corwin Hawkins, Gary Cervantes and Gregory Sierra
Shame (Wayans), a down-and-out private investigator, is hired to help a former colleague at the DEA find a woman (Pinkett) in the witness protection program.

MAD LOVE

Director: Antonia Bird; **Writer**: Paula Milne; **Director of Photography**: Fred Tammes; **Editor**: Jeff Freeman; **Music**: Andy Roberts; **Production Designer**: David Brisbin; **Producer**: David Manson
Buena Vista; PG-13; 99 minutes
Release: 5/95
Cast: Drew Barrymore, Chris O'Donnell and Joan Allen
Intelligent, responsible Matt Leland (O'Donnell) falls for the manic-depressive, suicidal new girl in town, Casey Roberts (Barrymore). Escaping Roberts's pending institutionalization, the couple road trip down the west coast, where Roberts's mental illness becomes frighteningly apparent to Leland.

THE MADNESS OF KING GEORGE

Director: Nicholas Hytner; **Writer**: Alan Bennett; **Director of Photography**: Andrew Dunn; **Editor**: Tariq Anwar; **Music**: Adapted from George Frideric Handel by George Fenton; **Production Designer**: Ken Adam;

Producers: Stephen Evans and David Parfitt
Samuel Goldwyn; NR; 105 minutes
Release: 12/94
Cast: Nigel Hawthorne, Helen Mirren, Rupert Graves, Ian Holm and Amanda Donohoe
Based on the play by Alan Bennett

A physical condition manifests itself in King George III's (Hawthorne) bizarre behavior. His sons and political adversaries scheme for his throne as he questions his own grip on reality, and the nature of reality.

MAJOR PAYNE

Director: Nick Castle; **Writers:** Dean Lorey, Damon Wayans and Gary Rosen; **Director of Photography:** Richard Bowen; **Editor:** Patrick Kennedy; **Music:** Craig Safan; **Production Designer:** Peter Larkin; **Producers:** Eric L. Gold and Michael Rachmil
MCA/Universal; PG-13; 97 minutes
Release: 3/95
Cast: Damon Wayans, Orlando Brown, Chris Owen and Karyn Parsons
Based on a story by Joe Connelly and Bob Mosher and a screenplay by William Roberts and Richard Alan Simmons
Stereotypical marine Maj. Benson Payne (Wayans) has been reassigned to teach in a junior R.O.T.C. boarding school for boys, who are resistant to his military-like lessons. The major and his cadets compromise in time to prepare for the annual R.O.T.C. games.

MAMMA ROMA

Director/Writer: Pier Paolo Pasolini; **Director of Photography:** Tonino Delli Colli; **Editor:** Nino Baragli; **Music:** Carlo Rustichelli; **Producer:** Alfredo Bini
Milestone Films; NR; 110 minutes
U.S. Release: 2/95; premiered in Italy in 1962
Cast: Anna Magnani, Ettore Garofolo, Franco Citti, Silvana Corsini, Luisa Orioli, Paolo Volponi, Luciano Gonini and Vittorio La Paglia
In Italian with English subtitles
When Mamma Roma's (Magnani) pimp Carmine (Citti) marries, she is free to pursue a respectable life. Roma and her son Ettore (Garofolo) move to the Italian countryside, but Carmine shows up and threatens Roma's new-found happiness.

THE MANGLER

Director: Tobe Hooper; **Writers:** Tobe Hooper, Stephen Brooks and Peter Welbeck; **Director of Photography:** Amnon Salomon; **Editor:** David Heitner; **Music:** Barrington Pheloung; **Production Designer:** David Barkham; **Producer:** Anant Singh
New Line; R; 106 minutes
Release: 3/95
Cast: Robert Englund, Ted Levine, Vanessa Pike, Demetre Phillips and Lisa Morris

Based on a short story by Stephen King
Bill Gartley (Englund) owns small-town Maine's Blue Ribbon Laundry, the site of gruesome death and injuries. One of his machines, an old speed iron, mangles one of the laundromat's workers. Police officer John Hunton (Levine) discovers that Gartley has a pact with the appliance.

A MAN OF NO IMPORTANCE

Director: Suri Krishnamma; **Writer:** Barry Devlin; **Director of Photography:** Ashley Rowe; **Editor:** David Freeman; **Music:** Julian Nott; **Production Designer:** Jamie Leonard; **Producer:** Johnathan Cavendish
Sony Pictures Classics; R; 98 minutes
Release: 12/94
Cast: Albert Finney, Brenda Fricker, Michael Gambon, Tara Fitzgerald and Rufus Sewell
Dublin bus conductor Alfie Byrne (Finney), a repressed homosexual in unrequited love with his colleague (Sewell), attempts to stage a play by his hero, Oscar Wilde.

MAN OF THE HOUSE

Director: James Orr; **Writers:** James Orr and Jim Cruickshank; **Director of Photography:** Jamie Anderson; **Editor:** Harry Keramidas; **Music:** Mark Mancina; **Production Designer:** Lawrence G. Paull; **Producers:** Bonnie Bruckheimer and Marty Katz
Walt Disney Pictures; PG; 98 minutes
Release: 3/95
Cast: Chevy Chase, Farrah Fawcett, Jonathan Taylor Thomas, George Wendt and Chief Leonard George
Based on the story by David Peckinpah and Richard Jefferies
Eleven-year-old Ben Archer (Thomas) is determined to come between his mother Sandy (Fawcett) and her fiancé Jack Sturges (Chase) by putting Sturges through living hell. Federal prosecutor Sturges must also deal with henchmen who are on his trail for putting away a gangster.

MARTHA AND ETHEL

Director: Jyll Johnstone; **Writers/Producers:** Jyll Johnstone and Barbara Ettinger; **Director of Photography:** Joseph Friedman; **Editor:** Toby Shimin
Sony Pictures Classics; G; 80 minutes
Release: 2/95
Cast: Jyll Johnstone, Barbara Ettinger, Martha Kneifel, Ethel Edwards and members of the Johnstone, Ettinger and Edwards families
Jyll Johnstone and Barbara Ettinger, while documenting life with their former nannies, unearth resentment they feel toward their parents.

MARTHA AND I

Director/Writer: Jiri Weiss; **Director of Photography:** Viktor Ruzicka; **Editor:** Gisela Haller; **Music:** Jiri Stivin; **Producers:** Marius Schwartz and Sabine Tettenborn
Cinema Four; NR; 107 minutes
Release: 3/95
Cast: Marianne Saegebrecht, Michel Piccoli, Vaclov

1994 NATIONAL BOARD OF REVIEW AWARDS

Best Picture (tie)
Pulp Fiction

Forrest Gump

Best Director
Quentin Tarantino, *Pulp Fiction*

Best Actor
Tom Hanks, *Forrest Gump*

Best Actress
Miranda Richardson, *Tom and Viv*

Best Supporting Actor
Gary Sinise, *Forrest Gump*

Best Supporting Actress
Rosemary Harris, *Tom and Viv*

Best Foreign Film
Eat Drink Man Woman

Best Documentary
Hoop Dreams

The Lion King received a special award for excellence in family film.

NATIONAL BOARD OF REVIEW'S TOP MOVIES OF 1994

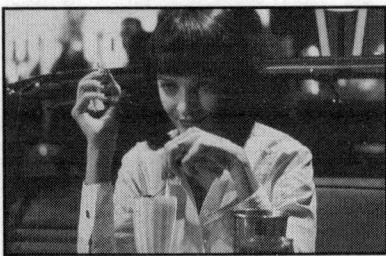

Pulp Fiction

1. *Pulp Fiction* and *Forrest Gump*
2. *Quiz Show*
3. *Four Weddings and a Funeral*
4. *Bullets Over Broadway*
5. *Ed Wood*
6. *Shawshank Redemption*
7. *Nobody's Fool*
8. *The Madness of King George*
9. *Tom and Viv*
10. *Heavenly Creatures*

Chalupa and Ondrej Vetchy
In German with English subtitles
When respected Jewish obstetrician Ernst (Piccoli) marries his gentile housekeeper Martha (Saegebrecht) in 1930s Czechoslovakia, he puts them both in grave danger as Nazism is on the march.

MARY SHELLEY'S FRANKENSTEIN

Director: Kenneth Branagh; **Writers:** Steph Lady, Frank Darabont; **Director of Photography**: Roger Pratt; **Editor:** Andrew Marcus; **Music:** Patrick Doyle; **Production Designer:** Tim Harvey; **Producers:** Francis Ford Coppola, James V. Hart, David Parfitt and John Veitch
TriStar; R; 159 minutes
Release: 11/94
Cast: Kenneth Branagh, Robert De Niro, Helena Bonham Carter, Tom Hulce, Aidan Quinn and John Cleese
Based on the novel by Mary Shelley
Victor Frankenstein (Branagh) goes to medical school planning to eradicate death, but instead creates life: the monster (De Niro), who turns against his creator.

MAYA LIN: A STRONG CLEAR VISION

Director/Writer: Freida Lee Mock; **Photography:** Eddie Marritz and Don Lenzer; **Editor:** William T. Cartwright, Sr.; **Music:** Charles Bernstein; **Producers:** Freida Lee Mock and Terry Sanders
Sanders & Mock; NR; 105 minutes
Release: 2/95
This documentary portrays visionary architect Maya Lin, who was 20 years old when she won a contest to design a Vietnam Veterans Memorial for Washington D.C. Originally criticized by some as too somber, her black wall covered with the names of those who died is now a place of pilgrimage.

MEET THE FEEBLES

Director: Peter Jackson; **Writers:** Danny Mulheron, Frances Walsh, Stephen Sinclair and Peter Jackson; **Director of Photography:** Murray Milne; **Editor:** Jamie Selkirk; **Music:** Peter Dasent; **Production Designer:** Mike Kane; **Puppet Designer:** Cameron Chittock; **Supervising Puppeteers:** Jonathan Acorn and Peter Jackson; **Producers:** Jim Booth and Peter Jackson
Greycat Films; NR; 94 minutes
Release: 2/95
Voices of: Donna Akersten, Stuart Devenie, Mark Hadlow, Ross Jolly, Brian Sergent, Peter Vere Jones and Mark Wright
The film industry is parodied here using puppets that represent show-biz types: a walrus producer, a worm stage manager, a fox director, a fly journalist (who puts a new spin on the term muck-raking) and a rabbit who has AIDS. The puppets bleed, have sex, retch and drool convincingly.

MIAMI RHAPSODY

Director/Writer: David Frankel; **Director of Photography:** Jack Wallner; **Editor:** Steven Weisberg; **Music:** Mark Isham; **Production Designer:** J. Mark Harrington; **Producers:** Barry Jossen and David Frankel
Hollywood Pictures; PG-13; 95 minutes
Release: 1/95
Cast: Sarah Jessica Parker, Gil Bellows, Antonio Banderas, Mia Farrow, Paul Mazursky, Kevin Pollak, Barbara Garrick, Carla Gugino, Bo Eason, Naomi Campbell and Kelly Bishop
A young woman (Parker) contemplates marriage, but is wary of commitment because of the infidelities in her sibilings' and parents' marriages.

MIDNIGHT DANCERS

Director: Mel Chionglo; **Writer:** Ricardo Lee; **Director of Photography:** George Tutanes; **Editor:** Jess Navarro; **Music:** Nonong Buenoamino; **Production Designer:** Edgar Martin Littaua; **Producer:** Richard Wong Tang
First Run Features; NR; 115 minutes
Release: 7/95
Cast: Alex Del Rosario, Gandong Cervantes, Lawrence David, Perla Bautista, Soxy Topacio and R. S. Francisco
In Filipino with English subtitles
Three Filipino brothers Sonny (David), Joel (Del Rosario) and Dennis (Cervantes) living in poverty in Manila work as male prostitutes in Club Exotica to support the family.

MIGHTY MORPHIN POWER RANGERS: THE MOVIE

Director: Bryan Spicer; **Writer:** Arne Olsen; **Director of Photography:** Paul Murphy; **Editor:** Wayne Wahrman; **Production Designer:** Craig Stearns; **Producers:** Haim Saban, Shuki Levy and Suzanne Todd
Twentieth Century-Fox; PG; 95 minutes
Release: 6/95
Cast: Karan Ashley, Johnny Yong Bosch, Steve Cardenas, Jason David Frank, Amy Jo Johnson, David Yost, Gabrielle Fitzpatrick and Paul Freeman
Based on a story by John Kamps and Arne Olsen
The six color-coded martial arts heroes made it to the big screen, but fighting a different villain than in the television series. Purple-faced Ivan Ooze (Freeman) has smashed the Rangers' command center, where they go to get orders from their leader, and they must travel to another planet for an alternative source of power.

MINA TANNENBAUM

Director/Writer: Martine Dugowson; **Director of Photography:** Dominique Chapuis; **Editors:** Martine Barraqué and Dominique Gallieni; **Music:** Peter Chase; **Production Designer:** Oury Milshtein; **Producer:** Georges Benayoun
New Yorker Films; NR; 128 minutes
Release: 3/95
Cast: Romane Bohringer, Elsa Zylberstein, Florence Thomassin and Nils Tavernier
In French with English subtitles

Mina (Bohringer) and Ethel (Zylberstein) were born only hours apart in a French hospital, and because they were both outcasts (though for different reasons) they developed a friendship that would see them through adolescence and adulthood.

MIRACLE ON 34TH STREET

Director: Les Mayfield; **Writers:** Valentine Davies, John Hughes and George Seaton; **Director of Photography:** Julio Macat; **Editor:** Raja Gosnell; **Music:** Bruce Broughton; **Production Designer:** Doug Kraner; **Producer:** John Hughes
Twentieth Century-Fox; PG; 114 minutes
Release: 11/94
Cast: Richard Attenborough, Elizabeth Perkins, Dylan McDermott, J.T. Walsh, James Remar, Mara Wilson, Robert Prosky, Jane Leeves, William Windom and Simon Jones
A remake of the 1947 *Miracle on 34th Street*
A department store Santa Claus (Attenborough) is put on trial for insanity because he insists he is the real thing.

MIXED NUTS

Director: Nora Ephron; **Writers:** Nora Ephron and Delia Ephron; **Director of Photography:** Sven Nykvist; **Editor:** Robert Reitano; **Music:** George Fenton; **Production Designer:** Bill Groom; **Producer:** Paul Junger Witt
TriStar; PG-13; 97 minutes
Release: 12/94
Cast: Steve Martin, Madeline Kahn, Robert Klein, Anthony LaPaglia, Juliette Lewis, Rob Reiner, Adam Sandler, Liev Schreiber, Rita Wilson, Parker Posey, Jon Stewart, Joely Fisher, Steven Wright, Garry Shandling and Victor Garber
Based on the French film *Le Père Noël Est une Ordure*
The less-than-stable staff of a Venice, California, suicide hot line deal with a night of depressing calls on Christmas Eve.

MOVING THE MOUNTAIN

Director/Writer: Michael Apted; **Director of Photography:** Maryse Alberti; **Editor:** Susanne Rostock; **Music:** Liu Sola; **Producer:** Trudie Styler
October Films; NR; 83 minutes
Release: 4/95
With: Wang Dan, Wang Chaohua, Wu'er Kaixi, Chai Ling and Li Lu
Dramatic sequences cast: Huang Yi-Ming and Zhang Jin-Ming
In Mandarin and English with English subtitles
Using interviews with radical students and television and video footage interspersed with dramatic flashbacks, Apted chronicles Beijing's 1989 Tiananmen Square uprising.

MRS. PARKER AND THE VICIOUS CIRCLE

Director: Alan Rudolph; **Writers:** Randy Sue Coburn and Alan Rudolph; **Director of Photography:** Jan Kiesser; **Editor:** Suzy Elmiger; **Music:** Mark Isham;

Production Designer: Francois Seguin; **Producer:** Robert Altman
Fine Line; R; 126 minutes
Release: 12/94
Cast: Jennifer Jason Leigh, Matthew Broderick, Lili Taylor Andrew McCarthy, Campbell Scott and Peter Gallagher

The literary wits of 1920s New York, including poet Dorothy Parker (Leigh) and novelist Robert Benchley (Scott), lunch together daily at the Algonquin Hotel restaurant and drink together nightly to talk, romance and mourn.

MURDER IN THE FIRST

Director: Marc Rocco; **Writer:** Dan Gordon; **Director of Photography:** Fred Murphy; **Editor:** Russell Livingstone; **Music:** Christopher Young; **Production Designer:** Kirk M. Petruccelli; **Producers:** Marc Frydman and Mark Wolper
Warner Bros.; R; 122 minutes
Release: 1/95
Cast: Christian Slater, Kevin Bacon, Gary Oldman, Embeth Davidtz, Brad Dourif, William H. Macy and R. Lee Ermey

An idealistic young attorney (Slater) defends Henri Young (Bacon), a prisoner at Alcatraz who after three years of solitary confinement, murders the inmate he thought had foiled his escape plan.

MURIEL'S WEDDING

Director/Writer: P.J. Hogan; **Director of Photography:** Martin McGrath; **Editor:** Jill Bilcock; **Music:** Peter Best; **Production Designer:** Patrick Reardon; **Producers:** Lynda House and Jocelyn Moorhouse
Miramax; R; 105 minutes
Release: 3/95
Cast: Toni Collette, Bill Hunter, Rachel Griffiths, Jeanie Drynan and Gennie Nevinson

No one in the small, dead-end town of Porpoise Spit, Australia, takes Muriel (Collette) very seriously: she's plain, giddy and large. The high-spirted

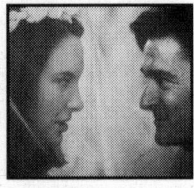

Muriel seizes a chance to leave behind the small-minded town and heads to metropolitan Sydney where her vacation becomes permanent and she gains confidence, a new name and lives an outrageous adventure.

MY FAMILY: MI FAMILIA

Director: Gregory Nava; **Writers:** Gregory Nava and Anna Thomas; **Director of Photography:** Edward Lachman; **Editor:** Nancy Richardson; **Folk Music:** Pepe Avila; **Orchestral Score:** Mark McKenzie; **Production Designer:** Barry Robison; **Producer:** Anna Thomas

New Line; R; 120 minutes
Release: 3/95
Cast: Jimmy Smits, Esai Morales, Eduardo López Rojas, Jenny Gago and Edward James Olmos

This epic saga follows through three generations the travails of the Latino Sanchezs from the 1920s through the 1980s. The problems in the family include drugs, prison, deportment and estrangement.

MY LIFE AND TIMES WITH ANTONIN ARTAUD

Director: Gérard Mordillat; **Writers:** Gérard Mordillat and Jérôme Prieur; **Director of Photography:** François Catonné; **Editor:** Sophie Rouffio; **Music:** Jean-Claude Petit; **Producer:** Denis Freyd
Leisure Time Features; NR; 93 minutes
Release: 7/95
Cast: Sami Frey, Marc Barbé, Julie Zézéquel and Valérie Jeannet
Based on the diaries of Jacques Prevel
In French with English subtitles

Poets Jacques Prevel (Barbé) and Antonin Artaud (Frey) began a friendship in 1946 Paris that was mutually beneficial, though they did care about each other. Artaud, a master poet, dispensed literary advice to the self-absorbed though untalented Prevel, and Prevel supplied the mentally ill Artaud numbing pills to alleviate the pain from cancer. Using Artaud as an example, the film implies that insanity and artistic brilliance are closely related.

THE MYSTERY OF RAMPO

Director: Kazuyoshi Okuyama; **Writers:** Kazuyoshi Okuyama and Yuhel Enoki; **Director of Photography:** Yasushi Sasakibara; **Editor:** Akimasa Kawashima; **Music:** Akira Senju; **Production Designer:** Kyoko Heya; **Producer:** Yoshihisa Nakagawa
Samuel Goldwyn; NR; 103 minutes
Release: 6/95
Cast: Masahiro Motoki, Naoto Takenaka, Michiko Hada, Teruyuki Kagawa and Mikijiro Hira
Based on the original story by Edogawa Rampo
In Japanese with English subtitles

Dreams and reality, fiction and nonfiction converge in this visually beautiful story of a Japanese mystery writer (Takenaka) whose work eerily comes to life in the real world.

NAKED KILLER

Director: Clarence Fok; **Writer/Producer:** Wong Jing; **Director of Photography:** Yim Wai Lun
Rim Film Distributors; NR; 95 minutes
Release: 3/95
Cast: Simon Yam, Chingmy Yau, Svenwara Madoka and Kelly Yao
In Cantonese with English subtitles

A group of lesbians embark on an assassination campaign, which involves the murder and genital mutilation of men. While detective Tinam (Yam) investigates the crimes, he finds that one of the women may be able to cure his impotence.

NELL

Director: Michael Apted; **Writer:** Miles Malleson; **Director of Photography:** Frederick A. Young; **Editor:** Jim Clark; **Music:** Edward German and Philip Braham; **Production Designer:** Jon Hutman; **Producers:** Jodie Foster and Renee Missel
Twentieth Century-Fox; PG-13; 118 minutes
Release: 12/94
Cast: Jodie Foster, Liam Neeson and Natasha Richardson
Based on the play by Mark Handley

Nell (Foster), a woman who grew up as a wild child with her own incomprehensible language, becomes the object of fascination and contention for the doctor (Neeson) and psychologist (Richardson) who study her. Much histrionics ensue.

THE NET

Director: Irwin Winkler; **Writers:** John Brancato and Michael Ferris; **Director of Photography:** Jack N. Green; **Editor:** Richard Halsey; **Music:** Mark Isham; **Production Designer:** Dennis Washington; **Producer:** Irwin Winkler
Columbia; PG-23; 118 minutes
Release: 7/95
Cast: Sandra Bullock and Jeremy Northam
Everyone's worst information-age nightmare comes true for Angela Bennett (Bullock): to be erased from existence by a simple keystoke. The computer hacker, who has spent the past four years living on the Internet having minimal face-to-face human interaction, stumbles across a program powerful enough to interfere with Wall Street, the federal government and air-traffic control. The owners of the program pursue her and change her name on all computer databases, and she must outwit them to regain her identity.

NEW JERSEY DRIVE

Director/Writer: Nick Gomez; **Director of Photography:** Adam Kimmel; **Editor:** Tracy S. Granger; **Music:** Dawn Soler; **Production Designer:** Lester Cohen; **Producers:** Larry Meistrich and Bob Gosse
Gramercy; NR; 100 minutes
Release: 3/95
Cast: Sharron Corley, Gabriel Casseus, Saul Stein and Andre Moore
Based on the story by Nick Gomez and Michel Marriott
Midget (Casseus) and Jason (Corley), two poor New Jersey black men, steal cars as much for the thrill and status as they do for the money. At the center of their life is racism, especially at the hands of police, who take pleasure in brutalizing the misguided teens.

1994 NATIONAL SOCIETY OF FILM CRITICS AWARDS

Best Picture
 Pulp Fiction

Best Director
 Quentin Tarantino, Pulp Fiction

Best Screenwriters
 Quentin Tarantino and Roger Avary, Pulp Fiction

Best Actor
 Paul Newman, Nobody's Fool

Best Actress
 Jennifer Jason Leigh, Mrs. Parker and the Vicious Circle

Quentin Tarantino

Best Supporting Actor
 Martin Landau, Ed Wood

Best Supporting Actress
 Dianne Wiest, Bullets Over Broadway

Best Foreign Film
 Red

Best Documentary
 Hoop Dreams

Best Cinematography
 Stefan Czapsky, Ed Wood

Special citations in the experimental category were given to Bela Tarr's Hungarian epic **Satantango** and Lewis Klahr's animated **The Pharaoh's Belt**.

1995 INDEPENDENT SPIRIT AWARDS

The 10th Independent Spirit Awards, honoring excellence in independent film, were presented on March 25, 1995 under a tent on Santa Monica beach by the Independent Feature Project/West. The I.F.P./West promotes filmmakers who work outside the studio system. This year the nominating committee had to revise their definition of independent film as many previously independent companies have been purchased by major studios: Disney owns Miramax, Turner Broadcasting System, Inc. owns New Line and Fine Line and Universal co-owns Gramercy. The regulations now allow the committee to consider films that have "a percentage of financing from non-studio sources, uniqueness of vision, economy of means and original, provocative subject matter."

Feature
  Pulp Fiction

First Feature
  David Russell, *Spanking the Monkey*

Male Lead
  Samuel L. Jackson, *Pulp Fiction*

Female Lead
  Linda Fiorentino, *The Last Seduction*

Supporting Male
  Chazz Palminteri, *Bullets Over Broadway*

Supporting Female
  Dianne Wiest, *Bullets Over Broadway*

Debut Performance
  Sean Nelson, *Fresh*

Director
  Quentin Tarantino, *Pulp Fiction*

Screenplay
  Quentin Tarantino and Roger Avary, *Pulp Fiction*

First Screenplay
  David Russell, *Spanking the Monkey*

Cinematography
  John Thomas, *Barcelona*

Foreign Film
  Red, Krzystzof Kieslowski

Special Distinction Prize
  Hoop Dreams

Dedicated Independent Spirit
  Samuel Goldwyn, Jr.

Someone to Watch Prize
  Lodge Kerrigan, *Clean, Shaven*

NINA TAKES A LOVER

Director/Writer: Alan Jacobs; **Director of Photography:** Phil Parmet; **Editor:** John Nutt; **Music:** Todd Boekelheide; **Production Designer:** Don De Fina; **Producers:** Jane Hernandez and Alan Jacobs
Triumph/TriStar; R; 100 minutes
Release: 5/95
Cast: Laura San Giacomo, Paul Rhys, Michael O'Keefe, Cristi Conaway and Fisher Stevens
While Nina's (San Giacomo) husband is away on business trip, she and a Welsh photographer (Rhys) have an affair after meeting in the park and teasing each other over the telephone. Nina's best friend (Conaway) is also having an affair, and Nina lets the couple use her apartment for a tryst, which causes Nina more trouble than she imagined.

NINE MONTHS

Director/Writer: Chris Columbus; **Director of Photography:** Donald McAlpine; **Editor:** Raja Gosnell; **Music:** Hans Zimmer; **Production Designer:** Angelo P. Graham; **Producers:** Anne Francois, Chris Columbus, Mark Radcliffe and Michael Barnathan
Twentieth Century-Fox; PG-13; 100 minutes
Release: 7/95
Cast: Hugh Grant, Julianne Moore, Tom Arnold, Joan Cusack, Jeff Goldblum and Robin Williams
Based on the French film *Neuf Mois*
With his performance in *Nine Months*, Grant passes his initiation into big-budget Hollywood comedy, although there wasn't much chance he would fail. Samuel Faulkner  (Grant), though in a relationship he cherishes, avoids marriage and children because of his work as a child psychologist. He gets a rude awakening when his girlfriend of five years (Moore) tells him she's pregnant. Though the pregnancy threatens the relationship, Faulkner does a complete 360 and evolves into a caring father and partner. Williams nearly steals the show as the flaky Russian obstetrician who delivers the baby.

NOBODY'S FOOL

Director/Writer: Robert Benton; **Director of Photography:** John Bailey; **Editor:** John Bloom; **Music:** Howard Shore; **Production Designer:** David  Gropman; **Producers:** Scott Rudin and Arlene Donovan
Paramount; R; 112 minutes
Release: 12/94
Cast: Paul Newman, Jessica Tandy, Bruce Willis and Melanie Griffith
Based on the novel by Richard Russo

A 60-year-old semi-employed construction worker (Newman) gets a chance to reconcile with the family he abandoned when his son was a baby.

OLEANNA

Director/Writer: David Mamet; **Director of Photography:** Andrzej Sekula; **Editor:** Barbara Tulliver; **Music:** Rebecca Pidgeon; **Producers:** Patricia Wolf and Sarah Green
Samuel Goldwyn; R; 89 minutes
Release: 11/94
Cast: William Macy and Debra Eisenstadt
Based on the play by David Mamet
A college student (Eisenstadt) seeks help from one of her professors (Macy) then accuses him of sexual harassment. Both points of view are articulated in an adaptation of a play that caused much discussion.

ONCE WERE WARRIORS

Director: Lee Tamahori; **Writer:** Riwia Brown; **Director of Photography:** Stuart Dryburgh; **Editor:** Michael Horton; **Music:** Murray McNabb and Murray Grindlay; **Production Designer:** Michael Dane; **Producer:** Robin Scholes
Fine Line; R; 108 minutes
Release: 2/95
Cast: Rena Owen, Temuera Morrison, Mamaengaroa Kerr-Bell, Julian "Sonny" Arahanga and Taungaroa Emile
Based on the novel by Alan Duff
Beth Heke (Owen) is having a bad day: her alcoholic husband (Morrison) lost his job and gave her a black eye — again, one son is heading to jail and the other had his  face completely tattooed. Director Tamahori offers a look at troubled New Zealand Maori culture and family life in the 1990s.

ONLY YOU

Director: Norman Jewison; **Writer:** Diane Drake; **Director of Photography:** Sven Nykvist; **Editor:** Stephen E. Rivkin; **Music:** Rachel Portman; **Production Designer:** Luciana Arrighi; **Producers:** Robert N. Fried, Norman Jewison, Charles Mulvehilll and Cary Woods
TriStar; PG; 108 minutes
Release: 10/94
Cast: Marisa Tomei, Robert Downey, Jr. and Bonnie Hunt
Faith Corvatch (Tomei) travels abroad days before her wedding in search of her dream man. She runs into a man (Downey) who, though not the man she had in mind, is the answer to her dreams.

OPERATION DUMBO DROP

Director: Simon Wincer; **Writers:** Gene Quintano and Jim Kouf; **Director of Photography:** Russell Boyd; **Editor:** O. Nicholas Brown; **Music:** David

1994 LOS ANGELES FILM CRITICS ASSOCIATION AWARDS

Best Picture
  Pulp Fiction

Best Director
  Quentin Tarantino, *Pulp Fiction*

Best Actor
  John Travolta, *Pulp Fiction*

Best Actress
  Jessica Lange, *Blue Sky*

Best Screenplay
  Quentin Tarantino, *Pulp Fiction*

Best Supporting Actor
  Martin Landau, *Ed Wood*

Best Supporting Actress
  Dianne Wiest, *Bullets Over Broadway*

1994 BOSTON SOCIETY OF FILM CRITICS AWARDS

Best Picture
  Pulp Fiction

Best Director
  Quentin Tarantino, *Pulp Fiction*

Best Screenplay
  Quentin Tarantino, *Pulp Fiction*

Best Actor
  Albert Finney, *The Browning Version*

Best Actress
  Julianne Moore, *Vanya on 42nd Street*

Best Supporting Actor
  Martin Landau, *Ed Wood*

Best Supporting Actress
  Kirsten Dunst, *Interview With the Vampire* and *Little Women*

Best Cinematography
  Stefan Czapsky, *Ed Wood*

Best Documentary
  Hoop Dreams

Best Foreign Film
  Red

A commendation was voted to founding member **David Brudnoy.**

1994 NEW YORK FILM CRITICS CIRCLE AWARDS

Quiz Show

Best Picture
Quiz Show

Best Director
Quentin Tarantino, *Pulp Fiction*

Best Screenwriter
Quentin Tarantino, *Pulp Fiction*

Best Actor
Paul Newman, *Nobody's Fool*

Best Actress
Linda Fiorentino, *The Last Seduction*

Best Supporting Actor
Martin Landau,
Ed Wood

Best Supporting Actress
Dianne Wiest, *Bullets Over Broadway*

Best Foreign Film
Red

Red

Best Documentary
Hoop Dreams

French director **Jean-Luc Godard** received a special award for his "influence on world cinema."

Darnell Martin, director of *I Like It Like That,* was honored as best first-time filmmaker — an award given only on a year-by-year basis.

Newman; **Production Designer:** Paul Peters;
Producers: Diane Nabatoff and David Madden
Walt Disney; PG; 108 minutes
Cast: Danny Glover, Ray Liotta, Denis Leary, Doug E. Doug, Corin Nemec and Dinh Thien Le
Based on the story by Maj. Jim Morris
In 1968, a North Vietnamese village's mascot, an elephant, was killed, and the death involved Capt. T. C. Doyle (Liotta) and a Nestlé Crunch candybar. To make amends, the Capt. Sam Chahill (Glover) suggests that the military replace the elephant. What follows is the challenge of making the airborne delivery.

OUTBREAK

Director: Wolfgang Petersen; **Writers:** Laurence Dworet and Robert Roy Pool; **Director of Photography:** Michael Balhaus; **Editors:** Neil Travis, Lynzee Klingman and William Hoy; **Music:** James Newton Howard; **Production Designer:** William Sandell; **Producers:** Arnold Kopelson, Wolfgang Petersen and Gail Katz
Warner Bros.; R; 125 minutes
Release: 3/95
Cast: Dustin Hoffman, Rene Russo, Morgan Freeman, Cuba Gooding, Jr., Patrick Dempsey, Donald Sutherland and Kevin Spacey
A killer virus first identified in the 1960s has resurfaced and wiped out an entire African village. Col. Sam Daniels, M.D. (Hoffman) wants to warn the United States that the virus could spread, but his commanding officer Gen. Billy Ford (Freeman) overrules him. Daniels' fears are realized — the disease strikes a Californian town. He and ex-wife Dr. Roberta Keough (Robby) team up (and Daniels hopes will reunite romantically) to save the country from the virus.

THE PAGEMASTER

Live Action Director: Joe Johnston; **Animation Director:** Maurice Hunt; **Writers:** David Casci, Ernie Contreras and David Kirschner; **Director of Photography:** Alexander Gruszunski; **Editor:** Kaja Fehr; **Music:** James Horner; **Production Designers:** Gay Lawrence, Roy Smith, Roy Forge Smith and Valerio Ventura; **Producers:** Paul Gertz and David Kirschner
Twentieth Century-Fox; G; 75 minutes
Release: 11/94
Cast: Macaulay Culkin, Christopher Lloyd, Ed Begley, Jr. and Mel Harris.
Voices of: Whoopi Goldberg, Patrick Stewart, Leonard Nimoy and Frank Welker
Ducking into a library to escape a rainstorm, a timid boy (Culkin) takes an animated trip with the book characters Adventure, Fantasy and Horror, who help him find courage.

PANTHER

Director: Mario Van Peebles; **Writer:** Melvin Van Peebles; **Director of Photography:** Eddie Pei; **Editor:** Earl Watson; **Music:** Larry Robinson; **Production Designer:** Richard Hoover; **Producers:** Preston

Holmes, Mario Van Peebles and Melvin Van Peebles
Gramercy; R; 125 minutes
Release: 5/95
Cast: Kadeem Hardison, Bokeem Woodbine, Courtney B. Vance, Marcus Chong, Anthony Griffith, Wesley Jonathan, Richard Dysart, Joe Don Baker and Mario Van Peebles
This docudrama traces the rise of the Black Panthers in the 1960s, from their early non-uni-formed days to their armed, black-clad days as militant fighters of oppression. Panthers' co-founders Bobby Seale (Vance) and Huey Newton (Chong) recruit an army of Oakland's black men to patrol the streets, looking for and confronting police brutality.

PARTY GIRL
Director: Daisy von Scherler Mayer; **Writers:** Daisy von Scherler Mayer and Harry Birckmayer; **Director of Photography**: Michael Slovis; **Editor:** Cara Silverman; **Music:** Bill Coleman; **Production Designer:** Kevin Thompson; **Producers:** Harry Birckmayer
First Look Pictures; R; 98 minutes
Release: 6/95
Cast: Parker Posey, Guillermo Diaz, Omar Townsend, Anthony DeSando, Donna Mitchell, Liev Schreiber and Sasha von Scherler
Ultimate 1990s party girl Mary (Posey) lives hard in Manhattan's Lower East Side until she is arrested for illegally selling alcohol. Facing limited options, she takes a job as a clerk in a branch of the New York Public Library, where she sacrifices her fast life for the Dewey Decimal System.

THE PEBBLE AND THE PENGUIN
Director: Don Bluth; **Writers:** Rachel Koretsky and Steve Whitestone; **Editor:** Thomas V. Moses; **Music:** Mark Watters; **Producer:** Russell Bond
MGM; G; 74 minutes
Release: 5/95
Voices of: Martin Short, James Belushi, Tim Curry and Annie Golden
Each male penguin in Antarctica must present his intended a perfect pebble for mating rights and as a symbol of his love. Hubie (Short) has his eye out for Marina (Golden), but can't seem to find the right stone. When he finally does, an evil pen-guin (Curry) nearly foils Hubie's engagement.

THE PEREZ FAMILY
Director: Mira Nair; **Writer:** Robin Swicord; **Director of Photography**: Stuart Dryburgh; **Editor:** Bob Estrin; **Music:** Jellybean Benitez; **Production Designer:** Mark Friedberg; **Producers:** Michael Nozik and Lydia Dean Pilcher
Samuel Goldwyn; R; 112 minutes
Release: 5/95
Cast: Alfred Molina, Marisa Tomei, Anjelica Huston, Chazz Palminteri and Trini Alvarado
Based on the novel by Christine Bell
Juan Perez (Molina), former owner of a Cuban

1994 CHICAGO FILM CRITICS AWARDS

Best Picture
Hoop Dreams

Best Actor
Tom Hanks, *Forrest Gump*

Best Actress
Jennifer Jason Leigh, *Mrs. Parker and the Vicious Circle*

Best Supporting Actor
Martin Landau, *Ed Wood*

Best Supporting Actress
Dianne Wiest, *Bullets Over Broadway*

Best Director
Quentin Tarantino, *Pulp Fiction*

Best Screenplay
Quentin Tarantino and Roger Avary, *Pulp Fiction*

Best Foreign Film
Three Colors: Blue, White and *Red,* Krzysztof Kieslowski

Best Musical Score
Hans Zimmer, *The Lion King*

Most Promising Actor
Hugh Grant

Most Promising Actress
Kirsten Dunst

Commitment to Chicago Award
William Petersen, co-founder of Chi's Remains Theatre Ensemble

Hugh Grant

sugar plantation, and Dottie Perez (Tomei), former prostitute, meet on their way to Miami as part of 1980's Mariel boatlift and pretend to be married to facilitate the immigration process. The optimistic Dottie anticipates a new life in Miami, and pessimistic Juan fears his wife Carmela (Huston) grew sick of waiting and abandoned him.

PICTURE BRIDE

Director: Kayo Hatta; **Writers:** Kayo Hatta and Mari Hatta; **Director of Photography**: Claudio Rocha; **Editors:** Lynzee Klingman and Mallori Gottlieb; **Producers:** Lisa Onodera and Diane Mei Lin Mark
Miramax; PG-13; 90 minutes
Release: 4/95
Cast: Youki Kudoh, Akira Takayama, Tamlyn Tomita and Toshiro Mifune
In Japanese and English with English subtitles
Sixteen-year-old Riyo (Kudoh), a Japanese picture bride, travels to Hawaii for the marriage her aunt arranged. She is shocked to see her future groom Matsuji (Takayama) is old enough to be her father. Riyo shows no affection for Matsuji and saves her paltry wages for a ticket home.

PLUTONIUM CIRCUS

Director/Producer/Editor: George Ratliff; **Director of Photography**: Judd Metni
NR; 73 minutes
Release: 6/95
When the cold war ended, the government sent the Amarillo, Texas, Pantex Plant an arsenal of nuclear weapons, including MIRVs and ICBMs, to be dismantled, apparently not worried that the plutonium could leak into the water supply that hydrates several states. This documentary includes interviews with local officials, businessmen and residents who are proud that the plant is in their town and appreciate the jobs it has created.

POCAHONTAS

Directors: Mike Gabriel and Eric Goldberg; **Writers:** Carl Binder, Susanna Grant and Philip LaZebnik; **Editor:** H. Lee Peterson; **Music:** Alan Menken; **Lyrics:** Stephen Schwartz; **Producer:** James Pentecost
Walt Disney Pictures; G; 81 minutes
Release: 6/95
Voices of: Irene Bedard, Judy Kuhn, Mel Gibson, David Ogden Stiers, John Kassir, Russell Means, Christian Bale, Linda Hunt, Danny Mann
White settlers led by gold-hungry Governor Ratcliffe (Stiers) reach the Virginia coast and start building a fort, christening it Jamestown after King James. Inquisitive scout John Smith (Gibson) meets Native American princess Pocahontas (Bedard) by a river, and they fall in love as fighting erupts between whites and Native Americans.

PONTIAC MOON

Director: Peter Medek; **Writer:** Finn Taylor; **Director of Photography:** Thomas Kloss; **Editor:** Anne V. Coates; **Music:** Randy Edelman; **Production Designer:** Jeffrey Beecroft; **Producers:** Youssef Vahabzadeh
Paramount; PG-13; 108 minutes
Release: 11/94
Cast: Ted Danson, Mary Steenburgen, Ryan Todd, Eric Schweig, Cathy Moriarty and Max Gail
Washington Bellamy (Danson), seeking to teach his son Andy (Todd) to dream big, takes the boy on a road trip the night before the Apollo XI moon launch. Bellamy plans to drive the distance between Earth and the moon in his classic Pontiac. Bellamy's agoraphobic wife Katherine (Steenburgen) stays behind, but summons the courage to follow her son and husband when she senses trouble.

POSTCARDS FROM AMERICA

Director/Writer: Steve McLean; **Director of Photography:** Ellen Kuras; **Editor:** Elizabeth Gazzara; **Music:** Stephen Endleman; **Production Designer:** Therese Deprez; **Producers:** Craig Paull and Christine Vachon
98 minutes
Release: 7/95
Cast: Jim Lyons, Michael Tighe, Olmo Tighe, Michael Imperioli, Michael Ringer and Maggie Low
Adapted from the writings of David Wojnarowicz
David (played at different stages in his life by Lyons, Michael Tighe, Olmo Tighe and Imperioli), flees his abusive suburban home, becomes a teenage New York hustler and as an adult hits the road, killing his pain with anonymous sex anywhere he can find it.

THE POSTMAN (IL POSTINO)

Director: Michael Radford; **Writers:** Anna Pavignano, Michael Radford, Furio Scarpelli, Giacomo Scarpelli and Massimo Troisi; **Director of Photography:** Franco Di Giacomo; **Editor:** Roberto Perpignani; **Music:** Luis Enrique Bacalov; **Production Designer:** Lorenzo Baraldi; **Producers:** Mario and Vittorio Cecchi Gori and Gaetano Daniele
Miramax; NR; 113 minutes
Release: 6/95
Cast: Massimo Troisi, Philippe Noiret, Maria Grazia Cucinotta, Linda Moretti and Renato Scarpa
Based on the novel *Burning Patience* by Antonio Skarmeta
In Italian with English subtitles
Mario Ruoppolo's (Troisi) life changes when exiled Chilean poet Pablo Neruda (Noiret) moves to the small Italian island where Ruoppolo lives. Ruoppolo delivers mail to Neruda by bicycle, and the men develop a mutual interest in each other's lives.

PRIEST

Director: Antonia Bird; **Writer:** Jimmy McGovern; **Director of Photography:** Fred Tammes; **Editor:** Susan Spivey; **Music:** Andy Roberts; **Production Designer:** Raymond Langhorn; **Producers:** George Faber and Josephine Ward
Miramax; R; 97 minutes
Release: 3/95
Cast: Linus Roache, Tom Wilkinson, Cathy Tyson and Robert Carlyle

One of the most controversial movies of 1995, and fodder for right-wing attacks against the entertainment industry, *Priest* portrays the inner turmoil of homosexual cleric Greg Pilkington (Roache), who struggles with temptation he cannot overcome and the confidentiality of the confessional, which his conscience tells him to disregard.

THE PROFESSIONAL

Director/Writer: Luc Besson; **Director of Photography:** Thierry Arbogast; **Editor:** Sylvie Landra; **Music:** Eric Serra; **Production Designer:** Dan Weil; **Producer:** Gaumont/Les Films du Dauphin
Columbia; R; 105 minutes
Release: 11/94
Cast: Jean Reno, Gary Oldman, Natalie Portman and Danny Aiello
An adolescent girl (Portman), whose family was murdered by a corrupt DEA agent (Oldman), befriends and brings out the sweet side of her neighbor (Reno), a hired killer.

PROFESSION: NEO-NAZI

Director/Writer: Winfried Bonengel; **Director of Photography:** Johann Feindt; **Editor:** Wolfram Kohler; **Producer:** Andrea Hoffman
Drift Releasing; NR; 83 minutes
Release: 5/95
This documentary follows 28-year-old Ewald Althans who considers himself a general in Ernst Zundel's neo-Nazi army as he travels from Canada to Germany to recruit youths into the Nazi cause, along the way proclaiming that the "Holocaust is a hoax."

PULP FICTION

Director: Quentin Tarantino; **Writers:** Quentin Tarantino and Roger Avary; **Director of Photography:** Andrzej Sekula; **Editor:** Sally Menke; **Music:** Karyn Rachtman; **Production Designer:** David Wasco; **Producer:** Lawrence Bender
Miramax; R; 149 minutes
Release: 11/94
Cast: John Travolta, Samuel L. Jackson, Uma Thurman, Harvey Keitel, Amanda Plummer, Rosanna Arquette, Maria de Medeiros, Bruce Willis, Eric Stoltz, Tim Roth, Ving Rhames and Christopher Walken

Three dark underworld tales intertwine and revolve around each other: Vincent (Travolta) and Jules (Jackson) are hitmen for mob boss Marsellus (Rhames); Vincent is hired to chaperone Marsellus's wife Mia (Thurman); and Willis is a palooka who wins the fight Marsellus orders him to lose. *Pulp Fiction* was 1994's surprise hit that elevated Tarantino from cult to mainstream fame.

THE PUPPET MASTERS

Director: Stuart Orme; **Writers:** Ted Elliot, David S. Gayer and Terry Rosio; **Director of Photography:** Clive Tickner; **Editor:** William Goldenberg; **Music:** Colin Towns; **Production Designer:** Daniel A. Lomino; **Producer:** Ralph Winter
Hollywood Pictures; R; 109 minutes
Release: 10/94
Cast: Donald Sutherland, Eric Thal, Julie Warner, Richard Belzer and Keith David
Based on the novel by Robert Heinlein
Heroic scientists battle parasitic aliens who try to control the planet by inhabiting human bodies and eliminating their personalities.

A PURE FORMALITY

Director/Editor: Giuseppe Tornatore; **Writers:** Giuseppe Tornatore and Pascale Quignard; **Director of Photography:** Blasco Giurato; **Music:** Ennio Morricone; **Producers:** Mario and Vittorio Cecchi Gori
Sony Pictures Classics; PG-13; 107 minutes
Release: 5/95
Cast: Gérard Depardieu and Roman Polanski
In French with English subtitles
Famous novelist and songwriter Onoff (Depardieu) becomes a murder suspect when police find him running in the woods on a rainy night. The Inspector (Polanski), who is conversant with Onoff's work, interrogates Onoff, who is not himself sure if he is guilty or innocent.

PUSHING HANDS

Director: Ang Lee; **Writers:** Ang Lee and James Schamus; **Director of Photography:** Jong Lin; **Editor:** Tim Squyres; **Music:** Xiao-Song Qu; **Producers:** Ted Hope, James Schamus, Emily Liu and Ang Lee
Cinepix Film Properties; NR; 100 minutes
Release: 6/95
Cast: Sihung Lung, Lai Wang, Bo Z. Wang and Deb Snyder
In Mandarin and English with English subtitles
Retired tai chi master Mr. Chu (Lung) moves from China to New York to live with his only son (Bo Z. Wang) and his family. Problems immediately arise between Mr. Chu and his Caucasian daughter-in-law Martha (Snyder), who has no interest in Mr.

1995 BRITISH ACADEMY OF FILM AND TELEVISION ARTS AWARDS

The BAFTA Awards, the British equivalent of our Oscar and Emmy awards (combined into one ceremony), were presented Sunday, April 23, 1995 at the London Palladium. Here are the winners in the film categories.

Film
Four Weddings and a Funeral

British Film of the Year
Shallow Grave

Actor
Hugh Grant, *Four Weddings and a Funeral*

Actress
Susan Sarandon, *The Client*

Supporting Actor
Samuel L. Jackson, *Pulp Fiction*

Supporting Actress
Kristen Scott Thomas, *Four Weddings and a Funeral*

Direction
Mike Newell, *Four Weddings and a Funeral*

Original Screenplay
Quentin Tarantino and Roger Avary, *Pulp Fiction*

Adapted Screenplay
Paul Attanasio, *Quiz Show*

Foreign Film
To Live

To Live

Billy Wilder received a special fellowship.

Chu's traditional Chinese lifestyle, while he does not understand the aspiring novelist's culinary tastes and her child-rearing philosophy.

A PYROMANIAC'S LOVE STORY
Director: Joshua Brand; **Writer:** Morgan Ward; **Director of Photography**: John Schwartzman; **Editor:** David Rosenbloom; **Music:** Rachel Portman; **Production Designer:** Dan Davis; **Producer:** Mark Gordon
Buena Vista; PG; 96 minutes
Release: 4/95
Cast: William Baldwin, John Leguizamo, Sadie Frost, Erika Eleniak, Joan Plowright and Armin Mueller-Stahl
Passions burn, as do flames, in this story of unrequited and new-found love. Pastry shop assistant Sergio (Leguizamo) loves Hattie (Frost) but has no chance with her unless he makes more money. He gets his chance when he is offered $25,000 to confess that he burned down the pastry shop in order to keep Garet (Baldwin) out of trouble.

QUEEN MARGOT
Director: Patrice Chéreau; **Writers:** Danièle Thompson and Patrice Chéreau; **Director of Photography**: Philippe Rousselot; **Editors:** Francois Gedigier and Helene Viard; **Music:** Goran Bregovic; **Production Designers:** Richard Peduzzi and Olivier Radot; **Producer:** Claude Berri
Miramax; R; 143 minutes
Release: 12/94
Cast: Isabelle Adjani, Daniel Auteuil, Jean-Hughes Anglade, Vincent Perez, Pascal Greggory, Julien Rassam and Virna Lisi
Based on the novel by Alexandre Dumas
A Catholic woman (Adjani) and a Protestant man (Auteuil) are forced into an arranged royal marriage intended to quell the religious wars of 16th-century France.

THE QUICK AND THE DEAD
Director: Sam Raimi; **Writer:** Simon Moore; **Director of Photography**: Dante Spinotti; **Editor:** Pietro Scalia; **Music:** Alan Silvestri; **Production Designer:** Patrizia von Brandenstein; **Producers:** Joshua Donen, Allen Shapiro and Patrick Markey
TriStar; R; 103 minutes
Release: 2/95
Cast: Sharon Stone, Gene Hackman, Russell Crowe, Leonardo DiCaprio, Pat Hingle, Gary Sinise and Woody Strode
Tough cowgirl Ellen (Stone) rides into Redemption looking like she means business. She is: she's out to avenge her father's death at the hands of evil mayor Herod (Hackman), whose mental and physical cruelty is limitless. Ellen and the undefeated Herod square off in one of the film's many gunfights.

RADIOLAND MURDERS
Director: Mel Smith; **Writers:** Willard Huyck, Gloria Katz, Jeff Reno, Ron Osborn and George Lucas; **Director of Photography:** David Tattersall; **Editor:** Paul Trejo; **Music:** Joel McNeely; **Production Designer:** Gavin Bocquet; **Producers:** Rick McCallum and Fred Ross
Universal; PG; 112 minutes
Release: 10/94
Cast: Brian Benben, Ned Beatty, Mary Stuart Masterson and Michael Lerner
A series of murders occur on the debut night of a new radio network in 1939 Chicago. When the network's head writer (Benben) becomes a suspect, he and his ex-wife (Masterson) try to find the real culprit.

READY TO WEAR (PRÊT-À-PORTER)
Director: Robert Altman; **Writers:** Robert Altman and Barbara Shulgasser; **Directors of Photography:** Pierre Mignot and Jean Lépine; **Editor:** Geraldine Peroni; **Music:** Michel Legrand; **Production Designer:** Stephen Altman; **Producer:** Robert Altman
Miramax; R; 133 minutes
Release: 12/94
Cast: Danny Aiello, Anouk Aimée, Lauren Bacall, Kim Basinger, Michel Blanc, Jean-Pierre Cassel, Rossy de Palma, Rupert Everett, Teri Garr, Richard E. Grant, Linda Hunt, Sally Kellerman, Ute Lemper, Sophia Loren, Lyle Lovett, Marcello Mastroianni, Stephen Rea, Sam Robards, Tim Robbins, Julia Roberts, Jean Rochefort, Lili Taylor, Tracey Ullman and Forest Whitaker
Following models, designers and reporters at Parisian couture shows, Altman gives an alternately funny and tedious behind-the-scenes look at the fashion industry.

RED
Director: Krzysztof Kieslowski; **Writers:** Krzysztof Kieslowski and Krzysztof Piesiewicz; **Director of Photography:** Piotr Sobocinski; **Editor:** Jacques Witta; **Music:** Zbigniew Preisner; **Production Designer:** Claude Lenoir; **Producer:** Marin Karmitz
Miramax; R; 99 minutes
Release: 12/94
Cast: Irene Jacob, Jean-Louis Trintignant, Frederique Feder and Jean-Pierre Lorit
In French with English subtitles
Red, the third in Kieslowski's triology based on the French tricolor flag, centers around the relationship between a young model Valentine (Jacob) and retired judge (Trintignant), who meet by chance when she runs over his dog. A technicality prevented *Red* from garnering a best foreign-language film Oscar nomination.

RED FIRECRACKER, GREEN FIRECRACKER
Director: He Ping; **Writer:** Da Ying; **Director of Photography:** Yang Lun; **Editor:** Yuan Hong; **Music:** Zhao Jiping; **Producers:** Chen Chunkeung and Yung Naiming
October Films; NR; 111 minutes
Release: 3/95
Cast: Ning Jing, Wu Gang and Zhao Xiaorui
Based on the story by Feng Jical
In Mandarin with English subtitles
Chun Zhi (Jing), the master of her family's firecracker empire, commands the respect and privileges normally reserved for men because of her position. One thing she is not allowed is marriage; her father forbade her from marrying, fearing that his estate would fall into another family's hands. Chun Zhi falls for an adventurous, impoverished artist (Gang), and her chief assistant becomes insanely jealous and will do anything to end the affair.

RICHIE RICH
Director: Donald Petrie; **Writers:** Tom S. Parker and Jim Jennewein; **Director of Photography:** Don Burgess; **Editor:** Malcolm Campbell; **Music:** Alan Silvestri; **Production Designer:** James Spencer; **Producers:** John Davis and Joel Silver
Warner Bros.; PG; 95 minutes
Release: 12/94
Cast: Macaulay Culkin, John Larroquette, Edward Herrmann, Jonathan Hyde, Christine Ebersole, Michael McShane and Stephi Lineburg
Based on the Harvey Comics series
Richie Rich (Culkin) is the wealthiest boy in the world; he has a roller coaster in his backyard and a McDonald's in his mansion. His father's advisor (Larroquette) schemes to rob the family of its fortune.

RIFT
Director/Writer: Edward S. Barkin; **Director of Photography:** Lee Daniel; **Editor:** Tryan George; **Music:** Tryan George, Eric Masunaga and Edward S. Barkin; **Production Designer:** Mark C. Andrews; **Producers:** Gabriel Fischbarg, Edward S. Barkin and Tryan George
Curb Entertainment International; NR; 87 minutes
Release: 6/95
Cast: William Sage, Timothy Cavanaugh, Jennifer Bransford and Alan Davidson
When Tom (Sage) falls for his best friend's (Cavanaugh) wife (Bransford), he starts having terrifying nightmares and therapy seems to only compound his problem.

RISK
Director/Writer: Deirdre Fishel; **Director of Photography:** Peter Pearce; **Editors:** Deirdre Fisher and Gordon McLennan; **Music:** John Paul Jones; **Production Designer:** Flavio Galuppo; **Producer:**

Gordon McLennan
Seventh Art Releasing; NR; 85 minutes
Release: 10/94
Cast: Karen Sillas, David Ilku, Molly Price, Jack Gwaltney, Christie MacFadyen, Phillip Clarke and Charlie Levi
A frustrated artist (Sillas) makes a living posing nude for art classes. A shy petty thief (Ilku) sees her on a bus and decides he must make love to her.

RIVER OF GRASS
Director/Writer: Kelly Reichardt; **Director of Photography:** Jim Denault; **Editor:** Larry Fessenden; **Production Designer:** Divid Doernberg; **Producers:** Jesse Hartman and Kelly Reichardt
Strand; NR; 80 minutes
Release: 8/95
Cast: Lisa Bowman, Larry Fessenden and Dick Russell
Based on a story by Kelly Reichardt and Jesse Hartman
In flat, lifeless south Florida, Cozy (Bowman) is trapped with a husband she can't stand and two children she doesn't love. Cozy and Lee Ray (Fessenden), a miserable loner who lives with his mother and grandmother, meet in a bar and go on a parody of a drunken spree that lands them in a motel, hiding from a murder that never happened. In the end, the two can't even steal a quarter for the toll to freedom.

THE ROAD TO WELLVILLE
Director/Writer: Alan Parker; **Director of Photography:** Peter Biziou; **Editor:** Gerry Hambling; **Music:** Rachel Portman; **Production Designer:** Brian Morris; **Producers:** Armyan Bernstein, Robert F. Colesberry and Alan Parker
Columbia; R; 120 minutes
Release: 10/94
Cast: Anthony Hopkins, John Cusack, Bridget Fonda and Matthew Broderick
Based on the novel by T. Coraghessan Boyle
Dr. Kellogg (Hopkins) runs the Battle Creek Sanitarium, a turn-of-the-century health spa particularly concerned with bodily functions. A couple (Broderick and Fonda) checks in to cure their ills, but end up cavorting with other guests. Though panned by critics, *The Road to Wellville* is a peculiarly funny exercise in scatology.

ROB ROY
Director: Michael Caton-Jones; **Writer:** Alan Sharp; **Director of Photography:** Karl Walter Lindenlaub; **Editor:** Peter Honess; **Music:** Carter Burwell; **Production Designer:** Assheton Gorton; **Producers:** Peter Broughan and Richard Jackson
United Artists; R; 134 minutes
Release: 4/95
Cast: Liam Neeson, Jessica Lange, John Hurt, Tim Roth, Eric Stoltz and Brian Cox
Cunningham (Roth), a n'er-do-well relation of the the Marquis of Montrose (Hurt) foils Rob Roy's

(Neeson) plan to protect his MacGregor clan and ensure its independence in early 16th-century Scotland. Cunningham discredits Roy in the eyes of the Marquis, rapes his wife and challenges Roy to a duel, which Roy must win to regain his credibility.

ROOMMATES
Director: Peter Yates; **Writers:** Max Apple and Stephen Metcalfe; **Director of Photography:** Mike Southon; **Editor:** John Tintori; **Music:** Elmer Bernstein; **Production Designer:** Dan Bishop; **Producers:** Ted Field, Scott Kroopf and Robert W. Cort
Buena Vista; PG; 109 minutes
Release: 3/95
Cast: Peter Falk, D. B. Sweeney, Julianne Moore and Ellen Burstyn
Based on the story by Max Apple
Rocky (Falk) raised his orphaned grandson Michael (Sweeney) since he was a child, and, behind his crankiness, Rocky knows that family watches out for family. Michael, an emergency-room doctor, and Rocky find themselves living together once again and share humorous ups and downs.

RUDYARD KIPLING'S THE JUNGLE BOOK
Director/Writer: Stephen Sommers; **Director of Photography:** Juan Ruiz-Anchia; **Editor:** Bob Ducsay; **Music:** Basil Poledouris; **Production Designer:** Allan Cameron; **Producer:** Edward S. Feldman
Walt Disney; PG; 111 minutes
Release: 12/94
Cast: Jason Scott Lee, Cary Elwes, Lena Headey, Sam Neill, John Cleese, Jason Flemyng and Stefan Kalipha
Based on characters from Rudyard Kipling's book Mowgli (Lee), a boy who was raised in the jungles of India by a pack of wolves, returns to civilization and is disappointed when he finds that people do not live by the rules of the jungle.

SAFE
Director/Writer: Todd Haynes; **Director of Photography:** Alex Nepomniaschy; **Editor:** James Lyons; **Producers:** Christine Vachon and Lauren Zalaznick
Sony Pictures Classics; R; 119 minutes
Release: 6/95
Cast: Julianne Moore, Xander Berkeley and James LeGros
Convinced her undiagnosed malady is an environmental illness, Carol (Moore) checks into a New Age spa run by "a chemically senstive person with AIDS" and finds comfort among others with the same allergy to the 20th century.

SAFE PASSAGE

Director: Robert Allan Ackerman; **Writer:** Deena Goldstone; **Director of Photography:** Ralf D. Bode; **Editor:** Rick Shaine; **Music:** Mark Isham; **Production Designer:** Dan Bishop; **Producer:** Gale Anne Hurd
New Line; PG-13; 97 minutes
Release: 1/95
Cast: Susan Sarandon, Sam Shepard, Nick Stahl, Marcia Gay Harden and Robert Sean Leonard

Based on the novel by Ellyn Bache
A mother (Sarandon) of seven sons plans to leave her suffocating marriage, but her plan is stalled when her Marine son is declared missing after a missile attack in the Middle East.

THE SANTA CLAUSE

Director: John Pasquin; **Writers:** Leo Benvenuti and Steve Rudnick; **Director of Photography:** Walt Lloyd; **Editor:** Larry Bock; **Music:** Michael Convertino; **Production Designer:** Carol Spier; **Producers:** Robert Newmyer, Brian Reilly and Jeffrey Silver
Walt Disney; PG; 97 minutes
Release: 11/94
Cast: Tim Allen, Judge Reinhold, Wendy Crewson, Eric Lloyd, David Krumholtz, Joyce Guy, Zach

McLemore, Nic Knight and Scott Wickware
When Santa Claus is knocked unconscious after a fall from a roof, divorced dad Scott Calvin (Allen) dons the suit and assumes Santa's responsibilities and appearance.

THE SCOUT

Director: Michael Ritchie; **Writers:** Andrew Bergman, Albert Brooks, Monica Johnson and Roger Angell; **Director of Photography:** Laszlo Kovacs; **Editors:** Pembroke J. Herring and Don Zimmerman; **Music:** Bill Conti; **Production Designer:** Stephen Hendrickson; **Producers:** Andre E. Morgan and Albert S. Ruddy
Twentieth Century-Fox; PG-13; 101 minutes
Release: 10/94
Cast: Albert Brooks, Brendan Fraser, Dianne Wiest, George M. Steinbrenner and Tony Bennett
A New York Yankees scout (Brooks) discovers a pitching phenomenon (Fraser) while on a recruiting trip in a Mexican village. The hurler's psychological problems jeopardize his big-league career.

SEARCH AND DESTROY

Director: David Salle; **Writer:** Michael Almereyda; **Director of Photography:** Bobby Bukowski; **Editor:** Michelle Gorchow; **Music:** Elmer Bernstein; **Production Designer:** Robin Standefer; **Producers:** Ruth Charny, Dan Lupovitz and Elie Cohn
October Films; R; 90 minutes
Release: 4/95
Cast: Griffin Dunne, Illeana Douglas, Dennis Hopper, Christopher Walken, John Turturro, Rosanna Arquette, Ethan Hawke and Nicole Burdette.
Based on the play by Howard Korder
When his life falls apart, down-and-out promoter Martin Mirkheim (Dunne) turns to cable television self-help guru Dr. Luthor Waxling (Hopper) and yearns to buy the film rights to Waxling's novel *Daniel Strong*. Thrown off course by financial problems, Mirkheim's interests turn to Waxler's secretary (Douglas) and her horror-story script.

THE SECRET OF ROAN INISH

Director/Writer/Editor: John Sayles; **Director of Photography:** Haskell Wexler; **Music:** Mason Daring; **Production Designer:** Adrian Smith; **Producers:** Sarah Green and Maggie Renzi
First Look Pictures; PG; 102 minutes
Release: 2/95
Cast: Jeni Courtney, Eileen Colgan, Mick Lally, Richard Sheridan and John Lynch
Based on the novel *Secret of the Ron Mor Skerry* by Rosalie K. Fry
A young Irish girl (Courtney) tries to convince her grandparents (Lally and Colgan) that her baby brother, who was carried out to sea and never found, is living in the sea with friendly seals.

SEX, DRUGS AND DEMOCRACY

Director/Director of Photography/Editor: Jonathan Blank; **Writers:** Barclay Powers and Jonathan Blank; **Music:** Philip Foxman; **Producers:** Jonathan Blank and Barclay Powers
Red Hat Productions; NR; 87 minutes
Release: 2/95
This portrait of the Netherlands examines the country's liberal social laws, which include a legalized sex industry, full equality for homosexuals and open marijuana sales.

S.F.W.

Director: Jefery Levy; **Writers:** Danny Rubin and Jefery Levy; **Director of Photography:** Peter Deming; **Editor:** Lauren Zuckerman; **Music:** Graeme Revell; **Production Designer:** Eve Cauley; **Producer:** Dale Pollock
Gramercy; R; 92 minutes
Release: 1/95
Cast: Stephen Dorff and Reese Witherspoon
Based on the novel by Andrew Wellman
A hostage (Dorff), held for 36 days in a convenience store, becomes an instant media celebrity when the ordeal is broadcast on network television.

SHALLOW GRAVE

Director: Danny Boyle; **Writer:** John Hodge; **Director of Photography:** Brian Tufano; **Editor:** Masahiro Hirakubo; **Music:** Simon Boswell; **Production Designer:** Kave Quinn; **Producer:** Andrew Macdonald
Film Four International; R; 92 minutes
Release: 2/95
Cast: Kerry Fox, Christopher Eccleston, Ewan McGregor and Keith Allen

When three roommates (Fox, Eccleston and McGregor) find their new fourth roommate (Allen) dead in his room with a suitcase full of money, they decide to keep the cash and get rid of the body.

SILENT FALL

Director: Bruce Beresford; **Writer:** Akiva Goldsman; **Director of Photography:** Peter James; **Editor:** Ian Crafford; **Music:** Stewart Copeland; **Production Designer:** John Stoddart; **Producer:** James G. Robinson
Warner Bros.; R; 106 minutes
Release: 10/94
Cast: Richard Dreyfuss, John Lithgow, Linda Hamilton, J.T. Walsh, Ben Faulkner and Liv Tyler
A psychologist (Dreyfuss) tries to help a nine-year-old autistic boy (Walsh) recount his recollection of his parents' brutal murder.

SISTER MY SISTER

Director: Nancy Meckler; **Writer:** Wendy Kesselman; **Director of Photography:** Ashley Rowpe; **Editor:** David Stiven; **Music:** Stephen Warbeck; **Producer:** Norma Heyman
Seventh Art Releasing; NR; 102 minutes
Release: 6/95
Cast: Joely Richardson, Jodhi May, Julie Walters and Sophie Thursfield
Based on a true story
This film explores the incestuous relationship between two working-class sisters Christine (Richardson) and Lea (May) in 1930s France. The girls work in isolation as housekeepers for Madame Danzard (Walters) and her grown daughter Isabelle (Thursfield). The sisters kill their employers, and it's still not clear what drove them to murder.

SMOKE

Director: Wayne Wang; **Writer:** Paul Auster; **Director of Photography:** Adam Holender; **Editor:** Maysie Hoy; **Music:** Rachel Portman; **Production Designer:** Kalina Ivanov; **Producers:** Greg Johnson, Peter Newman, Hisami Kuroiwa and Kenzo Horikoshi
Miramax; R; 112 minutes
Release: 6/95

Cast: Harvey Keitel, William Hurt, Harold Perrineau, Forest Whitaker, Stockard Channing and Ashley Judd
Unhappy parent-child relationships are exposed and introduced among Auggie (Keitel) and the customers of his Brooklyn tobacco shop. Auggie learns that he and a former girlfriend (Channing) have an 18-year-old crack-addicted, pregnant daughter (Judd).

Customer Paul (Hurt) befriends a young black man (Perrineau) who saves his life and is in town to track down his long-lost father (Whitaker).

SOMETHING TO TALK ABOUT

Director: Lasse Hallstrom; **Writer:** Callie Khouri; **Director of Photography:** Sven Nykvist; **Editor:** Mia Goldman; **Music:** Hans Zimmer and Graham Preskett; **Production Designer:** Mel Bourne; **Producers:** Anthea Sylbert and Paula Weinstein
Warner Bros.; R; 105 minutes
Release: 8/95
Cast: Julia Roberts; Dennis Quaid; Robert Duvall; Gena Rowlands, Kyra Sedgwick and Brett Cullen
Grace King Bichon (Roberts) rebels against her sedate southern life after she sees her charming husband (Quaid) kissing another woman. Bichon's parents (Duvall and Rowlands) offer their daughter no sympathy when she tells them of her philandering husband. Her quick-witted sister Emma Rae (Sedgwick) helps Bichon get her life together.

THE SPECIALIST

Director: Luis Llosa; **Writers:** Alexander Seros and John Shirley; **Director of Photography:** Jeffrey L. Kimball; **Editor:** Jack Hofstra; **Music:** John Barry; **Production Designer:** Walter P. Martishius; **Producer:** Jerry Weintraub
Warner Bros.; R; 110 minutes
Release: 10/94
Cast: Sharon Stone, Sylvester Stallone, Eric Roberts, Rod Steiger and James Woods
May Munro (Stone) recruits an explosives expert (Stallone) to avenge her parents' murder, which occurred 20 years earlier at the hands of the mob.

SPECIES

Director: Roger Donaldson; **Writer:** Dennis Feldman; **Director of Photography:** Andrzej Bartrowiak; **Editor:** Conrad Buff; **Music:** Christopher Young; **Production Designer:** John Muto; **Producers:** Frank Mancusoo, Jr. and Dennis Feldman
MGM; R; 151 minutes
Release: 7/95
Cast: Ben Kingsley, Michael Madsen, Alfred Molina, Forest Whitaker, Marg Helgenberger, Whip Hubley, Michele Williams and Natasha Henstridge
In 1974, government scientists thrust DNA information into space and 20 years later someone or

something replied with a new DNA sequence and instructions on how to combine it with Earth's. Scientist Xavier Fitch (Kingsley) created a being named Sil (Henstridge) who grows from an infant to a teen in only months. Realizing his creation is beyond their control, Fitch and his team (Whitaker, Molina and Helgenberger) try to capture Sil, who is leaving behind a trail of dead bodies in Los Angeles.

SPEECHLESS

Director: Ron Underwood; **Writer:** Robert King; **Director of Photography:** Don Peterman; **Editor:** Richard Francis-Bruce; **Music:** Marc Shaiman; **Production Designer:** Dennis Washington; **Producers:** Renny Harlin and Geena Davis
MGM; PG-13; 98 minutes
Release: 12/94

Cast: Michael Keaton, Geena Davis, Christopher Reeve and Bonnie Bedelia
Two speechwriters (Davis and Keaton) from opposing camps fall in love while working on a New Mexico Senate race.

SQUANTO: A WARRIOR'S TALE

Director: Xavier Koller; **Writer:** Darlene Craviotto; **Director of Photography:** Robbie Greenberg; **Editor:** Lisa Day; **Music:** Joel McNeely; **Production Designer:** Gemma Jackson; **Producer:** Kathryn F. Galan
Walt Disney; PG; 102 minutes
Release: 10/94
Cast: Adam Beach, Michael Gambon, Nathaniel Parker, Mandy Patinkin, Sheldon Peters Wolfchild, Irene Bedard, Eric Schweig, Leroy Peltier and Mark Margolis
Squanto (Beach), taken from his Native American home and brought to England as a slave, escapes and returns home to find his people have been decimated by disease. He is captured by pilgrims, and as they face starvation Squanto helps them survive and they celebrate the first Thanksgiving together.

STARGATE

Director: Roland Emmerich; **Writers:** Dean Derlin and Roland Emmench; **Director of Photography:** Karl Walter Lindenlamb; **Editors:** Derek Brechin and Michael J. Duthie; **Music:** David Arnold; **Production Designer:** Holger Gross; **Producers:** Dean Devlin, Oliver Eberle and Joel B. Michaels
MGM; PG-13; 121 minutes
Release: 10/94
Cast: Kurt Russell, James Spader and Jaye Davidson
An Egyptologist (Spader) and an Army colonel (Russell) team up on planet Abydos to defeat its extraterrestial ruler (Davidson).

STAR TREK GENERATIONS

Director: David Carson; **Writers:** Ronald D. Moore and Brannon Braga; **Director of Photography:** John A. Alonzo; **Editor:** Peter E. Berger; **Music:** Dennis McCarthy; **Production Designer:** Herman Zimmerman; **Producer:** Rick Berman
Paramount; PG; 110 minutes
Release: 11/94
Cast: William Shatner, Patrick Stewart, Malcolm McDowell and Whoopi Goldberg
Based on the story by Rick Berman, Ronald D. Moore and Brannon Braga and the television series *Star Trek*

A time warp brings together captains James Kirk (Shatner), Jean-Luc Picard (Stewart) and their crews, who join forces to stop the diabolical Soran (McDowell) from inciting chaos in the universe.

STRAWBERRY AND CHOCOLATE

Directors: Tomás Gutiérrez Alea and Juan Carlos Tabio; **Writer:** Senel Paz; **Director of Photography:** Mario Garcia Joya; **Editors:** Osvaldo Donatien, Rolando Martinez and Miriam Talavera; **Music:** José María Vitier
Miramax; NR; 111 minutes
Release 1/95
Cast: Jorge Perugorría, Vladimir Cruz, Mirta Ibarra, Francisco Gattorno, Jorge Angelino and Marilyn Solaya
In Spanish with English subtitles
Set in Havana, a 40-year-old gay man (Perugorría) falls in love with a 20-year-old heterosexual student (Cruz), and the men develop a platonic friendship.

STREET FIGHTER

Director/Writer: Steven E. de Souza; **Director of Photography:** William A. Fraker; **Editors:** Edward M. Abroms, Donn Aron, Anthony Redman and Robert F. Shugrue; **Music:** Graeme Revell; **Production Designer:** William J. Creber; **Producers:** Edward R. Pressman and Kenzo Tsujimoto
Universal; PG-13; 106 minutes
Release: 12/94
Cast: Jean-Claude Van Damme, Raul Julia, Ming-Na Wen, Damian Chapa, Kylie Minogue, Simon Callow, Roshan Seth, Wes Studi and Byron Mann
Based on the video game
The crazed Bison (Julia) kidnaps 52 workers from an international peace-keeping group and ransoms them to the world for $20 billion. Armed forces leader Colonel Guile (Van Damme) has 72 hours to find Bison.

STUART SAVES HIS FAMILY

Director: Harold Ramis; **Writer:** Al Franken; **Director of Photography:** Lauro Escorel; **Editors:** Pembroke Herring and Craig Herring; **Music:** Marc Shaiman; **Production Designer:** Joseph T. Garrity; **Producers:** Lorne Michaels and Trevor Albert
Paramount; PG-13; 100 minutes
Release: 4/95
Based on Al Franken's book and his *Saturday Night*

Live character
Cast: Al Franken, Laura San Giacomo, Vincent D'Onofrio, Shirley Knight and Harris Yulin
When New Age self-help expert Stuart Smalley loses his cable television show, he plies his trade on his family and tries to save his alcoholic father (Yulin), pot-smoking brother (D'Onofrio), enabling mother (Knight) and over-eating sister (Boone) from self-destruction.

THE SUM OF US
Directors: Kevin Dowling and Geoff Burton; **Writer:** David Stevens; **Director of Photography:** Geoff Burton; **Editor:** Frans Vandenburg; **Music:** Dave Faulkner; **Production Designer:** Graham (Grace) Walker; **Producer:** Hal McElroy
Samuel Goldwyn; NR; 95 minutes
Release: 3/95
Cast: Jack Thompson, Russell Crowe, John Polson and Deborah Kennedy
Based on the play by David Stevens
Harry Mitchell (Thompson) not only accepts his son Jeff's (Crowe) openly gay relationships, he encourages them. Though they annoy each other, Harry and Jeff maintain a touching father-son relationship filled with humor, trust and shared loneliness.

SUPER 8 1/2
Director/Writer: Bruce LaBruce; **Director of Photography:** Donna Mobbs; **Editors:** Manse James and Robert Kennedy; **Producers:** Jurgen Bruning, Bruce LaBruce, Jon Gerrans, Marcus Hu and Mike Thomas
Strand Releasing; NR; 100 minutes
Release: 3/95
Cast: Bruce LaBruce, Liza Lamonica, Chris Teen, Dirty Pillows, Mikey Mike, Klaus Von Brucker, Kate Ashley, Buddy Cole, Ben Weasel and Scott Thompson
Has-been porn god Bruce (LaBruce) downs pureed aspirin for breakfast, rinses his mouth with scotch and slides slowly downhill from love with young hunk Pierce (Von Brucker) to straitjacket, street-life lunacy. Lesbian experimental filmmaker Googie (LaMonica) captures it all in a wild documentary.

THE SWAN PRINCESS
Director: Richard Rich; **Writer:** Brian Nissen; **Art Directors:** Mike Hodgson and James Coleman; **Editors:** James Koford and Armetta Jackson-Hamlett; **Music:** Lex de Azevedo and David Zippel; **Producers:** Richard Rich and Jared F. Brown
New Line Cinema; G; 90 minutes
Release: 11/94
Voices of: Jack Palance, John Cleese, Steven Wright, Howard McGillin, Michelle Nicastro, Sandy Duncan and Liz Callaway
A beautiful princess (voices of Nicastro and Callaway) is turned into a swan by the local sorcerer (voice of Palance). Only the handsome prince's (voice of McGillin) promise of love can break the spell.

SWIMMING WITH SHARKS
Director/Writer: George Huang; **Director of Photography:** Steven Finestone; **Editor:** Ed Marx; **Music:** Tom Hiel; **Production Designers:** Cecil Gentry and Veronika Merlin; **Producers:** Steve Alexander and Joanne Moore
Trimark Pictures; R; 93 minutes
Release: 3/95
Cast: Kevin Spacey, Frank Whaley, Michelle Forbes and Benicio Del Toro
High-ranking movie producer Buddy Ackerman (Spacey) loves to yell, scream and insult just about everyone below him on the corporate ladder. Guy (Whaley), Ackerman's personal assistant, can endure only so much and one day snaps, seeking revenge on his insolent boss.

TALES FROM THE CRYPT PRESENTS DEMON KNIGHT
Director: Ernest Dickerson ("Crypt Keeper" sequences directed by Gilbert Adler); **Writer:** Ethan Reiff, Cyrus Voris and Mark Bishop; **Director of Photography:** Rick Bota; **Editor:** Stephen Lovejoy; **Music:** Ed Shearmur; **Production Designer:** Christiaan Wagener; **Producer:** Gilbert Adler
Universal; R; 93 minutes
Release: 1/95
Cast: Billy Zane, William Sadler, Jada Pinkett, Brenda Bakke, Thomas Haden Church, Dick Miller, C. C. H. Pounder and John Kassir
Based on the comic magazines originally published by William M. Gaines
The Collector (Zane), who works for the devil, chases a servant of Christ (Sadler) in pursuit of the seventh key, necessary to control the universe. It's a bloody, gory battle of good versus evil.

TALES FROM THE HOOD
Director: Rusty Cundieff; **Writers:** Rusty Cundieff and Darin Scott; **Director of Photography:** Anthony B. Richmond; **Editor:** Charles Bornstein; **Music:** Christopher Young; **Production Designer:** Stuart Platt; **Producer:** Darin Scott
Savoy Pictures; R; 98 minutes
Release: 5/95
Cast: Clarence Williams III, Joe Torry, Wings Hauser, Anthony Griffith, Paul Jai Parker, Corbin Bernsen, Rosalind Cash, Rusty Cundieff and David Alan Grier
With styling reminiscent of *The Twilight Zone,* each of the four tales included in the movie, "Rogue Cop Revelation," "Boys Do Get Bruised," "KKK Comeuppance" and "Hard Core Convert," all hosted by crazed mortician Mr. Simms (Williams), is based on earlier horror movies and involve racism and payback.

TALL TALE
Director: Jeremiah Chechik; **Writers:** Steven L. Bloom and Robert Rodat; **Director of Photography:** Janusz Kaminski; **Editor:** Richard Chew; **Music:** Randy Edelman; **Production Designer:** Eugenio

Zanetti; **Producers:** Joe Roth and Roger Birnbaum
Walt Disney; PG; 98 minutes
Release: 3/95
Cast: Patrick Swayze, Oliver Platt, Nick Stahl, Roger
Aaron Brown and Scott Glenn
When land-grabbers show interest in the Hackett
farm, Daniel Hackett (Stahl) runs away with the
deed to the land and embarks on a mythical jour-
ney. Pecos Bill (Swayze), Paul Bunyan (Platt) and
John Henry (Brown) guide him on his journey
and offer wise advice.

TANK GIRL

Director: Rachel Talalay; **Writer:** Tedi Sarafian;
Director of Photography: Gale Tattersall; **Editor:**
James R. Symons; **Music:** Graeme Revell;
Production Designer: Catherine Hardwicke;
Producers: Richard B. Lewis, Pen Densham and
John Watson
United Artists; R; 103 minutes
Release: 3/95
Cast: Lori Petty, Ice T, Naomi Watts, Don Harvey, Reg
E. Cathey, Jeff Kober and Malcolm McDowell
Based on the comic strip created by Alan Martin
and Jamie Hewlett

It's 2033 and the world is
thirsty. Feminist punk heroine Tank Girl (Petty) isn't
afraid to use her big guns
on anyone who gets in her
way, especially the ruthless
Kesslee (McDowell), who
controls most of the post-
apocalyptic world's water
supply.

TEMPTATION OF A MONK

Director: Clara Law; **Writers:** Eddie Fong Ling-Ching
and Lilian Lee; **Director of Photography:** Andrew
Lesnie; **Editor:** Jill Bilcock; **Music:** Tats Lau;
Production Designers: Timmy Yip, Yang Zhanjia and
William Lygratte; **Producer:** Teddy Robin Kwan
Northern Arts Entertainment; NR; 118 minutes
Release: 12/94
Cast: Joan Chen, Wu Hsin-Kuo, Zhang Fengyi,
Michael Lee and Lisa Lu
Based on the novella by Lilian Lee
In Mandarin with English subtitles
General Shi (Hsin-Kuo), fleeing the diabolical
ruler during the Tang Dynasty, disguises himself
as a monk and falls in love with Princess Scarlet
(Joan Chen).

THROUGH THE OLIVE TREES

Director/Writer/Editor/Producer: Abbas Kiarostami;
Directors of Photography: Hossein Djafarian and
Farhad Saba
Miramax; NR; 108 minutes
Release: 2/95
Cast: Hossein Rezai, Mohamed Ali Keshavarz, Farhad
Keradmand, Zarifeh Shiva and Tahereh Ladania

A sequel to 1992's . . . *And Life Goes On*
This film-within-a-film looks at the making of
. . . *And Life Goes On* in rural Iran and the problems the director encountered, which included
his leading man Hossein Rezai (playing himself)
falling in unrequited love with leading lady
Tahereh Ladania (playing herself).

TIGRERO: A FILM THAT WAS NEVER MADE

Director/Writer/Producer/Editor: Mika Kaurismaki;
Director of Photography: Jacques Cheuiche; **Music:**
Chuck Jonkey, Nana Vasconcelos and the Karaja
Indians; **Production Designer:** William O'Dwyer
Fogtman
Arrow Releasing; NR; 75 minutes
Release: 12/94
With: Samuel Fuller, Jim Jarmusch and the Karaja
Indians
In 1955, director Samuel Fuller was in a Brazilian
village filming a romantic adventure that would
have starred John Wayne, Ava Gardner and
Tyrone Power, but insuring the actors was pro-
hibitively expensive and the film was never
made. Almost 40 years later, Fuller and Jarmusch
return to the village to see how the Karaja
Indians have adapted to modernization.

TO LIVE

Director: Zhang Yimou; **Writers:** Yu Hua and Lu Wei;
Director of Photography: Lu Yue; **Editor:** Yuan Du;
Music: Zhao Jiping; **Production Designer:** Cao
Jiuping; **Producers:** Fu-Sheng Chiu, Funhong Kow
and Christophe Tseng
Samuel Goldwyn; NR; 125 minutes
Release: 12/94
Cast: Ge You, Gong Li, Niu Ben, Guo Tao, Jiang Wu,
Liu Tian Chi and Zhang Lu
Based on the novel by Yu Hua
In Mandarin with English
subtitles

A Chinese couple (You
and Li) survive three
turbulent decades, suf-
fering tragedy in their
personal lives and wit-
nessing their country's
political upheavals.

TOM AND VIV

Director: Brian Gilbert; **Writers:** Michael Hastings
and Adrian Hodges; **Director of Photography:** Martin
Fuhrer; **Editor:** Tony Lawson; **Music:** Debbie
Wiseman; **Production Designer:** Jamie Leonard;
Producers: Harvey Kass, Marc Samuelson and Peter
Samuelson
Miramax; R; 115 minutes
Release: 12/94
Cast: Willem Dafoe, Miranda Richardson, Tim
Dutton, Rosemary Harris and Nickolas Grace
Based on the play by Michael Hastings

This story of T. S. Eliot's (Dafoe) first wife Vivien Haigh-Wood (Richardson) focuses on her mental instability and its effect on their lives and his work. Eliot, with the help of friends and family, has Vivien institutionalized after 18 turbulent years of marriage.

TOMMY BOY

Director: Peter Segal; **Writers:** Bonnie Turner and Terry Turner; **Director of Photography:** Victor J. Kemper; **Editor:** William Kerr; **Music:** David Newman; **Production Designer:** Stephen J. Lineweaver; **Producer:** Lorne Michaels
Paramount; PG-13; 96 minutes
Release: 3/95
Cast: Chris Farley, David Spade, Brian Dennehy, Bo Derek, Rob Lowe and Dan Aykroyd
Tommy (Farley), who finishes college in just seven years, returns to his Ohio home to help save his family's car-parts business. Salesman Richard (Spade) takes him on the road to show him the ropes.

TOP DOG

Director: Aaron Norris; **Writer:** Ron Swanson; **Director of Photography:** Joao Fernandes; **Editor:** Peter Schink; **Music:** Hummie Mann; **Production Designer:** Norm Baron; **Producer:** Andy Howard
Live Entertainment; PG-13; 87 minutes
Release: 4/95
Cast: Chuck Norris and Peter Savard Moore
Based on the story by Aaron Norris and Tim Grayem
Suspended police lieutenant Jake Wilder (Norris) returns to the force to investigate the murder of a fellow officer and teams up with the dead cop's former partner, Reno, who happens to be a dog. The pair discover that the murder involves a terrorist neo-Nazi group.

TRAPPED IN PARADISE

Director/Writer: George Gallo; **Director of Photography:** Jack N. Green; **Editor:** Terry Rawlings; **Music:** Robert Folk; **Production Designer:** Bob Ziembicki; **Producers:** Jon Davison and George Gallo
Twentieth Century-Fox; PG-13; 111 minutes
Release: 12/94
Cast: Nicolas Cage, Jon Lovitz, Dana Carvey, Donald Moffat and Madchen Amick
The Firpo brothers (Cage and Lovitz), small-time New York City crooks, rob a bank in Paradise, Pennsylvania, on Christmas Eve and are trapped by a snowstorm in this town of sickeningly kind-hearted people.

TRUE BELIEVERS

Director/Editor/Producer: Robert Mugge; **Director of Photography:** Bill Burke; **Music Consultants:** Scott Billington, Keith Case and Peter Guralnick
Dakin Films; NR; 86 minutes
Release: 4/95
With: Marian Levy, Bill Nowlin, Ken Irwin, Bill Morrissey, Marcia Ball, Little Jimmy King, Steve Riley, Irma Thomas, Beau Jocque and Alison Krauss
This documentary celebrates the 25th anniversary of Cambridge, Massachusetts-based Rounder Records, a label that records blues, folk, bluegrass and other roots styles. Interviews with the founding owners Levy, Nowlin and Irwin reveal the label's commitment to finding and promoting quality roots artists such as Alison Krauss, Bill Morrissey, Marcia Ball and Little Jimmy King. Performances and interviews with the artists are interspersed throughout the film.

TSAHAL

Director/Writer: Claude Lanzmann; **Directors of Photography:** Dominique Chapuis, Pierre-Laurent Chenieux and Jean-Michel Humeau; **Editor:** Sabine Mamou; **Production Designer:** Eyal Sher; **Producers:** Les Productions Dussart, Les Films Aleph, France 2 Cinema and Bavaria Films
New Yorker Films; NR; Part 1, 170 minutes; Part 2, 130 minutes
Release: 3/95
Interviews with: Ariel Sharon, Avigdor Feldman, David Grossman, Amos Oz, Sgt. Avi Yaffe, Lt. Col. Yuval Neria, Maj. Meir Weisel, Brig. Gen. Avigdor Kahalani and others
In English, Hebrew and French with English subtitles
In this epic-length film about contemporary Jewish history, Lanzmann looks at the Israeli army and its effect on Israel and its citizens. Lanzmann interviews military officials and citizens, letting them speak freely and at length about the army, themselves and their country.

UNDER SIEGE 2: DARK TERRITORY

Director: Geoff Murphy; **Writers:** Richard Hatem and Matt Reeves; **Director of Photography:** Robbie Greenberg; **Editor:** Michael Tronick; **Music:** Basil Poledouris; **Production Designer:** Albert Brenner; **Producers:** Steven Seagal, Arnon Milchan and Steve Perry
Warner Bros.; R; 98 minutes
Release: 7/95
Cast: Steven Seagal, Eric Bogosian, Katherine Heigl, Morris Chestnut, Everett McGill, Nick Mancuso, Andy Romano, Dave Gianapoulos, Brenda Bakke and Peter Green
A sequel to 1992's *Under Siege*
When a distributor doesn't preview a movie for the press, it's guaranteed to be a bomb, and *Under Siege 2* is no exception. While aboard a passenger train with his recently orphaned

niece, martial arts expert Casey Ryback (Seagal), this time a culinary genius, too, learns that Travis Dane (Bogosian) is using the train as command central to hijack a satellite he designed for the government. It's Ryback to the rescue, and he must stop Dane from blowing up the Pentagon with the weaponry.

managing the family's Russian estate, sending all the profits from the farm to his sister and her ungrateful husband (Gaynes).

THE UNDERNEATH

Director: Steven Soderbergh; **Writers:** Sam Lowry and Daniel Fuchs; **Director of Photography**: Elliot Davis; **Editor:** Stan Salfas; **Music:** Cliff Martinez; **Production Designer:** Howard Cummings; **Producer:** John Hardy
Gramercy; R; 99 minutes
Release: 4/95
Cast: Peter Gallagher, Alison Elliott, William Fichtner, Adam Trese, Paul Dooley and Elisabeth Shue
A remake of the 1949 movie *Criss Cross*
Michael Chambers (Gallagher), who left his wife Rachel (Elliott) and mounting gambling debts several years earlier, returns to Austin, Texas, for his mother's wedding. Sparks reignite the flame with Rachel, and he tries to tear her away from sleazy club-owner Tommy (Fichtner). His quick fix does not go as planned and Chambers finds himself in the middle of an armed robbery. Flashbacks, flashforwards and color are masterfully used in this updated film noir.

UNZIPPED

Director: Douglas Keeve; **Director of Photography:** Ellen Kuras; **Editor:** Paula Heredia; **Producer:** Michael Alden
Miramax; R; 76 minutes
Release: 8/95
With: Isaac Mizrahi, Sarah Mizrahi, Kate Moss, Cindy Crawford, Naomi Campbell, Christy Turlington, Linda Evangelista and Polly Allen Mellen
Keeve's documentary on the fashion industry and designer Mizrahi does what *Ready to Wear* did not: it successfully captures the fashion world and one of its top designers behind-the-scenes as he prepares for the premiere of a new line. Mizrahi and his models, including Crawford, Campbell and Moss, speak candidly about the industry and themselves.

VANYA ON 42ND STREET

Director: Louis Malle; **Writer:** David Mamet; **Director of Photography:** Declan Quinn; **Editor:** Nancy Baker; **Music:** Joshua Redman; **Production Designer:** Eugene Lee; **Producer:** Fred Berner
Sony Pictures Classics; PG; 119 minutes
Release: 12/94
Cast: Wallace Shawn, Larry Pine, Julianne Moore, Brooke Smith, George Gaynes, Lynn Cohen, Phoebe Brane and Jerry Mayer
Based on Anton Chekov's play *Uncle Vanya*
Vanya On 42nd Street is a filmed rehearsal of the Broadway play *Uncle Vanya*, which dramatizes the life of Ivan Voinitsky, known as Uncle Vanya (Shawn). The embittered Vanya has spent his life

VILLAGE OF THE DAMNED

Director: John Carpenter; **Writer:** David Himmelstein; **Director of Photography:** Gary B. Kibbe; **Editor:** Edward A. Warschilka; **Music:** John Carpenter and Dave Davies; **Production Designer:** Rodger Maus; **Producers:** Michael Preger and Sandy King
Universal; R; 95 minutes
Release: 4/95
Cast: Christopher Reeve, Kirstie Alley, Linda Kozlowski, Michael Paré and Mark Hamill
Based on the novel *The Midwich Cuckoos* by John Wyndham and the 1960 screenplay by Stirling Silliphant, Wolf Rilla and George Barclay
Nine months after an entire English town falls into a trance, the women of Midwich simultaneously give birth to identical children. The precocious children all have platinum-blond hair, glowing eyes and order adults to commit gruesome suicides.

VIRTUOSITY

Director: Brett Leonard; **Writer:** Eric Bernt; **Director of Photography:** Gale Tattersall; **Editors:** B. J. Sears and Rob Kobrin; **Music:** Christopher Young; **Production Designer:** Nilo Rodis; **Producer:** Gary Lucchesi
Paramount; R; 120 minutes
Release: 8/95
Cast: Denzel Washington, Kelly Lynch, Russell Crowe and Stephen Spinella
Virtual reality and technology are the stories here as they easily surpass the narrative. Sid 6.7 (Crowe), an electronic serial killer with 200 criminal personalities, escapes from virtual reality with the help of his creator (Spinella) and rampages in real reality. Parker Barnes (Washington), a former cop who went nuts after his family was killed, also moves between the two realities in pursuit of Sid 6.7.

A WALK IN THE CLOUDS

Director: Alfonso Arau; **Writers:** Robert Mark Kamen, Mark Miller and Harvey Weitzman; **Director of Photography:** Emmanuel Lubezki; **Editor:** Don Zimmerman; **Music:** Maurice Jarre; **Production Designer:** David Gropman; **Producers:** Gil Netter, David Zucker and Jerry Zucker
Twentieth Century-Fox; PG-13; 100 minutes
Release: 8/95
Cast: Keanu Reeves, Aitana Sanchez-Gijon, Anthony Quinn and Giancarlo Giannini
Based on *Quattro Passi fra le Nuvole*, story and screenplay by Piero Tellini, Cesare Zavattini and Vittorio de Benedetti

Paul Sutton (Reeves), just returning home from military service in 1945, finds his formerly beautiful wife is a slattern. Disappointed, he takes a job as a traveling candy salesman and meets the lovely and pregnant Victoria (Sanchez-Gijon). Sutton poses as her husband to placate her suspicious, vineyard-owning father (Giannini).

THE WALKING DEAD

Director/Writer: Preston A. Whitmore II; **Director of Photography:** John L. Demps, Jr.; **Editors:** Don Brochu and William C. Carruth; **Music:** Gary Chang; **Production Designer:** George Costello; **Producers:** George Jackson, Douglas McHenry and Frank Price
Savoy Pictures; R; 90 minutes
Release: 2/95
Cast: Allen Payne, Eddie Griffin, Joe Morton, Vonte Sweet, Roger Floyd, Ion Overman, Kyley Jackman, Bernie Mac, Jean LeMarre and Lena Sang
Five marines (Morton, Griffin, Payne, Sweet and Floyd), all but one African American, search an abandoned Viet Cong P.O.W. camp for survivors. Flashbacks illustrate why each man enlisted.

THE WAR

Director: Jon Avnet; **Writer:** Kathy McWorter; **Director of Photography:** Geoffrey Simpson; **Editor:** Debra Neil; **Music:** Thomas Newman; **Production Designer:** Kristi Zea; **Producer:** Jordan Kerner
Universal; PG-13; 127 minutes
Release: 11/94
Cast: Elijah Wood, Kevin Costner, Mare Winningham and Lexi Randall

While Stephen Simmons (Costner) struggles to deal with his emotional and physical wounds from Vietnam, his children (Wood and Randall) fight their own battle over a tree house.

WATERWORLD

Director: Kevin Reynolds; **Writers:** Peter Rader and David Twohy; **Director of Photography:** Dean Semler; **Editor:** Peter Boyle; **Music:** James Newton Howard; **Production Designer:** Dennis Gassner; **Producers:** Kevin Costner and John Davis
Universal; PG-13; 120 minutes
Release: 8/95
Cast: Kevin Costner, Dennis Hopper, Jeanne Tripplehorn and Tina Majorino
The polar ice caps have melted in this post-apocalyptic world and its inhabitants, who live to find dry land, live on atolls made from scrap metal. The Mariner (Costner), a mutant with gills and webbed feet, faces off against the evil Smokers, who are led by the Deacon (Hopper), in their quest to find land. The Mariner takes as passengers Helen (Tripplehorn) and Enola (Majorino) after their establishment is nearly decimated by the Smokers. Tattooed on Enola's back is a map

to land, and the Mariner must protect her from the Deacon, who will go to any extreme to see the map. Waterworld, the most expensive movie of all time, reportedly cost between $175 and $235 million to produce.

WES CRAVEN'S NEW NIGHTMARE

Director/Writer: Wes Craven; **Director of Photography:** Mark Irwin; **Editor:** Patrick Lussier; **Music:** J. Peter Robinson; **Production Designer:** Cynthia Kay Charette; **Producer:** Marianne Maddalena
New Line; R; 112 minutes
Release: 10/94
Cast: Heather Langenkamp, Robert Englund, Miko Hughes, David Newsom, Matt Winston, Rob LaBelle, Wes Craven and Marianne Maddalena
Freddy Kruger (Englund) is back, this time spooking the creators of a new *Nightmare on Elm Street* series, including its creator Wes Craven and the actor who plays Freddy, Robert Englund.

WHILE YOU WERE SLEEPING

Director: John Turtletaub; **Writers:** Daniel G. Sullivan and Frederic Lebow; **Director of Photography:** Phedon Papamichael; **Editor:** Bruce Green; **Music:** Randy Edelman; **Production Designer:** Garret Stover; **Producers:** Joe Roth and Roger Birnbaum
Hollywood Pictures; PG; 98 minutes
Release: 4/95
Cast: Sandra Bullock, Bill Pullman, Peter Gallagher, Peter Boyle, Jack Warden, Glynis Johns, Nicole Mercurio, Jason Bernard, Michael Rispoli and Margaret Travolta
Lonely Chicago Transit Authority worker Lucy Moderatz (Bullock) saves unconscious Peter Callahan (Gallagher) from an approaching train. She meets his family at the hospital and is mistaken for his finaceé, which is fine with her as she fantasizes about Callahan. The trouble begins when she falls in love with Peter's brother (Pullman).

WIGSTOCK: THE MOVIE

Director/Writer: Barry Shils; **Director of Photography:** Wolfgang Held; **Editors:** Barry Shils, Tod Brody and Marlen Hecht; **Producers:** Dean Silvers and Marlen Hecht
Samuel Goldwyn; NR; 85 minutes
Release: 6/95
Cast: RuPaul, Lipsinka, Alexis Arquette, Daisy, the Lady Bunny, Jackie Beat, Mistress Formika and the Dueling Bankheads
This chronicle of the annual Manhattan festival celebrates drag queens, their performances and their fashions including the peacock style, sequins and, of course, wigs.

THE WILD BUNCH

Director: Sam Peckinpah; **Writers:** Walon Green and Sam Peckinpah; **Director of Photography:** Lucien Ballad; **Editor:** Lou Lombardo; **Music:** Jerry Fielding; **Producer:** Phil Feldman
Warner Bros.; R; 145 minutes
Release: 3/95
Cast: William Holden, Ernest Borgnine, Robert Ryan, Edmond O'Brien, Warren Oates, Ben Johnson, Jaime Sanchez, Strother Martin, L. Q. Jones, Albert Dekker, Emilio Fernandez and Dub Taylor
Director's cut of the 1969 film
A gang of outlaws led by Pike Bishop (Holden) attempt to pull off one last score in 1913 Texas before fleeing to Mexico, but they are ambushed and then find themselves in the middle of the Mexican Civil War.

WILD REEDS

Director: André Téchiné; **Writers:** André Téchiné, Gilles Taurand and Olivier Massart; **Directors of Photography:** Jeanne Lapoirie and Germain Desmoulins; **Editor:** Martine Giordano; **Production Designer:** Pierre Soula; **Producers:** Georges Benayoun and Alain Sarde
Ima Films; NR; 110 minutes
Release: 6/95
Cast: Elodie Bouchez, Gaël Morel, Stéphane Rideau, Frédéric Gorny, Michèle Moretti and Jacques Nolot
In French with English subtitles
Set in a French boarding school in 1962 at the end of the Algerian war, this is the coming-of-age story of François (Morel), who falls in love with classmate Serge (Rideau) and right-wing Algerian exile Henri (Gorny), who both fall for François's best friend Maïté (Bouchez).

WINDOW TO PARIS

Director: Yuri Mamin; **Writers:** Yuri Mamin and Arkadi Tigai; **Directors of Photography:** Sergei Nekrassov and Anatoly Lapchov; **Editors:** Olga Andrianova and Joele Van Effenterre; **Music:** Yuri Mamin and Aleksei Zalivalov; **Producer:** Guy Seligmann
Sony Pictures Classics; NR; 87 minutes
Release: 2/95
Cast: Agnes Soral, Sergei Donstov, Viktor Mikhailov and Nina Oussatova
In French and Russian with English subtitles
Nikolai (Donstov) accidentally discovers a gateway from a hidden window in his crowded Russian apartment to beautiful France. He and his roommates are in heaven and take full advantage of Paris's food, wine and clothing — items they must wait in line for if available at all in St. Petersburg. Frenchwoman Nicole (Soral), whose apartment they enter from the window, does not have such pleasant experiences in Russia when she passes out of France.

WINGS OF COURAGE

Director/Producer: Jean-Jacques Annaud; **Writers:** Alain Godard and Jean-Jacques Annaud; **Director of Photography:** Robert Fraisse; **Editor:** Louise Rubacky; **Production Designer:** Ian Thomas
Sony Pictures Classics; G; 40 minutes
Release: 4/95
Cast: Craig Sheffer, Elizabeth McGovern, Tom Hulce, Val Kilmer, Ken Pogue and Ron Sauve
In this first IMAX 3-D feature film, pathbreaking 1930s fliers Mermoz (Kilmer) and St. Exupery (Hulce) employ pilot Guillaumet (Sheffer) to shuttle mail between Santiago de Chile and Buenos Aires. Downed in the Andes on his first run, Guillaumet battles punishing cold while wife Noelle (McGovern) clings fiercely to faith in his survival.

THE WOODEN MAN'S BRIDE

Director: Huang Jianxin; **Writer:** Yang Zhengguang; **Director of Photography:** Zhang Xiaoguang; **Editor:** Lei Qin; **Music:** Zhang Dalong; **Producer:** Wang Ying Hsiang
Arrow Releasing; NR; 114 minutes
Release: 2/95
Cast: Chang Shih, Wang Lan, Ku Paoming, Want Yumei, Wang Fuli and Kao Mingjun
In Mandarin with English subtitles
When Young Mistress's (Lan) new husband dies trying to rescue his bride from kidnappers, Madame Liu (Yumei) insists that Young Mistress marry a wooden statue of her deceased bridegroom and live a life of celibacy. Young Mistress, bored with her lifestyle, has an affair with her servant Kui (Shih). ■

INTRODUCING...

THE EAST COAST

It appears the quakes, floods and riots have shaken quite a few Hollywood players. The recent exodus from the West Coast to the East Coast has seen Steven Spielberg, Jerry Seinfeld, Dennis Hopper, Rosie O'Donnell and Sylvester Stallone make the move. With Spielberg, Hopper and O'Donnell joining Winona Ryder, Julianne Moore and Ethan Hawke in New York, has Hollywood found a second home?

Variety's 1994 Domestic Box Office

Variety magazine tracked the box office gross of more than 450 films that appeared in domestic theaters in 1994. Here are their figures through December 31, 1994.

The Lion King

The Lion King	$298,879,911
Forrest Gump	298,096,620
True Lies	146,260,993
The Santa Clause	134,560,221
The Flintstones	130,522,921
Clear and Present Danger	121,715,132
Speed	121,248,145
The Mask	118,644,781
Maverick	101,631,272
Interview With the Vampire	100,006,085
The Client	92,115,211
Philadelphia	76,878,958
Ace Ventura: Pet Detective	72,217,396
Star Trek Generations	70,432,156
Stargate	68,228,515
Wolf	65,011,757
Pulp Fiction	62,391,023
Dumb and Dumber	59,072,700
The Specialist	55,834,548
Four Weddings and a Funeral	52,700,832
The Little Rascals	51,932,954
Naked Gun 33 1/3: The Final Insult	51,109,400
The Crow	50,693,162
Angels in the Outfield	50,236,831
Natural Born Killers	50,177,396

When a Man Loves a Woman	50,021,959
Disclosure	46,250,464
D2: The Mighty Ducks	45,610,410
The River Wild	45,167,745
Timecop	44,454,024
City Slickers II: The Legend of Curly's Gold	43,622,150
Beverly Hills Cop III	42,610,021
The Paper	38,824,341
On Deadly Ground	38,590,458
It Could Happen to You	37,939,757
The Shadow	32,060,771
I Love Trouble	30,806,194
Major League II	30,626,182
Blank Check	30,577,969
Blown Away	30,155,037
Junior	30,204,485
In the Army Now	28,864,707
Guarding Tess	27,058,304
A Low Down Dirty Shame	26,524,388
My Father, the Hero	25,479,558
Wyatt Earp	25,052,000
Renaissance Man	24,332,324
Blue Chips	22,354,402
Mary Shelley's Frankenstein	22,024,639
Quiz Show	21,840,003
Drop Zone	21,274,027
The Air up There	21,011,318
Iron Will	21,006,361
Reality Bites	20,982,557
Intersection	20,928,892
Jason's Lyric	20,452,161
The Cowboy Way	20,279,854
Corrina, Corrina	20,164,171
With Honors	20,043,254
Only You	20,042,048
Color of Night	19,721,814
8 Seconds	19,623,396
Little Giants	19,288,821
House Party 3	19,281,235

Richie Rich	19,175,387	The Puppet Masters	8,638,072
Getting Even With Dad	18,438,164	Bullets Over Broadway	8,482,052
Sugar Hill	18,272,447	Fresh	8,094,616
Love Affair	18,250,211	The Chase	8,009,329
The Professional	18,007,189	Blankman	7,941,977
Milk Money	17,837,658	Serial Mom	7,881,335
Street Fighter	17,662,440	Sirens	7,770,731
Wes Craven's New Nightmare	17,412,282	Surviving the Game	7,727,256
My Girl 2	17,359,799	Clean Slate	7,503,192
The Jungle Book	17,345,474	Clifford	7,411,659
Miracle on 34th Street	16,867,213	Barcelona	7,266,973
Baby's Day Out	16,827,402	North	7,182,747
Lightning Jack	16,821,273	Eat Drink Man Woman	7,015,697
André	16,819,465	Trial by Jury	6,971,777
Blink	16,696,219	Exit to Eden	6,841,570
The War	16,551,365	The Road to Wellville	6,507,514
Terminal Velocity	16,478,879	The House of the Spirits	6,265,311
Monkey Trouble	16,453,258	Widow's Peak	6,243,722
The Shawshank Redemption	16,424,889	Belle Époque	5,971,369
Above the Rim	16,192,320	Ed Wood	5,784,528
The Getaway	16,096,272	Trapped in Paradise	5,777,916
Little Women	15,999,996	Airheads	5,370,123
No Escape	15,339,030	Ready to Wear	5,249,097
Bad Girls	15,240,435	Mixed Nuts	5,130,493
Threesome	14,815,317	Little Buddha	4,858,139
Crooklyn	13,639,634	Black Beauty	4,630,377
Speechless	13,445,643	Wagons East	4,412,297
Greedy	13,145,977	P.C.U.	4,350,774
Little Big League	12,267,790	Brainscan	4,264,509
3 Ninjas Kick Back	11,798,854	Ghost in the Machine	3,775,773
The Ref	11,439,193	Jimmy Hollywood	3,692,874
Cops and Robbersons	11,391,093	Cabin Boy	3,662,459
Thumbelina	11,373,501	A Simple Twist of Fate	3,428,774
The Pagemaster	11,176,333		
Camp Nowhere	10,471,613		
I'll Do Anything	10,424,645		
The Adventures of Priscilla, Queen of the Desert	10,205,944		
You So Crazy	10,184,701		
I.Q.	10,148,571		
Lassie	9,979,683		
Nell	9,582,346		
Angie	9,398,308		
The Next Karate Kid	8,914,777		
The Inkwell	8,880,705		
White Fang 2	8,878,839		
The Swan Princess	8,740,247		

The Santa Clause

Gunmen	3,411,885
Squanto: A Warrior's Tale	3,337,685
Romeo Is Bleeding	3,275,585
Mi Vida Loca	3,269,420
Silent Fall	3,180,674
The Favor	3,134,081
Princess Caraboo	3,062,530
China Moon	3,038,499
The Hudsucker Proxy	2,869,369
The Scout	2,694,234
Blue Sky	2,415,094
Go Fish	2,408,311
Backbeat	2,392,599
The Last Seduction	2,359,228
Double Dragon	2,341,309
Red Rock West	2,331,411
Clerks	2,312,723
A Good Man in Africa	2,308,390
Leprechaun 2	2,260,622
Sankofa	2,181,305
The Endless Summer II	2,155,385
The Princess and the Goblin	2,144,238
Kika	2,093,370
Vertical Reality	2,000,007
Hoop Dreams	1,926,145
The Scent of Green Papaya	1,910,763
Bitter Moon	1,862,805
I Like It Like That	1,777,020
Even Cowgirls Get the Blues	1,708,873
Death Wish V	1,702,394
Chasers	1,596,687
Louis 19 — King of the Airwaves	1,569,021
32 Short Films About Glenn Gould	1,567,543
Being Human	1,519,366
White	1,464,625
Spanking the Monkey	1,359,736
Sick and Twisted Animation	1,347,529
Radioland Murders	1,309,607
Red (Rouge)	1,303,454
Heavenly Creatures	1,261,763
Car 54, Where Are You?	1,238,080
A Million to Juan	1,221,832
Ciao, Professore	1,113,435
Naked in New York	1,038,959
Mrs. Parker and the Vicious Circle	967,611
Matusalem	959,307
Mother's Boys	874,148

Clerks

Dazed and Confused	835,147
Queen Margot	813,583
RoboCop 3	786,087
Parenthood	740,970
Bhaji on the Beach	735,192
Drop Squad	734,693
Vanya on 42nd Street	714,911
Holy Matrimony	713,234
Exotica	704,244
The Advocate	667,078
Savage Nights	662,341
To Live	648,011
Cronos	621,392
Where the Rivers Flow North	595,505
Latchodrom	584,311
Immortal Beloved	492,978
My Fair Lady	462,466
The Wonderful, Horrible Life of Leni Reifenstahl	449,707
American Cyborg	447,784
Fiorile	429,184
Body Snatchers	428,868
The Browning Version	421,891
Killing Zoe	418,953
Caro Diario	415,465
Love and Human Remains	414,454
Golden Gate	395,105
Showdown	365,284
Nostradamus	364,164
The Blue Kite	355,974
Octobre	349,633
What Happened Was . . .	327,482
The Cement Garden	322,975
Trading Mom	319,123

Café au Lait	315,420	Sex and Zen	105,700
Legends of the Fall	312,427	L'enfant Lion	105,066
La Fille de D'Artagnan	311,922	Mouvements du Desir	104,288
The Slingshot	309,117	Suture	102,780
Rapa Nui	305,070	A Place in the World	100,986
Sex, Drugs and Democracy	276,174	Totally F***ed Up	98,967
That's Entertainment III	274,794	Salmonberries	96,717
Babyfever	269,904	A Man of No Importance	95,254
Nobody's Fool	258,233	A Man in Uniform	93,623
Dream Lover	256,264	In Custody	92,612
The Conformist	251,691	The Return of Tommy Tricker	92,605
I Don't Want to Talk About It	249,530	Imaginary Crimes	89,611
The New Age	246,217	Raining Stones	89,388
Cobb	241,776	A Simple Formality	88,606
Boy's Life	241,477	Gross Indecency	86,836
Fear of a Black Hat	238,230	Second Best	86,115
Á la Mode	236,090	Just Like a Woman	78,808
Colonel Chabert	222,408	Faster, Pussycat! Kill! Kill!	78,417
Zero Patience	217,225	Dialogues With Mad Women	77,789
Grief	215,428	Love After Love	75,473
The Wedding Gift	214,380	A Troll in Central Park	71,368
A Tale of Winter	213,687	Freedom on My Mind	71,176
Midnight Cowboy	205,150	It Runs in the Family	70,936
The Boys of St. Vincent	204,540	December Bride	70,298
Reckless Kelly	203,602	Diabolique	69,752
Federal Hill	196,588	Desperate Remedies	69,695
My Life's in Turnaround	196,383	Tom and Viv	66,255
Grosse Fatigue	195,536	An Unforgettable Summer	65,352
Crime Story	194,720	Leon the Pig Farmer	65,222
L'enfer	194,223	. . . And God Spoke	62,598
Dr. Strangelove	193,892	Silent Tongue	61,274
Camilla	183,385	It's Pat	60,822
Le Vent du Wyoming	169,880	The Madness of King George	58,142
Ivan and Abraham	164,628	Smoking/No Smoking	57,033
Sleep With Me	161,410	La Vengeance d'une blonde	56,218
Death and the Maiden	156,776	Le Sourire	55,497
Sunday's Children	151,881	Neuf Mois	52,849
High Lonesome	150,148	Woodstock	51,740
La Scorta	147,394	Apex	49,601
Burnt by the Sun	144,541	The Myth of the Male Orgasm	49,349
Police Academy 7: Mission to Moscow	126,247	The Secret Adventures of Tom Thumb	41,176
There Goes My Baby	125,169	Whale Music	39,129
Oleanna	124,693	Gordy	39,018
For the Moment	121,548		
Foreign Student	113,727	*Source:* Variety	
Mina Tannenbaum	111,307		

1994 Academy Awards

Tom Hanks accepting Best Actor Oscar©

BEST PICTURE
Forrest Gump, **Wendy Finerman, Steve Tisch and
    Steve Starkey, producers (Paramount)**

Four Weddings and a Funeral, Duncan Kenworthy,
    producer (Gramercy)

Pulp Fiction, Lawrence Bender, producer (Miramax)

Quiz Show, Robert Redford, Michael Jacobs, Julian
    Krainin and Michael Nozik, producers (Buena
    Vista)

The Shawshank Redemption, Niki Marvin, producer
    (Columbia)

ACTOR IN A LEADING ROLE
Morgan Freeman, *The Shawshank Redemption*

Tom Hanks, *Forrest Gump*

Nigel Hawthorne, *The Madness of King George*

Paul Newman, *Nobody's Fool*

John Travolta, *Pulp Fiction*

ACTRESS IN A LEADING ROLE
Jodie Foster, *Nell*

Jessica Lange, *Blue Sky*

Miranda Richardson, *Tom and Viv*

Winona Ryder, *Little Women*

Susan Sarandon, *The Client*

ACTOR IN A SUPPORTING ROLE
Samuel L. Jackson, *Pulp Fiction*

Martin Landau, *Ed Wood*

Chazz Palminteri, *Bullets Over Broadway*

Paul Scofield, *Quiz Show*

Gary Sinise, *Forrest Gump*

ACTRESS IN A SUPPORTING ROLE
Rosemary Harris, *Tom and Viv*

Helen Mirren, *The Madness of King George*

Uma Thurman, *Pulp Fiction*

Jennifer Tilly, *Bullets Over Broadway*

Dianne Wiest, *Bullets Over Broadway*

DIRECTING
Woody Allen, *Bullets Over Broadway*

Krzysztof Kieslowski, *Red*

Robert Redford, *Quiz Show*

Quentin Tarantino, *Pulp Fiction*

Robert Zemeckis, *Forrest Gump*

WRITING
SCREENPLAY WRITTEN DIRECTLY FOR THE SCREEN
Woody Allen and Douglas McGrath, *Bullets Over
    Broadway*

Richard Curtis, *Four Weddings and a Funeral*

Krzysztof Piesiewicz and Krzysztof Kieslowski, *Red*

Quentin Tarantino and Roger Avary, *Pulp Fiction*

Frances Walsh and Peter Jackson, *Heavenly Creatures*

SCREENPLAY BASED ON MATERIAL PREVIOUSLY PRODUCED OR PUBLISHED
Paul Attanasio, *Quiz Show*

Alan Bennett, *The Madness of King George*

Robert Benton, *Nobody's Fool*

Frank Darabont, *The Shawshank Redemption*

Eric Roth, *Forrest Gump*

CINEMATOGRAPHY
Don Burgess, *Forrest Gump*

Roger Deakins, *The Shawshank Redemption*

Owen Roizman, *Wyatt Earp*

Piotr Sobocinski, *Red*

John Toll, *Legends of the Fall*

ART DIRECTION
**Ken Adam, art direction; Carolyn Scott, set decora-
    tion, *The Madness of King George***

Rick Carter, art direction; Nancy Haigh, set
    decoration, *Forrest Gump*

Dante Ferretti, art direction; Francesca Lo Schiavo,
    set decoration, *Interview With the Vampire*

Lilly Kilvert, art direction; Dorree Cooper, set decoration, *Legends of the Fall*

Santo Loquasto, art direction; Susan Bode, set decoration, *Bullets Over Broadway*

SOUND

Gregg Landaker, Steve Maslow, Bob Beemer and David R. B. MacMillan, *Speed*

Robert J. Litt, Elliot Tyson, Michael Herbick and Willie Burton, *The Shawshank Redemption*

Paul Massey, David Campbell, Christopher David and Douglas Ganton, *Legends of the Fall*

Donald O. Mitchell, Michael Herbick, Frank A. Montano and Arthur Rochester, *Clear and Present Danger*

Randy Thom, Tom Johnson, Dennis Dands and William B. Kaplan, *Forrest Gump*

MUSIC
SONG

"Can You Feel the Love Tonight," *The Lion King*, Elton John, music; Tim Rice, lyrics

"Circle of Life," *The Lion King*, Elton John, music; Tim Rice, lyrics

"Hakuna Matata," *The Lion King*, Elton John, music; Tim Rice, lyrics

"Look What Love Has Done," *Junior*, Carol Bayer Sager, James Newton Howard, James Ingram and Patty Smyth, music and lyrics

Elton John

"Make Up Your Mind," *The Paper*, Randy Newman, music and lyrics

ORIGINAL SCORE

Elliot Goldenthal, *Interview With the Vampire*

Thomas Newman, *Little Women*

Thomas Newman, *The Shawshank Redemption*

Alan Silvestri, *Forrest Gump*

Hans Zimmer, *The Lion King*

FILM EDITING

Richard Francis-Bruce, *The Shawshank Redemption*

Frederick Marx, Steve James and Bill Haugse, *Hoop Dreams*

Sally Menke, *Pulp Fiction*

Arthur Schmidt, *Forrest Gump*

John Wright, *Speed*

CONTINUED ON PAGE 79 ▶

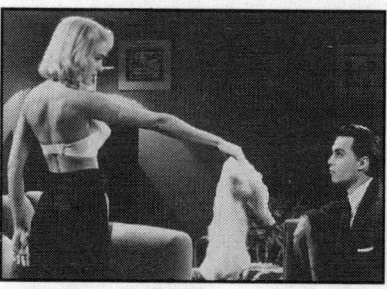

IPEA's
ALTERNATIVE OSCARS

Part of the enjoyment of Hollywood's annual celebration of itself is imagining that the only vote that mattered was yours. The editors of the IPEA, with the assistance of several contributing film writers and filmmakers, got together and argued, cajoled and orated in order to craft the list below.

Ed Wood

Best Picture
  Ed Wood

Best Actor
  Samuel L. Jackson, *Pulp Fiction*

Best Actress
  Julianne Moore,
  Vanya on 42nd Street

Best Supporting Actor
  Paul Scofield, *Quiz Show*

Best Supporting Actress
  Helen Mirren,
  The Madness of King George

Best Director
  Steve James, *Hoop Dreams*

Best Foreign Language Film
  To Live

Helen Mirren,
The Madness of
King George

Oscar's Big Night

DAVID LETTERMAN'S OPENING MONOLOGUE FOR THE 67TH ANNUAL ACADEMY AWARDS set the pace for the March evening: slow and uneventful. Most of his jokes fell flat, especially the Uma (Thurman) and Oprah (Winfrey) reference — "Umaaa, Oprahh. Umaaa, Oprahh." Sorry Dave, it wasn't funny and adding Keanu (Reeves) didn't help. The gimmick barely garnered a chuckle from the unamused audience. Drawing on his *Late Show* shtick, Letterman did find some success with the Stupid Pet Trick that had a dog run in head-spinning circles whenever the audience clapped, and clap they did. His top-10 list of signs that a film or actor will not win an Oscar, included a misspelling — "Dom DeLuise is Ghandi." (Oops.) Despite Letterman's performance, the show earned a 32.5 rating, the highest for an Oscarcast in 12 years.

Perhaps the biggest surprise of the otherwise predictable night was Susan Sarandon's and blue-alligator-tux-clad Tim Robbins's award presentation. Letterman introduced them by saying, "Pay attention, I'm sure they're pissed off about something." But they weren't; there was no harangue about their political cause du jour. Save for Robbins, the stars were conservatively attired. Armani was the rule for men, who mostly opted for the traditional black tux (though some did mix it up a bit with Nehru-style collars). A number of the women went with conservative but low-cut pastel Versace gowns. Jane Fonda ran away with the "What were you thinking?" award when she showed up on Ted Turner's arm wearing a big, black-and-white checkboard Versace that evoked memories of the Queen of Hearts in *Alice in Wonderland*. Holly Hunter followed in a close second with her white hip-hugger skirt and bra, which was topped with skin-tight white mesh.

Susan Sarandon, Ken Adam, Carolyn Scott and Tim Robbins

As last year, when Anna Paquin won the hearts of the audience when she received the Best Supporting Actress nod for *The Piano,* a child stole the 1995 show. This year, it was Nadia Mikhalkov, who while hoisted on her father Nikita's shoulder with her braids tied up with big, white ribbons, carried Nikita's Foreign Language Film Oscar for *Burnt by the Sun.*

Were it not for Nadia's bows and braids, a monkey would've been the night's biggest hit. Letterman, trying to convince the audience that his role as Earl Hofert in 1994's bomb *Cabin Boy* was coveted by other actors, showed a tape of other actors including Paul Newman, Rosie O'Donnell and Albert Brooks holding a cloth monkey and reciting his one line, "Do you wanna buy a monkey?" Sales of the sock monkey skyrocketed the day after the broadcast. Bobbi Patterson, a volunteer at New York City's Woman's Exchange where the dolls are sold, put a sign in the window reading "Do you wanna buy a monkey?," and immediately sold 10, a marked increase considering she normally sells 50 in a year.

Had the awards not been so predictable and safe, the 3½ hour ceremony would not have dragged so. But as always, Oscar is not one to take chances. ∎

◀ CONTINUED FROM PAGE 77

COSTUME DESIGN

Colleen Atwood, *Little Women*

Moidele Bickel, *Queen Margot*

April Ferry, *Maverick*

Lizzy Gardiner and Tim Chappel, *The Adventures of Priscilla, Queen of the Desert*

Jeffrey Kurland, *Bullets Over Broadway*

MAKEUP

Rick Baker, Ve Neill and Yolanda Toussieng, *Ed Wood*

Daniel Parker, Paul Engelen and Carol Hemming, *Mary Shelley's Frankenstein*

Daniel C. Striepeke, Hallie D'Amore and Judith A. Cory, *Forrest Gump*

VISUAL EFFECTS

John Bruno, Thomas L. Fisher, Jacques Stroweis and Patrick McClung, *True Lies*

Ken Ralston, George Murphy, Stephen Rosenbaum and Allen Hall, *Forrest Gump*

Scott Squires, Steve Williams, Tom Bertino and John Farhat, *The Mask*

SOUND EFFECTS EDITING

Gloria S. Borders and Randy Thom, *Forrest Gump*

Stephen Hunter Flick, *Speed*

Bruce Stambler and John Leveque, *Clear and Present Danger*

SHORT FILMS
ANIMATION

The Big Story (Tim Watts and David Stoten, producers; Spitting Image Production)

***Bob's Birthday* (Alison Snowden and David Fine, producers; Channel Four/National Film Board of Canada Production)**

The Janitor (Vanessa Schwartz, producer; Vanessa Schwartz Production)

The Monk and the Fish (Michael Dudok de Wit, producer; Folimage Valence Production)

Triangle (Erica Russell, producer; Gingco Ltd. Production)

LIVE ACTION

***Franz Kafka's It's a Wonderful Life* (Peter Capaldi and Ruth Kenley-Letts, producers; Conundrum Films Production)**

Kangaroo Court (Sean Astin and Christine Astin, producers; Lava Entertainment Production)

On Hope (JoBeth Williams and Michele McGuire, producers; Chanticleer Films Production)

Syrup (Paul Unwin and Nick Vivian, producers; First Choice Production)

Trevor (Peggy Rajski and Randy Stone, producers; Rajski/Stone Production)

DOCUMENTARY
SHORT SUBJECT

Blues Highway (Vince DiPersio and Bill Guttentag, producers; Half Court Pictures, Ltd./National Geographic Society Production)

89MM od Europy (89MM From Europe) (Marcel Lozinski, producer; Studio Filmowe "Kalejdoskop"/Telewizja Polska Production)

School for the Americas Assassins (Robert Richter, producer; Richter Production)

Straight From the Heart (Dee Mosbacher and Frances Reid, producers; Woman Vision Production)

***A Time for Justice* (Charles Guggenheim, producer; Guggenheim Productions, Inc. Production)**

FEATURE

Complaints of a Dutiful Daughter (Deborah Hoffmann, producer; D/D Production)

D-Day Remembered (Charles Guggenheim, producer; Guggenheim Productions, Inc. Production)

Freedom on My Mind (Connie Field and Marilyn Mulford, producers; Clarity Film Production)

A Great Day in Harlem (Jean Bach, producer; Jean Bach Production)

***Maya Lin: A Strong Clear Vision* (Freida Lee Mock and Terry Sanders, producers; American Film Foundation/Sanders and Mock Production)**

FOREIGN LANGUAGE FILM

Before the Rain, The Former Yugoslav Republic of Macedonia

***Burnt by the Sun,* Russia**

Eat Drink Man Woman, Republic of China on Taiwan

Farinelli: Il Castrato, Belgium

Strawberry and Chocolate, Cuba

IRVING G. THALBERG MEMORIAL AWARD

Clint Eastwood for a consistently high quality of motion picture production

JEAN HERSHOLT HUMANITARIAN AWARD

Quincy Jones

HONORARY AWARDS

Michelangelo Antonioni for lifetime achievement

Major International Film Festivals

Our around-the-globe round-up of cinematic scenes

Commercialism is to Cannes what content is to Berlin. Queer film traditionally finds a home here, as do verité docs and arthouse features. In its 45th year, the Berlin International Film Festival is undisputably one of the most established and powerful showcases for the world's newest cinema. More than 10,000 attended 1995's February 9–20 event, which runs in tandem with the European Film Market, representing 91 companies from 40 countries.

Unlike Telluride and its lovely, lofty mountain vistas, Berlin is hard work. Tension and high anxiety fill the air as European productions and American independents race from booth to booth trying to secure distribution deals and finishing funds. There's no time to waste. Coming three months before Cannes, Berlin is where the make-or-break buzz is first heard as to what's out there and what's going to show up in your local multiplex later in the year.

Wayne Wang

Twenty-seven films, 19 of them world premieres, headlined in 1995's high-profile Competition section. Some of the biggest titles were American entries: *Quiz Show* by Robert Redford — whose personal absence disappointed both audiences and festival organizers; Robert Benton's vehicle for Paul Newman, *Nobody's Fool;* Abel Ferrara's vampire-film, *The Addiction; Before Sunrise,* an intercontinental one-night stand by Richard Linklater; and Wayne Wang's *Smoke,* an ensemble drama starring William

Before Sunrise

Hurt and Harvey Keitel.

British-made *Butterfly Kiss,* a film about two lesbian serial killers, garnered critical raves and a distribution deal. Favorites with the audience, known for being more interested in discussing camera angles over coffee than market surveys over martinis, were French New Waver Agnes Varda's valentine to cinema's 100th anniversary, *A Hundred and One Nights,* Bernard Tavernier's street-tough *The Bait* and the hometown favorite, Margarethe von Trotta's ode to love and the Wall, *The Promise.*

This year was also marked by the increased presence of East Asian fare, most notably by Beijing Film Studio, aggressively wooed by festival organizers. Standouts were Hong Kong's period film *Red Rose White Rose* and Li Shaohong's *Blush,* the story of a mainland China call girl.

They came, they saw, they bought. On February 20, they went home. In May, most would see each other when the madness began all over again — with more glitz, more hype, and, for the unsigned, more to lose — at Cannes.

22ND TELLURIDE FILM FESTIVAL

The plot: A top-secret lineup turns little ol' Telluride into one of the jewels of the festival world. The set: A modest, pretty-as-a-picture ski town that is surrounded by the San Juan Range's 13,000-foot snow-covered peaks. The cast: At 5,000, the festival's audience more than quadruples the local population. In hopes of glimpsing the next *Blue Velvet*, *The Crying Game* or *The Piano* — films that world-premiered at Telluride — festival audiences every year bypass the ski slopes and Native American jewelry shops in favor of the hundreds of screenings scheduled over the four-day festival. As a Telluride regular, the legendary animator Chuck Jones, quipped last year of the 8,745 feet-altitude movie marathon, "it's the most fun you'll ever have without breathing."

Every Labor Day, sell-out crowds fly and drive into the former mining boom-town in Colorado without the slightest idea of what they will see. They simply buy a $400 festival pass and attend as many films as possible. Secrecy is one of the selling points of the 22-year-old event. "It's a film lover's festival. It's not concerned with star power or who's who as much as the art of film," explains Buck Lowe of Telluride's press office. Organizers were true to their word at 1995's event. The art of film was very much in evidence at the festival, which honored English director John Schlesinger, Chinese filmmaker Zhang Yimou and contemporary surrealist filmmakers including Czech Jan Svankmajer and the Brothers Quay. Schlesinger, whose most recent film *Cold Comfort Farm* was shown at the festival, is best known for 1969's *Midnight Cowboy*. Yimou, who

directed 1991's *Raise the Red Lantern*, made the rounds on the 1995 festival circuit with *Shanghai Triad*.

"I'm particularly happy with the way the tribute came together this year. More and more, we're finding it difficult to be imaginative, to find people we geniunely believe are in a class with filmmakers such as Andrei Tarkovsky and Abel Gance," said festival organizer Bill Pence. "We felt [the tribute to surrealists] would make a statement that cinema can be something other than grosses that are reported on weekly in *USA Today*."

Other highlights of the program included *On the Beat*, the third feature from China's Ning Ying; *Warrior Lanling*, the period piece from 34-year-old Sherwood Hu; *Amanda Root*, an adapatation of Jane Austen's *Persuasion* from British director Roger Michell; British writer/director Christopher Hampton's *Carrington*, which focuses on writer Lytton Strachey and painter Dora Carrington and stars Jonathan Pryce and Emma Thompson (many predicted another Best Actress Oscar for Thompson); Hampton also penned Agnieszka Holland's *Total Eclipse*, which depicts the turbulent relationship between French poets Arthur Rimbaud and Paul Verlaine; Gus van Sant, back on the festival scene after 1994's bomb *Even Cowgirls Get the Blues*, brought *To Die For*, starring Nicole Kidman and ever-emotionless Matt Dillon; this year's hometown film was Gary Fleder's *Things to Do in Denver When You're Dead*, starring Andy Garcia, Treat Williams and Christopher Walken; and the Jonathan Demme-recommended Generation X film *Desolation Angeles*.

One of the festival's greatest pleasures is an under-the-stars screening at the Abel Gance Open Air Cinema. Built in 1979 for the first showing since 1929 of the director's *Napoleon*, the theater was designed to accommodate the silent film's requisite three full-size screens and five projectors. These days, few films have these requirements, but single-screen viewings continue to draw audiences, who bring sleeping bags and wait under the stars for the show to begin. The evening could include a live appearance, a reprinted masterwork, a retrospective or a world premiere. Anything can happen in the dark at Telluride.

To Die For

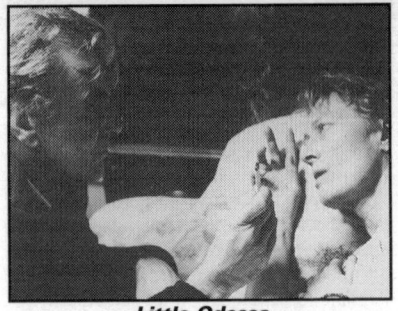

Little Odessa

The buzz starts here. Every January, Park City, Utah, sounds the call across America, and independents come running. Formerly synonymous with low-budget, fuzzy films about do-gooder subjects and the meaning of life, Sundance is now a full-blown, viable market for commercial hits. As founder Robert Redford explained, "There seems to be a maturing of the independent feature film. They're a little more mature, more sophisticated, more in tune with the times."

"See you in Park City," uttered unctuous studio exec Tim Robbins in *The Player,* immortalizing Sundance onscreen as a meet-and-greet must stop for Hollywood. Distributors such as Fine Line Features and Miramax came prepared to do business and buy, buy, buy at the premier shopping mall for America's up-and-coming picture-makers.

With 304 submissions for the dramatic competition alone, 1995's fest screened 100 features to some 5,000 Hollywood insiders and movie buffs from January 19–29.

The Grand Jury Prize for dramatic film went to *The Brothers McMullen,* written and directed by newcomer Edward Burns, whose own how-he-made-the-film story sent the publicity machine into overdrive. A former van driver for *Entertainment Tonight,* Burns shot the film over eight months on weekends at his parents' Long

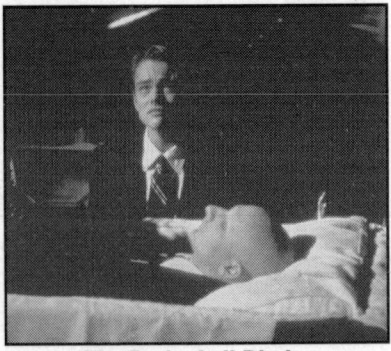

The Basketball Diaries

Island home and cast himself and his girlfriend in key roles. The film tells the story of three brothers in an Irish Catholic family who wrestle with issues of family, women and growing up. Critical acclaim and studio deals also marked two other features by first-timers: James Gray's *Little Odessa,* a stylized New York story about the Russian Mafia, and Scott Kalvert's *The Basketball Diaries,* Jim Carroll's chronicle of the descent of a young punk poet into heroin abuse. Yet another Sundance winner that would go on to define the 1995 cinematic landscape was *Crumb.* A portrait of twisted underground comic-book artist R. Crumb by Terry Zwigoff, *Crumb* took home the Grand Jury Prize for best documentary as well as the Cinematography Award.

Though untrustworthy, since ballots were easily obtainable early and often, the Audience Award for dramatic film went to Kayo Hatta's *Picture Bride,* which movingly created a historical portrait of the plight of Japanese mail-order brides in colonial Hawaii. Documentary Audience Awards went to *Unzipped,* Douglas Keeve's raucous, behind-the-scenes look at Isaac Mizrahi's annual fall fashion show, and to *Ballot Measure 9,* which chronicles Oregon's controversial 1992 ballot referendum restricting gay rights. The Filmmakers Trophy for dramatic film went to *Angela,* a psychological narrative about two sisters and their manic-depressive mother, written and directed by Rebecca Miller, the daughter of playwright Arthur Miller. Marlon T. Riggs was honored posthumously with the Filmmakers Trophy for documentary for his *Black Is . . . Black Ain't,* a discussion with African Americans about black identity.

Their resumes may be on the light side, but the chosen are no fly-by-night talents. Sundance winners tend to stick around in the limelight. The 17th Sundance Festival unveiled follow-up works by previous winners Todd Haines, Bryan Singer, Tom Noonan and Richard Linklater. Linklater, who became a household name after his Gen-X epic *Slackers,* received the coveted kickoff festival spot for *Before Sunrise.* A sweet tale in which American boy meets European girl, *Before Sunrise* went on to become an independent's dream — a box-office hit.

Amateur

1994 AND 1995 NEW YORK FILM FESTIVALS

The New York Film Festival is the Russian Tea Room of film festivals — only the elite need apply. Because it is small (only 30 films are featured), New York is not the place for unknowns to hope for a big break. The festival attracts the attention of cineastes worldwide by premiering features and shorts by top filmmakers, as well as audience favorites from recent film-festival screenings. Don't plan to see 16mm black-and-white art films at New York; expect the likes of Zhang Yimou's latest epic starring Gong Li.

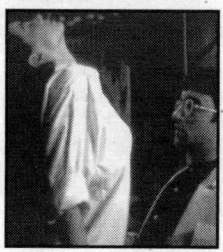

Exotica

The 1994 Festival kicked off with the much-awaited American premiere of *Pulp Fiction,* video-clerk-turned-superstar-hipster Quentin Taran-tino's mega-hit, and closed with the highly acclaimed true-life basketball epic *Hoop Dreams.* The festival's centerpiece was perennial favorite, New York neurotic Woody Allen's paean to thespian aspirations and backstage histrionics, *Bullets Over Broadway.*

Tim Burton's homage to schlockmeister *Ed Wood* also premiered, as did a number of indie productions: *Exotica,* a meditation on voyeurism, family and secrets by Canada's award-winning Atom Egoyan; Hal Hartley's patented brand of Long Island noir, *Amateur;* and Steve MacLean's *Postcards From America,* inspired by the work of the late artist and AIDS activist David Wojnarowicz. Documentary connoisseurs flocked to the strong lineup: in addition to *Hoop Dreams,* the festival screened *The Troubles We've Seen,* Marcel Ophuls' haunting look at war correspondents and their strategies for surviving the horrors of war, and Terry Zwigoff's *Crumb,* a disturbing look at the life and family of cartoonist and '60s icon R. Crumb, which would go on to be the year's doc discovery. The 1994 NYFF also screened the American premieres of a number of foreign-language films, including Krzyzstof Kieslowski's *Red* and Zhang Yimou's *To Live* (China).

The 1995 Festival opened with Yimou's lavish 1930s gangster flick, *Shanghai Triad.* The much-awaited closing night film was the ballyhooed *Carrington,* already widely discussed on the festival circuit, having earned Jonathan Pryce the best actor award at Cannes for his portrayal of Lytton Strachey. The centerpiece feature was Katherine Bigelow's *Strange Days* starring Ralph Fiennes and Angela Bassett. Independent filmmaker Hal Hartley also debuted *Flirt.*

Festival director Richard Peña balanced movies about cinema and the arts with political features that included Ken Loach's look at the Spanish Civil War, *Land and Freedom, Sixteen Oh Sixty,* a first feature by Brazilian director Vinicius Mainardi and *Dead Presidents,* a story of a Vietnam veteran's return by the Hughes Brothers.

Cinema's Center Ring

The IPEA asked a long-time Cannes festival-goer to give us an impressionistic view of the world's biggest cinema circus.

■ BY JEFF GROSS

EVERY YEAR, MY HOTEL OWNER TELLS ME that she thinks the Cannes film festival is getting worse. She has now given up. This year, no matter how I tried to provoke her into one of her annual diatribes, she would not let herself be enticed. She still goes to a film or two a year, but she's always disappointed. The French films are the worst, she says, the actors are bad and there are no new ideas. Small wonder, in such a climate, that she sees the festival going downhill.

At the bar of the Majestic Hotel, the tables are full at 10:30 A.M. A coffee costs $5, tea or soft drinks $6 and beer $9. It's the price a writer has to pay for the conversations, the ambiance, the show — during the day a constant parade of different types, and at night a lively sexual atmosphere of tuxedo-clad men and women with plenty of money and time to spare. For free, you get peanuts, crackers and olives, and a good chance to eavesdrop on a table full of French producers, all masters of unpopular cinema, all self-appointed saviors of culture from the clutches of the Hollywood dinosaur.

At every festival there is a buzz, fueled by the trade papers, influenced by the weather, by the briskness of business, by the quality of the films, by the mood of my hotel owner. This year's festival was condemned as *mou* (soft)

Nicole Kidman

early on, and never really recovered in spite of the generally excellent weather. A gloominess descended that seemed to be a continuation of a stubborn four-year slide. Although festival director Gilles Jacob claimed to have screened over 400 films to make the official selection, good films were few, and great films were nowhere to be seen. Not only that, but the festival seems to have become less glamorous. Less money, fewer stars, (the biggest appearance of the first week was Pamela Anderson of *Baywatch*), more hangers-on pushing to get into the parties. There they can take advantage of the free booze and talk to other people about the bad films they will make, the same films they criticize in the festival, the same films they hope to bring here next year.

Even in flush years, Cannes is a circus: packs of paparazzi prowling the beaches, producers-for-a-fortnight promising fame and fortune to gullible starlets in revealing dress. But this is just the sideshow. What Cannes is really about is the creators, the people on the fringe, the rebels, the first-timers, the wannabes. In this year of the 100th anniversary of cinema, the talk is about turning the slide around, about finding forms and themes and characters

**Elizabeth Hurley
and Hugh Grant**

to make people dream again. It's about taking audiences on a ride that they will never forget. It's about emotions and hope. It's about having a planet for our children to live on when they get older. These are the things you talk about at 2:30 in the morning in the Majestic bar, as the lights go low, the place slowly empties, and the waiters move through the room straightening up. This is Cannes, in years that some say are bad, in years which others say are good.

In years past, I sometimes saw as many as 35 films during the festival. This year I went to 12 films and walked out of seven. I liked Ken Loach's *Land and Freedom* because the actors, mostly Spanish non-professionals, made me forget that I was watching actors. I liked *Carrington* because Christopher Hampton's imaginative, insightful script is one of the few with dialogue that actually sounds true to my ear. I liked the imaginative madness of *Underground*, the film by Emir Kusturica that won the Palme d'Or, but found it much too long to sit through at 8:30 in the morning.

A detail: more than half the people in the festival had a cough for twelve days running. A detail: I was amused by an inscription on an arch inside the Chateau de la Napoule, where one of the trade magazines holds its yearly parties. It's a massive affair, a tremendous release after 10 days of no sleep, and a highly-coveted ticket, from which the 100 francs donation goes to an AIDS charity. The inscription reads: "Save me Marie, from gynocrat, scientist and democrat." A warning no one is sober enough to notice. It's an interesting notion to consider on the Monday after the festival, strolling down the Croisette for the thousandth time in 13 days, watching the cranes take down the large movie billboards on both sides and in the middle of the palm-lined sea-front avenue, watching the workmen roll up the disposable blue carpet, and load into their moving trucks the pavilions that housed the 48th Cannes Film Festival. ∎

Jeff Gross has lived in Paris for 13 years. He is the author of five novels and 14 screenplays, including collaborations on Roman Polanski's Frantic *and* Bitter Moon.

1995 CANNES FILM FESTIVAL WINNERS

Palme d'Or
Underground, Emir Kusturica
(France, Germany and Hungary)

Grand Prize
Ulysses' Gaze, Theo Angelopoulos
(Greece, France and Italy)

Best Actor
Jonathan Price, *Carrington*

Best Actress
Helen Mirren, *The Madness of King George*
(United Kingdom and United States)

Direction
Hate, Matthieu Kassovitz (France)

Special Jury Prize
Carrington, Christopher Hampton
(United Kingdom and France)

Jury Prize
Don't Forget You're Going to Die, Xavier Beauvois (France)

Camera d'Or for Film Debut
The White Balloon, Jafar Pahani (Iran)

Helen Mirren,
The Madness of
King George

Special Mention
Denise Calls Up (United States)

Technique
Shanghai Triad, Zhang Yimou

Palme d'Or for Short Film
Gagarine, Alexel Kharidiri (Russia)

Special Jury Prize for Short Film
Swinger, Gregor Jordon (Australia)

The Year in Film Preservation

Through the work of media groups such as the Film Foundation and the various archives devoted to film preservation, and through the appearance in theaters of newly restored prints of titles such as *My Fair Lady, Belle de Jour* and even *Faster Pussycat! Kill! Kill!*, the general public has been coming to understand the magnitude of the potential loss of our common movie heritage. We now know that up to 80 percent of silent film, the dawn of the new art form of the movies, has been lost due to neglect and lack of funds for restoration. Color films made just decades ago are subject to fading and image degradation. Millions of feet of film shot on unstable

Belle de Jour

nitrate stocks awaiting restoration represent history literally turning to dust before our eyes.

Gains are being made, though, as public consciousness grows. The UCLA Film and Television Archive presents an annual Festival of Preservation, now in its seventh year. The Festival of Preservation highlights the activities of one of the busiest archives, and, this year, the festival (held from April 6 to May 4, 1995) coincided with the Congress of the International Federation of Film Archives in Los Angeles, which celebrated the centennial of film. The IFAF creates collaborations between archives around the world and sponsors the Lumière Project, an initiative intended to rescue European film, to develop a Joint European Filmography and to search for lost titles. UCLA's festival included showings of Lumière's results: restorations of Abel Gance's *Mater Dolorosa* (France, 1917), Guido Brignone's *Maciste All'Inferno* (Italy, 1926), Giovanni Pastrone's *Cabiria* (Italy, 1914), Robert Wiese's *Cabinet of Dr. Caligari* (Germany, 1919), Danish film before Carl Dreyer and several others. The festival also unveiled this year's work of the UCLA Archive including a re-creation of the opening night of *The Better 'Ole* (1926), starring Sydney Chaplin and accompanied by vaudeville acts and Al Jolson musical shorts made a full year before *The Jazz Singer*, *The Bright Shawl* (1923), a re-creation of the Cuban revolution of 1850 featuring Richard Barthlemess and Dorothy Gish and early appearances by Mary Astor and William Powell; an opening-night debut of a stunning new print of Fred Zinneman's *A Man for All Seasons* (1966); and restoration prints of Harold Lloyd's *Safety Last* (1923) and Cecil B. DeMille's *Union Pacific* (1939).

CLASSICS

A THRILLING
FANTASTIC
PHOTO-PLAY

THE CABINET OF DR. CALIGARI

The Museum of Modern Art's six-person film archive staff has also been busy with international film preservation efforts, as they engaged in restoration of several titles obtained from foreign archives. Their work includes a big feature project, the restoration from two sources of a European *Alice in Wonderland* made in an obsolete color process. MOMA is also supervising work on *Don Q, Son of Zorro* (1925), a Douglas Fairbanks vehicle costarring Mary Astor and directed by Donald Crisp. It was the sequel to *The Mark of Zorro* (1920), Fairbanks's first costume epic.

The last year has seen extensive activity at the George Eastman House International Museum of Photography and Film. Movies restored include *The Price She Paid* (1924), an early Columbia feature and the earliest known use of the Columbia logo; *The Dollar Princess* (Germany, 1927), directed by Felix Basch and written by Walter Reisch, who had a long Hollywood career; *There It Is* (1928), one of the few Charlie Bowers films known to

Douglas Fairbanks

ALL-TIME BOX OFFICE

MOVIE	DISTRIBUTOR	YEAR	TOTAL DOMESTIC BOX OFFICE (IN MILLIONS)
1. *E.T. the Extra-Terrestrial*	Universal	1982	$399.8
2. *Jurassic Park*	Universal	1993	356.5
3. *Star Wars*	Fox	1977	322.7
4. *The Lion King*	Disney	1994	300.4
5. *Forrest Gump*	Paramount	1994	298.5
6. *Home Alone*	Fox	1990	285.8
7. *Return of the Jedi*	Fox	1983	263.7
8. *Jaws*	Universal	1975	260.0
9. *Batman*	Warner	1989	251.2
10. *Raiders of the Lost Ark*	Paramount	1981	242.4
11. *Beverly Hills Cop*	Paramount	1984	234.8
12. *The Empire Strikes Back*	Fox	1980	223.2
13. *Ghostbusters*	Columbia	1984	221.1
14. *Ghost*	Paramount	1990	217.5
15. *Aladdin*	Disney	1992	217.4

As of January 3, 1995

LEADERS IN FILM PRESERVATION

The following institutions are the most active in preserving America's film heritage.

American Movie Classics
150 Crossways Park W.
Woodbury, NY 11797
(516) 364-2222
Each year, the AMC network supports the cause of film preservation through the Film Foundation, a group of filmmakers, producers and individual archives. The network sponsors a telethon and Film Preservation Festival that raise money for the restoration institutions.

The International Museum of Photography at George Eastman House
900 East Ave.
Rochester, NY 14607
(716) 271-3361
Founded in 1947, the Eastman House is particularly noted for its work in the restoration of silent films, and it maintains one of the largest collections of silent film anywhere. The film department also acquires film-related artifacts and documents that are available to researchers.

The Library of Congress
Motion Picture, Broadcasting and Recorded Sound Division
Washington D.C. 20540
(202) 707-1000
Among the largest of research facilities in the world, the library houses more than 1 million films and 50,000 television programs. The library maintains its own lab facilities in Dayton, Ohio. Its collection includes nitrate prints from the 1930s to 1950s, foreign films from the World War II era, and "paper prints" (early motion pictures) dating from 1898.

Buster Keaton

survive anywhere in the world; and *Carmen* (Britain, 1943), a one-reel cartoon produced in an obsolete additive color process developed in England in the 1930s. Current projects include work with organizations such as Gaumont (on the Gaumont Chronochromes); silent film restoration in collaboration with the Library of Congress; work on an MGM musical with MOMA; several projects with Sony/Columbia, Turner Entertainment, Paramount, the Canadian National Film Archive and the Cineteca Del Commune di Bologna, Italy.

American Movie Classics cable network held its third annual film preservation festival in October. The on-air event not only screens restored titles and highlights the work of the film archives, but also raises money for film preservation through audience donations to the Film Foundation, a media industry initiative to support the work of film preservationists. This year's event highlighted comedy with a festival of restored comic films, and special salutes to the work of individual film comedians including Buster Keaton, Laurel and Hardy and Jerry Lewis.

This very brief summary of the work at just a few archives indicates the dimension of the international effort to preserve motion pictures. Though the results are promising and awareness is growing, time is the silent enemy and the amount of work to be done is great as our century's contribution to the arts fades to black. ∎

INTRODUCING...

EDWARD BURNS
The surprise of the 1995 Sundance Film Festival, Burns's *The Brothers McMullen* won the Grand Jury Prize and the writer/director/actor walked away with a distribution deal from Fox Searchlight. The former van driver for *Entertainment Tonight* has a knack for writing dry, Woody Allen-like dialogue and economizing on the set (he shot *The Brothers McMullen* for a little more than $20,000).

MTV AS MOVIE PRODUCER
The cable network that has made millions by appealing to the short attention span of teens is taking a whack at feature films. The first production from MTV will be *Joe's Apartment,* featuring 3,500 cockroaches that reek havoc on New Yorker Joe and his love life. Also in the works is an animated *Beavis and Butt-head* movie.

MICHAEL STIPE
Stipe is no newcomer to music fans. Surprise: he is to movies. Stipe's production company, Single Cell Productions, has a two-year, first-look deal with New Line. We can't expect to see a typical Hollywood film from his company as his favorite movies include the semi-independents *S.F.W., Drugstore Cowboy* and *Heathers.* "I just feel there's a huge chasm between independent film — the people who are really trying some wild shit — and Hollywood," he said. "I want to bridge that chasm." Stipe attributes his interest in film to his friendship with the late River Phoenix.

The Museum of Modern Art Film Department
Department of Film
11 W. 53rd St.
New York, NY 10019
(212) 708-9400
One of the first institutions to recognize film as an art form, MOMA oversees the acquisition of historical treasures of American film and important exhibition series. The collection also includes film stills and production materials.

The National Center for Film and Video Preservation at the American Film Institute
2021 N. Western Ave.
Los Angeles, CA 90027
(213) 856-7600
The center was established in 1984 by the American Film Institute and the National Endowment for the Arts. It coordinates the nation's preservation efforts, raises money, established the National Moving Image Data Base and publishes the AFI Catalog of Feature Films. The AFI has sponsored many restoration projects since its founding.

The UCLA Film and Television Archive
302 E. Melnitz Hall
University of California
405 Hilgard Ave.
Los Angeles, CA 90024
(310) 206-8013
The archive acquires, restores, transfers and maintains film and television works. It houses 25 million feet of nitrate film in need of preservation, half of which is pre-1950 Hearst Metronome newsreel footage. It has been responsible for many high-profile film restoration projects. The Archive's Festival of Preservation is a high point in the year's preservation activities.

The Academy Awards

The Oscars©, awarded annually by the Academy of Motion Picture Arts and Sciences showcase the best in movies and couture, and always stir controversy. Whether it be the omission of *Hoop Dreams* from the documentary category or *Red* from the foreign language film category, critics and movie fans take great pleasure in second-guessing the Academy's picks. Listed here is Oscar's 66-year history.

1927–1928

OUTSTANDING PICTURE
The Racket (Caddo; Paramount Famous Lasky)
7th Heaven (Fox)
Wings (Paramount Famous Lasky)

ARTISTIC QUALITY OF PRODUCTION
Chang (Paramount)
The Crowd (MGM)
Sunrise (Fox)

BEST ACTOR
Richard Barthelmess, *The Noose* and *The Patent Leather Kid*
Charles Chaplin, *The Circus* (Though nominated for best actor, the academy decided to remove Chaplin's name from the competitive classes, and instead award him a Special Award for writing, acting, directing and producing *The Circus.*)
Emil Jannings, *The Last Command* and *The Way of All Flesh*

BEST ACTRESS
Louise Dresser, *A Ship Comes In*
Janet Gaynor, *7th Heaven*, *Street Angel* and *Sunrise*
Gloria Swanson, *Sadie Thompson*

DIRECTING
DRAMATIC PICTURE
Frank Borzage, *7th Heaven*
Herbert Brenon, *Sorrell and Son*
King Vidor, *The Crowd*

COMEDY PICTURE
Charles Chaplin, *The Circus* (Though nominated for best director of a comedy picture, the academy decided to remove Chaplin's name from the competitive classes, and instead award him a Special Award for writing, acting, directing and producing *The Circus.*)
Lewis Milestone, *Two Arabian Knights*
Ted Wilde, *Speedy*

WRITING
ADAPTATION
Alfred Cohn, *The Jazz Singer*
Anthony Coldeway, *Glorious Betsy*
Benjamin Glazer, *7th Heaven*

ORIGINAL STORY
Lajos Biro, *The Last Command*
Ben Hecht, *Underworld*

TITLE WRITING
Gerald Duffy, *The Private Life of Helen of Troy*
Joseph Farnham
George Marion, Jr.

CINEMATOGRAPHY
George Barnes, *The Devil Dancer*, *The Magic Flame* and *Sadie Thompson*
Charles Rosher, *Sunrise*
Karl Struss, *Sunrise*

ART DIRECTION
Rochus Gliese, *Sunrise*
William Cameron Menzies, *The Dove* and *Tempest*
Harry Oliver, *7th Heaven*

ENGINEERING EFFECTS
Ralph Hammeras
Roy Pomeroy, *Wings*
Nugent Slaughter, *The Jazz Singer*

SPECIAL AWARDS
(Not necessarily given each year)
To **Warner Bros.** for producing *The Jazz Singer*, the outstanding pioneer talking picture, which has revolutionized the industry

To **Charles Chaplin** for versatility and genius in writing, acting, directing and producing *The Circus*

1928–1929

OUTSTANDING PICTURE
Alibi (Art Cinema; United Artists)
The Broadway Melody (MGM)
Hollywood Revue (MGM)
In Old Arizona (Fox)
The Patriot (Paramount Famous Lasky)

BEST ACTOR
George Bancroft, *Thunderbolt*
Warner Baxter, *In Old Arizona*
Chester Morris, *Alibi*
Paul Muni, *The Valiant*
Lewis Stone, *The Patriot*

Mary Pickford, *Coquette*

BEST ACTRESS
Ruth Chatterton, *Madame X*
Betty Compson, *The Barker*
Jeanne Eagels, *The Letter*
Corinne Griffith, *The Divine Lady*
Bessie Love, *The Broadway Melody*
Mary Pickford, *Coquette*

DIRECTING
Lionel Barrymore, *Madame X*
Harry Beaumont, *The Broadway Melody*
Irving Cummings, *In Old Arizona*
Frank Lloyd, *The Divine Lady*
Frank Lloyd, *Weary River* and *Drag*
Ernst Lubitsch, *The Patriot*

WRITING
Tom Barry, *In Old Arizona* and *The Valiant*
Elliott Clawson, *The Leatherneck, The Cop, Sal of Singapore* and *Skyscraper*
Josephine Lovett, *Our Dancing Daughters*
Hans Kraly, *The Last of Mrs. Cheyney*
Hans Kraly, *The Patriot*
Bess Meredyth, *Wonder of Women* and *A Woman of Affairs*

CINEMATOGRAPHY
George Barnes, *Our Dancing Daughters*
Clyde De Vinna, *White Shadows in the South Seas*
Arthur Edeson, *In Old Arizona*
Ernest Palmer, *Four Devils* and *Street Angel*
John Seitz, *The Divine Lady*

ART DIRECTION
Hans Dreier, *The Patriot*
Cedric Gibbons, *The Bridge of San Luis Rey* and other pictures
Mitchell Leisen, *Dynamite*
William Cameron Menzies, *Alibi* and *The Awakening*
Harry Oliver, *Street Angel*

1929–1930

OUTSTANDING PRODUCTION
***All Quiet on the Western Front* (Universal)**
The Big House (Cosmopolitan; MGM)
Disraeli (Warner Bros.)
The Divorcée (MGM)
The Love Parade (Paramount Famous Lasky)

BEST ACTOR
George Arliss, *Disraeli*
George Arliss, *The Green Goddess*
Wallace Beery, *The Big House*
Maurice Chevalier, *The Big Pond* and *The Love Parade*
Ronald Colman, *Bulldog Drummond* and *Condemned*
Lawrence Tibbett, *The Rogue Song*

BEST ACTRESS
Nancy Carroll, *The Devil's Holiday*
Ruth Chatterton, *Sarah and Son*
Greta Garbo, *Anna Christie* and *Romance*
Norma Shearer, *The Divorcée*
Norma Shearer, *Their Own Desire*
Gloria Swanson, *The Trespasser*

DIRECTING
Clarence Brown, *Anna Christie* and *Romance*
Robert Z. Leonard, *The Divorcée*
Ernst Lubitsch, *The Love Parade*
Lewis Milestone, *All Quiet on the Western Front*
King Vidor, *Hallelujah*

WRITING
George Abbott, Maxwell Anderson and Del Andrews, *All Quiet on the Western Front*
Howard Estabrook, *Street of Chance*
Julian Josephson, *Disraeli*
Frances Marion, *The Big House*
John Meehan, *The Divorcée*

CINEMATOGRAPHY
William Daniels, *Anna Christie*
Arthur Edeson, *All Quiet on the Western Front*
Gaetano Gaudio and Harry Perry, *Hell's Angels*
Victor Milner, *The Love Parade*
Joseph T. Rucker and Willard Van Der Veer, *With Byrd at the South Pole*

ART DIRECTION
Hans Dreier, *The Love Parade*
Hans Dreier, *The Vagabond King*
William Cameron Menzies, *Bulldog Drummond*
Jack Okey, *Sally*
Herman Rosse, *King of Jazz*

SOUND RECORDING

First National Studio Sound Dept., *Song of the Flame*
MGM Studio Sound Dept., *The Big House*
Paramount Famous Lasky Studio Sound Dept.,
    The Love Parade
RKO Radio Studio Sound Dept., *The Case of Sergeant Grischa*
United Artists Studio Sound Dept., *Raffles*

1930–1931

OUTSTANDING PRODUCTION

***Cimarron* (RKO Radio)**
East Lynne (Fox)
The Front Page (Caddo, United Artists)
Skippy (Paramount Publix)
Trader Horn (MGM)

BEST ACTOR

Lionel Barrymore, *A Free Soul*
Jackie Cooper, *Skippy*
Richard Dix, *Cimarron*
Fredric March, *The Royal Family of Broadway*
Adolphe Menjou, *The Front Page*

BEST ACTRESS

Marlene Dietrich, *Morocco*
Marie Dressler, *Min and Bill*
Irene Dunne, *Cimarron*
Ann Harding, *Holiday*
Norma Shearer, *A Free Soul*

DIRECTING

Clarence Brown, *A Free Soul*
Lewis Milestone, *The Front Page*
Wesley Ruggles, *Cimarron*
Norman Taurog, *Skippy*
Josef Von Sternberg, *Morocco*

WRITING

ADAPTATION

Howard Estabrook, *Cimarron*
Francis Faragoh and Robert N. Lee, *Little Caesar*
Horace Jackson, *Holiday*
Joseph L. Mankiewicz and Sam Mintz, *Skippy*
Seton Miller and Fred Niblo, Jr., *The Criminal Code*

ORIGINAL STORY

John Bright and Kubec Glasmon, *The Public Enemy*
Rowland Brown, *The Doorway to Hell*
Harry d'Abbadie d'Arrast, Douglas Doty and Donald Ogden
    Stewart, *Laughter*
Lucien Hubbard and Joseph Jackson, *Smart Money*
John Monk Saunders, *The Dawn Patrol*

CINEMATOGRAPHY

Edward Cronjager, *Cimarron*
Floyd Crosby, *Tabu*
Lee Garmes, *Morocco*
Charles Lang, *The Right to Love*
Barney "Chick" McGill, *Svengali*

ART DIRECTION

Richard Day, *Whoopee!*
Hans Dreier, *Morocco*
Stephen Goosson and Ralph Hammeras, *Just Imagine*
Anton Grot, *Svengali*
Max Ree, *Cimmaron*

SOUND RECORDING

MGM Studio Sound Department
Paramount Publix Studio Sound Department
RKO Radio Studio Sound Department
Samuel Goldwyn-United Artists Studio Sound Department

1931–1932

OUTSTANDING PRODUCTION

Arrowsmith (Goldwyn; United Artists)
Bad Girl (Fox)
The Champ (MGM)
Five Star Final (First National)
***Grand Hotel* (MGM)**
One Hour With You (Paramount Publix)
Shanghai Express (Paramount Publix)
The Smiling Lieutenant (Paramount Publix)

BEST ACTOR (TIE)

Wallace Beery, *The Champ*
Alfred Lunt, *The Guardsman*
Fredric March, *Dr. Jekyll and Mr. Hyde*

BEST ACTRESS

Marie Dressler, *Emma*
Lynn Fontanne, *The Guardsman*
Helen Hayes, *The Sin of Madelon Claudet*

DIRECTING

Frank Borzage, *Bad Girl*
King Vidor, *The Champ*
Josef Von Sternberg, *Shanghai Express*

WRITING

ADAPTATION

Edwin Burke, *Bad Girl*
Percy Heath and Samuel Hoffenstein, *Dr. Jekyll and Mr. Hyde*
Sidney Howard, *Arrowsmith*

ORIGINAL STORY

Lucien Hubbard, *The Star Witness*
Grover Jones and William Slavens McNutt, *Lady and Gent*
Frances Marion, *The Champ*
Adela Rogers St. Johns, *What Price Hollywood?*

CINEMATOGRAPHY
Lee Garmes, *Shanghai Express*
Ray June, *Arrowsmith*
Karl Struss, *Dr. Jekyll and Mr. Hyde*

ART DIRECTION
Richard Day, *Arrowsmith*
Lazare Meerson, *A Nous la Liberté*
Gordon Wiles, *Transatlantic*

SOUND RECORDING
MGM Studio Sound Dept.
Paramount Publix Studio Sound Department
RKO Radio Studio Sound Dept.
Warner Bros.-First National Studio Sound Dept.

SHORT SUBJECTS
CARTOON
Flowers and Trees **(*Silly Symphony Series*) (Walt Disney Productions; United Artists)**
It's Got Me Again (Leon Schlesinger, producer; Warner Bros.)
Mickey's Orphans (*Mickey Mouse Series*) (Walt Disney Productions; Columbia)

COMEDY
The Loud Mouth (Mack Sennett, producer; Paramount Publix)
The Music Box (*Laurel and Hardy Series*) (Hal Roach, producer; MGM)
Scratch-As-Catch-Can (*Headliner Series*) (RKO Radio)
Stout Hearts and Willing Hands (*Masquers Comedies Series*) (RKO Radio) (This film was originally announced as a nominee, but before the final voting, it was disqualified and replaced by *Scratch-As-Scratch-Can*.)

NOVELTY
Screen Souvenirs (Paramount Publix)
Swing High (*Sports Champion Series*) (MGM)
Wrestling Swordfish (*Cannibals of the Deep Series*) (Mack Sennett, producer; Educational)

SPECIAL AWARD
To **Walt Disney** for the creation of Mickey Mouse

1932–1933

OUTSTANDING PRODUCTION
Cavalcade (Fox)
A Farewell to Arms (Paramount)
42nd Street (Warner Bros.)
I Am a Fugitive From a Chain Gang (Warner Bros.)
Lady for a Day (Columbia)
Little Women (RKO Radio)
The Private Life of Henry VIII (London Films; United Artists)
She Done Him Wrong (Paramount)
Smilin' Through (MGM)
State Fair (Fox)

Katharine Hepburn, *Morning Glory*

BEST ACTOR
Leslie Howard, *Berkeley Square*
Charles Laughton, *The Private Life of Henry VIII*
Paul Muni, *I Am a Fugitive From a Chain Gang*

BEST ACTRESS
Katharine Hepburn, *Morning Glory*
May Robson, *Lady for a Day*
Diana Wynyard, *Cavalcade*

DIRECTING
Frank Capra, *Lady for a Day*
George Cukor, *Little Women*
Frank Lloyd, *Cavalcade*

WRITING
ADAPTATION
Paul Green and Sonya Levien, *State Fair*
Victor Heerman and Sarah Y. Mason, *Little Women*
Robert Riskin, *Lady for a Day*

ORIGINAL STORY
Robert Lord, *One Way Passage*
Charles MacArthur, *Rasputin and the Empress*
Frances Marion, *The Prizefighter and the Lady*

CINEMATOGRAPHY
George J. Folsey, *Reunion in Vienna*
Charles Bryant Lang, Jr., *A Farewell to Arms*
Karl Struss, *The Sign of the Cross*

ART DIRECTION
William S. Darling, *Cavalcade*
Hans Dreier and Roland Anderson, *A Farewell to Arms*
Cedric Gibbons, *When Ladies Meet*

SOUND RECORDING
Paramount Studio Sound Dept., *A Farewell to Arms*
Warner Bros. Studio Sound Dept., *42nd Street*
Warner Bros. Studio Sound Dept., *Gold Diggers of 1933*
Warner Bros. Studio Sound Dept., *I Am a Fugitive From a Chain Gang*

ASSISTANT DIRECTOR (TIE)

Al Alborn, Warner Bros.

Charles Barton, Paramount

Scott Beal, Universal

Sidney S. Brod, Paramount

Charles Dorian, MGM

Benny Dull, MGM

Fred Fox, United Artists

Gordon Hollingshead, Warner Bros.

Percy Ikerd, Fox

Arthur Jacobson, Paramount

Eddie Killey, RKO Radio

Joe McDonough, Universal

W. J. Reiter, Universal

Frank X. Shaw, Warner Bros.

Benjamin Silvey, United Artists

Dewey Starkey, RKO Radio

William Tummel, Fox

John S. Waters, MGM

SHORT SUBJECTS

CARTOON

Building a Building (*Mickey Mouse Series*) (Walt Disney
    Productions; United Artists)

The Merry Old Soul (*Oswald the Rabbit Series*) (Walter Lantz
    Productions; Universal)

The Three Little Pigs (***Silly Symphony Series***) (**Walt Disney
    Productions; United Artists**)

COMEDY

Mister Mugg (*Comedies Series*) (Warren Doane, producer;
    Universal)

A Preferred List (*Headliner Series #5*) (Louis Brock, producer;
    RKO Radio)

So This Is Harris (**Louis Brock, producer; RKO Radio**)

NOVELTY

Krakatoa (**Joe Rock, producer; Educational**)

Menu (*Oddities Series*) (Pete Smith, producer; MGM)

The Sea (*Battle for Life Series*) (Educational)

1934

OUTSTANDING PRODUCTON

The Barretts of Wimpole Street (MGM)

Cleopatra (Paramount)

Flirtation Walk (First National)

The Gay Divorcée (RKO Radio)

Here Comes the Navy (Warner Bros.)

The House of Rothschild (Twentieth Century; United Artists)

It Happened One Night (**Columbia**)

One Night of Love (Columbia)

The Thin Man (MGM)

Viva Villa! (MGM)

The White Parade (Jesse L. Lasky; Fox)

It Happened One Night

BEST ACTOR

Clark Gable, *It Happened One Night*

Frank Morgan, *The Affairs of Cellini*

William Powell, *The Thin Man*

BEST ACTRESS

Claudette Colbert, *It Happened One Night*

Bette Davis, *Of Human Bondage* (Write-in candidate, not an
    official nomination)

Grace Moore, *One Night of Love*

Norma Shearer, *The Barretts of Wimpole Street*

DIRECTING

Frank Capra, *It Happened One Night*

Victor Schertzinger, *One Night of Love*

W. S. Van Dyke, *The Thin Man*

WRITING

ADAPTATION

Frances Goodrich and Albert Hackett, *The Thin Man*

Ben Hecht, *Viva Villa!*

Robert Riskin, *It Happened One Night*

ORIGINAL STORY

Arthur Caesar, *Manhattan Melodrama*

Mauri Grashin, *Hide-Out*

Norman Krasna, *The Richest Girl in the World*

CINEMATOGRAPHY

George Folsey, *Operator 13*

Victor Milner, *Cleopatra*

Charles Rosher, *The Affairs of Cellini*

ART DIRECTION

Richard Day, *The Affairs of Cellini*

Cedric Gibbons and Frederic Hope, *The Merry Widow*

Van Nest Polglase and Carroll Clark, *The Gay Divorcée*

SOUND RECORDING

Columbia Studio Sound Dept., *One Night of Love*

Fox Studio Sound Dept., *The White Parade*

MGM Studio Sound Dept., *Viva Villa!*

Paramount Studio Sound Dept., *Cleopatra*

RKO Radio Studio Sound Dept., *The Gay Divorcée*

United Artists Studio Sound Dept., *The Affairs of Cellini*

Universal Studio Sound Dept., *Imitation of Life*

Warner Bros.-First National Studio Sound Dept.,
Flirtation Walk

ASSISTANT DIRECTOR

Scott Beal, *Imitation of Life*

Cullen Tate, *Cleopatra*

John Waters, *Viva Villa!*

MUSIC

SONG

"Carioca," *Flying Down to Rio,* Vincent Youmans, music;
Edward Eliscu and Gus Kahn, lyrics

**"The Continental," *The Gay Divorcée,* Con Conrad, music;
Herb Magidson, lyrics**

"Love in Bloom," *She Loves Me Not,* Ralph Rainger, music;
Leo Robin, lyrics

SCORE

Columbia Studio Music Dept., *One Night of Love*

RKO Radio Studio Music Dept., *The Gay Divorcée*

RKO Radio Studio Music Dept., *The Lost Patrol*

FILM EDITING

Anne Bauchens, *Cleopatra*

Gene Milford, *One Night of Love*

Conrad Nervig, *Eskimo*

SHORT SUBJECTS

CARTOON

Holiday Land (*Color Rhapsody Series*) (Screen Gems;
Columbia)

Jolly Little Elves (*Cartune Classic Series*) (Walter Lantz
Productions; Universal)

***The Tortoise and the Hare* (*Silly Symphony Series*) (Walt
Disney Productions; United Artists)**

COMEDY

***La Cucaracha* (Pioneer Pictures; RKO Radio)**

Men in Black (*The Three Stooges Series*) (Jules White,
producer; Columbia)

What, No Men! (*Broadway Brevities Series*) (Warner Bros.)

NOVELTY

Bosom Friends (*Treasure Chest Series*) (Skibo Productions;
Educational-Fox)

***City of Wax* (*Battle for Life Series*) (Skibo Productions;
Educational-Fox)**

Strikes and Spares (*Oddities Series*) (Pete Smith, producer;
MGM)

SPECIAL AWARD

To **Shirley Temple** in grateful recognition of her outstanding
contribution to screen entertainment during the year 1934

1935

OUTSTANDING PRODUCTION

Alice Adams (RKO Radio)

Broadway Melody of 1936 (MGM)

Captain Blood (Cosmopolitan; First National)

David Copperfield (MGM)

The Informer (RKO Radio)

Les Misérables (Twentieth Century; United Artists)

The Lives of a Bengal Lancer (Paramount)

A Midsummer Night's Dream (Warner Bros.)

***Mutiny on the Bounty* (MGM)**

Naughty Marietta (MGM)

Ruggles of Red Gap (Paramount)

Top Hat (RKO Radio)

BEST ACTOR

Clark Gable, *Mutiny on the Bounty*

Charles Laughton, *Mutiny on the Bounty*

Victor McLaglen, *The Informer*

Paul Muni, *Black Fury* (Write-in candidate, not an official
nomination)

Franchot Tone, *Mutiny on the Bounty*

BEST ACTRESS

Elisabeth Bergner, *Escape Me Never*

Claudette Colbert, *Private Worlds*

Bette Davis, *Dangerous*

Katharine Hepburn, *Alice Adams*

Miriam Hopkins, *Becky Sharp*

Merle Oberon, *The Dark Angel*

DIRECTING

Michael Curtiz, *Captain Blood* (Write-in candidate, not an
official nomination)

John Ford, *The Informer*

Henry Hathaway, *The Lives of a Bengal Lancer*

Frank Lloyd, *Mutiny on the Bounty*

WRITING

ORIGINAL STORY

Moss Hart, *Broadway Melody of 1936*

Don Hartman and Stephen Avery, *The Gay Deception*

Ben Hecht and Charles MacArthur, *The Scoundrel*

Gregory Rogers, *G-Men* (Write-in candidate, not an official
nomination)

SCREENPLAY

Achmed Abdullah, John L. Balderston and Waldemar Young,
screenplay; Jules Furthman, Talbot Jennings and Carey
Wilson, *Mutiny on the Bounty*

Grover Jones and William Slavens McNutt, adaptation, *The
Lives of a Bengal Lancer*

Dudley Nichols, *The Informer*

Casey Robinson, *Captain Blood* (Write-in candidate, not an
official nomination)

CINEMATOGRAPHY

Ray June, *Barbary Coast*

Victor Milner, *The Crusades*

Hal Mohr, *A Midsummer Night's Dream* (Write-in candidate, not an official nomination)

Gregg Toland, *Les Misérables*

ART DIRECTION

Carroll Clark and Van Nest Polglase, *Top Hat*

Richard Day, *The Dark Angel*

Hans Dreier and Roland Anderson, *The Lives of a Bengal Lancer*

SOUND RECORDING

Columbia Studio Sound Dept., *Love Me Forever*

MGM Studio Sound Dept., *Naughty Marietta*

Paramount Studio Sound Dept., *The Lives of a Bengal Lancer*

Republic Studio Sound Department, *$1,000 a Minute*

RKO Radio Studio Sound Dept., *I Dream Too Much*

Twentieth Century-Fox Studio Sound Dept., *Thanks a Million*

United Artists Studio Sound Dept., *The Dark Angel*

Universal Studio Sound Dept., *The Bride of Frankenstein*

Warner Bros.-First National Studio Sound Dept., *Captain Blood*

ASSISTANT DIRECTOR

Clem Beauchamp and Paul Wing, *The Lives of a Bengal Lancer*

Joseph Newman, *David Copperfield*

Sherry Shourds, *A Midsummer Night's Dream* (Write-in candidate, not an official nomination)

Eric Stacey, *Les Misérables*

MUSIC

SONG

"Cheek to Cheek," *Top Hat*, Irving Berlin, music and lyrics

"Lovely to Look At," *Roberta*, Jerome Kern, music; Dorothy Fields and Jimmy McHugh, lyrics

"Lullaby of Broadway," *Gold Diggers of 1935*, Harry Warren, music; Al Dubin, lyrics

SCORE

MGM Studio Music Dept., *Mutiny on the Bounty*

Paramount Studio Music Dept., *Peter Ibbetson*

RKO Radio Studio Music Dept., *The Informer*

Warner Bros.-First National Studio Music Dept., *Captain Blood*

FILM EDITING

Margaret Booth, *Mutiny on the Bounty*

Ralph Dawson, *A Midsummer Night's Dream*

George Hively, *The Informer*

Ellsworth Hoagland, *The Lives of a Bengal Lancer*

Robert J. Kern, *David Copperfield*

Barbara McLean, *Les Miserables*

DANCE DIRECTION

Busby Berkeley, "Lullaby of Broadway" and "The Words Are in My Heart," *Gold Diggers of 1935*

Bobby Connolly, "Latin From Manhattan," *Go Into Your Dance* and "Playboy From Paree," *Broadway Hostess*

Dave Gould, "I've Got a Feeling You're Fooling," *Broadway Melody of 1936* and "Straw Hat," *Folies Bergere*

Sammy Lee, "Lovely Lady" and "Too Good to Be True," *King of Burlesque*

Hermes Pan, "Piccolino" and "Top Hat, White Tie and Tails," *Top Hat*

LeRoy Prinz, "It's the Animal in Me," *Big Broadcast of 1936* and "Viennese Waltz," *All the King's Horses*

Benjamin Zemach, "Hall of Kings," *She*

SHORT SUBJECTS

CARTOON

The Calico Dragon (*Happy Harmonies Series*) (Harman-Ising; MGM)

***Three Orphan Kittens* (*Silly Symphony Series*) (Walt Disney Productions; United Artists)**

Who Killed Cock Robin? (*Silly Symphony Series*) (Walt Disney Productions; United Artists)

COMEDY

***How to Sleep* (*Miniature Series*) (Jack Chertok, producer; MGM)**

Oh, My Nerves (*Broadway Comedies Series*) (Jules White, producer; Columbia)

Tit for Tat (*Laurel and Hardy Series*) (Hal Roach, producer; MGM)

NOVELTY

Audioscopiks (Pete Smith, producer; MGM)

Camera Thrills (Universal)

***Wings Over Mt. Everest* (Gaumont British and Skibo Productions; Educational)**

SPECIAL AWARD

To **David Wark Griffith** for his distinguished creative achievements as director and producer and his invaluable initiative and lasting contributions to the progress of the motion picture arts

1936

OUTSTANDING PRODUCTION

Anthony Adverse (Warner Bros.)

Dodsworth (Goldwyn; United Artists)

***The Great Ziegfeld* (MGM)**

Libeled Lay (MGM)

Mr. Deeds Goes to Town (Columbia)

Romeo and Juliet (MGM)

San Francisco (MGM)

The Story of Louis Pasteur (Cosmopolitan; Warner Bros.-First National)

A Tale of Two Cities (MGM)

Three Smart Girls (Universal)

BEST ACTOR

Gary Cooper, *Mr. Deeds Goes to Town*

Walter Huston, *Dodsworth*

Paul Muni, *The Story of Louis Pasteur*

William Powell, *My Man Godfrey*

Spencer Tracy, *San Francisco*

BEST ACTRESS

Irene Dunne, *Theodora Goes Wild*
Gladys George, *Valiant Is the Word for Carrie*
Carole Lombard, *My Man Godfrey*
Luise Rainer, *The Great Ziegfeld*
Norma Shearer, *Romeo and Juliet*

ACTOR IN A SUPPORTING ROLE

Mischa Auer, *My Man Godfrey*
Walter Brennan, *Come and Get It*
Stuart Erwin, *Pigskin Parade*
Basil Rathbone, *Romeo and Juliet*
Akim Tamiroff, *The General Died at Dawn*

ACTRESS IN A SUPPORTING ROLE

Beulah Bondi, *The Gorgeous Hussy*
Alice Brady, *My Man Godfrey*
Bonita Granville, *These Three*
Maria Ouspenskaya, *Dodsworth*
Gale Sondergaard, *Anthony Adverse*

Mr. Deeds Goes to Town

DIRECTING

Frank Capra, *Mr. Deeds Goes to Town*
Gregory La Cava, *My Man Godfrey*
Robert Z. Leonard, *The Great Ziegfeld*
W. S. Van Dyke, *San Francisco*
William Wyler, *Dodsworth*

WRITING

ORIGINAL STORY

Pierre Collings and Sheridan Gibney, *The Story of Louis Pasteur*
Adele Comandini, *Three Smart Girls*
Robert Hopkins, *San Francisco*
Norman Krasna, *Fury*
William Anthony McGuire, *The Great Ziegfeld*

SCREENPLAY

Pierre Collings and Sheridan Gibney, *The Story of Louis Pasteur*
Frances Goodrich and Albert Hackett, *After the Thin Man*
Eric Hatch and Morris Ryskind, *My Man Godfrey*
Sidney Howard, *Dodsworth*
Robert Riskin, *Mr. Deeds Goes to Town*

CINEMATOGRAPHY

George Folsey, *The Gorgeous Hussy*
Gaetano Gaudio, *Anthony Adverse*
Victor Milner, *The General Died at Dawn*

ART DIRECTION

Albert S. D'Agostino and Jack Otterson, *The Magnificent Brute*
William S. Darling, *Lloyds of London*
Richard Day, *Dodsworth*
Perry Ferguson, *Winterset*
Cedric Gibbons, Frederic Hope and Edwin B. Willis, *Romeo and Juliet*
Cedric Gibbons, Eddie Imazu and Edwin B. Willis, *The Great Ziegfeld*
Anton Grot, *Anthony Adverse*

SOUND RECORDING

Columbia Studio Sound Dept., *Mr. Deeds Goes to Town*
Hal Roach Studio Sound Dept., *General Spanky*
MGM Studio Sound Dept., *San Francisco*
Paramount Studio Sound Dept., *The Texas Rangers*
RKO Radio Studio Sound Dept., *That Girl From Paris*
Twentieth Century-Fox Studio Sound Dept., *Banjo on My Knee*
United Artists Studio Sound Dept., *Dodsworth*
Universal Studio Sound Dept., *Three Smart Girls*
Warner Bros. Studio Sound Dept., *The Charge of the Light Brigade*

ASSISTANT DIRECTOR

Clem Beauchamp, *The Last of the Mohicans*
William Cannon, *Anthony Adverse*
Joseph Newman, *San Francisco*
Eric G. Stacey, *Garden of Allah*
Jack Sullivan, *The Charge of the Light Brigade*

MUSIC

SONG

"Did I Remember," *Suzy*, Walter Donaldson, music; Harold Adamson, lyrics
"I've Got You Under My Skin," *Born to Dance*, Cole Porter, music and lyrics
"A Melody From the Sky," *Trail of the Lonesome Pine*, Louis Alter, music; Sidney Mitchell, lyrics
"Pennies From Heaven," *Pennies From Heaven*, Arthur Johnston, music; Johnny Burke, lyrics
"The Way You Look Tonight," *Swing Time*, Jerome Kern, music; Dorothy Fields, lyrics
"When Did You Leave Heaven," *Sing, Baby Sing*, Richard A. Whiting, music; Walter Bullock, lyrics

SCORE

Paramount Studio Music Dept., *The General Died at Dawn*

RKO Radio Studio Music Dept., *Winterset*

Selznick International Pictures Music Dept., *The Garden of Allah*

Warner Bros. Studio Music Dept., *Anthony Adverse*

Warner Bros. Studio Music Dept., *The Charge of the Light Brigade*

FILM EDITING

Edward Curtiss, *Come and Get It*

Ralph Dawson, *Anthony Adverse*

William S. Gray, *The Great Ziegfeld*

Barbara McLean, *Lloyds of London*

Otto Meyer, *Theodora Goes Wild*

Conrad A. Nervig, *A Tale of Two Cities*

DANCE DIRECTION

Busby Berkeley, "Love and War," *Gold Diggers of 1937*

Bobby Connolly, "1,000 Love Songs," *Cain and Mabel*

Seymour Felix, "A Pretty Girl Is Like a Melody," *The Great Ziegfeld*

Dave Gould, "Swingin' the Jinx," *Born to Dance*

Jack Haskell, "Skating Ensemble," *One in a Million*

Russell Lewis, "The Finale," *Dancing Pirate*

Hermes Pan, "Bojangles of Harlem," *Swing Time*

SHORT SUBJECTS

CARTOON

***The Country Cousin* (*Silly Symphony Series*) (Walt Disney Productions; United Artists)**

Old Mill Pond (*Happy Harmonies Series*) (Harman-Ising; MGM)

Sinbad the Sailor (*Popeye Series*) (Paramount)

ONE-REEL

***Bored of Education* (*Our Gang Series*) (Hal Roach, producer; MGM)**

Moscow Moods (*Headliners Series*) (Paramount)

Wanted, A Master (*Pete Smith Specialties Series*) (Pete Smith, producer; MGM)

TWO-REEL

Double or Nothing (*Melody Masters Series*) (Warner Bros.)

Dummy Ache (*Edgar Kennedy Comedies Series*) (RKO Radio)

***The Public Pays* (*Crime Doesn't Pay Series*) (MGM)**

COLOR

***Give Me Liberty* (*Broadway Brevities Series*) (Warner Bros.)**

La Fiesta de Santa Barbara (*Musical Revues Series*) (Lewis Lewyn, producer; MGM)

Popular Science J-6-2 (*Popular Science Series*) (Paramount)

SPECIAL AWARDS

To the **March of Time** for its significance to motion pictures and for having revolutionized one of the most important branches of the industry — the newsreel

To **W. Howard Greene** and **Harold Rosson** for the color cinematography of the Selznick International Production, *The Garden of Allah*

1937

OUTSTANDING PRODUCTION

The Awful Truth (Columbia)

Captains Courageous (MGM)

Dead End (Goldwyn; United Artists)

The Good Earth (MGM)

In Old Chicago (Twentieth Century-Fox)

***The Life of Emile Zola* (Warner Bros.)**

Lost Horizon (Columbia)

One Hundred Men and a Girl (Universal)

Stage Door (RKO Radio)

A Star Is Born (Selznick International Pictures; United Artists)

BEST ACTOR

Charles Boyer, *Conquest*

Fredric March, *A Star Is Born*

Robert Montgomery, *Night Must Fall*

Paul Muni, *The Life of Emile Zola*

Spencer Tracy, *Captains Courageous*

BEST ACTRESS

Irene Dunne, *The Awful Truth*

Greta Garbo, *Camille*

Janet Gaynor, *A Star Is Born*

Luise Rainer, *The Good Earth*

Barbara Stanwyck, *Stella Dallas*

ACTOR IN A SUPPORTING ROLE

Ralph Bellamy, *The Awful Truth*

Thomas Mitchell, *The Hurricane*

Joseph Schildkraut, *The Life of Emile Zola*

H. B. Warner, *Lost Horizon*

Roland Young, *Topper*

ACTRESS IN A SUPPORTING ROLE

Alice Brady, *In Old Chicago*

Andrea Leeds, *Stage Door*

Anne Shirley, *Stella Dallas*

Claire Trevor, *Dead End*

Dame May Whitty, *Night Must Fall*

DIRECTING

William Dieterle, *The Life of Emile Zola*

Sidney Franklin, *The Good Earth*

Gregory La Cava, *Stage Door*

Leo McCarey, *The Awful Truth*

William Wellman, *A Star Is Born*

WRITING

ORIGINAL STORY

Niven Busch, *In Old Chicago*

Heinz Herald and Geza Herczeg, *The Life of Emile Zola*

Hans Kraly, *One Hundred Men and a Girl*

Robert Lord, *Black Legion*

William A. Wellman and Robert Carson, *A Star Is Born*

Spencer Tracy, *Captains Courageous*

SCREENPLAY

Alan Campbell, Robert Carson and Dorothy Parker, *A Star Is Born*

Vina Delmar, *The Awful Truth*

John Lee Mahin, Marc Connolly and Dale Van Every, *Captains Courageous*

Morris Ryskind and Anthony Veiller, *Stage Door*

CINEMATOGRAPHY

Karl Freund, *The Good Earth*

Gregg Toland, *Dead End*

Joseph Valentine, *Wings Over Honolulu*

ART DIRECTION

Carroll Clark, *A Damsel in Distress*

William S. Darling and David Hall, *Wee Willie Winkie*

Richard Day, *Dead End*

Hans Dreier and Roland Anderson, *Souls at Sea*

Cedric Gibbons and William Horning, *Conquest*

Stephen Goosson, *Lost Horizon*

Anton Grot, *The Life of Emile Zola*

Wiard Ihnen, *Every Day's a Holiday*

John Victor Mackay, *Manhattan Merry-Go-Round*

Jack Otterson, *You're a Sweetheart*

Alexander Toluboff, *Walter Wanger's Vogues of 1938*

Lyle Wheeler, *The Prisoner of Zenda*

SOUND RECORDING

Columbia Studio Sound Dept., *Lost Horizon*

Grand National Studio Sound Dept., *The Girl Said No*

Hal Roach Studio Sound Dept., *Topper*

MGM Studio Sound Dept., *Maytime*

Paramount Studio Sound Dept., *Wells Fargo*

RKO Radio Studio Sound Dept., *Hitting a New High*

Twentieth Century-Fox Studio Sound Dept., *In Old Chicago*

United Artists Studio Sound Dept., *The Hurricane*

Universal Studio Sound Dept., *One Hundred Men and a Girl*

Warner Bros. Studio Sound Dept., *The Life of Emile Zola*

ASSISTANT DIRECTOR

C. C. Coleman, Jr., *Lost Horizon*

Russ Saunders, *The Life of Emile Zola*

Eric Stacey, *A Star Is Born*

Hal Walker, *Souls at Sea*

Robert Webb, *In Old Chicago*

MUSIC

SONG

"Remember Me," *Mr. Dodd Takes the Air*, Harry Warren, music; Al Dubin, lyrics

"Sweet Leilani," *Waikiki Wedding*, Harry Owens, music and lyrics

"That Old Feeling," *Walter Wanger's Vogues of 1938*, Sammy Fain, music; Lew Brown, lyrics

"They Can't Take That Away From Me," *Shall We Dance*, George Gershwin, music; Ira Gershwin, lyrics

"Whispers in the Dark," *Artists and Models*, Frederick Hollander, music; Leo Robin, lyrics

SCORE

Columbia Studio Music Dept., *Lost Horizon*

Goldwyn Studio Music Dept., *The Hurricane*

Grand National Studio Music Dept., *Something to Sing About*

Hal Roach Studio Music Dept., *Way Out West*

MGM Studio Music Dept., *Maytime*

Paramount Studio Music Dept., *Souls at Sea*

Principal Productions, *Make a Wish*

Republic Studio Music Dept., *Portia on Trial*

RKO Radio Studio Music Dept., *Quality Street*

Selznick International Pictures Music Dept., *The Prisoner of Zenda*

Twentieth Century-Fox Studio Music Dept., *In Old Chicago*

Universal Studio Music Dept., *One Hundred Men and a Girl*

Walt Disney Studio Music Dept., *Snow White and the Seven Dwarfs*

Warner Bros. Studio Music Dept., *The Life of Emile Zola*

FILM EDITING

Bernard W. Burton, *One Hundred Men and a Girl*

Al Clark, *The Awful Truth*

Gene Havlick and Gene Milford, *Lost Horizon*

Elmo Vernon, *Captains Courageous*

Basil Wrangell, *The Good Earth*

DANCE DIRECTION

Busby Berkeley, "The Finale," *Varsity Show*

Bobby Connolly, "Too Marvelous for Words," *Ready, Willing and Able*

Dave Gould, "All God's Children Got Rhythm," *A Day at the Races*

Sammy Lee, "Swing Is Here to Stay," *Ali Baba Goes to Town*

Hermes Pan, "Fun House," *A Damsel in Distress*

LeRoy Prinz, "Luau," *Waikiki Wedding*

SHORT SUBJECTS

CARTOON

Educated Fish (*Color Classics Series*) (Paramount)

The Little Match Girl (Charles Mintz, producer; Columbia)

***The Old Mill* (Walt Disney Productions; RKO Radio)**

ONE-REEL

A Night at the Movies (*Robert Benchley Series*) (MGM)

The Private Life of the Gannetts (Skibo Productions; Educational)

Romance of Radium (*Pete Smith Specialties Series*) (Pete Smith, producer; MGM)

TWO-REEL

Deep South (*Radio Musical Comedies Series*) (RKO Radio)

Should Wives Work? (*Leon Errol Comedies Series*) (RKO Radio)

Torture Money (*Crime Doesn't Pay Series*) (MGM)

COLOR

The Man Without a Country (*Broadway Brevities Series*) (Warner Bros.)

Penny Wisdom (*Pete Smith Specialties Series*) (Pete Smith, producer; MGM)

Popular Science J-7-1 (*Popular Science Series*) (Paramount)

IRVING G. THALBERG MEMORIAL AWARD
(Not necessarily given each year)
Darryl F. Zanuck

SPECIAL AWARDS

To **Mack Sennett** for his lasting contribution to the comedy technique of the screen

To **Edgar Bergen** for his outstanding comedy creation, Charlie McCarthy

To the **Museum of Modern Art Film Library** for its significant work in collecting films dating from 1895 to the present, and for the first time making available to the public the means of studying the historical and aesthetic development of the motion picture as one of the major arts

To **W. Howard Greene** for the color photography of *A Star Is Born*

1938

OUTSTANDING PRODUCTION

The Adventures of Robin Hood (Warner Bros.-First National)

Alexander's Ragtime Band (Twentieth Century-Fox)

Boys Town (MGM)

The Citadel (MGM)

Four Daughters (Warner Bros.-First National)

Grand Illusion (Realization D'Art Cinematographique; World Pictures)

Jezebel (Warner Bros.)

Pygmalion (MGM)

Test Pilot (MGM)

You Can't Take It With You (Columbia)

BEST ACTOR

Charles Boyer, *Algiers*

James Cagney, *Angels With Dirty Faces*

Robert Donat, *The Citadel*

Leslie Howard, *Pygmalion*

Spencer Tracy, *Boys Town*

BEST ACTRESS

Fay Bainter, *White Banners*

Bette Davis, *Jezebel*

Wendy Hiller, *Pygmalion*

Norma Shearer, *Marie Antoinette*

Margaret Sullavan, *Three Comrades*

ACTOR IN A SUPPORTING ROLE

Walter Brennan, *Kentucky*

John Garfield, *Four Daughters*

Gene Lockhart, *Algiers*

Robert Morley, *Marie Antoinette*

Basil Rathbone, *If I Were King*

ACTRESS IN A SUPPORTING ROLE

Fay Bainter, *Jezebel*

Beulah Bondi, *Of Human Hearts*

Billie Burke, *Merrily We Live*

Spring Byington, *You Can't Take It With You*

Miliza Korjus, *The Great Waltz*

DIRECTING

Frank Capra, *You Can't Take It With You*

Michael Curtiz, *Angels With Dirty Faces*

Michael Curtiz, *Four Daughters*

Norman Taurog, *Boys Town*

King Vidor, *The Citadel*

WRITING
ORIGINAL STORY

Irving Berlin, *Alexander's Ragtime Band*

Rowland Brown, *Angels With Dirty Faces*

Marcella Burke and Frederick Kohner, *Mad About Music*

Eleanore Griffin and Dore Schary, *Boys Town*

John Howard Lawson, *Blockade*

Frank Wead, *Test Pilot*

SCREENPLAY

Lenore Coffee and Julius J. Epstein, *Four Daughters*

Ian Dalrymple, Elizabeth Hill and Frank Wead, *The Citadel*

Bette Davis, *Jezebel*

John Meehan and Dore Schary, *Boys Town*

Robert Riskin, *You Can't Take It With You*

George Bernard Shaw, writer; Ian Dalrymple, Cecil Lewis and W. P. Lipscomb, adaptation, *Pygmalion*

CINEMATOGRAPHY

Norbert Brodine, *Merrily We Live*

Robert de Grasse, *Vivacious Lady*

Ernest Haller, *Jezebel*

James Wong Howe, *Algiers*

Peverell Marley, *Suez*

Ernest Miller and Harry Wild, *Army Girl*

Victor Milner, *The Buccaneer*

Joseph Ruttenberg, *The Great Waltz*

Leon Shamroy, *The Young in Heart*

Joseph Valentine, *Mad About Music*

Joseph Walker, *You Can't Take It With You*

ART DIRECTION

Richard Day, *The Goldwyn Follies*

Hans Dreier and John Goodman, *If I Were King*

Cedric Gibbons, *Marie Antoinette*

Stephen Goosson and Lionel Banks, *Holiday*

Charles D. Hall, *Merrily We Live*

Bernard Herzbrun and Boris Leven, *Alexander's Ragtime Band*

Jack Otterson, *Mad About Music*

Van Nest Polglase, *Carefree*

Alexander Toluboff, *Algiers*

Carl J. Weyl, *The Adventures of Robin Hood*

Lyle Wheeler, *The Adventures of Tom Sawyer*

SOUND RECORDING

Columbia Studio Sound Dept., *You Can't Take It With You*

Hal Roach Studio Sound Dept., *Merrily We Live*

MGM Studio Sound Dept., *Sweethearts*

Paramount Studio Sound Dept., *If I Were King*

Republic Studio Sound Dept., *Army Girl*

RKO Radio Studio Sound Dept., *Vivacious Lady*

Twentieth Century-Fox Studio Sound Dept., *Suez*

United Artists Studio Sound Dept., *The Cowboy and the Lady*

Universal Studio Sound Dept., *That Certain Age*

Warner Bros. Studio Sound Dept., *Four Daughters*

MUSIC

SONG

"Always and Always," *Mannequin*, Edward Ward, music; Chet Forrest and Bob Wright, lyrics

"Change Partners," *Carefree*, Irving Berlin, music and lyrics

"The Cowboy and the Lady," *The Cowboy and the Lady*, Lionel Newman, music; Arthur Quenzer, lyrics

"Dust," *Under Western Stars*, Johnny Marvin, music and lyrics

"Jeepers Creepers," *Going Places*, Harry Warren, music; Johnny Mercer, lyrics

"Merrily We Live," *Merrily We Live*, Phil Charig, music; Arthur Quenzer, lyrics

"A Mist Over the Moon," *The Lady Objects*, Ben Oakland, music; Oscar Hammerstein II, lyrics

"My Own," *That Certain Age*, Jimmy McHugh, music; Harold Adamson, lyrics

"Now It Can Be Told," *Alexander's Ragtime Band*, Irving Berlin, music and lyrics

"Thanks for the Memory," *The Big Broadcast of 1938*, Ralph Rainger, music; Leo Robin, lyrics

SCORE

Victor Baravalle, *Carefree*

Cy Feuer, *Storm Over Bengal*

Marvin Hatley, *There Goes My Heart*

Boris Morros, *Tropic Holiday*

Alfred Newman, *Alexander's Ragtime Band*

Alfred Newman, *The Goldwyn Follies*

Charles Previn and Frank Skinner, *Mad About Music*

Max Steiner, *Jezebel*

Morris Stoloff and Gregory Stone, *Girls' School*

Herbert Stothart, *Sweethearts*

Franz Waxman, *The Young in Heart*

ORIGINAL SCORE

Russell Bennett, *Pacific Liner*

Richard Hageman, *If I Were King*

Marvin Hatley, *Block-heads*

Werner Janssen, *Blockade*

Erich Wolfgang Korngold, *The Adventures of Robin Hood*

Alfred Newman, *The Cowboy and the Lady*

Louis Silvers, *Suez*

Herbert Stothart, *Marie Antoinette*

Franz Waxman, *The Young in Heart*

Victor Young, *Army Girl*

Victor Young, *Breaking the Ice*

FILM EDITING

Ralph Dawson, *The Adventures of Robin Hood*

Tom Held, *The Great Waltz*

Tom Held, *Test Pilot*

Gene Havlick, *You Can't Take It With You*

Barbara McLean, *Alexander's Ragtime Band*

SHORT SUBJECTS

CARTOON

Brave Little Tailor (*Mickey Mouse Series*) (Walt Disney Productions; RKO Radio)

***Ferdinand the Bull* (Walt Disney Productions; RKO Radio)**

Good Scouts (*Donald Duck Series*) (Walt Disney Productions; RKO Radio)

Hunky and Spunky (Paramount)

Mother Goose Goes Hollywood (*Silly Symphony Series*) (Walt Disney Productions; RKO Radio)

ONE-REEL

The Great Heart (*Miniature Series*) (MGM)

***That Mothers Might Live* (*Miniature Series*) (MGM)**

Timber Toppers (*Ed Thorgensen-Sports Series*) (Twentieth Century-Fox)

TWO-REEL

***Declaration of Independence* (*Historical Featurette Series*) (Warner Bros.)**

Swingtime in the Movies (*Broadway Brevities Series*) (Warner Bros.)

They're Always Caught (*Crime Doesn't Pay Series*) (MGM)

IRVING G. THALBERG MEMORIAL AWARD
Hal B. Wallis

SPECIAL AWARDS

To **Deanna Durbin** and **Mickey Rooney** for their significant contribution in bringing to the screen the spirit and personification of youth, and as juvenile players setting a high standard of ability and achievement

To **Harry M. Warner** in recognition of patriotic service in the production of historical short subjects presenting significant episodes in the early struggle of the American people for liberty

To **Walt Disney** for *Snow White and the Seven Dwarfs*, recognized as a significant screen innovation which has charmed millions and pioneered a great new entertainment field for the motion picture cartoon

To **Oliver Marsh** and **Allen Davey** for the color cinematography of the MGM production *Sweethearts*

For outstanding achievement in creating special photographic and sound effects in the Paramount production, *Spawn of the North;* special effects by **Gordon Jenning**; assisted by **Jan Domela, Dev Jennings, Irmin Roberts** and **Art Smith;** transparencies by **Farciot Edouart;** assisted by **Loyal Griggs;** sound effects by **Loren Ryder;** assisted by **Harry Mills, Louis H. Mesenkop** and **Walter Oberst**

To **J. Arthur Ball** for his outstanding contributions to the advancement of color in motion picture photography

1939

OUTSTANDING PRODUCTION

Dark Victory (Warner Bros.-First National)
***Gone With the Wind* (Selznick International Pictures; MGM)**
Goodbye, Mr. Chips (MGM)
Love Affair (RKO Radio)
Mr. Smith Goes to Washington (Columbia)
Ninotchka (MGM)
Of Mice and Men (Hal Roach; United Artists)
Stagecoach (Walter Wanger; United Artists)
The Wizard of Oz (MGM)
Wuthering Heights (Goldwyn; United Artists)

BEST ACTOR

Robert Donat, *Goodbye, Mr. Chips*
Clark Gable, *Gone With the Wind*
Laurence Olivier, *Wuthering Heights*
Mickey Rooney, *Babes in Arms*
James Stewart, *Mr. Smith Goes to Washington*

BEST ACTRESS

Bette Davis, *Dark Victory*
Irene Dunne, *Love Affair*
Greta Garbo, *Ninotchka*
Greer Garson, *Goodbye, Mr. Chips*
Vivien Leigh, *Gone With the Wind*

ACTOR IN A SUPPORTING ROLE

Brian Aherne, *Juarez*
Harry Carey, *Mr. Smith Goes to Washington*

Brian Donlevy, *Beau Geste*
Thomas Mitchell, *Stagecoach*
Claude Rains, *Mr. Smith Goes to Washington*

ACTRESS IN A SUPPORTING ROLE

Olivia de Havilland, *Gone With the Wind*
Geraldine Fitzgerald, *Wuthering Heights*
Hattie McDaniel, *Gone With the Wind*
Edna May Oliver, *Drums Along the Mohawk*
Maria Ouspenskaya, *Love Affair*

DIRECTING

Frank Capra, *Mr. Smith Goes to Washington*
Victor Fleming, *Gone With the Wind*
John Ford, *Stagecoach*
Sam Wood, *Goodbye, Mr. Chips*
William Wyler, *Wuthering Heights*

WRITING

ORIGINAL STORY

Mildred Cram and Leo McCarey, *Love Affair*
Lewis R. Foster, *Mr. Smith Goes to Washington*
Felix Jackson, *Bachelor Mother*
Melchior Lengyel, *Ninotchka*
Lamar Trotti, *Young Mr. Lincoln*

SCREENPLAY

Charles Brackett, Walter Reisch and Billy Wilder, *Ninotchka*
Sidney Buchman, *Mr. Smith Goes to Washington*
Ben Hecht and Charles MacArthur, *Wuthering Heights*
Sidney Howard, *Gone With the Wind*
Eric Maschwitz, R. C. Sherriff and Claudine West, *Goodbye, Mr. Chips*

CINEMATOGRAPHY

BLACK-AND-WHITE

Joseph H. August, *Gunga Din*
Norbert Brodine, *Of Mice and Men*
George Folsey, *Lady of the Tropics*
Tony Gaudio, *Juarez*
Bert Glennon, *Stagecoach*
Arthur Miller, *The Rains Came*
Victor Milner, *The Great Victor Herbert*
Gregg Toland, *Intermezzo*
Gregg Toland, *Wuthering Heights*
Joseph Valentine, *First Love*
Joseph Walker, *Only Angels Have Wings*

COLOR

Ernest Haller and Ray Rennahan, *Gone With the Wind*
Georges Perinal and Osmond Borradaile, *Four Feathers*
Sol Polito and W. Howard Greene, *The Private Lives of Elizabeth and Essex*
Ray Rennahan and Bert Glennon, *Drums Along the Mohawk*
Hal Rosson, *The Wizard of Oz*
William V. Skall and Bernard Knowles, *The Mikado*

ART DIRECTION

Lionel Banks, *Mr. Smith Goes to Washington*
James Basevi, *Wuthering Heights*

Stagecoach

William Darling and George Dudley, *The Rains Came*
Hans Dreier and Robert Odell, *Beau Geste*
Cedric Gibbons and William A. Horning, *The Wizard of Oz*
Anton Grot, *The Private Lives of Elizabeth and Essex*
Charles D. Hall, *Captain Fury*
John Victor Mackay, *Man of Conquest*
Jack Otterson and Martin Obzina, *First Love*
Van Nest Polglase and Al Herman, *Love Affair*
Alexander Toluboff, *Stagecoach*
Lyle Wheeler, *Gone With the Wind*

SOUND RECORDING
Columbia Studio Sound Dept., *Mr. Smith Goes to Washington*
Denham Studio Sound Dept., *Goodbye, Mr. Chips*
Hal Roach Studio Sound Dept., *Of Mice and Men*
MGM Studio Sound Dept., *Balalaika*
Paramount Studio Sound Dept., *The Great Victor Herbert*
Republic Studio Sound Dept., *Man of Conquest*
RKO Radio Studio Sound Dept., *The Hunchback of Notre Dame*
Samuel Goldwyn Studio Sound Dept., *Gone With the Wind*
Twentieth Century-Fox Studio Sound Dept., *The Rains Came*
Universal Studio Sound Dept., *When Tomorrow Comes*
Warner Bros. Studio Sound Dept., *The Private Lives of Elizabeth and Essex*

MUSIC
SONG
"Faithful Forever," *Gulliver's Travels*, Ralph Rainger, music; Leo Robin, lyrics
"I Poured My Heart Into a Song," *Second Fiddle*, Irving Berlin, music and lyrics
"Over the Rainbow," *The Wizard of Oz*, Harold Arlen, music; E. Y. Harburg, lyrics
"Wishing," *Love Affair*, Buddy de Sylva, music and lyrics

SCORE
Phil Boutelje and Arthur Lange, *The Great Victor Herbert*
Aaron Copland, *Of Mice and Men*
Roger Edens and George E. Stoll, *Babes in Arms*
Cy Feuer, *She Married a Cop*
Lou Forbes, *Intermezzo*
Richard Hageman, Frank Harling, John Leipold and Leo Shuken, *Stagecoach*

Erich Wolfgang Korngold, *The Private Lives of Elizabeth and Essex*
Alfred Newman, *The Hunchback of Notre Dame*
Alfred Newman, *They Shall Have Music*
Charles Previn, *First Love*
Louis Silvers, *Swanee River*
Dimitri Tiomkin, *Mr. Smith Goes to Washington*
Victor Young, *Way Down South*

ORIGINAL SCORE
Anthony Collins, *Nurse Edith Cavell*
Aaron Copland, *Of Mice and Men*
Lud Gluskin and Lucien Moraweck, *The Man in the Iron Mask*
Werner Janssen, *Eternally Yours*
Alfred Newman, *The Rains Came*
Alfred Newman, *Wuthering Heights*
Max Steiner, *Dark Victory*
Max Steiner, *Gone With the Wind*
Herbert Stothart, *The Wizard of Oz*
Victor Young, *Golden Boy*
Victor Young, *Gulliver's Travels*
Victor Young, *Man of Conquest*

FILM EDITING
Charles Frend, *Goodbye, Mr. Chips*
Gene Havlick and Al Clark, *Mr. Smith Goes to Washington*
Hal C. Kern and James E. Newcom, *Gone With the Wind*
Otho Lovering and Dorothy Spencer, *Stagecoach*
Barbara McLean, *The Rains Came*

SPECIAL EFFECTS
John R. Cosgrove, Fred Albin and Arthur Johns, *Gone With the Wind*
Roy Davidson and Edwin C. Hahn, *Only Angels Have Wings*
Farciot Edouart, Gordon Jennings and Loren Ryder, *Union Pacific*
A. Arnold Gillespie and Douglas Shearer, *The Wizard of Oz*
E. H. Hansen and Fred Sersen, *The Rains Came*
Byron Haskin and Nathan Levinson, *The Private Lives of Elizabeth and Essex*
Roy Seawright, *Topper Takes a Trip*

SHORT SUBJECTS
CARTOON
Detouring America (*Merrie Melodies Series*) (Warner Bros.)
Peace on Earth (Hugh Harmon, producer; MGM)
The Pointer (*Mickey Mouse Series*) (Walt Disney Productions; RKO Radio)
***The Ugly Duckling* (*Silly Symphony Series*) (Walt Disney Productions; RKO Radio)**

ONE-REEL
***Busy Little Bears* (*Paragraphics Series*) (Paramount)**
Information Please (RKO Radio)
Prophet Without Honor (*Miniature Series*) (MGM)
Sword Fishing (*Vitaphone Variety Series*) (Warner Bros.)

TWO-REEL
Drunk Driving (*Crime Doesn't Pay Series*) (MGM)

Five Times Five (Pathé; RKO Radio)

Sons of Liberty (*Historical Featurette Series*) (Warner Bros.)

IRVING G. THALBERG MEMORIAL AWARD
David O. Selznick

SPECIAL AWARDS

To **Douglas Fairbanks** (Commemorative Award) recognizing the unique and outstanding contribution of Douglas Fairbanks, first president of the Academy, to the international development of the motion picture

To the **Motion Picture Relief Fund** acknowledging its outstanding services to the industry during the past year and its progressive leadership; presented to **Jean Hersholt**, president; **Ralph Morgan,** chairman of the executive committee; **Ralph Block,** first vice president; and **Conrad Nagel**

To **Judy Garland** for her outstanding performance as a screen juvenile during the past year

To **William Cameron Menzies** for outstanding achievement in the use of color for the enhancement of dramatic mood in the production of *Gone With the Wind*

To the **Technicolor Company** for its contributions in successfully bringing three-color feature production to the screen

1940

OUTSTANDING PRODUCTION

All This, and Heaven Too (Warner Bros.)

Foreign Correspondent (Walter Wanger; United Artists)

The Grapes of Wrath (Twentieth Century-Fox)

The Great Dictator (Charles Chaplin Productions; United Artists)

Kitty Foyle (RKO Radio)

The Letter (Warner Bros.)

The Long Voyage Home (Argosy-Wanger; United Artists)

Our Town (Sol Lesser; United Artists)

The Philadelphia Story (MGM)

***Rebecca* (Selznick International Pictures, United Artists)**

BEST ACTOR
Charles Chaplin, *The Great Dictator*

Preston Sturges

Henry Fonda, *The Grapes of Wrath*

Raymond Massey, *Abe Lincoln in Illinois*

Laurence Olivier, *Rebecca*

James Stewart, *The Philadelphia Story*

BEST ACTRESS

Bette Davis, *The Letter*

Joan Fontaine, *Rebecca*

Katharine Hepburn, *The Philadelphia Story*

Ginger Rogers, *Kitty Foyle*

Martha Scott, *Our Town*

ACTOR IN A SUPPORTING ROLE

Albert Basserman, *Foreign Correspondent*

Walter Brennan, *The Westerner*

William Gargan, *They Knew What They Wanted*

Jack Oakie, *The Great Dictator*

James Stephenson, *The Letter*

ACTRESS IN A SUPPORTING ROLE

Judith Anderson, *Rebecca*

Jane Darwell, *The Grapes of Wrath*

Ruth Hussey, *The Philadelphia Story*

Barbara O'Neil, *All This, and Heaven Too*

Marjorie Rambeau, *Primrose Path*

DIRECTING

George Cukor, *The Philadelphia Story*

John Ford, *The Grapes of Wrath*

Alfred Hitchcock, *Rebecca*

Sam Wood, *Kitty Foyle*

William Wyler, *The Letter*

WRITING
ORIGINAL STORY

Hugo Butler and Dore Schary, *Edison, the Man*

Benjamin Gazer and John S. Toldy, *Arise, My Love*

Stuart N. Lake, *The Westerner*

Leo McCarey, Bella Spewack and Samuel Spewack, *My Favorite Wife*

Walter Reisch, *Comrade X*

ORIGINAL SCREENPLAY

Charles Bennett and Joan Harrison, *Foreign Correspondent*

Norman Burnside, Heinz Herald and John Huston, *Dr. Ehrlich's Magic Bullet*

Charles Chaplin, *The Great Dictator*

Ben Hecht, *Angels Over Broadway*

Preston Sturges, *The Great McGinty*

SCREENPLAY

Nunnally Johnson, *The Grapes of Wrath*

Dudley Nichols, *The Long Voyage Home*

Robert E. Sherwood and Joan Harrison, *Rebecca*

Donald Ogden Stewart, *The Philadelphia Story*

Dalton Trumbo, *Kitty Foyle*

CINEMATOGRAPHY

BLACK-AND-WHITE

George Barnes, *Rebecca*

Gaetano Gaudio, *The Letter*

Ernest Haller, *All This, and Heaven Too*

James Wong Howe, *Abe Lincoln in Illinois*

Charles B. Lang, Jr., *Arise, My Love*

Rudolph Maté, *Foreign Correspondent*

Harold Rosson, *Boom Town*

Joseph Ruttenberg, *Waterloo Bridge*

Gregg Toland, *The Long Voyage Home*

Joseph Valentine, *Spring Parade*

COLOR

Oliver T. Marsh and Allen Davey, *Bitter Sweet*

Arthur Miller and Ray Rennahan, *The Blue Bird*

Victor Milner and W. Howard Greene, *Northwest Mounted Police*

Georges Perinal, *The Thief of Bagdad*

Leon Shamroy and Ray Rennahan, *Down Argentine Way*

Sidney Wagner and William V. Skall, *Northwest Passage*

ART DIRECTION

BLACK-AND-WHITE

Lionel Banks and Robert Peterson, *Arizona*

James Basevi, *The Westerner*

Richard Day and Joseph C. Wright, *Lillian Russell*

Hans Dreier and Robert Usher, *Arise, My Love*

John DuCasse Schulze, *My Son, My Son!*

Cedric Gibbons and Paul Groesse, *Pride and Prejudice*

Alexander Golitzen, *Foreign Correspondent*

Anton Grot, *The Sea Hawk*

John Victor Mackay, *The Dark Command*

John Otterson, *The Boys From Syracuse*

Van Nest Polglase and Mark-Lee Kirk, *My Favorite Wife*

Lewis J. Rachmil, *Our Town*

Lyle Wheeler, *Rebecca*

COLOR

Richard Day and Joseph C. Wright, *Down Argentine Way*

Hans Dreier and Roland Anderson, *Northwest Mounted Police*

Cedric Gibbons and John S. Detlie, *Bitter Sweet*

Vincent Korda, *The Thief of Bagdad*

SOUND RECORDING

Columbia Studio Sound Dept., *Too Many Husbands*

General Service Studio Sound Dept., *The Howards of Virginia*

Hal Roach Studio Sound Dept., *Captain Caution*

MGM Studio Sound Dept., *Strike Up the Band*

Paramount Studio Sound Dept., *Northwest Mounted Police*

Republic Studio Sound Dept., *Behind the News*

RKO Radio Studio Sound Dept., *Kitty Foyle*

Samuel Goldwyn Studio Sound Dept., *Our Town*

Twentieth Century-Fox Studio Sound Dept., *The Grapes of Wrath*

Universal Studio Sound Dept., *Spring Parade*

Warner Bros. Studio Sound Dept., *The Sea Hawk*

MUSIC

SONG

"Down Argentine Way," *Down Argentine Way*, Harry Warren, music; Mack Gordon, lyrics

"I'd Know You Anywhere," *You'll Find Out*, Jimmy McHugh, music; Johnny Mercer, lyrics

"It's a Blue World," *Music in My Heart*, Chet Forrest and Bob Wright, music and lyrics

"Love of My Life," *Second Chorus*, Artie Shaw, music; Johnny Mercer, lyrics

"Only Forever," *Rhythm on the River*, James Monaco, music; John Burke, lyrics

"Our Love Affair," *Strike Up the Band*, Roger Edens and Arthur Freed, music and lyrics

"Waltzing in the Clouds," *Spring Parade*, Robert Stolz; music; Gus Kahn, lyrics

"When You Wish Upon a Star," *Pinocchio*, **Leigh Harline, music; Ned Washington, lyrics**

"Who Am I?," *Hit Parade of 1941*, Jule Styne, music; Walter Bullock, lyrics

SCORE

Anthony Collins, *Irene*

Aaron Copland, *Our Town*

Cy Feuer, *Hit Parade of 1941*

Erich Wolfgang Korngold, *The Sea Hawk*

Alfred Newman, *Tin Pan Alley*

Charles Previn, *Spring Parade*

Artie Shaw, *Second Chorus*

Georgie Stoll and Roger Edens, *Strike Up the Band*

Victor Young, *Arise, My Love*

ORIGINAL SCORE

Aaron Copland, *Our Town*

Louis Gruenberg, *The Fight for Life*

Richard Hageman, *The Howards of Virginia*

Richard Hageman, *The Long Voyage Home*

Leigh Harline, Paul J. Smith and Ned Washington, *Pinocchio*

Werner Heymann, *One Million B.C.*

Alfred Newman, *The Mark of Zorro*

Miklos Rozsa, *The Thief of Bagdad*

Frank Skinner, *The House of Seven Gables*

Max Steiner, *The Letter*

Herbert Stothart, *Waterloo Bridge*

Franz Waxman, *Rebecca*

Roy Webb, *My Favorite Wife*

Meredith Willson, *The Great Dictator*

Victor Young, *Arizona*

Victor Young, *The Dark Command*

Victor Young, *Northwest Mounted Police*

FILM EDITING

Anne Bauchens, *Northwest Mounted Police*

Hal C. Kern, *Rebecca*

Warren Low, *The Letter*

Robert E. Simpson, *The Grapes of Wrath*

Sherman Todd, *The Long Voyage Home*

SPECIAL EFFECTS

Lawrence Butler, photography; Jack Whitney, sound, *The Thief of Bagdad*

Jack Cosgrove, photography; Arthur Johns, sound, *Rebecca*

Paul Eagler, photography; Thomas T. Moulton, sound, *Foreign Correspondent*

Farciot Edouart and Gordon Jennings, photography, *Dr. Cyclops*

Farciot Edouart and Gordon Jennings, photography; Loren Ryder, sound, *Typhoon*

John P. Fulton, photography; Bernard B. Brown and Joseph Lapis, sound, *The Boys From Syracuse*

John P. Fulton, photography; Bernard B. Brown and William Hedgecock, sound, *The Invisible Man Returns*

A. Arnold Gillespie, photography; Douglas Shearer, sound, *Boom Town*

Byron Haskin, photography; Nathan Levinson, sound, *The Sea Hawk*

R. T. Layton and R. O. Binger, photography; Thomas T. Moulton, sound, *The Long Voyage Home*

Howard J. Lydecker, William Bradford and Ellis J. Thackery, photography; Herbert Norsch, sound, *Women in War*

Roy Seawright, photography; Elmer Raguse, sound, *One Million B.C.*

Fred Sersen, photography; E.H. Hansen, sound, *The Blue Bird*

Vernon L. Walker, photography; John O. Aalberg, sound, *Swiss Family Robinson*

SHORT SUBJECTS
CARTOON
The Milky Way (Rudolph Ising Series) (MGM)

Puss Gets the Boot (*Cat and Mouse Series*) (MGM)

A Wild Hare (*Bugs Bunny Series*) (Leon Schlesinger, producer; Warner Bros.)

ONE-REEL
London Can Take It (*Vitaphone Varieties Series*) (Warner Bros.)

More About Nostradamus (Miniature Series) (MGM)

Quicker 'N a Wink (Pete Smith Specialties Series) (Pete Smith, producer; MGM)

Siege (*Reelism Series*) (RKO Radio)

TWO-REEL
Eyes of the Navy (*Crime Doesn't Pay Series*) (MGM)

Service With the Colors (*National Defense Series*) (Warner Bros.)

Teddy, the Rough Rider (Historical Featurette Series) (Warner Bros.)

SPECIAL AWARDS
To **Bob Hope** in recognition of his unselfish services to the motion picture industry

To **Colonel Nathan Levinson** for his outstanding service to the industry and the Army during the past nine years, which has made possible the present efficient mobilization of the motion picture industry facilities for the production of Army training films

1941

OUTSTANDING MOTION PICTURE
Blossoms in the Dust (MGM)

Citizen Kane (Mercury; RKO Radio)

Here Comes Mr. Jordan (Columbia)

Hold Back the Dawn (Paramount)

***How Green Was My Valley* (Twentieth Century-Fox)**

The Little Foxes (Goldwyn; RKO Radio)

The Maltese Falcon (Warner Bros.)

One Foot in Heaven (Warner Bros.)

Sergeant York (Warner Bros.)

Suspicion (RKO Radio)

BEST ACTOR
Gary Cooper, *Sergeant York*

Cary Grant, *Penny Serenade*

Walter Huston, *All That Money Can Buy*

Robert Montgomery, *Here Comes Mr. Jordan*

Orson Welles, *Citizen Kane*

BEST ACTRESS
Bette Davis, *The Little Foxes*

Olivia de Havilland, *Hold Back the Dawn*

Joan Fontaine, *Suspicion*

Greer Garson, *Blossoms in the Dust*

Barbara Stanwyck, *Ball of Fire*

ACTOR IN A SUPPORTING ROLE
Walter Brennan, *Sergeant York*

Charles Coburn, *The Devil and Miss Jones*

Donald Crisp, *How Green Was My Valley*

James Gleason, *Here Comes Mr. Jordan*

Sydney Greenstreet, *The Maltese Falcon*

ACTRESS IN A SUPPORTING ROLE
Sarah Allgood, *How Green Was My Valley*

Mary Astor, *The Great Lie*

Patricia Collinge, *The Little Foxes*

Teresa Wright, *The Little Foxes*

Margaret Wycherly, *Sergeant York*

DIRECTING
John Ford, *How Green Was My Valley*

Alexander Hall, *Here Comes Mr. Jordan*

Howard Hawks, *Sergeant York*

Orson Welles, *Citizen Kane*

William Wyler, *The Little Foxes*

WRITING
ORIGINAL STORY
Richard Connell and Robert Presnell, *Meet John Doe*

Monckton Hoffe, *The Lady Eve*

Thomas Monroe and Billy Wilder, *Ball of Fire*

Harry Segall, *Here Comes Mr. Jordan*

Gordon Wellesley, *Night Train*

ORIGINAL SCREENPLAY
Harry Chandlee, Abem Finkel, John Huston and Howard Koch, *Sergeant York*

Paul Jarrico, *Tom, Dick and Harry*

Norman Krasna, *The Devil and Miss Jones*

Herman J. Mankiewicz and Orson Welles, *Citizen Kane*

Karl Tunberg and Darrell Ware, *Tall, Dark and Handsome*

SCREENPLAY

Charles Brackett and Billy Wilder, *Hold Back the Dawn*

Sidney Buchman and Seton I. Miller, *Here Comes Mr. Jordan*

Philip Dunne, *How Green Was My Valley*

Lillian Hellman, *The Little Foxes*

John Huston, *The Maltese Falcon*

CINEMATOGRAPHY

BLACK-AND-WHITE

Edward Cronjager, *Sun Valley Serenade*

Karl Freund, *The Chocolate Soldier*

Charles Lang, *Sundown*

Rudolph Maté, *That Hamilton Woman*

Arthur Miller, *How Green Was My Valley*

Sol Polito, *Sergeant York*

Joseph Ruttenberg, *Dr. Jekyll and Mr. Hyde*

Gregg Toland, *Citizen Kane*

Leo Tover, *Hold Back the Dawn*

Joseph Walker, *Here Comes Mr. Jordan*

COLOR

Wilfred M. Cline, Karl Struss and William Snyder, *Aloma of the South Seas*

Karl Freund and W. Howard Greene, *Blossoms in the Dust*

Bert Glennon, *Dive Bomber*

Harry Hallenberger and Ray Rennahan, *Louisiana Purchase*

Ernest Palmer and Ray Rennahan, *Blood and Sand*

William V. Skall and Leonard Smith, *Billy the Kid*

ART DIRECTION

BLACK-AND-WHITE

Lionel Banks, art direction; George Montgomery, interior decoration, *Ladies in Retirement*

Richard Day and Nathan Juran, art direction; Thomas Little, interior decoration, *How Green Was My Valley*

Hans Dreier and Robert Usher, art direction; Sam Comer, interior decoration, *Hold Back the Dawn*

John DuCasse Schulze, art direction; Edward G. Boyle, interior decoration, *The Son of Monte Cristo*

Perry Ferguson and Van Nest Polglase, art direction; Al Fields and Darrell Silvera, interior decoration, *Citizen Kane*

Cedric Gibbons and Randall Duell, art direction; Edwin B. Willis, interior decoration, *When Ladies Meet*

Alexander Golitzen, art direction; Richard Irvine, interior decoration, *Sundown*

Stephen Goosson, art direction; Howard Bristol, interior decoration, *The Little Foxes*

John Hughes, art direction; Fred MacLean, interior decoration, *Sergeant York*

Vincent Korda, art direction; Julia Heron, interior decoration, *That Hamilton Woman*

Martin Obzina and Jack Otterson, art direction; Russell A. Gausman, interior decoration, *The Flame of New Orleans*

COLOR

Richard Day and Joseph C. Wright, art direction; Thomas Little, interior decoration, *Blood and Sand*

Raoul Pene du Bois, art direction; Stephen A. Seymour, interior decoration *Louisiana Purchase*

Cedric Gibbons and Urie McCleary, art direction; Edwin B. Willis, interior decoration, *Blossoms in the Dust*

John Ford

SOUND RECORDING

Columbia Studio Sound Dept., *The Men in Her Life*

General Service Sound Dept., *That Hamilton Woman*

Hal Roach Studio Sound Dept., *Topper Returns*

MGM Studio Sound Dept., *The Chocolate Soldier*

Paramount Studio Sound Dept., *Skylark*

Republic Studio Sound Dept., *The Devil Pays Off*

RKO Radio Studio Sound Dept., *Citizen Kane*

Samuel Goldwyn Studio Sound Dept., *Ball of Fire*

Twentieth Century-Fox Studio Sound Dept., *How Green Was My Valley*

Universal Studio Sound Dept., *Appointment for Love*

Warner Bros. Studio Sound Dept., *Sergeant York*

MUSIC

SONG

"Baby Mine," *Dumbo*, Frank Churchill, music; Ned Washington, lyrics

"Be Honest With Me," *Ridin' on a Rainbow*, Gene Autry and Fred Rose, music and lyrics

"Blues in the Night," *Blues in the Night*, Harold Arlen, music; Johnny Mercer, lyrics

"Boogie Woogie Bugle Boy of Company B," *Buck Privates*, Hugh Prince, music; Don Raye, lyrics

"Chattanooga Choo Choo," *Sun Valley Serenade,* Harry Warren, music; Mack Gordon, lyrics

"Dolores," *Las Vegas Nights*, Lou Alter, music; Frank Loesser, lyrics

"The Last Time I Saw Paris," *Lady Be Good*, Jerome Kern, music; Oscar Hammerstein II, lyrics

"Out of the Silence," *All-American Co-Ed*, Lloyd B. Norlind, music and lyrics

"Since I Kissed My Baby Goodbye," *You'll Never Get Rich*, Cole Porter, music and lyrics

SCORING OF A DRAMATIC PICTURE

Cy Feuer and Walter Scharf, *Mercy Island*

Louis Gruenberg, *So Ends Our Night*

Richard Hageman, *That Woman Is Mine*

Bernard Herrmann, *All That Money Can Buy*

Bernard Herrmann, *Citizen Kane*

Werner Heymann, *That Uncertain Feeling*

Edward Kay, *King of the Zombies*

Alfred Newman, *Ball of Fire*

Alfred Newman, *How Green Was My Valley*

Miklos Rozsa, *Lydia*

Miklos Rozsa, *Sundown*

Frank Skinner, *Back Street*

Max Steiner, *Sergeant York*

Morris Stoloff and Ernst Toch, *Ladies in Retirement*

Edward Ward, *Cheers for Miss Bishop*

Edward Ward, *Tanks a Million*

Franz Waxman, *Dr. Jekyll and Mr. Hyde*

Franz Waxman, *Suspicion*

Meredith Willson, *The Little Foxes*

Victor Young, *Hold Back the Dawn*

SCORING OF A MUSICAL PICTURE

Frank Churchill and Oliver Wallace, *Dumbo*

Anthony Collins, *Sunny*

Robert Emmett Dolan, *Birth of the Blues*

Cy Feuer, *Ice-Capades*

Emil Newman, *Sun Valley Serenade*

Charles Previn, *Buck Privates*

Heinz Roemheld, *The Strawberry Blonde*

Morris Stoloff, *You'll Never Get Rich*

Herbert Stothart and Bronislau Kaper, *The Chocolate Soldier*

Edward Ward, *All-American Co-Ed*

FILM EDITING

James B. Clark, *How Green Was My Valley*

William Holmes, *Sergeant York*

Harold F. Kress, *Dr. Jekyll and Mr. Hyde*

Daniel Mandell, *The Little Foxes*

Robert Wise, *Citizen Kane*

SPECIAL EFFECTS

Lawrence Butler, photography; William H. Wilmarth, sound, *That Hamilton Woman*

Farciot Edouart and Gordon Jennings, photography; Louis Mesenkop, sound, *Aloma of the South Seas*

Farciot Edouart and Gordon Jennings, photography; Louis Mesenkop, sound, *I Wanted Wings*

John Fulton, photography; John Hall, sound, *The Invisible Woman*

A. Arnold Gillespie, photography; Douglas Shearer, sound, *Flight Command*

Byron Haskin, photography; Nathan Levinson, sound, *The Sea Wolf* (This was not one of the original nominees; it replaced *Dive Bomber*, another Warner Bros. production.)

Roy Seawright, photography; Elmer Raguse, sound, *Topper Returns*

Fred Sersen, photography; E.H. Hansen, sound, *A Yank in the R.A.F.*

SHORT SUBJECTS

CARTOON

Boogie Woogie Bugle Boy of Company B (Walter Lantz Productions, Universal)

Hiawatha's Rabbit Hunt (*Merrie Melodies Series*) (Leon Schlesinger, producer; Warner Bros.)

How War Came (*Raymond Gram Swing Series*) (Columbia)

***Lend a Paw* (*Mickey Mouse Series*) (Walt Disney Productions; RKO Radio)**

The Night Before Christmas (*Tom and Jerry Series*) (MGM)

Rhapsody in Rivets (*Merrie Melodies Series*) (Leon Schlesinger, producer; Warner Bros.)

Rhythm in the Ranks (*George Pal Puppetoon Series*) (George Pal Productions; Paramount)

The Rookie Bear (*Bear Series*) (MGM)

Superman (*Superman Series #1*) (Max Fleischer, producer; Paramount)

Truant Officer Donald (*Donald Duck Series*) (Walt Disney Productions; RKO Radio)

ONE-REEL

Army Champions (*Pete Smith Specialties Series*) (Pete Smith, producer; MGM)

Beauty and the Beach (*Headliner Series*) (Paramount)

Down on the Farm (*Speaking of Animals Series*) (Paramount)

Forty Boys and a Song (*Melody Master Series*) (Warner Bros.)

Kings of the Turf (*Color Parade Series*) (Warner Bros.)

***Of Pups and Puzzles* (*Passing Parade Series*) (MGM)**

Sagebrush and Silver (*Magic Carpet Series*) (Twentieth Century-Fox)

TWO-REEL

Alive in the Deep (Woodard Productions, Inc.)

Forbidden Passage (*Crime Doesn't Pay Series*) (MGM)

The Gay Parisian (*Miniature Featurette Series*) (Warner Bros.)

***Main Street on the March!* (MGM)**

The Tanks Are Coming (*National Defense Series*) (U.S. Army; Warner Bros.)

DOCUMENTARY

SHORT SUBJECT

Adventures in the Bronx (Film Associates)

Bomber (U.S. Office for Emergency Management Film Unit; Motion Picture Committee Cooperating for National Defense)

Christmas Under Fire (British Ministry of Information; Warner Bros.)

***Churchill's Island* (National Film Board of Canada; United Artists)**

Letter From Home (British Ministry of Information; United Artists)

Life of a Thoroughbred (Truman Talley; Twentieth Century-Fox)

Norway in Revolt (March of Time; RKO Radio)

A Place to Live (Philadelphia Housing Authority; Philadelphia Housing Association)

Russian Soil (Amkino)

Soldiers of the Sky (Truman Talley; Twentieth Century-Fox)

War Clouds in the Pacific (National Film Board of Canada; MGM)

IRVING G. THALBERG MEMORIAL AWARD

Walt Disney

SPECIAL AWARDS

To **Rey Scott** for his extraordinary achievement in producing *Kukan*, the film record of China's struggle, including its photography with a 16mm camera under the most difficult and dangerous conditions

To the **British Ministry of Information** for its vivid and dramatic presentation of the heroism of the R.A.F. in the documentary film *Target for Tonight*

To **Leopold Stokowski** and his associates for their unique achievement in the creation of a new form of visualized music in Walt Disney's production, *Fantasia*, thereby widening the scope of the motion picture as entertainment and as an art form

To **Walt Disney, William Garity, John N. A. Hawkins** and the **RCA Manufacturing Company** for their outstanding contribution to the advancement of the use of sound in motion pictures through the production of *Fantasia*

1942

OUTSTANDING MOTION PICTURE
The Invaders (Ortus; Columbia)
Kings Row (Warner Bros.)
The Magnificent Ambersons (Mercury; RKO Radio)
Mrs. Miniver (MGM)
The Pied Piper (Twentieth Century-Fox)
The Pride of the Yankees (Goldwyn; RKO Radio)
Random Harvest (MGM)
The Talk of the Town (Columbia)
Wake Island (Paramount)
Yankee Doodle Dandy (Warner Bros.)

BEST ACTOR
James Cagney, *Yankee Doodle Dandy*
Ronald Colman, *Random Harvest*
Gary Cooper, *The Pride of the Yankees*
Walter Pidgeon, *Mrs. Miniver*
Monty Woolley, *The Pied Piper*

BEST ACTRESS
Bette Davis, *Now, Voyager*
Greer Garson, *Mrs. Miniver*
Katharine Hepburn, *Woman of the Year*
Rosalind Russell, *My Sister Eileen*
Teresa Wright, *The Pride of the Yankees*

Louis B. Mayer and Helen Hayes

ACTOR IN A SUPPORTING ROLE
William Bendix, *Wake Island*
Van Heflin, *Johnny Eager*
Walter Huston, *Yankee Doodle Dandy*
Frank Morgan, *Tortilla Flat*
Henry Travers, *Mrs. Miniver*

ACTRESS IN A SUPPORTING ROLE
Gladys Cooper, *Now, Voyager*
Agnes Moorehead, *The Magnificent Ambersons*
Susan Peters, *Random Harvest*
Dame May Whitty, *Mrs. Miniver*
Teresa Wright, Mrs. Miniver

DIRECTING
Michael Curtiz, *Yankee Doodle Dandy*
John Farrow, *Wake Island*
Mervyn LeRoy, *Random Harvest*
Sam Wood, *Kings Row*
William Wyler, *Mrs. Miniver*

WRITING
ORIGINAL MOTION PICTURE STORY
Irving Berlin, *Holiday Inn*
Robert Buckner, *Yankee Doodle Dandy*
Paul Gallico, *The Pride of the Yankees*
Sidney Harmon, *The Talk of the Town*
Emeric Pressburger, *The Invaders*

ORIGINAL SCREENPLAY
W. R. Burnett and Frank Butler, *Wake Island*
Frank Butler and Don Hartman, *Road to Morocco*
Michael Kanin and Ring Lardner, Jr., *Woman of the Year*
George Oppenheimer, *The War Against Mrs. Hadley*
Michael Powell and Emeric Pressburger, *One of Our Aircraft Is Missing*

SCREENPLAY
Rodney Ackland and Emeric Pressburger, *The Invaders*
Sidney Buchman and Irwin Shaw, *The Talk of the Town*
George Froeschel, James Hilton, Claudine West and Arthur Wimperis, *Mrs. Miniver*
George Froeschel, Claudine West and Arthur Wimperis, *Random Harvest*
Herman J. Mankiewicz and Jo Swerling, *The Pride of the Yankees*

CINEMATOGRAPHY
BLACK-AND-WHITE
Charles Clarke, *Moontide*
Stanley Cortez, *The Magnificent Ambersons*
Edward Cronjager, *The Pied Piper*
James Wong Howe, *Kings Row*
Rudolph Maté, *The Pride of the Yankees*
John Mescall, *Take a Letter, Darling*
Arthur Miller, *This Above All*
Joseph Ruttenberg, *Mrs. Miniver*
Leon Shamroy, *Ten Gentlemen From West Point*
Ted Tetzlaff, *The Talk of the Town*

COLOR

Edward Cronjager and William V. Skall, *To the Shores of Tripoli*

W. Howard Greene, *Jungle Book*

Milton Krasner, William V. Skall and W. Howard Greene, *Arabian Knights*

Victor Milner and William V. Skall, *Reap the Wild Wind*

Sol Polito, *Captains of the Clouds*

Leon Shamroy, *The Black Swan*

ART DIRECTION
BLACK-AND-WHITE

Lionel Banks and Rudolph Sternad, art direction; Fay Babcock, interior decoration, *The Talk of the Town*

Ralph Berger, art direction; Emile Kuri, interior decoration, *Silver Queen*

Albert S. D'Agostino, art direction; Al Fields and Darrell Silvera, interior decoration, *The Magnificent Ambersons*

Richard Day and Joseph Wright, art direction; Thomas Little, interior decoration, *This Above All*

Hans Dreier and Roland Anderson, art direction; Sam Comer, interior decoration, *Take a Letter, Darling*

Perry Ferguson, art direction; Howard Bristol, interior decoration, *The Pride of the Yankees*

Cedric Gibbons and Randall Duell, art direction; Edwin B. Willis and Jack Moore, interior decoration, *Random Harvest*

John B. Goodman and Jack Otterson, art direction; Russell A. Gausman and Boris Leven, art direction and interior decoration, *The Shanghai Gesture*

Max Parker and Mark-Lee Kirk, art direction; Casey Roberts, interior decoration, *George Washington Slept Here*

Edward R. Robinson, interior decoration, *The Spoilers*

COLOR

Richard Day and Joseph Wright, art direction; Thomas Little, interior decoration, *My Gal Sal*

Hans Dreier and Roland Anderson, art direction; George Sawley, interior decoration, *Reap the Wild Wind*

Alexander Golitzen and Jack Otterson, art direction; Russell A. Gausman and Ira S. Webb, interior decoration, *Arabian Nights*

Vincent Korda, art direction; Julia Heron, interior decoration, *Jungle Book*

Ted Smith, art direction; Casey Roberts, interior decoration, *Captains of the Clouds*

SOUND RECORDING

Columbia Studio Sound Dept., *You Were Never Lovelier*

MGM Studio Sound Dept., *Mrs. Miniver*

Paramount Studio Sound Dept., *Road to Morocco*

RCA Sound, *The Gold Rush*

Republic Studio Sound Dept., *Flying Tigers*

RKO Radio Studio Sound Dept., *Once Upon a Honeymoon*

Samuel Goldwyn Studio Sound Dept., *The Pride of the Yankees*

Sound Service, Inc., *Friendly Enemies*

Twentieth Century-Fox Studio Sound Dept., *This Above All*

Universal Studio Sound Dept., *Arabian Nights*

Walt Disney Studio Sound Dept., *Bambi*

Warner Bros. Studio Sound Dept., *Yankee Doodle Dandy*

MUSIC
SONG

"Always in My Heart," *Always in My Heart*, Ernesto Lecuona, music; Kim Gannon, lyrics

"Dearly Beloved," *You Were Never Lovelier*, Jerome Kern, music; Johnny Mercer, lyrics

"How About You?," *Babes on Broadway*, Burton Lane, music; Ralph Freed, lyrics

"It Seems I Heard That Song Before," *Youth on Parade*, Jule Styne, music; Sammy Cahn, lyrics

"I've Got a Gal in Kalamazoo," *Orchestra Wives*, Harry Warren, music; Mack Gordon, lyrics

"Love Is a Song," *Bambi*, Frank Churchill, music; Larry Morey, lyrics

"Pennies for Peppino," *Flying With Music*, Edward Ward, music; Chet Forrest and Bob Wright, lyrics

"Pig Foot Pete," *Hellzapoppin'*, Gene de Paul, music; Don Raye, lyrics (This song was declared ineligible because it does not appear in *Hellzapoppin'*. The song did appear in the 1941 film *Keep 'Em Flying*.)

"There's a Breeze on Lake Louise," *The Mayor of 44th Street*, Harry Revel, music; Mort Greene, lyrics

"White Christmas," *Holiday Inn*, Irving Berlin, music and lyrics

SCORING OF A DRAMATIC OR COMEDY PICTURE

Frank Churchill and Edward Plumb, *Bambi*

Richard Hageman, *The Shanghai Gesture*

Leigh Harline, *The Pride of the Yankees*

Werner Heymann, *To Be or Not to Be*

Frederick Hollander and Morris Stoloff, *The Talk of the Town*

Edward Kay, *Klondike Fury*

Alfred Newman, *The Black Swan*

Miklos Rozsa, *Jungle Book*

Frank Skinner, *Arabian Nights*

Max Steiner, *Now, Voyager*

Herbert Stothart, *Random Harvest*

Max Terr, *The Gold Rush*

Dimitri Tiomkin, *The Corsican Brothers*

Roy Webb, *I Married a Witch*

Roy Webb, *Joan of Paris*

Victor Young, *Flying Tigers*

Victor Young, *Silver Queen*

Victor Young, *Take a Letter, Darling*

SCORING OF A MUSICAL PICTURE

Roger Edens and Georgie Stoll, *For Me and My Gal*

Robert Emmett Dolan, *Holiday Inn*

Leigh Harline, *You Were Never Lovelier*

Ray Heindorf and Heinz Roemheld, *Yankee Doodle Dandy*

Alfred Newman, *My Gal Sal*

Charles Previn and Hans Salter, *It Started With Eve*

Walter Scharf, *Johnny Doughboy*

Edward Ward, *Flying With Music*

FILM EDITING

George Amy, *Yankee Doodle Dandy*

Harold F. Kress, *Mrs. Miniver*

Daniel Mandell, *The Pride of the Yankees*

Otto Meyer, *The Talk of the Town*

Walter Thompson, *This Above All*

SPECIAL EFFECTS

Lawrence Butler, photography; William H. Wilmarth, sound, *Jungle Book*

Jack Cosgrove and Ray Binger, photography; Thomas T. Moulton, sound, *The Pride of the Yankees*

Farciot Edouart, Gordon Jennings and William L. Pereira, photography; Louis Mesenkop, sound, *Reap the Wild Wind*

John Fulton, photography; Bernard B. Brown, sound, *Invisible Agent*

A. Arnold Gillespie and Warren Newcombe, photography; Douglas Shearer, sound, *Mrs. Miniver*

Byron Haskin, photography; Nathan Levinson, sound, *Desperate Journey*

Howard Lydecker, photography; Daniel J. Bloomberg, sound, *Flying Tigers*

Ronald Neame, photography; C. C. Stevens, sound, *One of Our Aircraft Is Missing*

Fred Sersen, photography; Roger Heman and George Leverett, sound, *The Black Swan*

Vernon L. Walker, photography; James G. Stewart, sound, *The Navy Comes Through*

SHORT SUBJECTS

CARTOON

All Out for "V" (*Terrytoons Series*) (Twentieth Century-Fox)

Blitz Wolf (MGM)

***Der Fuehrer's Face* (Walt Disney Productions; RKO Radio)**

Juke Box Jamboree (*Swing Symphony Series*) (Walter Lantz Productions; Universal)

Pigs in a Polka (*Blue Ribbon Series*) (Leon Schlesinger, producer; Warner Bros.)

Tulips Shall Grow (*George Pal Puppetoon Series*) (George Pal Productions, Paramount)

ONE-REEL

Desert Wonderland (*Magic Carpet Series*) (Twentieth Century-Fox)

Marines in the Making (*Pete Smith Specialties Series*) (Pete Smith, producer; MGM)

***Speaking of Animals and Their Families* (*Speaking of Animals Series*) (Paramount)**

United States Marine Band (*Melody Master Bands Series*) (Warner Bros.)

TWO-REEL

***Beyond the Line of Duty* (*Broadway Brevities Series*) (U.S. War Department; Warner Bros.)**

Don't Talk (*Crime Doesn't Pay Series*) (MGM)

Private Smith of the U.S.A. (*This Is America Series*) (RKO Radio)

DOCUMENTARY

Africa, Prelude to Victory (March of Time; Twentieth Century-Fox)

***The Battle of Midway* (U.S. Navy; Twentieth Century-Fox)**

Combat Report (U.S. Army Signal Corps)

Conquer by the Clock (*America Speaks Series*) (U.S. War Information Office; RKO Pathé)

The Grain That Built a Hemisphere (Walt Disney, producer; Office of the Coordinator of Inter-American Affairs)

The Battle of Midway

Henry Browne, Farmer (U.S. Department of Agriculture; Republic)

High Over the Borders (National Film Board of Canada)

High Stakes in the East (Netherlands Information Bureau; Netherlands Information Bureau/Service)

Inside Fighting China (*World in Action Series*) (National Film Board of Canada; United Artists)

It's Everybody's War (U.S. War Information Office; Twentieth Century-Fox)

***Kokoda Front Line!* (Australian News and Information Bureau)**

Listen to Britain (British Ministry of Information)

Little Belgium (Belgian Ministry of Information)

Little Isles of Freedom (*Broadway Brevities Series*) (Victor Stoloff and Edgar Loew, producers; Warner Bros.)

***Moscow Strikes Back* (Artkino; Republic)**

Mr. Blabbermouth! (U.S. War Information Office; MGM)

Mr. Gardenia Jones (U.S. War Information Office; MGM)

The New Spirit (Walt Disney, producer; U.S. Treasury Department)

***Prelude to War* (U.S. Army Special Services)**

The Price of Victory (U.S. War Information Office; Paramount)

A Ship Is Born (U.S. Merchant Marine; Warner Bros.)

Twenty-One Miles (British Ministry of Information)

We Refuse to Die (U.S. War Information Office; Paramount)

White Eagle (Concanen Films)

Winning Your Wings (U.S. Army Air Force; Warner Bros.)

IRVING G. THALBERG MEMORIAL AWARD

Sidney Franklin

SPECIAL AWARDS

To **Charles Boyer** for his progressive cultural achievement in establishing the French Research Foundation in Los Angeles as a source of reference for the Hollywood motion picture industry

To **Noel Coward** for his outstanding production achievement in *In Which We Serve*

To **MGM** for its achievement in representing the American way of life in the production of the *Andy Hardy* series of films

1943

OUSTANDING MOTION PICTURE
Casablanca (Warner Bros.)
For Whom the Bell Tolls (Paramount)
Heaven Can Wait (Twentieth Century-Fox)
The Human Comedy (MGM)
In Which We Serve (Two Cities; United Artists)
Madame Curie (MGM)
The More the Merrier (Columbia)
The Ox-Bow Incident (Twentieth Century-Fox)
The Song of Bernadette (Twentieth Century-Fox)
Watch on the Rhine (Warner Bros.)

BEST ACTOR
Humphrey Bogart, *Casablanca*
Gary Cooper, *For Whom the Bell Tolls*
Paul Lukas, *Watch on the Rhine*
Walter Pidgeon, *Madame Curie*
Mickey Rooney, *The Human Comedy*

BEST ACTRESS
Jean Arthur, *The More the Merrier*
Ingrid Bergman, *For Whom the Bell Tolls*
Joan Fontaine, *The Constant Nymph*
Greer Garson, *Madame Curie*
Jennifer Jones, *The Song of Bernadette*

ACTOR IN A SUPPORTING ROLE
Charles Bickford, *The Song of Bernadette*
Charles Coburn, *The More the Merrier*
J. Carrol Naish, *Sahara*
Claude Rains, *Casablanca*
Akim Tamiroff, *For Whom the Bell Tolls*

ACTRESS IN A SUPPORTING ROLE
Gladys Cooper, *The Song of Bernadette*
Paulette Goddard, *So Proudly We Hail!*
Katina Paxinou, *For Whom the Bell Tolls*

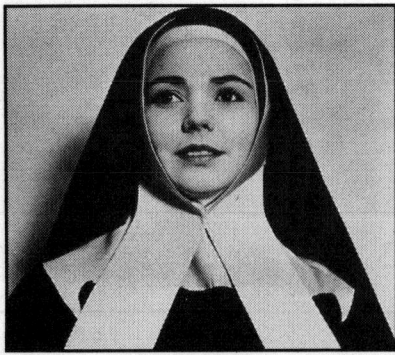

Jennifer Jones,
The Song of Bernadette

Anne Revere, *The Song of Bernadette*
Lucile Watson, *Watch on the Rhine*

DIRECTING
Clarence Brown, *The Human Comedy*
Michael Curtiz, *Casablanca*
Henry King, *The Song of Bernadette*
Ernst Lubitsch, *Heaven Can Wait*
George Stevens, *The More the Merrier*

WRITING
ORIGINAL MOTION PICTURE STORY
Steve Fisher, *Destination Tokyo*
Guy Gilpatric, *Action in the North Atlantic*
Gordon McDonell, *Shadow of a Doubt*
Frank Ross and Robert Russell, *The More the Merrier*
William Saroyan, *The Human Comedy*

ORIGINAL SCREENPLAY
Noel Coward, *In Which We Serve*
Lillian Hellman, *The North Star*
Norman Krasna, *Princess O'Rourke*
Dudley Nichols, *Air Force*
Allan Scott, *So Proudly We Hail!*

SCREENPLAY
Julius J. Epstein, Philip G. Epstein and Howard Koch, *Casablanca*
Richard Flournoy, Lewis R. Foster, Frank Ross and Robert Russell, *The More the Merrier*
Dashiell Hammett, *Watch on the Rhine*
Nunnally Johnson, *Holy Matrimony*
George Seaton, *The Song of Bernadette*

CINEMATOGRAPHY
BLACK-AND-WHITE
Arthur Edeson, *Casablanca*
Tony Gaudio, *Corvette K-225*
James Wong Howe, *The North Star*
James Wong Howe, Elmer Dyer and Charles Marshall, *Air Force*
Charles Lang, *So Proudly We Hail!*
Rudolph Maté, *Sahara*
Arthur Miller, *The Song of Bernadette*
Joseph Ruttenberg, *Madame Curie*
John Seitz, *Five Graves to Cairo*
Harry Stradling, *The Human Comedy*

COLOR
Charles G. Clarke and Allen Davey, *Hello, Frisco, Hello*
Edward Cronjager, *Heaven Can Wait*
George Folsey, *Thousands Cheer*
Hal Mohr and W. Howard Greene, *Phantom of the Opera*
Ray Rennahan, *For Whom the Bell Tolls*
Leonard Smith, *Lassie Come Home*

ART DIRECTION
BLACK-AND-WHITE
James Basevi and William Darling, art direction; Thomas Little, interior decoration, *The Song of Bernadette*

Albert S. D'Agostino and Carroll Clark, art direction; Darrell Silvera and Harley Miller, interior decoration, *Flight for Freedom*

Hans Dreier and Ernst Fegte, art direction; Bertram Granger, interior decoration, *Five Graves to Cairo*

Perry Ferguson, art direction; Howard Bristol, interior decoration, *The North Star*

Cedric Gibbons and Paul Groesse, art direction; Edwin B. Willis and Hugh Hunt, interior decoration, *Madame Curie*

Carl Weyl, art direction; George J. Hopkins interior decoration, *Mission to Moscow*

COLOR

James Basevi and Joseph C. Wright, art direction; Thomas Little, interior decoration, *The Gang's All Here*

Hans Dreier and Haldane Douglas, art direction; Bertram Granger, interior decoration, *For Whom the Bell Tolls*

Cedric Gibbons and Daniel Cathcart, art direction; Edwin B. Willis and Jacques Mersereau, interior decoration, *Thousands Cheer*

Alexander Golitzen and John B. Goodman, art direction; Russell A. Gausman and Ira S. Webb, interior decoration, Phantom of the Opera

John Hughes and Lt. John Koenig, art direction; George J. Hopkins, interior decoration, *This Is the Army*

SOUND RECORDING

Columbia Studio Sound Dept., *Sahara*

MGM Studio Sound Dept., *Madame Curie*

Paramount Studio Sound Dept., *Riding High*

RCA Sound, *So This Is Washington*

Republic Studio Sound Dept., *In Old Oklahoma*

RKO Radio Studio Sound Dept., This Land Is Mine

Samuel Goldwyn Studio Sound Dept., *The North Star*

Sound Service, Inc., *Hangmen Also Die*

Twentieth Century-Fox Studio Sound Dept., *The Song of Bernadette*

Universal Studio Sound Dept., *Phantom of the Opera*

Walt Disney Studio Sound Dept., *Saludos Amigos*

Warner Bros. Studio Sound Dept., *This Is the Army*

MUSIC

SONG

"Black Magic," *Star Spangled Rhythm,* Harold Arlen, music; Johnny Mercer, lyrics

"A Change of Heart," *Hit Parade of 1943,* Jule Styne, music; Harold Adamson, lyrics

"Happiness Is a Thing Called Joe," *Cabin in the Sky,* Harold Arlen, music; E. Y. Harburg, lyrics

"My Shining Hour," *The Sky's the Limit,* Harold Arlen, music; Johnny Mercer, music

"Saludos Amigos," *Saludos Amigos,* Charles Wolcott, music; Ned Washington, lyrics

"Say a Pray'r for the Boys Over There," *Hers to Hold,* Jimmy McHugh, music; Herb Magidson, lyrics

"They're Either Too Young or Too Old," *Thank Your Lucky Stars,* Arthur Schwartz, music; Frank Loesser, lyrics

"We Mustn't Say Goodbye," *Stage Door Canteen,* James Monaco, music; Al Dubin, lyrics

"You'd Be So Nice to Come Home To," *Something to Shout About,* Cole Porter, music and lyrics

"You'll Never Know," *Hello, Frisco, Hello,* Harry Warren, music; Mack Gordon, lyrics

SCORING OF A DRAMATIC OR COMEDY PICTURE

C. Bakaleinikoff and Roy Webb, *The Fallen Sparrow*

Philip Boutelje, *Hi Diddle Diddle*

Gerard Carbonara, *The Kansan*

Aaron Copland, *The North Star*

Hanns Eisler, *Hangmen Also Die*

Louis Gruenberg and Morris Stoloff, *Commandos Strike at Dawn*

Leigh Harline, *Johnny Come Lately*

Arthur Lange, *Lady of Burlesque*

Alfred Newman, The Song of Bernadette

Edward H. Plumb, Paul J. Smith and Oliver G. Wallace, *Victory Through Air Power*

Hans J. Salter and Frank Skinner, *The Amazing Mrs. Holliday*

Walter Scharf, *In Old Oklahoma*

Max Steiner, *Casablanca*

Herbert Stothart, *Madame Curie*

Dimitri Tiomkin, *The Moon and Sixpence*

Victor Young, *For Whom the Bell Tolls*

SCORING OF A MUSICAL PICTURE

Robert Emmett Dolan, *Star Spangled Rhythm*

Leigh Harline, *The Sky's the Limit*

Ray Heindorf, This Is the Army

Alfred Newman, *Coney Island*

Edward H. Plumb, Paul J. Smith and Charles Wolcott, *Saludos Amigos*

Frederic E. Rich, *Stage Door Canteen*

Walter Scharf, *Hit Parade of 1943*

Morris Stoloff, *Something to Shout About*

Herbert Stothart, *Thousands Cheer*

Edward Ward, *Phantom of the Opera*

FILM EDITING

George Amy, Air Force

Doane Harrison, *Five Graves to Cairo*

Owen Marks, *Casablanca*

Barbara McLean, *The Song of Bernadette*

Sherman Todd and John Link, *For Whom the Bell Tolls*

SPECIAL EFFECTS

Farciot Edouart and Gordon Jennings, photography; George Dutton, sound, *So Proudly We Hail!*

A. Arnold Gillespie and Donald Jahraus, photography; Michael Steinore, sound, *Stand by for Action*

Hans Koenekamp and Rex Wimpy, photography; Nathan Levinson, sound, *Air Force*

Fred Sersen, photography; Roger Heman, sound, Crash Dive

Clarence Slifer and R. O. Binger, photography; Thomas T. Moulton, sound, *The North Star*

Vernon L. Walker, photography; James G. Stewart and Roy Granville, sound, *Bombardier*

SHORT SUBJECTS

CARTOON

The Dizzy Acrobat (*Woody Woodpecker Series*) (Walter Lantz Productions; Universal)

The 500 Hats of Bartholomew Cubbins (*George Pal Puppetoon Series*) (George Pal Productions; Paramount)

Greetings, Bait! (*Merrie Melodies Series*) (Leon Schlesinger, producer; Warner Bros.)

Imagination (*Color Rhapsodies Series*) (Dave Fleischer, producer; Columbia)

Reason and Emotion (Walt Disney Productions; RKO Radio)

Yankee Doodle Mouse (**Tom and Jerry Series**) **(Frederick Quimby, producer; MGM)**

ONE-REEL

Amphibious Fighters (**Grantland Rice Spotlight Series**) **(Grantland Rice, producer; Paramount)**

Cavalcade of Dance With Veloz and Yolanda (*Melody Master Bands Series*) (Gordon Hollingshead, producer; Warner Bros.)

Champions Carry On (*Ed Thorgerson's Sports Reviews Series*) (Edmund Reek, producer; Twentieth Century-Fox)

Hollywood in Uniform (*Screen Snapshots Series*) (Ralph Staub, producer; Columbia)

Seeing Hands (*Pete Smith Specialties Series*) (Pete Smith, producer; MGM)

TWO-REEL

Heavenly Music **(Jerry Bresler and Sam Coslow, producers; MGM)**

Letter to a Hero (*This Is America Series*) (Frederic Ullman, Jr., producer; RKO Radio)

Mardi Gras (*Musical Parade Series*) (Walter MacEwen, producer; Paramount)

Women at War (*Technicolor Special Series*) (Gordon Hollingshead, producer; Warner Bros.)

DOCUMENTARY

SHORT SUBJECT

Children of Mars (*This Is America Series*) (RKO Radio)

December 7th **(U.S. Office of Strategic Services Field Photographic Bureau; U.S. Navy)**

Plan for Destruction (MGM)

Swedes in America (U.S. War Information Office Overseas Motion Picture Bureau)

To the People of the United States (Walter Wanger; U.S. Public Health Service)

Tomorrow We Fly (U.S. Navy Bureau of Aeronautics)

Youth in Crisis (*March of Time Series*) (Twentieth Century-Fox)

FEATURE

Baptism of Fire (*Fighting Men's Series*) (U.S. Army)

The Battle of Russia (Special Service Division of the U.S. War Department; Twentieth Century-Fox)

Desert Victory **(British Ministry of Information; Twentieth Century-Fox)**

Report From the Aleutians (*Combat Film Series*) (U.S. Army Pictorial Service)

War Department Report (Office of Strategic Services Field Photographic Bureau)

The following titles were originally announced as Feature nominees, but they did not appear on the final ballot.

For God and Country (U.S. Army Pictorial Service)

Silent Village (British Ministry of Information; Czechoslovak Ministry of Foreign Affairs)

We've Come a Long Way (Negro Marches On, Inc.)

IRVING G. THALBERG MEMORIAL AWARD

Hal B. Wallis

SPECIAL AWARD

To **George Pal** for the development of novel methods and techniques in the production of short subjects known as Puppetoons

1944

BEST MOTION PICTURE

Double Indemnity (Paramount)

Gaslight (MGM)

Going My Way (Paramount)

Since You Went Away (Selznick International Pictures; United Artists)

Wilson (Twentieth Century-Fox)

Ingrid Bergman, *Gaslight*

BEST ACTOR

Charles Boyer, *Gaslight*

Bing Crosby, *Going My Way*

Barry Fitzgerald, *Going My Way*

Cary Grant, *None but the Lonely Heart*

Alexander Knox, *Wilson*

BEST ACTRESS

Ingrid Bergman, *Gaslight*

Claudette Colbert, *Since You Went Away*

Bette Davis, *Mr. Skeffington*

Greer Garson, *Mrs. Parkington*

Barbara Stanwyck, *Double Indemnity*

ACTOR IN A SUPPORTING ROLE

Hume Cronyn, *The Seventh Cross*

Barry Fitzgerald, *Going My Way*

Claude Rains, *Mr. Skeffington*

Clifton Webb, *Laura*

Monty Woolley, *Since You Went Away*

ACTRESS IN A SUPPORTING ROLE

Ethel Barrymore, *None but the Lonely Heart*
Jennifer Jones, *Since You Went Away*
Angela Lansbury, *Gaslight*
Aline MacMahon, *Dragon Seed*
Agnes Moorehead, *Mrs. Parkington*

DIRECTING

Alfred Hitchcock, *Lifeboat*
Henry King, *Wilson*
Leo McCarey, *Going My Way*
Otto Preminger, *Laura*
Billy Wilder, *Double Indemnity*

WRITING

ORIGINAL MOTION PICTURE STORY

David Boehm and Chandler Sprague, *A Guy Named Joe*
Edward Doherty and Jules Schermer, *The Sullivans*
Leo McCarey, *Going My Way*
Alfred Neumann and Joseph Than, *None Shall Escape*
John Steinbeck, *Lifeboat*

ORIGINAL SCREENPLAY

Jerome Cady, *Wing and a Prayer*
Richard Connell and Gladys Lehman, *Two Girls and a Sailor*
Preston Sturges, *Hail the Conquering Hero*
Preston Sturges, *The Miracle of Morgan's Creek*
Lamar Trotti, *Wilson*

SCREENPLAY

John L. Balderston, Walter Reisch and John Van Druten, *Gaslight*
Irving Brecher and Fred F. Finkelhoffe, *Meet Me in St. Louis*
Frank Butler and Frank Cavett, *Going My Way*
Raymond Chandler and Billy Wilder, *Double Indemnity*
Jay Dratler, Samuel Hoffenstein and Betty Reinhardt, *Laura*

CINEMATOGRAPHY

BLACK-AND-WHITE

Stanley Cortez and Lee Garmes, *Since You Went Away*
George Folsey, *The White Cliffs of Dover*
Charles Lang, *The Uninvited*
Joseph LaShelle, *Laura*
Lionel Lindon, *Going My Way*
Glen MacWilliams, *Lifeboat*
Joseph Ruttenberg, *Gaslight*
John Seitz, *Double Indemnity*
Robert Surtees and Harold Rosson, *Thirty Seconds Over Tokyo*
Sidney Wagner, *Dragon Seed*

COLOR

Edward Cronjager, *Home in Indiana*
George Folsey, *Meet Me in St. Louis*
Rudolph Maté and Allen M. Davey, *Cover Girl*
Ray Rennahan, *Lady in the Dark*
Charles Rosher, *Kismet*
Leon Shamroy, *Wilson*

ART DIRECTION

BLACK-AND-WHITE

Lionel Banks and Walter Holscher, art direction; Joseph Kish, interior decoration, *Address Unknown*
Albert S. D'Agostino and Carroll Clark, art direction; Darrell Silvera and Claude Carpenter, interior decoration, *Step Lively*
Hans Dreier and Robert Usher, art direction; Sam Comer, interior decoration, *No Time for Love*
Perry Ferguson, art direction; Julia Heron, interior decoration, *Casanova Brown*
Cedric Gibbons and William Ferrari, art direction; Edwin B. Willis and Paul Huldschinsky, interior decoration, *Gaslight*
John J. Hughes, art direction; Fred MacLean, interior decoration, *The Adventures of Mark Twain*
Mark-Lee Kirk, art direction; Victor A. Gangelin, interior decoration, *Since You Went Away*
Lyle Wheeler and Leland Fuller, art direction; Thomas Little, interior decoration, *Laura*

COLOR

Lionel Banks and Cary Odell, art direction; Fay Babcock, interior decoration, *Cover Girl*
Hans Dreier and Raoul Pene du Bois, art direction; Ray Moyer, interior decoration, *Lady in the Dark*
Ernst Fegte, art direction; Howard Bristol, interior decoration, *The Princess and the Pirate*
Cedric Gibbons and Daniel B. Cathcart, art direction; Edwin B. Willis and Richard Pefferle, interior decoration, *Kismet*
John B. Goodman and Alexander Golitzen, art direction; Russell A. Gausman and Ira S. Webb, interior decoration, *The Climax*
Wiard Ihnen, art direction; Thomas Little, interior decoration, *Wilson*
Charles Novi, art direction; Jack McConaghy, interior decoration, *The Desert Song*

SOUND RECORDING

Columbia Studio Sound Dept., *Cover Girl*
MGM Studio Sound Dept., *Kismet*
Paramount Studio Sound Dept., *Double Indemnity*
RCA Sound, *Voice in the Wind*
Republic Studio Sound Dept., *Brazil*
RKO Radio Studio Sound Dept., *Music in Manhattan*
Samuel Goldwyn Studio Sound Department, *Casanova Brown*
Sound Service Inc., *It Happened Tomorrow*
Twentieth Century-Fox Studio Sound Dept., *Wilson*
Universal Studio Sound Dept., *His Butler's Sister*
Warner Bros. Studio Sound Dept., *Hollywood Canteen*

MUSIC

SONG

"I Couldn't Sleep a Wink Last Night," *Higher and Higher,* Jimmy McHugh, music; Harold Adamson, lyrics
"I'll Walk Alone," *Follow the Boys,* Jule Styne, music; Sammy Cahn, lyrics
"I'm Making Believe," *Sweet and Lowdown,* James V. Monaco, music; Mack Gordon, lyrics
"Long Ago and Far Away," *Cover Girl,* Jerome Kern, music; Ira Gershwin, lyrics

"Now I Know," *Up in Arms*, Harold Arlen, music; Ted Koehler, lyrics

"Remember Me to Carolina," *Minstrel Man*, Harry Revel, music; Paul Webster, lyrics

"Rio de Janeiro," *Brazil*, Ary Barroso, music; Ned Washington, lyrics

"Silver Shadows and Golden Dreams," *Lady, Let's Dance*, Lew Pollack, music; Charles Newman, lyrics

"Sweet Dreams Sweetheart," *Hollywood Canteen*, M. K. Jerome, music; Ted Koehler, lyrics

"Swinging on a Star," *Going My Way*, James Van Heusen, music; Johnny Burke, lyrics

"Too Much in Love," *Song of the Open Road*, Walter Kent, music; Kim Gannon, lyrics

"The Trolley Song," *Meet Me in St. Louis*, Ralph Blane and Hugh Martin, music and lyrics

SCORING OF A DRAMATIC OR COMEDY PICTURE

C. Bakaleinikoff and Hanns Eisler, *None but the Lonely Heart*

Karl Hajos, *Summer Storm*

Franke Harling, *Three Russian Girls*

Arthur Lange, *Casanova Brown*

Michel Michelet and Edward Paul, *The Hairy Ape*

Michel Michelet, *Voice in the Wind*

Alfred Newman, *Wilson*

Edward Paul, *Up in Mabel's Room*

Frederic E. Rich, *Jack London*

David Rose, *The Princess and the Pirate*

Miklos Rozsa, *Double Indemnity*

Miklos Rozsa, *Woman of the Town*

H. J. Salter, *Christmas Holiday*

Walter Scharf and Roy Webb, *The Fighting Seabees*

Max Steiner, *The Adventures of Mark Twain*

Max Steiner, *Since You Went Away*

Morris Stoloff and Ernst Toch, *Address Unknown*

Robert Stolz, *It Happened Tomorrow*

Herbert Stothart, *Kismet*

Dimitri Tiomkin, *The Bridge of San Luis Rey*

SCORING OF A MUSICAL PICTURE

C. Bakaleinikoff, *Higher and Higher*

Robert Emmett Dolan, *Lady in the Dark*

Carmen Dragon and Morris Stoloff, *Cover Girl*

Leo Erdody and Ferde Grofé, *Minstrel Man*

Louis Forbes and Ray Heindorf, *Up in Arms*

Ray Heindorf, *Hollywood Canteen*

Werner R. Heymann and Kurt Weill, *Knickerbocker Holiday*

Edward Kay, *Lady, Let's Dance*

Mahlon Merrick, *Sensations of 1945*

Alfred Newman, *Irish Eyes Are Smiling*

Charles Previn, *Song of the Open Road*

H. J. Salter, *The Merry Monahans*

Walter Scharf, *Brazil*

Georgie Stoll, *Meet Me in St. Louis*

FILM EDITING

Roland Gross, *None but the Lonely Heart*

Hal C. Kern and James E. Newcom, *Since You Went Away*

Owen Marks, *Janie*

Barbara McLean, *Wilson*

Leroy Stone, *Going My Way*

SPECIAL EFFECTS

David Allen, Ray Cory and Robert Wright, photography; Russell Malmgren and Harry Kusnick, sound, *Secret Command*

John R. Cosgrove, photography; Arthur Johns, sound, *Since You Went Away*

Paul Detlefsen and John Crouse, photography; Nathan Levinson, sound, *The Adventures of Mark Twain*

Farciot Edouart and Gordon Jennings, photography; George Dutton, sound, *The Story of Dr. Wassell*

A. Arnold Gillespie, Donald Jahraus and Warren Newcombe, photography; Douglas Shearer, sound, *Thirty Seconds Over Tokyo*

Fred Sersen, photography; Roger Heman, sound, *Wilson*

Vernon L. Walker, photography; James G. Steward and Roy Granville, sound, *Days of Glory*

SHORT SUBJECTS

CARTOON

And to Think I Saw It on Mulberry Street (*George Pal Puppetoon Series*) (George Pal Productions; Paramount)

Dog, Cat and Canary (*Color Rhapsody Series*) (Screen Gems; Columbia)

Fish Fry (*Cartunes*) (Walter Lantz Productions; Universal)

How to Play Football (*Goofy Series*) (Walt Disney Productions; RKO Radio)

Mouse Trouble (Tom and Jerry Series) (Frederick Quimby, producer; MGM)

My Boy Johnny (*Terrytoons Series*) (Paul Terry, producer; Twentieth Century-Fox)

Swooner Crooner (*Looney Tunes Series*) (Warner Bros.)

ONE-REEL

Blue Grass Gentlemen (*Ed Thorgerson's Sports Review Series*) (Edmund Reek, producer; Twentieth Century-Fox)

Jammin' the Blues (*Melody Master Bands Series*) (Gordon Hollingshead, producer; Warner Bros.)

Movie Pests (*Pete Smith's Specialties Series*) (Pete Smith, producer; MGM)

Screen Snapshots' 50th Anniversary of Motion Pictures (*Screen Snapshots Series*) (Ralph Staub, producer; Columbia)

Who's Who in Animal Land (Speaking of Animals Series) (Jerry Fairbanks, producer; Paramount)

TWO-REEL

Bombalera (*Musical Parade Series*) (Louis Harris, producer; Paramount)

I Won't Play (Featurette Series) (Gordon Hollingshead, producer; Warner Bros.)

Main Street Today (Jerry Bresler, producer; MGM)

DOCUMENTARY

SHORT SUBJECT

Arturo Toscanini (U.S. War Information Office Overseas Motion Picture Bureau)

New Americans (*This Is America Series*) (RKO Radio)

With the Marines at Tarawa (U.S. Marine Corps)

FEATURE
The Fighting Lady (U.S. Navy; Twentieth Century-Fox)
Resisting Enemy Interrogation (U.S. Army Air Force)

IRVING G. THALBERG MEMORIAL AWARD
Darryl F. Zanuck

SPECIAL AWARDS
To **Margaret O'Brien,** outstanding child actress of 1944

To **Bob Hope** for his many services to the Academy (a life membership in the Academy of Motion Picture Arts and Sciences)

1945

BEST MOTION PICTURE
Anchors Aweigh (MGM)
The Bells of St. Mary's (Rainbow Productions; RKO Radio)
***The Lost Weekend* (Paramount)**
Mildred Pierce (Warner Bros.)
Spellbound (Selznick International Pictures; United Artists)

BEST ACTOR
Bing Crosby, *The Bells of St. Mary's*
Gene Kelly, *Anchors Aweigh*
Ray Milland, *The Lost Weekend*
Gregory Peck, *The Keys of the Kingdom*
Cornel Wilde, *A Song to Remember*

BEST ACTRESS
Ingrid Bergman, *The Bells of St. Mary's*
Joan Crawford, *Mildred Pierce*
Greer Garson, *The Valley of Decision*
Jennifer Jones, *Love Letters*
Gene Tierny, *Leave Her to Heaven*

ACTOR IN A SUPPORTING ROLE
Michael Chekhov, *Spellbound*
John Dall, *The Corn Is Green*
James Dunn, *A Tree Grows in Brooklyn*
Robert Mitchum, *G. I. Joe*
J. Carrol Naish, *A Medal for Benny*

ACTRESS IN A SUPPORTING ROLE
Eve Arden, *Mildred Pierce*
Ann Blyth, *Mildred Pierce*
Angela Lansbury, *The Picture of Dorian Gray*
Joan Loring, *The Corn Is Green*
Anne Revere, *National Velvet*

DIRECTING
Clarence Brown, *National Velvet*
Alfred Hitchcock, *Spellbound*
Leo McCarey, *The Bells of St. Mary's*
Jean Renoir, *The Southerner*
Billy Wilder, *The Lost Weekend*

Joan Crawford, *Mildred Pierce*

WRITING
ORIGINAL MOTION PICTURE STORY
Alvah Bessie, *Objective, Burma!*
Charles G. Booth, *The House on 92nd Street*
Laszlo Gorog and Thomas Monroe, *The Affairs of Susan*
Ernst Marischka, *A Song to Remember*
John Steinbeck and Jack Wagner, *A Medal for Benny*

ORIGINAL SCREENPLAY
Myles Connolly, *Music for Millions*
Milton Holmes, *Salty O'Rourke*
Harry Kurnitz, *What Next, Corporal Hargrove?*
Richard Schweizer, *Marie-Louise*
Philip Yordan, *Dillinger*

SCREENPLAY
Leopold Atlas, Guy Endore and Philip Stevenson, *G. I. Joe*
Charles Brackett and Billy Wilder, *The Lost Weekend*
Frank Davis and Tess Slesinger, *A Tree Grows in Brooklyn*
Ranald MacDougall, *Mildred Pierce*
Albert Maltz, *Pride of the Marines*

CINEMATOGRAPHY
BLACK-AND-WHITE
George Barnes, *Spellbound*
Ernest Haller, *Mildred Pierce*
Arthur Miller, *The Keys of the Kingdom*
John F. Seitz, *The Lost Weekend*
Harry Stradling, *The Picture of Dorian Gray*

COLOR
George Barnes, *The Spanish Main*
Tony Gaudio and Allen M. Davey, *A Song to Remember*
Robert Planck and Charles Boyle, *Anchors Aweigh*
Leon Shamroy, *Leave Her to Heaven*
Leonard Smith, *National Velvet*

ART DIRECTION
BLACK-AND-WHITE
James Basevi and William Darling, art direction; Thomas Little and Frank E. Hughes, interior decoration, *The Keys of the Kingdom*

Albert S. D'Agostino and Jack Okey, art direction; Darrell Silvera and Claude Carpenter, interior decoration, *Experiment Perilous*

Hans Dreier and Roland Anderson, art direction; Sam Comer and Ray Moyer, interior decoration, *Love Letters*

Cedric Gibbons and Hans Peters, art direction; Edwin B. Willis, John Bonar and Hugh Hunt, interior decoration, *The Picture of Dorian Gray*

Wiard Ihnen, art direction; A. Roland Fields, interior decoration, *Blood on the Sun*

COLOR

Hans Dreier and Ernst Fegte, art direction; Sam Comer, interior decoration, *Frenchman's Creek*

Cedric Gibbons and Urie McCleary, art direction; Edwin B. Willis and Mildred Griffiths, interior decoration, *National Velvet*

Stephen Goosson and Rudolph Sternad, art direction; Frank Tuttle, interior decoration, *A Thousand and One Nights*

Ted Smith, art direction; Jack McConaghy, interior decoration, *San Antonio*

Lyle Wheeler and Maurice Ransford, art direction; Thomas Little, interior decoration, *Leave Her to Heaven*

SOUND RECORDING

Columbia Studio Sound Dept., *A Song to Remember*

General Service, *The Southerner*

MGM Studio Sound Dept., *They Were Expendable*

Paramount Studio Sound Dept., *The Unseen*

RCA Sound, *Three Is a Family*

Republic Studio Sound Dept., *Flame of Barbary Coast*

RKO Radio Studio Sound Dept., *The Bells of St. Mary's*

Samuel Goldwyn Studio Sound Dept., *Wonder Man*

Twentieth Century-Fox Studio Sound Dept., *Leave Her to Heaven*

Universal Studio Sound Dept., *Lady on a Train*

Walt Disney Studio Sound Dept., *The Three Caballeros*

Warner Bros. Studio Sound Dept., *Rhapsody in Blue*

MUSIC
SONG

"Accentuate the Positive," *Here Come the Waves*, Harold Arlen, music; Johnny Mercer, lyrics

"Anywhere," *Tonight and Every Night*, Jule Styne, music; Sammy Cahn, lyrics

"Aren't You Glad You're You," *The Bells of St. Mary's*, James Van Heusen, music; Johnny Burke, lyrics

"The Cat and the Canary," *Why Girls Leave Home*, Jay Livingston, music; Ray Evans, lyrics

"Endlessly," *Earl Carroll Vanities*, Walter Kent, music; Kim Gannon, lyrics

"I Fall in Love Too Easily," *Anchors Aweigh*, Jule Styne, music; Sammy Cahn, lyrics

"I'll Buy That Dream," *Sing Your Way Home*, Allie Wrubel, music; Herb Magidson, lyrics

"It Might as Well Be Spring," *State Fair*, Richard Rodgers, music; Oscar Hammerstein II, lyrics

"Linda," *G. I. Joe*, Ann Ronell, music and lyrics

"Love Letters," *Love Letters*, Victor Young, music; Eddie Heyman, lyrics

"More and More," *Can't Help Singing*, Jerome Kern, music; E. Y. Harburg, lyrics

"Sleighride in July," *Belle of the Yukon*, James Van Heusen, music; Johnny Burke, lyrics

"So in Love," *Wonder Man*, David Rose, music; Leo Robin, lyrics

"Some Sunday Morning," *San Antonio*, Ray Heindorf and M. K. Jerome, music; Ted Koehler, lyrics

SCORING OF A DRAMATIC OR COMEDY PICTURE

Daniele Amfitheatrof, *Guest Wife*

Louis Applebaum and Ann Ronell, *G. I. Joe*

Dale Butts and Morton Scott, *Flame of the Barbary Coast*

Robert Emmett Dolan, *The Bells of St. Mary's*

Lou Forbes, *Brewster's Millions*

Hugo Friedhofer and Arthur Lange, *The Woman in the Window*

Karl Hajos, *The Man Who Walked Alone*

Werner Janssen, *Captain Kidd*

Werner Janssen, *Guest in the House*

Werner Janssen, *The Southerner*

Edward J. Kay, *G. I. Honeymoon*

Alfred Newman, *The Keys of the Kingdom*

Miklos Rozsa, *The Lost Weekend*

Miklos Rozsa and Morris Stoloff, *A Song to Remember*

Miklos Rozsa, *Spellbound*

H. J. Salter, *This Love of Ours*

Herbert Stothart, *The Valley of Decision*

Alexander Tansman, *Paris, Underground*

Franz Waxman, *Objective, Burma*

Roy Webb, *The Enchanted Cottage*

Victor Young, *Love Letters*

SCORING OF A MUSICAL PICTURE

Robert Emmett Dolan, *Incendiary Blonde*

Lou Forbes and Ray Heindorf, *Wonder Man*

Walter Greene, *Why Girls Leave Home*

Ray Heindorf and Max Steiner, *Rhapsody in Blue*

Charles Henderson and Alfred Newman, *State Fair*

Edward J. Kay, *Sunbonnet Sue*

Jerome Kern and H. J. Salter, *Can't Help Singing*

Arthur Lange, *Belle of the Yukon*

Edward Plumb, Paul J. Smith and Charles Wolcott, *The Three Caballeros*

Morton Scott, *Hitchhike to Happiness*

Marlin Skiles and Morris Stoloff, *Tonight and Every Night*

Georgie Stoll, *Anchors Aweigh*

FILM EDITING

George Amy, *Objective, Burma!*

Doane Harrison, *The Lost Weekend*

Robert J. Kern, *National Velvet*

Harry Marker, *The Bells of St. Mary's*

Charles Nelson, *A Song to Remember*

SPECIAL EFFECTS

Lawrence W. Butler, photography; Ray Bomba, sound, *A Thousand and One Nights*

Jack Cosgrove, photography, *Spellbound*

John Fulton, photography; Arthur W. Johns, sound, *Wonder Man*

A. Arnold Gillespie, Donald Jahraus and Robert A. MacDonald, photography; Michael Steinore, sound, *They Were Expendable*

Fred Sersen and Sol Halprin, photography; Roger Heman and Harry Leonard, sound, *Captain Eddie*

SHORT SUBJECTS

CARTOON

Donald's Crime (*Donald Duck Series*) (Walt Disney Productions; RKO Radio)

Jasper and the Beanstalk (*George Pal Puppetoon-Jasper Series*) (George Pal Productions; Paramount)

Life With Feathers (*Merrie Melodies Series*) (Eddie Selzer, producer; Warner Bros.)

Mighty Mouse in Gypsy Life (*Terrytoon Series*) (Paul Terry, producer; Twentieth Century-Fox)

The Poet and Peasant (*Lantz Technicolor Cartune Series*) (Walter Lantz Productions; Universal)

Quiet Please! (*Tom and Jerry Series*) **(Frederick Quimby, producer; MGM)**

Rippling Romance (*Color Rhapsodies Series*) (Screen Gems; Columbia)

ONE-REEL

Along the Rainbow Trail (*Movietone Adventure Series*) (Edmund Reek, producer; Twentieth Century-Fox)

Screen Snapshots' 25th Anniversary (*Screen Snapshots Series*) (Ralph Staub, producer; Columbia)

Stairway to Light (*John Nesbitt Passing Parade Series*) **(Herbert Moulton, producer; MGM)**

Story of a Dog (*Vitaphone Varieties Series*) (Gordon Hollingshead, producer; Warner Bros.)

White Rhapsody (*Grantland Rice Spotlights Series*) (Grantland Rice, producer; Paramount)

Your National Gallery (*Variety Views Series*) (Joseph O'Brien and Thomas Mead, producers; Universal)

TWO-REEL

A Gun in His Hand (*Crime Doesn't Pay Series*) (Chester Franklin, producer; MGM)

The Jury Goes Round 'N' Round (*All Star Comedies Series*) (Jules White, producer; Columbia)

The Little Witch (*Musical Parade Series*) (George Templeton, producer; Paramount)

Star in the Night (*Broadway Brevities Series*) **(Gordon Hollingshead, producer; Warner Bros.)**

DOCUMENTARY

SHORT SUBJECT

Hitler Lives? (*Featurette Series*) **(Gordon Hollingshead, producer; Warner Bros.)**

Library of Congress (U.S. War Information Office Overseas Motion Picture Bureau)

To the Shores of Iwo Jima (U.S. Marine Corps.)

FEATURE

The Last Bomb (U.S. Army Air Force)

The True Glory **(Governments of Great Britain and the United States; Columbia)**

SPECIAL AWARDS

To **Walter Wanger** for his six years service as President of the Academy of Motion Picture Arts and Sciences

To **Peggy Ann Garner**, outstanding child actress of 1945

To **The House I Live In**, tolerance short subject; produced by Frank Ross and Mervyn LeRoy; directed by Mervyn LeRoy; screenplay by Albert Maltz; song "The House I Live In," music by Earl Robinson, lyrics by Lewis Allen; starring Frank Sinatra; released by RKO Radio

To **Republic Studio, Daniel J. Bloomberg** and the **Republic Sound Department** for the building of an outstanding musical scoring auditorium which provides optimum recording conditions and combines all elements of acoustic and engineering design

1946

BEST MOTION PICTURE

The Best Years of Our Lives (Goldwyn; RKO Radio)

Henry V (J. Arthur Rank-Two Cities Films; United Artists)

It's a Wonderful Life (Liberty Films; RKO Radio)

The Razor's Edge (Twentieth Century-Fox)

The Yearling (MGM)

BEST ACTOR

Fredric March, The Best Years of Our Lives

Laurence Olivier, *Henry V*

Larry Parks, *The Jolson Story*

Gregory Peck, *The Yearling*

James Stewart, *It's a Wonderful Life*

BEST ACTRESS

Olivia de Havilland, To Each His Own

Celia Johnson, *Brief Encounter*

Jennifer Jones, *Duel in the Sun*

Rosalind Russell, *Sister Kenny*

Jane Wyman, *The Yearling*

ACTOR IN A SUPPORTING ROLE

Charles Coburn, *The Green Years*

William Demarest, *The Jolson Story*

Claude Rains, *Notorious*

Harold Russell, The Best Years of Our Lives

Clifton Webb, *The Razor's Edge*

Fredric March, *The Best Years of Our Lives*

ACTRESS IN A SUPPORTING ROLE

Ethel Barrymore, *The Spiral Staircase*
Anne Baxter, *The Razor's Edge*
Lilian Gish, *Duel in the Sun*
Flora Robson, *Saratoga Trunk*
Gale Sondergaard, *Anna and the King of Siam*

DIRECTING

Clarence Brown, *The Yearling*
Frank Capra, *It's a Wonderful Life*
David Lean, *Brief Encounter*
Robert Siodmak, *The Killers*
William Wyler, *The Best Years of Our Lives*

WRITING

ORIGINAL MOTION PICTURE STORY

Charles Brackett, *To Each His Own*
Clemence Dane, *Vacation From Marriage*
Jack Patrick, *The Strange Love of Martha Ivers*
Vladimir Pozner, *The Dark Mirror*
Victor Trivas, *The Stranger*

ORIGINAL SCREENPLAY

Muriel Box and Sydney Box, *The Seventh Veil*
Raymond Chandler, *The Blue Dahlia*
Ben Hecht, *Notorious*
Norman Panama and Melvin Frank, *Road to Utopia*
Jacques Prévert, *Children of Paradise*

SCREENPLAY

Sergio Amidei and Federico Fellini, *Open City*
Sally Benson and Talbot Jennings, *Anna and the King of Siam*
Anthony Havelock-Allan, David Lean and Ronald Neame, *Brief Encounter*
Robert E. Sherwood, *The Best Years of Our Lives*
Anthony Veiller, *The Killers*

CINEMATOGRAPHY

BLACK-AND-WHITE

George Folsey, *The Green Years*
Arthur Miller, *Anna and the King of Siam*

COLOR

Charles Rosher, Leonard Smith and Arthur Arling, *The Yearling*
Joseph Walker, *The Jolson Story*

ART DIRECTION

BLACK-AND-WHITE

Richard Day and Nathan Juran, art direction; Thomas Little and Paul S. Fox, interior decoration, *The Razor's Edge*
Hans Dreier and Walter Tyler, art direction; Sam Comer and Ray Moyer, interior decoration, *Kitty*
Lyle Wheeler and William Darling, art direction; Thomas Little and Frank E. Hughes, interior decoration, *Anna and the King of Siam*

COLOR

John Bryan, art direction, *Caesar and Cleopatra*
Cedric Gibbons and Paul Groesse, art direction; Edwin B. Willis, interior decoration, *The Yearling*
Paul Sheriff and Carmen Dillon, art direction, *Henry V*

SOUND RECORDING

Columbia Studio Sound Dept., *The Jolson Story*
RKO Radio Studio Sound Dept., *It's a Wonderful Life*
Samuel Goldwyn Studio Sound Dept., *The Best Years of Our Lives*

MUSIC

SONG

"All Through the Day," *Centennial Summer*, Jerome Kern, music; Oscar Hammerstein II, lyrics
"I Can't Begin to Tell You," *The Dolly Sisters*, James Monaco, music; Mack Gordon, lyrics
"Ole Buttermilk Sky," *Canyon Passage*, Hoagy Carmichael, music; Jack Brooks, lyrics
"On the Atchison, Topeka and the Santa Fe," *The Harvey Girls*, Harry Warren, music; Johnny Mercer, lyrics
"You Keep Coming Back Like a Song," *Blue Skies*, Irving Berlin, music and lyrics

SCORING OF A DRAMATIC OR COMEDY PICTURE

Hugo Friedhofer, *The Best Years of Our Lives*
Bernard Herrmann, *Anna and the King of Siam*
Miklos Rozsa, *The Killers*
William Walton, *Henry V*
Franz Waxman, *Humoresque*

SCORING OF A MUSICAL PICTURE

Robert Emmett Dolan, *Blue Skies*
Lennie Hayton, *The Harvey Girls*
Ray Heindorf and Max Steiner, *Night and Day*
Alfred Newman, *Centennial Summer*
Morris Stoloff, *The Jolson Story*

FILM EDITING

Arthur Hilton, *The Killers*
William Hornbeck, *It's a Wonderful Life*
Harold Kress, *The Yearling*
William Lyon, *The Jolson Story*
Daniel Mandell, *The Best Years of Our Lives*

SPECIAL EFFECTS

Thomas Howard, visual, *Blithe Spirit*
William McGann, visual; Nathan Levinson, audible, *A Stolen Life*

SHORT SUBJECTS

CARTOON

The Cat Concerto (*Tom and Jerry Series*) (Frederick Quimby, producer; MGM)
Chopin's Musical Moments (*Musical Miniatures Series*) (Walter Lantz, producer; Universal)
John Henry and the Inky Poo (*George Pal Puppetoon Series*) (George Pal, producer; Paramount)
Squatter's Rights (*Mickey Mouse Series*) (Walt Disney Productions; RKO Radio)
Walky Talky Hawky (*Merrie Melodies Series*) (Edward Selzer, producer; Warner Bros.)

ONE-REEL

Dive-hi Champs (*Grantland Rice Spotlights Series*) (Jack Eaton, producer; Paramount)

Facing Your Danger (*Sports Parade Series*) (Gordon Hollingshead, producer; Warner Bros.)

Golden Horses (*Ed Thorgerson's Sports Review Series*) (Edmund Reek, producer; Twentieth Century-Fox)

Smart as a Fox (*Vitaphone Varieties Series*) (Gordon Hollingshead, producer; Warner Bros.)

Sure Cures (*Pete Smith Specialty Series*) (Pete Smith, producer; MGM)

TWO-REEL

A Boy and His Dog (*Featurettes Series*) (Gordon Hollingshead, producer; Warner Bros.)

College Queen (*Musical Parade Series*) (George B. Templeton, producer; Paramount)

Hiss and Yell (*All Star Comedies Series*) (Jules White, producer; Columbia)

The Luckiest Guy in the World (*Crime Doesn't Pay Series*) (Jerry Bresler, producer; MGM)

DOCUMENTARY

SHORT SUBJECT

Atomic Power (*March of Time Series*) (Twentieth Century-Fox)

Life at the Zoo (Artkino; Artkino Pictures)

Paramount News Issue #37 (*Twentieth Anniversary Issue! 1927–1947*) (Paramount)

Seeds of Destiny (U.S. War Department)

Traffic With the Devil (*Theatre of Life Series*) (Herbert Morgan, producer; MGM)

IRVING G. THALBERG MEMORIAL AWARD

Samuel Goldwyn

SPECIAL AWARDS

To **Laurence Olivier** for his outstanding achievement as actor, producer and director in bringing *Henry V* to the screen

To **Harold Russell** for bringing hope and courage to his fellow veterans through his appearance in *The Best Years of Our Lives*

To **Ernst Lubitsch** for his distinguished contributions to the art of the motion picture

To **Claude Jarman, Jr.**, outstanding child actor of 1946

1947

BEST MOTION PICTURE

The Bishop's Wife (Goldwyn; RKO Radio)

Crossfire (RKO Radio)

Gentleman's Agreement (Twentieth Century-Fox)

Great Expectations (J. Arthur Rank-Cineguild; Universal-International)

Miracle on 34th Street (Twentieth Century-Fox)

BEST ACTOR

Ronald Colman, *A Double Life*

John Garfield, *Body and Soul*

Gregory Peck, *Gentleman's Agreement*

William Powell, *Life With Father*

Michael Redgrave, *Mourning Becomes Electra*

BEST ACTRESS

Joan Crawford, *Possessed*

Susan Hayward, *Smash Up — The Story of a Woman*

Dorothy McGuire, *Gentleman's Agreement*

Rosalind Russell, *Mourning Becomes Electra*

Loretta Young, *The Farmer's Daughter*

ACTOR IN A SUPPORTING ROLE

Charles Bickford, *The Farmer's Daughter*

Thomas Gomez, *Ride the Pink Horse*

Edmund Gwenn, *Miracle on 34th Street*

Robert Ryan, *Crossfire*

Richard Widmark, *Kiss of Death*

ACTRESS IN A SUPPORTING ROLE

Ethel Barrymore, *The Paradine Case*

Gloria Grahame, *Crossfire*

Celeste Holm, *Gentleman's Agreement*

Marjorie Main, *The Egg and I*

Anne Revere, *Gentleman's Agreement*

Loretta Young, *The Farmer's Daughter*

DIRECTING

George Cukor, *A Double Life*

Edward Dmytryk, *Crossfire*

Elia Kazan, *Gentleman's Agreement*

Henry Koster, *The Bishop's Wife*

David Lean, *Great Expectations*

WRITING

ORIGINAL MOTION PICTURE STORY

Georges Chaperot and Rene Wheeler, *A Cage of Nightingales*

Herbert Clyde Lewis and Frederick Stephani, *It Happened on Fifth Avenue*

Valentine Davies, *Miracle on 34th Street*

Eleazar Lipsky, *Kiss of Death*

Dorothy Parker and Frank Cavett, *Smash Up — The Story of a Woman*

ORIGINAL SCREENPLAY

Sergio Amidei, Adolfo Franci, C. G. Viola and Cesare Zavattini, *Shoe-shine*

Charles Chaplin, *Monsieur Verdoux*

Ruth Gordon and Garson Kanin, *A Double Life*

Abraham Polonsky, *Body and Soul*

Sidney Sheldon, *The Bachelor and the Bobby-Soxer*

SCREENPLAY

Moss Hart, *Gentleman's Agreement*

David Lean, Ronald Neame and Anthony Havelock-Allan, *Great Expectations*

Richard Murphy, *Boomerang!*

John Paxton, *Crossfire*

George Seaton, *Miracle on 34th Street*

CINEMATOGRAPHY

BLACK-AND-WHITE

George Folsey, *Green Dolphin Street*

Guy Green, *Great Expectations*

Charles Lang, Jr., *The Ghost and Mrs. Muir*

COLOR

Jack Cardiff, *Black Narcissus*

Harry Jackson, *Mother Wore Tights*

Peverell Marley and William V. Skall, *Life With Father*

ART DIRECTION

BLACK-AND-WHITE

John Bryan, art direction; Wilfred Shingleton, set decoration, *Great Expectations*

Lyle Wheeler and Maurice Ransford, art direction; Thomas Little and Paul S. Fox, set decoration, *The Foxes of Harrow*

COLOR

Robert M. Haas, art direction; George James Hopkins, set decoration, *Life With Father*

Alfred Junge, art direction and set decoration, *Black Narcissus*

SOUND RECORDING

Samuel Goldwyn Studio Sound Department, *The Bishop's Wife*

MGM Studio Sound Department, *Green Dolphin Street*

Sound Service, Inc., *T-Men*

MUSIC

SONG

"A Gal in Calico," *The Time, the Place and the Girl*, Arthur Schwartz, music; Leo Robin, lyrics

"I Wish I Didn't Love You So," *The Perils of Pauline*, Frank Loesser, music and lyrics

"Pass That Peace Pipe," *Good News*, Ralph Blane, Hugh Martin and Roger Edens, music and lyrics

"You Do," *Mother Wore Tights*, Josef Myrow, music; Mack Gordon, lyrics

"Zip-a-Dee-Doo-Dah," *Song of the South*, Allie Wrubel, music; Ray Gilbert, lyrics

SCORING OF A DRAMATIC OR COMEDY PICTURE

Hugo Friedhofer, *The Bishop's Wife*

Alfred Newman, *Captain From Castile*

David Raksin, *Forever Amber*

Miklos Rozsa, *A Double Life*

Max Steiner, *Life With Father*

SCORING OF A MUSICAL PICTURE

Daniele Amfitheatrof, Paul J. Smith and Charles Wolcott, *Song of the South*

Robert Emmett Dolan, *Road to Rio*

Johnny Green, *Fiesta*

Ray Heindorf and Max Steiner, *My Wild Irish Rose*

Alfred Newman, *Mother Wore Tights*

FILM EDITING

Monica Collingwood, *The Bishop's Wife*

Harmon Jones, *Gentleman's Agreement*

Francis Lyon and Robert Parrish, *Body and Soul*

Fergus McDonnell, *Odd Man Out*

George White, *Green Dolphin Street*

SPECIAL EFFECTS

Farciot Edouart, Devereux Jennings, Gordon Jennings, Wallace Kelley and Paul Lerpae, visual; George Dutton, audible, *Unconquered*

A. Arnold Gillespie and Warren Newcombe, visual; Douglas Shearer and Michael Steinore, audible, *Green Dolphin Street*

SHORT SUBJECTS

CARTOON

Chip an' Dale (*Donald Duck Series*) (Walt Disney Productions; RKO Radio)

Dr. Jekyll and Mr. Mouse (*Tom and Jerry Series*) (Frederick Quimby, producer; MGM)

Pluto's Blue Note (*Pluto Series*) (Walt Disney Productions; RKO Radio)

Tubby the Tuba (*George Pal Puppetoon Series*) (George Pal, producer; Paramount)

Tweetie Pie (***Merrie Melodies Series***) (Edward Selzer, producer; Warner Bros.)**

ONE-REEL

Brooklyn, U.S.A. (*Variety View Series*) (Thomas Mead, producer; Universal-International)

Goodbye Miss Turlock (***John Nesbitt Passing Parade Series***) (Herbert Moulton, producer; MGM)**

Moon Rockets (*Popular Science Series*) (Jerry Fairbanks, producer; Paramount)

Now You See It (*Pete Smith Specialty Series*) (Pete Smith, producer; MGM)

So You Want to Be in Pictures (*Joe McDoakes Series*) (Gordon Hollingshead, producer; Warner Bros.)

TWO-REEL

Champagne for Two (*Musical Parade Featurette Series*) (Harry Grey, producer; Paramount)

Climbing the Matterhorn (***Color Series***) (Irving Allen, producer; Monogram)**

Fight of the Wild Stallions (*Featurette Series*) (Thomas Mead, producer; Universal-International)

Give Us the Earth (Herbert Morgan, producer; MGM)

A Voice Is Born: The Story of Niklos Gafni (*Musical Featurette Series*) (Ben Blake, producer; Columbia)

DOCUMENTARY

SHORT SUBJECT

First Steps (United Nations Division of Films and Visual Education)

Passport to Nowhere (*This Is America Series*) (Frederic Ullman, Jr., producer; RKO Pathé)

School in the Mailbox (Australian News and Information Bureau)

FEATURE

Design for Death (Theron Warth and Richard O. Fleischer, producers; RKO Radio)

Journey Into Medicine (U.S. State Department Office of Information and Educational Exchange)

The World Is Rich (Paul Rotha, producer; British Information Services)

SPECIAL AWARDS

To **James Baskett** for his able and heartwarming characterization of Uncle Remus, friend and storyteller to the children of the world in Walt Disney's *Song of the South*

To *Bill and Coo*, in which artistry and patience blended in a novel and entertaining use of the medium of motion pictures

To *Shoe-shine* — the high quality of this motion picture, brought to eloquent life in a country scarred by war, is proof to the world that the creative spirit can triumph over adversity.

To **Colonel William N. Selig, Albert E. Smith, Thomas Armat** and **George K. Spoor**, the small group of pioneers whose belief in a new medium, and whose contributions to its development, blazed the trail along which the motion picture has progressed, in their lifetime, from obscurity to world-wide acclaim

1948

BEST MOTION PICTURE

Hamlet, British (J. Arthur Rank-Two Cities; Universal-International)

Johnny Belinda (Warner Bros.)

The Red Shoes (J. Arthur Rank-Archers; Eagle-Lion)

The Snake Pit (Twentieth Century-Fox)

The Treasure of the Sierra Madre (Warner Bros.)

BEST ACTOR

Lew Ayres, *Johnny Belinda*

Montgomery Clift, *The Search*

Dan Dailey, *When My Baby Smiles at Me*

Laurence Olivier, *Hamlet*

Clifton Webb, *Sitting Pretty*

BEST ACTRESS

Ingrid Bergman, *Joan of Arc*

Olivia de Havilland, *The Snake Pit*

Irene Dunne, *I Remember Mama*

Barbara Stanwyck, *Sorry, Wrong Number*

Jane Wyman, *Johnny Belinda*

ACTOR IN A SUPPORTING ROLE

Charles Bickford, *Johnny Belinda*

José Ferrer, *Joan of Arc*

Laurence Olivier, *Hamlet*

Oscar Homolka, *I Remember Mama*

Walter Huston, *The Treasure of the Sierra Madre*

Cecil Kellaway, *The Luck of the Irish*

ACTRESS IN A SUPPORTING ROLE

Barbara Bel Geddes, *I Remember Mama*

Ellen Corby, *I Remember Mama*

Agnes Moorehead, *Johnny Belinda*

Jean Simmons, *Hamlet*

Claire Trevor, *Key Largo*

DIRECTING

John Huston, *The Treasure of the Sierra Madre*

Anatole Litvak, *The Snake Pit*

Jean Negulesco, *Johnny Belinda*

Laurence Olivier, *Hamlet*

Fred Zinnemann, *The Search*

WRITING

MOTION PICTURE STORY

Borden Chase, *Red River*

Frances Flaherty and Robert Flaherty, *Louisiana Story*

Emeric Pressburger, *The Red Shoes*

Richard Schweizer and David Wechsler, *The Search*

Malvin Wald, *The Naked City*

SCREENPLAY

Charles Brackett, Billy Wilder and Richard L. Breen, *A Foreign Affair*

John Huston, *The Treasure of the Sierra Madre*

Frank Partos and Millen Brand, *The Snake Pit*

Richard Schweizer and David Wechsler, *The Search*

Irmgard Von Cube and Allen Vincent, *Johnny Belinda*

CINEMATOGRAPHY

BLACK-AND-WHITE

Joseph August, *Portrait of Jennie*

William Daniels, *The Naked City*

Charles B. Lang, Jr., *A Foreign Affair*

Ted McCord, *Johnny Belinda*

Nicholas Musuraca, *I Remember Mama*

REFERENCE

COLOR
Charles G. Clarke, *Green Grass of Wyoming*
Robert Planck, *The Three Musketeers*
William Snyder, *The Loves of Carmen*
**Joseph Valentine, William V. Skall and Winton Hoch,
Joan of Arc**

ART DIRECTION
BLACK-AND-WHITE
**Roger K. Furse, art direction; Carmen Dillon, set decoration,
Hamlet**
Robert Haas, art direction; William Wallace, set decoration,
Johnny Belinda

COLOR
Richard Day, art direction; Edwin Casey Roberts and Joseph
Kish, set decoration, *Joan of Arc*
**Hein Heckroth, art direction; Arthur Lawson, set decoration,
The Red Shoes**

SOUND RECORDING
Republic Studio Sound Dept., *Moonrise*
Twentieth Century-Fox Studio Sound Dept., The Snake Pit
Warner Bros. Studio Sound Dept., *Johnny Belinda*

MUSIC
SONG
**"Buttons and Bows," The Paleface, Jay Livingston and Ray
Evans, music and lyrics**
"For Every Man There's a Woman," *Casbah*, Harold Arlen,
music; Leo Robin, lyrics
"It's Magic," *Romance on the High Seas*, Jule Styne, music;
Sammy Cahn, lyrics
"This Is the Moment," *That Lady in Ermine*, Frederick
Hollander, music; Leo Robin, lyrics
"The Woody Woodpecker Song," *Wet Blanket Policy*, Ramey
Idriss and George Tibbles, music and lyrics

SCORING OF A DRAMATIC OR COMEDY PICTURE
Brian Easdale, The Red Shoes
Hugo Friedhofer, *Joan of Arc*
Alfred Newman, *The Snake Pit*
Max Steiner, *Johnny Belinda*
William Walton, *Hamlet*

SCORING OF A MUSICAL PICTURE
Johnny Green and Roger Edens, Easter Parade
Lennie Hayton, *The Pirate*
Ray Heindorf, *Romance on the High Seas*
Alfred Newman, *When My Baby Smiles at Me*
Victor Young, *The Emperor Waltz*

FILM EDITING
Reginald Mills, *The Red Shoes*
Christian Nyby, *Red River*
Frank Sullivan, *Joan of Arc*
Paul Weatherwax, The Naked City
David Weisbart, *Johnny Belinda*

COSTUME DESIGN
BLACK-AND-WHITE
Roger K. Furse, Hamlet
Irene, *B.F.'s Daughter*

COLOR
Edith Head and Gile Steele, *The Emperor Waltz*
Dorothy Jeakins and Karinska, Joan of Arc

SPECIAL EFFECTS
**Paul Eagler, J. McMillan Johnson, Russell Shearman and
Clarence Slifer, visual; Charles Freeman and James G.
Stewart, audible, Portrait of Jennie**
Ralph Hammeras, Fred Sersen and Edward Snyder, visual;
Roger Heman, audible, *Deep Waters*

SHORT SUBJECTS
CARTOON
***The Little Orphan** (Tom and Jerry Series) (Frederick Quimby,
producer; MGM)*
Mickey and the Seal (Mickey Mouse Series) (Walt Disney
Productions; RKO Radio)
Mouse Wreckers (Merrie Melodies Series) (Edward Selzer,
producer; Warner Bros.)
Robin Hoodlum (Fox and Crow Series) (United Productions of
America; Columbia)
Tea for Two Hundred (Donald Duck Series) (Walt Disney
Productions; RKO Radio)

ONE-REEL
Annie Was a Wonder (John Nesbitt Passing Parade Series)
(Herbert Moulton, producer; MGM)
Cinderella Horse (Sports Parade Series) (Gordon Hollingshead,
producer; Warner Bros.)
So You Want to Be on the Radio (Joe McDoakes Series)
(Gordon Hollingshead, producer; Warner Bros.)
***Symphony of a City** (Movietone Specialty Series) (Edmund H.
Reek, producer; Twentieth Century-Fox)*
You Can't Win (Pete Smith Specialty Series) (Pete Smith, pro-
ducer; MGM)

TWO-REEL
Calgary Stampede (Technicolor Special Series) (Gordon
Hollingshead, producer; Warner Bros.)
Going to Blazes (Herbert Morgan, producer; MGM)
Samba-Mania (Musical Parade Featurette Series) (Harry Grey,
producer; Paramount)
***Seal Island** (True Life Adventure Series) (Walt Disney
Productions; RKO Radio)*
Snow Capers (Thomas Mead, producer; Universal-
International)

DOCUMENTARY
SHORT SUBJECT
Heart to Heart (Herbert Morgan, producer; Fact Film
Organization)
Operation Vittles (U.S. Army Air Force)
***Toward Independence** (U.S. Army)*

FEATURE
The Quiet One (Film Documents; Mayer-Burstyn)
***The Secret Land** (U.S. Navy; MGM)*

All the King's Men

IRVING G. THALBERG MEMORIAL AWARD
Jerry Wald

SPECIAL AWARDS
To **Monsieur Vincent** (France), voted by the Academy Board of Governors as the most outstanding foreign language film released in the United States during 1948

To **Ivan Jandl** for the outstanding juvenile performance of 1948 in *The Search*

To **Sid Grauman,** master showman, who raised the standard of exhibition of motion pictures

To **Adolph Zukor,** a man who has been called the father of the feature film in America, for his services to the industry over a period of forty years

To **Walter Wanger** for distinguished service to the industry in adding to its moral stature in the world community by his production of the picture *Joan of Arc*

1949

BEST MOTION PICTURE
All the King's Men (Robert Rossen Productions; Columbia)
Battleground (MGM)
The Heiress (Paramount)
A Letter to Three Wives (Twentieth Century-Fox)
Twelve O'Clock High (Twentieth Century-Fox)

BEST ACTOR
Broderick Crawford, All the King's Men
Kirk Douglas, *Champion*
Gregory Peck, *Twelve O'Clock High*
Richard Todd, *The Hasty Heart*
John Wayne, *Sands of Iwo Jima*

BEST ACTRESS
Jeanne Crain, *Pinky*
Olivia de Havilland, The Heiress

Susan Hayward, *My Foolish Heart*
Deborah Kerr, *Edward, My Son*
Loretta Young, *Come to the Stable*

ACTOR IN A SUPPORTING ROLE
John Ireland, *All the King's Men*
Dean Jagger, Twelve O'Clock High
Arthur Kennedy, *Champion*
Ralph Richardson, *The Heiress*
James Whitmore, *Battleground*

ACTRESS IN A SUPPORTING ROLE
Ethel Barrymore, *Pinky*
Celeste Holm, *Come to the Stable*
Elsa Lanchester, *Come to the Stable*
Mercedes McCambridge, All the King's Men
Ethel Waters, *Pinky*

DIRECTING
Joseph L. Mankiewicz, A Letter to Three Wives
Carol Reed, *The Fallen Idol*
Robert Rossen, *All the King's Men*
William A. Wellman, *Battleground*
William Wyler, *The Heiress*

WRITING
MOTION PICTURE STORY
Harry Brown, *Sands of Iwo Jima*
Virginia Kellogg, *White Heat*
Clare Boothe Luce, *Come to the Stable*
Douglas Morrow, The Stratton Story
Shirley W. Smith and Valentine Davies, *It Happens Every Spring*

SCREENPLAY
Carl Foreman, *Champion*
Graham Greene, *The Fallen Idol*
Joseph L. Mankiewicz, A Letter to Three Wives
Robert Rossen, *All the King's Men*
Cesare Zavattini, *The Bicycle Thief*

STORY AND SCREENPLAY
Sidney Buchman, *Jolson Sings Again*
T. E. B. Clarke, *Passport to Pimlico*
Alfred Hayes, Federico Fellini, Sergio Amidei, Marcello Pagliero and Roberto Rossellini, *Paisan*
Helen Levitt, Janice Loeb and Sidney Meyers, *The Quiet One*
Robert Pirosh, Battleground

CINEMATOGRAPHY
BLACK-AND-WHITE
Joseph LaShelle, *Come to the Stable*
Frank Planer, *Champion*
Leon Shamroy, *Prince of Foxes*
Leo Tover, *The Heiress*
Paul C. Vogel, Battleground
COLOR
Charles G. Clarke, *Sand*
Winton Hoch, She Wore a Yellow Ribbon

Robert Planck and Charles Schoenbaum, *Little Women*

William Snyder, *Jolson Sings Again*

Harry Stradling, *The Barkleys of Broadway*

ART DIRECTION
BLACK-AND-WHITE

Cedric Gibbons and Jack Martin Smith, art direction; Edwin B. Willis and Richard A. Pefferle, set decoration, *Madame Bovary*

John Meehan and Harry Horner, art direction; Emile Kuri, set decoration, *The Heiress*

Lyle Wheeler and Joseph C. Wright, art direction; Thomas Little and Paul S. Fox, set decoration, *Come to the Stable*

COLOR

Edward Carrere, art direction; Lyle Reifsnider, set decoration, *The Adventures of Don Juan*

Cedric Gibbons and Paul Groesse; Edwin B. Willis and Jack D. Moore, *Little Women*

Jim Morahan, William Kellner and Michael Relph, art direction, *Saraband*

SOUND RECORDING

Republic Studio Sound Department, *Sands of Iwo Jima*

Twentieth Century-Fox Studio Sound Department, *Twelve O'Clock High*

Universal-International Studio Sound Department, *Once More, My Darling*

MUSIC
SONG

"Baby, It's Cold Outside," *Neptune's Daughter*, Frank Loesser, music and lyrics

"It's a Great Feeling," *It's a Great Feeling*, Jule Styne, music; Sammy Cahn, lyrics

"Lavender Blue," *So Dear to My Heart*, Eliot Daniel, music; Larry Morey, lyrics

"My Foolish Heart," *My Foolish Heart*, Victor Young, music; Ned Washington, lyrics

"Through a Long and Sleepless Night," *Come to the Stable*, Alfred Newman, music; Mack Gordon, lyrics

SCORING OF A COMEDY OR DRAMATIC PICTURE

Aaron Copland, *The Heiress*

Max Steiner, *Beyond the Forest*

Dimitri Tiomkin, *Champion*

SCORING OF A MUSICAL PICTURE

Roger Edens and Lennie Hayton, *On the Town*

Ray Heindorf, *Look for the Silver Lining*

Morris Stoloff and George Duning, *Jolson Sings Again*

FILM EDITING

John Dunning, *Battleground*

Harry Gerstad, *Champion*

Frederic Knudtson, *The Window*

Robert Parrish and Al Clark, *All the King's Men*

Richard L. Van Enger, *Sands of Iwo Jima*

COSTUME DESIGN
BLACK-AND-WHITE

Edith Head and Gile Steele, *The Heiress*

Vittorio Nino Novarese, *Prince of Foxes*

COLOR

Kay Nelson, *Mother Is a Freshman*

Leah Rhodes, Travilla and Marjorie Best, *The Adventures of Don Juan*

SPECIAL EFFECTS

***Mighty Joe Young* (Arko Production; RKO Radio)**

Tulsa (Walter Wagner; Eagle Lion)

SHORT SUBJECTS
CARTOON

Canary Row (*Merrie Melodies Series*) (Warner Bros. Cartoons, Inc.; Warner Bros.) (Nomination withdrawn by producer.)

***For Scent-imental Reasons* (*Merrie Melodies Series*) (Warner Bros. Cartoons, Inc.; Warner Bros.)**

Hatch Up Your Troubles (*Tom and Jerry Series*) (Frederick Quimby, producer; MGM)

The Magic Fluke (*Fox and Crow Series*) (United Productions of America; Columbia)

Toy Tinkers (*Donald Duck Series*) (Walt Disney Productions; RKO Radio)

ONE-REEL

***Aquatic House-Party* (*Grantland Rice Sportlights Series*) (Jack Eaton, producer; Paramount)**

Roller Derby Girl (*Pacemaker Series*) (Justin Herman, producer; Paramount)

So You Think You're Not Guilty (*John McDoakes Series*) (Gordon Hollingshead, producer; Warner Bros.)

Spills and Chills (*Sports News Review Series*) (Walton C. Ament, producer; Warner Bros.)

Water Trix (*Pete Smith Specialties Series*) (Pete Smith, producer; MGM)

TWO-REEL

The Boy and the Eagle (William Lasky, producer; RKO Radio)

Chase of Death (Irving Allen Productions)

The Grass Is Always Greener (Gordon Hollingshead, producer; Warner Bros.)

Snow Carnival (*Two-reel Technicolor Series*) (Gordon Hollingshead, producer; Warner Bros.)

***Van Gogh* (Gaston Diehl and Robert Haeessens, producers; Canton-Weiner Films)**

DOCUMENTARY
SHORT SUBJECT (TIE)

***A Chance to Live* (*March of Time Series*) (Richard de Rochemont, producer; Twentieth Century-Fox)**

1848 (A. F. Films; French Cinema General Cooperative)

The Rising Tide (National Film Board of Canada; St. Francis-Xavier University)

***So Much for So Little* (Warner Bros. Cartoons, Inc.; Warner Bros.)**

FEATURE

***Daybreak in Udi* (British Information Services; Crown Film Unit)**

Kenji Comes Home (Paul F. Heard, producer; Protestant Film Commission)

SPECIAL AWARDS

To ***The Bicycle Thief***, voted by the Academy Board of Governors as the most outstanding foreign language film released in the United States during 1949

To **Bobby Driscoll,** outstanding juvenile actor of 1949

To **Fred Astaire** for his unique artistry and his contributions to the technique of musical pictures

To **Cecil B. DeMille,** distinguished motion picture pioneer, for 37 years of brilliant showmanship

To **Jean Hersholt** for distinguished service to the motion-picture industry

1950

BEST MOTION PICTURE

All About Eve (Twentieth Century-Fox)
Born Yesterday (Columbia)
Father of the Bride (MGM)
King Solomon's Mines (MGM)
Sunset Boulevard (Paramount)

BEST ACTOR

Louis Calhern, *The Magnificent Yankee*
José Ferrer, *Cyrano de Bergerac*
William Holden, *Sunset Boulevard*
James Stewart, *Harvey*
Spencer Tracy, *Father of the Bride*

BEST ACTRESS

Anne Baxter, *All About Eve*
Bette Davis, *All About Eve*
Judy Holliday, *Born Yesterday*
Eleanor Parker, *Caged*
Gloria Swanson, *Sunset Boulevard*

ACTOR IN A SUPPORTING ROLE

Jeff Chandler, *Broken Arrow*
Edmund Gwenn, *Mister 880*
Sam Jaffe, *The Asphalt Jungle*
George Sanders, *All About Eve*
Erich von Stroheim, *Sunset Boulevard*

ACTRESS IN A SUPPORTING ROLE

Hope Emerson, *Caged*
Celeste Holm, *All About Eve*
Josephine Hull, *Harvey*
Nancy Olson, *Sunset Boulevard*
Thelma Ritter, *All About Eve*

DIRECTING

George Cukor, *Born Yesterday*
John Huston, *The Asphalt Jungle*
Joseph L. Mankiewicz, *All About Eve*
Carol Reed, *The Third Man*
Billy Wilder, *Sunset Boulevard*

WRITING

MOTION PICTURE STORY

Edna Anhalt and Edward Anhalt, *Panic in the Streets*
William Bowers and Andre de Toth, *The Gunfighter*

All About Eve

Giuseppe De Santis and Carlo Lizzani, *Bitter Rice*
Sy Gomberg, *When Willie Comes Marching Home*
Leonard Spigelgass, *Mystery Street*

SCREENPLAY

Michael Blankfort, *Broken Arrow*
Frances Goodrich and Albert Hackett, *Father of the Bride*
Ben Maddow and John Huston, *The Asphalt Jungle*
Joseph L. Mankiewicz, *All About Eve*
Albert Mannheimer, *Born Yesterday*

STORY AND SCREENPLAY

**Charles Brackett, Billy Wilder and D. M. Marshman, Jr.,
    *Sunset Boulevard***
Carl Foreman, *The Men*
Ruth Gordon and Garson Kanin, *Adam's Rib*
Virginia Kellogg and Bernard C. Schoenfeld, *Caged*
Joseph L. Mankiewicz and Lesser Samuels, *No Way Out*

CINEMATOGRAPHY

BLACK-AND-WHITE

Robert Krasker, *The Third Man*
Milton Krasner, *All About Eve*
Victor Milner, *The Furies*
Harold Rosson, *The Asphalt Jungle*
John F. Seitz, *Sunset Boulevard*

COLOR

George Barnes, *Samson and Delilah*
Ernest Haller, *The Flame and the Arrow*
Ernest Palmer, *Broken Arrow*
Charles Rosher, *Annie Get Your Gun*
Robert Surtees, *King Solomon's Mines*

ART DIRECTION

BLACK-AND-WHITE

**Hans Dreier and John Meehan, art direction; Sam Comer and
    Ray Moyer, set decoration, *Sunset Boulevard***
Cedric Gibbons and Hans Peters, art direction; Edwin B. Willis
    and Hugh Hunt, set decoration, *The Red Danube*

Lyle Wheeler and George Davis, art direction; Thomas Little and Walter M. Scott, set decoration, *All About Eve*

COLOR

Hans Dreier and Walter Tyler, art direction; Sam Comer and Ray Moyer, set decoration, *Samson and Delilah*

Ernst Fegte, art direction; George Sawley, set decoration, *Destination Moon*

Cedric Gibbons and Paul Groesse, art direction; Edwin B. Willis and Richard A. Pefferle, set decoration, *Annie Get Your Gun*

SOUND RECORDING

Pinewood Studio Sound Dept., *Trio*

Samuel Goldwyn Studio Sound Dept., *Our Very Own*

Twentieth Century-Fox Studio Sound Department, *All About Eve*

Universal-International Studio Sound Dept., *Louisa*

Walt Disney Studio Sound Dept., *Cinderella*

MUSIC
SONG

"Be My Love," *The Toast of New Orleans*, Nicholas Brodszky, music; Sammy Cahn, lyrics

"Bibbidi-Bobbidi-Boo," *Cinderella*, Mack David, Al Hoffman and Jerry Livingston, music and lyrics

"Mona Lisa," *Captain Carey*, Ray Evans and Jay Livingston, music and lyrics

"Mule Train," *Singing Guns*, Fred Glickman, Hy Heath and Johnny Lange, music and lyrics

"Wilhelmina," *Wabash Avenue*, Josef Myrow, music; Mack Gordon, lyrics

SCORING OF A DRAMATIC OR COMEDY PICTURE

George Duning, *No Sad Songs for Me*

Alfred Newman, *All About Eve*

Max Steiner, *The Flame and the Arrow*

Franz Waxman, *Sunset Boulevard*

Victor Young, *Samson and Delilah*

SCORING OF A MUSICAL PICTURE

Adolph Deutsch and Roger Edens, *Annie Get Your Gun*

Ray Heindorf, *The West Point Story*

Lionel Newman, *I'll Get By*

André Previn, *Three Little Words*

Oliver Wallace and Paul J. Smith, *Cinderella*

FILM EDITING

Oswald Hafenrichter, *The Third Man*

Barbara McLean, *All About Eve*

James E. Newcom, *Annie Get Your Gun*

Arthur Schmidt and Doane Harrison, *Sunset Boulevard*

Ralph E. Winters and Conrad A. Nervig, *King Solomon's Mines*

COSTUME DESIGN
BLACK-AND-WHITE

Edith Head and Charles LeMaire, *All About Eve*

Jean Louis, *Born Yesterday*

Walter Plunkett, *The Magnificent Yankee*

COLOR

Edith Head, Dorothy Jeakins, Elois Jenssen, Gile Steele and Gwen Wakeling, *Samson and Delilah*

Walter Plunkett and Valles, *That Forsyte Woman*

Michael Whittaker, *The Black Rose*

SPECIAL EFFECTS

***Destination Moon* (George Pal Productions; Eagle Lion Classics)**

Samson and Delilah (Cecil B. DeMille Productions; Paramount)

SHORT SUBJECTS
CARTOON

***Gerald McBoing-Boing* (*Jolly Frolics Series*) (United Productions of America; Columbia)**

Jerry's Cousin (*Tom and Jerry Series*) (Frederick Quimby, producer; MGM)

Trouble Indemnity (*Mr. Magoo Series*) (United Productions of America; Columbia)

ONE-REEL

Blaze Busters (*Vitaphone Novelties Series*) (Robert Youngson, producer; Warner Bros.)

***Grandad of Races* (*Sports Parade Series*) (Gordon Hollingshead, producer; Warner Bros.)**

Wrong Way Butch (*Pete Smith Specialty Series*) (Pete Smith, producer; MGM)

TWO-REEL

Grandma Moses (Falcon Films, Inc.; A.F. Films)

***In Beaver Valley* (*True-Life Adventure Series*) (Walt Disney Productions; RKO Radio)**

My Country 'Tis of Thee (*Featurette Series*) (Gordon Hollingshead, producer; Warner Bros.)

DOCUMENTARY
SHORT SUBJECT

The Fight: Science Against Cancer (Medical Film Institute of the Association of American Medical Colleges; National Film Board of Canada)

The Stairs (Film Documents, Inc.)

***Why Korea?* (Twentieth Century-Fox Movietone; Twentieth Century-Fox)**

FEATURE

***The Titan: Story of Michelangelo* (Michelangelo Co.; Classics Pictures, Inc.)**

With These Hands (Jack Arnold and Lee Goodman, producers; Promotional Films Co., Inc.)

IRVING G. THALBERG MEMORIAL AWARD

Darryl F. Zanuck

HONORARY AWARDS

To **George Murphy** for his services in interpreting the film industry to the country at large

To **Louis B. Mayer** for distinguished service to the motion picture industry

To *The Walls of Malapaga* (France/Italy) voted by the Board of Governors as the most outstanding foreign language film released in the United States in 1950

1951

BEST MOTION PICTURE

***An American in Paris*, Arthur Freed, producer (MGM)**

Decision Before Dawn, Anatole Litvak and Frank McCarthy, producers (Twentieth Century-Fox)

A Place in the Sun, George Stevens, producer (Paramount)

Quo Vadis, Sam Zimbalist, producer (MGM)

A Streetcar Named Desire, Charles K. Feldman, producer (Warner Bros.)

BEST ACTOR

Humphrey Bogart, *The African Queen*

Marlon Brando, A Streetcar Named Desire

Montgomery Clift, A Place in the Sun

Arthur Kennedy, Bright Victory

Fredric March, Death of a Salesman

BEST ACTRESS

Katharine Hepburn, The African Queen

Vivien Leigh, *A Streetcar Named Desire*

Eleanor Parker, Detective Story

Shelley Winters, A Place in the Sun

Jane Wyman, The Blue Veil

ACTOR IN A SUPPORTING ROLE

Leo Genn, Quo Vadis

Karl Malden, *A Streetcar Named Desire*

Kevin McCarthy, Death of a Salesman

Peter Ustinov, Quo Vadis

Gig Young, Come Fill the Cup

ACTRESS IN A SUPPORTING ROLE

Joan Blondell, The Blue Veil

Mildred Dunnock, Death of a Salesman

Lee Grant, Detective Story

Kim Hunter, *A Streetcar Named Desire*

Thelma Ritter, The Mating Season

DIRECTING

John Huston, The African Queen

Elia Kazan, A Streetcar Named Desire

Vincente Minnelli, An American in Paris

Humphrey Bogart, *The African Queen*

George Stevens, *A Place in the Sun*

William Wyler, Detective Story

WRITING

MOTION PICTURE STORY

Budd Boetticher and Ray Nazarro, Bullfighter and the Lady

Paul Dehn and James Bernard, *Seven Days to Noon*

Alfred Hayes and Stewart Stern, Teresa

Oscar Millard, The Frogmen

Robert Riskin and Liam O'Brian, Here Comes the Groom

SCREENPLAY

James Agee and John Huston, The African Queen

Jacques Natanson and Max Ophuls, La Ronde

Tennessee Williams, A Streetcar Named Desire

Michael Wilson and Harry Brown, *A Place in the Sun*

Philip Yordan and Robert Wyler, Detective Story

STORY AND SCREENPLAY

Philip Dunne, David and Bathsheba

Clarence Greene and Russell Rouse, The Well

Alan Jay Lerner, *An American in Paris*

Robert Pirosh, Go for Broke!

Billy Wilder, Lesser Samuels and Walter Newman, The Big Carnival

CINEMATOGRAPHY

BLACK-AND-WHITE

Norbert Brodine, The Frogmen

Robert Burks, Strangers on a Train

William C. Mellor, *A Place in the Sun*

Frank Planer, Death of a Salesman

Harry Stradling, A Streetcar Named Desire

COLOR

Alfred Gilks and John Alton, *An American in Paris*

Charles Rosher, Show Boat

John F. Seitz and W. Howard Greene, When Worlds Collide

Leon Shamroy, David and Bathsheba

Robert Surtees and William V. Skall, Quo Vadis

ART DIRECTION

BLACK-AND-WHITE

Richard Day, art direction; George James Hopkins, set decoration, *A Streetcar Named Desire*

D'Eaubonne, art direction and set decoration, La Ronde

Cedric Gibbons and Paul Groesse, art direction; Edwin B. Willis and Jack D. Moore, set decoration, Too Young to Kiss

Lyle Wheeler and John DeCuir, art direction; Thomas Little and Paul S. Fox, set decoration, House on Telegraph Hill

Lyle Wheeler and Leland Fuller, art direction; Thomas Little and Fred J. Rode, set decoration, Fourteen Hours

COLOR

Cedric Gibbons and Preston Ames, art direction; Edwin B. Willis and Keogh Gleason, set decoration, *An American in Paris*

Hein Heckroth, art direction and set decoration, Tales of Hoffmann

William A. Horning, Cedric Gibbons and Edward Carfagno, art direction; Hugh Hunt, set decoration, Quo Vadis

Lyle Wheeler and George Davis, art direction; Thomas Little and Paul S. Fox, set decoration, *David and Bathsheba*

Lyle Wheeler and Leland Fuller, art direction; Joseph C. Wright, musical settings; Thomas Little and Walter M. Scott, set decoration, *On the Riviera*

SOUND RECORDING

MGM Studio Sound Dept., *The Great Caruso*

RKO Radio Studio Sound Dept., *Two Tickets to Broadway*

Samuel Goldwyn Studio Sound Dept., *I Want You*

Universal-International Studio Sound Dept., *Bright Victory*

Warner Bros. Studio Sound Dept., *A Streetcar Named Desire*

MUSIC

SONG

"In the Cool, Cool, Cool of the Evening," *Here Comes the Groom*, Hoagy Carmichael, music; Johnny Mercer, lyrics

"A Kiss to Build a Dream On," *The Strip*, Bert Kalmar, Harry Ruby and Oscar Hammerstein II, music and lyrics

"Never," *Golden Girl*, Lionel Newman, music; Eliot Daniel, lyrics

"Too Late Now," *Royal Wedding*, Burton Lane, music; Alan Jay Lerner, lyrics

"Wonder Why," *Rich, Young and Pretty*, Nicholas Brodszky, music; Sammy Cahn, lyrics

SCORING OF A DRAMATIC OR COMEDY PICTURE

Alfred Newman, *David and Bathsheba*

Alex North, *Death of a Salesman*

Alex North, *A Streetcar Named Desire*

Miklos Rozsa, *Quo Vadis*

Franz Waxman, *A Place in the Sun*

SCORING OF A MUSICAL PICTURE

Peter Herman Adler and Johnny Green, *The Great Caruso*

Adolph Deutsch and Conrad Salinger, *Show Boat*

Johnny Green and Saul Chaplin, *An American in Paris*

Alfred Newman, *On the Riviera*

Oliver Wallace, *Alice in Wonderland*

FILM EDITING

Adrienne Fazan, *An American in Paris*

William Hornbeck, *A Place in the Sun*

Chester Schaeffer, *The Well*

Dorothy Spencer, *Decision Before Dawn*

Ralph E. Winters, *Quo Vadis*

COSTUME DESIGN

BLACK-AND-WHITE

Lucinda Ballard, *A Streetcar Named Desire*

Edith Head, *A Place in the Sun*

Charles LeMaire and Renie, *The Model and the Marriage Broker*

Walter Plunkett and Gile Steele, *Kind Lady*

Edward Stevenson and Margaret Furse, *The Mudlark*

COLOR

Hein Heckroth, *Tales of Hoffmann*

Charles LeMaire and Edward Stevenson, *David and Bathsheba*

Herschel McCoy, *Quo Vadis*

Orry-Kelly, Walter Plunkett and Irene Sharaff, *An American in Paris*

Helen Rose and Gile Steele, *The Great Caruso*

SPECIAL EFFECTS

***When Worlds Collide* (Paramount)**

SHORT SUBJECTS

CARTOON

Lambert, the Sheepish Lion (Walt Disney Productions; RKO Radio)

Rooty Toot Toot (*Jolly Frolics Series*) (United Productions of America; Columbia)

***Two Mouseketeers* (*Tom and Jerry Series*) (Frederick Quimby, producer; MGM)**

ONE-REEL

Ridin' the Rails (*Grantland Rice Spotlight Series*) (Jack Eaton, producer; Paramount)

The Story of Time (Signal Films Production; Cornell Film Company)

***World of Kids* (*Vitaphone Novelties Series*) (Robert Youngson, producer; Warner Bros.)**

TWO-REEL

Balzac (Les Films du Compass; A.F. Films, Inc.)

Danger Under the Sea (Tom Mead, producer; Universal-International)

***Nature's Half Acre* (*True-Life Adventure Series*) (Walt Disney Productions; RKO Radio)**

DOCUMENTARY

SHORT SUBJECT

***Benjy* (Fred Zinnemann, producer; Paramount)**

One Who Came Back (U.S. Department of Defense; Association of Motion Picture Producers)

The Seeing Eye (Gordon Hollingshead, producer; Warner Bros.)

FEATURE

I Was a Communist for the F.B.I. (Bryan Foy, producer; Warner Bros.)

***Kon-Tiki* (Artfilm Production; RKO Radio)**

IRVING G. THALBERG MEMORIAL AWARD

Arthur Freed

HONORARY AWARDS

To **Gene Kelly** in appreciation of his versatility as an actor, singer, director and dancer, and specifically for his brilliant achievements in the art of choreography on film

To ***Rashomon*** (Japan) voted by the Board of Governors as the most outstanding foreign language film released in the United States during 1951

1952

BEST MOTION PICTURE

***The Greatest Show on Earth*, Cecil B. DeMille, producer (Paramount)**

High Noon, Stanley Kramer, producer (United Artists)

Ivanhoe, Pandro S. Berman, producer (MGM)

The Greatest Show on Earth

Moulin Rouge, John Huston, producer (United Artists)

The Quiet Man, John Ford and Merian C. Cooper, producers (Republic)

BEST ACTOR
Marlon Brando, *Viva Zapata!*

Gary Cooper, *High Noon*

Kirk Douglas, *The Bad and the Beautiful*

José Ferrer, *Moulin Rouge*

Alec Guinness, *The Lavender Hill Mob*

BEST ACTRESS
Shirley Booth, *Come Back, Little Sheba*

Joan Crawford, *Sudden Fear*

Bette Davis, *The Star*

Julie Harris, *The Member of the Wedding*

Susan Hayward, *With a Song in My Heart*

ACTOR IN A SUPPORTING ROLE
Richard Burton, *My Cousin Rachel*

Arthur Hunnicutt, *The Big Sky*

Victor McLaglen, *The Quiet Man*

Jack Palance, *Sudden Fear*

Anthony Quinn, *Viva Zapata!*

ACTRESS IN A SUPPORTING ROLE
Gloria Grahame, *The Bad and the Beautiful*

Jean Hagen, *Singin' in the Rain*

Colette Marchand, *Moulin Rouge*

Terry Moore, *Come Back, Little Sheba*

Thelma Ritter, *With a Song in My Heart*

DIRECTING
Cecil B. DeMille, *The Greatest Show on Earth*

John Ford, *The Quiet Man*

John Huston, *Moulin Rouge*

Joseph L. Mankiewicz, *Five Fingers*

Fred Zinnemann, *High Noon*

WRITING
MOTION PICTURE STORY
Edna Anhalt and Edward Anhalt, *The Sniper*

Frederic M. Frank, Theodore St. John and Frank Cavett, *The Greatest Show on Earth*

Martin Goldsmith and Jack Leonard, *The Narrow Margin*

Leo McCarey, *My Son John*

Guy Trosper, *The Pride of St. Louis*

SCREENPLAY
Carl Foreman, *High Noon*

Roger MacDougall, John Dighton and Alexander Mackendrick, *The Man in the White Suit*

Frank S. Nugent, *The Quiet Man*

Charles Schnee, *The Bad and the Beautiful*

Michael Wilson, *Five Fingers*

STORY AND SCREENPLAY
Sydney Boehm, *The Atomic City*

T. E. B. Clarke, *The Lavender Hill Mob*

Ruth Gordon and Garson Kanin, *Pat and Mike*

Terence Rattigan, *Breaking the Sound Barrier*

John Steinbeck, *Viva Zapata!*

CINEMATOGRAPHY
BLACK-AND-WHITE
Russell Harlan, *The Big Sky*

Charles B. Lang, Jr., *Sudden Fear*

Joseph LaShelle, *My Cousin Rachel*

Virgil E. Miller, *Navajo*

Robert Surtees, *The Bad and the Beautiful*

COLOR
George J. Folsey, *Million Dollar Mermaid*

Winton C. Hoch and Archie Stout, *The Quiet Man*

Leon Shamroy, *The Snows of Kilimanjaro*

Harry Stradling, *Hans Christian Andersen*

F. A. Young, *Ivanhoe*

ART DIRECTION
BLACK-AND-WHITE
Cedric Gibbons and Edward Carfagno, art direction; Edwin B. Willis and Keogh Gleason, set decoration, *The Bad and the Beautiful*

Matsuyama, art direction; H. Motsumoto, set decoration, *Rashomon*

Hal Pereira and Roland Anderson, art direction; Emile Kuri, set decoration, *Carrie*

Lyle Wheeler and John DeCuir, art direction; Walter M. Scott, set decoration, *My Cousin Rachel*

Lyle Wheeler and Leland Fuller, art direction; Thomas Little and Claude Carpenter, set decoration, *Viva Zapata!*

COLOR
Richard Day and Clave, art direction; Howard Bristol, set decoration, *Hans Christian Andersen*

Cedric Gibbons and Paul Groesse, art direction; Edwin B. Willis and Arthur Krams, set decoration, *The Merry Widow*

Frank Hotaling, art direction; John McCarthy, Jr. and Charles Thompson, set decoration, *The Quiet Man*

Paul Sheriff, art direction; Marcel Vertes, set decoration, *Moulin Rouge*

Lyle Wheeler and John DeCuir, art direction; Thomas Little and Paul S. Fox, set decoration, *The Snows of Kilimanjaro*

SOUND RECORDING

London Film Sound Dept., *Breaking the Sound Barrier*

Pinewood Studios Sound Dept., *The Promoter*

Republic Studio Sound Dept.; Daniel J. Bloomberg, *The Quiet Man*

Samuel Goldwyn Studio Sound Dept., *Hans Christian Andersen*

Twentieth Century-Fox Studio Sound Dept., Thomas T. Moulton, *With a Song in My Heart*

MUSIC
SONG

"Am I in Love," *Son of Paleface*, Jack Brooks, music

"Because You're Mine," *Because You're Mine*, Nicholas Brodszky, music; Sammy Cahn, lyrics

"High Noon" (Do Not Forsake Me, Oh My Darlin'), *High Noon*, Dimitri Tiomkin, music; Ned Washington, lyrics

"Thumbelina," *Hans Christian Andersen*, Frank Loesser, music and lyrics

"Zing a Little Zong," *Just for You*, Harry Warren, music; Leo Robin, lyrics

SCORING OF A DRAMATIC OR COMEDY PICTURE

Herschel Burke Gilbert, *The Thief*

Alex North, *Viva Zapata!*

Miklos Rozsa, *Ivanhoe*

Max Steiner, *The Miracle of Our Lady of Fatima*

Dimitri Tiomkin, *High Noon*

SCORING OF A MUSICAL PICTURE

Lennie Hayton, *Singin' in the Rain*

Ray Heindorf and Max Steiner, *The Jazz Singer*

Gian-Carlo Menotti, *The Medium*

Alfred Newman, *With a Song in My Heart*

Walter Scharf, *Hans Christian Andersen*

FILM EDITING

William Austin, *Flat Top*

Anne Bauchens, *The Greatest Show on Earth*

Ralph Kemplen, *Moulin Rouge*

Warren Low, *Come Back, Little Sheba*

Elmo Williams and Harry Gerstad, *High Noon*

COSTUME DESIGN
BLACK-AND-WHITE

Edith Head, *Carrie*

Charles LeMaire and Dorothy Jeakins, *My Cousin Rachel*

Jean Louis, *Affair in Trinidad*

Sheila O'Brien, *Sudden Fear*

Helen Rose, *The Bad and the Beautiful*

COLOR

Clave, Mary Wills and Madame Karinska, *Hans Christian Andersen*

Edith Head, Dorothy Jeakins and Miles White, *The Greatest Show on Earth*

Charles LeMaire, *With a Song in My Heart*

Helen Rose and Gile Steele, *The Merry Widow*

Marcel Vertes, *Moulin Rouge*

SPECIAL EFFECTS
Plymouth Adventure (MGM)

SHORT SUBJECTS
CARTOON

***Johann Mouse* (*Tom and Jerry Series*) (Frederick Quimby, producer; MGM)**

Little Johnny Jet (*MGM Series*) (Frederick Quimby, producer; MGM)

Madeline (*Jolly Frolics Series*) (United Productions of America; Columbia)

Pink and Blue Blues (*Mister Magoo Series*) (United Productions of America; Columbia)

Romance of Transportation (Tom Daly, producer; National Film Board of Canada)

ONE-REEL

Athletes of the Saddle (*Grantland Rice Sportlights Series*) (Jack Eaton, producer; Paramount)

Desert Killer (*Sports Parade Series*) (Gordon Hollingshead, producer; Warner Bros.)

***Light in the Window* (*Art Film Series*) (Art Film Productions; Twentieth Century-Fox)**

Neighbours (National Film Board of Canada; Arthur Mayer-Edward Kingsley, Inc.)

Royal Scotland (Crown Film Unit; British Information Services)

TWO-REEL

Bridge of Time (London Films; British Information Services)

Devil Take Us (*Theatre of Life Series*) (Herbert Morgan, producer; Theatre of Life Production)

Thar She Blows! (*Technicolor Special Series*) (Gordon Hollingshead, producer; Warner Bros.)

***Water Birds* (*True-Life Adventure Series*) (Walt Disney Productions; RKO Radio)**

DOCUMENTARY
SHORT SUBJECT

Devil Take Us (Herbert Morgan, producer; Theatre of Life Production)

The Garden Spider (Epeira Diadema) (Cristallo Films; I.F.E. Releasing Corp.)

Man Alive! (United Productions of America; American Cancer Society)

***Neighbours* (National Film Board of Canada; Arthur Mayer-Edward Kingsley, Inc.)**

FEATURE

The Hoaxters (Dore Schary, producer; MGM)

Navajo (Bartlett-Foster Productions; Lippert Pictures, Inc.)

***The Sea Around Us* (Irwin Allen, producer; RKO Radio)**

IRVING G. THALBERG MEMORIAL AWARD
Cecil B. DeMille

HONORARY AWARDS

To George **Alfred Mitchell** for the design and development of the camera which bears his name and for his continued and dominant presence in the field of cinematography

To Joseph **M. Schenck** for long and distinguished service to the motion picture industry

REFERENCE

To **Merian C. Cooper** for his many innovations and contributions to the art of motion pictures

To **Harold Lloyd,** master comedian and good citizen

To **Bob Hope** for his contribution to the laughter of the world, his service to the motion picture industry and his devotion to the American premise

To ***Forbidden Games*** (French), best foreign language film first released in the United States during 1952

1953

BEST MOTION PICTURE
From Here to Eternity, Buddy Adler, producer (Columbia)
Julius Caesar, John Houseman, producer (MGM)
The Robe, Frank Ross, producer (Twentieth Century-Fox)
Roman Holiday, William Wyler, producer (Paramount)
Shane, George Stevens, producer (Paramount)

BEST ACTOR
Marlon Brando, *Julius Caesar*
Richard Burton, *The Robe*
Montgomery Clift, *From Here to Eternity*
William Holden, *Stalag 17*
Burt Lancaster, *From Here to Eternity*

BEST ACTRESS
Leslie Caron, *Lili*
Ava Gardner, *Mogambo*
Audrey Hepburn, *Roman Holiday*
Deborah Kerr, *From Here to Eternity*
Maggie McNamara, *The Moon Is Blue*

ACTOR IN A SUPPORTING ROLE
Eddie Albert, *Roman Holiday*
Brandon de Wilde, *Shane*
Jack Palance, *Shane*
Frank Sinatra, *From Here to Eternity*
Robert Strauss, *Stalag 17*

From Here to Eternity

ACTRESS IN A SUPPORTING ROLE
Grace Kelly, *Mogambo*
Geraldine Page, *Hondo*
Marjorie Rambeau, *Torch Song*
Donna Reed, *From Here to Eternity*
Thelma Ritter, *Pickup on South Street*

DIRECTING
George Stevens, *Shane*
Charles Walters, *Lili*
Billy Wilder, *Stalag 17*
William Wyler, *Roman Holiday*
Fred Zinnemann, *From Here to Eternity*

WRITING
MOTION PICTURE STORY
Ray Ashley, Morris Engel and Ruth Orkin, *Little Fugitive*
Alec Coppel, *The Captain's Paradise*
Beirne Lay, Jr., *Above and Beyond*
Dalton Trumbo, *Roman Holiday*

SCREENPLAY
Eric Ambler, *The Cruel Sea*
Helen Deutsch, *Lili*
A. B. Guthrie, Jr., *Shane*
Ian McLellan Hunter and John Dighton, *Roman Holiday*
Daniel Taradash, *From Here to Eternity*

STORY AND SCREENPLAY
Charles Brackett, Walter Reisch and Richard Breen, *Titanic*
Betty Comden and Adolph Green, *The Band Wagon*
Millard Kaufman, *Take the High Ground*
Richard Murphy, *The Desert Rats*
Sam Rolfe and Harold Jack Bloom, *The Naked Spur*

CINEMATOGRAPHY
BLACK-AND-WHITE
Joseph C. Brun, *Martin Luther*
Burnett Guffey, *From Here to Eternity*
Hal Mohr, *The Four Poster*
Frank Planer and Henry Alekan, *Roman Holiday*
Joseph Ruttenberg, *Julius Caesar*

COLOR
Edward Cronjager, *Beneath the 12-Mile Reef*
George Folsey, *All the Brothers Were Valiant*
Loyal Griggs, *Shane*
Robert Planck, *Lili*
Leon Shamroy, *The Robe*

ART DIRECTION
BLACK-AND-WHITE
Cedric Gibbons and Edward Carfagno, art direction; Edwin B. Willis and Hugh Hunt, set decoration, *Julius Caesar*
Fritz Maurischat and Paul Markwitz, art direction and set decoration, *Martin Luther*
Hal Pereira and Walter Tyler, art direction and set decoration, *Roman Holiday*
Lyle Wheeler and Leland Fuller, art direction; Paul S. Fox, set decoration, *The President's Lady*

Lyle Wheeler and Maurice Ransford, art direction; Stuart Reiss, set decoration, *Titanic*

COLOR

Cedric Gibbons, Preston Ames, Edward Carfagno and Gabriel Scognamillo, art direction; Edwin B. Willis, Keogh Gleason, Arthur Krams and Jack D. Moore, set decoration, *The Story of Three Loves*

Cedric Gibbons and Paul Groesse, art direction; Edwin B. Willis and Arthur Krams, set decoration, *Lili*

Cedric Gibbons and Urie McCleary, art direction; Edwin B. Willis and Jack D. Moore, set decoration, *Young Bess*

Alfred Junge and Hans Peters, art direction; John Jarvis, set decoration, *Knights of the Round Table*

Lyle Wheeler and George W. Davis, art direction; Walter M. Scott and Paul S. Fox, set decoration, *The Robe*

SOUND RECORDING

Columbia Studio Sound Dept., John P. Livadary, *From Here to Eternity*

MGM Studio Sound Dept., *Knights of the Round Table*

Paramount Studio Sound Dept., *The War of the Worlds*

Universal-International Studio Sound Dept., *The Mississippi Gambler*

Warner Bros. Studio Sound Dept., William A. Mueller, *Calamity Jane*

MUSIC
SONG

"The Moon Is Blue," *The Moon Is Blue*, Herschel Burke Gilbert, music; Sylvia Fine, lyrics

"My Flaming Heart," *Small Town Girl*, Nicholas Brodszky, music; Leo Robin, lyrics

"Sadie Thompson's Song" (Blue Pacific Blues), *Miss Sadie Thompson*, Lester Lee, music; Ned Washington, lyrics

"Secret Love," *Calamity Jane*, Sammy Fain, music; Paul Francis Webster, lyrics

"That's Amore," *The Caddy*, Harry Warren, music; Jack Brooks, lyrics

SCORING OF A DRAMATIC OR COMEDY PICTURE

Louis Forbes, *This Is Cinerama*

Hugo Friedhofer, *Above and Beyond*

Bronislau Kaper, *Lili*

Miklos Rozsa, *Julius Caesar*

Morris Stoloff and George Duning, *From Here to Eternity*

SCORING OF A MUSICAL PICTURE

Adolph Deutsch, *The Band Wagon*

Ray Heindorf, *Calamity Jane*

Frederick Hollander and Morris Stoloff, *The 5,000 Fingers of Dr. T.*

Alfred Newman, *Call Me Madam*

André Previn and Saul Chaplin, *Kiss Me Kate*

FILM EDITING

Everett Douglas, *The War of the Worlds*

Otto Ludwig, *The Moon Is Blue*

William Lyon, *From Here to Eternity*

Robert Swink, *Roman Holiday*

Irvine (Cotton) Warburton, *Crazylegs*

COSTUME DESIGN
BLACK-AND-WHITE

Edith Head, *Roman Holiday*

Charles LeMaire and Renie, *The President's Lady*

Jean Louis, *From Here to Eternity*

Walter Plunkett, *The Actress*

Helen Rose and Herschel McCoy, *Dream Wife*

COLOR

Charles LeMaire and Emile Santiago, *The Robe*

Charles LeMaire and Travilla, *How to Marry a Millionaire*

Mary Ann Nyberg, *The Band Wagon*

Walter Plunkett, *Young Bess*

Irene Sharaff, *Call Me Madam*

SPECIAL EFFECTS

The War of the Worlds (Paramount)

SHORT SUBJECTS
CARTOON

Christopher Crumpet (*Jolly Frolics Series*) (United Productions of America; Columbia)

From A to Z-Z-Z-Z (*Loony Tunes Series*) (Warner Bros. Cartoons, Inc.; Warner Bros.)

Rugged Bear (*Donald Duck Series*) (Walt Disney Productions; RKO Radio)

The Tell Tale Heart (*UPA Cartoon Special Series*) (United Productions of America; Columbia)

Toot, Whistle, Plunk and Boom (*Adventures in Music Series*) (Walt Disney Productions; Buena Vista)

ONE-REEL

Christ Among the Primitives (Vincenzo Lucci-Chiarissi Production; I.F.E. Releasing Corp.)

Herring Hunt (*Canada Carries on Series*) (National Film Board of Canada; RKO Pathé, Inc.)

Joy of Living (*Art Film Series*) (Art Film Productions; Twentieth Century-Fox)

The Merry Wives of Windsor Overture (*Overture Series*) (Johnny Green, producer; MGM)

Wee Water Wonders (*Grantland Rice Spotlight Series*) (Jack Eaton, producer; Paramount)

TWO-REEL

Bear Country (*True Life Adventure Series*) (Walt Disney Productions; RKO Radio)

Ben and Me (Walt Disney Productions; Buena Vista)

Return to Glennascaul (Dublin Gate Theatre Production; Arthur Mayer-Edward Kingsley, Inc.)

Vesuvius Express (*CinemaScope Shorts Series*) (Otto Lang, producer; Twentieth Century-Fox)

Winter Paradise (*Technicolor Special Series*) (Cedric Francis, producer; Warner Bros.)

DOCUMENTARY
SHORT SUBJECT

The Alaskan Eskimo (Walt Disney Productions; RKO Radio)

The Living City (John Barnes, producer; Encyclopaedia Britannica Films, Inc.)

Operation Blue Jay (U.S. Army Signal Corps.)

They Planted a Stone (World Wide Pictures; British Information Services)

The Word (John Healy and John Adams, producers; Twentieth Century-Fox)

FEATURE

The Conquest of Everest (Countryman Films, Ltd. and Group 3 Ltd.; United Artists)

The Living Desert (*True Life Adventure Series*) (Walt Disney Productions; Buena Vista)

A Queen Is Crowned (J. Arthur Rank Organization Ltd.; Universal-International)

IRVING G. THALBERG MEMORIAL AWARD
George Stevens

HONORARY AWARDS

To **Pete Smith** for his witty and pungent observations on the American scene in his series of *Pete Smith Specialities*

To **Twentieth Century-Fox Film Corporation** in recognition of their imagination, showmanship and foresight in introducing the revolutionary process known as CinemaScope

To **Joseph I. Breen** for his conscientious, open-minded and dignified management of the Motion Picture Production Code

To **Bell and Howell Company** for their pioneering and basic achievements in the advancement of the motion picture industry

1954

BEST MOTION PICTURE

The Caine Mutiny, Stanley Kramer, producer (Columbia)
The Country Girl, William Perlberg, producer (Paramount)
On the Waterfront, Sam Spiegel, producer (Columbia)
Seven Brides for Seven Brothers, Jack Cummings, producer (MGM)
Three Coins in the Fountain, Sol C. Siegel, producer (Twentieth Century-Fox)

On the Waterfront

BEST ACTOR
Humphrey Bogart, *The Caine Mutiny*
Marlon Brando, On the Waterfront
Bing Crosby, *The Country Girl*
James Mason, *A Star Is Born*
Dan O'Herlihy, *Adventures of Robinson Crusoe*

BEST ACTRESS
Dorothy Dandridge, *Carmen Jones*
Judy Garland, *A Star Is Born*
Audrey Hepburn, *Sabrina*
Grace Kelly, The Country Girl
Jane Wyman, *Magnificent Obsession*

ACTOR IN A SUPPORTING ROLE
Lee J. Cobb, *On the Waterfront*
Karl Malden, *On the Waterfront*
Edmond O'Brien, The Barefoot Contessa
Rod Steiger, *On the Waterfront*
Tom Tully, *The Caine Mutiny*

ACTRESS IN A SUPPORTING ROLE
Nina Foch, *Executive Suite*
Katy Jurado, *Broken Lance*
Eva Maria Saint, On the Waterfront
Jan Sterling, *The High and the Mighty*
Claire Trevor, *The High and the Mighty*

DIRECTING
Alfred Hitchcock, *Rear Window*
Elia Kazan, On the Waterfront
George Seaton, *The Country Girl*
William Wellman, *The High and the Mighty*
Billy Wilder, *Sabrina*

WRITING

MOTION PICTURE STORY
François Boyer, *Forbidden Games*
Jed Harris and Tom Reed, *Night People*
Ettore Margadonna, *Bread, Love and Dreams*
Lamar Trotti, *There's No Business Like Show Business*
Philip Yordan, Broken Lance

SCREENPLAY
Albert Hackett, Frances Goodrich and Dorothy Kingsley, *Seven Brides for Seven Brothers*
John Michael Hayes, *Rear Window*
Stanley Roberts, *The Caine Mutiny*
George Seaton, The Country Girl
Billy Wilder, Samuel Taylor and Ernest Lehman, *Sabrina*

STORY AND SCREENPLAY
Valentine Davies and Oscar Brodney, *The Glenn Miller Story*
Joseph L. Mankiewicz, *The Barefoot Contessa*
Norman Panama and Melvin Frank, *Knock on Wood*
William Rose, *Genevieve*
Budd Schulberg, On the Waterfront

CINEMATOGRAPHY
BLACK-AND-WHITE
George Folsey, *Executive Suite*

Boris Kaufman, *On the Waterfront*

Charles Lang, Jr., *Sabrina*

John Seitz, *Rogue Cop*

John F. Warren, *The Country Girl*

COLOR
Robert Burks, *Rear Window*

George Folsey, *Seven Brides for Seven Brothers*

Milton Krasner, *Three Coins in the Fountain*

Leon Shamroy, *The Egyptian*

William V. Skall, *The Silver Chalice*

ART DIRECTION
BLACK-AND-WHITE
Richard Day, art direction and set decoration, *On the Waterfront*

Cedric Gibbons and Edward Carfagno, art direction; Edwin B. Willis and Emile Kuri, set decoration, *Executive Suite*

Max Ophuls, art direction and set decoration, *Le Plaisir*

Hal Pereira and Roland Anderson, art direction; Sam Comer and Grace Gregory, set decoration, *The Country Girl*

Hal Pereira and Walter Tyler, art direction; Sam Comer and Ray Moyer, set decoration, *Sabrina*

COLOR
Malcolm Bert, Gene Allen and Irene Sharaff, art direction; George James Hopkins, set decoration, *A Star Is Born*

Cedric Gibbons and Preston Ames, art direction; Edwin B. Willis and Keogh Gleason, set decoration, *Brigadoon*

John Meehan, art direction; Emile Kuri, set decoration, *20,000 Leagues Under the Sea*

Hal Pereira and Roland Anderson, art direction; Sam Comer and Ray Moyer, set decoration, *Red Garters*

Lyle Wheeler and Leland Fuller, art direction; Walter M. Scott and Paul S. Fox, set decoration, *Desirée*

SOUND RECORDING
Columbia Studio Sound Dept., *The Caine Mutiny*

MGM Studio Sound Dept., *Brigadoon*

Paramount Studio Sound Dept., *Rear Window*

RKO Radio Studio Sound Dept., *Susan Slept Here*

Universal-International Studio Sound Dept., *The Glenn Miller Story*

MUSIC
SONG
"Count Your Blessings Instead of Sheep," *White Christmas*, Irving Berlin, music and lyrics

"The High and the Mighty," *The High and the Mighty*, Dimitri Tiomkin, music; Ned Washington, lyrics

"Hold My Hand," *Susan Slept Here*, Jack Lawrence and Richard Myers, music and lyrics

"The Man That Got Away," *A Star Is Born*, Harold Arlen, music; Ira Gershwin, lyrics

"Three Coins in the Fountain," *Three Coins in the Fountain*, Jule Styne, music; Sammy Cahn, lyrics

SCORING OF A DRAMATIC OR COMEDY PICTURE
Larry Adler, *Genevieve*

Leonard Bernstein, *On the Waterfront*

Max Steiner, *The Caine Mutiny*

Dimitri Tiomkin, *The High and the Mighty*

Franz Waxman, *The Silver Chalice*

SCORING OF A MUSICAL PICTURE
Adolph Deutsch and Saul Chaplin, *Seven Brides for Seven Brothers*

Joseph Gershenson and Henry Mancini, *The Glenn Miller Story*

Herschel Burke Gilbert, *Carmen Jones*

Ray Heindorf, *A Star Is Born*

Alfred Newman and Lionel Newman, *There's No Business Like Show Business*

FILM EDITING
Ralph Dawson, *The High and the Mighty*

William A. Lyon and Henry Batista, *The Caine Mutiny*

Gene Milford, *On the Waterfront*

Elmo Williams, *20,000 Leagues Under the Sea*

Ralph E. Winters, *Seven Brides for Seven Brothers*

COSTUME DESIGN
BLACK-AND-WHITE
Georges Annenkov and Rosine Delamare, *The Earrings of Madame De…*

Christian Dior, *Indiscretion of an American Wife*

Edith Head, *Sabrina*

Jean Louis, *It Should Happen to You*

Helen Rose, *Executive Suite*

COLOR
Charles LeMaire and Rene Hubert, *Desirée*

Charles LeMaire, Travilla and Miles White, *There's No Business Like Show Business*

Jean Louis, Mary Ann Nyberg and Irene Sharaff, *A Star Is Born*

Irene Sharaff, *Brigadoon*

Sanzo Wada, *Gate of Hell*

SPECIAL EFFECTS
Hell and High Water (Twentieth Century-Fox)

Them! (Warner Bros.)

***20,000 Leagues Under the Sea* (Walt Disney Productions; Buena Vista)**

SHORT SUBJECTS
CARTOON
Crazy Mixed Up Pup (Walter Lantz Productions; Universal-International)

Pigs Is Pigs (Walt Disney Productions; RKO Radio)

Sandy Claws (*Looney Tunes Series*) (Warner Bros. Cartoons, Inc.; Warner Bros.)

Touché, Pussy Cat (*Tom and Jerry Series*) (Frederick Quimby, producer; MGM)

***When Magoo Flew* (*Mr. Magoo Series*) (United Productions of America; Columbia)**

ONE-REEL

The First Piano Quartette (Music Series) (Otto Lang, producer; Twentieth Century-Fox)

The Strauss Fantasy (Musical Gems Series) (Johnny Green, producer; MGM)

This Mechanical Age (Warner Variety Series) (Robert Youngson, producer; Warner Bros.)

TWO-REEL

Beauty and the Bull (Technicolor Specials Series) (Cedric Francis, producer; Warner Bros.)

Jet Carrier (Otto Lang, producer; Twentieth Century-Fox)

Siam (People and Places Series) (Walt Disney Productions; Buena Vista)

***A Time Out of War* (Denis Sanders and Terry Sanders, producers; Carnival Productions)**

DOCUMENTARY

SHORT SUBJECT

Jet Carrier (Otto Lang, producer; Twentieth Century-Fox)

Rembrandt: A Self-Portrait (Morrie Roizman Production; Distributors Corporation of America)

***Thursday's Children* (World Wide Pictures and Morse Films; British Information Services)**

FEATURE

The Stratford Adventure (National Film Board of Canada; Continental Distributing, Inc.)

***The Vanishing Prairie (True Life Adventure Series)* (Walt Disney Productions; Buena Vista)**

HONORARY AWARDS

To **Bausch and Lomb Optical Company** for their contributions to the advancement of the motion picture industry

To **Kemp R. Niver** for the development of the Renovare Process, which has made possible the restoration of the Library of Congress Paper Film Collection

To **Greta Garbo** for her unforgettable screen performances

To **Danny Kaye** for his unique talents, his service to the Academy, the motion picture industry and the American people

To **Jon Whiteley** for his outstanding juvenile performance in *The Little Kidnappers*

To **Vincent Winter** for his outstanding performance in *The Little Kidnappers*

To ***Gate of Hell*** (Japan) best foreign language film first released in the United States during 1954

1955

BEST MOTION PICTURE

Love Is a Many-Splendored Thing, Buddy Adler, producer (Twentieth Century-Fox)

***Marty*, Harold Hecht, producer (United Artists)**

Mister Roberts, Leland Hayward, producer (Warner Bros.)

Picnic, Fred Kohlmar, producer (Columbia)

The Rose Tattoo, Hal Wallis, producer (Paramount)

BEST ACTOR

Ernest Borgnine, *Marty*

James Cagney, *Love Me or Leave Me*

James Dean, *East of Eden*

Frank Sinatra, *The Man With the Golden Arm*

Spencer Tracy, *Bad Day at Black Rock*

BEST ACTRESS

Susan Hayward, *I'll Cry Tomorrow*

Katharine Hepburn, *Summertime*

Jennifer Jones, *Love Is a Many-Splendored Thing*

Anna Magnani, *The Rose Tattoo*

Eleanor Parker, *Interrupted Melody*

ACTOR IN A SUPPORTING ROLE

Arthur Kennedy, *Trial*

Jack Lemmon, *Mister Roberts*

Joe Mantell, *Marty*

Sal Mineo, *Rebel Without a Cause*

Arthur O'Connell, *Picnic*

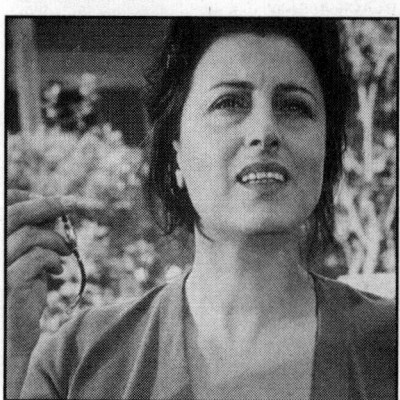

Anna Magnani, *The Rose Tattoo*

ACTRESS IN A SUPPORTING ROLE

Betsy Blair, *Marty*

Jo Van Fleet, *East of Eden*

Peggy Lee, *Pete Kelly's Blues*

Marisa Pavan, *The Rose Tattoo*

Natalie Wood, *Rebel Without a Cause*

DIRECTING

Elia Kazan, *East of Eden*

David Lean, *Summertime*

Joshua Logan, *Picnic*

Delbert Mann, *Marty*

John Sturges, *Bad Day at Black Rock*

WRITING

MOTION PICTURE STORY

Joe Connelly and Bob Mosher, *The Private War of Major Benson*

Daniel Fuchs, *Love Me or Leave Me*

Beirne Lay, Jr., *Strategic Air Command*

Jean Marsan, Henry Troyat, Jacques Perret, Henri Verneuil and Raoul Ploquin, *The Sheep Has Five Legs*

Nicholas Ray, *Rebel Without a Cause*

SCREENPLAY

Richard Brooks, *Blackboard Jungle*

Paddy Chayefsky, *Marty*

Daniel Fuchs and Isobel Lennart, *Love Me or Leave Me*

Millard Kaufman, *Bad Day at Black Rock*

Paul Osborn, *East of Eden*

STORY AND SCREENPLAY

Betty Comden and Adolph Green, *It's Always Fair Weather*

William Ludwig and Sonya Levien, *Interrupted Melody*

Melville Shavelson and Jack Rose, *The Seven Little Foys*

Milton Sperling and Emmet Lavery, *The Court-Martial of Billy Mitchell*

Jacques Tati and Henri Marquet, *Mr. Hulot's Holiday*

CINEMATOGRAPHY

BLACK-AND-WHITE

Arthur E. Arling, *I'll Cry Tomorrow*

Russell Harlan, *Blackboard Jungle*

James Wong Howe, *The Rose Tattoo*

Charles Lang, *Queen Bee*

Joseph LaShelle, *Marty*

COLOR

Robert Burks, *To Catch a Thief*

Harold Lipstein, *A Man Called Peter*

Leon Shamroy, *Love Is a Many-Splendored Thing*

Harry Stradling, *Guys and Dolls*

Robert Surtees, *Oklahoma!*

ART DIRECTION

BLACK-AND-WHITE

Cedric Gibbons and Malcolm Brown, art direction; Edwin B. Willis and Hugh B. Hunt, set decoration, *I'll Cry Tomorrow*

Cedric Gibbons and Randall Duell, art direction; Edwin B. Willis and Henry Grace, set decoration, *Blackboard Jungle*

Edward S. Haworth and Walter Simonds, art direction; Robert Priestley, set decoration, *Marty*

Hal Pereira and Tambi Larsen, art direction; Sam Comer and Arthur Krams, set decoration, *The Rose Tattoo*

Joseph C. Wright, art direction; Darrell Silvera, set decoration, *The Man With the Golden Arm*

COLOR

William Flannery and Jo Mielziner, art direction; Robert Priestley, set decoration, *Picnic*

Hal Pereira and Joseph McMillan Johnson, art direction; Sam Comer and Arthur Krams, set decoration, *To Catch a Thief*

Oliver Smith and Joseph C. Wright, art direction; Howard Bristol, set decoration, *Guys and Dolls*

Lyle Wheeler and George W. Davis, art direction; Walter M. Scott and Jack Stubbs, set decoration, *Love Is a Many-Splendored Thing*

Lyle Wheeler and John DeCuir, art direction; Walter M. Scott and Paul S. Fox, set decoration, *Daddy Long Legs*

SOUND RECORDING

MGM Studio Sound Dept., *Love Me or Leave Me*

RCA Sound Department, *Not As a Stranger*

Todd-AO Sound Department, *Oklahoma!*

Twentieth Century-Fox Studio Sound Dept., *Love Is a Many-Splendored Thing*

Warner Bros. Studio Sound Dept., *Mister Roberts*

MUSIC

SONG

"I'll Never Stop Loving You," *Love Me or Leave Me*, Nicholas Brodszky, music; Sammy Cahn, lyrics

"Love Is a Many-Splendored Thing," *Love Is a Many-Splendored Thing*, Sammy Fain, music; Paul Francis Webster, lyrics

"Something's Gotta Give," *Daddy Long Legs*, Johnny Mercer, music and lyrics

(Love Is) "The Tender Trap," *The Tender Trap*, James Van Heusen, music; Sammy Cahn, lyrics

"Unchained Melody," *Unchained*, Alex North, music; Hy Zaret, lyrics

SCORING OF A DRAMATIC OR COMEDY PICTURE

Elmer Bernstein, *The Man With the Golden Arm*

George Duning, *Picnic*

Alfred Newman, *Love Is a Many-Splendored Thing*

Alex North, *The Rose Tattoo*

Max Steiner, *Battle Cry*

SCORING OF A MUSICAL PICTURE

Robert Russell Bennett, Jay Blackton and Adolph Deutsch, *Oklahoma!*

Jay Blackton and Cyril J. Mockridge, *Guys and Dolls*

Percy Faith and George Stoll, *Love Me or Leave Me*

Alfred Newman, *Daddy Long Legs*

André Previn, *It's Always Fair Weather*

FILM EDITING

Warren Low, *The Rose Tattoo*

Alma Macrorie, *The Bridges at Toko-Ri*

Charles Nelson and William A. Lyon, *Picnic*

Gene Ruggiero and George Boemler, *Oklahoma!*

Ferris Webster, *Blackboard Jungle*

COSTUME DESIGN

BLACK-AND-WHITE

Beatrice Dawson, *The Pickwick Papers*

Edith Head, *The Rose Tattoo*

Tadaoto Kainoscho, *Ugetsu*

Jean Louis, *Queen Bee*

Helen Rose, *I'll Cry Tomorrow*

COLOR

Edith Head, *To Catch a Thief*

Charles LeMaire, *Love Is a Many-Splendored Thing*

Charles LeMaire and Mary Wills, *The Virgin Queen*

Helen Rose, *Interrupted Melody*

Irene Sharaff, *Guys and Dolls*

SPECIAL EFFECTS

The Bridges at Toko-Ri (Paramount)

The Dam Busters (Warner Bros.)

The Rains of Ranchipur (Twentieth Century-Fox)

SHORT SUBJECTS

CARTOON

Good Will to Men (*MGM Cartoon Series*) (Frederick Quimby, William Hanna and Joseph Barbera, producers; MGM)

The Legend of Rock-a-Bye Point (Walter Lantz Productions; Universal-International)

No Hunting (*Donald Duck Series*) (Walt Disney Productions; RKO Radio)

Speedy Gonzales (*Merrie Melodies Series*) (Warner Bros. Cartoons, Inc.; Warner Bros.)

ONE-REEL

Gadgets Galore (*Warner Varieties Series*) (Robert Youngson, producer; Warner Bros.)

Survival City (*Movietone CinemaScope Series*) (Edmund Reek, producer; Twentieth Century-Fox)

3rd Ave. El (Carson Davidson Productions; Ardee Films)

Three Kisses (*Topper Special Series*) (Justin Herman, producer; Paramount)

TWO-REEL

The Battle of Gettysburg (Dore Schary, producer; MGM)

The Face of Lincoln (University of Southern California Presentation; Cavalcade Pictures, Inc.)

On The Twelfth Day . . . (United Kingdom Series) (Go Pictures, Inc.; George Brest and Associates)

Switzerland (*People and Places Series*) (Walt Disney Productions; Buena Vista)

24-Hour Alert (Cedric Francis, producer; Warner Bros.)

DOCUMENTARY

SHORT SUBJECT

The Battle of Gettysburg (Dore Schary, producer; MGM)

The Face of Lincoln (University of Southern California Presentation; Cavalcade Pictures, Inc.)

Men Against the Arctic (*People and Places Series*) (Walt Disney Productions; Buena Vista)

FEATURE

Heartbreak Ridge (Rene Risacher Production; Tudor Pictures)

Helen Keller in Her Story (Nancy Hamilton, producer; Nancy Hamilton Presentation)

HONORARY AWARD

To *Samurai, The Legend of Musashi* (Japan), best foreign language film first released in the United States during 1955

1956

BEST MOTION PICTURE

Around the World in 80 Days, Michael Todd, producer (United Artists)

Friendly Persuasion, William Wyler, producer (Allied Artists)

Giant, George Stevens and Henry Ginsberg, producers (Warner Bros.)

The King and I, Charles Brackett, producer (Twentieth Century-Fox)

The Ten Commandments, Cecil B. DeMille, producer (Paramount)

Yul Brynner, *The King and I*

BEST ACTOR

Yul Brynner, *The King and I*

James Dean, *Giant*

Kirk Douglas, *Lust for Life*

Rock Hudson, *Giant*

Sir Laurence Olivier, *Richard III*

BEST ACTRESS

Carroll Baker, *Baby Doll*

Ingrid Bergman, *Anastasia*

Katharine Hepburn, *The Rainmaker*

Nancy Kelly, *The Bad Seed*

Deborah Kerr, *The King and I*

ACTOR IN A SUPPORTING ROLE

Don Murray, *Bus Stop*

Anthony Perkins, *Friendly Persuasion*

Anthony Quinn, *Lust for Life*

Mickey Rooney, *The Bold and the Brave*

Robert Stack, *Written on the Wind*

ACTRESS IN A SUPPORTING ROLE

Mildred Dunnock, *Baby Doll*

Eileen Heckart, *The Bad Seed*

Mercedes McCambridge, *Giant*

Patty McCormack, *The Bad Seed*

Dorothy Malone, *Written on the Wind*

DIRECTING

Michael Anderson, *Around the World in 80 Days*

Walter Lang, *The King and I*

George Stevens, *Giant*

King Vidor, *War and Peace*

William Wyler, *Friendly Persuasion*

WRITING

MOTION PICTURE STORY

Leo Katcher, *The Eddy Duchin Story*

Jean Paul Sartre, *The Proud and the Beautiful*

Dalton Trumbo, *The Brave One*

Cesare Zavattini, *Umberto D.*

SCREENPLAY, ADAPTED

Norman Corwin, *Lust for Life*

Fred Guiol and Ivan Moffat, *Giant*

James Poe, John Farrow and S.J. Perelman, *Around the World in 80 Days*

Tennessee Williams, *Baby Doll*

SCREENPLAY, ORIGINAL

Federico Fellini and Tullio Pinelli, *La Strada*

Albert Lamorisse, *The Red Balloon*

Robert Lewin, *The Bold and the Brave*

William Rose, *The Lady Killers*

Andrew L. Stone, *Julie*

CINEMATOGRAPHY

BLACK-AND-WHITE

Burnett Guffey, *The Harder They Fall*

Boris Kaufman, *Baby Doll*

Hal Rosson, *The Bad Seed*

Joseph Ruttenberg, *Somebody Up There Likes Me*

Walter Strenge, *Stagecoach to Fury*

COLOR

Jack Cardiff, *War and Peace*

Loyal Griggs, *The Ten Commandments*

Lionel Lindon, *Around the World in 80 Days*

Leon Shamroy, *The King and I*

Harry Stradling, *The Eddy Duchin Story*

ART DIRECTION

BLACK-AND-WHITE

Ross Bellah, art direction; William R. Kiernan and Louis Diage, set decoration, *The Solid Gold Cadillac*

Cedric Gibbons and Malcolm F. Brown, art direction; Edwin B. Willis and F. Keogh Gleason, set decoration, *Somebody Up There Likes Me*

Takashi Matsuyama, art direction and set decoration, *The Magnificent Seven*

Hal Pereira and A. Earl Hedrick, art direction; Samuel M. Comer and Frank R. McKelvy, set decoration, *The Proud and the Profane*

Lyle R. Wheeler and Jack Martin Smith, art direction; Walter M. Scott and Stuart A. Reiss, set decoration, *Teenage Rebel*

COLOR

Cedric Gibbons, Hans Peters and Preston Ames, art direction; Edwin B. Willis and F. Keogh Gleason, set decoration, *Lust for Life*

Boris Leven, art direction; Ralph S. Hurst, set decoration, *Giant*

Hal Pereira, Walter H. Tyler and Albert Nozaki, art direction; Sam M. Comer and Ray Moyer, set decoration, *The Ten Commandments*

James W. Sullivan and Ken Adam, art direction; Ross J. Dowd, set decoration, *Around the World in 80 Days*

Lyle R. Wheeler and John DeCuir, art direction; Walter M. Scott and Paul S. Fox, set decoration, *The King and I*

SOUND RECORDING

Columbia Studio Sound Dept., *The Eddy Duchin Story*

Paramount Studio Sound Dept., *The Ten Commandments*

RKO Radio Studio Sound Dept., *The Brave One*

Twentieth Century-Fox Studio Sound Dept., *The King and I*

Westrex Sound Services, Inc. and Samuel Goldwyn Studio Sound Dept., *Friendly Persuasion*

MUSIC

SONG

"Friendly Persuasion" (Thee I Love), *Friendly Persuasion*, Dimitri Tiomkin, music; Paul Francis Webster, lyrics

"Julie," *Julie*, Leith Stevens, music; Tom Adair, lyrics

"True Love," *High Society*, Cole Porter, music and lyrics

"Whatever Will Be, Will Be" (Que Será, Será), *The Man Who Knew Too Much*, Jay Livingston and Ray Evans, music and lyrics

"Written on the Wind," *Written on the Wind*, Victor Young, music; Sammy Cahn, lyrics

SCORING OF A DRAMATIC OR COMEDY PICTURE

Hugo Friedhofer, *Between Heaven and Hell*

Alfred Newman, *Anastasia*

Alex North, *The Rainmaker*

Dimitri Tiomkin, *Giant*

Victor Young, *Around the World in 80 Days*

SCORING OF A MUSICAL PICTURE

Johnny Green and Saul Chaplin, *High Society*

Alfred Newman and Ken Darby, *The King and I*

Lionel Newman, *The Best Things in Life Are Free*

George Stoll and Johnny Green, *Meet Me in Las Vegas*

Morris Stoloff and George Duning, *The Eddy Duchin Story*

FILM EDITING

Albert Akst, *Somebody Up There Likes Me*

Anne Bauchens, *The Ten Commandments*

William Hornbeck, Philip W. Anderson and Fred Bohanan, *Giant*

Gene Ruggiero and Paul Weatherwax, *Around the World in 80 Days*

Merrill G. White, *The Brave One*

COSTUME DESIGN

BLACK-AND-WHITE

Kohei Ezaki, *The Magnificent Seven*

Edith Head, *The Proud and the Profane*

Charles LeMaire and Mary Wills, *Teenage Rebel*

Jean Louis, *The Solid Gold Cadillac*

Helen Rose, *The Power and the Prize*

COLOR

Marie De Matteis, *War and Peace*

Edith Head, Ralph Jester, John Jensen, Dorothy Jeakins and Arnold Friberg, *The Ten Commandments*

Moss Mabry and Marjorie Best, *Giant*

Irene Sharaff, *The King and I*

Miles White, *Around the World in 80 Days*

SPECIAL EFFECTS

John Fulton, *The Ten Commandments*

A. Arnold Gillespie, Irving Ries and Wesley C. Miller, *Forbidden Planet*

SHORT SUBJECTS

CARTOON

Gerald McBoing-Boing on Planet Moo (*Jolly Frolics Series*) (United Productions of America; Columbia)

The Jay Walker (*UPA Special Series*) (United Productions of America; Columbia)

Mister Magoo's Puddle Jumper (*Mr. Magoo Series*) (United Productions of America; Columbia)

ONE-REEL

Crashing the Water Barrier (*The Sports Parade Series*) (Konstantin Kalser, producer; Warner Bros.)

I Never Forget a Face (*Warner Specials Series*) (Robert Youngson, producer; Warner Bros.)

Time Stood Still (*Scope Gems Series*) (Cedric Francis, producer; Warner Bros.)

TWO-REEL

The Bespoke Overcoat (Go Pictures, Inc.; Romulus Films)

Cow Dog (Walt Disney Productions; Buena Vista)

The Dark Wave (John Healy, producer; Twentieth Century-Fox)

Samoa (*People and Places Series*) (Walt Disney Productions; Buena Vista)

DOCUMENTARY

SHORT SUBJECT

A City Decides (Charles Guggenheim and Associates, Inc.)

The Dark Wave (John Healy, producer; Twentieth Century-Fox)

The House Without a Name (Valentine Davies, producer; Universal-International)

Man in Space (Walt Disney Productions; Buena Vista)

The True Story of the Civil War (Louis Clyde Stoumen, producer; Camera Eye Pictures, Inc.)

FEATURE

The Naked Eye (Camera Eye Pictures, Inc.; Film Representatives, Inc.)

The Silent World (Filmad-F.S.J.Y.C. Production; Columbia)

Where Mountains Float (Arno/Studios, Copenhagen; Brandon Films, Inc.)

FOREIGN LANGUAGE FILM

The Captain of Kopenick, Federal Republic of Germany – West

Gervaise, France

Harp of Burma, Japan

Qivitoq, Denmark

La Strada, Italy

IRVING G. THALBERG MEMORIAL AWARD
Buddy Adler

JEAN HERSHOLT HUMANITARIAN AWARD
(Not necessarily given each year)
Y. Frank Freeman

HONORARY AWARD
To **Eddie Cantor** for distinguished service to the film industry

1957

BEST MOTION PICTURE

The Bridge on the River Kwai, Sam Spiegel, producer (Columbia)

Peyton Place, Jerry Wald, producer (Twentieth Century-Fox)

Sayonara, William Goetz, producer (Warner Bros.)

12 Angry Men, Henry Fonda and Reginald Rose, producers (United Artists)

Witness for the Prosecution, Arthur Hornblow, Jr., producer (United Artists)

BEST ACTOR

Marlon Brando, *Sayonara*

Anthony Franciosa, *A Hatful of Rain*

Alec Guinness, *The Bridge on the River Kwai*

Charles Laughton, *Witness for the Prosecution*

Anthony Quinn, *Wild Is the Wind*

BEST ACTRESS

Deborah Kerr, *Heaven Knows, Mr. Allison*

Anna Magnani, *Wild Is the Wind*

Elizabeth Taylor, *Raintree County*

Lana Turner, *Peyton Place*

Joanne Woodward, *The Three Faces of Eve*

ACTOR IN A SUPPORTING ROLE

Red Buttons, *Sayonara*

Vittorio de Sica, *A Farewell to Arms*

Sessue Hayakawa, *The Bridge on the River Kwai*

Arthur Kennedy, *Peyton Place*

Russ Tamblyn, *Peyton Place*

ACTRESS IN A SUPPORTING ROLE

Carolyn Jones, *The Bachelor Party*

Elsa Lanchester, *Witness for the Prosecution*

Hope Lange, *Peyton Place*

Miyoshi Umeki, *Sayonara*

Diane Varsi, *Peyton Place*

Joanne Woodward, *The Three Faces of Eve*

DIRECTING

David Lean, *The Bridge on the River Kwai*

Joshua Logan, *Sayonara*

Sidney Lumet, *12 Angry Men*

Mark Robson, *Peyton Place*

Billy Wilder, *Witness for the Prosecution*

WRITING

SCREENPLAY BASED ON MATERIAL FROM ANOTHER MEDIUM

Pierre Boulle, Michael Wilson and Carl Foreman, *The Bridge on the River Kwai*

John Michael Hayes, *Peyton Place*

John Lee Mahin and John Huston, *Heaven Knows, Mr. Allison*

Paul Osborn, *Sayonara*

Reginald Rose, *12 Angry Men*

STORY AND SCREENPLAY WRITTEN DIRECTLY FOR THE SCREEN

Federico Fellini, Ennio Flaiano and Tullio Pinelli, story; Federico Fellini and Ennio Flaiano, screenplay, *Vitelloni*

Leonard Gershe, *Funny Face*

Barney Slater and Joel Kane, story; Dudley Nichols, screenplay, *The Tin Star*

George Wells, *Designing Woman*

Ralph Wheelright, story; R. Wright Campbell, Ivan Goff and Ben Roberts, screenplay, *Man of a Thousand Faces*

CINEMATOGRAPHY

Ellsworth Fredericks, *Sayonara*

Jack Hildyard, *The Bridge on the River Kwai*

Ray June, *Funny Face*

Milton Krasner, *An Affair to Remember*

William Mellor, *Peyton Place*

ART DIRECTION

Ted Haworth, art direction; Robert Priestley, set decoration, *Sayonara*

Walter Holscher, art direction; William Kiernan and Louis Diage, set decoration, *Pal Joey*

William A. Horning and Gene Allen, art direction; Edwin B. Willis and Richard Pefferle, set decoration, *Les Girls*

William A. Horning and Urie McCleary, art direction; Edwin B. Willis and Hugh Hunt, set decoration, *Raintree County*

Hal Pereira and George W. Davis, art direction; Sam Comer and Ray Moyer, set decoration, *Funny Face*

SOUND RECORDING

Columbia Studio Sound Dept., *Pal Joey*

MGM Studio Sound Dept., *Les Girls*

Paramount Studio Sound Dept., *Gunfight at the O.K. Corral*

Samuel Goldwyn Studio Sound Dept., *Witness for the Prosecution*

Warner Bros. Studio Sound Dept., *Sayonara*

MUSIC

SONG

"An Affair to Remember," *An Affair to Remember*, Harry Warren, music; Harold Adamson and Leo McCarey, lyrics

"All the Way," *The Joker Is Wild*, James Van Heusen, music; Sammy Cahn, lyrics

"April Love," *April Love*, Sammy Fain, music; Paul Francis Webster, lyrics

"Tammy," *Tammy and the Bachelor*, Ray Evans and Jay Livingston, music and lyrics

"Wild Is the Wind," *Wild Is the Wind*, Dimitri Tiomkin, music; Ned Washington, lyrics

SCORE

Malcolm Arnold, *The Bridge on the River Kwai*

Hugo Friedhofer, *An Affair to Remember*

Hugo Friedhofer, *Boy on a Dolphin*

Johnny Green, *Raintree County*

Paul Smith, *Perri*

FILM EDITING

Viola Lawrence and Jerome Thoms, *Pal Joey*

Warren Low, *Gunfight at the O.K. Corral*

Daniel Mandell, *Witness for the Prosecution*

Arthur P. Schmidt and Philip W. Anderson, *Sayonara*

Peter Taylor, *The Bridge on the River Kwai*

COSTUME DESIGN

Edith Head and Hubert de Givenchy, *Funny Face*

Charles LeMaire, *An Affair to Remember*

Jean Louis, *Pal Joey*

Orry-Kelly, *Les Girls*

Walter Plunkett, *Raintree County*

SPECIAL EFFECTS

Louis Lichtenfield, visual, *The Spirit of St. Louis*

Walter Rossi, audible, *The Enemy Below*

SHORT SUBJECTS

CARTOON

***Birds Anonymous* (*Tweety and Sylvester Series*) (Edward Selzer, producer; Warner Bros.)**

One Droopy Knight (*Droopy Series*) (William Hanna and Joseph Barbera, producers; MGM)

Tabasco Road (*Speedy Gonzales Series*) (Edward Selzer, producer; Warner Bros.)

Trees and *Jamaica Daddy* (*Ham and Hattie Series*) (United Productions of America; Columbia)

The Truth About Mother Goose (Walt Disney Productions; Buena Vista)

LIVE ACTION SUBJECTS

A Chairy Tale (National Film Board of Canada; Kingsley International)

City of Gold (National Film Board of Canada; Kingsley International)

Foothold on Antarctica (World Wide Pictures; Lester A. Shoenfeld Films)

Portugal (*People and Places Series*) (Walt Disney Productions; Buena Vista)

***The Wetback Hound* (Walt Disney Productions; Buena Vista)**

DOCUMENTARY

SHORT SUBJECT

No award given this year

FEATURE

***Albert Schweitzer* (Hill and Anderson Production; Louis de Rochemont Associates)**

On the Bowery (Lionel Rogosin Productions; Film Representations, Inc.)

Torero! (Producciones Barbachano Ponce; Columbia)

FOREIGN LANGUAGE FILM

The Devil Came at Night, Federal Republic of Germany – West

Gates of Paris, France

Mother India, India

The Nights of Cabiria, Italy

Nine Lives, Norway

JEAN HERSHOLT HUMANITARIAN AWARD

Samuel Goldwyn

HONORARY AWARDS

To **Charles Brackett** for outstanding service to the academy

To **B. B. Kahane** for distinguished service to the motion picture industry

To **Gilbert M. "Broncho Billy" Anderson**, motion picture pioneer, for his contributions to the development of motion pictures as entertainment

To the **Society of Motion Picture and Television Engineers** for their contributions to the advancement of the motion picture industry

1958

BEST MOTION PICTURE

Auntie Mame (Warner Bros.)

Cat on a Hot Tin Roof, Lawrence Weingarten, producer (MGM)

The Defiant Ones, Stanley Kramer, producer (United Artists)

Gigi, Arthur Freed, producer (MGM)

Separate Tables, Harold Hecht, producer (United Artists)

BEST ACTOR

Tony Curtis, *The Defiant Ones*

Paul Newman, *Cat on a Hot Tin Roof*

David Niven, *Separate Tables*

Sidney Poitier, *The Defiant Ones*

Spencer Tracy, *The Old Man and the Sea*

BEST ACTRESS

Susan Hayward, *I Want to Live!*

Deborah Kerr, *Separate Tables*

Shirley MacLaine, *Some Came Running*

Rosalind Russell, *Auntie Mame*

Elizabeth Taylor, *Cat on a Hot Tin Roof*

ACTOR IN A SUPPORTING ROLE

Theodore Bikel, *The Defiant Ones*

Lee J. Cobb, *The Brothers Karamazov*

Burl Ives, *The Big Country*

Arthur Kennedy, *Some Came Running*

Gig Young, *Teacher's Pet*

ACTRESS IN A SUPPORTING ROLE

Peggy Cass, *Auntie Mame*

Wendy Hiller, *Separate Tables*

Gigi

Martha Hyer, *Some Came Running*

Maureen Stapleton, *Lonelyhearts*

Cara Williams, *The Defiant Ones*

DIRECTING

Richard Brooks, *Cat on a Hot Tin Roof*

Stanley Kramer, *The Defiant Ones*

Vincente Minnelli, *Gigi*

Mark Robson, *The Inn of the Sixth Happiness*

Robert Wise, *I Want to Live!*

WRITING

SCREENPLAY BASED ON MATERIAL FROM ANOTHER MEDIUM

Richard Brooks and James Poe, *Cat on a Hot Tin Roof*

Nelson Gidding and Don Mankiewicz, *I Want to Live!*

Alec Guinness, *The Horse's Mouth*

Alan Jay Lerner, *Gigi*

Terence Rattigan and John Gay, *Separate Tables*

STORY AND SCREENPLAY WRITTEN DIRECTLY FOR THE SCREEN

Paddy Chayefsky, *The Goddess*

James Edward Grant and William Bowers, *The Sheepman*

Fay and Michael Kanin, *Teacher's Pet*

Melville Shavelson and Jack Rose, *Houseboat*

Nedrick Young and Harold Jacob Smith, *The Defiant Ones*

CINEMATOGRAPHY

BLACK-AND-WHITE

Daniel L. Fapp, *Desire Under the Elms*

Charles Lang, Jr., *Separate Tables*

Sam Leavitt, *The Defiant Ones*

Lionel Lindon, *I Want to Live!*

Joe MacDonald, *The Young Lions*

COLOR

William Daniels, *Cat on a Hot Tin Roof*

James Wong Howe, *The Old Man and the Sea*

Joseph Ruttenberg, *Gigi*

Leon Shamroy, *South Pacific*

Harry Stradling, Sr., *Auntie Mame*

ART DIRECTION

Malcolm Bert, art direction; George James Hopkins, set decoration, *Auntie Mame*

William A. Horning and Preston Ames, art direction; Henry Grace and Keogh Gleason, set decoration, *Gigi*

Cary Odell, art direction; Louis Diage, set decoration, *Bell, Book and Candle*

Hal Pereira and Henry Bumstead, art direction; Sam Comer and Frank McKelvy, set decoration, *Vertigo*

Lyle R. Wheeler and John DeCuir, art direction; Walter M. Scott and Paul S. Fox, set decoration, *A Certain Smile*

SOUND

Paramount Studio Sound Dept., *Vertigo*

Samuel Goldwyn Studio Sound Dept., *I Want to Live!*

Todd-AO Sound Dept., *South Pacific*

Twentieth Century-Fox Studio Sound Dept., *The Young Lions*

Universal-International Studio Sound Dept., *A Time to Love and a Time to Die*

MUSIC
SONG

"Almost in Your Arms" (Love Song From *Houseboat*), *Houseboat*, Jay Livingston and Ray Evans, music and lyrics

"A Certain Smile," *A Certain Smile*, Sammy Fain, music; Paul Francis Webster, lyrics

"Gigi," *Gigi*, Frederick Loewe, music; Alan Jay Lerner, lyrics

"To Love and Be Loved," *Some Came Running*, James Van Heusen, music; Sammy Cahn, lyrics

"A Very Precious Love," *Marjorie Morningstar*, Sammy Fain, music; Paul Francis Webster, lyrics

SCORING OF A DRAMATIC OR COMEDY PICTURE

Hugo Friedhofer, *The Young Lions*

Jerome Moross, *The Big Country*

David Raksin, *Separate Tables*

Dimitri Tiomkin, *The Old Man and the Sea*

Oliver Wallace, *White Wilderness*

SCORING OF A MUSICAL PICTURE

Yuri Faier and G. Rozhdestvensky, *The Bolshoi Ballet*

Ray Heindorf, *Damn Yankees*

Alfred Newman and Ken Darby, *South Pacific*

Lionel Newman, *Mardi Gras*

André Previn, *Gigi*

FILM EDITING

Adrienne Fazan, *Gigi*

William Hornbeck, *I Want to Live!*

Frederick Knudtson, *The Defiant Ones*

William A. Lyon and Al Clark, *Cowboy*

William Ziegler, *Auntie Mame*

COSTUME DESIGN
BLACK-AND-WHITE OR COLOR

Cecil Beaton, *Gigi*

Ralph Jester, Edith Head and John Jensen, *The Buccaneer*

Charles LeMaire and Mary Wills, *A Certain Smile*

Jean Louis, *Bell, Book and Candle*

Walter Plunkett, *Some Came Running*

SPECIAL EFFECTS

A. Arnold Gillespie, visual; Harold Humbrock, audible, *Torpedo Run*

Tom Howard, visual, *tom thumb*

SHORT SUBJECTS
CARTOON

Knighty Knight Bugs (*Bugs Bunny Series*) (John W. Burton, producer; Warner Bros.)

Paul Bunyan (Walt Disney Productions; Buena Vista)

Sidney's Family Tree (*Silly Sidney Series*) (Terrytoons; Twentieth Century-Fox)

LIVE ACTION

Grand Canyon (Walt Disney Productions; Buena Vista)

Journey Into Spring (British Transport Films; Lester A. Schoenfeld Films)

The Kiss (Cohay Productions; Continental Distributing, Inc.)

Snows of Aorangi (New Zealand Screen Board; George Brest and Associates)

T Is for Tumbleweed (James A. Lebenthal Productions; Continental Distributing, Inc.)

DOCUMENTARY
SHORT SUBJECT

AMA Girls (*People and Places Series*) (Walt Disney Productions; Buena Vista)

Employees Only (Kenneth G. Brown, producer; Hughes Aircraft Co.)

Journey Into Spring (British Transport Films; Lester A. Schoenfeld Films)

The Living Stone (Tom Daly, producer; National Film Board of Canada)

Overture (United Nations Film Services; Kingsley International Pictures)

FEATURE

Antarctic Crossing (World Wide Pictures; Lester A. Schoenfeld Films)

The Hidden World (Robert Snyder, producer; Small World Co.)

Psychiatric Nursing (Nathan Zucker, producer; Dynamic Films, Inc.)

White Wilderness (*True Life Adventure Series*) (Walt Disney Productions; Buena Vista)

FOREIGN LANGUAGE FILM

Arms and the Man, Federal Republic of Germany – West

La Venganza, Spain

My Uncle, France

The Road a Year Long, Yugoslavia

The Usual Unidentified Thieves, Italy

IRVING G. THALBERG MEMORIAL AWARD
Jack L. Warner

HONORARY AWARD

To **Maurice Chevalier** for his contributions to the world of entertainment for more than half a century

1959

BEST MOTION PICTURE

Anatomy of a Murder, Otto Preminger, producer (Columbia)

Ben-Hur, Sam Zimbalist, producer (MGM)

The Diary of Anne Frank, George Stevens, producer (Twentieth Century-Fox)

The Nun's Story, Henry Blanke, producer (Warner Bros.)

Room at the Top, John and James Woolf, producers (Continental)

BEST ACTOR

Laurence Harvey, *Room at the Top*

Charlton Heston, *Ben-Hur*

Jack Lemmon, *Some Like It Hot*

Paul Muni, *The Last Angry Man*

James Stewart, *Anatomy of a Murder*

Charlton Heston, *Ben-Hur*

BEST ACTRESS

Doris Day, *Pillow Talk*

Audrey Hepburn, *The Nun's Story*

Katharine Hepburn, *Suddenly, Last Summer*

Simone Signoret, *Room at the Top*

Elizabeth Taylor, *Suddenly, Last Summer*

ACTOR IN A SUPPORTING ROLE

Hugh Griffith, *Ben-Hur*

Arthur O'Connell, *Anatomy of a Murder*

George C. Scott, *Anatomy of a Murder*

Robert Vaughn, *The Young Philadelphians*

Ed Wynn, *The Diary of Anne Frank*

ACTRESS IN A SUPPORTING ROLE

Hermione Baddeley, *Room at the Top*

Susan Kohner, *Imitation of Life*

Juanita Moore, *Imitation of Life*

Thelma Ritter, *Pillow Talk*

Shelley Winters, *The Diary of Anne Frank*

DIRECTING

Jack Clayton, *Room at the Top*

George Stevens, *The Diary of Anne Frank*

Billy Wilder, *Some Like It Hot*

William Wyler, *Ben-Hur*

Fred Zinnemann, *The Nun's Story*

WRITING

SCREENPLAY BASED ON MATERIAL FROM ANOTHER MEDIUM

Robert Anderson, *The Nun's Story*

Wendell Mayes, *Anatomy of a Murder*

Neil Paterson, *Room at the Top*

Karl Tunberg, *Ben-Hur*

Billy Wilder and I. A. L. Diamond, *Some Like It Hot*

STORY AND SCREENPLAY WRITTEN DIRECTLY FOR THE SCREEN

Ingmar Bergman, *Wild Strawberries*

Ernest Lehman, *North by Northwest*

Russell Rouse and Clarence Greene, story; Stanley Shapiro and Maurice Richlin, screenplay, *Pillow Talk*

François Truffaut and Marcel Moussy, *The 400 Blows*

CINEMATOGRAPHY

BLACK-AND-WHITE

Charles Lang, Jr., *Some Like It Hot*

Joseph LaShelle, *Career*

Sam Leavitt, *Anatomy of a Murder*

William C. Mellor, *The Diary of Anne Frank*

Harry Stradling, Sr., *The Young Philadelphians*

COLOR

Daniel L. Fapp, *The Five Pennies*

Lee Garmes, *The Big Fisherman*

Franz Planer, *The Nun's Story*

Leon Shamroy, *Porgy and Bess*

Robert L. Surtees, *Ben-Hur*

ART DIRECTION

BLACK-AND-WHITE

Carl Anderson, art direction; William Kiernan, set decoration, *The Last Angry Man*

Ted Haworth, art direction; Edward G. Boyle, set decoration, *Some Like It Hot*

Oliver Messel and William Kellner, art direction; Scot Slimon, set decoration, *Suddenly, Last Summer*

Hal Pereira and Walter Tyler, art direction; Sam Comer and Arthur Krams, set decoration, *Career*

Lyle R. Wheeler and George W. Davis, art direction; Walter M. Scott and Stuart A. Reiss, set decoration, *The Diary of Anne Frank*

COLOR

John DeCuir, art direction; Julia Heron, set decoration, *The Big Fisherman*

William A. Horning, Robert Boyle and Merrill Pye, art direction; Henry Grace and Frank McKelvy, set decoration, *North by Northwest*

William A. Horning and Edward Carfagno, art direction; Hugh Hunt, set decoration, *Ben-Hur*

Richard H. Riedel, art direction; Russell A. Gausman and Ruby R. Levitt, set decoration, *Pillow Talk*

Lyle R. Wheeler, art direction, Franz Bachelin and Herman A. Blumenthal, set decoration; Walter M. Scott and Joseph Kish, *Journey to the Center of the Earth*

SOUND

MGM London Studio Sound Dept., *Libel!*

MGM Studio Sound Dept. *Ben-Hur*

Samuel Goldwyn Studio Sound Dept. and Todd-AO Sound Dept., *Porgy and Bess*

Twentieth Century-Fox Studio Sound Dept., *Journey to the Center of the Earth*

Warner Bros. Studio Sound Dept., *The Nun's Story*

MUSIC

SONG

"The Best of Everything," *The Best of Everything*, Alfred Newman, music; Sammy Cahn, lyrics

"The Five Pennies," *The Five Pennies*, Sylvia Fine, music and lyrics

"The Hanging Tree," *The Hanging Tree*, Jerry Livingston, music; Mack David, lyrics

"High Hopes," *A Hole in the Head*, James Van Heusen, music; Sammy Cahn, lyrics

"Strange Are the Ways of Love," *The Young Land*, Dimitri Tiomkin, music; Ned Washington, lyrics

SCORING OF A DRAMATIC OR COMEDY PICTURE

Frank DeVol, *Pillow Talk*

Ernest Gold, *On the Beach*

Miklos Rozsa, *Ben-Hur*

Franz Waxman, *The Nun's Story*

SCORING OF A MUSICAL PICTURE

George Bruns, *Sleeping Beauty*

Lionel Newman, *Say One for Me*

André Previn and Ken Darby, *Porgy and Bess*

Nelson Riddle and Joseph J. Lilley, *Li'l Abner*

Leith Stevens, *The Five Pennies*

FILM EDITING

Frederic Knudtson, *On the Beach*

Louis R. Loeffler, *Anatomy of a Murder*

Walter Thompson, *The Nun's Story*

George Tomasini, *North by Northwest*

Ralph E. Winters and John D. Dunning, *Ben-Hur*

COSTUME DESIGN

BLACK-AND-WHITE

Edith Head, *Career*

Charles LeMaire and Mary Wills, *The Diary of Anne Frank*

Orry-Kelly, *Some Like It Hot*

Helen Rose, *The Gazebo*

Howard Shoup, *The Young Philadelphians*

COLOR

Elizabeth Haffenden, *Ben-Hur*

Edith Head, *The Five Pennies*

Adele Palmer, *The Best of Everything*

Renie, *The Big Fisherman*

Irene Sharaff, *Porgy and Bess*

SPECIAL EFFECTS

L. B. Abbott and James G. Bordon, visual; Carl Faulkner, audible, *Journey to the Center of the Earth*

A. Arnold Gillespie and Robert MacDonald, visual; Milo Lory, audible, *Ben-Hur*

SHORT SUBJECTS

CARTOON

Mexicali Shmoes (*Speedy Gonzales Series*) (John W. Burton, producer; Warner Bros.)

Moonbird (Storyboard, Inc.; Edward Harrison)

Noah's Ark (Walt Disney Productions; Buena Vista)

The Violinist (Pintoff Productions; Kingsley International)

LIVE ACTION

Between the Tides (British Transport Films; Lester A. Schoenfeld Films)

The Golden Fish (Les Requins Associes; Columbia)

Mysteries of the Deep (Walt Disney Productions; Buena Vista)

The Running, Jumping and Standing-Still Film (Lion International Films; Kingsley-Union Films)

Skyscraper (Tishman Realty and Construction Co.; Burstyn Film Enterprises)

DOCUMENTARY

SHORT SUBJECT

Donald in Mathmagic Land (Walt Disney Productions; Buena Vista)

From Generation to Generation (Cullen Associates; Maternity Center Association)

Glass (Netherlands Government; George K. Arthur-Go Pictures, Inc.)

FEATURE

The Race for Space (David L. Wolper, producer; Wolper, Inc.)

Serengeti Shall Not Die (Okapia-Film GmbH Production; Transocean-Film)

FOREIGN LANGUAGE FILM

Black Orpheus, France

The Bridge, Federal Republic of Germany—West

The Great War, Italy

Paw, Denmark

The Village on the River, Netherlands

JEAN HERSHOLT HUMANITARIAN AWARD

Bob Hope

HONORARY AWARDS

To **Lee De Forest** for his pioneering inventions which brought sound to the motion picture

To **Buster Keaton** for his unique talents which brought immortal comedies to the screen

1960

BEST MOTION PICTURE

The Alamo, John Wayne, producer (United Artists)

***The Apartment*, Billy Wilder, producer (United Artists)**

Elmer Gantry, Bernard Smith, producer (United Artists)

Sons and Lovers, Jerry Wald, producer (Twentieth Century-Fox)

The Sundowners, Fred Zinnemann, producer (Warner Bros.)

The Apartment

BEST ACTOR
Trevor Howard, *Sons and Lovers*
Burt Lancaster, *Elmer Gantry*
Jack Lemmon, *The Apartment*
Laurence Olivier, *The Entertainer*
Spencer Tracy, *Inherit the Wind*

BEST ACTRESS
Greer Garson, *Sunrise at Campobello*
Deborah Kerr, *The Sundowners*
Shirley MacLaine, *The Apartment*
Melina Mercouri, *Never on Sunday*
Elizabeth Taylor, *Butterfield 8*

ACTOR IN A SUPPORTING ROLE
Peter Falk, *Murder, Inc.*
Jack Kruschen, *The Apartment*
Sal Mineo, *Exodus*
Peter Ustinov, *Spartacus*
Chill Wills, *The Alamo*

ACTRESS IN A SUPPORTING ROLE
Glynis Johns, *The Sundowners*
Shirley Jones, *Elmer Gantry*
Shirley Knight, *The Dark at the Top of the Stairs*
Janet Leigh, *Psycho*
Mary Ure, *Sons and Lovers*

DIRECTING
Jack Cardiff, *Sons and Lovers*
Jules Dassin, *Never on Sunday*
Alfred Hitchcock, *Psycho*
Billy Wilder, *The Apartment*
Fred Zinnemann, *The Sundowners*

WRITING
**SCREENPLAY BASED ON MATERIAL
FROM ANOTHER MEDIUM**
Richard Brooks, *Elmer Gantry*
James Kennaway, *Tunes of Glory*

Gavin Lambert and T. E. B. Clarke, *Sons and Lovers*
Isobel Lennart, *The Sundowners*
Nedrick Young and Harold Jacob Smith, *Inherit the Wind*

**STORY AND SCREENPLAY WRITTEN
DIRECTLY FOR THE SCREEN**
Jules Dassin, *Never on Sunday*
Marguérite Duras, *Hiroshima, Mon Amour*
Richard Gregson and Michael Craig, story; Bryan Forbes,
    screenplay, *The Angry Silence*
Norman Panama and Melvin Frank, *The Facts of Life*
Billy Wilder and I. A. L. Diamond, *The Apartment*

CINEMATOGRAPHY
BLACK-AND-WHITE
Freddie Francis, *Sons and Lovers*
Charles B. Lang, Jr., *The Facts of Life*
Joseph LaShelle, *The Apartment*
Ernest Laszlo, *Inherit the Wind*
John L. Russell, *Psycho*

COLOR
William H. Clothier, *The Alamo*
Sam Leavitt, *Exodus*
Joe MacDonald, *Pepe*
Russell Metty, *Spartacus*
Joseph Ruttenberg and Charles Harten, *Butterfield 8*

ART DIRECTION
BLACK-AND-WHITE
Joseph Hurley and Robert Clatworthy, art direction; George
    Milo, set decoration, *Psycho*
Joseph McMillan Johnson and Kenneth A. Reid, art direction;
    Ross Dowd, set decoration, *The Facts of Life*
Tom Morahan, art direction; Lionel Couch, set decoration,
    Sons and Lovers
Hal Pereira and Walter Tyler, art direction; Sam Comer and
    Arthur Krams, set decoration, *Visit to a Small Planet*
**Alexander Trauner, art direction; Edward G. Boyle, set
    decoration, *The Apartment***

COLOR
Edward Carrere, art direction; George James Hopkins, set
    decoration, *Sunrise at Campobello*
George W. Davis and Addison Hehr, art direction; Henry
    Grace, Hugh Hunt and Otto Siegel, set decoration,
    Cimarron
**Alexander Golitzen and Eric Orbom, art direction; Russell A.
    Gausman and Julia Heron, set decoration, *Spartacus***
Ted Haworth, art direction; William Kiernan, set decoration,
    Pepe
Hal Pereira and Roland Anderson, art direction; Sam Comer
    and Arrigo Breschi, set decoration, *It Started in Naples*

SOUND
Columbia Studio Sound Dept., *Pepe*
MGM Studio Sound Dept., *Cimarron*
**Samuel Goldwyn Studio Sound Dept. and Todd-AO Sound
    Dept., *The Alamo***
Samuel Goldwyn Studio Sound Dept., *The Apartment*
Warner Bros. Studio Sound Dept., *Sunrise at Campobello*

MUSIC

SONG

"The Facts of Life," *The Facts of Life*, Johnny Mercer, music and lyrics

"Faraway Part of Town," *Pepe*, André Previn, music; Dory Langdon, lyrics

"The Green Leaves of Summer," *The Alamo*, Dimitri Tiomkin, music; Paul Francis Webster, lyrics

"Never on Sunday," *Never on Sunday*, Manos Hadjidakis, music and lyrics

"The Second Time Around," *High Time*, James Van Heusen, music; Sammy Cahn, lyrics

SCORING OF A DRAMATIC OR COMEDY PICTURE

Elmer Bernstein, *The Magnificent Seven*

Ernest Gold, *Exodus*

Alex North, *Spartacus*

André Previn, *Elmer Gantry*

Dimitri Tiomkin, *The Alamo*

SCORING OF A MUSICAL PICTURE

Johnny Green, *Pepe*

Lionel Newman and Earle H. Hagen, *Let's Make Love*

André Previn, *Bells Are Ringing*

Nelson Riddle, *Can-Can*

Morris Stoloff and Harry Sukman, *Song Without End*

FILM EDITING

Stuart Gilmore, *The Alamo*

Frederic Knudtson, *Inherit the Wind*

Robert Lawrence, *Spartacus*

Viola Lawrence and Al Clark, *Pepe*

Daniel Mandell, *The Apartment*

COSTUME DESIGN

BLACK-AND-WHITE

Edith Head and Edward Stevenson, *The Facts of Life*

Howard Shoup, *The Rise and Fall of Legs Diamond*

Bill Thomas, *Seven Thieves*

Deni Vachlioti, *Never on Sunday*

Marik Vos, *The Virgin Spring*

COLOR

Marjorie Best, *Sunrise at Campobello*

Edith Head, *Pepe*

Irene, *Midnight Lace*

Irene Sharaff, *Can-Can*

Bill Thomas and Valles, *Spartacus*

SPECIAL EFFECTS

A.J. Lohman, visual, *The Last Voyage*

Gene Warren and Tim Baar, visual, *The Time Machine*

SHORT SUBJECTS

CARTOON

Goliath II (Walt Disney Productions; Buena Vista)

High Note (*Looney Tune Series*) (Warner Bros.)

Mouse and Garden (*Sylvester the Cat Series*) (Warner Bros.)

Munro (*Noveltoon Series*) (Rembrandt Films; Film Representations)

A Place in the Sun (Frantisek Vystrecil, producer; George K. Arthur-Go Pictures)

LIVE ACTION

The Creation of Woman (Trident Films, Inc.; Sterling World Distributors)

Day of the Painter (Little Movies; Kingsley-Union Films)

Islands of the Sea (*True Life Adventure Series*) (Walt Disney Productions; Buena Vista)

A Sport Is Born (*Sports Illustrated Series*) (Leslie Winik, producer; Paramount)

DOCUMENTARY

SHORT SUBJECT

Beyond Silence (U.S. Information Agency)

A City Called Copenhagen (Statens Filmcentral; Danish Government Film Office)

George Grosz' Interregnum (Charles Carey and Altina Carey, producers; Educational Communications Corp.)

Giuseppina (James Hill Production; Lester A. Schoenfeld Films)

Universe (National Film Board of Canada; Lester A. Schoenfeld Films)

FEATURE

The Horse With the Flying Tail (Walt Disney Productions; Buena Vista)

Rebel in Paradise (Robert D. Fraser, producer; Tiare Co.)

FOREIGN LANGUAGE FILM

Kapo, Italy

La Verité, France

Macario, Mexico

The Ninth Circle, Yugoslavia

The Virgin Spring, Sweden

JEAN HERSHOLT HUMANITARIAN AWARD

Sol Lesser

HONORARY AWARDS

To **Gary Cooper** for his many memorable screen performances and the international recognition he, as an individual, has gained for the motion picture industry

To **Stan Laurel** for his creative pioneering in the field of cinema comedy

To **Hayley Mills** for *Pollyana*, the most outstanding juvenile performance during 1960

1961

BEST MOTION PICTURE

Fanny, Joshua Logan, producer (Warner Bros.)

The Guns of Navarone, Carl Foreman, producer (Columbia)

The Hustler, Robert Rossen, producer (Twentieth Century-Fox)

Judgment at Nuremberg, Stanley Kramer, producer (United Artists)

West Side Story, Robert Wise, producer (United Artists)

BEST ACTOR

Charles Boyer, *Fanny*

Paul Newman, *The Hustler*

Sophia Loren, *Two Women*

Maximilian Schell, *Judgment at Nuremberg*
Spencer Tracy, *Judgment at Nuremberg*
Stuart Whitman, *The Mark*

BEST ACTRESS

Audrey Hepburn, *Breakfast at Tiffany's*
Piper Laurie, *The Hustler*
Sophia Loren, *Two Women*
Geraldine Page, *Summer and Smoke*
Natalie Wood, *Splendor in the Grass*

ACTOR IN A SUPPORTING ROLE

George Chakiris, *West Side Story*
Montgomery Clift, *Judgment at Nuremberg*
Peter Falk, *Pocketful of Miracles*
Jackie Gleason, *The Hustler*
George C. Scott, *The Hustler*

ACTRESS IN A SUPPORTING ROLE

Fay Bainter, *The Children's Hour*
Judy Garland, *Judgment at Nuremberg*
Lotte Lenya, *The Roman Spring of Mrs. Stone*
Una Merkel, *Summer and Smoke*
Rita Moreno, *West Side Story*

DIRECTING

Federico Fellini, *La Dolce Vita*
Stanley Kramer, *Judgment at Nuremberg*
Robert Rossen, *The Hustler*
J. Lee Thompson, *The Guns of Navarone*
Robert Wise and Jerome Robbins, *West Side Story*

WRITING

SCREENPLAY BASED ON MATERIAL FROM ANOTHER MEDIUM

George Axelrod, *Breakfast at Tiffany's*
Sidney Carroll and Robert Rossen, *The Hustler*
Carl Foreman, *The Guns of Navarone*
Ernest Lehman, *West Side Story*
Abby Mann, *Judgment at Nuremberg*

STORY AND SCREENPLAY WRITTEN DIRECTLY FOR THE SCREEN

Sergio Amidei, Diego Fabbri and Indro Montanelli, *General Della Rovere*
Federico Fellini, Tullio Pinelli, Ennio Flaiano and Brunello Rondi, *La Dolce Vita*
William Inge, *Splendor in the Grass*
Stanley Shapiro and Paul Henning, *Lover Come Back*
Valentin Yoshov and Grigori Chukhrai, *Ballad of a Soldier*

CINEMATOGRAPHY

BLACK-AND-WHITE

Edward Colman, *The Absent-Minded Professor*
Daniel L. Fapp, *One, Two, Three*
Ernest Laszlo, *Judgment at Nuremberg*
Franz F. Planer, *The Children's Hour*
Eugen Shuftan, *The Hustler*

COLOR

Jack Cardiff, *Fanny*
Daniel L. Fapp, *West Side Story*
Charles Lang, Jr., *One-Eyed Jacks*
Russell Metty, *Flower Drum Song*
Harry Stradling, Sr., *A Majority of One*

ART DIRECTION

BLACK-AND-WHITE

Fernando Carrere, art direction; Edward G. Boyle, set decoration, *The Children's Hour*
Carroll Clark, art direction; Emile Kuri and Hal Gausman, set decoration, *The Absent-Minded Professor*
Piero Gherardi, art direction and set decoration, *La Dolce Vita*
Harry Horner, art direction; Gene Callahan, set decoration, *The Hustler*
Rudolph Sternad, art direction; George Milo, set decoration, *Judgment at Nuremberg*

COLOR

Veniero Colasanti and John Moore, art direction and set decoration, *El Cid*
Alexander Golitzen and Joseph Wright, art direction; Howard Bristol, set decoration, *Flower Drum Song*
Boris Leven, art direction; Victor Gangelin, set decoration, *West Side Story*
Hal Pereira and Roland Anderson, art direction; Sam Comer and Ray Moyer, set decoration, *Breakfast at Tiffany's*
Hal Pereira and Walter Tyler, art direction; Sam Comer and Arthur Krams, set decoration, *Summer and Smoke*

SOUND

Revue Studio Sound Dept., Waldon O. Watson, sound director, *Flower Drum Song*
Samuel Goldwyn Studio Sound Dept., Gordon E. Sawyer, sound director, *The Children's Hour*
Shepperton Studio Sound Dept., John Cox, sound director, *The Guns of Navarone*
Todd-AO Sound Dept., Fred Hynes, sound director and Samuel Goldwyn Studio Sound Dept., Gordon E. Sawyer, sound director, *West Side Story*
Walt Disney Studio Sound Dept., Robert O. Cook, sound director, *The Parent Trap*

MUSIC

SONG

"Bachelor in Paradise," *Bachelor in Paradise*, Henry Mancini, music; Mack David, lyrics

"Love Theme From *El Cid*" (The Falcon and the Dove), *El Cid*, Miklos Rozsa, music; Paul Francis Webster, lyrics

"Moon River," *Breakfast at Tiffany's*, Henry Mancini, music; Johnny Mercer, lyrics

"Pocketful of Miracles," *Pocketful of Miracles*, James Van Heusen, music; Sammy Cahn, lyrics

"Town Without Pity," *Town Without Pity*, Dimitri Tiomkin, music; Ned Washington, lyrics

SCORING OF A DRAMATIC OR COMEDY PICTURE

Elmer Bernstein, *Summer and Smoke*

Henry Mancini, *Breakfast at Tiffany's*

Miklos Rozsa, *El Cid*

Morris Stoloff and Harry Sukman, *Fanny*

Dimitri Tiomkin, *The Guns of Navarone*

SCORING OF A MUSICAL PICTURE

George Bruns, *Babes in Toyland*

Saul Chaplin, Johnny Green, Sid Ramin and Irwin Kostal, *West Side Story*

Duke Ellington, *Paris Blues*

Alfred Newman and Ken Darby, *Flower Drum Song*

Dimitri Shostakovich, *Khovanshchina*

FILM EDITING

Philip W. Anderson, *The Parent Trap*

Frederic Knudtson, *Judgment at Nuremberg*

Alan Osbiston, *The Guns of Navarone*

William H. Reynolds, *Fanny*

Thomas Stanford, *West Side Story*

COSTUME DESIGN

BLACK-AND-WHITE

Piero Gherardi, *La Dolce Vita*

Dorothy Jeakins, *The Children's Hour*

Jean Louis, *Judgment at Nuremberg*

Yoshiro Muraki, *Yojimbo*

Howard Shoup, *Claudelle Inglish*

COLOR

Babes in Toyland, Bill Thomas

Back Street, Jean Louis

Flower Drum Song, Irene Sharaff

Pocketful of Miracles, Edith Head and Walter Plunkett

***West Side Story*, Irene Sharaff**

SPECIAL EFFECTS

Robert A. Mattey and Eustace Lycett, visual, *The Absent-Minded Professor*

Bill Warrington, visual; Vivian C. Greenham, audible, *The Guns of Navarone*

SHORT SUBJECTS

CARTOON

Aquamania (Walt Disney Productions; Buena Vista)

Beep Prepared (Roadrunner and Coyote Series) (Chuck Jones, producer; Warner Bros.)

***Ersatz (The Substitute)* (Zagreb Film; Herts-Lion International Corp.)**

Nelly's Folly (Nelly the Giraffe Series) (Chuck Jones, producer; Warner Bros.)

Pied Piper of Guadalupe (Speedy Gonzalez and Sylvester Series) (Friz Freleng, producer; Warner Bros.)

LIVE ACTION

Ballon Vole (Play Ball!) (Ciné-Documents; Kingsley International)

The Face of Jesus (Jenga Productions; Harry Stern, Inc.)

Rooftops of New York (Musical Travelbook Series) (McCarty-Rush Production in association with Robert Gaffney; Columbia)

***Seawards the Great Ships* (Templar Film Studios; Lester A. Schoenfeld Films)**

Very Nice, Very Nice (National Film Board of Canada; Kingsley International)

DOCUMENTARY

SHORT SUBJECT

Breaking the Language Barrier (Travel Adventure Series) (U.S. Air Force)

Cradle of Genius (Plough Productions; Irving M. Lesser Film Presentation)

Kahl (Dido Film GmbH; AEG-Filmdienst)

L'Uomo in Grigio (The Man in Gray) (Benedetto Benedetti, producer; Benedetto Benedetti Production)

***Project Hope* (MacManus, John and Adams, Inc./Klaeger Film Production; Ex-Cell-O Corp.)**

FEATURE

La Grande Olimpiade (Olympic Games 1960) (Dell Istituto Nazionale Luce, Comitato Organizzatore Del Giochi Della XVII Olimpiade; Cineriz)

***Le Ciel et la Boue (Sky Above and Mud Beneath)* (Ardennes Films and Michael Arthur Film Productions; Rank Films)**

FOREIGN LANGUAGE FILM

Harry and the Butler, Denmark

Immortal Love, Japan

The Important Man, Mexico

Placido, Spain

***Through a Glass Darkly*, Sweden**

IRVING G. THALBERG MEMORIAL AWARD

Stanley Kramer

JEAN HERSHOLT HUMANITARIAN AWARD

George Seaton

HONORARY AWARDS

To **William L. Hendricks** for his outstanding patriotic service in the conception, writing and production of the Marine Corps film, *A Force in Readiness*, which has brought honor to the Academy and the motion picture industry

To **Fred L. Metzler** for his dedication and outstanding service to the Academy of Motion Picture Arts and Sciences

To **Jerome Robbins** for his brilliant achievements in the art of choreography on film

1962

BEST PICTURE

Lawrence of Arabia, Sam Spiegel, producer (Columbia)

The Longest Day, Darryl F. Zanuck, producer (Twentieth Century-Fox)

Meredith Willson's the Music Man, Morton Da Costa, producer (Warner Bros.)

Mutiny on the Bounty, Aaron Rosenberg, producer (MGM)

To Kill a Mockingbird, Alan J. Pakula, producer (Universal-International)

BEST ACTOR

Burt Lancaster, *Birdman of Alcatraz*

Jack Lemmon, *Days of Wine and Roses*

Marcello Mastroianni, *Divorce — Italian Style*

Peter O'Toole, *Lawrence of Arabia*

Gregory Peck, *To Kill a Mockingbird*

BEST ACTRESS

Anne Bancroft, *The Miracle Worker*

Bette Davis, *What Ever Happened to Baby Jane?*

Katharine Hepburn, *Long Day's Journey Into Night*

Geraldine Page, *Sweet Bird of Youth*

Lee Remick, *Days of Wine and Roses*

ACTOR IN A SUPPORTING ROLE

Ed Begley, *Sweet Bird of Youth*

Victor Buono, *What Ever Happened to Baby Jane?*

Telly Savalas, *Birdman of Alcatraz*

Omar Sharif, *Lawrence of Arabia*

Terence Stamp, *Billy Budd*

ACTRESS IN A SUPPORTING ROLE

Mary Badham, *To Kill a Mockingbird*

Patty Duke, *The Miracle Worker*

Shirley Knight, *Sweet Bird of Youth*

Angela Lansbury, *The Manchurian Candidate*

Thelma Ritter, *Birdman of Alcatraz*

DIRECTING

Pietro Germi, *Divorce — Italian Style*

David Lean, *Lawrence of Arabia*

Robert Mulligan, *To Kill a Mockingbird*

Arthur Penn, *The Miracle Worker*

Frank Perry, *David and Lisa*

WRITING

SCREENPLAY BASED ON MATERIAL FROM ANOTHER MEDIUM

Robert Bolt, *Lawrence of Arabia*

Horton Foote, *To Kill a Mockingbird*

William Gibson, *The Miracle Worker*

Vladimir Nabokov, *Lolita*

Eleanor Perry, *David and Lisa*

STORY AND SCREENPLAY WRITTEN DIRECTLY FOR THE SCREEN

Ingmar Bergman, *Through a Glass Darkly*

Ennio de Concini, Alfredo Giannetti and Pietro Germi, *Divorce — Italian Style*

Charles Kaufman, story; Charles Kaufman and Wolfgang Reinhardt, screenplay, *Freud*

Alain Robbe-Grillet, *Last Year at Marienbad*

Stanley Shapiro and Nate Monaster, *That Touch of Mink*

CINEMATOGRAPHY

BLACK-AND-WHITE

Jean Bourgoin and Walter Wottitz, *The Longest Day*

Burnett Guffey, *Birdman of Alcatraz*

Ernest Haller, *What Ever Happened to Baby Jane?*

Russell Harlan, *To Kill a Mockingbird*

Ted McCord, *Two for the Seesaw*

COLOR

Russell Harlan, *Hatari!*

Harry Stradling, Sr., *Gypsy*

Robert L. Surtees, *Mutiny on the Bounty*

Paul C. Vogel, *The Wonderful World of the Brothers Grimm*

Fred A. Young, *Lawrence of Arabia*

ART DIRECTION

BLACK-AND-WHITE

George W. Davis and Edward Carfagno, art direction; Henry Grace and Dick Pefferle, set decoration, *Period of Adjustment*

Alexander Golitzen and Henry Bumstead, art direction; Oliver Emert, set decoration, *To Kill a Mockingbird*

Ted Haworth, Leon Barsacq and Vincent Korda, art direction; Gabriel Bechir, set decoration, *The Longest Day*

Hal Pereira and Roland Anderson, art direction; Sam Comer and Frank R. McKelvy, set decoration, *The Pigeon That Took Rome*

Joseph Wright, art direction; George James Hopkins, set decoration, *Days of Wine and Roses*

Gregory Peck, *To Kill a Mockingbird*

COLOR

John Box and John Stoll, art direction; Dario Simoni, set decoration, *Lawrence of Arabia*

George W. Davis and Edward Carfagno, art direction; Henry Grace and Dick Pefferle, set decoration, *The Wonderful World of the Brothers Grimm*

Alexander Golitzen and Robert Clatworthy, art direction; George Milo, set decoration, *That Touch of Mink*

Paul Groesse, art direction; George James Hopkins, set decoration, *Meredith Willson's The Music Man*

Hugh Hunt, set decoration, *Mutiny on the Bounty*

SOUND

Shepperton Studio Sound Dept., John Cox, sound director, *Lawrence of Arabia*

Universal City Studio Sound Dept., Waldon O.Watson, sound director, *That Touch of Mink*

Walt Disney Studio Sound Dept., Robert O. Cook, sound director, *Bon Voyage!*

Warner Bros. Studio Sound Dept. and Glen Glenn Sound Dept., Joseph Kelly, sound director, *What Ever Happened to Baby Jane?*

Warner Bros. Studio Sound Dept., George R. Groves, sound director, *Meredith Willson's The Music Man*

MUSIC
SONG

"Days of Wine and Roses," *Days of Wine and Roses*, Henry Mancini, music; Johnny Mercer, lyrics

"Love Song From *Mutiny on the Bounty*" (Follow Me), *Mutiny on the Bounty*, Bronislau Kaper, music; Paul Francis Webster, lyrics

"Song From *Two for the Seesaw*" (Second Chance), *Two for the Seesaw*, André Previn, music; Dory Langdon, lyrics

"Tender Is the Night," *Tender Is the Night*, Sammy Fain, music; Paul Francis Webster, lyrics

"Walk on the Wild Side," *Walk on the Wild Side*, Elmer Bernstein, music; Mack David, lyrics

MUSICAL SCORE, SUBSTANTIALLY ORIGINAL

Elmer Bernstein, *To Kill a Mockingbird*

Jerry Goldsmith, *Freud*

Maurice Jarre, *Lawrence of Arabia*

Bronislau Kaper, *Mutiny on the Bounty*

Franz Waxman, *Taras Bulba*

SCORING OF MUSIC, ADAPTATION OR TREATMENT

Leigh Harline, *The Wonderful World of the Brothers Grimm*

Ray Heindorf, *Meredith Willson's The Music Man*

Michel Magne, *Gigot*

Frank Perkins, *Gypsy*

George Stoll, *Billy Rose's Jumbo*

FILM EDITING

Samuel E. Beetley, *The Longest Day*

Anne Coates, *Lawrence of Arabia*

John McSweeney, Jr., *Mutiny on the Bounty*

Ferris Webster, *The Manchurian Candidate*

William Ziegler, *Meredith Willson's The Music Man*

COSTUME DESIGN
BLACK-AND-WHITE

Don Feld, *Days of Wine and Roses*

Edith Head, *The Man Who Shot Liberty Valance*

Norma Koch, *What Ever Happened to Baby Jane?*

Ruth Morley, *The Miracle Worker*

Denny Vachlioti, *Phaedra*

COLOR

Edith Head, *My Geisha*

Dorothy Jeakins, *Meredith Willson's The Music Man*

Orry-Kelly, *Gypsy*

Bill Thomas, *Bon Voyage!*

Mary Wills, *The Wonderful World of the Brothers Grimm*

SPECIAL EFFECTS

A. Arnold Gillespie, visual; Milo Lory, audible, *Mutiny on the Bounty*

Robert MacDonald, visual; Jacques Maumont, audible, *The Longest Day*

SHORT SUBJECTS
CARTOON

The Hole (Storyboard, Inc.; Brandon Films)

Icarus Montgolfier Wright (Format Films; United Artists)

Now Hear This (*Looney Tune Series*) (Warner Bros. Cartoons, Inc.; Warner Bros.)

Self-Defense — For Cowards (*Self-Help Series*) (Rembrandt Films; Film Representations)

Symposium on Popular Songs (Walt Disney Productions; Buena Vista)

LIVE ACTION

Big City Blues (Martina and Charles Huguenot van der Linden, producers; Mayfair Pictures)

The Cadillac (Robert Clouse Production; United Producers Releasing)

The Cliff Dwellers (Formerly titled *One Plus One*) (Group II Film Production; Lester A. Schoenfeld Films)

Heureux Anniversaire (Happy Anniversary) (C.A.P.A.C. Productions; Atlantic Pictures Corp.)

Pan (Herman van der Horst Production; Mayfair Pictures)

DOCUMENTARY
SHORT SUBJECT

Dylan Thomas (TWW Ltd.; Janus Films)

The John Glenn Story (U.S. Navy; Warner Bros.)

The Road to the Wall (CBS Films, Inc.; U.S. Department of Defense)

FEATURE

Alvorada (*Brazil's Changing Face*) (Hugo Niebeling, producer; MW Filmproduktion)

Black Fox (Image Productions, Inc.; Heritage Films, Inc.)

FOREIGN LANGUAGE FILM

Electra, Greece

The Four Days of Naples, Italy

Keeper of Promises (*The Given Word*) Brazil

Sundays and Cybèle, France

Tlayucan, Mexico

JEAN HERSHOLT HUMANITARIAN AWARD
Steve Broidy

1963

BEST PICTURE

America, America, Elia Kazan, producer (Warner Bros.)

Cleopatra, Walter Wanger, producer (Twentieth Century-Fox)

How the West Was Won, Bernard Smith, producer (MGM)

Lilies of the Field, Ralph Nelson, producer (United Artists)

Tom Jones, Tony Richardson, producer (United Artists-Lopert Pictures)

BEST ACTOR

Albert Finney, *Tom Jones*

Richard Harris, *This Sporting Life*

Rex Harrison, *Cleopatra*

Paul Newman, *Hud*

Sidney Poitier, *Lilies of the Field*

Sidney Poitier, *Lilies of the Field*

BEST ACTRESS

Leslie Caron, *The L-Shaped Room*

Shirley MacLaine, *Irma La Douce*

Patricia Neal, *Hud*

Rachel Roberts, *This Sporting Life*

Natalie Wood, *Love With the Proper Stranger*

ACTOR IN A SUPPORTING ROLE

Nick Adams, *Twilight of Honor*

Bobby Darin, *Captain Newman, M.D.*

Melvyn Douglas, *Hud*

Hugh Griffith, *Tom Jones*

John Huston, *The Cardinal*

ACTRESS IN A SUPPORTING ROLE

Diane Cilento, *Tom Jones*

Dame Edith Evans, *Tom Jones*

Joyce Redman, *Tom Jones*

Margaret Rutherford, *The V.I.P.s*

Lilia Skala, *Lilies of the Field*

DIRECTING

Federico Fellini, *Federico Fellini's 8-1/2*

Elia Kazan, *America, America*

Otto Preminger, *The Cardinal*

Tony Richardson, *Tom Jones*

Martin Ritt, *Hud*

WRITING

SCREENPLAY BASED ON MATERIAL FROM ANOTHER MEDIUM

Serge Bourguigon and Antoine Tudal, *Sundays and Cybèle*

Richard Breen, Phoebe Ephron and Henry Ephron, *Captain Newman, M.D.*

John Osborne, *Tom Jones*

James Poe, *Lilies of the Field*

Irving Ravetch and Harriet Frank, Jr., *Hud*

STORY AND SCREENPLAY WRITTEN DIRECTLY FOR THE SCREEN

Carlo Bernari, screenplay, *The Four Days of Naples*

Pasquale Festa Campanile, Massimo Franciosa, Vasco Pratolini and Nanni Loy, story; Pasquale Festa Campanile, Massimo Franciosa, Nanni Loy and James R. Webb, *How the West Was Won*

Federico Fellini, Ennio Flaiano, Tullio Pinelli and Brunello Rondi, *Federico Fellini's 8-1/2*

Elia Kazan, *America, America*

Arnold Schulman, *Love With the Proper Stranger*

CINEMATOGRAPHY

BLACK-AND-WHITE

Lucien Ballard, *The Caretakers*

George Folsey, *The Balcony*

Ernest Haller, *Lilies of the Field*

James Wong Howe, *Hud*

Milton Krasner, *Love With the Proper Stranger*

COLOR

William H. Daniels, Milton Krasner, Charles Lang, Jr. and Joseph LaShelle, *How the West Was Won*

Joseph LaShelle, *Irma La Douce*

Ernest Laszlo, *It's a Mad, Mad, Mad, Mad World*

Leon Shamroy, *The Cardinal*

Leon Shamroy, *Cleopatra*

ART DIRECTION

BLACK-AND-WHITE

Gene Callahan, art direction, *America, America*

George W. Davis and Paul Groesse, art direction; Henry Grace and Hugh Hunt, set decoration, *Twilight of Honor*

Piero Gherardi, art direction, *Federico Fellini's 8-1/2*

Hal Pereira and Tambi Larsen, art direction; Sam Comer and Robert Benton, set decoration, *Hud*

Hal Pereira and Roland Anderson, art direction; Sam Comer and Grace Gregory, set decoration, *Love With the Proper Stranger*

COLOR

Ralph Brinton, Ted Marshall and Jocelyn Herbert, art direction; Josie MacAvin, set decoration, *Tom Jones*

George W. Davis, William Ferrari and Addison Hehr, art direction; Henry Grace, Don Greenwood, Jr. and Jack Mills, set decoration, *How the West Was Won*

John DeCuir, Jack Martin Smith, Hilyard Brown, Herman Blumenthal, Elven Webb, Maurice Pelling and Boris Juraga, art direction; Walter M. Scott, Paul S. Fox and Ray Moyer, set decoration, *Cleopatra*

Hal Pereira and Roland Anderson, art direction; Sam Comer and James Payne, set decoration, *Come Blow Your Horn*

Lyle Wheeler, art direction; Gene Callahan, set decoration, *The Cardinal*

SOUND

Columbia Studio Sound Dept., *Bye Bye Birdie*

MGM Studio Sound Dept., *How the West Was Won*

Samuel Goldwyn Studio Sound Dept., *It's a Mad, Mad, Mad, Mad World*

Twentieth Century-Fox Studio Sound Dept. and Todd-AO Sound Dept., *Cleopatra*

Universal City Studio Sound Dept., *Captain Newman, M.D.*

MUSIC

SONG

"Call Me Irresponsible," *Papa's Delicate Condition*, James Van Heusen, music; Sammy Cahn, lyrics

"Charade," *Charade*, Henry Mancini, music; Johnny Mercer, lyrics

"It's a Mad, Mad, Mad, Mad World," *It's a Mad, Mad, Mad, Mad World*, Ernest Gold, music; Mack David, lyrics

"More," *Mondo Cane*, Riz Ortolani and Nino Oliviero, music; Norman Newell, lyrics

"So Little Time," *55 Days at Peking*, Dimitri Tiomkin, music; Paul Francis Webster, lyrics

MUSICAL SCORE, SUBSTANTIALLY ORIGINAL

John Addison, *Tom Jones*

Ernest Gold, *It's a Mad, Mad, Mad, Mad World*

Alfred Newman and Ken Darby, *How the West Was Won*

Alex North, *Cleopatra*

Dimitri Tiomkin, *55 Days at Peking*

SCORING OF MUSIC, ADAPTATION OR TREATMENT

George Bruns, *The Sword in the Stone*

John Green, *Bye Bye Birdie*

Maurice Jarre, *Sundays and Cybèle*

André Previn, *Irma La Douce*

Leith Stevens, *A New Kind of Love*

FILM EDITING

Frederic Knudtson, Robert C. Jones and Gene Fowler, Jr., *It's a Mad, Mad, Mad, Mad World*

Harold F. Kress, *How the West Was Won*

Louis R. Loeffler, *The Cardinal*

Dorothy Spencer, *Cleopatra*

Ferris Webster, *The Great Escape*

COSTUME DESIGN

BLACK-AND-WHITE

Piero Gherardi, *Federico Fellini's 8-1/2*

Edith Head, *Love With the Proper Stranger*

Edith Head, *Wives and Lovers*

Bill Thomas, *Toys in the Attic*

Travilla, *The Stripper*

COLOR

Donald Brooks, *The Cardinal*

Edith Head, *A New Kind of Love*

Walter Plunkett, *How the West Was Won*

Irene Sharaff, Vittorio Nino Novarese and Renie, *Cleopatra*

Piero Tosi, *The Leopard*

SPECIAL EFFECTS

Ub Iwerks, *The Birds*

Emil Kosa, Jr., *Cleopatra*

SOUND EFFECTS
(Not necessarily given each year)

Robert L. Bratton, *A Gathering of Eagles*

Walter G. Elliott, *It's a Mad, Mad, Mad, Mad World*

SHORT SUBJECTS

CARTOON

Automania 2000 (Halas and Batchelor Production; Pathé Contemporary Films)

***The Critic* (Pintoff-Crossbow Productions; Columbia)**

The Game (*Igra*) (Zagreb Film; Rembrandt Films-Film Representations)

My Financial Career (National Film Board of Canada; Walter Reade-Sterling-Continental Distributing)

Pianissimo (Carmen D'Avino Production; Cinema 16)

LIVE ACTION

The Concert (James A. King Corp.; George K. Arthur-Go Pictures)

Home-Made Car, BP (North American) Ltd.; Lester A. Schoenfeld Films)

***An Occurrence at Owl Creek Bridge* (Films du Centaure-Filmartic; Cappagariff-Janus Films)**

Six-Sided Triangle (Milesian Film Production, Ltd.; Lion International Films)

That's Me (Stuart Productions; Pathé Contemporary Films)

DOCUMENTARY

SHORT SUBJECT

***Chagall* (Auerbach Film Enterprises, Ltd.-Flag Films; Union Films)**

The Five Cities of June (George Stevens, Jr., producer; U.S. Information Agency)

The Spirit of America (Algernon G. Walker, producer; Spotlight News, Inc.)

Thirty Million Letters (Edgar Anstey, producer; British Transport Films)

To Live Again (Wilding, Inc.; St. Barnabas Hospital, Bronx, N.Y.)

FEATURE

***Robert Frost: A Lover's Quarrel With the World* (WGBH Educational Foundation; Holt, Reinhart and Winston, Inc.)**

Le Maillon et la Chaine (*The Link and the Chain*) (Paul de Roubaix, producer; Films Du Centaure-Filmartic)

Terminus (Edgar Anstey, producer; British Transport Films)

The Yanks Are Coming (Marshall Flaum, producer; David L. Wolper Productions)

FOREIGN LANGUAGE FILM
Federico Fellini's 8-1/2, Italy
Knife in the Water, Poland
Los Tarantos, Spain
The Red Lanterns, Greece
Twin Sisters of Kyoto, Japan

IRVING G. THALBERG MEMORIAL AWARD
Sam Spiegel

1964

BEST PICTURE
Becket, Hal B. Wallis, producer (Paramount)
Dr. Strangelove or: How I Learned to Stop Worrying and Love the Bomb, Stanley Kubrick, producer (Columbia)
Mary Poppins, Walt Disney and Bill Walsh, producers (Buena Vista)
My Fair Lady, Jack L. Warner, producer (Warner Bros.)
Zorba the Greek, Michael Cacoyannis, producer (International Classics)

BEST ACTOR
Richard Burton, *Becket*
Rex Harrison, *My Fair Lady*
Peter O'Toole, *Becket*
Anthony Quinn, *Zorba the Greek*
Peter Sellers, *Dr. Strangelove or: How I Learned to Stop Worrying and Love the Bomb*

My Fair Lady

BEST ACTRESS
Julie Andrews, *Mary Poppins*
Anne Bancroft, *The Pumpkin Eater*
Sophia Loren, *Marriage Italian Style*
Debbie Reynolds, *The Unsinkable Molly Brown*
Kim Stanley, *Seance on a Wet Afternoon*

ACTOR IN A SUPPORTING ROLE
John Gielgud, *Becket*
Stanley Holloway, *My Fair Lady*
Edmond O'Brien, *Seven Days in May*
Lee Tracy, *The Best Man*
Peter Ustinov, *Topkapi*

ACTRESS IN A SUPPORTING ROLE
Gladys Cooper, *My Fair Lady*
Dame Edith Evans, *The Chalk Garden*
Grayson Hall, *The Night of the Iguana*
Lila Kedrova, *Zorba the Greek*
Agnes Moorehead, *Hush . . . Hush, Sweet Charlotte*

DIRECTING
Michael Cacoyannis, *Zorba the Greek*
George Cukor, *My Fair Lady*
Peter Glenville, *Becket*
Stanley Kubrick, *Dr. Strangelove or: How I Learned to Stop Worrying and Love the Bomb*
Robert Stevenson, *Mary Poppins*

WRITING
SCREENPLAY BASED ON MATERIAL FROM ANOTHER MEDIUM
Edward Anhalt, *Becket*
Michael Cacoyannis, *Zorba the Greek*
Stanley Kubrick, Peter George and Terry Southern, *Dr. Strangelove or: How I Learned to Stop Worrying and Love the Bomb*
Alan Jay Lerner, *My Fair Lady*
Bill Walsh and Don DaGradi, *Mary Poppins*

STORY AND SCREENPLAY WRITTEN DIRECTLY FOR THE SCREEN
Age, Scarpelli and Mario Monicelli, *The Organizer*
S. H. Barnett, story; Peter Stone and Frank Tarloff, screenplay, *Father Goose*
Orville H. Hampton, story; Orville H. Hampton and Raphael Hayes, screenplay, *One Potato, Two Potato*
Alun Owen, *A Hard Day's Night*
Jean-Paul Rappeneau, Ariane Mnouchkine, Daniel Boulanger and Philippe De Broca, *That Man From Rio*

CINEMATOGRAPHY
BLACK-AND-WHITE
Joseph Biroc, *Hush . . . Hush, Sweet Charlotte*
Gabriel Figueroa, *The Night of the Iguana*
Milton Krasner, *Fate Is the Hunter*
Walter Lassally, *Zorba the Greek*
Philip H. Lathrop, *The Americanization of Emily*

COLOR
William H. Clothier, *Cheyenne Autumn*
Edward Colman, *Mary Poppins*
Daniel L. Fapp, *The Unsinkable Molly Brown*
Harry Stradling, *My Fair Lady*
Geoffrey Unsworth, *Becket*

ART DIRECTION

BLACK-AND-WHITE

George W. Davis, Hans Peters and Elliot Scott, art direction; Henry Grace and Robert R. Benton, set decoration, *The Americanization of Emily*

Vassilis Fotopoulos, *Zorba the Greek*

William Glasgow, art direction; Raphael Bretton, set decoration, *Hush . . . Hush, Sweet Charlotte*

Stephen Grimes, *The Night of the Iguana*

Cary Odell, art direction; Edward G. Boyle, set decoration, *Seven Days in May*

COLOR

Gene Allen and Cecil Beaton, art direction; George James Hopkins, set decoration, *My Fair Lady*

John Bryan and Maurice Carter, art direction; Patrick McLoughlin and Robert Cartwright, set decoration, *Becket*

Carroll Clark and William H. Tuntke, art direction; Emile Kuri and Hal Gausman, set decoration, *Mary Poppins*

George W. Davis and Preston Ames, art direction; Henry Grace and Hugh Hunt, set decoration, *The Unsinkable Molly Brown*

Jack Martin Smith and Ted Haworth, art direction; Walter M. Scott and Stuart A. Reiss, set decoration, *What a Way to Go!*

SOUND

MGM Studio Sound Dept., *The Unsinkable Molly Brown*

Shepperton Studio Sound Dept., *Becket*

Universal City Studio Sound Dept., *Father Goose*

Walt Disney Studio Sound Dept., *Mary Poppins*

Warner Bros. Studio Sound Dept., *My Fair Lady*

MUSIC

SONG

"Chim Chim Cher-ee," *Mary Poppins*, Richard M. Sherman and Robert B. Sherman, music and lyrics

"Dear Heart," *Dear Heart*, Henry Mancini, music; Jay Livingston and Ray Evans, lyrics

"Hush . . . Hush, Sweet Charlotte," *Hush . . . Hush, Sweet Charlotte*, Frank DeVol, music; Mack David, lyrics

"My Kind of Town," *Robin and the 7 Hoods*, James Van Heusen, music; Sammy Cahn, lyrics

"Where Love Has Gone," *Where Love Has Gone*, James Van Heusen, music; Sammy Cahn, lyrics

MUSICAL SCORE, SUBSTANTIALLY ORIGINAL

Frank DeVol, *Hush . . . Hush, Sweet Charlotte*

Henry Mancini, *The Pink Panther*

Laurence Rosenthal, *Becket*

Richard M. Sherman and Robert B. Sherman, *Mary Poppins*

Dimitri Tiomkin, *The Fall of the Roman Empire*

SCORING OF MUSIC, ADAPTATION OR TREATMENT

Robert Armbruster, Leo Arnaud, Jack Elliott, Jack Hayes, Calvin Jackson and Irwin Kostal, *Mary Poppins*

George Martin, *A Hard Day's Night*

André Previn, *My Fair Lady*

Nelson Riddle, *Robin and the 7 Hoods*

Leo Shuken, *The Unsinkable Molly Brown*

FILM EDITING

Anne Coates, *Becket*

Ted J. Kent, *Father Goose*

Michael Luciano, *Hush . . . Hush, Sweet Charlotte*

Cotton Warburton, *Mary Poppins*

William Ziegler, *My Fair Lady*

COSTUME DESIGN

BLACK-AND-WHITE

Edith Head, *A House Is Not a Home*

Rene Hubert, *The Visit*

Dorothy Jeakins, *The Night of the Iguana*

Norma Koch, *Hush . . . Hush, Sweet Charlotte*

Howard Shoup, *Kisses for My President*

COLOR

Cecil Beaton, *My Fair Lady*

Margaret Furse, *Becket*

Morton Haack, *The Unsinkable Molly Brown*

Edith Head and Moss Mabry, *What a Way to Go!*

Tony Walton, *Mary Poppins*

SPECIAL VISUAL EFFECTS

Jim Danforth, *7 Faces of Dr. Lao*

Peter Ellenshaw, Hamilton Luske and Eustace Lycett, *Mary Poppins*

SOUND EFFECTS

Robert L. Bratton, *The Lively Set*

Norman Wanstall, *Goldfinger*

SHORT SUBJECTS

CARTOON

Christmas Cracker (National Film Board of Canada; Favorite Films of California)

How to Avoid Friendship (Self-Help Series) (Rembrandt Films; Film Representations)

Nudnik #2 (Nudnik Series) (Rembrandt Films; Film Representations)

***The Pink Phink* (*Pink Panther Series*) (Mirisch-Geoffrey Productions; United Artists)**

LIVE ACTION SUBJECT

***Casals Conducts: 1964* (Thalia Films; Beckman Film Corp.)**

Help! My Snowman's Burning Down (Carson Davidson Productions; Pathé Contemporary Films)

The Legend of Jimmy Blue Eyes (Robert Clouse Associates; Topaz Film Corp.)

DOCUMENTARY

SHORT SUBJECT

Breaking the Habit (American Cancer Society; Modern Talking Picture Service)

Children Without (Guggenheim Productions; National Education Association)

Kenojuak (National Film Board of Canada)

***Nine From Little Rock* (Guggenheim Productions; U.S. Information Agency)**

140 Days Under the World (New Zealand National Film Unit; Rank Film Distributors of New Zealand)

FEATURE

The Finest Hours (Le Vien Films, Ltd.; Columbia)

Four Days in November (David L. Wolper Productions; United Artists)

The Human Dutch (Bert Haanstra, producer; Haanstra Filmproductie)

Jacques-Yves Cousteau's World Without Sun (Filmad Les Requins Associes-Orsay-CEIAP; Columbia)

Over There, 1914–18 (Zodiac Productions; Pathé Contemporary Films)

FOREIGN LANGUAGE FILM

Raven's End, Sweden

Sallah, Israel

The Umbrellas of Cherbourg, France

Woman in the Dunes, Japan

Yesterday, Today and Tomorrow, Italy

HONORARY AWARD

To **William Tuttle** for his outstanding makeup achievement for *7 Faces of Dr. Lao*

1965

The Sound of Music

BEST PICTURE

Darling, Joseph Janni, producer (Embassy Pictures Corp.)

Doctor Zhivago, Carlo Ponti, producer (MGM)

Ship of Fools, Stanley Kramer, producer (Columbia)

The Sound of Music, Robert Wise, producer (Twentieth Century-Fox)

A Thousand Clowns, Fred Coe, producer (United Artists)

BEST ACTOR

Richard Burton, *The Spy Who Came in From the Cold*

Lee Marvin, *Cat Ballou*

Laurence Olivier, *Othello*

Rod Steiger, *The Pawnbroker*

Oskar Werner, *Ship of Fools*

BEST ACTRESS

Julie Andrews, *The Sound of Music*

Julie Christie, *Darling*

Samantha Eggar, *The Collector*

Elizabeth Hartman, *A Patch of Blue*

Simone Signoret, *Ship of Fools*

ACTOR IN A SUPPORTING ROLE

Martin Balsam, *A Thousand Clowns*

Ian Bannen, *The Flight of the Phoenix*

Tom Courtenay, *Doctor Zhivago*

Michael Dunn, *Ship of Fools*

Frank Finlay, *Othello*

ACTRESS IN A SUPPORTING ROLE

Ruth Gordon, *Inside Daisy Clover*

Joyce Redman, *Othello*

Maggie Smith, *Othello*

Shelley Winters, *A Patch of Blue*

Peggy Wood, *The Sound of Music*

DIRECTING

David Lean, *Doctor Zhivago*

John Schlesinger, *Darling*

Hiroshi Teshigahara, *Woman in the Dunes*

Robert Wise, *The Sound of Music*

William Wyler, *The Collector*

WRITING

SCREENPLAY BASED ON MATERIAL FROM ANOTHER MEDIUM

Robert Bolt, *Doctor Zhivago*

Herb Gardner, *A Thousand Clowns*

Abby Man, *Ship of Fools*

Stanley Mann and John Kohn, *The Collector*

Walter Newman and Frank R. Pierson, *Cat Ballou*

STORY AND SCREENPLAY WRITTEN DIRECTLY FOR THE SCREEN

Age, Scarpelli, Mario Monicelli, Tonino Guerra, Giorgio Salvioni and Suso Cecchi D'Amico, *Casanova 70*

Franklin Coen and Frank Davis, *The Train*

Jack Davies and Ken Annakin, *Those Magnificent Men in Their Flying Machines*

Jacques Demy, *The Umbrellas of Cherbourg*

Frederic Raphael, *Darling*

CINEMATOGRAPHY

BLACK-AND-WHITE

Robert Burks, *A Patch of Blue*

Loyal Griggs, *In Harm's Way*

Burnett Guffey, *King Rat*

Conrad Hall, *Morituri*

Ernest Laszlo, *Ship of Fools*

COLOR

Russell Harlan, *The Great Race*

Ted McCord, *The Sound of Music*

William C. Mellor and Loyal Griggs, *The Greatest Story Ever Told*

Leon Shamroy, *The Agony and the Ecstasy*

Freddie Young, *Doctor Zhivago*

ART DIRECTION

BLACK-AND-WHITE

Robert Clatworthy, art direction; Joseph Kish, set decoration, *Ship of Fools*

George W. Davis and Urie McCleary, art direction; Henry Grace and Charles S. Thompson, set decoration, *A Patch of Blue*

Hal Pereira, Tambi Larsen and Edward Marshall, art direction; Josie MacAvin, set decoration, *The Spy Who Came in From the Cold*

Hal Pereira and Jack Poplin, art direction; Robert Benton and Joseph Kish, set decoration, *The Slender Thread*

Robert Emmet Smith, art direction; Frank Tuttle, set decoration, *King Rat*

COLOR

John Box and Terry Marsh, art direction; Dario Simoni, set decoration, *Doctor Zhivago*

Robert Clatworthy, art direction; George James Hopkins, set decoration, *Inside Daisy Clover*

Richard Day, William Creber and David Hall, art direction; Ray Moyer, Fred MacLean and Norman Rockett, set decoration, *The Greatest Story Ever Told*

John DeCuir and Jack Martin Smith, art direction; Dario Simoni, set decoration, *The Agony and the Ecstasy*

Boris Leven, art direction; Walter M. Scott and Ruby Levitt, set decoration, *The Sound of Music*

SOUND

MGM British Studio Sound Dept. and MGM Studio Sound Dept., *Doctor Zhivago*

Twentieth Century-Fox Studio Sound Dept., *The Agony and the Ecstasy*

Twentieth Century-Fox Studio Sound Dept. and Todd-AO Sound Dept., *The Sound of Music*

Universal City Studio Sound Dept., *Shenandoah*

Warner Bros. Studio Sound Dept., *The Great Race*

MUSIC

SONG

"The Ballad of Cat Ballou," *Cat Ballou*, Jerry Livingston, music; Mack David, lyrics

"I Will Wait for You," *The Umbrellas of Cherbourg*, Michel Legrand, music; Jacques Demy, lyrics

"The Shadow of Your Smile," *The Sandpiper*, Johnny Mandel, music; Paul Francis Webster, lyrics

"The Sweetheart Tree," *The Great Race*, Henry Mancini, music; Johnny Mercer, lyrics

"What's New, Pussycat?," *What's New, Pussycat?*, Burt Bacharach, music; Hal David, lyrics

MUSICAL SCORE, SUBSTANTIALLY ORIGINAL

Jerry Goldsmith, *A Patch of Blue*

Maurice Jarre, *Doctor Zhivago*

Michel Legrand and Jacques Demy, *The Umbrellas of Cherbourg*

Alfred Newman, *The Greatest Story Ever Told*

Alex North, *The Agony and the Ecstasy*

SCORING OF MUSIC, ADAPTATION OR TREATMENT

DeVol, *Cat Ballou*

Irwin Kostal, *The Sound of Music*

Michel Legrand, *The Umbrellas of Cherbourg*

Lionel Newman and Alexander Courage, *The Pleasure Seekers*

Don Walker, *A Thousand Clowns*

FILM EDITING

Michael Luciano, *The Flight of the Phoenix*

Charles Nelson, *Cat Ballou*

William Reynolds, *The Sound of Music*

Norman Savage, *Doctor Zhivago*

Ralph E. Winters, *The Great Race*

COSTUME DESIGN

BLACK-AND-WHITE

Julie Harris, *Darling*

Edith Head, *The Slender Thread*

Moss Mabry, *Morituri*

Howard Shoup, *A Rage to Live*

Bill Thomas and Jean Louis, *Ship of Fools*

COLOR

Phyllis Dalton, *Doctor Zhivago*

Edith Head and Bill Thomas, *Inside Daisy Clover*

Dorothy Jeakins, *The Sound of Music*

Vittorio Nino Novarese, *The Agony and the Ecstasy*

Vittorio Nino Novarese and Marjorie Best, *The Greatest Story Ever Told*

SPECIAL VISUAL EFFECTS

J. McMillan Johnson, *The Greatest Story Ever Told*

John Stears, *Thunderball*

SOUND EFFECTS EDITING

Tregoweth Brown, *The Great Race*

Walter A. Rossi, *Von Ryan's Express*

SHORT SUBJECTS

CARTOON

Clay or the Origin of Species (Harvard University; Pathé Contemporary Films)

The Dot and the Line (Chuck Jones and Les Goldman, producers; MGM)

The Thieving Magpie (*La Gazza Ladra*) (Giulio Gianni-Emanuele Luzzati; Allied Artists)

LIVE ACTION

The Chicken (Le Poulet) (Renn Productions; Pathé Contemporary Films)

Fortress of Peace (Lothar Wolff Productions for Farner-Looser Films; Cinerama)

Skaterdater (Byway Productions; United Artists)

Snow (British Transport Films in association with Geoffrey Jones, Ltd.; Manson Distributing)

Time Piece (Muppets, Inc.; Pathé Contemporary Films)

DOCUMENTARY

SHORT SUBJECT

Mural on Our Street (Henry Street Settlement; Pathé Contemporary Films)

Ouverture (Mafilm Studios Production; Hungarofilm-Pathé Contemporary Films)

Point of View (Vision Associates Production; National Tuberculosis Association)

To Be Alive! (Francis Thompson, producer; Johnson Wax)

Yeats Country (Patrick Carey and Joe Mendoza, producers; Aengus Films for the Dept. of External Affairs of Ireland)

FEATURE

The Battle of the Bulge . . . The Brave Rifles (Laurence E. Mascott, producer; Mascott Productions)

The Eleanor Roosevelt Story (Sidney Glazier Production; American International)

The Forth Road Bridge (Random Film Productions; Shell-Mex and B.P. Film Library)

Let My People Go (Marshall Flaum, producer; David L. Wolper Productions)

To Die in Madrid (Ancinex Productions; Altura Films International)

FOREIGN LANGUAGE FILM

Blood on the Land, Greece

Dear John, Sweden

Kwaidan, Japan

Marriage Italian Style, Italy

The Shop on Main Street, Czechoslovakia

IRVING G. THALBERG MEMORIAL AWARD
William Wyler

JEAN HERSHOLT HUMANITARIAN AWARD
Edmond L. DePatie

HONORARY AWARD
To **Bob Hope** for unique and distinguished service to our industry and the Academy

1966

BEST PICTURE

Alfie, Lewis Gilbert, producer (Paramount)

A Man for All Seasons, Fred Zinnemann, producer (Columbia)

The Russians Are Coming, The Russians Are Coming, Norman Jewison, producer (United Artists)

The Sand Pebbles, Robert Wise, producer (Twentieth Century-Fox)

Who's Afraid of Virginia Woolf? Ernest Lehman, producer (Warner Bros.)

BEST ACTOR

Alan Arkin, *The Russians Are Coming, The Russians Are Coming*

Richard Burton, *Who's Afraid of Virginia Woolf?*

Michael Caine, *Alfie*

Steve McQueen, *The Sand Pebbles*

Paul Scofield, A Man for All Seasons

BEST ACTRESS

Anouk Aimée, *A Man and a Woman*

Ida Kaminska, *The Shop on Main Street*

Lynn Redgrave, *Georgy Girl*

Elizabeth Taylor,
Who's Afraid of Virginia Woolf?

Vanessa Redgrave, *Morgan!*

Elizabeth Taylor, *Who's Afraid of Virginia Woolf?*

ACTOR IN A SUPPORTING ROLE

Mako, *The Sand Pebbles*

James Mason, *Georgy Girl*

Walter Matthau, *The Fortune Cookie*

George Segal, *Who's Afraid of Virginia Woolf?*

Robert Shaw, *A Man for All Seasons*

ACTRESS IN A SUPPORTING ROLE

Sandy Dennis, *Who's Afraid of Virginia Woolf?*

Wendy Hiller, *A Man for All Seasons*

Jocelyne Lagarde, *Hawaii*

Vivien Merchant, *Alfie*

Geraldine Page, *You're a Big Boy Now*

DIRECTING

Michelangelo Antonioni, *Blow-Up*

Richard Brooks, *The Professionals*

Claude Lelouch, *A Man and a Woman*

Mike Nichols, *Who's Afraid of Virginia Woolf?*

Fred Zinnemann, *A Man for All Seasons*

WRITING

SCREENPLAY BASED ON MATERIAL FROM ANOTHER MEDIUM

Robert Bolt, *A Man for All Seasons*

Richard Brooks, *The Professionals*

Ernest Lehman, *Who's Afraid of Virginia Woolf?*

Bill Naughton, *Alfie*

William Rose, *The Russians Are Coming, The Russians Are Coming*

STORY AND SCREENPLAY WRITTEN DIRECTLY FOR THE SCREEN

Michelangelo Antonioni, story; Michelangelo Antonioni, Tonino Guerra and Edward Bond, *Blow-Up*

Robert Ardrey, *Khartoum*

Clint Johnston and Don Peters, *The Naked Prey*

Claude Lelouch, story; Pierre Uytterhoeven and Claude Lelouch, screenplay, *A Man and a Woman*

Billy Wilder and I. A. L. Diamond, *The Fortune Cookie*

CINEMATOGRAPHY

BLACK-AND-WHITE

Marcel Grignon, *Is Paris Burning?*

Ken Higgins, *Georgy Girl*

James Wong Howe, *Seconds*

Joseph LaShelle, *The Fortune Cookie*

Haskell Wexler, *Who's Afraid of Virginia Woolf?*

COLOR

Conrad Hall, *The Professionals*

Russell Harlan, *Hawaii*

Ernest Laszlo, *Fanastic Voyage*

Joseph MacDonald, *The Sand Pebbles*

Ted Moore, *A Man for All Seasons*

ART DIRECTION

BLACK-AND-WHITE

George W. Davis and Paul Groesse, art direction; Henry Grace and Hugh Hunt, set decoration, *Mister Buddwing*

Willy Holt, art direction; Marc Frederix and Pierre Guffroy, set decoration, *Is Paris Burning?*

Robert Luthardt, art direction; Edward G. Boyle, set decoration, *The Fortune Cookie*

Luigi Scaccianoce, art direction, *The Gospel According to St. Matthew*

Richard Sylbert, art direction; George James Hopkins, set decoration, *Who's Afraid of Virginia Woolf?*

COLOR

Piero Gherardi, art direction, *Juliet of the Spirits*

Alexander Golitzen and George C. Webb, art direction; John McCarthy and John Austin, set decoration, *Gambit*

Boris Leven, art direction; Walter M. Scott, John Sturtevant and William Kiernan, set decoration, *The Sand Pebbles*

Hal Pereira and Arthur Lonergan, art direction; Robert Benton and James Payne, set decoration, *The Oscar*

Jack Martin Smith and Dale Hennesy, art direction; Walter M. Scott and Stuart A. Reiss, set decoration, *Fantastic Voyage*

SOUND

MGM Studio Sound Dept., *Grand Prix*

Samuel Goldwyn Studio Sound Dept., *Hawaii*

Twentieth Century-Fox Studio Sound Dept., *The Sand Pebbles*

Universal City Studio Sound Dept., *Gambit*

Warner Bros. Studio Sound Dept., *Who's Afraid of Virginia Woolf?*

MUSIC

SONG

"Alfie," *Alfie*, Burt Bacharach, music; Hal David, lyrics

"Born Free," *Born Free*, John Barry, music; Don Black, lyrics

"Georgy Girl," *Georgy Girl*, Tom Springfield, music; Jim Dale, lyrics

"My Wishing Doll," *Hawaii*, Elmer Bernstein, music; Mack David, lyrics

"A Time for Love," *An American Dream*, Johnny Mandel, music; Paul Francis Webster, lyrics

ORIGINAL MUSIC SCORE

John Barry, *Born Free*

Elmer Bernstein, *Hawaii*

Jerry Goldsmith, *The Sand Pebbles*

Toshiro Mayuzumi, *The Bible*

Alex North, *Who's Afraid of Virginia Woolf?*

SCORING OF MUSIC, ADAPTATION OR TREATMENT

Luis Enrique Bacalov, *The Gospel According to St. Matthew*

Elmer Bernstein, *Return of the Seven*

Al Ham, *Stop the World — I Want to Get Off*

Harry Sukman, *The Singing Nun*

Ken Thorne, *A Funny Thing Happened on the Way to the Forum*

FILM EDITING

Hal Ashby and J. Terry Williams, *The Russians Are Coming, The Russians Are Coming*

William B. Murphy, *Fantastic Voyage*

Sam O'Steen, *Who's Afraid of Virginia Woolf?*

William Reynolds, *The Sand Pebbles*

Fredric Steinkamp, Henry Berman, Stewart Linder and Frank Santillo, *Grand Prix*

COSTUME DESIGN

BLACK-AND-WHITE

Danilo Donati, *The Gospel According to St. Matthew*

Danilo Donati, *Mandragola*

Jocelyn Rickards, *Morgan!*

Helen Rose, *Mister Buddwing*

Irene Sharaff, *Who's Afraid of Virginia Woolf?*

COLOR

Piero Gherardi, *Juliet of the Spirits*

Elizabeth Haffenden and Joan Bridge, *A Man for All Seasons*

Edith Head, *The Oscar*

Dorothy Jeakins, *Hawaii*

Jean Louis, *Gambit*

SPECIAL VISUAL EFFECTS

Art Cruickshank, *Fantastic Voyage*

Linwood G. Dunn, *Hawaii*

SOUND EFFECTS

Gordon Daniel, *Grand Prix*

Walter Rossi, *Fantastic Voyage*

SHORT SUBJECTS

CARTOON

The Drag (National Film Board of Canada; Favorite Films of California)

***Herb Alpert and the Tijuana Brass Double Feature (I Feel Special Series)* (Hubley Studios; Paramount)**

The Pink Blueprint (*Pink Panther Series*) (Mirisch-Geoffrey-DePatie-Freleng; United Artists)

LIVE ACTION

Turkey the Bridge (Samaritan Productions; Schoenfeld Films)

***Wild Wings* (British Transport Films; Manson Distributing)**

The Winning Strain (*Sports in Action Series*) (Winik Films; Paramount)

DOCUMENTARY

SHORT SUBJECT

Adolescence (Marin Karmitz and Vladimir Forgency, producers; M.K. Productions)

Cowboy (Ahnemann /Schlosser Productions; U.S. Information Agency)

The Odds Against (Vision Associates Production; American Foundation Institute of Corrections)

Saint Matthew Passion (Mafilm Studios Production; Hungarofilm)

A Year Toward Tomorrow (Sun Dial Films, Inc.; Office of Economic Opportunity)

FEATURE

The Face of Genius (WBZ-TV, Group W, Boston)

Helicopter Canada (National Film Board of Canada Centennial Commission; National Film Board of Canada)

Le Volcan Interdit (*The Forbidden Volcano*) (Cine Documents Tazieff; Athos Films)

The Really Big Family (Alex Grasshoff, producer; David L. Wolper Production)

The War Game (BBC Production for the British Film Institute; Pathé Contemporary Films)

FOREIGN LANGUAGE FILM

The Battle of Algiers, Italy

Loves of a Blonde, Czechoslovakia

A Man and a Woman, France

Pharaoh, Poland

Three, Yugoslavia

IRVING G. THALBERG MEMORIAL AWARD
Robert Wise

JEAN HERSHOLT HUMANITARIAN AWARD
George Bagnall

HONORARY AWARDS

To **Y. Frank Freeman** for unusual and outstanding service to the Academy during his 30 years in Hollywood

To **Yakima Canutt** for achievements as a stuntman and for developing safety devices to protect stuntmen everywhere

1967

BEST PICTURE

Bonnie and Clyde, Warren Beatty, producer (Warner Bros.-Seven Arts)

Doctor Dolittle, Arthur P. Jacobs, producer (Twentieth Century-Fox)

The Graduate, Lawrence Turman, producer (Embassy Pictures)

Guess Who's Coming to Dinner?, Stanley Kramer, producer (Columbia)

In the Heat of the Night, Walter Mirisch, producer (United Artists)

BEST ACTOR

Warren Beatty, *Bonnie and Clyde*

Dustin Hoffman, *The Graduate*

Paul Newman, *Cool Hand Luke*

Rod Steiger, *In the Heat of the Night*

Spencer Tracy, *Guess Who's Coming to Dinner?*

BEST ACTRESS

Anne Bancroft, *The Graduate*

Faye Dunaway, *Bonnie and Clyde*

Dame Edith Evans, *The Whisperers*

Audrey Hepburn, *Wait Until Dark*

Katharine Hepburn, *Guess Who's Coming to Dinner?*

ACTOR IN A SUPPORTING ROLE

John Cassavetes, *The Dirty Dozen*

Gene Hackman, *Bonnie and Clyde*

Cecil Kellaway, *Guess Who's Coming to Dinner?*

George Kennedy, *Cool Hand Luke*

Michael J. Pollard, *Bonnie and Clyde*

ACTRESS IN A SUPPORTING ROLE

Carol Channing, *Thoroughly Modern Millie*

Mildred Natwick, *Barefoot in the Park*

Estelle Parsons, *Bonnie and Clyde*

Beah Richards, *Guess Who's Coming to Dinner?*

Katharine Ross, *The Graduate*

DIRECTING

Richard Brooks, *In Cold Blood*

Norman Jewison, *In the Heat of the Night*

Stanley Kramer, *Guess Who's Coming to Dinner?*

Mike Nichols, *The Graduate*

Arthur Penn, *Bonnie and Clyde*

WRITING

SCREENPLAY BASED ON MATERIAL FROM ANOTHER MEDIUM

Richard Brooks, *In Cold Blood*

Donn Pearce and Frank R. Pierson, *Cool Hand Luke*

Mike Nichols

Stirling Silliphant, *In the Heat of the Night*

Joseph Strick and Fred Haines, *Ulysses*

Calder Willingham and Buck Henry, *The Graduate*

STORY AND SCREENPLAY WRITTEN DIRECTLY FOR THE SCREEN

Robert Kaufman, story; Norman Lear, screenplay, *Divorce American Style*

David Newman and Robert Benton, *Bonnie and Clyde*

Frederic Raphael, *Two for the Road*

William Rose, *Guess Who's Coming to Dinner?*

Jorge Semprun, *La Guerre Est Finie*

CINEMATOGRAPHY

Burnett Guffey, *Bonnie and Clyde*

Conrad Hall, *In Cold Blood*

Richard H. Kline, *Camelot*

Robert Surtees, *Doctor Dolittle*

Robert Surtees, *The Graduate*

ART DIRECTION

Mario Chiari, Jack Martin Smith and Ed Graves, art direction; Walter M. Scott and Stuart A. Reiss, set decoration, *Doctor Dolittle*

Robert Clatworthy, art direction; Frank Tuttle, set decoration, *Guess Who's Coming to Dinner?*

Alexander Golitzen and George C. Webb, art direction; Howard Bristol, set decoration, *Thoroughly Modern Millie*

Renzo Mongiardino, John DeCuir, Elven Webb and Giuseppe Mariani, art direction; Dario Simoni and Luigi Gervasi, set decoration, *The Taming of the Shrew*

John Truscott and Edward Carrere, art direction; John W. Brown, set decoration, *Camelot*

SOUND

MGM Studio Sound Dept., *The Dirty Dozen*

Samuel Goldwyn Studio Sound Dept., *In the Heat of the Night*

Twentieth Century-Fox Studio Sound Dept., *Doctor Dolittle*

Universal City Studio Sound Dept., *Thoroughly Modern Millie*

Warner Bros.-Seven Arts Studio Sound Dept., *Camelot*

MUSIC

SONG

"The Bare Necessities," *The Jungle Book*, Terry Gilkyson, music and lyrics

"The Eyes of Love," *Banning*, Quincy Jones, music; Bob Russell, lyrics

"The Look of Love," *Casino Royale*, Burt Bacharach, music; Hal David, lyrics

"Talk to the Animals," *Doctor Dolittle*, Leslie Bricusse, music and lyrics

"Thoroughly Modern Millie," *Thoroughly Modern Millie*, James Van Heusen and Sammy Cahn, music and lyrics

ORIGINAL MUSIC SCORE

Richard Rodney Bennett, *Far From the Madding Crowd*

Elmer Bernstein, *Thoroughly Modern Millie*

Leslie Bricusse, *Doctor Dolittle*

Quincy Jones, *In Cold Blood*

Lalo Schifrin, *Cool Hand Luke*

SCORING OF MUSIC, ADAPTATION OR TREATMENT

DeVol, *Guess Who's Coming to Dinner?*

Alfred Newman and Ken Darby, *Camelot*

Lionel Newman and Alexander Courage, *Doctor Dolittle*

André Previn and Joseph Gershenson, *Thoroughly Modern Millie*

John Williams, *Valley of the Dolls*

FILM EDITING

Hal Ashby, *In the Heat of the Night*

Samuel E. Beetley and Marjorie Fowler, *Doctor Dolittle*

Robert C. Jones, *Guess Who's Coming to Dinner?*

Frank P. Keller, *Beach Red*

Michael Luciano, *The Dirty Dozen*

COSTUME DESIGN

Jean Louis, *Thoroughly Modern Millie*

Irene Sharaff and Danilo Donati, *The Taming of the Shrew*

Bill Thomas, *The Happiest Millionaire*

John Truscott, *Camelot*

Theadora Van Runkle, *Bonnie and Clyde*

SPECIAL VISUAL EFFECTS

L. B. Abbott, *Doctor Dolittle*

Howard A. Anderson, Jr. and Albert Whitlock, *Tobruk*

SOUND EFFECTS

John Poyner, *The Dirty Dozen*

James A. Richard, *In the Heat of the Night*

SHORT SUBJECTS

CARTOON

***The Box* (Murakami-Wolf Films; Brandon Films)**

Hypothese Beta (Films Orzeaux; Pathé Contemporary Films)

What on Earth! (National Film Board of Canada; Columbia)

LIVE ACTION

Paddle to the Sea (National Film Board of Canada; Favorite Films of California)

***A Place to Stand* (T.D.F. Production for the Ontario Department of Economics and Development; Columbia)**

Sky Over Holland (John Ferno Production for the Netherlands; Warner Bros.-Seven Arts)

Stop, Look and Listen (Len Janson and Chuck Menville, producers; MGM)

DOCUMENTARY

SHORT SUBJECT

Monument to the Dream (Charles E. Guggenheim, producer; Guggenheim Productions)

A Place to Stand (T.D.F. Production for the Ontario Department of Economics and Development; Columbia)

***The Redwoods* (Mark Harris and Trevor Greenwood, producers; King Screen Productions)**

See You at the Pillar (Robert Fitchett, producer; Associated British-Pathé Production)

While I Run This Race (Carl V. Ragsdale, producer; Sun Dial Films for VISTA)

FEATURE

***The Anderson Platoon* (French Broadcasting System)**

Festival (Patchke Productions)

Harvest (U.S. Information Agency)

A King's Story (Jack Le Vien Production)

A Time for Burning (Quest Productions for Lutheran Film Associates)

FOREIGN LANGUAGE FILM

Closely Watched Trains, Czechoslovakia

El Amor Brujo, Spain

I Even Met Happy Gypsies, Yugoslavia

Live for Life, France

Portrait of Chieko, Japan

IRVING G. THALBERG MEMORIAL AWARD

Alfred Hitchcock

JEAN HERSHOLT HUMANITARIAN AWARD

Gregory Peck

HONORARY AWARD

To **Arthur Freed** for distinguished service to the Academy and the production of six top-rated Awards telecasts

1968

BEST PICTURE

Funny Girl, Ray Stark, producer (Columbia)

The Lion in Winter, Martin Poll, producer (Avco Embassy)

Oliver!, John Woolf, producer (Columbia)

Rachel, Rachel, Paul Newman, producer (Warner Bros.- Seven Arts)

Romeo and Juliet, Anthony Havelock-Allan and John Brabourne, producers (Paramount)

BEST ACTOR

Alan Arkin, *The Heart Is a Lonely Hunter*

Alan Bates, *The Fixer*

Ron Moody, *Oliver!*

Peter O'Toole, *The Lion in Winter*

Cliff Robertson, *Charly*

BEST ACTRESS (TIE)

Katharine Hepburn, *The Lion in Winter*

Patricia Neal, *The Subject Was Roses*

Barbra Streisand, *Funny Girl*

Vanessa Redgrave, *Isadora*

Barbra Streisand, *Funny Girl*

Joanne Woodward, *Rachel, Rachel*

ACTOR IN A SUPPORTING ROLE

Jack Albertson, *The Subject Was Roses*

Seymour Cassel, *Faces*

Daniel Massey, *Star!*

Jack Wild, *Oliver!*

Gene Wilder, *The Producers*

ACTRESS IN A SUPPORTING ROLE

Lynn Carlin, *Faces*

Ruth Gordon, *Rosemary's Baby*

Sondra Locke, *The Heart Is a Lonely Hunter*

Kay Medford, *Funny Girl*

Estelle Parsons, *Rachel, Rachel*

DIRECTING

Anthony Harvey, *The Lion in Winter*

Stanley Kubrick, *2001: A Space Odyssey*

Gillo Pontecorvo, *The Battle of Algiers*

Carol Reed, *Oliver!*

Franco Zeffirelli, *Romeo and Juliet*

WRITING

SCREENPLAY BASED ON MATERIAL FROM ANOTHER MEDIUM

James Goldman, *The Lion in Winter*

Vernon Harris, *Oliver!*

Roman Polanski, *Rosemary's Baby*

Neil Simon, *The Odd Couple*

Stewart Stern, *Rachel, Rachel*

STORY AND SCREENPLAY WRITTEN DIRECTLY FOR THE SCREEN

Mel Brooks, *The Producers*

John Cassavetes, *Faces*

Stanley Kubrick and Arthur C. Clarke, *2001: A Space Odyssey*

Franco Solinas and Gillo Pontecorvo, *The Battle of Algiers*

Ira Wallach and Peter Ustinov, *Hot Millions*

CINEMATOGRAPHY

Pasqualino De Santis, *Romeo and Juliet*

Daniel L. Fapp, *Ice Station Zebra*

Ernest Laszlo, *Star!*

Oswald Morris, *Oliver!*

Harry Stradling, *Funny Girl*

ART DIRECTION

Mikhail Bogdanov and Gennady Myasnikov, art direction; G. Koshelev and V. Uvarov, set decoration, *War and Peace*

John Box and Terence Marsh, art direction; Vernon Dixon and Ken Muggleston, set decoration, *Oliver!*

George W. Davis and Edward Carfagno, art direction, *The Shoes of the Fisherman*

Boris Leven, art direction; Walter M. Scott and Howard Bristol, set decoration, *Star!*

Tony Masters, Harry Lange and Ernie Archer, art direction, *2001: A Space Odyssey*

SOUND

Columbia Studio Sound Dept., *Funny Girl*

Shepperton Studio Sound Dept., *Oliver!*

Twentieth Century-Fox Studio Sound Dept., *Star!*

Warner Bros.-Seven Arts Studio Sound Dept., *Bullitt*

Warner Bros.-Seven Arts Studio Sound Dept., *Finian's Rainbow*

MUSIC
SONG

"Chitty Chitty Bang Bang," *Chitty Chitty Bang Bang*, Richard M. Sherman and Robert B. Sherman, music and lyrics

"For Love of Ivy," *For Love of Ivy*, Quincy Jones, music; Bob Russell, lyrics

"Funny Girl," *Funny Girl*, Jule Styne, music; Bob Merrill, lyrics

"Star!," *Star!*, Jimmy Van Heusen, music; Sammy Cahn, lyrics

"The Windmills of Your Mind," *The Thomas Crown Affair*, Michel Legrand, music; Alan and Marilyn Bergman, lyrics

ORIGINAL SCORE FOR A MOTION PICTURE, NOT A MUSICAL

John Barry, *The Lion in Winter*

Jerry Goldsmith, *Planet of the Apes*

Michel Legrand, *The Thomas Crown Affair*

Alex North, *The Shoes of the Fisherman*

Lalo Schifrin, *The Fox*

SCORE OF A MUSICAL PICTURE, ORIGINAL OR ADAPTATION

John Green, *Oliver!*

Lennie Hayton, *Star!*

Ray Heindorf, *Finian's Rainbow*

Michel Legrand, music and adaptation; Jacques Demy, lyrics, *The Young Girls of Rochefort*

Walter Scharf, *Funny Girl*

FILM EDITING

Frank Bracht, *The Odd Couple*

Fred Feitshans and Eve Newman, *Wild in the Streets*

Frank P. Keller, *Bullitt*

Ralph Kemplen, *Oliver!*

Robert Swink, Maury Winetrobe and William Sands, *Funny Girl*

COSTUME DESIGN

Donald Brooks, *Star!*

Phyllis Dalton, *Oliver!*

Danilo Donati, *Romeo and Juliet*

Margaret Furse, *The Lion in Winter*

Morton Haack, *Planet of the Apes*

SPECIAL VISUAL EFFECTS

Stanley Kubrick, *2001: A Space Odyssey*

Hal Millar and J. McMillan Johnson, *Ice Station Zebra*

SHORT SUBJECTS
CARTOON

The House That Jack Built (National Film Board of Canada; Columbia)

The Magic Pear Tree (Murakami-Wolf Films; Bing Crosby Productions)

Windy Day (Hubley Studios; Paramount)

***Winnie the Pooh and the Blustery Day* (Walt Disney Productions; Buena Vista)**

LIVE ACTION

The Dove (Coe-Davis Ltd.; Schoenfeld Films Distributing Co.)

Duo (National Film Board of Canada; Columbia)

Prelude (Prelude Co.; Excelsior Distributing)

***Robert Kennedy Remembered* (Guggenheim Productions; National General Pictures)**

DOCUMENTARY
SHORT SUBJECT

The House That Ananda Built (Films Division, Government of India)

The Revolving Door (Vision Associates Production for the American Foundation Institute of Corrections)

A Space to Grow (Office of Economic Opportunity for Project Upward Bound)

A Way Out of the Wilderness (Dan E. Weisburd, producer; John Sutherland Productions)

***Why Man Creates* (Saul Bass, producer; Saul Bass and Associates)**

FEATURE

A Few Notes on Our Food Problem (James Blue, producer; U.S. Information Agency)

***Journey Into Self* (Bill McGaw, producer; Western Behavioral Sciences Institute) (At the April 14, 1968 awards ceremony, *Young Americans* was announced as the Documentary Feature winner. On May 7, 1969, the film was disqualified because it played in October 1967, therefore ineligible for a 1968 award. *Journey Into Self*, the first runner-up, was awarded the Oscar on May 8, 1969.)**

The Legendary Champions (William Cayton, producer; Turn of the Century Fights)

Other Voices (David H. Sawyer, producer; DHS Films)

Young Americans (Robert Cohn and Alex Grasshoff, producers; The Young Americans Production)

FOREIGN LANGUAGE FILM

The Boys of Paul Street, Hungary

The Fireman's Ball, Czechoslovakia

The Girl With the Pistol, Italy

Stolen Kisses, France

***War and Peace*, U.S.S.R.**

JEAN HERSHOLT HUMANITARIAN AWARD
Martha Raye

HONORARY AWARDS

To **John Chambers** for his outstanding makeup achievement for *Planet of the Apes*

To **Onna White** for her outstanding choreography achievement for *Oliver!*

1969

BEST PICTURE

Anne of the Thousand Days, Hal B. Wallis, producer (Universal)

Butch Cassidy and the Sundance Kid, John Foreman, producer (Twentieth Century-Fox)

Hello, Dolly!, Ernest Lehman, producer (Twentieth Century-Fox)

Midnight Cowboy, Jerome Hellman, producer (United Artists)

Z, Jacques Perrin and Hamed Rachedi, producers (Cinema V)

BEST ACTOR

Richard Burton, *Anne of the Thousand Days*

Dustin Hoffman, *Midnight Cowboy*

Peter O'Toole, *Goodbye, Mr. Chips*

Jon Voight, *Midnight Cowboy*

John Wayne, *True Grit*

BEST ACTRESS

Genevieve Bujold, *Anne of the Thousand Days*

Jane Fonda, *They Shoot Horses, Don't They?*

Liza Minnelli, *The Sterile Cuckoo*

Jean Simmons, *The Happy Ending*

Maggie Smith, *The Prime of Miss Jean Brodie*

ACTOR IN A SUPPORTING ROLE

Rupert Crosse, *The Reivers*

Elliott Gould, *Bob & Carol & Ted & Alice*

Jack Nicholson, *Easy Rider*

Anthony Quayle, *Anne of the Thousand Days*

Gig Young, *They Shoot Horses, Don't They?*

ACTRESS IN A SUPPORTING ROLE

Catherine Burns, *Last Summer*

Dyan Cannon, *Bob & Carol & Ted & Alice*

Goldie Hawn, *Cactus Flower*

Sylvia Miles, *Midnight Cowboy*

Susannah York, *They Shoot Horses, Don't They?*

DIRECTING

Costa-Gavras, *Z*

George Roy Hill, *Butch Cassidy and the Sundance Kid*

Arthur Penn, *Alice's Restaurant*

Sydney Pollack, *They Shoot Horses, Don't They?*

John Schlesinger, *Midnight Cowboy*

WRITING

SCREENPLAY BASED ON MATERIAL FROM ANOTHER MEDIUM

John Hale and Bridget Boland, screenplay; Richard Sokolove, adaptation, *Anne of the Thousand Days*

James Poe and Robert E. Thompson, *They Shoot Horses, Don't They?*

Waldo Salt, *Midnight Cowboy*

Arnold Schulman, *Goodbye, Columbus*

Jorge Semprun and Costa-Gavras, *Z*

STORY AND SCREENPLAY BASED ON MATERIAL NOT PREVIOUSLY PUBLISHED OR PRODUCED

Nicola Badalucco, story; Nicola Badalucco, Enrico Medioli and Luchino Visconti, screenplay, *The Damned*

Peter Fonda, Dennis Hopper and Terry Southern, *Easy Rider*

William Goldman, *Butch Cassidy and the Sundance Kid*

Walon Green and Roy N. Sickner, story; Walon Green and Sam Peckinpah, screenplay, *The Wild Bunch*

Paul Mazursky and Larry Tucker, *Bob & Carol & Ted & Alice*

Butch Cassidy and the Sundance Kid

CINEMATOGRAPHY

Daniel Fapp, *Marooned*

Conrad Hall, *Butch Cassidy and the Sundance Kid*

Arthur Ibbetson, *Anne of the Thousand Days*

Charles B. Lang, *Bob & Carol & Ted & Alice*

Harry Stradling, *Hello, Dolly!*

ART DIRECTION

Robert Boyle and George B. Chan, art direction; Edward Boyle and Carl Biddiscombe, set decoration, *Gaily, Gaily*

Maurice Carter and Lionel Couch, art direction; Patrick McLoughlin, set decoration, *Anne of the Thousand Days*

John DeCuir, Jack Martin Smith and Herman Blumenthal, art direction; Walter M. Scott, George Hopkins and Raphael Bretton, set decoration, *Hello, Dolly!*

Alexander Golitzen and George C. Webb, art direction; Jack D. Moore, set decoration, *Sweet Charity*

Harry Horner, art direction; Frank McKelvy, set decoration, *They Shoot Horses, Don't They?*

SOUND

John Aldred, *Anne of the Thousand Days*

William Edmundson and David Dockendorf, *Butch Cassidy and the Sundance Kid*

Les Fresholtz and Arthur Piantadosi, *Marooned*

Robert Martin and Clem Portman, *Gaily, Gaily*

Jack Solomon and Murray Spivack, *Hello, Dolly!*

MUSIC

SONG

"Come Saturday Morning," *The Sterile Cuckoo*, Fred Karlin, music; Dory Previn, lyrics

"Jean," *The Prime of Miss Jean Brodie*, Rod McKuen, music and lyrics

"Raindrops Keep Fallin' on My Head," *Butch Cassidy and the Sundance Kid*, Burt Bacharach, music; Hal David, lyrics

"True Grit," *True Grit*, Elmer Bernstein, music; Don Black, lyrics

"What Are You Doing the Rest of Your Life?," *The Happy Ending*, Michel Legrand, music; Alan and Marilyn Bergman, lyrics

ORIGINAL SCORE FOR A MOTION PICTURE, NOT A MUSICAL

Burt Bacharach, *Butch Cassidy and the Sundance Kid*

Georges Delerue, *Anne of the Thousand Days*

Jerry Fielding, *The Wild Bunch*

Ernest Gold, *The Secret of Santa Vittoria*

John Williams, *The Reivers*

SCORE OF A MUSICAL PICTURE, ORIGINAL OR ADAPTATION

Leslie Bricusse, music and lyrics; John Williams, score, *Goodbye, Mr. Chips*

Cy Coleman, *Sweet Charity*

John Green and Albert Woodbury, *They Shoot Horses, Don't They?*

Lennie Hayton and Lionel Newman, *Hello, Dolly!*

Nelson Riddle, *Paint Your Wagon*

FILM EDITING

Françoise Bonnot, *Z*

William Lyon and Earle Herdan, *The Secret of Santa Vittoria*

William Reynolds, *Hello, Dolly!*

Hugh A. Robertson, *Midnight Cowboy*

Fredric Steinkamp, *They Shoot Horses, Don't They?*

COSTUME DESIGN

Ray Aghayan, *Gaily, Gaily*

Donfeld, *They Shoot Horses, Don't They?*

Margaret Furse, *Anne of the Thousand Days*

Edith Head, *Sweet Charity*

Irene Sharaff, *Hello, Dolly!*

SPECIAL VISUAL EFFECTS

Eugene Lourie and Alex Weldon, *Krakatoa, East of Java*

Robbie Robertson, *Marooned*

SHORT SUBJECTS

CARTOON

***It's Tough to Be a Bird* (Walt Disney Productions; Buena Vista)**

Of Men and Demons (Hubley Studios; Paramount)

Walking (National Film Board of Canada; Columbia)

LIVE ACTION

Blake (National Film Board of Canada; Vaudeo, Inc.)

***The Magic Machines* (Fly-by-Night Productions; Manson Distributing)**

People Soup (Pangloss Productions; Columbia)

DOCUMENTARY

SHORT SUBJECT

***Czechoslovakia 1968* (Sanders-Fresco Film Makers for the U.S. Information Agency)**

An Impression of John Steinbeck: Writer (Donald Wrye Productions for the U.S. Information Agency)

Jenny Is a Good Thing (A.C.I. Prod. for Project Head Start)

Leo Beuerman (Arthur H. Wolf and Russell A. Mosser, producers; Centron Production)

The Magic Machines (Fly-By-Night Productions; Manson Distributing)

FEATURE

***Arthur Rubinstein — The Love of Life* (Bernard Chevry, producer; Midem Production)**

Before the Mountain Was Moved (Robert K. Sharpe Productions for the Office of Economic Opportunity)

In the Year of the Pig (Emile de Antonio, producer; Emile de Antonio Production)

The Olympics in Mexico (Film Section of the Organizing Committee for the XIX Olympic Games)

The Wolf Men (Irwin Rosten, producer; MGM)

FOREIGN LANGUAGE FILM (TIE)

Adalen '31, Sweden

The Battle of Neretva, Yugoslavia

***The Brothers Karamazov*, U.S.S.R.**

My Night With Maud, France

Z, Algeria

JEAN HERSHOLT HUMANITARIAN AWARD
George Jessel

HONORARY AWARD

To **Cary Grant** for his unique mastery of the art of screen acting with the respect and affection of his colleagues

1970

BEST PICTURE

Airport, Ross Hunter, producer (Universal)

Five Easy Pieces, Bob Rafelson and Richard Wechsler, producers (Columbia)

Love Story, Howard G. Minsky, producer (Paramount)

M*A*S*H, Ingo Preminger, producer (Twentieth Century-Fox)

***Patton*, Frank McCarthy, producer (Twentieth Century-Fox)**

BEST ACTOR

Melvyn Douglas, *I Never Sang for My Father*

James Earl Jones, *The Great White Hope*

Jack Nicholson, *Five Easy Pieces*

Ryan O'Neal, *Love Story*

George C. Scott, *Patton*

Patton

BEST ACTRESS

Jane Alexander, *The Great White Hope*

Glenda Jackson, *Women in Love*

Ali MacGraw, *Love Story*

Sarah Miles, *Ryan's Daughter*

Carrie Snodgress, *Diary of a Mad Housewife*

ACTOR IN A SUPPORTING ROLE

Richard Castellano, *Lovers and Other Strangers*

Chief Dan George, *Little Big Man*

Gene Hackman, *I Never Sang for My Father*

John Marley, *Love Story*

John Mills, *Ryan's Daughter*

ACTRESS IN A SUPPORTING ROLE

Karen Black, *Five Easy Pieces*

Lee Grant, *The Landlord*

Helen Hayes, *Airport*

Sally Kellerman, *M*A*S*H*

Maureen Stapleton, *Airport*

DIRECTING

Robert Altman, *M*A*S*H*

Federico Fellini, *Fellini Satyricon*

Arthur Hiller, *Love Story*

Ken Russell, *Women in Love*

Franklin J. Schaffner, *Patton*

WRITING

SCREENPLAY BASED ON MATERIAL FROM ANOTHER MEDIUM

Robert Anderson, *I Never Sang for My Father*

Larry Kramer, *Women in Love*

Ring Lardner, Jr., *M*A*S*H*

George Seaton, *Airport*

Renee Taylor, Joseph Bologna and David Zelag Goodman, *Lovers and Other Strangers*

ORIGINAL SCREENPLAY

Francis Ford Coppola and Edmund H. North, *Patton*

Bob Rafelson and Adrien Joyce, story; Adrien Joyce, screenplay, *Five Easy Pieces*

Eric Rohmer, *My Night at Maud's*

Erich Segal, *Love Story*

Norman Wexler, *Joe*

CINEMATOGRAPHY

Fred Koenekamp, *Patton*

Ernest Laszlo, *Airport*

Charles F. Wheeler, Osami Furuya, Sinsaku Himeda and Masamichi Satoh, *Tora! Tora! Tora!*

Billy Williams, *Women in Love*

Freddie Young, *Ryan's Daughter*

ART DIRECTION

Alexander Golitzen and E. Preston Ames, art direction; Jack D. Moore and Mickey S. Michaels, set decoration, *Airport*

Tambi Larsen, art direction; Darrell Silvera, set decoration, *The Molly Maguires*

Terry Marsh and Bob Cartwright, art direction; Pamela Cornell, set decoration, *Scrooge*

Urie McCleary and Gil Parrondo, art direction; Antonio Mateos and Pierre-Louis Thevenet, set decoration, *Patton*

Mickey S. Michaels, set decoration, *Airport*

Jack Martin Smith, Yoshiro Muraki, Richard Day and Taizoh Kawashima, art direction; Walter M. Scott, Norman Rockett and Carl Biddiscombe, set decoration, *Tora! Tora! Tora!*

SOUND

Gordon K. McCallum and John Bramall, *Ryan's Daughter*

Ronald Pierce and David Moriarty, *Airport*

Murray Spivack and Herman Lewis, *Tora! Tora! Tora!*

Dan Wallin and Larry Johnson, *Woodstock*

Douglas Williams and Don Bassman, *Patton*

MUSIC

SONG

"For All We Know," *Lovers and Other Strangers*, Fred Karlin, music; Robb Royer and James Griffin, lyrics

"Pieces of Dreams," *Pieces of Dreams*, Michel Legrand, music; Alan and Marilyn Bergman, lyrics

"Thank You Very Much," *Scrooge*, Leslie Bricusse, music and lyrics

"Till Love Touches Your Life," *Madron*, Riz Ortolani, music; Arthur Hamilton, lyrics

"Whistling Away the Dark," *Darling Lili*, Henry Mancini, music; Johnny Mercer, lyrics

ORIGINAL SCORE

Frank Cordell, *Cromwell*

Jerry Goldsmith, *Patton*

Francis Lai, *Love Story*

Henry Mancini, *Sunflower*

Alfred Newman, *Airport*

ORIGINAL SONG SCORE

The Beatles, *Let It Be*

Leslie Bricusse, music and lyrics; Ian Fraser and Herbert W. Spencer, adaptation, *Scrooge*

Fred Karlin and Tylwyth Kymry, *The Baby Maker*

Henry Mancini, music; Johnny Mercer, lyrics, *Darling Lili*

Rod McKuen and John Scott Trotter, music; Rod McKuen, Bill Melendez and Al Shean, lyrics; Vince Guaraldi, adaptation score, *A Boy Named Charlie Brown*

FILM EDITING

Hugh S. Fowler, *Patton*

Stuart Gilmore, *Airport*

Danford B. Greene, *M*A*S*H*

James E. Newcom, Pembroke J. Herring and Inoue Chikaya, *Tora! Tora! Tora!*

Thelma Schoonmaker, *Woodstock*

COSTUME DESIGN

Donald Brooks and Jack Bear, *Darling Lili*

Margaret Furse, *Scrooge*

Edith Head, *Airport*

Nino Novarese, *Cromwell*

Bill Thomas, *The Hawaiians*

SPECIAL VISUAL EFFECTS
A. D. Flowers and L. B. Abbott, *Tora! Tora! Tora!*

Alex Weldon, *Patton*

SHORT SUBJECTS
CARTOON
The Further Adventures of Uncle Sam: Part Two (Haboush Company; Goldstone Films)

Is It Always Right to Be Right? (Stephen Bosustow Productions; Lester A. Schoenfeld Films)

The Shepherd (Cameron Guess and Associates; Brandon Films)

LIVE ACTION
The Resurrection of Broncho Billy (University of Southern California, Department of Cinema; Universal)

Shut Up . . . I'm Crying (Robert Siegler Productions; Lester A. Schoenfeld Films)

Sticky My Fingers . . . Fleet My Feet (American Film Institute; Lester A. Schoenfeld Films)

DOCUMENTARY
SHORT SUBJECT
The Gifts (Robert McBride, producer; Richter-McBride Productions for the Water Quality Office of the Environmental Protection Agency)

Interviews With My Lai Veterans (Joseph Strick, producer; Laser Film Corp.)

A Long Way From Nowhere (Bob Aller, producer; Robert Aller Productions)

Oisin (Vivien Carey and Patrick Carey, producers; Aengus Films)

Time Is Running Out (Horst Dallmayr and Robert Menegoz, producers; Gesellschaft für bildende Filme)

FEATURE
Chariots of the Gods (Dr. Harald Reinl, producer; Terra-Filmkunst GmbH)

Jack Johnson (Jim Jacobs, producer; The Big Fights)

King: A Filmed Record . . . Montgomery to Memphis (Ely Landau, producer; Commonwealth United Corporation Production)

Say Goodbye (David H. Vowell, producer; David L. Wolper Productions)

Woodstock (Wadleigh-Maurice Ltd.; Warner Bros.)

FOREIGN LANGUAGE FILM
First Love, Switzerland

Hoa-Binh, France

Investigation of a Citizen Above Suspicion, Italy

Paix Sur Les Champs, Belgium

Tristana, Spain

IRVING G. THALBERG MEMORIAL AWARD
Ingmar Bergman

JEAN HERSHOLT HUMANITARIAN AWARD
Frank Sinatra

HONORARY AWARDS
To **Lillian Gish** for superlative artistry and for distinguished contribution to the progress of motion pictures

To **Orson Welles** for superlative artistry and versatility in the creation of motion pictures

1971

BEST PICTURE
A Clockwork Orange, Stanley Kubrick, producer (Warner Bros.)

Fiddler on the Roof, Norman Jewison, producer (United Artists)

The French Connection, Philip D'Antoni, producer (Twentieth Century-Fox)

The Last Picture Show, Stephen J. Friedman, producer (Columbia)

Nicholas and Alexandra, Sam Spiegel, producer (Columbia)

BEST ACTOR
Peter Finch, *Sunday Bloody Sunday*

Gene Hackman, The French Connection

Walter Matthau, *Kotch*

George C. Scott, *The Hospital*

Topol, *Fiddler on the Roof*

BEST ACTRESS
Julie Christie, *McCabe & Mrs. Miller*

Jane Fonda, Klute

Glenda Jackson, *Sunday Bloody Sunday*

Vanessa Redgrave, *Mary, Queen of Scots*

Janet Suzman, *Nicholas and Alexandra*

ACTOR IN A SUPPORTING ROLE
Jeff Bridges, *The Last Picture Show*

Leonard Frey, *Fiddler on the Roof*

Richard Jaeckel, *Sometimes a Great Notion*

Ben Johnson, The Last Picture Show

Roy Scheider, *The French Connection*

ACTRESS IN A SUPPORTING ROLE
Ellen Burstyn, *The Last Picture Show*

Barbara Harris, *Who Is Harry Kellerman and Why Is He Saying Those Terrible Things About Me?*

Cloris Leachman, The Last Picture Show

Margaret Leighton, *The Go-Between*

Ann-Margret, *Carnal Knowledge*

Lillian Gish

DIRECTING

Peter Bogdanovich, *The Last Picture Show*

William Friedkin, *The French Connection*

Norman Jewison, *Fiddler on the Roof*

Stanley Kubrick, *A Clockwork Orange*

John Schlesinger, *Sunday Bloody Sunday*

WRITING

SCREENPLAY BASED ON MATERIAL FROM ANOTHER MEDIUM

Bernardo Bertolucci, *The Conformist*

Stanley Kubrick, *A Clockwork Orange*

Larry McMurtry and Peter Bogdanovich, *The Last Picture Show*

Ugo Pirro and Vittorio Bonicelli, *The Garden of the Finzi-Continis*

Ernest Tidyman, *The French Connection*

ORIGINAL SCREENPLAY

Paddy Chayefsky, *The Hospital*

Penelope Gilliatt, *Sunday Bloody Sunday*

Andy Lewis and Dave Lewis, *Klute*

Elio Petri and Ugo Pirro, *Investigation of a Citizen Above Suspicion*

Herman Raucher, *Summer of '42*

CINEMATOGRAPHY

Oswald Morris, *Fiddler on the Roof*

Owen Roizman, *The French Connection*

Robert Surtees, *The Last Picture Show*

Robert Surtees, *Summer of '42*

Freddie Young, *Nicholas and Alexandra*

ART DIRECTION

John Box, Ernest Archer, Jack Maxsted and Gil Parrondo, art direction; Vernon Dixon, set decoration, *Nicholas and Alexandra*

Robert Boyle and Michael Stringer, art direction; Peter Lamont, set decoration, *Fiddler on the Roof*

Boris Leven and William Tuntke, art direction; Ruby Levitt, set decoration, *The Andromeda Strain*

John B. Mansbridge and Peter Ellenshaw, art direction; Emile Kuri and Hal Gausman, set decoration, *Bedknobs and Broomsticks*

Terence Marsh and Robert Cartwright, art direction; Peter Howitt, set decoration, *Mary, Queen of Scots*

SOUND

Bob Jones and John Aldred, *Mary, Queen of Scots*

Gordon K. McCallum and David Hildyard, *Fiddler on the Roof*

Gordon K. McCallum, John Mitchell and Alfred J. Overton, *Diamonds Are Forever*

Richard Portman and Jack Solomon, *Kotch*

Theodore Soderberg and Christopher Newman, *The French Connection*

MUSIC

SONG

"The Age of Not Believing," *Bedknobs and Broomsticks*, Richard M. Sherman and Robert B. Sherman, music and lyrics

"All His Children," *Sometimes a Great Notion*, Henry Mancini, music; Alan and Marilyn Bergman, lyrics

"Bless the Beasts and Children," *Bless the Beasts and Children*, Barry DeVorzon and Perry Botkin, Jr., music and lyrics

"Life Is What You Make It," *Kotch*, Marvin Hamlisch, music; Johnny Mercer, lyrics

"Theme From *Shaft*," *Shaft*, Isaac Hayes, music and lyrics

ORIGINAL DRAMATIC SCORE

John Barry, *Mary, Queen of Scots*

Richard Rodney Bennett, *Nicholas and Alexandra*

Jerry Fielding, *Straw Dogs*

Isaac Hayes, *Shaft*

Michel Legrand, *Summer of '42*

SCORING: ADAPTATION AND ORIGINAL SONG SCORE

Leslie Bricusse and Anthony Newley, song; Walter Scharf, adaptation, *Willy Wonka and the Chocolate Factory*

Peter Maxwell Davies and Peter Greenwell, *The Boy Friend*

Richard M. Sherman and Robert B. Sherman, song; Irwin Kostal, adaptation, *Bedknobs and Broomsticks*

Dimitri Tiomkin, *Tchaikovsky*

John Williams, *Fiddler on the Roof*

FILM EDITING

Folmar Blangsted, *Summer of '42*

Bill Butler, *A Clockwork Orange*

Stuart Gilmore and John W. Holmes, *The Andromeda Strain*

Jerry Greenberg, *The French Connection*

Ralph E. Winters, *Kotch*

COSTUME DESIGN

Yvonne Blake and Antonio Castillo, *Nicholas and Alexandra*

Margaret Furse, *Mary, Queen of Scots*

Morton Haack, *What's the Matter With Helen?*

Bill Thomas, *Bedknobs and Broomsticks*

Piero Tosi, *Death in Venice*

SPECIAL VISUAL EFFECTS

Jim Danforth and Roger Dicken, *When Dinosaurs Ruled the Earth*

Alan Maley, Eustace Lycett and Danny Lee, *Bedknobs and Broomsticks*

SHORT SUBJECTS

ANIMATED

***The Crunch Bird* (Maxwell-Petok-Petrovich Productions; Regency Film Distributing Corp.)**

Evolution (National Film Board of Canada; Columbia)

The Selfish Giant (Potterton Productions; Pyramid Films)

LIVE ACTION

Good Morning (E/G Films; Seymour Borde and Associates)

The Rehearsal (Cinema Verona Production; Schoenfeld Film Distributing Corp.)

***Sentinels of Silence* (Producciones Concord; Paramount)**

DOCUMENTARY

SHORT SUBJECT

Adventures in Perception (Hans van Gelder Filmproduktie; Netherlands Information Service)

Art Is . . . (Henry Strauss Associates; Sears, Roebuck Foundation)

The Numbers Start With the River (WH Picture; U.S. Information Agency)

Sentinels of Silence (Producciones Concord; Paramount)

Somebody Waiting (Snider Productions; University of California Medical Film Library)

FEATURE

Alaska Wilderness Lake (Alan Landsburg, producer; Alan Landsburg Productions)

The Hellstrom Chronicle (David L. Wolper Productions; Cinema 5, Ltd.)

On Any Sunday (Bruce Brown-Solar; Cinema 5, Ltd.)

The RA Expeditions (Swedish Broadcasting Company; Interwest Film Corp.)

The Sorrow and the Pity (Television Rencontre-Norddeutscher Rundfunk-Television Swiss Romande; Cinema 5, Ltd.)

FOREIGN LANGUAGE FILM

Dodes'Ka-Den, Japan

The Emigrants, Sweden

The Garden of the Finzi-Continis, Italy

The Policeman, Israel

Tchaikovsky, U.S.S.R.

HONORARY AWARD

To **Charles Chaplin** for the incalculable effect he has had in making motion pictures the art form of this century

1972

BEST PICTURE

Cabaret, Cy Feuer, producer (Allied Artists)

Deliverance, John Boorman, producer (Warner Bros.)

The Emigrants, Bengt Forslund, producer (Warner Bros.)

The Godfather, Albert S. Ruddy, producer (Paramount)

Sounder, Robert B. Radnitz, producer (Twentieth Century-Fox)

Sacheen Littlefeather accepts Marlon Brando's Best Actor Oscar

BEST ACTOR

Marlon Brando, *The Godfather*

Michael Caine, *Sleuth*

Laurence Olivier, *Sleuth*

Peter O'Toole, *The Ruling Class*

Paul Winfield, *Sounder*

BEST ACTRESS

Liza Minelli, *Cabaret*

Diana Ross, *Lady Sings the Blues*

Maggie Smith, *Travels With My Aunt*

Cicely Tyson, *Sounder*

Liv Ullman, *The Emigrants*

ACTOR IN A SUPPORTING ROLE

Eddie Albert, *The Heartbreak Kid*

James Caan, *The Godfather*

Robert Duvall, *The Godfather*

Joel Grey, *Cabaret*

Al Pacino, *The Godfather*

ACTRESS IN A SUPPORTING ROLE

Jeannie Berlin, *The Heartbreak Kid*

Eileen Heckart, *Butterflies Are Free*

Geraldine Page, *Pete 'n' Tillie*

Susan Tyrrell, *Fat City*

Shelley Winters, *The Poseidon Adventure*

DIRECTING

John Boorman, *Deliverance*

Francis Ford Coppola, *The Godfather*

Bob Fosse, *Cabaret*

Joseph L. Mankiewicz, *Sleuth*

Jan Troell, *The Emigrants*

WRITING

SCREENPLAY BASED ON MATERIAL FROM ANOTHER MEDIUM

Jay Allen, *Cabaret*

Lonne Elder, III, *Sounder*

Julius J. Epstein, *Pete 'n' Tillie*

Mario Puzo and Francis Ford Coppola, *The Godfather*

Jan Troell and Bengt Forslund, *The Emigrants*

ORIGINAL SCREENPLAY

Luis Buñuel, story and screenplay in collaboration with Jean-Claude Carrière, *The Discreet Charm of the Bourgeoisie*

Carl Foreman, *Young Winston*

Jeremy Larner, *The Candidate*

Louis Malle, *Murmur of the Heart*

Terence McCloy, Chris Clark and Suzanne de Passe, *Lady Sings the Blues*

CINEMATOGRAPHY

Charles B. Lang, *Butterflies Are Free*

Douglas Slocombe, *Travels With My Aunt*

Harold E. Stine, *The Poseidon Adventure*

Harry Stradling, Jr., *1776*

Geoffrey Unsworth, *Cabaret*

ART DIRECTION

Carl Anderson, art direction; Reg Allen, set decoration,
Lady Sings the Blues

Don Ashton, Geoffrey Drake, John Graysmark and William
Hutchinson, art direction; Peter James, set decoration,
Young Winston

John Box, Gil Parrondo and Robert W. Laing, art direction and
set decoration, *Travels With My Aunt*

William Creber, art direction; Raphael Bretton, set decoration,
The Poseidon Adventure

**Rolf Zehetbauer and Jurgen Kiebach, art direction; Herbert
Strabel, set decoration, *Cabaret***

SOUND

Bud Grenzbach, Richard Portman and Christopher Newman,
The Godfather

Robert Knudson and David Hildyard, *Cabaret*

Arthur Piantadosi and Charles Knight, *Butterflies Are Free*

Richard Portman and Gene Cantamessa, *The Candidate*

Theodore Soderberg and Herman Lewis, *The Poseidon
Adventure*

MUSIC

SONG

"Ben," *Ben*, Walter Scharf, music; Don Black, lyrics

"Come Follow, Follow Me," *The Little Ark*, Fred Karlin, music;
Marsha Karlin, lyrics

"Marmalade, Molasses & Honey," *The Life and Times of
Judge Roy Bean*, Maurice Jarre, music; Marilyn and Alan
Bergman, lyrics

**"The Morning After," *The Poseidon Adventure*, Al Kasha and
Joel Hirschhorn, music and lyrics**

"Strange Are the Ways of Love," *The Stepmother*, Sammy
Fain, music; Paul Francis Webster, lyrics

ORIGINAL DRAMATIC SCORE

John Addison, *Sleuth*

Buddy Baker, *Napoleon and Samantha*

Charles Chaplin, Raymond Rasch and Larry Russell, *Limelight*

John Williams, *Images*

John Williams, *The Poseidon Adventure*

SCORING: ADAPTATION AND ORIGINAL SCORE

Gil Askey, *Lady Sings the Blues*

Ralph Burns, *Cabaret*

Laurence Rosenthal, *Man of La Mancha*

FILM EDITING

David Bretherton, *Cabaret*

Frank P. Keller and Fred W. Berger, *The Hot Rock*

Harold F. Kress, *The Poseidon Adventure*

Tom Priestley, *Deliverance*

William Reynolds and Peter Zinner, *The Godfather*

COSTUME DESIGN

Anna Hill Johnstone, *The Godfather*

Bob Mackie, Ray Aghayan and Norma Koch, *Lady Sings the
Blues*

Anthony Mendleson, *Young Winston*

Anthony Powell, *Travels With My Aunt*

Paul Zastupnevich, *The Poseidon Adventure*

SHORT SUBJECTS

ANIMATED

***A Christmas Carol* (Richard Williams Production; American
Broadcasting Company Film Services)**

Kama Sutra Rides Again (Bob Godfrey Films, Ltd.; Lion
International Films)

Tup Tup (Zagreb Film-Corona Cinematografica Production;
Manson Distributing)

LIVE ACTION

Frog Story (Gidron Productions; Lester A. Schoenfeld Films)

***Norman Rockwell's World . . . An American Dream* (Concepts
Unlimited; Columbia)**

Solo (Pyramid Films; United Artists)

DOCUMENTARY

SHORT SUBJECT

Hundertwasser's Rainy Day (Argos Films-Peter Schamoni Film
Production)

K-Z (Giorgio Treves, producer; Nexus Film S.r.l. Production)

Selling Out (Tadeusz Jaworski, producer; Unit Productions
Film)

***This Tiny World* (Charles Huguenot van der Linden and
Martina Huguenot van der Linden, producers; Charles
Huguenot van der Linden Production)**

The Tide of Traffic (Humphrey Swingler, producer; BP-
Greenpark Production)

FEATURE

Ape and Super-Ape (Bert Haanstra Film Production;
Netherlands Ministry of Culture, Recreation and Social
Welfare)

Malcolm X (Marvin Worth Production; Warner Bros.)

Manson (Robert Hendrickson and Laurence Merrick,
producers; Merrick International Pictures)

***Marjoe* (Cinema X Production; Cinema 5, Ltd.)**

The Silent Revolution (Eckehard Munck, producer; Leonaris
Film Production)

FOREIGN LANGUAGE FILM

The Dawns Here Are Quiet, U.S.S.R.

***The Discreet Charm of the Bourgeoisie*, France**

I Love You Rosa, Israel

My Dearest Señorita, Spain

The New Land, Sweden

JEAN HERSHOLT HUMANITARIAN AWARD

Rosalind Russell

HONORARY AWARDS

To **Charles S. Boren**, leader for 38 years of the industry's
enlightened labor relations and architect of its policy of
nondiscrimination

To **Edward G. Robinson** who achieved greatness as a player, a
patron of the arts and a dedicated citizen . . . in sum, a
Renaissance man

SPECIAL ACHIEVEMENT AWARD

(Not necessarily given each year)

VISUAL EFFECTS

L. B. Abbott and A. D. Flowers, *The Poseidon Adventure*

1973

BEST PICTURE

American Graffiti, Francis Ford Coppola, producer; Gary Kurtz, co-producer (Universal)

Cries and Whispers, Ingmar Bergman, producer (New World Pictures)

The Exorcist, William Peter Blatty, producer (Warner Bros.)

The Sting, Tony Bill, Michael Phillips and Julia Phillips, producers (Universal)

A Touch of Class, Melvin Frank, producer (Avco Embassy)

BEST ACTOR

Marlon Brando, *Last Tango in Paris*

Jack Lemmon, Save the Tiger

Jack Nicholson, *The Last Detail*

Al Pacino, *Serpico*

Robert Redford, *The Sting*

BEST ACTRESS

Ellen Burstyn, *The Exorcist*

Glenda Jackson, A Touch of Class

Marsha Mason, *Cinderella Liberty*

Barbra Streisand, *The Way We Were*

Joanne Woodward, *Summer Wishes, Winter Dreams*

ACTOR IN A SUPPORTING ROLE

Vincent Gardenia, *Bang the Drum Slowly*

Jack Gilford, *Save the Tiger*

John Houseman, The Paper Chase

Jason Miller, *The Exorcist*

Randy Quaid, *The Last Detail*

ACTRESS IN A SUPPORTING ROLE

Linda Blair, *The Exorcist*

Candy Clark, *American Graffiti*

Madeline Kahn, *Paper Moon*

Tatum O'Neal, Paper Moon

Sylvia Sidney, *Summer Wishes, Winter Dreams*

DIRECTING

Ingmar Bergman, *Cries and Whispers*

Bernardo Bertolucci, *Last Tango in Paris*

William Friedkin, *The Exorcist*

George Roy Hill, The Sting

George Lucas, *American Graffiti*

WRITING

SCREENPLAY BASED ON MATERIAL FROM ANOTHER MEDIUM

William Peter Blatty, The Exorcist

James Bridges, *The Paper Chase*

Waldo Salt and Norman Wexler, *Serpico*

Alvin Sargent, *Paper Moon*

Robert Towne, *The Last Detail*

ORIGINAL SCREENPLAY

Ingmar Bergman, *Cries and Whispers*

Melvin Frank and Jack Rose, *A Touch of Class*

George Lucas, Gloria Katz and Willard Huyck, *American Grafitti*

Steve Shagan, *Save the Tiger*

David S. Ward, The Sting

CINEMATOGRAPHY

Jack Couffer, *Jonathan Livingston Seagull*

Sven Nykvist, Cries and Whispers

Owen Roizman, *The Exorcist*

Harry Stradling, Jr., *The Way We Were*

Robert Surtees, *The Sting*

ART DIRECTION

Henry Bumstead, art direction; James Payne, set decoration, The Sting

Stephen Grimes, art direction; William Kiernan, set decoration, *The Way We Were*

Philip Jefferies, art direction; Robert de Vestel, set decoration, *Tom Sawyer*

Bill Malley, art direction; Jerry Wunderlich, set decoration, *The Exorcist*

Lorenzo Mongiardino and Gianni Quaranta, art direction; Carmelo Patrono, set decoration, *Brother Sun Sister Moon*

SOUND

Robert Knudson and Chris Newman, The Exorcist

Donald O. Mitchell and Lawrence O. Jost, *The Paper Chase*

Ronald K. Pierce and Robert Bertrand, *The Sting*

Richard Portman and Les Fresholtz, *Paper Moon*

Richard Portman and Lawrence O. Jost, *The Day of the Dolphin*

MUSIC

SONG

"All That Love Went to Waste," *A Touch of Class*, George Barrie, music; Sammy Cahn, lyrics

"Live and Let Die," *Live and Let Die*, Paul McCartney and Linda McCartney, music and lyrics

"Love," *Robin Hood*, George Bruns, music; Floyd Huddleston, lyrics

"Nice to Be Around," *Cinderella Liberty*, John Williams, music; Paul Williams, lyrics

"The Way We Were," The Way We Were, Marvin Hamlisch, music; Alan and Marilyn Bergman, lyrics

ORIGINAL DRAMATIC SCORE

John Cameron, *A Touch of Class*

Georges Delerue, *The Day of the Dolphin*

Jerry Goldsmith, *Papillon*

Marvin Hamlisch, The Way We Were

John Williams, *Cinderella Liberty*

SCORING: ORIGINAL SONG SCORE AND ADAPTATION OR SCORING: ADAPTATION

Marvin Hamlisch, The Sting

André Previn, Herbert Spencer and Andrew Lloyd Webber, *Jesus Christ Superstar*

Richard M. Sherman and Robert B. Sherman, song; John Williams, adaptation, *Tom Sawyer*

Tatum O'Neal, *Paper Moon*

FILM EDITING

Verna Fields and Marcia Lucas, *American Graffiti*

Frank P. Keller and James Galloway, *Jonathan Livingston Seagull*

Ralph Kemplen, *The Day of the Jackal*

Jordan Leondopoulos, Bud Smith, Evan Lottman and Norman Gay, *The Exorcist*

William Reynolds, *The Sting*

COSTUME DESIGN

Donfeld, *Tom Sawyer*

Edith Head, *The Sting*

Dorothy Jeakins and Moss Mabry, *The Way We Were*

Piero Tosi, *Ludwig*

Marik Vos, *Cries and Whispers*

SHORT SUBJECTS

ANIMATED

***Frank Film* (Frank Mouris, producer; Frank Mouris Production)**

The Legend of John Henry (Nick Bosustow and David Adams, producers; Bosustow-Pyramid Films Production)

Pulcinella (Emanuele Luzzati and Guilio Gianini, producers; Luzzati-Gianini Production)

LIVE ACTION

***The Bolero* (Allan Miller and William Fertik, producers; Allan Miller Production)**

Clockmaker (Richard Gayer, producer; James Street Productions)

Life Times Nine (Pen Densham and John Watson, producers; Insight Productions)

DOCUMENTARY

SHORT SUBJECT

Background (Carmen D'Avino, producer; D'Avino and Fucci-Stone Productions)

Children at Work (*Paisti Ag Obair*) (Louis Marcus, producer; Gael-Linn Films)

Christo's Valley Curtain (Albert Maysles and David Maysles, producers; Maysles Films Production)

Four Stones for Kanemitsu (Terry Sanders and June Wayne, producers; Tamarind Production)

***Princeton: A Search for Answers* (Julian Krainin and DeWitt L. Sage, Jr., producers; Krainin-Sage Productions)**

FEATURE

Always a New Beginning (John D. Goodell, producer; Goodell Motion Pictures)

Battle of Berlin (Bengt von zur Muehlen, producer; Chronos Film GmbH)

***The Great American Cowboy* (Keith Merrill, producer; Keith Merrill Associates-Rodeo Film Productions)**

Journey to the Outer Limits (Alex Grasshoff, producer; National Geographic Society and Wolper Productions)

Walls of Fire (Gertrude Ross Marks and Edmund F. Penney, producers; Mentor Productions)

FOREIGN LANGUAGE FILM

Day for Night, France

The House of Chelouche Street, Israel

L'Invitation, Switzerland

The Pedestrian, Federal Republic of Germany – West

Turkish Delight, Netherlands

IRVING G. THALBERG MEMORIAL AWARD

Lawrence Weingarten

JEAN HERSHOLT HUMANITARIAN AWARD

Lew Wasserman

HONORARY AWARDS

To **Henri Langlois** for his devotion to the art of film, his massive contributions in preserving its past and his unswerving faith in its future

To **Groucho Marx** in recognition of his brilliant creativity and for the unequalled acheivements of the Marx Brothers in the art of motion picture comedy

1974

BEST PICTURE

Chinatown, Robert Evans, producer (Paramount)

The Conversation, Francis Ford Coppola, producer (Paramount)

***The Godfather Part II,* Francis Ford Coppola, producer; Gray Frederickson and Fred Roos, co-producers (Paramount)**

Lenny, Marvin Worth, producer (United Artists)

The Towering Inferno, Irwin Allen, producer (Twentieth Century-Fox/Warner Bros.)

BEST ACTOR

Art Carney, *Harry and Tonto*

Albert Finney, *Murder on the Orient Express*

Dustin Hoffman, *Lenny*

Jack Nicholson, *Chinatown*

Al Pacino, *The Godfather Part II*

BEST ACTRESS

Ellen Burstyn, *Alice Doesn't Live Here Anymore*

Diahann Carroll, *Claudine*

Faye Dunaway, *Chinatown*

Valerie Perrine, *Lenny*

Gena Rowlands, *A Woman Under the Influence*

Robert De Niro, *The Godfather Part II*

ACTOR IN A SUPPORTING ROLE
Fred Astaire, *The Towering Inferno*
Jeff Bridges, *Thunderbolt and Lightfoot*
Robert De Niro, *The Godfather Part II*
Michael V. Gazzo, *The Godfather Part II*
Lee Strasberg, *The Godfather Part II*

ACTRESS IN A SUPPORTING ROLE
Ingrid Bergman, *Murder on the Orient Express*
Valentina Cortese, *Day for Night*
Madeline Kahn, *Blazing Saddles*
Diane Ladd, *Alice Doesn't Live Here Anymore*
Talia Shire, *The Godfather Part II*

DIRECTING
John Cassavetes, *A Woman Under the Influence*
Francis Ford Coppola, *The Godfather Part II*
Bob Fosse, *Lenny*
Roman Polanski, *Chinatown*
François Truffaut, *Day for Night*

WRITING
ORIGINAL SCREENPLAY
Francis Ford Coppola, *The Conversation*
Robert Getchell, *Alice Doesn't Live Here Anymore*
Paul Mazursky and Josh Greenfeld, *Harry and Tonto*
Robert Towne, *Chinatown*
François Truffaut, Jean-Louis Richard and Suzanne Schiffman, *Day for Night*

SCREENPLAY ADAPTED FROM OTHER MATERIAL
Julian Barry, *Lenny*
Paul Dehn, *Murder on the Orient Express*
Francis Ford Coppola and Mario Puzo, *The Godfather Part II*
Mordecai Richler, screenplay; Lionel Chetwynd, adaptation, *The Apprenticeship of Duddy Kravitz*
Gene Wilder and Mel Brooks, *Young Frankenstein*

CINEMATOGRAPHY
John A. Alonzo, *Chinatown*
Fred Koenekamp and Joseph Biroc, *The Towering Inferno*
Philip Lathrop, *Earthquake*
Bruce Surtees, *Lenny*
Geoffrey Unsworth, *Murder on the Orient Express*

ART DIRECTION
William Creber and Ward Preston, art direction; Raphael Bretton, set decoration, *The Towering Inferno*
Peter Ellenshaw, John B. Mansbridge, Walter Tyler and Al Roelofs, art direction; Hal Gausman, set decoration, *The Island at the Top of the World*
Alexander Golitzen and E. Preston Ames, art direction; Frank McKelvy, set decoration, *Earthquake*
Richard Sylbert and W. Stewart Campbell, art direction; Ruby Levitt, set decoartion, *Chinatown*
Dean Tavoularis and Angelo Graham, art direction; George R. Nelson, set decoration, *The Godfather Part II*

SOUND
Bud Grenzbach and Larry Jost, *Chinatown*
Walter Murch and Arthur Rochester, *The Conversation*
Ronald Pierce and Melvin Metcalfe, Sr., *Earthquake*
Richard Portman and Gene Cantamessa, *Young Frankenstein*
Theodore Soderberg and Herman Lewis, *The Towering Inferno*

MUSIC
SONG
"Benji's Theme" (I Feel Love), *Benji*, Euel Box, music; Betty Box, lyrics
"Blazing Saddles," *Blazing Saddles*, John Morris, music; Mel Brooks, lyrics
"Little Prince," *The Little Prince*, Frederick Loewe, music; Alan Jay Lerner, lyrics
"We May Never Love Like This Again," *The Towering Inferno*, Al Kasha and Joel Hirschhorn, music and lyrics
"Wherever Love Takes Me," *Gold*, Elmer Bernstein, music; Don Black, lyrics

ORIGINAL DRAMATIC SCORE
Richard Rodney Bennett, *Murder on the Orient Express*
Jerry Goldsmith, *Chinatown*
Alex North, *Shanks*
Nino Rota and Carmine Coppola, *The Godfather Part II*
John Williams, *The Towering Inferno*

SCORING: ORIGINAL SONG SCORE AND ADAPTATION OR SCORING: ADAPTATION
Alan Jay Lerner and Frederick Loewe, song; Angela Morley and Douglas Gamley, adaptation, *The Little Prince*
Nelson Riddle, adaptation, *The Great Gatsby*
Paul Williams, song; George Aliceson Tipton and Paul Williams, adaptation, *Phantom of the Paradise*

FILM EDITING
John C. Howard and Danford Greene, *Blazing Saddles*
Harold F. Kress and Carl Kress, *The Towering Inferno*
Michael Luciano, *The Longest Yard*
Sam O'Steen, *Chinatown*
Dorothy Spencer, *Earthquake*

COSTUME DESIGN

Theoni V. Aldredge, *The Great Gatsby*

John Furness, *Daisy Miller*

Anthea Sylbert, *Chinatown*

Theadora Van Runkle, *The Godfather Part II*

Tony Walton, *Murder on the Orient Express*

SHORT FILMS
ANIMATED

Closed Mondays (Will Vinton and Bob Gardiner, producers; Lighthouse Productions)

The Family That Dwelt Apart (Yvon Mallette and Robert Verrall, producers; National Film Board of Canada)

Hunger (Peter Foldes and René Jodoin, producers; National Film Board of Canada)

Voyage to Next (Faith Hubley and John Hubley, producers; Hubley Studios)

Winnie the Pooh and Tigger Too (Wolfgang Reitherman, producer; Walt Disney Productions)

LIVE ACTION

Climb (Dewitt Jones, producer; Dewitt Jones Productions)

The Concert (Julian and Claude Chagrin, producers; The Black and White Colour Film Company, Ltd.)

One-Eyed Men Are Kings (Paul Claudon and Edmond Sechan, producers; C.A.P.A.C. Productions)

Planet Ocean (George V. Casey, producer; Graphic Films)

The Violin (Andrew Welsh and George Pastic, producers; Sincinkin, Ltd.)

DOCUMENTARY
SHORT SUBJECT

City Out of Wilderness (Francis Thompson, producer; Francis Thompson Inc.)

Don't (Robin Lehman, producer; R. A. Films)

Exploratorium (Jon Boorstin, producer; Jon Boorstin Production)

John Muir's High Sierra (Dewitt Jones and Lesley Foster, producers; Dewitt Jones Productions)

Naked Yoga (Ronald S. Kass and Mervyn Lloyd, producers; Filmshop Production)

FEATURE

Antonia: A Portrait of the Woman (Judy Collins and Jill Godmilow, producers; Rocky Mountain Productions)

The Challenge . . . A Tribute to Modern Art (Herbert Kline, producer; World View Production)

The 81st Blow (Jacquot Ehrlich, David Bergman and Haim Gouri, producers; Ghetto Fighters House Film)

Hearts and Minds (Touchstone-Audjeff-BBS Production; Howard Zucker/Henry Jaglom-Rainbow Pictures Presentation)

The Wild and the Brave (E.S.J. Productions in association with Tomorrow Entertainment Inc. and Jones/Howard Ltd.)

FOREIGN LANGUAGE FILM

Amarcord, Italy

Cats' Play, Hungary

The Deluge, Poland

Lacombe, Lucien, France

The Truce, Argentina

JEAN HERSHOLT HUMANITARIAN AWARD

Arthur B. Krim

HONORARY AWARDS

To **Howard Hawks,** a master American filmmaker whose creative efforts hold a distinguished place in world cinema

To **Jean Renoir,** a genius who, with grace, responsibility and enviable devotion through silent film, sound film, feature, documentary and television, has won the world's admiration

SPECIAL ACHIEVEMENT AWARD
VISUAL EFFECTS

Frank Brendel, Glen Robinson and Albert Whitlock, Earthquake

1975

BEST PICTURE

Barry Lyndon, Stanley Kubrick, producer (Warner Bros.)

Dog Day Afternoon, Martin Bregman and Martin Elfand, producers (Warner Bros.)

Jaws, Richard D. Zanuck and David Brown, producers (Universal)

Nashville, Robert Altman, producer (Paramount)

One Flew Over the Cuckoo's Nest, Saul Zaentz and Michael Douglas, producers (United Artists)

BEST ACTOR

Walter Matthau, *The Sunshine Boys*

Jack Nicholson, *One Flew Over the Cuckoo's Nest*

Al Pacino, *Dog Day Afternoon*

Maximilian Schell, *The Man in the Glass Booth*

James Whitmore, *Give 'em Hell, Harry!*

BEST ACTRESS

Isabelle Adjani, *The Story of Adele H.*

Louise Fletcher, *One Flew Over the Cuckoo's Nest*

Glenda Jackson, *Hedda*

Carol Kane, *Hester Street*

Ann-Margret, *Tommy*

Jack Nicholson,
One Flew Over the Cuckoo's Nest

ACTOR IN A SUPPORTING ROLE

George Burns, *The Sunshine Boys*

Brad Dourif, *One Flew Over the Cuckoo's Nest*

Burgess Meredith, *The Day of the Locust*

Chris Sarandon, *Dog Day Afternoon*

Jack Warden, *Shampoo*

ACTRESS IN A SUPPORTING ROLE

Ronee Blakley, *Nashville*

Lee Grant, *Shampoo*

Sylvia Miles, *Farewell, My Lovely*

Lily Tomlin, *Nashville*

Brenda Vaccaro, *Jacqueline Susann's Once Is Not Enough*

DIRECTING

Robert Altman, *Nashville*

Federico Fellini, *Amarcord*

Milos Forman, *One Flew Over the Cuckoo's Nest*

Stanley Kubrick, *Barry Lyndon*

Sidney Lumet, *Dog Day Afternoon*

WRITING

ORIGINAL SCREENPLAY

Ted Allan, *Lies My Father Told Me*

Federico Fellini and Tonino Guerra, *Amarcord*

Claude Lelouch and Pierre Uytterhoeven, *And Now My Love*

Frank Pierson, *Dog Day Afternoon*

Robert Towne and Warren Beatty, *Shampoo*

SCREENPLAY ADAPTED FROM OTHER MATERIAL

Lawrence Hauben and Bo Goldman, *One Flew Over the Cuckoo's Nest*

John Huston and Gladys Hill, *The Man Who Would Be King*

Stanley Kubrick, *Barry Lyndon*

Ruggero Maccari and Dino Risi, *Scent of a Woman*

Neil Simon, *The Sunshine Boys*

CINEMATOGRAPHY

John Alcott, *Barry Lyndon*

Conrad Hall, *The Day of the Locust*

James Wong Howe, *Funny Lady*

Robert Surtees, *The Hindenburg*

Haskell Wexler and Bill Butler, *One Flew Over the Cuckoo's Nest*

ART DIRECTION

Ken Adam and Roy Walker, art direction; Vernon Dixon, set decoration, *Barry Lyndon*

Albert Brenner, art direction; Marvin March, set decoration, *The Sunshine Boys*

Edward Carfagno, art direction; Frank McKelvy, set decoration, *The Hindenburg*

Richard Sylbert and W. Stewart Campbell, art direction; George Gaines, set decoration, *Shampoo*

Alexander Trauner and Tony Inglis, art direction; Peter James, set decoration, *The Man Who Would Be King*

SOUND

Robert L. Hoyt, Roger Heman, Earl Madery and John Carter, *Jaws*

Leonard Peterson, John A. Bolger, Jr., John Mack and Don K. Sharpless, *The Hindenburg*

Arthur Piantadosi, Les Fresholtz, Richard Tyler and Al Overton, Jr., *Bite the Bullet*

Richard Portman, Don MacDougall, Curly Thirlwell and Jack Solomon, *Funny Lady*

Harry W. Tetrick, Aaron Rochin, William McCaughey and Roy Charman, *The Wind and the Lion*

MUSIC

ORIGINAL SONG

"How Lucky Can You Get," *Funny Lady*, Fred Ebb and John Kander, music and lyrics

"I'm Easy," *Nashville*, Keith Carradine, music and lyrics

"Now That We're in Love," *Whiffs*, George Barrie, music; Sammy Cahn, lyrics

"Richard's Window," *The Other Side of the Mountain*, Charles Fox, music; Norman Gimbel, lyrics

"Theme From *Mahogany*" (Do You Know Where You're Going To), *Mahogany*, Michael Masser, music; Gerry Goffin, lyrics

ORIGINAL SCORE

Gerald Fried, *Birds Do It, Bees Do It*

Jerry Goldsmith, *The Wind and the Lion*

Jack Nitzsche, *One Flew Over the Cuckoo's Nest*

Alex North, *Bite the Bullet*

John Williams, *Jaws*

SCORING: ORIGINAL SONG SCORE AND ADAPTATION OR SCORING: ADAPTATION

Peter Matz, *Funny Lady*

Leonard Rosenman, *Barry Lyndon*

Peter Townshend, *Tommy*

FILM EDITING

Dede Allen, *Dog Day Afternoon*

Richard Chew, Lynzee Klingman and Sheldon Kahn, *One Flew Over the Cuckoo's Nest*

Verna Fields, *Jaws*

Russell Lloyd, *The Man Who Would Be King*

Frederic Steinkamp and Don Guidice, *Three Days of the Condor*

COSTUME DESIGN

Ray Aghayan and Bob Mackie, *Funny Lady*

Yvonne Blake and Ron Talsky, *The Four Musketeers*

Edith Head, *The Man Who Would Be King*

Henny Noremark and Karin Erskine, *The Magic Flute*

Ulla-Britt Soderlund and Milena Canonero, *Barry Lyndon*

SHORT FILMS

ANIMATED

***Great* (Grantstern Ltd.; British Lion Films Ltd.)**

Kick Me (Robert Swarthe, producer; Robert Swarthe Productions)

Monsieur Pointu (René Jodoin, Bernard Longpré and André Leduc, producers; National Film Board of Canada)

Sisyphus (Marcell Jankovics, producer; Hungarofilms)

LIVE ACTION

Angel and Big Joe (Bert Salzman, producer; Bert Salzman
Productions)

Conquest of Light (Louis Marcus, producer; Louis Marcus
Films Ltd.)

Dawn Flight (Lawrence M. Lansburgh and Brian Lansburgh,
producers; Lawrence M. Lansburgh Productions)

A Day in the Life of Bonnie Consolo (Barry Spinello, producer;
Barr Films)

Doubletalk (Alan Beattie, producer; Beattie Productions)

DOCUMENTARY
SHORT SUBJECT

Arthur and Lillie (Jon Else, Steven Kovacs and Kristine
Samuelson, producers; Stanford University Department of
Communication)

**The End of the Game (Claire Wilbur and Robin Lehman,
producers; Opus Films Ltd.)**

Millions of Years Ahead of Man (Manfred Baier, producer;
BASF)

Probes in Space (George V. Casey, producer; Graphic Films)

Whistling Smith (Barrie Howells and Michael Scott, producers;
National Film Board of Canada)

FEATURE

The California Reich (Walter F. Parkes and Keith F. Critchlow,
producers; Yasny Talking Pictures)

Fighting for Our Lives (Glen Pearcy, producer; Farm Worker
Film)

The Incredible Machine (National Geographic Society and
Wolper Productions)

**The Man Who Skied Down Everest (F. R. Crawley, James
Hager and Dale Hartleben, producers; Crawley Films
Presentation)**

The Other Half of the Sky: A China Memoir (Shirley MacLaine,
producer; MacLaine Productions)

FOREIGN LANGUAGE FILM

Dersu Uzala, U.S.S.R.

Land of Promise, Poland

Letters From Marusia, Mexico

Sandakan No. 8, Japan

Scent of a Woman, Italy

IRVING G. THALBERG MEMORIAL AWARD
Mervyn LeRoy

JEAN HERSHOLT HUMANITARIAN AWARD
Dr. Jules C. Stein

HONORARY AWARD

To **Mary Pickford** in recognition of her unique contributions to
the film industry and the development of film as an artistic
medium

SPECIAL ACHIEVEMENT AWARDS
SOUND EFFECTS
Peter Berkos, *The Hindenburg*

VISUAL EFFECTS
Albert Whitlock and Glen Robinson, *The Hindenburg*

1976

BEST PICTURE

All the President's Men, Walter Coblenz, producer (Warner
Bros.)

Bound for Glory, Robert F. Blumofe and Harold Leventhal,
producers (United Artists)

Network, Howard Gottfried, producer (MGM/United Artists)

***Rocky*, Irwin Winkler and Robert Chartoff, producers
(United Artists)**

Taxi Driver, Michael Phillips and Julia Phillips, producers
(Columbia)

BEST ACTOR

Robert De Niro, *Taxi Driver*

Peter Finch, *Network*

Giancarlo Giannini, *Seven Beauties*

William Holden, *Network*

Sylvester Stallone, *Rocky*

BEST ACTRESS

Marie-Christine Barrault, *Cousin, Cousine*

Faye Dunaway, *Network*

Talia Shire, *Rocky*

Sissy Spacek, *Carrie*

Liv Ullman, *Face to Face*

ACTOR IN A SUPPORTING ROLE

Ned Beatty, *Network*

Burgess Meredith, *Rocky*

Laurence Olivier, *Marathon Man*

Jason Robards, *All the President's Men*

Burt Young, *Rocky*

ACTRESS IN A SUPPORTING ROLE

Jane Alexander, *All the President's Men*

Jodie Foster, *Taxi Driver*

Lee Grant, *Voyage of the Damned*

Piper Laurie, *Carrie*

Beatrice Straight, *Network*

Rocky

DIRECTING

John G. Avildsen, *Rocky*

Ingmar Bergman, *Face to Face*

Sidney Lumet, *Network*

Alan J. Pakula, *All the President's Men*

Lina Wertmuller, *Seven Beauties*

WRITING

ORIGINAL SCREENPLAY

Walter Bernstein, *The Front*

Paddy Chayefsky, *Network*

Sylvester Stallone, *Rocky*

Jean-Charles Tacchella, story and screenplay; Daniele Thompson, adaptation, *Cousin, Cousine*

Lina Wertmuller, *Seven Beauties*

SCREENPLAY BASED ON MATERIAL FROM ANOTHER MEDIUM

Federico Fellini and Bernadino Zapponi, *Fellini's Casanova*

Robert Getchell, *Bound for Glory*

William Goldman, *All the President's Men*

Nicholas Meyer, *The Seven-Per-Cent Solution*

Steve Shagan and David Butler, *Voyage of the Damned*

CINEMATOGRAPHY

Richard H. Kline, *King Kong*

Ernest Laszlo, *Logan's Run*

Owen Roizman, *Network*

Robert Surtees, *A Star Is Born*

Haskell Wexler, *Bound for Glory*

ART DIRECTION

Robert F. Boyle, art direction; Arthur Jeph Parker, set decoration, *The Shootist*

Gene Callahan and Jack Collis, art direction; Jerry Wunderlich, set decoration, *The Last Tycoon*

Dale Hennessy, art direction; Robert de Vestel, set decoration, *Logan's Run*

George Jenkins, art direction; George Gaines, set decoration, *All the President's Men*

Elliot Scott and Norman Reynolds, art direction; Peter Howitt, set decoration, *The Incredible Sarah*

SOUND

Robert Knudson, Dan Wallin, Robert Glass and Tom Overton, *A Star Is Born*

Donald Mitchell, Douglas Williams, Richard Tyler and Hal Etherington, *Silver Streak*

Arthur Piantadosi, Les Fresholtz, Dick Alexander and Jim Webb, *All the President's Men*

Harry Warren Tetrick, William McCaughey, Aaron Rochin and Jack Solomon, *King Kong*

Harry Warren Tetrick, William McCaughey, Lyle Burbridge and Bud Alper, *Rocky*

MUSIC

ORIGINAL SONG

"Ave Satani," *The Omen*, Jerry Goldsmith, music and lyrics

"Come to Me," *The Pink Panther Strikes Again*, Henry Mancini, music; Don Black, lyrics

"Evergreen" (Love Theme From *A Star Is Born*), *A Star Is Born*, Barbra Streisand, music; Paul Williams, lyrics

"Gonna Fly Now," *Rocky*, Bill Conti, music; Carol Connors and Ayn Robbins, lyrics

"A World That Never Was," *Half a House*, Sammy Fain, music; Paul Francis Webster, lyrics

ORIGINAL SCORE

Jerry Fielding, *The Outlaw Josey Wales*

Jerry Goldsmith, *The Omen*

Bernard Herrmann, *Obsession*

Bernard Herrmann, *Taxi Driver*

Lalo Schifrin, *Voyage of the Damned*

ORIGINAL SONG SCORE AND ITS ADAPTATION OR ADAPTATION SCORE

Roger Kellaway, *A Star Is Born*

Leonard Rosenman, *Bound for Glory*

Paul Williams, *Bugsy Malone*

FILM EDITING

Richard Halsey and Scott Conrad, *Rocky*

Alan Heim, *Network*

Robert Jones and Pembroke J. Herring, *Bound for Glory*

Eve Newman and Walter Hannemann, *Two-Minute Warning*

Robert L. Wolfe, *All the President's Men*

COSTUME DESIGN

Alan Barrett, *The Seven-Per-Cent Solution*

Danilo Donati, *Fellini's Casanova*

Anthony Mendleson, *The Incredible Sarah*

William Theiss, *Bound for Glory*

Mary Wills, *The Passover Plot*

SHORT FILMS

ANIMATED

Dedalo (Manfredo Manfredi, producer; Cineteam Realizzazioni Production)

***Leisure* (Suzanne Baker, producer; Film Australia Production)**

The Street (Caroline Leaf and Guy Glover, producers; National Film Board of Canada)

LIVE ACTION

***In the Region of Ice* (Andre Guttfreund and Peter Werner, producers; American Film Institute)**

Kudzu (Marjorie Ann Short, producer; Short Productions)

The Morning Spider (Julian Chagrin and Claude Chagrin, producers; The Black and White Colour Film Company)

Nightlife (Claire Wilbur and Robin Lehman, producers; Opus Films Ltd.)

Number One (Dyan Cannon and Vince Cannon, producers; Number One Productions)

DOCUMENTARY

SHORT SUBJECT

American Shoeshine (Sparky Greene, producer; Titan Films)

Blackwood (Tony Ianzelo and Andy Thompson, producers; National Film Board of Canada)

The End of the Road (John Armstrong, producer; Pelican Films)

***Number Our Days* (Lynne Littman, producer; Community Television of Southern California)**

Universe (Lester Novros, producer; Graphic Films Corporation for NASA)

FEATURE

Harlan County, U.S.A. **(Barbara Kopple, producer; Cabin Creek Films)**

Hollywood on Trial (James Gutman and David Helpern, Jr., producers; October Films/Cinema Associates)

Off the Edge (Michael Firth, producer; Pentacle Films)

People of the Wind (Anthony Howarth and David Koff, producers; Elizabeth E. Rogers Productions)

Volcano: An Inquiry Into the Life and Death of Malcolm Lowry (Donald Brittain and Robert Duncan, producers; National Film Board of Canada)

FOREIGN LANGUAGE FILM

***Black and White in Color*, Ivory Coast**

Cousin, Cousine, France

Jacob, the Liar, German Democratic Republic – East

Nights and Days, Poland

Seven Beauties, Italy

IRVING G. THALBERG MEMORIAL AWARD

Pandro S. Berman

SPECIAL ACHIEVEMENT AWARDS

VISUAL EFFECTS

Carlo Rambaldi, Glen Robinson and Frank Van der Veer, *King Kong*

VISUAL EFFECTS

L.B. Abbott, Glen Robinson and Matthew Yuricich, *Logan's Run*

1977

BEST PICTURE

***Annie Hall*, Charles H. Joffe, producer (United Artists)**

The Goodbye Girl, Ray Stark, producer (MGM/Warner Bros.)

Julia, Richard Roth, producer (Twentieth Century-Fox)

Star Wars, Gary Kurtz, producer (Twentieth Century-Fox)

The Turning Point, Herbert Ross and Arthur Laurents, producers (Twentieth Century-Fox)

ACTOR IN A LEADING ROLE

Woody Allen, *Annie Hall*

Richard Burton, *Equus*

Richard Dreyfuss, *The Goodbye Girl*

Marcello Mastroianni, *A Special Day*

John Travolta, *Saturday Night Fever*

ACTRESS IN A LEADING ROLE

Anne Bancroft, *The Turning Point*

Jane Fonda, *Julia*

Diane Keaton, *Annie Hall*

Shirley MacLaine, *The Turning Point*

Marsha Mason, *The Goodbye Girl*

ACTOR IN A SUPPORTING ROLE

Mikhail Baryshnikov, *The Turning Point*

Peter Firth, *Equus*

Alec Guinness, *Star Wars*

Jason Robards, *Julia*

Maximilian Schell, *Julia*

ACTRESS IN A SUPPORTING ROLE

Leslie Browne, *The Turning Point*

Quinn Cummings, *The Goodbye Girl*

Melinda Dillon, *Close Encounters of the Third Kind*

Vanessa Redgrave, *Julia*

Tuesday Weld, *Looking for Mr. Goodbar*

DIRECTING

Woody Allen, *Annie Hall*

George Lucas, *Star Wars*

Herbert Ross, *The Turning Point*

Steven Spielberg, *Close Encounters of the Third Kind*

Fred Zinnemann, *Julia*

WRITING

ORIGINAL SCREENPLAY

Woody Allen and Marshall Brickman, *Annie Hall*

Robert Benton, *The Late Show*

Arthur Laurents, *The Turning Point*

George Lucas, *Star Wars*

Neil Simon, *The Goodbye Girl*

SCREENPLAY BASED ON MATERIAL FROM ANOTHER MEDIUM

Luis Buñuel and Jean-Claude Carrière, *That Obscure Object of Desire*

Larry Gelbart, *Oh, God!*

Gavin Lambert and Lewis John Carlino, *I Never Promised You a Rose Garden*

Alvin Sargent, *Julia*

Peter Shaffer, *Equus*

CINEMATOGRAPHY

William A. Fraker, *Looking for Mr. Goodbar*

Fred J. Koenekamp, *Islands in the Stream*

Douglas Slocombe, *Julia*

Robert Surtees, *The Turning Point*

Vilmos Zsigmond, *Close Encounters of the Third Kind*

Woody Allen

ART DIRECTION

Ken Adam and Peter Lamont, art direction; Hugh Scaife, set decoration, *The Spy Who Loved Me*

Joe Alves and Dan Lomino, art direction; Phil Abramson, set decoration, *Close Encounters of the Third Kind*

John Barry, Norman Reynolds and Leslie Dilley, art direction; Roger Christian, set decoration, *Star Wars*

Albert Brenner, art direction; Marvin March, set decoration, *The Turning Point*

George C. Webb, art direction; Mickey S. Michaels, set decoration, *Airport '77*

SOUND

Walter Goss, Dick Alexander, Tom Beckert and Robin Gregory, *The Deep*

Robert Knudson, Robert J. Glass, Don MacDougall and Gene S. Cantamessa, *Close Encounters of the Third Kind*

Robert Knudson, Robert J. Glass, Richard Tyler and Jean-Louis Ducarme, *Sorcerer*

Don MacDougall, Ray West, Bob Minkler and Derek Ball, *Star Wars*

Theodore Soderberg, Paul Wells, Douglas O. Williams and Jerry Jost, *The Turning Point*

MUSIC

ORIGINAL SONG

"Candle on the Water," *Pete's Dragon*, Al Kasha and Joel Hirschhorn, music and lyrics

"Nobody Does It Better," *The Spy Who Loved Me*, Marvin Hamlisch, music; Carole Bayer Sager, lyrics

"The Slipper and the Rose Waltz" (He Danced With Me/She Danced With Me), *The Slipper and the Rose — The Story of Cinderella*, Richard M. Sherman and Robert B. Sherman, music and lyrics

"Someone's Waiting for You," *The Rescuers,* Sammy Fain, music; Carol Connors and Ayn Robbins, lyrics

"You Light Up My Life," *You Light Up My Life*, Joseph Brooks, music and lyrics

ORIGINAL SCORE

Georges Delerue, *Julia*

Marvin Hamlisch, *The Spy Who Loved Me*

Maurice Jarre, *Mohammad — Messenger of God*

John Williams, *Close Encounters of the Third Kind*

John Williams, *Star Wars*

ORIGINAL SONG SCORE AND ITS ADAPTATION OR ADAPTATION SCORE

Al Kasha and Joel Hirschhorn, song; Irwin Kostal, adaptation, *Pete's Dragon*

Richard M. Sherman and Robert B. Sherman, song; Angela Morley, adaptation, *The Slipper and the Rose — The Story of Cinderella*

Jonathan Tunick, *A Little Night Music*

FILM EDITING

Walter Hannemann and Angelo Ross, *Smokey and the Bandit*

Paul Hirsch, Marcia Lucas and Richard Chew, *Star Wars*

Michael Kahn, *Close Encounters of the Third Kind*

Walter Murch, *Julia*

William Reynolds, *The Turning Point*

COSTUME DESIGN

Edith Head and Burton Miller, *Airport '77*

Florence Klotz, *A Little Night Music*

John Mollo, *Star Wars*

Irene Sharaff, *The Other Side of Midnight*

Anthea Sylbert, *Julia*

VISUAL EFFECTS

Roy Arbogast, Douglas Trumbull, Matthew Yuricich, Gregory Jein and Richard Yuricich, *Close Encounters of the Third Kind*

John Stears, John Dykstra, Richard Edlund, Grant McCune and Robert Blalack, *Star Wars*

SHORT FILMS

ANIMATED

The Bead Game (Ishu Patel, producer; National Film Board of Canada)

The Doonesbury Special (John Hubley, Faith Hubley and Garry Trudeau, producers; Hubley Studios)

Jimmy the C (James Picker, Robert Grossman and Craig Whitaker, producers; Motionpicker Production)

***The Sand Castle* (Co Hoedeman, producer; National Film Board of Canada)**

LIVE ACTION

The Absent-Minded Waiter (William E. McEuen, producer; Aspen Film Society)

Floating Free (Jerry Butts, producer; Trans World International)

***I'll Find a Way* (Beverly Shaffer and Yuki Yoshida, producers; National Film Board of Canada)**

Notes on the Popular Arts (Saul Bass, producer; Saul Bass Films)

Spaceborne (Philip Dauber, producer; Lawrence Hall of Science Production for the Regents of the University of California with the cooperation of NASA)

DOCUMENTARY

SHORT SUBJECT

Agueda Martinez: Our People, Our Country (Moctesuma Esparza, producer; Moctesuma Esparza Production)

First Edition (Helen Whitney and DeWitt L. Sage, Jr., producers; D.L. Sage Productions)

***Gravity Is My Enemy* (John Joseph and Jan Stussy, producers; John Joseph Production)**

Of Time, Tombs and Treasure (James R. Messenger and Paul N. Raimondi, producers; Charlie/Papa Productions, Inc.)

The Shetland Experience (Douglas Gordon, producer; Balfour Films)

FEATURE

The Children of Theatre Street (Robert Dornhelm and Earle Mack, producers; Mack-Vaganova Company)

High Grass Circus (Bill Brind, Torben Schioler and Tony Ianzelo, producers; National Film Board of Canada)

Homage to Chagall — The Colours of Love (Harry Rasky, producer; CBC Production)

Union Maids (James Klein, Julia Reichert and Miles Mogulescu, producers; Klein, Reichert, Mogulescu Production)

***Who Are the DeBolts? And Where Did They Get Nineteen Kids?* (Korty Films and Charles M. Schulz Creative Associates in association with Sanrio Films)**

FOREIGN LANGUAGE FILM

Iphigenia, Greece
Madame Rosa, France
Operation Thunderbolt, Israel
A Special Day, Italy
That Obscure Object of Desire, Spain

IRVING G. THALBERG MEMORIAL AWARD

Walter Mirisch

JEAN HERSHOLT HUMANITARIAN AWARD

Charlton Heston

HONORARY AWARDS

To **Margaret Booth** for her exceptional contribution to the art
of film editing in the motion picture industry

To **Gordon E. Sawyer** in appreciation for outstanding service
and dedication in upholding the high standards of the
Academy of Motion Picture Arts and Sciences

To **Sidney P. Solow** in appreciation for outstanding service
and dedication in upholding the high standards of the
Academy of Motion Picture Arts and Sciences

SPECIAL ACHIEVEMENT AWARDS

SOUND EFFECTS EDITING

Frank E. Warner, *Close Encounters of the Third Kind*

To **Benjamin Burtt, Jr.** for the creation of the alien, creature
and robot voices in *Star Wars*

1978

BEST PICTURE

Coming Home, Jerome Hellman, producer (United Artists)
The Deer Hunter, Barry Spikings, Michael Deeley, Michael
   Cimino and John Peverall, producers (Universal)
Heaven Can Wait, Warren Beatty, producer (Paramount)
Midnight Express, Alan Marshall and David Puttnam, produc-
   ers (Columbia)
An Unmarried Woman, Paul Mazursky and Tony Ray, produc-
   ers (Twentieth Century-Fox)

ACTOR IN A LEADING ROLE

Warren Beatty, *Heaven Can Wait*
Gary Busey, *The Buddy Holly Story*
Robert De Niro, *The Deer Hunter*
Laurence Olivier, *The Boys From Brazil*
Jon Voight, Coming Home

ACTRESS IN A LEADING ROLE

Ingrid Bergman, *Autumn Sonata*
Ellen Burstyn, *Same Time, Next Year*
Jill Clayburgh, *An Unmarried Woman*
Jane Fonda, Coming Home
Geraldine Page, *Interiors*

Christopher Walken, *The Deer Hunter*

ACTOR IN A SUPPORTING ROLE

Bruce Dern, *Coming Home*
Richard Farnsworth, *Comes a Horseman*
John Hurt, *Midnight Express*
Christopher Walken, *The Deer Hunter*
Jack Warden, *Heaven Can Wait*

ACTRESS IN A SUPPORTING ROLE

Dyan Cannon, *Heaven Can Wait*
Penelope Milford, *Coming Home*
Maggie Smith, *California Suite*
Maureen Stapleton, *Interiors*
Meryl Streep, *The Deer Hunter*

DIRECTING

Woody Allen, *Interiors*
Hal Ashby, *Coming Home*
Warren Beatty and Buck Henry, *Heaven Can Wait*
Michael Cimino, *The Deer Hunter*
Alan Parker, *Midnight Express*

WRITING

SCREENPLAY WRITTEN DIRECTLY FOR THE SCREEN

Woody Allen, *Interiors*
Ingmar Bergman, *Autumn Sonata*
Michael Cimino, Deric Washburn, Louis Garfinkle and Quinn K.
   Redeker, story; Deric Washburn, screenplay, *The Deer
   Hunter*
**Nancy Dowd, story; Waldo Salt and Robert C. Jones,
   screenplay, Coming Home**
Paul Mazursky, *An Unmarried Woman*

SCREENPLAY BASED ON MATERIAL FROM ANOTHER MEDIUM

Elaine May and Warren Beatty, *Heaven Can Wait*
Walter Newman, *Bloodbrothers*
Neil Simon, *California Suite*
Bernard Slade, *Same Time, Next Year*
Oliver Stone, *Midnight Express*

CINEMATOGRAPHY

Nestor Almendros, *Days of Heaven*

William A. Fraker, *Heaven Can Wait*

Oswald Morris, *The Wiz*

Robert Surtees, *Same Time, Next Year*

Vilmos Zsigmond, *The Deer Hunter*

ART DIRECTION

Mel Bourne, art direction; Daniel Robert, set decoration, *Interiors*

Albert Brenner, art direction; Marvin March, set decoration, *California Suite*

Paul Sylbert and Edwin O'Donovan, art direction; George Gaines, set decoration, *Heaven Can Wait*

Dean Tavoularis and Angelo Graham, art direction; George R. Nelson and Bruce Kay, set decoration, *The Brink's Job*

Tony Walton and Philip Rosenberg, art direction; Edward Stewart and Robert Drumheller, set decoration, *The Wiz*

SOUND

Robert Knudson, Robert J. Glass, Don MacDougall and Jack Solomon, *Hooper*

Gordon K. McCallum, Graham Hartstone, Nicholas Le Messurier and Roy Charman, *Superman*

Richard Portman, William McCaughey, Aaron Rochin and Darin Knight, *The Deer Hunter*

Tex Rudloff, Joel Fein, Curly Thirlwell and Willie Burton, *The Buddy Holly Story*

John K. Wilkinson, Robert W. Glass, Jr., John T. Reitz and Barry Thomas, *Days of Heaven*

MUSIC
ORIGINAL SONG

"Hopelessly Devoted to You," *Grease*, John Farrar, music and lyrics

"Last Dance," *Thank God It's Friday*, Paul Jabara, music and lyrics

"The Last Time I Felt Like This," *Same Time, Next Year*, Marvin Hamlisch, music; Alan and Marilyn Bergman, lyrics

"Ready to Take a Chance Again," *Foul Play*, Charles Fox, music; Norman Gimbel, lyrics

"When You're Loved," *The Magic of Lassie*, Richard M. Sherman and Robert B. Sherman, music and lyrics

ORIGINAL SCORE

Jerry Goldsmith, *The Boys From Brazil*

Dave Grusin, *Heaven Can Wait*

Giorgio Moroder, *Midnight Express*

Ennio Morricone, *Days of Heaven*

John Williams, *Superman*

ADAPTATION SCORE

Quincy Jones, *The Wiz*

Joe Renzetti, *The Buddy Holly Story*

Jerry Wexler, *Pretty Baby*

FILM EDITING

Stuart Baird, *Superman*

Gerry Hambling, *Midnight Express*

Robert E. Swink, *The Boys From Brazil*

Don Zimmerman, *Coming Home*

Peter Zinner, *The Deer Hunter*

COSTUME DESIGN

Renie Conley, *Caravans*

Patricia Norris, *Days of Heaven*

Anthony Powell, *Death on the Nile*

Tony Walton, *The Wiz*

Paul Zastupnevich, *The Swarm*

SHORT FILMS
ANIMATED

Oh My Darling (Nico Crama, producer; Nico Crama Productions)

Rip Van Winkle (Will Vinton, producer; Will Vinton Productions)

***Special Delivery* (Eunice Macaulay and John Weldon, producers; National Film Board of Canada)**

LIVE ACTION

A Different Approach (Jim Belcher and Fern Field, producers; Jim Belcher/Brookfield Production)

Mandy's Grandmother (Andrew Sugerman, producer; Illumination Films)

Strange Fruit (Seth Pinsker, producer; American Film Institute)

***Teenage Father* (Taylor Hackford, producer; New Visions Inc. for the Children's Home Society of California)**

DOCUMENTARY
SHORT SUBJECT

The Divided Trail: A Native American Odyssey (Jerry Aronson, producer; Jerry Aronson Production)

An Encounter With Faces (K. K. Kapil, producer; Films Division, Government of India)

***The Flight of the Gossamer Condor* (Jacqueline Phillips Shedd and Ben Shedd, producers; Shedd Production)**

Goodnight Miss Ann (August Cinquegrana, producer; August Cinquegrana Films Production)

Squires of San Quentin (J. Gary Mitchell, producer; J. Gary Mitchell Film Company)

FEATURE

The Lovers' Wind (Ministry of Culture and Arts of Iran)

Mysterious Castles of Clay (Survival Anglia Ltd. Production)

Raoni (Franco-Brazilian Production)

***Scared Straight!* (Golden West Television Production)**

With Babies and Banners: Story of the Women's Emergency Brigade (Women's Labor History Film Project Production)

FOREIGN LANGUAGE FILM

***Get Out Your Handkerchiefs*, France**

The Glass Cell, German Federal Republic – West

Hungarians, Hungary

Viva Italia!, Italy

White Bim Black Ear, U.S.S.R.

JEAN HERSHOLT HUMANITARIAN AWARD

Leo Jaffe

HONORARY AWARDS

To **Walter Lantz** for bringing joy and laughter to every part of the world through his unique animated motion pictures

To **Laurence Olivier** for the full body of his work, for the unique achievements of his entire career and his lifetime of contribution to the art of film

To **King Vidor** for his incomparable achievements as a cinematic creator and innovator

To the **Museum of Modern Art Department of Film** for the contribution it has made to the public's perception of movies as an art form

To **Linwood G. Dunn, Loren L. Ryder** and **Waldon O. Watson** in appreciation for outstanding service and dedication in upholding the high standards of the Academy of Motion Picture Arts and Sciences

SPECIAL ACHIEVEMENT AWARD
VISUAL EFFECTS
Les Bowie, Colin Chilvers, Denys Coop, Roy Field, Derek Meddings and Zoran Perisic, *Superman*

1979

BEST PICTURE

All That Jazz, Robert Alan Aurthur, producer (Twentieth Century-Fox)

Apocalypse Now, Francis Coppola, producer; Fred Roos, Gray Frederickson and Tom Sternberg, co-producers (United Artists)

Breaking Away, Peter Yates, producer (Twentieth Century-Fox)

***Kramer vs. Kramer*, Stanley R. Jaffe, producer (Columbia)**

Norma Rae, Tamara Asseyev and Alex Rose, producers (Twentieth Century-Fox)

ACTOR IN A LEADING ROLE
Dustin Hoffman, *Kramer vs. Kramer*
Jack Lemmon, *The China Syndrome*
Al Pacino, *. . . And Justice for All*
Roy Scheider, *All That Jazz*
Peter Sellers, *Being There*

ACTRESS IN A LEADING ROLE
Jill Clayburgh, *Starting Over*
Sally Field, *Norma Rae*
Jane Fonda, *The China Syndrome*
Marsha Mason, *Chapter Two*
Bette Midler, *The Rose*

Kramer vs. Kramer

ACTOR IN A SUPPORTING ROLE
Melvyn Douglas, *Being There*
Robert Duvall, *Apocalypse Now*
Frederic Forrest, *The Rose*
Justin Henry, *Kramer vs. Kramer*
Mickey Rooney, *The Black Stallion*

ACTRESS IN A SUPPORTING ROLE
Jane Alexander, *Kramer vs. Kramer*
Barbara Barrie, *Breaking Away*
Candice Bergen, *Starting Over*
Mariel Hemingway, *Manhattan*
Meryl Streep, *Kramer vs. Kramer*

DIRECTING
Robert Benton, *Kramer vs. Kramer*
Francis Coppola, *Apocalypse Now*
Bob Fosse, *All That Jazz*
Edouard Molinaro, *La Cage aux Folles*
Peter Yates, *Breaking Away*

WRITING
SCREENPLAY WRITTEN DIRECTLY FOR THE SCREEN
Woody Allen and Marshall Brickman, *Manhattan*
Robert Alan Aurthur and Bob Fosse, *All That Jazz*
Valerie Curtin and Barry Levinson, *. . . And Justice for All*
Mike Gray, T.S. Cook and James Bridges, *The China Syndrome*
Steve Tesich, *Breaking Away*

SCREENPLAY BASED ON MATERIAL FROM ANOTHER MEDIUM
Robert Benton, *Kramer vs. Kramer*
Allan Burns, *A Little Romance*
John Milius and Francis Coppola, *Apocalypse Now*
Irving Ravetch and Harriet Frank, Jr., *Norma Rae*
Francis Veber, Edouard Molinaro, Marcello Danon and Jean Poiret, *La Cage Aux Folles*

CINEMATOGRAPHY
Nestor Almendros, *Kramer vs. Kramer*
William A. Fraker, *1941*
Frank Phillips, *The Black Hole*
Giuseppe Rotunno, *All That Jazz*
Vittorio Storaro, *Apocalypse Now*

ART DIRECTION
George Jenkins, art direction; Arthur Jeph Parker, set decoration, *The China Syndrome*
Harold Michelson, Joe Jennings, Leon Harris and John Vallone, art direction; Linda DeScenna, set decoration, *Star Trek — The Motion Picture*
Philip Rosenberg and Tony Walton, art direction; Edward Stewart and Gary Brink, set decoration, *All That Jazz*
Michael Seymour, Les Dilley and Roger Christian, art direction; Ian Whittaker, set decoration, *Alien*
Dean Tavoularis and Angelo Graham, art direction; George R. Nelson, set decoration, *Apocalypse Now*

SOUND

Robert Knudson, Robert J. Glass, Don MacDougall and Gene S. Cantamessa, *1941*

William McCaughey, Aaron Rochin, Michael J. Kohut and Jack Solomon, *Meteor*

Walter Murch, Mark Berger, Richard Beggs and Nat Boxer, *Apocalypse Now*

Arthur Piantadosi, Les Fresholtz, Michael Minkler and Al Overton, *The Electric Horseman*

Theodore Soderberg, Douglas Williams, Paul Wells and Jim Webb, *The Rose*

MUSIC

ORIGINAL SONG

"I'll Never Say 'Goodbye'," *The Promise*, David Shire, music; Alan and Marilyn Bergman, lyrics

"It Goes Like It Goes," *Norma Rae*, music by David Shire; lyrics by Norman Gimbel

"It's Easy to Say," *10*, Henry Mancini, music; Robert Wells, lyrics

"The Rainbow Connection," *The Muppet Movie*, Paul Williams and Kenny Ascher, music and lyrics

"Through the Eyes of Love," *Ice Castles*, Marvin Hamlisch, music; Carole Bayer Sager, lyrics

ORIGINAL SCORE

Georges Delerue, *A Little Romance*

Jerry Goldsmith, *Star Trek — The Motion Picture*

Dave Grusin, *The Champ*

Henry Mancini, *10*

Lalo Schifrin, *The Amityville Horror*

ORIGINAL SONG SCORE AND ITS ADAPTATION OR ADAPTATION SCORE

Ralph Burns, *All That Jazz*

Patrick Williams, *Breaking Away*

Paul Williams and Kenny Ascher, song; Paul Williams, adaptation, *The Muppet Movie*

FILM EDITING

Robert Dalva, *The Black Stallion*

Jerry Greenberg, *Kramer vs. Kramer*

Alan Heim, *All That Jazz*

Richard Marks, Walter Murch, Gerald B. Greenberg and Lisa Fruchtman, *Apocalypse Now*

Robert L. Wolfe and C. Timothy O'Meara, *The Rose*

COSTUME DESIGN

Judy Moorcroft, *The Europeans*

Shirley Russell, *Agatha*

William Ware Theiss, *Butch and Sundance: The Early Days*

Piero Tosi and Ambra Danon, *La Cage aux Folles*

Albert Wolsky, *All That Jazz*

VISUAL EFFECTS

Peter Ellenshaw, Art Cruickshank, Eustace Lycett, Danny Lee, Harrison Ellenshaw and Joe Hale, *The Black Hole*

William A. Fraker, A. D. Flowers and Gregory Jein, *1941*

H.R. Giger, Carlo Rambaldi, Brian Johnson, Nick Allder and Denys Ayling, *Alien*

Derek Meddings, Paul Wilson and John Evans, *Moonraker*

Douglas Trumbull, John Dykstra, Richard Yuricich, Robert Swarthe, Dave Stewart and Grant McCune, *Star Trek — The Motion Picture*

SHORT FILMS

ANIMATED

Dream Doll (Bob Godfrey Films/Zagreb Films/Halas and Batchelor; FilmWright)

***Every Child* (Derek Lamb, producer; National Film Board of Canada)**

It's So Nice to Have a Wolf Around the House (Paul Fierlinger, producer; AR&T Productions for Learning Corporation of America)

LIVE ACTION

***Board and Care* (Sarah Pillsbury and Ron Ellis, producers; Ron Ellis Films)**

Bravery in the Field (Roman Kroitor and Stefan Wodoslawsky, producers; National Film Board of Canada)

Oh Brother, My Brother (Carol Lowell and Ross Lowell, producers; Pyramid Films, Inc.)

The Solar Film (Saul Bass and Michael Britton, producers; Wildwood Enterprises Inc.)

Solly's Diner (Harry Mathias, Jay Zukerman and Larry Hankin, producers; Mathias/Zukerman/Hankin Productions)

DOCUMENTARY

SHORT SUBJECT

Dae (Risto Teofilovski, producer; Vardar Film/Skopje)

Koryo Celadon (Donald A. Connolly and James R. Messenger, producers; Charlie/Papa Productions, Inc.)

Nails (Phillip Borsos, producer; National Film Board of Canada)

***Paul Robeson: Tribute to an Artist* (Saul J. Turell, producer; Janus Films, Inc.)**

Remember Me (Dick Young, producer; Dick Young Productions, Ltd.)

FEATURE

***Best Boy* (Ira Wohl, producer; Only Child Motion Pictures, Inc.)**

Generation on the Wind (David A. Vassar, producer; More Than One Medium)

Going the Distance (Paul Cowan and Jacques Bobet, producers; National Film Board of Canada)

The Killing Ground (Steve Singer and Tom Priestley, producers; ABC News Closeup Unit)

The War at Home (Glenn Silber and Barry Alexander Brown, producers; Catalyst Films/Madison Film Production Co.)

FOREIGN LANGUAGE FILM AWARD

The Maids of Wilko, Poland

Mama Turns a Hundred, Spain

A Simple Story, France

***The Tin Drum*, Federal Republic of Germany – West**

To Forget Venice, Italy

IRVING G. THALBERG MEMORIAL AWARD

Ray Stark

JEAN HERSHOLT HUMANITARIAN AWARD

Robert Benjamin

HONORARY AWARDS

To **Hal Elias** for his dedication and distinguished service to the Academy of Motion Picture Arts and Sciences

To **Alec Guinness** for advancing the art of screen acting through a host of memorable and distinguished performances

John O. Aalberg, Charles G. Clarke and **John G. Frayne** in appreciation for outstanding service and dedication in upholding the high standards of the Academy of Motion Picture Arts and Sciences

SPECIAL ACHIEVEMENT AWARD
SOUND EDITING
Alan Splet, *The Black Stallion*

1980

BEST PICTURE

Coal Miner's Daughter, Bernard Schwartz, producer (Universal)

The Elephant Man, Jonathan Sanger, producer (Paramount)

***Ordinary People*, Ronald L. Schwary, producer (Paramount)**

Raging Bull, Irwin Winkler and Robert Chartoff, producers (United Artists)

Tess, Claude Berri, producer; Timothy Burrill, co-producer (Columbia)

ACTOR IN A LEADING ROLE

Robert De Niro, *Raging Bull*
Robert Duvall, *The Great Santini*
John Hurt, *The Elephant Man*
Jack Lemmon, *Tribute*
Peter O'Toole, *The Stunt Man*

ACTRESS IN A LEADING ROLE

Ellen Burstyn, *Resurrection*
Goldie Hawn, *Private Benjamin*
Mary Tyler Moore, *Ordinary People*
Gena Rowlands, *Gloria*
Sissy Spacek, *Coal Miner's Daughter*

Ordinary People

ACTOR IN A SUPPORTING ROLE

Judd Hirsch, *Ordinary People*
Timothy Hutton, *Ordinary People*
Michael O'Keefe, *The Great Santini*
Joe Pesci, *Raging Bull*
Jason Robards, *Melvin and Howard*

ACTRESS IN A SUPPORTING ROLE

Eileen Brennan, *Private Benjamin*
Eva Le Gallienne, *Resurrection*
Cathy Moriarty, *Raging Bull*
Diana Scarwid, *Inside Moves*
Mary Steenburgen, *Melvin and Howard*

DIRECTING

David Lynch, *The Elephant Man*
Roman Polanski, *Tess*
Robert Redford, *Ordinary People*
Richard Rush, *The Stunt Man*
Martin Scorsese, *Raging Bull*

WRITING
SCREENPLAY WRITTEN DIRECTLY FOR THE SCREEN

Bo Goldman, *Melvin and Howard*
Christopher Gore, *Fame*
Jean Gruault, *Mon Oncle D'Amerique*
Nancy Meyers, Charles Shyer and Harvey Miller, *Private Benjamin*
W. D. Richter, screenplay; W. D. Richter and Arthur Ross, story, *Brubaker*

SCREENPLAY BASED ON MATERIAL FROM ANOTHER MEDIUM

Christopher DeVore, Eric Bergren and David Lynch, *The Elephant Man*
Jonathan Hardy, David Stevens and Bruce Beresford, *Breaker Morant*
Lawrence B. Marcus and Richard Rush, *The Stunt Man*
Tom Rickman, *Coal Miner's Daughter*
Alvin Sargent, *Ordinary People*

CINEMATOGRAPHY

Nestor Almendros, *The Blue Lagoon*
Ralf D. Bode, *Coal Miner's Daughter*
Michael Chapman, *Raging Bull*
James Crabe, *The Formula*
Geoffrey Unsworth and Ghislain Cloquet, *Tess*

ART DIRECTION

John W. Corso, art direction; John M. Dwyer, set decoration, *Coal Miner's Daughter*

Stuart Craig and Bob Cartwright, art direction; Hugh Scaife, set decoration, *The Elephant Man*

Pierre Guffroy and Jack Stephens, art direction, *Tess*

Yoshiro Muraki, art direction, *Kagemusha (The Shadow Warrior)*

Norman Reynolds, Leslie Dilley, Harry Lange and Alan Tomkins, art direction; Michael Ford, set decoration, *The Empire Strikes Back*

SOUND

Michael J. Kohut, Aaron Rochin, Jay M. Harding and Chris Newman, *Fame*

Donald O. Mitchell, Bill Nicholson, David J. Kimball and Les Lazarowitz, *Raging Bull*

Arthur Piantadosi, Les Fresholtz, Michael Minkler and Willie D. Burton, *Altered States*

Richard Portman, Roger Heman and Jim Alexander, *Coal Miner's Daughter*

Bill Varney, Steve Maslow, Gregg Landaker and Peter Sutton, *The Empire Strikes Back*

MUSIC

ORIGINAL SONG

"Fame," *Fame*, Michael Gore, music; Dean Pitchford, lyrics

"Nine to Five," *Nine to Five*, Dolly Parton, music and lyrics

"On the Road Again," *Honeysuckle Rose*, Willie Nelson, music and lyrics

"Out Here on My Own," *Fame*, Michael Gore, music; Lesley Gore, lyrics

"People Alone," *The Competition*, Lalo Schifrin, music; Wilbur Jennings, lyrics

ORIGINAL SCORE

John Corigliano, *Altered States*

Michael Gore, *Fame*

John Morris, *The Elephant Man*

Philippe Sarde, *Tess*

John Williams, *The Empire Strikes Back*

FILM EDITING

David Blewitt, *The Competition*

Anne V. Coates, *The Elephant Man*

Gerry Hambling, *Fame*

Arthur Schmidt, *Coal Miner's Daughter*

Thelma Schoonmaker, *Raging Bull*

COSTUME DESIGN

Jean-Pierre Dorleac, *Somewhere in Time*

Patricia Norris, *The Elephant Man*

Anthony Powell, *Tess*

Anna Senior, *My Brilliant Career*

Paul Zastupnevich, *When Time Ran Out*

SHORT FILMS

ANIMATED

All Nothing (Frédéric Back, producer; Société Radio Canada)

The Fly (Ferenc Rofusz, producer; Pannonia Film)

History of the World in Three Minutes Flat (Michael Mills, producer; Michael Mills Productions Ltd.)

DRAMATIC LIVE ACTION

The Dollar Bottom (Rocking Horse Films, Ltd.; Paramount)

Fall Line (Bob Carmichael and Greg Lowe, producers; Sports Imagery, Inc.)

A Jury of Her Peers (Sally Heckel, producer; Sally Heckel Productions)

DOCUMENTARY

SHORT SUBJECT

Don't Mess With Bill (John Watson and Pen Densham, producers; John Watson and Pen Densham's Insight Productions Inc.)

The Eruption of Mount St. Helens (George Casey, producer; Graphic Films Corporation)

It's the Same World (Dick Young, producer; Dick Young Productions, Ltd.)

Karl Hess: Toward Liberty (Roland Hallé and Peter W. Ladue, producers; Hallé/Ladue, Inc.)

Luther Metke at 94, U.C.L.A. (Richard Hawkins and Jorge Preloran, producers; U.C.L.A. Ethnographic Film Program)

FEATURE

Agee (Ross Spears, producer; James Agee Film Project)

The Day After Trinity (Jon Else, producer; Jon Else Productions)

From Mao to Mozart: Isaac Stern in China (Murray Lerner, producer; The Hopewell Foundation)

Front Line (David Bradbury, producer; David Bradbury Productions)

The Yellow Star — The Persecution of the Jews in Europe, 1933–45 (Bengt von zur Muehlen and Arthur Cohn, producers; Chronos Film GmbH)

FOREIGN LANGUAGE FILM

Confidence, Hungary

Kagemusha (*The Shadow Warrior*), Japan

The Last Metro, France

Moscow Does Not Believe in Tears, U.S.S.R.

The Nest, Spain

SPECIAL ACHIEVEMENT AWARD
VISUAL EFFECTS

Brian Johnson, Richard Edlund, Dennis Muren and Bruce Nicholson, *The Empire Strikes Back*

HONORARY AWARDS

To **Henry Fonda**, the consummate actor, in recognition of his brilliant accomplishments and enduring contribution to the art of motion pictures

To **Fred Hynes** in appreciation for outstanding service and dedication in upholding the high standards of the Academy of Motion Picture Arts and Sciences

1981

BEST PICTURE

Atlantic City, Denis Heroux and John Kemeny, producers (Paramount)

Chariots of Fire, David Puttnam, producer (The Ladd Co.; Warner Bros.)

On Golden Pond, Bruce Gilbert, producer (Universal)

Raiders of the Lost Ark, Frank Marshall, producer (Paramount)

Reds, Warren Beatty, producer (Paramount)

ACTOR IN A LEADING ROLE

Warren Beatty, *Reds*

Henry Fonda, *On Golden Pond*

Burt Lancaster, *Atlantic City*

Dudley Moore, *Arthur*

Paul Newman, *Absence of Malice*

ACTRESS IN A LEADING ROLE

Katharine Hepburn, *On Golden Pond*
Diane Keaton, *Reds*
Marsha Mason, *Only When I Laugh*
Susan Sarandon, *Atlantic City*
Meryl Streep, *The French Lieutenant's Woman*

ACTOR IN A SUPPORTING ROLE

James Coco, *Only When I Laugh*
John Gielgud, *Arthur*
Ian Holm, *Chariots of Fire*
Jack Nicholson, *Reds*
Howard E. Rollins, Jr., *Ragtime*

ACTRESS IN A SUPPORTING ROLE

Melinda Dillon, *Absence of Malice*
Jane Fonda, *On Golden Pond*
Joan Hackett, *Only When I Laugh*
Elizabeth McGovern, *Ragtime*
Maureen Stapleton, *Reds*

DIRECTING

Warren Beatty, *Reds*
Hugh Hudson, *Chariots of Fire*
Louis Malle, *Atlantic City*
Mark Rydell, *On Golden Pond*
Steven Spielberg, *Raiders of the Lost Ark*

WRITING

SCREENPLAY WRITTEN DIRECTLY FOR THE SCREEN

Warren Beatty and Trevor Griffiths, *Reds*
Steve Gordon, *Arthur*
John Guare, *Atlantic City*
Kurt Luedtke, *Absence of Malice*
Colin Welland, *Chariots of Fire*

SCREENPLAY BASED ON MATERIAL FROM ANOTHER MEDIUM

Jay Presson Allen and Sidney Lumet, *Prince of the City*
Harold Pinter, *The French Lieutenant's Woman*
Dennis Potter, *Pennies From Heaven*
Ernest Thompson, *On Golden Pond*
Michael Weller, *Ragtime*

CINEMATOGRAPHY

Miroslav Ondricek, *Ragtime*
Douglas Slocombe, *Raiders of the Lost Ark*
Vittorio Storaro, *Reds*
Alex Thomson, *Excalibur*
Billy Williams, *On Golden Pond*

ART DIRECTION

Assheton Gorton, art direction; Ann Mollo, set decoration, *The French Lieutenant's Woman*
John Graysmark, Patrizia Von Brandenstein and Anthony Reading; art direction; George de Titta, Sr., George de Titta, Jr. and Peter Howitt, set decoration, *Ragtime*
Tambi Larsen, art direction; Jim Berkey, set decoration, *Heaven's Gate*

Henry Fonda, *On Golden Pond*

Norman Reynolds and Leslie Dilley, art direction; Michael Ford, set decoration, *Raiders of the Lost Ark*
Richard Sylbert, art direction; Michael Seirton, set decoration, *Reds*

SOUND

Michael J. Kohut, Jay M. Harding, Richard Tyler and Al Overton, *Pennies From Heaven*
Richard Portman and David Ronne, *On Golden Pond*
Bill Varney, Steve Maslow, Gregg Landaker and Roy Charman, *Raiders of the Lost Ark*
Dick Vorisek, Tom Fleischman and Simon Kaye, *Reds,*
John K. Wilkinson, Robert W. Glass, Jr., Robert M. Thirlwell and Robin Gregory, *Outland*

MUSIC

ORIGINAL SONG

"Arthur's Theme" (Best That You Can Do), *Arthur*, Burt Bacharach, Carole Bayer Sager, Christopher Cross and Peter Allen, music and lyrics
"Endless Love," *Endless Love*, Lionel Richie, music and lyrics
"The First Time It Happens," *The Great Muppet Caper*, Joe Raposo, music and lyrics
"For Your Eyes Only," *For Your Eyes Only*, Bill Conti, music; Mick Leeson, lyrics
"One More Hour," *Ragtime*, Randy Newman, music and lyrics

ORIGINAL SCORE

Dave Grusin, *On Golden Pond*
Randy Newman, *Ragtime*
Alex North, *Dragonslayer*
Vangelis, *Chariots of Fire*
John Williams, *Raiders of the Lost Ark*

FILM EDITING

Dede Allen and Craig McKay, *Reds*
John Bloom, *The French Lieutenant's Woman*
Michael Kahn, *Raiders of the Lost Ark*
Terry Rawlings, *Chariots of Fire*
Robert L. Wolfe, *On Golden Pond*

MAKEUP

Rick Baker, *An American Werewolf in London*

Stan Winston, *Heartbeeps*

VISUAL EFFECTS

Richard Edlund, Kit West, Bruce Nicholson and Joe Johnston, *Raiders of the Lost Ark*

Dennis Muren, Phil Tippett, Ken Ralston and Brian Johnson, *Dragonslayer*

SHORT FILMS

ANIMATION

Crac (Frédéric Back, producer; Société Radio Canada)

The Creation (Will Vinton, producer; Will Vinton Productions)

The Tender Tale of Cinderella Penguin (Janet Perlman, producer; National Film Board of Canada)

LIVE ACTION

Couples and Robbers (Christine Oestreicher, producer; Flamingo Pictures Ltd.)

First Winter (John N. Smith, producer; National Film Board of Canada)

Violet (Paul Kemp and Shelley Levinson, producers; American Film Institute)

DOCUMENTARY

SHORT SUBJECT

Americas in Transition (Obie Benz, producer; Americas in Transition, Inc.)

Close Harmony (Nigel Noble, producer; Noble Enterprise)

Journey for Survival (Dick Young, producer; Dick Young Productions, Ltd.)

See What I Say (Linda Chapman, Pam LeBlanc and Freddi Stevens, producers; Michigan Women Filmmakers Productions)

Urge to Build (Roland Hallé and John Hoover, producers; Roland Hallé Productions, Inc.)

FEATURE

Against Wind and Tide: A Cuban Odyssey (Suzanne Bauman, Paul Neshamkin and Jim Burroughs, producers; Seven League Productions, Inc.)

Brooklyn Bridge (Ken Burns, producer; Florentine Films Production)

Eight Minutes to Midnight: A Portrait of Dr. Helen Caldicott (Mary Benjamin, Susanne Simpson and Boyd Estus, producers; The Caldicott Project)

El Salvador: Another Vietnam (Glenn Silber and Tete Vasconcellos, producers; Catalyst Media Productions)

Genocide (Arnold Schwartzman and Rabbi Marvin Hier, producers; Arnold Schwartzman Productions, Inc.)

FOREIGN LANGUAGE FILM

The Boat Is Full, Switzerland

Man of Iron, Poland

Mephisto, Hungary

Muddy River, Japan

Three Brothers, Italy

IRVING G. THALBERG AWARD

Albert R. Broccoli

JEAN HERSHOLT HUMANITARIAN AWARD

Danny Kaye

HONORARY AWARD

To **Barbara Stanwyck** for superlative creativity and unique contribution to the art of screen acting

SPECIAL ACHIEVEMENT AWARD
SOUND EFFECTS EDITING

Benjamin P. Burtt, Jr. and Richard L. Anderson, *Raiders of the Lost Ark*

1982

BEST PICTURE

E.T. the Extra-Terrestrial, Steven Spielberg and Kathleen Kennedy, producers (Universal)

Gandhi, Richard Attenborough, producer (Columbia)

Missing, Edward Lewis and Mildred Lewis, producers (Universal)

Tootsie, Sydney Pollack and Dick Richards, producers (Columbia)

The Verdict, Richard D. Zanuck and David Brown, producers (Twentieth Century-Fox)

ACTOR IN A LEADING ROLE

Dustin Hoffman, *Tootsie*

Ben Kingsley, Gandhi

Jack Lemmon, *Missing*

Paul Newman, *The Verdict*

Peter O'Toole, *My Favorite Year*

ACTRESS IN A LEADING ROLE

Julie Andrews, *Victor/Victoria*

Jessica Lange, *Frances*

Sissy Spacek, *Missing*

Meryl Streep, Sophie's Choice

Debra Winger, *An Officer and a Gentleman*

ACTOR IN A SUPPORTING ROLE

Charles Durning, *The Best Little Whorehouse in Texas*

Louis Gossett, Jr., An Officer and a Gentleman

John Lithgow, *The World According to Garp*

James Mason, *The Verdict*

Robert Preston, *Victor/Victoria*

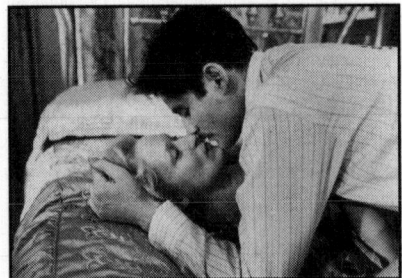

Meryl Streep, *Sophie's Choice*

ACTRESS IN A SUPPORTING ROLE

Glenn Close, *The World According to Garp*

Teri Garr, *Tootsie*

Jessica Lange, *Tootsie*

Kim Stanley, *Frances*

Lesley Ann Warren, *Victor/Victoria*

DIRECTING

Richard Attenborough, *Gandhi*

Sidney Lumet, *The Verdict*

Wolfgang Petersen, *Das Boot*

Sidney Pollack, *Tootsie*

Steven Spielberg, *E.T. the Extra-Terrestrial*

WRITING

SCREENPLAY WRITTEN DIRECTLY FOR THE SCREEN

John Briley, *Gandhi*

Larry Gelbart and Murray Schisgal, screenplay; Don McGuire and Larry Gelbart, story, *Tootsie*

Barry Levinson, *Diner*

Melissa Mathison, *E.T. the Extra-Terrestrial*

Douglas Day Stewart, *An Officer and a Gentleman*

SCREENPLAY BASED ON MATERIAL FROM ANOTHER MEDIUM

Blake Edwards, *Victor/Victoria*

Costa-Gavras and Donald Stewart, *Missing*

David Mamet, *The Verdict*

Alan J. Pakula, *Sophie's Choice*

Wolfgang Petersen, *Das Boot*

CINEMATOGRAPHY

Nestor Almendros, *Sophie's Choice*

Allen Daviau, *E.T. the Extra-Terrestrial*

Owen Roizman, *Tootsie*

Jost Vacano, *Das Boot*

Billy Williams and Ronnie Taylor, *Gandhi*

ART DIRECTION

Stuart Craig and Bob Laing, art direction; Michael Seirton, set decoration, *Gandhi*

Dale Hennesy, art direction; Marvin March, set decoration, *Annie*

Rodger Maus, Tim Hutchinson and William Craig Smith, art direction; Harry Cordwell, set decoration, *Victor/Victoria*

Lawrence G. Paull and David L. Snyder, art direction; Linda DeScenna, set decoration, *Blade Runner*

Franco Zeffirelli, art direction; Gianni Quaranta, set decoration, *La Traviata*

SOUND

Milan Bor, Trevor Pyke and Mike Le-Mare, *Das Boot*

Gerry Humphreys, Robin O'Donoghue, Jonathan Bates and Simon Kaye, *Gandhi*

Buzz Knudson, Robert Glass, Don Digirolamo and Gene Cantamessa, *E.T. the Extra-Terrestrial*

Michael Minkler, Bob Minkler, Lee Minkler and Jim La Rue, *Tron*

Arthur Piantadosi, Les Fresholtz, Dick Alexander and Les Lazarowitz, *Tootsie*

MUSIC

SONG

"Eye of the Tiger," *Rocky III*, Jim Peterik and Frankie Sullivan III, music and lyrics

"How Do You Keep the Music Playing?," *Best Friends*, Michel Legrand, music; Alan and Marilyn Bergman, lyrics

"If We Were in Love," *Yes, Giorgio*, John Williams, music; Alan and Marilyn Bergman, lyrics

"It Might Be You," *Tootsie*, Dave Grusin, music; Alan and Marilyn Bergman, lyrics

"Up Where We Belong," *An Officer and a Gentleman*, Jack Nitzsche and Buffy Sainte-Marie, music; Will Jennings, lyrics

ORIGINAL SCORE

Jerry Goldsmith, *Poltergeist*

Marvin Hamlisch, *Sophie's Choice*

Jack Nitzsche, *An Officer and a Gentleman*

Ravi Shankar and George Fenton, *Gandhi*

John Williams, *E.T. the Extra-Terrestrial*

ORIGINAL SONG SCORE AND ITS ADAPTATION OR ADAPTATION SCORE

Leslie Bricusse and Henry Mancini, *Victor/Victoria*

Ralph Burns, *Annie*

Tom Waits, *One From the Heart*

FILM EDITING

John Bloom, *Gandhi*

Carol Littleton, *E.T. the Extra-Terrestrial*

Hannes Nikel, *Das Boot*

Fredric Steinkamp and William Steinkamp, *Tootsie*

Peter Zinner, *An Officer and a Gentleman*

COSTUME DESIGN

Elois Jenssen and Rosanna Norton, *Tron*

John Mollo and Bhanu Athaiya, *Gandhi*

Patricia Norris, *Victor/Victoria*

Piero Tosi, *La Traviata*

Albert Wolsky, *Sophie's Choice*

MAKEUP

Sarah Monzani and Michèle Burke, *Quest for Fire*

Tom Smith, *Gandhi*

VISUAL EFFECTS

Richard Edlund, Michael Wood and Bruce Nicholson, *Poltergeist*

Carlo Rambaldi, Dennis Murren and Kenneth F. Smith, *E.T. the Extra-Terrestrial*

Douglas Trumbull, Richard Yuricich and David Dryer, *Blade Runner*

SOUND EFFECTS EDITING

Charles L. Campbell and Ben Burtt, *E.T. the Extra-Terrestrial*

Stephen Hunter Flick and Richard L. Anderson, *Poltergeist*

Mike Le-Mare, *Das Boot*

SHORT FILMS
ANIMATED

The Great Cognito (Will Vinton, producer; Will Vinton Productions)

The Snowman (John Coates, producer; Snowman Enterprises Ltd.)

Tango (Zbigniew Rybczynski, producer; Film Polski Production)

LIVE ACTION

Ballet Robotique (Bob Rogers, producer; Bob Rogers and Co.)

A Shocking Accident (Christine Oestreicher, producer; Flamingo Pictures, Ltd.)

The Silence (Michael Toshiyuki Uno and Joseph Benson, producers; American Film Institute)

Split Cherry Tree (Jan Saunders, producer; Learning Corporation of America)

Sredni Vashtar (Andrew Birkin, producer; Laurentic Film Productions, Ltd.)

DOCUMENTARY
SHORT SUBJECT

Gods of Metal (Robert Richter, producer; Richter Productions)

If You Love This Planet (Edward Le Lorrain and Terri Nash, producers; National Film Board of Canada)

The Klan: A Legacy of Hate in America (Charles Guggenheim and Werner Schumann, producers; Guggenheim Productions, Inc.)

To Live or Let Die (Freida Lee Mock, producer; American Film Foundation)

Traveling Hopefully (John G. Avildsen, producer; Arnuthfonyus Films, Inc.)

FEATURE

After the Axe (Sturla Gunnarsson and Steve Lucas, producers; National Film Board of Canada)

Ben's Mill (John Karol and Michel Chalufour, producers; Public Broadcasting Associates – ODYSSEY)

In Our Water (Meg Switzgable, producer; Foresight Films Production)

Just Another Missing Kid (John Zaritsky, producer; Canadian Broadcasting Corp.)

A Portrait of Giselle (ABC Video Enterprises, Inc. in association with Wishupon Productions)

FOREIGN LANGUAGE FILM

Alsino and the Condor, Nicaragua

Coup de Torchon (*Clean Slate*), France

The Flight of the Eagle, Sweden

Private Life, U.S.S.R.

Volver a Empezar (To Begin Again), Spain

JEAN HERSHOLT HUMANITARIAN AWARD
Walter Mirisch

HONORARY AWARD
To **Mickey Rooney** for 60 years of versatility in a variety of memorable film performances

1983

BEST PICTURE

The Big Chill, Michael Shamberg, producer (Columbia)

The Dresser, Peter Yates, producer (Columbia)

The Right Stuff, Irwin Winkler and Robert Chartoff, producers (The Ladd Co. through Warner Bros.)

Tender Mercies, Philip S. Hobel, producer (Universal)

Terms of Endearment, James L. Brooks, producer (Paramount)

ACTOR IN A LEADING ROLE

Michael Caine, *Educating Rita*

Tom Conti, *Reuben, Reuben*

Tom Courtenay, *The Dresser*

Robert Duvall, *Tender Mercies*

Albert Finney, *The Dresser*

ACTRESS IN A LEADING ROLE

Jane Alexander, *Testament*

Shirley MacLaine, *Terms of Endearment*

Meryl Streep, *Silkwood*

Julie Walters, *Educating Rita*

Debra Winger, *Terms of Endearment*

ACTOR IN A SUPPORTING ROLE

Charles Durning, *To Be or Not to Be*

John Lithgow, *Terms of Endearment*

Jack Nicholson, *Terms of Endearment*

Sam Shepard, *The Right Stuff*

Rip Torn, *Cross Creek*

ACTRESS IN A SUPPORTING ROLE

Cher, *Silkwood*

Glenn Close, *The Big Chill*

Linda Hunt, *The Year of Living Dangerously*

Amy Irving, *Yentl*

Alfre Woodard, *Cross Creek*

DIRECTING

Bruce Beresford, *Tender Mercies*

Ingmar Bergman, *Fanny & Alexander*

James L. Brooks, *Terms of Endearment*

Mike Nichols, *Silkwood*

Peter Yates, *The Dresser*

WRITING
SCREENPLAY WRITTEN DIRECTLY FOR THE SCREEN

Ingmar Bergman, *Fanny & Alexander*

Nora Ephron and Alice Arlen, *Silkwood*

Horton Foote, *Tender Mercies*

Lawrence Kasdan and Barbara Benedek, *The Big Chill*

Lawrence Lasker and Walter F. Parkes, *WarGames*

SCREENPLAY BASED ON MATERIAL FROM ANOTHER MEDIUM

James L. Brooks, *Terms of Endearment*

Julius J. Epstein, *Reuben, Reuben*

Ronald Harwood, *The Dresser*

Harold Pinter, *Betrayal*

Willy Russell, *Educating Rita*

CINEMATOGRAPHY

Caleb Deschanel, *The Right Stuff*

William A. Fraker, *WarGames*

Sven Nykvist, *Fanny & Alexander*

Don Peterman, *Flashdance*

Gordon Willis, *Zelig*

ART DIRECTION

Anna Asp, art direction and set decoration, *Fanny & Alexander*

Geoffrey Kirkland, Richard J. Lawrence, W. Stewart Campbell and Peter Romero, art direction; Pat Pending and George R. Nelson, set decoration, *The Right Stuff*

Polly Platt and Harold Michelson, art direction; Tom Pedigo and Anthony Mondello, set decoration, *Terms of Endearment*

Norman Reynolds, Fred Hole and James Schoppe, art direction; Michael Ford, set decoration, *Return of the Jedi*

Roy Walker and Leslie Tomkins, art direction; Tessa Davies, set decoration, *Yentl*

SOUND

Mark Berger, Tom Scott, Randy Thom and David MacMillan, *The Right Stuff*

Ben Burtt, Gary Summers, Randy Thom and Tony Dawe, *Return of the Jedi*

Michael J. Kohut, Carlos de Larios, Aaron Rochin and Willie D. Burton, *WarGames*

Donald O. Mitchell, Rick Kline, Kevin O'Connell and Jim Alexander, *Terms of Endearment*

Alan R. Splet, Todd Boekelheide, Randy Thom and David Parker, *Never Cry Wolf*

MUSIC
SONG

"Flashdance . . . What a Feeling," *Flashdance*, Giorgio Moroder, music; Keith Forsey and Irene Cara, lyrics

"Maniac," *Flashdance*, Michael Sembello and Dennis Matkosky, music and lyrics

"Over You," *Tender Mercies*, Austin Roberts and Bobby Hart, music and lyrics

"Papa, Can You Hear Me?," *Yentl*, Michel Legrand, music; Alan and Marilyn Bergman, lyrics

"The Way He Makes Me Feel," *Yentl*, Michel Legrand, music; Alan and Marilyn Bergman, lyrics

ORIGINAL SCORE

Bill Conti, *The Right Stuff*

Jerry Goldsmith, *Under Fire*

Michael Gore, *Terms of Endearment*

Leonard Rosenman, *Cross Creek*

John Williams, *Return of the Jedi*

ORIGINAL SONG SCORE OR ADAPTATION SCORE

Elmer Bernstein, *Trading Places*

Michel Legrand, Alan and Marilyn Bergman, *Yentl*

Lalo Schifrin, *The Sting II*

FILM EDITING

Glenn Farr, Lisa Fruchtman, Stephen A. Rotter, Douglas Steward and Tom Rolf, *The Right Stuff*

Richard Marks, *Terms of Endearment*

Frank Morriss and Edward Abroms, *Blue Thunder*

Sam O'Steen, *Silkwood*

Bud Smith and Walt Mulconery, *Flashdance*

COSTUME DESIGN

Santo Loquasto, *Zelig*

Anne-Marie Marchand, *The Return of Martin Guerre*

Joe I. Tompkins, *Cross Creek*

Marik Vos, *Fanny & Alexander*

William Ware Theiss, *Heart Like a Wheel*

SOUND EFFECTS EDITING

Jay Boekelheide, *The Right Stuff*

Ben Burtt, *Return of the Jedi*

SHORT FILMS
ANIMATED

Mickey's Christmas Carol (Burny Mattinson, producer; Walt Disney Productions)

Sound of Sunshine — Sound of Rain (Eda Godel Hallinan, producer; Hallinan Plus! Production)

***Sundae in New York* (Jimmy Picker, producer; Motionpicker Productions)**

LIVE ACTION

***Boys and Girls* (Janice L. Platt, producer; Atlantis Films Ltd. Production)**

Goodie-Two-Shoes (Timeless Films Production; Paramount)

Overnight Sensation (Jon N. Bloom, producer; Bloom Film Production)

DOCUMENTARY
SHORT SUBJECT

***Flamenco at 5:15* (Cynthia Scott and Adam Symansky, producers; National Film Board of Canada)**

In the Nuclear Shadow: What Can the Children Tell Us? (Vivienne Verdon-Roe and Eric Thiermann, producers; Impact Production)

Shirley MacLaine, *Terms of Endearment*

Sewing Woman (Arthur Dong, producer; DeepFocus Productions)

Spaces: The Architecture of Paul Rudoph (Robert Eisenhardt, producer; Eisenhardt Productions)

You Are Free (*Ihr Zent Frei*) (Dea Brokman and Ilene Landis, producers; Brokman/Landis Production)

FEATURE

Children of Darkness (Richard Kotuk and Ara Chekmayan, producers; Children of Darkness Production)

First Contact (Bob Connolly and Robin Anderson, producers; Arundel Production)

He Makes Me Feel Like Dancin' (Emile Ardolino, producer; **Edgar J. Scherick Associates Production**)

The Profession of Arms, (*War Series Film #3*) (Michael Bryan and Tina Viljoen, producers; National Film Board of Canada)

Seeing Red (James Klein and Julia Reichert, producers; Heartland Production)

FOREIGN LANGUAGE FILM

Carmen, Spain

Entre Nous, France

Fanny & Alexander, Sweden

Job's Revolt, Hungary

Le Bal, Algeria

JEAN HERSHOLT HUMANITARIAN AWARD

M. J. Frankovich

HONORARY AWARD

To **Hal Roach** in recognition of his unparalleled record of distinguished contributions to the motion picture art form

SPECIAL ACHIEVEMENT AWARDS

VISUAL EFFECTS

Richard Edlund, Dennis Muren, Ken Ralston and Phil Tippett, Return of the Jedi

1984

BEST PICTURE

Amadeus, Saul Zaentz, producer (Orion)

The Killing Fields, David Puttnam, producer (Warner Bros.)

A Passage to India, John Brabourne and Richard Goodwin, producer (Columbia)

Places in the Heart, Arlene Donovan, producer (TriStar)

A Soldier's Story, Norman Jewison, Ronald L. Schwary and Patrick Palmer, producers (Columbia)

ACTOR IN A LEADING ROLE

F. Murray Abraham, *Amadeus*

Jeff Bridges, *Starman*

Albert Finney, *Under the Volcano*

Tom Hulce, *Amadeus*

Sam Waterston, *The Killing Fields*

ACTRESS IN A LEADING ROLE

Judy Davis, *A Passage to India*

Sally Field, *Places in the Heart*

Fanny & Alexander

Jessica Lange, *Country*

Vanessa Redgrave, *The Bostonians*

Sissy Spacek, *The River*

ACTOR IN A SUPPORTING ROLE

Adolph Caesar, *A Soldier's Story*

John Malkovich, *Places in the Heart*

Noriyuki "Pat" Morita, *The Karate Kid*

Haing S. Ngor, *The Killing Fields*

Ralph Richardson, *Greystoke: The Legend of Tarzan, Lord of the Apes*

ACTRESS IN A SUPPORTING ROLE

Peggy Ashcroft, *A Passage to India*

Glenn Close, *The Natural*

Lindsay Crouse, *Places in the Heart*

Christine Lahti, *Swing Shift*

Geraldine Page, *The Pope of Greenwich Village*

DIRECTING

Woody Allen, *Broadway Danny Rose*

Robert Benton, *Places in the Heart*

Milos Forman, *Amadeus*

Roland Joffe, *The Killing Fields*

David Lean, *A Passage to India*

WRITING

SCREENPLAY WRITTEN DIRECTLY FOR THE SCREEN

Woody Allen, *Broadway Danny Rose*

Robert Benton, *Places in the Heart*

Lowell Ganz, Babaloo Mandel and Bruce Jay Friedman, screenplay; Bruce Jay Friedman; screen story, *Splash*

Gregory Nava and Anna Thomas, *El Norte*

Daniel Petrie, Jr., screenplay; Danilo Bach and Daniel Petrie, Jr., story, *Beverly Hills Cop*

SCREENPLAY BASED ON MATERIAL FROM ANOTHER MEDIUM

Charles Fuller, *A Soldier's Story*

David Lean, *A Passage to India*

Bruce Robinson, *The Killing Fields*

Peter Shaffer, *Amadeus*

P.H. Vazak and Michael Austin, *Greystoke: The Legend of Tarzan, Lord of the Apes*

CINEMATOGRAPHY

Ernest Day, *A Passage to India*

Caleb Deschanel, *The Natural*

Chris Menges, *The Killing Fields*

Miroslav Ondricek, *Amadeus*

Vilmos Zsigmond, *The River*

ART DIRECTION

John Box and Leslie Tomkins, art direction; Hugh Scaife, set decoration, *A Passage to India*

Albert Brenner, art direction; Rick Simpson, set decoration, *2010*

Angelo Graham and Mel Bourne, James J. Murakami and Speed Hopkins, art direction; Bruch Weintraub, set decoration, *The Natural*

Richard Sylbert, art direction; George Gaines and Les Bloom, set decoration, *The Cotton Club*

Patrizia Von Brandenstein, art direction; Karel Cerny, set decoration, *Amadeus*

SOUND

Nick Alphin, Robert Thirwell, Richard Portman and David Ronne, *The River*

Mark Berger, Tom Scott, Todd Boekelheide and Chris Newman, *Amadeus*

Graham V. Hartstone, Nicolas Le Messurier, Michael A. Carter and John Mitchell, *A Passage to India*

Michael J. Kohut, Aaron Rochin, Carlos De Larios and Gene S. Cantamessa, *2010*

Bill Varney, Steve Maslow, Kevin O'Connell and Nelson Stoll, *Dune*

MUSIC

ORIGINAL SONG

"Against All Odds" (Take a Look at Me Now), *Against All Odds*, Phil Collins, music and lyrics

"Footloose," *Footloose*, Kenny Loggins and Dean Pitchford, music and lyrics

"Ghostbusters," *Ghostbusters*, Ray Parker, Jr., music and lyrics

"I Just Called to Say I Love You," *The Woman in Red*, Stevie Wonder, music and lyrics

"Let's Hear It for the Boy," *Footloose*, Dean Pitchford and Tom Snow, music and lyrics

ORIGINAL SCORE

Maurice Jarre, *A Passage to India*

Randy Newman, *The Natural*

Alex North, *Under the Volcano*

John Williams, *Indiana Jones and the Temple of Doom*

John Williams, *The River*

ORIGINAL SONG SCORE

Kris Kristofferson, *Songwriter*

Jeffrey Moss, *The Muppets Take Manhattan*

Prince, *Purple Rain*

FILM EDITING

Donn Cambern and Frank Morriss, *Romancing the Stone*

Jim Clark, *The Killing Fields*

Nena Danevic and Michael Chandler, *Amadeus*

David Lean, *A Passage to India*

Barry Malkin and Robert Q. Lovett, *The Cotton Club*

COSTUME DESIGN

Jenny Beavan and John Bright, *The Bostonians*

Judy Moorcroft, *A Passage to India*

Patricia Norris, *2010*

Theodor Pistek, *Amadeus*

Ann Roth, *Places in the Heart*

MAKEUP

Rick Baker and Paul Engelen, *Greystoke: The Legend of Tarzan, Lord of the Apes*

Paul LeBlanc and Dick Smith, *Amadeus*

Michael Westmore, *2010*

VISUAL EFFECTS

Richard Edlund, John Bruno, Mark Vargo and Chuck Gasper, *Ghostbusters*

Richard Edlund, Neil Krepela, George Jenson and Mark Stetson, *2010*

Dennis Muren, Michael McAlister, Lorne Peterson and George Gibbs, *Indiana Jones and the Temple of Doom*

SHORT FILMS

ANIMATED

***Charade* (Jon Minnis, producer; Sheridan College Production)**

Doctor De Soto (Morton Schindel and Michael Sporn, producers; Michael Sporn Animation, Inc.)

Paradise (Ishu Patel, producer; National Film Board of Canada)

LIVE ACTION

The Painted Door (Atlantis Films Ltd. in association with the National Film Board of Canada)

Tales of Meeting and Parting (Sharon Oreck and Lesli Linka Glatter, producers; American Film Institute — Directing Workshop for Women)

***Up* (Mike Hoover, producer; Pyramid Films)**

DOCUMENTARY

SHORT SUBJECT

The Children of Soong Ching Ling (Gary Bush and Paul T.K. Lin, producers; UNICEF and the Soong Ching Ling Foundation)

Code Gray: Ethical Dilemmas in Nursing (Ben Achtenberg and Joan Sawyer, producers; The Nursing Ethics Project/Fanlight Productions)

The Garden of Eden (Lawrence R. Hott and Roger M. Sherman, producers; Florentine Films Production)

Recollections of Pavlovsk (Irina Kalinina, producer; Leningrad Documentary Film Studio)

***The Stone Carvers* (Marjorie Hunt and Paul Wagner, producers, Paul Wagner Productions)**

FEATURE

High Schools (Charles Guggenheim and Nancy Sloss, producers; Guggenheim Productions)

In the Name of the People (Alex W. Drehsler and Frank Christopher, producers; Pan American Films)

Marlene (Zev Braun Pictures, Inc.; OKO Film Produktion)

Streetwise (Cheryl McCall, producer; Bear Creek Productions, Inc.)

The Times of Harvey Milk (Robert Epstein and Richard Schmiechen, producers; Black Sand Educational Productions, Inc.)

FOREIGN LANGUAGE FILM

Beyond the Walls, Israel

Camila, Argentina

***Dangerous Moves*, Switzerland**

Double Feature, Spain

Wartime Romance, U.S.S.R.

JEAN HERSHOLT HUMANITARIAN AWARD
David L. Wolper

HONORARY AWARDS

To the **National Endowment for the Arts** in recognition of its 20th anniversary and its dedication to fostering artistic and creative activity and excellence in every area of the arts

To **James Stewart** for 50 years of memorable performances and for his high ideals, both on and off the screen, with the respect and affection of his colleagues

SPECIAL ACHIEVEMENT AWARD
SOUND EFFECTS EDITING
Kay Rose, *The River*

1985

BEST PICTURE

The Color Purple, Steven Spielberg, Kathleen Kennedy, Frank Marshall and Quincy Jones, producers (Warner Bros.)

Kiss of the Spider Woman, David Weisman, producer (Island Alive)

***Out of Africa*, Sydney Pollack, producer (Universal)**

Prizzi's Honor, John Foreman, producer (Twentieth Century-Fox)

Witness, Edward S. Feldman, producer (Paramount)

ACTOR IN A LEADING ROLE

Harrison Ford, *Witness*

James Garner, *Murphy's Romance*

William Hurt, *Kiss of the Spider Woman*

Jack Nicholson, *Prizzi's Honor*

Jon Voight, *Runaway Train*

ACTRESS IN A LEADING ROLE

Anne Bancroft, *Agnes of God*

Whoopi Goldberg, *The Color Purple*

Jessica Lange, *Sweet Dreams*

Geraldine Page, *The Trip to Bountiful*

Meryl Streep, *Out of Africa*

ACTOR IN A SUPPORTING ROLE

Don Ameche, *Cocoon*

Klaus Maria Brandauer, *Out of Africa*

William Hickey, *Prizzi's Honor*

Robert Loggia, *Jagged Edge*

Eric Roberts, *Runaway Train*

ACTRESS IN A SUPPORTING ROLE

Margaret Avery, *The Color Purple*

Anjelica Huston, *Prizzi's Honor*

Amy Madigan, *Twice in a Lifetime*

Meg Tilly, *Agnes of God*

Oprah Winfrey, *The Color Purple*

DIRECTING

Hector Babenco, *Kiss of the Spider Woman*

John Huston, *Prizzi's Honor*

Akira Kurosawa, *Ran*

Sydney Pollack, *Out of Africa*

Peter Weir, *Witness*

WRITING
SCREENPLAY WRITTEN DIRECTLY FOR THE SCREEN

Woody Allen, *The Purple Rose of Cairo*

Terry Gilliam, Tom Stoppard and Charles McKeown, *Brazil*

Luis Puenzo and Aida Bortnik, *The Official Story*

Earl W. Wallace and William Kelley, screenplay; William Kelley, Pamela Wallace and Earl W. Wallace, story, *Witness*

Robert Zemeckis and Bob Gale, *Back to the Future*

SCREENPLAY BASED ON MATERIAL FROM ANOTHER MEDIUM

Richard Condon and Janet Roach, *Prizzi's Honor*

Horton Foote, *The Trip to Bountiful*

Kurt Luedtke, *Out of Africa*

Menno Meyjes, *The Color Purple*

Leonard Schrader, *Kiss of the Spider Woman*

CINEMATOGRAPHY

Allen Daviau, *The Color Purple*

William A. Fraker, *Murphy's Romance*

Takao Saito, Masaharu Ueda and Asakazu Nakai, *Ran*

John Seale, *Witness*

David Watkin, *Out of Africa*

ART DIRECTION

Norman Garwood, art direction; Maggie Gray, set decoration, *Brazil*

Stephen Grimes, art direction; Josie MacAvin, set decoration, *Out of Africa*

Stan Jolley, art direction; John Anderson, set decoration, *Witness*

Yoshiro Muraki and Shinobu Muraki, art direction, *Ran*

J. Michael Riva and Robert W. Welch, art direction; Linda DeScenna, set decoration, *The Color Purple*

SOUND

Les Fresholtz, Dick Alexander, Vern Poore and Bud Alper, *Ladyhawke*

Chris Jenkins, Gary Alexander, Larry Stensvold and Peter Handford, *Out of Africa*

Donald O. Mitchell, Rick Kline, Kevin O'Connell and David Ronne, *Silverado*

Donald O. Mitchell, Rick Kline, Michael Minkler, Gerry Humphreys and Chris Newman, *A Chorus Line*

Bill Varney, B. Tennyson Sebastian II, Robert Thirlwell and William B. Kaplan, *Back to the Future*

MUSIC

SONG

"Miss Celie's Blues" (Sister), *The Color Purple*, Quincy Jones and Rod Temperton, music; Quincy Jones, Rod Temperton and Lionel Richie, lyrics

"The Power of Love," *Back to the Future*, Chris Hayes and Johnny Colla, music; Huey Lewis, lyrics

"Say You, Say Me," *White Nights*, Lionel Richie, music and lyrics

"Love Theme From *White Nights*" (Separate Lives), *White Nights*, Stephen Bishop, music and lyrics

"Surprise, Surprise," *A Chorus Line*, Marvin Hamlisch, music; Edward Kleban, lyrics

ORIGINAL SCORE

John Barry, *Out of Africa*

Bruce Broughton, *Silverado*

George Delerue, *Agnes of God*

Quincy Jones, Jeremy Lubbock, Rod Temperton, Caiphus Semenya, Andrae Crouch, Chris Boardman, Jorge Calandrelli, Joel Rosenbaum, Fred Steiner, Jack Hayes, Jerry Hey and Randy Kerber, *The Color Purple*

Maurice Jarre, *Witness*

FILM EDITING

John Bloom, *A Chorus Line*

Rudi Fehr and Kaja Fehr, *Prizzi's Honor*

Thom Noble, *Witness*

Henry Richardson, *Runaway Train*

Fredric Steinkamp, William Steinkamp, Pembroke Herring and Sheldon Kahn, *Out of Africa*

COSTUME DESIGN

Milena Canonero, *Out of Africa*

Donfeld, *Prizzi's Honor*

Aggie Guerard Rodgers, *The Color Purple*

Emi Wada, *Ran*

Albert Wolksy, *The Journey of Natty Gann*

MAKEUP

Ken Chase, *The Color Purple*

Carl Fullerton, *Remo Williams: The Adventure Begins*

Michael Westmore and Zoltan Elek, *Mask*

Angelica Huston, *Prizzi's Honor*

VISUAL EFFECTS

Dennis Muren, Kit West, John Ellis and David Allen, *Young Sherlock Holmes*

Ken Ralston, Ralph McQuarrie, Scott Farrar and David Berry, *Cocoon*

Will Vinton, Ian Wingrove, Zoran Perisic and Michael Lloyd, *Return to Oz*

SOUND EFFECTS EDITING

Frederick J. Brown, *Rambo: First Blood Part II*

Charles L. Campbell and Robert Rutledge, *Back to the Future*

Bob Henderson and Alan Murray, *Ladyhawke*

SHORT FILMS

ANIMATED

Anna & Bella (Cilia Van Dijk, producer; Netherlands)

The Big Snit (Richard Condie and Michael Scott, producers; National Film Board of Canada)

Second Class Mail (Alison Snowden, producer; National Film and Television School)

LIVE ACTION

Graffiti (Dianna Costello, producer; American Film Institute)

Molly's Pilgrim (Jeff Brown and Chris Pelzer, producers; Phoenix Films)

Rainbow War (Bob Rogers, producer; Bob Rogers and Co.)

DOCUMENTARY

SHORT SUBJECT

The Courage to Care (Robert Gardner, producer; United Way)

Keats and His Nightingale: A Blind Date (Michael Crowley and James Wolpaw, producers; Rhode Island Committee for the Humanities)

Making Overtures — The Story of a Community Orchestra (Barbara Willis Sweete, producer; Rhombus Media, Inc.)

Witness to War: Dr. Charlie Clements (David Goodman, producer; Skylight Picture Production)

The Wizard of the Strings (Alan Edelstein, producer; Seventh Hour Production)

FEATURE

Broken Rainbow (Maria Florio and Victoria Mudd, producers; Earthworks Films Production)

Las Madres — The Mothers of Plaza de Mayo (Susana Muñoz and Lourdes Portillo, producers; Film Arts Foundation)

Soldiers in Hiding (Japhet Asher, producer; Filmworks, Inc. Production)

The Statue of Liberty (Ken Burns and Buddy Squires, producers; Florentine Films Production)

Unfinished Business (Steven Okazaki, producer; Mouchette Films Production)

FOREIGN LANGUAGE FILM

Angry Harvest, Federal Republic of Germany – West

Colonel Redl, Hungary

The Official Story, Argentina

Three Men and a Cradle, France

When Father Was Away on Business, Yugoslavia

JEAN HERSHOLT HUMANITARIAN AWARD

Charles "Buddy" Rogers

HONORARY AWARDS

To **Paul Newman** in recognition of his many memorable and compelling screen performances and for his personal integrity and dedication to his craft

To **Alex North** in recognition of his brilliant artistry in the creation of memorable music for a host of distinguished motion pictures

To **John H. Whitney, Sr.** for cinematic pioneering

1986

BEST PICTURE

Children of a Lesser God, Burt Sugarman and Patrick Palmer, producers (Paramount)

Hannah and Her Sisters, Robert Greenhut, producer (Orion)

The Mission, Fernando Ghia and David Puttnam, producers (Warner Bros.)

***Platoon*, Arnold Kopelson, producer (Orion)**

A Room With a View, Ismail Merchant, producer (Cinecom Pictures)

ACTOR IN A LEADING ROLE

Dexter Gordon, *'Round Midnight*

Bob Hoskins, *Mona Lisa*

William Hurt, *Children of a Lesser God*

Paul Newman, *The Color of Money*

James Woods, *Salvador*

ACTRESS IN A LEADING ROLE

Jane Fonda, *The Morning After*

Marlee Matlin, *Children of a Lesser God*

Sissy Spacek, *Crimes of the Heart*

Kathleen Turner, *Peggy Sue Got Married*

Sigourney Weaver, *Aliens*

ACTOR IN A SUPPORTING ROLE

Tom Berenger, *Platoon*

Michael Caine, *Hannah and Her Sisters*

Willem Dafoe, *Platoon*

Denholm Elliott, *A Room With a View*

Dennis Hopper, *Hoosiers*

ACTRESS IN A SUPPORTING ROLE

Tess Harper, *Crimes of the Heart*

Piper Laurie, *Children of a Lesser God*

Mary Elizabeth Mastrantonio, *The Color of Money*

Maggie Smith, *A Room With a View*

Dianne Wiest, *Hannah and Her Sisters*

DIRECTING

Woody Allen, *Hannah and Her Sisters*

James Ivory, *A Room With a View*

Roland Joffe, *The Mission*

David Lynch, *Blue Velvet*

Oliver Stone, *Platoon*

WRITING

SCREENPLAY WRITTEN DIRECTLY FOR THE SCREEN

Woody Allen, *Hannah and Her Sisters*

Paul Hogan, story; Paul Hogan, Ken Shadie and John Cornell, screenplay, *"Crocodile" Dundee*

Hanif Kureishi, *My Beautiful Laundrette*

Oliver Stone, *Platoon*

Oliver Stone and Richard Boyle, *Salvador*

SCREENPLAY BASED ON ANOTHER MEDIUM

Hesper Anderson and Mark Medoff, *Children of a Lesser God*

Raynold Gideon and Bruce A. Evans, *Stand By Me*

Beth Henley, *Crimes of the Heart*

Ruth Prawer Jhabvala, *A Room With a View*

Richard Price, *The Color of Money*

CINEMATOGRAPHY

Jordan Cronenweth, *Peggy Sue Got Married*

Chris Menges, *The Mission*

Don Peterman, *Star Trek IV: The Voyage Home*

Tony Pierce-Roberts, *A Room With a View*

Robert Richardson, *Platoon*

ART DIRECTION

Stuart Craig, art direction; Jack Stephens, set decoration, *The Mission*

Peter Lamont, art direction; Crispian Sallis, set decoration, *Aliens*

Boris Leven, art direction; Karen A. O'Hara, set decoration, *The Color of Money*

Gianni Quaranta and Brian Ackland-Snow, art direction; Brian Savegar and Elio Altramura, set decoration, *A Room With a View*

Stuart Wurtzel, art direction; Carol Joffe, set decoration, *Hannah and Her Sisters*

SOUND

Les Fresholtz, Dick Alexander, Vern Poore and William Nelson, *Heartbreak Ridge*

Graham V. Hartstone, Nicolas Le Messurier, Michael A. Carter and Roy Charman, *Aliens*

Donald O. Mitchell, Kevin O'Connell, Rick Kline and William B. Kaplan, *Top Gun*

Terry Porter, Dave Hudson, Mel Metcalfe and Gene S. Cantamessa, *Star Trek IV: The Voyage Home*

John Wilkinson, Richard Rogers, Charles "Bud" Grenzbach and Simon Kaye, *Platoon*

MUSIC

SONG

"Glory of Love," *The Karate Kid Part II*, Peter Cetera and David Foster, music; Peter Cetera and Diane Nini, lyrics

"Life in a Looking Glass," *That's Life*, Henry Mancini, music; Leslie Bricusse, lyrics

"Mean Green Mother From Outer Space," *Little Shop of Horrors*, Alan Menken, music; Howard Ashman, lyrics

"Somewhere Out There," *An American Tail*, James Horner and Barry Mann, music; Cynthia Weil, lyrics

"Take My Breath Away," *Top Gun*, Giorgio Moroder, music; Tom Whitlock, lyrics

ORIGINAL SCORE

Jerry Goldsmith, *Hoosiers*

Herbie Hancock, *'Round Midnight*

James Horner, *Aliens*

Ennio Morricone, *The Mission*

Leonard Rosenman, *Star Trek IV: The Voyage Home*

FILM EDITING

Jim Clark, *The Mission*

Ray Lovejoy, *Aliens*

Susan E. Morse, *Hannah and Her Sisters*

Claire Simpson, *Platoon*

Billy Weber and Chris Lebenzon, *Top Gun*

COSTUME DESIGN

Anna Anni and Maurizio Millenotti, *Otello*

Jenny Beaven and John Bright, *A Room With a View*

Anthony Powell, *Pirates*

Enrico Sabbatini, *The Mission*

Theadora Van Runkle, *Peggy Sue Got Married*

MAKEUP

Rob Bottin and Peter Robb-King, *Legend*

Chris Walas and Stephan Dupuis, *The Fly*

Michael G. Westmore and Michèle Burke, *The Clan of the Cave Bear*

VISUAL EFFECTS

Lyle Conway, Brian Ferren and Martin Gutteridge, *Little Shop of Horrors*

Richard Edlund, John Bruno, Garry Waller and William Neil, *Poltergeist II: The Other Side*

Robert Skotak, Stan Winston, John Richardson and Suzanne Benson, *Aliens*

SOUND EFFECTS EDITING

Cecelia Hall and George Watters II, *Top Gun*

Mark Mangini, *Star Trek IV: The Voyage Home*

Don Sharpe, *Aliens*

SHORT FILMS

ANIMATED

The Frog, the Dog and the Devil (Bob Stenhouse, producer; New Zealand National Film Unit)

***A Greek Tragedy* (Linda Van Tulden and Willem Thijssen producers; CineTe pvba)**

Luxo Jr. (John Lasseter and William Reeves, producers; Pixar Productions)

LIVE ACTION

Exit (Stefano Reali and Pino Quartullo, producers; Rai Radiotelevisione Italiana/RAI-UNO)

Love Struck (Fredda Weiss, producer; Rainy Day Productions)

***Precious Images* (Chuck Workman, producer; Calliope Films, Inc.)**

DOCUMENTARY

SHORT SUBJECT

Debonair Dancers (Alison Nigh-Strelich, producer; Alison Nigh-Strelich Production)

The Masters of Disaster (Sonya Friedman, producer; Indiana University Audio Visual Center)

Red Grooms: Sunflower in a Hothouse (Thomas L. Neff and Madeline Bell, producers; Polaris Entertainment Production)

Sam (Aaron D. Weisblatt Production)

***Women — for America, for the World* (Vivienne Verdon-Roe, producer; Educational Film & Video Project)**

FEATURE

Artie Shaw: Time Is All You've Got (Brigitte Berman, producer; Bridge Film Production)

Chile: Hasta Cuando? (David Bradbury, producer; David Bradbury Productions)

***Down and Out in America* (Joseph Feury and Milton Justice, producers; Joseph Feury Production)**

Isaac in America: A Journey With Isaac Bashevis Singer (Kirk Simon and Amram Nowak, producers; Amram Nowak Associates)

Witness to Apartheid (Sharon I. Sopher, producer; Production of Developing News, Inc.)

FOREIGN LANGUAGE FILM

***The Assault*, Netherlands**

Betty Blue, France

The Decline of the American Empire, Canada

My Sweet Little Village, Czechoslovakia

"38", Austria

IRVING G. THALBERG MEMORIAL AWARD

Steven Spielberg

HONORARY AWARD

To **Ralph Bellamy** for his unique artistry and his distinguished service to the profession of acting

To **E.M. (Al) Lewis** in appreciation for outstanding service and dedication in upholding the high Academy standards

Steven Spielberg

1987

BEST PICTURE

Broadcast News, James L. Brooks, producer (Twentieth Century-Fox)

Fatal Attraction, Stanley R. Jaffe and Sherry Lansing, producers (Paramount)

Hope and Glory, John Boorman, producer (Columbia)

The Last Emperor, Jeremy Thomas, producer (Columbia)

Moonstruck, Patrick Palmer and Norman Jewison, producers (MGM)

ACTOR IN A LEADING ROLE

Michael Douglas, *Wall Street*

William Hurt, *Broadcast News*

Marcello Mastroianni, *Dark Eyes*

Jack Nicholson, *Ironweed*

Robin Williams, *Good Morning, Vietnam*

ACTRESS IN A LEADING ROLE

Cher, *Moonstruck*

Glenn Close, *Fatal Attraction*

Holly Hunter, *Broadcast News*

Sally Kirkland, *Anna*

Meryl Streep, *Ironweed*

ACTOR IN A SUPPORTING ROLE

Albert Brooks, *Broadcast News*

Sean Connery, *The Untouchables*

Morgan Freeman, *Street Smart*

Vincent Gardenia, *Moonstruck*

Denzel Washington, *Cry Freedom*

ACTRESS IN A SUPPORTING ROLE

Norma Aleandro, *Gaby — A True Story*

Anne Archer, *Fatal Attraction*

Olympia Dukakis, *Moonstruck*

Anne Ramsey, *Throw Momma From the Train*

Ann Sothern, *The Whales of August*

DIRECTING

Bernardo Bertolucci, *The Last Emperor*

John Boorman, *Hope and Glory*

Lasse Hallström, *My Life as a Dog*

Norman Jewison, *Moonstruck*

Adrian Lyne, *Fatal Attraction*

WRITING

SCREENPLAY WRITTEN DIRECTLY FOR THE SCREEN

Woody Allen, *Radio Days*

John Boorman, *Hope and Glory*

James L. Brooks, *Broadcast News*

Louis Malle, *Au Revoir les Enfants*

John Patrick Shanley, *Moonstruck*

SCREENPLAY BASED ON MATERIAL FROM ANOTHER MEDIUM

James Dearden, *Fatal Attraction*

The Last Emperor

Lasse Hallström, Reidar Jönsson, Brasse Brännström and Per Berglund, *My Life as a Dog*

Tony Huston, *The Dead*

Stanley Kubrick, Michael Herr and Gustav Hasford, *Full Metal Jacket*

Mark Peploe and Bernardo Bertolucci, *The Last Emperor*

CINEMATOGRAPHY

Michael Ballhaus, *Broadcast News*

Allen Daviau, *Empire of the Sun*

Philippe Rousselot, *Hope and Glory*

Vittorio Storaro, *The Last Emperor*

Haskell Wexler, *Matewan*

ART DIRECTION

Santo Loquasto, art direction; Carol Joffe, Les Bloom and George DeTitta, Jr., set decoration, *Radio Days*

Anthony Pratt, art direction; Joan Woolard, set decoration, *Hope and Glory*

Norman Reynolds, art direction; Harry Cordwell, set decoration, *Empire of the Sun*

Ferdinando Scarfiotti, art direction; Bruno Cesari and Osvaldo Desideri, set decoration, *The Last Emperor*

Patrizia Von Brandenstein and William A. Elliot, art direction; Hal Gausman, set decoration, *The Untouchables*

SOUND

Wayne Artman, Tom Beckert, Tom Dahl and Art Rochester, *The Witches of Eastwick*

Les Fresholtz, Dick Alexander, Vern Poore and Bill Nelson, *Lethal Weapon*

Robert Knudson, Don Digirolamo, John Boyde and Tony Dawe, *Empire of the Sun*

Michael J. Kohut, Carlos DeLarios, Aaron Rochin and Robert Wald, *RoboCop*

Bill Rowe and Ivan Sharrock, *The Last Emperor*

MUSIC

SONG

"Cry Freedom," *Cry Freedom*, George Fenton and Jonas Gwangwa, music and lyrics

(I've Had) "The Time of My Life," *Dirty Dancing*, Franke Previte, John DeNicola and Donald Markowitz, music; Franke Previte, lyrics

"Nothing's Gonna Stop Us Now," *Mannequin*, Albert Hammond and Diane Warren, music and lyrics

"Shakedown," *Beverly Hills Cop II*, Harold Faltermeyer and Keith Forsey, music; Harold Faltermeyer, Keith Forsey and Bob Seger, lyrics

"Storybook Love," *The Princess Bride*, Willy DeVille, music and lyrics

ORIGINAL SCORE

George Fenton and Jonas Gwangwa, *Cry Freedom*

Ennio Morricone, *The Untouchables*

Ryuichi Sakamoto, David Byrne and Cong Su, *The Last Emperor*

John Williams, *Empire of the Sun*

John Williams, *The Witches of Eastwick*

FILM EDITING

Gabriella Cristiani, *The Last Emperor*

Michael Kahn, *Empire of the Sun*

Michael Kahn and Peter E. Berger, *Fatal Attraction*

Richard Marks, *Broadcast News*

Frank J. Urioste, *RoboCop*

COSTUME DESIGN

James Acheson, *The Last Emperor*

Jenny Beavan and John Bright, *Maurice*

Dorothy Jeakins, *The Dead*

Bob Ringwood, *Empire of the Sun*

Marilyn Vance-Straker, *The Untouchables*

MAKEUP

Rick Baker, *Harry and the Hendersons*

Bob Laden, *Happy New Year*

VISUAL EFFECTS

Joel Hynek, Robert M. Greenberg, Richard Greenberg and Stan Winston, *Predator*

Dennis Muren, William George, Harley Jessup and Kenneth Smith, *Innerspace*

SHORT FILMS
ANIMATED

George and Rosemary (Eunice Macaulay, producer; National Film Board of Canada)

The Man Who Planted Trees (Frédéric Back, producer; Société Radio-Canada/Canadian Broadcasting Corporation)

Your Face (Bill Plympton, producer; Bill Plympton Productions)

LIVE ACTION

Making Waves (Ann Wingate, producer; The Production Pool Ltd.)

Ray's Male Heterosexual Dance Hall (Jonathan Sanger and Jana Sue Memel, producers; Chanticleer Films)

Shoeshine (Robert A. Katz, producer; Tom Abrams Productions)

DOCUMENTARY
SHORT SUBJECT

Frances Steloff: Memoirs of a Bookseller (Deborah Dickson,

producer; Winterlude Films, Inc. Production)

In the Wee Wee Hours . . . (Dr. Frank Daniel and Izak Ben-Meir, producers; University of Southern California School of Cinema/Television)

Languge Says It All (Megan Williams, producer; Tripod Production)

Silver Into Gold (Lynn Mueller, producer; Stanford University Department of Communications)

Young at Heart (Sue Marx and Pamela Conn, producers; Sue Marx Films, Inc. Production)

FEATURE

Eyes on the Prize: America's Civil Rights Years/Bridge to Freedom 1965 (Callie Crossley and James A. DeVinney, producers; Blackside, Inc. Production)

Hellfire: A Journey From Hiroshima (John Junkerman and John W. Dower, producers; Muraki Film Project)

Radio Bikini (Robert Stone, producer; Crossroads Film Project, Ltd.)

A Stitch for Time (Barbara Herbich and Cyril Christo, producers; Peace Quilters Production Company, Inc.)

The Ten-Year Lunch: The Wit and Legend of the Algonquin Round Table (Aviva Slesin, producer; Aviva Films)

FOREIGN LANGUAGE FILM

Au Revoir les Enfants (Goodbye, Children), France

Babette's Feast, Denmark

Course Completed, Spain

The Family, Italy

Pathfinder, Norway

IRVING G. THALBERG MEMORIAL AWARD
Billy Wilder

SPECIAL ACHIEVEMENT AWARD
SOUND EFFECTS EDITING
Stephen Flick and John Pospisil, *RoboCop*

1988

BEST PICTURE

The Accidental Tourist, Lawrence Kasdan, Charles Okun and Michael Grillo, producers (Warner Bros.)

Dangerous Liaisons, Norma Heyman and Hank Moonjean, producers (Warner Bros.)

Mississippi Burning, Frederick Zollo and Robert F. Colesberry, producers (Orion)

Rain Man, Mark Johnson, producer (United Artists)

Working Girl, Douglas Wick, producer (Twentieth Century-Fox)

ACTOR IN A LEADING ROLE

Gene Hackman, *Mississippi Burning*

Tom Hanks, *Big*

Dustin Hoffman, *Rain Man*

Edward James Olmos, *Stand and Deliver*

Max von Sydow, *Pelle the Conqueror*

ACTRESS IN A LEADING ROLE

Glenn Close, *Dangerous Liaisons*

Jodie Foster, *The Accused*

Melanie Griffith, *Working Girl*

Meryl Streep, *A Cry in the Dark*

Sigourney Weaver, *Gorillas in the Mist*

ACTOR IN A SUPPORTING ROLE

Alec Guinness, *Little Dorrit*

Kevin Kline, *A Fish Called Wanda*

Martin Landau, *Tucker the Man and His Dream*

River Phoenix, *Running on Empty*

Dean Stockwell, *Married to the Mob*

ACTRESS IN A SUPPORTING ROLE

Joan Cusack, *Working Girl*

Geena Davis, *The Accidental Tourist*

Frances McDormand, *Mississippi Burning*

Michelle Pfeiffer, *Dangerous Liaisons*

Sigourney Weaver, *Working Girl*

DIRECTING

Charles Crichton, *A Fish Called Wanda*

Barry Levinson, *Rain Man*

Mike Nichols, *Working Girl*

Alan Parker, *Mississippi Burning*

Martin Scorsese, *The Last Temptation of Christ*

WRITING

SCREENPLAY WRITTEN DIRECTLY FOR THE SCREEN

Ronald Bass and Barry Morrow, screenplay; Barry Morrow, story, *Rain Man*

John Cleese, screenplay; John Cleese and Charles Crichton, story, *A Fish Called Wanda*

Naomi Foner, *Running on Empty*

Gary Ross and Anne Spielberg, *Big*

Ron Shelton, *Bull Durham*

SCREENPLAY BASED ON MATERIAL FROM ANOTHER MEDIUM

Jean-Claude Carrière and Philip Kaufman, *The Unbearable Lightness of Being*

Christine Edzard, *Little Dorrit*

Frank Galati and Lawrence Kasdan, *The Accidental Tourist*

Christopher Hampton, *Dangerous Liaisons*

Anna Hamilton Phelan, screenplay; Anna Hamilton Phelan and Tab Murphy, story, *Gorillas in the Mist*

CINEMATOGRAPHY

Peter Biziou, *Mississippi Burning*

Dean Cundey, *Who Framed Roger Rabbit*

Conrad L. Hall, *Tequila Sunrise*

Sven Nykvist, *The Unbearable Lightness of Being*

John Seale, *Rain Man*

ART DIRECTION

Albert Brenner, art direction; Garrett Lewis, set decoration, *Beaches*

Stuart Craig, art direction; Gerard James, set decoration, *Dangerous Liaisons*

Ida Random, art direction; Linda DeScenna, set decoration, *Rain Man*

Elliot Scott, art direction; Peter Howitt, set decoration, *Who Framed Roger Rabbit*

Dean Tavoularis, art direction; Armin Ganz, set decoration, *Tucker the Man and His Dream*

SOUND

Don Bassman, Kevin F. Cleary, Richard Overton and Al Overton, *Die Hard*

Les Fresholtz, Dick Alexander, Vern Poore and Willie D. Burton, *Bird*

Robert Knudson, John Boyd, Don Digirolamo and Tony Dawe, *Who Framed Roger Rabbit*

Robert Litt, Elliot Tyson, Rick Kline and Danny Michael, *Mississippi Burning*

Andy Nelson, Brian Saunders and Peter Handford, *Gorillas in the Mist*

MUSIC

SONG

"Calling You," *Bagdad Cafe*, Bob Telson, music and lyrics

"Let the River Run," *Working Girl*, Carly Simon, music and lyrics

"Two Hearts," *Buster*, Lamont Dozier, music; Phil Collins, lyrics

ORIGINAL SCORE

George Fenton, *Dangerous Liaisons*

Dave Grusin, *The Milagro Beanfield War*

Maurice Jarre, *Gorillas in the Mist*

John Williams, *The Accidental Tourist*

Hans Zimmer, *Rain Man*

FILM EDITING

Stuart Baird, *Gorillas in the Mist*

Gerry Hambling, *Mississippi Burning*

Stu Linder, *Rain Man*

Arthur Schmidt, *Who Framed Roger Rabbit*

Frank J. Urioste and John F. Link, *Die Hard*

COSTUME DESIGN

James Acheson, *Dangerous Liaisons*

Milena Canonero, *Tucker the Man and His Dream*

Deborah Nadoolman, *Coming to America*

Patricia Norris, *Sunset*

Jane Robinson, *A Handful of Dust*

MAKEUP

Rick Baker, *Coming to America*

Tom Burman and Bari Dreiband-Burman, *Scrooged*

Ve Neill, Steve La Porte and Robert Short, *Beetlejuice*

VISUAL EFFECTS

Richard Edlund, Al DiSarro, Brent Boates and Thaine Morris, *Die Hard*

Dennis Muren, Michael McAlister, Phil Tippett and Chris Evans, *Willow*

Ken Ralston, Richard Williams, Edward Jones and George Gibbs, *Who Framed Roger Rabbit*

SOUND EFFECTS EDITING

Ben Burtt and Richard Hymns, *Willow*

Charles L. Campbell and Louis L. Edemann, *Who Framed Roger Rabbit*

Stephen H. Flick and Richard Shorr, *Die Hard*

Jessica Tandy, *Driving Miss Daisy*

SHORT FILMS
ANIMATION
The Cat Came Back (Cordell Barker, producer; National Film Board of Canada)

Technological Threat (Bill Kroyer and Brian Jennings, producers; Kroyer Films, Inc.)

Tin Toy (John Lasseter and William Reeves, producers; Pixar)

LIVE ACTION
The Appointments of Dennis Jennings (Dean Parisot and Steven Wright, producer; Schooner Productions, Inc.)

Cadillac Dreams (Matia Karrell and Abbee Goldstein, producers; Cadillac Dreams Production)

Gullah Tales (George deGolian and Gary Moss, producers; Georgia State University)

DOCUMENTARY
SHORT SUBJECT
The Children's Storefront (Karen Goodman, producer; Simon and Goodman Picture Company Production)

Family Gathering (Lise Yasui and Ann Tegnell, producers; Lise Yasui Production)

Gang Cops (Thomas B. Fleming and Daniel J. Marks, producers; University of Southern California Center for Visual Anthropology and the School of Cinema/Television)

Portrait of Imogen (Nancy Hale and Meg Partridge, producers; Pacific Pictures Production)

You Don't Have to Die (William Guttentag and Malcolm Clarke, producers; Tiger Rose Production in association with Filmworks, Inc.)

FEATURE
The Cry of Reason — Beyers Naude: An Afrikaner Speaks Out (Robert Bilheimer and Ronald Mix, producers; Worldwide Documentaries, Inc.)

Hotel Terminus: The Life and Times of Klaus Barbie (Marcel Ophuls, producer; The Memory Pictures Company)

Let's Get Lost (Bruce Weber and Nan Bush, producers; Little Bear Films, Inc.)

Promises to Keep (Ginny Durrin, producer; Durrin Productions, Inc.)

Who Killed Vincent Chin? (Renee Tajima and Christine Choy, producers; Film News Now Foundation and Detroit Educational Television Foundation Production)

FOREIGN LANGUAGE FILM
Hanussen, Hungary

The Music Teacher, Belgium

Pelle the Conqueror, Denmark

Salaam Bombay!, India

Women on the Verge of a Nervous Breakdown, Spain

SPECIAL ACHIEVEMENT AWARDS
ANIMATION DIRECTION
Richard Williams, *Who Framed Roger Rabbit*

HONORARY AWARDS
To the **National Film Board of Canada** in recognition of its 50th anniversary and its dedicated commitment to originate artistic, creative and technological activity and excellence in every area of filmmaking

To **Eastman Kodak Company** in recognition of the company's fundamental contributions to the art of motion pictures during the first century of film history

1989

BEST PICTURE
Born on the Fourth of July, A. Kitman Ho and Oliver Stone, producers (Universal)

Dead Poets Society, Steven Haft, Paul Junger Witt and Tony Thomas, producers (Buena Vista)

Driving Miss Daisy, Richard D. Zanuck and Lili Fini Zanuck, producers (Warner Bros.)

Field of Dreams, Lawrence Gordon and Charles Gordon, producers (Universal)

My Left Foot, Noel Pearson, producers (Miramax)

ACTOR IN A LEADING ROLE
Kenneth Branagh, *Henry V*

Tom Cruise, *Born on the Fourth of July*

Daniel Day-Lewis, *My Left Foot*

Morgan Freeman, *Driving Miss Daisy*

Robin Williams, *Dead Poets Society*

ACTRESS IN A LEADING ROLE
Isabelle Adjani, *Camille Claudel*

Pauline Collins, *Shirley Valentine*

Jessica Lange, *Music Box*

Michelle Pfeiffer, *The Fabulous Baker Boys*

Jessica Tandy, *Driving Miss Daisy*

ACTOR IN A SUPPORTING ROLE
Danny Aiello, *Do the Right Thing*

Dan Aykroyd, *Driving Miss Daisy*

Marlon Brando, *A Dry White Season*

Martin Landau, *Crimes and Misdemeanors*

Denzel Washington, *Glory*

ACTRESS IN A SUPPORTING ROLE
Brenda Fricker, *My Left Foot*

Anjelica Huston, *Enemies, A Love Story*

Lena Olin, *Enemies, A Love Story*

Julia Roberts, *Steel Magnolias*

Dianne Wiest, *Parenthood*

DIRECTING

Woody Allen, *Crimes and Misdemeanors*

Kenneth Branagh, *Henry V*

Jim Sheridan, *My Left Foot*

Oliver Stone, *Born on the Fourth of July*

Peter Weir, *Dead Poets Society*

WRITING

SCREENPLAY WRITTEN DIRECTLY FOR THE SCREEN

Woody Allen, *Crimes and Misdemeanors*

Nora Ephron, *When Harry Met Sally . . .*

Spike Lee, *Do the Right Thing*

Tom Schulman, *Dead Poets Society*

Steven Soderbergh, *sex, lies and videotape*

SCREENPLAY BASED ON MATERIAL FROM ANOTHER MEDIUM

Phil Alden Robinson, *Field of Dreams*

Jim Sheridan and Shane Connaughton, *My Left Foot*

Roger L. Simon and Paul Mazursky, *Enemies, A Love Story*

Oliver Stone and Ron Kovic, *Born on the Fourth of July*

Alfred Uhry, *Driving Miss Daisy*

CINEMATOGRAPHY

Michael Ballhaus, *The Fabulous Baker Boys*

Freddie Francis, *Glory*

Robert Richardson, *Born on the Fourth of July*

Mikael Salomon, *The Abyss*

Haskell Wexler, *Blaze*

ART DIRECTION

Leslie Dilley, art direction; Anne Kuljian, set decoration, *The Abyss*

Dante Ferretti, art direction; Francesca Lo Schiavo, set decoration, *The Adventures of Baron Munchausen*

Anton Furst, art direction; Peter Young, set decoration, *Batman*

Norman Garwood, art direction; Garrett Lewis, set decoration, *Glory*

Bruno Rubeo, art direction; Crispian Sallis, set decoration, *Driving Miss Daisy*

SOUND

Don Bassman, Kevin F. Cleary, Richard Overton and Lee Orloff, *The Abyss*

Ben Burtt, Gary Summers, Shawn Murphy and Tony Dawe, *Indiana Jones and the Last Crusade*

Michael Minkler, Gregory H. Watkins, Wylie Stateman and Tod A. Maitland, *Born on the Fourth of July*

Donald O. Mitchell, Kevin O'Connell, Greg P. Russell and Keith A. Wester, *Black Rain*

Donald O. Mitchell, Gregg C. Rudloff, Elliot Tyson and Russell Williams II, *Glory*

MUSIC

SONG

"After All," *Chances Are*, Tom Snow, music; Dean Pitchford, lyrics

"The Girl Who Used to Be Me," *Shirley Valentine*, Marvin Hamlisch, music; Alan and Marilyn Bergman, lyrics

Denzel Washington, *Glory*

"I Love to See You Smile," *Parenthood*, Randy Newman, music and lyrics

"Kiss the Girl," *The Little Mermaid*, Alan Menken, music; Howard Ashman, lyrics

"Under the Sea," *The Little Mermaid*, Alan Menken, music; Howard Ashman, lyrics

ORIGINAL SCORE

David Grusin, *The Fabulous Baker Boys*

James Horner, *Field of Dreams*

Alan Menken, *The Little Mermaid*

John Williams, *Born on the Fourth of July*

John Williams, *Indiana Jones and the Last Crusade*

FILM EDITING

Noëlle Boisson, *The Bear*

David Brenner and Joe Hutshing, *Born on the Fourth of July*

Steven Rosenblum, *Glory*

William Steinkamp, *The Fabulous Baker Boys*

Mark Warner, *Driving Miss Daisy*

COSTUME DESIGN

Phyllis Dalton, *Henry V*

Elizabeth McBride, *Driving Miss Daisy*

Gabriella Pescucci, *The Adventures of Baron Munchausen*

Theodor Pistek, *Valmont*

Joe I. Tompkins, *Harlem Nights*

MAKEUP

Manlio Rocchetti, Lynn Barber and Kevin Haney, *Driving Miss Daisy*

Dick Smith, Ken Diaz and Greg Nelson, *Dad*

Maggie Weston and Fabrizio Sforza, *The Adventures of Baron Munchausen*

VISUAL EFFECTS

John Bruno, Dennis Muren, Hoyt Yeatman and Dennis Skotak, *The Abyss*

Richard Conway and Kent Houston, *The Adventures of Baron Munchausen*

Ken Ralston, Michael Lantieri, John Bell and Steve Gawley, *Back to the Future Part II*

SOUND EFFECTS EDITING

Milton C. Burrow and William L. Manger, *Black Rain*

Ben Burtt and Richard Hymns, *Indiana Jones and the Last Crusade*

Robert Henderson and Alan Robert Murray, *Lethal Weapon 2*

SHORT FILMS
ANIMATION

***Balance* (Christoph Lauenstein and Wolfgang Lauenstein, producers; Lauenstein Production)**

The Cow (Alexander Petrov, producer; The "Pilot" Co-op Animated Film Studio with VPTO Videofilm)

The Hill Farm (Mark Baker, producer; National Film and Television School)

LIVE ACTION

Amazon Diary (Robert Nixon, producer; Determined Productions, Inc.)

The Childeater (Jonathan Tammuz, producer; Stephen-Tammuz Productions, Ltd.)

***Work Experience* (James Hendrie, producer; North Inch Production Ltd.)**

DOCUMENTARY
SHORT SUBJECT

Fine Food, Fine Pastries, Open 6 to 9 (David Petersen, producer; David Petersen Productions)

***The Johnstown Flood* (Charles Guggenheim, producer; Guggenheim Productions)**

Yad Vashem: Preserving the Past to Ensure the Future (Ray Errol Fox, producer; Ray Errol Fox Production)

FEATURE

Adam Clayton Powell (Richard Killberg and Yvonne Smith, producers; RKB Productions)

***Common Threads: Stories From the Quilt* (Robert Epstein and Bill Couturie, producers; Telling Pictures and the Couturie Company Production)**

Crack USA: County Under Siege (Vince DiPersio and William Guttentag, producers; Half-Court Productions, Ltd.)

For All Mankind (Al Reinert and Betsy Broyles Breier, producers; Apollo Associates/FAM Productions Inc.)

Super Chief: The Life and Legacy of Earl Warren (Judith Leonard and Bill Jersey; Quest Production)

FOREIGN LANGUAGE FILM

Camille Claudel, France

***Cinema Paradiso*, Italy**

Jesus of Montreal, Canada

Waltzing Regitze, Denmark

What Happened to Santiago, Puerto Rico

JEAN HERSHOLT HUMANITARIAN AWARD
Howard W. Koch

HONORARY AWARDS

To **Akira Kurosawa** for accomplishments that have inspired, delighted, enriched and entertained audiences and influenced filmmakers throughout the world

The Academy of Motion Picture Arts and Sciences' Board of Governors commends the contributions of the members of the engineering committees of **The Society of Motion Picture and Television Engineers (SMPTE)**. By establishing industry standards, they have greatly contributed to making film a primary form of international communication.

1990

BEST PICTURE

Awakenings, Walter F. Parkes and Lawrence Lasker, producers (Columbia)

***Dances With Wolves*, Jim Wilson and Kevin Costner, producers (Orion)**

Ghost, Lisa Weinstein, producer (Paramount)

The Godfather Part III, Francis Ford Coppola, producer (Paramount)

Good Fellas, Irwin Winkler, producer (Warner Bros.)

ACTOR IN A LEADING ROLE

Kevin Costner, *Dances With Wolves*

Robert De Niro, *Awakenings*

Gérard Depardieu, *Cyrano de Bergerac*

Richard Harris, *The Field*

Jeremy Irons, *Reversal of Fortune*

ACTRESS IN A LEADING ROLE

Kathy Bates, *Misery*

Anjelica Huston, *The Grifters*

Julia Roberts, *Pretty Woman*

Meryl Streep, *Postcards From the Edge*

Joanne Woodward, *Mr. & Mrs. Bridge*

ACTOR IN A SUPPORTING ROLE

Bruce Davison, *Longtime Companion*

Andy Garcia, *The Godfather Part III*

Graham Greene, *Dances With Wolves*

Al Pacino, *Dick Tracy*

Joe Pesci, *Good Fellas*

ACTRESS IN A SUPPORTING ROLE

Annette Bening, *The Grifters*

Lorraine Bracco, *Good Fellas*

Whoopi Goldberg, *Ghost*

Diane Ladd, *Wild at Heart*

Mary McDonnell, *Dances With Wolves*

Dances With Wolves

DIRECTING

Francis Ford Coppola, *The Godfather Part III*

Kevin Costner, *Dances With Wolves*

Stephen Frears, *The Grifters*

Barbet Schroeder, *Reversal of Fortune*

Martin Scorsese, *Good Fellas*

WRITING

SCREENPLAY WRITTEN DIRECTLY FOR THE SCREEN

Woody Allen, *Alice*

Barry Levinson, *Avalon*

Bruce Joel Rubin, *Ghost*

Whit Stillman, *Metropolitan*

Peter Weir, *Green Card*

SCREENPLAY BASED ON MATERIAL FROM ANOTHER MEDIUM

Michael Blake, *Dances With Wolves*

Nicholas Kazan, *Reversal of Fortune*

Nicholas Pileggi and Martin Scorsese, *Good Fellas*

Donald E. Westlake, *The Grifters*

Steven Zaillian, *Awakenings*

CINEMATOGRAPHY

Allen Daviau, *Avalon*

Philippe Rousselot, *Henry & June*

Dean Semler, *Dances With Wolves*

Vittorio Storaro, *Dick Tracy*

Gordon Willis, *The Godfather Part III*

ART DIRECTION

Jeffrey Beecroft, art direction; Lisa Dean, set decoration, *Dances With Wolves*

Dante Ferretti, art direction; Francesca Lo Schiavo, set decoration, *Hamlet*

Ezio Frigerio, art direction; Jacques Rouxel, set decoration, *Cyrano de Bergerac*

Richard Sylbert, art direction; Rick Simpson, set decoration, *Dick Tracy*

Dean Tavoularis, art direction; Gary Fettis, set decoration, *The Godfather Part III*

SOUND

Don Bassman, Richard Overton, Kevin F. Cleary and Richard Bryce Goodman, *The Hunt for Red October*

Chris Jenkins, David E. Campbell, D. M. Hemphill and Thomas Causey, *Dick Tracy*

Michael J. Kohut, Carlos de Larios, Aaron Rochin and Nelson Stoll, *Total Recall*

Donald O. Mitchell, Rick Kline, Kevin O'Connell and Charles Wilborn, *Days of Thunder*

Jeffrey Perkins, Bill W. Benton, Greg Watkins and Russell Williams II, *Dances With Wolves*

MUSIC

SONG

"Blaze of Glory," *Young Guns II*, Jon Bon Jovi, music and lyrics

"I'm Checkin' Out," *Postcards From the Edge*, Shel Silverstein, music and lyrics

"Promise Me You'll Remember," *The Godfather Part III*, Carmine Coppola, music; John Bettis, lyrics

"Somewhere in My Memory," *Home Alone*, music by John Williams; lyrics by Leslie Bricusse

"Sooner Or Later" (I Always Get My Man), *Dick Tracy*, Stephen Sondheim, music and lyrics

ORIGINAL SCORE

John Barry, *Dances With Wolves*

David Grusin, *Havana*

Maurice Jarre, *Ghost*

Randy Newman, *Avalon*

John Williams, *Home Alone*

FILM EDITING

Barry Malkin, Lisa Fruchtman and Walter Murch, *The Godfather Part III*

Walter Murch, *Ghost*

Thelma Schoonmaker, *Good Fellas*

Neil Travis, *Dances With Wolves*

Dennis Virkler, John Wright, *The Hunt for Red October*

COSTUME DESIGN

Milena Canonero, *Dick Tracy*

Gloria Gresham, *Avalon*

Maurizio Millenotti, *Hamlet*

Franca Squarciapino, *Cyrano de Bergerac*

Elsa Zamparelli, *Dances With Wolves*

MAKEUP

Michèle Burke and Jean-Pierre Eychenne, *Cyrano de Bergerac*

John Caglione, Jr. and Doug Drexler, *Dick Tracy*

Ve Neill and Stan Winston, *Edward Scissorhands*

SOUND EFFECTS EDITING

Charles L. Campbell and Richard Franklin, *Flatliners*

Stephen H. Flick, *Total Recall*

Cecelia Hall and George Watters II, *The Hunt for Red October*

SHORT FILMS

ANIMATION

***Creature Comforts* (Nick Park, producer; Aardman Animations Ltd. Production)**

A Grand Day Out (Nick Park, producer; National Film and Television School)

Grasshoppers (Cavallette) (Bruno Bozzetto, producer; Bruno Bozzetto Production)

LIVE ACTION

Bronx Cheers (Raymond De Felitta and Matthew Gross, producers; American Film Institute)

Dear Rosie (Peter Cattaneo and Barnaby Thompson, producers; World's End Production)

***The Lunch Date* (Adam Davidson, producer; Adam Davidson Production)**

Senzeni Na? (What Have We Done?) (Bernard Joffa and Anthony E. Nicholas, producers; American Film Institute)

12:01 P.M. (Hillary Ripps and Jonathan Heap, producers; Chanticleer Films)

DOCUMENTARY

SHORT SUBJECT

Burning Down Tomorrow (Kit Thomas, producer; Interscope Communications Inc.)

Chimps: So Like Us (Karen Goodman and Kirk Simon, producers; Simon and Goodman Picture Company)

Days of Waiting (Steven Okazaki, producer; Mouchette Films Production)

Journey Into Life: The World of the Unborn (Derek Bromhall, producer; ABC/Kane Productions International, Inc.)

Rose Kennedy: A Life to Remember (Sanders and Mock Productions and American Film Foundation)

FEATURE

American Dream (Barbara Kopple and Arthur Cohn, producers; Cabin Creek Films)

Berkeley in the Sixties (Mark Kitchell, producer; Berkeley in the Sixties Production Partnership)

Building Bombs (Mark Mori and Susan Robinson, producers; Mori/Robinson Production)

Forever Activists: Stories From the Veterans of the Abraham Lincoln Brigade (Judith Montell, producer; Judith Montell Production)

Waldo Salt: A Screenwriter's Journey (Robert Hillmann and Eugene Corr, producers; Waldo Productions, Inc.)

FOREIGN LANGUAGE FILM

Cyrano de Bergerac, France

Journey of Hope, Switzerland

Ju Dou, People's Republic of China

The Nasty Girl, Germany

Open Doors, Italy

IRVING G. THALBERG MEMORIAL AWARD

David Brown and Richard D. Zanuck

SPECIAL ACHIEVEMENT AWARDS

VISUAL EFFECTS

Eric Brevig, Rob Bottin, Tim McGovern and Alex Funke, *Total Recall*

HONORARY AWARDS

To **Sophia Loren,** one of the genuine treasures of world cinema who, in a career rich with memorable performances, has added permanent luster to our art form

To **Myrna Loy,** in recognition of her extraordinary qualities both on screen and off, with appreciation for a lifetime's worth of indelible performances

To **Roderick T. Ryan, Don Trumbull** and **Geoffrey H. Williamson** in appreciation for outstanding service and dedication in upholding the high standards of the Academy of Motion Picture Arts and Sciences

1991

BEST PICTURE

Beauty and the Beast, Don Hahn, producer (Buena Vista)

Bugsy, Barry Levinson and Warren Beatty, producers (TriStar)

JFK, A. Kitman Ho and Oliver Stone, producers (Warner Bros.)

**Anthony Hopkins,
*The Silence of the Lambs***

The Prince of Tides, Barbra Streisand and Andrew Karsch, producers (Columbia)

The Silence of the Lambs, Edward Saxon, Kenneth Utt and Ron Bozman, producers (Orion)

ACTOR IN A LEADING ROLE

Warren Beatty, *Bugsy*

Robert De Niro, *Cape Fear*

Anthony Hopkins, *The Silence of the Lambs*

Nick Nolte, *The Prince of Tides*

Robin Williams, *The Fisher King*

ACTRESS IN A LEADING ROLE

Geena Davis, *Thelma & Louise*

Laura Dern, *Rambling Rose*

Jodie Foster, *The Silence of the Lambs*

Bette Midler, *For the Boys*

Susan Sarandon, *Thelma & Louise*

ACTOR IN A SUPPORTING ROLE

Tommy Lee Jones, *JFK*

Harvey Keitel, *Bugsy*

Ben Kingsley, *Bugsy*

Michael Lerner, *Barton Fink*

Jack Palance, *City Slickers*

ACTRESS IN A SUPPORTING ROLE

Diane Ladd, *Rambling Rose*

Juliette Lewis, *Cape Fear*

Kate Nelligan, *The Prince of Tides*

Mercedes Ruehl, *The Fisher King*

Jessica Tandy, *Fried Green Tomatoes*

DIRECTING

Jonathan Demme, *The Silence of the Lambs*

Barry Levinson, *Bugsy*

Ridley Scott, *Thelma & Louise*

John Singleton, *Boyz N the Hood*

Oliver Stone, *JFK*

WRITING

SCREENPLAY WRITTEN DIRECTLY FOR THE SCREEN

Lawrence Kasdan and Meg Kasdan, *Grand Canyon*

Callie Khouri, *Thelma & Louise*

Richard LaGravenese, *The Fisher King*

John Singleton, *Boyz N the Hood*

James Toback, *Bugsy*

SCREENPLAY BASED ON MATERIAL PREVIOUSLY PRODUCED OR PUBLISHED

Pat Conroy and Becky Johnston, *The Prince of Tides*

Fannie Flagg and Carol Sobieski, *Fried Green Tomatoes*

Agnieszka Holland, *Europa Europa*

Oliver Stone and Zachary Sklar, *JFK*

Ted Tally, *The Silence of the Lambs*

CINEMATOGRAPHY

Adrian Biddle, *Thelma & Louise*

Allen Daviau, *Bugsy*

Stephen Goldblatt, *The Prince of Tides*

Adam Greenberg, *Terminator 2: Judgment Day*

Robert Richardson, *JFK*

ART DIRECTION

Mel Bourne, art direction; Cindy Carr, set decoration, *The Fisher King*

Norman Garwood, art direction; Garrett Lewis, set decoration, *Hook*

Dennis Gassner, art direction; Nancy Haigh, set decoration, *Barton Fink*

Dennis Gassner, art direction; Nancy Haigh, set decoration, *Bugsy*

Paul Sylbert, art direction; Caryl Heller, set decoration, *The Prince of Tides*

SOUND

Tom Fleischman and Christopher Newman, *The Silence of the Lambs*

Tom Johnson, Gary Rydstrom, Gary Summers and Lee Orloff, *Terminator 2: Judgment Day*

Michael Minkler, Gregg Landaker and Tod A. Maitland, *JFK*

Terry Porter, Mel Metcalfe, David J. Hudson and Doc Kane, *Beauty and the Beast*

Gary Summers, Randy Thom, Gary Rydstrom and Glenn Williams, *Backdraft*

MUSIC

SONG

"Beauty and the Beast," *Beauty and the Beast*, Alan Menken, music; Howard Ashman, lyrics

"Belle," *Beauty and the Beast*, Alan Menken, music; Howard Ashman, lyrics

"Be Our Guest," *Beauty and the Beast*, Alan Menken, music; Howard Ashman, lyrics

(Everything I Do) "I Do It for You," *Robin Hood: Prince of Thieves*, Michael Kamen, music; Bryan Adams and Robert John Lange, lyrics

"When You're Alone," *Hook*, John Williams, music; Leslie Bricusse, lyrics

ORIGINAL SCORE

George Fenton, *The Fisher King*

James Newton Howard, *The Prince of Tides*

Alan Menken, *Beauty and the Beast*

Ennio Morricone, *Bugsy*

John Williams, *JFK*

FILM EDITING

Conrad Buff, Mark Goldblatt and Richard A. Harris, *Terminator 2: Judgment Day*

Gerry Hambling, *The Commitments*

Joe Hutshing and Pietro Scalia, *JFK*

Craig McKay, *The Silence of the Lambs*

Thom Noble, *Thelma & Louise*

COSTUME DESIGN

Richard Hornung, *Barton Fink*

Corinne Jorry, *Madame Bovary*

Ruth Myers, *The Addams Family*

Anthony Powell, *Hook*

Albert Wolsky, *Bugsy*

MAKEUP

Michael Mills, Edward French and Richard Snell, *Star Trek VI: The Undiscovered Country*

Christina Smith, Monty Westmore and Greg Cannom, *Hook*

Stan Winston and Jeff Dawn, *Terminator 2: Judgment Day*

VISUAL EFFECTS

Eric Brevig, Harley Jessup, Mark Sullivan and Michael Lantieri, *Hook*

Dennis Muren, Stan Winston, Gene Warren, Jr. and Robert Skotak, *Terminator 2: Judgment Day*

Mikael Salomon, Allen Hall, Clay Pinney and Scott Farrar, *Backdraft*

SOUND EFFECTS EDITING

Gary Rydstrom and Gloria S. Borders, *Terminator 2: Judgment Day*

Gary Rydstrom and Richard Hymns, *Backdraft*

George Watters II and F. Hudson Miller, *Star Trek VI: The Undiscovered Country*

SHORT FILMS

ANIMATION

Blackfly (Christopher Hinton, producer; National Film Board of Canada)

***Manipulation* (Daniel Greaves, producer; Tandem Films Production)**

Strings (Wendy Tilby, producer; National Film Board of Canada)

LIVE ACTION

Birch Street Gym (Stephen Kessler and Thomas R. Conroy, producers; Chanticleer Films)

Last Breeze of Summer (David M. Massey, producer; American Film Institute)

***Session Man* (Seth Winston and Rob Fried, producers; Chanticleer Films)**

DOCUMENTARY

SHORT SUBJECT

Birdnesters of Thailand (Shadow Hunters) (Antenne 2/National Geographic Society/M.D.I./Wind Horse Production)

***Deadly Deception: General Electric, Nuclear Weapons and Our Environment* (Debra Chasnoff, producer; Women's Educational Media, Inc. Production)**

A Little Vicious (Immy Humes, producer; Film and Video Workshop, Inc. Production)

The Mark of the Maker (David McGowan, producer; McGowan Film and Video, Inc. Production)

Memorial: Letters From American Soldiers (Bill Couturie and Bernard Edelman, producers; Couturie Company Production)

FEATURE

Death on the Job (Vince DiPersio and William Guttentag, producers; Half-Court Pictures, Ltd. Production)

Doing Time: Life Inside the Big House (Alan Raymond and Susan Raymond, producers; Video Verité Production)

In the Shadow of the Stars **(Allie Light and Irving Saraf, producers; Light-Saraf Films Production)**

The Restless Conscience (Hava Kohav Beller, producer; Hava Kohav Beller Production)

Wild by Law (Lawrence Hott and Diane Garey, producers; Florentine Films Production)

FOREIGN LANGUAGE FILM

Children of Nature, Iceland

The Elementary School, Czechoslovakia

Mediterraneo, **Italy**

The Ox, Sweden

Raise the Red Lantern, Hong Kong

IRVING G. THALBERG MEMORIAL AWARD

George Lucas

HONORARY AWARDS

To **Satyajit Ray,** in recognition of his rare mastery of the art of motion pictures, and of his profound humanitarian outlook, which has had an indelible influence on filmmakers and audiences throughout the world

To **Pete Comandini, Richard T. Dayton, Donald Hagans** and **Richard T. Ryan** of YCM Laboratories for the creation and development of a motion picture film restoration process using liquid gate and registration correction on a contact printer

To **Richard J. Stumpf** and **Joseph Westheimer** for outstanding service and dedication in upholding the high standards of the Academy of Motion Picture Arts and Sciences

1992

BEST PICTURE

The Crying Game, Stephen Woolley, producer (Miramax)

A Few Good Men, David Brown, Rob Reiner and Andrew Scheinman, producers (Columbia)

Howards End, Ismail Merchant, producer (Sony Pictures Classics)

Scent of a Woman, Martin Brest, producer (Universal)

Unforgiven, **Clint Eastwood, producer (Warner Bros.)**

ACTOR IN A LEADING ROLE

Robert Downey, Jr., *Chaplin*

Clint Eastwood, *Unforgiven*

Al Pacino, *Scent of a Woman*

Stephen Rea, *The Crying Game*

Denzel Washington, *Malcolm X*

ACTRESS IN A LEADING ROLE

Catherine Deneuve, *Indochine*

Emma Thompson, *Howards End*

Mary McDonnell, *Passion Fish*

Michelle Pfeiffer, *Love Field*

Susan Sarandon, *Lorenzo's Oil*

Emma Thompson, *Howards End*

ACTOR IN A SUPPORTING ROLE

Jaye Davidson, *The Crying Game*

Gene Hackman, *Unforgiven*

Jack Nicholson, *A Few Good Men*

Al Pacino, *Glengarry Glen Ross*

David Paymer, *Mr. Saturday Night*

ACTRESS IN A SUPPORTING ROLE

Judy Davis, *Husbands and Wives*

Joan Plowright, *Enchanted April*

Vanessa Redgrave, *Howards End*

Miranda Richardson, *Damage*

Marisa Tomei, *My Cousin Vinny*

DIRECTING

Robert Altman, *The Player*

Martin Brest, *Scent of a Woman*

Clint Eastwood, *Unforgiven*

James Ivory, *Howards End*

Neil Jordan, *The Crying Game*

WRITING

SCREENPLAY WRITTEN DIRECTLY FOR THE SCREEN

Woody Allen, *Husbands and Wives*

Neil Jordan, *The Crying Game*

George Miller and Nick Enright, *Lorenzo's Oil*

John Sayles, *Passion Fish*

David Webb Peoples, *Unforgiven*

SCREENPLAY BASED ON MATERIAL PREVIOUSLY PRODUCED OR PUBLISHED

Peter Barnes, *Enchanted April*

Richard Friedenberg, *A River Runs Through It*

Bo Goldman, *Scent of a Woman*

Ruth Prawer Jhabvala, *Howards End*

Michael Tolkin, *The Player*

CINEMATOGRAPHY

Stephen H. Burum, *Hoffa*

Robert Fraisse, *The Lover*

Jack N. Green, *Unforgiven*

Tony Pierce-Roberts, *Howards End*

Philippe Rousselot, *A River Runs Through It*

ART DIRECTION

Luciana Arrighi, art direction; Ian Whittaker, set decoration, *Howards End*

Henry Bumstead, art direction; Janice Blackie-Goodine, set decoration, *Unforgiven*

Stuart Craig, art direction; Chris A. Butler, set decoration, *Chaplin*

Thomas Sanders, art direction; Garrett Lewis, set decoration, *Bram Stoker's Dracula*

Ferdinando Scarfiotti, art direction; Linda DeScenna, set decoration, *Toys*

SOUND

Les Fresholtz, Vern Poore, Dick Alexander and Rob Young, *Unforgiven*

Chris Jenkins, Doug Hemphill, Mark Smith and Simon Kaye, *The Last of the Mohicans*

Don Mitchell, Frank A. Montano, Rick Hart and Scott Smith, *Under Siege*

Kevin O'Connell, Rick Kline and Bob Eber, *A Few Good Men*

Terry Porter, Mel Metcalfe, David J. Hudson and Doc Kane, *Aladdin*

MUSIC

SONG

"Beautiful Maria of My Soul," *The Mambo Kings*, Robert Kraft, music; Arne Glimcher, lyrics

"Friend Like Me," *Aladdin*, Alan Menken, music; Howard Ashman, lyrics

"I Have Nothing," *The Bodyguard*, David Foster, music; Linda Thompson, lyrics

"Run to You," *The Bodyguard*, Jud Friedman, music; Allan Rich, lyrics

"A Whole New World," *Aladdin*, Alan Menken, music; Tim Rice, lyrics

ORIGINAL SCORE

John Barry, *Chaplin*

Jerry Goldsmith, *Basic Instinct*

Mark Isham, *A River Runs Through It*

Alan Menken, *Aladdin*

Richard Robbins, *Howards End*

FILM EDITING

Joel Cox, *Unforgiven*

Robert Leighton, *A Few Good Men*

Kant Pan, *The Crying Game*

Geraldine Peroni, *The Player*

Frank J. Urioste, *Basic Instinct*

COSTUME DESIGN

Jenny Beavan and John Bright, *Howards End*

Ruth Carter, *Malcolm X*

Eiko Ishioka, *Bram Stoker's Dracula*

Sheena Napier, *Enchanted April*

Albert Wolsky, *Toys*

MAKEUP

Greg Cannom, Michèle Burke and Matthew W. Mungle, *Bram Stoker's Dracula*

Ve Neill, Greg Cannom and John Blake, *Hoffa*

Ve Neill, Ronnie Specter and Stan Winston, *Batman Returns*

VISUAL EFFECTS

Richard Edlund, Alec Gillis, Tom Woodruff, Jr. and George Gibbs, *Alien³*

Michael Fink, Craig Barron, John Bruno and Dennis Skotak, *Batman Returns*

Ken Ralston, Doug Chiang, Doug Smythe and Tom Woodruff, Jr., *Death Becomes Her*

SOUND EFFECTS EDITING

John Leveque and Bruce Stambler, *Under Siege*

Mark Mangini, *Aladdin*

Tom C. McCarthy and David E. Stone, *Bram Stoker's Dracula*

SHORT FILMS

ANIMATION

Adam (Peter Lord, producer; Aardman Animations Ltd. Production)

***Mona Lisa Descending a Staircase* (Joan C. Gratz, producer; Joan C. Gratz Production)**

Reci, Reci, Reci . . . (Words, Words, Words) (Michaela Pavlátová, producer; Krátky Film Production)

The Sandman (Paul Berry, producer; Batty Berry Mackinnon Production)

Screen Play (Barry J.C. Purves, producer; Bare Boards Film Production)

LIVE ACTION

Contact (Jonathan Darby and Jana Sue Memel, producers; Chanticleer Films)

Cruise Control (Matt Palmieri, producer; Palmieri Pictures Production)

The Lady in Waiting (Christian M. Taylor, producer; Taylor Made Films Production)

***Omnibus* (Sam Karmann, producer; Lazennec tout court/Le C.R.R.A.V. Production)**

Swan Song (Kenneth Branagh and David Parfitt, producers; Renaissance Film PLC Production)

DOCUMENTARY

SHORT SUBJECT

At the Edge of Conquest: The Journey of Chief Wai-Wai (Geoffrey O'Connor, producer; Realis Pictures Inc. Production)

Beyond Imagining: Margaret Anderson and the "Little Review" (Wendy L. Weinberg, producer; Wendy L. Weinberg Production)

The Colours of My Father: A Portrait of Sam Borenstein (Imageries P.B. Ltd. Production in coproduction with the National Film Board of Canada)

***Educating Peter* (Thomas C. Goodwin and Gerardine Wurzburg, producers; State of the Art, Inc. Production)**

When Abortion Was Illegal: Untold Stories (Dorothy Fadiman, producer; Concentric Media Production)

FEATURE

Changing Our Minds: The Story of Dr. Evelyn Hooker (David Haugland, producer; Intrepid Production)

Fires of Kuwait (Black Sun Films, Ltd./IMAX Corporation Production)

Liberators: Fighting on Two Fronts in World War II (William Miles and Nina Rosenblum, producers; Miles Educational Film Productions, Inc.)

Music for the Movies: Bernard Herrmann (Alternate Current Inc./Les Films d'Ici Production)

The Panama Deception (Barbara Trent and David Kasper, producers; Empowerment Project Production)

FOREIGN LANGUAGE FILM

Close to Eden, Russia

Daens, Belgium

Indochine, France

A Place in the World, Uruguay (This film was declared ineligible and removed from the final ballot because it had insufficient Uruguayian artistic control.)

Schtonk, Germany

JEAN HERSHOLT HUMANITARIAN AWARD

Audrey Hepburn

Elizabeth Taylor

HONORARY AWARDS

To **Federico Fellini** in appreciation of one of the screen's master storytellers

To **Petro Vlahos** in appreciation for outstanding service and dedication in upholding the high standards of the Academy of Motion Picture Arts and Sciences

1993

PICTURE

The Fugitive, Arnold Kopelson, producer (Warner Bros.)

In the Name of the Father, Jim Sheridan, producer (Universal)

The Piano, Jan Chapman, producer (Miramax)

The Remains of the Day, Mike Nichols, John Calley and Ismail Merchant, producers (Columbia)

Schindler's List, Stephen Spielberg, Gerald R. Molen and Branko Lustig, producers (Universal)

ACTOR IN A LEADING ROLE

Daniel Day-Lewis, *In the Name of the Father*

Laurence Fishburne, *What's Love Got to Do With It*

Tom Hanks, *Philadelphia*

Anthony Hopkins, *The Remains of the Day*

Liam Neeson, *Schindler's List*

ACTRESS IN A LEADING ROLE

Angela Bassett, *What's Love Got to Do With It*

Stockard Channing, *Six Degrees of Separation*

Holly Hunter, *The Piano*

Emma Thompson, *The Remains of the Day*

Debra Winger, *Shadowlands*

ACTOR IN A SUPPORTING ROLE

Leonardo DiCaprio, *What's Eating Gilbert Grape*

Ralph Fiennes, *Schindler's List*

Tommy Lee Jones, *The Fugitive*

John Malkovich, *In the Line of Fire*

Pete Postlethwaite, *In the Name of the Father*

ACTRESS IN A SUPPORTING ROLE

Holly Hunter, *The Firm*

Anna Paquin, *The Piano*

Rosie Perez, *Fearless*

Winona Ryder, *The Age of Innocence*

Emma Thompson, *In the Name of the Father*

DIRECTING

Robert Altman, *Short Cuts*

Jane Campion, *The Piano*

James Ivory, *The Remains of the Day*

Jim Sheridan, *In the Name of the Father*

Steven Spielberg, *Schindler's List*

WRITING

SCREENPLAY WRITTEN DIRECTLY FOR THE SCREEN

Jane Campion, *The Piano*

Nora Ephron, David S. Ward and Jeff Arch, screenplay; Jeff Arch, story, *Sleepless in Seattle*

Jeff Maguire, *In the Line of Fire*

Ron Nyswaner, *Philadelphia*

Gary Ross, *Dave*

SCREENPLAY BASED ON MATERIAL PREVIOUSLY PRODUCED OR PUBLISHED

Jay Cocks and Martin Scorsese, *The Age of Innocence*

Terry George and Jim Sheridan, *In the Name of the Father*

Ruth Prawer Jhabvala, *The Remains of the Day*

William Nicholson, *Shadowlands*

Steven Zaillian, *Schindler's List*

CINEMATOGRAPHY

Gu Changwei, *Farewell My Concubine*

Michael Chapman, *The Fugitive*

Stuart Dryburgh, *The Piano*

Conrad L. Hall, *Searching for Bobby Fischer*

Janusz Kaminski, *Schindler's List*

ART DIRECTION

Ken Adam, art direction; Marvin March, set decoration, *Addams Family Values*

Luciana Arrighi, art direction; Ian Whittaker, set decoration, *The Remains of the Day*

Dante Ferretti, art direction; Robert J. Franco, set decoration, *The Age of Innocence*

Allan Starski, art direction; Ewa Braun, set decoration, *Schindler's List*

Ben Van Os and Jan Roelfs, art direction, *Orlando*

SOUND

Chris Carpenter, D. M. Hemphill, Bill W. Benton and Lee Orloff, *Geronimo: An American Legend*

Michael Minkler, Bob Beemer and Tim Cooney, *Cliffhanger*

Donald O. Mitchell, Michael Herbick, Frank A. Montaño and Scott D. Smith, *The Fugitive*

Andy Nelson, Steve Pederson, Scott Millan and Ron Judkins, *Schindler's List*

Gary Summers, Gary Rydstrom, Shawn Murphy and Ron Judkins, *Jurassic Park*

MUSIC
SONG

"Again," *Poetic Justice*, Janet Jackson, James Harris III and Terry Lewis, music and lyrics

"The Day I Fall in Love," *Beethoven's 2nd*, Carole Bayer Sager, James Ingram and Clif Magness, music and lyrics

"Philadelphia," *Philadelphia*, Neil Young, music and lyrics

"Streets of Philadelphia," *Philadelphia*, Bruce Springsteen, music and lyrics

"A Wink and a Smile," *Sleepless in Seattle*, Marc Shaiman, music; Ramsey McLean, lyrics

ORIGINAL SCORE

Elmer Bernstein, *The Age of Innocence*

Dave Grusin, *The Firm*

James Newton Howard, *The Fugitive*

Richard Robbins, *The Remains of the Day*

John Williams, *Schindler's List*

FILM EDITING

Anne V. Coates, *In the Line of Fire*

Gerry Hambling, *In the Name of the Father*

Veronika Jenet, *The Piano*

Michael Kahn, *Schindler's List*

Dennis Virkler, David Finfer, Dean Goodhill, Don Brochu, Richard Nord and Dov Hoenig, *The Fugitive*

COSTUME DESIGN

Jenny Beavan and John Bright, *The Remains of the Day*

Anna Biedrzycka-Sheppard, *Schindler's List*

Janet Patterson, *The Piano*

Gabriella Pescucci, *The Age of Innocence*

Sandy Powell, *Orlando*

MAKEUP

Greg Cannom, Ve Neill and Yolanda Toussieng, *Mrs. Doubtfire*

Carl Fullerton and Alan D'Angerio, *Philadelphia*

Christina Smith, Matthew Mungle and Judy Alexander Cory, *Schindler's List*

VISUAL EFFECTS

Pete Kozachik, Eric Leighton, Ariel Velasco Shaw and Gordon Baker, *The Nightmare Before Christmas*

Neil Krepela, John Richardson, John Bruno and Pamela Easley, *Cliffhanger*

Dennis Muren, Stan Winston, Phil Tippett and Michael Lantieri, *Jurassic Park*

SOUND EFFECTS EDITING

John Leveque and Bruce Stambler, *The Fugitive*

Gary Rydstrom and Richard Hymns, *Jurassic Park*

Wylie Stateman and Gregg Baxter, *Cliffhanger*

SHORT FILMS
ANIMATION

Blindscape (Stephen Palmer, producer; National Film and Television School)

The Mighty River (Frédéric Back and Hubert Tison, producers; Canadian Broadcasting Corporation/Société Radio-Canada Production)

Small Talk (Bob Godfrey and Kevin Baldwin, producers; Bob Godfrey Films, Ltd.)

The Village (Mark Baker, producer; Pizazz Pictures Production)

The Wrong Trousers (Nick Park, producer; Aardman Animations Limited Production)

LIVE ACTION

Black Rider (*Schwarzfahrer*) (Pepe Danquart, producer; Trans-Film GmbH Production)

Down on the Waterfront (Stacy Title and Jonathan Penner, producers; Stacy Title/Jonathan Penner Production)

The Dutch Master (Susan Seidelman and Jonathan Brett, producers; Regina Ziegler Film Production)

Partners (Peter Weller and Jana Sue Memel, producers; Chanticleer Films)

The Screw (La Vis) (Didier Flamand, producer; Perla Films Production)

DOCUMENTARY
SHORT SUBJECT

Blood Ties: The Life and Work of Sally Mann (Steven Cantor and Peter Spirer, producers; Moving Target Production)

Chicks in White Satin (Elaine Holliman and Jason Schneider, producers; University of Southern California School of Cinema/Television)

Defending Our Lives (Margaret Lazarus and Renner Wunderlich, producers; Cambridge Documentary Films Production)

FEATURE

The Broadcast Tapes of Dr. Peter (David Paperny and Arthur Ginsberg, producers; Canadian Broadcasting Corporation/HBO Films Production)

Children of Fate (Susan Todd and Andrew Young, producers; Young/Friedson Production)

For Better or for Worse (David Collier and Betsy Thompson, producers; David Collier Production)

I Am a Promise: The Children of Stanton Elementary School (Susan Raymond and Alan Raymond, Verité Films Production)

The War Room (D. A. Pennebaker and Chris Hegedus, producers; R. J. Cutler/Wendy Ettinger/Frazer Pennebaker Production)

FOREIGN LANGUAGE FILM

Belle Époque, Spain

Farewell My Concubine, Hong Kong

Hedd Wyn, United Kingdom

The Scent of Green Papaya, Vietnam

The Wedding Banquet, Republic of China on Taiwan

JEAN HERSHOLT HUMANITARIAN AWARD

Paul Newman

HONORARY AWARDS

To **Deborah Kerr** in appreciation for a full career's worth of elegant and beautifully crafted performances

Cannes Film Festival Winners

The Cannes International Film Festival, held annually in May on the French Riviera, attracts the glitterati for its parties as much as for its screenings. Directors, producers and agents work the crowds in pursuit of big, lucrative movie deals. The winners at Cannes often emerge as the year's most talked about films.

The Lost Weekend

1946

GRAND PRIX
The Red Earth, Lau Lauritzen (Denmark)
The Lost Weekend, Billy Wilder (United States)
Symphonie Pastorale, Jean Delannoy (France)
Brief Encounter, David Lean (United Kingdom)
Neecha Nagar, Chetan Anand (India)
Open City, Roberto Rossellini (Italy)
Maria Candelaria, Emilio Fernandez (Mexico)
The Prize, Alf Sjoberg (Sweden)
The Last Chance, Leopold Lindtberg (Switzerland)
Men Without Wings, M. Cap (Czechoslovakia)
The Great Turning Point, Friedrich Ermler (U.S.S.R.)

SPECIAL JURY PRIZE
Battle of the Rails, Rene Clement (France)

BEST ACTOR
Ray Milland, *The Lost Weekend* (United States)

BEST ACTRESS
Michele Morgan, *Symphonie Pastorale* (France)

DIRECTION
Rene Clement, *Battle of the Rails* (France)

SCREENPLAY
Tchirskov, *The Great Turning Point* (U.S.S.R.)

CINEMATOGRAPHY
Gabriel Figueroa, *Maria Candelaria* and *The Three Musketeers* (Mexico)

MUSIC
Georges Auric

COLOR
The Stone Flower, Alexander Ptouchko (U.S.S.R.)

DOCUMENTARY
Berlin, J. Raisman (U.S.S.R.)

ANIMATION
Make Mine Music, Walt Disney (United States)

GRAND PRIX FOR PEACE
The Last Chance, Leopold Lindtberg (Switzerland)

CIDALC PRIZE
Epaves, Jacques Yves Cousteau, Frederic Dumas, Philippe Tailliez and Roger Gary (France)

1947

PSYCHOLOGICAL AND LOVE FILM
Antoine et Antoinette, Jacques Becker (France)

ADVENTURE AND DETECTIVE FILM
The Damned, Rene Clement (France)

SOCIAL FILM
Crossfire, Edward Dmytryk (United States)

MUSICAL
Ziegfeld Follies, Vincente Minnelli (United States)

ANIMATED FILM
Dumbo, Ben Sharpsteen for Walt Disney (United States)

1948

The festival was not held due to lack of funding.

1949

GRAND PRIX
The Third Man, Carol Reed (United Kingdom)

BEST ACTOR
Edward G. Robinson, *House of Strangers* (United States)

BEST ACTRESS
Isa Miranda, *The Walls of Malapaga* (France/Italy)

DIRECTION
Rene Clement, *The Walls of Malapaga* (France/Italy)

SCREENPLAY
Virginia Shaler and Eugene Ling, *Lost Boundaries* (United States)

MUSIC
Pueblerina, Emilio Fernandez (Mexico)

DECOR
Oh, Amelia, Claude Autant-Lara (France)

1950

The festival was not held due to lack of funds and other problems in France's film industry.

1951

GRAND PRIX
Miracle in Milan, Vittorio De Sica (Italy)
Miss Julie, Alf Sjoberg (Sweden)

SPECIAL JURY PRIZE
All About Eve, Joseph L. Mankiewicz (United States)

BEST ACTOR
Michael Redgrave, *The Browning Version* (United Kingdom)

BEST ACTRESS
Bette Davis, *All About Eve* (United States)

DIRECTION
Luis Buñuel, *Los Olvidados* (Mexico)

SCREENPLAY
Terence Rattigan, *The Browning Version* (United Kingdom)

CINEMATOGRAPHY
Luis-Maria Beltran, *La Caravelle Isabel Partira ce Soir* (Venezuela)

MUSIC
Joseph Kosma, *Juliette ou la Clef Des Songes* (France)

DECOR
Moussorgsky, Souvorov A. Veksler (U.S.S.R.)

SPECIAL PRIZE FOR ORIGINALITY OF LYRICAL ADAPTATION TO FILM
Tales of Hoffman, Michael Powell and Emeric Pressburger (United Kingdom)

SPECIAL AWARD
To the entire selection of films presented at the festival by Italy

1952

GRAND PRIX
Two Pennyworth of Hope, Renato Castellani (Italy)
Othello, Orson Welles (Morocco)

SPECIAL JURY PRIZE
We Are All Murderers, Andre Cayatte (France)

BEST ACTOR
Marlon Brando, *Viva Zapata!* (United States)

BEST ACTRESS
Lee Grant, *Detective Story* (United States)

DIRECTION
Christian-Jaque, *Fanfan la Tulipe* (France)

SCREENPLAY
Piero Fellini, *Cops and Robbers* (Italy)

PHOTOGRAPHY AND COMPOSITION
Kohei Sugiyama, *A Tale of Genji* (Japan)

MUSIC
Sven Skold, *One Summer of Happiness* (Sweden)

FILM LYRICISM
The Medium, Gian Carlo Menotti (United States)

1953

GRAND PRIX
The Wages of Fear, Henri-Georges Clouzot (France/Italy)

BEST ACTOR
Charles Vanel, *The Wages of Fear* (France/Italy)

BEST ACTRESS
Shirley Booth, *Come Back Little Sheba* (United States)

SCREENPLAY
Luis Berlanga, *Bienvenudo, Mister Marshall* (Spain)

MUSIC
O Cangaceiro, Lima Barreto (Spain)

ADVENTURE FILM
O Cangaceiro, Lima Barreto (Brazil)

ENTERTAINMENT FILM
Lili, Charles Walters (United States)

DRAMATIC FILM
Come Back Little Sheba, Daniel Mann (United States)

MYTHICAL FILM
The White Reindeer, Erik Blomberg (United States)

EXPLORATION FILM
Magia Verde, Gian Gaspare Napolitano (Italy)

COLOR FILM
Magia Verde, Gian Gaspare Napolitano (Italy)

PRIZE FOR GOOD HUMOR
Bienvenudo, Mister Marshall, Luis Berlanga (Spain)

LE MIEUX RACONTE PAR L'IMAGE
The Net, Emilio Fernandez (Mexico)

SPECIAL HOMAGE
To Walt Disney for the entire ensemble of his work
Duende y Misterio del Flamenco, Edgar Neville (Spain)

1954

GRAND PRIX
Gate of Hell, Teinosuke Kinugasa (Japan)

SPECIAL JURY PRIZE
Rene Clement, *Knave of Hearts* (United Kingdom)

INTERNATIONAL PRIZE
The Last Bridge, Helmut Kautner (Austria)
Maria Schell for her performance in *The Last Bridge* (Austria)

NATIONAL RECOGNITION AWARDS
The Living Desert, James Algar for Walt Disney (United States)
Avant le Deluge, Andre Cayatte (France)

Two Acres of Land, Bimal Roy (India)

Neapolitan Carousel, Ettore Gianinni (Italy)

Chronicle of Poor Lovers, Carlo Lizzani (Italy)

Five Boys From Barska Street, Aleksander Ford (Poland)

The Great Adventure, Arne Sucksdorff (Sweden)

The Great Warrior, Skanderberg, Serge Youtkevitch (U.S.S.R.)

SPECIAL RECOGNITION PRIZE
From Here to Eternity, Fred Zinnemann (United States)

1955

PALME D'OR
Marty (United States)

> Particular praise for the following contributions to *Marty:*
> Paddy Chayevsky, screenplay
> Delbert Mann, direction
> Ernest Borgnine and Betsy Blair, performances

SPECIAL JURY PRIZE
The Lost Continent, Leonardo Bonzi, Mario Craveri, Enrico
Gras, F. Lavagnino and G. Moser (Italy)

PERFORMANCES
Spencer Tracy, *Bad Day at Black Rock* (United States)

The ensemble of actors in *The Big Family,* Joseph Heifitz
(U.S.S.R.)

DIRECTION
Sergei Vassiliev, *The Heroes of Shipka* (Bulgaria)

Jules Dassin, *Rififi* (France)

FILM LYRICISM
Romeo and Juliet, L. Arnchtam and L. Lavrovsky (U.S.S.R.)

DRAMATIC FILM
East of Eden, Elia Kazan (United States)

SPECIAL JURY MENTIONS
Baby Naaz, *Boot Polish* (India)

Haya Havarit, *Hill 24 Doesn't Answer* (Israel)

Ladislao Vajda, *Marcelino Pan y Vino* (Spain

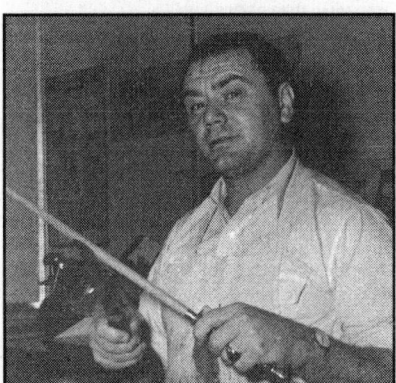

Marty

1956

PALME D'OR
The Silent World, Jacques Yves Cousteau and Louis Malle
(France)

SPECIAL JURY PRIZE
The Mystery of Picasso, Henri-Georges Clouzot (France)

BEST ACTRESS
Susan Hayward, *I'll Cry Tomorrow* (United States)

DIRECTION
Serge Youtkevitch, *Othello* (U.S.S.R.)

POETIC HUMOR FILM
Smiles of a Summer Night, Ingmar Bergman (Sweden)

HUMAN DOCUMENT
Pather Panchali, Satyajit Ray (India)

1957

PALME D'OR
Friendly Persuasion, William Wyler (United States)

SPECIAL JURY PRIZE
Kanal, Andrzej Wajda (Poland)

The Seventh Seal, Ingmar Bergman (Sweden)

SPECIAL PRIZE
The Forty-First, Grigori Chukhrai (U.S.S.R.)

BEST ACTOR
John Kitzmiller, *Valley of Faces* (Yugoslavia)

BEST ACTRESS
Giuletta Masina, *Nights of Cabiria* (Italy/France)

DIRECTION
Robert Bresson, *A Man Escaped* (France)

DOCUMENTARY
The Roof of Japan, Sadao Imamura (Japan)

Qivitoq, Erik Balling (Denmark)

SPECIAL MENTION
Gotoma the Buddha, Rajbans Khanna (India)

COUNTRY SELECTION: FRANCE
He Who Must Die, Jules Dassin

A Man Escaped, Robert Bresson

Toute la Memoire du Monde, Alain Resnais

Noik, Edmond Sechan

1958

PALME D'OR
The Cranes Are Flying, Mikhail Kalatozov
with an Honorary Award to Tatiana Samoilova
for her superb performance (U.S.S.R.)

SPECIAL JURY PRIZE
My Uncle, Jacques Tati (France)

BEST ACTOR
Paul Newman, *The Long Hot Summer* (United States)

BEST ACTRESS
Bibi Andersson, Eva Dahlbeck, Ingrid Thulin and Barbro
Hiort-Af-Ornas for their combined performances in
Brink of Life (Sweden)

DIRECTION
Ingmar Bergman, *Brink of Life* (Sweden)

ORIGINAL SCREENPLAY
Pier Paolo Pasolini, Massimo Franciosa and P. Festa
    Campanile, *Young Husbands* (Italy)

SPECIAL PRIZES
Goha, Jacques Baratier (Tunisia)
Bronze Faces, Bernard Taisant (Switzerland)

FIPRESCI AWARD
Vengeance, Juan Bardem (Spain)

1959

PALME D'OR
Black Orpheus, Marcel Camus (France)

SPECIAL JURY PRIZE
Stars, Konrad Wolf (Bulgaria)

INTERNATIONAL PRIZE
Nazarin, Luis Buñuel (Mexico)

BEST ACTOR
Dean Stockwell, Bradford Dillman and Orson Welles for
    their combined performances in *Compulsion*
    (United States)

BEST ACTRESS
Simone Signoret, *Room at the Top* (United Kingdom)

DIRECTION
The 400 Blows, François Truffaut (France)

COMEDY
Policarpo, Mario Soldati (Italy)

SPECIAL MENTION
The White Heron, Teinosuke Kinugasa (Japan)

FIPRESCI AWARD
Hiroshima Mon Amour, Alain Resnais (France/Japan)
Araya, Margot Benaceraf (Venezuela)

CATHOLIC FILM OFFICE AWARD
The 400 Blows, François Truffaut (France)

FILM WRITERS AWARD
Margerite Duras and Alain Resnais, *Hiroshima Mon Amour*
    (France/Japan)

1960

PALME D'OR
La Dolce Vita, Federico Fellini (Italy)

SPECIAL JURY PRIZES
Ballad of a Soldier, Grigori Chukrai (U.S.S.R.)
Lady With a Pet Dog, Josef Heifitz (U.S.S.R.)
Kagi, Kon Ichikawa (Japan)
L'Avventura, Michelangelo Antonioni (Italy)

BEST ACTRESS
Melina Mercouri, *Never on Sunday* (Greece)
Jeanne Moreau, *Moderato Cantabile* (France)

SPECIAL HOMAGE AWARDS
Ingmar Bergman, *The Virgin Spring* (Sweden)
Luis Buñuel, *The Young One* (Mexico)

La Dolce Vita

1961

PALME D'OR
Viridiana, Luis Buñuel (Spain)
A Long Absence, Henri Colpi (France/Italy)

SPECIAL JURY PRIZE
Mother Joan of the Angels, Jerzy Kawalerowicz (Poland)

BEST ACTOR
Anthony Perkins, *Goodbye Again* (France/United States)

BEST ACTRESS
Sophia Loren, *Two Women* (France/Italy)

DIRECTION
Julia Solntzeva, *History of the Burning Years* (U.S.S.R.)

GARY COOPER AWARD FOR HUMAN VALUES
A Raisin in the Sun, Daniel Petrie (United States)

FIPRESCI AWARDS
Hands in the Trap, Leopoldo Torre Nilsson (Argentina)
Chronicle of a Summer, Jean Rouch (France)

CATHOLIC FILM OFFICE AWARD
The Hoodlum Priest, Irvin Kershner (United States)

NATIONAL SELECTION: ITALY
Nebbia, Raffaele Andreassi
Giovedì: Passegiata, Vincenzo Gamma
Girl With a Suitcase, Valerio Zurlini
Che Gioia Vivere, Rene Clement
The Love Makers, Mauro Bolognini

1962

PALME D'OR
The Given Word, Anselmo Duarte (Brazil)

SPECIAL JURY PRIZE
The Trial of Joan of Arc, Robert Bresson (France)
L'Eclisse, Michelangelo Antonioni (Italy/France)

PERFORMANCES
The combined performances of Katharine Hepburn, Ralph
    Richardson, Jason Robards, Jr. and Dean Stockwell
    in *Long Day's Journey Into Night* (United States)
The combined performances of Rita Tushingham and Murray
    Melvin in *A Taste of Honey* (United Kingdom)

ADAPTATION
Electra, Michael Cacoyannis (Greece)

COMEDY
Divorce — Italian Style, Pietro Germi (Italy)

FIPRESCI AWARD
The Exterminating Angel, Luis Buñuel (Mexico)

CATHOLIC FILM OFFICE AWARD
L'Eclisse, Michelangelo Antonioni (Italy/France)

1963

PALME D'OR
The Leopard, Luchino Visconti (France/Italy)

SPECIAL JURY PRIZE
Harakiri, Masaki Kobayashi (Japan)
A Cat, Vojtech Jasny (Czechoslovakia)

BEST ACTOR
Richard Harris, *This Sporting Life* (United Kingdom)

BEST ACTRESS
Marina Vlady, *The Conjugal Bed* (Italy)

SCREENPLAY
Yves Jamiaque, Dumuitru Carabat and Henri Colpi,
    Codine (Romania)

EVOCATION D'UNWE EPOPEE REVOLUTIONNAIRE
The Optimistic Tragedy (U.S.S.R.)

GARY COOPER AWARD FOR HUMAN VALUES
To Kill a Mockingbird, Robert Mulligan (United States)

FIPRESCI AWARDS
This Sporting Life, Lindsay Anderson (United Kingdom)
Le Joli Mai, Chris Marker (France)

CATHOLIC FILM OFFICE AWARD
The Fiances, Ermanno Olmi (Italy)

1964

PALME D'OR
The Umbrellas of Cherbourg, Jacques Demy
    (France/Germany)

SPECIAL JURY PRIZE
Woman of the Dunes, Hiroshi Teshigahara (Japan)

BEST ACTOR
Antal Pager, *Pacsirta* (Hungary)
Saro Urzi, *Seduced and Abandoned* (Italy)

BEST ACTRESS
Anne Bancroft, *The Pumpkin Eater* (United States)
Barbara Barrie, *One Potato-Two Potato* (United States)

SPECIAL HOMAGE
Andrzej Munk, *The Passenger* (Poland)

SPECIAL JURY MENTION
Jaromil Jires, *Krik* (Czechoslovakia)
Georgui Danelia, *Romance a Moscou* (U.S.S.R.)
Manuel Summers, *La Nina de Luto* (Spain)

FIPRESCI AWARD
The Passenger, Andrzej Munk (Poland)

CATHOLIC FILM OFFICE AWARD
The Umbrellas of Cherbourg, Jacques Demy (France)
Sterile Lives, Nelson Pereira dos Santos (Brazil)

1965

PALME D'OR
The Knack, Richard Lester (United Kingdom)

SPECIAL JURY PRIZE
Kwaidan, Masaki Kobayashi (Japan)

BEST ACTOR AND BEST ACTRESS
Samantha Eggar and Terence Stamp, *The Collector*
    (United States)

DIRECTION
Liviu Ciulei, *The Lost Forest* (Romania)

SCREENPLAY
Ray Rigby, *The Hill* (United Kingdom)
Pierre Schoendoerffer, *317th Section* (France)

SPECIAL JURY MENTIONS
Josef Kroner (Czechoslovakia)
Ida Kaminska (Czechoslovakia)
Vera Kouznetsova (U.S.S.R.)

FIPRESCI PRIZE
Tarahumara, Luis Alcoriza (Mexico)

CATHOLIC FILM OFFICE AWARDS
Yoyo, Pierre Etaix (France)
Tokyo Olympics, Kon Ichikawa (Japan)

1966

PALME D'OR
A Man and a Woman, Claude Lelouch (France)
The Birds, the Bees and the Italians, Pietro Germi
    (France/Italy)

SPECIAL JURY PRIZE
Alfie, Lewis Gilbert (United Kingdom)

BEST ACTOR
Per Oscarsson, *Hunger* (Denmark)

BEST ACTRESS
Vanessa Redgrave, *Morgan!* (United Kingdom)

DIRECTION
Serge Youtkevitch, *Portrait of Lenin* (U.S.S.R.)

DIRECTORIAL DEBUT
Rascoala, Mircea Muresan (Romania)

SPECIAL ACTING MENTION
Toto (Italy)

FIPRESCI PRIZE
Young Torless, Volker Schloendorff (Germany)
The War Is Over, Alain Resnais (France)

CATHOLIC FILM OFFICE AWARD
A Man and a Woman, Claude Lelouch (France)

20TH ANNIVERSARY TRIBUTE
To Orson Welles in recognition of his outstanding
contribution to cinema

1967

PALME D'OR
Blow-Up, Michelangelo Antonioni (United Kingdom/Italy)

SPECIAL JURY PRIZE
Accident, Joseph Losey (United Kingdom)
I Even Met Happy Gypsies, Aleksandar Petrovic (Yugoslavia)

BEST ACTOR
Odded Kotler, *Three Days and a Child* (Israel)

BEST ACTRESS
Pia Degermark, *Elvira Madigan* (Denmark)

DIRECTION
Ferenc Kosa, *Ten Thousand Suns* (Hungary)

SCREENPLAY
Alain Jessua, *The Killing Game* (France)
Elio Petri and Ugo Pirro, *We Still Kill the Old Way* (Italy)

FILM DEBUT
Le Vent des Aures, Mohammed Lakhdar Hamina (Algeria)

SPECIAL HOMAGE AWARD
Robert Bresson

1968

The festival was canceled because of the unstable political climate in Paris.

1969

PALME D'OR
If, Lindsay Anderson (United Kingdom)

SPECIAL JURY PRIZE
Adalen 31, Bo Widerberg (Sweden)

BEST ACTOR
Jean-Louis Trintignant, *Z* (France)

BEST ACTRESS
Vanessa Redgrave, *Isadora* (United Kingdom)

DIRECTION
Antonio das Mortes, Glauber Rocha (Brazil)
All Good Citizens, Vojtech Jasny (Czechoslovakia)

FILM DEBUT
Easy Rider, Dennis Hopper (United States)

JURY PRIZE
Z, Constantin Costa-Gavras (France)

FIPRESCI PRIZE
Andrei Roublev, Andrei Tarkovsky (U.S.S.R.)

1970

PALME D'OR
M*A*S*H, Robert Altman (United States)

SPECIAL JURY PRIZE
Investigation of a Citizen Above Suspicion, Elio Petri (Italy)

BEST ACTOR
Marcello Mastroianni, *Drama of Jealousy* (Italy)

BEST ACTRESS
Ottavia Piccolo, *Metello* (Italy)

DIRECTION
John Boorman, *Leo the Last* (United Kingdom)

FILM DEBUT
Hoa-Binh, Raoul Coutard (France)

JURY PRIZES
The Falcons, Istvan Gal (Hungary)
The Strawberry Statement, Stuart Hagmann (United States)

1971

PALME D'OR
The Go-Between, Joseph Losey (United Kingdom)

SPECIAL JURY PRIZE
Taking Off, Milos Forman (United States)
Johnny Got His Gun, Dalton Trumbo (United States)

BEST ACTOR
Riccardo Cucciolla, *Sacco and Vanzetti* (Italy)

BEST ACTRESS
Kitty Winn, *Panic in Needle Park* (United States)

FILM DEBUT
By Grace Received, Nino Manfredi (Italy)

JURY PRIZE
Love, Karoly Makk with a special mention for
the performances of Lily Darvas and
Mari Torocsik (Hungary)
Joe Hill, Bo Widerberg (Sweden)

25TH ANNIVERSARY PRIZE
To Luchino Visconti for *Death in Venice* (Italy) and his complete oeuvre

1972

PALME D'OR
The Mattei Affair, Francesco Rosi with a Special Jury Mention
for the performance of Gian Maria Volonte (Italy)
The Working Class Go to Heaven, Elio Petri (Italy)

SPECIAL JURY PRIZE
Solaris, Andrei Tarkovsky (U.S.S.R.)

BEST ACTOR
Jean Yanne, *We Will Not Grow Old Together* (France)

BEST ACTRESS
Susannah York, *Images* (Ireland)

DIRECTION
Red Psalm, Miklos Jancso (Hungary)

JURY PRIZE
Slaughterhouse-Five, George Roy Hill (United States)

1973

PALME D'OR
Scarecrow, Jerry Schatzberg (United States)
The Hireling, Alan Bridges (United Kingdom)

SPECIAL JURY PRIZE
The Mother and the Whore, Jean Eustache (France)

Taxi Driver

BEST ACTOR
Giancarlo Giannini, *Love and Anarchy* (Italy)

BEST ACTRESS
Joanne Woodward, *The Effect of Gamma Rays on Man-in-the-Moon Marigolds* (United States)

SPECIAL PRIZE
La Planete Sauvage, Rene Laloux (France)

FILM DEBUT
Jeremy, Arthur Barron (United States)

JURY PRIZE
Hour Glass Sanatorium, Wojciech Has (Poland)
The Invitation, Claude Goretta (Switzerland)

FIPRESCI PRIZE
The Mother and the Whore, Jean Eustache (France)
La Grande Bouffe, Marco Ferreri (France)

1974

PALME D'OR
The Conversation, Francis Ford Coppola (United States)

SPECIAL JURY PRIZE
One Thousand and One Nights, Pier Paolo Pasolini (Italy)

BEST ACTOR
Jack Nicholson, *The Last Detail* (United States)

BEST ACTRESS
Marie-Jose Nat, *Les Violons du Bal* (France)

SCREENPLAY
Hal Barwood and Matthew Robbins, *The Sugarland Express* (United States)

TECHNIQUE
Mahler, Ken Russell (United Kingdom)

JURY PRIZE
Carlos Saura, *Cousin Angelica* (Spain)

SPECIAL TRIBUTE
To Charles Boyer for his portrayal in *Stavisky* (France)

FIPRESCI PRIZE
Lancelot of the Lake, Robert Bresson (France)
Fear Eats the Soul, Rainer Werner Fassbiner (Germany)

1975

PALME D'OR
Chronicle of the Burning Years, Mohammed Lakhdar-Hamina (Algeria)

SPECIAL JURY PRIZE
Every Man for Himself and God Against All, Werner Herzog (Germany)

BEST ACTOR
Vittorio Gassman, *Scent of a Woman* (Italy)

BEST ACTRESS
Valerie Perrine, *Lenny* (United States)

DIRECTION
Constantin Costa-Gavras, *Special Section* (France)
Michel Brault, *The Order* (Canada)

HONORABLE MENTION
Delphine Seyrig

FIPRESCI PRIZE
Every Man for Himself and God Against All, Werner Herzog (Germany)

ECUMENICAL PRIZE (MIXED CATHOLIC AND PROTESTANT JURY)
Every Man for Himself and God Against All, Werner Herzog (Germany)

1976

PALME D'OR
Taxi Driver, Martin Scorsese (United States)

SPECIAL JURY PRIZE
Cria Cuervos, Carlos Saura (Spain)
The Marquise of O, Eric Rohmer (Germany/France)

BEST ACTOR
José Luis Gomez, *Pascual Duarte* (Spain)

BEST ACTRESS
Dominique Sanda, *The Inheritance* (Italy)
Mari Toroscik, *Mrs. Dery, Where Are You?* (Hungary)

DIRECTION
Ettore Scola, *Ugly, Dirty, and Mean* (Italy)

FIPRESCI PRIZE
Ferdinand the Strongman, Alexander Kluge (Germany)
Kings of the Road, Wim Wenders (Germany)

1977

PALME D'OR
Padre Padrone, Paolo and Vittorio Taviani (Italy)

BEST ACTOR
Fernando Rey, *Elisa, My Love* (Spain)

BEST ACTRESS
Shelley Duvall, *Three Women* (United States)
Monique Mercure, *J. A. Martin, Photographer* (Canada)

MUSICAL SCORE
Norman Whitfield, *Car Wash* (United States)

FILM DEBUT
The Duellists, Ridley Scott (United Kingdom)

FIPRESCI PRIZE
Padre Padrone, Paolo and Vittorio Taviani (Italy)

ECUMENICAL AWARD (MIXED CATHOLIC AND PROTESTANT JURY)
The Lacemaker, Claude Goretta (Switzerland)

1978

PALME D'OR
The Tree of Wooden Clogs, Ermanno Olmi (Italy)

SPECIAL JURY PRIZE
Bye Bye Monkey, Marco Ferreri (Italy)
The Shout, Jerzy Skolimowski (United Kingdom)

BEST ACTOR
Jon Voight, *Coming Home* (United States)

BEST ACTRESS
Jill Clayburgh, *An Unmarried Woman* (United States)
Isabelle Huppert, *Violette* (France)

DIRECTION
Nagisa Oshima, *Empire of Passion* (Japan)

FIPRESCI PRIZE
Man of Marble, Andrzej Wajda (Poland)
Smell of Wild Flowers, Srdan Karanovic (Italy)

ECUMENICAL AWARD (MIXED CATHOLIC AND PROTESTANT JURY)
The Tree of Wooden Clogs, Ermanno Olmi (Italy)

1979

PALME D'OR
The Tin Drum, Volker Schloendorff (Germany)
Apocalypse Now, Francis Ford Coppola (United States)

SPECIAL JURY PRIZE
Siberaid, Andrei Mikhalkov Kontchalovksy (U.S.S.R.)

BEST ACTOR
Jack Lemmon, *The China Syndrome* (United States)

Sally Field, *Norma Rae*

BEST ACTRESS
Sally Field, *Norma Rae* (United States)

DIRECTION
Terrence Malick, *Days of Heaven* (United States)

BEST SUPPORTING ACTOR
Stefano Madia, *Dear Papa* (Italy)

BEST SUPPORTING ACTRESS
Eva Mattes, *Woyzeck* (Germany)

CAMERA D'OR FOR FILM DEBUT
Northern Lights, John Hanson and Rob Nilsson
    (United States)

TECHNIQUE
Norma Rae, Martin Ritt (United States)

SPECIAL HOMAGE
Miklos Jancso in recognition of his ensemble of work

FIPRESCI PRIZE
COMPETING FILM
Apocalypse Now, Francis Ford Coppola (United States)
NON-COMPETING FILMS
Angi Vera, Pal Gabor (Hungary)
Black Jack, Ken Loach (United Kingdom)

ECUMENICAL AWARD (MIXED CATHOLIC AND PROTESTANT JURY)
Rough Treatment, Andrzej Wajda (Poland)

1980

PALME D'OR
Kagemusha, Akira Kurosawa (Japan)
All That Jazz, Bob Fosse (United States)

SPECIAL JURY PRIZE
Mon Oncle D'Amerique, Alain Resnais (France)

BEST ACTOR
Michel Piccoli, *Leap Into the Void* (Italy)

BEST ACTRESS
Anouk Aimeé, *Leap Into the Void* (Italy)

SUPPORTING ACTOR
Jack Thompson, *Breaker Morant* (Austria)

SUPPORTING ACTRESS
Carla Gravina, *The Terrace* (Italy)
Milena Dravic, *Special Therapy* (Yugoslavia)

DIRECTION
Krzysztof Zanussi, *The Constant Factor* (Poland)

SCREENPLAY
Ettore Scola, Agenore Incrocci and Furio Scarpelli, *The Terrace* (Italy)

CAMERA D'OR FOR FILM DEBUT
Historie d'Adrien, Jean-Pierre Denis (France)

TECHNIQUE
Le Risque de Vivre, Gerald Calderon (France)

FIPRESCI PRIZE
Mon Oncle D'Amerique, Alain Resnais (France)
Provincial Actors, Agniezka Holland (Poland)

1981

PALME D'OR
Man of Iron, Andrzej Wajda (Poland)

SPECIAL JURY PRIZE
Light Years Away, Alain Tanner (France/Switzerland)

BEST ACTOR
Ugo Tognazzi, *The Tragedy of a Ridiculous Man* (Italy)

BEST ACTRESS
Isabelle Adjani, *Quartet* (United Kingdom/France) and
    Possession (France/Germany)

SUPPORTING ACTOR
Ian Holm, *Chariots of Fire* (United Kingdom)

SUPPORTING ACTRESS
Elena Solovei, *Blood Group Zero* (U.S.S.R.)

SCREENPLAY
Istvan Szabo and Peter Dobai, *Mephisto* (Hungary)

**ARTISTIC CONTRIBUTION TO THE POETICS
OF CINEMA**
John Boorman, *Excalibur* (Ireland)

CAMERA D'OR FOR FILM DEBUT
Desperado City, Vadim Glowna (Germany)

TECHNIQUE
Les Uns et les Autres, Claude Lelouch (France)

CONTEMPORARY CINEMA
Looks and Smiles, Ken Loach (United Kingdom)
Neige, Juliet Berto and Jean-Henri Roger (France)

FIPRESCI PRIZE
Mephisto, Istvan Szabo (Hungary)

1982

PALME D'OR
Missing, Constantin Costa-Gavras (United States)
Yol, Yilmaz Guney (Turkey)

SPECIAL JURY PRIZE
Night of the Shooting Stars, Paolo and Vittorio Taviani (Italy)

BEST ACTOR
Jack Lemmon, *Missing* (United States)

BEST ACTRESS
Jadwiga Jankowska-Cieslak, *Another Way* (Hungary)

DIRECTION
Werner Herzog, *Fitzcarraldo* (Germany)

SCREENPLAY
Jerzy Skolimowski, *Moonlighting* (United Kingdom)

ARTISTIC CONTRIBUTION
For the photography of Bruno Nuytten in *Invitation au Voyage*
    (France)

CAMERA D'OR FOR FILM DEBUT
Mourir a Trente Ans, Romain Goupil (France)

TECHNIQUE
Passion, Raoul Coutard, photography (France)

FIPRESCI PRIZE
Yol, Yilmaz Guney (Turkey)

SPECIAL AWARDS
Another Way, Karoly Makk (Hungary)
Les Fleurs Sauvages (Canada)

SPECIAL 35TH ANNIVERSARY AWARD
Michelangelo Antonioni, *Identification of a Woman* (Italy)

1983

PALME D'OR
The Ballad of Narayama, Shohei Imamura (Japan)

SPECIAL JURY PRIZE
Monty Python — The Meaning of Life, Terry Jones (United
    Kingdom)

GRAND PRIX DU CINEMA DE CREATION
Robert Bresson, *L'Argent* (France)
Andrei Tarkovsky, *Nostalghia* (Italy)

BEST ACTOR
Gian Maria Volonte, *The Death of Mario Ricci*
    (Switzerland/France)

BEST ACTRESS
Hanna Schygulla, *The Story of Piera* (Italy)

ARTISTIC CONTRIBUTION
Carmen, Carlos Saura, screenplay (Spain)

CAMERA D'OR FOR FILM DEBUT
La Princesse, Pal Erdoss (Hungary)

TECHNIQUE
Carmen, Carlos Saura (Spain)

JURY PRIZE
Kharij, Mrinal Sen (India)

FIPRESCI PRIZE
Nostalghia, Andrei Tarkovsky (Italy)
Szerencses Daniel, Pal Sandor (Hungary)

1984

PALME D'OR
Paris, Texas, Wim Wenders (Germany)

SPECIAL JURY PRIZE
Naplo, Marta Meszaros (Hungary)

BEST ACTOR
Alfredo Landa and Francisco Rabal, *The Holy Innocents*
    (Spain)

BEST ACTRESS
Helen Mirren, *Cal* (Ireland)

DIRECTION
Bertrand Tavernier, *A Sunday in the Country* (France)

SCREENPLAY
Theo Angelopoulos, Theo Valtinos and Tonino Guerra, *Vogage
    to Cythera* (Greece)

ARTISTIC CONTRIBUTION
Peter Biziou for the cinematography of *Another Country*
    (United Kingdom)

CAMERA D'OR FOR FILM DEBUT
Stranger Than Paradise, Jim Jarmusch (United States)

TECHNIQUE
The Element of Crime, Lars von Trier (Denmark)

The Mission

FIPRESCI PRIZE
Paris, Texas, Wim Wenders (Germany/France)
Voyage to Cythera, Theo Angelopoulos (Greece)

1985

PALME D'OR
When Father Was Away on Business, Emir Kusturica
(Yugoslavia)

SPECIAL JURY PRIZE
Birdy, Alan Parker (United States)

BEST ACTOR
William Hurt, *Kiss of the Spider Woman* (United States/Brazil)

BEST ACTRESS
Norma Aleandro, *The Official Story* (Argentina)
Cher, *Mask* (United States)

DIRECTION
André Téchiné, *Rendez-vous* (France)

ARTISTIC CONTRIBUTION
John Bailey, visual concept; Eiko Ishioka, set design; and Philip
Glass, music, *Mishima* (United States)

CAMERA D'OR FOR FILM DEBUT
Oriane, Fina Torres (Venezuela/France)

TECHNIQUE
Insignificance, Nicholas Roeg (United States)

JURY PRIZE
Colonel Redl, Istvan Szabo (Hungary/Germany/Austria)

PALME D'OR FOR SHORT FILM
Marriage, Slav Bakalov and Roman Petkov

FIPRESCI PRIZE
COMPETING FILM
When Father Was Away on Business, Emir Kusturica
(Yugoslavia)

NON-COMPETING FILM
The Purple Rose of Cairo, Woody Allen (United States)

1986

PALME D'OR
The Mission, Roland Joffe (United Kingdom)

SPECIAL JURY PRIZE
The Sacrifice, Andrei Tarkovsky (Sweden)

BEST ACTOR
Michel Blanc, *Tenue de Soiree* (France)
Bob Hoskins, *Mona Lisa* (United Kingdom)

BEST ACTRESS
Barbara Sukowa, *Rosa Luxemburg* (Germany)
Fernanda Torres, *Speak to Me of Love* (Brazil)

DIRECTION
Martin Scorsese, *After Hours* (United States)

ARTISTIC CONTRIBUTION
Sven Nykvist, cinematographer, *The Sacrifice* (Sweden)

CAMERA D'OR FOR FILM DEBUT
Claire Devers, *Noir et Blanc* (France)

TECHNIQUE
The Mission, Roland Joffe (United Kingdom)

JURY PRIZE
Therèsè, Alain Cavalier (France)

PALME D'OR FOR SHORT FILM
Peel, Jane Campion (Australia)

JURY PRIZE FOR SHORT FILM (ANIMATION)
Gaidouk, Y. Katsap and L. Gorokhov (U.S.S.R.)

JURY PRIZE FOR SHORT FILM (FICTION)
The Little Magicians, Vincent Mercier and Yves Robert
(Switzerland)

1987

PALME D'OR
Under Satan's Sun, Maurice Pialat (France)

SPECIAL JURY PRIZE
Repentance, Tengiz Abuladze (U.S.S.R.)

BEST ACTOR
Marcello Mastroianni, *Dark Eyes* (Italy)

BEST ACTRESS
Barbara Hershey, *Shy People* (United States)

DIRECTION
Wim Wenders, *Wings of Desire* (Germany/France)

ARTISTIC CONTRIBUTION
Stanley Myers, music, *Prick Up Your Ears* (United Kingdom)

CAMERA D'OR FOR FILM DEBUT
Nana Dzhordzhadze, *My English Grandfather* (U.S.S.R.)

TECHNIQUE
Le Cinema dans les Yeux, Gilles Jacob and Laurent Jacob
(France)

JURY PRIZE
Souleymane Cisse, *Yeelen (La Lumière)* (Mali)
Rentaro Mikuni, *Shinran* (Japan)

PALME D'OR FOR SHORT FILM
Palisade, Laurie McInnes

40TH ANNIVERSARY PRIZE
Federico Fellini, *Intervista* (Italy)

1988

PALME D'OR
Pelle the Conqueror, Bille August (Denmark/Sweden)

SPECIAL JURY PRIZE
A World Apart, Chris Menges (United States)

BEST ACTOR
Forest Whitaker, *Bird* (United States)

BEST ACTRESS
Barbara Hershey, Jodhi May and Linda Mvusi, *A World Apart*
(United States)

DIRECTION
Fernando E. Solanas, *The South* (Argentina)

ARTISTIC COLLABORATION
Peter Greenaway, *Drowning by Numbers* (United Kingdom)

CAMERA D'OR FOR FILM DEBUT
Salaam, Bombay!, Mira Nair (United Kingdom/India)

TECHNIQUE
Bird, Clint Eastwood (United States)

JURY PRIZE
Krzysztof Kieslowski, *Thou Shall Not Kill* (Poland)

PALME D'OR FOR SHORT FILM
Fioritures, Gary Bardine (U.S.S.R.)

JURY PRIZE FOR SHORT FILM (ANIMATION)
Ab Ovo/Traces de Sable, Ferenc Cako

JURY PRIZE FOR SHORT FILM (FICTION)
Physical Sculpture, Yann Piquer and Jean-Marie Maddeddu

FIPRESCI PRIZE
BEST OFFICIAL FILM
Thou Shall Not Kill, Krzysztof Kieslowski (Poland)
Hotel Terminus, Marcel Ophuls (France)
BEST UNOFFICIAL FILM
Distant Voices, Still Lives, Terence Davies (United Kingdom)

1989

PALME D'OR
sex, lies and videotape, Steven Soderbergh (United States)

SPECIAL JURY PRIZE
Trop Belle Pour Toi, Bertrand Blier (France)
Cinéma Paradiso, Giuseppe Tornatore (Italy/France)

BEST ACTOR
James Spader, *sex, lies and videotape* (United States)

BEST ACTRESS
Meryl Streep, *A Cry in the Dark* (United States/Australia)

DIRECTION
Emir Kusturica, *Time of the Gypsies* (Yugoslavia)

ARTISTIC CONTRIBUTION
Jim Jarmusch, *Mystery Train* (United States)

CAMERA D'OR FOR FILM DEBUT
My Twentieth Century, Ildiko Enyedi (Hungary)

TECHNIQUE
Black Rain, Shohei Imamura (Japan)

JURY PRIZE
Jesus of Montreal, Denys Arcand (Canada/France)

PALME D'OR FOR SHORT FILM
50 Years, Gilles Carle, representing the continuing efforts of
the National Film Board of Canada in the area of short film

1990

PALME D'OR
Wild at Heart, David Lynch (United States)

GRAND PRIX (TIE)
Shi no Toge, Kohei Oguri
Tilaï, Idrissa Ouedraogo (Burkina Faso/Switzerland/France)

BEST ACTOR
Gérard Depardieu, *Cyrano de Bergerac* (France)

BEST ACTRESS
Krystyna Janda, *Interrogation* (Poland)

sex, lies and videotape

DIRECTION
Pavel Lounguine, *Taxi Blues* (U.S.S.R./France)

ARTISTIC CONTRIBUTION
Gleb Panfilov, *Matj (Zaprechtchionnye Lioudi)* (U.S.S.R.)

CAMERA D'OR FOR FILM DEBUT
Freeze, Die, Come to Life, Vitali Kanevski (U.S.S.R.)

TECHNIQUE
Cyrano de Bergerac, Pierre Lhomme, director of photography
(France)

JURY PRIZE
Hidden Agenda, Ken Loach (United Kingdom)

PALME D'OR FOR SHORT FILM
The Lunch Date, Adam Davidson

FIPRESCI PRIZE
Shi no Toge, Kohei Oguri (Japan)

FIPRESCI SPECIAL PRIZE
Manoel de Oliveira for his body of work

1991

PALME D'OR
Barton Fink, Joel Coen and Ethan Coen (United States)

GRAND PRIX
La Belle Noiseuse, Jacques Rivette (France)

BEST ACTOR
John Turturro, *Barton Fink* (United States)

BEST ACTRESS
Irène Jacob, *The Double Life of Veronique* (Poland/France)

DIRECTION
Joel Coen, *Barton Fink* (United States)

BEST SUPPORTING ROLE
Samuel Jackson, *Jungle Fever* (United States)

CAMERA D'OR FOR FILM DEBUT
Toto the Hero, Jaco van Dormael (Belgium/France/Germany)

TECHNIQUE
Europa, Lars von Trier (Denmark)

JURY PRIZE
Europa, Lars von Trier (Denmark)
Hors la Vie, Maroun Bagdadi (France/Italy/Germany)

PALME D'OR FOR SHORT FILM
Avec les Mains en l'Air, Mitko Panov (Yugoslavia)

JURY PRIZE FOR SHORT FILM
Push Comes to Shove, Bill Plympton (United States)

FIPRESCI PRIZE
The Double Life of Veronique, Krzysztof Kieslowski
   (Poland/France)

1992

PALME D'OR
The Best Intentions, Bille August (Sweden)

GRAND PRIX
Il Ladro di Bambini (Stolen Children), Gianni Amelio
   (Italy/France)

BEST ACTOR
Tim Robbins, *The Player* (United States)

BEST ACTRESS
Pernilla August, *The Best Intentions* (Sweden)

DIRECTION
Robert Altman, *The Player* (United States)

CAMERA D'OR FOR FILM DEBUT
Mac, John Turturro (United States)

TECHNIQUE
El Viaje, Fernando Solanas (Argentina/France)

JURY PRIZE
El Sol Del Membrillo, Victor Erice (Spain)
An Independent Life, Vitali Kanevski (Russia)

PALME D'OR FOR SHORT FILM
Omnibus, Sam Karmann (France)

SPECIAL JURY PRIZE FOR SHORT FILM
La Sensation, Manuel Poutte (Belgium)

FIPRESCI PRIZE
El Sol del Membrillo, Victor Erice (Spain)

45TH ANNIVERSARY PRIZE
Howards End, James Ivory (United Kingdom)

1993

PALME D'OR
The Piano, Jane Campion (Australia/France)
Farewell, My Concubine, Chen Kaige (China/Hong Kong)

GRAND PRIX
Faraway, So Close!, Wim Wenders (Germany)

BEST ACTOR
David Thewlis, *Naked* (United Kingdom)

BEST ACTRESS
Holly Hunter, *The Piano* (Australia/France)

DIRECTION
Mike Leigh, *Naked* (United Kingdom)

CAMERA D'OR FOR FILM DEBUT
The Scent of Green Papaya, Tran Anh Hung (France/Vietnam)

TECHNIQUE
Mazeppa, Jean Gargonne and Vincent Arnardi (France)

JURY PRIZE
The Puppetmaster, Hou Hsiao Hsien (Taiwan)
Raining Stones, Ken Loach (United Kingdom)

SPECIAL MENTION
Friends, Elaine Proctor (South Africa)

PALME D'OR FOR SHORT FILM
Coffee and Cigarettes, Jim Jarmusch (United States)

FIPRESCI PRIZE
Farewell, My Concubine, Chen Kaige (China)

1994

PALME D'OR
Pulp Fiction, Quentin Tarantino (United States)

GRAND PRIX
Burnt by the Sun, Nikita Mikhalkov (Russia/France)
To Live, Zhang Yimou (China/Hong Kong)

BEST ACTOR
Ge You, *To Live* (China/Hong Kong)

BEST ACTRESS
Virna Lisi, *Queen Margot* (France)

DIRECTION
Nanni Moretti, *Caro Diario* (Italy)

SCREENPLAY
Michel Blanc, *Grosse Fatigue* (France)

JURY PRIZE
Queen Margot, Patrice Chéreau (France)

CAMERA D'OR FOR FILM DEBUT
Petits Arrangements Avec les Morts, Pascale Ferran
   (France)

SPECIAL MENTION
Les Silences du Palais, Moufida Tlatli (Tunisia)

TECHNIQUE
Grosse Fatigue, Pitof (France)

PALME D'OR FOR SHORT FILM
El Héroe, Carlos Carrera (Mexico)

SPECIAL JURY PRIZE FOR SHORT FILM
Lemming Aid, Grant Lahood

The Best Conservative Movies

Spencer Warren compiled a list of the Best Conservative Movies for the October 24, 1994 issue of *National Review*. The films he selected honor family values, celebrate the American Dream and reveal the evils of Communism.

Best Pictures Celebrating Religion and Faith
A Man for All Seasons (1966)
Chariots of Fire (1981)
Thérèse (1986)
King of Kings (1927)
The Ten Commandments (1956)
The Sign of the Cross (1932)

Best Scenes Dramatizing Faith
Johnny Belinda (1948)
Quo Vadis? (1950)

**Best Pictures Indicting the Spiritual
Barrenness of Hedonistic Yuppieism**
Carnal Knowledge (1971)
Ten (1979)

Best Picture Indicting the Sixties Counterculture
Forrest Gump (1994)

Best Picture Dramatizing Individual Conscience
On the Waterfront (1954)

Best Pictures About Personal Redemption
Tender Mercies (1983)
Three Godfathers (1948)

Best Picture About the Relation of Property to the Human Soul
The Bicycle Thief (1949)

**Best Picture About Personal Achievement
Against Heavy Odds**
My Left Foot (1989)

Best Pictures About Inner-City Youth Overcoming Heavy Odds
Stand and Deliver (1988)
Lean on Me (1989)

Best Pictures Celebrating Family Life
Meet Me in St. Louis (1944)
Little Women (1933)

Best Scene Celebrating Family Life
Opening scene in *Since You Went Away* (1944)

Best Baby Scene
Penny Serenade (1941)

Best Pictures Commemorating Tradition and Community
How Green Was My Valley (1941)
Fort Apache (1947)
She Wore a Yellow Ribbon (1948)
Rio Grande (1950)
The Quiet Man (1952)
The Life and Death of Colonel Blimp (1943)
A Canterbury Tale (1944)
I Know Where I'm Going (1945)

Best Conservative Animal Pictures
Dumbo (1941)
The Yearling (1946)

Special Lifetime Achievement
Frank Capra (1897–1991)

Best Picture Celebrating the American Dream
An American Romance (1944)

Best Picture Commemorating the Settling of America
My Darling Clementine (1946)

Best Scene of the American Idea
Since You Went Away (1944)

Best Picture About Defending America
Sergeant York (1941)

Best Fourth of July Movie
Yankee Doodle Dandy (1942)

Pictures to Make the Patriotic Blood Boil
The Hanoi Hilton (1987)
Heartbreak Ridge (1986)
Rambo: First Blood Part II (1985)
The Deer Hunter (1979)
Red Dawn (1984)
Thirty Seconds Over Tokyo (1944)
Wake Island (1942)

Winston Churchill's Favorite Movie
That Hamilton Woman (1941)

Ronald Reagan's Greatest Movies
King's Row (1942)
Knute Rockne — All American (1940)

Best Pictures Depicting the Evils of Communism
Repentance (1987)
The Inner Circle (1992)

Best Picture Predicting the Collapse of Communism
Ninotchka (1939)

Best Pictures Depicting the Inhumanity of Mass Revolution
Marie Antoinette (1938)
A Tale of Two Cities (1935)
Viva Villa! (1934)
Knight Without Armor (1937)

Best Pictures on the Limits of Good Intentions
There Was a Crooked Man (1971)
Heavens Above (1963)
Forbidden Planet (1956)

Best Movie Critique of Journalism
The Big Carnival (1951)

Yankee Doodle Dandy

Film Comment's Guilty Pleasures

Guilty Pleasures began when Richard Corliss, then-editor of *Film Comment*, needed a *New Times* filler column during a slow movie season in May 1978. It was an annotated list of 10 films — among them *The Bobo, School Girl, Tenth Avenue Angel, Unknown World* — "films you hear universally reviled, if they're ever discussed at all, until your small, cracking voice can be heard saying, 'Well, I liked it.' " Corliss transferred the idea to *Film Comment* that summer; the first contributors were Roger Ebert, Martin Scorsese and David Newman, and the feature has continued irregularly since then. Some contributors fessed up; others picked fights. Here's a selection.

The Trip

Joe Bob Briggs
Hundra (1983)
White Star (1985)
How to Make a Doll (1968)
The Hills Have Eyes (1977)
Billy Jack (1971)
Caged Heat (1974)
The Wild Angels (1966)
The Trip (1967)
Naughty Dallas (1964)
Funny Girl (1968)

Vincent Canby
Tarzan, the Ape Man (1932)
The Last Days of Pompeii (1935)
The Sign of the Cross (1932)
The Adventures of Robin Hood (1938)
Death Takes a Holiday (1934)
Topper (1937)
Mom and Dad (1944)
Rain (1932)
Captain From Castile (1947)
Ecstasy (1933)

Joe Dante
Attack of the 50 Ft. Woman (1958)
Blood and Black Lace (1964)
Confessions of an Opium Eater (1962)
Exorcist II: The Heretic (1977)
The Sadist (1962)
Frankenstein Meets the Wolf Man (1943)
Invaders From Mars (1952)
The Gamma People (1955)
Truck Turner (1974)
Long John Silver (1954)
It's a Gift (1934)
Tomb of Ligeia (1965)

Brian De Palma
El Topo (1971)
The Naked Kiss (1964)
White Dog (1982)
Homicidal (1961)
The Tenant (1976)
David Holzman's Diary (1968)
Night Dreams (1981)
Nightmare Alley (1947)
Two Rode Together (1961)
Get Carter (1971)
Savage Grace (1985)
The Damned (1969)
Ludwig (1973)

Christopher Durang
Going My Way (1944)
The Song of Bernadette (1943)
The Bells of St. Mary's (1945)
The Nun's Story (1959)
There's No Business Like Show Business (1954)
Woman's World (1954)
Pope Joan (1972)
Teorema (1968)
Until They Sail (1957)
Since You Went Away (1943)
Waterloo Bridge (1940)
Strangers When We Meet (1960)

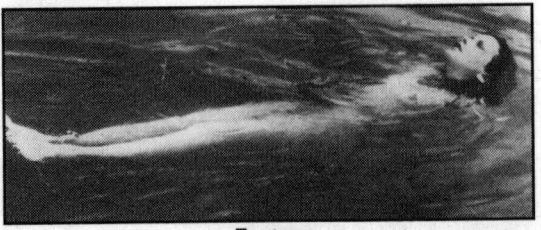

Ecstasy

Stephen King

Bring Me the Head of Alfredo Garcia (1974)
Bloody Mama (1970)
Killers Three (1968)
Sorcerer (1977)
The Horror of Party Beach (1964)
The Amityville Horror (1979)
The Wild Angels (1966)
Suspiria (1977)
Night of the Juggler (1980)

John Milius

The Wild One (1953)
The Losers (1970)
The Texas Chainsaw Massacre (1974)
Return to Paradise (1953)

Andrew Sarris

Sweet Adeline (1935)
South Riding (1937)
Mr. Lucky (1943)
The Adventuress (1947)
Love Letters (1945)
The Clouded Yellow (1951)
My Foolish Heart (1949)
Music for Millions (1944)
Her Highness and the Bellboy (1945)
Two Sisters From Boston (1946)
Miss Tatlock's Millions (1948)
I Know Where I'm Going (1947)
Vacation From Marriage (1945)
I Married an Angel (1942)

Paul Schrader

Scorpio Rising (1963)
Wavelength (1983)
Two Thousand Maniacs (1964)
The Heart Is a Rebel (1958)
True Heart Suzie (1919)
Decision at Sundown (1957)
The Brain That Wouldn't Die (1963)
Peeping Tom (1969)
I, the Jury (1953)
Last Year at Marienbad (1961)
Reflections in a Golden Eye (1967)
Abbott and Costello Go to Mars (1953)

Martin Scorsese

Land of the Pharaohs (1955)
Khartoum (1966)
The Ten Commandments (1956)
The Silver Chalice (1954)
Hell's Angels (1930)
The Counterfeit Traitor (1962)
Play Dirty (1969)
Twelve O'Clock High (1949)

Death Race 2000

In Harm's Way (1965)
Lady in the Dark (1944)
My Dream Is Yours (1949)
The Man I Love (1946)
Always Leave Them Laughing (1949)
The Road to Zanzibar (1941)
Blue Skies (1946)
Lost in a Harem (1944)
Abbott and Costello Go to Mars (1953)
House of Wax (1953)
The Uninvited (1944)
Frankenstein Created Woman (1967)
Exorcist II: The Heretic (1977)
One-Eyed Jacks (1961)
I Walk Alone (1947)
Night and the City (1950)
Station Six — Sahara (1963)
Dark of the Sun (1968)
Guns Don't Argue (1957)
Murder by Contract (1958)
The Magic Box (1951)

Julia Sweeney

Mahogany (1975)
The Parent Trap (1961)
The Trouble With Angels (1966)
Yours, Mine and Ours (1968)
The Singing Nun (1966)
Bless the Beasts and the Children (1971)
Brother Sun, Sister Moon (1973)
Divorce American Style (1967)
How to Save a Marriage and Ruin Your Life (1968)
The Last Married Couple in America (1980)
A Touch of Class (1973)
The Harrad Experiment (1973)
For Singles Only (1968)
Cactus Flower (1969)
Bob & Carol & Ted & Alice (1969)
How to Commit Marriage (1969)
The Love Bug (1969)
Herbie Rides Again (1974)

John Waters

Interiors (1978)
The films of Marguerite Duras
Brink of Life (1958)
Night Games (1966)
Teorema (1968)
Salo (1977)
A Cold Wind in August (1961)
Mademoiselle (1966)
Lancelot du Lac (1974)
Anything by Fassbinder

James Woods

Zontar, the Thing From Venus (1966)
R.P.M. (1970)
Believe in Me (1971)
Death Race 2000 (1975)
Gidget movies
Prime Cut (1972)
Earthquake (1973)
Dreamer (1978)
PT 109 (1963)
Fantastic Voyage (1966)

Robert Zemeckis

Macabre (1958)
House on Haunted Hill (1958)
The Tingler (1959)
13 Ghosts (1960)
I Saw What You Did (1965)
Two on a Guillotine (1965)
You'll Like My Mother (1972)
The Texas Chainsaw Massacre (1974)
The Beginning of the End (1957)
Nevada Smith (1960)
Hell Is for Heroes (1962)
The Great Escape (1963)
Where Eagles Dare (1969)

The Hollywood Walk of Fame

The Hollywood Walk of Fame is a permanent tribute to the entertainment industry's most famous and influential figures. More than 2,000 bronze stars line the Walk, which covers 2 1/2 miles of sidewalk on Hollywood Boulevard and Vine Street. Inscribed into each star is the person's name and the field or fields in which he or she was honored. Criteria for inclusion include achievement, community service and the promise to attend the dedication ceremony. The Walk of Fame Committee dedicates between 15 and 20 stars each year.

Gracie Allen

A

Abbott, Bud: *movies, radio, TV*
Abdul, Paula: *music*
Ackerman, Harry: *TV*
Acord, Art: *movies*
Acuff, Roy: *music*
Adoree, Renee: *movies*
Aherne, Brian: *TV*
Ahn, Philip: *movies*
Albanese, Licia: *music*
Albert, Eddie: *TV*
Albertson, Frank: *movies*
Albertson, Jack: *TV*
Aldrin, Edwin (Buzz): *TV*
Allen, Debbie: *TV*
Allen, Fred: *radio, TV*
Allen, Gracie: *TV*
Allen, Rex: *movies*
Allen, Steve: *radio, TV*
Alexander, Ben: *movies, TV*
Allison, Fran: *TV*
Allyson, June: *movies*
Alpert, Herb: *music*
Alvarado, Don: *movies*
Ameche, Don: *radio, TV*
Ames, Adrienne: *movies*
Amsterdam, Morey: *movies*
Anderson, Bronco Billy: *movies*
Anderson, Leroy: *music*
Anderson, Marian: *music*
Anderson, Mary: *movies*
Andrews Sisters, The: *music*
Andrews, Julie: *movies*
Angel, Heather: *movies*
Anka, Paul: *movies*
Ansara, Michael: *TV*

Anthony, Ray: *music*
Arbuckle, Roscoe: *movies*
Archerd, Army: *TV*
Arden, Eve: *radio, TV*
Arkoff, Samuel Z.: *movies*
Arlen, Richard: *movies*
Arliss, George: *movies*
Armstrong, Louis: *movies*
Armstrong, Neil: *TV*
Arnaz, Desi: *movies, TV*
Arness, James: *TV*
Arnold, Eddy: *radio*
Arnold, Edward: *music*
Arnold, Roseanne: *TV*
Arquette, Cliff: *radio*
Arthur, Jean: *movies*
Arzner, Dorothy: *movies*
Asner, Edward: *TV*
Astaire, Fred: *movies*
Asther, Nils: *movies*
Astor, Mary: *movies*
Austin, Gene: *music*
Autry, Gene: *movies, music, radio, TV, theater*
Ayres, Agnes: *movies*
Ayres, Lew: *movies, radio*

B

Bacall, Lauren: *movies*
Backus, Jim: *TV*
Bacon, Lloyd: *movies*
Baggot, King: *movies*
Bailey, Jack: *radio, TV*
Bailey, Pearl: *music*
Bainter, Fay: *movies*
Baker, Anita: *music*
Baker, Art: *radio*
Baker, Carroll: *movies*
Baker, Kenny: *radio*
Baker, Phil: *Radio*
Ball, Lucille: *movies, TV*
Bancroft, Anne: *TV*
Bankhead, Tallulah: *movies*
Banky, Vilma: *movies*
Bara, Theda: *movies*
Bari, Lynn: *movies, TV*
Barker, Bob: *TV*
Barnes, Binnie: *movies*
Barrie, Mona: *movies*
Barrie, Wendy: *movies*
Barriscale, Bessie: *movies*

Barron, Blue: *music*
Barry, Gene: *theater*
Barrymore, Ethel: *movies*
Barrymore, John: *movies*
Barrymore, John Drew: *TV*
Barrymore, Lionel: *movies, radio*
Barthelmes, Richard: *movies*
Bartholomew, Freddie: *movies*
Barty, Billy: *TV*
Basehart, Richard: *movies*
Basie, Count: *music*
Basinger, Kim: *movies*
Basquette, Lina: *movies*
Baxter, Anne: *movies*
Baxter, Dr. Frank C.: *TV*
Baxter, Les: *music*
Baxter, Warner: *movies*
Bayne, Beverly: *movies*
Beach Boys, The: *music*
Beatles, The: *music*
Beaudine, William: *movies*
Bee Gees: *music*
Beery, Noah Jr.: *TV*
Beery, Wallace: *movies*
Beirne, Brian: *radio*
Belafonte, Harry: *music*
Bellamy, Madge: *movies*
Bellamy, Ralph: *TV*
Benaderet, Bea: *TV*
Benchley, Robert: *movies*
Bendix, William: *radio, TV*
Beneke, Tex: *music*
Bennett, Belle: *movies*
Bennett, Constance: *movies*
Bennett, Joan: *movies*
Bennett, Tony: *music*
Benny, Jack: *movies, radio, TV*
Beradino, John: *TV*

Theda Bara

Fanny Brice

Bergen, Edgar: *movies, radio, TV*
Bergman, Ingrid: *movies*
Berle, Milton: *radio, TV*
Berlin, Irving: *music*
Bernardi, Ernani: *music*
Bernhardt, Sarah: *movies*
Bernie, Ben: *radio*
Bernstein, Leonard: *music*
Berry, Chuck: *music*
Best, Edna: *movies*
Bickford, Charles: *movies, TV*
Big Bird: *TV*
Biggs, E. Powers: *music*
Binney, Constance: *movies*
Blackmer, Sidney: *movies*
Blackwell, Carlyle: *movies*
Blanc, Mel: *radio*
Blondell, Joan: *movies*
Blue, Monte: *movies*
Blyth, Ann: *movies*
Blythe, Betty: *movies*
Boardman, Eleanor: *movies*
Bogart, Humphrey: *movies*
Boland, Mary: *movies*
Boles, John: *movies*
Boleslawski, Richard: *movies*
Bolger, Ray: *movies, TV*
Bond, Ford: *radio*
Bond, Ward: *TV*
Bondi, Beulah: *movies*
Boone, Pat: *music, TV*
Booth, Shirley: *movies*
Borden, Olive: *movies*
Borgnine, Ernest: *movies*
Borzage, Frank: *movies*
Bosworth, Hobart: *movies*
Bow, Clara: *movies*
Bowers, John: *movies*
Bowes, Major: *radio*
Boyd, Bill: *radio*
Boyd, Jimmy: *music*
Boyd, William: *movies*
Boyer, Charles: *movies, TV*
Bracken, Eddie: *radio, TV*
Brady, Alice: *movies*
Brando, Marlon: *movies*
Breneman, Tom: *radio*
Brennan, Walter: *movies*
Brent, Evelyn: *movies*
Brent, George: *movies, TV*
Brewer, Teresa: *music*
Brian, David: *TV*
Brian, Mary: *movies*
Brice, Fanny: *movies, radio*
Bridges, Jeff: *movies*

Bridges, Lloyd: *TV*
Briem, Ray: *radio*
Britt, Elton: *music*
Britton, Barbara: *TV*
Broccoli, Cubby: *movies*
Bronson, Charles: *movies*
Brooke, Hillary: *TV*
Brooks, Richard: *movies*
Brown, Cecil: *radio*
Brown, Clarence: *movies*
Brown, Harry Joe: *movies*
Brown, Joe E.: *movies*
Brown, Johnny Mack: *movies*
Brown, Les: *music*
Brown, Tom: *movies*
Brown, Vanessa: *movies, TV*
Browning, Tod: *movies*
Brubeck, Dave: *music*
Brynner, Yul: *movies*
Bunny, Bugs: *movies*
Bunny, John: *movies*
Burke, Billie: *movies*
Burke, Sonny: *music*
Burnett, Carol: *TV*
Burnette, Smiley: *movies*
Burns, Bob: *movies, radio*
Burns, George: *movies, TV, theater*
Burr, Raymond: *TV*
Burrud, Bill: *TV*
Burton, Levar: *TV*
Busch, Mae: *movies*
Bushman, Francis X.: *movies*
Butler, David: *movies*
Butterworth, Charles: *movies*
Buttons, Red: *TV*
Buttram, Pat: *TV*
Byington, Spring: *movies, TV*

C

Caan, James: *movies*
Caesar, Sid: *TV*
Cagney, James: *movies*
Cahn, Sammy, *music*
Calhoun, Alice: *movies*
Calhoun, Rory: *movies, TV*
Callas, Maria: *music*
Cameron, Rod: *TV*
Campbell, Glenn: *TV*
Cannell, Stephen J.: *TV*
Cannon, Dyan: *movies*
Canova, Judy: *movies, radio*
Cantinflas: *movies*
Cantor, Eddie: *movies, radio, TV*
Canutt, Yakima: *movies*
Capra, Frank: *movies*
Carey, Harry: *movies*
Carey, Harry Jr.: *TV*
Carey, McDonald: *TV*
Carle, Frankie: *music*
Carlin, George: *theater*
Carlisle, Kitty: *movies*
Carlisle, Mary: *movies*
Carlson, Richard: *TV*
Carmichael, Hoagy: *TV*
Carney, Art: *TV*
Carpenter, Ken: *radio*
Carpenters, The: *music*

Carr, Vicki: *music*
Carradine, John: *movies*
Carradine, Keith: *TV*
Carrillo, Leo: *movies, TV*
Carroll, Diahann: *music*
Carroll, Madeleine: *movies*
Carroll, Nancy: *movies*
Carson, Jack: *radio, TV*
Carson, Jeannie: *TV*
Carson, Johnny: *TV*
Carter, Benny: *music*
Caruso, Enrico: *music*
Casadesus, Robert: *music*
Cash, Johnny: *music*
Castle, Peggie: *TV*
Cates, Gil: *movies*
Caulfield, Joan: *TV*
Catlett, Walter: *movies*
Cavallaro, Carmen: *music*
Cerf, Bennett: *TV*
Chaliapin, Feodor: *music*
Chambers, John: *movies*
Chambers, Stan: *TV*
Champion, Gower: *movies*
Champion, Marge: *TV*
Chandler, Jeff: *movies*
Channing, Carol: *TV*
Chaney, Lon: *movies*
Chaplin, Charles: *movies*
Chapman, Marguerite: *TV*
Charisse, Cyd: *movies*
Charles, Ray: *music*
Chase, Charley: *movies*
Chase, Chevy: *movies*
Chase, Ilka: *movies, TV*
Chatterton, Ruth: *movies*
Cherrill, Virginia: *movies*
Chevalier, Maurice: *movies*
Chicago: *music*
Christie, Al: *movies*
Christie, Charles: *movies*
Claire, Ina: *movies*
Clark, Buddy: *music*
Clark, Dane: *TV*
Clark, Dick: *TV*
Clark, Fred: *TV*
Clark, Marguerite: *movies*
Clark, Roy: *music*
Clayton, Ethel: *movies*
Clayton, Jan: *TV*
Cleveland, Rev. James: *music*
Clift, Montgomery: *movies*
Clooney, Rosemary: *music*
Clyde, Andy: *movies*
Coburn, Charles: *movies*

Charles Chaplin

Coburn, James: *movies*
Coca, Imogene: *TV*
Cochran, Steve: *TV*
Cody, Iron Eyes: *TV*
Cohan, George M.: *movies*
Cohn, Arthur: *movies*
Colbert, Claudette: *movies*
Cole, Natalie: *music*
Cole, Nat "King": *music, TV*
Collier, Constance: *movies*
Collier, William: *movies*
Collins, Gary: *TV*
Collins, Joan: *Movies*
Collins, Michael: *TV*
Collyer, Bud: *radio*
Colman, Ronald: *movies, TV*
Colonna, Jerry: *radio*
Como, Perry: *music, radio, TV*
Compson, Betty: *movies*
Compton, Joyce: *movies*
Conklin, Chester: *movies*
Conklin, Heinie: *movies*
Connors, Chuck: *TV*
Conreid, Hans: *TV*
Conte, John: *TV*

Kirk Douglas

Conti, Bill: *movies*
Conway, Jack: *movies*
Conway, Tom: *TV*
Conway, Tim: *TV*
Coogan, Jackie: *movies*
Cook, Clyde: *movies*
Cook, Donald: *movies*
Cooke, Sam: *music*
Cooke, Alistair: *TV*
Cooley, Spade: *radio*
Cooper, Gary: *movies*
Cooper, Jackie: *movies*
Cooper, Jeanne: *TV*
Cooper, Meriam C.: *movies*
Corey, Wendell: *TV*
Corman, Roger: *movies*
Cornell, Don: *music*
Correll, Charles "Andy": *radio*
Cortez, Ricardo: *movies*
Cosby, Bill: *TV*
Costello, Dolores: *movies*
Costello, Helene: *movies*
Costello, Lou: *movies, radio, TV*
Costello, Maurice: *movies*
Cotten, Joseph: *movies*
Cowan, Jerome: *TV*
Cox, Wally: *TV*
Crabbe, Buster: *TV*

Crawford, Broderick: *movies, TV*
Crawford, Joan: *movies*
Cregar, Laird: *movies*
Crenna, Richard: *movies*
Crews, Laura Hope: *movies*
Crisp, Donald: *movies*
Cromwell, John: *movies*
Cromwell, Richard: *movies*
Crooks, Richard: *music*
Crosby, Bing: *movies, music, radio*
Crosby, Bob: *radio, TV*
Crosby, Norm: *TV*
Crosby, Stills & Nash: *music*
Cross, Milton: *radio*
Cruise, Tom: *movies*
Crumit, Frank: *radio*
Cruze, James: *movies*
Crystal, Billy: *movies*
Cugat, Xavier: *music, TV*
Cukor, George: *movies*
Cummings, Constance: *movies*
Cummings, Irving: *movies*
Cummings, Robert: *movies, TV*
Cunningham, Bill: *radio*
Curtis, Alan: *movies*
Curtis, Tony: *movies*
Curtiz, Michael: *movies*
Crothers, Scatmen: *TV*
Cruz, Celia: *music*

D

Dahl, Arlene: *movies*
Daley, Cass: *radio*
Dale, Cass: *TV*
Dalton, Dorothy: *movies*
Daly, John: *TV*
Damone, Vic: *music*
Dana, Viola: *movies*
Dandridge, Dorothy: *movies*
Dane, Karl: *movies*
Daniels, Bebe: *movies*
Daniels, Billy: *music*
Danza, Tony: *TV*
Darin, Bobby: *music*
Darnell, Linda: *movies*
Darwell, Jane: *movies*
Daves, Delmer L.: *movies*
Davies, Marion: *movies*
Davis, Ann B.: *TV*
Davis, Bette: *movies, TV*
Davis, Gail: *TV*
Davis, Jim: *TV*
Davis, Joan: *movies, radio*
Davis, Sammy Jr.: *music*
Day, Dennis: *radio, TV*
Day, Doris: *movies, music*
Day, Laraine: *movies*
Dead End Kids: *movies*
Dean, James: *movies*
DeCamp, Rosemary: *TV*
DeCarlo, Yvonne: *movies, TV*
Dee, Frances: *movies*
Dees, Rick: *radio*
DeFore, Don: *TV*
DeForest, Lee: *movies*
DeHaven, Carter: *movies*
DeHaven, Gloria: *movies*

DeHavilland, Olivia: *movies*
Dekker, Albert: *TV*
De La Motte, Marguerite: *movies*
De Leath, Vaughn: *radio*
Del Rio, Dolores: *movies*
Del Ruth, Roy: *movies*
DeLuise, Dom: *movies*
Demarest, William: *movies*
DeMille, Cecil B.: *movies, radio*
DeMille, William: *movies*
DeSylva, Buddy: *music*
Denning, Richard: *TV*
Denny, Reginald: *movies*
Derek, John: *TV*
Devine, Andy: *radio, TV*
Dexter, Elliott: *movies*
Deiterle, William: *movies*
Dickinson, Angie: *TV*
Dietrich, Marlene: *movies*
Diller, Phyllis: *TV*
Disney, Walt: *movies, TV*
Dix, Richard: *movies*
Dmytryk, Edward: *movies*
Dodd, Jimmie: *TV*
Domingo, Placido: *theater*
Domino, Fats: *music*
Donald, Peter: *TV*
Donat, Robert: *movies*
Donlevy, Brian: *TV*
Doro, Marie: *movies*
Dorsey, Jimmy: *music*
Dorsey, Tommy: *music*
Douglas, Jack: *TV*
Douglas, Kirk: *movies*
Douglas, Melvyn: *movies, TV*
Douglas, Mike: *TV*
Douglas, Paul: *movies, TV*
Dove, Billie: *movies*
Downey, Morton: *radio*
Downs, Cathy: *TV*
Dragon, Carmen: *radio*
Dragonette, Jessica: *radio*
Drake, Frances: *movies*
Dresser, Louise: *movies*
Dressler, marie: *movies*
Drew, Ellen: *movies*
Drew, Mr. & Mrs. Sidney: *movies*
Driscoll, Bobby: *movies*
Dru, Joanne: *TV*
Duff, Howard: *TV*
Dunn, James: *movies, TV*
Dunne, Irene: *movies*
Dunne, Philip: *movies*
Dunnock, Mildred: *movies*
Dunphy, Jerry: *TV*
Durante, Jimmy: *movies, radio*
Duran, Duran: *music*
Durbin, Deanna: *movies*
Duryea, Dan: *TV*
Dvorak, Ann: *movies*
Dwan, Allan: *movies*

E

Eastman, George: *movies*
Ebsen, Buddy: *movies*
Eckstine, Billy: *music*
Eddy, Nelson: *movies, music, radio*

Eden, Barbara: *TV*
Edeson, Robert: *movies*
Edison, Thomas A.: *movies*
Edwards, Blake: *movies*
Edwards, Ralph: *radio, TV*
Ellington, Duke: *music*
Elman, Mischa: *music*
Emerson, Faye: *movies, TV*
Ericson, John: *TV*
Errol, Leon: *movies*
Erwin, Stu: *TV*
Estefan, Gloria: *music*
Etting, Ruth: *movies*
Evans, Dale: *radio, TV*
Evans, Linda: *TV*
Evans, Madge: *movies*
Everett, Chad: *TV*
Everly Brothers, The: *music*

F

Fabray, Nanette: *TV*
Factor, Max: *movies*
Fadiman, Clifton: *radio*
Fairbanks, Douglas Sr.: *movies*
Fairbanks, Douglas Jr.: *movies, radio, TV*
Fairbanks, Jerry: *movies*
Faith, Percy: *music*
Falkenburg, Jinx: *TV*
Farnum, Dustin: *movies*
Farnum, William: *movies*
Farr, Jamie: *TV*
Farrar, Geraldine: *movies, music*
Farrell, Charles: *movies*
Farrell, Charlie: *TV*
Farrell, Glenda: *movies*
Farrow, John: *movies*
Faversham, William: *movies*
Fawcett, Farrah: *TV*
Fay, Frank: *movies, radio*
Faye, Alice: *movies*
Faye, Julia: *movies*
Faylen, Frank: *TV*
Fazenda, Louise: *movies*
Fedderson, Don: *TV*
Feliciano, Jose: *music*
Felton, Verna: *TV*
Fenneman, George: *TV*
Ferguson, Helen: *movies*
Ferrer, Jose: *movies*
Ferrer, Mel: *movies*
Fetchit, Stepin: *movies*
Fidler, Jimmie: *radio*
Fiedler, Arthur: *music*
Field, Virginia: *TV*
Fields, Gracie: *radio*
Fields, W. C.: *movies, radio*
5th Dimension, The Original: *music*
Finch, Flora: *movies*
Fisher, Eddie: *music, TV*
Fisher, George: *radio*
Fishman, Hal: *TV*
Fitzgerald, Barry: *movies, TV*
Fitzgerald, Ella: *music*
Fitzgerald, Geraldine: *movies*
Fitzmaurice, George: *movies*
Fitzpatrick, James A.: *movies*
Flagsrad, Kirsten: *music*
Fleetwood Mac: *music*

Annette Funicello

Fleming, Rhonda: *movies*
Fleming, Victor: *movies*
Flynn, Errol: *movies, TV*
Foch, Nina: *movies, TV*
Foley, Red: *music, TV*
Fonda, Henry: *movies*
Fontaine, Joan: *movies*
Foran, Dick: *TV*
Forbes, Scott: *TV*
Ford, Glenn: *movies*
Ford, Harrison: *movies*
Ford, John: *movies*
Ford, Tennessee Ernie: *music, radio, TV*
Foster, Preston: *TV*
Forsythe, John: *TV*
Four Step Brothers, The: *theater*
Fox, William: *movies*
Foy, Eddie: *movies*
Frampton, Peter: *music*
Francescatti, Zino: *music*
Francis, Anne: *TV*
Francis, Arlene: *radio, TV*
Frances, Kay: *movies*
Franklin, Aretha: *music*
Franklin, Sidney: *movies*
Frawley, William: *movies*
Freberg, Stan: *music*
Frederick, Pauline: *movies*
Freed, Alan: *radio*
Freeman, Y. Frank: *movies*
Fries, Charles: *TV*
Frizzell, Lefty: *music*
Froman, Jane: *music, radio, TV*
Fuller, Robert: *TV*
Funicello, Annette: *movies*
Furness, Betty: *movies, TV*

G

Gable, Clark: *movies*
Gabor, Eva: *TV*
Gabor, Zsa Zsa: *TV*
Gahagan, Helen: *movies*
Galli-Curci, Amelita: *music*
Garbo, Greta: *movies*
Gardner, Ava: *movies*
Gardner, Ed: *radio, TV*
Garfield, John: *movies*
Garland, Beverly: *TV*
Garland, Judy: *movies, music*
Garner, Errol: *music*
Garner, James: *TV*

Garner, Peggy Ann: *movies*
Garnett, Tay: *movies*
Garroway, Dave: *radio, TV*
Garson, Greer: *movies*
Gaye, Marvin: *music*
Gaynor, Janey: *movies*
Gaynor, Mitzi: *movies*
Gibbons, Floyd: *radio*
Gibbs, Georgia: *music*
Gibson, Hoot: *movies*
Gigli, Beniamino: *music*
Gilbert, Billy: *movies*
Gilbert, John: *movies*
Gilbert, Melissa: *TV*
Gilbert, Paul: *TV*
Gilley, Mickey: *music*
Gish, Dorothy: *movies*
Gish, Lillian: *movies*
Glaum, Louise: *movies*
Gleason, Jackie: *music, TV*
Gleason, James: *movies*
Globetrotters: *TV*
Gobel, George: *TV*
Goddard, Paulette: *movies*
Godfrey, Arthur: *music, radio, TV*
Godwin, Earl: *radio*
Gold, Earnest: *Composer/Conductor*
Goldberg, Leonard: *TV*
Goldman, Edwin F.: *radio*
Goldwyn, Samuel: *movies*
Goodman, Al: *music*
Goodman, Benny: *music*
Goodson, Mark: *TV*
Goodwin, Bill: *radio*
Gordon, Gale: *radio*
Gore, Mike: *movies*
Gorme, Edie and Steve Lawrence: *music*
Gosden, Freeman "Amos": *radio*
Gossett, Jr., Louis: *movies*
Goudal, Jetta: *movies*
Gould, Morton: *music*
Goulet, Robert: *music*
Grable, Betty: *movies*
Graham, Billy: *radio*
Grahame, Gloria: *movies*
Granger, Farley: *TV*
Grey, Joel: *theater*
Grant, Cary: *movies*
Grant, Johnny: *TV*
Granville, Bonita: *movies*
Grauman, Sid: *movies*
Gray, Gilda, *movies*
Gray, Glen: *music*
Grayson, Kathryn: *movies*
Green, Alfred: *movies*
Green, John: *movies*
Green, Mitzi: *movies*
Greene, Lorne: *TV*
Greenwood, Charlotte: *radio*
Greer, Jane: *movies*
Griffin, Merv: *TV*
Griffith, Andy: *TV*
Griffith, Corinne: *movies*
Griffith, David W.: *movies*
Griffith, Raymond: *movies*
Guillaume, Robert: *TV*
Guinan, Texas: *movies*
Guinness, Alec: *movies*
Gwenn, Edmund: *movies*

H

Hadley, Reed: *TV*
Hagen, Jean: *TV*
Haggerty, Dan: *TV*
Haggerty, Don: *TV*
Hagman, Larry: *TV*
Haines, William: *movies*
Hairston, Jester: *TV*
Hale, Alan: *movies*
Hale, Alan Jr.: *TV*
Hale, Barbara: *TV*
Hale, Creighton: *movies*
Haley, Bill: *music*
Haley, Jack: *radio*
Hall, Arsenio: *TV*
Hall, Jon: *movies, TV*
Hall, Monty: *TV*
Hamblen, Stuart: *radio*
Hamer, Rusty: *TV*
Hamilton, Lloyd: *movies*
Hamilton, Neil: *movies*
Hampton, Lionel: *music*
Hancock, Herbie: *music*
Hanks, Tom: *movies*
Hanna-Barbera: *TV*
Harding, Ann: *movies, TV*
Hardwicke, Sir Cedric: *movies, TV*
Hardy, Oliver: *movies*
Harlow, Jean: *movies*
Harris, Arlene: *radio*
Harris, Mildred: *movies*
Harris, Phil: *music, radio*
Harrison, Rex: *movies, TV*
Hart, John: *TV*
Hart, Mary: *TV*
Hart, William S.: *movies*
Hartley, Mariette: *TV*
Hasso, Signe: *movies*
Hathaway, Henry: *movies*
Hatton, Raymond: *movies*
Haver, June: *movies*
Havoc, June: *movies, TV*
Hawk, Bob: *TV*
Hawks, Howard: *movies*
Hay, Bill: *radio*
Hayakawa, Sessue: *movies*
Hayes, George "Gabby": *radio, TV*
Hayes, Helen: *movies, radio*
Hayman, Richard: *music*
Haymes, Dick: *music, radio*
Haynes, Dick: *radio*

Tom Hanks

Hays, Will H.: *movies*
Hayward, Louis: *movies, TV*
Hayward, Susan: *movies*
Hayworth, Rita: *movies*
Head, Edith: *movies*
Healy, Jim: *radio*
Hearn, Chick: *radio*
Heckart, Eileen: *movies*
Heflin, Van: *movies, TV*
Hefner, Hugh: *TV*
Heidt, Horace: *radio, TV*
Heifetz, Jascha: *music*
Hendrix, Jimi: *music*
Henie, Sonia: *movies*
Henreid, Paul: *movies, TV*
Henson, Jim: *TV*
Hepburn, Audrey: *movies*
Hepburn, Katharine: *movies*
Herbert, Hugh: *movies*
Herman, Jerry: *theater*
Herman, Pee-Wee: *movies*
Herman, Woody: *music*
Hersholt, Jean: *movies, radio*
Hervey, Irene: *movies*
Heston, Charlton: *movies*
Heywood, Eddie: *music*
Hibbler, Al: *music*
Hicks, George: *radio*
Hildegarde: *radio*
Hitchcock, Alfred: *movies, TV*
Hodiak, John: *radio*
Hoffa, Portland: *radio*
Holden, William: *movies*
Holiday, Billie: *music*
Holliday, Judy: *movies*
Holliman, Earl: *TV*
Hollingshead, Gordon: *movies*
Holm, Celeste: *movies, TV*
Holmes, Burton: *movies*
Holmes, Phillips: *movies*
Holmes, Taylor: *movies*
Holt, Jack: *movies*
Hope, Bob: *movies, radio, TV, theater*
Hopkins, Mariam: *movies*
Hopkins, Miriam: *TV*
Hopper, Hedda: *movies*
Horne, Lena: *movies, music*
Horton, Edward Everett: *movies*
Horowitz, Vladimir: *music*
Houdini, Harry: *movies*
Howard, Eddy: *music*
Howard, John: *TV*
Howard, Leslie: *movies*
Howard, Ron: *TV*
Howard, William K.: *movies*
Hudson, Rochelle: *movies*
Hudson, Rock: *movies*
Hull, Josephine: *movies*
Hull, Warren: *radio, TV*
Humberstone, Bruce: *movies*
Humperdinck, Engelbert: *music*
Hunt, Frazier: *radio*
Hunt, Marsha: *TV*
Hunt, Pee Wee: *music*
Hunter, Jeffrey: *TV*
Hunter, Kim: *movies, TV*
Hunter, Tab: *music*
Hurt, Marlin: *radio*
Husing, Ted: *radio*
Husky, Ferlin: *music*
Hussey, Ruth: *movies*

Huston, John: *movies*
Huston, Walter: *movies*
Hutton, Betty: *movies*

I

Iglesias, Julio: *music*
Ince, Thomas: *movies*
Infante, Pedro: *music*
Ingram, Rex: *movies*
Ireland, Jill: *movies*
Ireland, John: *TV*
Iturbi, Jose: *music*

J

Jackson, Janet: *music*
Jackson, Mahalia: *music*
Jackson, Michael: *music, radio*
Jackson, Sherry: *TV*
Jacksons, The: *music*
Jagger, Dean: *movies*
Jam, Jimmy & Terry Lewis: *music*
James, Dennis: *TV*
James, Harry: *music*
James, Joni: *music*
James, Sonny: *music*
Janis, Elsie: *movies*
Jannings, Emil: *movies*
Janssen, David: *TV*
Jarre, Maurice: *movies*
Jeffreys, Ann: *TV*
Jenkins, Gordon: *music*
Jergens, Adele: *TV*
Jessel, George: *movies*
Jewell, Isabel: *movies*
Jewison, Norman: *movies*
John, Elton: *music*
Johnson, Ben: *movies*
Johnson, Nunnally: *movies*
Johnson, Van: *movies*
Jolson, Al: *movies, music, radio*
Jones, Allan: *music*
Jones, Buck: *movies*
Jones, Chuck: *movies*
Jones, Dick: *TV*
Jones, Gordon: *TV*
Jones, Jack: *music*
Jones, Jennifer: *movies*
Jones, Quincy: *music*
Jones, Shirley: *movies*
Jones, Spike: *music, radio, TV*
Jones, Tom: *music*
Jones, Tommy Lee: *movies*
Jourdan, Louis: *music, TV*
Jory, Victor: *movies*
Joy, Leatrice: *movies*
Jurado, Katy: *movies*

K

Kallen, Kitty: *music*
Kalmus, Herbert: *movies*
Karloff, Boris: *movies, TV*

Kasem, Casey: *radio*
Kaye, Danny: *movies, music*
Kaye, Sammy: *music, radio, TV*
Kazan, Elia: *movies*
Keaton, Buster: *movies, TV*
Keel, Howard: *movies*
Keeler, Ruby: *movies*
Keene, Bill: *TV*
Keeshan, Bob: *TV*
Kellerman, Annette: *movies*
Kelley, Deforest: *movies*
Kelly, Gene: *movies*
Kelly, Grace: *movies*
Kelly, Nancy: *movies*
Kelly, Patsy: *movies*
Kennedy, Arthur: *movies, TV*
Kennedy, John B.: *radio*
Kennedy, Edgar: *movies*
Kennedy, George: *movies*
Kennedy, Madge: *movies*
Kenton, Stan: *music*
Kerr, Deborah: *movies*
Kerrigan, J. M.: *movies*
Kerry, Norman: *movies*
Kilgallen, Dorothy: *TV*
King, Andrea: *TV*
King, B. B.: *music*
King, Henry: *movies*
King, John Reed: *radio*
King, Pee Wee: *music*
King, Peggy: *TV*
King, Wayne: *radio*
Kirkwood, Joe Jr.: *TV*
Kirsten, Dorothy: *music*
Kitt, Eartha: *music*
Klugman, Jack: *TV*
Knight, June: *movies*
Knight, Evelyn: *music*
Knight, Raymond: *radio*
Knight, Ted: *TV*
Knowles, Patric: *TV*
Knudsen, Peggy: *TV*
Kosloff, Theodore: *movies*
Kostelanetz, Andre: *music*
Koster, Henry: *movies*
Kovacs, Ernie: *TV*
Kramer, Stanley: *movies*
Kreisler, Fritz: *music*
Krueger, Kurt: *movies*
Kruger, Otto: *movies, TV*
Kyser, Kay: *music, radio*

L

Labelle, Patti: *music*
Laboe, Art: *radio*
LaCava, Gregory: *movies*
Ladd, Alan: *movies*
Ladd, Sue Carol: *movies*
Laemmle, Carl: *movies*
Laine, Frankie: *music, TV*
Lake, Alice: *movies*
Lake, Arthur: *radio*
Lake, Veronica: *movies*
Lamarr, Barbara: *movies*
Lamarr, Hedy: *movies*
Lamour, Dorothy: *movies, radio*
Lancaster, Burt: *movies*

Landi, Elissa: *movies*
Landis, Carole: *movies*
Lane, Abbe: *TV*
Lane, Dick: *TV*
Lanfield, Sidney: *movies*
Lang, Fritz: *movies*
Lang, Walter: *movies*
Langdon, Harry: *movies*
Landon, Michael: *TV*
Langford, Frances: *movies, radio*
Landsberg, Klaus: *TV*
Lansbury, Angela: *movies, TV*
Lansing, Joi: *TV*
Lantz, Walter: *movies*
Lanza, Mario: *movies, music*
LaPlante, Laura: *movies*
LaRocque, Rod: *movies*
LaRosa, Julius: *TV*
Larson, Glen: *TV*
Lasky, Jesse: *movies*
Lassie: *movies*
Laughton, Charles: *movies*
Laurel, Stan: *movies*
Lawford, Peter: *TV*
Lawrence, Barbara: *TV*
Lawrence, Carol: *theater*
Lawrence, Steve and Edie **Gorme:** *music*
Lear, Norman: *TV*

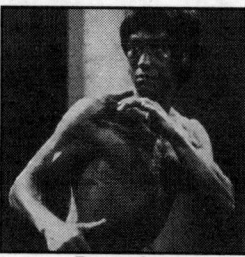

Bruce Lee

Leiber and Stoller: *music*
Lederer, Francis: *movies*
Lee, Anna: *movies*
Lee, Bruce: *movies*
Lee, Lila: *movies*
Lee, Peggy: *music*
Lee, Gypsy Rose: *movies*
Lee, Pinky: *TV*
Lee, Roland: *movies*
Leachman, Cloris: *TV*
Lehmann, Lottie: *music*
Leigh, Janet: *movies*
Leigh, Vivien: *movies*
Leisen, Mitchell: *movies*
Lemmon, Jack: *movies*
Lennon, John: *music*
Lennon Sisters, The: *TV*
Leonard, Robert Z.: *movies*
LeRoy, Mervyn: *movies*
Lescoulie, Jack: *TV*
Leslie, Joan: *TV*
Lesser, Sol: *movies*
Levant, Oscar: *music*
Lewis, Fulton: *radio*
Lewis, Jerry: *movies, TV*

Lewis, Jerry Lee: *music*
Lewis, Robert Q.: *TV*
Lewis, Sheri: *TV*
Leyden, Bill: *TV*
Liberace: *music, TV*
Lichtman, Al: *movies*
Lillie, Beatrice: *movies*
Lincoln, Elmo: *movies*
Linden, Eric: *movies*
Lindsay, Margaret: *movies*
Linkletter, Art: *radio, TV*
Little, Cleavon: *movies*
Little, Little Jack: *radio*
Little, Rich: *TV*
Litvak, Anatole: *movies*
Livingston and Evans: *music*
Livingston, Mary: *radio*
Lloyd, Frank: *movies*
Lloyd, Harold: *movies*
Lockhart, Gene: *movies, TV*
Lockhart, June: *movies, TV*
Lockhart, Kathleen: *movies*
Loew, Marcus: *movies*
Logan, Joshua: *movies*
Lohman & Barkley: *radio*
Lombard, Carole: *movies*
Lombardo, Guy: *music, radio, TV*
London, Julie: *music*
Lopez, Vincent: *radio*
Lord, Marjorie: *TV*
Lord, Philips: *radio*
Loren, Sophia: *movies*
Lorre, Peter: *movies*
Louise, Anita: *movies*
Love, Bessie: *movies*
Lovejoy, Frank: *TV*
Lowe, Edmund: *movies, TV*
Lowe, Jim: *music*
Loy, Myrna: *movies*
Lubin, Sigmund: *movies*
Lubitsch, Ernst: *movies*
Luboff, Norman: *music*
Ludden, Allen: *TV*
Lugosi, Bela: *movies*
Lukas, Paul: *movies*
Luke, Keye: *movies*
Lumiere, Auguste: *movies*
Lumiere, Louis: *movies*
Luna, Humberto: *TV*
Lunda, Art: *music*
Lupino, Ida: *movies, TV*
Lupton, John: *TV*
Luther, Frank: *music*
Lyles, A. C.: *movies*
Lymon, Frankie: *music*
Lynn, Diana: *movies, TV*
Lynn, Loretta: *music*
Lyon, Ben: *movies*
Lytell, Bert: *movies*

M

MacDonald, Jeanette: *movies, music*
MacDonald, Katherine: *movies*
Mack, Helen: *movies*
Mack, Ted: *TV*
Mackenzie, Gisele: *TV*
MacLaine, Shirley: *movies*

MacLane, Barton: *TV*
MacMurray, Fred: *movies*
MacPherson, Jeanie: *movies*
MacRae, Gordon: *radio*
Maddox, Johnny: *music*
Madison, Guy: *radio, TV*
Magnani, Anna: *movies*
Majors, Lee: *TV*
Mako: *movies*
Malden, Karl: *movies*
Malone, Dorothy: *movies*
Malone, Ted: *radio*
Mamoulian, Rouben: *movies*
Mancini, Henry: *music*
Manilow, Barry: *music*
Mankiewicz, Joseph L.: *movies*
Mann, Anthony: *movies*
Mann, Delbert: *movies*
Mann, Hank: *movies*
Mansfield, Jayne: *movies*
Mantovani: *music*
March, Fredric: *movies*
March, Hal: *radio, TV*
Margret, Ann: *movies*
Marley, J. Peverell: *movies*
Marsh, Mae: *movies*
Marshall, Garry: *TV*
Marshall, George: *movies*
Marshall, Herbert: *movies*
Martin, Dean: *music, TV*
Martin, Freddy: *music*
Martin, Marion: *movies*
Martin, Mary: *music, radio*
Martin, Quinn: *TV*
Martin, Tony: *movies, music, radio, TV*
Marx, Groucho: *radio, TV*
Mason, James: *TV*
Massey, Ilona: *movies*
Massey, Raymond: *movies, TV*
Mathis, Johnny: *music*
Matthau, Walter: *movies*
Mature, Victor: *movies*
Mayer, Louis B.: *movies*
Maynard, Ken: *movies*
Mayo, Archie: *movies*
Mayo, Virginia: *TV*
McAvoy, May: *movies*
McBride, Mary Margaret: *radio*
McCalla, Irish: *TV*
McCambridge, Mercedes: *movies, TV*
McCarey, Leo: *movies*
McCarthy, Clem: *radio*
McConnell, Smilin' Ed: *radio*
McCormack, Patty: *movies*
McCoy, Clyde: *music*
McCoy, Tim, *movies*
McCrary, Tex: *TV*
McCrea, Joel: *movies, radio*
McDaniel, Hattie: *movies, radio*
McDowall, Roddy: *TV*
McFarland, Spanky: *movies*
McGee, Fibber & Molly: *radio*
McGraw, Charles: *TV*
McGuire, Dorothy: *movies*
McKuen, Rod: *music*
McLaglen, Victor: *movies*
McLeod, Norman Z.: *movies*
McMahon, Ed: *TV*
McNamee, Graham: *radio*
McNeill, Don: *radio*
McQueen, Steve: *movies*

Meadow, Audrey: *TV*
Meek, Donald: *movies*
Meeker, George: *movies*
Meighan, Thomas: *movies*
Meiklejohn: *movies*
Melachrino: *music*
Melchior, Lauritz: *music*
Melton, James: *music, radio*
Mendez, Rafael: *music*
Menjou, Adolphe: *movies*
Menuhin, Yehudi: *music*
Mercer, Johnny: *TV*
Meredith, Burgess: *movies*
Merkel, Una: *movies*
Merman, Ethel: *movies, music*
Merrill, Robert: *music*
Micheaux, Oscar: *movies*
Midler, Bette: *music*
Miles, Vera: *TV*
Milestone, Lewis: *movies*
Milland, Ray: *movies, TV*
Miller, Ann: *movies*
Miller, Glenn: *music*
Miller, Marilyn: *movies*
Miller, Marvin: *TV*
Miller, Mitch: *music*
Miller Band, The Steve: *music*

Dean Martin

Mills Brothers: *music*
Milstein, Nathan: *music*
Minnelli, Liza: *theater*
Minnelli, Vincente: *movies*
Minter, Mary Miles: *movies*
Minyard, Ken & Bob Arthur: *radio*
Miranda, Carmen: *movies*
Mitchell, Everett: *radio*
Mitchell, Guy: *music*
Mitchell, Thomas: *movies, TV*
Mitchum, Robert: *movies*
Mix, Tom: *movies*
Mohr, Hal: *movies*
Monk, Thelonious: *music*
Monkees, The: *music*
Monroe, Marilyn: *movies*
Monroe, Vaughn: *music, radio*
Montalban, Ricardo: *TV*
Monteux, Pierre: *music*
Montgomery, George: *TV*
Montgomery, Robert: *TV*
Mooney, Art: *music*
Moore, Clayton/Lone Ranger: *TV*
Moore, Colleen: *movies*
Moore, Constance: *movies*
Moore, Del: *TV*
Moore, Dudley: *movies*

Moore, Garry: *radio, TV*
Moore, Grace: *movies*
Moore, Mary Tyler: *TV*
Moore, Matt: *movies*
Moore, Owen, *movies*
Moore, Terry: *movies*
Moore, Tom: *movies*
Moore, Victor: *movies*
Moorehead, Agnes: *movies*
Moran, Polly: *movies*
Moreno, Antonio: *movies*
Morgan, Frank: *movies, radio*
Morgan, Henry: *radio*
Morgan, Michele: *movies*
Morgan, Ralph: *movies*
Morgan, Robert W.: *radio*
Morgan, Russ: *music*
Morita, Pat: *movies*
Morse, Carlton E.: *radio*
Morse, Ella Mae: *music*
Mouse, Mickey: *movies*
Muir, Jean: *movies*
Mulhall, Jack: *movies*
Mulligan, Richard: *TV*
Muni, Paul: *movies*
Munson, Ona: *movies*
Murphy, Audie: *movies*
Murphy, George: *movies*
Murphy, Charlie: *movies*
Murray, Anne: *music*
Murray, Don: *movies*
Murray, Jan: *TV*
Murray, Ken: *radio*
Murray, Mae: *movies*
Murrow, Edward R.: *radio, TV*
Myers, Carmel: *movies*

N

Nabors, Jim: *theater*
Nagel, Conrad: *movies, radio, TV*
Naish, J. Carrol: *TV*
Naldi, Nita: *movies*
Nash, Ogden: *TV*
Nazimova: *movies*
Nederlander, James: *theater*
Negri, Pola: *movies*
Negulesco, Jean: *movies*
Neilan, Marshall: *movies*
Nelson, Barry: *TV*
Nelson, Gene: *movies*
Nelson, Harriet: *TV*
Nelson, Ozzie: *TV*
Nelson, Ozzie & Harriet: *radio*
Nelson, Rick: *music*
Nesbitt, John: *movies, radio*
Newman, Alfred: *music*
Newman, Paul: *movies*
Newton, Wayne: *music*
Newton-John, Olivia: *music*
Niblo, Fred: *movies*
Nichols, Nichelle: *TV*
Nicholas Brothers: *movies*
Nielson, Leslie: *movies*
Niles, Ken: *radio*
Niles, Wendell: *radio*
Nilsson, Anna Q.: *movies*
Nimoy, Leonard: *movies*
Niven, David: *movies, TV*

Nixon, Marian: *movies*
Nolan, Lloyd: *TV*
Normand, Mabel: *movies*
Norris, Chuck: *movies*
Novak, Kim: *movies*
Navarro, Ramon: *movies*

O

Oakie, Jack: *movies*
Oberon, Merle: *movies*
O'Brian, Hugh: *TV*
O'Brien, Dave: *movies*
O'Brien, Edmond: *movies, TV*
O'Brien, Eugene: *movies*
O'Brien, George: *movies*
O'Brien, Margaret: *movies, TV*
O'Brien, Pat: *movies, TV*
O'Connor, Donald: *movies, TV*
O'Day, Molly: *movies*
O'Hanlon, George: *movies*
O'Hara, Maureen: *movies*
O'Keefe, Walter: *radio*
Oliver, Edna May: *movies*
Olivier, Laurence: *movies*
Olmos, Edward James: *movies*
Orlando, Tony: *music*
Ormandy, Eugene: *music*
O'Neill, Henry: *movies*
O'Shea, Michael: *TV*
O'Sullivan, Maureen: *movies*
Owens, Buck: *music*
Owens, Gary: *radio*

P

Parr, Jack: *TV*
Paderewski: *music*
Page, Anita: *movies*
Page, Patti: *music*
Paige, Janis: *movies*
Pal, George: *movies*
Palance, Jack: *TV*
Pallette, Eugene: *movies*
Palmer, Lilli: *TV*
Pangborn, Franklin: *movies*
Parker, Eleanor: *movies*
Parker, Frank: *radio*
Parker, Jean: *movies*
Parkyakarkus: *radio*

Rin-Tin-Tin

Parrish, Helen: *movies*
Parsons, Louella O.: *movies, radio*
Parton, Dolly: *music*
Pasternak, Joe: *movies*
Paul, Les & Mary Ford: *music*
Paxinou, Katrina: *movies*
Payne, John: *movies, TV*
Pearce, Al: *radio*
Pearl, Jack: *radio*
Pearson, Drew: *radio*
Peary, Harold: *radio, TV*
Peck, Gregory: *movies*
Peerce, Jan: *music*
Penner, Joe: *radio*
Peppard, George: *movies*
Perkins, Anthony: *movies, TV*
Perreau, Gigi: *movies*
Perrin, Jack: *movies*
Peters, Brock: *theater*
Peters, House: *movies*
Peters, Susan: *movies*
Petrova, Olga: *movies*
Phillips, Dorothy: *movies*
Pickford, Jack: *movies*
Pickford, Mary: *movies*
Pidgeon, Walter: *movies*
Pierce, Webb: *music*
Pinza, Ezio: *music*
Pitts, Zasu: *movies*
Pointer Sisters, *music*
Poitier, Sidney: *movies*
Pollard, Snub: *movies*
Pons, Lily: *music*
Potter, H.C.: *movies*
Powell, David: *movies*
Powell, Dick: *movies, radio, TV*
Powell, Eleanor: *movies*
Powell, Jane: *movies*
Powell, William: *movies*
Power, Tyrone: *movies*
Powers, Mala: *TV*
Powers, Stefanie: *TV*
Prado, Perez: *music*
Preminger, Otto: *movies*
Presley, Elvis: *music*
Prevost, Marie: *movies*
Price, Vincent: *movies, TV*
Primrose, William: *music*
Pringle, Aileen: *movies*
Provost, Jon: *TV*
Pryor, Richard: *movies*
Puente, Tito: *music*
Putnam, George: *TV*

Q

Quinn, Anthony: *movies*

R

Raft, George: *movies, TV*
Rainer, Luise: *movies*
Raines, Ella: *movies*
Rains, Claude: *movies*
Raitt, John: *theater*
Ralston, Esther: *movies*

Ralston, Vera: *movies*
Rambeau, Marjorie: *movies*
Rathbone, Basil: *movies, radio, TV*
Ratoff, Gregory: *movies*
Rawlinson, Herbert: *movies*
Rawls, Lou: *music*
Ray, Charles: *movies*
Ray, Johnie: *music*
Raye, Martha: *movies., TV*
Raymond, Gene: *movies, TV*
Reagan, Ronald: *TV*
Reddy, Helen: *music*
Reed, Donna: *movies*
Reese, Della: *TV*
Reeves, George: *TV*
Reid, Wallace: *movies*
Reiner, Carl: *TV*
Reis, Irving: *movies*
Remick, Lee: *movies*
Renaldo, Duncan: *TV*
Rene, Henri: *music*
Rennahan, Ray: *movies*
Renoir, Jean: *movies*
Reynolds, Burt: *movies*
Reynolds, Debbie: *movies*
Reynolds, Marjorie: *TV*
Reynolds, Quentin: *radio*
Rice, Grantland: *radio*
Rich, Irene: *movies, radio*
Richard, Little: *music*
Riddle, Nelson: *music*
Riggs, Tommy & Betty Lou: *radio*
Rin-Tin-Tin: *movies*
Ripley, Robert: *radio*
Ritter, John: *TV*
Ritter, Tex: *music*
Ritz Brothers: *movies*
Rivers, Joan: *TV*
Roach, Hal: *movies*
Robbins, Gale: *TV*
Robbins, Harold: *movies*
Robbins, Marty: *music*
Roberts, Theodore: *movies*
Robertson, Cliff: *movies*
Robertson, Dale: *TV*
Robeson, Paul: *movies*
Robinson, Edward G.: *movies*
Robinson, Smokey: *music*
Robson, Mark: *movies*
Rochester: *radio*
Roddenberry, Gene: *TV*
Rodgers, Kenny: *music*
Rogers, Buddy: *movies*
Rogers, Ginger: *movies*
Rogers, Roy: *movies, radio, TV*
Rogers, Will: *movies, radio*
Roland, Gilbert: *movies*
Roland, Ruth: *movies, TV*
Romero, Cesar: *movies, TV*
Rooney, Mickey: *movies, radio, TV*
Rose, David: *music*
Ross, Diana: *music*
Ross, Lanny: *radio*
Rossen, Robert: *movies*
Roth, Lillian: *movies*
Rowland, Henry: *TV*
Rowland, Richard: *movies*
Rubens, Alma: *movies*
Rubinstein, Arthur: *music*
Rudie, Evelyn: *TV*
Ruggles, Charles: *movies, radio*

Ruggles, Charlie: *TV*
Ruggles, Wesley: *movies*
Russell, Gail: *movies*
Russell, Harold: *movies*
Russell, Jane: *movies*
Russell, Rosalind: *movies*
Rutherford, Ann: *movies, TV*

S

Sabu: *movies*
Saint, Eva Marie: *movies, TV*
St. John, Adela: *movies*
St. John, Al: *movies*
Sajak, Pat: *TV*
Sanders, George: *movies, TV*
Sanderson, Julia: *radio*
Sandrich, Mark: *movies*
Sands, Tommy: *music*
Savalas, Telly: *movies*
Schenck, Joseph: *movies*
Schertzinger, Victor: *movies*
Schifrin, Lalo: *music*
Schildkraut, Joseph: *movies*
Schlatter, George: *TV*
Schoedsack, Ernest: *movies*
Schulberg, B. P.: *movies*
Schumann-Heink: *music*
Schwarzenegger, Arnold: *movies*
Scott, Lizabeth: *movies*
Scott, Martha: *theater*
Scott, Randolph: *movies*
Scott, Zachary: *movies*
Scully, Vin: *radio*
Seaton, George: *movies*
Sebastian, Dorothy: *movies*
Sedaka, Neil: *music*
Sedgwick, Edward: *movies*
Seger, Bob & The Silver Bullet Band: *music*
Seiter, William: *movies*
Selig, William: *movies*
Selleck, Tom: *movies*
Selznick, Lewis J.: *movies*
Semon, Larry: *movies*
Sennett, Mack: *movies*
Serkin, Rudolf: *music*
Serling, Rod: *TV*
Serrurier, Mark: *movies*
Shamroy, Leon: *movies*
Shatner, William: *TV*
Shaw, Artie: *music*
Shaw, Robert: *music*
Shearer, Norma: *movies*
Shearing, George: *music*
Sheen, Charlie: *movies*
Sheen, Martin: *movies*
Sheldon, Sidney: *TV*
Shepherd, Cybill: *TV*
Sheridan, Ann: *movies*
Sherman Brothers: *movies*
Sherwood, Bobby: *TV*
Shirley, Anne: *movies*
Shore, Dinah: *music, radio, TV*
Sidney, George: *movies*
Sidney, Sylvia: *movies*
Sills, Beverly: *music*
Sills, Milton: *movies*

Silver, Joel: *movies*
Silverheels, Jay: *TV*
Simms, Ginny: *radio*
Sinatra, Frank: *movies, music, TV*
Singleton, Penny: *movies, radio*
Skelton, Red: *radio, TV*
Sloane, Everett: *TV*
Small, Edward: *movies*
Smith, C. Aubrey: *movies*
Smith, Carl: *music*
Smith, Jack: *radio*
Smith, Jaclyn: *TV*
Smith, Kate: *music, radio*
Smith, Pete: *movies*
Smothers Brothers, The: *TV*
Snow White: *movies*
Sons of the Pioneers: *music*
Sothern, Ann: *movies, TV*
Sousa, John Philip: *music*
Spelling, Aaron: *TV*
Spiegel, Arthur: *movies*
Spinners, The: *music*
Spitalny, Phil: *radio*
Stack, Robert: *movies*
Stafford, Hanley: *radio*
Stafford, Jo: *music, radio, TV*
Stahl, John: *movies*

Frank Sinatra

Stallone, Sylvester: *movies*
Stanwyck, Barbara: *movies*
Starke, Pauline: *movies*
Starr, Kay: *music*
Staub, Ralph: *movies*
Steber, Eleanor: *music*
Stein, Jules C.: *movies*
Steinberg, William: *music*
Steiner, Max: *movies*
Sterling, Ford: *movies*
Sterling, Jan: *movies*
Sterling, Robert: *TV*
Stern, Bill: *radio*
Stern, Isaac: *music*
Steve Miller Band, The: *music*
Stevens, Connie: *TV*
Stevens, George: *movies*
Stevens, Mark: *TV*
Stevens, Onslow: *movies*
Stewart, Anita: *movies*
Stewart, James: *movies*
Stiller, Maurice: *movies*
Stock, Frederick: *music*
Stockwell, Dean: *movies*
Stokowski, Leopold: *music*
Stoloff, Morris: *music*
Stone, Andrew L.: *movies*

Stone, Cliffie: *radio*
Stone, Ezra: *radio*
Stone, Fred: *movies*
Stone, George E.: *movies*
Stone, Lewis: *movies*
Stone, Milburn: *movies*
Storey, Edith: *movies*
Storm, Gale: *music, radio, TV*
Stout, Bill: *TV*
Strasberg, Lee: *movies*
Stravinsky, Igor: *radio*
Streisand, Barbra: *movies*
Strongheart: *movies*
Sturges, John: *movies*
Sturges, Preston: *movies*
Sullavan, Margaret: *movies*
Sullivan, Barry: *movies, TV*
Sullivan, Ed: *TV*
Sumac, Yma: *music*
Summer, Donna: *music*
Summerville, Slim: *movies*
Supremes, The: *music*
Swain, Mack: *movies*
Swanson, Gloria: *movies*
Swarthout, Gladys: *music*
Sweet, Blanche: *movies*
Swit, Loretta: *TV*
Szigeti, Joseph: *music*

T

Takei, George: *TV*
Taliaferro, Mabel: *movies*
Talmadge, Constance: *movies*
Talmadge, Norma: *movies*
Tamiroff, Akim: *movies*
Tandy, Jessica: *movies*
Taurog, Norman: *movies*
Taylor, Elizabeth: *movies*
Taylor, Estelle: *movies*
Taylor, Kent: *movies, TV*
Taylor, Rip: *theater*
Taylor, Robert: *movies*
Taylor, Ruth Ashton: *TV*
Tebaldi, Renata: *music*
Temple, Shirley: *movies*
Templeton, Alec: *radio*
Temptations, The: *music*
Terry, Alice: *movies*
Tesh, John: *TV*
Thalberg, Irving: *movies*
Thaxter, Phyllis: *movies*
Thebom, Blanche: *music*
Thomas, Bob: *movies*
Thomas, Danny: *TV*
Thomas, Jay: *radio*
Thomas, John Carlos: *music*
Thomas, Lowell: *movies, radio*
Thomas, Marlo: *movies*
Thompson, Bill: *radio*
Thomson, Fred: *movies*
Thorpe, Richard: *movies*
Three Stooges, The: *movies*
Tibbett, Lawrence: *music*
Tierney, Gene: *movies*
Tobin, Genevieve: *movies*
Todd, Thelma: *movies*
Tone, Franchot: *movies*

Lupe Velez

Toomey, Regis: *movies*
Torme, Mel: *music*
Torrence, David: *movies*
Torrence, Ernest: *movies*
Toscanini, Arturo: *music, radio*
Tourner, Maurice: *movies*
Tracy, Lee: *movies*
Tracy, Spencer: *movies*
Traubel, Helen: *music*
Travolta, John: *movies*
Treacher, Arthur: *movies*
Trevor, Claire: *movies*
Trimble, Laurence: *movies*
Truex, Ernest: *TV*
Tubb, Ernest: *music*
Tucker, Forrest: *movies*
Tucker, Sophie: *movies*
Tully, Thomas L.: *movies*
Tuna, Charlie: *radio*
Tune, Tommy: *theater*
Turner, Lana: *movies*
Turner, Tina, *music*
Turpin, Ben: *movies*
Tuttle, Lurene: *radio, TV*
Twelvetrees, Helen: *movies*

V

Vague, Vera: *movies, radio*
Valens, Ritchie: *music*
Valenti, Jack: *movies*
Valentino, Rudolph: *movies*
Vallee, Rudy: *radio*
Valli, Virginia: *movies*
Vance, Vivian: *TV*
Van Doren, Mamie: *movies*
Van Dyke, Dick: *TV*
Van Dyke, W.S.: *movies*
Van Fleet, Jo: *movies*
Van Patten, Dick: *TV*
Vaughan, Sarah: *music*
Velez, Lupe: *movies*
Venable, Evelyn: *movies*
Vera, Billy: *music*
Vera-Ellen: *movies*
Verdugo, Elena: *TV*
Vernon, Bobby: *movies*
Vidor, Charles: *movies*
Vidor, King: *movies*
Vincent, Gene: *music*
Vinson, Helen: *movies*
Vinton, Bobbie: *music*

Von Sternberg, Josef: *movies*
Von Stroheim, Erich: *movies*
Von Zell, Harry: *radio*

W

Wagner, Lindsay: *TV*
Wagner, Robert: *music*
Wakely, Jimmy: *music*
Walker, Clint: *TV*
Walker, Robert: *movies*
Wallace, Mike: *TV*
Wallace, Richard: *movies*
Wallington, James: *radio*
Walsh, Raoul: *movies*
Walter, Bruno: *music*
Walters, Charles: *movies*
Walthall, Henry B.: *movies*
Waring, Fred: *music, radio, TV*
Warner, H. B.: *movies*
Warner, Harry: *movies*
Warner, Jack: *movies*
Warner, Sam: *movies*
Warrick, Ruth: *movies*
Warwick, Dionne: *music*
Waterman, Willard: *radio*
Wayne, John: *movies*
Weaver, Dennis: *TV*
Webb, Clifton: *movies*
Webb, Jack: *radio, TV*
Webb, Richard: *TV*
Webber, Sir Andrew Lloyd: *theater*
Weber, Lois: *movies*
Weems, Ted: *music*
Weintraub, Jerry: *movies*
Weissmuller, Johnny: *TV*
Welk, Lawrence: *music, TV*
Welles, Orson: *movies, radio*
Wellman, William: *movies*
Welsh, Bill: *TV*
West, Mae: *movies*
Weston, Paul: *music*
White, Alice: *movies*
White, Betty: *TV*
White, Jack: *movies*
White, Jules: *movies*
White, Pearl: *movies*
Whiteman, Paul: *music, radio*
Whiting, Barbara: *TV*
Whiting, Margaret: *music*
Whitman, Slim: *music*
Whitmore, James: *TV*
Whittinghill, Dick: *radio*
Widmark, Richard: *movies*
Wilcoxon, Henry: *movies*
Wilde, Cornel: *movies*
Wilder, Billy: *movies*
Wilkerson Kassel, Tichi: *movies*
William, Warren: *movies*
Williams, Andy: *music*
Williams, Bill: *TV*
Williams, Billy Dee: *movies*
Williams, Earle: *movies*
Williams, Esther: *movies*
Williams, Hank: *music*
Williams, Joe: *music*
Williams, Kathlyn: *movies*
Williams, Paul: *music*

Williams, Robin: *movies*
Williams, Roger: *music*
Williams, Tex: *radio*
Willock, Dave: *TV*
Wills, Chill: *movies*
Willson, Meredith: *radio*
Wilson, Carey: *movies*
Wilson, Don: *radio*
Wilson, Lois: *movies*
Wilson, Marie: *movies, radio, TV*
Wilson, Nancy: *music*
Winchell, Paul: *TV*
Winchell, Walter: *Radio, TV*
Windsor, Claire: *movies*
Windsor, Marie: *movies*
Wing, Toby: *movies*
Winkler, Henry: *TV*
Winninger, Charles: *radio*
Winterhalter, Hugo: *music*
Winters, Jonathan: *TV*
Winters, Shelley: *movies*
Wise, Robert: *movies*
Withers, Jane: *movies*
Wolper, David: *TV*
Wonder, Stevie: *music*
Wong, Anna May: *movies*
Wood, Natalie: *movies*
Wood, Sam: *movies*
Woodpecker, Woody: *movies*
Woods, Donald: *TV*
Woodward, Joanne: *movies*
Woolley, Monty: *movies*
Wray, Fay: *movies*
Wright, Teresa: *movies, TV*
Wyatt, Jane: *TV*
Wyler, William: *movies*
Wyman, Jane: *movies, TV*
Wynn, Ed: *movies, radio, TV*
Wynn, Keenan: *TV*

Y

Young, Alan: *radio*
Young, Carleton: *radio*
Young, Clara Kimball: *movies*
Young, Gig: *TV*
Young, Loretta: *movies, TV*
Young, Robert: *movies, radio, TV*
Young, Roland: *movies, TV*
Young, Victor: *music*

Z

Zabach, Florian: *TV*
Zanuck, Darryl: *movies*
Zanuck, Richard: *movies*
Zimbalist, Efrem Jr.: *TV*
Zinneman, Fred: *movies*
Zukor, Adolph: *movies*

Major Motion Picture Producers and Distributors

Buena Vista Pictures Distribution
3900 W. Alameda Ave.
Tower Building, Suite 2400
Burbank, CA 91521-0021
(818) 567-5000

Carolco Pictures Inc.
8800 Sunset Blvd.
Los Angeles, CA 90069
(310) 859-8800

Castle Hill Productions, Inc.
1414 Ave. of the Americas
New York, NY 10019
(212) 888-0080

Castle Rock Entertainment
335 N. Maple Drive, Suite 2300
Beverly Hills, CA 90210
(310) 285-2300

Columbia Pictures
10202 W. Washington Blvd.
Culver City, CA 90232
(310) 280-8000

Walt Disney Pictures
500 S. Buena Vista St.
Burbank, CA 91521
(818) 560-1000

DreamWorks SKG
100 Universal Plaza, Building 601
Universal City, CA 91608
(818) 733-7000

Fine Line Features
888 Seventh Ave., 20th Floor
New York, NY 10106
(212) 649-4900

The Samuel Goldwyn Co.
810203 Santa Monica Blvd., Suite 500
Los Angeles, CA 90067
(310) 552-2255

Gramercy Pictures
9247 Alden Drive
Beverly Hills, CA 90210
(310) 777-1960

Hemdale
7966 Beverly Blvd.
Los Angeles, CA 90048
(213) 966-3700

Hollywood Pictures
500 S. Buena Vista St.
Burbank, CA 91521
(818) 560-6990

Home Box Office
81100 Ave. of the Americas
New York, NY 10036
(212) 512-1000

Imagine Entertainment
1925 Century Park E., 23rd Floor
Los Angeles, CA 90067
(310) 277-1665

Interscope
10900 Wilshire Blvd., Suite 1400
Los Angeles, CA 90024
(310) 208-8525

Largo Entertainment
2029 Century Park E., Suite 920
Los Angeles, CA 90067
(310) 203-0055

Lucasfilm, Ltd.
P.O. Box 2459
San Rafael, CA 94912
(415) 662-1800

MCA Inc.
100 Universal City Plaza
Universal City, CA 91608
(818) 777-1000

Merchant Ivory Productions
250 W. 57th St., Suite 1913A
New York, NY 10107
(212) 582-8049

Metro-Goldwyn-Mayer Inc.
2500 Broadway St.
Santa Monica, CA 90404-3061
(310) 449-3000

Miramax Films Corp.
375 Greenwich St.
New York, NY 10013
(212) 941-3800

New Line Cinema Corp.
888 Seventh Ave., 20th Floor
New York, NY 10106
(212) 649-4900

October Films
65 Bleecker St., 2nd Floor
New York, NY 10012
(212) 539-4000

Orion Pictures Corp.
304 Park Ave. S.
New York, NY 10010
(212) 505-0051

Paramount Pictures
1515 Broadway, 3rd Floor
New York, NY 10019
(212) 654-7000

Edward R. Pressman Film Corp.
445 N. Bedford Drive, Penthouse
Beverly Hills, CA 90210
(310) 271-8383

Republic Pictures Corp.
5700 Wilshire Blvd., Suite 525
Los Angeles, CA 90036
(213) 965-6900

Sony Pictures Entertainment, Inc.
10202 W. Washington Blvd.
Culver City, CA 90232
(310) 280-8000

Touchstone Pictures
500 S. Buena Vista St.
Burbank, CA 91521
(818) 560-1000

TriStar Pictures
10202 W. Washington Blvd.
Culver City, CA 90232
(310) 280-7700

Troma, Inc.
733 Ninth Ave.
New York, NY 10019
(212) 757-4555

Twentieth Century-Fox
P.O. Box 900
Beverly Hills, CA 90213
(310) 277-2211

Universal Pictures
445 Park Ave.
New York, NY 10022
(212) 759-7500

Warner Bros. Inc.
75 Rockefeller Plaza
New York, NY 10019
(212) 484-8000

Film Museums and Archives

Academy of Motion Picture Arts and Sciences
Center for Motion Picture Study
Academy Film Archive
333 S. La Cienega Blvd.
Beverly Hills, CA 90211
(310) 247-3000

American Museum of the Moving Image
35th Ave. at 36th St.
Astoria, NY 11106
(718) 784-4520

American Cinematheque
Hollywood Roosevelt Hotel
7000 Hollywood Blvd.
Hollywood, CA 90028
(213) 466-3456

**American Film Institute/National Center
for Film and Video Preservation**
John F. Kennedy Center for the Performing Arts
Washington D.C. 20566
(202) 828-4000

George Eastman House/International Museum of Photography
900 East Ave.
Rochester, NY 14607
(716) 271-3361

Harvard Film Archive
Carpenter Center for the Visual Arts
Harvard University
24 Quincy St.
Cambridge, MA 02138
(617) 495-4700

Library of Congress
Motion Picture, Broadcasting and Recorded Sound Division
Washington D.C. 20540
(202) 707-5840

Museum of Modern Art
Department of Film
11 W. 53rd St.
New York, NY 10019
(212) 708-9602

National Museum of Natural History/Human Studies Film Archives
Smithsonian Institute, Room E307
Washington D.C. 20560
(202) 357-3349

Pacific Film Archive
University Art Museum
2625 Durant Ave.
Berkeley, CA 94720
(510) 642-1412

UCLA Film and Television Archive
302 E. Melnitz Hall
University of California
405 Hilgard Ave.
Los Angeles, CA 90024
(310) 206-8013

Wisconsin Center for Film and Theater Research
816 State St.
Madison, WI 53706
(608) 264-6466

MOVIE TIME LINE

1824
Scientist Peter Mark Rogêt first identifies persistence of vision, the ability of the brain to retain an image captured by the retina one-twentieth to one-fifth of a second after the image has disappeared. When moving at a certain speed, persistence of vision allows the human eye to "see" a group of individual still pictures as one continuous moving image.

1889
In search of a visual counterpart to the phonograph, which he invented in 1877, Thomas Alva Edison commissions his lab assistant, **William Kennedy Laurie Dickson, to design a machine to process strips of celluloid film.** Dickson builds the first motion-picture camera and names it the Kinetograph.

1894
The Edison Corporation establishes a Kinetograph production center, the first motion-picture studio, nick-named the Black Maria (at the time, a slang word for a police van). To meet the new demand, Dickson produces, directs and shoots hundreds of short 50-foot-long movies (with running times of less than one minute).

U.S. Colleges and Universities Offering Degree Programs in Film

ALABAMA

BACHELOR'S DEGREE, FILM
University of North Alabama
Department of Communication and
Theater
Box 5007
University Station
Florence, AL 35632-0001
(205) 760-4247

ARIZONA

BACHELOR'S DEGREE, FILM
University of Arizona
College of Fine Arts
Department of Media Arts
Tucson, AZ 85721
(602) 621-7352

CALIFORNIA

BACHELOR'S DEGREE, FILM
Art Center College of Design
Department of Film
1700 Lida
Pasadena, CA 91103-1999
(818) 584-5035

Brooks Institute of Photography
Media Center
801 Alston Road
Santa Barbara, CA 93108
(805) 966-3888 ext. 217 or ext. 218

California Institute of the Arts
School of Film and Video
24700 McBean Parkway
Santa Clarita, CA 91355-2397
(805) 255-1050

California State University —
Northridge
Department of Radio, Television and
Film
18111 Nordhoff St.
Northridge, CA 91330-8317
(818) 885-3192

Humboldt State University
Theater Arts Department
Arcata, CA 95521-8299
(707) 826-4402

Loyola Marymount University
Department of Film
Loyola Blvd. at W. 80th St.
Los Angeles, CA 90045
(310) 338-2750

Pitzer College
Department of Film
1050 N. Mills Ave.
Claremont, CA 91711-6110
(909) 621-8000

San Diego State University
College of Professional Studies
Department of Telecommunications
5500 Campanile Drive
San Diego, CA 92182-0771
(619) 594-5450

San Francisco Art Institute
Filmmaking Department
800 Chestnut St.
San Francisco, CA 94133-2299
(415) 771-7020

San Francisco State University
Cinema Department
1600 Holloway Ave.
San Francisco, CA 94132-1722
(415) 338-1629

San Jose State University
Department of Radio, Film and
Television
1 Washington Square
San Jose, CA 95192-0001
(408) 924-4543

University of California — Irvine
Department of Film Studies
Humanities Hall
Irvine, CA 92717-1425
(714) 824-5386

University of California — Los Angeles
Department of Film and Television
102 E. Melnitz Hall
405 Hilgard Ave.
Los Angeles, CA 90024-1301
(310) 206-8441

University of California — San Diego
Department of Visual Arts
9500 Gilman Drive
La Jolla, CA 92093-0327
(619) 534-2860

University of California — Santa
Barbara
Film Studies
University of California
Santa Barbara, CA 93106
(805) 893-2347

University of Southern California
Student Affairs
School of Cinema-Television
Los Angeles, CA 90089-0911
(213) 740-2911

MASTER'S DEGREE, FILM
American Film Institute Center for
Advanced Film
and Television Studies
2021 N. Western Ave.
Los Angeles, CA 90027
(213) 856-7000

1894

The first Kinetoscope parlor is opened at 1155 Broadway in New York City. Films can be viewed by spectators individually for 25 cents.

1895

In France, the first screening for a private audience is held by Auguste and Louis

Lumière, soon after they invent the Cinémato-graph, a combination camera and projector. The image of an oncoming train is said to have caused a stampede.

1896

George Méliès, a professional magician in France, becomes film's first independent filmmaker, going on to serve

as producer, director and cameraman on some 500 films. Editing is invented when his camera jams while he is shooting a procession, accidentally superimposing two images.

1903

Edison Corporation mechanic turned cameraman, director and producer, Edwin S.

Porter makes *The Great Train Robbery.* As its 14 shots cut to and from events happening at the same time, this 12-minute short, in addition to being the first Western, establishes the shot as the basic element of film and editing as one of the medium's most powerful narrative devices.

Brooks Institute of Photography
Media Center
801 Alston Road
Santa Barbara, CA 93108
(805) 966-3888 ext. 217 or ext. 218

California Institute of the Arts
School of Film and Video
24700 McBean Parkway
Santa Clarita, CA 91355-2397
(805) 255-1050

Humboldt State University
Theater Arts Department
Arcata, CA 95521-8299
(707) 826-4402

Loyola Marymount University
Graduate School
Department of Film
Loyola Blvd. at W. 80th St.
Los Angeles, CA 90045
(310) 338-2750

San Francisco Art Institute
Filmmaking Department
800 Chestnut St.
San Francisco, CA 94133-2299
(415) 771-7020

San Francisco State University
Cinema Department
1600 Holloway Ave.
San Francisco, CA 94132-1722
(415) 338-1629

University of California — Los Angeles
Graduate Division of Department of Film
and Television
102 E. Melnitz Hall
405 Hilgard Ave.
Los Angeles, CA 90024-1301
(310) 206-8441

University of Southern California
Student Affairs
School of Cinema-Television
Los Angeles, CA 90089-0911
(213) 740-2911

DOCTORATE, FILM
University of California — Los Angeles
Graduate Department of Film and
Television
102 E. Melnitz Hall
405 Hilgard Ave.
Los Angeles, CA 90024-1301
(310) 206-8441

University of Southern California
Student Affairs
School of Cinema-Television
Los Angeles, CA 90089-0911
(213) 740-2911

COLORADO

BACHELOR'S DEGREE, FILM
University of Colorado — Boulder
Office of Film Studies
Campus Box 316
Boulder, CO 80309-0316
(303) 492-7574

CONNECTICUT

BACHELOR'S DEGREE, FILM
Yale University
Film Studies Program
New Haven, CT 06520
(203) 432-0152

DISTRICT OF COLUMBIA

BACHELOR'S DEGREE, FILM
The American University
School of Communications
4400 Massachusetts Ave. N.W.
Washington D.C. 20016-8001
(202) 885-2060

Gallaudet University
Department of Television, Film and
Photography
800 Florida Ave. N.E.
Washington D.C. 20002-3625
(202) 651-5115

MASTER'S DEGREE, FILM
The American University
School of Communications
4400 Massachusetts Ave. N.W.
Washington D.C. 20016-8001
(202) 885-2061

FLORIDA

BACHELOR'S DEGREE, FILM
Florida State University
School of Motion Picture, Television
and Recording Arts
1346 University Center
Tallahassee, FL 32306-2084
(904) 644-8747

University of Central Florida
Motion Picture Division
PC3-201
P.O. Box 16,3120
Orlando, FL 32816-3120
(407) 823-3456

University of Florida
School of Fine Arts
Gainesville, FL 32611
(904) 392-2038

MASTER'S DEGREE, FILM
Florida State University
School of Motion Picture, Television
and Recording Arts
1346 University Center
Tallahassee, FL 32306-2084
(904) 644-8747

University of Miami
School of Communication
P.O. Box 248127
Coral Gables, FL 33124
(305) 284-2265

GEORGIA

BACHELOR'S DEGREE, FILM
Georgia State University
Department of Communication
Film and Video
Atlanta, GA 30303
(404) 651-3200

Savannah College of Art and Design
Hamilton Hall's Video Department
522 Indian St.
Savannah, GA 31401
(912) 238-2407

ILLINOIS

BACHELOR'S DEGREE, FILM
Columbia College
Department of Film and Video
600 S. Michigan Ave.
Chicago, IL 60605
(312) 663-1600 ext. 129

Northwestern University
Department of Radio, Television and
Film
1905 Sheridan Road
Evanston, IL 60201
(708) 491-7315

1909

The first film review is published in the *New York Times* about D.W. Griffith's *Pippa Passes*.

1909

Hollywood begins its Golden Age as filmmakers flee the East Coast and its concentration of power and wealth for the land of sunshine.

1911

The first feature film is screened when the two reels of D.W. Griffith's *Enoch Arden* are released together.

1914

In his technically brilliant though ideologically condemned Civil War epic, *The Birth of a Nation*, D.W. Griffith

introduces the narrative close-up and the flashback, in addition to discovering and advancing elements that endure as the definitive structural principles of narrative filmmaking.

1925

Influenced by his Soviet colleague Lev Kuleshov's editing experiments concluding

that "real" time is subordinate to the shot sequence, a process he called montage, director Sergei Eisenstein makes *Potemkin*, a revolutionary portrait of a mutiny aboard a battleship and its violent repercussions. In the hands of Eisenstein, montage is raised to the highest structural role in filmmaking, serving as

Southern Illinois University — Carbondale
Department of Cinema and Photography
Carbondale, IL 62901-6610
(618) 453-2365

University of Illinois — Chicago
Department of Photography, Film and Electronic Media
929 W. Harrison St.
Jefferson Hall, Room 106
M-C036
Chicago, IL 60607
(312) 996-3337

MASTER'S DEGREE, FILM
Columbia College
Department of Film and Video
600 S. Michigan Ave.
Chicago, IL 60605
(312) 663-1600 ext. 300

Northwestern University
Department of Radio, Television and Film
1905 Sheridan Road
Evanston, IL 60201
(708) 491-7315

Southern Illinois University — Carbondale
Department of Cinema and Photography
Carbondale, IL 62901-6610
(618) 453-2365

University of Illinois — Chicago
Department of Photography, Film and Electronic Media
929 W. Harrison St.
Jefferson Hall, Room 106
M-C036
Chicago, IL 60607
(312) 996-3337

DOCTORATE, FILM
Northwestern University
Department of Radio, Television and Film
1905 Sheridan Road
Evanston, IL 60201
(708) 491-7315

INDIANA

BACHELOR'S DEGREE, FILM
Indiana State University
Department of Communication
105 BCSB
Terre Haute, IN 47809
(812) 237-3245

University of Notre Dame
Department of Communication and Theater
105 BCSB
Notre Dame, IN 46556
(219) 631-5134

IOWA

MASTER'S DEGREE, FILM
University of Iowa
College of Liberal Arts
Department of Communication Studies
Iowa City, IA 52242
(319) 335-0575

DOCTORATE, FILM
University of Iowa
College of Liberal Arts
Department of Communication Studies
Iowa City, IA 52242
(319) 335-0575

KANSAS

BACHELOR'S DEGREE, FILM
Southwestern College
Media Center
100 College St.
Winfield, KS 67156-2499
(316) 221-8266

University of Kansas
Department of Theater and Film
356 Murphy Hall
Lawrence, KS 66045
(913) 864-3511

MASTER'S DEGREE, FILM
University of Kansas
Department of Theater and Film
356 Murphy Hall
Lawrence, KS 66045
(913) 864-3511

DOCTORATE, FILM
University of Kansas
Department of Theater and Film
356 Murphy Hall
Lawrence, KS 66045
(913) 864-3511

LOUISIANA

BACHELOR'S DEGREE, FILM
Northeast Louisiana University
Department of Radio, Television and Film
156A Dubbs Hall
Monroe, LA 71209
(318) 342-1419

MASSACHUSETTS

BACHELOR'S DEGREE, FILM
Boston University
School of Broadcasting and Film
640 Commonwealth Ave.
Boston, MA 02215
(617) 353-3483

Clark University
Department of Visual and Performing Arts
950 Main St.
Worcester, MA 01610
(508) 793-7113

Emerson College
Department of Mass Communications
100 Beacon St.
Boston, MA 02116
(617) 578-8800

Hampshire College
School of Humanities and Art
Emily Dickinson Hall
Amherst, MA 01002
(413) 582-5361

School of the Museum of Fine Arts
Department of Film Animation
230 The Fenway
Boston, MA 02115
(617) 267-3678

MASTER'S DEGREE, FILM
Boston University
School of Broadcasting and Film
640 Commonwealth Ave.
Boston, MA 02215
(617) 353-3483

---

the unifying element of the medium. No longer a borrower from the other arts's methods and techniques, film can communicate on its own terms for the first time.

1927
Thanks to Vitaphone sound-on-disk technology, the silent film *Don Juan*, starring John Barrymore, is released with an orchestral score.

1929
Popular vaudevillian Al Jolson introduced his nightclub act in *The Jazz Singer*, astounding audiences attending the first feature-length talkie. The industry-wide conversion to sound cost an estimated $300 million.

1935
Although a primitive, two-color process was first used in 1922, audiences didn't respond until the introduction of Technicolor's three-color system in 1935's *Becky Sharp*, Rouben Mamoulian's take on William Makepeace Thackeray's novel, *Vanity Fair*. This is basically the same process used in 1939's *The Wizard of Oz* and *Gone With the Wind*.

1939
An unbeatable year for Hollywood and film, 1939 saw the release of *The Wizard of Oz, Gone With the Wind* and *Wuthering Heights*.

MICHIGAN

BACHELOR'S DEGREE, FILM

Central Michigan University
Department of Film Studies
Moore Hall, Room 340
Mount Pleasant, MI 48859
(517) 774-3851

Eastern Michigan University
Department of Communication and
Theater Arts
124 Quirk
Ypsilanti, MI 48197
(313) 487-3131

Grand Valley State University
School of Communications
121 Lake Superior Hall
Allendale, MI 49401
(616) 895-3668

Northern Michigan University
Department of Art and Design
1401 Presque Isle Ave.
Marquette, MI 49855
(906) 227-2194

University of Michigan
Film and Video Studies
2512 Frieze Building
Ann Arbor, MI 48109-1282
(313) 764-0147

Wayne State University
Department of Film
585 Manoogian Building
906 W. Warren Ave.
Detroit, MI 48202
(313) 577-2943

MASTER'S DEGREE, FILM

Central Michigan University
Department of Film Studies
Moore Hall, Room 340
Mount Pleasant, MI 48859
(517) 774-3851

MISSISSIPPI

BACHELOR'S DEGREE, FILM

University of Southern Mississippi
Department of Film Studies
Box 5141
Hattiesburg, MS 39406
(601) 266-4281

MISSOURI

BACHELOR'S DEGREE, FILM

Central Missouri State University
Department of Communication
Martin 1136
Warrensburg, MO 64093
(816) 543-4840

NEW HAMPSHIRE

BACHELOR'S DEGREE, FILM

Dartmouth College
Department of Film Studies
319 Wilson Hall
Hanover, NH 03755
(603) 646-3402

Keene State College
Department of Film
229 Main St.
Keene, NH 03435
(603) 358-2765

NEW YORK

BACHELOR'S DEGREE, FILM

Bard College
Department of Film
Annandale-on-Hudson, NY 12504
(914) 758-6822

**City University of New York —
Brooklyn College**
Department of Film
2900 Bedford Ave.
Brooklyn, NY 11210
(718) 951-5664

**City University of New York — City
College**
Department of Film and Video
Convent Ave. at 138th St.
New York, NY 10031
(212) 650-6560

**City University of New York — College
of Staten Island**
Department of Film
2800 Victory Blvd.
Staten Island, NY 10314
(718) 982-2523

**City University of New York — Hunter
College**
Department of Film
695 Park Ave.
New York, NY 10021
(212) 772-5148

**City University of New York
— Queens College**
Department of Film Studies
65-30 Kissena Blvd.
Flushing, NY 11367-1597
(718) 997-5748

Ithaca College
Department of Cinema and Photography
School of Communication
350 Roy H. Park Hall
Ithaca, NY 14850-7251
(607) 274-3896

**Long Island University
— C.W. Post Center**
Department of Visual and Performing
Arts
Brookville, NY 11548
(516) 299-2353

New York University
Tisch School of the Arts
721 Broadway, 9th Floor
New York, NY 10003
(212) 998-1700

Pratt Institute
Department of Film
200 Willoughby Ave.
Brooklyn, NY 11205
(718) 636-3767

Rochester Institute of Technology
College of Imagine Arts and Sciences
School of Photography
Gannett Building, Room 2143
70 Lomb Memorial Drive
Rochester, NY 14623
(716) 475-2779

School of Visual Arts
Department of Film Studies
209 E. 23rd St.
New York, NY 10010
(212) 592-2180

**State University of New York —
Binghamton**
Department of Cinema
Student Wing, Room B11
Bestal Parkway E.
P.O. Box 6000
Binghamton, NY 13902
(607) 777-4998

1939

Mise-en-scène (a
French term referring to
the incorporation of cin-
ematic elements such
as action, set design
and lighting within one
shot rather than relying
on a sequence of shots)
reaches new heights in
The Rules of the Game,
Jean Renoir's ironic tale
of desire and deceit

during a country-week-
end hunting party. With
long takes and deep-
focus photography,
Renoir looks beyond
montage to create a
new aesthetic in which
the close-up, middle
shot and long shot exist
within the same frame,
establishing the single
shot as a powerful unit
of storytelling.

1941

In *Citizen Kane*, Orson
Welles subordinates all
previous technological
and cinematic accom-
plishments to his own
essentially cinematic
vision. Using newly
developed film stocks
and a wider, faster lens,
Welles pushes the
boundaries of montage
and mise-en-scène, as

well as sound, redefin-
ing the medium.

1945

Roberto Rossellini's
Neorealist ode to the
Italian Resistance,
Rome, Open City, pre-
sents an alternative to
Hollywood with its use
of street cinematogra-
phy, grainy black-and-
white stocks and

State University of New York — Purchase
Department of Film
735 Anderson Hill Road
Purchase, NY 10577-1400
(914) 251-6860

Syracuse University
Department of Radio,
Television and Film
362 Newhouse II
215 University Place
Syracuse, NY 13244
(315) 443-1944

University of Rochester
Department of Film
Rush Rhees, Room 427
Rochester, NY 14627
(716) 275-5757

MASTER'S DEGREE, FILM
Bard College
Department of Film
Annandale-on-Hudson, NY 12504
(914) 758-6822

City University of New York — College of Staten Island
Department of Film
2800 Victory Blvd.
Staten Island, NY 10314
(718) 982-2523

City University of New York — Queens College
Department of Film
65-30 Kissena Blvd.
Flushing, NY 11367-1597
(718) 997-5748

Columbia University
Graduate School of Arts and Sciences
Department of Film
513 C Dodge
New York, NY 10027
(212) 854-2815

New York University
Tisch School of the Arts
721 Broadway, 9th Floor
New York, NY 10003
(212) 998-1700

Syracuse University
Department of Radio, Television and Film
362 Newhouse II
215 University Place
Syracuse, NY 13244
(315) 443-1944

University of Rochester
Department of Film
Rush Rhees, Room 427
Rochester, NY 14627
(716) 275-5757

DOCTORATE, FILM
New York University
Tisch School of the Arts
721 Broadway, 9th Floor
New York, NY 10003
(212) 998-1700

Syracuse University
Department of Radio, Television and Film
362 Newhouse II
215 University Place
Syracuse, NY 13244
(315) 443-1944

NORTH CAROLINA

BACHELOR'S DEGREE, FILM
University of North Carolina — Greensboro
Division of Broadcasting and Cinema
Greensboro, NC 27412
(910) 334-5360

MASTER'S DEGREE, FILM
University of North Carolina — Greensboro
Division of Broadcasting and Cinema
Greensboro, NC 27412
(910) 334-5360

OHIO

BACHELOR'S DEGREE, FILM
Denison University
Department of Arts and Cinema
Granville, OH 43023
(614) 587-6234

University of Toledo
Department of Theater, Film and Dance
2801 W. Bancroft St.
Toledo, OH 43606
(419) 537-2202

Wright State University
Department of Theater
Dayton, OH 45435
(513) 873-3072

MASTER'S DEGREE, FILM
Ohio University
School of Film
378 Lindley Hall
Athens, OH 45701
(614) 593-1323

OKLAHOMA

BACHELOR'S DEGREE, FILM
University of Oklahoma
Department of Film
Dale Hall Tower, Room 806
College of Arts and Sciences
Norman, OK 73019
(405) 325-3020

MASTER'S DEGREE, FILM
University of Oklahoma
Department of Film
Dale Hall Tower, Room 806
College of Arts and Sciences
Norman, OK 73019
(405) 325-3020

PENNSYLVANIA

BACHELOR'S DEGREE, FILM
Drexel University
Nesbitt College of Design Arts, Film and Video
Philadelphia, PA 19104
(215) 895-1960

Pennsylvania State University — University Park Campus
Department of Film and Video
201 Carnegie Building
University Park, PA 16802
(814) 865-6597

Pittsburgh Filmmakers
3712 Sorbes Ave., 2nd Floor
Pittsburgh, PA 15213
(412) 681-5449

Temple University
Department of Radio, Television and Film
Annenberg Hall, Room 9
Philadelphia, PA 19122
(215) 204-8423

---

untrained actors, lyrically capturing the despair and confusion of post-World War II Europe.

1953
To counteract the threat of television, Hollywood thinks big and develops wide-screen processes such as CinemaScope, first seen in *The Robe*.

1955
70mm film is introduced with *Oklahoma!*

1959
Jean-Luc Godard's *Breathless*, typical of the French New Wave use of the jump cut, the hand-held camera and loose, improvised direction, is made for $90,000 in just four weeks. The

jump cut's assault on seamless editing and the presumption of time continuity opens new possibilities for filmmakers.

1962
Government regulations force studios out of the talent agency business.

1964
Bonnie and Clyde and *Red Desert* make spectacular use of the recently perfected zoom lens, which increases the optical mobility of a shot and its expressive capacities.

University of Pittsburgh
Department of Film
Cathedral of Learning, Room 526
Pittsburgh, PA 15260
(412) 624-6564

University of the Arts
Department of Film
333 S. Broad St.
Philadelphia, PA 19102
(215) 875-1020

MASTER'S DEGREE, FILM
Pennsylvania State University —
University Park Campus
Department of Film and Video
201 Carnegie Building
University Park, PA 16802
(814) 865-6597

RHODE ISLAND

BACHELOR'S DEGREE, FILM
Rhode Island College
Department of Film Studies
Providence, RI 02908
(401) 456-8027

Rhode Island School of Design
Department of Film and Video
Providence, RI 02903-2784
(401) 454-6233

SOUTH CAROLINA

BACHELOR'S DEGREE, FILM
Bob Jones University
Department of Unusual Films
1700 Wade Hampton Blvd.
Greenville, SC 29615
(803) 242-5100 ext. 2742

MASTER'S DEGREE, FILM
Bob Jones University
Department of Unusual Films
1700 Wade Hampton Blvd.
Greenville, SC 29615
(803) 242-5100 ext. 2742

TEXAS

BACHELOR'S DEGREE, FILM
Sam Houston State University
Department of Photography and
Technology
P.O. Box 2266
Huntsville, TX 77341
(409) 294-1191

Southern Methodist University
Center for Communication Arts
3300 Dyer
Dallas, TX 75275
(214) 768-3607

Texas Christian University
Department of Radio, Television and
Film
P.O. Box 30793
Fort Worth, TX 76129
(817) 921-7630

University of North Texas
Department of Radio, Television and
Film
Box 13108
Denton, TX 76203
(817) 565-2537

University of Texas — Austin
Department of Radio, Television and
Film
College of Communication
Austin, TX 78712
(512) 471-4071

MASTER'S DEGREE, FILM
University of North Texas
Department of Radio, Television and
Film
Box 13108
Denton, TX 76203
(817) 565-2537

University of Texas — Austin
Department of Radio, Television and
Film
College of Communication
Austin, TX 78712
(512) 471-4071

UTAH

BACHELOR'S DEGREE, FILM
University of Utah
Department of Film
206 Pab Building
Salt Lake City, UT 84112
(801) 581-6448

VERMONT

BACHELOR'S DEGREE, FILM
Marlboro College
Department of Film Studies
Marlboro, VT 05344
(802) 257-4333

Middlebury College
Department of Film Studies
Middlebury, VT 05753-6000
(802) 388-3190

VIRGINIA

MASTER'S DEGREE, FILM
Virginia Commonwealth University
School of the Arts
Department of Design
Program in Photography/Film
Richmond, VA 23284
(804) 828-0100

WISCONSIN

BACHELOR'S DEGREE, FILM
University of Wisconsin — Milwaukee
Department of Film
P.O. Box 413
Milwaukee, WI 53201
(414) 229-6015

University of Wisconsin — Oshkosh
Department of Radio, Television and
Film
Arts and Communication West 112
Oshkosh, WI 54901
(414) 424-3131

MASTER'S DEGREE, FILM
University of Wisconsin — Milwaukee
Department of Film
P.O. Box 413
Milwaukee, WI 53201
(414) 229-6015

1976
The Steadicam is used for the first time in *Rocky*.

1977
Saturday Night Fever sparks the disco inferno and the popularity of movie soundtracks.

1988
Foreign box office receipts for American movies reach 40% of total receipts, prompting studios to make movies more easily understood and marketed overseas.

1993
Lost in Yonkers is edited on an Avid Media Composer system, the first non-linear-editing system to allow viewing at film's required "real-time"-viewing rate of 24 frames per second. By converting film into digital bits, film can now be cut on a computer.

Movie Palaces

American Movie Classics network and *American Movie Classics* magazine regularly highlight some of the country's finest restored movie palaces. These "everyman palaces," typically dating from the 1920s, evoked as much magic as the doings on the screen. The grande dames of American entertainment halls have been restored by local organizations determined to preserve their contribution to American architecture and society, in many cases establishing them as the home base for today's community performing arts groups. This very brief list is meant to encourage a visit if you're passing by; there's probably a movie palace near you waiting to inspire wonder.

Paul Bowen/Courtesy of the Augusta Arts Council, Inc.

Augusta Theatre

AUGUSTA THEATRE
523 State St.
Augusta, KS 67010
(316) 775-3661

Christened in 1935, this late-period venue, adorned with colorful murals of classical scenes, is an exemplary model of art deco style. Architect L.P. Larson was chosen for his emphasis on neon lighting; the Augusta was the first theater to be lit completely by neon. The theater is now operated by the Augusta Arts Council.

CASTRO THEATRE
429 Castro St.
San Francisco, CA 94114
(415) 621-6350

Long considered to be one of the finest 1920s movie palaces on the West Coast, the Castro remains a thriving movie house. Each evening's performance includes musical interludes with performances on the Wurlitzer Opus organ. Architect Timothy Pflueger marked the beginning of his theater design career with the Castro, and he created what amounts to a Spanish colonial cathedral. The 1922 opening revealed frescoed murals, gilt mirrors and grand staircases; the exterior reflects the Spanish theme with an elaborate mullioned window.

THE 5TH AVENUE THEATRE

1308 5th Ave.
Seattle, WA 98101
(206) 625-1900

Bucking the trend of French and Spanish baroque styling, architect Robert Reamer and designer Gustav Liljestrom opted for an eye-popping Chinese excursion. Reamer and Liljestrom modeled their work on the Temple of Heavenly Peace, including Foo dogs, Ho-Ho birds in the plaster work and a magnificent dome that replicates the dome of the throne room at Peking's Imperial Palace.

THE FOX THEATRE

660 Peach Tree St. NE
Atlanta, GA 30365
(404) 881-2100

Opening only a few months after the 1929 stock market crash, The Fox offered relief from the dismal times. An Egyptian/Moorish fantasy greets visitors with minarets, bronze onion domes and Moorish arches. A night sky of twinkling stars and drifting clouds creates a dreamy embrace, and a striped canopy covers the balcony area. Mighty Mo, the enormous Moller organ, still thunders and emulates exotic animals and bird whistles.

THE OHIO THEATRE

55 E. State St.
Columbus, OH 43215
(614) 469-1045

Renowned movie palace architect Thomas Lamb created his signature Spanish baroque atmosphere in this 1928 theater. A jewel box of gold leaf and Moroccan touches, the lower lounge even contained decorations obtained on safari for the "African Corner." The theater is now operated by the Columbus Association for the Performing Arts.

THE PARAMOUNT THEATRE

352 Cypress St.
Abilene, TX 79601
(915) 676-9620

Texas's Spanish heritage is echoed in Spanish mission-bell towers that flank the stage and the conquistadors' helmets that grace the exterior of this 1921 palace. Projected clouds move lazily over a ceiling containing thousands of electric stars. The award-winning restoration was completed in 1987, and the Paramount now houses ballet, opera, theater and a classic film series.

D. R. Goff/Courtesy of Columbus Association for the Performing Arts

The Ohio Theatre

The Rialto Square Theatre

THE RIALTO SQUARE THEATRE
102 N. Chicago St.
Joliet, IL 60431
(815) 726-7171

The jewel of Joliet is considered by many to be among the 10 most beautiful theaters in the country. Seven different styles of architecture from classical Greek and Roman to Renaissance and Baroque are seen in the building and its appointments. A Sicilian sculptor created classical statuary for the exterior. The 1926 palace features a grand hall fashioned after Versailles's Hall of Mirrors and the Arc de Triomphe. The lobby lit-

erally sparkles with the "Duchess," still the largest hand-cut crystal chandelier in the country. The many dazzling details were restored to their former luster in 1981.

THE SENATOR THEATRE
5904 York Road
Baltimore, MD 21212
(410) 435-8338

Though not an enormous palace, this friendly neighborhood theater presents a splendid example of art deco architecture. The Senator was voted one of the nation's four best movie theaters in 1991 by *USA Today*. It continues to operate as a movie theater run by the grandson of Frank Durkee, the man who brought the flickers to Baltimore in 1909.

THE STATE THEATRE
805 Hennepin Ave.
Minneapolis, MN 55402
(612) 339-0075

THE ORPHEUM THEATRE
910 Hennepin Ave.
Minneapolis, MN 55403
(612) 339-0075

The recent restoration of The State and The Orpheum theaters brought to life a once rundown area. The Orpheum boasts a Beaux Arts majesty contained in its grand stairways, friezes and columns. The State glories in a gilded Italian Renaissance glitter. Both theaters date from 1921, and were once among the largest theaters on the country's vaudeville circuit. Now both theaters present musical theater and classic film festivals.

George Heinrich

The State Theatre

Syracuse Area Landmark Theater

SYRACUSE AREA LANDMARK THEATER
362 S. Salina St.
Syracuse, NY 13201
(315) 475-7979

Thomas Lamb has described his 1928 baroque creation as "European, Byzantine, Romanesque — the Orient as it came to us through the mer-

George Heinrich

The Orpheum Theatre

chants of Venice." A chandelier by Louis Tiffany adorns the lobby and illuminates several murals. The theater also contained a Musician's Gallery and a fish pond with a Japanese pagoda fountain. Now the home of the Syracuse Symphony, it was the anchor of 1977's downtown revitalization efforts.

WANG CENTER FOR THE PERFORMING ARTS
268 Tremont St.
Boston, MA 02116
(617) 482-9393

When the Metropolitan, known today as the Wang Center for the Performing Arts, opened in 1925, it occupied a full city block and extended five stories into the sky. Architect Clarence Blackall succeeding in creating Boston's cultural center. His masterpiece housed a 70-piece orchestra that rose from the basement as it played an overture. Acres of marble cover the lobby and ornamental statuary depicting themes from the performing arts adorn the baroque interior. The theater presented both movies and vaudeville, and was visited by the cream of jazz entertainers and bands. It currently presents Broadway touring shows, ballet, concerts and occasional film series.

THE WARNER THEATRE
1299 Pennsylvania Ave.
Washington D.C. 20004
(202) 783-4000

This opulent auditorium was meticulously restored using original materials — right down to replicating carpet fragments and fabric swatches. The neoclassical palace opened in 1924 for both movies and vaudeville. Its gold-leafed ceiling was illuminated by a 15-by-6 chandelier, and the basement housed a restaurant and ballroom. The Warner now presents theater, music and film.

Movie Magazines and Journals

AFI Guide to College Courses in Film and Television
American Film Institute, Education Services
2021 N. Western Ave.
Los Angeles, CA 90027-1625
(213) 856-7600

American Cinematographer
A.S.C. Holding Corp.
1782 N. Orange Drive
Los Angeles, CA 90028
(213) 876-5080

American Movie Classics Magazine
Working Media, Inc.
18 Shawmut St.
Boston, MA 02116
(800) 669-1002

Black Film Review
Sojourner Productions, Inc.
2025 Eye St., N.W.
Washington DC 20006
(202) 466-2753

Bright Lights
P.O. Box 420987
San Francisco, CA 94142-0987
(415) 989-9841

Camera Obscura: A Journal of Feminism and Film Theory
Indiana University Press
601 N. Morton St.
Bloomington, IN 47404
(812) 855-9449

Cineaste
200 Park Ave. S., Suite 1601
New York, NY 10003
(212) 982-1241

Cinefantastique
P.O. Box 270
Oak Park, IL 60303
(708) 366-5566

Cinefex
Box 20027
Riverside, CA 92516-0027
(909) 781-1917

Director's Guild of America, Directory of Members
Directors Guild of America, Inc.
7920 Sunset Blvd.
Hollywood, CA 90046-3388
(310) 289-2073

East-West Film Journal
University of Hawaii Press
2840 Kolowalu St.
Honolulu, HI 96822-1888
(808) 956-8833

Entertainment Weekly
1675 Broadway
New York, NY 10019
(212) 522-5600

Fangoria
Starlog Group
475 Park Ave. S.
New York, NY 10016-6989
(212) 689-2830

Film Comment
Film Society of Lincoln Center
165 W. 65th St.
New York, NY 10023-6910
(212) 875-5610

Filmfax
Box 1900
Evanston, IL 60204-1900
(708) 866-7155

Filmmaker Magazine
Independent Feature Project
104 W. 29th St., 12th Floor
New York, NY 10001
(212) 465-2243

Film Quarterly
University of California Press
2120 Berkeley Way
Berkeley, CA 94702
(510) 642-4247

Films in Review
P. O. Box 589
New York, NY 10021
(212) 628-1594

Film Threat Video Guide
Film Threat Video Inc.
2805 Magnolia Blvd.
Burbank, CA 91505
(818) 848-8971

Independent
Foundation for Independent Video and Film
625 Broadway, 9th Floor
New York, NY 10012-2611
(212) 473-3400

Millennium Film Journal
66 E. Fourth St.
New York, NY 10003
(212) 673-0090

Millimeter
Penton Publishing
1100 Superior Ave.
Cleveland, OH 44114
(216) 696-7000

Movieline
1141 S. Beverly Drive
Los Angeles, CA 90035-1155
(619) 745-2809

Outré
Box 1900
Evanston, IL 60204-1900
(708) 866-7155

Premiere
K-III Communications
2 Park Ave., 11th Floor
New York, NY 10016
(212) 545-3500

Spectator-USC Journal of Film and Television Criticism
USC School of Cinema and TV
Division of Critical Studies
University of Southern California
Los Angeles, CA 90089-2211
(213) 740-3334

Velvet Light Trap
University of Texas Press
Box 7819
Austin, TX 78713-7819
(512) 471-4531

Movie Glossary

aspect ratio The width-to-height ratio of a movie frame and screen. Standard aspect ratio is 1.33 to 1; CinemaScope uses 2.35 to 1.

assistant director The person on a film crew who manages production issues and scheduling; not generally a collaborator in the artistic work of directing.

auteur A filmmaker, usually a director, with a recognizable, strong personal style.

backlighting A style of lighting that illuminates a subject from behind creating a silhouetting effect.

best boy The chief assistant to the gaffer on a set.

biopic A film or television biography, often with fictionalized episodes.

boom A movable arm that holds a microphone over actors' heads during filming.

B picture A low-budget movie that accompanied the main feature in a double bill.

celluloid A colorless, flammable material made from nitrocellulose and camphor that is used to make photographic film.

cineaste A film or movie enthusiast.

CinemaScope The trademark used for an anamorphic wide-screen process.

cinéma vérité A style of filmmaking that stresses unbiased realism and often contains unedited sequences.

coverage The shots, including close-ups and reverse angles, that a director takes in addition to the master shot.

cut 1. The instruction to stop the camera and the action in front of the camera. **2.** The process of editing a film or shortening a scene.

cutaway A brief shot that interrupts the continuity of the main action of a film, often used to depict related matter or indicate concurrent action.

day for night A shot filmed during the day, which appears on the screen to be a night scene.

depth of field The area in which objects are in focus using a given camera lens.

diffusion The reduction of the harshness or intensity of light achieved by using a screen, glass filter or smoke.

director of photography The movie photographer responsible for camera technique and lighting during production. Also called **cinematographer**.

dissolve The gradual transformation of one scene to the next by overlapping a fade-out with a fade-in.

dolly shot A moving shot that uses a wheeled camera platform known as a dolly.

editor The person often responsible for the final structure of a film.

exterior A scene shot outside a sound stage.

extras The non-speaking actors used to populate the backgrounds of scenes.

eyelight A small lighting instrument used to highlight an actor's eyes.

fade-in A gradual transition from complete black to full exposure.

fade-out A gradual transition from full exposure to complete black.

film noir A term for a genre of film typically set in a squalid urban environment and involving dark passions and violence.

finder A device, similar in appearance to a small camera lens, used to indicate the approximate field of view of a lens.

first run The distribution of a new film to a select number of showcase theaters.

flag v. To direct light and prevent unwanted reflection and lens flare. **n.** The opaque material used to flag.

frame An individual unit of movie film. The American standard film speed is 24 frames per second; there are 16 frames per foot of 35mm film.

freeze-frame A still picture during a movie, made by running a series of identical frames.

gaffer The main electrician and supervisor of lighting on a set.

grip A member of a crew who adjusts scenery, flags lights and often operates the camera cranes and dollies.

gross The amount of revenue a film generates from rental and ticket receipts before deducting expenses.

jump cut A cut made in the middle of a continuous shot rather than between shots creating discontinuity in time and drawing attention to the film itself instead of its content.

key grip The head grip who supervises the grip crew and receives orders from the gaffer or the head lighting technician.

kinescope A film made of a transmitted television program. It was generally used to preserve programs made before videotape was widely available.

klieg light A powerful carbon-arc lamp producing an intense light that is commonly used in filmmaking. It is sometimes used outside Hollywood theaters to promote premieres. Named after John H. Kliegl (1869–1959) and his brother Anton T. Kliegl (1870–1970), German-born American lighting experts.

looping The re-creation of movie dialogue in a sound stage to replace unusable passages from the original takes.

Lumière, Auguste Marie Louis Nicolas (1862–1954) French chemist, inventor and cinematography pioneer who, with his brother Louis Jean Lumière (1864–1948), gave the first public showing of a cinematic film in 1895.

master shot A continuous take that covers the entire set or all of the action in a scene.

matte shote A partially opaque shot in the frame area. The shot can be printed with another frame, hiding unwanted content and permitting the addition of another scene on a reverse matte.

montage The creation of narrative sense from a series of individual shots.

new wave A movement in French cinema in the 1960s, led by directors such as Jean-Luc Godard and François Truffaut, that abandoned traditional narrative techniques in favor of greater use of symbolism and abstraction and dealt with themes of social alienation, psychopathology and sexual love.

outtake A shot or scene that is shot but not used in the final print of the film.

pan A horizontal movement of the camera from a fixed point.

point of view A shot that depicts the outlook or position of a character.

postproduction A final stage in the production of a film or a television program, typically involving editing and the addition of soundtracks. Also called **post**.

preproduction The planning stage of a film involving budgeting, scheduling, casting, design and location selection.

rough-cut The first assembly of a film and soundtrack.

rushes The print of the camera footage from one day's shooting. Also called **dailies**.

scene A succession of shots that convey a unified element of a movie's story.

screenplay The script of a movie that contains both dialogue and action in continuous form.

second run The second distribution of a film to a large number of theaters usually in less exclusive theaters than a first run.

sequence A succession of scenes that comprise a dramatic unit of the film.

shot The basic building block of film narrative, the single unedited piece of film.

silver nitrate A poisonous, colorless crystalline compound, $AgNO3$, that becomes grayish-black when exposed to light in the presence of organic matter and was used in manufacturing photographic film. It was replaced by celluloid safety film.

slate The digital board that is held in front of the camera and identifies shot number, director, cameraperson, studio and title. The data was originally written with chalk on a piece of slate. This footage is used in the laboratory and editing room to identify the shot.

sound stage A soundproof room or studio used in movie production.

spaghetti Western A low-budget Western movie usually made by an Italian film company.

speed The call that indicates that the both camera and audio recorder have reached proper operating speed. The assistant camera operator and tape operator make the call before the director requests action.

sprocket A cylinder with a toothed rim that engages the perforations of photographic or movie film to pull it through a camera or projector.

SteadiCam A hydraulically-balanced apparatus that harnesses a camera to an operator's body providing smooth tracking shots without using a track.

storyboard The rough sketches depicting plot, action and characters in the sequential scenes of a film, television show or advertisement.

take The filming of a shot in particular camera setup. The director usually films several takes before approving the shot.

tilt A vertical camera movement from a fixed position.

tracking shot A shot that moves in one plane by moving the camera dolly along fixed tracks.

trailer A short filmed preview or advertisement for a movie.

treatment A detailed synopsis of a movie's story, with action and character rendered in prose form.

wild wall The removable wall on an interior set that moves out of the way of the camera.

Music

Boyz II Men

Jerry Garcia

R.E.M.

Mick Jagger

Courtney Love

Change Your Mind

■ BY TIM RILEY

Tim Riley's books include *Tell Me Why: A Beatles Commentary* (Knopf, 1988), *Hard Rain: A Dylan Commentary* (Knopf, 1992) and *Madonna: Illustrated* (Hyperion 1992). He is also editor of *millennium pop*, a journal of the popular arts.

THE 1990S ROUNDED ITS MID-DECADE CURVE with pop audiences rehashing old questions about fame, integrity and dinosaurs. For most rockers, the question was moot. Except for the obligatory noises about the hazards of touring, mainstream rock was aging comfortably (read: profitably). But for punk rock, which finally found its commercial triumph in the Seattle band Nirvana, the dilemma of fame may have been its undoing.

Within weeks of his suicide on April 5, 1994, Kurt Cobain had taken his place in the pantheon his mother had warned him about: "that stupid club" of dead rock stars. And Cobain's loss cast a shadow on the rest of 1994, right up through the release of Nirvana's *Unplugged* performance in December. Everyone from fans to newspaper columnists to network commentators spewed pieties about today's price of fame. Neil Young, who had seen his share of waste, was moved to memorialize Cobain's anguished "sacrifice" in "Sleeps With Angels" (his "Change Your Mind" could also be heard this way).

MUSIC

Nirvana's saga stretched back to 1992, when "Smells Like Teen Spirit" became punk's first bona fide smash. It carried its album, *Nevermind*, past triple platinum, and selling more than seven million units into 1995. Led by Cobain, a dirty blond with unruly bangs and a cackling voice that caught an epic exasperation, Nirvana's alienated thrash was festooned with catchy melodies. The success of "Teen Spirit" ridiculed the superficial styles that had dominated popular music since the mid-'80s. "Here we are now, entertain us," went the refrain, casting its audience as mummies buying shock therapy. The lyric was sarcasm on a stick; the sound was revenge drenched in hilarity.

But for Cobain, the whole process of becoming famous rubbed hard against punk's anti-corporate integrity. And since he made the simplistic equation that popularity meant selling out, and the matter was quickly out of his hands, he spoke as if it was a tragic fluke of fate that so many had responded to his music. Cobain seemed to fear that too much popularity might turn him into a freak, into a grunge Michael Jackson. During its heady 1992–1994 reign, Nirvana worked up an excitement in pop that had been missing since the glory days of the Clash in the early 1980s. But behind every hope were rumors of despondency, an air of desperation that the music couldn't forestall. Cobain was in and out of drug rehabs, and his daughter Frances Bean was said to have been conceived while Cobain and his wife, Courtney Love of Hole, were using heroin. Disabled by a chronic stomach ailment, Cobain's canceled shows earned him a professional reputation for being unreliable. There was enough goodwill (and cashola) to keep the machine churning, but Cobain took every opportunity to describe how much he hated stardom, how distanced he felt from listeners and how the precious Seattle scene had been corrupted by unwelcome gate-crashers and corporate raiders.

Charlie Hoselton/Retna

Kurt Cobain and Courtney Love

A
lthough discomfort with rock fame is hardly a new dilemma, part of what was charming about Cobain was the way he acted as if his quandary was original. There were times when it seemed all he really needed was a long sit-down with Pete Townshend, who had made such matters the stuff of great Who songs (and uneven rock operas) back in the 1960s and 1970s. The more commonplace comparison was to Beatle John Lennon, who complained about success just as he became the most famous man in the world in 1966 and compared The Beatles' success to Jesus Christ.

Before the band's final European stint in early 1994, Nirvana gathered in New York City to shoot MTV's *Unplugged*. With the massive success of Eric Clapton's *Unplugged* in 1992 — it sold more than four million copies, making it the best-selling title of Clapton's 30-year career — MTV's forum had become a rite of passage for careerists. In the brief history of the *Unplugged* series, Neil Young was suddenly born-again, R.E.M. got even hipper (as if that were possible) and acts like Paul McCartney, Bruce Springsteen and a reunited Led Zeppelin treated the "acoustic" format as a platform for the new rock "respectability" (read: aging process). Nobody asked self-reliant pioneers like Randy Newman or Richard Thompson to appear; *Unplugged* was about king-crowning, not star-making.

But Nirvana's *Unplugged* surpassed even "Smells Like Teen Spirit" as the band's finest moment. Mixing wariness about its massive audience with a belief in how far the music could redeem their situation, the set is now a modern classic. With Cobain mumbling an apology for opening with a sleeper ("About a Girl," from the band's first album on Sub Pop), and moving through a sober cover of David Bowie's "The Man Who Sold the World" (a blueprint for Cobain's cosmic despair), Nirvana made its venom compelling at the level of a whisper, and Cobain got even more out of his hushed growl than his considerable yammer. But there's a fatalism to Nirvana's *Unplugged* that's hard to miss; by this point the jig was basically up. Four months later, Cobain overdosed in Rome and emerged from a coma requesting a milkshake. Shortly after his family got him into his final California rehab in March of 1994, Love called the police to their home when Cobain locked himself in a room with a gun. Talk of an American tour was put aside until Cobain could commit himself to the road with confidence.

At the end of March, within a week after being admitted, Cobain escaped from rehab, spent a few days missing, and turned up dead in his Seattle guest house lying next to the shotgun he had swallowed. The cable man found him, and called the local radio station before the police. MTV took on the story as if it were the Kennedy assassination. It broadcast its bank of Nirvana interviews and clips in heavy rotation, interviewed *Rolling Stone* writers such as Nirvana

Nirvana on MTV's *Unplugged*

biographer Michael Azerrad and David Fricke, who trotted out the easy Lennon analogies. Thousands gathered for a public memorial in Seattle, and a shaken Courtney Love addressed Cobain's fans, reading his suicide note aloud.

Most editors settled for the usual lame commentary about how fame had killed another angry young man, and didn't even bother to dig up sudden-success showbiz precedents like the young comic Freddie Prinze, who shot himself in the flush of his sudden success at age 26 in 1977, or punker Ian Curtis of Joy Division, who hung himself in 1980. Instead, the Lennon comparisons resurfaced with a vengeance, never mind that Lennon had built an 18-year career and Cobain's lasted barely three. Never mind that Cobain actively chose to leave behind a wife and a daughter whose legacy now included the statistical caution that children of suicides kill themselves as well. Cobain was sainted as the new pop martyr for Generation X, the generation that had resisted needing anything of the kind. A lavish, glossy memorial book appeared collecting Nirvana coverage from *Rolling Stone*. Everything the man had to say was suddenly drowned in the very media frenzy he had used as an excuse to check out.

As the dust settled, Cobain's suicide, which was even more violent and resentful than most of his music, seemed less symptomatic of the cost of fame than of our culture's blindness regarding addiction illnesses. The prevailing myth surrounding heroin users, drug addicts and alcoholics continues to be that they are troubled arty types whose bad habits "force" them to self-destruct. That a growing self-help, sobriety culture had come of age in the late 1980s and crossed over into sitcoms like the *John Laroquette Show* and movies like *When a Man Loves a Woman* seemed irrelevant to most eulogizers. Cobain, the great misunderstood kid, was somehow more gifted and thus "sicker" than all the others. The subtext of

Courtney Love and Kurt Cobain with daughter Frances Bean

most of the adoring commentary was that he was too good for this world.

Nirvana's *Unplugged* tells a different story: it's the transparent, quietly riveting sound of a man set on killing himself, no matter how far the music transports him out of his isolation. (Key lyrics like "I swear I don't have a gun," from "Come as You Are," still sting like blisters.) Broken up with asides to his band ("I didn't fuck it up" Cobain marveled after "The Man Who Sold the World"), the set has the disjointed pace of a band finding its way for an audience intent on giving it all the room it needs to get there. *Unplugged* demonstrates how Cobain threw away an inestimable opportunity to snub convention and stand for something larger than the pettiness of showbiz.

Everything that happened in the wake of Cobain's death seemed anticlimactic, and proof that the opportunity he abandoned was pretty well lost, at least for the time being. Pearl Jam ascended to top dog, acting as Nirvana's heir apparent, although not a single song emerged from Vedder and Co. that came close to the hilarious disgust and resignation of Nirvana's "Smells Like Teen Spirit," "In Bloom," "Serving the Servants" or "All Apologies." And whether you liked Pearl Jam or not, the band was not a punk act (though singer Eddie Vedder sought contact with punk roots on tour with forefather Mike Watt). Taking on Ticketmaster before Congress for excessive service charges and throwing in with the Hollywood elite for the animal-lover vote made Vedder seem like a man of caus-

Pearl Jam

No Alternative!

Steve Rapport/Retna

Mike Mills

On January 6, 1995 R.E.M. kicked off its *Monster* world tour, which was interrupted in May when drummer Bill Berry suffered a near-fatal brain aneurysm, again in July when Mike Mills required emergency abdominal surgery and again in August when Michael Stipe underwent a hernia operation. National Public Radio's Joe Richman interviewed the band just before they left for Australia, the first leg of the tour. Richman, suggesting that alternative is now equated with big business, asked the band what they thought the term means in today's music scene.

"Alternative actually meant something when it was an option," said bassist Mills. "But now alternative generally tends to mean three white guys with long hair playing guitars. That's sort of  the connotation it has now. And what's alternative music now? Well, you have to go look for it. You have to find it. You can't go and say, 'Well, I'd like some alternative music please.' That's bogus." ∎

Major Music Festivals

by Ted Drozdowski

BEN & JERRY'S NEWPORT FOLK FESTIVAL
NEWPORT, R.I

The mother of all folk festivals returned in 1988 thanks to the sponsorship of the Vermont-based ice cream moguls. The three-day 1995 lineup included such luminaries as Bill Morrissey, Cheryl Wheeler, John Hiatt, the Indigo Girls, Joan Baez, Bob Weir and Rob Wasserman. The festival began Friday, August 4, in the old-world Newport Casino, and spilled onto the sea-surrounded, expansive lawn of Ft. Adams State Park on Saturday and Sunday. When the weather cooperates, this is a beautiful summer affair, with sailboats circling the concert grounds. And each year's festival has a special theme. In 1995 it was contemporary Irish folk, with Luka Bloom, Mary Black and others performing. Despite a charming seacoast and its industrial-era mansions, however, downtown Newport is overpriced and overpopulated during summer.

> Ben & Jerry's Newport Folk Festival
> P.O. Box 605
> Newport, RI 02840
> (401) 847-3700

CHICAGO BLUES FESTIVAL
GRANT PARK
CHICAGO, ILLINOIS

Held each year in early June in Chicago's Grant Park on the shores of Lake Michigan, this is the country's largest blues festival. Its three stages host plenty of hometown talent — from heroes like Buddy Guy and Otis Rush to obscure bar-crawlers like Little Smokey Smothers — and players from across the globe. Some of the deepest, most authentic performances occur on the "front porch" stage, where Mississippi hill-country greats Junior Kimbrough and R.L. Burnside held court in 1995. But when performers such as Rush, Koko Taylor or Etta James take the main stage, some 360,000 listeners can flood the surrounding fields. Fresh roasted corn, barbecued sausages and other Midwestern fare are available. At night, as usual, Chicago's blues clubs are crawling with musicians and revelers. Recommended venues include Buddy Guy's Legends and the bars dotting Halstead St., including the popular Kingston Mines and B.L.U.E.S. and Theresa's on the south side.

> Chicago Blues Festival
> Mayor's Office of Special Events
> 121 N. LaSalle St., Room 703
> Chicago, IL 60602
> (312) 744-3315 or (800) ITS-CHGO

es, not ideas. Pearl Jam became America's answer to U2 on a decade-delay tape loop, with Vedder aping Bono's Last Good Man routine. When asked if Vedder had ever cracked a good joke, one fan responded indignantly: "No. Things are different these days. . . ."

Three dinosaur rock tours defined the corporate pop machine and two of them seemed completely fossilized: Pink Floyd, behind a torpid comeback album called *The Division Bell*, and then a live set, *Pulse*; and the Eagles, with an inert stage act that made their tour slogan "Hell Freezes Over" seem all too descriptive. The Rolling Stones, on the other hand, upped the ante with a lavish arena show that outdid even their triumphant 1989 *Steel Wheels* jaunt. Mick Jagger seemed more famous and less troubled about it than ever. So did Barbra Streisand, whose CEO tour outpriced them all.

The comebacks continued, including such unlikely old hands as Television, Steely Dan, Traffic and King Crimson. Nobody was holding their breath for Supertramp, but with radio formats probing the outer limits of cryogenics, and Kansas, Peter Frampton, hell, even Jason and the Scorchers among the hopefuls, Supertramp's return is probably imminent. And the charts threw off more derivative piffle in Sheryl Crow's "All I Wanna Do" smash, which sounded like Rickie Lee Jones covering Cyndi Lauper. Rock wasn't moving forward as much as it was repeating old orbits at varying altitudes.

Which is not to say that fame didn't

The Rolling Stones

Michael Jackson

ensnare some big fish. To the casual observer, Michael Jackson's child molestation suit, which upstaged even the Woody Allen-Mia Farrow scandal, was only the *hors d'oeuvre* to the main course: the O.J. Simpson double murder case, which broke in June 1994. Just weeks before, Jackson's payoff to his child-molestation accuser was announced by Johnnie Cochrane, who parlayed the exposure into a seat on O.J.'s $10 million defense dream team.

O.J. was clearly the best thing that could have happened to obscure Jackson's reputed $15 million settlement from the public mind, but Jackson persisted. Months after collapsing from exhaustion and pharmaceutical dependency during a European tour, he married Lisa Marie Presley in a bizarre elopement in August 1994. This caused tabloid stupefaction: Compared to what O.J. was accused of doing, Jackson's eccentricities, however abusive, seemed of a piece with Hollywood life. Now, as if he needed to regain the center of attention, Jackson acted as if getting married was part of the PR scheme of the century when, basically, few were left who cared.

Unexpectedly, the one act that resisted abandoning what Cobain had stood for and refused to let 1994 be defined by Cobain's death, was Hole, led by Cobain's wife, Courtney Love. Love didn't play the widow with the finesse of a Yoko Ono, who straddled the line between grief as performance art and tasteless exploitation. Ending a two-

CHICAGO JAZZ FESTIVAL
GRANT PARK
CHICAGO, ILLINOIS

Each fall visitors from all over the world attend this venerable event, one of the country's largest jazz festivals, which acknowledges the contributions of Chicago's strong jazz community and the African-American musical tradition in general. Local legends such as Lester Bowie, Joseph Jarman and other pillars of the AACM draw large crowds to Grant Park. And they're joined by many of the biggest names in jazz. In recent years neo-trad heroes such as Wynton Marsalis and Cyrus Chestnut have appeared, as have avant-grade major-leaguers including Cecil Taylor and Don Byron and aggressive generalists like David Murray. The 1995 festival ran from September 1 to 3, and fans kept clubs such as local favorite Andy's and the more prestigious Jazz Showcase hopping throughout.

Chicago Jazz Festival
Mayor's Office of Special Events
121 N. LaSalle St., Room 703
Chicago, IL 60602
(312) 744-3315 or (800) ITS-CHGO

FAN FAIR
NASHVILLE, TENNESSEE

The reunion of George Jones and Tammy Wynette, country music's legendary dysfunctional duo, was the big news at last 1995's Fan Fair, where an army of fans descended on the Tennessee State Fairground to catch dozens of live performances, get autographs signed by stars including Wynonna, Alan Jackson, Billy Ray Cyrus and Brooks & Dunn and devour souvenirs and junk food. There's camping, with enough trailers and mobile homes on site to earn a spot in the *Guinness* book. And the atmosphere's plain, middle-American crazy. Country music stars and their fans do have a genuine love affair, and each June, this is where they let it all hang out. Add the Country Music Hall of Fame, the Grand Ole Opry, Ryman Auditorium and the gift shops of the stars surrounding Hope and Commerce streets to your agenda while in town.

Fan Fair
2804 Opryland Drive
Nashville, TN 37214
(615) 889-7503

CONTINUED ON NEXT PAGE ▶

FESTIVAL INTERNATIONAL DE JAZZ DE MONTREAL
MONTREAL, QUEBEC, CANADA

With bookings as richly international as Montreal itself, this nine-day extravaganza is a favorite of festival hoppers. Roots rock, R&B, fusion, folk music, salsa, African highlife and soukous all have room on the stages that dot the city's streets, parks, clubs and theaters for this early July event. Each year a theme is built around a series of major performances. In '95, festival organizers paid homage to tenor-sax giant David Murray and eclectic pianist Randy Weston. Murray played with a different ensemble for the first five nights of the festival — a big band, the World Saxophone Quartet, a foursome with pianist Hilton Ruiz, bassist Fred Hopkins and drummer Idris Muhammed, and finally in duets with Weston, who himself headlined the last four nights with small groups, a big band and a clan of Gnawan master musicians. If nine days of music seems overwhelming, there are the delights of Old Montreal, shops, fine restaurants and all the other amenities a truly world-class city offers.

> Festival International de Jazz de Montreal
> 822 Rue Sherbrooke Est
> Montreal, Quebec
> Canada H2L 1K4
> (514) 523-3378

JVC JAZZ FESTIVAL
NEW YORK CITY

This is the granddaddy of American jazz fests. It began in Newport, Rhode Island, in 1954, moved to New York in the '70s and by the '90s had satellite events in Chicago; Dallas; Atlanta; Concord and Hollywood, California; Saratoga, New York; and back at Newport. The big kahuna is in New York City, however, with an international audience attracted as much by the music as by the Big Apple's bright lights. This year's festival, held from June 23 to July 2, mixed outdoor shows with gigs at such historic sites as Avery Fisher and Carnegie halls. And the music offered bristling highs: Ray Charles and his Orchestra in an R&B tag-team blowout with Maceo Parker (whose volatile playing was the apex of many of 1995's summer festivals); a historic pairing of the Carnegie Hall Jazz Band and the Lincoln Center Jazz Orchestra directed by Wynton Marsalis and a night of Latin fire uniting Celia Cruz, Arturo Sandoval and Oscar DeLeon's band.

> JVC Jazz Festival New York
> P.O. Box 1169
> Ansonia Station
> New York, NY 10023
> (212) 787-2020

Retna/Bill Schwab

Hole at Lollapalooza

year absence from the music business during which she married Cobain and had his child, Love released a prescient set of songs on an album she completed just before Cobain's suicide called *Live Through This*. This was punk without the hilarity, but enough deadpan wisecracks to keep the ironies jumping. Love, a former stripper, could make a simple dress look like derision itself. "Go on take everything, take everything, I want you to" Love sang in "Violet," and it meant something different each time you heard it. Love's punk didn't revel in revenge fantasies, instead it piled on the petty insults until you began to appreciate her weary feminist taunts.

Then, in June 1994, just two months after Cobain died, Hole's bassist Kristen Pfaff was found dead of a heroin overdose in her bathtub. Undaunted, Love hired Melissa Auf der Maur, a resourceful player and a vivid singer, and kept moving. Hole began touring in Europe in August, just as the dinosaurs began straying offstage, and built its reputation with an unsteady persistence. Reports of odd onstage confrontations and off-stage mishaps dogged the band. By the time it reached America, the resolute ironies of *Live Through This* had won over a lot of skeptics, and the album was selling respectably (peaking at number 55 on the *Billboard* charts). Earning her fame in spite of who she was, and what Cobain had done, Love made his death seem all the more wasteful for the music they might have made together. By New Years' 1995, Love trounced the competition for Album of the Year in the *Village Voice*'s annual critics' poll, which tallies votes from upwards of 300 critics nationwide.

By May of 1995, when Courtney Love took the stage for her own *Unplugged*, the appearance was charged with passing-the-torch symbolism, and the world sat up to take notice. Sitting on a stool and running through her set matter-of-factly, Love's manner seemed coy for a punk-rocker, but that may have just been her way of being nervous. By now her record had grown familiar, and her deadpan delivery only made her better lines leap out with greater force: "When you get what you want/And you never want it again. . . ." (again from "Violet"). Halfway through the set, Love introduced her defining cover, Gerry Goffin's and Carole King's "He Hit Me, and It Felt Like a Kiss." Phil Spector produced the song for The Crystals back in 1962, pulled it defensively just after its release, and it resurfaced on the Spector box set *Back to Mono* almost 30 years later in 1991.

Love's version wrought a wizened resolve from the song's abject fear and antiquated sexism, and turned it into a kind of cleansing-away, as if to say "This is the dark ages where feminism and female rock started. This is chocolate cake compared to what I've been through." (A similar cultural barometer of the season was Urge Overkill's deliciously wry cover of "Girl, You'll Be a Woman Soon," a 1967 Neil Diamond hit, which Quentin Tarantino used as the score to Uma Thurman's death dance in *Pulp Fiction*.)

When Love appeared on the cover of *Vanity Fair* soon afterward, and stirred up 1995's Lollapalooza with fistfights and clothes-shredding dives into the audience, the concept of sellout was so remote it was never uttered. Instead, her success seemed merely the just desserts of a woman who had somehow danced her way through an avalanche.

Other big events of 1995 were greatest hits packages from two veterans: Bruce Springsteen, who reunited with his E Street Band and finally put out "Murder Incorporated" (a much-bootlegged *Born in the U.S.A.* song about

LOLLAPALOOZA

This traveling three-stage, summertime rock and roll circus has become America's premiere youth-culture event, with performances, films, galleries, artisans, technology, dance music and politics woven into its lively mix. Organized six years ago by Los Angeles rocker Perry Farrell as a grand farewell tour for his band Jane's Addiction, it has grown to embrace nearly every trend, from body piercing to virtual reality, but the main attraction is still the groups on its big stage. The 1995 revue was headlined by trailblazers Sonic Youth and Courtney Love's raw, emotional band Hole. But Farrell's embrace included the rap of Cypress Hill, lo-fi indie-popsters Pavement and the raw, raging Jesus Lizard.

Date information can be obtained through local promoters or via the Internet at http://lollapalooza.com

MACINTOSH NEW YORK MUSIC FESTIVAL NEW YORK CITY

After the biz-intensive New Music Seminar collapsed beneath the heft of its irrelevance in 1994, Knitting Factory club owner Michael Dorf stepped in to pick up the slack — and keep the city's major rock rooms full during otherwise fallow July. He dropped the conference aspect of the event, found a sponsor in Apple and organized a coalition of 15 New York City clubs to keep alive the week of performances (July 17–22) the seminar used to host. This was the best part of the Seminar anyway, and now nobody has to wear a name tag. In its inaugural year, the Macintosh New York Music Festival hosted more than 250 performers, including such known commodities as Laurie Anderson, the Young Gods, Yo La Tengo, Olatunji, Todd Rundgren, Mutabaruka and Buffalo Tom and special events like Queer Night, with gay-themed rock acts packing the Knitting Factory. Participating clubs range from such holes-in-the-walls as Brownie's and the Mercury Lounge to hall-size venues such as the Academy and Irving Plaza. A 1995 festival pass cost $75, and a limited number of single-show tickets were available for certain acts.

Macintosh New York Music Festival
285 W. Broadway, Suite 630
New York, NY 10013
(212) 343-9290

CONTINUED ON NEXT PAGE ▶

MISSISSIPPI DELTA BLUES FESTIVAL
GREENVILLE, MISSISSIPPI

Each fall — after the summer heat has passed — the heart of the Delta opens up to accommodate as many as 100,000 fans for this event, which primarily draws its talent from home. Held on September 16, the no-frills 1995 festival embraced artists from Jackson, Mississippi's big-selling Malaco Records stable, slicks such as Latimore and Vasti Jackson, to more obscure players like rough-as-a-cob Belzoni guitarist/singer Paul "Wine" Jones, whose daddy, K.C. Jones, was a juke joint operator and old running buddy of Sonny Boy Williamson. There's barbecue and fried catfish at the festival. And Greenville itself, a literary center of the old South, offers plenty of affordable chain hotels, mall shopping, museums and brown tap water — a legacy of life on the muddy Mississippi River. It's also the home of the original Doe's Eat Place, a downhome cookery with a two-item dinner menu: a pile of plump Gulf shrimp, or a steak twice as big as your head. Both are delicious.

M.A.C.E.
119 S. Theobold
Greenville, Mississippi 38701
(601) 335-3523

NEW ORLEANS JAZZ AND HERITAGE FESTIVAL

From its humble beginnings as a daylong celebration of local music and culture in the French Quarter's Congo Square 26 years ago, the New Orleans Jazz and Heritage Festival has become the nation's premier musical and folk-culture event. Now spanning the last weekend in April and the first in May, it fills the sprawling New Orleans Fairgrounds, off Gentilly Boulevard with hundreds of artists performing concurrently on 10 stages, dozens of vendors providing regional delicacies at bargain prices and artisans and craftspeople selling their wares and offering workshops. The real treats are appearances of local R&B legends like Allen Toussaint, Snooks Eaglin and Ernie K. Doe or the deep-swamp Cajun, zydeco and old-time country musicians who come to the city for their annual day in the warm southern sun. But expect to also see pop greats like Bonnie Raitt, Bob Dylan and the Allman Brothers Band. At night, the festival spills into the city's many clubs and music halls, the best of which are the local landmark Tipitina's (named after Professor Longhair's signature song) in the warehouse district, the House of Blues on the edge of the French Quarter and the Mid-City Lanes, a.k.a. Rock 'n' Bowl, where live music, bowling and good 'n' greasy eats can be had simultaneously. Of course, there's enough time between Festival shlepping and club-hopping to enjoy the Crescent City's other delights, from boozing and decadence on Bourbon Street to the world-

Bruce Springsteen

the mob), and Michael Jackson on the rehab circuit. With his raucous appearance on Letterman, Springsteen prevailed; Jackson miscalculated: *HIStory* was a double CD with 30 tracks, half of which were greatest hits, begging the question of why a self-proclaimed "King of Pop" needed to hitch his new material to the stuff everybody already owned.

The most promising collaboration among heavyweights came in the summer, when Neil Young released *Mirror Ball*, his album with Pearl Jam, the result of jamming together at the 1995 Rock 'n' Roll Hall of Fame induction ceremony. This seemed in character for Young, a relentless drifter, and hopeful for the band. It's fun to think about Young coaching Vedder through the messianic undertones of "Piece of Crap."

Between dinosaur comebacks and Pearl Jam's off-and-on road success backing *Vitalogy,* 1994's ticket receipts were the largest in the history of music. Without all the dinosaurs, 1995's live receipts dipped, but R.E.M., in its first tour in six years, returned as elder statesmen (ironic?) to play stadiums as if they were oversized garages. This was consistent with the general recoiling from mass adulation that Cobain's suicide represented in its most extreme form. Suddenly, bands that deserved wider audiences, like Pavement (*Wowee Zowee*) and Guided by Voices (*Alien Lanes* and their upcoming album produced by Kim Deal of The Breeders), released fetchingly lo-fi CDs that betrayed an ambivalence toward fame bordering on pathological. Pavement's inspired stream-of-consciousness method resisted packaging, and Guided by Voices' brief, heady songs shrank the pop process into a series of fragments, pieces of ideas that refused to coalesce.

This gave the season's true conquering heroine an edge: Courtney Love was a genuine songwriter, not just a widow, but a new brand of feminist who refused to play rock star as role model. Love stood apart not just from the punk rock tradition her husband enlivened, but also from the stream of girl acts like Babes in Toyland, Liz Phair, Belly, Lucious Jackson and the Northwest riot grrrrl press phenom.

If 1994 began by immortalizing Cobain as the rock star who died for his dignity, it progressed to discover that he was just another talented addict who copped out. Michael Jackson is at the opposite end of the spectrum, courting the coverage he supposedly despises; he's addicted to his celebrity in a way Cobain detested. But neither's self-destructive urges are heroic or enviable. Fame brings its share of unspeakable humiliations, but then, so do plenty of other jobs. For some real lessons on the price of fame and how healthy celebrity ambivalence can be, listen to Hole's *Live Through This*, a landmark of rock feminism, survivalism and how immersion in craft can see you through times of utter peril. ■

class cuisine, including K-Paul's Louisiana Kitchen, the eatery run by chef Paul Prodhomme, whose blackening process put the redfish on the endangered list.

New Orleans Jazz and Heritage Festival
1205 N. Rampart St.
New Orleans, LA 70116
(504) 522-4786

SOUTH BY SOUTHWEST MUSIC AND MEDIA CONFERENCE AUSTIN, TEXAS

Even before the New York City-based New Music Seminar wheezed to its death in 1994, this five-day fête in hospitable Austin had become the must-attend annual event for smart music-biz insiders. Last year it became a fan's haven as well for two reasons. First, a special pass gets you into nearly every club in Austin — from the Sixth Street strip to the suburbs — which the conference's wide embrace fills with everything from Tex-Mex border music to country to folk, grunge, jazz and meat-and-potatoes rock. Second, Austin is beautiful in springtime, with its rolling hills and appealing riverbeds, strong artists' community and world-class down-home eateries like Threadgill's, where Janis Joplin used to sing for her supper, and La Zona Rosa, where fantastic Mexican fare is served along with great music and Day of the Dead decor. Explore — otherwise you'll miss spots like the Broken Spoke, the last of Austin's classic honky-tonks, with sawdusted floors, picnic benches, beer in cans and patrons aged 21 to 75 two-stepping to the best of country music. As usual, this year's SXSW began on March 15 with the Austin Music Awards, an opportunity to see many of the city's estimable talents (including rocking songwriter Joe Ely, guitar wiz Eric Johnson and psychedelic-rock cult hero Roky Erickson). The biggest buzzes among fans and pros in 1995 were wall-shaking shows from country rockers Wilco, hometowners the Charlie Sexton Sextet (actually a guitar-heavy quartet led by the photogenic rock chameleon) and — as always — the great Flaco Jiminez, king of *conjunto* accordion and member of Lone Star State supergroup the Texas Tornados. The music biz stuff's at the Austin Convention Center, but with so many distractions . . .

South by Southwest
P.O. Box 4999
Austin, TX 78765
(512) 467-7979

Ted Drozdowski writes about music for Rolling Stone *and* Pulse *and is the arts editor of the* Boston Phoenix.

1994 Billboard Chart Toppers

Each week, *Billboard* publishes music charts based on nationwide airplay and sales data using a point system and information compiled by Broadcast Data Systems (airplay) and SoundScan (retail sales). Here are the recordings that topped the charts and received the most points in 1994.

Top 100 Albums

Deniz Kalkavan/Retna

Ace of Base

1. **The Sign**
   Ace of Base
   (Arista)

2. **Music Box**
   Mariah Carey
   (Columbia)

3. **Doggy Style**
   Snoop Doggy Dogg
   (Death Row/Interscope)

4. **The Lion King**
   Soundtrack
   (Walt Disney)

5. **August and Everything After**
   Counting Crows
   (DGC)

6. **Vs.**
   Pearl Jam
   (Epic)

7. **Toni Braxton**
   Toni Braxton
   (LaFace)

8. **janet**
   Janet Jackson
   (Virgin)

9. **Bat Out of Hell II: Back Into Hell**
   Meat Loaf
   (MCA)

10. **The One Thing**
    Michael Bolton
    (Columbia)

11. **12 Play**
    R. Kelly
    (Jive)

12. **Not a Moment Too Soon**
    Tim McGraw
    (Curb)

13. **Purple**
    Stone Temple Pilots
    (Atlantic)

14. **Greatest Hits**
    Tom Petty and the Heartbreakers
    (MCA)

15. **Siamese Dream**
    Smashing Pumpkins
    (Virgin)

16. **The Colour of My Love**
    Celine Dion
    (550 Music)

17. **So Far So Good**
    Bryan Adams
    (A&M)

18. **Very Necessary**
    Salt-N-Pepa
    (Next Plateau/London)

19. **Superunknown**
    Soundgarden
    (A&M)

20. **The Division Bell**
    Pink Floyd
    (Columbia)

21. **Get a Grip**
    Aerosmith
    (Geffen)

22. **II**
    Boyz II Men
    (Motown)

23. **Duets**
    Frank Sinatra
    (Capitol)

24. **Dookie**
    Green Day
    (Reprise)

25. **Common Thread: The Songs of the Eagles**
    Various artists
    (Giant)

26. **Candlebox**
    Candlebox
    (Maverick/Sire)

27. **The Bodyguard**
    Soundtrack
    (Arista)

Counting Crows

28. **Forrest Gump**
Soundtrack
(Epic Soundtrax)

29. **In Pieces**
Garth Brooks
(Liberty)

30. **Chant**
Benedictine Monks of
Santo Domingo de Silos
(Angel)

31. **Above the Rim**
Soundtrack
(Death Row/Interscope)

32. **Regulate ... G Funk Era**
Warren G
(Violator/RAL)

33. **In Utero**
Nirvana
(DGC)

34. **River of Dreams**
Billy Joel
(Columbia)

35. **Kickin' It Up**
John Michael Montgomery
(Atlantic)

Eric Clapton

36. **Greatest Hits Volume Two**
Reba McEntire
(MCA)

37. **Smash**
Offspring
(Epitaph)

38. **Live at the Acropolis**
Yanni
(Private Music)

39. **All-4-One**
All-4-One
(Blitzz/Atlantic)

40. **Reality Bites**
Soundtrack
(RCA)

41. **Diary of a Mad Band**
Jodeci
(Uptown)

42. **The Cross of Changes**
Enigma
(Charisma)

43. **Lethal Injection**
Ice Cube
(Priority)

44. **I'm Ready**
Tevin Campbell
(Qwest)

45. **Everybody Else Is Doing It,
So Why Can't We?**
The Cranberries
(Island)

46. **The Crow**
Soundtrack
(Interscope/Atlantic)

47. **MTV Unplugged**
10,000 Maniacs
(Elektra)

48. **A Lot About Livin' (And a
Little 'Bout Love)**
Alan Jackson
(Arista)

49. **The Beavis and Butt-Head
Experience**
Beavis and Butt-Head
(Geffen)

50. **Core**
Stone Temple Pilots
(Atlantic)

51. **Breathless**
Kenny G
(Arista)

52. **Jar of Flies**
Alice in Chains
(Columbia)

53. **God Shuffled His Feet**
Crash Test Dummies
(Arista)

54. **New Miserable Experience**
Gin Blossoms
(A&M)

55. **Longing in Their Hearts**
Bonnie Raitt
(Capitol)

56. **Sleepless in Seattle**
Soundtrack
(Epic Soundtrax)

57. **Yes I Am**
Melissa Etheridge
(Island)

58. **Ten**
Pearl Jam
(Epic)

59. **The Downward Spiral**
Nine Inch Nails
(Nothing/TVT-Interscope)

60. **Tuesday Night Music Club**
Sheryl Crow
(A&M)

61. **The Spaghetti Incident**
Guns N' Roses
(Geffen)

62. **Voodoo Lounge**
The Rolling Stones
(Virgin)

63. **Ill Communication**
Beastie Boys
(Capitol)

64. **From the Cradle**
Eric Clapton
(Duck/Reprise)

65. **Read My Mind**
Reba McEntire
(MCA)

66. **Unplugged ... and Seated**
Rod Stewart
(Warner Bros.)

67. **Monster**
R.E.M.
(Warner Bros.)

68. **Hints, Allegations and
Things Left Unsaid**
Collective Soul
(Atlantic)

69. **Philadelphia**
Soundtrack
(Epic Soundtrax)

70. **Who I Am**
Alan Jackson
(Arista)

71. **Metallica**
Metallica
(Elektra)

72. **For the Cool in You**
Babyface
(Epic)

73. **Hard Workin' Man**
Brooks and Dunn
(Arista)

74. **Age Ain't Nothing
but a Number**
Aaliyah
(Blackground)

75. **Rhythm of Love**
Anita Baker
(Elektra)

76. **Easy Come, Easy Go**
George Strait
(MCA)

Mary Chapin Carpenter

77. *When Love Finds You*
Vince Gill
(MCA)

78. *Hummin' Comin' at 'Cha*
Xscape
(So So Def)

79. *Murder Was the Case*
Soundtrack
(Death Row/Interscope)

80. *Rhythm Country and Blues*
Various Artists
(MCA)

81. *Blind Melon*
Blind Melon
(Capitol)

82. *Far Beyond Driven*
Pantera
(EastWest)

83. *It's On (Dr. Dre 187 Um) Killa*
Eazy E
(Ruthless)

84. *Nevermind*
Nirvana
(DGC)

85. *Both Sides*
Phil Collins
(Atlantic)

86. *This Time*
Dwight Yoakam
(Reprise)

87. *Come On Come On*
Mary Chapin Carpenter
(Columbia)

88. *When My Heart Finds Christmas*
Harry Connick, Jr.
(Columbia)

89. *Under the Pink*
Tori Amos
(Atlantic)

90. *Creepin On Ah Come Up*
Bone Thugs N Harmony
(Ruthless)

91. *Big Time*
Little Texas
(Warner Bros.)

92. *Seal*
Seal
(ZTT/Sire)

93. *MCMXC A.D.*
Enigma
(Charisma)

94. *Mellow Gold*
Beck
(DGC)

95. *I Still Believe in You*
Vince Gill
(MCA)

96. *Barney's Favorites Vol. 1*
Barney
(SBK)

97. *Pure Country*
(Soundtrack)
George Strait
(MCA)

98. *Black Sunday*
Cypress Hill
(Ruffhouse)

99. *Phantom of the Opera Highlights*
Original London Cast
(Polydor)

100. *Shaq Diesel*
Shaquille O'Neal
(Jive)

Hot 50 Singles

1. "The Sign"
Ace of Base
(Arista)

2. "I Swear"
All-4-One
(Blitzz)

3. "I'll Make Love to You"
Boyz II Men
(Motown)

4. "The Power of Love"
Celine Dion
(550 Music)

5. "Hero"
Mariah Carey
(Columbia)

6. "Stay" (I Missed You)
(From the motion picture *Reality Bites*)
Lisa Loeb and Nine Stories
(RCA)

7. "Breathe Again"
Toni Braxton
(LaFace)

8. "All for Love"
Bryan Adams, Rod Stewart and Sting
(A&M)

9. "All That She Wants"
Ace of Base
(Arista)

10. "Don't Turn Around"
Ace of Base
(Arista)

11. "Bump N' Grind"
R. Kelly
(Jive)

12. "Again"
Janet Jackson
(Virgin)

13. "I'll Remember"
(From the motion picture *With Honors*)
Madonna
(Maverick/Sire)

14. "Whatta Man"
Salt-N-Pepa featuring En Vogue
(Next Plateau/London)

15. "Wild Night"
John Mellencamp with Me'Shell Ndegeocello
(Mercury)

16. "Without You/Never Forget You"
Mariah Carey
(Columbia)

17. "You Mean the World to Me"
Toni Braxton
(LaFace)

18. "Can You Feel the Love Tonight"
(From the animated movie *The Lion King*)
Elton John
(Hollywood)

19. "The Most Beautiful Girl in the World"
The Artist Formerly Known as Prince
(NPG)

20. "Fantastic Voyage"
Coolio
(Tommy Boy)

TOP 10 TOURING ACTS OF 1994

	ACT	GROSS RECEIPTS	TOTAL ATTENDANCE	# OF SHOWS
1.	Pink Floyd	$103,666,142	3,043,233	59
2.	The Rolling Stones	93,831,264	1,981,585	44
3.	Billy Joel	78,217,615	2,003,721	73
4.	Eagles	74,377,442	1,369,818	50
5.	Elton John	56,192,500	1,205,403	28
6.	The Grateful Dead	49,086,048	1,732,952	77
7.	Barbra Streisand	45,359,825	268,779	20
8.	Phil Collins	33,694,293	1,072,428	64
9.	Smashing Pumpkins	24,450,427	918,238	63
10.	Reba McEntire	18,739,616	834,671	71

Source: Amusement Business

Boyz II Men

21. "Baby I Love Your Way"
(From the motion picture *Reality Bites*)
Big Mountain
(RCA)

22. "Regulate"
(From the motion picture *Above the Rim*)
Warren G and Nate Dogg
(Death Row)

23. "If You Go"
Jon Secada
(SBK)

24. "Back and Forth"
Aaliyah
(Blackground)

25. "Now and Forever"
Richard Marx
(Capitol)

26. "When Can I See You"
Babyface
(Epic)

27. "Please Forgive Me"
Bryan Adams
(A&M)

28. "So Much in Love"
All-4-One
(Blitzz)

29. "Shoop"
Salt-N-Pepa
(Next Plateau/London)

30. "Any Time, Any Place/And On and On"
Janet Jackson
(Virgin)

31. "Shine"
Collective Soul
(Atlantic)

32. "Said I Loved You . . . but I Lied"
Michael Bolton
(Columbia)

33. "Return to Innocence"
Enigma
(Virgin)

34. "All I Wanna Do"
Sheryl Crow
(A&M)

35. "MMM MMM MMM MMM"
Crash Test Dummies
(Arista)

36. "Can We Talk"
Tevin Campbell
(Qwest)

37. "Funkdafied"
Da Brat
(So So Def)

38. "I'd Do Anything for Love (But I Won't Do That)"
Meat Loaf
(MCA)

39. "Gangsta Lean"
DRS
(Capitol)

40. "Because the Night"
10,000 Maniacs
(Elektra)

41. "Cantaloop" (Flip Fantasia)
US3
(Blue Note)

42. "Whoomp!" (There It Is)
Tag Team
(Life)

43. "Come to My Window"
Melissa Etheridge
(Island)

44. "Stroke You Up"
Changing Faces
(Spoiled Rotten/Big Beat)

45. "I'm Ready"
Tevin Campbell
(Qwest)

46. "100% Pure Love"
Crystal Waters
(Mercury)

47. "Anytime You Need a Friend"
Mariah Carey
(Columbia)

48. "Because of Love"
Janet Jackson
(Virgin)

49. "Linger"
The Cranberries
(Island)

50. "Loser"
Beck
(DGC)

Top 20 Hot Modern Rock Tracks

1. "Black Hole Sun"
Soundgarden
(A&M)

2. "Come Out and Play"
Offspring
(Epitaph)

3. "Longview"
Green Day
(Reprise)

Green Day, *Dookie*

4. **"Basket Case"**
   Green Day
   (Reprise)

5. **"Fall Down"**
   Toad the Wet Sprocket
   (Columbia)

6. **"Selling the Drama"**
   Live
   (Radioactive)

7. **"Vasoline"**
   Stone Temple Pilots
   (Atlantic)

8. **"Loser"**
   Beck
   (DGC)

9. **"Interstate Love Song"**
   Stone Temple Pilots
   (Atlantic)

10. **"Einstein on the Beach"**
    Counting Crows
    (DGC)

11. **"Self Esteem"**
    Offspring
    (Epitaph)

12. **"Closer"**
    Nine Inch Nails
    (Nothing/TVT)

13. **"Shine"**
    Collective Soul
    (Atlantic)

14. **"All I Wanna Do"**
    Sheryl Crow
    (A&M)

15. **"God"**
    Tori Amos
    (Atlantic)

16. **"What's the Frequency, Kenneth?"**
    R.E.M.
    (Warner Bros.)

17. **"MMM MMM MMM MMM"**
    Crash Test Dummies
    (Arista)

18. **"Fade Into You"**
    Mazzy Star
    (Capitol)

19. **"Return to Innocence"**
    Enigma
    (Virgin)

20. **"Undone — The Sweater Song"**
    Weezer
    (DGC)

Top 20 Hot Album Rock Tracks

1. **"Shine"**
   Collective Soul
   (Atlantic)

2. **"Black Hole Sun"**
   Soundgarden
   (A&M)

3. **"Far Behind"**
   Candlebox
   (Maverick/Sire)

4. **"No Excuses"**
   Alice in Chains
   (Columbia)

5. **"Backwater"**
   Meat Puppets
   (London)

6. **"Vasoline"**
   Stone Temple Pilots
   (Atlantic)

7. **"Daughter"**
   Pearl Jam
   (Epic)

Live

8. **"Keep Talking"**
   Pink Floyd
   (Columbia)

9. **"Deuces Are Wild"**
   Aerosmith
   (Geffen)

10. **"Big Empty"**
    Stone Temple Pilots
    (Atlantic)

11. **"Mr. Jones"**
    Counting Crows
    (DGC)

12. **"Interstate Love Song"**
    Stone Temple Pilots
    (Atlantic)

13. **"Spoonman"**
    Soundgarden
    (A&M)

14. **"Mary Jane's Last Dance"**
    Tom Petty and the
    Heartbreakers
    (MCA)

15. **"All Apologies"**
    Nirvana
    (DGC)

16. **"Creep"**
    Stone Temple Pilots
    (Atlantic)

17. **"Bad Thing"**
    Cry of Love
    (Columbia)

18. **"Cold Fire"**
    Rush
    (Atlantic)

19. **"Low"**
    Cracker
    (Virgin)

20. **"Found Out About You"**
    Gin Blossoms
    (A&M)

Top 50 R&B Albums

1. ***Doggy Style***
   Snoop Doggy Dogg
   (Death Row/Interscope)

2. ***12 Play***
   R. Kelly
   (Jive)

3. ***Toni Braxton***
   Toni Braxton
   (LaFace)

4. *Above the Rim*
Soundtrack
(Death Row/Interscope)

5. *I'm Ready*
Tevin Campbell
(Qwest)

6. *Diary of a Mad Band*
Jodeci
(Uptown)

7. *Lethal Injection*
Ice Cube
(Priority)

8. *Music Box*
Mariah Carey
(Columbia)

9. *Regulate . . . G Funk Era*
Warren G
(Violator/RAL)

10. *II*
Boyz II Men
(Motown)

11. *Age Ain't Nothing but a Number*
Aaliyah
(Blackground)

12. *For the Cool in You*
Babyface
(Epic)

13. *Very Necessary*
Salt-N-Pepa
(Next Plateau/London)

14. *Murder Was the Case*
Soundtrack
(Death Row/Interscope)

15. *janet*
Janet Jackson
(Virgin)

16. *Rhythm of Love*
Anita Baker
(Elektra)

17. *Creepin On Ah Come Up*
Bone Thugs N Harmony
(Ruthless)

18. *Southernplayalisti-cadillacmuzik*
Outkast
(LaFace)

19. *We Come Strapped*
MC Eight featuring CMW
(Epic Street)

20. *Hummin' Comin' at 'Cha*
Xscape
(So So Def)

21. *The Truth*
Aaron Hall
(Silas)

22. *Enter the Wu-Tang (36 Chambers)*
Wu-Tang Clan
(Loud)

23. *Funkdafied*
Da Brat
(So So Def/Chaos)

24. *Midnight Marauders*
A Tribe Called Quest
(Jive)

25. *Get Up on It*
Keith Sweat
(Elektra)

26. *Nuttin' but Love*
Heavy D and The Boyz
(Uptown)

27. *The Diary*
Scarface
(Rap-A-Lot)

28. *Get In Where You Fit In*
Too Short
(Jive)

29. *Somethin' Serious*
Big Mike
(Rap-A-Lot)

30. *The Bodyguard*
Soundtrack
(Arista)

31. *Pronounced Jah-Nay*
Zhane
(Illtown)

32. *Blackstreet*
Blackstreet
(Interscope)

33. *Jason's Lyric*
Soundtrack
(Mercury)

34. *It's On (Dr. Dre 187 Um) Killa*
Eazy-E
(Ruthless)

35. *The Funky Headhunter*
Hammer
(Giant)

36. *Ready to Die*
The Notorious B.I.G.
(Bad Boy)

37. *Domino*
Domino
(Outburst/Chaos)

38. *Black Reign*
Queen Latifah
(Motown)

39. *The Icon Is Love*
Barry White
(A&M)

40. *Groove On*
Gerald Levert
(EastWest)

41. *Breathless*
Kenny G
(Arista)

42. *Illmatic*
NAS
(Columbia)

43. *Songs*
Luther Vandross
(LV)

44. *All the Greatest Hits*
Zapp and Roger
(Reprise)

45. *Gems*
Patti LaBelle
(MCA)

46. *Sons of Soul*
Tony! Toni! Tone!
(Wing)

47. *Queen of the Pack*
Patra
(Epic)

48. *Christmas Interpretations*
Boyz II Men
(Motown)

49. *Back to Basics*
Maze featuring Frankie Beverly
(Warner Bros.)

50. *Shock of the Hour*
MC Ren
(Ruthless)

Janet Jackson

These are the songs and albums that topped the charts in the United Kingdom and Japan in July 1995.

TOP OF THE POPS

Singles

1. "Boom Boom Boom," Outhere Brothers (Stip/Eternal)
2. "Alright/Time," Supergrass (Parlophone)
3. "Shy Guy," Diana King (Work/Columbia)
4. "A Girl Like You," Edwyn Collins (Setanta)
5. "In the Summertime," Shaggy featuring Rayvon (Virgin)
6. "Hold Me, Thrill Me, Kiss Me, Kill Me," U2 (Island/Atlantic)
7. "Unchained Melody/White Cliffs of Dover," Robson Green and Jerome Flynn (RCA)
8. "Kiss From a Rose/I'm Alive," Seal (ZTT)
9. "You Do Something to Me!," Paul Weller (Go!Discs)
10. "3 Is Family," Dana Dawson (EMI)

Albums

1. *These Days*, Bon Jovi (Mercury)
2. *I Should Coco*, Supergrass (Parlophone)
3. *HIStory: Past, Present and Future — Book 1*, Michael Jackson (Epic)
4. *Picture This*, Wet Wet Wet (Precious Organisation)
5. *Singles*, Alison Moyet (Columbia)
6. *The Colour of My Love*, Celine Dion (Epic)
7. *Stanley Road*, Paul Weller (Go!Discs)
8. *Gorgeous George*, Edwyn Collins (Setanta)
9. *Bizarre Fruit*, M People (Deconstruction)
10. *No Need to Argue*, The Cranberries (Island)

BIG IN JAPAN

Singles

1. "Love Me, I Love You," B'Z (BMG Rooms)
2. "Tomorrow," Mayo Okamoto (Tokuma Japan)
3. "Namida Ga Kirari," Spitz (Polydor)
4. "Zurui Onna," Sharanq (BMG Victor)
5. "Anonatsu Wo Sagasite," Tube (Sony)
6. "Aoi Usagi," Noriko Sakai (Victor)
7. "Robbinson," Spitz (Polydor)
8. "Anata Dakewo," Southern All Stars (Victor)
9. "Man and Woman," My Little Woman (Toy's Factory)
10. "Negai," B'Z (BMG Rooms)

Albums

1. *She Loves You*, Misato Watanabe (Epic Sony)
2. *Smap 007*, Smap (Victor)
3. *Hyper Mix 4*, TRF (Avex Trax)
4. *Code Name 1*, Chage and Aska (Pony Canyon)
5. *Pan*, Blue Hearts (Eastwest Japan)
6. *Electromanger*, Daisuke Asakura (Fun House)
7. *M. Collection Kazewo Sagashiteru*, Masaharu Fukuyama (BMG Victor)
8. *Konoyono Dokokade*, Eikichi Yazawa (Toshiba/EMI)
9. *History: Past, Present and Future — Book 1*, Michael Jackson (Sony)
10. *Yuzurenai Natsu*, Tube (Sony)

Source: Billboard

Toni Braxton

Hot 50 R&B Singles

1. "Bump N' Grind"
   R. Kelly
   (Jive)

2. "Back and Forth"
   Aaliyah
   (Blackground)

3. "I'll Make Love to You"
   Boyz II Men
   (Motown)

4. "Can We Talk"
   Tevin Campbell
   (Qwest)

5. "Cry for You"
   Jodeci
   (Uptown)

6. "I Miss You"
   Aaron Hall
   (Silas)

7. "Any Time, Any Place/And On and On"
   Janet Jackson
   (Virgin)

8. "Never Keeping Secrets"
   Babyface
   (Epic)

9. "Your Body's Callin'"
   R. Kelly
   (Jive)

10. "U Send Me Swingin'"
    Mint Condition
    (Perspective)

11. "Stroke You Up"
    Changing Faces
    (Spoiled Rotten/Big Beat)

12. "I'm Ready"
    Tevin Campbell
    (Qwest)

13. **"Willing to Forgive"**
Aretha Franklin
(Arista)

14. **"Funkdafied"**
Da Brat
(So So Def/Chaos)

15. **"You Mean the World to Me"**
Toni Braxton
(LaFace)

16. **"Anything"**
(From the motion picture *Above the Rim*)
SWV
(RCA)

17. **"The Most Beautiful Girl in the World"**
The Artist Formerly Known as Prince
(NPG)

18. **"Sending My Love"**
Zhane
(Illtown)

19. **"Understanding"**
Xscape
(So So Def)

20. **"Groove Thang"**
Zhane
(Illtown)

21. **"The Right Kinda Lover"**
Patti LaBelle
(MCA)

22. **"Got Me Waiting"**
Heavy D and the Boyz
(Uptown)

23. **"At Your Best (You Are Love)"**
Aaliyah
(Blackground)

Salt-N-Pepa

24. **"I Wanna Be Down"**
Brandy
(Atlantic)

25. **"Feenin'"**
Jodeci
(Uptown)

26. **"Gangsta Lean"**
DRS
(Capitol)

27. **"Breathe Again"**
Toni Braxton
(LaFace)

28. **"Body and Soul"**
Anita Baker
(Elektra)

29. **"When Can I See You"**
Babyface
(Epic)

30. **"Getto Jam"**
Domino
(Outburst/RAL)

31. **"Never Lie"**
Immature
(MCA)

32. **"I'm Not Over You"**
Ce Ce Peniston
(A&M)

33. **"Flava in Ya Ear"**
Craig Mack
(Bad Boy)

34. **"Believe in Love"**
Teddy Pendergrass
(Elektra)

35. **"(Lay Your Head on My) Pillow"**
Tony! Toni! Tone!
(Wing)

36. **"Whatta Man"**
Salt-N-Pepa featuring En Vogue
(Next Plateau/London)

37. **"Shoop"**
Salt-N-Pepa
(Next Plateau/London)

38. **"Tootsee Roll"**
69 Boyz
(Rip-It)

39. **"I'd Give Anything"**
Gerald Levert
(EastWest)

40. **"Regulate"**
(From the motion picture *Above the Rim*)
Warren G and Nate Dogg
(Death Row)

41. **"Always in My Heart"**
Tevin Campbell
(Qwest)

Alan Jackson

42. **"I'm in the Mood"**
Ce Ce Peniston
(A&M)

43. **"Treat U Rite"**
Angela Winbush
(Elektra)

44. **"Hero"**
Mariah Carey
(Columbia)

45. **"Here Comes the Hotstepper"**
Ini Kamoze
(Columbia)

46. **"Just Kickin' It"**
Xscape
(So So Def)

47. **"Always on My Mind"**
SWV
(RCA)

48. **"Practice What You Preach"**
Barry White
(A&M)

49. **"Never Should've Let You Go"**
(From the motion picture *Sister Act 2*)
Hi-Five
(Jive)

50. **"U.N.I.T.Y."**
Queen Latifah
(Motown)

Top 50 Country Albums

1. ***Not a Moment Too Soon***
Tim McGraw
(Curb)

Wynonna

2. **Common Thread: The Songs of the Eagles**
Various artists
(Giant)

3. **In Pieces**
Garth Brooks
(Liberty)

4. **Kickin' It Up**
John Michael Montgomery
(Atlantic)

5. **Greatest Hits Volume Two**
Reba McEntire
(MCA)

6. **A Lot About Livin' (And a Little 'Bout Love)**
Alan Jackson
(Arista)

7. **Read My Mind**
Reba McEntire
(MCA)

8. **Who I Am**
Alan Jackson
(Arista)

9. **Hard Workin' Man**
Brooks and Dunn
(Arista)

10. **Easy Come, Easy Go**
George Strait
(MCA)

11. **When Love Finds You**
Vince Gill
(MCA)

12. **Rhythm Country and Blues**
Various artists
(MCA)

13. **I Still Believe in You**
Vince Gill
(MCA)

14. **This Time**
Dwight Yoakam
(Reprise)

15. **Big Time**
Little Texas
(Warner Bros.)

16. **Come On Come On**
Mary Chapin Carpenter
(Columbia)

17. **Pure Country**
(Soundtrack)
George Strait
(MCA)

18. **Clay Walker**
Clay Walker
(Giant)

19. **Let There Be Peace on Earth**
Vince Gill
(MCA)

20. **Tell Me Why**
Wynonna
(Curb)

21. **No Fences**
Garth Brooks
(Liberty)

22. **No Time to Kill**
Clint Black
(RCA)

23. **Take Me As I Am**
Faith Hill
(Warner Bros.)

24. **Life's a Dance**
John Michael Montgomery
(Atlantic)

25. **Confederate Railroad**
Confederate Railroad
(Atlantic)

26. **Ten Feet Tall and Bulletproof**
Travis Tritt
(Warner Bros.)

27. **Brand New Man**
Brooks and Dunn
(Arista)

28. **The Song Remembers When**
Trisha Yearwood
(MCA)

29. **What a Crying Shame**
The Mavericks
(MCA)

30. **Honky Tonk Attitude**
Joe Diffie
(Epic)

31. **Toby Keith**
Toby Keith
(Mercury)

32. **Almost Goodbye**
Mark Chesnutt
(MCA)

33. **Blackhawk**
Blackhawk
(Arista)

34. **Garth Brooks**
Garth Brooks
(Liberty)

35. **Cheap Seats**
Alabama
(RCA)

36. **Extremes**
Collin Raye
(Epic)

37. **No Doubt About It**
Neal McCoy
(Atlantic)

38. **8 Seconds**
Soundtrack
(MCA)

39. **Stones in the Road**
Mary Chapin Carpenter
(Columbia)

40. **Haunted Heart**
Sammy Kershaw
(Mercury)

41. **Only What I Feel**
Patty Loveless
(Epic)

42. **Thinkin' Problem**
David Ball
(Warner Bros.)

43. **Soon**
Tanya Tucker
(Liberty)

44. **Ropin' the Wind**
Garth Brooks
(Liberty)

45. **It Won't Be the Last**
Billy Ray Cyrus
(Mercury)

46. **The Way That I Am**
Martina McBride
(RCA)

47. **Notorious**
Confederate Railroad
(Atlantic)

48. **Some Gave All**
Billy Ray Cyrus
(Mercury)

49. **Call of the Wild**
Aaron Tippin
(RCA)

50. **You Might Be a Redneck If . . .**
Jeff Foxworthy
(Warner Bros.)

Vince Gill

Hot 50 Country Singles and Tracks

1. **"I Swear"**
   John Michael Montgomery
   (Atlantic)
2. **"Wink"**
   Neal McCoy
   (Atlantic)
3. **"Third Rock From the Sun"**
   Joe Diffie
   (Epic)
4. **"Dreaming With My Eyes Open"**
   Clay Walker
   (Giant)
5. **"Down on the Farm"**
   Tim McGraw
   (Curb)
6. **"XXX's and OOO's" (An American Girl)**
   Trisha Yearwood
   (MCA)
7. **"Summertime Blues"**
   Alan Jackson
   (Arista)
8. **"What the Cowgirls Do"**
   Vince Gill
   (MCA)
9. **"Love a Little Stronger"**
   Diamond Rio
   (Arista)
10. **"Foolish Pride"**
    Travis Tritt
    (Warner Bros.)

11. **"That Ain't No Way to Go"**
    Brooks and Dunn
    (Arista)
12. **"Whenever You Come Around"**
    Vince Gill
    (MCA)
13. **"Every Once in a While"**
    Blackhawk
    (Arista)
14. **"Little Rock"**
    Collin Raye
    (Epic)
15. **"No Doubt About It"**
    Neal McCoy
    (Atlantic)
16. **"He Thinks He'll Keep Her"**
    Mary Chapin Carpenter
    (Columbia)
17. **"Rock My World" (Little Country Girl)**
    Brooks and Dunn
    (Arista)
18. **"I Just Wanted You to Know"**
    Mark Chesnutt
    (MCA)
19. **"State of Mind"**
    Clint Black
    (RCA)
20. **"A Good Run of Bad Luck"**
    Clint Black
    (RCA)
21. **"Walking Away a Winner"**
    Kathy Mattea
    (Mercury)
22. **"Piece of My Heart"**
    Faith Hill
    (Warner Bros.)
23. **"My Love"**
    Little Texas
    (Warner Bros.)
24. **"Whisper My Name"**
    Randy Travis
    (Warner Bros.)
25. **"I've Got It Made"**
    John Anderson
    (BNA)
26. **"Wish I Didn't Know Now"**
    Toby Keith
    (Mercury)
27. **"They Don't Make 'Em Like That Anymore"**
    Boy Howdy
    (Curb)
28. **"Be My Baby Tonight"**
    John Michael Montgomery
    (Atlantic)

29. **"I Try to Think About Elvis"**
    Patty Loveless
    (Epic)
30. **"Don't Take the Girl"**
    Tim McGraw
    (Curb)
31. **"Tryin' to Get Over You"**
    Vince Gill
    (MCA)

Clint Black

32. **"If the Good Die Young"**
    Tracy Lawrence
    (Atlantic)
33. **"National Working Woman's Holiday"**
    Sammy Kershaw
    (Mercury)
34. **"Who's That Man"**
    Toby Keith
    (Polydor)
35. **"If Bubba Can Dance" (I Can Too)**
    Shenandoah
    (RCA)
36. **"Spilled Perfume"**
    Pam Tillis
    (Arista)
37. **"Before You Kill Us All"**
    Randy Travis
    (Warner Bros.)
38. **"A Little Less Talk and a Lot More Action"**
    Toby Keith
    (Mercury)
39. **"Rock Bottom"**
    Wynonna
    (Curb)
40. **"I'm Holding My Own"**
    Lee Roy Parnell
    (Arista)

Tony Bennett

41. "Your Love Amazes Me"
John Berry
(Liberty)

42. "I Take My Chances"
Mary Chapin Carpenter
(Columbia)

43. "Why Haven't I Heard
From You"
Reba McEntire
(MCA)

44. "Live Until I Die"
Clay Walker
(Giant)

45. "Rope the Moon"
John Michael Montgomery
(Atlantic)

46. "Hangin' In"
Tanya Tucker
(Liberty)

47. "John Deere Green"
Joe Diffie
(Epic)

48. "How Can I Help You Say
Goodbye"
Patty Loveless
(Epic)

49. "The Man in Love With You"
George Strait
(MCA)

50. "I Can't Reach Her
Anymore"
Sammy Kershaw
(Mercury)

Top 20 Jazz Albums

1. *Steppin' Out*
Tony Bennett
(Columbia)

2. *MTV Unplugged*
Tony Bennett
(Columbia)

3. *25*
Harry Connick, Jr.
(Columbia)

4. *Blue Light 'til Dawn*
Cassandra Wilson
(Blue Note)

5. *All My Tomorrows*
Grover Washington, Jr.
(Columbia)

6. *Swing Kids*
Soundtrack
(Hollywood)

7. *Heart to Heart*
Diane Schuur and B.B. King
(GRP)

8. *Wish*
Joshua Redman
(Warner Bros.)

9. *The Best of the Songbooks*
Ella Fitzgerald
(Verve)

10. *We'll Be Together Again*
Lena Horne
(Blue Note)

11. *Mystery Lady*
Etta James
(Private)

12. *I Can See Your House From
Here*
John Scofield and Pat
Metheny
(Blue Note)

13. *Billie's Best*
Billie Holiday
(Verve)

14. *Mood Swing*
Joshua Redman Quartet
(Warner Bros.)

15. *With the Tenors of Our Time*
Roy Hargrove Quintet
(Verve)

16. *The Billie Holiday
Songbook*
Terence Blanchard
(Columbia)

17. *Live at Montreux*
Miles Davis and Quincy
Jones
(Warner Bros.)

18. *A Single Woman*
Nina Simone
(Elektra)

19. *Gershwin for Lovers*
Marcus Roberts
(Columbia)

20. *Invitation*
Joe Sample
(Warner Bros.)

Hot 25 Rap Singles

1. "Funkdafied"
Da Brat
(So So Def/Chaos)

2. "Tootsee Roll"
69 Boyz
(Rip-It)

3. "Flava in Ya Ear"
Craig Mack
(Bad Boy)

4. "Dunkie Butt"
(Please Please Please)
12 Gauge
(Street Life)

5. "Getto Jam"
Domino
(Outburst/Chaos)

6. "Player's Ball"
Outkast
(LaFace)

7. "Regulate"
Warren G and Nate Dogg
(Death Row/Interscope)

8. "Gin and Juice"
Snoop Doggy Dogg
(Death Row/Interscope)

9. "Got Me Waiting"
Heavy D and The Boyz
(Uptown)

10. "Fantastic Voyage"
Coolio
(Tommy Boy)

11. "Keep Ya Head Up"
2Pac
(Interscope)

12. "Whatta Man"
Salt-N-Pepa featuring En
Vogue
(Next Plateau/London)

13. "Whoomp!" (There It Is)
Tag Team
(Life)

14. "Juicy/Unbelievable"
The Notorious B.I.G.
(Bad Boy)

15. "Back in the Day"
Ahmad
(Giant/Reprise)

16. **"Pumps and a Bump"**
    Hammer
    (Giant/Reprise)

17. **"U.N.I.T.Y."**
    Queen Latifah
    (Motown)

18. **"Shoop"**
    Salt-N-Pepa
    (Next Plateau/London)

19. **"Thuggish Ruggish Bone"**
    Bone Thugs N Harmony
    (Ruthless)

20. **"Cantaloop" (Flip Fantasia)**
    US3
    (Blue Note)

21. **"Born to Roll"**
    Masta Ace Incorporated
    (Delicious Vinyl/EastWest)

22. **"This D.J."**
    Warren G
    (Violator/RAL)

23. **"What's My Name?"**
    Snoop Doggy Dogg
    (Death Row/Interscope)

24. **"It's All Good"**
    Hammer
    (Giant/Reprise)

25. **"You Know How We Do It"**
    Ice Cube
    (Priority)

Top 10 World Music Albums

1. *Love and Liberté*
   Gipsy Kings
   (Elektra Musician)

2. *Talking Timbuktu*
   Ali Farka Toure with
   Ry Cooder
   (Hannibal)

3. *Aye*
   Angelique Kidjo
   (Mango)

4. *Island Angel*
   Altan
   (Green Linnet)

5. *Hope*
   Hugh Masekela
   (Triloka)

6. *Banba*
   Clannad
   (Atlantic)

7. *The Mansa of Mali
   — A Retrospective*
   Salif Keita
   (Mango)

8. *The World Sings Goodnight*
   Various artists
   (Silver Wave)

9. *Sabsylma*
   Zap Mama
   (Luaka Bop)

10. *Still on the Journey*
    Sweet Honey in the Rock
    (Earth Beat)

Top 15 Classical Albums

1. *Chant*
   Benedictine Monks of
   Santo Domingo de Silos
   (Angel)

2. *The Three Tenors in
   Concert 1994*
   Carreras, Domingo and
   Pavarotti (Mehta)
   (Atlantic)

3. *In Concert*
   Carreras, Domingo, Pavarotti
   (Mehta)
   (London)

4. *Gershwin Plays Gershwin*
   Gershwin/Wodehouse
   (Nonesuch)

5. *Gorecki: Symphony No. 3*
   Upshaw/Zinman
   (Nonesuch)

6. *The Nutcracker*
   NYC Ballet (Zinman)
   (Nonesuch)

7. *Ti Amo*
   Luciano Pavarotti
   (London)

8. *Arvo Part: Te Deum*
   Tallinn Chamber Orchestra
   (Kaljuste)
   (ECM)

9. *My Heart's Delight*
   Luciano Pavarotti
   (London)

10. *If You Love Me*
    Cecilia Bartoli
    (London)

11. *Mozart Portraits*
    Cecilia Bartoli
    (London)

12. *The Impatient Lover*
    Bartoli/Schiff
    (London)

13. *Great Studio Recordings*
    Luciano Pavarotti
    (London)

14. *Amore*
    Luciano Pavarotti
    (London)

15. *On Yoolis Night*
    Anonymous 4
    (Harmonia Mundi/France)

Top 10 New Age Albums

1. *Hours Between Night
   and Day*
   Ottmar Liebert and Luna
   Negra
   (Epic)

2. *Shepherd Moons*
   Enya
   (Reprise)

3. *Live at the Acropolis*
   Yanni
   (Private Music)

4. *Nothing Above My
   Shoulders but the Evening*
   Ray Lynch
   (Windham Hill)

5. *Another Star in the Sky*
   David Arkenstone
   (Narada)

6. *Windham Hill Sampler '94*
   Various artists
   (Windham Hill)

7. *Bridge of Dreams*
   David Lanz and Paul Speer
   (Narada)

8. *Acoustic Highway*
   Craig Chaquico
   (Higher Octave)

9. *Watermark*
   Enya
   (Reprise)

10. *Turn of the Tide*
    Tangerine Dream
    (Miramar)

Top 10 Gospel Albums

1. **It Remains to Be Seen**
   Mississippi Mass Choir
   (Malaco)

2. **Kirk Franklin and Family**
   Kirk Franklin and the Family
   (Gospo-Centric)

3. **I Will Trust in the Lord**
   Rev. James Moore
   (Malaco)

4. **Stand Still**
   Shirley Caesar
   (Word)

5. **Save the World**
   Yolanda Adams
   (Tribute)

6. **Live and in Praise II**
   Rudolph Stanfield and
   New Revelation
   (Sound of Gospel)

7. **Shekinah Glory**
   Lashun Pace
   (Savoy)

8. **Live in Memphis**
   The Canton Spirituals
   (Blackberry)

9. **Nothing Can Be Better**
   Luther Barnes and The Red
   Budd Gospel Choir
   (Atlanta International)

10. **Through God's Eyes**
    Rev. Milton Brunson and
    The Thompson Community
    Singers
    (Word)

Top 10 Latin Albums

1. **Mi Tierra**
   Gloria Estefan
   (Epic)

2. **Segundo Romance**
   Luis Miguel
   (WEA Latina)

3. **Love and Liberté**
   Gipsy Kings
   (Elektra Musician)

4. **Amor Prohibido**
   Selena
   (EMI Latin)

5. **Donde Jugarán los Niños**
   Maná
   (WEA Latina)

6. **Pura Sangre**
   Bronco
   (Fonovisa)

7. **Gipsy Kings**
   Gipsy Kings
   (Elektra)

8. **Romance**
   Luis Miguel
   (WEA Latina)

9. **Inalcanzable**
   M. A. Solís y Los Bukis
   (Fonovisa)

10. **Vida**
    La Mafia
    (Sony)

Top 10 Reggae Albums

1. **Queen of the Pack**
   Patra
   (Epic)

2. **Promises and Lies**
   UB40
   (Virgin)

3. **Cool Runnings**
   Soundtrack
   (Chaos)

4. **Bad Boys**
   Inner Circle
   (Big Beat)

5. **Kids From Foreign**
   Born Jamericans
   (Delicious Vinyl/EastWest)

6. **Yaga Yaga**
   Terror Fabulous
   (EastWest)

7. **Big Blunts**
   Various artists
   (Tommy Boy)

8. **Songs of Freedom**
   Bob Marley
   (Tuff Gong)

9. **Voice of Jamaica**
   Buju Banton
   (Mercury)

10. **All She Wrote**
    Chaka Demus and Pliers
    (Mango)

Top 10 Contemporary Christian Albums

1. **Free at Last**
   DC Talk
   (Forefront)

2. **First Decade 1983–1993**
   Michael W. Smith
   (Reunion)

3. **The Standard**
   Carman
   (Sparrow)

4. **Beyond a Dream**
   Twila Paris
   (Starsong)

5. **Songs From the Loft**
   Various artists
   (Reunion)

6. **Heaven in the Real World**
   Steven Curtis Chapman
   (Sparrow)

7. **Susan Ashton**
   Susan Ashton
   (Sparrow)

8. **Joy in the Journey**
   Michael Card
   (Sparrow)

9. **God Is Able**
   Ron Kenoly
   (Integrity)

10. **Michael Sweet**
    Michael Sweet
    (Benson)

Top 20 Concert Grosses of 1994

Amusement Business annually ranks domestic and international concert grosses and touring acts. Here are 1994's top money-makers.

	HEADLINER/ SUPPORTING ACT	GROSS TICKET SALES	TOTAL ATTENDANCE	TICKET PRICE	VENUE, CITY
1.	Barbra Streisand	$16,488,900	94,284	$350, $125, $50	Madison Square Garden, New York, NY
2.	Billy Joel/Elton John	$14,889,127	293,539	$85, $46	Giants Stadium, East Rutherford, NJ
3.	Barbra Streisand	$12,400,650	77,130	$350, $125, $50	Arrowhead Pond, Anaheim, CA
4.	The Rolling Stones/ Counting Crows	$9,531,214	201,547	$50, $25	Giants Stadium, East Rutherford, NJ
5.	The Rolling Stones/ Seal	$9,431,700	199,285	$50, $25	Oakland–Alameda Co. Stadium, Oakland, CA
6.	Phil Collins	$8,730,842	225,113	$38.70	Niedersachsenstadion, Hannover, Germany
7.	Barbra Streisand	$7,780,700	45,160	$350, $125, $50	Palace of Auburn Hills, MI
8.	Billy Joel/Elton John	$7,315,495	150,511	$85, $46	Veterans Stadium, Philadelphia, PA
9.	Paul McCartney	$6,564,416	101,910	$125, $56.25, $28.13	Hermanos Rodriguez Autodromo, Mexico City, Mexico
10.	The Rolling Stones/ Buddy Guy/Red Hot Chili Peppers	$6,153,301	119,140	$55, $25	Rose Bowl Pasadena, CA
11.	Luis Miguel	$5,543,982	150,000	$60.42, $18.13	National Auditorium Mexico City, Mexico
12.	Pink Floyd	$5,301,117	187,302	$69.50, $23.50	Montreal, Quebec Olympic Stadium
13.	Pink Floyd	$5,249,778	155,662	$60, $22.50	Oakland-Alameda Co. Stadium, Oakland, CA
14.	Pink Floyd	$5,235,862	90,476	$125, $28.13	Hermanos Rodriguez Autodromo, Mexico City, Mexico
15.	Eagles	$5,129,091	92,777	$97, $79.50, $59.50, $45.50	Great Woods Center for the Performing Arts, Mansfield, MA
16.	Eagles/ Sheryl Crow	$5,115,545	115,181	$75, $40	Giants Stadium, East Rutherford, NJ
17.	Pink Floyd	$5,091,120	152,264	$60, $22.50	Veterans Stadium, Philadelphia, PA
18.	Eagles	$5,077,875	75,000	$115, $75, $35	Irvine Meadows Amphitheatre, Irvine, CA
19.	Pink Floyd	$4,975,365	137,175	$60, $25	Foxboro, MA Stadium
20.	Eagles	$4,840,000	100,000	$75, $35	Shoreline Amphitheatre, Mountain View, CA

IPEA's Significant Recordings of 1994–1995

These are the recordings (released in the United States between October 1994 and October 1995) that caught our ears. Our selections are alphabetical, unscientific and highly opinionated, and meant to direct you to releases you may have missed.

GERI ALLEN
Twenty One
Blue Note

Here's a terrific lineup: pianist Allen in an energetic mode backed by Ron Carter on bass and Tony Williams on drums. The originals are fiery and her evocations of Monk are insightful.

THE ARTIST FORMERLY KNOWN AS PRINCE
The Black Album
Warner Bros.

When the bootlegs of this album appeared in 1987, they were shockingly raw and a thrilling return to form. It was a disappointment when The Artist Then Known as Prince changed his mind and released the relatively benign *Lovesexy* instead. Now the fabled recording is out, and it still sounds snotty and funky. That beats his last recording, *Come*.

BAND OF SUSANS
Wired for Sound (1986–1993)
Restless

This two-disk (vocal songs and instrumentals) retrospective makes clear that the fascination with pure guitar sound and massed guitar voicings had expression beyond that of the oft-cited manipulations of Sonic Youth or the near-metal of Helmet. Forsaking random experimentation for exploration of harmonic structure and overtone, Band of Susans can still kick a rock song (listen to their signature song, "Hope Against Hope").

SAMUEL BARBER
The Complete Songs (1910–1981)
Thomas Hampson, Cheryl Studer and Emerson String Quartet
Deutsche Grammophon

The ongoing rediscovery of Barber's work now yields a two-disk set of his complete songs. The settings of text by writers such as Theodore Roethke, James Joyce, W.H. Davies and others in performances by Hampson and Studer confirm Barber's preeminence in the form.

THE BEATLES
The Beatles Live at the BBC
Apple/Capitol

Take them down from the pedestals in rock's Valhalla and the Beatles are revealed — at least in their early days — to be a rollicking good bar band. These 56 performances culled from appearances on BBC programs from 1962 to 1965 document the Fab Four's fascination with American R&B as well as their talent as songwriters and Top 40 interpreters. They cover everyone from Arthur Alexander to Ann-Margret to Carl Perkins to the obscure Eddie Fontaine and it still sounds fresh to us.

BIG AUDIO DYNAMITE
Higher Power
Columbia

Big Audio Dynamite first released *Higher Power* under the name Big Audio, but changed the name back halfway through its 1994 tour. Good thing, because *Higher Power* proves the old goats still have substance in their sound. Combining several influences — dance, reggae, hip hop and funk — the album melds into a rhythmic rock rich in melody and substance.

BJORK
Post
Elektra

The former vocalist for Iceland's playfully weird Sugarcubes made a big solo debut with 1994's *Debut*, a multimillion seller. Though she could have simply remade her previous success, Bjork has lent her characteristic whoops to a challenging range of sounds from industrial clangor to orchestral interludes to a Betty Hutton chestnut.

JEFF BUCKLEY
Grace
Columbia

Singer/songwriter Buckley captured the imagination of the most jaded rockers with his emotional renditions of Leonard Cohen's "Hallelujah" and his own stirring songs. His vocalizations of intimate emotion may not be to everyone's taste, but the authenticity of feeling is unmistakable.

BETTY CARTER
Feed the Fire
Verve

Carter has long been a supporter of younger players, and this live set showcases her supple vocals backed by an unbeatable combo of Geri Allen, Dave Holland and Jack DeJohnette.

JOHNNY CASH
American Recordings
American Recordings

The Man in Black caught the ears of country fans — and also those of young grunge rockers — with a stark set of growling and picking produced by Rick Rubin. Accompanied by only an acoustic guitar, *American Recordings* exposes Cash's honesty and craft.

MARY CHAPIN CARPENTER
Stones in the Road
Columbia

That Carpenter has beguiled the country audience is something of a surprise as she hews closer to the folk side of singer/songwriter terrain (though in her live performances she rocks closer to Melissa Etheridge's anthemic territory) and her politcial sympathies would confound the flag-waving crowd. This set of new Carpenter songs mines troubled emotional territory ("House of Cards") and includes a beautiful story song ("John Doe #24") and a spunky come-hither "Shut Up and Kiss Me."

CYRUS CHESTNUT
The Dark Before the Dawn
Atlantic

At the forefront of the young pianists who explore jazz tradition — in this case, the modal jazz of Coltrane with McCoy Tyner's articulation — Chestnut swings with a near-rhythm-and-blues drive, even when essaying a Bach keyboard invention.

THE CHIEFTAINS
The Long Black Veil
RCA

Finally, after 30-odd years, *The Long Black Veil* may turn the Chieftains into rock stars. Though revered for years by musicians and anyone else whose heart could be touched by the haunting beauty of Irish music, this album contains once-in-a-lifetime partnerships with luminaries such as The Rolling Stones, Marianne Faithfull, Van Morrison, Sting, Sinead O'Connor and Ry Cooder.

ERIC CLAPTON
From the Cradle
Duck/Reprise

For many rock fans, Eric Clapton's work with John Mayall's Bluesbreakers, the Yardbirds or Derek and the Dominos was their introduction to the electric blues of Muddy Waters, Elmore James or Willie Dixon. Clapton has since been revered as godlike: here he shows the source of his inspiration. His tribute to the blues is a heartfelt showcase for some of the best guitar work to be heard anywhere, and his efforts are more than a star turn. The players, including pianist Chris Stainton, guitarist Andy Fairweather-Low and harmonica player Jerry Portnoy, sound like a band and there are plenty of instrumental pyrotechnics to go around.

GUY CLARK
Dublin Blues
Asylum

One of the seemingly endless supply of Texas songwriters, Clark traveled to Ireland to record an impressive set of new songs. The result is a celebration of the simple pleasures in the work of a man and his guitar.

COMBUSTIBLE EDISON
I, Swinger
Sub Pop

Along with the Bar None reissue of Esquivel's sonic experimentations on *Space Age Bachelor Pad Music*, this was the record that led the new cocktail generation back to the lounges. The easy-listening music of their parents (grandparents?!) held a witty allure after the ceaseless

din of a thousand sound-alike alternarock bands. Combustible Edison produces an arch, knowing take on exotica that, yes, swings. Why shouldn't we *all* be fabulous?

THE CRANBERRIES
No Need to Argue
Island

Dolores O'Riordan translates her bitterness into art with a singular voice. Though cliché-ridden, her songs weave dark romantic tales and lash out at Ireland's political quagmire, both past and present. Most notable on the album is "Yeats's Grave," the story of William Butler Yeat's unrequited love for Maud Gonne.

IRIS DeMENT

My Life
Warner Bros.

From Arkansas comes a yearning voice that reaches back to parents, family and the costs of love and growing up for a classic country recording. Plainspoken and somber, these are essential stories made for country music.

DINOSAUR JR
Without a Sound
Sire/Reprise

J Mascis led the parade (Sebadoh and Buffalo Tom followed) of dispirited guitar strummers who took alternative rock down a peculiarly enervated path. Drone and volume took the place of melody and rhythm, but there is undeniable majesty in much of Dinosaur's output. *Without a Sound*, essentially a Mascis solo album, sounds like the last gasp of the shoegazers. It did feature an amazing single, though, in "Feel the Pain."

BOB DYLAN
MTV Unplugged
Columbia

Dylan's appearance at Woodstock '94 was a spiritual high point and a reaching across the generations. It was also an open-hearted, giving performance — not always a guarantee with Dylan. The same band accompanies him on his *Unplugged* outing and the same spirit prevails. Need a Dylan greatest hits collection? You could do worse.

MARTY EHRLICH
Can You Hear a Motion?
Enja

Thoughtful compositions and well-crafted soloing mark this quartet session fronted by reed-player Ehrlich. He's joined up front by sax player Stan Strickland.

8 BOLD SOULS
Ant Farm
Arabesque Jazz

Saxophonist Ed Wilkerson, Jr., the leading light of the younger wing of Chicago's AACM movement, uses this octet to work out compositions for a larger ensemble. The Souls emphasize the lower registers, featuring baritone sax, tuba, trombone and cello. Just 'cause it's low doesn't mean it can't swing with a burning intensity.

ELASTICA
Elastica
Geffen

The juxtaposition of jaunty pop punk with a sharp tongue and a nasty disposition makes this a stellar debut. This reminds us of the legendary Buzzcocks, and that ain't bad.

DUKE ELLINGTON
The Far East Suite: Special Mix
Bluebird

Yet another milestone in Ellington's career when it was released in 1967 (how many peaks did Ellington and Strayhorn climb?), this new version includes four alternate takes that were never released, and it has been remixed to alleviate distortion.

MARIANNE FAITHFULL
A Secret Life
Island

Faithfull's mournful delivery gets a lush, sympathetic setting by producer Angelo Badalamenti. The record presents what are essentially cabaret songs informed by rock history and a deep well of personal experience.

FOO FIGHTERS
Foo Fighters
Roswell/Capitol

This was one of the most anticipated records of the year. Music fans were understandably anxious to hear the next projects from members of Nirvana, and they followed Dave Grohl (now on guitar and vocals) and Nirvana sideman Pat Smear as Foo Fighters toured with Mike Watt.

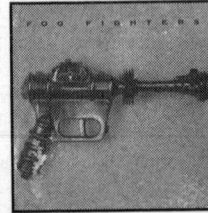

The record started to leak out before release and then ascended immediately to the top of the modern rock charts. Does it sound like Nirvana? Some, but why shouldn't it? If it lacks the bitter edge, maybe that means Dave Grohl will be around long enough to grow into the expectations the world has for him.

BILL FRISELL
Go West
The High Sign/One Week
Nonesuch/Elektra

Guitarist Frisell blends composition and improvisation on his two-disk contemplation of Buster Keaton silents of the early 1920s. The melancholy humor of Keaton seems an inspirational foil for Frisell's imagination that throws off excursions into jazz, country, blues and rock. The trio includes Joey Baron on drums and bassist Kermit Driscoll.

FUGAZI
Red Medicine
Dischord

Fugazi has long been the hero of the independent rock scene because it is one of the few bands to remain steadfastly independent, running its own label, setting low ticket prices, generally refusing to pander. From its first EP, Fugazi showed the way out of the formulaic cul-de-sac that plagued hardcore. With this new release, the band takes another step, finding new voices and new sounds to express warning and alarm. Though Fugazi never hit the charts before *Red Medicine*, it influenced musicians from all over the independent sector, and will again with *Red Medicine*.

WARREN G
Regulate . . . G Funk Era
Island

Warren G extends the dominance of Dr. Dre and his partner Snoop Doggy Dog as the smooth sound of Long Beach now rules over the wrenching rap of the Compton gangsters. The reality is equally grim and terrifying, but the G Funk sound may provide the missing link back to the wellspring of the soul and funk pioneers.

LISA GERMANO
Geek the Girl
4AD

Germano, former John Mellencamp violinist, has made a name for herself with *Geek the Girl* and her brighter first album *Happiness*. She tackles some tough emotional issues — alienation, date rape and emotional abuse — with honesty and simplicity.

GUIDED BY VOICES
Alien Lanes
Matador

What if the Beatles were never lifted out of the Cavern Club by Brian Epstein and they continued to record material on home two-track decks for fun? What if those songs made it to disk in 1995? Would you recognize the genius on those scratchy reels? Guided by Voices may be the next best thing, and there is certainly genius on these disks. Imagine the most glorious pop chorus you've ever heard, that exultant 20 seconds that makes life worth living. Now repeat. Repeat again. Now add scratches, warbles, snoring and other random low-fi glitches. Now make it stop before the chorus gets tired or you lose interest. You just conjured up Guided by Voices's *Alien Lanes*. The frontier into radio-ready production is rumored to be crossed by their forthcoming disk. Recorded by the Breeders' Kim Deal with an assist by Steve Albini, the January 1996 release reportedly features a cleaner sound, actual verses and choruses and more pop genius.

BUTCH HANCOCK
Eats Away the Night
Sugar Hill

We have a bias, and it's this: We believe that Butch Hancock is one of the greatest songwriters of our time. The Lubbock, Texas, native fueled the songbooks of the legendary Flatlanders and compadres Jimmie Dale Gilmore and Joe Ely. This outing, Hancock gets a real band and real production — as opposed to the homemade cassettes and low-budget treatment he has gotten in the past. It even includes the much-covered, but always welcome, "If You Were a Bluebird."

HERBIE HANCOCK
Dis Is Da Drum
Mercury

Since *Head Hunters*, Hancock has been mixing up jazz inflections with soul and funk rhythms. His latest uses 1970s-style keyboards and integrates African instrumentation, hip hop and acoustic jazz. A new fusion built on the acid-jazz phenomenon?

PJ HARVEY
To Bring You My Love
Island

Polly Jean Harvey manages to slash and tear at the heart with the sparest possible arrangements. With no aural trickery and song structures that border on the blues, Harvey exposes the barbed wire that waits for unaware lovers and makes powerful prayers for the restoration of love that's lost.

HELMET
Betty
Interscope

All the hoopla that surrounded the signing of Helmet to a lucrative major-label contract seemed calculated to make the music itself seem more important. Why more worthy than Band of Susans (former employers of front man Page Hamilton) or Sonic Youth? *Betty* was the payoff. The thought is apparent, the influences impressive (Coltrane, Branca) and the record steams ahead with purposeful abandon.

TISH HINOJOSA
Frontejas
Rounder

The achingly beautiful ballads and *corridas* found here grew out of work Hinojosa undertook with a historian and anthropologist. The traditions of the border culture come through in Hinojosa's warm vocals and the able back-up of accordionists Flaco and Santiago Jiminez, Peter Rowan and Brave Combo.

CHRIS ISAAK
Forever Blue
Reprise

It's been a long time since 1989's *Heart-Shaped World*'s "Wicked Game" made Isaak and his Roy Orbison quaver the choice of hopeless romantics everywhere. Pursuing a career as a screen heartthrob hasn't dimmed Isaak's appeal, and the time off has made this a must-listen.

MICHAEL JACKSON
HIStory
Epic

Can anyone truly hear the music through the headline-grabbing static? The Diane Sawyer interview, the anti-Semitic lines rerecorded: It all seemed rote, part of the high-stakes campaign for the millions in sales needed to maintain global supremacy. The new material's stridency seems forced and nearly humorous, like Bambi wearing a fright wig. It doesn't help that the only good track is "Scream," a duet with sister Janet that moves in on her territory, or that the package includes a greatest hits compilation, forcing a fond look backwards.

THE JAYHAWKS
Tomorrow the Green Grass
American Recordings

After being trammeled by the baroque blandness of the middle-aged Eagles and being co-opted by the louder wing of the resurgent country music scene, country-rock has made a sterling comeback on *Tomorrow the Green Grass*. Minneapolis's Jayhawks have been chummy with the alternative crowd for years, and they lend a little street

cred to a genre that had languished. Heart-rending harmonies, chiming guitars and a reliable tick-tock, two-step rhythm reward every listening. Gram Parsons would be proud.

TOM JONES
The Lead and How to Swing It
Interscope

The last couple of years have seen the rediscovery of pop icons and lounge lizards (as in MTV's Tony Bennett *Unplugged* session). Can any of this, particularly the return of Tom Jones, be greeted with anything other than an ironic giggle? Well, maybe. Jones may be high camp, but he undeniably does know how to swing it. This is the soundtrack for young hipsters.

CHRIS KNOX
Songs of You and Me
Caroline

Not for everyone, but the once and future Tall Dwarf ventures into territory seldom explored by the run-of-the-mill alternative rocker. His solo ruminations co-opt genres and surprise with every track.

ALISON KRAUSS
Now That I've Found You
Rounder Records

The passing of the torch to a new generation of bluegrass artists has found its most renowned exponent in a young woman whose fiddle playing enlivens gospel, trad bluegrass and some surprising takes on rock songs such as the Association's "Baby, Now That I've Found You" and Bad Company's "Oh, Atlanta."

THE KRONOS QUARTET
Performs Philip Glass
Elektra/Nonesuch

Philip Glass's music came bursting out of downtown New York with the volume and urgency of arena rock, electronic keyboards hammering out pulsing ostinatos. Now new-music champions The Kronos Quartet lend elegant, cutting sonorities to four Glass quartets. The intricacies and sudden tempo changes inherent in Glass's music pose a challenge to string instruments, but Kronos navigates its way with precision and grace.

ANNIE LENNOX
Medusa
Arista

This has got to stop. Rock stars must stop sliding into middle age by co-opting the pop standards that made their parents (or even their older siblings) swing. If they can't stop, the vaults should be locked and the key thrown away. And yet this torpid slice of dreck sold mil lions. Did Neil Young, the Temptations, or poor Al Green, who has seen "Take Me to the River" covered for the nine billionth time here, ever imagine their work easing the hours baby boomers spend burping their babies? No. No. A thousand times no. Especially as tired output from formerly adventurous artists. And that goes double for you, Elvis Costello. And triple for Duran Duran. Quadruple for Chicago.

LETTERS TO CLEO
Auroragoryalice
Giant

THE REMBRANDTS
L.P.
East/West

Witness the power of television over the record charts (and note also the continuing power of the movies: *The Lion King* soundtrack was the top seller of 1994). Boston's Letters to Cleo ascended to the upper reaches of the charts with their first album after many viewers asked, "Who's the band that plays over the credits on *Melrose Place?*" The music on their major-label debut, and its follow-up, *Wholesale Meats and Fish* fits with this year's phenomenon of little girl voices being paired with blaring guitars (Belly, Juliana Hatfield, Veruca Salt). The only artistry the Rembrandts can claim is an artful placement over the opening credits of NBC's *Friends*.

LYLE LOVETT
I Love Everybody
MCA

For those who think Lovett's best work can be found in the records that featured just his voice and guitar, rather than the jump-blues, big-band stylings, this is a welcome return to the stark simplicity that best showcases his often bent perspective on the world. The songs themselves are a return in another sense as they mark Lovett's rethinking of songs he wrote when he was an itinerant folk singer and before his recording debut in 1987.

SHANE MACGOWAN AND THE POPES
The Snake
ZTT

Fans of the Pogues had reason to despair of ever seeing another set of Shane MacGowan's teary rants. After years of abuse, he had dropped out of the Pogues and attempts at new beginnings seemed dim and pale. This is a welcome-back with a new group, traditional melodies and fresh exorcisms.

THE MAVERICKS
What a Crying Shame
MCA

This was a banner year for resurgent country rock — and the best of the lot was made far from the Nashville factories by the Jayhawks, Wilco and The Mavericks. Miami-based The Mavericks feature a Cuban lead singer with a sound that recalls the heart-stopping ache of Roy Orbison and a fun-loving band that finds that intersection where country veered off into rock. The Maverick's summer 1995 release *Music for All Occasions* continues the band's love affair with 1950's rock and tex-mex.

CHRISTIAN MCBRIDE
Gettin' to It
Verve

Christian McBride is another jazz prodigy drawn to the sounds of the jazz heritage, and the 22-year-old bassman already shows the steady hand of a master. A sweet, on-the-money tone and accurate bowing lift the six originals on this maiden voyage played with contemporaries that include Joshua Redman and Cyrus Chestnut. Check out "Splanky," an outing with idols Ray Brown, Milt Hinton and Redman that reads like a happy-go-lucky homage.

MOBY
Everything Is Wrong
Elektra

Those who remain suspicious of techno's trance-like allure need to check out one-man band Moby's rocking melange of screaming guitars, odd-ball raps and machine-gun beats. And the guy quietly espouses a Christian philosophy. Bob Dole: get on it.

MORPHINE
yes
Rykodisc

The third release from the leading (read: only) exponents of low rock — cocktail drum set, two-string slide bass, baritone sax and Mark Sandman's smoky purr — should find the unfamiliar lineup waning in interest. But instead, it's becoming clearer that great rock is in the inspiration and execution, not the instrumentation.

DEIDRE MURRAY AND FRED HOPKINS
Stringology
Black Saint

Two of the premier string players in jazz (Murray on cello, Hopkins on bass) join forces for a resonant set.

NIRVANA
MTV Unplugged in New York
DGC

MTV's innovative rock platform has yielded some oddities (Tony Bennett *unplugged?* What was he before?). On its face, Nirvana's excursion would seem one of them: here's the band that made the yammer and howl of punk palatable for the masses being deprived of their raw power. Yet, *MTV Unplugged in New York* may stand as the finest testament to Kurt Cobain's song writing. Unadorned, his taste and his skill with songs such as "All Apologies" and a dead-on cover of David Bowie's "The Man Who Sold the World" speak with undeniable strength.

OASIS
Definitely Maybe
Epic

After the punk revival comes what? Beatle-inflected, new wave power pop, naturally. Oasis joined the ranks of its British brethren (with Blur, London Suede) given the big sendoff at home on its way to conquer America, only to wash back humbled. Being heralded as the "next big thing" in the British press is a virtual assurance of "same old shit."

PASSION
Original Broadway Cast Recording
Music and lyrics: Stephen Sondheim
Book and direction: James Lapine
Angel Records

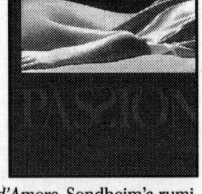

Based on Ettore Scola's romantic film, *Passione d'Amore*, Sondheim's rumination on the unpredictable ways of the heart is touching and ambitiously operatic. An exercise in unabashed emotion and soaring melody.

PAVEMENT
Crooked Rain, Crooked Rain
Wowee Zowee
Matador

Pavement has resolutely resisted being defined by any easy classification of rock — though their willful obscurity made them awfully hard to love. *Crooked Rain* marked a step forward. The songs cohered into an understandable whole, and the music itself flirted with the previously dreaded country rock. *Wowee Zowee* continued the momentum, even the acoustic wanderings, yet turned away from easier listening. Whither Pavement?

PEARL JAM
Vitalogy
Epic

The cover of *Vitalogy* looks like it could be a Small Faces outing from the early '70s, and let's face it, that's just about right. That Pearl Jam became the banner-carrier of alternative rock reveals the emptiness of the label. Alternative to what? This band is destined for classic rock because they possess the qualities of the best bands in history: memorable melodies, sterling musicianship and a lead singer whose emotive vocals catch the imagination of a generation of kids. Anyone who has seen Pearl Jam live marvels at the bond Eddie Vedder forms with his audience. Those kids know that Pearl Jam will be theirs forever.

DANILO PEREZ
The Journey
Novus

A rewarding excursion through Afro-Cuban rhythmic territory courtesy of Perez's muscular piano work. This is no museum piece, though; Perez and saxophonist David Sanchez plumb their own imaginations and experience for a unique vision of Latin jazz.

PORTISHEAD
Dummy
Go!Discs/London

Lounge crooners for the lush life of a new generation, singer Beth Gibbons and songwriter Geoff Barrows create lots of space around their mournful lyrics and pin the meaning with nearly ambient techno beats and movie-soundtrack samples. They were curiously ubiquitous on MTV for a while; try Massive Attack for more "trip hop."

PULP FICTION
The Motion Picture Soundtrack
MCA

In the avalanche of pop-compilation soundtrack recordings, particularly those that settle for an easy response to musical memories, it's refreshing to sample a soundtrack record that not only is inextricably tied to the action of the film — and therefore allows you to relive the movie's highlights — but also reawakens interest in a favorite genre of music, in this case surf guitar.

R.E.M.
Monster
Warner Bros.

"What's the frequency, Michael?" was the question more than a few R.E.M. fans asked as the group, heralded as the best rock band in America by *Rolling Stone*, wandered in the acoustic, self-absorbed (though multimillion selling) margins of rock. With *Monster*, they've knocked down the door and claimed their mantle once again. Peter Buck takes center stage with squalling feedback and deft touches, and Michael Stipe comes clean with clearer statements and an authoritative tone. "What's the Frequency, Kenneth?," "Bang and Blame" and "Crush With Eyeliner" make great radio tunes; what more can you ask of your favorite band than great singles and a confident, absorbing set of tunes?

ROYAL TRUX
Thank You
Virgin

Hailed as the up-from-the-underground noise-merchant version of The Rolling Stones' malevolent barroom rock, the Trux appeared on a major label somewhat tidier, but no less entertaining.

KEVIN SALEM
Soma City
Roadrunner

Former guitar sideman with Freedy Johnson and others, Salem moves into the spotlight with his first solo album. The poetry of his musings on love and loss and the straightforward take on the guitar-rock style make this a memorable debut.

SEBADOH
Bake Sale
Sub Pop

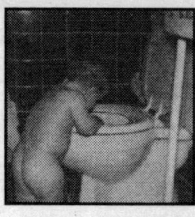

Wading through Lou Barlow's musings to sift out the gems has always been a hallmark of listening to Sebadoh. This record was a breakthrough. Not only was the proportion of listenable songs high, Barlow and his compatriots Jason Loewenstein and Bob Fay play with assurance and clarity. Barlow has always been interesting for his ability to plumb his emotional life in an often-cynical alternative rock environment. Now the wider world has caught on.

SELENA
Dreaming of You
EMI Latin

At just 23 years old, Selena had already sold 3 million records, all *tejano* hits unheard by the mainstream outside the Southwest border territory. When she was murdered by a former associate, the beloved queen of *tejano*'s records hit the charts in a too-late burst of morbid enthusiasm. *Dreaming of You* made Selena the fastest-selling female artist of all time, moving an estimated 400,000 copies in its first week of release. The hype doesn't dampen her obvious talent and the music itself, a heart-rending blend of *conjunto*, an accordion-based dance music, Mexican folk and pop.

SHELLAC
Live at Action Park
Touch and Go

There's no mistaking that Steve Albini fuels this recording with its corrosively metronomic guitar sound and lacerating vocals. But fellow travelers Bob Weston and Tod Trainor add a little more jump — dare we say swing — than found on previous Albini projects such as Big Black.

SMASHING PUMPKINS
Pisces Iscariot
Virgin

Coming off huge success with *Siamese Dream*, the Pumpkins had high expectations to fulfill. Unlike so many bands that can't follow up a hit with another winner, the band came through with this compilation of B-sides. The acoustic ballads showcase Billy Corgan's songwriting prowess. Especially pleasing are "Soothe," "La Dolly Vita" and the Fleetwood Mac cover "Landslide."

JON SPENCER BLUES EXPLOSION
Orange
Matador

Spencer's trash blues and funk sounds like nothing else around. Jon and crew pack more into one post-modern mongrel of a song — radical changes in direction, wordless howls, theremin whoops, guitar pounding — than most bands put in an entire record. These guys are huge. Also check out the experimental remix disk.

SPIRITUALIZED
Pure Phase
Arista

Whispering, slow, insinuating — this is rock music that moves at a glacial pace (mostly) and yet has the impressive heft of a colossus that builds momentum to rave-up speed. An intriguing branch of alternative rock that's just as much classic pop as ambient trance.

BRUCE SPRINGSTEEN
Greatest Hits
Columbia

Just when it seemed that the fantasies fueled by rock — freedom, romance, community with kindred souls — end inevitably in disillusionment, if not suicide, along comes a Springsteen collection that reminds us of when those yearnings were a priceless part of every adolescence. It's startling to hear Springsteen's radio hits now sound as quaint as Stephen Foster, relics of an innocent age. The three new songs with the E Street Band sound flabby; the much-requested "Murder Incorporated" from 1982 sounds just right. No "Rosalita," but there's "Hungry Heart." Baffling.

STEREOLAB
Mars Audiac Quartet
Elektra

Near-ambient synthesizer burbles, organ washes and extended trance-inducing rhythms aren't the sole domain of the techno crowd. Sterolab's distention of what are essentially guitar-and-organ pop masterpieces makes this an intriguing new sound. The mystifying lyrics (particularly those in French) add to the allure.

DAWN UPSHAW
I Wish It So
Elektra/Nonesuch

Upshaw's clear and compelling voice elevated Gorecki's *Third Symphony* to a nearly religious experience and made a bestseller of Samuel Barber. Here she turns her attention to Broadway, with some not-so-obvious choices of material (Weill, Blitzstein, Bernstein and less-well-known Sondheim), and makes the horde of other classical crossover recordings seem merely starstruck.

VARIOUS ARTISTS
Afro-Peruvian Classics: The Soul of Black Peru
Luaka Bop/Warner Bros.

David Byrne and Yale Evelev venture to the Andes for a sound that melds flamenco sounds with Afro-Cuban rhythms. The various artists they found will satisfy those who appreciate Byrne's other south-of-the-border explorations.

VARIOUS ARTISTS
Celtic Graces: A Best of Ireland
Hemisphere

This primer for the softer side of Irish music includes standout tracks from Clannad, Christy Moore with Planxty, The Bothy Band and Donal Lunny. The mix of traditional songs with the craft of Ireland's finest songwriters and performers makes a fine introduction to contemporary Irish music.

VARIOUS
The Envelope Please . . . Academy Award Winning Songs (1934–1993)
Rhino

A five-CD set (with nicely produced companion booklet) that covers everything from 1934's "The Continental" to Richie Havens's take on "Streets of Philadelphia" from 1993. Among the nicest aspects of this prodigious effort is discovering the way our musical history can be traced through its appearance in the movies. Fascinating.

VARIOUS ARTISTS
Till the Night Is Gone: A Tribute to Doc Pomus
Rhino/Forward

Tribute records are beginning to be a stale idea, but when the subject has provided songs of the caliber of "This Magic Moment," "Save the Last Dance for Me" and "Viva Las Vegas," it makes a worthy project. The list of performers is impressive as well, including Bob Dylan, Lou Reed, Shawn Colvin, John Hiatt and Dr. John.

WILCO
A.M.
Reprise/Sire

Picking up the pieces from Missouri's Uncle Tupelo, guitarist Jeff Tweedy recruited Tupelo's bassist John Stirratt, drummer Ken Coomer, jack-of-all-trades Max Johnston and pulled in Midwestern guitarist Brian Henneman to form the country-rock band Wilco. Tweedy's laid-back, baritone vocals and his poetic songs create a back-porch feel enhanced by Johnston's nimble fingers on the guitar, banjo, mandolin and other instruments.

VAUGHN WILLIAMS/ LONDON PHILHARMONIC CONDUCTED BY SIR ADRIAN BOULT
Symphony No. 2 "A London Symphony"
Belart

One of the benefits (one of the only benefits?) of the compact-disk era in recorded music is the continuing surprise as dimly remembered treasures come to the fore one after the other. We have always cherished an old, scratchy LP of Boult's 1952 — not the 1971 — rendition of Ralph Vaughn Williams's "London," though with the purchase of a CD player, it has made its appearance on woefully rare occasions. Now it can take its place once more in the most-played section of the shelf. The sonorous slow movement is justifiably renowned, and the orchestra's affection for its leader and the composer for his subject is evident throughout.

PAUL WELLER
Stanley Road
Go!Discs/London

Once the leader of the Jam, mod revivalists in the early post-punk days, and Style Council, a sleek dance-pop combo, Weller's seemingly disparate interests never fail to exhibit a real feeling of soul. Now a rock hero in Britain, Weller has released a rhythm-and-blues-tinged recording that ponders personal themes while finding a dignified use for the classic sound of rock.

VICTORIA WILLIAMS
Loose
Mammoth/Atlantic

A songwriter who refuses to be bound by expectations, Williams came to the attention of a wider audience through the benefit album, *Sweet Relief*, which her musician pals made to help pay the bills for her multiple sclerosis treatment. Reissues of previous work followed, and then the release of her first new recording in

four years. *Loose* spans musical genres and partakes of Williams's Southern roots, all in a sunny style uniquely hers. A must-have.

NEIL YOUNG AND PEARL JAM
Mirror Ball
Reprise

The collaboration between the irrepressible and unpredictable Young and the biggest stars of a generation 20 years younger yields a truly astonishing collection. The quickly recorded (nearly live in the studio) set of Young songs burns with the intensity of rock's truest believer.

Between Rock and a Hard Place

For the Jayhawks, the price for dancing on the threshold of rock 'n' roll fame is compromise and debt to the tune of $1 million.

■ BY FRED GOODMAN

O N VALENTINE'S DAY 1995, AMERICAN RECORDINGS RELEASED *Tomorrow the Green Grass,* the make-or-break fourth album from baby-boom country rockers the Jayhawks. It's a pinnacle only a handful of the tens of thousands of bands in the highly competitive world of rock 'n' roll ever reach. After years of sleeping on floors and mooching off friends, the Jayhawks now will live out the fantasy of everyone who ever stood up with a guitar in a bar: touring the country to support a well-promoted record from a glamorous label.

But the Minneapolis band's permanent members — three college-educated friends in their 30s — are profoundly torn over the price of their success. And this ambivalence is no artistic pose. So deep in debt they may never make money from their music, the Jayhawks are an object lesson in the weird economics of rock 'n' roll, a $5 billion industry in which everyone makes a decent living except most musicians.

Even if *Tomorrow* goes platinum (that is, if it sells 1 million copies), the Jayhawks likely won't see much of the resulting cash avalanche. That's because the band owes more than $700,000 to American Recordings and has other debts to various managers. In the decade they've been together, the most band members have put aside for themselves is $250 a week each, and that was just for a few months in 1993.

THE MUSIC BUSINESS

None of the Jayhawks has bought a house in Los Angeles, their new base. None drives a rock-star car. Unless they're being wined and dined by record-company executives, they generally eat at diners and modest restaurants. While the band's following has grown steadily — its previous album, *Hollywood Town Hall,* sold 200,000 copies worldwide — it's possible the Jayhawks will be in their 40s before they find out whether playing music can ever pay the bills. And that's not unusual, even for very successful artists. Such well-known rockers as Bonnie Raitt and Boston's J. Geils Band toured for more than a decade before making more than pocket change. Before she died of cancer in 1992, Motown singer Mary Wells relied on donations from Diana Ross, Bruce Springsteen and others to pay for her care.

On the other hand, once a band makes it the rewards can grow enormous over time: Witness The Rolling Stones' hugely lucrative tour last year, for which the band earned $120 million. "It's survival of the fittest," says Gary Borman, the Jayhawks' well-regarded manager. "If a band is prepared to sacrifice early and sustain that over time until everything else catches up, then on the back end it can win exponentially." But in the meantime, bands must make wrenching decisions as they wait for the break that may never come. The Jayhawks have changed their sound to be more commercial. They've ditched a stockbroker friend who used to manage them. They've parted ways with a band member.

Y et for all the moral grappling, the band still lives without many basic comforts and securities that most professionals take for granted — a point that was pounded home when Victoria Williams, the 35-year-old singer-songwriter who is married to Jayhawk guitarist Mark Olson, was diagnosed with multiple sclerosis. Friends rallied to the couple's support with benefit concerts and *Sweet Relief,* a popular album that so far has raised more than $350,000 to offset her medical expenses and help other hard-pressed musicians. Williams's condition has improved with treatment, but the crisis was a reminder of how financially shaky life can be even for recognized musicians.

The Jayhawks

Saddled with mounting bills, increasing age and decreasing patience, the Jayhawks may finally reach a breaking point in 1995. If *Tomorrow the Green Grass* can't attract a big audience — or at least sell enough to suggest that the next album will be a hit — American Recordings could drop the band and shatter what's left of its members' idealism.

Not so long ago, Jayhawk guitarist and former architect Gary Louris refused to do an ad for Levi's 501 jeans that could have earned the band as much as $200,000. Mildly irked but still good humored, his bandmates dubbed him Mr. Integrity. Louris, a tall, rail-thin man with a perpetual air of troubled concentration, sighs: "There are times when you say 'Wow, we could really use the money.' But I imagined how it would feel singing, '501, 501. . . .'"

That may have been the Jayhawks' last moral stand. If *Tomorrow the Green Grass* is a hit, selling a half million or more, the group could begin to erase its debt and settle into comfortable lives. But as the band's rough-hewn producer, George Drakoulias, says in a cruel joke: If this album bombs, it's time to do as many Levi's ads as possible.

When stockbroker Charlie Pine saw the Jayhawks warming up for cult rocker Alex Chilton at a Minneapolis club in 1985, the 30-year-old music fan was bowled over by the local quartet's straightforward country rock and heartfelt lyrics. "They were very rough, but I thought the music was amazing," he remembers. "It wasn't attitude, it wasn't angst. It was songs."

Pine visited the band's rehearsal space in a run-down Minneapolis warehouse, and the conversation turned to the business of running a band. At the time, Mark Olson — who had formed the group — was making ends meet as a cook and child-care worker. But he was also lining up all the Jayhawks' gigs himself, and it was proving a heavy burden. Pine quickly offered his services to Olson, whose tousled brown hair frames the kind of open face that would be at home on a Midwestern farm.

The Jayhawks
Tomorrow the Green Grass

Pine, now 39, was hardly a seasoned pro: His previous experience in music was limited to managing a record store and working at his college radio station. But the short, slight man was an aggressive broker with a small local firm, Engler and Budd, and he began channeling that drive into making the Jayhawks more than a mildly successful bunch of part-timers. Together with the band, Pine formed a homegrown record label called Bunkhouse Records. Over ten days and for $12,000 of Pine's money, they recorded a debut album as bait for a major-league deal. Pine used his brokerage's WATS line to promote the band to radio stations.

The next step was touring — except that Louris didn't relish the idea of spending time away from home. He had been through that once already, with a failed rockabilly band called Safety Last. "I'd see other people and think about how they were going home to have a barbecue or go to bed," he says. So the Jayhawks played just short tours of the East and West Coasts — mostly to get the band in front of major-label folks in New York and Los Angeles. They traveled by van and slept in friends' homes, but there was no chance of making money. In Minneapolis, where their following was strongest, the Jayhawks could command as much as $700 a night. On the road, however, they rarely made more than a few hundred bucks to cover expenses — and sometimes worked for much less. "You might as well write CBGB's a check," says Pine of the legendary New York dive. "You don't make anything. We were told to come back and pick up $25. And by then the van had been broken into on the street."

Despite strong reviews in grassroots publications such as *College Media Journal* and *Rockpool*, the Jayhawks had trouble attracting a record company. Still, Pine got some nibbles. In 1988, A&M Records, whose roster includes such artists as Sting and Soundgarden, gave the band $1,000 to record some demos. The Jayhawks put their heart into the effort, but A&M hemmed, hawed and passed.

It was a devastating experience for the band and a personal low point for Louris, who had just been in a car accident. Although not seriously hurt, the incident rekindled all the guitarist's old doubts about the rock 'n' roll life. Deciding he'd had enough of the financial uncertainty and the traveling, he returned to full-time work at an architectural firm, throwing the Jayhawks' very existence in doubt.

Desperate to make a quick deal, Pine shopped the band's A&M demos to Twin/Tone, a local label that always seemed short of cash — but that had launched the career of Jayhawk pals Soul Asylum. The tapes were polished up, a few songs quickly added and Twin/Tone released the result as the Jayhawks' second album, *Blue Earth*. Despite the inexpensive, off-the-cuff manner of assembly (the album cost a paltry $10,000 to complete), the band was justifiably proud of the results; Olson believes it features some of his best work as a songwriter. "It showed that we had something going on," he says.

To cap the triumph, Louris, who came down to the studio to overdub a few of his old parts, found his way back into the band. The reunited Jayhawks hit the road in a refitted ambulance named Bula — the name came from blocking out some of the letters in ambulance, which was emblazoned on the van's front. But the band was soon dissatisfied with Twin/Tone's ability to promote them. "Twin/Tone did less at radio [stations] than I did by myself when I was working the first record," says Pine, who concluded that the Jayhawks had to find a bigger label.

In this respect, Twin/Tone actually proved helpful. It had cultivated a reputation as the farm team for major record companies — Soul Asylum had gone to A&M and then Columbia, for example, the Replacements to Sire. In spring of 1990, the label hooked the Jayhawks up with an American Recordings producer named George Drakoulias, who had just scored a hit album with the Black Crowes. "George was the first person who liked us who was also big enough in his company to sign us," says Louris. "He asked us to make a demo for him, and he went crazy."

Charlie Pine was skeptical. American wasn't known for its largesse, he warned, and the country-inflected group would have a hard time getting noticed by American's brass, who are more closely associated with speed-metal and rap acts. He urged the Jayhawks to go slow and told them of feelers from Atlantic Records, Geffen and CBS. "Their time was almost there," he says now. But the group signed with American Recordings anyway, for $25,000 — a small bonus by industry standards, but far more than the meager $5,000 they heard Drakoulias had paid the Black Crowes.

As is usual in the music world, the money came with a price. Drakoulias told the band to fire Pine and hire someone who knew the L.A. music scene. "It didn't really bother anyone," says drummer Ken Callahan. "The Jayhawks wanted to do what was right for the Jayhawks. Goodbye, Charlie."

The band rented modest apartments in Los Angeles for about $200 a week and, along with Drakoulias, went into the studio to begin work on *Hollywood Town Hall.* Unlike their previous albums, which were recorded on a shoestring budget, this one had to be polished enough to attract a wide audience. It wasn't an easy transition.

American Recordings is backed by industry giant Warner Brothers, but the label is very much the expression of founder Rick Rubin. An arresting figure who's all sunglasses, beard and long hair, Rubin has a hot reputation as producer of such diverse acts as the Red Hot Chili Peppers, the Beastie Boys and Johnny Cash. Although he looks like a biker, Rubin rarely fails to think like a banker: Even his label's promotional freebies bear the half-joking legend "Now you owe us." American is one of the most highly touted startups in U.S. music since David Geffen made his reputation with Asylum Records during the 1970s.

Drakoulias is Rubin's housemate, cut from the same raw cloth as his mentor. Heavyset and imposing, he looks more like a pirate than a producer. When he signed the Jayhawks, Drakoulias had only produced one other band — the Black Crowes, whose debut album, *Shake Your Money*

CONTINUED ON NEXT PAGE ▶

◤ CONTINUED FROM PREVIOUS PAGE

Extreme
http://www.hear.com/extreme

Extreme offers a unique collection of eclectic music from around the globe with sound clips and ordering information.

Harmony Music List
http://orpheus.ucsd.edu/webmaster/harmony/index.html

Music buff Michael Breen has done an amazing job of creating an encyclopedic list of available music, covering the spectrum of genres. He also categorized radio stations, magazines, resources, studios, events, instruments and equipment and has compiled discographies. Also worth a look is **Harmony List: Artists** (http://orpheus.ucsd.edu/webmaster/artists.html), which lists artists with web sites. The list is divided into three categories: industry, independent and marching bands.

Internet Underground Music Archive
http://www.iuma.com/IUMA–2.0/pages/home_page/homepage.html

Undoubtedly the most popular underground music archive on the Net, the IUMA represents more than 600 unsigned, independent bands and artists. IUMA also provides information on labels, publications and bands. Users can download sound clips from any of the bands.

The Mammoth Music Meta-list
http://www.pathfinder.com/@@RdOwOAAAAAAAAAcuc/vibe/mmm/music.html

The MMM is a good place to see the Web's music resources. This index to other sites has links to most genres, including Russian and Bhangra music, radio stations, performances, music schools and libraries, on-line music mags and much, much more.

Musi-Cal!
http://www.automatrix.com/concerts

A calendar database, Mus-Cal! provides up-to-date, worldwide live music information. The database is searchable by performer, city, state, country, genre and date.

OLGA — The On-line Guitar Archive
ftp://ftp.nevada.edu/pub/guitar

OLGA lists guitar tablatures for thousands of songs.

Rocktropolis
http://underground.net/Rocktropolis

Whether you want the latest scoop on your favorite rocker or need to find out tour dates, this rock 'n' roll site has it all. Rocktropolis provides you with entertainment news, concert schedules, downloadable audio/video clips and much more.

Maker, rose to No. 4 on the *Billboard* charts. While he may have known what he wanted from his new hires musically, the intense rookie wasn't adept at putting it into words.

"George was not a great communicator," says drummer Callahan. "Somebody is always his favorite, and he always picks on one person. To be honest, I had a really horrible time." The band also began to realize just how expensive a commercial album can be. By the time they finished *Hollywood Town Hall*, the Jayhawks' signing bonus was long gone — spent on basic living expenses — and they owed $250,000 to American for studio time, about average for a top-drawer act. That was just the start. American launched a long-term campaign to position the Jayhawks as "catalog" artists — a band that doesn't have huge hits but gets critical praise and sells lots of albums over time.

"American couldn't have worked any harder," says Callahan. "Everyone else in the industry would say, 'You guys are so lucky.' We'd go to dinner with our lawyers and start bitching, and they'd say, 'You guys don't know how lucky you are — most bands don't get this kind of money.' "

But in fact, none of the money was flowing into the Jayhawks' pockets. If the band ever succeeds, it will actually flow out of their pockets. In an arrangement typical in the music industry, American decides how much to invest in a band, gambling that the act will be able to pay it all back. Despite having no money, therefore, the Jayhawks are on the hook for half the cost of their videos — that's $75,000 owed for the three clips made to promote *Hollywood Town Hall*, for example. And they're responsible for all the money American advanced them to tour with the Black Crowes, an additional $200,000. Their own shows also lost money, even after they ditched a tour bus and traveled again by van to cut costs. The only bright spot was a $25,000 advance from Brockum, a merchandising company that makes T-shirts and other souvenirs. The band lived off that for three months.

Emotionally, the grind began to wear on the band members. Worse, they began to wear on each other. "I was drinking myself to sleep every night," says Callahan. "I need to be physically active, but we never even had time for a walk. You're always being transported somewhere on a bus, or you have an interview to do — never any time for yourself." After spending all their waking hours together while touring to support the modest success of *Hollywood Town Hall*, the Jayhawks decided separate hotel rooms were essential. They'd owe more, but they needed their sanity.

By the time a new album loomed strains were showing. Callahan felt like an outsider: At one point, American had even proposed a publicity push that focused exclusively on the songwriting duo of Olson and Louris. The Jayhawks nixed that idea, but bad feelings festered and Callahan's playing suffered. Frustrated and skeptical that the band would ever make it, the disenchanted 31-year-old finally quit.

"I didn't want to be 36 and in the same boat I'm in now," he says. "Starting over. No health insurance. I want a home. And it just didn't seem feasible. None of it did."

When they started recording *Tomorrow the Green Grass* in the spring of 1994, the Jayhawks bore little resemblance to the bunch of friends who played bars for fun in Minneapolis; they had become a business. Rather than replace Callahan, the three remaining members opted to hire drummer Tim O'Reagan as an employee who will play on tours. They have a similar salary relationship with keyboardist Karen Grotberg, who played on the last two albums and tours with the band.

"It's just an easier way to deal with all the contracts," says Louris. "And if we hit it big and feel like it makes sense, then we'll cut people in." Actually, by the standards of just about every amateur musician, the Jayhawks are already huge. Still, they can't match the comfort that friends back in Minneapolis enjoy by working as bankers — or as investment brokers like former manager Charlie Pine, who now works for R.J. Steichen & Co. and limits his musical involvement to visiting the record store. "We're in a really weird place," says Olson. "Sometimes it makes me not want to pick up my guitar."

Yet the money side can work out. For proof, the Jayhawks need only look to their buddies in Soul Asylum, who sold about 2 million albums in the U.S. and became

Sub Pop
http://www.subpop.com/

Though we tried to stay away from promoting record labels' sites, Sub Pop's site merits inclusion. It features a complete discography of its bands, news, tour diaries, ordering info and an always interesting monthly column.

The Ultimate Band List
http://american.recordings.com/wwwofmusic/ubl/ull.shtml

This site claims to be the largest interactive list of music links, and it probably is. Included are a master list of bands, bands grouped by genre and a resource section, which covers newsgroups, mailing lists, frequently asked questions, lyrics, guitar tablatures, digitized songs and links to other Web sites.

World-Wide Internet Live Music Archive
http://underground.net/Wilma

This is the place to go for information — dates, reviews and venues — on live performances all over the world. Venues are listed by state, and tours are listed alphabetically.

Web Wide World of Music
http://american.recordings.com/wwwofmusic

The Ultimate Band List (see above) is the main attraction to this site, but it does offer much more, including the NEWSstand, a comprehensive electronic magazine list, and music charts and polls.

WWW Music Database
http://www.gcms.com/~burnett/MDB

Another database of recordings, this compendium has more than 5,200 that are searchable by album, artists, track, band member, style, language and country.

Yahoo Entertainment: Music
http://www.yahoo.com/Entertainment/Music

This is where we've had the best luck tracking down music-related information. Yahoo's Entertainment page provides links to just about every genre and resource imaginable. Especially helpful and informative is **Yahoo's Entertainment: Music: Events: Festivals** site (http://www.yahoo.com/Entertainment/Music/Events/Festivals), which lists dozens of international festivals and provides links to those home pages.

huge money-spinners after their single "Runaway Train" hit it big. Soul Asylum leader Dave Pirner, a former roommate of Jayhawk bassist Marc Perlman, now dates actress Winona Ryder, who starred in *The Age of Innocence* and *Bram Stoker's Dracula.*

Soul Asylum

To join Soul Asylum on "the next level," the Jayhawks need *Tomorrow the Green Grass* to sell substantially more than the 200,000 that *Hollywood Town Hall* did. Otherwise, American may cut its losses. Until such a reckoning, however, the cash keeps flowing and the band slips further into hock. The new album cost about $300,000 more in studio time, and the Jayhawks are once more making videos and touring. The band's debt will likely top $1 million before starting to shrink.

American's anxiety over the Jayhawks became clear as *Tomorrow* was being recorded in Hollywood. At one point, the band was relaxing in a lounge with friend Charlie Sexton, who had dropped by to add a slide-guitar part to a new Jayhawks track. As the men talked and jammed gently together, they looked up in surprise to discover an American engineer wheeling in microphones to get it all on tape — just in case anyone stumbled on an idea for the hit that could push the Jayhawks over the top.

Unsurprisingly in such an atmosphere, *Tomorrow the Green Grass* is more mainstream than anything the Jayhawks have done before. A bit more "classic rock," says Louris from behind his curly, shoulder-length mane. Still, *Tomorrow* is a decent record, showcasing the band's facility with straightforward rock 'n' roll. And Louris is evidently proud he navigated the strait between art and commerce without giving up too much. "After a few beers at night it sounds pretty good" is his final judgment.

Among those rooting for *Tomorrow the Green Grass* to become a huge hit, count Ken Callahan number one. Having returned to Minneapolis, the former Jayhawk has made bittersweet peace with the music industry. Abandoning the drums except for fun, he set up a furniture-making shop; now he's aiming to be a blacksmith, too.

After years on the edge, Callahan is optimistic about his financial future. Indeed, he's already got some prestigious customers. "The guys in Soul Asylum just got money and bought houses," he says. "So I built new kitchen cabinets for [drummer] Grant Young. I think I'll sell my furniture to Pirner and Winona — and the Black Crowes, and all these people I've met who do have money."

Callahan may turn out to be the first Jayhawk to crack the secret of a business that nearly sucked him dry. "That's how I'm going to cash in," he says. "I'm gonna try and get their money." ∎

1995 Grammy Awards

The 37th Annual Grammy Awards were presented at Los Angeles's Shrine Auditorium on March 1, 1995.

Record of the Year
"All I Wanna Do," Sheryl Crow

Album of the Year
MTV Unplugged, Tony Bennett (Columbia)

Song of the Year
"Streets of Philadelphia" (Theme from *Philadelphia*),
    Bruce Springsteen, songwriter

Best New Artist
Sheryl Crow

Best Pop Vocal Performance, Male
"Can You Feel the Love Tonight," Elton John

Best Pop Vocal Performance, Female
"All I Wanna Do," Sheryl Crow

Best Pop Performance by a Duo or Group With Vocal
"I Swear," All-4-One

Best Traditional Pop Vocal Performance
MTV Unplugged, Tony Bennett

Best Pop Instrumental Performance
"Cruisin'," Booker T and the MG's

Best Pop Vocal Collaboration
"Funny How Time Slips Away," Al Green and
    Lyle Lovett

Best Pop Album
Longing in Their Hearts, Bonnie Raitt (Capitol)

Best Rock Album
Voodoo Lounge, The Rolling Stones (Virgin)

Best Rock Gospel Album
Wake-Up Call, Petra (Dayspring)

Best Rock Song
"Streets of Philadelphia," Bruce Springsteen,
    songwriter

Best Rock Vocal Performance, Male

Scott Weiner/Retna

Sheryl Crow

"Streets of Philadelphia," Bruce Springsteen

Best Rock Vocal Performance, Female
"Come to My Window," Melissa Etheridge

Best Rock Performance by a Duo or Group With Vocal
"Crazy," Aerosmith

Tony Bennett

Best Rock Instrumental Performance
"Marooned," Pink Floyd

Best Hard Rock Performance
"Black Hole Sun," Soundgarden

Best Metal Performance
"Spoonman," Soundgarden

Best Alternative Music Performance
Dookie, Green Day

Best Rhythm and Blues Album
II, Boyz II Men (Motown)

Best Rhythm and Blues Song
"I'll Make Love to You," Babyface, songwriter

Best Rhythm and Blues Vocal Performance, Male
"When Can I See You," Babyface

Best Rhythm and Blues Vocal Performance, Female
"Breathe Again," Toni Braxton

Best Rhythm and Blues Performance by a Duo or Group With Vocal
"I'll Make Love to You," Boyz II Men

Best Rap Solo Performance
"U.N.I.T.Y.," Queen Latifah

Best Rap Performance by a Duo or Group
"None of Your Business," Salt-N-Pepa

Best Jazz Vocal Performance
Mystery Lady (Songs of Billie Holiday), Etta James

Best Jazz Instrumental Solo
"Prelude to a Kiss," Benny Carpenter

Best Jazz Instrumental Performance, Individual or Group
A Tribute to Miles, Ron Carter, Herbie Hancock, Wallace Roney, Wayne Shorter and Tony Williams

Best Contemporary Jazz Performance
"Out of the Loop," Brecker Brothers

Best Large Jazz Ensemble Performance
"Journey," McCoy Tyner Big Band

Best Latin Jazz Performance
"Danzon," Arturo Sandoval

Best Country Album
Stones in the Road, Mary Chapin Carpenter (Columbia)

Best Country Song
"I Swear," Gary Baker and Frank J. Meyers, songwriters

Best Country Vocal Performance, Male
"When Love Finds You," Vince Gill

Best Country Vocal Performance, Female
"Shut Up and Kiss Me," Mary Chapin Carpenter

Best Country Performance by a Duo or Group With Vocal
"Blues for Dixie," Asleep at the Wheel with Lyle Lovett

Best Country Vocal Collaboration
"I Fall to Pieces," Aaron Neville and Trisha Yearwood

Best County Instrumental Performance
"Young Thing," Chet Atkins

Best Bluegrass Album
The Great Dobro Sessions, various artists (Sugar Hill)

Best Traditional Soul Gospel Album
Songs of the Church — Live in Memphis, Albertina Walker (Benson)

Best Contemporary Soul Gospel Album
Join the Band, Take 6 (Reprise/Warner Alliance)

Best Pop/Contemporary Gospel Album
Mercy, Andrae Crouch (Qwest/Warner Alliance)

Best Southern Gospel, Country Gospel or Bluegrass Gospel Album
I Know Who Holds Tomorrow, Alison Krauss and the Cox Family (Rounder)

Best Gospel Album by a Choir or Chorus (tie)
Through God's Eyes, Thompson Community Singers; Rev. Milton Brunson, choir director (Word)

Live in Atlanta at Morehouse College, Love Fellowship Crusade Choir; Hezekiah Walker, choir director (Benson)

Best Latin Pop Performance
"Segundo Romance," Luis Miguel

Best Tropical Latin Performance
Master Sessions Volume 1, Chachao

Best Mexican-American Performance
"Recuerdo a Javier Solis," Vikki Carr

Best Traditional Blues Album
From the Cradle, Eric Clapton (Reprise)

Best Contemporary Blues Album
Father Father, Pops Staples (Pointblank)

Best Traditional Folk Album
World Gone Wrong, Bob Dylan (Columbia)

Best Contemporary Folk Album
American Recordings, Johnny Cash (American Recordings)

Best Reggae Album
Crucial! Roots Classics, Bunny Wailer (Shanachie)

Best New Age Album
Prayer for the Wild Things, Paul Winter (Living Music Records)

Best World Music Album
Talking Timbuktu, Ali Farka Toure with Ry Cooder (Hannibal)

Best Polka Album
Music & Friends, Walter Ostanek Band (WRS)

Best Instrumental Arrangement
"Three Cowboy Songs," Dave Grusin, arranger

Best Instrumental Arrangement With Accompanying Vocal(s)
"Circle of Life," Lebo Morake and Hans Zimmer, arrangers

Best Instrumental Composition
"African Skies," Michael Brecker, composer

Best Musical Show Album
Passion, Original Broadway cast (Angel)

Bruce Springsteen

Best Instrumental Composition Written for a Motion Picture or for Television
Schindler's List, John Williams, composer

Best Song Written Specifically for a Motion Picture or for Television
"Streets of Philadelphia" (From *Philadelphia*), Bruce Springsteen, songwriter

Best Classical Contemporary Composition
"Cello Concerto," Stephen Albert, composer

Best Classical Album
Bartok, *Concerto for Orchestra; Four Orchestral Pieces, Op. 12*, Pierre Boulez conducting Chicago Symphony Orchestra (Deutsche Grammophon)

Best Chamber Music Performance
Beethoven and Mozart, *Quintets*, Daniel Barenboim, piano; Dale Clevenger, horn; Larry Combs, clarinet; Daniele Damiano, bassoon; Hansjorg Schellenberger, oboe

Best Classical Performance, Instrumental Soloist(s) (With Orchestra)
The New York Album (Works of Albert, Bartok and Bloch), David Zinman conducting Baltimore Symphony Orchestra; Yo-Yo Ma, cellist and alto violinist

Best Classical Performance, Instrumental Soloist(s) (Without Orchestra)
Haydn, *Piano Sonatas nos. 32, 47, 53 and 59*, Emmanuel Ax, pianist

Best Orchestral Performance
Bartok, *Concerto for Orchestra; Four Orchestral Pieces, Op. 12*, Pierre Boulez, conducting Chicago Symphony Orchestra

Best Opera Recording
Floyd, *Susannah,* Kent Nagano conducting Orchestra and Chorus of Opera de Lyon; solos: Studer, Hadley, Ramey and Chester (Virgin Classics)

Best Performance of a Choral Work
Berlioz, *Messe Solennelle*, John Eliot Gardiner, choir director, the Monteverdi Choir, Orchestra Revolutionnaire et Romantique and various artists

Best Classical Vocal Performance
The Impatient Lover (Italian Songs by Beethoven, Schubert, Mozart, etc.), Cecilia Bartoli, mezzo-soprano; Andras Schiff, piano

Best Spoken Comedy Album
Live From Hell, Sam Kinison (Priority Records)

Best Spoken Word or Non-Musical Album
Get in the Van: On the Road With Black Flag, Henry Rollins (Time Warner Audiobooks)

Ella Fitzgerald

Best Musical Album for Children
The Lion King — Original Motion Picture Soundtrack, various artists (Walt Disney Records)

Best Spoken Word Album for Children
The Lion King Read-Along, original cast (Walt Disney Records)

Best Recording Package
Tribute to the Music of Bob Willis and the Texas Playboys, Buddy Jackson, art director (Liberty)

Best Recording Package—Boxed
The Complete Ella Fitzgerald Song Books, Chris Thompson, art director (Verve)

Best Album Notes
Louis Armstrong: Portrait of the Artist as a Young Man, 1923–1934, Dan Morgenstern and Loren Schoenberg, album notes writers (Columbia/Legacy/Smithsonian)

Best Historical Album
The Complete Ella Fitzgerald Song Books on Verve (Verve)

Best Music Video, Short Form
"Love Is Strong," The Rolling Stones

Best Music Video, Long Form
Zoo TV: Live From Sydney, U2

Producer of the Year (Non-Classical)
Don Was

Classical Producer of the Year
Andrew Cornall

1995 Rolling Stone Music Awards

Each year, *Rolling Stone* polls its readers and writers to illuminate the year's shining stars in contemporary music. Here's what they had to say.

READERS' PICKS

1995

Artist of the Year
Nirvana

Best Album
Dookie, Green Day
(Reprise/Warner Bros.)

Best Single
"Closer," Nine Inch Nails

Best Band
Pearl Jam

Best New Band
Green Day

Best Male Singer
Eddie Vedder, Pearl Jam

Best Female Singer
Courtney Love, Hole

Best New Male Singer
Billie Joe Armstrong, Green Day

Best New Female Singer
Sheryl Crow

Best Songwriter
Kurt Cobain

Best Metal Band
Soundgarden

Best Rap Group
Beastie Boys

Best Rapper
Snoop Doggy Dogg

Best R&B Artist
Boyz II Men

Best Country Artist
Garth Brooks

Best Jazz Artist
Harry Connick, Jr.

Best Video
"Sabotage," Beastie Boys

Best Album Cover
Dookie, Green Day
(Reprise/Warner Bros.)

Best Reissue Album
Woodstock, Jimi Hendrix (MCA)

Best Movie Soundtrack
The Crow (Interscope)

Best Tour
The Rolling Stones

Hype of the Year
Woodstock '94

Comeback of the Year
The Rolling Stones

Best Character on MTV's *The Real World*
Puck

Best-Dressed Artist
Courtney Love

Biggest Poseur
Madonna

Best Radio Station, Large Market
WHTZ, New York, New York

Best Radio Station, Medium Market
WBRU, Providence,
Rhode Island

Best Radio Station, Small Market
WAPL, Appleton, Wisconsin

CRITICS' PICKS

1995

Artist of the Year
Courtney Love

Best Album
Live Through This, Hole
(DGC/Geffen)

Best Single
"Loser," Beck

Best Band
R.E.M.

Best New Band
Green Day

Best Male Singer
Grant Lee Phillips, Grant Lee
Buffalo

Best Female Singer
Sam Phillips

Best New Male Singer
Jeff Buckley

Best New Female Singer
Sheryl Crow

Best Songwriter
Freedy Johnston

Best Metal Band
Soundgarden

Best Rap Group
Salt-N-Pepa

Best Rapper
Snoop Doggy Dogg

Best R&B Artist
Boyz II Men

Best Country Artist
Johnny Cash

Best Jazz Artist
Joshua Redman

Best Producer
Rick Rubin

Best Video
"Sabotage," Beastie Boys

Best Album Cover
Live Through This, Hole
(DGC/Geffen)

Best Reissue Album
Here, My Dear, Marvin Gaye
(Motown)

Best Rock Book
Last Train to Memphis, Peter
Guralnick

Best Tour or Show
Lollapalooza

Hype of the Year
Woodstock '94

Comeback of the Year
Johnny Cash

Most Unwelcome Comeback
Woodstock '94

Best Unsigned Band
Black Velvet Flag

The Millionaire Selects the Smoothest

■ BY MICHAEL "THE MILLIONAIRE" CUDAHY

Friend, how many times have you dismissed a strain of song as Elevator Music? Do the words Easy Listening make you wince? It just doesn't sound "cool," does it? It's the kind of music your parents or even your *grandparents* listened to. Guess again! One of the most welcome trends in recent years has been the rediscovery and rehabilitation of Easy Listening, Lounge Music . . . call it what you will. I've always been partial to the suave imagery of Cocktail Music, which implies the relaxing yet intoxicating qualities to be found in the best of this swank and luxuriant field; a style of music that belies the consensus that music must be loud, aggressive or even emotional to be powerful. Cast off the shackles of received hipness, and behold the jeweled pantheon

Combustible Edison

COLLECTING

that is Cocktail Music! Cocktail Music is not so much a single genre, but a number of distinct yet related genres and sub-genres and, as in any first foray into an unfamiliar musical style, finding your way to the gems while avoiding the dross can initially seem daunting. Fortunately for the novice, there are a few things about Easy Listening which make acquiring a deeper knowledge of the form a little easier.

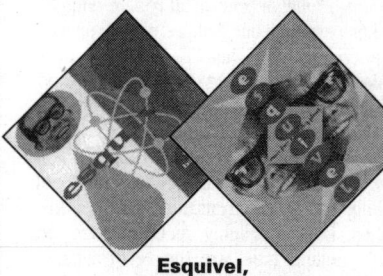

**Esquivel,
*Spaceage Bachelor Pad
Music* and *Music From a
Sparkling Planet***

First, the savvy music enthusiast will benefit from the general disfavor into which Cocktail Music has fallen. Yard sales, thrift stores and the aforementioned parents' or grandparents' attics can yield a virtually unlimited supply of fresh sounds, although it is wise to keep an eye out for the condition of the records. These glorious slabs of hi-fi heaven are not generally available on CD, and scratches, pops and hiss are the occasional tradeoff for acquiring an argosy of musical opulence with only a few dollars. I tend not to pay more than a dollar a record, a dollar a song being my absolute limit.

Second, despite what Bo Diddley and proverbial wisdom might have to say on the subject, you *can* quite often judge a record by its cover. In fact, for many people, including myself, this is what first drew them into the phantasmagorical sonic wonderland of smooth sounds. Look for colorful, dramatic scenes of faux-primitive rituals, tableaux of sophisticated seduction or exciting vistas of exotic faraway lands, the mysterious deep and outer space. The words Percussion or Hi-Fi in the title are a good sign as well.

To aid the intrepid neophyte in his or her quest of discovery, here are a few informed recommendations.

Some of what is perceived as Cocktail Music is still in print or readily available today and in some cases still popular and well respected. The Sinatra/Sammy/Dino "rat pack" school of Vegas cool needs no introduction from me. Herb Alpert and the Tijuana Brass's *Whipped Cream and Other Delights* is not only immediately recognizable musically, but has provoked dozens of parodies of its cover, a cream-smeared beauty wearing nothing else but a coy, come-hither look. *Whipped Cream* has also received dubious distinction: It was determined to be the one record most frequently found in Salvation Army bins. A more "jazzy" sort of legitimacy still surrounds the

1995 MTV MUSIC VIDEO AWARDS

The 1995 MTV Music Video Awards were presented September 7, 1995 at New York City's Radio City Music Hall.

Best Video of the Year
"Waterfalls," TLC

Viewers' Choice Award
"Waterfalls," TLC

Breakthrough Video
"Buddy Holly," Weezer

Best Male Video
"You Don't Know How It Feels," Tom Petty

Best Female Video
"Take a Bow," Madonna

Best Group Video
"Waterfalls," TLC

Best Rap Video
"Keep Their Heads Ringin'," Dr. Dre

Best Dance Video
"Scream," Michael Jackson and Janet Jackson

Best Hard Rock Video
"More Human Than Human," White Zombie

Best Alternative Video
"Buddy Holly," Weezer

Best New Artist in a Video
"Hold My Hand," Hootie and the Blowfish

Best Video From a Film
"Kiss From a Rose," Seal

Best R&B Video
"Waterfalls," TLC

Best Direction
Spike Jonze, "Buddy Holly"

Best Choreography
"Scream," Michael Jackson and Janet Jackson

Best Special Effects in a Video
"Love Is Strong," The Rolling Stones

Best Editing
Eric Zumbrunnen, "Buddy Holly"

Best Cinematography
Gary Waller, "Love Is Strong"

Michael Jackson Video Vanguard Award
R.E.M.

mellow Bossa Nova stylings of Antonio Carlos Jobim and Astrud Gilberto, whose rendition of *The Girl From Ipanema* on Verve's *Getz/Gilberto* record is a Lounge Anthem.

Esquivel, *Other Worlds Other Sounds*

The iconoclastic innovator of Space Age Bachelor Pad Music is Mr. Juan Garcia Esquivel. His music features drastic dynamic juxtapositions, zany combinations of unusual instruments (e.g., buzzimba, theremin, jaw harp, boobams, harpsichord, ondioline and out-of-control steel guitar) and frequently, vocal groups interjecting fragments of lyrics, nonsense syllables like "zu zu zu" or sudden ejaculations the likes of "pow! pow!" A familiar standard in Esquivel's hands becomes an unpredictable ride through a musical funhouse. New Jersey's Bar/None Records has released two compilations of his music, now available for the first time on CD. Look for *Space Age Bachelor Pad Music* and *Music for a Sparkling Planet* at your local record emporium. Less extreme but definitely more prolific is Enoch Light and his Command Records stable of artists. Light's *Provocative* and *Persuasive Percussion* series are a scintillating concoction of jaunty pop favorites in arrangements vacillating between elegant and wacky, infused with a kaleidoscopic array of rattling, banging percussion and bongos, bongos, bongos. Highly recommended on the Command label are the recordings of Dick Hyman, a tonally adventurous organist with a wry sense of humor. On RCA, Dick Schory's New Percussion Ensemble continued the percussion craze, providing listening that can't *quite* be categorized as Easy, while at the same time testing the tracking and response of your hi-fi rig with such collections as *Music for Bang, Baroom and Harp* and *Music to Break Any Mood.* Jack Costanza, the "King of the Bongos" led an orchestra that made every instrument seem percussive.

Enoch Light and Esquivel both proudly touted the up-to-date technical innovations of their hi-fi recording, but RCA's Stereo Action series went them one better: "The Sound Your Eyes Can Follow" itself was the star, while the orchestras (some of the finest that Cocktail Music has to offer) were relegated to a supporting role. In a few instances the technical inventiveness of these recordings rivals anything of the present day. Case in point: Benny Green's *Futura* LP boasts a version of the pop tango *Kiss of Fire* in which the trumpet melody was spliced together on tape, *a note at a time!*

For a taste of the alluring, imaginary "Orient" and beyond, try the sonic Tiki travelogues of Martin Denny and Yma Sumac. Denny merged the urbane swing of George

Juan Garcia Esquivel

Shearing's cocktail hour piano-and-vibraphone sound with exotic percussion and tropical sound effects to produce a style he called Exotica. His hit record *Quiet Village* is an ideal place to acquaint yourself with his foreign yet familiar sound. Yma Sumac was an alleged Peruvian princess with a breathtaking five-octave vocal range who performed bizarre orchestral "Exoti-Cantatas" depicting the majesty and splendor of the ancient Incan civilization and impressionistic musical interpretations of the savage jungle. *Jivaro, Voice of the Xtabay* and *Legend of the Sun Virgin* are all prime slices of her jungle-ripe Exotica. *Mirages,* her late 1960s contribution, was a fascinatingly incongruous mixture of Sumac's feats of vocal derring-do with wah-wah guitars and wailing organs. It forms the missing link between Exotica and Psychedelia.

Jackie Gleason presents *Music, Martinis, and Memories*

Aficionados of Ease have always been fascinated with new sounds and frontiers; synthesizers made early inroads into the world of Cocktail Music before they were commonly used in rock. Jean Jacques Perrey and Gershon Kingsley made a pair of records (*In Sounds From Way Out* and *Kaleidoscopic Vibrations*) that utilized the synth's fiberglass tonalities in perky, humorous ditties. Where the Swingle Singers performed J. S. Bach as swinging vocalese, ideal for accompanying a fondue party or a chilled glass of Fino sherry, Wendy Carlos performed a musical double whammy with *Switched on Bach.* Musical masterworks of two centuries hence were now transfigured as the perfect soundtrack to Martinis on Mars. The space theme had been prevalent for years prior, however, with such titles as Les Baxter's *Music From Out of the Moon* and *Space Escapade.*

Martin Denny, *Quiet Village*

For those with a penchant for more limpid and sonorous (some might even say "soporific") tones, explore the oeuvre of The Great One himself. Jackie Gleason released dozens of albums with titles like *Oooo!, Music to Make You Misty* and *Music, Martinis and Memories.* His *Lonesome Echo* features a cover painting commissioned from Salvador Dali. The 101 Strings (The Sound of Magnificence!) and Mystic Moods orchestras both account for hundreds of hours of soothing, hypnotic listening.

Sometimes the novelty of a single otherwise familiar instrument set in an Easy Listening context could launch a whole career. Jerry Murad's Harmonicats, Dick Contino (on accordion), Robert Maxwell (a harpist and composer of such instantly recognizable-but-maybe-not-by-name hits as *EbbTide* and *Solfeggio* (a/k/a *Song of the Nairobi Trio*) and Muzzy Marcelino (one of a *very* select group of professional whistlers) all add a new dimension to their respective instruments.

There you have a few of the high points of the fabulous, glittering world of style and enchantment afforded the listener of taste and discrimination by Smooth Music. Avanti! ■

Michael "The Millionaire" Cudahy leads a swinging combo known as Combustible Edison that brings cocktail music to the masses via Sub Pop Records. He was also responsible for the soundtrack to Quentin Tarantino's segment of the anthology film, Four Rooms.

Rock and Roll Hall of Fame and Museum

A group of music industry insiders in 1983 formed the Rock and Roll Hall of Fame Foundation, which recognizes those who have contributed to the energy and evolution of the genre. Members of the foundation then began a nationwide search to find the perfect location for the Rock and Roll Hall of Fame and Museum. They selected Cleveland, and 12 years later their dream became a reality. Prior to the grand opening of the museum, the founda-

The Rock and Roll Hall of Fame

tion conducted all of its business — organizing the nomination process, planning the annual induction event and dealing with the press — from a cramped New York office.

To celebrate the completion of their new digs and the museum, the foundation hosted several events over 1995's Labor Day weekend, including the historic Concert for the Hall of Fame, which brought together at Cleveland Municipal Stadium rock and roll greats Bruce Springsteen, Al Green, Aretha Franklin, John Mellencamp, Melissa Etheridge, Alice in Chains, Johnny Cash, the Pretenders, Little Richard, Jon Bon Jovi and Richie Sambora, Martha and the Vandellas, Chuck Berry, Soul Asylum, Dr. Dre and Snoop Doggy Dog, James Brown, the Kinks, Booker T. and the MG's, George Clinton, John Fogerty, Annie Lennox, Jerry Lee Lewis, Natalie Merchant, the Artist Formerly Known as Prince and Robbie Robertson. Music and entertainment heavyweights were on hand for the September 1 parade and ribbon-cutting ceremony, which marked the official opening of the world's first museum dedicated to the living heritage and worldwide impact of rock music.

Renowned architect I. M. Pei added splendor to the facility when he designed the ultra-modern 150,000-square-foot building that sits on the shore of Lake Erie. Pei describes the $92 million building as a composition of geometric forms and cantilevered spaces that are anchored by a 162-foot tower, which supports a dual-triangular-shaped glass "tent" that extends onto an impressive 65,000-square-foot plaza.

"In designing this building, it was my intention

1995 INDUCTEES TO THE ROCK AND ROLL HALL OF FAME

The Allman Brothers Band

The Allman Brothers Band

Al Green

Janis Joplin

Led Zeppelin

Martha and the Vandellas

Neil Young

Frank Zappa

Nonperformer
Paul Ackerman

Early Influence
The Orioles

Johnny Cash

to echo the energy of rock and roll," Pei said. His designs include the expansion of the Louvre, the National Gallery of Art's East Building and the John F. Kennedy Library in Boston. "I have consciously used an architectural vocabulary that is bold and new, and I hope the building will become a dramatic landmark for the city of Cleveland and for fans of rock and roll around the world."

The contents of the museum are just as impressive as its edifice. The exhibits chronicle the history of rock and roll using state-of-the-art interactive and multimedia technology and showcase musicians, scenes in rock history and the music's influence on society. The museum also offers a working studio for visiting DJ's, exhibits on R&B, soul, folk, blues and country music, a 200-seat indoor theater, an outdoor concert area, a two-floor gallery for the Rock and Roll Hall of Fame and a full-service library and archival facility.

Other exhibits highlight regional music that exploded to form new genres of rock — Detroit during the Motown era, San Francisco's psychedelic scene, New York's rap and grunge in Seattle. An interactive database features the "500 Songs That Shaped Rock and Roll." Also on display is the foundation's impressive collection of rock and roll memorabilia, which includes Elvis's stage outfit and guitar from NBC's 1968 "Comeback" special, Grace Slick's dress from Woodstock, John Lennon's Rickenbacker guitar and Keith Moon's report card, which indicated promise in music. ■

1994 COUNTRY MUSIC ASSOCIATION AWARDS

The 28th Annual Country Music Association Awards were presented October 5, 1994 at the Grand Ole Opry House in Nashville, Tennessee.

Entertainer of the Year
Vince Gill

Single of the Year
"I Swear," John Michael Montgomery

Album of the Year
Common Thread: The Songs of the Eagles, John Anderson, Clint Black, Suzy Bogguss, Brooks and Dunn, Billy Dean, Diamond Rio, Vince Gill, Alan Jackson, Little Texas, Lorrie Morgan, Travis Tritt, Tanya Tucker and Trisha Yearwood (Giant)

Song of the Year
"Chattahoochee," Alan Jackson and Jim McBride, songwriters

Male Vocalist of the Year
Vince Gill

Female Vocalist of the Year
Pam Tillis

Vocal Group of the Year
Diamond Rio

Vocal Duo of the Year
Brooks and Dunn

Vocal Event of the Year
"Does He Love You," Reba McEntire with Linda Davis

Horizon Award
John Michael Montgomery

Musician of the Year
Mark O'Connor, Fiddle

Music Video of the Year
"Independence Day," Martina McBride

1994 INDUCTEE TO THE COUNTRY MUSIC HALL OF FAME

Merle Haggard

1994 Down Beat Poll Results

Down Beat's **annual Readers Poll appears in the December issue of the magazine and the Critics Poll in the August issue. Both polls nominate inductees to the Jazz Hall of Fame. TDWR, which appears as a category in the Critics Poll, indicates Talent Deserving Wider Recognition. Beyond categories, found in both the Readers and Critics polls, honor performers beyond the jazz world.**

READERS POLL

Jazz Musician of the Year
Joshua Redman

Jazz Album of the Year
Joshua Redman, *Wish*
(Warner Bros.)

Male Singer
Joe Williams

Female Singer
Cassandra Wilson

Vocal Group
Take 6

Jazz Acoustic Group
Charlie Haden and Quartet West

Jazz Electric Group
John Scofield

Jazz Big Band
McCoy Tyner

Arranger
Carla Bley

Composer
Henry Threadgill

Soprano Saxophone
Steve Lacy

Alto Saxophone
Phil Woods

Eric Antoniou

Joshua Redman

JAZZ HALL OF FAME

1994 Readers Poll
Dave Brubeck

1994 Critics Poll
Frank Zappa

Tenor Saxophone
Joe Henderson

Baritone Saxophone
Gerry Mulligan

Clarinet
Don Byron

Flute
James Newton

Trumpet
Wynton Marsalis

Trombone
J.J. Johnson

Synthesizer
Joe Zawinul

Piano
Keith Jarrett

Organ
Jimmy Smith

Acoustic Guitar
John McLaughlin

Electric Guitar
John Scofield

Acoustic Bass
Charlie Haden

Electric Bass
Steve Swallow

Drums
Max Roach

Percussion
Tito Puente

Vibes
Milt Jackson

Violin
Stephane Grappelli

Miscellaneous Instrument
Toots Thielemans, Harmonica

Blues/Soul/Rhythm and Blues Musician of the Year
B.B. King

Blues/Soul/Rhythm and Blues Album of the Year
B.B. King, *Blues Summit* (MCA)

Blues/Soul/Rhythm and Blues Group
B.B. King

Beyond Musician of the Year
Sting

Beyond Album of the Year
Bruce Hornsby, *Harbor Lights*
(RCA)

Beyond Group
Neville Brothers

Lifetime Achievement Award
Marian McPartland

Jazz Artist of the Year
Wynton Marsalis
TDWR
Joshua Redman

Jazz Album of the Year
Charlie Haden, *Always Say Goodbye* (Verve)

Reissue of the Year
Ornette Coleman, *Beauty Is a Rare Thing: The Complete Atlantic Recordings* (Rhino/Atlantic)

Male Jazz Singer
Joe Williams
TDWR
Kevin Mahogany

Male Non-Jazz Singer
Aaron Neville
TDWR
Salif Keita

Female Jazz Singer
Betty Carter
TDWR
Cassandra Wilson

Female Non-Jazz Singer
Aretha Franklin
TDWR
Jane Siberry

Vocal Jazz Group
Take 6

Eric Antoniou

Ornette Coleman

TDWR
New York Voices

Acoustic Jazz Group
Wynton Marsalis
TDWR
Bobby Watson

Electric Jazz Group
John Scofield
TDWR
Naked City

Big Band
Count Basie
TDWR
Maria Schneider

Arranger
Carla Bley
TDWR
Bob Belden

Composer
Randy Weston
TDWR
Bobby Watson

Soprano Saxophone
Steve Lacy
TDWR
Jane Bunnett

Alto Saxophone
Jackie McLean
TDWR
Vincent Herring

Tenor Saxophone
Joe Henderson
TDWR
Joshua Redman

Baritone Saxophone
Gerry Mulligan
TDWR
Mwata Bowden

Clarinet
Don Byron
TDWR
Ken Peplowski

Flute
James Newton
TDWR
Kent Jordan

Trumpet
Wynton Marsalis
TDWR
Nicholas Payton

Trombone
J. J. Johnson
TDWR
Frank Lacy

Acoustic Piano
Tommy Flanagan
TDWR
Geri Allen

Organ
Jimmy Smith
TDWR
Joey DeFrancesco

Electric Keyboard
Joe Zawinul

Eric Antoniou

Geri Allen

TDWR
Lyle Mays

Acoustic Guitar
John McLaughlin
TDWR
Fareed Haque

Electric Guitar
John Scofield
TDWR
Mike Stern

Acoustic Bass
Charlie Haden
TDWR
Christian McBride

Electric Bass
Steve Swallow
TDWR
Bill Laswell

Drums
Max Roach

Mark Morelli

Charlie Haden

TDWR
Lewis Nash

Percussion
Trilok Gurtu
TDWR
Giovanni Hidalgo

Vibes
Milt Jackson

TDWR
Steve Nelson

Violin
Stephane Grappelli
TDWR
Mark Feldman

Miscellaneous Instrument
Toots Thielemans, Harmonica
TDWR
Steve Turre, Conch Shells

Blues Artist of the Year
B.B. King
TDWR
Lucky Peterson

Blues Album of the Year
B.B. King, *Blues Summit* (MCA)

Blues Group
B.B. King
TDWR
Cheatham's Sweet Baby Blues
      Band

Beyond Artist of the Year
George Clinton
TDWR
Salif Keita

Beyond Album of the Year
A. F. Toure and Ry Cooder, *Talking
      Timbuktu* (Hannibal)

Beyond Group
Neville Brothers
TDWR
Morphine

Record Label of the Year
Verve

Record Producer
Michael Cuscuna
TDWR
Hal Willner

INTRODUCING...

BUDDHISM
Several musicians and actors are beginning to embrace Tibetan Buddhism. In addition to avowed Buddhists Richard Gere and Uma Thurman, Natalie Merchant, Laurie Anderson, David Byrne, Jimmie Dale Gilmore and Adam Yauch of the Beastie Boys are practitioners. The Beastie Boys even brought Tibetan monks along on 1994's Lollapalooza tour.

LAURA LOVE
Love, a former homeless Seattle singer/songwriter, produces an eclectic mix of folk, blues, soul and jazz. *Billboard* listed her as one of the country's top 10 unsigned artists and the *New York Times* gave her high praise for her performance at 1994's New York Singer-Songwriter Festival. Look for her to be signed by a major label.

CONTEMPORARY CHRISTIAN MUSIC
If interest in Contemporary Christian music continues to rapidly flourish, the market will most likely double in two to five years, a impressive feat in an industry that is tough to break. Currently, the music accounts for 3.3% of the music market, which places it ahead of jazz and classical, according to the Recording Industry Association of America.

1995 Down Beat Critics Poll

Jazz Artist of the Year
Joe Lovano
TDWR
James Carter

Jazz Album of the Year
Joe Lovano and Gunther Schuller,
    Rush Hour (Blue Note)

Reissue of the Year
Bud Powell, *The Complete Bud
    Powell on Verve* (Verve)

Male Vocalist
Joe Williams
TDWR
Kevin Mahogany

Female Jazz Singer
Betty Carter
TDWR
Patricia Barber

Vocal Jazz Group
Take 6
TDWR
Zap Mama

Acoustic Jazz Group
Charlie Haden's Quartet West
TDWR
Joshua Redman

Electric Jazz Group
John Scofield
TDWR
Medeski Martin and Wood

Big Band
McCoy Tyner Big Band
TDWR
Either/Orchestra

Arranger
Toshiko Akiyosha
TDWR
Maria Schneider

Composer
Henry Threadgill
TDWR
Ed Wilkerson

Soprano Saxophone
Steve Lacy
TDWR
Jane Bunnett

Alto Saxophone
Jackie McLean
TDWR
Sonny Simmons

Tenor Saxophone
Sonny Rollins
TDWR
James Carter

Baritone Saxophone
Gerry Mulligan
TDWR
James Carter

Clarinet
Don Byron
TDWR
Ken Peplowski

Flute
James Newton
TDWR
Kent Jordan

Trumpet
Wynton Marsalis
TDWR
Nicholas Payton

Trombone
J. J. Johnson
TDWR
Robin Eubanks

Piano
Tommy Flanagan

TDWR
Cyrus Chestnut

Organ
Jimmy Smith
TDWR
Amina Claudine Myers

Electric Keyboard
Herbie Hancock
TDWR
Wayne Horvitz

Acoustic Guitar
John McLaughlin
TDWR
Howard Alden

Electric Guitar
John Scofield
TDWR
Mark Whitfield

Acoustic Bass
Charlie Haden
TDWR
Christian McBride

Electric Bass
Steve Swallow
TDWR
Bill Laswell

Drums
Elvin Jones

Eric Antoniou

Wynton Marsalis

305

TDWR
Leon Parker

Percussion
Trilok Gurtu
TDWR
Kahil El'Zabar

Vibes
Milt Jackson
TDWR
Steve Nelson

Violin
Stephane Grappelli
TDWR
Mark Feldman

Miscellaneous Instrument
Toots Thielemans, Harmonica
TDWR
Howard Johnson, Tuba

Blues Artist of the Year
Buddy Guy

Toots Theilemans

TDWR
R. L. Burnside

Blues Album of the Year
Buddy Guy, *Slippin' In*
(Silvertone)

Blues Group
B.B. King
TDWR
Lucky Peterson

Beyond Artist of the Year
Eddie Palmieri
TDWR
Steve Tibbetts

Beyond Album of the Year
Maleem Mahmoud Ghania and
Pharoah Sanders, *The
Trance of Seven Colors*
(Axiom)

Beyond Group
Jerry Gonzalez Fort Apache
Band
TDWR
Wayne Horvitz's Pigpen

Record Label of the Year
Verve

Record Producer
Michael Cuscuna
TDWR
Delfeayo Marsalis

INTRODUCING...

GUIDED BY VOICES
This low-fi band came on strong in 1995 with *Alien Lanes, Box* and their much-anticipated follow-up, which was produced by The Breeder's Kim Deal with engineering by Steve Albini. We expect them to continue to produce the psychedelic, The Beatles-influenced pop that appeals to both mainstream and alternative audiences.

BLOCKBUSTER AS MUSIC OUTLET
Facing a potential threat from video-on-demand and an increased number of cable channels, expect Blockbuster to start stocking its video store shelves with music CDs as well as videos. Blockbuster already has almost 550 music outlets across the country.

HURRICANE
The Beastie Boys may have lost their DJ to a solo career. Hurricane (Wendell Fite) released *The Hura* on the Beasties's Grand Royal label and the record, featuring plenty of scratching and bad rhymes, has been favorably reviewed.

WADE HAYES
Ignoring his dream for years in fear that he would fall victim to shady record deals, Hayes finally decided to follow his heart and give country music a try. His debut album *Old Enough to Know Better,* released in December 1994, went on to be number one on *Billboard's* Heatseekers chart and break the top 100 on The *Billboard* 200.

1994 Gramophone Awards

The 1994 Gramophone Awards were presented October 6, 1994 at London's Dorchester Hotel.

INSTRUMENTAL (RECORD OF THE YEAR)
Debussy, *Préludes,* Krystian Zimerman (Deutsche Grammophon)

BAROQUE VOCAL
Monteverdi, *Quarto Libro dei Madrigali,* Concerto Italiano / Rinaldo Alessandrini (Opus 111)

BAROQUE NON-VOCAL
Bach, *Goldberg Variations,* Pierre Hantaï (Opus 111)

CHAMBER
Tchaikovsky, *String Quartets nos. 1–3,* Borodin Quartet (Teldec)

CHORAL
Delius, *Sea Drift, Songs of Sunset, etc.,* Richard Hickox conducting Bournemouth Symphony Orchestra; solos: Terfel and Burgess (Chandos)

CONCERTO
Bartók, *Violin Concerto No. 2,* Simon Rattle conducting City of Birmingham Symphony Orchestra; solo: Chung (EMI)

CONTEMPORARY
Holloway, *Second Concerto for Orchestra,* Oliver Knussen conducting BBC Symphony Orchestra (NMC)

EARLY MUSIC
Rore, *Missa Praeter Rerum Seriem,* Peter Phillips conducting the Tallis Scholars (Gimell)

ENGINEERING
Dutilleux, *Symphonies 1 and 2,* Yan Pascal Tortelier conducting BBC Philharmonic Orchestra (Chandos)

HISTORIC VOCAL
Britten, Peter Grimes, *Rape of Lucretia, Folksong Arrangements,* Reginald Goodall conducting Benjamin Britten Orchestra; solos: Cross, Pears, Evans and Wyss (EMI)

HISTORIC NON-VOCAL
Schubert, Schoenberg, *Verklärte Nacht, String Quartet,* Kurt Reher, Hollywood String Quartet (Testament)

MUSIC THEATER AND VIDEO
Leonard Bernstein, *On the Town,* Michael Tilson Thomas conducting London Symphony Orchestra and London Voices (DG)

OPERA
Britten, *Gloriana,* Charles Mackerras conducting Welsh National Opera Chorus and Orchestra (Argo)

ORCHESTRAL
Koechlin, *Jungle Book,* David Zinman conducting Berlin Radio Symphony Orchestra (RCA)

SOLO VOCAL
Barber, *Complete Songs,* Emerson String Quartet; solos: Studer, Hampson and Browning (DG)

BEST-SELLING RECORD
Canto Gregoriano, *Coro del Monasterio Benedictino de Santo Domingo de Silos* (EMI)

SPECIAL ACHIEVEMENT
Richter, *The Authorized Recordings,* Richter (Philips)

ARTIST OF THE YEAR
John Eliot Gardiner

YOUNG ARTIST OF THE YEAR
Maxim Vengerov

LIFETIME ACHIEVEMENT
Klaus Tennstedt

1995 PULITZER PRIZE IN MUSIC

The Pulitzer Prizes were awarded April 18, 1995 by Columbia University.

STRING MUSIC
Morton Gould

The Grammy Awards

The Grammy Awards, presented annually by the National Academy of Recording Arts and Sciences (NARAS), are considered the most coveted of the many contemporary music awards. Despite the honor the awards carry and the ratings success of the televised awards show, many industry insiders consider the Grammys to be merely a reflection of mainstream commercial success.

Count Basie

1958

Record of the Year
"Nel Blu Dipinto di Blu" (Volare), Domenico Modugno

Album of the Year
The Music From Peter Gunn, Henry Mancini (RCA)

Song of the Year
"Nel Blu Dipinto di Blu," Domenico Modugno, songwriter

Best Vocal Performance, Male
"Catch a Falling Star," Perry Como

Best Vocal Performance, Female
Ella Fitzgerald Sings the Irving Berlin Song Book, Ella Fitzgerald

Best Performance by a Vocal Group or Chorus
"That Old Black Magic," Louis Prima and Keely Smith

Best Rhythm and Blues Performance
"Tequila," Champs

Best Jazz Performance, Individual
Ella Fitzgerald Sings the Duke Ellington Song Book, Ella Fitzgerald

Best Jazz Performance, Group
Basie, Count Basie

Best Performance by a Dance Band
Basie, Count Basie

Best Country and Western Performance
"Tom Dooley," Kingston Trio

Best Performance by an Orchestra
Billy May's Big Fat Brass, Billy May

Best Arrangement
The Music From Peter Gunn, Henry Mancini, arranger

Best Musical Composition First Recorded and Released in 1958 (More Than Five Minutes)
"Cross Country Suite," Nelson Riddle, composer

Best Original Cast Album, Broadway or Television
The Music Man, Meredith Willson (Capitol)

Best Soundtrack Album, Dramatic Picture Score or Original Cast
Gigi, André Previn (MGM)

Best Classical Performance, Orchestra
Gaîté Parisienne, Felix Slatkin conducting Hollywood Bowl Symphony Orchestra

Best Classical Performance, Chamber Music (Including Chamber Orchestra)
Beethoven, *Quartet 130*, Hollywood String Quartet

Best Classical Performance, Instrumental (With Concerto Scale Accompaniment)
Tchaikovsky, *Concerto No. 1 in B-Flat Minor, Op. 23*, Van Cliburn, pianist; Kiril Kondrashin Symphony Orchestra

Best Classical Performance, Instrumental (Other Than Concerto Scale)
Segovia Golden Jubilee, Andrés Segovia

Best Classical Performance, Operatic or Choral
Virtuoso, Roger Wagner Chorale

Best Classical Performance, Vocal Soloist (With or Without Orchestra)
Operatic Recital, Renata Tebaldi

Best Comedy Performance
"The Chipmunk Song," David Seville

Best Performance, Documentary or Spoken Word
The Best of the Stan Freberg Shows, Stan Freberg

Best Recording for Children
"The Chipmunk Song," David Seville (Liberty)

Best Album Cover
Only the Lonely, Frank Sinatra (Capitol)

1959

Record of the Year
"Mack the Knife," Bobby Darin

Album of the Year
Come Dance With Me, Frank Sinatra (Capitol)

Song of the Year
"The Battle of New Orleans," Jimmy Driftwood, songwriter

Best Artist of 1959
Bobby Darin

Best Performance by a "Top 40" Artist
"Midnight Flyer," Nat King Cole

Best Vocal Performance, Male
Come Dance With Me, Frank Sinatra

Best Vocal Performance, Female
"But Not for Me," Ella Fitzgerald

Best Performance by a Chorus
"Battle Hymn of the Republic," Mormon Tabernacle Choir

Best Rhythm and Blues Performance
"What a Diff'rence a Day Makes," Dinah Washington

Best Jazz Performance, Soloist
Ella Swings Lightly, Ella Fitzgerald

Best Jazz Performance, Group
I Dig Chicks, Jonah Jones

Best Performance by a Dance Band
Anatomy of a Murder, Duke Ellington

Best Country and Western Performance
"The Battle of New Orleans," Johnny Horton

Best Performance, Folk
The Kingston Trio at Large, Kingston Trio

Best Performance by an Orchestra
Like Young, David Rose and His Orchestra With André Previn

Best Arrangement
Come Dance With Me, Billy May, arranger

Best Musical Composition First Recorded and Released in 1959 (More Than Five Minutes)
Anatomy of a Murder, Duke Ellington, composer

Best Broadway Show Album (tie)
Gypsy, Ethel Merman (Columbia)
Redhead, Gwen Verdon (RCA)

Best Soundtrack Album, Original Cast, Motion Picture or Television
Porgy and Bess, André Previn and Ken Darby (Columbia)

Best Soundtrack Album, Background Score From Motion Picture or Television
Anatomy of a Murder, Duke Ellington (Columbia)

Best Classical Performance, Orchestra
Debussy, Images for Orchestra, Charles Munch conducting Boston Symphony Orchestra

Best Classical Performance, Chamber Music (Including Chamber Orchestra)
Beethoven, Sonata No. 21 in C, Op. 53; Waldstein Sonata No. 18 in E-Flat, Op. 31, No. 3, Artur Rubinstein, pianist

Best Classical Performance, Concerto or Instrumental Soloist (Full Orchestra)
Rachmaninoff, Piano Concerto No. 3, Van Cliburn, pianist; Kiril Kondrashin conducting Symphony of the Air

Best Classical Performance, Instrumental Soloist (Other Than Full Orchestral Accompaniment)
Beethoven, Sonata No. 21 in C, Op. 53; Waldstein Sonata No. 18 in E-Flat, Op. 31, No. 3, Artur Rubinstein, pianist

Best Classical Performance, Opera Cast or Choral
Mozart, The Marriage of Figaro, Erich Leinsdorf conducting Vienna Philharmonic Orchestra

Best Classical Performance, Vocal Soloist (With or Without Orchestra)
Björling in Opera, Jussi Björling

Best Comedy Performance, Spoken Word
Inside Shelley Berman, Shelley Berman

Best Comedy Performance, Musical
The Battle of Kookamonga, Homer and Jethro

Best Performance, Documentary or Spoken Word (Other Than Comedy)
A Lincoln Portrait, Carl Sandburg

Best Recording for Children
Peter and the Wolf, Peter Ustinov, narrating; Herbert von Karajan conducting Philharmonia Orchestra (Angel)

Best Album Cover
Shostakovich, Symphony No. 5, Robert M. Jones, art director (RCA)

1960

Record of the Year
"Theme From A Summer Place," Percy Faith

Album of the Year
Button Down Mind, Bob Newhart (Warner Bros.)

Song of the Year
"Theme From Exodus," Ernest Gold, songwriter

Best New Artist of 1960
Bob Newhart

Best Performance by a Pop Single Artist
"Georgia on My Mind," Ray Charles

Best Vocal Performance Single Record or Track, Male
"Georgia on My Mind," Ray Charles (ABC)

Best Vocal Performance Single Record or Track, Female
"Mack the Knife," Ella Fitzgerald (Verve)

Best Vocal Performance, Album, Male
Genius of Ray Charles, Ray Charles (Atlantic)

Best Vocal Performance, Album, Female
Mack the Knife — Ella in Berlin, Ella Fitzgerald (Verve)

Best Performance by a Vocal Group
"We Got Us," Eydie Gormé and Steve Lawrence

Best Performance by a Chorus
Songs of the Cowboy, Norman Luboff Choir

Best Rhythm and Blues Performance
"Let the Good Times Roll," Ray Charles

Best Jazz Performance, Solo or Small Group
West Side Story, André Previn

Best Jazz Performance, Large Group
Blues and the Beat, Henry Mancini

Best Jazz Composition of More Than Five Minutes
Sketches of Spain, Miles Davis and Gil Evans, composers

Best Performance by a Band for Dancing
Dance With Basie, Count Basie

Best Country and Western Performance
"El Paso," Marty Robbins

Best Performance, Folk
"Swing Dat Hammer," Harry Belafonte

Best Performance by an Orchestra
Mr. Lucky, Henry Mancini

Best Arrangement
Mr. Lucky, Henry Mancini, arranger

Best Show Album (Original Cast)
The Sound of Music, Richard Rodgers and Oscar Hammerstein, composers (Columbia)

Best Soundtrack Album or Recording of Music Score From Motion Picture or Television
Exodus, Ernest Gold, composer (RCA)

Best Soundtrack Album or Recording of Original Cast From Motion Picture or Television
Can-Can, Cole Porter, composer (Capital)

Best Classical Performance, Orchestra
Bartók, Music for Strings, Percussion and Celeste, Fritz Reiner conducting Chicago Symphony

Best Classical Performance, Vocal or Instrumental Chamber Music
Conversations With the Guitar, Laurindo Almeida

Best Classical Performance, Concerto or Instrumental Soloist
Brahms, *Piano Concerto No. 2 in B-Flat,* Sviatoslav Richter; Erich Leinsdorf conducting Chicago Symphony

Best Classical Performance, Instrumental Soloist or Duo (Other Than Orchestral)
The Spanish Guitars of Laurindo Almeida, Laurindo Almeida

Best Classical Opera Production
Puccini, *Turandot,* Erich Leinsdorf conducting Rome Opera House Chorus and Orchestra; solos: Tebaldi, Nilsson, Björling and Tozzi

Best Classical Performance, Choral (Including Oratorio)
Handel, *The Messiah,* Sir Thomas Beecham conducting Royal Philharmonic Orchestra and Chorus

Best Classical Performance, Vocal Soloist
A Program of Song, Leontyne Price

Best Contemporary Classical Composition
Orchestral Suite From Tender Land Suite, Aaron Copland, composer

Best Comedy Performance (Spoken Word)
Button Down Mind Strikes Back, Bob Newhart

Best Comedy Performance (Musical)
Jonathan and Darlene Edwards in Paris, Jo Stafford and Paul Weston

Best Performance, Documentary or Spoken Word (Other Than Comedy)
F.D.R. Speaks, Robert Bialek

Best Album Created for Children
Let's All Sing With the Chipmunks, David Seville (Liberty)

Best Album Cover
Latin a la Lee, Marvin Schwartz, art director (Capitol)

1961

Record of the Year
"Moon River," Henry Mancini

Album of the Year
Judy at Carnegie Hall, Judy Garland (Capitol)

Song of the Year
"Moon River," Henry Mancini and Johnny Mercer, songwriters

Henry Mancini

Best New Artist of 1961
Peter Nero

Best Solo Vocal Performance, Male
"Lollipops and Roses," Jack Jones

Best Solo Vocal Performance, Female
Judy at Carnegie Hall, Judy Garland

Best Performance by a Vocal Group
High Flying, Lambert, Hendricks and Ross

Best Performance by a Chorus
Great Band With Great Voices, Johnny Mann Singers and Si Zentner Orchestra

Best Rock and Roll Recording
Let's Twist Again, Chubby Checker (Parkway)

Best Rhythm and Blues Recording
Hit the Road Jack, Ray Charles (ABC/Paramount)

Best Jazz Performance, Soloist or Small Group (Instrumental)
André Previn Plays Harold Arlen, André Previn

Best Jazz Performance, Large Group
West Side Story, Stan Kenton

Best Original Jazz Composition
"African Waltz," Galt MacDermott, composer

Best Country and Western Recording
Big Bad John, Jimmy Dean (Columbia)

Best Gospel or Other Religious Recording
Everytime I Feel the Spirit, Mahalia Jackson (Columbia)

Best Folk Recording
Belafonte Folk Singers at Home and Abroad, Belafonte Folk Singers (RCA)

Best Performance by an Orchestra for Dancing
Up a Lazy River, Si Zentner

Best Performance by an Orchestra for Other Than Dancing
Breakfast at Tiffany's, Henry Mancini

Best Arrangement
"Moon River," Henry Mancini, arranger

Best Instrumental Theme or Instrumental Version of a Song
"African Waltz," Galt MacDermott, composer

Best Original Cast Show Album
How to Succeed in Business Without Really Trying, Frank Loesser, composer (RCA)

Best Soundtrack Album or Recording of Score From a Motion Picture or Television
Breakfast at Tiffany's, Henry Mancini (RCA)

Best Soundtrack Album or Recording of Original Cast From a Motion Picture or Television
West Side Story, Johnny Green, Saul Chaplin, Sid Ramin and Irwin Kostal (Columbia)

Album of the Year, Classical
Stravinsky Conducts, 1960: Le Sacre du Printemps; Petrouchka, Igor Stravinsky conducting Columbia Symphony (Columbia)

Best Classical Performance, Orchestra
Ravel, *Daphnis et Chloe,* Charles Munch conducting Boston Symphony Orchestra

Best Classical Performance, Chamber Music
Beethoven, *Serenade, Op. 8;* Kodaly, *Duo for Violin and Cello, Op. 7,* Jascha Heifetz, Gregor Piatigorsky and William Primrose

Best Classical Performance, Instrumental Soloist (With Orchestra)
Bartók, *Concerto No. 1 for Violin and Orchestra,* Isaac Stern; Eugene Ormandy conducting Philharmonic Orchestra

Best Classical Performance, Instrumental Soloist or Duo (Without Orchestra)
Reverie for Spanish Guitars, Laurindo Almeida

Best Opera Recording
Puccini, *Madame Butterfly,* Gabriele Santini conducting Rome Opera Chorus and Orchestra (Capitol)

Best Classical Performance, Choral
Bach, *B Minor Mass,* Robert Shaw conducting Robert Shaw Chorale

Best Classical Performance, Vocal Soloist
The Art of the Prima Donna, Joan Sutherland; Francesco Molinari-Pradelli conducting Royal Opera House Orchestra

Best Contemporary Classical Composition (tie)
Discantus, Laurindo Almeida, composer
Movements for Piano and Orchestra, Igor Stravinsky, composer

Best Comedy Performance
An Evening With Mike Nichols and Elaine May, Mike Nichols and Elaine May

Best Documentary or Spoken Word Recording (Other Than Comedy)
Humor in Music, Leonard Bernstein conducting New York Philharmonic Symphony (Columbia)

Best Recording for Children
Prokofiev, *Peter and the Wolf,* Leonard Bernstein conducting New York Philharmonic Orchestra (Columbia)

Best Album Cover
Judy at Carnegie Hall, Jim Silke, art director (Capitol)

Best Album Cover, Classical
Puccini, *Madame Butterfly,* Marvin Schwartz, art director (Angel)

1962

Record of the Year
"I Left My Heart in San Francisco," Tony Bennett

Album of the Year
The First Family, Vaughn Meader (Cadence)

Song of the Year
"What Kind of Fool Am I," Leslie Bricusse and Anthony Newley, songwriters

Best New Artist of 1962
Robert Goulet

Best Solo Vocal Performance, Male
I Left My Heart in San Francisco, Tony Bennett

Best Solo Vocal Performance, Female
Ella Swings Brightly With Nelson Riddle, Ella Fitzgerald

Best Performance by a Vocal Group
"If I Had a Hammer," Peter, Paul and Mary

Best Performance by a Chorus
Presenting the New Christy Minstrels, New Christy Minstrels

Best Rock and Roll Recording
"Alley Cat," Bent Fabric (Atco)

Best Rhythm and Blues Recording
"I Can't Stop Loving You," Ray Charles (ABC)

Best Jazz Performance, Soloist or Small Group (Instrumental)
"Desafinado," Stan Getz

Best Jazz Performance, Large Group (Instrumental)
Adventures in Jazz, Stan Kenton

Best Original Jazz Composition
"Cast Your Fate to the Winds," Vince Guaraldi, composer

Best Country and Western Recording
"Funny Way of Laughin'," Burl Ives (Decca)

Best Gospel or Other Religious Recording
Great Songs of Love and Faith, Mahalia Jackson (Columbia)

Best Folk Recording
"If I Had a Hammer," Peter, Paul and Mary (Warner Bros.)

Best Performance by an Orchestra for Dancing
Fly Me to the Moon Bossa Nova, Joe Harnell

Best Performance by an Orchestra or Instrumentalist With Orchestra, Not for Jazz or Dancing
The Colorful Peter Nero, Peter Nero

Best Instrumental Arrangement
"Baby Elephant Walk," Henry Mancini, arranger

Best Background Arrangement
"I Left My Heart in San Francisco," Marty Manning, arranger

Best Instrumental Theme
"A Taste of Honey," Bobby Scott and Ric Marlow, composers

Best Original Cast Show Album
No Strings, Richard Rodgers, composer (Capitol)

Album of the Year, Classical
Columbia Records Presents Vladimir Horowitz, Vladimir Horowitz (Columbia)

Best Classical Performance, Orchestra
Stravinsky, *The Firebird Ballet,* Igor Stravinsky conducting Columbia Symphony

Tony Bennett

Best Classical Performance, Chamber Music
The Heifetz-Piatigorsky Concerts With Primrose, Pennario and Guests, Jascha Heifetz, Gregor Piatigorsky and William Primrose

Best Classical Performance, Instrumental Soloist(s) (With Orchestra)
Stravinsky, *Concerto in D for Violin,* Isaac Stern; Igor Stravinsky conducting Columbia Symphony

Best Classical Performance, Instrumental Soloist or Duo (Without Orchestra)
Columbia Records Presents Vladimir Horowitz, Vladimir Horowitz

Best Opera Recording
Verdi, *Aïda,* Georg Solti conducting Rome Opera House Orchestra and Chorus; solos: Price, Vickers, Gorr, Merrill and Tozzi (RCA)

Best Classical Performance, Choral
Bach, *St. Matthew Passion,* Philharmonia Choir, Wilhelm Pitz, choral director; Otto Klemperer conducting Philharmonic Orchestra

Best Classical Performance, Vocal Soloist (With or Without Orchestra)
Wagner, *Götterdamerung Brunnhilde's Immolation Scene; Wesendonck, Songs,* Eileen Farrell; Leonard Bernstein conducting New York Philharmonic

Best Classical Composition by Contemporary Composer
The Flood, Igor Stravinsky, composer

Best Comedy Performance
The First Family, Vaughn Meader

Best Documentary or Spoken Word Recording (Other Than Comedy)
The Story-Teller: A Session With Charles Laughton, Charles Laughton (Capitol)

Best Recording for Children
Saint-Saëns, *Carnival of the Animals;* Britten, *Young Person's Guide to the Orchestra,* Leonard Bernstein (Columbia)

Best Album Cover
Lena . . . Lovely and Alive, Robert Jones, art director (RCA)

Best Album Cover, Classical
The Intimate Bach, Marvin Schwartz, art director (Capitol)

1963

Record of the Year
"The Days of Wine and Roses," Henry Mancini

Album of the Year
The Barbra Streisand Album, Barbra Streisand (Columbia)

Song of the Year
"The Days of Wine and Roses," Henry Mancini and Johnny Mercer, composers

Best New Artist of 1963
Swingle Singers

Best Vocal Performance, Male
"Wives and Lovers, " Jack Jones

Best Vocal Performance, Female
The Barbra Streisand Album, Barbra Streisand

Best Performance by a Vocal Group
"Blowin' in the Wind," Peter, Paul and Mary

Best Performance by a Chorus
Bach's Greatest Hits, Swingle Singers

Best Rock and Roll Recording
"Deep Purple," Nino Tempo and April Stevens (Atco)

Best Rhythm and Blues Recording
"Busted," Ray Charles (ABC/Paramount)

Best Instrumental Jazz Performance, Soloist or Small Group
Conversations With Myself, Bill Evans

Best Instrumental Jazz Performance, Large Group
Encore: Woody Herman, 1963, Woody Herman Band

Best Original Jazz Composition
"Gravy Waltz," Steve Allen and Ray Brown, composers

Best Country and Western Recording
"Detroit City," Bobby Bare (RCA)

Best Gospel or Other Religious Recording (Musical)
"Dominique," Soeur Sourire (The Singing Nun) (Philips)

Best Folk Recording
"Blowin' in the Wind," Peter, Paul and Mary (Warner Bros.)

Best Performance by an Orchestra for Dancing
This Time by Basie! Hits of the 50's and 60's, Count Basie

Best Performance by an Orchestra or Instrumentalist With Orchestra, Not for Jazz or Dancing
"Java," Al Hirt

Best Instrumental Arrangement
"I Can't Stop Loving You," Quincy Jones, arranger

Best Background Arrangement
"The Days of Wine and Roses," Henry Mancini, arranger

Best Instrumental Theme
"More" (Theme From *Mondo Cane*), Norman Newell, Nino Oliviero and Riz Ortolani, composers

Best Original Score From a Motion Picture or Television Show
Tom Jones, John Addison, composer

Best Score From an Original Cast Show Album
She Loves Me, Jerry Bock and Sheldon Harnick, composers (MGM)

Album of the Year, Classical
Britten, *War Requiem,* Benjamin Britten conducting London Symphony Orchestra and Chorus (London)

Most Promising New Classical Recording Artist
André Watts, pianist

Best Classical Performance, Orchestra
Bartók, *Concerto for Orchestra,* Erich Leinsdorf conducting Boston Symphony Orchestra

Best Classical Performance, Chamber Music
Evening of Elizabethan Music, Julian Bream Consort

Best Classical Performance, Instrumental Soloist(s) (With Orchestra)
Tchaikovsky, *Concerto No. 1 in B-Flat Minor for Piano and Orchestra,* Artur Rubinstein; Erich Leinsdorf conducting Boston Symphony Orchestra

Best Classical Performance, Instrumental Soloist or Duo (Without Orchestra)
The Sound of Horowitz, Vládimir Horowitz

The Beatles

Best Opera Recording
Puccini, *Madama Butterfly,* Erich Leinsdorf conducting RCA Italiana Opera Orchestra and Chorus; solos: Price, Tucker and Elias (RCA)

Best Classical Performance, Choral
Britten, *War Requiem,* David Willcocks directing Bach Choir; Edward Chapman directing Highgate School Choir; Benjamin Britten conducting London Symphony Orchestra and Chorus

Best Classical Performance, Vocal Soloist (With or Without Orchestra)
Great Scenes From Gershwin's Porgy and Bess, Leontyne Price

Best Classical Composition by Contemporary Composer
War Requiem, Benjamin Britten, composer

Best Comedy Performance
Hello Mudduh, Hello Faddah, Allan Sherman

Best Documentary, Spoken Word or Drama Recording (Other Than Comedy)
Who's Afraid of Virginia Woolf?, Edward Albee (Warner Bros.)

Best Recording for Children
Bernstein Conducts for Young People, Leonard Bernstein conducting New York Philharmonic (Columbia)

Best Album Cover, Other Than Classical
The Barbra Streisand Album, John Berg, art director. (Columbia)

Best Album Cover, Classical
Puccini, *Madama Butterfly,* Robert Jones, art director (RCA)

Best Album Notes
The Ellington Era, Stanley Dance and Leonard Feather, annotators (Columbia)

1964

Record of the Year
"The Girl From Ipanema," Stan Getz and Astrud Gilberto

Album of the Year
Getz/Gilberto, Stan Getz and Joao Gilberto (Verve)

Song of the Year
"Hello, Dolly!," Jerry Herman, songwriter

Best New Artist of 1964
The Beatles

Most Promising New Recording Artist
Marilyn Horne

Best Vocal Performance, Male
"Hello, Dolly!," Louis Armstrong

Best Vocal Performance, Female
"People," Barbra Streisand

Best Performance by a Vocal Group
A Hard Day's Night, The Beatles

Best Performance by a Chorus
The Swingle Singers Going Baroque, Swingle Singers

Best Rock and Roll Recording
"Downtown," Petula Clark (Warner Bros.)

Best Rhythm and Blues Recording
"How Glad I Am," Nancy Wilson (Capitol)

Best Instrumental Jazz Performance, Small Group or Soloist With Small Group
Getz/Gilberto, Stan Getz

Best Instrumental Jazz Performance, Large Group or Soloist With Large Group
Guitar From Ipanema, Laurindo Almeida

Best Original Jazz Composition
"The Cat," Lalo Schifrin, composer

Music by Mail

Here are some places to turn if you can't find a recording at your local store.

Alternative Press
P.O. Box 17136
N. Hollywood, CA 91615
(818) 760-8520

Arhoolie
Arhoolie Productions, Inc.
10341 San Pablo Ave.
El Cerrito, CA 94530
(510) 525-2129

Cadence Magazine
P.O. Box 56604
Boulder, CO 80322
(800) 289-0484

Classics
P.O. Box 64502
St. Paul, MN 55164-0502
(800) 949-9999

Footlight Records
113 E. 12th St.
New York, NY 10003
(212) 533-1572

Grateful Dead Catalog and Newsletter
Grateful Dead Mercantile Co.
P.O. Box X
Novato, CA 94948
(800) 225-3323

Pulse! Magazine
2500 Del Monte St.
Building C
West Sacramento, CA 95691-3820
(916) 373-2450

Rara Avis
77 Wittenberg Road
Bearsville, NY 12409
(914) 679-1054

Request Magazine
Musicland Group
10400 Yellow Circle Drive
Minnetonka, MN 55343
(612) 931-8800

Rhino
Rhino Records, Inc.
10635 Santa Monica Blvd.
Los Angeles, CA 90025-4900
(800) 546-3670

Rounder Mail Order
1 Camp St.
Cambridge, MA 02140
(800) 443-4727

Wireless Audio
P.O. Box 64422
St. Paul, MN 55164-0422
(800) 726-8742

Best Country and Western Single
"Dang Me," Roger Miller

Best Country and Western Album
Dang Me/Chug-a-Lug, Roger Miller (Smash)

Best Country and Western Song
"Dang Me," Roger Miller, songwriter

Best Country and Western Vocal Performance, Male
"Dang Me," Roger Miller

Best Country and Western Vocal Performance, Female
"Here Comes My Baby," Dottie West

Best New Country and Western Artist of 1964
Roger Miller

Best Gospel or Other Religious Recording (Musical)
Great Gospel Songs, Tennessee Ernie Ford (Capitol)

Best Folk Recording
We'll Sing in the Sunshine, Gale Garnett (RCA)

Best Instrumental Arrangement
"*The Pink Panther* Theme," Henry Mancini, arranger

Best Accompaniment Arrangement for Vocalist(s) or Instrumentalist(s)
"People," Peter Matz, arranger

Best Instrumental Composition (Other Than Jazz)
"*The Pink Panther* Theme," Henry Mancini, composer

Best Instrumental Performance, Non-Jazz
"*The Pink Panther* Theme," Henry Mancini

Best Score From an Original Cast Show Album
Funny Girl, Jule Styne and Bob Merrill, composers (Capitol)

Best Original Score Written for a Motion Picture or Television Show
Mary Poppins, Richard M. Sherman and Robert B. Sherman, composers

Album of the Year, Classical
Bernstein, *Symphony No. 3 ("Kaddish"),* Leonard Bernstein conducting New York Philharmonic Orchestra (Columbia)

Best Classical Performance, Orchestra
Mahler, *Symphony No. 5 in C-Sharp Minor;* Berg, *"Wozzeck"* *Excerpts,* Erich Leinsdorf conducting Boston Symphony

Best Chamber Performance, Instrumental
Beethoven, *Trio No. 1 in E-Flat, Op. 1, No. 1,* Jascha Heifetz and Gregor Piatigorsky; Jacob Lateiner, pianist

Best Chamber Music Performance, Vocal
It Was a Lover and His Lass, Morley, Byrd and others; Noah Greenberg conducting New York Pro Musica

Best Classical Performance, Instrumental Soloist(s) (With Orchestra)
Prokofiev, *Concerto No. 1 in D Major for Violin,* Isaac Stern; Eugene Ormandy conducting Philadelphia Orchestra

Best Performance, Instrumental Soloist (Without Orchestra)
Vladimir Horowitz Plays Beethoven, Debussy, Chopin (Beethoven, *Sonata No. 8 "Pathetique";* Debussy, *Preludes;* Chopin, *Etudes and Scherzos 1–4),* Vladimir Horowitz

Best Opera Recording
Bizet, *Carmen,* Herbert von Karajan conducting Vienna Philharmonic Orchestra and Chorus; solos: Price, Corelli, Merrill and Freni (RCA)

Best Classical Choral Performance (Other Than Opera)
Britten, *A Ceremony of Carols,* Robert Shaw conducting Robert Shaw Chorale

Best Classical Vocal Soloist Performance (With or Without Orchestra)
Berlioz, *Nuits d'Ete Falla: El Amor Brujo,* Leontyne Price; Fritz Reiner conducting Chicago Symphony

Best Classical Composition by a Contemporary Composer
Samuel Barber, *Concerto*

Tom Jones

Best Comedy Performance
I Started Out as a Child, Bill Cosby

Best Documentary, Spoken Word or Drama Recording (Other Than Comedy)
BBC Tribute to John F. Kennedy, That Was the Week That Was, cast (Decca)

Best Recording for Children
Mary Poppins, Julie Andrews and Dick Van Dyke (Buena Vista)

Best Album Cover
People, Robert Cato, art director; Don Bronstein, photographer (Columbia)

Best Album Cover, Classical
Saint-Saëns, *Carnival of the Animals;* Britten, *Young Person's Guide to the Orchestra,* Robert Jones, art director; Jan Balet, graphic artist (RCA)

Best Album Notes
Mexico (Legacy Collection), Stanton Catlin and Carleton Beals, annotators (Columbia)

1965

Record of the Year
"A Taste of Honey," Herb Alpert and the Tijuana Brass

Album of the Year
September of My Years, Frank Sinatra (Reprise)

Song of the Year
"The Shadow of Your Smile" (Love Theme From *The Sandpiper*), Paul Francis Webster and Johnny Mandel, songwriters

Best New Artist
Tom Jones

Most Promising New Recording Artist
Peter Serkin, pianist

Best Vocal Performance, Male
"It Was a Very Good Year," Frank Sinatra

Best Vocal Performance, Female
My Name Is Barbra, Barbra Streisand

Best Performance by a Vocal Group
We Dig Mancini, Anita Kerr Singers

Best Performance by a Chorus
Anyone for Mozart?, Swingle Singers

Best Contemporary (Rock and Roll) Single
"King of the Road," Roger Miller

Best Contemporary (Rock and Roll) Vocal Performance, Male
"King of the Road," Roger Miller

Best Contemporary (Rock and Roll) Vocal Performance, Female
"I Know a Place," Petula Clark

Best Contemporary (Rock and Roll) Performance Group (Vocal or Instrumental)
"Flowers on the Wall," Statler Brothers

Best Rhythm and Blues Recording
"Papa's Got a Brand New Bag," James Brown (King)

Best Instrumental Jazz Performance, Small Group or Soloist With Small Group
The "In" Crowd, Ramsey Lewis Trio

Best Instrumental Jazz Performance, Large Group or Soloist With Large Group
Ellington '66, Duke Ellington Orchestra

Best Original Jazz Composition
Jazz Suite on the Mass Texts, Lalo Shifrin, composer

Best Country and Western Single
"King of the Road," Roger Miller

Best Country and Western Album
The Return of Roger Miller, Roger Miller (Smash)

Best Country and Western Song
"King of the Road," Roger Miller, songwriter

Best Country and Western Vocal Performance, Male
"King of the Road," Roger Miller

Best Country and Western Vocal Performance, Female
"Queen of the House," Jody Miller

Best New Country and Western Artist
Statler Brothers

Best Gospel or Other Religious Recording (Musical)
Southland Favorites, George Beverly Shea and the Anita Kerr Quartet (RCA)

Best Folk Recording
An Evening With Belafonte/Makeba, Harry Belafonte and Miriam Makeba (RCA)

Best Instrumental Arrangement
"A Taste of Honey," Herb Alpert, arranger

Best Arrangement Accompanying a Vocalist or Instrumentalist
"It Was a Very Good Year," Gordon Jenkins, arranger

Best Instrumental Performance, Non-Jazz
"A Taste of Honey," Herb Alpert and the Tijuana Brass

Best Score From an Original Show Album
On a Clear Day, Alan Lerner and Burton Lane (RCA)

Best Original Score Written for a Motion Picture or Television Show
The Sandpiper, Johnny Mandel, composer (Mercury)

Album of the Year, Classical
Horowitz at Carnegie Hall, An Historic Return, Vladimir Horowitz (Columbia)

Best Classical Performance, Orchestra
Ives, Symphony No. 4, Leopold Stokowski conducting American Symphony Orchestra

Best Classical Chamber Music Performance, Instrumental or Vocal
Bartók, The Six String Quartets, Juilliard String Quartet

Best Classical Performance, Instrumental Soloist(s) (With Orchestra)
Beethoven, Concerto No. 4 in G Major for Piano and Orchestra, Artur Rubinstein; Erich Leinsdorf conducting Boston Symphony

Best Classical Performance, Instrumental Soloist (Without Orchestra)
Horowitz at Carnegie Hall, An Historic Return, Vladimir Horowitz

Best Opera Recording
Berg, Wozzeck, Karl Bohm conducting Orchestra of German Opera, Berlin; solos: Fisher-Dieskau, Lear and Wunderlich (Deutsche Grammophon)

Best Classical Choral Performance (Other Than Opera)
Stravinsky, Symphony of Psalms; Poulenc, Gloria, Robert Shaw conducting Robert Shaw Chorale and RCA Victor Symphony Orchestra

Best Classical Vocal Performance, With or Without Orchestra
Strauss, Salome ("Dance of the Seven Veils," Interlude, Final Scene); The Egyptian Helen (Awakening Scene), Leontyne Price

Best Composition by a Contemporary Classical Composer
Symphony No. 4, Charles Ives, composer

Best Comedy Performance
Why Is There Air?, Bill Cosby

Best Spoken Word or Drama Recording
John F. Kennedy: As We Remember Him (Columbia)

Best Recording for Children
Dr. Seuss Presents "Fox in Sox" and "Green Eggs and Ham," Marvin Miller (RCA)

Best Album Cover, Graphic Arts
Bartók, Concerto No. 2 for Violin; Stravinsky, Concerto for Violin, James Alexander, graphic artist; George Estes, art director (RCA)

Best Album Cover, Photography
Jazz Suite on the Mass Texts, Ken Whitmore, photographer; Bob Jones, art director (RCA)

Best Album Notes
September of My Years, Stan Cornyn, annotator (Reprise)

1966

Record of the Year
"Strangers in the Night," Frank Sinatra

Album of the Year
Sinatra: A Man and His Music, Frank Sinatra (Reprise)

Song of the Year
"Michelle," John Lennon and Paul McCartney, songwriters

Best Vocal Performance, Male
"Strangers in the Night," Frank Sinatra

Best Vocal Performance, Female
"If He Walked Into My Life," Eydie Gormé

Best Performance by a Vocal Group
"A Man and a Woman," Anita Kerr Singers

Best Performance by a Chorus
"Somewhere, My Love" (Lara's Theme From Dr. Zhivago), Ray Conniff and Singers

Best Contemporary (Rock and Roll) Recording
"Winchester Cathedral," New Vaudeville Band (Fontana)

Best Contemporary (Rock and Roll) Solo Vocal Performance, Male or Female
"Eleanor Rigby," Paul McCartney

Mamas and the Papas

Best Contemporary (Rock and Roll) Group Performance, Vocal or Instrumental
"Monday, Monday," Mamas and the Papas

Best Rhythm and Blues Recording
"Crying Time," Ray Charles (ABC/Paramount)

Best Rhythm and Blues Solo Vocal Performance, Male or Female
"Crying Time," Ray Charles

Best Rhythm and Blues Group, Vocal or Instrumental
"Hold It Right There," Ramsey Lewis

Best Instrumental Jazz Performance, Group or Soloist With Group
"Goin' Out of My Head," Wes Montgomery

Best Original Jazz Composition
"In the Beginning God," Duke Ellington, composer

Best Country and Western Song
"Almost Persuaded," Billy Sherrill and Glenn Sutton, songwriters

Best Country and Western Recording
"Almost Persuaded," David Houston (Epic)

Best Country and Western Vocal Performance, Male
"Almost Persuaded," David Houston

Best Country and Western Vocal Performance, Female
"Don't Touch Me," Jeannie Seely

Best Sacred Recording (Musical)
Grand Old Gospel, Porter Wagoner and the Blackwood Brothers (RCA)

Best Folk Recording
Blues in the Street, Cortelia Clark (RCA)

Best Instrumental Arrangement
"What Now My Love," Herb Alpert, arranger

Best Arrangement Accompanying a Vocalist or Instrumentalist
"Strangers in the Night," Ernie Freeman, arranger

Best Instrumental Theme
"*Batman* Theme," Neal Hefti, composer

Best Instrumental Performance (Other Than Jazz)
"What Now My Love," Herb Alpert and the Tijuana Brass

Best Score From an Original Cast Show Album
Mame, Jerry Herman, composer (Columbia)

Best Original Score Written for a Motion Picture or Television Show
Dr. Zhivago, Maurice Jarre, composer

Album of the Year, Classical
Ives, *Symphony No. 1 in D Minor,* Morton Gould conducting Chicago Symphony (RCA)

Best Classical Performance, Orchestra
Mahler, *Symphony No. 6 in A Minor,* Eric Leinsdorf conducting Boston Symphony

Best Chamber Music Performance, Instrumental or Vocal
Boston Symphony Chamber Players, Boston Symphony Chamber Players

Best Classical Music Performance, Instrumental Soloist(s) (With or Without Orchestra)
Baroque Guitar, Julian Bream

Best Opera Recording
Wagner, *Die Walkure,* Georg Solti conducting Vienna Philharmonic; solos: Nilsson, Crespin, Ludwig, King and Hotter (London)

Best Classical Choral Performance (Other Than Opera) (tie)
Handel, *Messiah,* Robert Shaw conducting Robert Shaw Chorale and Orchestra

Ives, *Music for Chorus,* Gregg Smith conducting Columbia Chamber Orchestra, Gregg Smith Singers and Ithaca College Concert Choir; George Bragg conducting Texas Boys Choir

Best Classical Vocal Soloist Performance (With or Without Orchestra)
Prima Donna, Leontyne Price; Francesco Molinari-Pradelli conducting RCA Italiana Opera Orchestra

Best Comedy Performance
Wonderfulness, Bill Cosby

Best Spoken Word, Documentary or Drama Recording
Edward R. Murrow: A Reporter Remembers — Vol. I The War Years, Edward R. Murrow (Columbia)

Best Recording for Children
Dr. Seuss Presents: "If I Ran the Zoo" and "Sleep Book," Marvin Miller (RCA)

Best Album Cover, Graphic Arts
Revolver, Klaus Voormann, graphic artist (Capitol)

Best Album Cover, Photography
Confessions of a Broken Man, Les Leverette, photographer; Robert Jones, art director (RCA)

Best Album Notes
Sinatra at the Sands, Stan Cornyn, annotator (Reprise)

1967

Record of the Year
"Up, Up and Away," 5th Dimension

Album of the Year
Sgt. Pepper's Lonely Hearts Club Band, The Beatles (Capitol)

Song of the Year
"Up, Up and Away," Jimmy L. Webb, songwriter

Best New Artist
Bobbie Gentry

Best Vocal Performance, Male
"By the Time I Get to Phoenix," Glen Campbell

Best Vocal Performance, Female
"Ode to Billie Joe," Bobbie Gentry

Best Performance by a Vocal Group (Two to Six Persons)
"Up, Up and Away," 5th Dimension

Best Performance by a Chorus (Seven or More Persons)
"Up, Up and Away," Johnny Mann Singers

Best Contemporary Single
"Up, Up and Away," 5th Dimension

Best Contemporary Album
Sgt. Pepper's Lonely Hearts Club Band, The Beatles (Capitol)

Best Contemporary Male Solo Vocal Performance
"By the Time I Get to Phoenix," Glen Campbell

Best Contemporary Female Solo Vocal Performance
"Ode to Billie Joe," Bobbie Gentry

Best Contemporary Group Performance, Vocal or Instrumental
"Up, Up and Away," 5th Dimension

Best Rhythm and Blues Recording
"Respect," Aretha Franklin (Atlantic)

Best Rhythm and Blues Solo Vocal Performance, Male
"Dead End Street," Lou Rawls

Best Rhythm and Blues Solo Vocal Performance, Female
"Respect," Aretha Franklin

Best Rhythm and Blues Group Performance, Vocal or Instrumental (Two or More)
"Soul Man," Sam and Dave

Best Instrumental Jazz Performance, Small Group or Soloist With Small Group
Mercy, Mercy, Mercy, Cannonball Adderley Quintet

Best Instrumental Jazz Performance, Large Group or Soloist With Large Group
"Far East Suite," Duke Ellington

Best Country and Western Song
"Gentle on My Mind" John Hartford, songwriter

Best Country and Western Recording
"Gentle on My Mind," Glen Campbell (Capitol)

Best Country and Western Solo Vocal Performance, Male
"Gentle on My Mind," Glen Campbell

Best Country and Western Solo Vocal Performance, Female
"I Don't Wanna Play House," Tammy Wynette

Best Country and Western Performance, Duet, Trio or Group (Vocal or Instrumental)
"Jackson," Johnny Cash and June Carter

Best Gospel Performance
More Grand Old Gospel, Porter Wagoner and the Blackwood Brothers

Best Sacred Performance
How Great Thou Art, Elvis Presley

Best Folk Performance
"Gentle on My Mind," John Hartford

Best Instrumental Arrangement
Alfie, Burt Bacharach, arranger

Best Arrangement Accompanying Vocalist(s) or Instrumentalist(s)
"Ode to Billie Joe," Jimmie Haskell, arranger

Best Instrumental Theme
"Mission: Impossible," Lalo Schifrin, composer

Best Instrumental Performance
"Chet Atkins Picks the Best," Chet Atkins

Best Score From an Original Cast Show Album
Cabaret, Fred Ebb and John Kander, composers (Columbia)

Best Original Score Written for a Motion Picture or Television Show
"Mission: Impossible," Lalo Schifrin, composer

Duke Ellington

Album of the Year, Classical (tie)
Berg, *Wozzeck,* Pierre Boulez conducting Paris National Opera; solos: Berry, Strauss, Uhl and Doench (Columbia)

Mahler, *Symphony No. 8 in E-Flat Major ("Symphony of a Thousand"),* Leonard Bernstein conducting London Symphony Orchestra (Columbia)

Best Classical Performance, Orchestra
Stravinsky, *Firebird and Petrouchka Suites,* Igor Stravinsky conducting Columbia Symphony

Best Chamber Music Performance
West Meets East, Ravi Shanker and Yehudi Menuhin

Best Classical Performance, Instrumental Soloist(s) (With or Without Orchestra)
Horowitz in Concert, Vladimir Horowitz

Best Opera Recording
Berg, *Wozzeck,* Pierre Boulez conducting Paris National Opera; solos: Berry, Strauss, Uhl and Doench (Columbia)

Best Classical Choral Performance (tie)
Mahler, *Symphony No. 8 in E-Flat Major ("Symphony of a Thousand"),* Leonard Bernstein conducting London Symphony Orchestra

Orff, *Catulli Carmina,* Robert Page conducting Temple University Chorus; Eugene Ormandy conducting Philadelphia Orchestra

Best Classical Vocal Soloist Performance
Prima Donna, Vol. 2, Leontyne Price; Francesco Molinari-Pradelli conducting RCA Italiana Opera Orchestra

Best Comedy Recording
Revenge, Bill Cosby (Warner Bros.-Seven Arts)

Best Spoken Word, Documentary or Drama Recording
Gallant Men, Sen. Everett M. Dirksen (Capitol)

Best Recording for Children
Dr Seuss: How the Grinch Stole Christmas, Boris Karloff (MGM)

Best Album Cover, Graphic Arts
Sgt. Pepper's Lonely Hearts Club Band, Peter Blake and Jann Haworth, art directors (Capitol)

Best Album Cover, Photography
Bob Dylan's Greatest Hits, Roland Scherman, photographer; John Berg and Bob Cato, art directors (Columbia)

Best Album Notes
Suburban Attitudes in Country Verse, John O. Loudermilk, annotator (RCA)

1968

Record of the Year
"Mrs. Robinson," Simon and Garfunkel

Album of the Year
By the Time I Get to Phoenix, Glen Campbell (Capitol)

Song of the Year
"Little Green Apples," Bobby Russell, songwriter

Best New Artist of 1968
José Feliciano

Best Contemporary Pop Vocal Performance, Male
"Light My Fire," José Feliciano

Best Contemporary Pop Vocal Performance, Female
"Do You Know the Way to San Jose," Dionne Warwick

Best Contemporary Pop Vocal Performance, Duo or Group
"Mrs. Robinson," Simon and Garfunkel

Best Contemporary Pop Performance, Chorus
"Mission Impossible/Norwegian Wood" (medley), Alan
 Copeland Singers

Best Contemporary Pop Performance, Instrumental
"Classical Gas," Mason Williams

Best Rhythm and Blues Song
(Sittin' On) "The Dock of the Bay," Otis Redding and Steve
 Cropper, songwriters

Best Rhythm and Blues Vocal Performance, Male
(Sittin' On) "The Dock of the Bay," Otis Redding

Best Rhythm and Blues Vocal Performance, Female
"Chain of Fools," Aretha Franklin

**Best Rhythm and Blues Performance by a Duo or Group, Vocal
or Instrumental**
"Cloud Nine," The Temptations

**Best Instrumental Jazz Performance, Small Group or Soloist
With Small Group**
Bill Evans at the Montreux Jazz Festival, Bill Evans Trio

**Best Instrumental Jazz Performance, Large Group or Soloist
With Large Group**
"And His Mother Called Him Bill," Duke Ellington

Best Country Song
"Little Green Apples," Bobby Russell, songwriter

Best Country Vocal Performance, Male
"Folsom Prison Blues," Johnny Cash

Best Country Vocal Performance, Female
"Harper Valley P.T.A.," Jeannie C. Riley

**Best Country Performance, Duo or Group Vocal or
Instrumental**
"Foggy Mountain Breakdown," Flatt and Scruggs

Best Sacred Performance
"Beautiful Isle of Somewhere," Jack Hess

Best Gospel Performance
The Happy Gospel of the Happy Goodmans, Happy Goodman
 Family

Best Soul Gospel Performance
"The Soul of Me," Dottie Rambo

Best Folk Performance
"Both Sides Now," Judy Collins

Best Instrumental Arrangement
"Classical Gas," Mike Post, arranger

Best Arrangement Accompanying Vocalist(s)
"MacArthur Park," Jimmy L. Webb, arranger

Best Instrumental Theme
"Classical Gas," Mason Williams, composer

Aretha Franklin

Best Score From an Original Cast Show Album
Hair, Gerome Ragni, James Rado and Galt MacDermott, composers (RCA)

**Best Original Score Written for a Motion Picture or a
Television Special**
The Graduate, Paul Simon and Dave Grusin, composers

Best Classical Performance, Orchestra
Boulez Conducts Debussy, Pierre Boulez conducting New
 Philharmonia Orchestra

Best Chamber Music Performance
Gabrieli, *Canzoni for Brass, Winds, Strings and Organ,*
 E. Power Biggs with Edward Tarr Ensemble and Gabrieli
 Consort; Vittorio Negri, conductor

**Best Classical Performance, Instrumental Soloist(s) (With or
Without Orchestra)**
Horowitz on Television, Vladimir Horowitz

Best Opera Recording
Mozart, *Cosi fan Tutte,* Erich Leinsdorf conducting New
 Philharmonia Orchestra and Ambrosian Opera Chorus; solos:
 Price, Raskin, Troyanos, Milnes, Shirley and Flagello (RCA)

Best Choral Performance (Other Than Opera)
The Glory of Gabrieli, Vittorio Negri conducting Gregg Smith
 Singers and Texas Boys Choir; George Bragg directing
 Edward Tarr Ensemble with E. Power Biggs

Best Classical Vocal Soloist Performance
Rossini Rarities, Montserrat Caballe; Carlo Felice Cillario conducting RCA Italiana Opera Orchestra and Chorus

Best Comedy Recording
To Russell, My Brother, Whom I Slept With, Bill Cosby (Warner
 Bros.)

Best Spoken Word Recording
Lonesome Cities, Rod McKuen (Warner Bros.-Seven Arts)

Best Album Cover
Underground, John Berg and Richard Mantel, art directors
 (Columbia)

Best Album Notes
Johnny Cash at Folsom Prison, Johnny Cash, annotator

1969

Record of the Year
"Aquarius/Let the Sunshine In," 5th Dimension

Album of the Year
Blood, Sweat and Tears, Blood, Sweat and Tears (Columbia)

Song of the Year
"Games People Play," Joe South, songwriter

Best New Artist of 1969
Crosby, Stills and Nash

Best Contemporary Song
"Games People Play," Joe South, songwriter

Best Contemporary Vocal Performance, Male
"Everybody's Talkin'," Harry Nilsson

Best Contemporary Vocal Performance, Female
"Is That All There Is," Peggy Lee

Best Contemporary Vocal Performance by a Group
"Aquarius/Let the Sunshine In," 5th Dimension

Best Contemporary Performance by a Chorus
"Love Theme From *Romeo and Juliet,*" Percy Faith Orchestra and Chorus

Best Contemporary Instrumental Performance
"Variations on a Theme by Eric Satie," Blood, Sweat and Tears

Best Rhythm and Blues Song
"Color Him Father," Richard Spencer, songwriter

Best Rhythm and Blues Vocal Performance, Male
"The Chokin' Kind," Joe Simon

Best Rhythm and Blues Vocal Performance, Female
"Share Your Love With Me," Aretha Franklin

Best Rhythm and Blues Vocal Performance by a Group or Duo
"It's Your Thing," Isley Brothers

Best Rhythm and Blues Instrumental Performance
"Games People Play," King Curtis

Best Instrumental Jazz Performance, Small Group or Soloist With Small Group
Willow Weep for Me, Wes Montgomery

Best Instrumental Jazz Performance, Large Group or Soloist With Large Group
"Walking in Space," Quincy Jones

Best Country Song
"A Boy Named Sue," Shel Silverstein, songwriter

Best Country Vocal Performance, Male
"A Boy Named Sue," Johnny Cash

Best Country Vocal Performance, Female
Stand by Your Man, Tammy Wynette

Best Country Performance by a Duo or Group
"MacArthur Park," Waylon Jennings and the Kimberlys

Best Country Instrumental Performance
The Nashville Brass Featuring Danny Davis Play More Nashville Sounds, Danny Davis and the Nashville Brass

Best Gospel Performance
"In Gospel Country," Porter Wagoner and the Blackwood Brothers

Best Soul Gospel Performance
Oh Happy Day, Edwin Hawkins Singers

Best Sacred Performance
"Ain't That Beautiful Singing," Jake Hess

Best Folk Performance
Clouds, Joni Mitchell

Best Instrumental Arrangement
"Love Theme From *Romeo and Juliet,*" Henry Mancini, arranger

Best Arrangement Accompanying Vocalist(s)
"Spinning Wheel," Fred Lipsius, arranger

Best Instrumental Theme
Midnight Cowboy, John Barry, composer

Best Score From an Original Cast Show Album
Promises, Promises, Burt Bacharach and Hal Davis, composers (Liberty)

Best Original Score Written for Motion Picture or Television
Butch Cassidy and the Sundance Kid, Burt Bacharach, composer

Album of the Year, Classical
Switched-On Bach, Walter Carlos (Columbia)

Best Classical Performance, Orchestra
Boulez Conducts Debussy, Vol. 2 "Images Pour Orchestre," Pierre Boulez conducting Cleveland Orchestra

Best Chamber Music Performance
Gabrieli, *Antiphonal Music of Gabrieli (Canzoni for Brass Choirs),* the Philadelphia, Cleveland and Chicago Brass ensembles

Best Classical Performance, Instrumental Soloist(s) (With or Without Orchestra)
Switched-On Bach, Walter Carlos

Best Opera Recording
Wagner, *Siegfried,* Herbert von Karajan conducting Berlin Philharmonic; solos: Thomas, Stewart, Stolze, Dernesch, Keleman, Dominguez, Gayer and Ridderbusch (Deutsche Grammophon)

Best Choral Performance (Other Than Opera)
Berio, *Sinfonia,* Swingle Singers; Ward Swingle, choral master; Luciano Berio conducting New York Philharmonic

Best Vocal Soloist Performance, Classical
Barber, *Two Scenes From "Antony and Cleopatra";* Knoxville, *Summer of 1915,* Leontyne Price; Thomas Schippers conducting New Philharmonia

Best Comedy Recording
Bill Cosby, Bill Cosby (Uni)

Best Spoken Word Recording
We Love You, Call Collect, Art Linkletter and Diane (Word/Capitol)

Best Recording for Children
Peter, Paul and Mommy, Peter, Paul and Mary (Warner Bros.)

Best Album Cover
America the Beautiful, Evelyn J. Kelbish, painting; David Stahlberg, graphics (Skye)

Best Album Notes
Nashville Skyline, Johnny Cash, annotator (Columbia)

1970

Record of the Year
"Bridge Over Troubled Water," Simon and Garfunkel

Album of the Year
Bridge Over Troubled Water, Simon and Garfunkel (Columbia)

Song of the Year
"Bridge Over Troubled Water," Paul Simon, songwriter

Best New Artist of the Year
Carpenters

Best Contemporary Song
"Bridge Over Troubled Water," Paul Simon, songwriter

Best Contemporary Vocal Performance, Male
"Everything Is Beautiful," Ray Stevens

Best Contemporary Vocal Performance, Female
I'll Never Fall in Love Again, Dionne Warwick

Best Contemporary Vocal Performance by a Group
"Close to You," Carpenters

Best Contemporary Instrumental Performance
Theme From Z and Other Film Music, Henry Mancini

Best Rhythm and Blues Song
"Patches," Ronald Dunbar and General Johnson, songwriters

Best Rhythm and Blues Vocal Performance, Male
"The Thrill Is Gone," B.B. King

Best Rhythm and Blues Vocal Performance, Female
"Don't Play That Song," Aretha Franklin

Simon and Garfunkel

Best Rhythm and Blues Vocal Performance by a Duo or Group
"Didn't I" (Blow Your Mind This Time), Delfonics

Best Jazz Performance, Small Group or Soloist With Small Group
Alone, Bill Evans

Best Jazz Performance, Large Group or Soloist With Large Group
Bitches Brew, Miles Davis

Best Country Song
"My Woman, My Woman, My Wife," Marty Robbins, songwriter

Best Country Vocal Performance, Male
"For the Good Times," Ray Price

Best Country Vocal Performance, Female
"Rose Garden," Lynn Anderson

Best Country Performance by a Duo or Group
"If I Were a Carpenter," Johnny Cash and June Carter

Best Country Instrumental Performance
Me and Jerry, Chet Atkins and Jerry Reed

Best Gospel Performance (Other Than Soul Gospel)
"Talk About the Good Times," Oak Ridge Boys

Best Soul Gospel Performance
"Every Man Wants to Be Free," Edwin Hawkins Singers

Best Sacred Performance
"Everything Is Beautiful," Jake Hess

Best Ethnic or Traditional Recording
"Good Feelin'," T-Bone Walker (Polydor)

Best Instrumental Arrangement
"Theme From Z," Henry Mancini, arranger

Best Arrangement Accompanying Vocalist(s)
"Bridge Over Troubled Water," Paul Simon, Arthur Garfunkel, Jimmie Haskell, Ernie Freeman and Larry Knechtel, arrangers

Best Instrumental Composition
"*Airport* Love Theme," Alfred Newman, composer

Best Score From an Original Cast Show Album
Company, Stephen Sondheim, composer (Columbia)

Best Original Score Written for a Motion Picture or Television Special
Let It Be, John Lennon, Paul McCartney, George Harrison and Ringo Starr, composers

Album of the Year, Classical
Berlioz, *Les Troyens,* Colin Davis conducting Royal Opera House Orchestra and Chorus; solos: Vickers, Veasey and Lindholm (Philips)

Best Classical Performance, Orchestra
Stravinsky, *Le Sacre du Printemps,* Pierre Boulez conducting Cleveland Orchestra

Best Chamber Music Performance
Beethoven, *The Complete Piano Trios,* Eugene Istomin, Isaac Stern and Leonard Rose

Best Classical Performance, Instrumental Soloist(s) (With or Without Orchestra)
Brahms, *Double Concerto (Concerto in A Minor for Violin and Cello),* David Oistrakh and Mstislav Rostropovich

Best Choral Performance (Other Than Opera)
New Music of Charles Ives, Gregg Smith conducting Gregg Smith Singers and Columbia Chamber Ensemble

Best Opera Recording
Berlioz, *Les Troyens,* Colin Davis conducting Royal Opera House Orchestra and Chorus; solos: Vickers, Veasey and Lindholm (Philips)

Best Vocal Soloist Performance, Classical
Schubert, *Lieder,* Dietrich Fischer-Dieskau

Best Comedy Recording
The Devil Made Me Buy This Dress, Flip Wilson (Little David)

Best Spoken Word Recording
Why I Oppose the War in Vietnam, Dr. Martin Luther King, Jr. (Black Forum)

Best Recording for Children
Sesame Street, Sesame Street cast (Columbia)

Best Album Cover
Indianola Mississippi Seeds, Robert Lockart, cover design; Ivan Nagy, photography (ABC)

Best Album Notes
The World's Greatest Blues Singer, Chris Albertson, annotator (Columbia)

1971

Record of the Year
"It's Too Late," Carole King

Album of the Year
Tapestry, Carole King (Ode)

Song of the Year
"You've Got a Friend," Carole King, songwriter

Best New Artist of the Year
Carly Simon

Best Pop Vocal Performance, Male
"You've Got a Friend," James Taylor

Best Pop Vocal Performance, Female
Tapestry, Carole King

Best Pop Vocal Performance by a Group
Carpenters, Carpenters

Best Pop Instrumental Performance
Smackwater Jack, Quincy Jones

Best Rhythm and Blues Song
"Ain't No Sunshine," Bill Withers, songwriter

Best Rhythm and Blues Vocal Performance, Male
"A Natural Man," Lou Rawls

Best Rhythm and Blues Vocal Performance, Female
"Bridge Over Troubled Water," Aretha Franklin

Best Rhythm and Blues Vocal Performance by a Group
"Proud Mary," Ike and Tina Turner

Best Jazz Performance by a Soloist
The Bill Evans Album, Bill Evans

Best Jazz Performance by a Group
The Bill Evans Album, Bill Evans Trio

Best Jazz Performance by a Big Band
"New Orleans Suite," Duke Ellington

Best Country Song
"Help Me Make It Through the Night," Kris Kristofferson, songwriter

Best Country Vocal Performance, Male
"When You're Hot, You're Hot," Jerry Reed

Best Country Vocal Performance, Female
"Help Me Make It Through the Night," Sammi Smith

Best Country Vocal Performance by a Group
"After the Fire Is Gone," Conway Twitty and Loretta Lynn

Best Country Instrumental Performance
"Snowbird," Chet Atkins

Best Gospel Performance (Other Than Soul Gospel)
"Let Me Live," Charley Pride

Best Soul Gospel Performance
Put Your Hand in the Hand of the Man From Galilee, Shirley Caesar

Best Sacred Performance
Did You Think to Pray, Charley Pride

Best Ethnic or Traditional Recording
They Call Me Muddy Waters, Muddy Waters (Chess)

Best Instrumental Arrangement
"Theme From *Shaft,*" Isaac Hayes and Johnny Allen, arrangers

Best Arrangement Accompanying Vocalist(s)
"Uncle Albert/Admiral Halsey," Paul McCartney, arranger

Best Instrumental Composition
"Theme From *Summer of '42,*" Michel Legrand, composer

Best Score From an Original Cast Show Album
Godspell, Stephen Schwartz, composer and producer (Bell)

Best Original Score Written for a Motion Picture or Television Special
Shaft, Isaac Hayes, composer

Album of the Year, Classical
Horowitz Plays Rachmaninoff, Vladimir Horowitz (Columbia)

Best Classical Performance, Orchestra
Mahler, *Symphony No. 1 in D Major,* Carlo Maria Giulini conducting Chicago Symphony Orchestra

Carole King

Best Chamber Music Performance
Debussy, *Quartet in G Minor,* Ravel, *Quartet in F Major,* Juilliard Quartet

Best Classical Performance, Instrumental Soloist(s) (With Orchestra)
Villa-Lobos, *Concerto for Guitar,* Julian Bream; André Previn conducting London Symphony

Best Classical Performance, Instrumental Soloist(s) (Without Orchestra)
Horowitz Plays Rachmaninoff, Vladimir Horowitz

Best Opera Recording
Verdi, *Aïda,* Erich Leinsdorf conducting London Symphony Orchestra; solos: Price, Domingo, Milnes, Bumbry and Raimondi (RCA)

Best Choral Performance, Classical (Other Than Opera)
Berlioz, *Requiem,* Colin Davis conducting London Symphony Orchestra; Russell Burgess conducting Wandsworth School Boys Choir; Arthur Oldham conducting London Symphony Chorus

Best Classical Vocal Soloist Performance
Leontyne Price Sings Robert Schumann, Leontyne Price

Best Comedy Recording
This Is a Recording, Lily Tomlin (Polydor)

Best Spoken Word Recording
Desiderata, Les Crane (Warner Bros.)

Best Recording for Children
Bill Cosby Talks to Kids About Drugs, Bill Cosby (Uni)

Best Album Cover
Pollution, Dean O. Torrance, album design; Gene Brownell, art director (Prophesy)

Best Album Notes
Sam, Hard and Heavy, Sam Samudio, annotator (Atlantic)

1972

Record of the Year
"The First Time Ever I Saw Your Face," Roberta Flack

Album of the Year
The Concert for Bangla Desh, George Harrison, Ravi Shanker, Bob Dylan, Leon Russell, Ringo Starr, Billy Preston, Eric Clapton and Klaus Voormann (Apple)

Song of the Year
"The First Time Ever I Saw Your Face," Ewan MacColl, songwriter

Best New Artist of the Year
America

Best Pop Vocal Performance, Male
"Without You," Nilsson

Best Pop Vocal Performance, Female
"I Am Woman," Helen Reddy

Best Pop Vocal Performance by a Duo, Group or Chorus
"Where Is the Love," Roberta Flack and Donny Hathaway

Best Pop Instrumental Performance by an Instrumental Performer
"Outa-Space," Billy Preston

Best Pop Instumental Performance With Vocal Coloring
Black Moses, Isaac Hayes

Best Rhythm and Blues Song
"Papa Was a Rolling Stone," Barrett Strong and Norman Whitfield, songwriters

Best Rhythm and Blues Vocal Performance, Male
"Me and Mrs. Jones," Billy Paul

Best Rhythm and Blues Vocal Performance, Female
Young, Gifted and Black, Aretha Franklin

Roberta Flack

Best Rhythm and Blues Vocal Performance by a Duo, Group, or Chorus
"Papa Was a Rolling Stone," Temptations

Best Jazz Performance by a Soloist
"Alone at Last," Gary Burton

Best Jazz Performance by a Group
"First Light," Freddie Hubbard

Best Jazz Performance by a Big Band
"Toga Brava Suite," Duke Ellington

Best Country Vocal Performance, Female
"Happiest Girl in the Whole USA," Donna Fargo

Best Country Vocal Performance, Male
Charley Pride Sings Heart Songs, Charley Pride

Best Country Vocal Performance by a Duo or Group
"Class of '57," Statler Brothers

Best Country Instrumental Performance
Charlie McCoy/The Real McCoy, Charlie McCoy

Best Country Song
"Kiss an Angel Good Mornin'," Ben Peters, songwriter

Best Gospel Performance
L-O-V-E, Blackwood Brothers

Best Soul Gospel Performance
"Amazing Grace," Aretha Franklin

Best Inspirational Performance
He Touched Me, Elvis Presley

Best Ethnic or Traditional Recording
The London Muddy Waters Session, Muddy Waters (Chess)

Best Instrumental Arrangement
"Theme From *The French Connection*," Don Ellis, arranger

Best Arrangement Accompanying Vocalist
"What Are You Doing the Rest of Your Life," Michel Legrand, arranger

Best Instrumental Composition
"Brian's Song," Michel Legrand, composer

Best Score From an Original Cast Show Album
Don't Bother Me, I Can't Cope, Micki Grant, composer (Polydor)

Best Original Score Written for a Motion Picture or a Television Special
The Godfather, Nino Rota, composer

Album of the Year, Classical
Mahler, *Symphony No. 8 in E-Flat Major (Symphony of a Thousand),* Sir Georg Solti conducting Chicago Symphony Orchestra, Vienna Boys Choir, Vienna State Opera Chorus, Vienna Singverein Chorus and Soloists (London)

Best Classical Performance, Orchestra
Mahler, *Symphony No. 7 in E Minor,* Sir Georg Solti conducting Chicago Symphony Orchestra

Best Chamber Music Performance
Julian and John, Julian Bream and John Williams

Best Instrumental Soloist Performance, Classical (With Orchestra)
Brahms, *Concerto No. 2,* Artur Rubinstein

Best Instrumental Soloist Performance, Classical (Without Orchestra)
Horowitz Plays Chopin, Vladimir Horowitz

Best Opera Recording
Berlioz, *Benvenuto Cellini,* Colin Davis conducting BBC Symphony and Chorus of Covent Garden (Philips)

Best Choral Performance, Classical
Mahler, *Symphony No. 8 in E-Flat Major (Symphony of a Thousand),* Sir Georg Solti conducting Chicago Symphony Orchestra, Vienna Boys Choir, Vienna State Opera Chorus, Vienna Singverein Chorus and Soloists

Best Vocal Soloist Performance, Classical
Brahms, *Die Schöne Magelone,* Dietrich Fischer-Dieskau

Best Comedy Recording
FM and AM, George Carlin (Little David)

Best Spoken Word Recording
Lenny, Original Cast (Blue Thumb)

Best Recording for Children
The Electric Company, Lee Chamberlin, Bill Cosby and Rita Moreno (Warner Bros.)

Best Album Cover
The Siegel Schwall Band, Acy Lehman, art director; Harvey Dinnerstein, artist (Wooden Nickel)

Best Album Notes
Tom T. Hall's Greatest Hits, Tom T. Hall, annotator (Mercury)

Best Album Notes, Classical
Williams, *Symphony No. 2,* James Lyons, annotator (RCA)

1973

Record of the Year
"Killing Me Softly With His Song," Roberta Flack

Album of the Year
Innervisions, Stevie Wonder (Tamla/Motown)

Song of the Year
"Killing Me Softly With His Song," Norman Gimbel and Charles Fox, songwriters

Best New Artist of the Year
Bette Midler

Best Pop Vocal Performance, Male
"You Are the Sunshine of My Life," Stevie Wonder

Best Pop Vocal Performance, Female
"Killing Me Softly With His Song," Roberta Flack

Best Pop Vocal Performance by a Duo, Group or Chorus
"Neither One of Us" (Wants to Be the First to Say Goodbye), Gladys Knight and the Pips

Best Pop Instrumental Performance
"Also Sprach Zarathustra (2001)," Eumir Deodato

Best Rhythm and Blues Song
"Superstition," Stevie Wonder, songwriter

Best Rhythm and Blues Vocal Performance, Male
"Superstition," Stevie Wonder

Best Rhythm and Blues Vocal Performance, Female
"Master of Eyes," Aretha Franklin

Best Rhythm and Blues Vocal Performance by a Duo, Group or Chorus
"Midnight Train to Georgia," Gladys Knight and the Pips

Best Rhythm and Blues Instrumental Performance
"Hang on Sloopy," Ramsey Lewis

Best Jazz Performance by a Soloist
God Is in the House, Art Tatum

Best Jazz Performance by a Group
Supersax Plays Bird, Supersax

Best Jazz Performance by a Big Band
Giant Steps, Woody Herman

Best Country Song
"Behind Closed Doors," Kenny O'Dell, songwriter

Best Country Vocal Performance, Male
"Behind Closed Doors," Charlie Rich

Best Country Vocal Performance, Female
"Let Me Be There," Olivia Newton-John

Best Country Vocal Performance by a Duo or Group
"From the Bottle to the Bottom," Kris Kristofferson and Rita Coolidge

Best Country Instrumental Performance
"Dueling Banjos," Eric Weissberg and Steve Mandell

Best Gospel Performance
Release Me (From My Sin), Blackwood Brothers

Best Soul Gospel Performance
"Loves Me Like a Rock," Dixie Hummingbirds

Best Inspirational Performance
Let's Just Praise the Lord, Bill Gaither Trio

Best Ethnic or Traditional Recording
Then and Now, Doc Watson (United Artists)

Best Instrumental Arrangement
"Summer in the City," Quincy Jones, arranger

Best Arrangement Accompanying Vocalist
"Live and Let Die," George Martin, arranger

Best Instrumental Composition
"Last Tango in Paris," Gato Barbiera, composer

Best Score From an Original Cast Show Album
A Little Night Music, Stephen Sondheim, composer

Best Original Score Written for a Motion Picture or a Television Special
Jonathan Livingston Seagull, Neil Diamond, composer

Album of the Year, Classical
Bartók, *Concerto for Orchestra,* Pierre Boulez conducting New York Philharmonic Orchestra (Columbia)

Best Classical Performance, Orchestra
Bartók, *Concerto for Orchestra,* Pierre Boulez conducting New York Philharmonic Orchestra

Best Chamber Music Performance
Joplin, *The Red Back Book,* Gunther Schuller and the New England Conservatory Ragtime Ensemble

Best Classical Performance, Instrumental Soloist (With Orchestra)
Beethoven, *Concerti (5) for Piano and Orchestra,* Vladimir Ashkenazy; Sir Georg Solti conducting Chicago Symphony

Best Classical Performance, Instrumental Soloist (Without Orchestra)
Scriabin, *Horowitz Plays Scriabin,* Vladimir Horowitz

Best Opera Recording
Bizet, *Carmen,* Leonard Bernstein conducting The Metropolitan Opera Orchestra and Manhattan Opera Chorus; solos: Horne, McCracken, Maliponte and Krause (Deutsche Grammophon/Polydor)

Best Choral Performance, Classical
Walton, *Belshazzar's Feast,* André Previn conducting London Symphony Orchestra; Arthur Oldham conducting London Symphony Orchestra Chorus

Best Classical Vocal Soloist Performance
Puccini, *Heroines (La Boheme, Tosca, Manon Lescaut),* Leontyne Price; Downes conducting New Philharmonia

Best Comedy Recording
Los Cochinos, Cheech and Chong (Ode)

Best Spoken Word Recording
Jonathan Livingston Seagull, Richard Harris (Columbia)

Best Recording for Children
Sesame Street Live, Sesame Street cast (Columbia)

Best Album Package
Tommy, Wilkes and Braun, Inc., art director (Ode)

Best Album Notes
God Is in the House, Dan Morgenstern, annotator (Onyx)

Best Album Notes, Classical
Hindemith, *Sonatas for Piano (Complete),* Glenn Gould, annotator (Columbia)

1974

Record of the Year
"I Honestly Love You," Olivia Newton-John

Album of the Year
Fulfillingness' First Finale, Stevie Wonder (Tamla/Motown)

Song of the Year
"The Way We Were," Marilyn and Alan Bergman and Marvin Hamlisch, songwriters

Best New Artist of the Year
Marvin Hamlisch

Best Pop Vocal Performance, Male
Fulfillingness' First Finale, Stevie Wonder

Best Pop Vocal Performance, Female
"I Honestly Love You," Olivia Newton-John

Best Pop Vocal Performance by a Duo, Group or Chorus
"Band on the Run," Paul McCartney and Wings

Best Pop Instrumental Performance
"The Entertainer," Marvin Hamlisch

Best Rhythm and Blues Song
"Living for the City," Stevie Wonder, songwriter

Stevie Wonder

Best Rhythm and Blues Vocal Performance, Male
"Boogie on Reggae Woman," Stevie Wonder

Best Rhythm and Blues Vocal Performance, Female
"Ain't Nothing Like the Real Thing," Aretha Franklin

Best Rhythm and Blues Vocal Performance by a Duo, Group or Chorus
"Tell Me Something Good," Rufus

Best Rhythm and Blues Instrumental Performance
"TSOP" (The Sound of Philadelphia), MFSB

Best Jazz Performance by a Soloist
First Recordings!, Charlie Parker

Best Jazz Performance by a Group
The Trio, Oscar Peterson, Joe Pass and Niels Pedersen

Best Jazz Performance by a Big Band
Thundering Herd, Woody Herman

Best Country Song
"A Very Special Love Song," Norris Wilson and Billy Sherrill, songwriters

Best Country Vocal Performance, Male
"Please Don't Tell Me How the Story Ends," Ronnie Milsap

Best Country Vocal Performance, Female
Love Song, Anne Murray

Best Country Vocal Performance by a Duo or Group
"Fairytale," Pointer Sisters

Best Country Instrumental Performance
The Atkins-Travis Traveling Show, Chet Atkins and Merle Travis

Best Gospel Performance
"The Baptism of Jesse Taylor," Oak Ridge Boys

Best Soul Gospel Performance
In the Ghetto, James Cleveland and the Southern California Community Choir

Best Inspirational Performance
"How Great Thou Art," Elvis Presley

Best Ethnic or Traditional Recording
Two Days in November, Doc and Merle Watson

Best Instrumental Arrangement
"Threshold," Pat Williams, arranger

Best Arrangement Accompanying Vocalists
"Down to You," Joni Mitchell and Tom Scott, arrangers

Best Instrumental Composition
"Tubular Bells" (Theme From *The Exorcist*), Mike Oldfield, composer

Best Score From an Original Cast Show Album
Raisin, Judd Woldin and Robert Britten, composers (Columbia)

Album of Best Original Score Written for a Motion Picture or a Television Special
The Way We Were, Marvin Hamlisch and Alan and Marilyn Bergman, composers (Columbia)

Album of the Year, Classical
Berlioz, *Symphonie Fantastique,* Sir Georg Solti conducting Chicago Symphony (London)

Best Classical Performance, Orchestra
Berlioz, *Symphonie Fantastique,* Sir Georg Solti conducting Chicago Symphony

Best Chamber Music Performance
Brahms and Schumann Trios, Artur Rubinstein, Henryk Szeryng and Pierre Fournier

Best Classical Performance, Instrumental Soloist(s) (With Orchestra)
Shostakovich, *Violin Concerto No. 1,* David Oistrakh

Best Classical Performance, Instrumental Soloist(s) (Without Orchestra)
Albeniz, *Iberia,* Alicia de Larrocha

Captain and Tennille

Best Opera Recording
Puccini, *La Boheme,* Sir Georg Solti conducting London Philharmonic; solos: Caballé, Domingo, Milnes, Blegen and Raimondi (RCA)

Best Choral Performance, Classical (Other Than Opera)
Berlioz, *The Damnation of Faust,* Colin Davis conducting London Symphony Orchestra and Chorus, Ambrosian Singers and Wandsworth School Boys' Choir; solos: Gedda, Bastin, Veasey and Van Allen

Best Classical Vocal Soloist Performance
Leontyne Price Sings Richard Strauss, Leontyne Price

Best Comedy Recording
That Nigger's Crazy, Richard Pryor (Partee/Stax)

Best Spoken Word Recording
Good Evening, Peter Cook and Dudley Moore (Island)

Best Recording for Children
Winnie the Pooh and Tigger Too, Sebastian Cabot, Sterling Holloway and Paul Winchell (Disneyland)

Best Album Package
Come and Gone, Ed Thrasher and Christopher Whorf, art directors (Warner Bros.)

Best Album Notes (tie)
For the Last Time, Charles R. Townsend, annotator (United Artists)

The Hawk Flies, Dan Morgenstern, annotator (Milestone)

Best Album Notes, Classical
The Classic Erich Wolfgang Korngold, Rory Guy, annotator (Angel)

Best Producer of the Year
Thom Bell

1975

Record of the Year
"Love Will Keep Us Together," Captain and Tennille

Album of the Year
Still Crazy After All These Years, Paul Simon (Columbia)

Song of the Year
"Send in the Clowns," Stephen Sondheim, songwriter

Best New Artist of the Year
Natalie Cole

Best Pop Vocal Performance, Male
Still Crazy After All These Years, Paul Simon

Best Pop Vocal Performance, Female
"At Seventeen," Janis Ian

Best Pop Vocal Performance by a Duo, Group or Chorus
"Lyin' Eyes," Eagles

Best Pop Instrumental Performance
"The Hustle," Van McCoy and the Soul City Symphony

Best Rhythm and Blues Song
"Where Is the Love," Harry Wayne Casey, Richard Finch,
    Willie Clarke and Betty Wright, songwriters

Best Rhythm and Blues Vocal Performance, Male
"Living for the City," Ray Charles

Best Rhythm and Blues Vocal Performance, Female
"This Will Be," Natalie Cole

Best Rhythm and Blues Vocal Performance by a Duo, Group or Chorus
"Shining Star," Earth, Wind and Fire

Best Rhythm and Blues Instrumental Performance
"Fly, Robin, Fly," Silver Convention

Best Jazz Performance by a Soloist
Oscar Peterson and Dizzy Gillespie, Dizzy Gillespie

Best Jazz Performance by a Group
No Mystery, Chick Corea and Return to Forever

Best Jazz Performance by a Big Band
Images, Phil Woods with Michel Legrand and His Orchestra

Best Country Song
(Hey Won't You Play) "Another Somebody Done Somebody
    Wrong Song," Chips Moman and Larry Butler,
    songwriters

Best Country Vocal Performance, Male
"Blue Eyes Crying in the Rain," Willie Nelson

Best Country Vocal Performance, Female
"I Can't Help It" (If I'm Still in Love With You), Linda Ronstadt

Best Country Vocal Performance by a Duo or Group
"Lover Please," Kris Kristofferson and Rita Coolidge

Best Country Instrumental Performance
"The Entertainer," Chet Atkins

Best Gospel Performance
No Shortage, Imperials

Best Soul Gospel Performance
Take Me Back, Andrae Crouch and the Disciples

Best Latin Recording
Sun of Latin Music, Eddie Palmieri (Coco)

Best Inspirational Performance
Jesus, We Just Want to Thank You, Bill Gaither Trio

Best Ethnic or Traditional Recording
The Muddy Waters Woodstock Album, Muddy Waters (Chess)

Best Instrumental Arrangement
"The Rockford Files," Mike Post and Pete Carpenter,
    arrangers

Best Arrangement Accompanying Vocalists
"Misty," Ray Stevens, arranger

Best Instrumental Composition
"Images," Michel Legrand, composer

Best Cast Show Album
The Wiz, Charlie Smalls, composer (Atlantic)

Album of Best Original Score Written for a Motion Picture or a Television Special
Jaws, John Williams, composer (MCA)

Album of the Year, Classical
Beethoven, *Symphonies Complete,* Sir Georg Solti conducting
    Chicago Symphony Orchestra (London)

Best Classical Performance, Orchestra
Ravel, *Daphnis et Chloè (Complete Ballet),* Pierre Boulez con-
    ducting New York Philharmonic

Best Chamber Music Performance (Instrumental or Vocal)
Schubert, *Trios nos. 1 in B-Flat Major, ops. 99 and 2 in E-Flat
    Major, Op. 11 (The Piano Trios),* Artur Rubinstein, Henryk
    Szeryng and Pierre Fournier

Best Classical Performance, Instrumental Soloist (With Orchestra)
Ravel, *Concerto for Left Hand and Concerto for Piano in G
    Major;* Fauré, *Fantaisie for Piano and Orchestra,* Alicia de
    Lorrocha; De Burgos and Foster conducting London
    Philharmonic

Best Classical Performance, Instrumental Soloist (Without Orchestra)
Bach, *Sonatas and Partitas for Violin Unaccompanied,* Nathan
    Milstein

Best Opera Recording
Mozart, *Cosi fan Tutte,* Colin Davis conducting Royal Opera
    House, Covent Garden; principle solos: Caballé, Baker,
    Gedda, Ganzarolli, Van Allan and Cotrubas (Philips)

Best Choral Performance, Classical
Orff, *Carmina Burana,* Robert Page directing the Cleveland
    Orchestra Chorus and Boys Choir; Michael Tilson Thomas
    conducting Cleveland Orchestra; soloists: Blegen, Binder
    and Riegel

Best Classical Vocal Soloist Performance
Mahler, *Kindertotenlieder,* Janet Baker; Leonard Bernstein
    conducting Israel Philharmonic

Best Comedy Recording
Is It Something I Said?, Richard Pryor (Reprise)

Best Spoken Word Recording
Give 'Em Hell Harry, James Whitmore (United Artists)

Best Recording for Children
The Little Prince, Richard Burton, narrator (RIP)

Best Album Package
Honey, Jim Ladwig, art director (Mercury)

Best Album Notes (Non-Classical)
Blood on the Tracks, Pete Hamill, annotator (Columbia)

Best Album Notes, Classical
Footlifters, Gunther Schuller, annotator (Columbia)

Best Producer of the Year
Arif Mardin

1976

Record of the Year
"This Masquerade," George Benson

Album of the Year
Songs in the Key of Life, Stevie Wonder (Tamla/Motown)

Song of the Year
"I Write the Songs," Bruce Johnston, songwriter

Best New Artist of the Year
Starland Vocal Band

Best Pop Vocal Performance, Male
Songs in the Key of Life, Stevie Wonder

Best Pop Vocal Performance, Female
Hasten Down the Wind, Linda Ronstadt

Best Pop Vocal Performance by a Duo, Group or Chorus
"If You Leave Me Now," Chicago

Best Pop Instrumental Performance
Breezin', George Benson

Best Rhythm and Blues Song
"Lowdown," Boz Scaggs and David Paich, songwriters

Best Rhythm and Blues Vocal Performance, Male
"I Wish," Stevie Wonder

Best Rhythm and Blues Vocal Performance, Female
"Sophisticated Lady" (She's a Different Lady), Natalie Cole

Best Rhythm and Blues Vocal Performance by a Duo, Group or Chorus
"You Don't Have to Be a Star" (To Be in My Show), Marilyn McCoo and Billy Davis, Jr.

Best Rhythm and Blues Instrumental Performance
"Theme From *Good King Bad*," George Benson

Best Jazz Vocal Performance
Fitzgerald & Pass Again, Ella Fitzgerald

Best Jazz Performance by a Soloist
Basie and Zoot, Count Basie

Best Jazz Performance by a Big Band
The Ellington Suites, Duke Ellington

Best Country Song
"Broken Lady," Larry Gatlin, songwriter

Best Country Vocal Performance, Male
(I'm a) "Stand by My Woman Man," Ronnie Milsap

Best Country Vocal Performance, Female
Elite Hotel, Emmylou Harris

Best Country Vocal Performance by a Duo or Group
"The End Is Not in Sight" (The Cowboy Tune), Amazing Rhythm Aces

Best Country Instrumental Performance
Chester and Lester, Chet Atkins and Les Paul

Best Gospel Performance
"Where the Soul Never Dies," Oak Ridge Boys

Best Soul Gospel Performance
How I Got Over, Mahalia Jackson

Best Latin Recording
Unfinished Masterpiece, Eddie Palmieri (Coco)

Best Inspirational Performance
The Astonishing, Outrageous, Amazing, Incredible, Unbelievable, Different World of Gary S. Paxton, Gary S. Paxton

Best Ethnic or Traditional Recording
Mark Twang, John Hartford (Flying Fish)

Best Instrumental Arrangement
"Leprechaun's Dream," Chick Corea, arranger

Vladimir Horowitz

Best Arrangement Accompanying Vocalists
"If You Leave Me Now," Jimmy Haskell and James William Guercio, arrangers

Best Arrangement for Voices
"Afternoon Delight," Starland Vocal Band, arrangers

Best Instrumental Composition
Bellavia, Chuck Mangione, composer

Best Cast Show Album
Bubbling Brown Sugar, various composers (H&L)

Album of Best Original Score Written for a Motion Picture or a Television Special
Car Wash, Norman Whitfield, composer (MCA)

Album of the Year, Classical
Beethoven, *Five Piano Concertos*, Artur Rubinstein; Daniel Barenboim conducting London Philharmonic (RCA)

Best Classical Orchestral Performance
Strauss, *Also Sprach Zarathustra*, Sir Georg Solti conducting Chicago Symphony

Best Chamber Music Performance
The Art of Courtly Love, David Munrow conducting Early Music Consort of London

Best Classical Performance, Instrumental Soloist (With Orchestra)
Beethoven, *The Five Piano Concertos*, Artur Rubinstein; Daniel Barenboim conducting London Philharmonic

Best Classical Performance, Instrumental Soloist (Without Orchestra)
Horowitz Concerts 1975/76, Vladimir Horowitz

Best Opera Recording
Gershwin, *Porgy and Bess*, Lorin Maazel conducting Cleveland Orchestra and Chorus (London)

Best Choral Performance, Classical
Rachmaninoff, *The Bells*, Arthur Oldham, Chorus master of London Symphony Chorus; André Previn conducting London Symphony Orchestra

Best Classical Vocal Soloist Performance
Music of Victor Herbert, Beverly Sills

Best Comedy Recording
Bicentennial Nigger, Richard Pryor (Warner Bros.)

Best Spoken Word Recording
Great American Documents, Orson Welles, Henry Fonda, Helen Hayes and James Earl Jones (CBS)

Best Recording for Children
Prokofiev, *Peter and the Wolf*; Saint-Saëns, *Carnival of the Animals*, Hermione Gingold, narrator; Karl Bohm, conductor (Deutsche Grammophon)

Best Album Package
Chicago X, John Berg, art director (Columbia)

Best Album Notes
The Changing Face of Harlem, the Savoy Sessions, Dan Morgenstern, annotator (Savoy)

Best Producer of the Year
Stevie Wonder

1977

Record of the Year
"Hotel California," Eagles

Album of the Year
Rumours, Fleetwood Mac (Warner Bros.)

Song of the Year (tie)
"Love Theme From *A Star Is Born*" (Evergreen), Barbra Streisand and Paul Williams, songwriters
"You Light Up My Life," Joe Brooks, songwriter

Best New Artist of the Year
Debby Boone

Best Pop Vocal Performance, Male
"Handy Man," James Taylor

Best Pop Vocal Performance, Female
"Love Theme From *A Star Is Born*" (Evergreen),
Barbra Streisand

Best Pop Vocal Performance by a Duo, Group or Chorus
"How Deep Is Your Love," Bee Gees

Best Pop Instrumental Performance
Star Wars, John Williams conducting London
Symphony Orchestra

Best Rhythm and Blues Song
"You Make Me Feel Like Dancing," Leo Sayer and
Vini Poncia, songwriters

Best Rhythm and Blues Vocal Performance, Male
Unmistakably Lou, Lou Rawls

Best Rhythm and Blues Vocal Performance, Female
"Don't Leave Me This Way," Thelma Houston

Best Rhythm and Blues Vocal Performance by a Duo, Group or Chorus
"Best of My Love," Emotions

Best Rhythm and Blues Instrumental Performance
"Q," Brothers Johnson

Best Jazz Vocal Performance
Look to the Rainbow, Al Jarreau

Best Jazz Performance by a Soloist
The Giants, Oscar Peterson

Best Jazz Performance by a Group
The Phil Woods Six — Live From the Showboat, Phil Woods

Best Jazz Performance by a Big Band
Prime Time, Count Basie and His Orchestra

Best Country Song
"Don't It Make My Brown Eyes Blue," Richard Leigh,
songwriter

Best Country Vocal Performance, Male
"Lucille," Kenny Rogers

Best Country Vocal Performance, Female
"Don't It Make My Brown Eyes Blue," Crystal Gayle

Best Country Vocal Performance by a Duo or Group
"Heaven's Just a Sin Away," The Kendalls

Best Country Instrumental Performance
Country Instrumentalist of the Year, Hargus "Pig" Robbins

Best Gospel Performance, Contemporary or Inspirational
Sail On, Imperials

Best Gospel Performance, Traditional
"Just a Little Talk With Jesus," Oak Ridge Boys

Best Soul Gospel Performance, Contemporary
Wonderful!, Edwin Hawkins and the Edwin Hawkins Singers

Best Soul Gospel Performance, Traditional
James Cleveland Live at Carnegie Hall, James Cleveland

Best Latin Recording
Dawn, Mongo Santamaria (Vaya)

Best Inspirational Performance
Home Where I Belong, B.J. Thomas

Best Ethnic or Traditional Recording
Hard Again, Muddy Waters (Blue Sky/CBS)

Best Instrumental Arrangement
"Nadia's Theme" (The Young and the Restless), Harry Betts,
Perry Botkin, Jr. and Barry De Vorzon, arrangers

Eagles

Best Arrangement Accompanying Vocalist(s)
"Love Theme From *A Star Is Born*" (Evergreen), Ian Freebairn-
Smith, arranger

Best Arrangement for Voices
"New Kid in Town," Eagles, arrangers

Best Instrumental Composition
"Main Title From *Star Wars,*" John Williams, composer

Best Cast Show Album
Annie, Charles Strouse and Martin Charnin, composers
(Columbia)

Best Original Score Written for a Motion Picture or Television Special
Star Wars, John Williams, composer (20th Century)

Album of the Year, Classical
Concert of the Century, Leonard Bernstein, Vladimir Horowitz,
Isaac Stern, Mstislav Rostropovich, Dietrich Fischer-
Dieskau, Yehudi Menuhin and Lyndon Woodside
(Columbia)

Best Classical Orchestral Performance
Mahler, *Symphony No. 9,* Carlo Maria Giulini conducting
Chicago Symphony Orchestra

Best Chamber Music Performance
Schoenberg, *Quartets for Strings,* Juilliard Quartet

Best Classical Performance, Instrumental Soloist(s) (With Orchestra)
Vivaldi, *The Four Seasons,* Itzhak Perlman, violin; Itzhak
Perlman conducting London Philharmonic Orchestra

Best Classical Performance Instrumental Soloist(s) (Without Orchestra)
Beethoven, *Sonata for Piano No. 18;* Schumann,
Fantasiestücke, Artur Rubinstein, piano

Best Opera Recording
Gershwin, *Porgy and Bess,* John De Main conducting Sherwin
M. Goldman Houston Grand Opera Production; solos:
Albert, Dale, Smith, Shakesnider, Lane, Brice and Smalls
(RCA)

Best Choral Performance, Classical (Other Than Opera)
Verdi, *Requiem,* Sir Georg Solti conducting Chicago Symphony
Orchestra; Margaret Hillis, choral director of the Chicago
Symphony Chorus

Best Classical Vocal Soloist Performance
Bach, *Arias,* Janet Baker; Neville Marriner conducting
Academy of St. Martin-in-the-Fields

Best Comedy Recording
Let's Get Small, Steve Martin (Warner Bros.)

Best Spoken Word Recording
The Belle of Amherst, Julie Harris (Credo)

Best Recording for Children
Aren't You Glad You're You, Sesame Street cast and Muppets (Sesame Street)

Best Album Package
Simple Dreams, Kosh, art director (Asylum)

Best Album Notes
Bing Crosby: A Legendary Performer, George T. Simon, annotator (RCA)

Best Producer of the Year
Peter Asher

1978

Record of the Year
"Just the Way You Are," Billy Joel

Album of the Year
Saturday Night Fever, Bee Gees, David Shire, Yvonne Elliman, Tevares, Kool and the Gang, K.C. and the Sunshine Band, MFSB, Trammps, Walter Murphy and Ralph MacDonald (RSO)

Song of the Year
"Just the Way You Are," Billy Joel, songwriter

Best New Artist of the Year
A Taste of Honey

Best Pop Vocal Performance, Male
"Copacabana" (At the Copa), Barry Manilow

Best Pop Vocal Performance, Female
"You Needed Me," Anne Murray

Best Pop Vocal Performance by a Duo, Group or Chorus
Saturday Night Fever, Bee Gees

Best Pop Instrumental Performance
Children of Sanchez, Chuck Mangione Group

Best Rhythm and Blues Song
"Last Dance," Paul Jabara, songwriter

Best Rhythm and Blues Vocal Performance, Male
"On Broadway," George Benson

Best Rhythm and Blues Vocal Performance, Female
"Last Dance," Donna Summer

Best Rhythm and Blues Vocal Performance by a Duo, Group or Chorus
All 'n All, Earth, Wind and Fire

Best Rhythm and Blues Instrumental Performance
"Runnin'," Earth, Wind and Fire

Best Jazz Vocal Performance
All Fly Home, Al Jarreau

Best Jazz Instrumental Performance, Soloist
Montreux '77 Oscar Peterson Jam, Oscar Peterson

Best Jazz Instrumental Performance, Group
Friends, Chick Corea

Best Jazz Instrumental Performance, Big Band
Live in Munich, Thad Jones and Mel Lewis

Best Country Song
"The Gambler," Don Schlitz, songwriter

Best Country Vocal Performance, Male
"Georgia on My Mind," Willie Nelson

Best Country Vocal Performance, Female
Here You Come Again, Dolly Parton

Best Country Vocal Performance by a Duo or Group
"Mamas Don't Let Your Babies Grow Up to Be Cowboys," Waylon Jennings and Willie Nelson

Billy Joel

Best Country Instrumental Performance
"One O'Clock Jump," Asleep at the Wheel

Best Gospel Performance, Contemporary or Inspirational
"What a Friend," Larry Hart

Best Gospel Performance, Traditional
Refreshing, Happy Goodman Family

Best Soul Gospel Performance, Contemporary
Live in London, Andrae Crouch and the Disciples

Best Soul Gospel Performance, Traditional
Live and Direct, Mighty Clouds of Joy

Best Latin Recording
Homenaje a Beny Moré, Tito Puente (Tico)

Best Inspirational Performance
Happy Man, B.J. Thomas

Best Ethnic or Traditional Recording
I'm Ready, Muddy Waters (Blue Sky)

Best Instrumental Arrangement
"Main Title" (Overture Part One, *The Wiz* Original Soundtrack), Quincy Jones and Robert Freedman, arrangers

Best Arrangement Accompanying Vocalist(s)
"Got to Get You Into My Life," Maurice White, arranger

Best Arrangement for Voices
"Stayin' Alive," Bee Gees, arrangers

Best Instrumental Composition
"Theme From *Close Encounters of the Third Kind*," John Williams, composer

Best Cast Show Album
Ain't Misbehavin', Thomas "Fats" Waller and others, composers (RCA Red Seal)

Best Album of Original Score Written for a Motion Picture or a Television Special
Close Encounters of the Third Kind, John Williams, composer (Arista)

Album of the Year, Classical
Brahms, *Concerto for Violin in D Major*, Itzhak Perlman; Carlo Maria Giulini conducting Chicago Symphony (Angel)

Best Classical Orchestral Performance
Beethoven, *Symphonies (Complete)*, Herbert von Karajan conducting Berlin Philharmonic

Best Chamber Music Performance
Beethoven, *Sonatas for Violin and Piano (Complete)*, Itzhak Perlman and Vladimir Ashkenazy

Best Classical Performance, Instrumental Soloist(s) (With Orchestra)
Rachmaninoff, *Concerto No. 3 in D Minor for Piano (Horowitz Golden Jubilee),* Vladimir Horowitz; Eugene Ormandy conducting Philadelphia Orchestra

Best Classical Performance, Instrumental Soloist(s) (Without Orchestra)
The Horowitz Concerts 1977/78, Vladimir Horowitz

Best Opera Recording
Lehar, *The Merry Widow,* Julius Rudel conducting New York City Opera Orchestra and Chorus; solos: Sills and Titus (Angel)

Best Choral Performance, Classical (Other Than Opera)
Beethoven, *Missa Solemnis,* Sir Georg Solti, conductor and Margaret Hillis, choral director, Chicago Symphony Orchestra and Chorus

Best Classical Vocal Soloist Performance
Luciano Pavarotti — Hits From Lincoln Center, Luciano Pavarotti

Best Comedy Recording
A Wild and Crazy Guy, Steve Martin (Warner Bros.)

Best Spoken Word Recording
Citizen Kane (Original Motion Picture Soundtrack), Orson Welles (Mark 56)

Best Recording for Children
The Muppet Show, Jim Henson (Arista)

Best Album Package
Boys in the Trees, Johnny Lee and Tony Lane, art directors (Elektra)

Best Album Notes
A Bing Crosby Collection, vols. I and II, Michael Brooks, annotator (Columbia)

Best Historical Repackage Album
Lester Young Story Vol. 3 (Columbia)

Best Producers of the Year
Bee Gees, Albhy Galuten and Karl Richardson

1979

Record of the Year
"What a Fool Believes," Doobie Brothers

Album of the Year
52nd Street, Billy Joel (Columbia)

Gloria Gaynor

Song of the Year
"What a Fool Believes," Kenny Loggins and Michael McDonald, songwriters

Best New Artist
Rickie Lee Jones

Best Pop Vocal Performance, Male
52nd Street, Billy Joel

Best Pop Vocal Performance, Female
"I'll Never Love This Way Again," Dionne Warwick

Best Pop Vocal Performance by a Duo, Group or Chorus
Minute by Minute, Doobie Brothers

Best Pop Instrumental Performance
"Rise," Herb Alpert

Best Rock Vocal Performance, Male
"Gotta Serve Somebody," Bob Dylan

Best Rock Vocal Performance, Female
"Hot Stuff," Donna Summer

Best Rock Vocal Performance by a Duo or Group
"Heartache Tonight," Eagles

Best Rock Instrumental Performance
"*Rockestra* Theme," Wings

Best Rhythm and Blues Song
"After the Love Has Gone," David Foster, Jay Graydon and Bill Champlin, songwriters

Best Rhythm and Blues Vocal Performance, Male
"Don't Stop 'Til You Get Enough," Michael Jackson

Best Rhythm and Blues Vocal Performance, Female
"Deja Vu," Dionne Warwick

Best Rhythm and Blues Vocal Performance by a Duo, Group or Chorus
"After the Love Has Gone," Earth, Wind and Fire

Best Rhythm and Blues Instrumental Performance
"Boogie Wonderland," Earth, Wind and Fire

Best Disco Recording
"I Will Survive," Gloria Gaynor (Polydor)

Best Jazz Vocal Performance
Fine and Mellow, Ella Fitzgerald

Best Jazz Instrumental Performance, Soloist
Jousts, Oscar Peterson

Best Jazz Instrumental Performance, Group
Duet, Gary Burton and Chick Corea

Best Jazz Instrumental Performance, Big Band
At Fargo, 1940 Live, Duke Ellington

Best Jazz Fusion Performance, Vocal or Instrumental
8:30, Weather Report

Best Country Song
"You Decorated My Life," Debbie Hupp and Bob Morrison, songwriters

Best Country Vocal Performance, Male
"The Gambler," Kenny Rogers

Best Country Vocal Performance, Female
Blue Kentucky Girl, Emmylou Harris

Best Country Vocal Performance by a Duo or Group
"The Devil Went Down to Georgia," Charlie Daniels Band

Best Country Instrumental Performance
"Big Sandy/Leather Britches," Doc and Merle Watson

Best Gospel Performance, Contemporary or Inspirational
Heed the Call, Imperials

Best Gospel Performance, Traditional
Lift Up the Name of Jesus, Blackwood Brothers

Best Soul Gospel Performance, Contemporary
I'll Be Thinking of You, Andrae Crouch

Best Soul Gospel Performance, Traditional
Changing Times, Mighty Clouds of Joy

Best Latin Recording
Irakere, Irakere (Columbia)

Best Inspirational Performance
You Gave Me Love (When Nobody Gave Me a Prayer), B.J. Thomas

Best Ethnic or Traditional Recording
Muddy "Mississippi" Waters Live, Muddy Waters (Sky/CBS)

Best Instrumental Arrangement
"Soulful Strut," Claus Ogerman, arranger

Best Arrangement Accompanying Vocalist(s)
"What a Fool Believes," Michael McDonald, arranger

Best Instrumental Composition
"Main Title Theme From *Superman,*" John Williams, composer

Best Cast Show Album
Sweeney Todd, Stephen Sondheim, composer and lyricist (RCA)

Best Album of Original Score Written for a Motion Picture or a Television Special
Superman, John Williams, composer (Warner Bros.)

Best Classical Album
Brahms, *Symphonies Complete,* Sir Georg Solti conducting Chicago Symphony Orchestra (London)

Best Classical Orchestral Recording
Brahms, *Symphonies Complete,* Sir Georg Solti conducting Chicago Symphony Orchestra (London)

Best Chamber Music Performance
Copland, *Appalachian Spring,* Dennis Russell Davies conducting St. Paul Chamber Orchestra

Best Classical Performance, Instrumental Soloist(s) (With Orchestra)
Bartók, *Concertos for Piano nos. 1 and 2,* Maurizio Pollini; Abbado conducting Chicago Symphony Orchestra

Best Classical Performance, Instrumental Soloist(s) (Without Orchestra)
The Horowitz Concerts 1978/79, Vladimir Horowitz

Best Opera Recording
Britten, *Peter Grimes,* Colin Davis conducting Orchestra and Chorus of the Royal Opera House, Covent Garden; solos: Vickers, Harper and Summers (Philips)

Best Choral Performance, Classical (Other Than Opera)
Brahms, *A German Requiem,* Sir Georg Solti, conductor and Margaret Hillis, choral director, Chicago Symphony Chorus and Orchestra

Best Classical Vocal Soloist Performance
O Sole Mio, Luciano Pavarotti

Best Comedy Recording
Reality . . . What a Concept, Robin Williams (Casablanca)

Best Spoken Word, Documentary or Drama Recording
Ages of Man (Readings From Shakespeare), Sir John Gielgud (Caedmon)

Best Recording for Children
The Muppet Movie, Jim Henson, creator (Atlantic)

Best Album Package
Breakfast in America, Mike Doud and Mick Haggerty, art directors (A&M)

Best Album Notes
Charlie Parker: The Complete Savoy Sessions, Bob Porter and James Patrick, annotators (Savoy)

Best Historical Reissue
Billie Holiday (Giants of Jazz) (Time Life)

Producer of the Year (Non-Classical)
Larry Butler

Classical Producer of the Year
James Mallinson

1980

Record of the Year
"Sailing," Christopher Cross

Album of the Year
Christopher Cross, Christopher Cross (Warner Bros.)

Song of the Year
"Sailing," Christopher Cross, songwriter

Best New Artist
Christopher Cross

Best Pop Vocal Performance, Male
"This Is It," Kenny Loggins

Best Pop Vocal Performance, Female
"The Rose," Bette Midler

Best Pop Performance by a Duo or Group With Vocal
"Guilty," Barbra Streisand and Barry Gibb

Best Pop Instrumental Performance
One on One, Bob James and Earl Klugh

Best Rock Vocal Performance, Male
Glass Houses, Billy Joel

Best Rock Vocal Performance, Female
Crimes of Passion, Pat Benatar

Best Rock Performance by a Duo or Group With Vocal
Against the Wind, Bob Seger and the Silver Bullet Band

Best Rock Instrumental Performance
"Reggatta de Blanc," Police

Best Rhythm and Blues Song
"Never Knew Love Like This Before," Reggie Lucas and James Mtume, songwriters

Best Rhythm and Blues Performance, Male
Give Me the Night, George Benson

Best Rhythm and Blues Vocal Performance, Female
"Never Knew Love Like This Before," Stephanie Mills

Best Rhythm and Blues Performance by a Duo or Group With Vocal
"Shining Star," Manhattans

Best Rhythm and Blues Instrumental Performance
"Off Broadway," George Benson

Best Jazz Vocal Performance, Male
"Moody's Mood," George Benson

Best Jazz Vocal Performance, Female
A Perfect Match/Ella and Basie, Ella Fitzgerald

Best Jazz Instrumental Performance, Soloist
I Will Say Goodbye, Bill Evans

Best Jazz Instrumental Performance, Group
We Will Meet Again, Bill Evans

Best Jazz Instrumental Performance, Big Band
On the Road, Count Basie and Orchestra

Best Jazz Fusion Performance, Vocal or Instrumental
"Birdland," Manhattan Transfer

Best Country Song
"On the Road Again," Willie Nelson, songwriter

Best Country Vocal Performance, Male
"He Stopped Loving Her Today," George Jones

Best Country Vocal Performance, Female
"Could I Have This Dance," Anne Murray

Best Country Performance by a Duo or Group With Vocal
"That Lovin' You Feelin' Again," Roy Orbison and Emmylou Harris

Best Country Instrumental Performance
"Orange Blossom Special/Hoedown," Gilley's Urban Cowboy Band

Yoko Ono and John Lennon

Best Gospel Performance, Contemporary or Inspirational
The Lord's Prayer, Reba Rambo, Dony McGuire, B.J. Thomas, Andrae Crouch, the Archers, Walter and Tramiane Hawkins and Cynthia Clawson

Best Gospel Performance, Traditional
We Come to Worship, Blackwood Brothers

Best Soul Gospel Performance, Contemporary
Rejoice, Shirley Caesar

Best Soul Gospel Performance, Traditional
Lord, Let Me Be an Instrument, James Cleveland and the Charles Fold Singers

Best Latin Recording
La Onda Va Bien, Cal Tjader (Concord Jazz)

Best Inspirational Performance
With My Song I Will Praise Him, Debby Boone

Best Ethnic or Traditional Recording
Rare Blues, Dr. Isaiah Ross, Maxwell Street Jimmy, Big Joe Williams, Son House, Rev. Robin Wilkins, Little Brother Montgomery and Sunnyland Slim (Takoma)

Best Instrumental Arrangement
"Dinorah, Dinorah," Quincy Jones and Jerry Hey, arrangers

Best Arrangement Accompanying Vocalist(s)
"Sailing," Michael Omatian and Christopher Cross, arrangers

Best Arrangement for Voices
"Birdland," Janis Siegel, arranger

Best Instrumental Composition
The Empire Strikes Back, John Williams, composer

Best Cast Show Album
Evita — Premier American Recording, Andrew Lloyd Webber, composer; Tim Rice, lyricist (MCA)

Best Album of Original Score Written for a Motion Picture or a Television Special
The Empire Strikes Back, John Williams, composer (RSO)

Best Classical Album
Berg, *Lulu (Complete Version),* Pierre Boulez conducting Orchestre de l'Opera de Paris; solos: Stratas, Minton, Mazura and Blankenheim (Deutsche Grammophon)

Best Classical Orchestral Recording
Bruckner, *Symphony No. 6 in A Major,* Sir Georg Solti conducting Chicago Symphony Orchestra (London)

Best Chamber Music Performance
Music for Two Violins (Moszkowski, *Suite for Two Violins;* Shostakovich, *Duets;* Prokofiev, *Sonata for Two Violins*), Itzhak Perlman and Pinchas Zukerman

Best Classical Performance, Instrumental Soloist(s) (With Orchestra) (tie)
Berg, *Concerto for Violin and Orchestra;* Stravinsky, *Concerto in D Major for Violin and Orchestra,* Itzhak Perlman; Seiji Ozawa conducting Boston Symphony Orchestra

Brahms, *Concerto in A Minor for Violin and Cello (Double Concerto),* Itzhak Perlman and Mstislav Rostropovich; Bernard Haitink conducting Concertgebouw Orchestra

Best Classical Performance Instrumental Soloist(s) (Without Orchestra)
The Spanish Album, Itzhak Perlman

Best Opera Recording
Berg, *Lulu (Complete Version),* Pierre Boulez conducting Orchestre de l'Opera de Paris; solos: Stratas, Minton, Mazura and Blankenheim

Best Choral Performance, Classical (Other Than Opera)
Mozart, *Requiem,* Carlo Maria Giulini, conductor and Norbert Balatsch, chorus master, Philharmonia Chorus and Orchestra (Deutsche Grammophon)

Best Classical Vocal Soloist Performance
Prima Donna, Volume 5 Great Soprano Arias From Handel to Britten, Leontyne Price; Henry Lewis conducting Philharmonia Orchestra

Best Comedy Recording
No Respect, Rodney Dangerfield (Casablanca)

Best Spoken Word, Documentary or Drama Recording
Gertrude Stein, Gertrude Stein, Gertrude Stein, Pat Carroll (Caedmon)

Best Recording for Children
In Harmony/A Sesame Street Record, Doobie Brothers, James Taylor, Carly Simon, Bette Midler, Muppets, Al Jarreau, Linda Ronstadt, Wendy Waldman, Libby Titus and Dr. John, Livingston Taylor, George Benson and Pauline Wilson, Lucy Simon, Kate Taylor and the Simon/Taylor Family (Sesame Street/Warner Bros.)

Best Album Package
Against the Wind, Roy Kohara, art director (Capitol)

Best Album Notes
Trilogy: Past, Present and Future, David McClintick, annotator (Reprise/Warner Bros.)

Best Historical Reissue Album
Segovia — The EMI Recordings 1927–39 (Angel)

Producer of the Year (Non-Classical)
Phil Ramone

Classical Producer of the Year
Robert Woods

1981

Record of the Year
"Bette Davis Eyes," Kim Carnes

Album of the Year
Double Fantasy, John Lennon and Yoko Ono (Warner Bros./Geffen)

Song of the Year
"Bette Davis Eyes," Donna Weiss and Jackie DeShannon, songwriters

Best New Artist
Sheena Easton

Best Pop Vocal Performance, Male
Breakin Away, Al Jarreau

Best Pop Vocal Performance, Female
Lena Horne: The Lady and Her Music Live On Broadway, Lena Horne

Ella Fitzgerald

Best Pop Vocal Performance by a Duo or Group With Vocal
"Boy From New York City," Manhattan Transfer

Best Pop Instrumental Performance
"The Theme From *Hill Street Blues*," Mike Post featuring Larry Carlton

Best Rock Vocal Performance, Male
"Jessie's Girl," Rick Springfield

Best Rock Vocal Performance, Female
"Fire and Ice," Pat Benatar

Best Rock Performance by a Duo or Group With Vocal
"Don't Stand So Close to Me," Police

Best Rock Instrumental Performance
"Behind My Camel," Police

Best Rhythm and Blues Song
"Just the Two of Us," Bill Withers, William Salter and Ralph MacDonald, songwriters

Best Rhythm and Blues Performance, Male
"One Hundred Ways," James Ingram

Best Rhythm and Blues Vocal Performance, Female
"Hold On I'm Comin'," Aretha Franklin

Best Rhythm and Blues Performance by a Duo or Group With Vocal
The Dude, Quincy Jones

Best Rhythm and Blues Instrumental Performance
"All I Need Is You," David Sanborn

Best Jazz Vocal Performance, Male
"Blue Rondo a la Turk," Al Jarreau

Best Jazz Vocal Performance, Female
Digital III at Montreux, Ella Fitzgerald

Best Jazz Vocal Performance, Duo or Group
"Until I Met You" (Corner Pocket), Manhattan Transfer

Best Jazz Instrumental Performance, Soloist
Bye Bye Blackbird, John Coltrane

Best Jazz Instrumental Performance, Group
Chick Corea and Gary Burton in Concert, Zurich, October 28, 1979, Chick Corea and Gary Burton

Best Jazz Instrumental Performance, Big Band
Walk on the Water, Gerry Mulligan and His Orchestra

Best Jazz Fusion Performance, Vocal or Instrumental
Winelight, Grover Washington, Jr.

Best Country Song
"9 to 5," Dolly Parton, songwriter

Best Country Vocal Performance, Male
(There's) "No Gettin' Over Me," Ronnie Milsap

Best Country Vocal Performance, Female
"9 to 5," Dolly Parton

Best Country Performance by a Duo or Group With Vocal
"Elvira," Oak Ridge Boys

Best Country Instrumental Performance
Country, After All These Years, Chet Atkins

Best Gospel Performance, Contemporary or Inspirational
Priority, Imperials

Best Gospel Performance, Traditional
The Masters V, J.D. Sumner, James Blackwood, Hovie Lister, Rosie Rozell and Jake Hess

Best Soul Gospel Performance, Contemporary
Don't Give Up, Andrae Crouch

Best Soul Gospel Performance, Traditional
The Lord Will Make a Way, Al Green

Best Latin Recording
"Guajira Pa la Jeva," Clare Fischer (Pausa)

Best Inspirational Performance
Amazing Grace, B.J. Thomas

Best Ethnic or Traditional Recording
There Must Be a Better World Somewhere, B.B. King (MCA)

Best Arrangement of an Instrumental Recording
"Velas," Quincy Jones and Johnny Mandel, arrangers

Best Instrumental Arrangement Accompanying Vocal(s)
"Ai No Corrida," Quincy Jones and Jerry Hey, arrangers

Best Vocal Arrangement for Two or More Voices
"A Nightingale Sang in Berkeley Square," Gene Puerling, arranger

Best Instrumental Composition
"The Theme From *Hill Street Blues*," Mike Post, composer

Best Cast Show Album
Lena Horne: The Lady and Her Music Live on Broadway, various composers and lyricists (Qwest/Warner Bros.)

Best Album of Original Score Written for a Motion Picture or a Television Special
Raiders of the Lost Ark, John Williams, composer (Columbia/CBS)

Best Classical Album
Mahler, *Symphony No. 2 in C Minor,* Sir Georg Solti conducting Chicago Symphony Orchestra and Chorus (London)

Best Classical Orchestral Recording
Mahler, *Symphony No. 2 in C Minor,* Sir Georg Solti conducting Chicago Symphony Orchestra and Chorus (London)

Best Chamber Music Performance
Tchaikovsky, *Piano Trio in A Minor,* Itzhak Perlman, Lynn Harrell and Vladimir Ashkenazy

Best Classical Performance, Instrumental Soloist(s) (With Orchestra)
Isaac Stern 60th Anniversary Celebration, Isaac Stern, Itzhak Perlman and Pinchas Zukerman; Zubin Mehta conducting New York Philharmonic Orchestra

Best Classical Performance, Instrumental Soloist(s) (Without Orchestra)
The Horowitz Concerts 1979/80, Vladimir Horowitz

Best Opera Recording
Janácek, *From the House of the Dead,* Sir Charles Mackerras conducting Vienna Philharmonic; solos: Zahradnicek, Zitek and Zidek (London)

Best Choral Performance (Other Than Opera)
Haydn, *The Creation,* Neville Marriner conducting Chorus of Academy of St. Martin-in-the-Fields

Best Classical Vocal Soloist Performance
Live From Lincoln Center, Sutherland-Horne-Pavarotti, Joan
  Sutherland, Marilyn Horne and Luciano Pavarotti

Best Comedy Recording
Rev. Du Rite, Richard Pryor (Laff)

Best Spoken Word, Documentary or Drama Recording
Donovan's Brain, Orson Welles (Radiola)

Best Recording for Children
Sesame Country, Muppets, Glen Campbell, Crystal Gayle,
  Loretta Lynn, Tanya Tucker; Jim Henson (Sesame Street)

Best Album Package
Tatoo You, Peter Corriston, art director (Rolling
  Stones/Atlantic)

Best Album Notes
Erroll Garner, Master of the Keyboard, Dan Morgenstern,
  annotator (Book-of-the-Month Records)

Best Historical Album
Hoagy Carmichael: From "Star Dust" to "Ole Buttermilk Sky"
  (Book-of-the-Month Records)

Video of the Year
"Michael Nesmith in Elephant Parts," Michael Nesmith

Producer of the Year (Non-Classical)
Quincy Jones

Classical Producer of the Year
James Mallinson

1982

Record of the Year
"Rosanna," Toto

Album of the Year
Toto IV, Toto (Columbia)

Song of the Year
"Always on My Mind," Johnny Christopher, Mark James and
  Wayne Carson, songwriters

Best New Artist
Men at Work

Best Pop Vocal Performance, Male
"Truly," Lionel Richie

Best Pop Vocal Performance, Female
"You Should Hear How She Talks About You," Melissa
  Manchester

Best Pop Performance by a Duo or Group With Vocal
"Up Where We Belong," Joe Cocker and Jennifer Warnes

Best Pop Instrumental Performance
"*Chariots of Fire* Theme" (dance version), Ernie Watts

Best Rock Vocal Performance, Male
"Hurts So Good," John Cougar

Best Rock Vocal Performance, Female
"Shadows of the Night," Pat Benatar

Best Rock Performance by a Duo or Group With Vocal
"Eye of the Tiger," Survivor

Best Rock Instrumental Performance
"D.N.A.," A Flock of Seagulls

Hard-to-Find Classical Recordings

**Having trouble locating a classical title? The following stores accept mail and
telephone orders.**

A Classical Record
547 W. 27th St.
New York, NY 10001
(212) 675-8010

Academy Record Store
12 W. 18th St.
New York, NY 10011
(212) 242-3000

Acoustic Sounds
Box 2043
Salina, KS 67402-2043
(800) 525-1630

Benedikt & Salmon
3020 Meade Ave.
San Diego, CA 92116
(619) 281-3345

Briggs & Briggs
1270 Massachusetts Ave.
Cambridge, MA 02138
(617) 547-2007

Canterbury Records
805 E. Colorado
Pasadena, CA 91101
(818) 792-7184

Encore Productions
P.O. Box 2240
Stamford, CT 06906-0240
(800) 546-2968

Footlight Records
113 E. 12th St.
New York, NY 10003
(212) 533-1572

H & B Recordings Direct
12037 Starcrest
San Antonio, TX 78247
(800) 222-6872

**Harvey Gilman
Rediscoveries**
243 W. 76th St.
New York, NY 10023
(212) 496-1681

Music for All
2908 E. Third Ave.
Denver, CO 80206
(800) 222-4544

Music Revolution
4055 S. Dale Mabry
Tampa, FL 33611
(813) 831-8889

Nathan Muchnick Inc.
1725 Chesnut St.
Philadelphia, PA 19103
(800) 373-9873

Opera World
P.O. Box 800
Concord, MA 01742
(800) 996-7372

Parnassus Records
56 Parnassus Lane
Saugerties, NY 12477
(914) 246-3332

Rara Avis
77 Wittenberg Road
Bearsville, NY 12409
(914) 679-1054

SKR Classical
539 E. Liberty
Ann Arbor, MI 48104
(800) 272-4506

Tower Records
Tower Records Mail Order
22 E. Fourth St., Suite 302
New York, NY 10003
(800) 648-4844

Yankee Music Search
P.O. Box 1143
Flushing, NY 11354
(718) 463-1702

Best Rhythm and Blues Song
"Turn Your Love Around," Jay Graydon, Steve Lukather and Bill Champlin, songwriters

Best Rhythm and Blues Vocal Performance, Male
"Sexual Healing," Marvin Gaye

Best Rhythm and Blues Performance, Female
"And I Am Telling You I'm Not Going," Jennifer Holliday

Best Rhythm and Blues Performance by a Duo or Group With Vocal (tie)
"Let It Whip," Dazz Band
"Wanna Be With You," Earth, Wind and Fire

Best Rhythm and Blues Instrumental Performance
"Sexual Healing," Marvin Gaye

Best Jazz Vocal Performance, Male
An Evening With George Shearing and Mel Tormé, Mel Tormé

Best Vocal Jazz Performance, Female
Gershwin Live!, Sarah Vaughan

Best Jazz Vocal Performance, Duo or Group
"Route 66," Manhattan Transfer

Best Jazz Instrumental Performance, Soloist
We Want Miles, Miles Davis

Best Jazz Instrumental Performance, Group
"More" Live, Phil Woods Quartet

Best Jazz Instrumental Performance, Big Band
Warm Breeze, Count Basie and His Orchestra

Best Jazz Fusion Performance, Vocal or Instrumental
Offramp, Pat Metheny Group

Best Country Song
"Always on My Mind," Johnny Christopher, Mark James and Wayne Carson, songwriters

Best Country Vocal Performance, Male
"Always on My Mind," Willie Nelson

Best Country Vocal Performance, Female
"Break It to Me Gently," Juice Newton

Best Country Performance by a Duo or Group With Vocal
Mountain Music, Alabama

Best Country Instrumental Performance
"Alabama Jubilee," Roy Clark

Best Gospel Performance, Contemporary
Age to Age, Amy Grant

Best Gospel Performance, Traditional
I'm Following You, Blackwood Brothers

Best Soul Gospel Performance, Contemporary
Higher Plane, Al Green

Best Soul Gospel Performance, Traditional
Precious Lord, Al Green

Best Latin Recording
Machito and His Salsa Big Band '82, Machito (Timeless)

Best Inspirational Performance
He Set My Life to Music, Barbara Mandrell

Best Traditional Blues Recording
Alright Again, Clarence Gatemouth Brown (Rounder)

Best Ethnic or Traditional Folk Recording
Queen Ida and the Bon Temps Zydeco Band on Tour, Queen Ida (GNR/Crescendo)

Best Arrangement on an Instrumental Recording
"Flying," John Williams, arranger

Best Instrumental Arrangement Accompanying Vocal(s)
"Rosanna," Jerry Hey, David Paich and Jeff Porcaro, arrangers

Best Vocal Arrangement for Two or More Voices
"Rosanna," David Paich, arranger

Best Instrumental Composition
"Flying" (Theme From *E.T. the Extra-Terrestrial*), John Williams, composer

Best Cast Show Album
Dreamgirls, Henry Krieger, composer; Tom Eyen, lyricist (Geffen/Warner Bros.)

Best Album of Original Score Written for a Motion Picture or a Television Special
E.T. the Extra-Terrestrial, John Williams, composer (MCA)

Best Classical Album
Bach, *The Goldberg Variations,* Glenn Gould (CBS)

Best Classical Orchestral Recording
Mahler, *Symphony No. 7 in E Minor,* James Levine conducting Chicago Symphony Orchestra (RCA)

Best Chamber Music Performance
Brahms, *The Sonatas for Clarinet and Piano, Op. 120,* Richard Stoltzman and Richard Goode

Best Classical Performance, Instrumental Soloist(s) (With Orchestra)
Elgar, *Concerto for Violin in B Minor,* Itzhak Perlman; Daniel Barenboim conducting Chicago Symphony

Best Classical Performance, Instrumental Soloist(s) (Without Orchestra)
Bach, *The Goldberg Variations,* Glenn Gould

Best Opera Recording
Wagner, *Der Ring des Nibelungen,* Pierre Boulez conducting Bayreuth Festival Orchestra; solos: Jones, Altmeyer, Wenkel, Hofmann, Jung, Jerusalem, Zednik, McIntrye, Salminen and Becht (Philips)

Best Choral Performance (Other Than Opera)
Berlioz, *La Damnation de Faust,* Sir Georg Solti conducting Chicago Symphony Orchestra; Margaret Hillis, chorus director, Chicago Symphony Chorus

Best Classical Vocal Soloist Performance
Leontyne Price Sings Verdi, Leontyne Price; Zubin Mehta conducting Israel Philharmonic Orchestra

Best Comedy Recording
Live on the Sunset Strip, Richard Pryor (Warner Bros.)

Best Spoken Word, Documentary or Drama Recording
Raiders of the Lost Ark: The Movie on Record (Columbia)

Best Recording for Children
In Harmony 2, Billy Joel, Bruce Springsteen, James Taylor, Kenny Loggins, Carly and Lucy Simon, Teddy Pendergrass, Crystal Gayle, Lou Rawls, Deniece Williams, Janis Ian and Dr. John (CBS)

Best Album Package
Get Closer, Kosh and Ron Larson, art directors (Elektra/Asylum)

Best Album Notes
Bunny Berigan (Giants of Jazz), John Chilton and Richard Sudhalter, art directors (Time Life)

Best Historical Album
The Tommy Dorsey/Frank Sinatra Sessions vols. 1, 2 and 3 (RCA)

Video of the Year
"Olivia Physical," Olivia Newton-John

Producer of the Year (Non-Classical)
Toto

Classical Producer of the Year
Robert Woods

1983

Record of the Year
"Beat It," Michael Jackson

Album of the Year
Thriller, Michael Jackson (Epic/CBS)

Song of the Year
"Every Breath You Take," Sting, songwriter

Best New Artist
Culture Club

Best Pop Vocal Performance, Male
Thriller, Michael Jackson

Best Pop Vocal Performance, Female
"Flashdance: What a Feeling," Irene Cara

Best Pop Performance by a Duo or Group With Vocal
"Every Breath You Take," Police

Best Pop Instrumental Performance
"Being With You," George Benson

Best Rock Vocal Performance, Male
"Beat It," Michael Jackson

Best Rock Vocal Performance, Female
"Love Is a Battlefield," Pat Benatar

Best Rock Performance by a Duo or Group With Vocal
Synchronicity, Police

Best New Rhythm and Blues Song
"Billie Jean," Michael Jackson, songwriter

Best Rhythm and Blues Vocal Performance, Male
"Billie Jean," Michael Jackson

Best Rhythm and Blues Vocal Performance, Female
Chaka Khan, Chaka Khan

Best Rhythm and Blues Vocal Performance by a Duo or Group With Vocal
"Ain't Nobody," Rufus and Chaka Khan

Best Rhythm and Blues Instrumental Performance
"Rockit," Herbie Hancock

Best Jazz Vocal Performance, Male
Top Drawer, Mel Tormé

Best Jazz Vocal Performance, Female
The Best Is Yet to Come, Ella Fitzgerald

Best Jazz Vocal Performance, Duo or Group
"Why Not!," Manhattan Transfer

Best Jazz Instrumental Performance, Soloist
Think of One, Wynton Marsalis

Best Jazz Instrumental Performance, Group
At the Vanguard, Phil Woods Quartet

Best Jazz Instrumental Performance, Big Band
All in Good Time, Rob McConnell and the Boss Brass

Michael Jackson

Best Jazz Fusion Performance, Vocal or Instrumental
Travels, Pat Metheny Group

Best New Country Song
"Stranger in My House," Mike Reid, songwriter

Best Country Vocal Performance, Male
"I.O.U.," Lee Greenwood

Best Country Vocal Performance, Female
"A Little Good News," Anne Murray

Best Country Performance by a Duo or Group With Vocal
The Closer You Get, Alabama

Best Country Instrumental Performance
"Fireball," New South (Ricky Skaggs, Jerry Douglas, Tony Rice, J.D. Crowe and Todd Phillips)

Best Gospel Performance, Male
Walls of Glass, Russ Taff

Best Gospel Performance, Female
"Ageless Medley," Amy Grant

Best Gospel Performance by a Duo or Group
"More Than Wonderful," Sandi Patti and Larnelle Harris

Best Soul Gospel Performance, Male
I'll Rise Again, Al Green

Best Soul Gospel Performance, Female
We Sing Praises, Sandra Crouch

Best Soul Gospel Performance by a Duo or Group
"I'm So Glad I'm Standing Here Today," Bobby Jones with Barbara Mandrell

Best Latin Pop Performance
Me Enamore, José Feliciano

Best Tropical Latin Performance
On Broadway, Tito Puente and His Latin Ensemble

Best Inspirational Performance
"He's a Rebel," Donna Summer

Best Traditional Blues Recording
Blues 'n Jazz, B.B. King (MCA)

Best Mexican-American Performance
"Anselma," Los Lobos

Best Ethnic or Traditional Folk Recording
I'm Here, Clifton Chenier and His Red Hot Louisiana Band (Alligator)

Best Arrangement on an Instrumental
"Summer Sketches '82," Dave Grusin, arranger

Best Instrumental Arrangement Accompanying Vocal(s)
"What's New," Nelson Riddle, arranger

Best Vocal Arrangement for Two or More Voices
"Be Bop Medley," Arif Mardin and Chaka Khan, arrangers

Best Instrumental Composition
"Love Theme From *Flashdance*," Giorgio Moroder, composer

Best Cast Show Album
Cats (Complete Original Broadway Cast Recording), Andrew Lloyd Webber, producer (Geffen/Warner Bros.)

Best Album of Original Score Written for a Motion Picture or a Television Special
Flashdance, Giorgio Moroder, Keith Forsey, Irene Cara, Shandi Sinnamon, Ronald Magness, Douglas Cotler, Richard Gilbert, Michael Boddicker, Jerry Hey, Phil Ramone, Michael Sembello, Kim Carnes, Duane Hitchings, Craig Krampf and Dennis Matkosky, songwriters (Casablanca/Polygram)

Best Classical Album
Mahler, *Symphony No. 9 in D Major*, Sir Georg Solti conducting Chicago Symphony Orchestra and Chorus (London)

Best Classical Orchestral Recording
Mahler, *Symphony No. 9 in D Major,* Sir Georg Solti conducting
   Chicago Symphony Orchestra (London)

Best Chamber Music Performance
Brahms, *Sonata for Cello and Piano in E Minor, Op. 38 and
   Sonata in F Major, Op. 99,* Mstislav Rostropovich and
   Rudolf Serkin

**Best Classical Performance, Instrumental Soloist(s) (With
Orchestra)**
Haydn, *Concerto for Trumpet and Orchestra in E-Flat Major;* L.
   Mozart, *Concerto for Trumpet and Orchestra in D Major;*
   Hummel, *Concerto for Trumpet and Orchestra in E-Flat
   Major,* Wynton Marsalis; Raymond Leppard conducting
   National Philharmonic Orchestra

**Best Classical Performance, Instrumental Soloist(s) (Without
Orchestra)**
Beethoven, *Sonata for Piano No. 12 in A-Flat Major, Op. 26 and
   No. 13 in E-Flat Major, Op. 27, No. 1,* Glenn Gould

Best Opera Recording (tie)
Mozart, *Le Nozzi de Figaro,* Sir Georg Solti conducting London
   Philharmonic; solos: Kanawa, Popp, Ramey, Allen, Moll
   and von Stade (London)

Verdi, *La Traviata* (Original Soundtrack), James Levine conducting The Metropolitan Opera Orchestra and Chorus;
   solos: Stratas, Domingo and MacNeil (Elektra)

Best Choral Performance (Other Than Opera)
Haydn, *The Creation,* Sir Georg Solti conducting Chicago
   Symphony Orchestra; Margaret Hillis, choral director,
   Chicago Symphony Chorus

Best Classical Vocal Soloist Performance
Leontyne Price and Marilyn Horne in Concert at The Met,
   Leontyne Price and Marilyn Horne; James Levine con-
   ducting The Metropolitan Opera Orchestra

Best Comedy Recording
Eddie Murphy, Comedian, Eddie Murphy (The Entertainment
   Co./Columbia)

Best Spoken Word or Non-Musical Recording
Copland, *A Lincoln Portrait,* William Warfield (Mercury/Philips)

Best Recording for Children
E.T. the Extra-Terrestrial, Michael Jackson, narration and
   vocals (MCA)

Best Album Package
Speaking in Tongues, Robert Rauschenberg, art director
   (Sire/Warner Bros.)

Best Album Notes
The "Interplay" Sessions, Orrin Keepnews, annotator
   (Milestone)

Best Historical Album
*The Greatest Recordings of Arturo Toscanini Symphonies Vol.
   I,* Arturo Toscanini (Franklin Mint)

Best Video, Short Form
"Girls on Film/Hungry Like the Wolf," Duran Duran

Producers of the Year (Non-Classical)
Quincy Jones and Michael Jackson

Classical Producers of the Year
Marc J. Aubort and Joanna Nickrenz

1984

Record of the Year
"What's Love Got to Do With It," Tina Turner

Album of the Year
Can't Slow Down, Lionel Richie (Motown)

Bruce Springsteen

Song of the Year
"What's Love Got to Do With It," Graham Lyle and Terry
   Britten, songwriters

Best New Artist
Cyndi Lauper

Best Pop Vocal Performance, Male
"Against All Odds" (Take a Look at Me Now), Phil Collins

Best Pop Vocal Performance, Female
"What's Love Got to Do With It," Tina Turner

Best Pop Performance by a Duo or Group With Vocal
"Jump" (For My Love), Pointer Sisters

Best Pop Instrumental Performance
"Ghostbusters" (instrumental version), Ray Parker, Jr.

Best Rock Vocal Performance, Male
"Dancing in the Dark," Bruce Springsteen

Best Rock Vocal Performance, Female
"Better Be Good to Me," Tina Turner

Best Rock Performance by a Duo or Group With Vocal
Purple Rain — Music From the Motion Picture, Prince and the
   Revolution

Best Rock Instrumental Performance
"Cinema," Yes

Best New Rhythm and Blues Song
"I Feel for You," Prince, songwriter

Best Rhythm and Blues Vocal Performance, Male
"Caribbean Queen" (No More Love on the Run), Billy Ocean

Best Rhythm and Blues Vocal Performance, Female
"I Feel for You," Chaka Khan

**Best Rhythm and Blues Performance by a Duo or Group With
Vocal**
"Yah Mo B There," James Ingram and Michael McDonald

Best Rhythm and Blues Instrumental Performance
Sound-System, Herbie Hancock

Best Jazz Vocal Performance
Nothin' but the Blues, Joe Williams

Best Jazz Instrumental Performance, Soloist
Hot House Flowers, Wynton Marsalis

Best Jazz Instrumental Performance, Group
"New York Scene," Art Blakey

Best Jazz Instrumental Performance, Big Band
88 Basie Street, Count Basie and His Orchestra

Best Jazz Fusion Performance, Vocal or Instrumental
First Circle, Pat Metheny Group

Best Country Song
"City of New Orleans," Steve Goodman, songwriter

Best Country Vocal Performance, Male
"That's the Way Love Goes," Merle Haggard

Best Country Vocal Performance, Female
"In My Dreams," Emmylou Harris

Best Country Performance by a Duo or Group With Vocal
"Mama He's Crazy," Judds

Best Country Instrumental Performance
"Wheel Hoss," Ricky Skaggs

Best Gospel Performance, Male
Michael W. Smith, Michael W. Smith

Best Gospel Performance, Female
"Angels," Amy Grant

Best Gospel Performance by a Duo or Group
"Keep the Flame Burning," Debby Boone and Phil Driscoll

Best Soul Gospel Performance, Male
"Always Remember," Andrae Crouch

Best Soul Gospel Performance, Female
Sailin', Shirley Caesar

Best Soul Gospel Performance by a Duo or Group
"Sailin' on the Sea of Your Love," Shirley Caeser and Al Green

Best Latin Pop Performance
Always in My Heart (Siempre en mi Corazón), Placido Domingo

Best Tropical Latin Performance
Palo Pa Rumba, Eddie Palmieri

Best Mexican/American Performance
"Me Gustas Tal Como Eres," Sheena Easton and Luis Miguel

Best Inspirational Performance
"Forgive Me," Donna Summer

Best Traditional Blues Recording
Blues Explosion, John Hammond, Stevie Ray Vaughan and Double Trouble, Sugar Blue, Koko Taylor and the Blues Machine, Luther "Guitar Junior" Johnson and J.B. Hutto and the New Hawks (Atlantic)

Best Ethnic or Traditional Folk Recording
Elizabeth Cotten Live!, Elizabeth Cotten (Arhoolie)

Best Reggae Recording
Anthem, Black Uhuru (Island)

Best Arrangement on an Instrumental
"Grace" (Gymnastics Theme), Quincy Jones and Jeremy Lubbock, arrangers

Best Instrumental Arrangement Accompanying Vocal(s)
"Hard Habit to Break," David Foster and Jeremy Lubbock, arrangers

Best Vocal Arrangement for Two or More Voices
"Automatic," Pointer Sisters, arrangers

Best Instrumental Composition (tie)
"The Natural," Randy Newman, composer

"Olympic Fanfare and Theme," John Williams, composer

Best Cast Show Album
Sunday in the Park With George, Stephen Sondheim, composer and lyricist (RCA)

Best Album of Original Score Written for a Motion Picture or a Television Special
Purple Rain, Prince, John L. Nelson, Lisa and Wendy, songwriters (Warner Bros.)

Best New Classical Composition
Antony and Cleopatra, Samuel Barber, composer

Best Classical Album
Amadeus (Original Soundtrack), Neville Marriner conducting the Academy of St. Martin-in-the-Fields; Ambrosian Opera Chorus; Choristers of Westminster Abbey (Fantasy)

Best Classical Orchestral Recording
Prokofiev, *Symphony No. 5 in B-Flat, Op. 100,* Leonard Slatkin conducting Saint Louis Symphony (RCA)

Best Chamber Music Performance
Beethoven, *The Late String Quartets,* Juilliard String Quartet

Best Classical Performance, Instrumental Soloist(s) (With Orchestra)
Wynton Marsalis, Edita Gruberova: *Handel, Purcell, Torelli, Fasch, Molter,* Wynton Marsalis and Edita Gruberova; Raymond Leppard conducting English Chamber Orchestra

Best Classical Performance, Instrumental Soloist(s) (Without Orchestra)
Bach, *The Unaccompanied Cello Suites,* Yo-Yo Ma

Best Opera Recording
Bizet, *Carmen* (Original Soundtrack), Lorin Maazel conducting Orchestre National de France; Choeurs et Maitrise de Radio France; solos: Johnson, Esham, Domingo and Raimondi (Erato)

Best Choral Performance (Other Than Opera)
Brahms, *A German Requiem,* James Levine conducting Chicago Symphony Orchestra; Margaret Hillis, choral director, Chicago Symphony Chorus

Best Classical Vocal Soloist Performance
Ravel, *Songs of Maurice Ravel,* Jessye Norman, Jose Van Dam and Heather Harper; Pierre Boulez conducting the Members of Ensemble Intercontemporain and BBC Symphony Orchestra

Best Comedy Recording
Eat It, "Weird Al" Yankovic (Rock & Roll)

Best Spoken Word or Non-Musical Recording
The Words of Gandhi, Ben Kingsley (Caedmon)

Best Recording for Children
Where the Sidewalk Ends, Shel Silverstein (Columbia)

Best Album Package
She's So Unusual, Janet Perr, art director (Portrait/CBS)

Best Album Notes
Big Band Jazz, Gunther Schuller and Martin Williams, songwriters (Smithsonian)

Best Historical Album
Big Band Jazz, Paul Whiteman, Fletcher Henderson, Chick Webb, Tommy Dorsey, Count Basie, Benny Goodman and others (Smithsonian)

Best Video, Short Form
"David Bowie," David Bowie

Best Video Album
Making Michael Jackson's Thriller, Michael Jackson (Vestron Music Video)

Producers of the Year (Non-Classical) (tie)
David Foster

Lionel Richie and James Anthony Carmichael

Classical Producer of the Year
Steven Epstein

1985

Record of the Year
"We Are the World," USA for Africa

Album of the Year
No Jacket Required, Phil Collins (Atlantic)

Song of the Year
"We Are the World," Michael Jackson and Lionel Richie, songwriters

Best New Artist
Sade

Best Pop Vocal Performance, Male
No Jacket Required, Phil Collins

Best Pop Vocal Performance, Female
"Saving All My Love for You," Whitney Houston

Best Pop Performance by a Duo or Group With Vocal
"We Are the World," USA for Africa

Best Pop Instrumental Performance
"Miami Vice Theme," Jan Hammer

Best Rock Vocal Performance, Male
"The Boys of Summer," Don Henley

Best Rock Vocal Performance, Female
"One of the Living," Tina Turner

Best Rock Performance by a Duo or Group With Vocal
"Money for Nothing," Dire Straits

Best Rock Instrumental Performance
"Escape," Jeff Beck

Best Rhythm and Blues Song
"Freeway of Love," Narada Michael Walden and Jeffrey Cohen, songwriters

Best Rhythm and Blues Vocal Performance, Male
In Square Circle, Stevie Wonder

Best Rhythm and Blues Vocal Performance, Female
"Freeway of Love," Aretha Franklin

Best Rhythm and Blues Performance by a Duo or Group With Vocal
"Nightshift," Commodores

Best Rhythm and Blues Instrumental Performance
Musician, Ernie Watts

Best Jazz Vocal Performance, Male
"Another Night in Tunisia," Jon Hendricks and Bobby McFerrin

Best Jazz Vocal Performance, Female
Cleo at Carnegie (The 10th Anniversary Concert), Cleo Laine

Best Jazz Vocal Performance, Duo or Group
Vocalese, Manhattan Transfer

Best Jazz Instrumental Performance, Soloist
Black Codes From the Underground, Wynton Marsalis

Best Jazz Instrumental Performance, Group
Black Codes From the Underground, Wynton Marsalis Group

Best Jazz Instrumental Performance, Big Band
The Cotton Club — Original Motion Picture Soundtrack, John Barry and Bob Wilber

Best Jazz Fusion Performance, Vocal or Instrumental
Straight to the Heart, David Sanborn

Best Country Song
"Highwayman," Jimmy L. Webb, songwriter

Best Country Vocal Performance, Male
"Lost in the Fifties Tonight" (In the Still of the Night), Ronnie Milsap

Best Country Vocal Performance, Female
"I Don't Know Why You Don't Want Me," Rosanne Cash

Best Country Performance by a Duo or Group With Vocal
Why Not Me, Judds

Best Country Instrumental Performance
"Cosmic Square Dance," Chet Atkins and Mark Knopfler

Best Gospel Performance, Male
"How Excellent Is Thy Name," Larnelle Harris

Best Gospel Performance, Female
Unguarded, Amy Grant

Best Soul Gospel Performance, Male
"Bring Back the Days of Yea and Nay," Marvin Winans

Best Soul Gospel Performance, Female
"Martin," Shirley Caesar

Best Soul Gospel Performance by a Duo or Group
Tomorrow, Winans

Best Latin Pop Performance
Ec Facil Amar, Lani Hall

Best Tropical Latin Performance (tie)
Mambo Diablo, Tito Puente and His Latin Ensemble

Solito, Eddie Palmieri

Phil Collins

Best Mexican/American Performance
Simplemente Mujer, Vikki Carr

Best Inspirational Performance
"Come Sunday," Jennifer Holliday

Best Traditional Blues Recording
"My Guitar Sings the Blues," B.B. King (MCA)

Best Ethnic or Traditional Folk Recording
"My Toot Toot," Rockin' Sidney (Maison De Soul)

Best Reggae Recording
Cliff Hanger, Jimmy Cliff (Columbia/CBS)

Best Polka Recording
70 Years of Hits, Frank Yankovic (Cleveland International/CBS)

Best Arrangement on an Instrumental
"Early A.M. Attitude," Dave Grusin and Lee Ritenour, arrangers

Best Instrumental Arrangement Accompanying Vocal(s)
"Lush Life," Nelson Riddle, arranger

Best Vocal Arrangement for Two or More Voices
"Another Night in Tunisia," Cheryl Bentyne and Bobby McFerrin, arrangers

Best Instrumental Composition
"Miami Vice Theme," Jan Hammer, composer

Best Cast Show Album
West Side Story, Stephen Sondheim, lyricist; Leonard Bernstein, composer (Deutsche Grammophone)

Best Album of Original Score Written for a Motion Picture or Television Special
Beverly Hills Cop, Sharon Robinson, Jon Gilutin, Bunny Hull, Hawk, Howard Hewett, Micki Free, Sue Sheridan, Howie Rice, Keith Forsey, Harold Faltermeyer, Allee Willis, Dan Sembello, Marc Benno and Richard Theisen, composers and songwriters (MCA)

Best Contemporary Composition
Requiem, Andrew Lloyd Webber, composer (Angel)

Best Classical Album
Berlioz, Requiem, Robert Shaw conducting Atlanta Symphony Orchestra and Chorus; solo: Aler (Telarc)

Best New Classical Artist
Chicago Pro Musica

Best Classical Orchestral Recording
Fauré, Pelléas et Mélisande, Robert Shaw conducting Atlanta Symphony Orchestra

Best Chamber Music Performance
Brahms, Cello and Piano Sonatas in E Minor and F Major, Emanuel Ax and Yo-Yo Ma

Best Classical Performance, Instrumental Soloist(s) (With Orchestra)
Elgar, Cello Concerto, Op. 85; Walton, Concerto for Cello and Orchestra, Yo-Yo Ma; André Previn conducting London Symphony Orchestra

Best Classical Performance, Instrumental Soloist(s) (Without Orchestra)
Ravel, Gaspard de la Nuit, Pavane Pour Une Infant Defunte, Valses Nobles et Sentimentales, Vladimir Ashkenazy

Best Opera Recording
Schoenberg, Moses und Aron, Sir Georg Solti conducting Chicago Symphony Orchestra and Chorus; solos: Mazura and Langridge (London)

Best Choral Performance (Other Than Opera)
Berlioz, Requiem, Robert Shaw conducting Atlanta Symphony Chorus and Orchestra

Best Classical Vocal Soloist Performance
Berlioz, Requiem, John Aler; Robert Shaw conducting Atlanta Symphony Orchestra and Chorus

Best Comedy Recording
Whoopi Goldberg (Original Broadway Show Recording), Whoopi Goldberg (Geffen)

Best Spoken Word or Non-Musical Recording
Ma Rainey's Black Bottom, Original Broadway cast (Manhattan)

Best Recording for Children
Follow That Bird (Original Motion Picture Soundtrack), Jim Henson's Muppets and the Sesame Street cast (RCA)

Best Album Package
Lush Life, Kosh and Ron Larson, art directors (Asylum)

Best Album Notes
Sam Cooke Live at the Harlem Square Club, 1963, Peter Guralnick, annotator (RCA)

Best Historical Album
RCA/MET — 100 Singers-100 Years, Melba, Schumann-Heink, Caruso, Price, Verrett, Domingo and 94 others (RCA Red Seal)

Best Music Video, Short Form
"We Are the World, the Video Event," USA for Africa

Best Music Video, Long Form
"Huey Lewis and the News: The Heart of Rock 'n Roll," Huey Lewis and the News

Producers of the Year (Non-Classical)
Phil Collins and Hugh Padgham

Classical Producer of the Year
Robert Woods

1986

Record of the Year
"Higher Love," Steve Winwood

Album of the Year
Graceland, Paul Simon (Warner Bros.)

Song of the Year
"That's What Friends Are For," Burt Bacharach and Carole Bayer Sager, songwriters

Best New Artist
Bruce Hornsby and the Range

Best Pop Vocal Performance, Male
"Higher Love," Steve Winwood

Best Pop Vocal Performance, Female
The Broadway Album, Barbra Streisand

Best Pop Performance by a Duo or Group With Vocal
"That's What Friends Are For," Dionne Warwick and Friends Featuring Elton John, Gladys Knight and Stevie Wonder

Best Pop Instrumental Performance (Orchestra, Group or Soloist)
"Top Gun" Anthem," Harold Faltermeyer and Steve Stevens

Best Rock Vocal Performance, Male
"Addicted to Love," Robert Palmer

Best Rock Vocal Performance, Female
"Back Where You Started," Tina Turner

Best Rock Performance by a Duo or Group With Vocal
"Missionary Man," Eurythmics

Best Rock Instrumental Performance (Orchestra, Group or Soloist)
"Peter Gunn," Art of Noise featuring Duane Eddy

Best Rhythm and Blues Song
"Sweet Love," Anita Baker, Louis A. Johnson and Gary Bias, songwriters

Best Rhythm and Blues Vocal Performance, Male
"Living in America," James Brown

Best Rhythm and Blues Vocal Performance, Female
Rapture, Anita Baker

Best Rhythm and Blues Performance by a Duo or Group With Vocal
"Kiss," Prince and the Revolution

Best Rhythm and Blues Instrumental Performance (Orchestra, Group or Soloist)
"And You Know That," Yellowjackets

Best Jazz Vocal Performance, Male
"Round Midnight," Bobby McFerrin

Best Jazz Vocal Performance, Female
Timeless, Diane Schuur

Best Jazz Vocal Performance, Duo or Group
Free Fall, 2 + 2 Plus (Clare Fischer and His Latin Jazz Sextet)

Best Jazz Instrumental Performance, Soloist
Tutu, Miles Davis

Best Jazz Instrumental Performance, Group
J Mood, Wynton Marsalis

Best Jazz Instrumental Performance, Big Band
The Tonight Show Band With Doc Severinsen, The Tonight Show Band With Doc Severinsen

Best Jazz Fusion Performance, Vocal or Instrumental
Double Vision, Bob James and David Sanborn

Best Country Song
"Grandpa" (Tell Me 'Bout the Good Old Days), Jamie O'Hara, songwriter

Best Country Vocal Performance, Male
Lost in the Fifties Tonight, Ronnie Milsap

Best Country Vocal Performance, Female
"Whoever's in New England," Reba McEntire

Best Country Performance by a Duo or Group With Vocal
"Grandpa" (Tell Me 'Bout the Good Old Days), Judds

Best Country Instrumental Performance (Orchestra, Group or Soloist)
"Raisin' the Dickens," Ricky Skaggs

Best Gospel Performance, Male
Triumph, Philip Bailey

Best Gospel Performance, Female
Morning Like This, Sandi Patti

Best Gospel Performance by a Duo or Group, Choir or Chorus
"They Say," Sandi Patti and Deniece Williams

Best Soul Gospel Performance, Male
"Going Away," Al Green

Best Soul Gospel Performance, Female
"I Surrender All," Deniece Williams

Best Soul Gospel Performance by a Duo or Group, Choir or Chorus
Let My People Go, Winans

Best Latin Pop Performance
"Lelolai," José Feliciano

Best Tropical Latin Performance
Escenas, Ruben Blades

Best Mexican/American Performance
Ay Te Dejo en San Antonio, Flaco Jimenez

Best Traditional Blues Recording
Showdown!, Albert Collins, Robert Cray and Johnny Copeland (Alligator)

Best Traditional Folk Recording
Riding the Midnight Train, Doc Watson (Sugar Hill)

Best Contemporary Folk Recording
Tribute to Steve Goodman, Arlo Guthrie, John Hartford, Richie Havens, Bonnie Koloc, Nitty Gritty Dirt Band, John Prine and others (Red Pajamas)

Best Reggae Recording
Babylon the Bandit, Steel Pulse (Elektra)

Best New Age Recording
Down to the Moon, Andreas Vollenweider (FM/CBS)

Best Polka Recording (tie)
Another Polka Celebration, Eddie Blazonczyk's Versatones (Bel Aire)

I Remember Warsaw, Jimmy Sturr and His Orchestra (Starr)

Best Arrangement on an Instrumental
"Suite Memories," Patrick Williams, arranger

Best Instrumental Arrangement Accompanying Vocal(s)
"Somewhere," David Foster, arranger

Best Instrumental Composition
Out of Africa (Original Motion Picture Soundtrack), John Barry, composer

Best Musical Cast Show Album
Follies in Concert (RCA)

Best Classical Album
Horowitz: The Studio Recordings, New York 1985, Vladimir Horowitz (Deutsche Grammophon)

Best Contemporary Composition
Symphony No. 3, Witold Lutoslawski, composer

Best Classical Orchestral Recording
Liszt, *A Faust Symphony,* Sir Georg Solti conducting the Chicago Symphony Orchestra (London)

Best Chamber Music Performance, Instrumental or Vocal
Beethoven, *Cello and Piano Sonata No. 4 in C Major and Variations,* Yo-Yo Ma and Emanuel Ax

Best Classical Performance, Instrumental Soloist(s) (With or Without Orchestra)
Horowitz, *The Studio Recordings, New York 1985,* Vladimir Horowitz

Best Opera Recording
Bernstein, *Candide,* John Mauceri conducting New York City Opera Chorus and Orchestra; solos: Mills, Eisler, Lankston, Castle, Reeve, Harrold, Billings and Clement (New World)

Best Choral Performance (Other Than Opera)
Orff, *Carmina Burana,* James Levine conducting Chicago Symphony Orchestra and Chorus

Best Classical Vocal Soloist Performance
Mozart, *Kathleen Battle Sings Mozart,* Kathleen Battle

Best Comedy Recording
Those of You With or Without Children, You'll Understand, Bill Cosby (Geffen)

Best Spoken Word or Non-Musical Recording
Interviews From the Class of '55 Recording Sessions, Carl Perkins, Jerry Lee Lewis, Roy Orbison, Johnny Cash, Sam Phillips, Rick Nelson and Chips Moman (America Record Corp.)

Best Recording for Children
The Alphabet, Sesame Street Muppets; Jim Henson (Golden Books)

Best Album Package
Tutu, Eiko Ishioka, art director (Warner Bros.)

Best Album Notes
The Voice, the Columbia Years 1943–1952, Gary Giddins, Wilfrid Sheed, Jonathan Schwartz, Murray Kempton, Andrew Sarris, Stephen Holden and Frank Conroy, annotators (Columbia/CBS)

Best Historical Album
Atlantic Rhythm and Blues 1947–1974 vols. 1–7, various artists (Atlantic)

Best Music Video, Short Form (VHS)
"Dire Straits Brothers in Arms," Dire Straits

Best Music Video, Short Form (VHS) (Beta) (Disk)
"Bring on the Night," Sting

Producers of the Year (Non-Classical)
Jimmy Jam and Terry Lewis

Classical Producer of the Year
Thomas Frost

1987

Record of the Year
"Graceland," Paul Simon

Album of the Year
Joshua Tree, U2 (Island)

Song of the Year
"Somewhere Out There," James Horner, Barry Mann and Cynthia Weil, songwriters

Best New Artist
Jody Watley

Best Pop Vocal Performance, Male
Bring on the Night, Sting

Best Pop Vocal Performance, Female
"I Wanna Dance With Somebody" (Who Loves Me), Whitney Houston

Best Pop Performance by a Duo or Group With Vocal
(I've Had) "The Time of My Life," Bill Medley and Jennifer Warnes

Best Pop Instrumental Performance (Orchestra, Group or Soloist)
"Minute by Minute," Larry Carlton

Best Rock Vocal Performance, Solo
Tunnel of Love, Bruce Springsteen

Best Rock Performance by a Duo or Group With Vocal
The Joshua Tree, U2

Best Rock Instrumental Performance (Orchestra, Group or Soloist)
Jazz From Hell, Frank Zappa

Best Rhythm and Blues Song
"Lean on Me," Bill Withers, songwriter

Best Rhythm and Blues Vocal Performance, Male
"Just to See Her," Smokey Robinson

Best Rhythm and Blues Vocal Performance, Female
Aretha, Aretha Franklin

Best Rhythm and Blues Performance by a Duo or Group With Vocal
"I Knew You Were Waiting" (For Me), Aretha Franklin and George Michael

Best Rhythm and Blues Instrumental Performance (Orchestra, Group or Soloist)
"Chicago Song," David Sanborn

Best Jazz Vocal Performance, Male
"What Is This Thing Called Love," Bobby McFerrin

Best Jazz Vocal Performance, Female
Diane Schuur and the Count Basie Orchestra, Diane Schuur

Best Jazz Instrumental Performance, Soloist
The Other Side of Round Midnight, Dexter Gordon

Best Jazz Instrumental Performance, Group
Marsalis Standard Time, Volume 1, Wynton Marsalis

Best Jazz Instrumental Performance, Big Band
Digital Duke, Duke Ellington Orchestra conducted by Mercer Ellington

Best Jazz Fusion Performance, Vocal or Instrumental
Still Life (Talking), Pat Metheny Group

Best Country Song
"Forever and Ever, Amen," Paul Overstreet and Don Schlitz, songwriters

Best Country Vocal Performance, Male
Always and Forever, Randy Travis

Best Country Vocal Performance, Female
"80's Ladies," K.T. Oslin

Best Country Performance by a Duo or Group With Vocal
Trio, Dolly Parton, Linda Ronstadt and Emmylou Harris

Best Country Vocal Performance, Duet
"Make No Mistake, She's Mine," Ronnie Milsap and Kenny Rogers

Best Country Instrumental Performance (Orchestra, Group or Soloist)
"String of Pars," Asleep at the Wheel

Best Gospel Performance, Male
The Father Hath Provided, Larnelle Harris

Best Gospel Performance, Female
"I Believe in You," Deniece Williams

Best Gospel Performance by a Duo, Group, Choir or Chorus
Crack the Sky, Mylon LeFevre and Broken Heart

Best Soul Gospel Performance, Male
"Everything's Gonna Be Alright," Al Green

Best Soul Gospel Performance, Female
"For Always," CeCe Winans

Best Soul Gospel Performance by a Duo, Group, Choir or Chorus
"Ain't No Need to Worry," Winans and Anita Baker

Best Latin Pop Performance
Un Hombre Solo, Julio Iglesias

Best Tropical Latin Performance
La Verdad — The Truth, Eddie Palmieri

Best Mexican/American Performance
Gracias! America sin Fronteras, Los Tigres Del Norte

Best Traditional Blues Recording
Houseparty New Orleans Style, Professor Longhair (Rounder)

Best Contemporary Blues Recording
Strong Persuader, Robert Cray Band (Mercury/Hightone)

Best Traditional Folk Recording
Shaka Zulu, Ladysmith Black Mambazo (Warner Bros.)

Best Contemporary Folk Recording
Unfinished Business, Steve Goodman (Red Pajamas)

Best Reggae Recording
No Nuclear War, Peter Tosh (EMI-America)

Best New Age Performance
Yusef Lateef's Little Symphony, Yusef Lateef

Best Polka Recording
A Polka Just for Me, Jimmy Sturr and His Orchestra (Starr)

Best Arrangement on an Instrumental
"Take the "A" Train," Bill Holman, arranger

Best Instrumental Arrangement Accompanying Vocal(s)
"Deedle's Blues," Frank Foster, arranger

Best Instrumental Composition
"Call Sheet Blues," Dexter Gordon, Wayne Shorter, Herbie Hancock, Ron Carter and Billy Higgins, composers

Sting

Best Musical Cast Show Album
Les Miserables (Geffen)

Best Album of Original Instrumental Background Score Written for a Motion Picture or Television
The Untouchables (Original Motion Picture Soundtrack), Ennio Morricone, composer (A&M)

Best Song Written Specifically for a Motion Picture or Television
"Somewhere Out There" (From the animated movie *An American Tale*), James Horner, Barry Mann and Cynthia Weil, songwriters

Best Contemporary Composition
Cello Concerto No. 2, Krzysztof Penderecki, composer

Best Classical Album
Horowitz in Moscow, Vladimir Horowitz (Deutsche Grammophon)

Best Orchestral Recording
Beethoven, *Symphony No. 9 in D Minor (Choral),* Sir Georg Solti conducting Chicago Symphony Orchestra (London)

Best Chamber Music Performance, Instrumental or Vocal
Beethoven, *The Complete Piano Trios,* Itzhak Perlman, Lynn Harrell and Vladimir Ashkenazy

Best Classical Performance, Instrumental Soloist(s) (With Orchestra)
Mozart, *Violin Concertos nos. 2 and 4 in D,* Itzhak Perlman; James Levine conducting Vienna Philarmonic

Best Classical Performance, Instrumental Soloist(s) (Without Orchestra)
Horowitz in Moscow, Vladimir Horowitz, piano

Best Opera Recording
Strauss, *Ariadne auf Naxos,* James Levine conducting Vienna Philharmonic; solos: Tomowa-Sintow, Battle, Baltsa, Lakes and Prey (Deutsche Grammophon)

Best Choral Performance (Othen Than Opera)
Hindemith, *When Lilacs Last in the Dooryard Bloom'd (A Requiem for Those We Love);* Robert Shaw conducting Atlanta Symphony Chorus and Orchestra

Best Classical Vocal Soloist Performance
Kathleen Battle, Salzburg Recital, Kathleen Battle; James Levine, accompanist

Best Comedy Recording
A Night at The Met, Robin Williams (Columbia/CBS)

Best Spoken Word or Non-Musical Recording
Lake Wobegon Days, Garrison Keillor (PHC)

Best Recording for Children
The Elephant's Child, Jack Nicholson, narrator; Bobby McFerrin, music (Windham Hill)

Best Album Package
King's Record Shop, Bill Johnson, art director (Columbia/CBS)

Best Album Notes
Thelonious Monk, the Complete Riverside Recordings, Orrin Keepnews, annotator (Riverside)

Best Historical Album
Thelonious Monk, the Complete Riverside Recordings, Thelonious Monk (Riverside)

Best Performance Music Video
The Prince's Trust All-Star Rock Concert, Elton John, Tina Turner, Sting and others

Best Concept Music Video
"Land of Confusion," Genesis

Producer of the Year (Non-Classical)
Narada Michael Walden

Classical Producer of the Year
Robert Woods

Robert Palmer

1988

Record of the Year
"Don't Worry Be Happy," Bobby McFerrin

Album of the Year
Faith, George Michael (Columbia/CBS)

Song of the Year
"Don't Worry Be Happy," Bobby McFerrin, songwriter

Best New Artist
Tracy Chapman

Best Pop Vocal Performance, Male
"Don't Worry Be Happy," Bobby McFerrin

Best Pop Vocal Performance, Female
"Fast Car," Tracy Chapman

Best Pop Vocal Performance by a Duo or Group With Vocal
Brasil, Manhattan Transfer

Best Pop Instrumental Performance (Orchestra, Group or Soloist)
Close-up, David Sanborn

Best Rock Vocal Performance, Male
"Simply Irresistible," Robert Palmer

Best Rock Vocal Performance, Female
Tina Live in Europe, Tina Turner

Best Rock Instrumental Performance by a Duo or Group With Vocal
"Desire," U2

Best Rock Instrumental Performance (Orchestra, Group or Soloist)
Blues for Salvador, Carlos Santana

Best Hard Rock/Metal Performance, Vocal or Instrumental
Crest of a Knave, Jethro Tull

Best Rhythm and Blues Song
"Giving You the Best That I Got," Anita Baker, Skip Scarborough and Randy Holland, songwriters

Best Rhythm and Blues Vocal Performance, Male
Introducing the Hardline According to Terence Trent D'Arby, Terence Trent D'Arby

Best Rhythm and Blues Vocal Performance, Female
"Giving You the Best That I Got," Anita Baker

Best Rhythm and Blues Performance by a Duo or Group With Vocal
"Love Overboard," Gladys Knight and the Pips

Best Rhythm and Blues Instrumental Performance (Orchestra, Group or Soloist)
"Light Years," Chick Corea

Best Rap Performance
"Parents Just Don't Understand," D.J. Jazzy Jeff and the Fresh Prince

Best Jazz Vocal Performance, Male
Brothers, Bobby McFerrin

Best Jazz Vocal Performance, Female
Look What I Got!, Betty Carter

Best Jazz Vocal Performance, Duo or Group
"Spread Love," Take 6

Best Jazz Instrumental Performance, Soloist on a Jazz Recording
Don't Try This at Home, Michael Brecker

Best Jazz Instrumental Performance, Group
Blues for Coltrane, A Tribute to John Coltrane, McCoy Tyner, Pharoah Sanders, David Murray, Cecil McBee and Roy Haynes

Best Jazz Instrumental Performance, Big Band
Bud and Bird, Gil Evans and the Monday Night Orchestra

Best Jazz Fusion Performance
Politics, Yellowjackets

Best Country Song
"Hold Me," K.T. Oslin, songwriter

Best Country Vocal Performance, Male
Old 8 x 10, Randy Travis

Best Country Vocal Performance, Female
"Hold Me," K.T. Oslin

Best Country Performance by a Duo or Group With Vocal
"Give a Little Love," Judds

Best Country Vocal Collaboration
"Crying," Roy Orbison and k.d. lang

Best Country Instrumental Performance (Orchestra, Group or Soloists)
"Sugarfoot Rag," Asleep at the Wheel

Best Bluegrass Recording (Vocal or Instrumental)
Southern Flavor, Bill Monroe (MCA)

Best Gospel Performance, Male
Christmas, Larnelle Harris

Best Gospel Performance, Female
Lead Me On, Amy Grant

Best Gospel Performance by a Duo or Group, Choir or Chorus
The Winans Live at Carnegie Hall, Winans

Best Soul Gospel Performance, Male
"Abundant Life," BeBe Winans

Best Soul Gospel Performance, Female
One Lord, One Faith, One Baptism, Aretha Franklin

Best Soul Gospel Performance by a Duo or Group, Choir or Chorus
Take Six, Take 6

Best Latin Pop Performance
Roberto Carlos, Roberto Carlos

Best Tropical Latin Performance
Antecedente, Rubén Blades

Best Mexican/American Performance
Canciones de Mi Padre, Linda Ronstadt

Best Traditional Blues Recording
Hidden Charms, Willie Dixon (Bug/Capitol)

Best Contemporary Blues Recording
"Don't Be Afraid of the Dark," Robert Cray Band (Mercury)

Best Traditional Folk Recording
Folkways: A Vision Shared — A Tribute to Woody Guthrie and Leadbelly, various artists (Columbia/CBS)

Best Contemporary Folk Recording
Tracy Chapman, Tracy Chapman (Elektra)

Best Reggae Recording
Conscious Party, Ziggy Marley and the Melody Makers (Virgin)

Best New Age Performance
Folksongs for a Nuclear Village, Shadowfax

Best Polka Recording
Born to Polka, Jimmy Sturr and His Orchestra (Starr)

Best Arrangement on an Instrumental
"Memos From Paradise," Roger Kellaway, arranger

Best Instrumental Arrangement Accompanying Vocal(s)
"No One Is Alone," Jonathan Tunick, arranger

Best Instrumental Composition
"The Theme From L.A. Law," Mike Post, composer

Best Musical Cast Show Album
Into the Woods, Stephen Sondheim, composer and lyricist (RCA)

Best Album of Original Instrumental Background Score Written for a Motion Picture or Television
The Last Emperor, Ryuichi Sakamoto, David Byrne and Cong Su, composers (Virgin)

Best Song Written Specifically for a Motion Picture or Television
"Two Hearts" (From the motion picture Buster), Phil Collins and Lamont Dozier, songwriters (Atlantic)

Best Contemporary Composition
Nixon in China, John Adams, composer

Best Classical Album
Verdi, Requiem and Operatic Choruses, Robert Shaw conducting Atlanta Symphony Orchestra and Chorus (Telarc)

Best Orchestral Recording
Rorem, String Symphony; Sunday Morning, Eagles; Robert Shaw conducting Atlanta Symphony Orchestra: String Symphony;Louis Lane conducting Atlanta Symphony Orchestra: Sunday Morning and Eagles (New World)

Best Chamber Music Performance (Instrumental or Vocal)
Bartók, Sonata for Two Pianos and Percussion; Brahms, Variation on a Theme by Joseph Haydn for Two Pianos, Murray Perahia and Sir Georg Solti, pianos; David Corkhill and Evelyn Glennie, percussion

Best Classical Performance, Instrumental Soloist(s) (With Orchestra)
Mozart, Piano Concerto No. 23 in A, Vladimir Horowitz, piano; Giulini conducting LaScala Opera Orchestra

Best Classical Performance, Instrumental Soloist(s) (Without Orchestra)
Albéniz, Iberia; Navarra; Suite Espagnola, Alicia de Larrocha

Best Opera Recording
Wagner, Lohengrin, Sir Georg Solti conducting Vienna State Opera Choir and Vienna Philharmonic; solos: Domingo, Norman, Randova, Nimsgern, Sotin and Fischer-Dieskau (London)

Best Choral Performance (Other Than Opera)
Verdi, Requiem and Operatic Choruses, Robert Shaw conducting Atlanta Symphony Chorus and Orchestra

Best Classical Vocal Soloist Performance
Luciano Pavarotti in Concert, Luciano Pavarotti

Best Comedy Recording
Good Morning Vietnam, Robin Williams (A&M)

Bonnie Raitt

Best Spoken Word or Non-Musical Recording
"Speech by Rev. Jesse Jackson (July 27)," Rev. Jesse Jackson (Arista)

Best Recording for Children
Pecos Bill, Robin Williams, narrator; Ry Cooder, music (Windham Hill)

Best Album Package
Tired of Runnin', Bill Johnson, art director (Columbia/CBS)

Best Album Notes
Crossroads, Anthony DeCurtis, annotator (Polydor)

Best Historical Album
Crossroads, Eric Clapton (Polydor)

Best Performance Music Video
"Where the Streets Have No Name," U2

Best Concept Music Video
"Fat," "Weird Al" Yankovic

Producer of the Year (Non-Classical)
Neil Dorfsman

Classical Producer of the Year
Robert Woods

1989

Record of the Year
"Wind Beneath My Wings," Bette Midler

Album of the Year
Nick of Time, Bonnie Raitt (Capitol)

Song of the Year
"Wind Beneath My Wings," Larry Henley and Jeff Silbar, song-writers

Best Pop Vocal Performance, Male
"How Am I Supposed to Live Without You," Michael Bolton

Best Pop Vocal Performance, Female
"Nick of Time," Bonnie Raitt

Best Pop Performance by a Duo or Group With Vocal
"Don't Know Much," Linda Ronstadt and Aaron Neville

Best Pop Instrumental Performance
"Healing Chant," Neville Brothers

Best Rock Vocal Performance, Male
The End of the Innocence, Don Henley

Best Rock Vocal Performance, Female
Nick of Time, Bonnie Raitt

Best Rock Performance by a Duo or Group With Vocal
Traveling Wilburys Volume One, Traveling Wilburys

Best Rock Instrumental Performance
Jeff Beck's Guitar Shop With Terry Bozzio and Tony Hymas, Jeff Beck, Terry Bozzio and Tony Hymas

Best Hard Rock Performance
"Cult of Personality," Living Colour

Best Metal Performance
"One," Metallica

Best Rhythm and Blues Song
"If You Don't Know Me by Now," Kenny Gamble and Leon Huff, songwriters

Best Rhythm and Blues Vocal Performance, Male
"Every Little Step," Bobby Brown

Best Rhythm and Blues Vocal Performance, Female
Giving You the Best That I Got, Anita Baker

Best Rhythm and Blues Performance by a Duo or Group With Vocal
"Back to Life," Soul II Soul featuring Caron Wheeler

Best Rhythm and Blues Instrumental Performance
"African Dance," Soul II Soul

Best Rap Performance
"Bust a Move," Young MC

Best Jazz Vocal Performance, Male
When Harry Met Sally, Harry Connick, Jr.

Best Jazz Vocal Performance, Female
Blues on Broadway, Ruth Brown

Best Jazz Vocal Performance, Duo or Group
"Makin' Whoopee," Dr. John and Rickie Lee Jones

Best Jazz Instrumental Performance, Soloist on a Jazz Recording
Aura, Miles Davis (Columbia/CBS)

Best Jazz Instrumental Performance, Group
Chick Corea Akoustic Band, Chick Corea Akoustic Band

Best Jazz Instrumental Performance, Big Band
Aura, Miles Davis

Best Jazz Fusion Performance
Letter From Home, Pat Metheny Group

Best Country Song
"After All This Time," Rodney Crowell, songwriter

Best Country Vocal Performance, Male
Lyle Lovett and His Large Band, Lyle Lovett

Best Country Vocal Performance, Female
Absolute Torch and Twang, k.d. lang

Best Country Performance by a Duo or Group With Vocal
Will the Circle Be Unbroken Volume Two, Nitty Gritty Dirt Band

Best Country Vocal Collaboration
"There's a Tear in My Beer," Hank Williams, Jr. and Hank Williams, Sr.

Best Country Instrumental Performance
"Amazing Grace," Randy Scruggs

Best Bluegrass Recording
"The Valley Road," Bruce Hornsby and the Nitty Gritty Dirt Band (Universal)

Best Gospel Vocal Performance, Male
"Meantime," BeBe Winans

Best Gospel Vocal Performance, Female
"Don't Cry," CeCe Winans

Best Gospel Vocal Performance by a Duo or Group, Choir or Chorus
"The Savior Is Waiting," Take 6

Best Soul Gospel Vocal Performance, Male or Female
"As Long as We're Together," Al Green

Best Soul Gospel Vocal Performance by a Duo or Group, Choir or Chorus
"Let Brotherly Love Continue," Daniel Winans and Choir

Best Latin Pop Performance
"Cielito Lindo," José Feliciano

Best Tropical Latin Performance
Ritmo en el Corazon, Celia Cruz and Ray Barretto

Best Mexican/American Performance
La Pistola y el Corazon, Los Lobos

Best Traditional Blues Recording
"I'm in the Mood," John Lee Hooker and Bonnie Raitt (Chameleon Music Group)

Best Contemporary Blues Recording
In Step, Stevie Ray Vaughan and Double Trouble (Epic)

Best Traditional Folk Recording
Le Mystère des Voix Bulgares, Vol. II, Bulgarian State Female Vocal Choir (Elektra/Nonesuch)

Best Contemporary Folk Recording
Indigo Girls, Indigo Girls (Epic)

Best Reggae Recording
One Bright Day, Ziggy Marley and the Melody Makers (Virgin)

Best New Age Performance
Passion (Music from *The Last Temptation of Christ),* Peter Gabriel

Best Polka Recording
All in My Love for You, Jimmy Sturr and His Orchestra (Starr)

Best Arrangement on an Instrumental
"Suite From *The Milagro Beanfield War,*" Dave Grusin, arranger

Best Instrumental Arrangement Accompanying Vocal(s)
"My Funny Valentine," Dave Grusin, arranger

Best Instrumental Composition
"The *Batman* Theme," Danny Elfman, composer

Best Musical Cast Show Album
Jerome Robbins' Broadway, Jason Alexander, Debbie Shapiro and Robert La Fasse (RCA Victor)

Best Album of Original Instrumental Background Score Written for a Motion Picture or Television
The Fabulous Baker Boys, Dave Grusin, composer (GRP)

Best Song Written Specifically for a Motion Picture or Television
Let the River Run (From the motion picture *Working Girl),* Carly Simon, composer (Arista)

Best Contemporary Composition
Different Trains, Steve Reich, composer

Best Classical Album
Bartók, *6 String Quartets,* Emerson String Quartet (Deutsche Grammophon)

Best Orchestral Performance
Mahler, *Symphony No. 3 in D Minor,* Leonard Bernstein and the New York Philharmonic

Best Chamber Music Performance
Bartók, *6 String Quartets,* Emerson String Quartet

Best Classical Performance, Instrumental Soloist(s) (With Orchestra)
Barber, *Cello Concerto, Op. 22;* Britten, *Symphony for Cello and Orchestra, Op. 68,* Yo-Yo Ma, cellist; David Zinman conducting Baltimore Symphony Orchestra

Best Classical Performance, Instrumental Soloist(s) (Without Orchestra)
Bach, *English Suites, BMV 806–11,* Andras Schiff, pianist

Best Opera Recording
Wagner, *Die Walkuere,* James Levine conducting Metropolitan Opera Orchestra; solos: Lakes, Moll, Morris, Norman, Behrens and Ludwig (Deutsche Grammophon)

Best Choral Performance (Other Than Opera)
Britten, *War Requiem,* Robert Shaw conducting Atlanta Symphony Orchestra and Chorus and Atlanta Boys Choir

Best Classical Vocal Soloist Performance
Knoxville, *Summer of 1915 (Music of Barber, Menott, Harbison and Stravinsky),* Dawn Upshaw, soprano; David Zinman conducting Orchestra of St. Luke's

Best Comedy Recording
P.D.Q. Bach, *1712 Overture and Other Musical Assaults,* Professor Peter Schickele (Telarc)

Best Spoken Word or Non-Musical Recording
It's Always Something, Gilda Radner (Simon & Schuster Audio)

Best Recording for Children
The Rock-a-Bye Collection Vol. I, Tanya Goodman (Jaba)

Best Album Package
Sound + Vision, Roger Gorman, art director (Rykodisc)

Best Album Notes
Bird: The Complete Charlie Parker on Verve, Phil Schaap, annotator (Verve)

Best Historical Album
Chuck Berry — The Chess Box, Chuck Berry (Chess/MCA)

Best Music Video, Short Form
"Leave Me Alone," Michael Jackson

Best Music Video, Long Form
"Rhythm Nation 1814," Janet Jackson

Producer of the Year (Non-Classical)
Peter Asher

Classical Producer of the Year
Robert Woods

1990

Record of the Year
"Another Day in Paradise," Phil Collins

Album of the Year
Back on the Block, Quincy Jones (Qwest/Warner Bros.)

Song of the Year
"From a Distance," Julie Gold, songwriter

Best New Artist
Mariah Carey

Best Pop Vocal Performance, Male
"Oh Pretty Woman," Roy Orbison

Best Pop Vocal Performance, Female
"Vision of Love," Mariah Carey

Best Pop Performance by a Duo or Group With Vocal
"All My Life," Linda Ronstadt with Aaron Neville

Best Pop Instrumental Performance
"*Twin Peaks* Theme," Angelo Badalamenti

Best Rock/Contemporary Gospel Album
Beyond Belief, Petra (Dayspring/Word)

Best Rock Vocal Performance, Male
"Bad Love," Eric Clapton

Best Rock Vocal Performance, Female
"Black Velvet," Alannah Myles

Best Pop Performance by a Duo or Group With Vocal
"Janie's Got a Gun," Aerosmith

Best Rock Instrumental Performance
"D/FW," Vaughan Brothers

Best Hard Rock Performance
Time's Up, Living Colour

Best Metal Performance
"Stone Cold Crazy," Metallica

Best Alternative Music Performance
I Do Not Want What I Haven't Got, Sinead O'Connor

Best Rhythm and Blues Song
"U Can't Touch This," Rick James, Alonzo Miller and M.C. Hammer, songwriters

Best Rhythm and Blues Vocal Performance, Male
"Here and Now," Luther Vandross

Best Rhythm and Blues Vocal Performance, Female
Compositions, Anita Baker

Best Rhythm and Blues Performance by a Duo or Group With Vocal
"I'll Be Good to You," Ray Charles and Chaka Khan

Best Rap Solo Performance
"U Can't Touch This," M.C. Hammer

Best Rap Performance by a Duo or Group
"Back on the Block," Ice T, Melle Mel, Big Daddy Kane, Kool Moe Dee, Quincy D. III and Quincy Jones

Best Jazz Vocal Performance, Male
We Are in Love, Harry Connick, Jr.

Best Jazz Vocal Performance, Female
All That Jazz, Ella Fitzgerald

Best Jazz Instrumental Performance, Soloist
The Legendary Oscar Peterson Trio Live at the Blue Note, Oscar Peterson

Best Jazz Instrumental Performance, Group
The Legendary Oscar Peterson Trio Live at the Blue Note, Oscar Peterson Trio

Best Jazz Instrumental Performance, Big Band
"Basie's Bag," George Benson featuring the Count Basie Orchestra

Best Jazz Fusion Performance
"Birdland," Quincy Jones

Best Country Song
"Where've You Been," Jon Vezner and Don Henry, songwriters

Best Country Vocal Performance, Male
"When I Call Your Name," Vince Gill

Best Country Vocal Performance, Female
"Where've You Been," Kathy Mattea

Best Country Performance by a Duo or Group With Vocal
Pickin' on Nashville, Kentucky Headhunters

Best Country Vocal Collaboration
"Poor Boy Blues," Chet Atkins and Mark Knopfler

Best Country Instrumental Performance
"So Soft, Your Goodbye," Chet Atkins and Mark Knopfler

Best Bluegrass Recording
I've Got That Old Feeling, Alison Krauss (Rounder)

Best Traditional Soul Gospel Album
Tramaine Hawkins Live, Tramaine Hawkins (Sparrow Corp.)

Best Contemporary Soul Gospel Album
So Much 2 Say, Take 6 (Reprise/Warner/Alliance)

Best Pop Gospel Album
Another Time . . . Another Place, Sandi Patti (A&M/Word)

Best Southern Gospel Album
The Great Exchange, Bruce Carroll (Word)

Best Gospel Album by a Choir or Chorus
Having Church, Rev. James Cleveland (Savoy)

Best Latin Pop Performance
"Por Que Te Tengo Que Olvidar?," José Feliciano

Best Tropical Latin Performance
"Lambada Timbales," Tito Puento

Best Mexican/American Performance
"Soy de San Luis," Texas Tornados

Best Traditional Blues Recording
Live at San Quentin, B.B. King (MCA)

Best Contemporary Blues Recording
Family Style, Vaughan Brothers (Epic Associated)

Best Traditional Folk Recording
On Praying Ground, Doc Watson (Sugar Hill)

Best Contemporary Folk Recording
Steady On, Shawn Colvin (Columbia/CBS)

Best Reggae Recording
Time Will Tell — A Tribute to Bob Marley, Bunny Wailer (Shanachie)

Best New Age Performance
Mark Isham, Mark Isham

Best Polka Recording
When It's Polka Time at Your House, Jimmy Sturr and His Orchestra (Starr)

Best Arrangement on an Instrumental
"Birdland," Quincy Jones, Ian Prince, Rod Temperton and Jerry Hey, arrangers

Best Instrumental Arrangement Accompanying Vocal(s)
"The Places You Find Love," Jerry Hey, Glen Ballard, Clif Magness and Quincy Jones, arrangers

Best Instrumental Composition
"Change of Heart" Pat Metheny, composer

Best Musical Cast Show Album
Les Miserables, The Complete Symphonic Recording (Relativity)

Best Instrumental Composition Written for a Motion Picture or for Television
Glory, James Horner, composer (Virgin)

Best Song Written Specifically for a Motion Picture or for Television
"Under the Sea" (From *The Little Mermaid*), Alan Menken and Howard Ashman, composers

Best Contemporary Composition
Arias and Barcarolles, Leonard Bernstein, composer

Best Classical Album
Ives, *Symphony No. 2 and Three Short Works*, Leonard Bernstein conducting New York Philharmonic (Deutsche Grammophon)

Best Chamber Music or Other Small Ensemble Performance
Brahms, *The Three Violin Sonatas*, Itzhak Perlman, violinist; Daniel Barenboim, pianist

Best Classical Performance, Instrumental Soloist(s) (With Orchestra)
Shostakovich, *Violin Concerto No. 1*; Glazunov, *Violin Concerto*, Itzhak Perlman, violinist; Zubin Mehta conducting Israel Philharmonic

Best Classical Performance, Instrumental Soloist(s) (Without Orchestra)
The Last Recording (Chopin, Haydn, Liszt and Wagner), Vladimir Horowitz

Best Opera Recording
Wagner, *Das Rheingold*, James Levine conducting The Metropolitan Opera Orchestra; solos: Morris, Ludwig, Jerusalem, Wlaschiha, Moll, Zednik and Rootering (Deutsche Grammophon)

Best Choral Performance (Other Than Opera)
Walton, *Belshazzar's Feast*; Bernstein, *Chichester Psalms, Missa Brevis*, Robert Shaw conducting Atlanta Symphony Orchestra and Chorus

Best Classical Vocal Performance
Carreras, Domingo and Pavarotti in Concert, José Carreras, Placido Domingo and Luciano Pavarotti, tenors; Zubin Mehta conducting Orchestra del Maggio Musicale Fiorentino and Orchestra del teatro dell'Opera di Roma

Best Comedy Recording
P.D.Q. Bach, *Oedipus Tex and Other Choral Calamities,* Professor Peter Shickele (Telarc)

Best Spoken Word or Non-Musical Recording
Gracie: A Love Story, George Burns (Simon & Schuster Audio)

Best Recording for Children
The Little Mermaid — Original Motion Picture Soundtrack, Howard Ashman and Alan Menken, composers (Disneyland Records)

Best Album Package
Days of Open Hand (Special Edition Hologram Digapack), Len Peltier, Jeffrey Gold and Suzanne Vega, art directors (A&M)

Best Album Notes
Brownie: The Complete Emarcy Recordings of Clifford Brown, Dan Morgenstern, annotator (Emarcy)

Best Historical Album
Robert Johnson: The Complete Recordings, Robert Johnson (Columbia/CBS)

Best Music Video, Short Form
"Opposites Attract," Paula Abdul

Best Music Video, Long Form
"Please Hammer Don't Hurt 'Em the Movie," M.C. Hammer

Producer of the Year (Non-Classical)
Quincy Jones

Classical Producer of the Year
Adam Stern

1991

Record of the Year
"Unforgettable," Natalie Cole with Nat King Cole

Album of the Year
Unforgettable, Natalie Cole with Nat King Cole (Elektra)

Song of the Year
"Unforgettable," Irving Gordon, songwriter

Best New Artist
Marc Cohn

Best Pop Vocal Performance, Male
"When a Man Loves a Woman," Michael Bolton

Best Pop Vocal Performance, Female
"Something to Talk About," Bonnie Raitt

Best Pop Performance by a Duo or Group With Vocal
"Losing My Religion," R.E.M.

Best Traditional Pop Performance
"Unforgettable," Natalie Cole with Nat King Cole

Best Pop Instrumental Performance
Robin Hood: Prince of Thieves, Michael Kamen conducting Greater Los Angeles Orchestra

Best Rock/Contemporary Gospel Album
Under Their Influence, Russ Taff (Myrrh)

Best Rock Song
"Soul Cages," Sting, songwriter

Best Rock Vocal Performance, Solo
Luck of the Draw, Bonnie Raitt

Best Rock Performance by a Duo or Group With Vocal
"Good Man, Good Woman," Bonnie Raitt and Delbert McClinton

Natalie Cole

Best Rock Instrumental Performance
"Cliffs of Dover," Eric Johnson

Best Hard Rock Performance With Vocal
For Unlawful Carnal Knowledge, Van Halen

Best Metal Performance With Vocal
Metallica, Metallica

Best Alternative Music Album
Out of Time, R.E.M. (Warner Bros.)

Best Rhythm and Blues Song
"Power of Love/Love Power," Luther Vandross, Marcus Miller and Teddy Vann, songwriters

Best Rhythm and Blues Vocal Performance, Male
Power of Love, Luther Vandross

Best Rhythm and Blues Vocal Performance, Female (tie)
Burnin', Patti LaBelle

"How Can I Ease the Pain," Lisa Fischer

Best Rhythm and Blues Performance by a Duo or Group With Vocal
Cooleyhigh Harmony, Boyz II Men

Best Rap Solo Performance
"Mama Said Knock You Out," L.L. Cool J

Best Rap Performance by a Duo or Group
"Summertime," D.J. Jazzy Jeff and the Fresh Prince

Best Jazz Vocal Performance
He Is Christmas, Take 6

Best Jazz Instrumental, Solo
"I Remember You," Stan Getz

Best Jazz Instrumental Performance, Group
Saturday Night at the Blue Note, Oscar Peterson Trio

Best Large Jazz Ensemble Performance
Live at the Royal Festival Hall, Dizzy Gillespie and the United Nation Orchestra

Best Contemporary Jazz Performance
"Sassy," Manhattan Transfer

Best Country Song
"Love Can Build a Bridge," Naomi Judd, John Jarvis and Paul Overstreet, songwriters

Best Country Vocal Performance, Male
Ropin' the Wind, Garth Brooks

Best Country Vocal Performance, Female
"Down at the Twist and Shout," Mary Chapin Carpenter

Best Country Performance by a Duo or Group With Vocal
"Love Can Build a Bridge," Judds

Best Country Vocal Collaboration
"Restless," Steve Wariner, Ricky Skaggs and Vince Gill

Best Country Instrumental Performance
The New Nashville Cats, Mark O'Conner

Best Bluegrass Album
Spring Training, Carl Jackson and John Starling (and the Nash
    Ramblers) (Sugar Hill)

Best Pop Gospel Album
For the Sake of the Call, Steven Curtis Chapman (Sparrow)

Best Traditional Soul Gospel Album
Pray for Me, Mighty Clouds of Joy (Word)

Best Contemporary Soul Gospel Album
Different Lifestyles, BeBe and CeCe Winans (Capitol/Sparrow)

Best Southern Gospel Album
Homecoming, Gaither Vocal Band (Star Song)

Best Gospel Album by a Choir or Chorus
The Evolution of Gospel, Sounds of Blackness; Gary Hines,
    choir director (Perspective/A&M)

Best Latin Pop Album
Cosas del Amor, Vikki Carr (Sony Discos International)

Best Tropical Latin Album
Bachata Rosa, Juan Luis Guerra 4.40 (Karen)

Best Mexican/American Album
16 de Septiembre, Little Joe (Sony Discos International)

Best Traditional Blues Album
Live at the Apollo, B.B. King (GRP)

Best Contemporary Blues Album
Damn Right, I've Got the Blues, Buddy Guy (Silvertone)

Best Traditional Folk Album
The Civil War (Original Soundtrack), various artists
    (Elektra/Nonesuch)

Best Contemporary Folk Album
The Missing Years, John Prine (Oh Boy)

Best Reggae Album
As Raw as Ever, Shabba Ranks (Epic)

Best New Age Album
Fresh Aire 7, Mannheim Steamroller (American Gramaphone)

Best World Music Album
Planet Drum, Mickey Hart (Rykodisc)

Best Polka Album
Live! At Gilley's, Jimmy Sturr and His Orchestra (Starr)

Best Arrangement on an Instrumental
"Medley: Bess You Is My Woman/I Love You Porgy," Dave
    Grusin, arranger

Best Instrumental Arrangement Accompanying Vocal(s)
"Unforgettable," Johnny Mandel, arranger

Best Instrumental Composition
"Basque," Elton John, composer

Best Musical Show Album
The Will Rogers Follies (Original Broadway Cast Album), Keith
    Carradine and cast (Columbia)

**Best Instrumental Composition Written Specifically for a
Motion Picture or for Television**
Dances With Wolves, John Barry, composer

**Best Song Written Specifically for a Motion Picture or for
Television**
(Everything I Do) "I Do It for You" (From *Robin Hood: Prince of
    Thieves),* Bryan Adams, Robert John "Mutt" Lange and
    Michael Kamen, songwriters (A&M/Morgan Creek)

Best Contemporary Composition
Symphony No. 1, John Corigliano, composer

Eric Clapton

Best Classical Album
Bernstein, *Candide,* Leonard Bernstein conducting London
    Symphony Orchestra; solos: Hadley, Anderson, Ludwig,
    Green, Gedda and Jones (Deutsche Grammophon)

Best Orchestral Performance
Corigliano, *Symphony No. 1,* Daniel Barenboim conducting
    Chicago Symphony Orchestra

Best Chamber Music Performance
Brahms, *Piano Quartets,* Isaac Stern and Jamime Laredo, vio-
    linists; Yo-Yo Ma, cellist; Emanuel Ax, pianist

**Best Classical Performance, Instrumental Soloist(s) (With
Orchestra)**
Barber, *Piano Concertos,* John Browning, pianist; Leonard
    Slatkin conducting St. Louis Symphony Orchestra

**Best Classical Performance, Instrumental Soloist(s) (Without
Orchestra)**
Granados, *Goyescas, Allegro de Concierto, Danza Lenta,* Alicia
    de Larrocha, pianist

Best Opera Recording
Wagner, *Götterdammerung,* James Levine conducting The
    Metropolitan Opera Orchestra and Choir; solos: Behrens,
    Studer, Schwartz, Goldberg, Weikl, Wlaschiha and
    Salminen (Deutsche Grammophon)

Best Performance of a Choral Work
Bach, *Mass in B Minor,* Sir Georg Solti conducting Chicago
    Symphony Chorus and Orchestra; Margaret Hills, choral
    director

Best Classical Vocal Performance
The Girl With Orange Lips, De Falla, Ravel, Kim, Stravinsky and
    Delage; Dawn Upshaw, soprano

Best Comedy Album
P.D.Q. Bach, *WTWP Classical Talkity-Talk Radio,* Professor
    Peter Schickele (Telarc)

Best Spoken Word or Non-Musical Album
The Civil War (Geoffrey Ward With Rick Burns and Ken Burns),
    Ken Burns (Sound Editions)

Best Album for Children
A Cappella Kids, Marantha! Kids (Marantha)

Best Album Package
Billie Holiday, The Complete Decca Recordings, Vartan, art
    director (GRP)

Best Album Notes
Star Time, James Brown, Cliff White, Harry Weinger, Nelson
    George and Alan M. Leeds, annotators (Polydor)

Best Historical Album
Billie Holiday, The Complete Decca Recordings, Billie Holiday (GRP)

Best Music Video, Short Form
"Losing My Religion," R.E.M.

Best Music Video, Long Form
Madonna: Blonde Ambition World Tour Live, Madonna

Producer of the Year (Non-Classical)
David Foster

Classical Producer of the Year
James Mallinson

1992

Record of the Year
"Tears in Heaven," Eric Clapton

Album of the Year
Unplugged, Eric Clapton (Reprise)

Song of the Year
"Tears in Heaven," Eric Clapton, songwriter

Best New Artist
Arrested Development

Best Pop Vocal Performance, Male
"Tears in Heaven," Eric Clapton

Best Pop Vocal Performance, Female
"Constant Craving," k.d. lang

Best Pop Performance by a Duo or Group With Vocal
"Beauty and the Beast," Celine Dion and Peabo Bryson

Best Traditional Pop Vocal Performance
Perfectly Frank, Tony Bennett

Best Pop Instrumental Performance
"Beauty and the Beast," Richard Kaufman conducting Nurenberg Symphony Orchestra

Best Rock/Contemporary Gospel Album
Unseen Power, Petra (Dayspring)

Best Rock Song
"Layla," Eric Clapton and Jim Gordon, songwriters

Best Rock Vocal Performance, Male
Unplugged, Eric Clapton

Best Rock Vocal Performance, Female
"Ain't It Heavy," Melissa Etheridge

Best Rock Performance by a Duo or Group With Vocal
Achtung Baby, U2

Best Rock Instrumental Performance
"Little Wing," Stevie Ray Vaughan and Double Trouble

Best Hard Rock Performance With Vocal
"Give It Away," Red Hot Chili Peppers

Best Metal Performance With Vocal
"Wish," Nine Inch Nails

Best Alternative Music Album
Bone Machine, Tom Waits (Island)

Best Rhythm and Blues Song
"End of the Road," L.A. Reid, Babyface and Daryl Simmons, songwriters

Best Rhythm and Blues Vocal Performance, Male
Heaven and Earth, Al Jarreau

Best Rhythm and Blues Vocal Performance, Female
The Woman I Am, Chaka Khan

Best Rhythm and Blues Performance by a Duo or Group With Vocal
"End of the Road," Boys II Men

Best Rhythm and Blues Instrumental Performance
Doo-Bop, Miles Davis

Best Rap Solo Performance
"Baby Got Back," Sir Mix-A-Lot

Best Rap Performance by a Duo or Group
"Tennessee," Arrested Development

Best Jazz Vocal Performance
"'Round Midnight," Bobby McFerrin

Best Jazz Instrumental Performance, Solo
"Lush Life," Joe Henderson

Best Jazz Instrumental Performance, Individual or Group
I Heard You Twice the First Time, Branford Marsalis

Best Large Jazz Ensemble Performance
The Turning Point, McCoy Tyner Big Band

Best Contemporary Jazz Performance, Instrumental
Secret Story, Pat Metheny

Best Country Song
"I Still Believe in You," Vince Gill and John Barlow Jarvis, songwriters

Best Country Vocal Performance, Male
I Still Believe in You, Vince Gill

Best Country Vocal Performance, Female
"I Feel Lucky," Mary Chapin Carpenter

Best Country Performance by a Duo or Group With Vocal
Emmylou Harris and the Nash Ramblers at the Ryman, Emmylou Harris and the Nash Ramblers at the Ryman

Best Country Vocal Collaboration
"The Whiskey Ain't Workin'," Travis Tritt and Marty Stuart

Best Country Instrumental Performance
Sneakin' Around, Chet Atkins and Jerry Reed

Best Bluegrass Album
Every Time You Say Goodbye, Alison Krauss and Union Station (Rounder)

Best Traditional Soul Gospel Album
He's Working It Out for You, Shirley Caesar (Word)

Best Contemporary Soul Gospel Album
Handel's Messiah — A Soulful Celebration, various artists (Reprise)

Best Pop Gospel Album
The Great Adventure, Steven Curtis Chapman (Sparrow)

Best Southern Gospel Album
Sometimes Miracles Hide, Bruce Carroll (Word)

Melissa Etheridge

Best Gospel Album by a Choir or Chorus
Edwin Hawkins Music and Arts Seminar Mass Choir — Recorded Live in Los Angeles, Music and Arts Seminar Mass Choir; Edwin Hawkins, choir director (Fixit)

Best Latin Pop Album
Otro Dia Mas Sin Verte, Jon Secada (Capitol-EMI-Latin)

Best Tropical Latin Album
Frenesi, Linda Ronstadt (Elektra Entertainment)

Best Mexican/American Album
Mas Canciones, Linda Ronstadt (Elektra)

Best Traditional Blues Album
Goin' Back to New Orleans, Dr. John (Warner Bros.)

Best Contemporary Folk Album
Another Country, Chieftains (RCA Victor)

Best Contemporary Blues Album
The Sky Is Crying, Stevie Ray Vaughan and Double Trouble (Epic)

Best Traditional Folk Album
An Irish Evening Live at the Grand Opera House, Belfast, Chieftains (RCA Victor)

Best Reggae Album
X-Tra Naked, Shabba Ranks (Epic)

Best New Age Album
Shepherd Moons, Enya (Reprise)

Best World Music Album
Brasileiro, Sergio Mendes (Elektra Entertainment)

Best Polka Album
35th Anniversary, Walter Ostanek (World Renowned Sounds)

Best Arrangement on an Instrumental
"Strike Up the Band," Rob McConnell, arranger

Best Instrumental Arrangement Accompanying Vocal(s)
"Here's to Life," Johnny Mandel, arranger

Best Instrumental Composition
"Harlem Renaissance Suite," Benny Carter, composer

Best Musical Show Album
Guys and Dolls — The New Broadway Cast Recording, New Broadway cast (RCA Victor)

Best Instrumental Composition Written for a Motion Picture or for Television
Beauty and the Beast, Alan Menken, composer

Best Song Written Specifically for a Motion Picture or for Television
"Beauty and the Beast," Howard Ashman and Alan Menken, songwriters

Best Contemporary Composition
The Lovers, Samuel Barber, composer

Best Classical Album
Mahler, *Symphony No. 9,* Leonard Bernstein conducting Berlin Philharmonic Orchestra (Deutsche Grammophon)

Best Orchestral Performance
Mahler, *Symphony No. 9,* Leonard Bernstein conducting Berlin Philharmonic Orchestra

Best Chamber Music Performance
Brahms, *Sonatas for Cello and Piano,* Yo-Yo Ma, cello; Emanuel Ax, piano

Best Classical Performance, Instrumental Soloist(s) (With Orchestra)
Prokofiev, *Sinfonia Concertante;* Tchaikovsky, *Variations on a Rococo Theme,* Yo-Yo Ma, cello; Lorin Maazel conducting Pittsburgh Symphony Orchestra

Best Classical Performance, Instrumental Soloist(s) (Without Orchestra)
Horowitz — Discovered Treasures (Chopin, Clementi, Liszt, Scarlatti and Scriabin), Vladimir Horowitz, piano

Aerosmith

Best Opera Recording
Strauss, *Die Frau Ohne Schatten,* Sir Georg Solti conducting Vienna Philharmonic; solos: Domingo, Varady, Van Dam, Behrens, Runkel and Jo (London)

Best Performance of a Choral Work
Orff, *Carmina Burana,* Herbert Blomstedt conducting San Francisco Girls and Boys Chorus, SFS Chorus and San Francisco Symphony Orchestra

Best Classical Vocal Performance
Kathleen Battle at Carnegie Hall (Handel, Mozart, Liszt, Strauss, Charpentier, etc.), Kathleen Battle, soprano; Margo Garrett, accompanist

Best Comedy Album
P.D.Q. Bach, *Music for an Awful Lot of Winds and Percussion,* Professor Peter Schickele (Telarc)

Best Spoken Word or Non-Musical Album
What You Can Do to Avoid AIDS, Earvin "Magic" Johnson and Robert O'Keefe (Random House Audiobooks)

Best Album for Children
Beauty and the Beast — Original Motion Picture Soundtrack, various artists (Walt Disney)

Best Album Package
Spellbound — Compact (Special Package), Melanie Nissen, art director (Capitol/Virgin)

Best Album Notes
Queen of Soul — The Atlantic Recordings, Dave Marsh, Jerry Wexler, David Ritz, Thulani Davis, Ahmet Ertegun, Tom Dowd and Arif Mardin, annotators (Rhino)

Best Historical Album
The Complete Capitol Recordings of the Nat King Cole Trio, Nat King Cole Trio (Mosaic)

Best Music Video, Short Form
"Digging in the Dirt," Peter Gabriel

Best Music Video, Long Form
"Diva," Annie Lennox

Producers of the Year (Non-Classical) (tie)
Daniel Lanois and Brian Eno

L.A. Reid and Babyface

Classical Producer of the Year
Michael Fine

1993

Record of the Year
"I Will Always Love You," Whitney Houston

Album of the Year
The Bodyguard — Original Soundtrack Album, Whitney Houston (Arista)

Song of the Year
"A Whole New World" (Theme From *Aladdin*), Alan Menken and Tim Rice, songwriters

Best New Artist
Toni Braxton

Best Pop Vocal Performance, Male
"If I Ever Lose My Faith in You," Sting

Best Pop Vocal Performance, Female
"I Will Always Love You," Whitney Houston

Best Pop Performance by a Duo or Group With Vocal
"A Whole New World" (Theme From *Aladdin*), Peabo Bryson and Regina Belle

Best Traditional Pop Vocal Performance
Steppin' Out, Tony Bennett

Best Pop Instrumental Performance
"Barcelona Mona," Bruce Hornsby and Branford Marsalis

Best Rock Gospel Album
Free at Last, DC Talk (ForeFront)

Best Rock Song
"Runaway Train," David Pirner, songwriter

Best Rock Vocal Performance, Solo
"I'd Do Anything for Love" (But I Won't Do That), Meat Loaf

Best Rock Performance by a Duo or Group With Vocal
"Livin' on the Edge," Aerosmith

Best Rock Instrumental Performance
"Sofa," Zappa's Universe Rock Group Featuring Steve Vai

Best Hard Rock Performance With Vocal
"Plush," Stone Temple Pilots

Best Metal Performance With Vocal
"I Don't Want to Change the World," Ozzy Osbourne

Best Alternative Music Album
Zooropa, U2 (Island)

Best Rhythm and Blues Song
"That's the Way Love Goes," Janet Jackson, James Harris III and Terry Lewis, songwriters

Best Rhythm and Blues Vocal Performance, Male
"A Song for You," Ray Charles

Best Rhythm and Blues Vocal Performance, Female
"Another Sad Love Song," Toni Braxton

Best Rhythm and Blues Performance by a Duo or Group With Vocal
"No Ordinary Love," Sade

Best Rap Solo Performance
"Let Me Ride," Dr. Dre

Best Rap Performance by a Duo or Group
"Rebirth of Slick" (Cool Like Dat), Digable Planets

Best Jazz Vocal Performance
Take a Look, Natalie Cole

Best Jazz Instrumental Solo
"Miles Ahead," Joe Henderson

Best Jazz Instrumental Performance, Individual or Group
So Near, So Far (*Musings for Miles*), Joe Henderson

Best Contemporary Jazz Performance (Instrumental)
The Road to You, Pat Metheny Group

Best Large Jazz Ensemble Performance
Miles and Quincy Live at Montreux, Miles Davis and Quincy Jones

Best Country Song
"Passionate Kisses," Lucinda Williams, songwriter

Best Country Vocal Performance, Male
"Ain't That Lonely Yet," Dwight Yoakam

Best Country Vocal Performance, Female
"Passionate Kisses," Mary Chapin Carpenter

Best Country Performance by a Duo or Group With Vocal
"Hard Workin' Man," Brooks and Dunn

Best Country Vocal Collaboration
"Does He Love You," Reba McEntire and Linda Davis

Best Country Instrumental Performance
"Red Wing," Asleep at the Wheel featuring Eldon Shamblin, Johnny Gimble, Chet Atkins, Vince Gill, Marty Stuart and Reuben "Lucky Orleans" Gosfield

Best Bluegrass Album
Waitin' for the Hard Times to Go, Nashville Bluegrass Band (Sugar Hill)

Best Traditional Soul Gospel Album
Stand Still, Shirley Caesar (Word Record and Music)

Best Contemporary Soul Gospel Album
All Out, Winans (Qwest/Warner Alliance)

Best Pop/Contemporary Gospel Album
The Live Adventure, Steven Curtis Chapman (Sparrow)

Best Southern Gospel, Country Gospel or Bluegrass Gospel Album
Good News, Kathy Mattea (Mercury)

Best Gospel Album by a Choir or Chorus
Live . . . We Come Rejoicing, Brooklyn Tabernacle Choir; Carol Cymbala, choir director (Warner Alliance)

Best Latin Pop Album
Aries, Luis Miguel (WEA Latina)

Best Tropical Latin Album
Mi Tierra, Gloria Estefan (Epic)

Best Mexican/American Album
Live, Selena (Capitol/EMI Latin)

Best Traditional Blues Album
Blues Summit, B.B. King (MCA)

Best Contemporary Blues Album
Feels Like Rain, Buddy Guy (Silvertone)

Whitney Houston

Maurice Rinaldi

Selena

Best Traditional Folk Album
The Celtic Harp, Chieftains (RCA Victor)

Best Contemporary Folk Album
Other Voices/Other Rooms, Nanci Griffith (Elektra)

Best Reggae Album
Bad Boys, Inner Circle (Big Beat/Atlantic)

Best New Age Album
Spanish Angel, Paul Winter Consort (Living Music)

Best World Music Album
A Meeting by the River, Ry Cooder and V.M. Bhatt (Walter Lily
Acoustics)

Best Polka Album
Accordionally Yours, Walter Ostanek and His Band (WRS)

Best Arrangement on an Instrumental
"Mood Indigo," Dave Grusin, arranger

Best Instrumental Arrangement Accompanying Vocal(s)
"When I Fall in Love," Jeremy Lubbock and David Foster,
arrangers

Best Instrumental Composition
"Forever in Love," Kenny G, composer

Best Musical Show Album
The Who's Tommy — Original Cast Recording, original cast
(RCA Victor)

**Best Instrumental Composition Written for a Motion Picture or
for Television**
Aladdin, Alan Menken, composer

Best Song Written for a Motion Picture or for Television
"A Whole New World" (Theme From *Aladdin),* Alan Menken
and Tim Rice, songwriters

Best Contemporary Composition
Violin Concerto, Elliott Carter, composer

Best Classical Album
Bartók, *The Wooden Prince and Cantata Profana,* Pierre
Boulez conducting Chicago Symphony Orchestra and
Chorus; John Aler, tenor; John Tomlinson, baritone
(Deutsche Grammophon)

Best Chamber Music Performance
Ives, *String Quartets nos. 1 and 2;* Barber *String Quartet Op. 11
(American Originals),* Emerson String Quartet

**Best Classical Performance, Instrumental Soloist(s) (With
Orchestra)**
Berg, *Violin Concerto;* Rihm, *Time Chant,* Anne-Sophie Mutter,
violinist; James Levine conducting Chicago Symphony
Orchestra

**Best Classical Performance, Instrumental Soloist(s) (Without
Orchestra)**
Barber, *The Complete Solo Piano Music,* John Browning,
pianist

Best Orchestral Performance
Bartók, *The Wooden Prince,* Pierre Boulez conducting Chicago
Symphony

Best Opera Recording
Handel, *Semele,* John Nelson conducting English Chamber
Orchestra and Ambrosian Opera Chorus; solos: Battle,
Horne, Ramey, Aler, McNair, Chance, Mackie and Doss
(Deutsche Grammophon)

Best Performance of a Choral Work
Bartók, *Cantata Profana,* Pierre Boulez conducting Chicago
Symphony Orchestra and Chorus; Margaret Hillis, choral
director

Best Classical Vocal Performance
*The Art of Arleen Auger (Works of Larsen, Purcell, Schumann,
Mozart),* Arleen Auger, soprano; Joel Revzen, accompa-
nist

Best Spoken Comedy Album
Jammin' in New York, George Carlin (Eardrum/Atlantic)

Best Spoken Word or Non-Musical Album
On the Pulse of Morning, Maya Angelou (Random House Audio
Books)

Best Musical Album for Children
Aladdin (Original Motion Picture Soundtrack), various artists
(Walt Disney Records)

Best Spoken Word Album for Children
Audrey Hepburn's Enchanted Tales, Audrey Hepburn (Dove
Audio)

Best Recording Package
The Complete Billie Holiday on Verve 1945–1959, David Lau, art
director (Verve)

Best Album Notes
The Complete Billie Holiday on Verve 1945–1959, Buck Clayton,
Phil Schaap and Joel E. Siegel, annotators (Verve)

Best Historical Album
The Complete Billie Holiday on Verve 1945–1959, Billie Holiday
(Verve)

Best Music Video, Short Form
"Steam," Peter Gabriel

Best Music Video, Long Form
"Ten Summoner's Tales," Sting

Producer of the Year (Non-Classical)
David Foster

Classical Producer of the Year
Judith Sherman

MTV's Top Videos of All Time

Each year, MTV's programming department assembles a list of the 100 best videos of all time (the music video era is 1981–1995). The programmers compile the list based on viewer requests, airplay, artist popularity, album sales and their own opinions. This year they could only come up with 90 videos, surely not for lack of selection.

Nirvana

1. **Smells Like Teen Spirit**
   Nirvana

2. **Thriller**
   Michael Jackson

3. **Janie's Got a Gun**
   Aerosmith

4. **Basketcase**
   Green Day

5. **Under the Bridge**
   Red Hot Chili Peppers

6. **I'll Make Love to You**
   Boyz II Men

7. **November Rain**
   Guns N' Roses

8. **Jeremy**
   Pearl Jam

9. **Vogue**
   Madonna

10. **Cryin'**
    Aerosmith

11. **Plush**
    Stone Temple Pilots

12. **Nuthin' but "G" Thang**
    Dr. Dre

13. **No Rain**
    Blind Melon

14. **Whatta Man**
    Salt-N-Pepa featuring
    En Vogue

15. **Right Now**
    Van Halen

16. **I Will Always Love You**
    Whitney Houston

17. **When I Come Around**
    Green Day

18. **Enter Sandman**
    Metallica

19. **Again**
    Janet Jackson

20. **Sledgehammer**
    Peter Gabriel

21. **Come As You Are**
    Nirvana

22. **Gin and Juice**
    Snoop Doggy Dogg

23. **Losing My Religion**
    R.E.M.

24. **Self Esteem**
    The Offspring

25. **Amazing**
    Aerosmith

26. **End of the Road**
    Boyz II Men

27. **Sweet Child of Mine**
    Guns N' Roses

28. **Billie Jean**
    Michael Jackson

29. **Sabotage**
    Beastie Boys

30. **With or Without You**
    U2

31. **Shoop**
    Salt-N-Pepa

32. **Jump**
    Van Halen

33. **Give It Away**
    Red Hot Chili Peppers

34. **If**
    Janet Jackson

35. **Black Hole Sun**
    Soundgarden

36. **Express Yourself**
    Madonna

37. **Free Fallin'**
    Tom Petty

38. **Fantastic Voyage**
    Coolio

39. **Even Flow**
    Pearl Jam

40. **Money for Nothin'**
    Dire Straits

41. **On Bended Knee**
    Boyz II Men

42. **Walk This Way**
    Run DMC

43. **Interstate Love Song**
    Stone Temple Pilots

44. **Everything I Do**
    Bryan Adams

45. **Dre Day**
    Dr. Dre

46. **Heart Shaped Box**
    Nirvana

Madonna

Beastie Boys

Country Music Association Awards

The Country Music Association Awards, presented annually in the first week of October, are considered the most coveted awards in the country music industry. Voting is limited to current CMA members, who select winners in a two-round balloting process.

Johnny Cash

1967

Entertainer of the Year
Eddy Arnold

Single of the Year
"There Goes My Everything," Jack Greene

Album of the Year
There Goes My Everything, Jack Greene (Decca)

Song of the Year (Songwriter's Award)
"There Goes My Everything," Dallas Frazier

Male Vocalist of the Year
Jack Greene

Female Vocalist of the Year
Loretta Lynn

Vocal Group of the Year
The Stoneman Family

Instrumental Group of the Year
The Buckaroos

Comedian of the Year
Don Bowman

Musician of the Year
Chet Atkins

1968

Entertainer of the Year
Glen Campbell

Single of the Year
"Harper Valley P.T.A.," Jeannie C. Riley

Album of the Year
Johnny Cash at Folsom Prison, Johnny Cash (Columbia)

Song of the Year (Songwriter's Award)
"Honey," Bobby Russell

Male Vocalist of the Year
Glen Campbell

Female Vocalist of the Year
Tammy Wynette

Vocal Group of the Year
Porter Wagoner and Dolly Parton

Instrumental Group of the Year
The Buckaroos

Comedian of the Year
Ben Colder

Musician of the Year
Chet Atkins

1969

Entertainer of the Year
Johnny Cash

Single of the Year
"A Boy Named Sue," Johnny Cash

Album of the Year
Johnny Cash at San Quentin Prison, Johnny Cash (Columbia)

Song of the Year (Songwriter's Award)
"Carroll County Accident," Bob Ferguson

Male Vocalist of the Year
Johnny Cash

Female Vocalist of the Year
Tammy Wynette

Vocal Group of the Year
Johnny Cash and June Carter

Instrumental Group of the Year
Danny Davis and the Nashville Brass

Comedian of the Year
Archie Campbell

Musician of the Year
Chet Atkins

1970

Entertainer of the Year
Merle Haggard

Single of the Year
"Okie From Muskogee," Merle Haggard

Album of the Year
Okie From Muskogee, Merle Haggard (Capitol)

Song of the Year (Songwriter's Award)
"Sunday Morning Coming Down," Kris Kristofferson

Male Vocalist of the Year
Merle Haggard

Female Vocalist of the Year
Tammy Wynette

Vocal Group of the Year
The Glaser Brothers

Vocal Duo of the Year
Porter Wagoner and Dolly Parton

Instrumental Group of the Year
Danny Davis and the Nashville Brass

Comedian of the Year
Roy Clark

Musician of the Year
Jerry Reed

1971

Entertainer of the Year
Charley Pride

Single of the Year
"Help Me Make It Through the Night," Sammi Smith

Album of the Year
I Won't Mention It Again, Ray Price (Columbia)

Song of the Year (Songwriter's Award)
"Easy Loving," Freddie Hart

Male Vocalist of the Year
Charley Pride

Female Vocalist of the Year
Lynn Anderson

Loretta Lynn

Vocal Group of the Year
The Osborne Brothers

Vocal Duo of the Year
Porter Wagoner and Dolly Parton

Instrumental Group of the Year
Danny Davis and the Nashville Brass

Musician of the Year
Jerry Reed

1972

Entertainer of the Year
Loretta Lynn

Single of the Year
"The Happiest Girl in the Whole U.S.A.,"
Donna Fargo

Album of the Year
Let Me Tell You About a Song, Merle
Haggard (Capitol)

Song of the Year (Songwriter's Award)
"Easy Loving," Freddie Hart

Male Vocalist of the Year
Charley Pride

Female Vocalist of the Year
Loretta Lynn

Vocal Group of the Year
Statler Brothers

Vocal Duo of the Year
Conway Twitty and Loretta Lynn

Instrumental Group of the Year
Danny Davis and the Nashville Brass

Musician of the Year
Charlie McCoy

1973

Entertainer of the Year
Roy Clark

Single of the Year
"Behind Closed Doors," Charlie Rich

Album of the Year
Behind Closed Doors, Charlie Rich
(Epic)

Song of the Year (Songwriter's Award)
"Behind Closed Doors," Kenny O'Dell

Male Vocalist of the Year
Charlie Rich

Female Vocalist of the Year
Loretta Lynn

Vocal Group of the Year
Statler Brothers

Vocal Duo of the Year
Conway Twitty and Loretta Lynn

Instrumental Group of the Year
Danny Davis and the Nashville Brass

Musician of the Year
Charlie McCoy

1974

Entertainer of the Year
Charlie Rich

Single of the Year
"Country Bumpkin," Cal Smith

Album of the Year
A Very Special Love Song, Charlie Rich
(Epic)

Song of the Year (Songwriter's Award)
"Country Bumpkin," Don Wayne

Male Vocalist of the Year
Ronnie Milsap

Female Vocalist of the Year
Olivia Newton-John

Vocal Group of the Year
Statler Brothers

Vocal Duo of the Year
Conway Twitty and Loretta Lynn

Instrumental Group of the Year
Danny Davis and the Nashville Brass

Musician of the Year
Don Rich

1975

Entertainer of the Year
John Denver

Single of the Year
"Before the Next Teardrop Falls,"
Freddy Fender

Album of the Year
A Legend in My Time, Ronnie Milsap
(RCA)

Song of the Year (Songwriter's Award)
"Back Home Again," John Denver

Male Vocalist of the Year
Waylon Jennings

Female Vocalist of the Year
Dolly Parton

Vocal Group of the Year
Statler Brothers

Vocal Duo of the Year
Conway Twitty and Loretta Lynn

Instrumental Group of the Year
Roy Clark and Buck Trent

Musician of the Year
Johnny Gimble

1976

Entertainer of the Year
Mel Tillis

Single of the Year
"Good Hearted Woman," Waylon
Jennings and Willie Nelson

Album of the Year
Wanted — The Outlaws, Waylon
Jennings, Willie Nelson, Tompall
Glaser and Jesse Colter (RCA)

Song of the Year (Songwriter's Award)
"Rhinestone Cowboy," Larry Weiss

Male Vocalist of the Year
Ronnie Milsap

Female Vocalist of the Year
Dolly Parton

Vocal Group of the Year
Statler Brothers

Vocal Duo of the Year
Waylon Jennings and Willie Nelson

Instrumental Group of the Year
Roy Clark and Buck Trent

Musician of the Year
Hargus "Pig" Robbins

1977

Entertainer of the Year
Ronnie Milsap

Single of the Year
"Lucille," Kenny Rogers

Album of the Year
Ronnie Milsap Live, Ronnie Milsap
(RCA)

Willie Nelson

Song of the Year (Songwriter's Award)
"Lucille," Roger Bowling and Hal Bynum

Male Vocalist of the Year
Ronnie Milsap

Female Vocalist of the Year
Crystal Gayle

Vocal Group of the Year
Statler Brothers

Vocal Duo of the Year
Jim Ed Brown and Helen Cornelius

Instrumental Group of the Year
The Original Texas Playboys

Musician of the Year
Roy Clark

1978

Entertainer of the Year
Dolly Parton

Single of the Year
"Heaven's Just a Sin Away," The
Kendalls

Album of the Year
It Was Almost Like a Song, Ronnie
Milsap (RCA)

Song of the Year (Songwriter's Award)
"Don't It Make My Brown Eyes Blue,"
Richard Leigh

Male Vocalist of the Year
Don Williams

Female Vocalist of the Year
Crystal Gayle

Vocal Group of the Year
Oak Ridge Boys

Vocal Duo of the Year
Kenny Rogers and Dottie West

Instrumental Group of the Year
Oak Ridge Boys

Musician of the Year
Roy Clark

1979

Entertainer of the Year
Willie Nelson

Single of the Year
"The Devil Went Down to Georgia,"
Charlie Daniels Band

Album of the Year
The Gambler, Kenny Rogers (United
Artists)

Song of the Year (Songwriter's Award)
"The Gambler," Don Schlitz

Male Vocalist of the Year
Kenny Rogers

Female Vocalist of the Year
Barbara Mandrell

Vocal Group of the Year
Statler Brothers

Vocal Duo of the Year
Kenny Rogers and Dottie West

Instrumental Group of the Year
Charlie Daniels Band

Musician of the Year
Charlie Daniels

1980

Entertainer of the Year
Barbara Mandrell

Single of the Year
"He Stopped Loving Her Today," George
Jones

Album of the Year
*Coal Miner's Daughter — Original
Motion Picture Soundtrack* (MCA)

Song of the Year (Songwriter's Award)
"He Stopped Loving Her Today," Bobby
Braddock and Curly Putman

Male Vocalist of the Year
George Jones

Female Vocalist of the Year
Emmylou Harris

Vocal Group of the Year
Statler Brothers

Vocal Duo of the Year
Moe Bandy and Joe Stampley

Instrumental Group of the Year
Charlie Daniels Band

Musician of the Year
Roy Clark

1981

Entertainer of the Year
Barbara Mandrell

Single of the Year
"Elvira," Oak Ridge Boys

Album of the Year
I Believe in You, Don Williams (MCA)

Song of the Year (Songwriter's Award)
"He Stopped Loving Her Today," Bobby
Braddock and Curly Putman

Male Vocalist of the Year
George Jones

Female Vocalist of the Year
Barbara Mandrell

Vocal Group of the Year
Alabama

Vocal Duo of the Year
David Frizzell and Shelly West

Instrumental Group of the Year
Alabama

Horizon Award
Terri Gibbs

Musician of the Year
Chet Atkins

1982

Entertainer of the Year
Alabama

Single of the Year
"Always on My Mind," Willie Nelson

Album of the Year
Always on My Mind, Willie Nelson
(Columbia)

Song of the Year (Songwriter's Award)
"Always on My Mind," Johnny
Christopher, Wayne Carson and
Mark James

Male Vocalist of the Year
Ricky Skaggs

Female Vocalist of the Year
Janie Frickie

Vocal Group of the Year
Alabama

Vocal Duo of the Year
David Frizzell and Shelly West

Instrumental Group of the Year
Alabama

Horizon Award
Ricky Skaggs

Barbara Mandrell

Musician of the Year
Chet Atkins

1983

Entertainer of the Year
Alabama

Single of the Year
"Swingin'," John Anderson

Album of the Year
The Closer You Get, Alabama (RCA)

Song of the Year (Songwriter's Award)
"Always on My Mind," Johnny
Christopher, Wayne Carson and
Mark James

Male Vocalist of the Year
Lee Greenwood

Female Vocalist of the Year
Janie Frickie

Vocal Group of the Year
Alabama

Vocal Duo of the Year
Merle Haggard and Willie Nelson

Instrumental Group of the Year
The Ricky Skaggs Band

Horizon Award
John Anderson

Musician of the Year
Chet Atkins

1984

Entertainer of the Year
Alabama

Single of the Year
"A Little Good News," Anne Murray

Album of the Year
A Little Good News, Anne Murray
(Capitol)

Song of the Year (Songwriter's Award)
"Wind Beneath My Wings," Larry
Henley and Jeff Silbar

Male Vocalist of the Year
Lee Greenwood

Female Vocalist of the Year
Reba McEntire

Vocal Group of the Year
Statler Brothers

Vocal Duo of the Year
Willie Nelson and Julio Iglesias

Instrumental Group of the Year
The Ricky Skaggs Band

Horizon Award
Judds

Musician of the Year
Chet Atkins

1985

Entertainer of the Year
Ricky Skaggs

Single of the Year
"Why Not Me," Judds

Album of the Year
Does Fort Worth Ever Cross Your Mind,
George Strait (MCA)

Song of the Year (Songwriter's Award)
"God Bless the U.S.A.," Lee Greenwood

Male Vocalist of the Year
George Strait

Female Vocalist of the Year
Reba McEntire

Vocal Group of the Year
Judds

Vocal Duo of the Year
Anne Murray and Dave Loggins

Instrumental Group of the Year
The Ricky Skaggs Band

Horizon Award
Sawyer Brown

Musician of the Year
Chet Atkins

Music Video of the Year
"All My Rowdy Friends Are Coming
    Over Tonight," Hank Williams, Jr.

Reba McEntire

1986

Entertainer of the Year
Reba McEntire

Single of the Year
"Bop," Dan Seals

Album of the Year
Lost in the Fifties Tonight, Ronnie
    Milsap (RCA)

Song of the Year (Songwriter's Award)
"On the Other Hand," Paul Overstreet
    and Don Schlitz

Male Vocalist of the Year
George Strait

Female Vocalist of the Year
Reba McEntire

Vocal Group of the Year
Judds

Vocal Duo of the Year
Dan Seals and Marie Osmond

Instrumental Group of the Year
Oak Ridge Boys

Horizon Award
Randy Travis

Musician of the Year
Johnny Gimble

Music Video of the Year
"Who's Gonna Fill Their Shoes," George
    Jones

1987

Entertainer of the Year
Hank Williams, Jr.

Single of the Year
"Forever and Ever, Amen," Randy Travis

Album of the Year
Always and Forever, Randy Travis
    (Warner Bros.)

Song of the Year (Songwriter's Award)
"Forever and Ever, Amen," Paul
    Overstreet and Don Schlitz

Male Vocalist of the Year
Randy Travis

Female Vocalist of the Year
Reba McEntire

Vocal Group of the Year
Judds

Vocal Duo of the Year
Ricky Skaggs and Sharon White

Horizon Award
Holly Dunn

Musician of the Year
Johnny Gimble

Music Video of the Year
"My Name Is Bocephus," Hank
    Williams, Jr.

1988

Entertainer of the Year
Hank Williams, Jr.

Single of the Year
"Eighteen Wheels and a Dozen Roses,"
    Kathy Mattea

Album of the Year
Born to Boogie, Hank Williams, Jr.
    (Warner Bros.)

Song of the Year (Songwriter's Award)
'80's Ladies," K.T. Oslin

Male Vocalist of the Year
Randy Travis

Female Vocalist of the Year
K.T. Oslin

Vocal Group of the Year
Highway 101

Vocal Duo of the Year
Judds

Vocal Event of the Year
Trio, Dolly Parton, Emmylou Harris and
    Linda Ronstadt

Horizon Award
Ricky Van Shelton

Musician of the Year
Chet Atkins

1989

Entertainer of the Year
George Strait

Single of the Year
"I'm No Stranger to the Rain," Keith
    Whitley

Album of the Year
Will the Circle Be Unbroken Volume II,
    Nitty Gritty Dirt Band (Universal)

Song of the Year (Songwriter's Award)
"Chiseled in Stone," Max D. Barnes and
    Vern Gosdin

Male Vocalist of the Year
Ricky Van Shelton

Female Vocalist of the Year
Kathy Mattea

Vocal Group of the Year
Highway 101

Vocal Duo of the Year
Judds

Vocal Event of the Year
"There's a Tear in My Beer," Hank
    Williams, Jr. and Hank Williams, Sr.

Horizon Award
Clint Black

Musician of the Year
Johnny Gimble

Music Video of the Year
"There's a Tear in My Beer," Hank
    Williams, Jr.

1990

Entertainer of the Year
George Strait

Single of the Year
"When I Call Your Name," Vince Gill

Album of the Year
Pickin' on Nashville, Kentucky
    HeadHunters (Mercury)

Song of the Year (Songwriter's Award)
"Where've You Been," Jon Vezner and
    Don Henry

Male Vocalist of the Year
Clint Black

Female Vocalist of the Year
Kathy Mattea

Vocal Group of the Year
Kentucky HeadHunters

Vocal Duo of the Year
Judds

Vocal Event of the Year
"Till a Tear Becomes a Rose," Lorrie
    Morgan and Keith Whitley

Horizon Award
Garth Brooks

Musician of the Year
Johnny Gimble

Music Video of the Year
"The Dance," Garth Brooks

1991

Entertainer of the Year
Garth Brooks

Single of the Year
"Friends in Low Places," Garth Brooks

Album of the Year
No Fences, Garth Brooks (Capitol Nashville)

Song of the Year (Songwriter's Award)
"When I Call Your Name," Vince Gill and Tim DuBois

Male Vocalist of the Year
Vince Gill

Female Vocalist of the Year
Tanya Tucker

Vocal Group of the Year
Kentucky HeadHunters

Vocal Duo of the Year
Judds

Vocal Event of the Year
Mark O'Connor and the New Nashville Cats, Mark O'Connor and the New Nashville Cats (featuring Vince Gill, Ricky Skaggs and Steve Wariner)

Horizon Award
Travis Tritt

Musician of the Year
Mark O'Connor

Music Video of the Year
"The Thunder Rolls," Garth Brooks

1992

Entertainer of the Year
Garth Brooks

Single of the Year
"Achy Breaky Heart," Billy Ray Cyrus

Album of the Year
Ropin' the Wind, Garth Brooks (Liberty)

Song of the Year (Songwriter's Award)
"Look at Us," Vince Gill and Max D. Barnes

Male Vocalist of the Year
Vince Gill

Female Vocalist of the Year
Mary Chapin Carpenter

Vocal Group of the Year
Diamond Rio

Vocal Duo of the Year
Brooks and Dunn

Vocal Event of the Year
"The Whiskey Ain't Workin'," Marty Stuart and Travis Tritt

Horizon Award
Suzy Bogguss

Musician of the Year
Mark O'Connor

Music Video of the Year
"Midnight in Montgomery," Alan Jackson

1993

Entertainer of the Year
Vince Gill

Single of the Year
"Chattahoochee," Alan Jackson

Album of the Year
I Still Believe in You, Vince Gill (MCA)

Song of the Year (Songwriter's Award)
"I Still Believe in You," Vince Gill

Male Vocalist of the Year
Vince Gill

Female Vocalist of the Year
Mary Chapin Carpenter

Vocal Group of the Year
Diamond Rio

Vocal Duo of the Year
Brooks and Dunn

Vocal Event of the Year
"I Don't Need Your Rocking Chair," George Jones with Vince Gill, Mark Chesnutt, Garth Brooks, Travis Tritt, Joe Diffie, Alan Jackson, Pam Tillis, T. Graham Brown, Patty Loveless and Clint Black

Horizon Award
Mark Chesnutt

Musician of the Year
Mark O'Connor

Music Video of the Year
"Chattahoochee," Alan Jackson

Garth Brooks

1994

Entertainer of the Year
Vince Gill

Single of the Year
"I Swear," John Michael Montgomery

Album of the Year
Common Thread: The Songs of the Eagles, John Anderson, Clint Black, Suzy Bogguss, Brooks and Dunn, Billy Dean, Diamond Rio, Vince Gill, Alan Jackson, Little Texas, Lorrie Morgan, Travis Tritt, Tanya Tucker and Trisha Yearwood (Giant)

Song of the Year (Songwriter's Award)
"Chattahoochee," Alan Jackson

Male Vocalist of the Year
Vince Gill

Female Vocalist of the Year
Pam Tillis

Vocal Group of the Year
Diamond Rio

Vocal Duo of the Year
Brooks and Dunn

Vocal Event of the Year
"Does He Love You," Reba McEntire and Linda Davis

Horizon Award
John Michael Montgomery

Musician of the Year
Mark O'Connor

Music Video of the Year
"Independence Day," Martina McBride

Vince Gill

Down Beat Polls and Hall of Fame

Each year, *Down Beat* magazine polls its readers and a group of international music critics to recognize those who have achieved excellence in the jazz world. The Critics Poll appears in the August issue and the Readers Poll in December. Both readers and critics polls annually nominate inductees to the Jazz Hall of Fame, which appears in the magazine with the polls. Talent Deserving Wider Recognition (TDWR), unique to the Critics Poll, allows critics to cite young, emerging talent and overlooked established talent. Here are the winners.

Readers Poll

1936

Favorite Soloist
Benny Goodman

Big Band
Benny Goodman

Sweet Band
Ray Noble

Clarinet
Benny Goodman

Trumpet
Bix Beiderbecke

Trombone
Tommy Dorsey

Piano
Teddy Wilson

Guitar
Eddie Lang

Bass
Pops Foster

Drums
Gene Krupa

1937

Favorite Soloist
Benny Goodman

Female Vocalist
Ella Fitzgerald

Big Band
Benny Goodman

Sweet Band
Hal Kemp

Alto Saxophone
Jimmy Dorsey

Tenor Saxophone
Chu Berry

Clarinet
Benny Goodman

Trumpet
Harry James

Trombone
Tommy Dorsey

Piano
Teddy Wilson

Guitar
Carmen Mastren

Bass
Bob Haggart

Drums
Gene Krupa

1938

Favorite Soloist
Benny Goodman

Female Vocalist
Ella Fitzgerald

Jazz Group
Benny Goodman

Big Band
Artie Shaw

Sweet Band
Casa Loma

Arranger/Composer
Larry Clinton

Alto Saxophone
Jimmy Dorsey

Tenor Saxophone
Bud Freeman

Clarinet
Benny Goodman

Trumpet
Harry James

Trombone
Tommy Dorsey

Piano
Bob Zurke

Guitar
Benny Heller

Bass
Bob Haggart

Drums
Gene Krupa

1939

Favorite Soloist
Benny Goodman

Male Vocalist
Bing Crosby

Female Vocalist
Ella Fitzgerald

Benny Goodman

Jazz Group
Benny Goodman

Big Band
Benny Goodman

Sweet Band
Tommy Dorsey

Arranger/Composer
Fletcher Henderson

Alto Saxophone
Jimmy Dorsey

Tenor Saxophone
Coleman Hawkins

Clarinet
Benny Goodman

Trumpet
Harry James

Trombone
Tommy Dorsey

Piano
Jess Stacy

Guitar
Charlie Christian

Bass
Bob Haggart

Drums
Gene Krupa

1940

Favorite Soloist
Benny Goodman

Male Vocalist
Bing Crosby

Female Vocalist
Helen O'Connell

Jazz Group
Benny Goodman

Big Band
Benny Goodman

Sweet Band
Glenn Miller

Arranger/Composer
Fletcher Henderson

Alto Saxophone
Johnny Hodges

Tenor Saxophone
Eddie Miller

Clarinet
Irving Fazola

Trumpet
Ziggy Elman

Trombone
Jack Jenney

Piano
Jess Stacy

Guitar
Charlie Christian

Bass
Bob Haggart

Drums
Ray Bauduc

1941

Favorite Soloist
Harry James

Male Vocalist
Frank Sinatra

Female Vocalist
Helen O'Connell

Jazz Group
Benny Goodman

Big Band
Benny Goodman

Sweet Band
Glenn Miller

Arranger/Composer
Sy Oliver

Alto Saxophone
Johnny Hodges

Tenor Saxophone
Tex Beneke

Clarinet
Irving Fazola

Trumpet
Ziggy Elman

Trombone
J. C. Higginbotham

Piano
Jess Stacy

Guitar
Charlie Christian

Bass
Bob Haggart

Drums
Buddy Rich

1942

Favorite Soloist
Benny Goodman

Male Vocalist
Frank Sinatra

Female Vocalist
Helen Forrest

Jazz Group
Benny Goodman

Big Band
Duke Ellington

Sweet Band
Tommy Dorsey

Arranger/Composer
Sy Oliver

Alto Saxophone
Johnny Hodges

Tenor Saxophone
Tex Beneke

Clarinet
Pee Wee Russell

Trumpet
Roy Eldridge

Trombone
J. C. Higginbotham

Piano
Jess Stacy

Guitar
Eddie Condon

Bass
Bob Haggart

Drums
Buddy Rich

1943

Favorite Soloist
Benny Goodman

Male Vocalist
Frank Sinatra

Female Vocalist
Jo Stafford

Jazz Group
Roy Eldridge

Big Band
Benny Goodman

Sweet Band
Tommy Dorsey

Arranger/Composer
Sy Oliver

Alto Saxophone
Johnny Hodges

Tenor Saxophone
Vido Musso

Clarinet
Pee Wee Russell

Trumpet
Ziggy Elman

Trombone
J. C. Higginbotham

Piano
Mel Powell

Guitar
Eddie Condon

Bass
Artie Bernstein

Drums
Gene Krupa

1944

Favorite Soloist
Benny Goodman

Male Vocalist
Bing Crosby

Female Vocalist
Dinah Shore

Male Vocalist With Band
Bob Eberly

Female Vocalist With Band
Anita O'Day

Vocal Group
Pied Pipers

Jazz Group
Nat King Cole

Big Band
Duke Ellington

Sweet Band
Charlie Spivak

Arranger/Composer
Sy Oliver

Alto Saxophone
Johnny Hodges

Tenor Saxophone
Lester Young

Baritone Saxophone
Harry Carney

Clarinet
Pee Wee Russell

Trumpet
Ziggy Elman

Trombone
J. C. Higginbotham

Piano
Mel Powell

Guitar
Allan Reuss

Bass
Bob Haggart

Drums
Buddy Rich

1945

Favorite Soloist
Benny Goodman

Male Vocalist
Bing Crosby

Female Vocalist
Jo Stafford

Male Vocalist With Band
Stuart Foster

Female Vocalist With Band
Anita O'Day

Vocal Group
Pied Pipers

Jazz Group
Nat King Cole

Big Band
Woody Herman

Sweet Band
Tommy Dorsey

Arranger/Composer
Sy Oliver

Alto Saxophone
Johnny Hodges

Tenor Saxophone
Charlie Ventura

Baritone Saxophone
Harry Carney

Clarinet
Buddy DeFranco

Trumpet
Ziggy Elman

Trombone
Bill Harris

Piano
Mel Powell

Guitar
Oscar Moore

Bass
Chubby Jackson

Drums
Dave Tough

1946

Favorite Soloist
Benny Goodman

Male Vocalist
Frank Sinatra

Female Vocalist
Peggy Lee

Male Vocalist With Band
Art Lund

Female Vocalist With Band
June Christy

Vocal Group
Pied Pipers

Jazz Group
Nat King Cole

Frank Sinatra

Big Band
Duke Ellington

Sweet Band
Duke Ellington

Arranger/Composer
Billy Strayhorn

Alto Saxophone
Johnny Hodges

Tenor Saxophone
Vido Musso

Baritone Saxophone
Harry Carney

Clarinet
Buddy DeFranco

Trumpet
Roy Eldridge

Trombone
Bill Harris

Piano
Mel Powell

Guitar
Oscar Moore

Bass
Eddie Safranski

Drums
Dave Tough

1947

Favorite Soloist
Duke Ellington

Male Vocalist
Frank Sinatra

Female Vocalist
Sarah Vaughan

Male Vocalist With Band
Buddy Stewart

Female Vocalist With Band
June Christy

Vocal Group
Pied Pipers

Jazz Group
Nat King Cole

Big Band
Stan Kenton

Arranger/Composer
Pete Rugolo

Alto Saxophone
Johnny Hodges

Tenor Saxophone
Vido Musso

Baritone Saxophone
Harry Carney

Clarinet
Buddy DeFranco

Trumpet
Ziggy Elman

Trombone
Bill Harris

Piano
Mel Powell

Guitar
Oscar Moore

Bass
Eddie Safranski

Drums
Shelly Manne

1948

Favorite Soloist
Benny Goodman

Male Vocalist
Billy Eckstine

Female Vocalist
Sarah Vaughan

Male Vocalist With Band
Al Hibbler

Female Vocalist With Band
June Christy

Vocal Group
Pied Pipers

Jazz Group
Charlie Ventura

Big Band
Duke Ellington

Arranger/Composer
Billy Strayhorn

Alto Saxophone
Johnny Hodges

Tenor Saxophone
Flip Phillips

Baritone Saxophone
Harry Carney

Clarinet
Buddy DeFranco

Trumpet
Charlie Shavers

Trombone
Bill Harris

Piano
Erroll Garner

Guitar
Oscar Moore

Bass
Eddie Safranski

Drums
Shelly Manne

1949

Male Vocalist
Billy Eckstine

Female Vocalist
Sarah Vaughan

Male Vocalist With Band
Al Hibbler

Female Vocalist With Band
Mary Ann McCall

Vocal Group
Pied Pipers

Jazz Group
George Shearing

Big Band
Woody Herman

Duke Ellington

Arranger/Composer
Pete Rugolo

Alto Saxophone
Johnny Hodges

Tenor Saxophone
Flip Phillips

Baritone Saxophone
Serge Chaloff

Clarinet
Buddy DeFranco

Trumpet
Howard McGhee

Trombone
Bill Harris

Piano
Oscar Peterson

Guitar
Billy Bauer

Bass
Eddie Safranski

Drums
Shelly Manne

Alto Saxophone
Charlie Parker

Tenor Saxophone
Stan Getz

Baritone Saxophone
Serge Chaloff

Clarinet
Buddy DeFranco

Trumpet
Maynard Ferguson

Trombone
Bill Harris

Piano
Oscar Peterson

Guitar
Billy Bauer

Bass
Eddie Safranski

Drums
Shelly Manne

Miscellaneous Instrument
Terry Gibbs, Vibes

1950

Male Vocalist
Billy Eckstine

Female Vocalist
Sarah Vaughan

Male Vocalist With Band
Jay Johnson

Female Vocalist With Band
June Christy

Vocal Group
Mills Brothers

Jazz Group
George Shearing

Big Band
Stan Kenton

Arranger/Composer
Pete Rugolo

1951

Favorite Soloist
Charlie Parker

Male Vocalist
Billy Eckstine

Female Vocalist
Sarah Vaughan

Male Vocalist With Band
Jay Johnson

Female Vocalist With Group
Lucy Ann Polk

Vocal Group
Mills Brothers

Jazz Group
George Shearing

Big Band
Stan Kenton

Arranger/Composer
Pete Rugolo

Alto Saxophone
Charlie Parker

Tenor Saxophone
Stan Getz

Baritone Saxophone
Serge Chaloff

Clarinet
Buddy DeFranco

Trumpet
Maynard Ferguson

Trombone
Bill Harris

Piano
Oscar Peterson

Guitar
Les Paul

Bass
Eddie Safranski

Drums
Shelly Manne

Miscellaneous Instrument
Terry Gibbs, Vibes

1952

Male Vocalist
Billy Eckstine

Female Vocalist
Sarah Vaughan

Male Vocalist With Band
Tommy Mercer

Female Vocalist With Band
Lucy Ann Polk

Vocal Group
Mills Brothers

Jazz Group
George Shearing

Big Band
Stan Kenton

Arranger/Composer
Ralph Burns

Alto Saxophone
Charlie Parker

Tenor Saxophone
Stan Getz

Baritone Saxophone
Harry Carney

Clarinet
Buddy DeFranco

Trumpet
Maynard Ferguson

Trombone
Bill Harris

Piano
Oscar Peterson

Guitar
Les Paul

Bass
Eddie Safranski

Drums
Gene Krupa

CONTINUED ON NEXT PAGE ▶

D O W N   B E A T   P O L L S

Down Beat's Jazz Hall of Fame

READERS POLL

1952
Louis Armstrong

1953
Glenn Miller

1954
Stan Kenton

1955
Charlie Parker

1956
Duke Ellington

1957
Benny Goodman

1958
Count Basie

1959
Lester Young

1960
Dizzy Gillespie

1961
Billie Holiday

1962
Miles Davis

1963
Thelonious Monk

1964
Eric Dolphy

1965
John Coltrane

1966
Bud Powell

1967
Billy Strayhorn

1968
Wes Montgomery

1969
Ornette Coleman

1970
Jimi Hendrix

1971
Charles Mingus

1972
Gene Krupa

1973
Sonny Rollins

1974
Buddy Rich

1975
Cannonball Adderley

1976
Woody Herman

1977
Paul Desmond

1978
Joe Venuti

1979
Ella Fitzgerald

1980
Dexter Gordon

1981
Art Blakey

1982
Art Pepper

1983
Stephane
  Grappelli

1984
Oscar Peterson

1985
Sarah Vaughan

1986
Stan Getz

1987
Lionel Hampton

1988
Jaco Pastorius

1989
Woody Shaw

1990
Red Rodney

1991
Lee Morgan

1992
Maynard Ferguson

1993
Gerry Mulligan

CRITICS POLL

1961
Coleman Hawkins

1962
Bix Beiderbecke

1963
Jelly Roll Morton

1964
Art Tatum

1965
Earl Hines

1966
Charlie Christian

1967
Bessie Smith

1968
Sidney Bechet/Fats Waller

1969
Pee Wee Russell/Jack
  Teagarden

1970
Johnny Hodges

1971
Roy Eldridge/Django
  Reinhardt

1972
Clifford Brown

Louis Armstrong

1973
Fletcher Henderson

1974
Ben Webster

1975
Cecil Taylor

1976
King Oliver

1977
Benny Carter

1978
Rahsaan Roland Kirk

1979
Lennie Tristano

1980
Max Roach

1981
Bill Evans

1982
Fats Navarro

1983
Albert Ayler

1984
Sun Ra

1985
Zoot Sims

1986
Gil Evans

1987
Johnny Dodds

1988
Kenny Clarke

1989
Chet Baker

1990
Mary Lou Williams

1991
John Carter

1992
James P. Johnson

1993
Edward Blackwell

Vibes
Terry Gibbs

Accordion
Art Van Damme

Miscellaneous Instrument
Art Van Damme, Accordion

1953

Male Vocalist
Nat Cole

Female Vocalist
Ella Fitzgerald

Male Vocalist With Group
Tommy Mercer

Female Vocalist With Group
Lucy Ann Polk

Vocal Group
Four Freshmen

Jazz Group
Dave Brubeck

Big Band
Stan Kenton

Dance Band
Les Brown

Arranger/Composer
Ralph Burns

Alto Saxophone
Charlie Parker

Tenor Saxophone
Stan Getz

Baritone Saxophone
Gerry Mulligan

Clarinet
Buddy DeFranco

Trumpet
Chet Baker

Trombone
Bill Harris

Piano
Oscar Peterson

Guitar
Les Paul

Bass
Ray Brown

Drums
Gene Krupa

Vibes
Terry Gibbs

Accordion
Art Van Damme

Miscellaneous Instrument
Don Elliott, Mellophone

1954

Male Vocalist
Frank Sinatra

Female Vocalist
Ella Fitzgerald

Male Vocalist With Group
Tommy Mercer

Female Vocalist With Group
Lucy Ann Polk

Vocal Group
Four Freshmen

Jazz Group
Dave Brubeck

Big Band
Stan Kenton

Dance Band
Les Brown

Arranger/Composer
Pete Rugolo

Alto Saxophone
Charlie Parker

Tenor Saxophone
Stan Getz

Baritone Saxophone
Gerry Mulligan

Clarinet
Buddy DeFranco

Trumpet
Chet Baker

Trombone
Bill Harris

Piano
Oscar Peterson

Guitar
Johnny Smith

Bass
Ray Brown

Drums
Shelly Manne

Vibes
Terry Gibbs

Accordion
Art Van Damme

Miscellaneous Instrument
Don Elliott, Mellophone

1955

Male Vocalist
Frank Sinatra

Female Vocalist
Ella Fitzgerald

Male Vocalist With Group
Joe Williams

Female Vocalist With Group
Ann Richards

Vocal Group
Four Freshmen

Jazz Group
Modern Jazz Quartet

Big Band
Count Basie

Dance Band
Les Brown

Arranger/Composer
Pete Rugolo

Alto Saxophone
Paul Desmond

Tenor Saxophone
Stan Getz

Baritone Saxophone
Gerry Mulligan

Clarinet
Buddy DeFranco

Trumpet
Miles Davis

Trombone
J. J. Johnson

Piano
Erroll Garner

Guitar
Johnny Smith

Bass
Ray Brown

Drums
Max Roach

Vibes
Milt Jackson

Accordion
Art Van Damme

Miscellaneous Instrument
Don Elliott, Mellophone

1956

Male Vocalist
Frank Sinatra

Female Vocalist
Ella Fitzgerald

Vocal Group
Four Freshmen

Jazz Group
Modern Jazz Quartet

Big Band
Count Basie

Dance Band
Les Brown

Arranger/Composer
John Lewis

Alto Saxophone
Paul Desmond

Tenor Saxophone
Stan Getz

Baritone Saxophone
Gerry Mulligan

Clarinet
Tony Scott

Flute
Bud Shank

Trumpet
Dizzy Gillespie

Trombone
J. J. Johnson

Piano
Erroll Garner

Guitar
Barney Kessel

Bass
Ray Brown

Drums
Shelly Manne

Vibes
Milt Jackson

Accordion
Art Van Damme

Miscellaneous Instrument
Don Elliott, Mellophone

1957

Male Vocalist
Frank Sinatra

Female Vocalist
Ella Fitzgerald

Vocal Group
Hi-Lo's

Jazz Group
Modern Jazz Quartet

Big Band
Count Basie

Dance Band
Les Brown

Arranger/Composer
Duke Ellington

Alto Saxophone
Paul Desmond

Tenor Saxophone
Stan Getz

Ella Fitzgerald

Baritone Saxophone
Gerry Mulligan

Clarinet
Jimmy Giuffre

Flute
Herbie Mann

Trumpet
Miles Davis

Trombone
J. J. Johnson

Piano
Erroll Garner

Guitar
Barney Kessel

Bass
Ray Brown

Drums
Shelly Manne

Vibes
Milt Jackson

Accordion
Art Van Damme

Miscellaneous Instrument
Don Elliott, Mellophone

1958

Male Vocalist
Frank Sinatra

Female Vocalist
Ella Fitzgerald

Vocal Group
Four Freshmen

Jazz Group
Modern Jazz Quartet

Big Band
Count Basie

Dance Band
Les Brown

Arranger/Composer
Duke Ellington

Alto Saxophone
Paul Desmond

Tenor Saxophone
Stan Getz

Baritone Saxophone
Gerry Mulligan

Clarinet
Tony Scott

Flute
Herbie Mann

Trumpet
Miles Davis

Trombone
J. J. Johnson

Piano
Oscar Peterson

Guitar
Barney Kessel

Bass
Ray Brown

Drums
Shelly Manne

Vibes
Milt Jackson

Accordion
Art Van Damme

Miscellaneous Instrument
Don Elliott, Mellophone

1959

Male Vocalist
Frank Sinatra

Female Vocalist
Ella Fitzgerald

Vocal Group
Lambert, Hendricks and
Ross

Jazz Group
Dave Brubeck

Big Band
Count Basie

Dance Band
Les Brown

Arranger/Composer
Gil Evans

Alto Saxophone
Paul Desmond

Tenor Saxophone
Stan Getz

Baritone Saxophone
Gerry Mulligan

Clarinet
Tony Scott

Flute
Herbie Mann

Trumpet
Miles Davis

Trombone
J. J. Johnson

Piano
Oscar Peterson

Guitar
Barney Kessel

Bass
Ray Brown

Drums
Shelly Manne

Vibes
Milt Jackson

Accordion
Art Van Damme

Miscellaneous Instrument
Don Elliott, Mellophone

1960

Male Vocalist
Frank Sinatra

Female Vocalist
Ella Fitzgerald

Vocal Group
Lambert, Hendricks and
Ross

Jazz Group
Modern Jazz Quartet

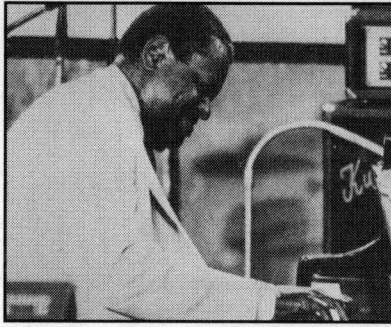

Oscar Peterson

Big Band
Count Basie

Dance Band
Les Brown

Arranger/Composer
Gil Evans

Alto Saxophone
Cannonball Adderley

Tenor Saxophone
John Coltrane

Baritone Saxophone
Gerry Mulligan

Clarinet
Buddy DeFranco

Flute
Herbie Mann

Trumpet
Miles Davis

Trombone
J. J. Johnson

Piano
Oscar Peterson

Guitar
Barney Kessel

Bass
Ray Brown

Drums
Shelly Manne

Vibes
Milt Jackson

Miscellaneous Instrument
Don Elliott, Mellophone

1961

Male Vocalist
Frank Sinatra

Female Vocalist
Ella Fitzgerald

Vocal Group
Lambert, Hendricks and
Ross

Jazz Group
Modern Jazz Quartet

Big Band
Count Basie

Dance Band
Count Basie

Arranger/Composer
Gil Evans

Alto Saxophone
Cannonball Adderley

Tenor Saxophone
John Coltrane

Baritone Saxophone
Gerry Mulligan

Clarinet
Buddy DeFranco

Flute
Herbie Mann

Trumpet
Miles Davis

Trombone
J. J. Johnson

Piano
Oscar Peterson

Guitar
Wes Montgomery

Bass
Ray Brown

Drums
Max Roach

Vibes
Milt Jackson

Miscellaneous Instrument
John Coltrane, Soprano
Saxophone

1962

Male Vocalist
Frank Sinatra

Female Vocalist
Ella Fitzgerald

Vocal Group
Lambert, Hendricks and Ross

Jazz Group
Dave Brubeck

Big Band
Duke Ellington

Dance Band
Count Basie

Dave Brubeck

Arranger/Composer
Gil Evans

Alto Saxophone
Paul Desmond

Tenor Saxophone
Stan Getz

Baritone Saxophone
Gerry Mulligan

Clarinet
Buddy DeFranco

Flute
Herbie Mann

Trumpet
Miles Davis

Trombone
J. J. Johnson

Piano
Oscar Peterson

Guitar
Wes Montgomery

Bass
Ray Brown

Drums
Joe Morello

Vibes
Milt Jackson

Miscellaneous Instrument
(tie)
Jimmy Smith, Organ
John Coltrane, Soprano
    Saxophone
Roland Kirk, Manzello and
    Stritch

1963

Male Vocalist
Ray Charles

Female Vocalist
Ella Fitzgerald

Vocal Group
Lambert, Hendricks and Ross

Jazz Group
Dave Brubeck

Big Band
Duke Ellington

Dance Band
Count Basie

Arranger/Composer
Duke Ellington

Alto Saxophone
Paul Desmond

Tenor Saxophone
Stan Getz

Baritone Saxophone
Gerry Mulligan

Clarinet
Buddy DeFranco

Flute
Herbie Mann

Trumpet
Miles Davis

Trombone
J. J. Johnson

Piano
Oscar Peterson

Guitar
Charlie Byrd

Bass
Ray Brown

Drums
Joe Morello

Vibes
Milt Jackson

Miscellaneous Instrument
(tie)
Roland Kirk, Manzello and
    Stritch
Jimmy Smith, Organ

1964

Male Vocalist
Ray Charles

Female Vocalist
Ella Fitzgerald

Vocal Group
Double Six

Jazz Group
Dave Brubeck

Big Band
Duke Ellington

Dance Band
Count Basie

Arranger/Composer
Duke Ellington

Alto Saxophone
Paul Desmond

Tenor Saxophone
John Coltrane

Baritone Saxophone
Gerry Mulligan

Clarinet
Jimmy Giuffre

Flute
Herbie Mann

Trumpet
Miles Davis

Trombone
J. J. Johnson

Piano
Bill Evans

Guitar
Jim Hall

Bass
Charles Mingus

Drums
Joe Morello

Vibes
Milt Jackson

Miscellaneous Instrument
(tie)
Roland Kirk, Manzello and
    Stritch
John Coltrane, Soprano
    Saxophone

1965

Jazzman of the Year
John Coltrane

Jazz Album of the Year
John Coltrane, *A Love
    Supreme* (MCA)

Male Vocalist
Frank Sinatra

Female Vocalist
Ella Fitzgerald

Vocal Group
Double Six

Jazz Group
Dave Brubeck

Big Band
Duke Ellington

Dance Band
Count Basie

Arranger
Gil Evans

Composer
Duke Ellington

Alto Saxophone
Paul Desmond

Tenor Saxophone
John Coltrane

Baritone Saxophone
Gerry Mulligan

Clarinet
Buddy DeFranco

Flute
Herbie Mann

Trumpet
Miles Davis

Trombone
J. J. Johnson

Piano
Oscar Peterson

Guitar
Jim Hall

Bass
Charles Mingus

Drums
Elvin Jones

Vibes
Milt Jackson

Miscellaneous Instrument
Roland Kirk, Manzello and
    Stritch

1966

Jazzman of the Year
Ornette Coleman

Jazz Album of the Year
Ornette Coleman, *At the
    Golden Circle Vol. 1*
    (Blue Note)

Male Vocalist
Frank Sinatra

Female Vocalist
Ella Fitzgerald

Vocal Group
Double Six

Jazz Group
Miles Davis

Big Band
Duke Ellington

Arranger
Gil Evans

Composer
Duke Ellington

Alto Saxophone
Paul Desmond

Tenor Saxophone
John Coltrane

Baritone Saxophone
Gerry Mulligan

Clarinet
Buddy DeFranco

Flute
Herbie Mann

Trumpet
Miles Davis

Trombone
J. J. Johnson

Piano
Oscar Peterson

Guitar
Wes Montgomery

Bass
Ray Brown

Drums
Elvin Jones

Vibes
Milt Jackson

Miscellaneous Instrument
Roland Kirk, Manzello and
Stritch

1967

Jazzman of the Year
Charles Lloyd

Jazz Album of the Year
Miles Davis, *Miles Smiles*
(Columbia)

Male Vocalist
Lou Rawls

Female Vocalist
Ella Fitzgerald

Vocal Group
The Beatles

Jazz Group
Miles Davis

Big Band
Duke Ellington

Arranger
Oliver Nelson

Composer
Duke Ellington

Alto Saxophone
Paul Desmond

Tenor Saxophone
Stan Getz

Baritone Saxophone
Gerry Mulligan

Clarinet
Buddy DeFranco

Flute
Herbie Mann

Trumpet
Miles Davis

Trombone
J. J. Johnson

Piano
Oscar Peterson

Guitar
Wes Montgomery

Bass
Ray Brown

Drums
Buddy Rich

Vibes
Milt Jackson

Miscellaneous Instrument
Roland Kirk, Manzello and
Stritch

1968

Jazzman of the Year
Gary Burton

Jazz Album of the Year
Don Ellis, *Electric Bath* (GNP
Crescendo)

Male Vocalist
Ray Charles

Female Vocalist
Ella Fitzgerald

Vocal Group
The Beatles

Jazz Group
Miles Davis

Big Band
Duke Ellington

Arranger
Oliver Nelson

Composer
Duke Ellington

Alto Saxophone
Cannonball Adderley

Tenor Saxophone
Stan Getz

Baritone Saxophone
Gerry Mulligan

Clarinet
Pee Wee Russell

Ray Charles

Flute
Herbie Mann

Trumpet
Miles Davis

Trombone
J. J. Johnson

Piano
Herbie Hancock

Guitar
Kenny Burrell

Bass
Richard Davis

Drums
Elvin Jones

Vibes
Gary Burton

Miscellaneous Instrument
Roland Kirk, Manzello and
Stritch

1969

Jazzman of the Year
Miles Davis

Jazz Album of the Year
Miles Davis, *Filles de
Killimanjaro* (Columbia
Jazz Contemporary
Masters)

Male Vocalist
Ray Charles

Female Vocalist
Ella Fitzgerald

Vocal Group
Blood, Sweat and Tears

Jazz Group
Miles Davis

Big Band
Duke Ellington

Arranger
Duke Ellington

Composer
Duke Ellington

Soprano Saxophone
Joe Farrell

Alto Saxophone
Cannonball Adderley

Tenor Saxophone
Stan Getz

Baritone Saxophone
Gerry Mulligan

Clarinet
Jimmy Hamilton

Flute
Herbie Mann

Trumpet
Miles Davis

Trombone
J. J. Johnson

Piano
Herbie Hancock

Guitar
Kenny Burrell

Bass
Richard Davis

Drums
Elvin Jones

Vibes
Gary Burton

Miscellaneous Instrument
Roland Kirk, Manzello and
Stritch

John Coltrane and Count Basie

1970

Jazzman of the Year
Miles Davis

Jazz Album of the Year
Miles Davis, *Bitches Brew*
(Columbia Jazz
Masterpieces)

Male Vocalist
Leon Thomas

Female Vocalist
Ella Fitzgerald

Vocal Group
Blood, Sweat and Tears

Jazz Group
Miles Davis

Big Band
Duke Ellington

Arranger
Quincy Jones

Composer
Duke Ellington

Soprano Saxophone
Wayne Shorter

Alto Saxophone
Cannonball Adderley

Tenor Saxophone
Stan Getz

Baritone Saxophone
Gerry Mulligan

Clarinet
Rahsaan Roland Kirk

Flute
Herbie Mann

Trumpet
Miles Davis

Trombone
J. J. Johnson

Piano
Herbie Hancock

Guitar
Kenny Burrell

Bass
Richard Davis

Drums
Buddy Rich

Vibes
Gary Burton

Miscellaneous Instrument
Rahsaan Roland Kirk,
Manzello and Stritch

Rock/Blues Musician
Frank Zappa

Rock/Blues Album of the Year
Blood, Sweat and Tears, *B, S and T 3* (Columbia)

1971

Jazzman of the Year
Miles Davis

Jazz Album of the Year
Weather Report, *Weather Report* (Columbia)

Male Vocalist
Leon Thomas

Female Vocalist
Roberta Flack

Vocal Group
Blood, Sweat and Tears

Jazz Group
Miles Davis

Big Band
Duke Ellington

Arranger
Quincy Jones

Miles Davis

Composer
Duke Ellington

Soprano Saxophone
Wayne Shorter

Alto Saxophone
Cannonball Adderley

Tenor Saxophone
Stan Getz

Baritone Saxophone
Gerry Mulligan

Clarinet
Rahsaan Roland Kirk

Flute
Hubert Laws

Trumpet
Miles Davis

Trombone
J. J. Johnson

Piano
Herbie Hancock

Guitar
Kenny Burrell

Bass
Richard Davis

Drums
Buddy Rich

Vibes
Gary Burton

Violin
Jean-Luc Ponty

Miscellaneous Instrument
Rahsaan Roland Kirk,
Manzello and Stritch

Rock/Blues Musician
Frank Zappa

Rock/Blues Album of the Year
Chase, *Chase* (Epic)

1972

Jazzman of the Year
Ornette Coleman

Jazz Album of the Year
Mahavishnu Orchestra,
Inner Mounting Flame
(Columbia)

Male Vocalist
Leon Thomas

Female Vocalist
Roberta Flack

Vocal Group
Mahavishnu Orchestra

Jazz Group
Weather Report

Big Band
Thad Jones and Mel Lewis

Arranger
Quincy Jones

Composer
Duke Ellington

Soprano Saxophone
Wayne Shorter

Alto Saxophone
Ornette Coleman

Tenor Saxophone
Sonny Rollins

Baritone Saxophone
Gerry Mulligan

Clarinet
Rahsaan Roland Kirk

Flute
Hubert Laws

Trumpet
Miles Davis

Trombone
J. J. Johnson

Herbie Hancock

Piano
Oscar Peterson

Guitar
John McLaughlin

Bass
Richard Davis

Drums
Buddy Rich

Vibes
Gary Burton

Violin
Jean-Luc Ponty

Miscellaneous Instrument
Rahsaan Roland Kirk,
  Manzello and Stritch

Rock/Blues Musician
Frank Zappa

**Rock/Blues Album of the
Year**
Mahavishnu Orchestra,
  Inner Mounting Flame
  (Columbia)

1973

Jazzman of the Year
Chick Corea

Jazz Album of the Year
Mahavishnu Orchestra,
  Birds of Fire (Columbia)

Male Vocalist
Leon Thomas

Female Vocalist
Roberta Flack

Vocal Group
Mahavishnu Orchestra

Jazz Group
Weather Report

Big Band
Thad Jones and Mel Lewis

Arranger
Quincy Jones

Composer
Duke Ellington

Soprano Saxophone
Wayne Shorter

Alto Saxophone
Ornette Coleman

Tenor Saxophone
Sonny Rollins

Baritone Saxophone
Gerry Mulligan

Clarinet
Benny Goodman

Flute
Hubert Laws

Trumpet
Freddie Hubbard

Trombone
J. J. Johnson

Piano
Chick Corea

Guitar
John McLaughlin

Bass
Ron Carter

Drums
Billy Cobham

Vibes
Gary Burton

Violin
Jean-Luc Ponty

Miscellaneous Instrument
Rahsaan Roland Kirk,
  Manzello and Stritch

Rock/Blues Musician
Stevie Wonder

**Rock/Blues Album of the
Year**
Mahavishnu Orchestra,
  Birds of Fire (Columbia)

1974

Jazzman of the Year
Herbie Hancock

Jazz Album of the Year
Weather Report, *Mysterious
  Traveller* (Columbia)

Male Vocalist
Stevie Wonder

Female Vocalist
Flora Purim

Vocal Group
Pointer Sisters

Jazz Group
Weather Report

Big Band
Thad Jones and Mel Lewis

Arranger
Gil Evans

Composer
Chick Corea

Soprano Saxophone
Wayne Shorter

Alto Saxophone
Ornette Coleman

Tenor Saxophone
Sonny Rollins

Baritone Saxophone
Gerry Mulligan

Clarinet
Rahsaan Roland Kirk

Flute
Hubert Laws

Trumpet
Freddie Hubbard

Trombone
Garnett Brown

Synthesizer
Herbie Hancock

Piano
McCoy Tyner

Guitar
John McLaughlin

Bass
Ron Carter

Electric Bass
Stanley Clarke

Drums
Billy Cobham

Percussion
Airto Moreira

Vibes
Gary Burton

Violin
Jean-Luc Ponty

Miscellaneous Instrument
Rahsaan Roland Kirk,
  Manzello and Stritch

Rock/Blues Musician
Stevie Wonder

**Rock/Blues Album of the
Year**
Stevie Wonder,
  *Fulfillingness' First
  Finale* (Motown)

Rock/Blues Group
Frank Zappa

1975

Jazzman of the Year
McCoy Tyner

Jazz Album of the Year
Weather Report, *Tail
  Spinnin'* (Columbia)

Male Vocalist
Stevie Wonder

Female Vocalist
Flora Purim

Vocal Group
Pointer Sisters

Jazz Group
Weather Report

Big Band
Thad Jones and Mel Lewis

Arranger
Gil Evans

Composer
Chick Corea

Soprano Saxophone
Wayne Shorter

Alto Saxophone
Phil Woods

Tenor Saxophone
Sonny Rollins

Baritone Saxophone
Gerry Mulligan

Clarinet
Rahsaan Roland Kirk

Flute
Hubert Laws

Trumpet
Miles Davis

Trombone
Bill Watrous

Synthesizer
Herbie Hancock

Piano
McCoy Tyner

Electric Piano
Chick Corea

Guitar
Joe Pass

Bass
Ron Carter

Electric Bass
Stanley Clarke

Drums
Billy Cobham

Percussion
Airto Moreira

Vibes
Gary Burton

Violin
Jean-Luc Ponty

Miscellaneous Instrument
Rahsaan Roland Kirk,
  Manzello and Stritch

Rock/Blues Musician
Stevie Wonder

**Rock/Blues Album of the
Year**
Jeff Beck, *Blow by Blow* (Epic)

Rock/Blues Group
Earth, Wind and Fire

Frank Zappa

Chick Corea

1976

Jazzman of the Year
McCoy Tyner

Jazz Album of the Year
Weather Report, *Black Market* (Columbia)

Male Vocalist
Mel Torme

Female Vocalist
Flora Purim

Vocal Group
Pointer Sisters

Jazz Group
Weather Report

Big Band
Thad Jones and Mel Lewis

Arranger
Gil Evans

Composer
Chick Corea

Soprano Saxophone
Wayne Shorter

Alto Saxophone
Phil Woods

Tenor Saxophone
Sonny Rollins

Baritone Saxophone
Gerry Mulligan

Clarinet
Benny Goodman

Flute
Hubert Laws

Trumpet
Freddie Hubbard

Trombone
Bill Watrous

Synthesizer
Joe Zawinul

Piano
McCoy Tyner

Electric Piano
Chick Corea

Organ
Jimmy Smith

Guitar
George Benson

Bass
Ron Carter

Electric Bass
Stanley Clarke

Drums
Billy Cobham

Percussion
Airto Moreira

Vibes
Gary Burton

Violin
Jean-Luc Ponty

Miscellaneous Instrument
Rahsaan Roland Kirk, Manzello and Stritch

Rock/Blues Musician
Jeff Beck

Rock/Blues Album of the Year
Jeff Beck, *Wired* (Epic)

Rock/Blues Group
Earth, Wind and Fire

1977

Jazzman of the Year
McCoy Tyner

Jazz Album of the Year
Weather Report, *Heavy Weather* (Columbia)

Male Vocalist
Al Jarreau

Female Vocalist
Flora Purim

Vocal Group
Earth, Wind and Fire

Jazz Group
Weather Report

Big Band
Thad Jones and Mel Lewis

Arranger
Gil Evans

Composer
Chick Corea

Soprano Saxophone
Wayne Shorter

Alto Saxophone
Phil Woods

Tenor Saxophone
Dexter Gordon

Baritone Saxophone
Gerry Mulligan

Clarinet
Anthony Braxton

Flute
Hubert Laws

Trumpet
Dizzy Gillespie

Trombone
Bill Watrous

Synthesizer
Joe Zawinul

Piano
McCoy Tyner

Electric Piano
Chick Corea

Organ
Jimmy Smith

Guitar
Joe Pass

Bass
Ron Carter

Electric Bass
Stanley Clarke

Drums
Elvin Jones

Percussion
Airto Moreira

Vibes
Gary Burton

Violin
Jean-Luc Ponty

Miscellaneous Instrument
Rahsaan Roland Kirk, Manzello and Stritch

Rock/Blues Musician
Stevie Wonder

Rock/Blues Album of the Year
Stevie Wonder, *Songs in the Key of Life* (Motown)

Rock/Blues Group
Earth, Wind and Fire

1978

Jazz Musician of the Year
Dexter Gordon

Jazz Album of the Year
Woody Shaw, *Rosewood* (Muse)

Male Vocalist
Al Jarreau

Female Vocalist
Flora Purim

Vocal Group
Steely Dan

Jazz Group
Weather Report

Big Jazz Band
Toshiko Akiyoshi and Lew Tabackin

Arranger
Toshiko Akiyoshi

Composer
Chick Corea

Soprano Saxophone
Wayne Shorter

Alto Saxophone
Phil Woods

Tenor Saxophone
Dexter Gordon

Baritone Saxophone
Gerry Mulligan

Clarinet
Benny Goodman

Flute
Hubert Laws

Trumpet
Woody Shaw

Trombone
Bill Watrous

Synthesizer
Joe Zawinul

Acoustic Piano
McCoy Tyner

Electric Piano
Chick Corea

Organ
Jimmy Smith

Guitar
Joe Pass

Acoustic Bass
Ron Carter

Electric Bass
Jaco Pastorius

Drums
Elvin Jones

Percussion
Airto Moreira

Vibes
Gary Burton

Violin
Jean-Luc Ponty

Miscellaneous Instrument
Toots Thielemans, Harmonica

Rock/Blues Musician
Stevie Wonder

Rock/Blues Album of the Year
Steely Dan, *Aja* (MCA)

Rock/Blues Group
Steely Dan

1979

Jazz Musician of the Year
Charles Mingus

Jazz Album of the Year
Joni Mitchell, *Mingus*
(Elektra)

Male Vocalist
Al Jarreau

Female Vocalist
Sarah Vaughan

Vocal Group
Steely Dan

Jazz Group
Weather Report

Big Jazz Band
Toshiko Akiyoshi and Lew
Tabackin

Arranger
Toshiko Akiyoshi

Composer
Charles Mingus

Soprano Saxophone
Wayne Shorter

Alto Saxophone
Phil Woods

Tenor Saxophone
Dexter Gordon

Baritone Saxophone
Gerry Mulligan

Clarinet
Anthony Braxton

Flute
Hubert Laws

Trumpet
Dizzy Gillespie

Trombone
Bill Watrous

Synthesizer
Joe Zawinul

Acoustic Piano
McCoy Tyner

Electric Piano
Chick Corea

Organ
Jimmy Smith

Guitar
Joe Pass

Acoustic Bass
Ron Carter

Electric Bass
Jaco Pastorius

Drums
Tony Williams

Percussion
Airto Moreira

Vibes
Gary Burton

Violin
Jean-Luc Ponty

Miscellaneous Instrument
Toots Thielemans,
Harmonica

Rock/Blues Musician
B.B. King

Rock/Blues Group
Steely Dan

1980

Jazz Musician of the Year
Dexter Gordon

Jazz Album of the Year
Jack DeJohnette, *Special
Edition* (ECM)

Male Vocalist
Al Jarreau

Female Vocalist
Sarah Vaughan

Vocal Group
Manhattan Transfer

Jazz Group
Weather Report

Big Jazz Band
Toshiko Akiyoshi and Lew
Tabackin

Arranger
Toshiko Akiyoshi

Composer
Toshiko Akiyoshi

Soprano Saxophone
Wayne Shorter

Alto Saxophone
Phil Woods

Tenor Saxophone
Dexter Gordon

Baritone Saxophone
Gerry Mulligan

Clarinet
Anthony Braxton

Flute
Hubert Laws

Trumpet
Woody Shaw

Trombone
Bill Watrous

Synthesizer
Joe Zawinul

Acoustic Piano
McCoy Tyner

Electric Piano
Chick Corea

Organ
Jimmy Smith

Guitar
Joe Pass

Acoustic Bass
Ron Carter

Electric Bass
Jaco Pastorius

Drums
Jack DeJohnette

Percussion
Airto Moreira

Vibes
Gary Burton

Dizzy Gillespie

Violin
Stephane Grappelli

Miscellaneous Instrument
Toots Thielemans,
Harmonica

**Rock/Blues Musician of the
Year**
Stevie Wonder

Rock/Blues Album
Clash, *London Calling*
(Columbia)

Rock/Blues Group
Earth, Wind and Fire

1981

Jazz Musician of the Year
Miles Davis

Jazz Album of the Year
Miles Davis, *Man With the
Horn* (Columbia)

Male Vocalist
Al Jarreau

Female Vocalist
Sarah Vaughan

Vocal Group
Manhattan Transfer

Jazz Group
Weather Report

Big Jazz Band
Toshiko Akiyoshi and Lew
Tabackin

Arranger
Toshiko Akiyoshi

Composer
Toshiko Akiyoshi

Soprano Saxophone
Wayne Shorter

Alto Saxophone
Phil Woods

Tenor Saxophone
Dexter Gordon

Baritone Saxophone
Gerry Mulligan

Clarinet
Anthony Braxton

Flute
Lew Tabackin

Trumpet
Freddie Hubbard

Trombone
Jimmy Knepper

Synthesizer
Josef Zawinul

Acoustic Piano
Oscar Peterson

Electric Piano
Chick Corea

Organ
Jimmy Smith

Guitar
Joe Pass

Acoustic Bass
Ron Carter

Electric Bass
Jaco Pastorius

Drums
Jack DeJohnette

Percussion
Airto Moreira

Vibes
Gary Burton

Violin
Stephane Grappelli

Miscellaneous Instrument
Toots Thielemans, Harmonica

**Rock/Blues Musician of the
Year**
Stevie Wonder

**Rock/Blues Album of the
Year**
Steely Dan, *Gaucho* (MCA)

Rock/Blues Group
Steely Dan

1982

Jazz Musician of the Year
Wynton Marsalis

Jazz Album of the Year
Wynton Marsalis, *Wynton Marsalis* (Columbia)

Male Vocalist
Al Jarreau

Female Vocalist
Sarah Vaughan

Vocal Group
Manhattan Transfer

Jazz Group
Weather Report

Jazz Big Band
Toshiko Akiyoshi and Lew Tabackin

Arranger
Toshiko Akiyoshi

Composer
Toshiko Akiyoshi

Soprano Saxophone
Wayne Shorter

Alto Saxophone
Phil Woods

Tenor Saxophone
Sonny Rollins

Baritone Saxophone
Pepper Adams

Clarinet
Benny Goodman

Flute
Lew Tabackin

Trumpet
Wynton Marsalis

Trombone
Jimmy Knepper

Synthesizer
Joe Zawinul

Acoustic Piano
Oscar Peterson

Electric Piano
Chick Corea

Organ
Jimmy Smith

Guitar
Joe Pass

Acoustic Bass
Ron Carter

Electric Bass
Jaco Pastorius

Drums
Jack DeJohnette

Percussion
Airto Moreira

Vibes
Gary Burton

Violin
Stephane Grappelli

Miscellaneous Instrument
Toots Thielemans, Harmonica

Rock/Blues Musician of the Year
Stevie Wonder

Rock/Blues Album of the Year
Police, *Ghost in the Machine* (A&M)

Rock/Blues Group
Earth, Wind and Fire

1983

Jazz Musician of the Year
Wynton Marsalis

Jazz Album of the Year
Miles Davis, *Star People* (Columbia)

Male Vocalist
Al Jarreau

Female Vocalist
Sarah Vaughan

Vocal Group
Manhattan Transfer

Acoustic Jazz Group
Art Blakey's Jazz Messengers

Electric Jazz Group
Weather Report

Big Band
Count Basie

Sarah Vaughan

Arranger
Gil Evans

Composer
Carla Bley

Soprano Saxophone
Wayne Shorter

Alto Saxophone
Phil Woods

Tenor Saxophone
Sonny Rollins

Baritone Saxophone
Gerry Mulligan

Clarinet
Benny Goodman

Flute
James Newton

Trumpet
Wynton Marsalis

Trombone
Jimmy Knepper

Synthesizer
Joe Zawinul

Acoustic Piano
Oscar Peterson

Electric Piano
Chick Corea

Organ
Jimmy Smith

Guitar
Pat Metheny

Acoustic Bass
Ron Carter

Electric Bass
Jaco Pastorius

Drums
Jack DeJohnette

Percussion
Nana Vasconcelos

Vibes
Gary Burton

Violin
Stephane Grappelli

Miscellaneous Instrument
Toots Thielemans, Harmonica

Pop/Rock Musician of the Year
Donald Fagen

Pop/Rock Album of the Year
Police, *Synchronicity* (A&M)

Pop/Rock Group
Police

Soul/R&B Musician of the Year
Michael Jackson

Soul/R&B Album of the Year
Michael Jackson, *Thriller* (Epic)

Soul/R&B Group
Earth, Wind and Fire

1984

Jazz Musician of the Year
Wynton Marsalis

Jazz Album of the Year
Miles Davis, *Decoy* (Columbia)

Male Vocalist
Bobby McFerrin

Female Vocalist
Sarah Vaughan

Vocal Group
Manhattan Transfer

Acoustic Jazz Group
Wynton Marsalis Quintet

Electric Jazz Group
Weather Report

Big Band
Count Basie

Arranger
Gil Evans

Composer
Carla Bley

Soprano Saxophone
Wayne Shorter

Alto Saxophone
Phil Woods

Tenor Saxophone
Sonny Rollins

Baritone Saxophone
Gerry Mulligan

Clarinet
Buddy De Franco

Flute
James Newton

Trumpet
Wynton Marsalis

Trombone
Jimmy Knepper

Synthesizer
Joe Zawinul

Acoustic Piano
Oscar Peterson

Electric Piano
Chick Corea

Organ
Jimmy Smith

Guitar
Joe Pass

Acoustic Bass
Charlie Haden

Electric Bass
Jaco Pastorius

Drums
Jack DeJohnette

Percussion
Nana Vasconcelos

Vibes
Gary Burton

Violin
Stephane Grappelli

Miscellaneous Instrument
Toots Thielemans, Harmonica

Pop/Rock Musician of the Year
Michael Jackson

Bobby McFerrin

Pop/Rock Album of the Year
Bruce Springsteen, *Born in the U.S.A.* (Columbia)

Pop/Rock Group
Police

Soul/R&B Musician of the Year
Prince

Soul/R&B Album of the Year
Prince, *Purple Rain* (Warner Bros.)

Soul/R&B Group
Earth, Wind and Fire

1985

Jazz Musician of the Year
Wynton Marsalis

Jazz Album of the Year
Jack DeJohnette, *Album Album* (ECM)

Male Vocalist
Bobby McFerrin

Female Vocalist
Sarah Vaughan

Vocal Group
Manhattan Transfer

Acoustic Jazz Group
Phil Woods

Electric Jazz Group
Miles Davis

Big Band
Count Basie

Arranger
Gil Evans

Composer
Carla Bley

Soprano Saxophone
Wayne Shorter

Alto Saxophone
Phil Woods

Tenor Saxophone
Sonny Rollins

Baritone Saxophone
Gerry Mulligan

Clarinet
Buddy DeFranco

Flute
James Newton

Trumpet
Wynton Marsalis

Trombone
J. J. Johnson

Synthesizer
Joe Zawinul

Acoustic Piano
Oscar Peterson

Electric Piano
Chick Corea

Organ
Jimmy Smith

Guitar
Stanley Jordan

Acoustic Bass
Ron Carter

Electric Bass
Steve Swallow

Drums
Jack DeJohnette

Percussion
Airto Moreira

Vibes
Milt Jackson

Violin
Stephane Grappelli

Miscellaneous Instrument
Toots Thielemans, Harmonica

Pop/Rock Musician of the Year
Sting

Pop/Rock Album of the Year
Sting, *The Dream of the Blue Turtles* (A&M)

Pop/Rock Group
Sting

Soul/R&B Musician of the Year
Stevie Wonder

Soul/R&B Album of the Year
Prince, *Around the World in a Day* (Warner Bros.)

Soul/R&B Group
Prince

1986

Jazz Musician of the Year
Wynton Marsalis

Jazz Album of the Year
Pat Metheny and Ornette Coleman, *Song X* (Geffen)

Male Vocalist
Bobby McFerrin

Female Vocalist
Sarah Vaughan

Vocal Group
Manhattan Transfer

Acoustic Jazz Group
Art Blakey and The Jazz Messengers

Electric Jazz Group
Miles Davis

Big Band
Count Basie

Arranger
Gil Evans

Composer
Toshiko Akiyoshi

Soprano Saxophone
Wayne Shorter

Alto Saxophone
Phil Woods

Tenor Saxophone
Sonny Rollins

Baritone Saxophone
Gerry Mulligan

Clarinet
Eddie Daniels

Flute
James Newton

Trumpet
Wynton Marsalis

Trombone
J. J. Johnson

Synthesizer
Joe Zawinul

Acoustic Piano
Oscar Peterson

Electric Piano
Chick Corea

Organ
Jimmy Smith

Guitar
Pat Metheny

Acoustic Bass
Ron Carter

Electric Bass
Steve Swallow

Drums
Jack DeJohnette

Percussion
Airto Moreira

Vibes
Gary Burton

Violin
Stephane Grappelli

Miscellaneous Instrument
Toots Thielemans, Harmonica

Pop/Rock Musician of the Year
Sting

Pop/Rock Album of the Year
Whitney Houston, *Whitney Houston* (Arista)

Pop/Rock Group
Sting

Soul/R&B Musician of the Year
Stevie Wonder

Soul/R&B Album of the Year
Stevie Wonder, *In Square Circle* (Motown)

Soul/R&B Group
Neville Brothers

1987

Jazz Musician of the Year
Ornette Coleman

Jazz Album of the Year
Michael Brecker, *Michael Brecker* (Impulse)

Male Vocalist
Bobby McFerrin

Female Vocalist
Sarah Vaughan

Vocal Group
Manhattan Transfer

Acoustic Jazz Group
Art Blakey and The Jazz Messengers

Electric Jazz Group
Pat Metheny Group

Big Band
Gil Evans

Arranger
Gil Evans

Composer
Carla Bley

Soprano Saxophone
Wayne Shorter

Alto Saxophone
Phil Woods

Tenor Saxophone
Michael Brecker

Baritone Saxophone
Gerry Mulligan

Clarinet
Eddie Daniels

Flute
James Newton

Trumpet
Wynton Marsalis

Trombone
J. J. Johnson

Synthesizer
Joe Zawinul

Acoustic Piano
McCoy Tyner

Electric Piano
Chick Corea

Organ
Jimmy Smith

Guitar
Pat Metheny

Acoustic Bass
Charlie Haden

Electric Bass
Marcus Miller

Drums
Jack DeJohnette

Percussion
Nana Vasconcelos

Vibes
Milt Jackson

Violin
Stephane Grappelli

Miscellaneous Instrument
Toots Thielemans,
Harmonica

Pop/Rock Musician of the Year
Paul Simon

Pop/Rock Album of the Year
Paul Simon, *Graceland*
(Warner Bros.)

Pop/Rock Group
Sting

Soul/R&B Musician of the Year
Robert Cray

Soul/R&B Album of the Year
Robert Cray, *Strong Persuader*
(Mercury/Hightone)

Soul/R&B Group
Robert Cray

1988

Jazz Musician of the Year
Wynton Marsalis

Jazz Album of the Year
Wynton Marsalis, *Standard
Time* (Columbia)

Male Vocalist
Bobby McFerrin

Female Vocalist
Sarah Vaughan

Vocal Group
Manhattan Transfer

Acoustic Jazz Group
Phil Woods

Electric Jazz Group
Chick Corea Elektric Band

Big Band
Count Basie

Arranger
Gil Evans

Composer
Henry Threadgill

Soprano Saxophone
Steve Lacy

Alto Saxophone
Phil Woods

Tenor Saxophone
Michael Brecker

Baritone Saxophone
Gerry Mulligan

Clarinet
Eddie Daniels

Flute
James Newton

Trumpet
Wynton Marsalis

Trombone
J. J. Johnson

Synthesizer
Joe Zawinul

Acoustic Piano
Oscar Peterson

Electric Piano
Chick Corea

Organ
Jimmy Smith

Guitar (tie)
Pat Metheny
John Scofield

Acoustic Bass
Charlie Haden

Electric Bass
Steve Swallow

Drums
Jack DeJohnette

Percussion
Airto Moreira

Vibes
Milt Jackson

Violin
Stephane Grappelli

Miscellaneous Instrument
Toots Thielemans,
Harmonica

Pop/Rock Musician of the Year
Sting

Pop/Rock Album of the Year
Sting, *Nothing Like the Sun*
(A&M)

Pop/Rock Group
Sting

Soul/R&B Musician of the Year
Robert Cray

Soul/R&B Album of the Year
Stevie Wonder, *Characters*
(Motown)

Soul/R&B Group
Robert Cray

Betty Carter

1989

Jazz Musician of the Year
Wynton Marsalis

Jazz Album of the Year
Pat Metheny, *Letter From
Home* (Geffen)

Male Vocalist
Bobby McFerrin

Female Vocalist
Betty Carter

Vocal Group
Take 6

Acoustic Jazz Group
Phil Woods

Electric Jazz Group
Miles Davis

Big Band
Sun Ra

Arranger
Toshiko Akiyoshi

Composer
Henry Threadgill

Soprano Saxophone
Branford Marsalis

Alto Saxophone
Phil Woods

Tenor Saxophone
Sonny Rollins

Baritone Saxophone
Gerry Mulligan

Clarinet
Eddie Daniels

Flute
James Newton

Trumpet
Wynton Marsalis

Trombone
J. J. Johnson

Synthesizer
Joe Zawinul

Acoustic Piano
Oscar Peterson

Organ
Jimmy Smith

Guitar
Pat Metheny

Acoustic Bass
Charlie Haden

Electric Bass
Steve Swallow

Drums
Jack DeJohnette

Percussion
Tito Puente

Vibes
Milt Jackson

Violin
Stephane Grappelli

Miscellaneous Instrument
Toots Thielemans, Harmonica

Pop/Rock Musician of the Year
Sting

Pop/Rock Album of the Year
Prince, *Batman* (Warner Bros.)

Pop/Rock Group
Sting

Soul/R&B Musician of the Year
Robert Cray

Soul/R&B Album of the Year
Neville Brothers, *Yellow
Moon* (A&M)

Soul/R&B Group
Neville Brothers

1990

Jazz Musician of the Year
Wynton Marsalis

Jazz Album of the Year
Miles Davis, *Aura* (Columbia)

Male Vocalist
Joe Williams

Female Vocalist
Betty Carter

Vocal Group
Take 6

Acoustic Jazz Group
Red Rodney

Electric Jazz Group
Chick Corea Elektric Band

Big Band
Count Basie

Arranger
Benny Carter

Composer
Benny Carter

Soprano Saxophone
Steve Lacy

Alto Saxophone
Phil Woods

Tenor Saxophone
Sonny Rollins

Baritone Saxophone
Gerry Mulligan

Clarinet
Eddie Daniels

Flute
James Newton

Trumpet
Wynton Marsalis

Trombone
Steve Turre

Synthesizer
Joe Zawinul

Acoustic Piano
Tommy Flanagan

Organ
Jimmy Smith

Acoustic Guitar
Jim Hall

Electric Guitar
Pat Metheny

Acoustic Bass
Charlie Haden

Electric Bass
Steve Swallow

Drums
Jack DeJohnette

Percussion
Airto Moreira

Vibes
Milt Jackson

Violin
Stephane Grappelli

Miscellaneous Instrument
Toots Thielemans, Harmonica

Pop/Rock Musician of the Year
Elvis Costello

Pop/Rock Album of the Year
Bonnie Raitt, Nick of Time (Capitol)

Rock Group
The Rolling Stones

Blues/Soul/R&B Musician of the Year
B.B. King

Blues/Soul/R&B Album of the Year
John Lee Hooker, The Healer (Chameleon)

Blues/Soul/R&B Group
Neville Brothers

Rap Musician of the Year
M. C. Hammer

Rap Album of the Year
Public Enemy, Fear of a Black Planet (Def Jam)

Rap Group
Public Enemy

World Beat Musician of the Year
Peter Gabriel

World Beat Album of the Year
Peter Gabriel, Passion (Geffen)

World Beat Group
Jerry Gonzalez

1991

Jazz Musician of the Year
Wynton Marsalis

Jazz Album of the Year
Charlie Haden's Liberation Music Orchestra, Dream Keeper (Blue Note)

Male Vocalist
Joe Williams

Female Vocalist
Betty Carter

Vocal Group
Take 6

Jazz Acoustic Combo
Phil Woods

Jazz Electric Combo
Miles Davis

Jazz Big Band
Count Basie Orchestra

Arranger
Carla Bley

Composer
Carla Bley

Soprano Saxophone
Steve Lacy

Alto Saxophone
Phil Woods

Tenor Saxophone
Sonny Rollins

Baritone Saxophone
Gerry Mulligan

Clarinet
Eddie Daniels

Flute
James Newton

Trumpet
Wynton Marsalis

Trombone
J. J. Johnson

Synthesizer
Joe Zawinul

Acoustic Piano
Keith Jarrett

Organ
Jimmy Smith

Acoustic Guitar
John McLaughlin

Electric Guitar
Pat Metheny

Acoustic Bass
Charlie Haden

Electric Bass
Steve Swallow

Drums
Jack DeJohnette

Percussion
Tito Puente

Vibes
Milt Jackson

Violin
Stephane Grappelli

Miscellaneous Instrument
Toots Thielemans, Harmonica

Pop/Rock Musician of the Year
Sting

Pop/Rock Album of the Year
Sting, The Soul Cages (A&M)

Pop/Rock Group
Living Colour

Blues/Soul/R&B Musician of the Year
B.B. King

Blues/Soul/R&B Album of the Year
Neville Brothers, Brother's Keeper (A&M)

Blues/Soul/R&B Group
Neville Brothers

World Beat Musician of the Year
Milton Nascimento

World Beat Album of the Year
Paul Simon, The Rhythm of the Saints (Warner Bros.)

World Beat Group
Tito Puente

1992

Jazz Musician of the Year
Joe Henderson

Jazz Album of the Year
Joe Henderson, Lush Life (Verve)

Male Vocalist
Joe Williams

Female Vocalist
Betty Carter

Vocal Group
Take 6

Jazz Acoustic Combo
Wynton Marsalis

Jazz Electric Combo
John Scofield

Jazz Big Band
Count Basie Band

Arranger
Carla Bley

Composer (tie)
Muhal Richard Abrams
Carla Bley

Soprano Saxophone
Steve Lacy

Alto Saxophone
Phil Woods

Tenor Saxophone
Joe Henderson

Baritone Saxophone
Gerry Mulligan

Clarinet
Eddie Daniels

Flute
James Newton

Trumpet
Wynton Marsalis

Trombone
J. J. Johnson

Synthesizer
Joe Zawinul

Acoustic Piano
Kenny Barron

Organ
Jimmy Smith

Acoustic Guitar
John McLaughlin

Electric Guitar
John Scofield

Acoustic Bass
Charlie Haden

Electric Bass
Steve Swallow

Drums
Jack DeJohnette

Percussion
Airto Moreira

Vibes
Milt Jackson

Violin
Stephane Grappelli

Miscellaneous Instrument
Toots Thielemans, Harmonica

Pop/Rock Musician of the Year
Sting

Pop/Rock Album of the Year
Bonnie Raitt, Luck of the Draw (Capitol)

Pop/Rock Group
U2

Blues/Soul/R&B Musician of the Year
Prince

Blues/Soul/R&B Album of the Year
Buddy Guy, *Damn Right I Got the Blues* (Silvertone)

Blues/Soul/R&B Group
Neville Brothers

World Beat Musician of the Year
Tito Puente

World Beat Album of the Year
Mickey Hart, *Planet Drum* (Rykodisc)

World Beat Group
Tito Puente

1993

Jazz Musician of the Year
Joe Henderson

Jazz Album of the Year
Joe Henderson, *So Near, So Far (Musings for Miles)* (Verve)

Male Vocalist
Joe Williams

Female Vocalist
Betty Carter

Vocal Group
Take 6

Jazz Acoustic Combo
Red Rodney

Jazz Electric Combo
John Scofield

Jazz Big Band
Count Basie Band

Arranger
Bob Belden

Composer
Henry Threadgill

Soprano Saxophone
Steve Lacy

Alto Saxophone
Phil Woods

Tenor Saxophone
Joe Henderson

Baritone Saxophone
Gerry Mulligan

Clarinet
Don Byron

Flute
James Newton

Trumpet
Wynton Marsalis

Trombone
J. J. Johnson

Synthesizer
Joe Zawinul

Piano
Tommy Flanagan

Organ
Jimmy Smith

Acoustic Guitar
John McLaughlin

Electric Guitar
John Scofield

Acoustic Bass
Charlie Haden

Electric Bass
Steve Swallow

Drums
Max Roach

Percussion
Airto Moreira

Vibes
Milt Jackson

Violin
Stephane Grappelli

Miscellaneous Instrument
Toots Thielemans, Harmonica

Blues/Soul/R&B Musician of the Year
B.B. King

Blues/Soul/R&B Album of the Year
John Lee Hooker, *Boom Boom* (Pointblank)

Blues/Soul/R&B Group
B.B. King

Max Roach

Beyond Artist of the Year
Sting

Beyond Album of the Year
Sting, *Ten Summoner's Tales* (A&M)

Beyond Group
Los Lobos

Critics Poll

1953

Male Singer
Louis Armstrong
TDWR
Jackie Paris

Female Singer
Ella Fitzgerald
TDWR (tie)
Annie Ross
Jeri Southern

Combo
Dave Brubeck

Big Band
Duke Ellington

Alto Saxophone
Charlie Parker
TDWR
Paul Desmond

Tenor Saxophone
Stan Getz
TDWR
Paul Quinichette

Baritone Saxophone
Harry Carney
TDWR
Gerry Mulligan

Clarinet
Buddy DeFranco
TDWR
Tony Scott

Trumpet
Louis Armstrong
TDWR
Chet Baker

Trombone
Bill Harris
TDWR (tie)
Bob Brookmeyer
Carl Fontana
Frank Rosolino

Acoustic Piano
Oscar Peterson
TDWR
Billy Taylor

Guitar
Barney Kessel
TDWR
Johnny Smith

Acoustic Bass
Oscar Pettiford
TDWR (tie)
Charles Mingus
Red Mitchell

Drums
Buddy Rich
TDWR
Art Blakey

1954

Male Singer
Louis Armstrong
TDWR
Clancy Hayes

Female Singer
Ella Fitzgerald
TDWR
Carmen McRae

Combo
Modern Jazz Quartet

Big Band
Count Basie

Alto Saxophone
Charlie Parker
TDWR
Bud Shank

Tenor Saxophone
Stan Getz
TDWR
Frank Wess

Baritone Saxophone
Harry Carney
TDWR
Lars Gullin

Clarinet
Buddy DeFranco
TDWR
Sam Most

Trumpet
Dizzy Gillespie
TDWR
Clifford Brown

Trombone
Bill Harris
TDWR
Urbie Green

Acoustic Piano
Art Tatum
TDWR
Horace Silver

Guitar
Jimmy Raney
TDWR
Tal Farlow

Acoustic Bass
Ray Brown
TDWR
Percy Heath

Drums
Buddy Rich
TDWR
Osie Johnson

Vibes
Lionel Hampton
TDWR
Teddy Charles

Louis Armstrong

1955

Male Singer
Louis Armstrong
TDWR
Joe Williams

Female Singer
Ella Fitzgerald
TDWR
Teddi King

Combo
Modern Jazz Quartet

Big Band
Count Basie

Alto Saxophone
Benny Carter
TDWR
Herb Geller

Tenor Saxophone
Stan Getz
TDWR
Bill Perkins

Baritone Saxophone
Gerry Mulligan
TDWR
Bob Gordon

Clarinet
Tony Scott
TDWR
Jimmy Giuffre

Trumpet (tie)
Dizzy Gillespie
Miles Davis
TDWR
Ruby Braff

Trombone
J. J. Johnson
TDWR
Jimmy Cleveland

Acoustic Piano
Art Tatum
TDWR
Randy Weston

Guitar
Jimmy Raney
TDWR
Howard Roberts

Acoustic Bass
Oscar Pettiford
TDWR
Wendell Marshall

Drums
Art Blakey
TDWR
Joe Morello

Vibes
Milt Jackson
TDWR
Cal Tjader

1956

Male Singer
Louis Armstrong
TDWR
Joe Turner

Female Singer
Ella Fitzgerald
TDWR
Barbara Lea

Combo
Modern Jazz Quartet

Big Band
Count Basie

Alto Saxophone
Benny Carter
TDWR
Phil Woods

Tenor Saxophone
Lester Young
TDWR
Bobby Jaspar

Baritone Saxophone
Harry Carney
TDWR
Jimmy Giuffre

Clarinet
Benny Goodman
TDWR
Buddy Collette

Trumpet
Dizzy Gillespie
TDWR
Thad Jones

Trombone
J. J. Johnson
TDWR
Benny Powell

Acoustic Piano
Art Tatum
TDWR
Hampton Hawes

Guitar
Tal Farlow
TDWR
Dick Garcia

Acoustic Bass
Oscar Pettiford
TDWR
Paul Chambers

Drums
Jo Jones
TDWR
Chico Hamilton

Vibes
Milt Jackson
TDWR
Terry Pollard

1957

Male Singer
Frank Sinatra

Female Singer
Ella Fitzgerald

Combo
Modern Jazz Quartet

Big Band
Count Basie

Alto Saxophone
Lee Konitz
TDWR
Art Pepper

Tenor Saxophone
Stan Getz
TDWR
Sonny Rollins

Baritone Saxophone
Gerry Mulligan
TDWR
Pepper Adams

Clarinet
Tony Scott

Trumpet
Dizzy Gillespie
TDWR
Donald Byrd

Trombone
J. J. Johnson
TDWR
Frank Rehak

Acoustic Piano
Erroll Garner
TDWR
Eddie Costa

Guitar
Tal Farlow
TDWR
Kenny Burrell

Acoustic Bass
Oscar Pettiford
TDWR
Leroy Vinnegar

Drums
Max Roach
TDWR
Philly Joe Jones

Vibes
Milt Jackson
TDWR
Eddie Costa

1958

Male Singer
Jimmy Rushing
TDWR
Ray Charles

Female Singer
Ella Fitzgerald

Combo
Modern Jazz Quartet

Big Band
Duke Ellington

Alto Saxophone
Lee Konitz

Tenor Saxophone
Stan Getz
TDWR
Benny Golson

Baritone Saxophone
Gerry Mulligan
TDWR
Tony Scott

Clarinet
Tony Scott

Trumpet
Miles Davis
TDWR
Art Farmer

Trombone
J. J. Johnson
TDWR
Jimmy Knepper

Acoustic Piano
Thelonious Monk
TDWR
Bill Evans

Guitar
Freddie Green
TDWR
Jim Hall

Acoustic Bass
Ray Brown
TDWR
Wilbur Ware

Drums
Max Roach

Vibes
Milt Jackson
TDWR
Victor Feldman

Aretha Franklin

1959

Male Singer
Jimmy Rushing
TDWR
Jon Hendricks

Female Singer
Ella Fitzgerald
TDWR
Ernestine Anderson

Combo
Modern Jazz Quartet
TDWR
Mastersounds

Big Band
Duke Ellington
TDWR
Maynard Ferguson

Arranger/Composer
Duke Ellington
TDWR
Benny Golson

Alto Saxophone
Johnny Hodges
TDWR
Cannonball Adderley

Tenor Saxophone
Coleman Hawkins
TDWR
Benny Golson

Baritone Saxophone
Harry Carney
TDWR
Ronnie Ross

Clarinet
Tony Scott
TDWR
Bob Wilber

Trumpet
Miles Davis
TDWR
Lee Morgan

Trombone
J. J. Johnson
TDWR
Curtis Fuller

Acoustic Piano
Thelonious Monk
TDWR
Bill Evans

Guitar
Barney Kessel
TDWR
Charlie Byrd

Acoustic Bass
Ray Brown
TDWR
Scott LaFaro

Drums
Max Roach
TDWR (tie)
Elvin Jones
Ed Thigpen

Vibes
Milt Jackson
TDWR
Buddy Montgomery

Miscellaneous Instrument
Frank Wess, Flute

1960

Male Singer
Jimmy Rushing
TDWR
Bill Henderson

Female Singer
Ella Fitzgerald

Vocal Group
Lambert, Hendricks and Ross

Combo
Modern Jazz Quartet
TDWR (tie)
Art Farmer
Benny Golson

Big Band
Duke Ellington
TDWR
Quincy Jones

Arranger/Composer
Duke Ellington
TDWR
Quincy Jones

Alto Saxophone
Cannonball Adderley
TDWR
Ornette Coleman

Tenor Saxophone
Coleman Hawkins
TDWR
Johnny Griffin

Baritone Saxophone
Gerry Mulligan

Clarinet
Buddy DeFranco
TDWR
Pete Fountain

Flute
Frank Wess
TDWR
Les Spann

Trumpet
Dizzy Gillespie
TDWR
Nat Adderley

Trombone
J. J. Johnson
TDWR
Al Grey

Acoustic Piano
Thelonious Monk
TDWR
Ray Bryant

Guitar
Kenny Burrell
TDWR
Wes Montgomery

Acoustic Bass
Ray Brown
TDWR
Sam Jones

Drums
Max Roach
TDWR
Billy Higgins

Vibes
Milt Jackson
TDWR
Lem Winchester

Miscellaneous Instrument
Julius Watkins, French Horn
TDWR
Steve Lacy, Soprano
   Saxophone

1961

Male Singer
Ray Charles
TDWR
Jimmy Witherspoon

Female Singer
Ella Fitzgerald
TDWR
Aretha Franklin

Vocal Group
Lambert, Hendricks and Ross
TDWR
Double Six

Combo
Modern Jazz Quartet
TDWR
John Coltrane

Big Band
Duke Ellington
TDWR
Gerry Mulligan

Arranger/Composer
Duke Ellington
TDWR
George Russell

Alto Saxophone
Cannonball Adderley
TDWR
Eric Dolphy

Tenor Saxophone
John Coltrane
TDWR
Charlie Rouse

Baritone Saxophone
Gerry Mulligan
TDWR
Sahib Shihab

Coleman Hawkins

Clarinet
Buddy DeFranco
TDWR
Rolf Kuhn

Flute
Frank Wess
TDWR
Leo Wright

Trumpet
Dizzy Gillespie
TDWR
Freddie Hubbard

Trombone
J. J. Johnson
TDWR
Julian Priester

Acoustic Piano
Thelonious Monk
TDWR
Junior Mance

Guitar
Wes Montgomery
TDWR
Les Spann

Acoustic Bass
Ray Brown
TDWR
Charlie Haden

Drums
Max Roach
TDWR
Louis Hayes

Vibes
Milt Jackson
TDWR
Mike Mainieri

Miscellaneous Instrument
Julius Watkins, French Horn
TDWR
John Coltrane, Soprano
    Saxophone

1962

Male Singer
Ray Charles
TDWR
Lightnin' Hopkins

Female Singer
Ella Fitzgerald
TDWR
Abbey Lincoln

Vocal Group
Lambert, Hendricks and
    Ross
TDWR
Staple Singers

Combo
Miles Davis
TDWR (tie)
Al Grey
Billy Mitchell

Big Band
Duke Ellington
TDWR
Terry Gibbs

Arranger/Composer
Duke Ellington
TDWR
Oliver Nelson

Alto Saxophone
Johnny Hodges
TDWR
Leo Wright

Tenor Saxophone
Sonny Rollins
TDWR
Wayne Shorter

Baritone Saxophone
Gerry Mulligan
TDWR
Cecil Payne

Clarinet
Pee Wee Russell
TDWR
Jimmy Hamilton

Flute
Frank Wess
TDWR
Eric Dolphy

Trumpet
Dizzy Gillespie
TDWR
Don Ellis

Trombone
J. J. Johnson
TDWR (tie)
Dave Baker
Slide Hampton

Acoustic Piano
Bill Evans
TDWR
Cecil Taylor

Guitar
Wes Montgomery
TDWR
Grant Green

Acoustic Bass
Ray Brown
TDWR
Art Davis

Drums
Philly Joe Jones
TDWR (tie)
Roy Haynes
Mel Lewis

Vibes
Milt Jackson
TDWR
Walt Dickerson

Miscellaneous Instrument
John Coltrane, Soprano
    Saxophone
TDWR
Roland Kirk, Manzello and
    Stritch

1963

Male Singer
Ray Charles
TDWR
Mark Murphy

Thelonious Monk

Female Singer
Ella Fitzgerald
TDWR
Sheila Jordan

Vocal Group
Lambert, Hendricks and
    Bavan
TDWR
Stars of Faith

Combo
Miles Davis
TDWR (tie)
Clark Terry
Bobby Brookmeyer

Big Band
Duke Ellington
TDWR
Gerald Wilson

Arranger/Composer
Duke Ellington
TDWR
Gary McFarland

Alto Saxophone
Johnny Hodges
TDWR
Jackie McLean

Tenor Saxophone
Sonny Rollins
TDWR
Dexter Gordon

Baritone Saxophone
Gerry Mulligan
TDWR
Jay Cameron

Clarinet
Pee Wee Russell
TDWR
Phil Woods

Flute
Frank Wess
TDWR
Roland Kirk

Trumpet
Dizzy Gillespie
TDWR
Don Cherry

Trombone
J. J. Johnson
TDWR
Roswell Rudd

Acoustic Piano
Bill Evans
TDWR
McCoy Tyner

Guitar (tie)
Jim Hall
Wes Montgomery
TDWR
Joe Pass

Acoustic Bass
Charles Mingus
TDWR
Gary Peacock

Drums
Elvin Jones
TDWR
Pete LaRoca

Vibes
Milt Jackson
TDWR
Dave Pike

Miscellaneous Instrument
John Coltrane, Soprano
    Saxophone
TDWR
Eric Dolphy, Bass Clarinet

Billie Holiday

1964

Male Singer
Ray Charles
TDWR
Muddy Waters

Female Singer
Ella Fitzgerald
TDWR (tie)
Nancy Wilson
Jeanne Lee

Vocal Group
Double Six
TDWR
Swingle Singers

Combo
Thelonious Monk
TDWR
Art Farmer

Big Band
Duke Ellington
TDWR
Henry James

Arranger/Composer
Duke Ellington
TDWR (tie)
Cecil Taylor
Gerald Wilson

Alto Saxophone
Johnny Hodges
TDWR
Jimmy Woods

Tenor Saxophone
John Coltrane
TDWR
Booker Ervin

Baritone Saxophone
Gerry Mulligan
TDWR
Charles Davis

Clarinet
Pee Wee Russell
TDWR
Bill Smith

Flute
Frank Wess
TDWR
Yusef Lateef

Trumpet
Miles Davis
TDWR
Carmell Jones

Trombone
J. J. Johnson
TDWR
Grachan Moncur III

Acoustic Piano
Bill Evans
TDWR
Don Friedman

Organ
Jimmy Smith
TDWR
Freddie Roach

Guitar
Jim Hall
TDWR
Gabor Szabo

Acoustic Bass
Charles Mingus
TDWR
Steve Swallow

Drums
Elvin Jones
TDWR
Tony Williams

Vibes
Milt Jackson
TDWR
Bobby Hutcherson

Miscellaneous Instrument
Roland Kirk, Manzello and
   Stritch
TDWR
Yusef Lateef, Oboe

1965

Record of the Year
John Coltrane, *A Love
   Supreme* (MCA/Impulse)

Male Singer
Louis Armstrong
TDWR
Johnny Hartman

Female Singer
Ella Fitzgerald
TDWR
Cleo Laine

Vocal Group
Double Six

Combo
Miles Davis
TDWR
Al Cohn and Zoot Sims

Big Band
Duke Ellington
TDWR
Johnny Dankworth

Arranger
Gil Evans
TDWR
Clare Fischer

Composer
Duke Ellington
TDWR
Ornette Coleman

Alto Saxophone
Johnny Hodges
TDWR
Charlie Marlano

Tenor Saxophone
John Coltrane
TDWR
Archie Shepp

Baritone Saxophone
Harry Carney
TDWR
Jerome Richardson

Clarinet
Pee Wee Russell
TDWR
Paul Horn

Flute
Roland Kirk
TDWR
James Moody

Trumpet
Miles Davis
TDWR
Johnny Coles

Trombone
J. J. Johnson
TDWR
Albert Mangelsdorff

Acoustic Piano
Bill Evans
TDWR
Andrew Hill

Organ
Jimmy Smith
TDWR
John Patton

Guitar
Jim Hall
TDWR
Bola Sete

Acoustic Bass
Charles Mingus
TDWR
Ron Carter

Drums
Elvin Jones
TDWR (tie)
Alan Dawson
Dannie Richmond

Vibes
Milt Jackson
TDWR
Gary Burton

Miscellaneous Instrument
Roland Kirk, Manzello and
   Stritch
TDWR
Stuff Smith, Violin

1966

Record of the Year
Ornette Coleman, *At the
   Golden Circle Vol. 1*
   (Blue Note)

Muddy Waters

Reissue of the Year
Billie Holiday, *The Golden Years Vol. 2* (Columbia)

Male Singer
Louis Armstrong
TDWR
Lou Rawls

Female Singer
Ella Fitzgerald
TDWR
Carol Sloane

Vocal Group
Double Six

Combo
Miles Davis
TDWR
Denny Zeitlin

Big Band
Duke Ellington
TDWR
Thad Jones and Mel Lewis

Arranger
Gil Evans
TDWR
Rod Levitt

Composer
Duke Ellington
TDWR
Carla Bley

Alto Saxophone
Johnny Hodges
TDWR (tie)
John Handy
John Tchical

Tenor Saxophone
John Coltrane
TDWR
Charles Lloyd

Baritone Saxophone
Harry Carney
TDWR
Ronnie Cuber

Clarinet
Pee Wee Russell
TDWR
Edmond Hall

Flute
Roland Kirk
TDWR
Charles Lloyd

Trumpet
Miles Davis
TDWR
Ted Curson

Trombone
J. J. Johnson
TDWR
Buster Cooper

Acoustic Piano
Earl Hines
TDWR
Jaki Byard

Organ
Jimmy Smith
TDWR
Larry Smith

Guitar
Wes Montgomery
TDWR
Rene Thomas

Acoustic Bass
Charles Mingus
TDWR
Richard Davis

Drums
Elvin Jones
TDWR
Sonny Murray

Vibes
Milt Jackson
TDWR
Roy Ayres

Miscellaneous Instrument
Roland Kirk, Manzello and Stritch
TDWR
Jean-Luc Ponty, Violin

1967

Record of the Year (tie)
Duke Ellington, *The Popular Ellington* (RCA)
Miles Davis, *Miles Smiles* (Columbia)

Reissue of the Year
Johnny Hodges and Rex Stewart, *Things Ain't What They Used To Be* (Victrola)

Male Singer
Louis Armstrong
TDWR
Richard Boone

Female Singer
Ella Fitzgerald
TDWR
Lorez Alexandria

Combo
Miles Davis
TDWR
Charles Lloyd

Big Band
Duke Ellington
TDWR
Don Ellis

Arranger
Duke Ellington
TDWR
Thad Jones

Composer
Duke Ellington
TDWR
Herbie Hancock

Alto Saxophone
Ornette Coleman
TDWR
Charles McPherson

Tenor Saxophone
Sonny Rollins
TDWR
Joe Henderson

Sonny Rollins

Baritone Saxophone
Harry Carney
TDWR
Pepper Adams

Clarinet
Pee Wee Russell
TDWR
Perry Robinson

Flute
James Moody
TDWR
Jeremy Steig

Trumpet
Miles Davis
TDWR
Jimmy Owens

Trombone
J. J. Johnson
TDWR
Garnett Brown

Acoustic Piano
Earl Hines
TDWR
Keith Jarrett

Organ
Jimmy Smith
TDWR
Don Patterson

Guitar
Wes Montgomery
TDWR
George Benson

Acoustic Bass
Richard Davis
TDWR
David Izenson

Drums
Elvin Jones
TDWR
Milford Graves

Vibes
Milt Jackson
TDWR
Tommy Vig

Miscellaneous Instrument
Roland Kirk, Manzello and Stritch
TDWR
Michael White, Violin

Rock/Blues Group
The Beatles
TDWR
Supremes

1968

Record of the Year
Duke Ellington, *Far East Suite* (Bluebird)

Reissue of the Year
Johnny Hodges, *Hodge Podge* (Encore)

Male Singer (tie)
Louis Armstrong
Ray Charles
TDWR
Jimmy Witherspoon

Female Singer
Ella Fitzgerald
TDWR
Aretha Franklin

Combo
Miles Davis
TDWR
Gary Burton

Big Band
Duke Ellington
TDWR
Buddy Rich

Arranger
Duke Ellington
TDWR
Tom McIntosh

Composer
Duke Ellington
TDWR
Wayne Shorter

Alto Saxophone
Johnny Hodges
TDWR
Sonny Criss

Tenor Saxophone
Sonny Rollins
TDWR
Joe Farrell

Baritone Saxophone
Harry Carney
TDWR
Cecil Payne

Clarinet
Pee Wee Russell
TDWR
Eddie Daniels

Flute
James Moody
TDWR
Hubert Laws

Trumpet
Miles Davis
TDWR
Charles Tolliver

Trombone
J. J. Johnson
TDWR
Carl Fontana

Acoustic Piano
Bill Evans
TDWR
Roger Kellaway

Organ
Jimmy Smith
TDWR (tie)
Odell Brown
Eddy Louiss

Guitar
Kenny Burrell
TDWR
Larry Coryell

Acoustic Bass
Richard Davis
TDWR
Eddie Gomez

Drums
Elvin Jones
TDWR
Billy Higgins

Vibes
Milt Jackson
TDWR
Karl Berger

Miscellaneous Instrument
Jean-Luc Ponty, Violin
TDWR
Howard Johnson, Tuba

Rock/Blues Group
Muddy Waters
TDWR
Jr. Wells

1969

Record of the Year
Duke Ellington, . . . And His
   Mother Called Him Bill
   (Bluebird)

Reissue of the Year
Louis Armstrong, V.S.O.P.
   Vol. 1 (Encore)

Male Singer
Ray Charles
TDWR
Jon Hendricks

Female Singer
Ella Fitzgerald
TDWR
Karin Krog

Combo
Miles Davis
TDWR
Elvin Jones Trio

Big Band
Duke Ellington
TDWR
Kenny Clarke and Francy
   Boland

Arranger
Duke Ellington
TDWR
Francy Boland

Composer
Duke Ellington
TDWR
Mike Westbrook

Soprano Saxophone
Lucky Thompson
TDWR
John Surman

Alto Saxophone
Johnny Hodges
TDWR
Lee Konitz

Tenor Saxophone
Sonny Rollins
TDWR
Albert Ayler

Baritone Saxophone
Harry Carney
TDWR
John Surman

Clarinet
Jimmy Hamilton
TDWR
Roland Kirk

Flute
James Moody
TDWR
Joe Farrell

Trumpet
Miles Davis
TDWR
Randy Brecker

Trombone
J. J. Johnson
TDWR
Lester Lashley

Acoustic Piano
Earl Hines
TDWR
Chick Corea

Organ
Jimmy Smith
TDWR
Lonnie Smith

Guitar
Kenny Burrell
TDWR
Pat Martino

Acoustic Bass
Richard Davis
TDWR
Niels-Henning Ørsted
   Pedersen

Drums
Elvin Jones
TDWR
Daniel Humair

Vibes
Bobby Hutcherson
TDWR
Red Norvo

Miscellaneous Instrument
Jean-Luc Ponty, Violin
TDWR
Ray Nance, Violin

Rock/Blues Group
Muddy Waters
TDWR (tie)
Canned Heat
J. B. Hutto

1970

Record of the Year
Miles Davis, Bitches Brew
   (Columbia Jazz
   Masterpieces)

Reissue of the Year
Various artists, Blue Note's
   Three Decades of Jazz,
   Vol. 1 (Blue Note)

Male Singer
Louis Armstrong
TDWR
Leon Thomas

Female Singer
Ella Fitzgerald
TDWR
Jeanne Lee

Combo
Miles Davis
TDWR
Phil Woods' European
   Rhythm Machine

Big Band
Duke Ellington
TDWR
Mike Westbrook

Arranger
Duke Ellington
TDWR
Duke Pearson

Composer
Duke Ellington
TDWR
Mike Gibbs

Soprano Saxophone
Wayne Shorter
TDWR
Tom Scott

Alto Saxophone
Phil Woods
TDWR
Eric Kloss

Tenor Saxophone
Sonny Rollins
TDWR (tie)
Paul Gonsalves
Pharoah Sanders

Baritone Saxophone
Harry Carney
TDWR
Nick Brignola

Clarinet
Russell Procope
TDWR (tie)
Frank Chase
Bob Wilber

Flute
James Moody
TDWR
Norris Turney

Trumpet
Miles Davis
TDWR (tie)
Woody Shaw
Kenny Wheeler

Earl Hines

Trombone
J. J. Johnson
TDWR (tie)
Malcolm Griffiths
Eje Thelin

Acoustic Piano
Earl Hines
TDWR
Stanley Cowell

Organ
Jimmy Smith
TDWR
Lou Bennett

Guitar
Kenny Burrell
TDWR
Sonny Sharrock

Acoustic Bass
Richard Davis
TDWR
Miroslav Vitous

Drums
Elvin Jones
TDWR
Jack DeJohnette

Vibes
Milt Jackson
TDWR
Dave Pike

Miscellaneous Instrument
Jean-Luc Ponty, Violin
TDWR
Stephane Grappelli, Violin

Rock/Blues Group
B. B. King
TDWR
Ike and Tina Turner

1971

Record of the Year
Duke Ellington, *New Orleans Suite* (Atlantic)

Reissue of the Year
Bessie Smith series of reissues on Columbia

Male Singer
Louis Armstrong
TDWR
Richard Boone

Female Singer
Ella Fitzgerald
TDWR
Betty Carter

Combo
Miles Davis
TDWR
Art Ensemble of Chicago

Big Band
Duke Ellington
TDWR
Sun Ra

Arranger
Duke Ellington
TDWR
Herbie Hancock

Composer
Duke Ellington
TDWR
Carla Bley

Soprano Saxophone
Wayne Shorter
TDWR
Budd Johnson

Alto Saxophone
Phil Woods
TDWR
Frank Strozier

Tenor Saxophone
Dexter Gordon
TDWR
Harold Ashby

Baritone Saxophone
Harry Carney
TDWR
Pat Patrick

Clarinet
Russell Procope
TDWR
Bob Wilber

Flute
James Moody
TDWR
Norris Turney

Trumpet
Dizzy Gillespie
TDWR
Roy Eldridge

Trombone
Vic Dickenson
TDWR (tie)
Vic Dickenson
Bill Watrous

Acoustic Piano
Earl Hines
TDWR (tie)
Jaki Byard
Tommy Flanagan

Organ
Jimmy Smith
TDWR
Eddy Louis

Guitar
Kenny Burrell
TDWR
Dennis Budimir

Acoustic Bass
Richard Davis
TDWR
Miroslav Vitous

Drums
Elvin Jones
TDWR
Gus Johnson

Vibes
Bobby Hutcherson
TDWR (tie)
Roy Ayers
Karl Berger

Violin
Jean-Luc Ponty
TDWR
Michael White

Ike and Tina Turner

Miscellaneous Instrument
Rahsaan Roland Kirk, Manzello and Stritch
TDWR
Russ Whitman, Bass Saxophone

Rock/Blues Group
B.B. King
TDWR
Soft Machine

1972

Record of the Year
Jimmy Rushing, *The You and Me That Used to Be* (Bluebird)

Reissue of the Year
Genius of Louis Armstrong, Vol. 1 (Columbia)

Male Singer
Jimmy Rushing
TDWR
Richard Boone

Female Singer
Ella Fitzgerald
TDWR (tie)
Dee Dee Bridgewater
Asha Puthli

Combo
World's Greatest Jazz Band
TDWR
JPJ Quartet

Big Band
Duke Ellington
TDWR
Sun Ra

Arranger
Duke Ellington
TDWR
Alan Broadbent

Composer
Duke Ellington
TDWR
Carla Bley

Soprano Saxophone
Wayne Shorter
TDWR
Joseph Jarman

Alto Saxophone
Ornette Coleman
TDWR
Gary Bartz

Tenor Saxophone
Sonny Rollins
TDWR
Gato Barbieri

Baritone Saxophone
Harry Carney
TDWR
Ronnie Cuber

Clarinet
Russell Procope
TDWR
Bob Wilber

Flute
James Moody
TDWR
Norris Turney

Trumpet
Dizzy Gillespie
TDWR
Lester Bowie

REFERENCE

Joe Williams

Trombone
Vic Dickenson
TDWR
Bill Watrous

Acoustic Piano
Earl Hines
TDWR
Randy Weston

Organ
Jimmy Smith
TDWR
Eddy Louiss

Guitar
Kenny Burrell
TDWR (tie)
Tiny Grimes
Pat Martino

Acoustic Bass
Richard Davis
TDWR
Dave Holland

Drums
Elvin Jones
TDWR
Harold Jones

Vibes
Gary Burton
TDWR
Roy Ayers

Violin
Jean-Luc Ponty
TDWR
Michael White

Miscellaneous Instrument
Rahsaan Roland Kirk,
    Manzello and Stritch
TDWR
Airto Moreira, Percussion

Rock/Blues Group
B.B. King
TDWR
Mahavishnu Orchestra

1973

Record of the Year (tie)
McCoy Tyner, *Sahara*
    (Fantasy/OJC)
Sonny Stitt, *Constellation*
    (Muse)

Reissue of the Year
Art Tatum, *God Is in the
    House* (Onyx)

Male Singer
Ray Charles
TDWR
Joe Lee Wilson

Female Singer
Sarah Vaughan
TDWR
Anita O'Day

Combo
Mahavishnu Orchestra
TDWR
Art Ensemble of Chicago

Big Band
Duke Ellington
TDWR
Gil Evans

Arranger
Duke Ellington
TDWR
Sy Oliver

Composer
Duke Ellington
TDWR
Chick Corea

Soprano Saxophone
Wayne Shorter
TDWR
Kenny Davern

Alto Saxophone
Ornette Coleman
TDWR
Anthony Braxton

Tenor Saxophone
Sonny Rollins
TDWR
John Klemmer

Baritone Saxophone
Harry Carney
TDWR
Howard Johnson

Clarinet
Russell Procope
TDWR
Bobby Jones

Flute
James Moody
TDWR
Jeremy Steig

Trumpet
Dizzy Gillespie
TDWR
Bill Hardman

Trombone
Vic Dickenson
TDWR
Dicky Wells

Acoustic Piano
Earl Hines
TDWR
Jan Hammer

Organ
Jimmy Smith
TDWR
Eddy Louiss

Guitar
Kenny Burrell
TDWR (tie)
George Benson
Attila Zoller

Acoustic Bass
Richard Davis
TDWR
Stanley Clarke

Drums
Elvin Jones
TDWR
Oliver Jackson

Vibes
Milt Jackson
TDWR
David Friedman

Violin
Jean-Luc Ponty
TDWR
Michael White

Miscellaneous Instrument
Rahsaan Roland Kirk,
    Manzello and Stritch
TDWR
Howard Johnson, Tuba

Rock/Blues Group
B.B. King
TDWR
War

1974

Record of the Year
Keith Jarrett, *Solo Concerts*
    (ECM)

Reissue of the Year
*Thelonious Monk and John
    Coltrane* (Fantasy/OJC)

Male Singer
Joe Williams
TDWR (tie)
Roy Eldridge
Stevie Wonder

Female Singer
Ella Fitzgerald
TDWR
Flora Purim

Vocal Group
Pointer Sisters
TDWR
Pointer Sisters

Combo
McCoy Tyner
TDWR
Ruby Braff and George Barnes

Big Band
Thad Jones and Mel Lewis
TDWR
Gil Evans

Arranger
Gil Evans
TDWR
Bill Stapleton

Composer
Duke Ellington
TDWR
McCoy Tyner

Soprano Saxophone
Wayne Shorter
TDWR
Gerry Niewood

Alto Saxophone
Ornette Coleman
TDWR
Anthony Braxton

Tenor Saxophone
Sonny Rollins
TDWR
Billy Harper

Baritone Saxophone
Gerry Mulligan
TDWR
Howard Johnson

Clarinet
Rahsaan Roland Kirk
TDWR
Kalaparusha Ara Difda

Flute
James Moody
TDWR
Jeremy Steig

Trumpet
Dizzy Gillespie
TDWR
Jon Faddis

Trombone
Vic Dickenson
TDWR
Garnett Brown

Acoustic Piano (tie)
Keith Jarrett
McCoy Tyner
TDWR
Muhal Richard Abrams

384

DOWN BEAT POLLS

Organ
Jimmy Smith
TDWR
Eddy Louiss

Guitar
Jim Hall
TDWR
Ralph Towner

Acoustic Bass
Richard Davis
TDWR
Stanley Clarke

Electric Bass
Stanley Clarke
TDWR
Stanley Clarke

Drums
Elvin Jones
TDWR
Billy Hart

Percussion
Airto Moreira
TDWR
Dom Um Romao

Vibes
Gary Burton
TDWR
Karl Berger

Violin
Jean-Luc Ponty
TDWR
Leroy Jenkins

Miscellaneous Instrument
Rahsaan Roland Kirk,
    Manzello and Stritch
TDWR
Howard Johnson, Tuba

Rock/Blues Group
B.B. King
TDWR
Jimmy Dawkins

1975

Record of the Year
Cecil Taylor, *Silent Tongues*
    (Arista/Freedom)

Reissue of the Year (tie)
Charlie Parker, *First
    Recordings* (Onyx)
Art Tatum, *Solo
    Masterpieces* (Pablo)

Male Singer
Joe Williams
TDWR
Eddie Jefferson

Female Singer
Sarah Vaughan
TDWR
Dee Dee Bridgewater

Vocal Group
Jackie and Roy
TDWR
Jackie and Roy

Combo
McCoy Tyner
TDWR
Oregon

Big Band
Thad Jones and Mel Lewis
TDWR
Clark Terry

Arranger
Gil Evans
TDWR
Michael Gibbs

Composer
Keith Jarrett
TDWR
Randy Weston

Soprano Saxophone
Wayne Shorter
TDWR
Gerry Niewood

Alto Saxophone
Phil Woods
TDWR
Sonny Fortune

Tenor Saxophone
Sonny Rollins
TDWR
Billy Harper

Baritone Saxophone
Gerry Mulligan
TDWR (tie)
John Surman
Pat Patrick

Clarinet
Rahsaan Roland Kirk
TDWR
Perry Robinson

Flute
Hubert Laws
TDWR
Sam Rivers

Trumpet
Dizzy Gillespie
TDWR
Jon Faddis

Trombone
Roswell Rudd
TDWR
Bruce Fowler

Synthesizer
Sun Ra
TDWR
George Duke

Piano
Keith Jarrett
TDWR
Dollar Brand

Organ
Jimmy Smith
TDWR
Sun Ra

Guitar
Joe Pass
TDWR
John Abercrombie

Acoustic Bass
Ron Carter
TDWR
George Mraz

Electric Bass
Stanley Clarke
TDWR
Steve Swallow

Drums
Elvin Jones
TDWR
Billy Higgins

Percussion
Airto Moreira
TDWR
Joe Evans

Vibes
Gary Burton
TDWR (tie)
Karl Berger
Dave Friedman

Violin
Jean-Luc Ponty
TDWR
Michal Urbaniak

Miscellaneous Instrument
Rahsaan Roland Kirk,
    Manzello and Stritch
TDWR
Howard Johnson, Tuba

Blues/R&B Group
B.B. King
TDWR (tie)
Blackbyrds
Otis Rush

1976

Record of the Year
*Oscar Peterson and Dizzy
    Gillespie* (Pablo)

Reissue of the Year
Herbie Nichols, *The Third
    World* (Blue Note)

Male Singer (tie)
Mel Tormé
Joe Williams
TDWR
Joe Lee Wilson

Female Singer
Sarah Vaughan
TDWR
Betty Carter

Vocal Group
Jackie and Roy
TDWR
Novi Singers

Combo
McCoy Tyner
TDWR
Lookout Farm

Big Band
Thad Jones and Mel Lewis
TDWR
Toshiko Akiyoshi and Lew
    Tabackin

Arranger
Gil Evans
TDWR
Toshiko Akiyoshi

Composer
Charles Mingus
TDWR
Michael Gibbs

Soprano Saxophone
Wayne Shorter
TDWR
Jan Garbarek

Alto Saxophone
Phil Woods
TDWR
Sonny Fortune

Tenor Saxophone
Sonny Rollins
TDWR
Jan Garbarek

Charles Mingus

Lester Young

Baritone Saxophone
Gerry Mulligan
TDWR
Howard Johnson

Clarinet
Benny Goodman
TDWR
Perry Robinson

Flute
Hubert Laws
TDWR
Sam Rivers

Trumpet
Dizzy Gillespie
TDWR
Jon Faddis

Trombone
Bill Watrous
TDWR
George Lewis

Synthesizer
Joe Zawinul
TDWR
Jan Hammer

Acoustic Piano
McCoy Tyner
TDWR
Don Pullen

Electric Piano
Chick Corea
TDWR
George Duke

Organ
Jimmy Smith
TDWR
Shirley Scott

Guitar
Jim Hall
TDWR
John Abercrombie

Acoustic Bass
Ron Carter
TDWR
Niels-Henning Ørsted

Electric Bass
Stanley Clarke
TDWR
Jaco Pastorius

Drums
Elvin Jones
TDWR
Philip Wilson

Percussion
Airto Moreira
TDWR
Guilherme Franco

Vibes
Milt Jackson
TDWR
Karl Berger

Violin
Jean-Luc Ponty
TDWR
Michal Urbaniak

Miscellaneous Instrument
Rahsaan Roland Kirk,
    Manzello and Stritch
TDWR
Paul McCandless, Oboe

Soul/R&B Artist
Stevie Wonder
TDWR
Bob Marley and the Wailers

Record Label of the Year
Pablo

Record Producer of the Year
Manfred Eicher (ECM)

1977

Record of the Year
Anthony Braxton, *Creative
    Orchestra Music 1976*
    (Arista)

Reissue of the Year
Lester Young, *Lester Young
    Story, Vol. 1* (Columbia)

Male Singer
Joe Williams
TDWR
Joe Lee Wilson

Female Singer
Sarah Vaughan
TDWR
Sheila Jordan

Vocal Group
Jackie and Roy
TDWR
Jackie and Roy

Combo
McCoy Tyner
TDWR
Air

Big Band
Thad Jones and Mel Lewis
TDWR
Toshiko Akiyoshi and Lew
    Tabackin

Arranger
Gil Evans
TDWR
Toshiko Akiyoshi

Composer
Charles Mingus
TDWR
Toshiko Akiyoshi

Soprano Saxophone
Wayne Shorter
TDWR
Zoot Sims

Alto Saxophone
Phil Woods
TDWR
Art Pepper

Tenor Saxophone
Dexter Gordon
TDWR
Billy Harper

Baritone Saxophone
Gerry Mulligan
TDWR
Henry Threadgill

Clarinet
Anthony Braxton
TDWR
Perry Robinson

Flute
Hubert Laws
TDWR
Sam Rivers

Trumpet
Dizzy Gillespie
TDWR
Woody Shaw

Trombone
Bill Watrous
TDWR
George Lewis

Synthesizer
Jan Hammer
TDWR
Richard Teitelbaum

Acoustic Piano
McCoy Tyner
TDWR
Don Pullen

Electric Piano
Joe Zawinul
TDWR
Patrice Rushen

Organ
Jimmy Smith
TDWR
Shirley Scott

Guitar
Jim Hall
TDWR
Derek Bailey

Acoustic Bass
Ron Carter
TDWR
Malachi Favors

Electric Bass
Stanley Clarke
TDWR
Steve Swallow

Drums
Elvin Jones
TDWR
Steve McCall

Pat Metheny

Percussion
Airto Moreira
TDWR
Don Moye

Vibes
Milt Jackson
TDWR
Karl Berger

Violin
Joe Venuti
TDWR
Michal Urbaniak

Miscellaneous Instrument
Howard Johnson, Tuba
TDWR
Anthony Braxton,
   Contrabass Saxophone

Soul/R&B Artist
Stevie Wonder
TDWR
Son Seals

Record Label of the Year
Pablo

Record Producer of the Year
Norman Granz

1978

Record of the Year (tie)
Toshiko Akiyoshi and Lew
   Tabackin, *Insights* (RCA)
Ornette Coleman, *Dancing in
   Your Head* (Horizon)
Dexter Gordon, *Sophisticated
   Giant* (Columbia)
Dexter Gordon, *Homecoming*
   (Columbia)
Roscoe Mitchell, *Nonaah*
   (Nessa)

Reissue of the Year
Lester Young, *The Lester
   Young Story vols. II and
   III* (Columbia)

Male Singer
Joe Williams
TDWR
Joe Lee Wilson

Female Singer
Sarah Vaughan
TDWR
Sheila Jordan

Vocal Group
Jackie and Roy
TDWR
Wild Tchoupitoulas

Combo
Weather Report
TDWR
Air

Big Band
Thad Jones and Mel Lewis
TDWR
Gil Evans

Arranger
Gil Evans
TDWR
Michael Gibbs

Composer
Charles Mingus
TDWR
Carla Bley

Soprano Saxophone
Wayne Shorter
TDWR
Jan Garbarek

Alto Saxophone
Phil Woods
TDWR
Oliver Lake

Tenor Saxophone
Dexter Gordon
TDWR
Scott Hamilton

Baritone Saxophone
Gerry Mulligan
TDWR
John Surman

Clarinet
Anthony Braxton
TDWR
Perry Robinson

Flute
Hubert Laws
TDWR
Sam Rivers

Trumpet
Dizzy Gillespie
TDWR
Kenny Wheeler

Trombone
Roswell Rudd
TDWR
George Lewis

Synthesizer
Joe Zawinul
TDWR
Brian Eno

Acoustic Piano
Cecil Taylor
TDWR (tie)
Jimmie Rowles
Randy Weston

Electric Piano
Joe Zawinul
TDWR
Kenny Barron

Organ
Jimmy Smith
TDWR
Jasper Van't Hof

Guitar
Joe Pass
TDWR
Pat Metheny

Acoustic Bass
Ron Carter
TDWR
Fred Hopkins

Electric Bass
Jaco Pastorius
TDWR
Eberhard Weber

Dexter Gordon

Drums
Elvin Jones
TDWR
Barry Altschul

Percussion
Airto Moreira
TDWR
Don Moye

Vibes
Milt Jackson
TDWR
Gunter Hampel

Violin
Stephane Grappelli
TDWR
Michal Urbaniak

Miscellaneous Instrument
Howard Johnson, Tuba
TDWR
Paul McCandless, Oboe and
   English Horn

Soul/R&B Artist
Stevie Wonder
TDWR
Otis Rush

Record Label of the Year
Columbia

Record Producer of the Year
Norman Granz

1979

Record of the Year
Charles Mingus, *Cumbia and
   Jazz Fusion* (Atlantic)

Reissue of the Year
Charlie Parker, *The Savoy
   Sessions* (Arista/Savoy)

Jazz Group
Phil Woods Quartet
TDWR
Air

Male Singer
Mel Torme
TDWR
Eddie Jefferson

Female Singer
Sarah Vaughan
TDWR (tie)
Norma Winstone
Helen Humes

Vocal Group
Jackie and Roy
TDWR
Anita Kerr Singers

Big Band
Toshiko Akiyoshi and Lew
   Tabackin
TDWR
Carla Bley

Arranger
Toshiko Akiyoshi
TDWR
Michael Gibbs

Composer
Charles Mingus
TDWR
Carla Bley

Soprano Saxophone
Wayne Shorter
TDWR
Jan Garbarek

Alto Saxophone
Phil Woods
TDWR
Arthur Blythe

Tenor Saxophone
Dexter Gordon
TDWR
Scott Hamilton

Baritone Saxophone
Pepper Adams
TDWR
Henry Threadgill

Clarinet
Anthony Braxton
TDWR
Perry Robinson

Flute
Sam Rivers
TDWR
James Newton

Trumpet
Dizzy Gillespie
TDWR
Kenny Wheeler

Trombone
Roswell Rudd
TDWR
Jimmy Knepper

Synthesizer
Joe Zawinul
TDWR
Richard Teitelbaum

Acoustic Piano
Cecil Taylor
TDWR
Joanne Brackeen

Electric Piano
Chick Corea
TDWR
Kenny Barron

Organ
Jimmy Smith
TDWR
Richard Tee

Guitar
Jim Hall
TDWR
Philip Catherine

Acoustic Bass
Ron Carter
TDWR
David Friesen

Electric Bass
Jaco Pastorius
TDWR
Eberhard Weber

Drums
Elvin Jones
TDWR
Steve McCall

Percussion
Airto Moreira
TDWR (tie)
Nana Vasconcelos
Collin Walcott

Vibes
Milt Jackson
TDWR
David Friedman

Violin
Stephane Grappelli
TDWR
L. Shankar

Miscellaneous Instrument
Toots Thielemans, Harmonica
TDWR
Bob Stewart, Tuba

Soul/R&B Artist
Stevie Wonder
TDWR
Junior Wells

Record Label of the Year
Inner City

Record Producer
Michael Cuscuna

1980

Record of the Year
Air, *Air Lore* (Arista/Novus)

Reissue of the Year
Charles Mingus, *Mingus at
Antibes* (Atlantic)

Jazz Group
Art Ensemble of Chicago
TDWR
World Saxophone Quartet

Male Singer
Joe Williams
TDWR
Joe Lee Wilson

Female Singer
Sarah Vaughan
TDWR
Sheila Jordan

Vocal Group
Manhattan Transfer
TDWR
Manhattan Transfer

Big Band
Toshiko Akiyoshi and Lew
Tabackin
TDWR
Globe Unity Orchestra

Arranger
Gil Evans
TDWR
Slide Hampton

Composer
Carla Bley
TDWR
Roscoe Mitchell

Soprano Saxophone
Steve Lacy
TDWR
John Surman

Alto Saxophone
Art Pepper
TDWR
Arthur Blythe

Tenor Saxophone
Sonny Rollins
TDWR
Chico Freeman

Baritone Saxophone
Pepper Adams
TDWR
Ronnie Cuber

Clarinet
Anthony Braxton
TDWR
Perry Robinson

Flute
Lew Tabackin
TDWR
James Newton

Trumpet
Dizzy Gillespie
TDWR
Leo Smith

Art Ensemble of Chicago

Trombone
Albert Mangelsdorff
TDWR
George Lewis

Synthesizer
Joe Zawinul
TDWR
Denny Zeitlin

Acoustic Piano
Cecil Taylor
TDWR
Anthony Davis

Electric Piano
Chick Corea
TDWR (tie)
Kenny Barron
Richard Belrach
Paul Bley

Organ
Jimmy Smith
TDWR
Amina Claudine Myers

Guitar
Joe Pass
TDWR
James "Blood" Ulmer

Acoustic Bass
Charlie Haden
TDWR
Fred Hopkins

Electric Bass
Jaco Pastorius
TDWR
Jamaaladeen Tacuma

Drums
Max Roach
TDWR
Billy Hart

Percussion
Airto Moreira
TDWR
Nana Vasconcelos

Vibes
Milt Jackson
TDWR
Jay Hoggard

Violin
Stephane Grappelli
TDWR
John Blake

Miscellaneous Instrument
Toots Thielemans, Harmonica
TDWR
Abdul Wadud, Cello

Soul/R&B Artist
Stevie Wonder
TDWR
Jimmy Johnson

Record Label (tie)
ECM
Inner City

Record Producer
Michael Cuscuna

1981

**Lifetime Achievement
Award**
John Hammond

Record of the Year (tie)
Art Ensemble of Chicago,
Full Force (ECM)
Archie Shepp and Horace
Parlan, *Trouble in Mind*
(SteepleChase)
Cecil Taylor, *One Too Many
Salty Swift and Not
Goodbye* (hat Hut)

Reissue of the Year
Lennie Tristano, *Requiem*
(Atlantic)

Jazz Group
Art Ensemble of Chicago
TDWR
World Saxophone Quartet

Male Singer
Joe Williams

Female Singer
Sarah Vaughan
TDWR
Carol Sloane

Vocal Group
Manhattan Transfer
TDWR
Hendricks Family

Big Band
Toshiko Akiyoshi and Lew
   Tabackin
TDWR
Globe Unity

Arranger
Gil Evans
TDWR
Jimmy Knepper

Composer
Toshiko Akiyoshi
TDWR
Kenny Wheeler

Soprano Saxophone
Steve Lacy
TDWR
John Surman

Alto Saxophone
Phil Woods
TDWR
Arthur Blythe

Tenor Saxophone
Dexter Gordon
TDWR
Ricky Ford

Baritone Saxophone
Pepper Adams
TDWR
Henry Threadgill

Clarinet
Anthony Braxton
TDWR
John Carter

Flute
Lew Tabackin
TDWR
James Newton

Trumpet
Dizzy Gillespie
TDWR
Wynton Marsalis

Trombone
Jimmy Knepper
TDWR
Ray Anderson

Synthesizer
Joe Zawinul
TDWR
George Lewis

Acoustic Piano
Cecil Taylor
TDWR
Anthony Davis

Electric Piano
Joe Zawinul
TDWR
Kenny Barron

Organ
Jimmy Smith
TDWR
Amina Claudine Myers

Guitar
Joe Pass
TDWR
James "Blood" Ulmer

Acoustic Bass
Niels-Henning Ørsted
TDWR
Aladar Pege

Electric Bass
Jaco Pastorius
TDWR
Jamaaladeen Tacuma

Drums
Max Roach
TDWR
Billy Hart

Percussion
Airto Moreira
TDWR
Nana Vasconcelos

Vibes
Milt Jackson
TDWR
Jay Hoggard

Violin
Stephane Grappelli
TDWR
Billy Bang

Miscellaneous Instrument
Toots Thielemans,
   Harmonica
TDWR
Abdul Wadud, Cello

Soul/R&B Artist
Stevie Wonder
TDWR
Otis Rush

Record Label
Concord

Record Producer
Michael Cuscuna

1982

**Lifetime Achievement
Award**
George Theodore Wein

Record of the Year
Old and New Dreams,
   Playing (ECM)

Reissue of the Year (tie)
Steve Lacy, *Evidence*
   (Prestige)
Charles Mingus,
   *Pithecanthropus
   Erectus* (Atlantic)
Ben Webster, *Giants of Jazz*
   (Time-Life)

Jazz Group
Art Ensemble of Chicago
TDWR
Old and New Dreams

Male Singer
Joe Williams
TDWR
Joe Lee Wilson

Female Singer
Sarah Vaughan
TDWR
Sheila Jordan

Vocal Group
Manhattan Transfer
TDWR
Hendricks Family

Big Band
Toshiko Akiyoshi and Lew
   Tabackin
TDWR
Globe Unity

Arranger
Toshiko Akiyoshi
TDWR
Muhal Richard Abrams

Composer
Toshiko Akiyoshi
TDWR
Muhal Richard Abrams

Soprano Saxophone
Steve Lacy
TDWR
Ira Sullivan

Alto Saxophone
Phil Woods
TDWR
Richie Cole

Tenor Saxophone
Archie Shepp
TDWR
Ricky Ford

Baritone Saxophone
Pepper Adams
TDWR
Henry Threadgill

Clarinet
Anthony Braxton
TDWR
John Carter

Flute
James Newton
TDWR
Ira Sullivan

Trumpet
Lester Bowie
TDWR
Wynton Marsalis

Trombone
Jimmy Knepper
TDWR
Ray Anderson

Synthesizer
Joe Zawinul
TDWR
George Lewis

Acoustic Piano
Cecil Taylor
TDWR
JoAnne Brackeen

Electric Piano
Chick Corea
TDWR
Lyle Mays

Organ
Sun Ra
TDWR
Amina Claudine Myers

Guitar
Jim Hall
TDWR
Emily Remler

Acoustic Bass
Charlie Haden
TDWR
Fred Hopkins

Electric Bass
Steve Swallow
TDWR
Jamaaladeen Tacuma

Drums
Max Roach
TDWR
Ronald Shannon Jackson

Percussion
Airto Moreira
TDWR
Famoudou Don Moye

Vibes
Milt Jackson
TDWR
Jay Hoggard

Manhattan Transfer

Dr. Billy Taylor

Violin
Stephane Grappelli
TDWR
Billy Bang

Miscellaneous Instrument
Toots Thielemans, Harmonica
TDWR
John Clark, French Horn

Soul/R&B Artist
Stevie Wonder
TDWR (tie)
Clifton Chenier
Otis Rush

Record Label (tie)
Concord Jazz
hat Hut

Record Producer (tie)
Giovanni Bonandrini (Black
    Saint/Soul Note)
Carl Jefferson (Concord Jazz)

1983

**Lifetime Achievement
Award**
Leonard Feather

Record of the Year
Muhal Richard Abrams, *Blues
    Forever* (Black Saint)

Reissue of the Year
Pee Wee Russell, *Pied Piper
    of Jazz* (Columbia)

Acoustic Jazz Group
Art Blakey
TDWR
Air

Electric Jazz Group
Weather Report
TDWR
Ronald Shannon Jackson

Male Singer
Joe Williams
TDWR
Bobby McFerrin

Female Singer
Sarah Vaughan
TDWR
Sheila Jordan

Vocal Group
Manhattan Transfer
TDWR
Rare Silk

Big Band
Toshiko Akiyoshi and Lew
    Tabackin
TDWR
Muhal Richard Abrams

Arranger
Gil Evans
TDWR
Rob McConnell

Composer
Carla Bley
TDWR
Anthony Davis

Soprano Saxophone
Steve Lacy
TDWR
Jane Ira Bloom

Alto Saxophone
Phil Woods
TDWR
Paquito D'Rivera

Tenor Saxophone
Sonny Rollins
TDWR
Ricky Ford

Baritone Saxophone
Pepper Adams
TDWR
John Surman

Clarinet
Anthony Braxton
TDWR
Alvin Batiste

Flute
James Newton
TDWR
Ira Sullivan

Trumpet
Wynton Marsalis
TDWR
Olu Dara

Trombone
Jimmy Knepper
TDWR
Ray Anderson

Synthesizer
Joe Zawinul
TDWR
Lyle Mays

Acoustic Piano
Cecil Taylor
TDWR
John Hicks

Electric Piano
Joe Zawinul
TDWR
Lyle Mays

Organ
Jimmy Smith
TDWR
Amina Claudine Myers

Guitar
Jimmy Hall
TDWR (tie)
Bruce Forman
Emily Remler

Acoustic Bass (tie)
Charlie Haden
Fred Hopkins

Electric Bass (tie)
Steve Swallow
Bill Laswell

Drums
Max Roach
TDWR
Ronald Shannon Jackson

Percussion
Nana Vasconcelos
TDWR
Famoudou Don Moye

Vibes
Gary Burton
TDWR
Walt Dickerson

Violin
Stephane Grappelli
TDWR
John Blake

Miscellaneous Instrument
Howard Johnson, Tuba
TDWR
Abdul Wadud, Cello

Pop/Rock Artist
Donald Fagan
TDWR
King Sunny Adé

Soul/R&B Artist
Ray Charles
TDWR
Johnny Copeland

Record Label
Elektra Musician

Record Producer
Giovanni Bonandrini

1984

**Lifetime Achievement
Award**
Dr. Billy Taylor

Record of the Year
Charlie Haden, *The Ballad of
    the Fallen* (ECM)

Reissue of the Year
Thelonious Monk, *The
    Complete Blue Note
    Recordings of Thelonious
    Monk* (Mosaic)

Acoustic Jazz Group
Art Blakey
TDWR
Sphere

Electric Jazz Group
Weather Report
TDWR
Ronald Shannon Jackson

Male Singer
Joe Williams
TDWR
Bobby McFerrin

Female Singer
Sarah Vaughan
TDWR
Tania Maria

Vocal Group
Manhattan Transfer
TDWR
Rare Silk

Big Band
Count Basie
TDWR
Vienna Art Orchestra

Arranger
Gil Evans
TDWR (tie)
Bob Moses
David Murray
Mathias Rüegg

Composer
Carla Bley
TDWR
Anthony Davis

Soprano Saxophone
Steve Lacy
TDWR
Jane Ira Bloom

Alto Saxophone
Phil Woods
TDWR
Eddie "Cleanhead" Vinson

Tenor Saxophone
Sonny Rollins
TDWR
Branford Marsalis

Baritone Saxophone
Pepper Adams
TDWR
John Surman

Clarinet
John Carter
TDWR
Perry Robinson

Flute
James Newton
TDWR
Henry Threadgill

Trumpet
Wynton Marsalis
TDWR
Olu Dara

Trombone
Jimmy Knepper
TDWR
Craig Harris

Synthesizer
Joe Zawinul
TDWR
Lyle Mays

Acoustic Piano
Cecil Taylor
TDWR
Michel Petrucciani

Electric Piano
Joe Zawinul
TDWR
Jasper Van't Hof

Organ
Jimmy Smith
TDWR
Amina Claudine Myers

Guitar
Joe Pass
TDWR
Emily Remler

Acoustic Bass
Charlie Haden
TDWR
Fred Hopkins

Electric Bass
Steve Swallow
TDWR (tie)
Bill Laswell
Jamaaladeen Tacuma

Drums
Max Roach
TDWR
Ronald Shannon Jackson

Percussion
Nana Vasconcelos
TDWR
Mino Cinelu

Vibes
Milt Jackson
TDWR
Jay Hoggard

Violin
Stephane Grappelli
TDWR
John Blake

Miscellaneous Instrument
Toots Thielemans,
    Harmonica
TDWR (tie)
Andy Narell, Steel Drums
Abdul Wadud, Cello

Pop/Rock Artist
Police
TDWR
UB40

Soul/R&B Artist
Ray Charles
TDWR
Buddy Guy

Record Label
Black Saint/Soul Note

Record Producer
Giovanni Bonandrini

1985

Lifetime Achievement Award
Dr. Lawrence Berk

Record of the Year
Various artists, *That's the Way I Feel Now (A Tribute to Thelonious Monk)* (A&M)

Reissue of the Year
Clifford Brown, *The Complete Blue Note and Pacific Jazz Recordings* (Mosaic)

Acoustic Jazz Group
Art Ensemble of Chicago
TDWR
Henry Threadgill Sextet

Electric Jazz Group
Miles Davis
TDWR
Ronald Shannon Jackson and Decoding Society

Male Singer
Joe Williams
TDWR
Bobby McFerrin

Female Singer
Sarah Vaughan
TDWR
Sheila Jordan

Vocal Group
Manhattan Transfer
TDWR
Rare Silk

Big Band
Sun Ra
TDWR
Vienna Art Orchestra

Arranger
Gil Evans
TDWR
Mathias Rüegg

Composer
Carla Bley
TDWR
Anthony Davis

Soprano Saxophone
Steve Lacy
TDWR
Branford Marsalis

Alto Saxophone
Phil Woods
TDWR (tie)
Paquito D'Rivera
Donald Harrison

Tenor Saxophone
Sonny Rollins
TDWR
Branford Marsalis

Baritone Saxophone
Pepper Adams
TDWR
John Surman

Clarinet
John Carter
TDWR
Alvin Batiste

Flute
James Newton
TDWR
Ira Sullivan

Trumpet
Wynton Marsalis
TDWR
Terence Blanchard

Trombone
Jimmy Knepper
TDWR
Craig Harris

Synthesizer
Joe Zawinul
TDWR
John Surman

Acoustic Piano
Cecil Taylor
TDWR
Kenny Kirkland

Electric Piano
Chick Corea
TDWR
Jasper Van't Hof

Organ
Jimmy Smith
TDWR
Amina Claudine Myers

Guitar
Jim Hall
TDWR
Emily Remler

Acoustic Bass
Charlie Haden
TDWR
Fred Hopkins

Electric Bass
Steve Swallow
TDWR
Jamaaladeen Tacuma

Drums
Max Roach
TDWR
Marvin "Smitty" Smith

Percussion
Nana Vasconcelos
TDWR
Günter Sommer

Vibes
Milt Jackson
TDWR
Walt Dickerson

Violin
Stephane Grappelli
TDWR
John Blake

Miscellaneous Instrument
Toots Thielemans, Harmonica
TDWR
Abdul Wadud, Cello

Pop/Rock Group
Stevie Wonder
TDWR
Los Lobos

Cecil Taylor

Soul/R&B Artist
Ray Charles
TDWR
Neville Brothers

Record Label
Black Saint/Soul Note

Record Producer
Giovanni Bonandrini

1986

Lifetime Achievement Award
Orrin Keepnews

Record of the Year
James Newton, *The African Flower* (Blue Note)

Reissue of the Year (tie)
Charles Mingus, *The Complete Candid Recordings* (Mosaic)
Ben Webster, *The Complete Ben Webster on EmArcy* (EmArcy/PolyGram)

Acoustic Jazz Group
Art Blakey's Jazz Messengers
TDWR
Adams/Pullen Quintet

Electric Jazz Group
Miles Davis
TDWR
Jamaaladeen Tacuma

Male Singer
Joe Williams
TDWR
Dave Frishberg

Female Singer
Sarah Vaughan
TDWR
Sheila Jordan

Vocal Group
Manhattan Transfer
TDWR
The Nylons

Big Band
Count Basie
TDWR
Willem Breuker Kollektief

Arranger
Gil Evans
TDWR
Mathias Rüegg

Composer
Carla Bley
TDWR
Henry Threadgill

Soprano Saxophone
Steve Lacy
TDWR
Jane Ira Bloom

Alto Saxophone
Ornette Coleman
TDWR
Steve Coleman

Tenor Saxophone
Sonny Rollins
TDWR
Bennie Wallace

Baritone Saxophone
Pepper Adams
TDWR
John Surman

Clarinet
John Carter
TDWR
Kenny Davern

Flute
James Newton
TDWR
Ira Sullivan

Trumpet
Lester Bowie
TDWR
Terence Blanchard

Trombone
Jimmy Knepper
TDWR
Ray Anderson

Synthesizer
Joe Zawinul
TDWR
John Surman

Acoustic Piano
Cecil Taylor
TDWR
Geri Allen

Electric Piano
Chick Corea
TDWR
Lyle Mays

Organ
Jimmy Smith
TDWR
Amina Claudine Myers

Guitar
John Scofield
TDWR
Bill Frisell

Acoustic Bass
Charlie Haden
TDWR
Cecil McBee

Electric Bass
Steve Swallow
TDWR
Gerald Veasley

Drums
Max Roach
TDWR
Marvin "Smitty" Smith

Percussion
Nana Vasconcelos
TDWR
Famoudou Don Moye

Vibes
Milt Jackson
TDWR
Walt Dickerson

Violin
Stephane Grappelli
TDWR
John Blake

Miscellaneous Instrument
Toots Thielemans, Harmonica
TDWR
Andy Narell, Steel Drums

Pop/Rock Group
Stevie Wonder
TDWR
Laurie Anderson

Soul/R&B Group
Ray Charles
TDWR
Neville Brothers

Record Label
Black Saint/Soul Note

Record Producer
Michael Cuscuna

1987

Lifetime Achievement Award
David Baker

Record of the Year
Pat Metheny and Ornette Coleman, *Song X* (Geffen)

Reissue of the Year (tie)
Duke Ellington, *The Blanton/Webster Years* (RCA/Bluebird)
Thelonious Monk, *The Complete Riverside Recordings* (Riverside)

Acoustic Jazz Group
Art Blakey's Jazz Messengers
TDWR
Blanchard/Harrison Quintet

Electric Jazz Group
Ornette Coleman and Prime Time
TDWR
Bass Desires

Male Singer
Bobby McFerrin
TDWR
Dave Frishberg

Female Singer
Sarah Vaughan
TDWR
Sheila Jordan

Vocal Group
Manhattan Transfer
TDWR
Sweet Honey in the Rock

Big Band
Gil Evans
TDWR
Willem Breuker Kollektief

Arranger
Gil Evans
TDWR
Mathias Rüegg

Composer
Carla Bley
TDWR
Henry Threadgill

Soprano Saxophone
Steve Lacy
TDWR
Jane Ira Bloom

Alto Saxophone
Ornette Coleman
TDWR
Steve Coleman

Tenor Saxophone
Sonny Rollins
TDWR
Bennie Wallace

Baritone Saxophone
Gerry Mulligan
TDWR
John Surman

Clarinet
John Carter
TDWR
Eddie Daniels

Flute
James Newton
TDWR
Henry Threadgill

Trumpet
Lester Bowie
TDWR
Tom Harrell

Trombone (tie)
Ray Anderson
Jimmy Knepper
TDWR
Steve Turre

Synthesizer
Sun Ra
TDWR
John Surman

Neville Brothers

Eric Antoniou

Cassandra Wilson

Acoustic Piano
Cecil Taylor
TDWR
Geri Allen

Electric Piano
Chick Corea
TDWR
Lyle Mays

Organ
Jimmy Smith
TDWR
Amina Claudine Myers

Guitar
Jim Hall
TDWR (tie)
Bill Frisell
Stanley Jordan

Acoustic Bass
Charlie Haden
TDWR
Charnett Moffett

Electric Bass
Steve Swallow
TDWR
Marcus Miller

Drums
Max Roach
TDWR
Marvin "Smitty" Smith

Percussion
Nana Vasconcelos
TDWR
Han Bennink

Vibes
Milt Jackson
TDWR
Jay Haggard

Violin
Stephane Grappelli
TDWR
Didier Lockwood

Miscellaneous Instrument
Toots Thielemans, Harmonica
TDWR
David Murray, Bass Clarinet

Pop/Rock Group
Paul Simon
TDWR
Brave Combo

Soul/R&B Group
Ray Charles
TDWR
Neville Brothers

Record Label
Black Saint/Soul Note

Record Producer
Giovanni Bonandrini

1988

Lifetime Achievement Award
Congressman John
    Conyers, Jr.

Record of the Year
Ornette Coleman, *In All
    Languages* (Caravan of
    Dreams)

Reissue of the Year
Herbie Nichols, *The
    Complete Blue Note
    Recordings* (Mosaic)

Acoustic Jazz Group
Phil Woods Quintet
TDWR
Henry Threadgill Sextet

Electric Jazz Group
Ornette Coleman and Prime
    Time
TDWR
Bass Desires

Male Singer
Bobby McFerrin
TDWR
Dave Frishberg

Female Singer
Sarah Vaughan
TDWR
Cassandra Wilson

Vocal Group
Manhattan Transfer
TDWR
Ladysmith Black Mambazo

Big Band
Sun Ra
TDWR
Willem Breuker Kollektief

Arranger
Gil Evans
TDWR
Willem Breuker Kollektief

Composer
Henry Threadgill
TDWR
Willem Breuker Kollektief

Soprano Saxophone
Steve Lacy
TDWR
Jane Ira Bloom

Alto Saxophone
Phil Woods
TDWR
Frank Morgan

Tenor Saxophone
Sonny Rollins
TDWR
Ricky Ford

Baritone Saxophone
Gerry Mulligan
TDWR
John Surman

Clarinet
John Carter
TDWR
Jimmy Hamilton

Flute
James Newton
TDWR
Sam Rivers

Trumpet
Wynton Marsalis
TDWR
Wallace Roney

Trombone
Ray Anderson
TDWR
Steve Turre

Synthesizer
Joe Zawinul
TDWR
John Surman

Acoustic Piano
Cecil Taylor
TDWR
Mulgrew Miller

Electric Piano
Chick Corea
TDWR
Lyle Mays

Organ
Jimmy Smith
TDWR
Amina Claudine Myers

Guitar
Jim Hall
TDWR
Bill Frisell

Acoustic Bass
Charlie Haden
TDWR
Charnett Moffett

Electric Bass
Steve Swallow
TDWR
Gerald Veasley

Drums
Max Roach
TDWR
Terri Lynn Carrington

Percussion
Nana Vasconcelos
TDWR
Mino Cinelu

Vibes
Milt Jackson
TDWR
Khan Jamal

Violin
Stephane Grappelli
TDWR
Claude Williams

Miscellaneous Instrument
Toots Thielemans, Harmonica
TDWR
John Surman, Bass Clarinet

Pop/Rock Group
Sting
TDWR
Ladysmith Black Mambazo

Soul/R&B Group
Ray Charles
TDWR
Kinsey Report

Record Label
Black Saint/Soul Note

Record Producer
Giovanni Bonandrini

1989

Lifetime Achievement Award
Norman Granz

Record of the Year (tie)
Jack DeJohnette, *Audio
    Visualscapes* (Impulse!)
Charlie Haden, Paul Motian
    and Geri Allen, *Etudes*
    (Soul Note)

Reissue of the Year
Charlie Parker, *The Complete
    Charlie Parker on Verve*
    (Verve)

Acoustic Jazz Group
Phil Woods
TDWR
8 Bold Souls

Electric Jazz Group
Miles Davis
TDWR
Bass Desires

Male Singer
Joe Williams
TDWR
Dave Frishberg

Female Singer
Betty Carter
TDWR
Cassandra Wilson

Vocal Group
Manhattan Transfer
TDWR
Take 6

Big Band
Sun Ra
TDWR
Willem Breuker Kollektief

Arranger
Benny Carter
TDWR
John Zorn

Composer
Henry Threadgill
TDWR
Henry Threadgill

Soprano Saxophone
Steve Lacy
TDWR
Jane Ira Bloom

Alto Saxophone
Phil Woods
TDWR
Bobby Watson

Tenor Saxophone
Sonny Rollins
TDWR (tie)
Courtney Pine
George Adams

Baritone Saxophone
Gerry Mulligan
TDWR
John Surman

Clarinet
John Carter
TDWR
Jimmy Hamilton

Flute
James Newton
TDWR
Sam Rivers

Trumpet
Wynton Marsalis
TDWR
Tom Harrell

Trombone
Ray Anderson
TDWR
Robin Eubanks

Synthesizer
Sun Ra
TDWR
John Surman

Acoustic Piano
Cecil Taylor
TDWR
Marcus Roberts

Organ
Jimmy Smith
TDWR
Amina Claudine Myers

Guitar
John Scofield
TDWR
Emily Remler

Acoustic Bass
Charlie Haden
TDWR
Charnett Moffett

Electric Bass
Steve Swallow
TDWR
Marcus Miller

Drums
Max Roach
TDWR
Marvin "Smitty" Smith

Percussion
Nana Vasconcelos
TDWR
Mino Cinelu

Vibes
Milt Jackson
TDWR
Steve Nelson

Violin
Stephane Grappelli
TDWR
Claude Williams

Miscellaneous Instrument
Toots Thielemans, Harmonica
TDWR
Hank Roberts, Cello

Pop/Rock Group
Sting
TDWR
Ray Charles

Soul/R&B Group
Ray Charles
TDWR
Jeannie Cheatham

Record Label
Black Saint/Soul Note

Record Producer
Giovanni Bonandrini

1990

Lifetime Achievement Award
Rudy Van Gelder

Jazz Album of the Year
Cecil Taylor, *In Berlin* (FMP)

Reissue of the Year
Clifford Brown, *Brownie: The Complete Emarcy Recordings* (Emarcy)

Acoustic Jazz Group
Phil Woods Quintet
TDWR
Harper Brothers

Jimmy Smith

Bruce Hilliard

Electric Jazz Group
Ornette Coleman's Prime Time
TDWR
John Zorn's Naked City

Male Jazz Singer
Joe Williams
TDWR
Mark Murphy

Male Non-Jazz Singer
Aaron Neville
TDWR
Harry Connick, Jr.

Female Jazz Singer
Betty Carter
TDWR
Cassandra Wilson

Female Non-Jazz Singer
Bonnie Raitt
TDWR
Sinead O'Connor

Vocal Jazz Group
Take 6
TDWR
Ladysmith Black Mambazo

Big Band
Sun Ra and His Arkestra
TDWR
Willem Breuker Kollektief

Arranger
Toshiko Akiyoshi
TDWR
Don Sickler

Composer
Henry Threadgill
TDWR
Bobby Previte

Soprano Saxophone
Steve Lacy
TDWR
Jane Ira Bloom

Alto Saxophone
Phil Woods
TDWR
Bobby Watson

Tenor Saxophone
Sonny Rollins
TDWR
Ralph Moore

Baritone Saxophone
Hamiet Bluiett
TDWR
John Surman

Clarinet
John Carter
TDWR
Don Byron

Flute
James Newton
TDWR
Frank Wess

Trumpet
Lester Bowie
TDWR
Wallace Roney

Trombone
Ray Anderson
TDWR
Robin Eubanks

Synthesizer
Sun Ra
TDWR
John Surman

Acoustic Piano
Cecil Taylor
TDWR
Geri Allen

Organ
Jimmy Smith
TDWR
Barbara Dennerlein

Acoustic Guitar
Jim Hall
TDWR
Emily Remler

Electric Guitar
Bill Frisell
TDWR
Sonny Sharrock

Acoustic Bass
Charlie Haden
TDWR
Fred Hopkins

Electric Bass
Steve Swallow
TDWR
Bill Laswell

Drums
Max Roach
TDWR
Marvin "Smitty" Smith

Percussion
Nana Vasconcelos
TDWR
Marilyn Mazur

Vibes
Milt Jackson
TDWR
Jay Hoggard

Violin
Stephane Grappelli
TDWR
Terry Jenoure

Miscellaneous Instrument
Toots Thielemans, Harmonica
TDWR
Hank Roberts, Cello

Rock Artist of the Year
Elvis Costello
TDWR
John Hiatt

Rock Group
Rolling Stones
TDWR
Living Colour

R&B Soul Artist of the Year
Ray Charles
TDWR
Barrence Whitfield

R&B/Soul Group
Neville Brothers
TDWR
Barrence Whitfield and the
    Savages

Blues Group
Kinsey Report
TDWR
Saffire

Rap Artist/Group of the Year
Public Enemy
TDWR
Jon Faddis

World Beat Artist of the Year
Youssou N'Dour
TDWR
Nusrat Fateh Ali Khan

Record Label
Blue Note

Record Producer
Michael Cuscuna
TDWR
Willem Breuker Kollektief

1991

**Lifetime Achievement
Award**
Bill Cosby

Jazz Artist of the Year
Wynton Marsalis
TDWR
Geri Allen

Jazz Album of the Year
Charlie Haden and the
    Liberation Music
    Orchestra, *Dream
    Keeper* (Blue Note)

Reissue of the Year
Robert Johnson, *The
    Complete Recordings*
    (Columbia/Legacy)

Acoustic Jazz Group
Phil Woods
TDWR
Harper Brothers

Electric Jazz Group
John Scofield Group
TDWR
Steve Coleman and Five
    Elements

Male Jazz Singer
Joe Williams
TDWR
Harry Connick, Jr.

Male Non-Jazz Singer
Aaron Neville
TDWR
Harry Connick, Jr.

Ornette Coleman

Female Jazz Singer
Betty Carter
TDWR
Cassandra Wilson

Female Non-Jazz Singer
Aretha Franklin
TDWR
Tracy Chapman

Vocal Jazz Group
Take 6
TDWR (tie)
New York Voices
Sweet Honey in the Rock

Big Band
Count Basie Orchestra
TDWR
Peter Apfelbaum and the
    Hieroglyphics Ensemble

Arranger
Carla Bley
TDWR
John Zorn

Composer
Henry Threadgill
TDWR
Ed Wilkerson, Jr.

Soprano Saxophone
Steve Lacy
TDWR
Jane Ira Bloom

Alto Saxophone
Frank Morgan
TDWR
Bobby Watson

Tenor Saxophone
Sonny Rollins
TDWR
Joe Lovano

Baritone Saxophone
Hamiet Bluiett
TDWR
John Surman

Clarinet
John Carter
TDWR
Don Byron

Flute
James Newton
TDWR
Kent Jordan

Trumpet
Wynton Marsalis
TDWR
Roy Hargrove

Trombone
Ray Anderson
TDWR
Robin Eubanks

Synthesizer
Sun Ra
TDWR
John Surman

Acoustic Piano
Cecil Taylor
TDWR
Geri Allen

Organ
Jimmy Smith
TDWR
Barbara Dennerlein

Acoustic Guitar
Jim Hall
TDWR
Egberto Gismonti

Electric Guitar
John Scofield
TDWR (tie)
Kevin Eubanks
Sonny Sharrock

Acoustic Bass
Charlie Haden
TDWR
Ray Drummond

Bill Cosby

Paul Robicheau

Sonny Sharrock

Electric Bass
Steve Swallow
TDWR
Bill Laswell

Drums
Max Roach
TDWR
Marvin "Smitty" Smith

Percussion
Nana Vasconcelos
TDWR
Jerry Gonzalez

Vibes
Milt Jackson
TDWR
Steve Nelson

Violin
Stephane Grappelli
TDWR
Terry Jenoure

Miscellaneous Instrument
Toots Thielemans, Harmonica
TDWR
Steve Turre, Conch Shells

Rock Artist of the Year
Paul Simon
TDWR
Richard Thompson

Rock Album of the Year
Neil Young and Crazy Horse,
    Ragged Glory (Reprise)

Rock Group
Living Colour
TDWR
Fishbone

R&B/Soul Artist of the Year
Ray Charles
TDWR
Maceo Parker

R&B/Soul Album of the Year
Maceo Parker, Roots
    Revisited (Verve)

R&B/Soul Group
Neville Brothers
TDWR
J. B. Horns

Blues Artist of the Year
B.B. King
TDWR
Joe Louis Walker

Blues Album of the Year
Charles Brown, All My Life
    (Bullseye
    Blues/Rounder)

Blues Group
Kinsey Report
TDWR
Lil' Ed and the Blues Imperials

**World Beat Artist of the
Year**
Milton Nascimento
TDWR
Jerry Gonzalez

**World Beat Album of the
Year**
Paul Simon, The Rhythm of the
    Saints (Warner Bros.)

World Beat Group
Mahlathini and the
    Mahotella Queens
TDWR
Jerry Gonzalez and the Fort
    Apache Band

Record Label of the Year
Blue Note

Record Producer
Michael Cuscuna
TDWR
Delfeayo Marsalis

1992

**Lifetime Achievement
Award**
Rich Matteson

Jazz Artist of the Year
Joe Henderson
TDWR
Don Byron

Jazz Album of the Year
Joe Henderson, Lush Life
    (Verve)

Reissue of the Year
Nat King Cole, The Complete
    Capitol Recordings of
    the Nat King Cole Trio
    (Mosaic)

Acoustic Jazz Group
Wynton Marsalis
TDWR
Ralph Peterson Fo'tet

Electric Jazz Group
Ornette Coleman
TDWR
Naked City

Male Jazz Singer
Joe Williams
TDWR
David Frishberg

Male Non-Jazz Singer
Aaron Neville
TDWR
Lyle Lovett

Female Jazz Singer
Betty Carter
TDWR
Cassandra Wilson

Female Non-Jazz Singer
Bonnie Raitt
TDWR
Diamanda Galas

Vocal Jazz Group
Take 6
TDWR
New York Voices

Big Band
Sun Ra Arkestra
TDWR (tie)
Willem Breuker Kollektief
George Gruntz Concert Band

Arranger
Carla Bley
TDWR
Bob Belden

Composer
Muhal Richard Abrams
TDWR
Ed Wilkerson

Soprano Saxophone
Steve Lacy
TDWR
Jane Bunnett

Alto Saxophone
Phil Woods
TDWR
Bobby Watson

Tenor Saxophone
Joe Henderson
TDWR
Ralph Moore

Baritone Saxophone
Hamiet Bluiett
TDWR
Nick Brignola

Clarinet
Don Byron
TDWR
Don Byron

Flute
James Newton
TDWR
Kent Jordan

Trumpet
Wynton Marsalis
TDWR
Roy Hargrove

Trombone
Ray Anderson
TDWR
Robin Eubanks

Synthesizer
Sun Ra
TDWR
Wayne Horvitz

Acoustic Piano
Tommy Flanagan
TDWR
Geri Allen

Organ
Jimmy Smith
TDWR
Don Pullen

Acoustic Guitar
John McLaughlin
TDWR
Howard Alden

Electric Guitar
John Scofield
TDWR
Sonny Sharrock

Acoustic Bass
Charlie Haden
TDWR
Anthony Cox

Electric Bass
Steve Swallow
TDWR
Gerald Veasley

Drums
Max Roach
TDWR
Ralph Peterson, Jr.

Percussion
Airto Moriera
TDWR
Poncho Sanchez

Vibes
Milt Jackson
TDWR
Steve Nelson

Violin
Stephane Grappelli
TDWR
Claude Williams

Miscellaneous Instrument
Toots Thielemans, Harmonica
TDWR
Diedre Murray, Cello

Rock Artist of the Year
Neil Young
TDWR
Dave Alvin

Rock Album of the Year
Neil Young, *Arc/Weld*
  (Reprise)

Rock Group
Grateful Dead
TDWR
NRBQ

R&B/Soul Artist of the Year
Ray Charles
TDWR
Charles Brown

R&B/Soul Album of the Year
Prince, *Diamonds and
  Pearls* (Paisley
  Park/Warner Bros.)

R&B/Soul Group
Neville Brothers

Blues Artist of the Year
B.B. King
TDWR
Joe Louis Walker

Blues Album of the Year
Buddy Guy, *Damn Right I Got
  the Blues* (Silvertone)

Blues Group
B.B. King
TDWR
Holmes Brothers

**World Beat Artist of the
Year**
Milton Nascimento
TDWR
Margareth Menezes

**World Beat Album of the
Year**
Mickey Hart, *Planet Drum*
  (Rykodisc)

Steven J. Sherman

Stephane Grappelli

World Beat Group
Ladysmith Black Mambazo
TDWR
Jerry Gonzalez and the Fort
  Apache Band

Record Label of the Year
Blue Note

Record Producer
Michael Cuscuna
TDWR
Delfeayo Marsalis

1993

Lifetime Achievement Award
Gunther Schuller

Jazz Artist of the Year
Joe Henderson
TDWR
Joe Lovano

Jazz Album of the Year
Joe Henderson, *So Near, So
  Far (Musings for Miles)*
  (Verve)

Reissue Album of the Year
Billy Holiday, *The Complete
  Billy Holiday on Verve*
  (Verve)

Male Jazz Singer
Joe Williams
TDWR
Mark Murphy

Male Non-Jazz Singer
Aaron Neville
TDWR
Harry Connick, Jr.

Female Jazz Singer
Betty Carter
TDWR
Cassandra Wilson

Female Non-Jazz Singer
Bonnie Raitt
TDWR
Lucinda Williams

Vocal Jazz Group
Take 6
TDWR
Sweet Honey in the Rock

Acoustic Jazz Group
Wynton Marsalis
TDWR
Bobby Watson

Electric Jazz Group
John Scofield
TDWR
Sonny Sharrock

Big Band
Count Basie
TDWR
Either/Orchestra

Arranger
Carla Bley
TDWR
Bob Belden

Composer
Muhal Richard Abrams
TDWR
Bobby Watson

Soprano Saxophone
Steve Lacy
TDWR
Jane Bunnett

Alto Saxophone
Jackie McLean
TDWR
Kenny Garrett

Tenor Saxophone
Joe Henderson
TDWR
Joshua Redman

Baritone Saxophone
Hamiet Bluiett
TDWR
Gary Smulyan

Clarinet
Don Byron
TDWR
Marty Ehrlich

Flute
James Newton
TDWR
Dave Valentin

Trumpet (tie)
Lester Bowie
Wynton Marsalis
TDWR
Roy Hargrove

Trombone
J. J. Johnson
TDWR
Frank Lacy

Acoustic Piano
Kenny Barron
TDWR (tie)
Geri Allen
Gonzalo Rubalcaba

Organ
Jimmy Smith
TDWR
Barbara Dennerlein

Acoustic Guitar
John McLaughlin
TDWR
Howard Alden

Electric Guitar
John Scofield
TDWR
Mike Stern

Acoustic Bass
Charlie Haden
TDWR
Christian McBride

Electric Bass
Steve Swallow
TDWR
Gerald Vessiey

Drums
Max Roach
TDWR
Lewis Nash

Percussion
Airto Moriera
TDWR
Jerry Gonzalez

Vibes
Milt Jackson
TDWR
Steve Nelson

Violin
Stephane Grappelli
TDWR
Regina Carter

Miscellaneous Instrument
Toots Thielemans,
  Harmonica
TDWR
Don Byron, Bass Clarinet

Blues Artist of the Year
B.B. King
TDWR
Lil' Ed

Blues Album of the Year
John Lee Hooker, *Boom Boom*
  (Pointblank/Virgin)

Blues Group
B.B. King
TDWR
Little Charlie and the Nightcats

Beyond Artist of the Year
Tom Waits
TDWR
Lyle Lovett

Beyond Album of the Year
Mario Bauza, *Tanga*
  (Messidor)

Beyond Group (tie)
Kronos Quartet
Los Lobos
TDWR
Greg Osby

Record Label of the Year
Verve

Record Producer
Michael Cuscuna
TDWR
Delfeayo Marsalis

Pulitzer Prizes in Music

Aaron Copland

1943
*Secular Cantata No. 2,
A Free Song,* William Schuman

1944
Symphony No. 4 (Op. 34), Howard
Hanson

1945
Appalachian Spring, Aaron Copland

1946
The Canticle of the Sun, Leo Sowerby

1947
Symphony No. 3, Charles Ives

1948
Symphony No. 3, Walter Piston

1949
Louisiana Story Music, Virgil Thomson

1950
The Consul, Gian Carlo Menotti

1951
*Music for Opera Giants
in the Earth,* Douglas Stuart Moore

1952
Symphony Concertante, Gail Kubik

1953
No award

1954
*Concerto for Two Pianos and
Orchestra,* Quincy Porter

1955
The Saint of Bleecker Street,
Gian Carlo Menotti

1956
Symphony No. 3, Ernst Toch

1957
Meditations on Ecclesiastes,
Norman Dello Joio

1958
Vanessa, Samuel Barber

1959
Concerto for Piano and Orchestra,
John La Montaine

1960
Second String Quartet, Elliott Carter

1961
Symphony No. 7, Walter Piston

1962
The Crucible, Robert Ward

1963
Piano Concerto No. 1, Samuel Barber

1964
No award

1965
No award

1966
Variations for Orchestra, Leslie
Bassett

1967
Quartet No. 3, Leon Kirchner

1968
Echoes of Time and the River, George
Crumb

1969
String Quartet No. 3, Karel Husa

1970
Time's Encomium, Charles Wuorinen

1971
*Synchronisms No. 6 for Piano and
Electronic Sound,* Mario
Davidowsky

1972
Windows, Jacob Druckman

1973
String Quartet No. 3, Elliott Carter

1974
Notturno, Donald Martino

1975
From the Diary of Virginia Woolf,
Dominick Argento

1976
Air Music, Ned Rorem

1977
Visions of Terror and Wonder,
Richard Wernick

1978
*Deja Vu for Percussion Quartet and
Orchestra,* Michael Colgrass

1979
Aftertones of Infinity, Joseph
Schwantner

1980
In Memory of a Summer Day, David
Del Tredici

1981
No award

1982
Concerto for Orchestra, Roger
Sessions

1983
Three Movements for Orchestra,
Ellen T. Zwilich

1984
Canti del Sole, Bernard Rands

1985
Symphony RiverRun, Stephen Albert

1986
Wind Quintet IV, George Perle

1987
The Flight Into Egypt, John Harbison

1988
12 New Etudes for Piano, William
Bolcom

Samuel Barber

1989
Whispers Out of Time, Roger
Reynolds

1990
*Duplicates: A Concerto for Two
Pianos and Orchestra,*
Mel Powell

1991
Symphony, Shulamit Ran

1992
*The Face of the Night, the Heart
of the Dark,* Wayne Peterson

1993
Trombone Concerto, Christopher
Rouse

1994
*Of Reminiscences and
Reflections,* Gunther Schuller

Gramophone Awards

The *Gramophone* Awards, presented each October at London's Dorchester Hotel, are widely regarded as the most important and influential classical music awards in the world. *Gramophone* critics select nominees from a pool of more than 2,000 reviews that appeared in the magazine throughout the year and choose the winners after a two-round balloting process. Each year a Record of the Year is selected from the list of winners.

Beethoven

1977

CHAMBER
Shostakovich, *String Quartets nos. 4 and 12*, Fitzwilliam Quartet (Decca)

CHORAL
Elgar, *Coronation Ode*; Parry, *I Was Glad*, Philip Ledger conducting Kings College Choir and New Philharmonia Orchestra (EMI)

CONCERTO
Mozart, *Piano Concerto No. 22*, Neville Marriner conducting Academy of St. Martin-in-the-Fields; solo: Brendel (Philips)

CONTEMPORARY
Berio, *Concerto for Two Pianos*, Pierre Boulez conducting London Symphony Orchestra and Luciano Berio conducting BBC Symphony Orchestra (RCA Red Seal)

EARLY MUSIC
Dowland, *Lute Works*, Julian Bream (RCA Red Seal)

HISTORICAL
Various artists, *Record of Singing*, various artists (HMV)

INSTRUMENTAL
Beethoven, *Piano Sonatas nos. 27–32*, Maurizio Pollini (Deutsche Grammophon)

OPERATIC (RECORD OF THE YEAR)
Janácek, *Kata Kabanova*, Charles Mackerras conducting Vienna State Opera and Vienna Philharmonic Orchestra (Decca)

ORCHESTRAL
Elgar, *Symphony No. 1*, Sir Adrian Boult conducting London Philharmonic Orchestra (EMI)

SOLO VOCAL
Shostakovich, *Suite, Six Songs to Lyrics, etc.*, Maxim Shostakovich conducting Moscow Radio Symphony Orchestra (HMV Melodiya)

1978

CHAMBER
Bartók, *Sonata for 2 Pianos*; Debussy, *En Blanc*; Mozart, *Andante With 5 Variations for Piano*, Martha Argerich, Stephen Bishop-Kovacevich, Willy Goudswaard and Michael de Roo (Philips)

CHORAL
Handel, *Dixit Dominus*, John Eliot Gardiner conducting Monteverdi Choir and Orchestra (Erato)

CONCERTO
Prokofiev, *Piano Concerto No. 1*, Simon Rattle conducting London Symphony Orchestra; solo: Gavrilov (EMI Studio Plus)

CONTEMPORARY
Webern, *Complete Works*, Pierre Boulez conducting Juilliard String Quartet and London Symphony Orchestra (Sony)

EARLY MUSIC
Handel, *Acis and Galatea*, John Eliot Gardiner conducting English Baroque Soloists (Archiv)

HISTORICAL
Gluck, *Orfeo ed Euridice*, Charles Bruck conducting Netherlands Opera Chorus and Orchestra (EMI)

INSTRUMENTAL
Liszt, *Piano Works*, Alfred Brendel (Philips)

OPERATIC (RECORD OF THE YEAR)
Puccini, *La Fanciulla del West*, Zubin Mehta conducting Royal Opera House Choir and Orchestra (Deutsche Grammophon)

ORCHESTRAL
Mozart, *Symphonies nos. 25 and 29*, Benjamin Britten conducting English Chamber Orchestra (Decca)

SOLO VOCAL
Chausson, *Poeme*; Duparc, *Melodies*, André Previn conducting London Symphony Orchestra; solo: Baker (HMV)

1979

CHAMBER (RECORD OF THE YEAR)
Haydn, *Piano Trios*, Beaux Arts Trio (Philips)

CHORAL
Schoenberg, *Gurrelieder*, Seiji Ozawa conducting Tanglewood Festival Chorus and Boston Symphony Orchestra (Philips)

CONCERTO
Bartók, *Piano Concertos nos. 1 and 2*, Claudio Abbado conducting Chicago Symphony Orchestra; solo: Pollini (Deutsche Grammophon)

CONTEMPORARY
Maxwell Davies, *Symphony No. 1*, Simon Rattle conducting Philharmonia Orchestra (Decca)

EARLY MUSIC
Mozart, *Symphonies Vol. 3*, Christopher Hogwood conducting Academy of Ancient Music (L'Oiseau-Lyre)

ENGINEERING
Debussy, *Images, Prélude à l'après-midi*, André Previn conducting London Symphony Orchestra (EMI)

HISTORICAL
Various artists, *Record of Singing Vol. 2*, various artists (HMV)

INSTRUMENTAL
Bach, *Organ Works Vol. 3*, Peter Hurford (Argo)

OPERATIC
Berg, *Lulu*, Pierre Boulez conducting Paris Opera Orchestra (Deutsche Grammophon)

ORCHESTRAL
Debussy, *Images, Prélude à l'après-midi*, André Previn conducting London Symphony Orchestra (EMI)

SOLO VOCAL
Grechaninov, etc., *Five Children's Songs*, Elisabeth Söderström and Vladimir Ashkenazy (Decca)

Brahms

HISTORICAL NON-VOCAL
Bartók, *Contrasts for Clarinet, Violin and Piano*, Bela Bartók, Joseph Szigeti and Benny Goodman (Sony)

INSTRUMENTAL
Brahms, *Piano Sonatas nos. 1 and 2*, Krystian Zimerman (Deutsche Grammophon)

OPERATIC (RECORD OF THE YEAR)
Janácek, *From the House of the Dead*, Sir Charles Mackerras conducting Vienna State Opera and Vienna Philharmonic Orchestra (Decca)

ORCHESTRAL
Debussy, *Nocturnes, Jeux*, Bernard Haitink conducting Concertgebouw Orchestra (Philips)

SOLO VOCAL
Various artists, *A Shropshire Lad*, Graham Trew and Roger Vignoles (Meridian)

1980

CHAMBER
Brahms, *Piano Quintet*, Quartetto Italiano; solo: Pollini (Deutsche Grammophon)

CHORAL
Handel, *L'Allegro, il Penseroso*, John Eliot Gardiner conducting Monteverdi Choir (Erato)

CONCERTO
Ravel, *Piano Concerto in G*, Lorin Maazel conducting French National Orchestra; solo: Collard (HMV)

CONTEMPORARY
Birtwistle, *Punch and Judy*, David Atherton conducting London Sinfonietta (Etcetera)

EARLY MUSIC
C.P.E. Bach, *Sinfonias*, Trevor Pinnock conducting The English Concert (Archiv)

ENGINEERING
Debussy, *Nocturnes, Jeux*, Bernard Haitink conducting Concertgebouw Orchestra (Philips)

HISTORICAL VOCAL
Various artists, *Gramophone Co. Recordings*, Fernando de Lucia (Rubini)

1981

CHAMBER
Bartók, *String Quartets nos. 1–6*, Tokyo Quartet (Deutsche Grammophon)

CHORAL
Delius, *Fenby Legacy*, Eric Fenby conducting Royal Philharmonia Orchestra (Unicorn-Kanchan)

CONCERTO
Beethoven, *Violin Concerto in D Minor*, Carlo Maria Giulini conducting Philharmonia; solo: Perlman (EMI)

CONTEMPORARY
Tippett, *King Priam*, David Atherton conducting London Sinfonietta (Decca)

EARLY MUSIC
Various artists, *German Chamber Music*, Cologne Music Antiqua (Archiv)

ENGINEERING
Massenet, *Werther*, Sir Colin Davis conducting Royal Opera House Orchestra (Philips)

HISTORICAL VOCAL
Various artists, *Hugo Wolf Society Lieder*, various artists (HMV)

HISTORICAL NON-VOCAL
Brahms, *Chamber Works,* Busch Quartet, Rudolf Serkin, Reginald Kell and Aubrey Brain (World Records)

INSTRUMENTAL
Liszt, *Piano Works,* Alfred Brendel (Philips)

OPERATIC (RECORD OF THE YEAR)
Wagner, *Parsifal,* Herbert von Karajan conducting Deutsche Opera and Berlin Philharmonic Orchestra (Deutsche Grammophon)

ORCHESTRAL
Mahler, *Symphony No. 9,* Herbert von Karajan conducting Berlin Philharmonic Orchestra (Deutsche Grammophon)

SOLO VOCAL
Liszt, *Lieder,* Dietrich Fischer-Dieskau and Daniel Barenboim (Deutsche Grammophon)

1982–1983

CHAMBER
Borodin, *String Quartets nos. 1 and 2,* Borodin Quartet (EMI)

CHORAL
Bach, *Mass in B Minor,* Joshua Rifkin conducting Bach Ensemble (Elektra-Nonesuch)

CONCERTO (RECORD OF THE YEAR)
Tippett, *Triple Concerto,* Sir Colin Davis conducting London Symphony Orchestra (Philips)

CONTEMPORARY
Boulez, *Pli Selon Pli,* Pierre Boulez conducting BBC Symphony Orchestra; solo: Bryn-Jolson (Erato)

EARLY-BAROQUE
Charpentier, *Acteon,* William Christie conducting Les Arts Florissants Vocal (Harmonia Mundi)

EARLY-MEDIEVAL
Hildegard of Binge, *Sequences and Hymns,* Christopher Page conducting Gothic Voices (Hyperion)

ENGINEERING
Shostakovich, *Symphony No. 5,* Bernard Haitink conducting Concertgebouw Orchestra (Decca)

HISTORICAL VOCAL
Schubert, *Historical Recordings of Lieder,* various artists (HMV)

HISTORICAL NON-VOCAL
Bartók, *At the Piano Vol. 1,* Béla Bartók (Hungaraton)

INSTRUMENTAL
Liszt, *Piano Sonata in B Minor,* Alfred Brendel (Philips)

OPERATIC
Janácek, *Cunning Little Vixen,* Sir Charles Mackerras conducting Vienna State Opera and Vienna Philharmonic Orchestra (Decca)

ORCHESTRAL
Strauss, *Metamorphosen,* Herbert von Karajan conducting Berlin Philharmonic Orchestra (Deutsche Grammophon)

SOLO VOCAL
Brahms, *Lieder,* Kurt Masur conducting Leipzig Gewandhaus Orchestra; solo: Norman (Philips)

1984

CHAMBER
Beethoven, *String Quartets nos. 12–16,* Lindsay Quartet (ASV)

CHORAL
Mozart, *Requiem,* Peter Schreier conducting Staatskapelle Dresden (Philips)

CONCERTO
Mozart, *Piano Concertos nos. 15 and 16,* Murray Perahia conducting English Chamber Orchestra (CBS Master)

CONTEMPORARY
Carter and Harvey, *String Quartets,* Arditti Quartet (RCA Red Seal)

EARLY-BAROQUE
Bach, *Chamber Works,* Reinhard Goebel conducting Cologne Musica Antiqua (Archiv)

EARLY-MEDIEVAL
Dunstable, *Motets,* Paul Hillier conducting Hilliard Ensemble (HMV)

ENGINEERING
Bax, *Symphony No. 4, Tintagel,* Bryden Thomson conducting Ulster Orchestra (Chandos)

HISTORICAL VOCAL
Brahms and Schumann, *Historical Recordings of Lieder,* various artists (HMV)

HISTORICAL NON-VOCAL
Beethoven, *Piano Sonatas nos. 30–32,* Egon Petri (dell'Arte)

INSTRUMENTAL
Beethoven, *Piano Sonata No. 29,* Emil Gilels (Deutsche Grammophon)

OPERATIC
Janácek, *Jenufa,* Sir Charles Mackerras conducting Vienna State Opera and Vienna Philharmonic Orchestra (Decca)

ORCHESTRAL (RECORD OF THE YEAR)
Mahler, *Symphony No. 9,* Herbert von Karajan conducting Berlin Philharmonic Orchestra (Deutsche Grammophon)

SOLO VOCAL
Strauss, *Four Last Songs,* Kurt Masur conducting Leipzig Gewandhaus Orchestra; solo: Norman (Philips)

1985

CHAMBER
Beethoven, *String Quartets nos. 12–16,* Alban Berg Quartet (EMI)

CHORAL
Fauré, *Requiem,* John Rutter conducting Cambridge Singers and City of London Sinfonia members (Collegium)

CONCERTO (RECORD OF THE YEAR)
Elgar, *Violin Concerto in B Minor,* Vernon Handley conducting London Philharmonic Orchestra; solo: Kennedy (EMI)

CONTEMPORARY
Kurtag, *Messages;* Birtwistle, *. . . agm . . .,* Pierre Boulez conducting John Alldis Choir (Erato)

EARLY-BAROQUE
Charpentier, *Medée,* William Christie conducting Arts Florissants Chorus and Orchestra (Harmonia Mundi)

Mahler

EARLY-MEDIEVAL
Victoria, *Masses and Motets*, David Hill conducting Westminster Cathedral Choir (Hyperion)

ENGINEERING
Ravel, *Ma Mère l'Oye*, Charles Dutoit conducting Montreal Symphony Orchestra (Decca)

HISTORICAL VOCAL
Various artists, *Opera Arias and Songs*, Claudio Muzio, Molajoli and Refice (EMI Références)

HISTORICAL NON-VOCAL
Nielsen, *Symphonies nos. 1–6*, Erik Tuxen and Thomas Jensen conducting Danish Radio Symphony (Danacord)

INSTRUMENTAL
Liszt, *Années de Pèlerinage*, Jorge Bolet (Decca)

OPERATIC
Mozart, *Don Giovanni*, Bernard Haitink conducting Glyndebourne Choir and London Philharmonic Orchestra (EMI)

ORCHESTRAL
Prokofiev, *Symphony No. 6*, Neeme Järvi conducting Scottish National Orchestra (Chandos)

SOLO VOCAL
Sibelius, *Songs*, Elisabeth Söderström and Vladimir Ashkenazy (Argo)

1986

CHAMBER
Fauré, *Piano Quartets nos. 1 and 2*, Domus (Hyperion)

CHORAL
Janáček, *Glagolitic Mass*, Sir Charles Mackerras conducting Czech Philharmonic Orchestra and Choir (Supraphon)

CONCERTO
Beethoven, *Piano Concertos nos. 3 and 4*, Bernard Haitink conducting Concertgebouw Orchestra; solo: Perahia (CBS Masterworks)

CONTEMPORARY
Lutoslawski, *Symphony No. 3*, Esa-Pekka Salonen conducting Los Angeles Philharmonic Orchestra; solo: Shirley-Quirk (CBS Masterworks)

EARLY-BAROQUE
Bach, *Art of Fugue*, Davitt Moroney (Harmonia Mundi)

EARLY-MEDIEVAL
Various artists, *Chansons de Toile*, Esther Lamandier (Alienor)

ENGINEERING
Respighi, *Belkis, Queen of Sheba*, Geoffrey Simon conducting Philharmonia Orchestra (Chandos)

HISTORICAL VOCAL
Various artists, *Record of Singing Vol. 3*, various artists (HMV)

HISTORICAL NON-VOCAL
Beethoven, *String Quartets nos. 9, 11–12 and 15*, Busch Quartet (HMV)

INSTRUMENTAL
Mozart, *Sonata for 2 Pianos*; Schubert, *Fantasia*, Murray Perahia and Radu Lupu (Sony)

OPERATIC (RECORD OF THE YEAR)
Rossini, *Il Viaggio a Reims*, Claudio Abbado conducting Prague Philharmonic Chorus and Chamber Orchestra Europe (Deutsche Grammophon)

ORCHESTRAL
Williams, *Sinfonia Antartica*, Bernard Haitink conducting London Philharmonic Orchestra; solo: Armstrong (EMI)

RE-MASTERED CD
Britten, *Peter Grimes*, Benjamin Britten conducting Royal Opera House Chorus and Orchestra (Decca)

SOLO VOCAL
Schubert, *Winterreise*, Peter Schreier and Sviatoslav Richter (Philips)

1987

CHAMBER
Chausson, *Concerto for Piano, etc.*, Muir Quartet; solos: Collard and Dumay (EMI)

CHORAL
Handel, *Athalia*, Christopher Hogwood conducting Academy of Ancient Music and New College Choir Oxford (L'Oiseau-Lyre)

CONCERTO
Hummel, *Piano Concertos in A Minor and B Minor*, Bryden Thomson conducting English Chamber Orchestra; solo: Hough (Chandos)

CONTEMPORARY
Tippett, *Mask of Time*, Andrew Davis conducting BBC Symphony Orchestra and Chorus (EMI)

EARLY MUSIC (RECORD OF THE YEAR)
Desprez, *Masses*, Peter Phillips conducting Tallis Scholars (Gimell)

ENGINEERING
Holst, *Planets*, Charles Dutoit conducting Montreal Symphony Orchestra (Decca)

HISTORICAL VOCAL
Various artists, *Art of Tito Schipa*, Tito Schipa (EMI Treasury)

HISTORICAL NON-VOCAL
Schubert, *String Quartets, Piano Trio, etc.*, Busch Quartet; solo: Serkin (EMI)

INSTRUMENTAL
Haydn, *Complete Piano Sonatas*, Alfred Brendel (Philips)

OPERATIC
Verdi, *La Forza del Destino*, Guiseppe Sinopoli conducting Philharmonia Orchestra and Ambrosian Opera Chorus (Deutsche Grammophon)

ORCHESTRAL
Mahler, *Symphony No. 8,* Klaus Tennstedt conducting London
Philharmonic Orchestra and Choir (EMI)

PERIOD PERFORMANCE
Beethoven, *Symphonies nos. 2 and 8,* Roger Norrington conducting London Classical Players (EMI)

RE-MASTERED CD
Delius, *Beecham Conducts Delius,* Sir Thomas Beecham conducting Royal Philharmonic Orchestra (EMI)

SOLO VOCAL
Liszt and Strauss, *Lieder,* Brigitte Fassbaender and Irwin Gage
(Deutsche Grammophon)

1988

CHAMBER
Mendelssohn, *Violin Sonatas in F Major and F Minor,* Shlomo
Mintz and Paul Ostrovsky (Deutsche Grammophon)

CHORAL
Verdi, *Messa da Requiem, Choruses,* Robert Shaw conducting
Atlanta Symphony Orchestra and Choir (Telarc)

CONCERTO
Tchaikovsky, *Piano Concerto No. 2,* Rudolf Barshai conducting
Bournemouth Symphony Orchestra; solo: Donohoe (EMI)

CONTEMPORARY
Birtwistle, *Carmen Arcadiae Mechanicae,* Elgar Howarth conducting London Sinfonietta (Etcetera)

EARLY-BAROQUE
Leclair, *Scylla et Glaucus,* John Eliot Gardiner conducting
Monteverdi Choir (Erato)

EARLY-MEDIEVAL
Various artists, *Service of Venus and Mars,* Christopher Page
conducting Gothic Voices (Hyperion)

ENGINEERING (RECORD OF THE YEAR)
Mahler, *Symphony No. 2,* Simon Rattle conducting City of
Birmingham Symphony Orchestra (EMI)

HISTORICAL VOCAL
Various artists, *Feodor Chaliapin,* Feodor Chaliapin (EMI Treasury)

HISTORICAL NON-VOCAL
Brahms and Sibelius, *Violin Concertos,* Walter Susskind con-
ducting Philharmonia Orchestra; solo: Neveu (EMI
Références)

INSTRUMENTAL
Poulenc, *Piano Works,* Pascal Rogé (Decca)

OPERATIC
Britten, *Paul Bunyan,* Philip Brunelle conducting Plymouth
Choir and Orchestra (Virgin Classics)

ORCHESTRAL (RECORD OF THE YEAR)
Mahler, *Symphony No. 2,* Simon Rattle conducting City of
Birmingham Symphony Orchestra (EMI)

PERIOD PERFORMANCE
Haydn, *Mass in D Minor, etc.,* Trevor Pinnock conducting The
English Concert and Choir (Archiv)

RE-MASTERED CD
Strauss, *Der Rosenkavalier,* Herbert von Karajan conducting
Philharmonia Orchestra (EMI)

SOLO VOCAL
Schubert, *Die Schöne Müllerin,* Olaf Bär and Geoffrey Parsons
(EMI)

1989

CHAMBER (RECORD OF THE YEAR)
Bartók, *String Quartets nos. 1–6,* Emerson Quartet (Deutsche
Grammophon)

CHORAL
Handel, *Jephtha,* John Eliot Gardiner conducting Monteverdi
Choir and English Baroque Soloists (Philips)

CONCERTO
Nielsen and Sibelius, *Violin Concertos,* Esa-Pekka Salonen conducting Swedish Radio Symphony Orchestra; solo: Lin (Sony)

CONTEMPORARY
Simpson, *Symphony No. 9,* Vernon Handley conducting
Bournemouth Symphony Orchestra (Hyperion)

EARLY-BAROQUE
Corelli, *12 Concerti Grossi,* Trevor Pinnock conducting The
English Concert (Archiv)

EARLY-MEDIEVAL
Various artists, *A Song for Francesca,* Christopher Page conducting Gothic Voices (Hyperion)

Mozart

ENGINEERING
Tubin, *Symphonies nos. 3 and 8,* Neeme Järvi conducting
Swedish Radio Symphony Orchestra (Bis)

HISTORICAL VOCAL
Various artists, *Record of Singing Vol. 4,* various artists (EMI)

HISTORICAL NON-VOCAL
Mahler, *Symphony No. 9,* Bruno Walter conducting Vienna
Philharmonic Orchestra (EMI Références)

INSTRUMENTAL
Mozart, *Complete Piano Sonatas,* Mitsuko Uchida (Philips)

MUSIC THEATRE
Kern and Hammerstein, *Show Boat,* John McGlinn conducting
London Sinfonietta (EMI)

OPERATIC
Gershwin, *Porgy and Bess,* Simon Rattle conducting London
Philharmonic Orchestra and Glyndebourne Chorus (EMI)

ORCHESTRAL
Schubert, *Symphonies nos. 1–6, 8 and 9,* Claudio Abbado con-
ducting Chamber Orchestra of Europe (Deutsche
Grammophon)

Bach

RE-MASTERED CD
Ravel, *L'enfant et les Sortilèges,* Lorin Maazel conducting French Radio National Orchestra (Deutsche Grammophon)

SOLO VOCAL
Schubert, *Lieder Vol. 1,* Dame Janet Baker and Graham Johnson (Hyperion)

1990

BAROQUE VOCAL
Bach, *St. Matthew Passion,* John Eliot Gardiner conducting Monteverdi Choir and English Baroque Soloists (Archiv)

BAROQUE NON-VOCAL
Bach, *Orchestral Suites,* Ton Koopman conducting Amsterdam Baroque Orchestra (DHM)

CHAMBER
Respighi, *Violin Sonata in B Minor,* Kyung-Wha Chung and Krystian Zimerman (Deutsche Grammophon)

CHORAL
Shumann, *Das Paradise und die Peri,* Armin Jordan conducting Suisse Romande Chamber Choir and Orchestra (Erato)

CONCERTO
Shostakovich, *Violin Concertos nos. 1 and 2,* Neeme Järvi conducting Scottish National Orchestra; solo: Mordkovitch (Chandos)

CONTEMPORARY
Benjamin, *Antara;* Boulez, *Dérive, etc.,* George Benjamin conducting London Sinfonietta (Nimbus)

EARLY MUSIC
Giovanni and Andrea Gabrieli, *A Venetian Coronation,* Paul McCreesh conducting Gabrieli Consort and Players (Virgin Classics)

ENGINEERING
Britten, *Prince of the Pagodas,* Oliver Knussen conducting London Sinfonietta (Virgin Classics)

HISTORICAL VOCAL
Massenet, *Werther,* Elie Cohen conducting Paris Opéra-Comique (EMI Références)

HISTORICAL NON-VOCAL
Delius, *Orchestral Works,* Sir Thomas Beecham conducting London Philharmonic Orchestra (Beecham Trust)

INSTRUMENTAL
Debussy, *Piano Works,* Zoltan Kocsis (Philips)

MUSIC THEATRE
Porter, *Anything Goes,* John McGlinn conducting Ambrosian Chorus and London Symphony Orchestra (EMI)

OPERA (RECORD OF THE YEAR)
Prokofiev, *The Love for Three Oranges,* Kent Nagano conducting Lyon Opera and Orchestra (Virgin Classics)

ORCHESTRAL
Williams, *A Sea Symphony,* Bernard Haitink conducting London Philharmonic Orchestra (EMI)

SOLO VOCAL
Schubert, *Schwanengesang,* Peter Schreier and Andras Schiff (Decca)

SPECIAL ACHIEVEMENT
Bach, *Sacred Cantatas vols. 1–45,* Nikolaus Harnoncourt and Gustav Leonhardt (Teldec)

1991

BAROQUE VOCAL
Handel, *Susanna,* Nicholas McGegan conducting Philharmonia Baroque Orchestra (Harmonia Mundi)

BAROQUE NON-VOCAL
Biber, *Mystery Sonatas,* Tragiccomedia, John Holloway and Davitt Moroney (Virgin Classics)

CHAMBER
Brahms, *Piano Quartets nos. 1–3,* Isaac Stern, Jamie Laredo, Yo-Yo Ma and Emanuel Ax (Sony Classical)

CHORAL (RECORD OF THE YEAR)
Beethoven, *Missa Solemnis,* John Eliot Gardiner conducting Monteverdi Choir (Archiv)

CONCERTO
Sibelius, *Violin Concerto,* Osmo Vänskä conducting Lahti Symphony Orchestra; solo: Kavakos (Bis)

CONTEMPORARY
Casken, *Golem,* Richard Bernas conducting Music Projects London (Virgin Classics)

EARLY MUSIC
Palestrina, *Masses and Motets,* Peter Phillips conducting The Tallis Scholars (Gimell)

ENGINEERING
Wordsworth, *Symphonies nos. 2 and 3,* Nicholas Braithwaite conducting London Philharmonic Orchestra (Lyrita)

HISTORICAL VOCAL
Fauré and Chausson, *French Songs,* Gerard Souzay and Jaqueline Bonneau (Decca)

HISTORICAL NON-VOCAL
Berg, *Violin Concerto, Lyric Suite,* Fritz Busch conducting BBC Symphony Orchestra and Galimir Quartet; solo: Krasner (Continuum)

INSTRUMENTAL
Shostakovich, *24 Preludes and Fugues,* Tatyana Nikolaieva (Hyperion)

MUSIC THEATRE
Sondheim, *Into the Woods,* Original London cast (RCA Red Seal)

OPERA
Mozart, *Idomeneo,* John Eliot Gardiner conducting English Baroque Soloists and Monteverdi Choir (Archiv)

ORCHESTRAL
Nielsen, *Symphonies nos. 2 and 3,* Herbert Blomstedt conducting San Francisco Symphony Orchestra (Decca)

SOLO VOCAL
Schubert, *Die Schöne Müllerin,* Peter Schreier and Andras Schiff (Decca)

SPECIAL ACHIEVEMENT
Mozart, *Complete Edition,* various artists (Philips)

1992

BAROQUE VOCAL
Handel, *Giulio Cesare,* Rene Jacobs conducting Concerto Cologne (Harmonia Mundi)

BAROQUE NON-VOCAL
Rameau, *Harpsichord Works,* Christophe Rousset (L'Oiseau-Lyre)

CHAMBER
Szymanowski, *String Quartets nos. 1 and 2,* Carmina Quartet (Denon)

CHORAL
Britten, *War Requiem,* Richard Hickox conducting London Symphony Orchestra and St. Paul's Cathedral Choir (Chandos)

CONCERTO
Medtner, *Piano Concertos nos. 2 and 3,* Nikolai Demidenko and Jerzy Maksymiuk, (Hyperion)

CONTEMPORARY
Tavener, *Protecting Veil,* Gennadi Rozhdestvensky conducting London Symphony Orchestra; solo: Isserlis (Virgin Classics)

EARLY MUSIC
Various artists, *Rose and the Ostrich Feather,* Harry Christophers conducting The Sixteen (Collins Classics)

ENGINEERING
Britten, *War Requiem,* Richard Hickox conducting St. Paul's Cathedral Choir and London Symphony Orchestra (Chandos)

HISTORICAL VOCAL
Various artists, *Covent Garden on Record,* various artists (Pearl)

HISTORICAL NON-VOCAL
Elgar, *Elgar Edition Vol. 1,* Sir Edward Elgar conducting London Symphony Orchestra and Royal Albert Hall Orchestra (EMI)

INSTRUMENTAL
Alkan, *25 Preludes;* Shostakovich, *24 Preludes,* Olli Mustonen (Decca)

MUSIC THEATRE
Bernstein, *Candide,* Leonard Bernstein conducting London Symphony Orchestra (Deutsche Grammophon)

Leonard Bernstein

OPERA
Strauss, *Die Frau Ohne Schatten,* Sir Georg Solti conducting Vienna State Opera and Vienna Philharmonic Orchestra (Decca)

ORCHESTRAL (RECORD OF THE YEAR)
Beethoven, *Symphonies nos. 1–9,* Nikolaus Harnoncourt conducting Chamber Orchestra of Europe (Teldec)

SOLO VOCAL
Schubert, *Lieder,* Brigitte Fassbaender and Aribert Reimann (Deutsche Grammophon)

1993

BAROQUE VOCAL
Stradella, *San Giovanni Battista,* Marc Minkowski conducting Louvre Musiciens du Louvre (Erato)

BAROQUE NON-VOCAL
Heinichen, *Dresden Concertos,* Reinhard Goebel conducting Musica Antiqua Köln (Archiv)

CHAMBER
Haydn, *String Quartets,* Quator Mosaïques (Astrée Auvidis)

CHORAL
Mendelssohn, *Elijah,* Kurt Masur conducting Israel Philharmonic Orchestra (Teldec)

CONCERTO
Brahms, *Piano Concerto No. 1,* Wolfgang Sawallisch conducting London Philharmonic Orchestra; solo: Kovacevich (EMI)

CONTEMPORARY
MacMillan, *Confession of Isabel Gowdie,* Jerzy Maksymiuk conducting BBC Scottish Symphony (Koch Schwann)

EARLY MUSIC
Various artists, *Venetian Vespers,* Paul McCreesh conducting Gabrieli Consort and Players (Archiv)

ENGINEERING
Debussy, *Le Martyr de Saint Sébastien,* Michael Tilson Thomas conducting London Symphony Orchestra (Sony Classical)

HISTORICAL VOCAL
Various artists, *Singers of Imperial Russia vols. 1–4,* various artists (Pearl)

HISTORICAL NON-VOCAL
Rachmaninov, *Complete Recordings,* Sergei Rachmaninov (RCA)

INSTRUMENTAL
Various artists, *80th Birthday Carnegie Hall,* Shura Cherkassky (Decca)

MUSIC THEATRE
Gershwin, *Lady, Be Good!,* Eric Stern (Elektra Nonesuch)

OPERA
Poulenc, *Dialogues des Carmelites,* Kent Nagano conducting Opera de Lyon Chorus and Orchestra (Virgin Classics)

ORCHESTRAL
Hindemith, *Kammermusik,* Riccardo Chailly conducting Royal Concertgebouw Orchestra (Decca)

SOLO VOCAL (RECORD OF THE YEAR)
Grieg, *Songs,* Anne Sofie von Otter and Bengt Forsberg (Deutsche Grammophon)

All-Time Billboard Charts

For its 100th anniversary, *Billboard* staff members undertook the monumental task of tracing every chart ever published in the magazine to determine the greatest hits of all time. In order to compile the most accurate charts, the lists below are based on a point system rather than reflecting retail sales or airplay as the buying audience is much larger today than it was when *Billboard* started tracking recordings. The dates listed above each chart indicate the period when *Billboard* monitored the progress of each recording.

Most Popular Albums

MARCH 24, 1956
TO JUNE 25, 1994

1. *Thriller*
   Michael Jackson
2. *My Fair Lady*
   Original Cast
3. *Calypso*
   Harry Belafonte
4. *Rumours*
   Fleetwood Mac
5. *West Side Story*
   Soundtrack
6. *South Pacific*
   Soundtrack
7. *Please Hammer Don't Hurt 'Em*
   M.C. Hammer
8. *Purple Rain*
   (Soundtrack)
   Prince and the Revolution
9. *Dirty Dancing*
   Soundtrack
10. *Saturday Night Fever*
    (Soundtrack)
    Bee Gees
11. *Born in the U.S.A.*
    Bruce Springsteen
12. *The Bodyguard*
    (Soundtrack)
    Whitney Houston
13. *Blue Hawaii*
    (Soundtrack)
    Elvis Presley
14. *Ropin' the Wind*
    Garth Brooks
15. *The Sound of Music*
    Soundtrack
16. *Some Gave All*
    Billy Ray Cyrus

17. *Synchronicity*
    The Police
18. *The Sound of Music*
    Original Cast
19. *Mary Poppins*
    Soundtrack
20. *The Button-Down Mind of Bob Newhart*
    Bob Newhart
21. *Faith*
    George Michael
22. *The Music Man*
    Original Cast
23. *Whitney Houston*
    Whitney Houston
24. *Mariah Carey*
    Mariah Carey
25. *Tapestry*
    Carole King
26. *Sgt. Pepper's Lonely Hearts Club Band*
    The Beatles
27. *Around the World in 80 Days*
    Soundtrack
28. *Forever Your Girl*
    Paula Abdul
29. *More of the Monkees*
    The Monkees
30. *Frampton Comes Alive!*
    Peter Frampton
31. *Hi Infidelity*
    REO Speedwagon
32. *To the Extreme*
    Vanilla Ice
33. *Business as Usual*
    Men At Work
34. *The Kingston Trio at Large*
    Kingston Trio
35. *Peter, Paul and Mary*
    Peter, Paul and Mary
36. *Slippery When Wet*
    Bon Jovi
37. *Songs in the Key of Life*
    Stevie Wonder

Michael Jackson

38. *Whipped Cream and Other Delights*
    Herb Alpert's Tijuana Brass
39. *Modern Sounds in Country and Western Music*
    Ray Charles
40. *The Wall*
    Pink Floyd
41. *Hysteria*
    Def Leppard
42. *The Monkees*
    The Monkees
43. *Days of Wine and Roses*
    Andy Williams
44. *A Hard Day's Night*
    The Beatles/Soundtrack
45. *Hair*
    Original Cast
46. *Camelot*
    Original Cast
47. *Elvis Presley*
    Elvis Presley
48. *4*
    Foreigner
49. *Gigi*
    Soundtrack

50. **The Music From Peter Gunn**
Henry Mancini

51. **Blood, Sweat and Tears**
Blood, Sweat and Tears

52. **Appetite for Destruction**
Guns N' Roses

53. **Grease**
Soundtrack

54. **Dr. Zhivago**
Soundtrack

55. **Girl You Know It's True**
Milli Vanilli

56. **Abbey Road**
The Beatles

57. **Judy at Carnegie Hall**
Judy Garland

58. **Sing Along With Mitch**
Mitch Miller and the Gang

59. **Bad**
Michael Jackson

60. **Sold Out**
Kingston Trio

61. **Whitney**
Whitney Houston

62. **Can't Slow Down**
Lionel Richie

63. **Don't Be Cruel**
Bobby Brown

64. **What Now My Love**
Herb Alpert and the Tijuana Brass

65. **Brothers in Arms**
Dire Straits

66. **Music Box**
Mariah Carey

67. **Hotel California**
Eagles

68. **Going Places**
Herb Alpert and the Tijuana Brass

69. **The First Family**
Vaughn Meader

70. **Asia**
Asia

Elvis Presley

71. **The Graduate**
(Soundtrack)
Simon and
Garfunkel

72. **The Joshua
Tree**
U2

73. **Tchaikovsky:
Piano
Concerto**
Van Cliburn

74. **Meet The
Beatles**
The Beatles

75. **No Jacket
Required**
Phil Collins

76. **Miami Vice**
TV Soundtrack

77. **The King and I**
Soundtrack

78. **Belafonte**
Harry Belafonte

79. **Footloose**
Soundtrack

80. **Love Is the Thing**
Nat King Cole

81. **Johnny's Greatest Hits**
Johnny Mathis

82. **Calcutta**
Lawrence Welk

83. **Janet Jackson's
Rhythm Nation 1814**
Janet Jackson

84. **The Long Run**
Eagles

85. **G.I. Blues**
(Soundtrack)
Elvis Presley

86. **Here We Go Again!**
Kingston Trio

87. **Led Zeppelin II**
Led Zeppelin

88. **The Singing Nun**
The Singing Nun

89. **Goodbye Yellow Brick Road**
Elton John

90. **Bridge Over Troubled Water**
Simon and Garfunkel

91. **Tattoo You**
The Rolling Stones

92. **Abraxas**
Santana

93. **Cosmo's Factory**
Creedence Clearwater Revival

94. **American Fool**
John Cougar

95. **Unplugged**
Eric Clapton

96. **Breakfast in America**
Supertramp

Boyz II Men

97. **Jesus Christ Superstar**
Various

98. **Oklahoma!**
Soundtrack

99. **Glass Houses**
Billy Joel

100. **janet**
Janet Jackson

Hot 100

**AUGUST 4, 1958
TO JUNE 25, 1994**

1. **"I Will Always Love You"**
Whitney Houston

2. **"End of the Road"**
Boyz II Men

3. **"The Sign"**
Ace of Base

4. **"You Light Up My Life"**
Debby Boone

5. **"Physical"**
Olivia Newton-John

6. **"The Twist"**
Chubby Checker

7. **"Mack the Knife"**
Bobby Darin

8. **"Endless Love"**
Diana Ross and Lionel Richie

9. **"Hey Jude"**
The Beatles

10. **"Bette Davis Eyes"**
Kim Carnes

11. **"That's the Way Love Goes"**
Janet Jackson

12. **"The Theme From a
Summer Place"**
Percy Faith

13. **"Jump"**
Kris Kross

14. "Can't Help Falling in Love With You"
    UB40

15. "Dreamlover"
    Mariah Carey

16. "Every Breath You Take"
    The Police

17. "Night Fever"
    Bee Gees

18. "Eye of the Tiger"
    Survivor

19. "Tossin' and Turnin' "
    Bobby Lewis

20. "I Want to Hold Your Hand"
    The Beatles

21. "Tonight's the Night" (Gonna Be Alright)
    Rod Stewart

22. "Informer"
    Snow

23. "Shadow Dancing"
    Andy Gibb

24. "Say Say Say"
    Paul McCartney and Michael Jackson

25. "Battle of New Orleans"
    Johnny Horton

26. "I Love Rock 'N Roll"
    Joan Jett and the Blackhearts

27. "Ebony and Ivory"
    Paul McCartney and Stevie Wonder

28. "Flashdance . . . What a Feeling"
    Irene Cara

29. "Le Freak"
    Chic

30. "I'm a Believer"
    The Monkees

31. "Baby Got Back"
    Sir Mix-a-Lot

32. "Freak Me"
    Silk

Janet Jackson

33. "Call Me"
    Blondie

34. "Whoomp! (There It Is)
    Tag Team

35. "Billie Jean"
    Michael Jackson

36. (Everything I Do) "I Do It for You"
    Bryan Adams

37. "I Heard It Through the Grapevine"
    Marvin Gaye

38. "Lady"
    Kenny Rogers

39. "Aquarius/Let the Sun Shine In"
    The 5th Dimension

40. "Black or White"
    Michael Jackson

41. "It's All in the Game"
    Tommy Edwards

42. "Centerfold"
    J. Geils Band

43. "My Sharona"
    The Knack

44. "Are You Lonesome Tonight?"
    Elvis Presley

45. "I'd Do Anything for Love" (But I Won't Do That)
    Meatloaf

46. "Alone Again" (Naturally)
    Gilbert O'Sullivan

47. "Stayin' Alive"
    Bee Gees

48. "Save the Best for Last"
    Vanessa Williams

49. "I Just Want to Be Your Everything"
    Andy Gibb

50. "The Power of Love"
    Celine Dion

51. "Hero"
    Mariah Carey

52. "The First Time Ever I Saw Your Face"
    Roberta Flack

53. "Nel Blu Dipinto di Blu" (Volare)
    Domenico Modugno

54. "Another One Bites the Dust"
    Queen

55. "Joy to the World"
    Three Dog Night

56. "Hot Stuff"
    Donna Summer

57. (Just Like) "Starting Over"
    John Lennon

58. "I'll Be There"
    The Jackson 5

Bee Gees

59. "I Can't Stop Loving You"
    Ray Charles

60. "Bridge Over Troubled Water"
    Simon and Garfunkel

61. "When Doves Cry"
    Prince

62. "Silly Love Songs"
    Wings

63. "Upside Down"
    Diana Ross

64. "Bump N' Grind"
    R. Kelly

65. "Maggie May/Reason To Believe"
    Rod Stewart

66. "All Night Long" (All Night)
    Lionel Richie

67. "Sugar, Sugar"
    The Archies

68. "Bad Girls"
    Donna Summer

69. "Again"
    Janet Jackson

70. "Sugar Shack"
    Jimmy Gilmer and the Fireballs

71. "Like a Virgin"
    Madonna

72. "Love Is Blue"
    Paul Mauriat

73. "Venus"
    Frankie Avalon

74. "Cathy's Clown"
    Everly Brothers

75. "It's Now or Never"
    Elvis Presley

76. "How Deep Is Your Love"
    Bee Gees

77. "Weak"
    SWV

78. "In the Year 2525"
    Zager and Evans

79. "Big Bad John"
    Jimmy Dean

80. **"Big Girls Don't Cry"**
Four Seasons

81. **"Jump"**
Van Halen

82. **"I Will Survive"**
Gloria Gaynor

83. **"If I Ever Fall in Love"**
Shai

84. **"To Sir With Love"**
Lulu

85. **"Crazy Little Thing Called Love"**
Queen

86. **"All for Love"**
Bryan Adams/
Rod Stewart/Sting

87. **"It's Too Late/I Feel the Earth Move"**
Carole King

88. **"Rush Rush"**
Paula Abdul

89. **"Raindrops Keep Falling on My Head"**
B.J. Thomas

90. **"People Got to Be Free"**
The Rascals

91. **"Total Eclipse of the Heart"**
Bonnie Tyler

92. **"Knock Three Times"**
Dawn

93. **"My Sweet Lord/Isn't It a Pity"**
George Harrison

94. **"Abracadabra"**
Steve Miller Band

95. **"American Pie"**
Don McLean

96. **"All That She Wants"**
Ace of Base

R.E.M.

97. **"Another Brick in the Wall (Part II)"**
Pink Floyd

98. **"Da Ya Think I'm Sexy?"**
Rod Stewart

99. **"Maneater"**
Darryl Hall and John Oates

l00. **"I Swear"**
All-4-One

Modern Rock Tracks

SEPTEMBER 10, 1988 TO JUNE 25, 1994

1. **"Into Your Arms"**
The Lemonheads

2. **"Mysterious Ways"**
U2

3. **"Orange Crush"**
R.E.M.

4. **"Cuts You Up"**
Peter Murphy

5. **"Regret"**
New Order

6. **"Fascination Street"**
The Cure

7. **"So Alive"**
Love and Rockets

8. **"Losing My Religion"**
R.E.M.

9. **"The More You Ignore Me ... the Closer I Get"**
Morrissey

10. **"Soul to Squeeze"**
Red Hot Chili Peppers

11. **"Rush"**
Big Audio Dynamite II

12. **"Love and Anger"**
Kate Bush

13. **"The Devil You Know"**
Jesus Jones

14. **"Kiss Them for Me"**
Siouxsie and the Banshees

15. **"Pets"**
Porno for Pyros

16. **"Loser"**
Beck

17. **"More"**
Sisters of Mercy

18. **"Smells Like Teen Spirit"**
Nirvana

19. **"The Mayor of Simpleton"**
XTC

20. **"Come Anytime"**
Hoodoo Gurus

Album Rock Tracks

MARCH 22, 1985 TO JUNE 25, 1994

1. **"Start Me Up"**
The Rolling Stones

2. **"Mysterious Ways"**
U2

3. **"Remedy"**
Black Crowes

4. **"Daughter"**
Pearl Jam

5. **"Livin' on the Edge"**
Aerosmith

6. **"Every Breath You Take"**
The Police

U2

CONTINUED ON PAGE 411

Musician Magazine's 57 Artists and Records That Changed Their Life

Musician asked 57 recording artists representing a broad range of genres to list the record that changed their life or led them down the path to a career in music.

Tony Bennett

1. Dave Alvin
Heart of Saturday Night, Tom Waits

2. Tori Amos
Led Zeppelin I, II and III, Led Zeppelin

3. Chet Atkins
A Django Reinhardt "reissue on Capitol around 1950"

4. Tony Bennett
Trees, Al Hibbler

5. Frank Black
Flood, They Might Be Giants

6. Edie Brickell
Greatest Hits, Volume 2, Al Green

7. Jackson Browne
Bringing It All Back Home, Bob Dylan

8. Peter Buck
Exile on Main Street, The Rolling Stones

9. Lindsay Buckingham
Smile, Beach Boys

10. Don Byron
Stravinsky Chamber Pieces, Igor Stravinsky
Delightfulee, Lee Morgan

11. J. J. Cale
"Baby Let's Play House," Elvis Presley

12. Ron Carter
The Brandenburg Concertos, J. S. Bach

13. Neneh Cherry
Songs in the Key of Life, Stevie Wonder
What's Going On, Marvin Gaye
Germ-Free Adolescents, X-Ray Spex

14. Marshall Crenshaw
The Bop That Just Won't Stop, Gene Vincent
The World Is Still Waiting for the Sunrise, Les Paul and Mary Ford
The Sun Collection, Elvis Presley

15. Steve Cropper
"Honky Tonk," Bill Doggett

16. Chuck D. (Public Enemy)
Raising Hell, Run-DMC

17. Dick Dale
"Sing Sing Sing," Gene Krupa

18. Danny Elfman
The Rite of Spring, Igor Stravinsky

19. Melissa Etheridge
Tommy, Pete Townshend with the London Symphony Orchestra

20. Perry Farrell
Fun House, The Stooges

21. Tommy Flanagan
Billie Holiday Collection, Billie Holiday

22. Buddy Guy
"Three O'Clock Blues," B.B. King

23. Herbie Hancock
Miles Ahead, Miles Davis

24. Paul Hartnoll (Orbital)
Fresh Fruit for Rotting Vegetables, Dead Kennedys

25. John Hiatt
Blonde on Blonde, Bob Dylan
Axis: Bold as Love, The Jimi Hendrix Experience

26. John Lee Hooker
"I Got My Mojo Workin'," Muddy Waters

27. Alan Jackson
"Rose Colored Glasses," John Conlee

28. Carole King
"There Goes My Baby," Ben E. King

29. Curt Kirkwood (The Meat Puppets)
Abbey Road, The Beatles

30. Lenny Kravitz
Innervisions, Stevie Wonder

31. Bill Laswell
Are You Experienced, The Jimi Hendrix Experience

32. David Lowery (Cracker)
West of Rome, Vic Chesnutt

33. John Mellencamp
Highway 61 Revisited, Bob Dylan

34. Willie Nelson
"Back in the Saddle Again," Gene Autry

35. Liz Phair
Psychocandy, Jesus and Mary Chain

36. Q-Tip (A Tribe Called Quest)
Run-DMC, Run-DMC

37. Bonnie Raitt
Blues at Newport — '63, various artists

38. Joey Ramone
Meet The Beatles, The Beatles

39. Joshua Redman
Songs in the Key of Life, Stevie Wonder

40. Jim Reid (Jesus and Mary Chain)
Never Mind the Bollocks, Sex Pistols

41. Teddy Riley
"Neither One of Us" (Wants to Be the First to Say Goodbye), Gladys Knight and the Pips

42. Terry Riley
Ragas of Morning and Night, Pandit Pran Nath

43. Ed Roland (Collective Soul)
"Kentucky Rain," Elvis Presley
"Mona Lisas and Mad Hatters," Elton John

44. Sonny Rollins
"I'm Gonna Sit Right Down and Write Myself a Letter," Fats Waller

Slash

45. Ryuichi Sakamato
"The record of Claude Debussy's String
Quartet and Ravel's String Quartet"
as played by the Budapest Quartet
Headhunters, Herbie Hancock

46. Slash
Aerosmith Rocks, Aerosmith

47. Michael Stipe
Horses, Patti Smith

48. Richard Thompson
*Scottish Dance Music by Pipe Major
John Burgess*

49. Lars Ulrich (Metallica)
Fireball, Deep Purple

50. Jimmie Vaughan
*Folk Festival of the Blues (Blues From
Big Bill's Coca Cabana),* Various
Artists

51. Don Was
Pet Sounds, Brian Wilson

52. Paul Westerberg
*A Nod is as Good as a Wink . . . to a
Blind Horse,* Faces

53. Barry White
"I Only Have Eyes for You," Flamingos

54. Victoria Williams
Sounds of Silence, Simon and Garfunkel

55. Tammy Wynette
"'Til I Can Make It on My Own," Tammy
Wynette

56. Adam Yauch (The Beastie Boys)
Bad Brains, Bad Brains

57. Dwight Yoakum
Songs That Made Him Famous, Johnny
Cash
"Candyman," Roy Orbison
Get Yer Ya-Yas Out, The Rolling Stones

◀ CONTINUED FROM
PAGE 409

7. **"Separate Ways"**
Journey

8. **"Jump"**
Van Halen

9. **"Photograph"**
Def Leppard

10. **"Cryin'"**
Aerosmith

11. **"How About That"**
Bad Company

12. **"Pride and Joy"**
Coverdale/Page

13. **"The Voice"**
The Moody Blues

14. **"Everybody Wants You"**
Billy Squier

15. **"Keep Talking"**
Pink Floyd

16. **"Hotel Illness"**
Black Crowes

17. **"Boys of Summer"**
Don Henley

18. **"Are You Gonna Go My Way"**
Lenny Kravitz

19. **"All This Time"**
Sting

20. **"Dancing in the Dark"**
Bruce Springsteen

Top R&B Albums

**JANUARY 30, 1965
TO JUNE 25, 1994**

1. *Thriller*
Michael Jackson

2. *Please Hammer Don't Hurt 'Em*
M.C. Hammer

3. *Just Like the First Time*
Freddie Jackson

4. *Whitney Houston*
Whitney Houston

5. *Bad*
Michael Jackson

6. *Don't Be Cruel*
Bobby Brown

7. *Rock Me Tonight*
Freedie Jackson

8. *Can't Slow Down*
Lionel Richie

9. *Off the Wall*
Michael Jackson

10. *Purple Rain*
(Soundtrack)
Prince and the Revolution

11. *Street Songs*
Rick James

12. *Songs in the Key of Life*
Stevie Wonder

13. *Tender Love*
Babyface

14. *Hot Buttered Soul*
Isaac Hayes

15. *The Temptations Sing Smokey*
The Temptations

16. *Lady Soul*
Aretha Franklin

17. *Lou Rawls Live!*
Lou Rawls

18. *Temptin' Temptations*
The Temptations

19. *I Never Loved a Man the Way
I Loved You*
Aretha Franklin

20. *Aretha Now*
Aretha Franklin

21. *Control*
Janet Jackson

22. *Puzzle People*
The Temptations

23. *What's Going On*
Marvin Gaye

24. *Shaft*
(Soundtrack)
Isaac Hayes

25. *Rapture*
Anita Baker

26. *Private Dancer*
Tina Turner

27. *The Chronic*
Dr. Dre

28. *The Temptations Greatest Hits*
The Temptations

29. *Toni Braxton*
Toni Braxton

30. *Cloud Nine*
The Temptations

31. *Diana Ross and the Supremes
Greatest Hits*
Diana Ross and
the Supremes

32. *Hotter Than July*
Stevie Wonder

Isaac Hayes

33. *Dangerous*
Michael Jackson

34. *Lou Rawls Soulin'*
Lou Rawls

35. *The Isaac Hayes Movement*
Isaac Hayes

36. *Give Me the Reason*
Luther Vandross

37. *In Square Circle*
Stevie Wonder

38. *Curtis*
Curtis Mayfield

39. *Third Album*
The Jackson 5

40. *Promise*
Sade

41. *To Be Continued*
Isaac Hayes

42. *Commodores*
Commodores

43. *ABC*
The Jackson Five

44. *Lionel Richie*
Lionel Richie

45. *Guy*
Guy

46. *I'm Your Baby Tonight*
Whitney Houston

47. *The Bodyguard*
(Soundtrack)
Whitney Houston

48. *Back on the Block*
Quincy Jones

49. *Forever My Lady*
Jodeci

50. *Make It Last Forever*
Keith Sweat

Hot R&B Singles

OCTOBER 20, 1958
TO JUNE 25, 1994

1. "Bump N' Grind"
R. Kelly

2. "Tossin' and Turnin' "
Bobby Lewis

3. "I Will Always Love You"
Whitney Houston

4. "Baby" (You've Got What It Takes)
Dinah Washington
and Brook Benton

5. "Sexual Healing"
Marvin Gaye

6. "That Girl"
Stevie Wonder

7. "I Can't Help Myself"
Four Tops

8. "Billie Jean"
Michael Jackson

9. "Lonely Teardrops"
Jackie Wilson

10. "I Can't Stop Loving You"
Ray Charles

11. "Kiddio"
Brook Benton

12. "It's Just a Matter of Time"
Brook Benton

13. "Shop Around"
The Miracles

14. "Please Mr. Postman"
The Marvelettes

15. "Let's Stay Together"
Al Green

16. "When Doves Cry"
Prince

17. "Right Here" (Human Nature)/Downtown
SWV

18. "He Will Break Your Heart"
Jerry Butler

19. "Ain't Too Proud to Beg"
The Temptations

20. "Juicy Fruit"
Mtume

21. "Endless Love"
Diana Ross and Lionel Richie

22. "Let's Groove"
Earth, Wind and Fire

23. "Master Blaster" (Jammin')
Stevie Wonder

24. "Papa's Got a Brand New Bag" (Part I)
James Brown

25. "Rock With You"
Michael Jackson

26. "Can We Talk"
Tevin Campbell

27. "Let's Get Serious"
Jermaine Jackson

28. "All Night Long" (All Night)
Lionel Richie

29. "Respect"
Aretha Franklin

30. "Soul Man"
Sam and Dave

31. "One Nation Under a Groove" (Part I)
Funkadelic

32. "Float On"
The Floaters

33. "Serpentine Fire"
Earth, Wind and Fire

34. "Kansas City"
Wilbert Harrison

35. "Gangsta Lean"
DRS

36. "Stagger Lee"
Lloyd Price

Billy Ray Cyrus

37. "I Got You" (I Feel Good)
James Brown

38. "Good Times"
Chic

39. "634-5789"
Wilson Pickett

40. "Celebration"
Kool and the Gang

41. "Knockin' Da Boots"
H-Town

42. "I Heard It Through the Grapevine"
Marvin Gaye

43. "The Love You Save"
The Jackson 5

44. "Rock Me Tonight" (For Old Times Sake)
Freedie Jackson

45. "I've Got Love on My Mind"
Natalie Cole

46. "I've Never Loved a Man the Way I Love You"
Aretha Franklin

47. "Disco Lady"
Johnnie Taylor

48. "It's Ecstasy When You Lay Down Next to Me"
Barry White

49. "Green Onions"
Booker T. and the MG's

50. "I Can't Get Next to You"
The Temptations

Top Country Albums

JANUARY 11, 1964
TO JUNE 25, 1994

1. *No Fences*
Garth Brooks

2. *Always and Forever*
Randy Travis

3. *Killin' Time*
Clint Black

4. *Some Gave All*
Billy Ray Cyrus

5. *Ropin' the Wind*
Garth Brooks

6. *Mountain Music*
Alabama

7. *Behind Closed Doors*
Charlie Rich

8. *Somewhere Over the Rainbow*
Willie Nelson

9. *Greatest Hits*
Waylon Jennings

10. *The Gambler*
Kenny Rogers

11. *Always on My Mind*
Willie Nelson

12. *Garth Brooks*
Garth Brooks

13. *Old 8 x 10*
Randy Travis

14. *Kenny*
Kenny Rogers

15. *The Closer You Get*
Alabama

16. *Roll On*
Alabama

17. *Storms of Life*
Randy Travis

18. *Johnny Cash at San Quentin*
Johnny Cash

19. *Brand New Man*
Brooks and Dunn

20. *Loving Proof*
Ricky Van Shelton

21. *40 Hour Week*
Alabama

22. *Kenny Rogers' Greatest Hits*
Kenny Rogers

23. *Stardust*
Willie Nelson

24. *The Chase*
Garth Brooks

25. *Wichita Lineman*
Glen Campbell

26. *The Best of Charley Pride*
Charley Pride

27. *Back Home Again*
John Denver

28. *I've Got a Tiger by the Tail*
Buck Owens

29. *No Holdin' Back*
Randy Travis

30. *Greatest Hits III*
Hank Williams, Jr.

Musician Magazine's 100 Greatest Guitarists of the 20th Century

THE CREAM OF THE CROP
Jeff Beck
Jimi Hendrix
Jimmy Page
Allan Holdsworth
Edward Van Halen
Frank Zappa
John McLaughlin

PRIME MOVERS
Chuck Berry
Charlie Christian
Maybelle Carter
Bo Diddley
Django Reinhardt
Chet Atkins
Rev. Gary Davis
Charley Patton
Scotty Moore
Freddie Green
John Lee Hooker
Merle Travis
Duane Eddy
Hank Garland
Muddy Waters
Elizabeth Cotton
Wes Montgomery
Andres Segovia
Eldon Shamblin

PROTOTYPES
Jimmy Nolen
Dr. Nico
Tony Iommi
Jim Hall
Keith Richards
Curtis Mayfield
Gabby Pahinui
Duane Allman
Pete Townshend
Steve Cropper
James Burton
Dick Dale

JAZZ
Pat Metheny
Larry Coryell
George Benson
Pat Martino
John Scofield
Emily Remler
Joe Pass
Barney Kessel
Sonny Sharrock
Stanley Jordan
Pete Cosey

Jimi Hendrix

FINGERPRINTS
Carlos Santana
Ry Cooder
Neil Young
Steve Morse
Clarence White
Albert Lee
Randy Rhoads
Yngwie Malmsteen
Jerry Garcia
Eric Johnson
Al Di Meola
Mark Knopfler
Richard Thompson

ACOUSTIC
John Fahey
Leo Kottke
Lonnie Johnson
Paco De Lucia
Jorma Kaukonen
Martin Carthy
Doc Watson

TEAM PLAYERS
The Beatles
Robbie Robertson
James Honeyman-Scott
Ross Garnick
Tommy Tedesco
Nils Lofgren
Mike Campbell
Al Anderson
Ricky Skaggs

PUNK AND POST-PUNK
Johnny Ramone
Cheetah Chrome
Tom Verlaine
Richard Lloyd
The Edge

BLUES
B.B. King
Elmore James
Eric Clapton
Albert King
Stevie Ray Vaughan
Robben Ford
Mississippi John Hurt
T-Bone Walker
Buddy Guy
Otis Rush
Albert Collins

POST 20TH CENTURY
Steve Vai
Joe Satriani
Bill Frisell
Fred Frith
Dave Tronzo
Michael Hedges
Vernon Reid

31. **Rose Garden**
Lynn Anderson

32. **Charley Pride Sings Heart Songs**
Charley Pride

33. **For the Good Times**
Ray Price

34. **Poncho and Lefty**
Merle Haggard and
Willie Nelson

35. **My World**
Eddy Arnold

36. **The Best of Charley Pride, Vol. II**
Charley Pride

37. **Ocean Front Property**
George Strait

38. **Ring of Fire (The Best of Johnny Cash)**
Johnny Cash

39. **Eyes That See in the Dark**
Kenny Rogers

40. **Put Yourself in My Shoes**
Clint Black

41. **Pickin' On Nashville**
Kentucky Headhunters

42. **Five-0**
Hank Williams, Jr.

43. **A Lot About Livin' (And a Little 'Bout Love)**
Alan Jackson

44. **Common Thread: The Songs of the Eagles**
Various Artists

45. **In Pieces**
Garth Brooks

46. **Waylon and Willie**
Waylon Jennings and
Willie Nelson

47. **Right or Wrong**
George Strait

48. **Reba**
Reba McEntire

49. **Turn the World Around**
Eddy Arnold

50. **The Best of Jim Reeves**
Jim Reeves

Top Jazz Albums

**MARCH 11, 1962
TO JUNE 25, 1994**

1. **Magic Touch**
Stanley Jordan

2. **A Day in the Life**
Wes Montgomery

3. **Bitches' Brew**
Miles Davis

4. **Memphis Underground**
Herbie Mann

5. **Winelight**
Grover Washington, Jr.

6. **Breezin'**
George Benson

7. **Diane Schuur and the Count Basie Orchestra**
Diane Schuur and the Count Basie Orchestra

8. **Head Hunters**
Herbie Hancock

9. **Breakin' Away**
Al Jarreau

10. **Hot Buttered Soul**
Isaac Hayes

11. **Black Byrd**
Donald Byrd

12. **Backstreet**
David Sanborn

13. **Smackwater Jack**
Quincy Jones

14. **The Isaac Hayes Movement**
Isaac Hayes

15. **To Be Continued**
Isaac Hayes

16. **Michael Brecker**
Michael Brecker

17. **Offramp**
Pat Metheny Group

Miles Davis

18. **Hot House Flowers**
Wynton Marsalis

19. **Feels So Good**
Chuck Mangione

20. **Steppin' Out**
Tony Bennett

21. **The Other Side of Round Midnight**
Dexter Gordon

22. **Mister Magic**
Grover Washington, Jr.

23. **The Electrifying Eddie Harris**
Eddie Harris

24. **Swiss Movement**
Les McCann and Eddie Harris

25. **Shaft**
(Soundtrack)
Isaac Hayes

26. **Street Life**
The Crusaders

27. **We Are in Love**
Harry Connick, Jr.

28. **Fool on the Hill**
Sergio Mendes and Brasil '66

29. **In Your Eyes**
George Benson

30. **25**
Harry Connick, Jr.

31. **Blue Light, Red Light**
Harry Connick, Jr.

32. **Think of One**
Wynton Marsalis

33. **Push Push**
Herbie Mann

34. **Jarreau**
Al Jarreau

35. **When Harry Met Sally . . .**
Harry Connick, Jr.

36. **Talkin' About You**
Diane Schuur

37. **Give Me the Night**
George Benson

38. **Two of a Kind**
Earl Klugh and
Bob James

39. **Down Here on the Ground**
Wes Montgomery

40. **As We Speak**
David Sanborn

41. **Weekend in L.A.**
George Benson

42. **Chapter Two**
Roberta Flack

43. **Dancing in the Sun**
George Howard

44. **In Flight**
George Benson

45. **Soulful Strut**
Young-Holt Limited

46. **California Dreaming**
Wes Montgomery

47. **Here's to Life**
Shirley Horn with Strings

48. **Body Heat**
Quincy Jones

49. **Free as the Wind**
The Crusaders

50. **December**
George Winston

Hot Rap Singles

**MARCH 11, 1989
TO JUNE 25, 1994**

1. **"Self-Destruction"**
Stop the Violence Movement

2. **"Expression"**
Salt-N-Pepa

Salt-N-Pepa

3. **"Me Myself and I"**
De la Soul

4. **"Player's Ball"**
OutKast

5. **"Getto Jam"**
Domino

6. **"Me So Horny"**
2 Live Crew

7. **"The Humpty Dance"**
Digital Underground

8. **"Fight the Power"**
Public Enemy

9. **"The Phuncky Feel One/
How I Could Just Kill a Man"**
Cypress Hill

10. **"Knockin' Boots"**
Candyman

11. **"Jump"**
Kris Kross

12. **"It's Funky Enough"**
The D.O.C.

13. **"Around the Way Girl"**
L.L. Cool J

14. **"Treat 'Em Right"**
Chubb Rock

15. **"Got Me Waiting"**
Heavy D. and the Boyz

16. **"Dunkie Butt"**
(Please Please Please)
12 Gauge

17. **"Shoop"**
Salt-N-Pepa

18. **"Smooth Operator"**
Big Daddy Kane

19. **"I'll Do 4 U"**
Father M.C.

20. **"Whatta Man"**
Salt-N-Pepa
featuring En Vogue

Hot World Music Albums

**MAY 19, 1990
TO JUNE 25, 1994**

1. **Planet Drum**
Mickey Hart

2. **The Source**
Ali Farka Toure

3. **Love and Liberte**
Gipsy Kings

4. **Logozo**
Angelique Kidjo

5. **Cruel, Crazy, Beautiful World**
Johnny Clegg and Savuka

6. **Amen**
Salif Keita

7. **Primal Magic**
Strunz and Farah

8. **Adventures in Afropea I**
Zap Mama

9. **Songs of Freedom**
Bob Marley

10. **Banba**
Clannad

Top Classical Albums

**APRIL 18, 1964
TO JUNE 25, 1994**

1. **Switched-On Bach**
Walter Carlos and Benjamin
Folkman

2. **Pachelbel: Kanon**
Paillard Chamber Orchestra
(Andre)

3. **The Three Tenors
in Concert**
Carreras, Domingo and Pavarotti

4. **Suite for Flute and Jazz Piano**
Jean-Pierre Rampal and
Claude Bolling

5. **Horowitz in Moscow**
Vladimir Horowitz

6. **My Favorite Chopin**
Van Cliburn

7. **Mozart Concertos 17 and 21
(Elvira Madigan)**
Anda and Camerata
of the Salzburg Mozarteum
Academica

8. **Bach: Goldberg Variations**
Glenn Gould

9. **2001: A Space Odyssey**
Soundtrack

10. **Gorecki: Symphony No. 3**
Upshaw and Zinman

11. **Bernstein: Mass**
Leonard Bernstein

12. **Scott Joplin: The Red Black Book**
New England Conservatory
Ragtime Ensemble (Schuller)

13. **O Sole Mio — Favorite Neopolitan
Songs**
Luciano Pavarotti

14. **Piano Rags by Scott Joplin, Vol. I**
Joshua Rifkin

15. **The Movies Go to the Opera**
Various

16. **Pavarotti's Greatest Hits**
Luciano Pavarotti

17. **The Last Recording**
Vladimir Horowitz

18. **Annie's Song and Other Galway
Favorites**
James Galway with National
Philharmonic Orchestra

19. **Haydn/Hummel/Mozart:
Trumpet Concertos**
Wynton Marsalis with Raymond
Leonard and National Philharmonic
Orchestra

20. **Bernstein: West Side Story**
Kiri Te Kanawa and
Jose Carreras

21. **Verdi and Puccini: Arias**
Kiri Te Kanawa

22. **Bravo Pavarotti**
Luciano Pavarotti

23. **Horowitz: The Last Romantic**
Vladimir Horowitz

24. **Amadeus**
(Soundtrack)
Neville Marriner

25. **West Meets East**
Yehudi Menuhin
and Ravi Shankar

26. **Horowitz at Home**
Vladimir Horowitz

27. **Mahler: Symphony No. 8**
London Symphony Orchestra

28. **Baroque Music for Trumpets**
Wynton Marsalis

29. **Baroque Duet**
Kathleen Battle and
Wynton Marsalis

30. **Piano Rags by Scott Joplin, Vol. II**
Joshua Rifkin

31. **The Well-Tempered Synthesizer**
Walter Carlos

32. **Hits From Lincoln Center**
Luciano Pavarotti

33. **Horowitz Plays Mozart**
Vladimir Horowitz

34. **60th Anniversary Gala**
Stern, Perlman,
Zuckerman and New York
Philharmonic (Mehta)

35. **Webber: Requiem**
Placido Domingo and
Sarah Brightman (Maazel)

36. **Beethoven: Symphony No. 9**
Leonard Bernstein

37. **Blue Skies**
Kiri Te Kanawa (Riddle)

38. **Horowitz: The Studio Recordings**
Vladimir Horowitz

39. **Pleasures of Their Company**
Kathleen Battle and
Christopher Parkening

40. **If You Love Me**
Cecelia Bartoli

41. **Pachelbel: Kanon**
Academy of Ancient Music

42. **Mamma**
Luciano Pavarotti (Mancini)

43. **Greatest Hits of 1720**
Richard Kapp

44. **Live From Lincoln Center**
New York City Opera

45. **The Great Pavarotti**
Luciano Pavarotti

46. **Golden Jubilee Concert:
Rachmaninoff Concerto No. 3**
Vladimir Horowitz and Eugene
Ormandy and New York
Philharmonic

47. **Pachelbel Kanon: The Record
That Made It Famous and
Other Baroque Favorites**
Stuttgart Chamber Orchestra

48. **Canteloube: Songs of the
Auvergne**
Kiri Te Kanawa with Jeffrey Tate
and English Chamber Orchestra
(Munchinger)

49. **Pieces of Africa**
Kronos Quartet

50. **Kathleen Battle Sings
Mozart**
Kathleen Battle

Top Christian Contemporary Albums

**MARCH 29, 1980
TO JUNE 25, 1994**

1. **Age to Age**
Amy Grant

2. **Morning Like This**
Sandi Patti

3. **Straight Ahead**
Amy Grant

4. **The Collection**
Amy Grant

5. **More Than Wonderful**
Sandi Patti

6. **Go West Young Man**
Michael W. Smith

7. **Free at Last**
DC Talk

8. **Unguarded**
Amy Grant

9. **Heart in Motion**
Amy Grant

10. **Lead Me On**
Amy Grant

Top Music Videos

**MARCH 30, 1985
TO JUNE 25, 1994**

1. **The Three Tenors in Concert**
Carreras, Domingo and Pavarotti

2. **Comedy Video Classics**
Ray Stevens

3. **$19.98 Home Vid Cliff 'Em All!**
Metallica

4. **Hangin' Tough**
New Kids on the Block

5. **Bon Jovi — Breakout**
Bon Jovi

6. **Historia**
Def Leppard

Amy Grant

7. **The No. 1 Video Hits**
Whitney Houston

8. **Wham! The Video**
Wham!

9. **Garth Brooks**
Garth Brooks

10. **Moonwalker**
Michael Jackson

11. **This Is Garth Brooks**
Garth Brooks

12. **Step by Step**
New Kids on the Block

13. **Madonna**
Madonna

14. **Our First Video**
Mary-Kate and Ashley Olsen

15. **The Virgin Tour — Madonna Live**
Madonna

16. **Faith**
George Michael

17. **Slippery When Wet —
The Videos**
Bon Jovi

18. **Hangin' Tough Live**
New Kids on the Block

19. **Control — The Videos**
Janet Jackson

20. **Prince and the Revolution Live**
Prince and the Revolution

IPEA's Recordings You Should Own

One of the pleasures of life in the post-CD era is reassessing your record collection. The enormous volume of back-catalog recordings being released and compilations being assembled on disk means that music fans can more easily explore new types of music.

To help in that exploration, we've assembled a list of recordings you should consider. There have been literally millions of musical performances recorded since the advent of audio tape, and thousands are worthy of your attention. Our list is meant to suggest genres, time periods and artists that should be represented in your CD collection. The list is historical; we assume you're keeping up with current artists (and you've already read our survey of this year's significant recordings). Many of the artists have had their work compiled into greatest hits collections that you may want to purchase. We've avoided them (except when a collection is the most commonly available or desirable form) in order to suggest interesting periods in the artists' development.

CLASSICAL

Various, *Ancient Music for a Modern Age*, Sequentia (RCA Red Label)

Pachelbel, Handel, Vivaldi, Gluck, *Various Compositions*, Academy of Ancient Music/Christopher Hogwood (L'Oiseau Lyre)

Bach, *Goldberg Variations* (1955), Glenn Gould (Columbia)

Bach, *Brandenburg Concertos*, Amsterdam Baroque Orchestra/Tom Koopman (Erato)

Bach, *Unaccompanied Cello Suites*, Yo-Yo Ma (Columbia)

Mozart, *Don Giovanni*, Wachter, Sutherland, others; Philharmonia Orchestra and Chorus/Carlo Maria Giulini (EMI)

Mozart, *Requiem*, Academy of St. Martin's-in-the-Fields/Neville Marriner (London)

Beethoven, **Nine Symphonies** (complete cycle), Academy of Ancient Music/Christopher Hogwood (L'Oiseau Lyre) (This is a period instruments reading; classicists may want to consider the redoubtable Bruno Walter/Columbia 1959 cycle.)

Beethoven, **The Late String Quartets,** Guarneri Quartet (RCA Victor Gold Seal)

Schubert, *Symphony No. 8 (Unfinished)*, Royal Concertgebouw Orchestra/Leonard Bernstein (Deutsche Grammophon)

Wagner

Brahms, *Symphony No. 1*, Berlin Philharmonic/Claudio Abbado (Deutsche Grammophon)

Bellini, *Norma*, Sutherland, Pavarotti, Caballe, Chorus and Orchestra of the Welsh National Opera/Bonynge (London)

MUSIC TIME LINE

ca. 1430–1600

From 1430 to 1600, Europe undergoes a rebirth in music, art and intellect known as the Renaissance. Josquin Desprez and Orlando di Lasso are among the great Renaissance composers.

ca. 1600–1750

The Baroque period, characterized by strict musical forms and highly ornamental works, flourishes from 1600 to 1750 in Europe.

1607

Italian master composer Claudio Monteverdi writes the opera *Orfeo, Favola in Musica*, a

work deemed to be a prime example of the early Baroque musical form.

1685

Johann Sebastian Bach and George Frederick Handel are born. They become principle classical composers of the late Baroque period. Bach explores musical forms associated with the church and Handel works as a dramatic composer.

1750

Bach dies. The end of the Baroque period is often seen in conjunction with his death.

Verdi, *Falstaff*, Bruson, Ricciarelli, Nucci, Los Angeles Philharmonic/Giulini (Deutsche Grammophon)

Wagner, *Tristan und Isolde*, Nilsson, Ludwig, Wachter, Chorus and Orchestra of the Bayreuth Festival/Bohm (Deutsche Grammophon)

Puccini, *Turandot*, Pavarotti, Sutherland, Caballe, London Philharmonic Orchestra/Mehta (London)

Stravinsky, *The Rite of Spring*, Cleveland Orchestra/Boulez (CBS Masterworks)

Schoenberg, *Verklarte Nacht*, Juilliard Quartet With Yo-Yo Ma (Sony Classical)

Weill, *The Threepenny Opera*, Ute Lemper, Berlin Sinfonietta (London)

Barber, *Complete Songs*, Thomas Hampson, Cheryl Studer, Emerson String Quartet (Deutsche Grammophon)

Ives, *Three Places in New England*, Boston Symphony Orchestra/Thomas (Deutsche Grammophon)

Gershwin, *Rhapsody in Blue*, Columbia Symphony/Bernstein (CBS Masterworks)

Reich, *Music for 18 Musicians*, Steve Reich Ensemble (ECM)

Glass, *Einstein on the Beach (1993)*, Philip Glass Ensemble (Elektra Nonesuch)

Pärt, *Tabula Rasa*, Gidon Kremer (ECM)

Duke Ellington and Billy Strayhorn

Gorecki, *Symphony No. 3*, London Sinfonietta with Dawn Upshaw/Zinman (Elektra Nonesuch)

JAZZ/BLUES

Louis Armstrong, *Hot Fives and Sevens 1927–1928* (Columbia)

Fats Waller, *The Complete Fats Waller, vols. 1–4* (Bluebird/RCA)

Duke Ellington, *The Blanton-Webster Band 1940–1942* (Bluebird)

Billie Holiday, *The Quintessential Billie Holiday 1940–1942* (Columbia)

Charlie Parker, *The Complete Charlie Parker Savoy Studio Sessions* (Savoy)

Charlie Parker, *Bird: The Complete Charlie Parker on Verve* (Verve)

Thelonious Monk, *The Genius of Modern Music 1947–1952* (Blue Note)

Miles Davis, *Kind of Blue* (Columbia)

Dave Brubeck, *Time Out* (Columbia)

Duke Ellington, *The Far East Suite: Special Mix* (Bluebird)

John Coltrane, *A Love Supreme* (Impulse)

John Coltrane, *My Favorite Things* (Impulse)

Ornette Coleman, *The Shape of Jazz to Come* (Atlantic)

Chet Baker, *Best of Chet Baker Sings* (Pacific Jazz)

Frank Sinatra, *Songs for Swinging Lovers* (Capitol)

Louis Armstrong

1750–ca. 1825

The highly ornate style of the Baroque period gives rise to the more simple, clarified styles of the Classical period. Franz Josef Haydn, considered to be the father of the Classical period, and Wolfgang Amadeus Mozart emerge as masters of this period.

1803

Ludwig van Beethoven, one of the great Romantic composers, produces his third symphony, *Eröica*. This piece marks the beginning of the Romantic period (1803–1900), in which the formality of the Classical period is replaced by subjectivity. Composers begin to appeal to the sensory response in audiences, rather than the purely intellectual.

ca. 1860

The slave trade introduces West African rhythms, work songs, chants and spirituals to America, which strongly influence the Blues and jazz.

1877

Thomas Edison invents sound recording.

1878

Thomas Edison patents the phonograph.

RECORDINGS YOU SHOULD OWN

Ella Fitzgerald, *The Best of the Songbooks* (Verve)

Charles Mingus, *Mingus Ah-Um* (Columbia)

Miles Davis, *Bitches Brew* (Columbia)

Wynton Marsalis, *Hot House Flowers* (Columbia)

Robert Johnson, *The Complete Recordings* (Columbia)

Charlie Patton, *Founder of the Delta Blues* (Yazoo)

Son House, *Son House* (Arhoolie)

Bessie Smith, *The Complete Recordings* (Columbia)

Muddy Waters, *Folksinger* (Chess/MCA)

Muddy Waters, *The Chess Box* (Chess/MCA)

Professor Longhair, *Rock 'n' Roll Gumbo* (A&M)

John Lee Hooker, *John Lee Hooker Plays and Sings the Blues* (Chess/MCA)

Albert King, *Born Under a Bad Sign* (Atlantic)

ROCK

Elvis Presley, *Elvis Presley* (RCA)

Sam Cooke, *The Man and His Music* (RCA)

Chuck Berry, *St. Louis to Liverpool* (Chess)

The Rolling Stones

The Rolling Stones, *High Tide and Green Grass* (ABKCO)

The Beach Boys, *Pet Sounds* (Capitol)

The Byrds, *The Byrds* (Columbia)

Bob Dylan, *Blonde on Blonde* (Columbia)

Simon and Garfunkel, *Parsley, Sage, Rosemary and Thyme* (Columbia)

Jefferson Airplane, *Surrealistic Pillow* (RCA)

Big Brother and the Holding Company, *Cheap Thrills* (Columbia)

Cream, *Disraeli Gears* (Polydor)

Jimi Hendrix, *Are You Experienced?* (Reprise)

Funkadelic, *Cosmic Slop* (Westbound)

James Brown, *Star Time* (Polydor)

Van Morrison, *Astral Weeks* (Warner Bros.)

The Four Tops, *Anthology* (Motown)

The Supremes, *Anthology* (Motown)

The Band, *The Band* (Capitol)

Creedance Clearwater Revival, *Willie and the Poor Boys* (Fantasy)

Elvis Presley, *Elvis (TV Special)* (RCA)

Neil Young, *After the Gold Rush* (Reprise)

The Allman Brothers, *At Fillmore East* (Capricorn)

Derek and the Dominoes, *Layla and Other Assorted Love Songs* (RSO)

Aerosmith, *Toys in the Attic* (CBS)

Sex Pistols

The Drifters, *1959–1965 All-Time Greatest Hits and More* (Atlantic)

Buddy Holly, *The Complete Buddy Holly* (MCA)

Phil Spector/Various, *Back to Mono* (ABKCO)

The Beatles, *Revolver* (Capitol)

The Beatles, *Sgt. Pepper's Lonely Hearts Club Band* (Capitol)

1896

Ragtime, a combination of West Indian rhythm and European musical form, is born. Scott Joplin is one of Ragtime's main composers.

1908

A major change in classical music style comes about with the release of Arnold Schoenberg's,

Book of Hanging Gardens. The harmony and tonality characteristic of classical music are replaced by dissonance, creating what many listeners consider to be noise.

1919

After moving from its southern rural roots, jazz establishes Chicago as its capital.

The city will become home to such jazz greats as trumpeter Louis Armstrong and pianist Jelly Roll Morton.

1921

The first recording by a black performer, at the time referred to as a "race" record, is released.

1923

"Queen of the Blues" Bessie Smith records her first song, "Down Hearted Blues," which becomes an immediate success. Other Blues masters include Muddy Waters, John Lee Hooker, B.B. King and Blind Lemon Jefferson.

Woody Guthrie

The Rolling Stones, *Exile on Main Street* (Rolling Stones)

The Who, *Live at Leeds* (MCA)

The Doors, *Morrison Hotel* (Elektra)

David Bowie, *Hunky Dory* (Rykodisc)

The Stooges, *Fun House* (Elektra)

Stevie Wonder, *Songs in the Key of Life* (Motown)

Marvin Gaye, *Let's Get It On* (Tamla)

Al Green, *Let's Stay Together* (Motown)

Sex Pistols, *Never Mind the Bollocks, Here's the Sex Pistols* (Warner Bros.)

The Clash, *London Calling* (Epic)

The Buzzcocks, *Singles Going Steady* (IRS)

Talking Heads, *Talking Heads '77* (Sire)

Elvis Costello, *Get Happy!* (Columbia)

Wire, *Chairs Missing* (Restless reissue)

Gang of Four, *Entertainment!* (Warner Bros.)

Blondie, *Plastic Letters* (Chrysalis)

Devo, *Q: Are We Not Men? A: We Are Devo* (Warner Bros.)

X, *Los Angeles* (Slash)

The Gun Club, *Fire of Love* (Ruby)

Tom Petty and the Heartbreakers, *Damn the Torpedoes* (MCA)

AC/DC, *Back in Black* (Atlantic)

U2, *The Joshua Tree* (Island)

R.E.M., *Murmur* (IRS)

Peter Gabriel, *So* (Geffen)

Tom Waits, *Swordfish Trombones* (Island)

Bruce Springsteen, *Greetings From Asbury Park* or *Darkness at the Edge of Town* (Columbia)

FOLK/COUNTRY

Jimmie Rodgers, *The Early Years 1928–1929* (Rounder)

The Carter Family, *My Clinch Mountain Home* (Rounder)

Bill Monroe, *The Original Bluegrass Band* (Rounder)

Hank Williams, eight-volume Polydor reissue (Polydor)

Patsy Cline, *The Patsy Cline Collection* (MCA)

George Jones, *The Best of George Jones* (Rhino)

Johnny Cash, *Johnny Cash at Folsom Prison* (Columbia)

Merle Haggard, *Sing Me Back Home* (Capitol)

Emmylou Harris, *Luxury Liner* (Warner Bros.)

Woody Guthrie, *The Greatest Songs of Woody Guthrie* (Vanguard)

Leadbelly, *Midnight Special, Gwine Dig a Hole to Put the Devil In* or *Let It Shine on Me* (three CDs; Rounder)

The Carter Family

1932

Jazz composer Duke Ellington writes "It Don't Mean a Thing, If It Ain't Got That Swing," a song that presaged the swing era of the 1930s and 1940s. Glenn Miller, the Dorsey Brothers, Benny Goodman and Cab Calloway led other major swing bands.

1948

Columbia Records introduces the 33 1/3 LP ("long playing") record at the New York's Waldorf-Astoria Hotel. It allows listeners to enjoy an unprecedented 25 minutes of music per side, compared to the four minutes per side of the standard 78 rpm record.

1954

Bill Haley and the Comets begin writing hit songs. As a white band using black-derived forms, they venture into what will be known as "rock 'n' roll."

1956

With many hit singles (including "Heartbreak Hotel"), Elvis Presley emerges as one of the world's first rock stars. During 1956, the gyrating rock'n'roller also enjoys fame on the stages of the Milton Berle, Steve Allen and Ed Sullivan shows, as well as in the first of his many movies, *Love Me Tender*.

Doc Watson, **The Doc Watson Family** (Smithsonian/Folkways)

Various, **Jubilation Volume: Great Gospel Performances** (Rhino)

Phil Ochs, **Phil Ochs in Concert** (Elektra)

Clifton Chenier, **Bogalusa Boogie** (Arhoolie)

Joan Baez, **Joan Baez 5** (Vanguard)

The Chieftains

Joni Mitchell, **Blue** (Reprise)

Tim Hardin, **Reason to Believe** (Polydor)

WORLD MUSIC

Planxty, **Planxty** (Shanachie)

The Bothy Band, **The Best of the Bothy Band** (Green Linnet)

The Chieftains, **The Long Black Veil** (RCA)

Altan, **Island Angel** (Green Linnet)

De Dannan, **De Dannan** (Shanachie)

Ewan MacColl, **Black and White** (Green Linnet)

The Oyster Band, **From Little Rock to Leipzig** (Rykodisc)

Kate and Anna McGarrigle, **French Record** (Hannibal)

Various, **Rai Rebels** (Earthworks)

Paco de Lucia, **Almoraima** (Philips)

Don Byron, **Don Byron Plays the Music of Mickey Katz** (Nonesuch)

Nusrat Fatah Ali Khan, **En Concert à Paris** (Harmonia Mundi)

Sabri Brothers, **Ya Habib** (Real World)

Ustad Ali Akbar Khan, **Signature Series Vol.1** (AMMP)

Dr. L. Subramaniam, **Raga Hemavati** (Nimbus)

Ramnad Krishnan, **Vidwan — Songs of the Carnatic Tradition** (Nonesuch)

Youssou N'Dour, **Eyes Open** (Columbia)

King Sunny Ade, **Juju Music** (Island)

Various, **Juju Roots 1930s–1950s** (Rounder)

Various, **The Indestructible Beat of Soweto** (Earthworks)

Mahlatini and the Mahotella Queens, **The Lion Roars** (Shanachie)

Various, **Zimbabwe Frontline** (Earthworks)

Thomas Mapfumo, **The Chimurenga Singles** (Shanachie)

The Bhundu Boys, **Jit Jive** (Mango)

Bob Marley and the Wailers, **Natty Dread** (Tuff Gong)

Gamelan of Pura Pakualaman, **Javanese Court Gamelan** (Nonesuch)

Various, **Bali: Gamelan and Kecak** (Nonesuch)

Fong Naam, **The Hang Hong Suite** (Nimbus)

Kohachiro Miyata, **Shakuhachi — The Japanese Flute** (Nonesuch)

Various, **Cuba Classics Vol. 1–3** (Luaka Bop)

Los Munequitos de Matanzas, **Rumba Caliente** (Qbadisc)

Various, **Konbit: Burning Rhythms of Haiti** (A&M)

Various, **Zouk Attack** (Rounder)

Los Pinguinos del Norte, **Conjuntos Nortenos** (Arhoolie)

Steve Jordan, **The Many Sounds of Steve Jordan** (Arhoolie)

Various, **Beliza Tropical: Brazil Classics** (Luaka Bop)

Various: **O Samba: Brazil Classics** (Luaka Bop)

Joao Gilberto, **Joao Gilberto** (Polygram)

Astor Piazzolla, **Zero Hour** (American Clave)

Various, **Vintage Hawaiian Music: Steel Guitar Masters** 1928–1934 (Rounder)

1959

The National Academy of Recording Ars and Sciences sponsors the first Grammy Award ceremony for music recorded in 1958.

1963

A wave of Beatlemania hits the U.K. The Beatles, a British band composed of John Lennon, George Harrison, Ringo Starr and Paul McCartney, take Britain by storm in a performance at the London Palladium, which launches them to international fame.

1964

Folk musician Bob Dylan becomes increasingly popular during this time of social protest, with songs expressing objection to the condition of American society. Psychedelic bands such as the Grateful Dead and Jefferson Airplane also enjoy great success during this time, with songs celebrating the counterculture of the '60s.

1969

In August, more than half a million people gather in the small, upstate New York town of Woodstock for four days of rain, sex, drugs and rock 'n' roll. Performers include Janis Joplin, Jimi Hendrix, the Who, Joan Baez, Crosby, Stills, Nash and Young, Jefferson Airplane and Sly and the Family Stone.

CONTINUED ON PAGE 423 ▶

The Rock and Roll Hall of Fame

The Rock and Roll Hall of Fame was founded in 1986 by the Hall of Fame Foundation. To be eligible for inclusion, musicians and bands must have released a record at least 25 years prior to the year of induction. A committee of 29 music historians and critics nominates 15 contenders, and a group of 600 music-industry figures makes the final cut.

1986
Chuck Berry
James Brown
Ray Charles
Sam Cooke
Fats Domino
The Everly Brothers
Buddy Holly
Jerry Lee Lewis
Elvis Presley
Little Richard
Nonperformers
Alan Freed
Sam Phillips
Early Influences
Robert Johnson
Jimmie Rodgers
Jimmy Yancey
Lifetime Achievement
John Hammond

1987
The Coasters
Eddie Cochran
Bo Diddley
Aretha Franklin
Marvin Gaye
Bill Haley
B.B. King
Clyde McPhatter
Ricky Nelson
Roy Orbison
Carl Perkins
Smokey Robinson
Joe Turner
Muddy Waters
Jackie Wilson

Nonperformers
Leonard Chess
Ahmet Ertegun
Jerry Leiber and Mike
    Stoller
Jerry Wexler
Early Influences
Louis Jordan
T-Bone Walker
Hank Williams

1988
The Beach Boys
The Beatles
The Drifters
Bob Dylan
The Supremes
Nonperformer
Berry Gordy, Jr.
Early Influences
Woody Guthrie
Leadbelly
Les Paul

1989
Dion
Otis Redding
The Rolling Stones
The Temptations
Stevie Wonder
Nonperformer
Phil Spector
Early Influences
The Ink Spots
Bessie Smith
The Soul Stirrers

1990
Hank Ballard
Bobby Darin

The Four Seasons
The Four Tops
The Kinks
The Platters
Simon & Garfunkel
The Who
Nonperformers
Gerry Goffin and Carole King
Brian Holland, Eddie Holland
    and Lamont Dozier
Early Influences
Louis Armstrong
Charlie Christian
May Rainey

1991
LaVern Baker
The Byrds
John Lee Hooker
The Impressions
Wilson Pickett
Jimmy Reed
Ike and Tina Turner
Nonperformers
Dave Bartholomew
Ralph Bass
Early Influence
Howlin' Wolf
**Lifetime Achievement
Award**
Nesuhi Ertegun

1992
Bobby "Blue" Bland
Booker T. and the MG's
Johnny Cash
Jimi Hendrix Experience
The Isley Brothers
Sam and Dave
The Yardbirds

Nonperformers
Leo Fender
Bill Graham
Doc Pomus
Early Influences
Elmore James
Professor Longhair

1993
Ruth Brown
Cream
Creedence Clearwater
    Revival
The Doors
Etta James
Frankie Lymon and
    The Teenagers
Van Morrison
Sly and The Family Stone
Nonperformers
Dick Clark
Milt Gabler
Early Influence
Dinah Washington

1994
The Animals
The Band
Duane Eddy
The Grateful Dead
Elton John
John Lennon
Bob Marley
Rod Stewart
Nonperformer
Johnny Otis
Early Influence
Willie Dixon

Buddy Holly

Bob Dylan

The Beatles

The Country Music Hall of Fame

The Country Music Hall of Fame, founded in 1961 by the Country Music Association, is located on Music Row in Nashville. Inductees are selected annually by an anonymous panel of 200 electors, each of whom has been an active participant in the music business for at least 15 years and has made a major contribution to the industry.

Hank Williams

1961
Jimmie Rodgers
Fred Rose
Hank Williams

1962
Roy Acuff

1963
Elections were held but no candidate received enough votes to qualify for induction.

1964
Tex Ritter

1965
Ernest Tubb

1966
Eddy Arnold
James R. Denny
George D. Hay
Uncle Dave Macon

1967
Red Foley
J.L. Frank
Jim Reeves
Stephen H. Sholes

1968
Bob Wills

1969
Gene Autry

1970
Original Carter Family
Bill Monroe

1971
Arthur Edward Satherley

1972
Jimmie H. Davis

1973
Chet Atkins
Patsy Cline

1974
Owen Bradley
Frank "Pee Wee" King

1975
Minnie Pearl

1976
Paul Cohen
Kitty Wells

1977
Merle Travis

1978
Grandpa Jones

1979
Hubert Long
Hank Snow

1980
Connie B. Gay
Johnny Cash
Original Sons of the Pioneers

1981
Vernon Dalhart
Grant Turner

1982
Lefty Frizzell
Ray Horton
Marty Robbins

1983
Little Jimmy Dickens

1984
Ralph Sylvester Peer
Floyd Tillman

1985
Lester Flatt and Earl Scruggs

1986
Whitey Ford
Wesley H. Rose

1987
Rod Brasfield

1988
Loretta Lynn
Roy Rogers

1989
Jack Stapp
Cliffie Stone
Hank Thompson

1990
Tennessee Ernie Ford

1991
Boudleaux and Felice Bryant

1992
George Jones
Frances Williams Preston

1993
Willie Nelson

Patsy Cline

1974

Patti Smith releases what is considered to be the first punk rock single, "Hey Joe." Punk roars out of Britain during the mid-'70s, with bands such as the Sex Pistols and the Clash expressing nihilistic and anarchistic views in response to a lack of opportunity in Britain, boredom and antipathy for the bland music of the day.

1979

The Sugar Hill Gang releases the first commercial rap hit, "Rapper's Delight," bringing rap off the New York streets and into the popular music scene. Rap originates in the mid 1970s as rhyme spoken over an instrumental track provided by snatches of music from records. Over the decades, raps grows to become one of the most important commercial and artistic branches of pop music, reflecting the fast paced, chaotic nature of life in the '90s.

1981

MTV goes on the air running around the clock music videos, debuting with "Video Killed the Radio Star."

1982

Michael Jackson releases *Thriller*, **which sells more than 20 million copies, becoming the biggest-selling album in history.**

Major Record Labels

A&M Records
1416 LaBrea Ave.
Hollywood, CA 90028
(213) 469-2411

American Recordings
3500 W. Olive Ave.,
Suite 1550
Burbank, CA 91505
(818) 973-4545

**Angel/EMI Classics/
Virgin Classics**
810 Seventh Ave.
New York, NY 10019
(212) 603-8600

Arista Records
6 W. 57th St.
New York, NY 10019
(212) 489-7400

Atlantic Records
75 Rockefeller Plaza
New York, NY 10019
(212) 275-2000

Blue Note
1290 Ave. of the Americas
New York, NY 10019
(212) 492-5300

Capitol Records
1290 Ave. of the Americas
New York, NY 10019
(212) 492-5300

Chrysalis Records
1290 Ave. of the Americas
New York, NY 10104
(212) 492-1200

Columbia Records
550 Madison Ave.
New York, NY 10022
(212) 833-8000

East/West Records
75 Rockefeller Plaza
New York, NY 10019
(212) 275-2500

Elektra Entertainment
75 Rockefeller Plaza
New York, NY 10019
(212) 275-2500

EMI Records
1290 Ave. of the Americas
New York, NY 10104
(212) 492-1800

Epic Records
550 Madison Ave.
New York, NY 10022-3211
(212) 833-8000

Geffen Record Co. (DGC)
9130 Sunset Blvd.
Los Angeles, CA 90069
(310) 278-9010

Giant Records
8900 Wilshire Blvd., Suite 200
Beverly Hills, CA 90211
(310) 289-5500

Gramophone Records
P.O. Box 910
Beverly Hills, CA 90213
(213) 276-2726

Interscope Records
10900 Wilshire Blvd.,
Suite 1230
Los Angeles, CA 90024
(310) 208-6547

I.R.S. Records
3939 Lankershim Blvd.
Universal City, CA 91604
(818) 508-3130

Island Records
825 Eighth Ave.
New York, NY 10019
(212) 333-8000

Mammoth Records
Carr Mill, 2nd Floor
Carrboro, NC 27510
(919) 932-1882

Matador Records
676 Broadway, 4th Floor
New York, NY 10012
(212) 995-5882

MCA Records
70 Universal City Plaza
Universal City, CA 91608
(818) 777-4500

Mercury Records
825 Eighth Ave.
New York, NY 10019
(212) 333-8000

Motown Record Co.
5750 Wilshire Blvd., Suite 300
Los Angeles, CA 90036
(213) 634-3500

Nonesuch Records
590 Fifth Ave., 16th Floor
New York, NY 10036
(212) 575-6720

Polygram Label Group
825 Eighth Ave.
New York, NY 10019
(212) 333-8000

RCA Records
1540 Broadway, 9th Floor
New York, NY 10036
(212) 930-4000

Reprise Records
3300 Warner Blvd.
Burbank, CA 91505
(818) 953-3750

Rhino Entertainment Co.
10635 Santa Monica Blvd.,
2nd Floor
Los Angeles, CA 90025-4900
(310) 474-4778

Rounder Records
1 Camp St.
Cambridge, MA 02140
(617) 354-0700

Rykodisc
Shetland Park
27 Congress St.
Salem, MA 01970
(508) 744-7678

Sire Records
75 Rockefeller Plaza
New York, NY 10019
(212) 275-4560

Verve Records
825 Eighth Ave.
New York, NY 10019
(212) 333-8000

Virgin Records
338 N. Foothill Road
Beverly Hills, CA 90210
(213) 278-1181

Warner Bros. Records
3300 Warner Blvd.
Burbank, CA 91505
(818) 846-9090

Windham Hill
P.O. Box 9388
Stanford, CA 94309
(415) 329-0647

1983

With the introduction of noise-free compact disks, the record begins its demise.

1987

Though African, Latin American and other genres of international music have been around for centuries, a group of small, London-based labels coin the term "World Music," which helps record sellers find rack space for the eclectic blend of music.

1991

Seattle band Nirvana releases the song "Smells Like Teen Spirit" on the LP *Nevermind* and enjoys instant success. With Nirvana's hit comes the grunge movement, which is characterized by distorted guitars, dispirited vocals and lots of flannel.

1992

Compact disks surpass cassette tapes as the preferred medium for recorded music.

Music Magazines and Journals

The Acoustic Guitar
String Letter Press
Box 767
San Anselmo, CA 94979-0767
(415) 485-6946

Alternative Press
P.O. Box 17136
N. Hollywood, CA 91615
(818) 760-8520

The American Organist
American Guild of Organists
475 Riverside Drive, #1260
New York, NY 10115-0122
(212) 870-2310

Bass Player
Miller Freeman Publications
600 Harrison St.
San Francisco, CA 94107
(415) 905-2200

Billboard
Billboard Publications, Inc.
1515 Broadway, 15th Floor
New York, NY 10036
(212) 764-7300

Bluegrass Unlimited
P.O. Box 111
Broad Run, VA 22014-0111
(703) 349-8181

Blues Access
1455 Chestnut Place
Boulder, CO 80304-3153
(303) 443-7245

Buddy, The Original Texas Music Magazine
Buddy, Inc.
501 N. Good Latimer Expressway
Dallas, TX 75204-5899
(214) 484-9010

CD Review
Connell Communications, Inc.
86 Elm St.
Peterborough, NH 03458
(603) 924-7271

CMJ New Music Report
College Media Inc.
1 Middle Neck Road, Suite 400
Great Neck, NY 11021
(516) 466-6000

Cadence: The Review of Jazz and Blues
Cadence Building
Redwood, NY 13679
(315) 287-2852

Computer Music Journal
MIT Press
55 Hayward St.
Cambridge, MA 02142
(617) 253-2889

Country America
Meredith Corp.
1716 Locust St.
Des Moines, IA 50309
(515) 284-3790

Down Beat
102 N. Haven
Elmhurst, IL 60126
(708) 941-2030

Electronic Musician (Polyphony)
6400 Hollis St., #12
Emeryville, CA 94608
(510) 653-3307

Entertainment Weekly
1675 Broadway
New York, NY 10019
(212) 522-5600

Ethnomusicology
Society for Ethnomusicology
Morrison Hall 005
Bloomington, IN 47405-2502
(812) 855-6672

Fanfare
P. O. Box 720
Tenafly, NY 07670
(201) 567-3908

Goldmine
Krause Publications, Inc.
700 E. State St.
Iola, WI 54990-0001
(715) 445-2214

Guitar Player
Miller Freeman, Inc.
1515 Broadway
New York, NY 10036
(212) 869-1300

Guitar for the Practicing Musician
Cherry Lane Music Co.
10 Midland Ave.
Port Chester, NY 10573
(914) 935-5200

Guitar World
Harris Publications, Inc.
1115 Broadway, 8th Floor
New York, NY 10010
(212) 807-7100

Hot Wire: Journal of Women's Music & Culture
Empty Closet Enterprises
5210 N. Wayne
Chicago, IL 60640-2223
(312) 769-9009

Jazz Times (Radio Free Jazz)
7961 Eastern Ave., Suite 303
Silver Spring, MD 20910
(301) 588-4114

Jazziz Magazine
3620 N.W. 43rd St.
Gainesville, FL 32606
(904) 375-3705

Keyboard (Contemporary Keyboard)
Miller Freeman, Inc.
1515 Broadway
New York, NY 10036
(408) 446-1105

Living Blues
301 Hill Hall
University, MS 38677
(601) 232-5742

millenium pop
173 Morrison Avenue
Somerville, MA 02144
http://mirror.wwa.com/mirror/atlantis/millpop/homepage.htm

Mix, The Recording Industry Magazine
6400 Hollis St., #12
Emeryville, CA 94608-1028
(510) 653-3307

Modern Drummer
12 Old Bridge Road
Cedar Grove, NJ 07009
(201) 239-4140

Music City News
50 Music Square W., #601
Nashville, TN 37203
(615) 329-2200

Musician
Billboard Publications, Inc.
1515 Broadway
New York, NY 10036
(800) 347-6969

New Schwann Record and Tape Guide
(Schwann/Record & Tape Guide)
Schwann Publications
440 Cerrillos Road, Suite C
Santa Fe, NM 87501-2644
(505) 988-2045

Option: Music Alternatives
1522 B Clover Field Boulevard
Santa Monica, CA 90404
(310) 449-0120

Pollstar
4333 N. West Avenue
Fresno, CA 93705
(209) 224-2631

Pulse! Magazine
2500 Del Monte St.
Building C
West Sacramento, CA 95691-3820
(916) 373-2450

Raygun
2110 Main Street #100
Santa Monica, CA 90405
(310) 452-6222

Relix
P.O. Box 94
Brooklyn, NY 11229
(718) 258-0009

Rolling Stone
1290 Ave. of the Americas
New York, NY 10104
(212) 484-1616

Schwann "Opus"
Stereophile
Box 5529
Santa Fe, NM 87502-5529
(505) 988-2045

Schwann "Spectrum"
Stereophile
Box 5529
Santa Fe, NM 87502-5529
(505) 988-2045

Sing Out! The Folk Song Magazine
125 E. Third St.
Bethlehem, PA 18015-0253
(610) 865-5366

The Source
594 Broadway, Suite 510
New York, NY 10012
(212) 274-0464

Spin Magazine
6 W. 18th St.
New York, NY 10011
(212) 633-8200

Stereo Review Compact Disc Buyers Guide
Hachette Filipacchi Magazines, Inc.
1633 Broadway, 42nd Floor
New York, NY 10019
(212) 767-6000

TuTTi
4612 LeJeune Road
Coral Gables, FL 33134
(305) 663-0077

Vibe
Time/Warner Inc.
75 Rockefeller Plaza
New York, NY 10020-1300
(212) 484-8000

Music Glossary

AAA (adult album alternative) The rapidly growing radio format that presents a combination of more adventurous rock with folk and world music and is marketed primarily to aging baby-boomer rock fans with expanding musical interests.

AOR (album-oriented rock) The radio format that presents a blend of heavy rock standards with the more traditional current practitioners of the genre.

a cappella A vocal performance without instrumental accompaniment.

accompaniment A vocal or instrumental part that supports another, often solo, part.

adagio adj. In a slow tempo, usually considered slower than andante but faster than larghetto.
n. A slow passage, movement or work.

air A simple melody for an instrument or a voice.

allegretto In a moderately quick tempo, slower than allegro but faster than andante.

allegro In a lively, fast tempo.

alternative The radio format that features guitar-based rock with desultory male vocalists or chirpy female vocalists. It grew in response to the last gasp of dinosaur bands from the seventies and from the commercial success of bands such as Nirvana and Pearl Jam. Also known as **modern rock**.

andante adj. In a moderately slow tempo, usually considered slower than allegretto but faster than adagio.
n. An andante passage or movement.

appoggiatura An embellishing note, usually one step above or below the note it precedes.

atonality The absence of a tonal center and of harmonies derived from a diatonic scale.

ballad A popular narrative song, especially of a romantic or sentimental nature.

barcarole A Venetian gondolier's song with a rhythm suggestive of rowing.

barrelhouse An early style of jazz characterized by free group improvisation and an accented two-beat rhythm.

bluegrass An early form of country music that combines the gospel-tinged vocals of the Blue Ridge Mountain region with folk melodies. Instrumentation generally includes guitars, banjos, mandolins and fiddles.

blue note A flatted note, especially the third or seventh note of a chord.

blues A style of music evolved from southern African-American secular songs and usually distinguished by slow tempo and flatted thirds and sevenths. Blues is an important stream of American music that fed the development of rock, rhythm and blues and country music.

boogie-woogie A style of jazz piano characterized by a repeated rhythmic and melodic pattern in the bass and a series of improvised variations in the treble.

bop A style of jazz characterized by rhythmic and harmonic complexity, improvised solo performances, and a virtuoso execution.

breve A note equivalent to two whole notes.

cadenza An unaccompanied instrumental passage generally occurring near the end of a concerto movement. Earlier cadenzas of the classical period were improvised but are now typically written.

calypso A type of music that originated in the West Indies and is characterized by humorous, improvised lyrics often on topical subjects.

canon A contrapuntal technique in which the melody line is exactly imitated and overlapped by other voices.

canticle A song or chant, especially a non-metrical hymn with words taken from a biblical text.

chaconne 1. A slow, stately dance of the 18th century or the music for it. 2. A form consisting of variations based on a reiterated harmonic pattern.

chamber music Music written for small ensembles and meant to be played in smaller rooms; a string quartet is the most common ensemble.

chord Three or more notes that form a harmony.

chromatic scale 1. Twelve notes in a scale that progress in semitones. See **key**. 2. Chromatic music includes the work of Wagner, Bartók and Schoenberg.

clef The indication on each staff of higher (treble) parts, or lower (bass) parts.

concerto A composition for an orchestra and one or more soloist instruments, usually violin or piano, generally in three movements.

concertmaster/concertmistress The first male or female violinist and assistant conductor in a symphony orchestra.

counterpoint Melodic material that is added above or below an existing melody, or the technique of combining two or more melodic lines in such a way that they establish a harmonic relationship.

diminuendo The indication to grow softer.

dissonance An instability between notes or chords that suggests tension when played together. Traditional harmony requires dissonant passages to resolve to consonance.

doo-wop A style of music popularized in the 1950s with words and nonsense syllables sung in harmony by small groups.

downbeat The first beat in a measure.

Euterpe The Muse of lyric poetry and music.

fantasia A free composition structured according to the composer's fancy.

flat The musical sign to lower a pitch by a semitone.

forte The indication for a loud, forceful passage.

funk A type of popular music combining elements of jazz, blues and soul and characterized by syncopated rhythm and a heavy, repetitive bass line.

gamelan An Indonesian orchestra composed mainly of tuned percussion instruments such as bamboo xylophones, wooden or metal chimes and gongs.

gangsta rap A form of rap music that reflects the violent nature of inner-city streets.

gospel music American religious music that is associated with evangelism and is based on the simple melodies of folk music blended with melodic and rhythmic elements of spirituals and the blues.

grunge The label applied to a rock form featuring distorted guitars, whining vocals and flannel-shirt-wearing band members. Popularized by and associated primarily with Seattle bands such as Nirvana and Alice in Chains.

gutbucket An early type of jazz characterized by a strong beat and rollicking delivery, similar to barrelhouse.

harmonic series A series of tones consisting of a fundamental tone and the overtones produced by it, and whose frequencies are consecutive integral multiples of the frequency of the fundamental.

harmony One of the basic elements of music involving the relationship of notes and chord progression.

heavy metal A ponderous rock form characterized by brittle, flashy guitar work, unnaturally high-pitched male vocals and an adolescent fascination with the darker side of human experience. Born in the late 1960s of bands such as Deep Purple and Black Sabbath, heavy metal is currently

associated with bands such as Metallica, and MTV's Beavis and Butthead. Also called **metal** and **speed metal**.

hip-hop The cultural context of rap music found in the urban style of dress, speech and art.

interval The distance on the scale between notes, usually measured in semitones.

jazz American music born in the early part of the century from African rhythms and slave chants. It has spread from its African-American roots to a worldwide audience. Jazz developed from early ensemble improvisation to big band swing to the soloing brilliance of bop to thorny atonality and back to the current re-articulation of melody and harmony.

key A scale of seven tones often found in the major or minor mode with a tonal center on the tonic or key note. Indicated in written music by its pattern of flats and sharps.

klezmer The Eastern European Jewish folk music played by small, traditionally itinerant bands, once played mostly at weddings, now increasingly popular concert music.

larghetto In a dignified style and slow tempo, usually considered to be slightly faster than largo but slower than adagio.

largo In a very slow tempo and with great dignity, usually considered to be slower than adagio.

madrigal A contrapuntal vocal composition for three or more voices, usually sung without accompaniment.

mbira An African instrument consisting of a hollow gourd or wooden resonator and a number of usually metal strips that vibrate when plucked.

melody One of the basic elements of music; a recognizable progression of notes that form a musical line.

meter The pattern of beats, organized in Western music into units of measure containing a set number of beats.

minimalism Contemporary music marked by extreme simplification of rhythms and patterns, prolonged chordal or melodic repetitions and often the achievement of a trancelike effect.

mode A scale, usually of five or seven notes. Most often used to indicate scales other than major or minor, for example, Dorian, Lydian or Mixolydian.

REFERENCE

modulation The movement from one key to another.

natural A note that is not sharped or flatted.

note The name given, in letters from A to G, of a particular pitch.

octave The musical interval in which the pitch of a note doubles, representing the eighth step in a scale. A note remains the same in each octave while the pitch changes in each octave.

orchestration The assignment of written music to particular instruments or sections of an orchestra.

organum Vocal polyphonic music, in two, three or four parts, of the 9th to the early 13th century.

passacaglia A musical form of the 17th and 18th centuries consisting of continuous variations on a ground bass in 3/4 time and similar to the chaconne.

passing note A note that is not part of a particular chord but is placed between two chords to provide a smooth melodic transition from one to the other. Also called passing tone.

piano The indication for a soft passage.

pitch The frequency of vibrations of a tone.

plainsong Monophonic music, including Gregorian chant, employed by the Catholic Church during the Middle Ages.

polyphony The combination of two or more melodic lines.

polyrhythm The simultaneous combination of different meters in one composition, employed by modernist composers and found in the music of Africa and Latin America.

punk A rock form characterized by aggressive volume, short, angry vocals and often bitter political or hopeless emotional content. Born as a reaction to the bland, corporate rock of the 1970s. Early exponents of punk include Sex Pistols, The Clash, The Ramones and The Buzzcocks. Punk's recent revival is attributed to the dominance of sound-alike "alternative" bands.

raga A traditional form in Hindu music, consisting of a theme that expresses an aspect of religious feeling and sets forth a tonal system on which variations are improvised within a framework of progressions, melodic formulas and rhythmic patterns.

ragtime A style of jazz with elaborately syncopated rhythm in the melody and a steadily accented accompaniment.

rap Urban, typically African-American music that features spoken lyrics, often reflecting current social or political issues, over a background of sampled sounds or scratched records.

reggae Popular music of Jamaican origin having elements of Calypso, soul and rock and characterized by a strongly accentuated offbeat.

rest A pause in the music for an indicated number of beats.

rhythm One of the basic elements of music, a pattern in a composition formed by a series of long and short tones in a given amount of time.

rhythm and blues The all-encompassing term used to describe the African-American wellspring of postwar popular music. From rhythm and blues has come rock, soul, funk, rap and regional and stylistic offshoots. Critics consider rhythm and blues's birth to coincide with the decline of big bands and jazz's turn toward the bop emphasis on soloing. Rhythm and blues retained an emphasis on vocals while adding a more pronounced beat characteristic of the blues.

riff n. A repeated rhythmic or melodic phrase in jazz or pop.
v. To improvise on a melodic or rhythmic theme.

rock Perhaps the most popular form of 20th-century music, a combination of African-American rhythms, urban blues, folk and country music of the rural South. It has developed since the early 1950s into hundreds of subgenres, each with its own audience, record labels and radio formats. Though for the first three decades of its existence, each generation seemed to recreate rock music for itself, rock currently seems to be in a baroque phase of restatement and an ornamentation of previous achievements.

salsa A popular form of Latin-American dance music, characterized by Afro-Caribbean rhythms, Cuban big-band dance melodies and elements of jazz and rock.

scale An arrangement of notes in intervals that indicate a key or mode.

score The written form of a musical composition either complete or for an individual part.

scratching To manipulate a record rhythmically on a turntable creating background sound. It is often used in rap music.

sharp The indication that a note is to be raised by a semitone.

ska A brisk form of Jamaican-born rock derived from reggae and rock energy. It was popularized in the early 1980s by British "black-and-white" multiracial bands that formed a lighter faction of the punk movement.

skiffle Folk music played by performers who use unconventional instruments, such as kazoos, washboards or jugs.

soca A West Indian style of music that is a blend of soul and calypso.

sonata A multimovement instrumental composition for one or more solo instruments.

soul The name for a type of rhythm and blues built on elements of gospel and spiritual music. Often, practitioners such as Sam Cooke, maintained two careers simultaneously in gospel and popular music.

string quartet 1. A chamber music ensemble consisting of two violins, a viola and a cello. 2. The music written for such a group.

symphony 1. A sonata for orchestra. 2. Any large-scale work for orchestra.

tempo The speed of a basic beat pattern.

tempered scale A scale, as the chromatic scale, in which all notes are an equal distance apart.

theremin An electronic instrument that creates eerie effects and is played by moving the hands near its two antennas.

timbre The quality of a sound that distinguishes it from other sounds of the same pitch and volume.

vamp The repeated phrase in jazz or pop over which an instrument or vocalist solos.

zydeco Music of Louisiana's bayous that blends Cajun rhythms with rhythm and blues. Instrumentation includes washboards and accordions, though more generally electric instruments. Clifton Chenier is an early example of a zydeco musician. Boozoo Chavis currently reigns as king.

TV&
Radio

The X–Files

Lisa Marie &
Michael,
PrimeTime Live

Prime
Suspect

ER

Reality Bites

Media Person, aka Lewis Grossberger, writes a weekly column for *MediaWeek* magazine and is the author of *Read My Clips: Media Person Cuts Up.*

■ BY LEWIS GROSSBERGER

I**T'S NEVER EASY TO PREDICT THE FUTURE,** but if Media Person had to, he'd guess that the 1994–1995 television season will be remembered as the year of O.J. and *ER*. Which is to say that nothing of earth-shaking significance occurred on the tube.

As usual. Little ever does, since television in the United States is used mainly for two purposes: 1. Making more money for people who already have a lot of it, and 2. Keeping the rest of us amused and indoors. It does both well, though we are often loath to admit it in the case of No. 2.

TELEVISION

Without a doubt, the most amusing, thus unforgettable, show on TV all decade was the famous low-speed chase in which celebrity murder suspect O.J. Simpson and the faithful driver of his white Ford Bronco, Al Cowlings, led a phalanx of cop cars over the Los Angeles freeway system for several suspenseful hours. Camcopters shot from on high and electrified viewers all over the country phoned their friends and cried, "Are you watching this?"

"Unbelievable!," came the typical reply.

The dreamlike, surreal episode made for a great show, the kind of show only television can present, the most memorable live TV drama since Ruby shot Oswald, and yet it was unscheduled, unsponsored, unwritten, unedited, ran only once and didn't win a single post-season award.

More important, it marked the beginning of O.J. Simpson's yearlong domination of the nation's favorite appliance. Soon came the spinoff, *The O.J. Trial.* This epic maxiseries made stars of schizoid California Judge Lance Ito (sometimes lenient, sometimes stern), prosecutor Marcia Clark, defense lawyers Robert Shapiro and Johnnie Cochran, allegedly racist LAPD detective Mark Fuhrman and professional houseguest Brian (Kato) Kaelin, who later

O.J. Simpson

Chicago Hope

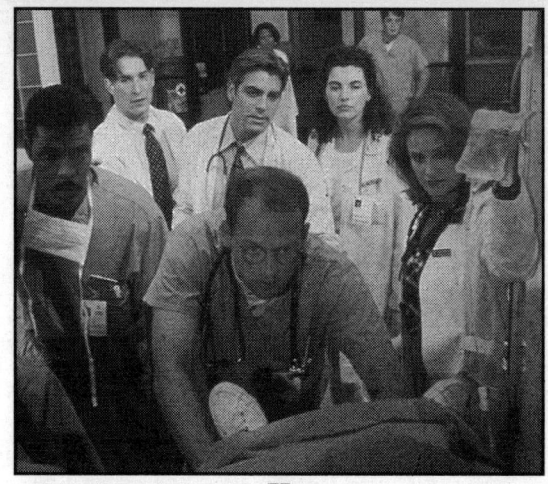

ER

graduated to a book deal and a radio show. The O.J. saga took up more airtime on the nightly newscasts of the three major networks than any other news event. It provided crates of low-budget programming and made millions for the Courtroom Television Network and CNN and more important, gave the average citizen a new understanding of and contempt for American jurisprudence. Viewers saw Cochran calling Clark hysterical and Clark calling Cochran a sexist while Judge Ito gazed passively on. They witnessed the six-day cross-examination of a lowly functionary whose job was bagging crime-scene evidence. The double murder at the heart of the case seemed long forgotten, and no observer could ever again view a courtroom without a powerful desire to retch.

Gory wounds, which figured prominently in the plot of *The O.J. Trial*, were also a staple of *ER*, a runaway hit from the moment it debuted on NBC. Thoughtful, discerning viewers (i.e., Media Person) were surprised to find themselves hooked on *ER*, rather than CBS's rival hospital drama, *Chicago Hope*. The latter boasted established stars and the battle-tested brain of David E. Kelley, who for several seasons had masterminded *L.A. Law*, a show both literate and popular. *ER* offered a mostly unknown cast, often predictable plotting and sometimes pedestrian dialogue and acting.

What made all that irrelevant was its creators' exquisite sense of pace. Just as *Rowan and Martin's Laugh-In* had pseudo-revolutionized TV comedy in the '70s by ratcheting up vaudeville jokes and skits to warp speed, *ER* retooled the hoary hospital-drama format by flinging in the viewer's face a weekly hour of rat-a-tat editing and dizzying, nerve-jangling motion (plus the fun of a bloody life-and-death soap opera). Gurneys fly down crowded hallways propelled by sprinting interns frantically shouting indecipherable commands to nurses as arteries spurt and the camera whirls and darts in. Then before you're even sure what disease the patient has, you're jerked into a different chaos in another hellish part of the thrill-a-minute hospital.

Chicago Hope was classical; *ER* was rock and roll. It set a record as the highest rated first-year series on TV, and remained the nation's top-ranked show through much of the season, earning 20 Emmy nominations. *Chicago Hope* limped off to another night to bandage its wounds.

Seinfeld

Meanwhile, it seemed as though the rest of network prime time was clogged with cute, young, wise-cracking urbanoids. This was primarily the fault of *Seinfeld*. That show had decisively captured America's 18 to 45-year-old money spenders, so its aura of casual, quirky, young, smart-ass, coed palhood was furiously replicated. *Ellen* was *Seinfeld* with a woman. *Mad About You* was *Seinfeld* with a marriage license. *Friends* was *Seinfeld* with non-Jews. None was quite as funny or inventive but then

Ricki Lake

again, neither was *Seinfeld*, which began to show subtle but unmistakable signs of series fatigue.

If nighttime had moved upscale with smart, hip sitcoms, daytime was sliding dramatically toward the nether regions. Once game shows dominated, then soaps. Now arose the talk show, a genre not only rapidly proliferating but undergoing an ominous change. Previously, it had been enough to present America's saddest cases: the abused and confused, the neurotic and psychotic, the addicted and afflicted, the dejected and rejected, the dumb and dumber. Now, given the increased competition, it became necessary to add conflict and confrontation. Tormentor and tormented, perp and vic, Christian and lion were hauled under the bright lights and, egged on by a howling studio audience, thrown together in screaming combat.

The pioneer here was the show named after Ricki Lake, a formerly rotund actress who had achieved renown in the realm of weight loss. Lake doubled her ratings and leaped to second place in the talk-show pack (after *Oprah*) by featuring young people with screwed-up relationships who were encouraged to shout and growl at each other. The competition was quick to copy, and daytime soon became a seething mass of trailer trash and ghetto goons ranting out their dysfunctional disputes and angst while the spectators hooted and cheered. An apotheosis of some sort was finally reached when one guest of the *Jenny Jones Show* shot and killed another (not on the show itself, though that wouldn't have surprised anyone) after the latter had revealed he had a crush on the former, who apparently disapproved of overt homosexual longing. This set off a burst of media consternation. "Are Talk Shows Out of Control?," the headlines brayed insistently for the week or so before the furor blew over and daytime TV reverted to business as usual.

Connie Chung

Another major headline frenzy followed the messy parting of CBS and its star anchor, Connie Chung. For two years, Chung had coanchored with Dan Rather the *CBS Evening News*. Network panjandrums had hoped that the popular and amiable Chung would help the show's ratings as well as unchain Rather from his anchor desk now and then to ramble off and play reporter, a role dear to his heart. But the show slipped to No. 3 in the ratings, and people kept carping about how stiff and ill at ease the two were together. "No chemistry," was the damning consensus.

Dan Rather

Worse for CBS's hopes, Chung got into embarrassing on-air pickles and did low-class celebrity interviews (including several O.J.-related ones) that damaged her already shaky image. Network anchors are supposed to have "gravitas" — a quality that prevents one from breaking out in giggles at inappropriate moments — whereas Chung was suspected of lightweight tendencies. Indeed, the dread word "tabloid" was sometimes hurled in her direction. Most notorious was her interview with the mother of Newt Gingrich, the speaker of the House, who blurted out, after what seemed to many viewers like an undue amount of coy cajolery by Chung, that her son had once described the first lady, Hillary Rodham Clinton, as "a bitch." Well! Consternation swept the land.

The denouement came when Chung was dispatched to Oklahoma City to cover the bombing of the federal office building there. Rather was reportedly peeved that he hadn't gotten the call, despite being on vacation at the time. Furthermore, some of Chung's ad-lib remarks offended the locals and she had to apologize. Shortly thereafter, CBS informed Chung she was being demoted. She quit, demanded the $2 million remaining on her contract and charged the network with sexist motives.

This was just what CBS didn't need at the moment: more trouble. The once lustrous "Tiffany network" was already badly tarnished. The *New York Times* pronounced it "in bad, perhaps desperate shape." CBS's feeble programming and hapless executives had become the frequent target of David Letterman monologues. It had not created a single breakout hit in the '90s. It had lost several affiliates. Ratings were down for both news and entertainment shows. And there were persistent rumors that CBS's owner, Laurence Tisch, was trying to sell the network. Even worse, there were persistent rumors that no one wanted to buy until Westinghouse followed fellow appliance manufacturer General Electric into the network fray. Though most observers failed to credit Chung's sexism charges, the media consensus was that CBS had been guilty of mismanaging her career by trying to position her simultaneously as serious newsperson and celebrity chaser and of hiring her for all the wrong reasons in the first place. Ultimately, the episode served mainly as another emblem of the network's pathetic state.

And who was luring away those deserting CBS affiliates? The upstart Fox network, commanded by would-be planetary ruler of all media Rupert Murdoch, who is dedicated to the proposition that Youth Must Be Served. But with the 1994–1995 season came a new wrinkle. Added to the familiar Fox staples of racy sitcoms and even racier hunk-and-babe melodramas was an onslaught of the

1994 GOLDEN GLOBE AWARDS

The 52nd Golden Globe Awards honoring excellence in film and television were presented January 21, 1995 at Los Angeles's Beverly Hilton Hotel.

TELEVISION AWARDS

Best Television Series
The X-Files (Fox)

Best Actor in a Drama
Dennis Franz, NYPD Blue

Best Actress in a Drama
Claire Danes, My So-Called Life

Best Series, Musical or Comedy (tie)
Frasier (NBC)
Mad About You (NBC)

Best Actor, Musical or Comedy
Tim Allen, Home Improvement

Best Actress, Musical or Comedy
Helen Hunt, Mad About You

Best Miniseries or Movie Made for Television
The Burning Season (HBO)

Best Actor in a Miniseries or Movie Made for Television
Raul Julia, The Burning Season

Best Actress in a Miniseries or Movie Made for Television
Joanne Woodward, Breathing Lessons: A Hallmark Hall of Fame Presentation

Best Supporting Actor in a Series, Miniseries or Movie Made for Television
Edward James Olmos, The Burning Season

Best Supporting Actress in a Series, Miniseries or Movie Made for Television
Miranda Richardson, Fatherland

Oustanding Directorial Achievement in a Musical or Variety Special
Dwight Hemion, Barbra Streisand: The Concert

Outstanding Directorial Achievement in a Daytime Drama
Jesus Salvador Trevino, P.O.W.E.R.: The Eddie Matos Story

The X-Files

The DGA Awards, which honor excellence in film and television direction, were announced in bi-coastal ceremonies at Los Angeles's Beverly Hilton Hotel and New York's Marriott Marquis on March 11, 1995. Here are the television awards.

Outstanding Directorial Achievement in a Dramatic Special
Rod Holcomb, *ER:* pilot

Outstanding Directorial Achievement in a Dramatic Series
Charles Haid, *ER:* "Into That Good Night"

Outstanding Directorial Achievement in a Comedy Series
David Lee, *Frasier:* "The Matchmaker"

Outstanding Directorial Achievement in a Musical or Variety Special
Dwight Hemion, *Barbra Streisand: The Concert*

Outstanding Directorial Achievement in a Daytime Drama
Jesus Salvador Trevino, *P.O.W.E.R.: The Eddie Matos Story*

1994 GEORGE FOSTER PEABODY AWARDS

The annual Peabody Awards, administered by the University of Georgia's Henry W. Grady College of Journalism and Mass Communication, honor excellence in both radio and television broadcasting.

RADIO AWARDS
Tobacco Stories (NPR)

Schizophrenia: Voices of an Illness (Lichtenstein Creative Media, New York, NY)

Wade in the Water: African-American Sacred Music Traditions (NPR and the Smithsonian Institution)

D-Day and 50 Years (WVXU-FM, Cincinnati, OH)

The Rise and Fall of Vee-Jay (WRKS-FM, New York, NY)

Fascinatin' Rhythm (WXXI-FM, Rochester, NY)

TELEVISION AWARDS
PrimeTime Live: "Rush to Read" (ABC)

CBS Reports: "D-Day" (CBS)

Rwanda (KGO-TV, San Francisco, CA)

The Atomic Bombshell (KSEE-TV, Fresno, CA)

Fat Chance (National Film Board of Canada)

Sewer Solvent Scandal (KGAN-TV, Cedar Rapids, IA)

---

eerie: science-fiction shows.

In its second season, *The X-Files*, the fastest growing show on TV, levitated from cult fave to certified major hit. And this despite its having two of the most depressed stars ever glimpsed, the glum FBI agents Fox (!) Mulder and Dana Sculley (David Duchovny and Gillian Anderson), permanently pounding the weirdness beat and apparently without a Prozac tablet between them. Talk about tabloid television! Every supernatural tabloid favorite from alien UFO pilots to yetis in the woods bedevil Sculley and Mulder, while a sinister conspiracy within the FBI constantly thwarts their efforts to bring the various boogie men to official notice — just like real life! About the only traditional tabloid menace left for them to encounter is Elvis, and Media Person has no doubt he will turn up soon.

Fox tried to reproduce *The X-Files*'s success by cobbling together two new sci-fi shows, *Sliders* (physics geek discovers a gateway to parallel universes) and *V.R. 5* (sexy blond computer hacker discovers a gateway to other people's subconscious minds), but both died even though the latter, starring Daryl Hannah look-alike Lori Singer, offered a touch of psychological complexity, some imaginative, surreal fantasy images and a running mystery involving her late — or was he? — father.

Of course, canceling high-quality programming is a wonderful old television tradition. Frequently, the best shows in any given season are those killed, those limping along on anemic ratings, waiting to be put out of their misery or those eking out obscure lives on the margins of the medium. The classic example this year was *My So-Called Life*, one of the best dramas in television history. This nonviolent, laugh-trackless ABC series limned the life and times of a smart and sensitive, though often confused and tormented, i.e. typical, 15-year-old girl played by a talented newcomer, Claire Danes. It regularly delivered poignant, sometimes hard-edged truths about contemporary teenage life in America. And it died, despite write-in and on-line campaigns by hard-core fans and the showcasing of reruns on MTV.

A more successful show, if only because

on cable it could thrive with a smaller audience, was *Absolutely Fabulous,* a BBC hit snatched up by Comedy Central. This rollicking sitcom braved a risky genre the Brits seem to excel in and the American networks fear: the show featuring an unsympathetic, perhaps even monstrous protagonist. *Ab Fab,* as it became known, starred two female reprobates, middle-aged pals who are totally irresponsible, grotesquely self-centered, slaves to every passing fashion, sex-crazed and given to abusing any and all substances. They frequently tumble down stairs, out of cars and even into open graves at funerals. It was hilarious, funnier than anything on the networks, with the possible exception of the long-running, subversive cartoon series, *The Simpsons.*

Other things happened on television, but they were of no importance. For instance, two new networks, UPN and WB, premiered with a panoply of new shows. No one watched.

Off television was another story.

In Washington, right-wing members of Congress were working hard to annihilate public television by cutting off government funding. They admonished PBS officials to go out and pay their own way as any other organization (though not Congress, of course) must. This, unfortunately, was impossible without destroying public television, since the whole point of the institution was to provide Americans with programming that doesn't attract advertisers and thus doesn't get on the commercial stations. The same legislators were also busily trying to pass a new telecommunications deregulation bill that would, among other things, permit cable companies to raise their rates, make it harder for TV stations to lose their licenses and help big companies form juicy new monopolies. Inevitably, such developments off the tube would be bound to affect what is put on the tube and hardly for the public interest. But for the moment, so long as no one interrupted their favorite shows, most of the viewers hardly cared. They wanted only to be amused. ∎

The American Experience: The Battle of the Bulge (WGBH-TV, Boston, MA)

Just Because: Tales of Violence, Dreams of Peace (KSBW-TV, Salinas, CA)

20/20: "The Hunger Inside" (ABC)

The American Experience: FDR (WGBH-TV, Boston, MA)

Normandy: The Great Crusade (Discovery Communications, Bethesda, MD)

China: Beyond the Clouds (WETA, Washington D.C. and Channel 4, London, England)

The American Experience: Malcolm X: Make It Plain (WGBH-TV, Boston, MA)

Buddy Check 12 (WTLV-TV, Jacksonville, FL)

Reflections on Elephants (National Geographic Television, Washington D.C., for the Public Broadcasting Service)

Fourways Farm (Channel 4, London, England)

Break the Silence: Kids Against Child Abuse (CBS)

Nick News (Nickelodeon)

ER (NBC)

American Playhouse: Armistead Maupin's Tales of the City (Channel 4, London, England)

Frasier (NBC)

MTV Unplugged (MTV)

Mad About You (NBC)

Barbra Streisand: The Concert (HBO)

Moon Shot (Turner Entertainment Networks)

1994–1995 DAYTIME EMMY AWARDS

The 1994–1995 Daytime Emmy Awards were presented May 21, 1995 at New York's Marriott Marquis. Here is a partial list of winners.

Outstanding Children's Series
Nick News (Nickelodeon)

Outstanding Children's Special
A Child Betrayed: The Calvin Mire Story (HBO)

Outstanding Animated Program
Where on Earth Is Carmen Sandiego? (PBS)

Outstanding Game/Audience Participation Show
Jeopardy (Syndicated)

Outstanding Talk/Service Show
Oprah Winfrey Show (Syndicated)

1994–1995 Prime-Time Broadcast Television Premieres

ALL AMERICAN GIRL

ABC
Fall Debut
Wednesday
8:30–9:00 P.M.
Cast: Margaret Cho, Jodi Long, Clyde Kusatsu, B.D. Wong, J.B. Quon and Amy Hill
A young, Korean-American college graduate (Cho) tries to balance her contemporary American lifestyle with the Korean traditions her immigrant parents encourage.

AMAZING GRACE

NBC
Spring Mid-Season Debut
Saturday 8:00–9:00 P.M.
Cast: Patty Duke, Joe Spano, Dan Lauria, Robin Gammell, Lorraine Toussaint, Gavin Harrison, Marguerite Moreau and Justin Garms
A pill-popping, emergency-room nurse (Duke) encounters a near-death experience that convinces her it's time to make some major changes in her life. The divorced mother of two takes up the cloth and faces new responsibilities and pressures as an ordained minister.

THE BOYS ARE BACK

CBS
Fall Debut
Wednesday 8:00–8:30 P.M.; moved to Saturday 9:00–9:30 P.M. spring season; on hiatus spring mid-season
Cast: Hal Linden, Suzanne Pleshette, Kevin Crowley, George Newbern and Bess Meyer
When Fred (Linden) and Jackie (Pleshette) Hansen send their youngest son off to college they think they finally have the house to themselves. Their hopes are soon dashed when two of their sons, a daughter-in-law and three grandchildren move in with them.

BLUE SKIES

ABC
Fall Debut
Monday 8:30–9:00 P.M.; on hiatus fall season
Cast: Matt Roth, Corey Parker and Julia Campbell
Two friends (Roth and Parker), partners in a mail-order business, fall in love with the Harvard MBA (Campbell) they hire to boost flagging sales.

CHICAGO HOPE

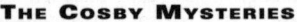

CBS
Fall Debut
Thursday 10:00–11:00 P.M.; moved to Monday 10:00–11:00 P.M. spring season
Cast: Mandy Patinkin, Adam Arkin, E.G. Marshall, Roxanne Hart, Peter MacNicol, Roma Maffia and Hector Elizondo
Personal and professional dramas unfold within the halls of the high-profile Chicago Hope Hospital where the renowned doctors and surgeons are as protective of their reputations as they are of their patients.

THE COSBY MYSTERIES

NBC
Fall Debut
Wednesday 8:00–9:00 P.M.
Cast: Bill Cosby, James Naughton, Rita Moreno, Lynn Whitfield and Dante Beze
When forensics expert Guy Hanks (Cosby) wins the New York lottery, he takes early retirement but is lured back into the criminal-investigation field when he finds he can't stay away from crime solving.

THE CRITIC

Fox
Spring Mid-Season Debut
Sunday 8:30–9:00 P.M.; on hiatus late spring
Formerly on ABC
Voices of: Jon Lovitz, Park Overall, Judith Ivey, Gerrit Graham, Nancy Cartwright, Christine Cavanaugh, Kath Soucie, Maurice LaMarche and Nick Jameson
Jay Sherman (voice of Lovitz), a bitter New York film critic, loathes the movies he reviews for the cable television show *Coming Attractions* almost as much as he hates being unattached. Sherman's critiques, including *Dennis the Menace II Society* and *The Nightmare Before Hanukkah*, parody real-life films.

CYBILL

CBS
Spring Debut
Monday 9:30–10:00 P.M.
Cast: Cybill Sheperd, Alan Rosenberg, Tom Wopat, Christine Baranski, Dedee Pfeiffer and Alicia Witt
Fortysomething, stop-start actress Cybill (Shepherd) leads a roller-coaster life complicated by her eccentric family: Her two ex-husbands still love her and are very involved in her life, her conservative daughter is pregnant and her other, 16-year-old daughter drives her crazy.

DADDY'S GIRLS

CBS
Fall Debut
Wednesday 8:30–9:00 P.M.; canceled fall season
Cast: Dudley Moore, Stacy Galina, Meredith Scott Lynn, Keri Russell, Harvey Fierstein, Alan Ruck and Phil Buckman
Dudley Walker (Moore) struggles to put his life back together after his wife and his business partner leave him for each other. His life is further challenged when his three daughters step in to help him but rely on him for help with their problems.

DOUBLE RUSH

CBS
Spring Debut
Wednesday 9:00–9:30 P.M.; moved to 8:30–9:00 P.M. mid-season
Cast: Robert Pastorelli, David Arquette, Corinne Bohrer, Adam Goldberg, D.L. Hughley, Phil Leeds and Sam Lloyd
Johnny Verona (Pastorelli), a 1960s rock star who almost made it big, owns a struggling Manhattan bicycle messenger service. Verona plays father figure to his employees, who range from a 75-year-old career messenger to a Harvard Business School graduate.

DREAM ON

Fox
Spring Debut
Sunday 9:30–10:00 P.M.
Cast: Brian Benben, Wendie Malick, Denny Dillon and Chris Demetral
An HBO series edited and adapted for broadcast television
New York book editor Martin Tupper (Benben), a divorced single father, tries to manage his career, care for his son and reenter the dating scene. Clips from old movies and television shows intrude on TV-weaned Tupper's feelings and thoughts.

DUE SOUTH

CBS
Fall Debut
Thursday 8:00–9:00 P.M.
Cast: Paul Gross and David Marciano
Personalities clash when nice-guy Canadian mountie Constable Fraser (Gross) is assigned to work with street-smart Detective Vecchio (Marciano) at Chicago's Canadian consulate.

EARTH 2

NBC
Fall Debut
Sunday 7:00–8:00 P.M.
Cast: Tim Curry, Antonio Sabato, Jr., Jessica Steen, Terry O'Quinn, Debrah Farentino, Clancy Brown, J. Madison

Wright, Rockmond Dunbar, Sullivan Walker, LaTanya Richardson, Joey Zimmerman, Rebecca Gayheart and John Gegenhuber
Set 200 years in the future, a group of humans led by Devon Adair (Farentino) leave their space station to establish an alternative civilization, Earth 2. Mystical events, menacing creatures and personal squabbles threaten their progress.

ER

NBC
Fall Debut
Thursday 10:00–11:00 P.M.
Cast: Anthony Edwards, George Clooney, Sherry Stringfield, Noah Wyle and Eriq LaSalle
Young, overworked emergency-room residents of General Memorial Hospital daily face life-and-death decisions and cope with their own personal traumas. *ER*, an instant smash hit, made history as the highest-rated, first-year show.

THE FIVE MRS. BUCHANANS

CBS
Fall Debut
Saturday 9:00–9:30 P.M.; moved to 9:30–10:00 P.M. spring season
Cast: Eileen Heckart, Judith Ivey, Beth Broderick, Harriet Sansom Harris and Charlotte Ross
Four women, all married to a Buchanan brother, develop unlikely friendships while trying to contend with their overbearing mother-in-law.

EXTREME

ABC
Spring Debut
Thursday 8:00–9:00 P.M.
Cast: James Brolin, Tom Wright, Cameron Bancroft, Elizabeth Gracen, Justin Lazar, Jule Bowen, Micah Dyer and Danny Masterson
The Steep Mountain Rescue Group, a search-and-rescue team, will tackle any obstacle — from treacherous white water to ice-covered moun-

1995 CableACE Awards

The 1995 CableACE Awards were presented in two ceremonies in Los Angeles: January 13, 1995 at the Century Plaza Hotel and January 15, 1995 at the Wiltern Theater.

Movie or Miniseries
Cracker: To Say I Love You (A&E Network)

Actor in a Movie or Miniseries
Robbie Coltrane, *Cracker: To Say I Love You*

Actress in a Movie or Miniseries
Amy Madigan, *And Then There Was One*

Supporting Actor in a Movie or Miniseries
Ian McKellan, *And the Band Played On*

Supporting Actress in a Movie or Miniseries
Ja'net DuBois, *Other Women's Children*

Directing in a Movie or Miniseries
Andy Wilson, *Cracker: To Say I Love You*

Writing in a Movie or Miniseries
Arnold Schulman, *And the Band Played On*

Direction of Photography and/or Lighting Direction in a Dramatic or Theatrical Special, Movie or Miniseries
Kenneth MacMillan, *Zelda*

Art Direction in a Dramatic Special or Series, Theatrical Special, Movie or Miniseries
David Crank and Paul J. Peters, *Heart of Darkness*

Editing a Dramatic Special or Series, Theatrical Special, Movie or Miniseries
Michael Ornstein, *Amelia Earhart: The Final Flight*

Makeup
Karen Stephens and Ron Wild, *Adventures in Wonderland*

Costume Design
Thierry Bosquet, *Capriccio*

Comedy Special
Merry Christmas, Mr. Bean (HBO)

Stand-up Comedy Special
HBO Comedy Half-Hour: "Chris Rock" (HBO)

Performance in a Comedy Special
Tracey Ullman, *Tracey Ullman: Takes on New York*

Directing a Comedy Special
John Birkin, *Merry Christmas, Mr. Bean*

---

tains — to save people caught in life-threatening situations. Call it the *Baywatch* of the mountains.

FORTUNE HUNTER
Fox
Fall Debut
Sunday 7:00–8:00 P.M.; canceled fall season
Cast: Mark Frankel and John Robert Hoffman
Agent-for-hire Carlton Dial (Frankel), a former government spy, specializes in recovering much-sought-after items such as classified information, weapons systems and endangered species. With the help of computer wizard Harry Flack (Hoffman), Dial maintains a perfect record.

FRIENDS
NBC
Fall Debut
Thursday 8:30–9:00 P.M.;
moved to 9:30–10:00 P.M.
spring season
Cast: Jennifer Aniston,
Courteney Cox, Lisa
Kudrow, Matt LeBlanc,
Matthew Perry and
David Schwimmer

Six twentysomething friends living in Manhattan look to each other for advice and comic relief while struggling with career frustration and troubled love lives. Amazingly, none of the beautiful characters have become romantically involved with each other.

THE GEORGE WENDT SHOW
CBS
Spring Mid-Season Debut
Wednesday 8:00–8:30 P.M.
Cast: George Wendt and Pat Finn
Wendt and his brother (Finn) host a radio show, *Points and Plugs,* dispensing automotive advice to callers from their repair shop. The show is loosely based on National Public Radio's *Cartalk* hosted by Tom and Ray Magliozzi.

GET SMART
Fox
Spring Debut
Sunday 7:30–8:00 P.M.; on hiatus mid-season
Cast: Don Adams, Andy Dick, Barbara Feldon and Elaine Hendrix
The special agents of the 1960s are back, this time with their son Zach (Dick), solving cases with high-tech gadgets.

HARDBALL
Fox
Fall Debut
Sunday 8:30–9:00 P.M.; canceled fall season
Cast: Bruce Greenwood, Mike Starr, Joe Rogan, Chris Browning, Dann Florek and Alexandra Wentworth

The players and management of the Pioneers, a major-league baseball team, let their conflicts and often offensive idiosyncrasies go wild in this locker-room look at baseball.

HOPE AND GLORIA
NBC
Spring Mid-Season Debut
Thursday 8:30–9:00 P.M.
Cast: Cynthia Stevenson, Jessica Lundy, Alan Thicke and Enrico Colantoni
Hope (Stevenson) and Gloria (Lundy) live in the same Philadelphia brownstone, work together on a talk 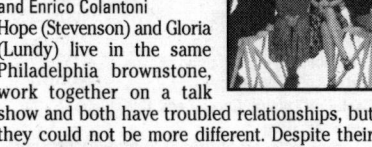 show and both have troubled relationships, but they could not be more different. Despite their personality differences, the women find they can turn to each other for advice and support.

HOUSE OF BUGGIN'
Fox
Spring Debut
Sunday 8:30–9:00 P.M.; on hiatus mid-season; returned late spring
Cast: John Leguizamo, Jorge Luis Abreu, Waleska Coindet, Tammi Cubilette, Yelba Osorio, Sixto Ramos, Luis Guzman, Rosie Perez, Fisher Stevens, Reid Asato, George K. Gee, William E. Massof and Andrew Pappas
The Latino equivalent of *In Living Color*, the *House of Buggin'* ensemble cast parodies contemporary urban life and popular culture.

IN THE HOUSE
NBC
Spring Mid-Season Debut
Monday 8:30–9:00 P.M.
Cast: Debbie Allen, L.L. Cool J, Lisa Arrindell, Maia Campbell, Jeffrey Wood and Arva Holt
A mother of two (Allen), forced back to work after her husband cleans her out in a messy divorce, relies on her football-star landlord Marion (Cool J) to baby-sit her children.

LEGEND
UPN
Spring Mid-Season Debut
Tuesday 8:00–9:00 P.M.
Cast: Richard Dean Anderson, John de Lancie, Mark Adair Rios, Stephanie Beacham, Katherine Moffat and Bob Balaban
Hard-drinking dime novelist Ernest Pratt (Anderson) pens western adventure books that readers believe are nonfiction. With the help of eccentric inventor Janos Bartok (de Lancie), Pratt reluctantly assumes the role of his fictional hero Nicodemus Legend.

Writing an Entertainment Special
Drew Carey, *Drew Carey: Human Cartoon*

Entertainment Host
Bill Maher, *Politically Incorrect*

Comedy Series
The Larry Sanders Show (HBO)

Stand-up Comedy Series
Caroline's Comedy Hour (A&E Network)

Actor in a Comedy Series
Rip Torn, *The Larry Sanders Show*

Actress in a Comedy Series
Denny Dillon, *Dream On*

Directing in a Comedy Series
Todd Holland, *The Larry Sanders Show:*
  "Hank's Night in the Sun"

Writing in a Comedy Series
Peter Tolan, *The Larry Sanders Show:*
  "Hank's Night in the Sun"

Art Direction in a Comedy or Music Special or Series
Roy Bennett, *1993 MTV Video Music Awards*

Editing a Comedy or Music Special or Series
Craig Ridenour, *Dream On:* "Silent Night, Holy Cow"

International Dramatic or Comedy Special or Series, Movie or Miniseries
Whose Line Is It Anyway? (Comedy Central)

Sports Information Special
Outside the Lines: Ali — Still the Greatest (ESPN)

Sports Information Series
The Sporting Life With Jim Huber (CNN)

Sports Event Coverage Special
NHL Stanley Cup Finals (ESPN)

Sports Events Coverage Series
New York Rangers Hockey (Madison Square Garden Network)

Sports News Series
NFL Game Day (ESPN)

Sports Host
Chris Berman, *NFL Game Day, Sunday Night NFL Halftime, SportsCenter* and *The Nickname Show*

Sports Play-by-Play Announcer
Marv Albert, New York Knicks Basketball

Sports Commentator/Analyst
Dick Vitale, NCAA Basketball

Directing a Live Sports Event Coverage, Special or Series
Doug Holmes, NHL Stanley Cup Finals

Children's Programming Special Six and Younger
The Tailor of Gloucester (Family Channel)

CONTINUED ON NEXT PAGE ▶

Children's Programming Series Six and Younger
Madeline (Family Channel)

Children's Programming Special Seven and Older
The Whipping Boy (Disney Channel)

Children's Programming Series Seven and Older
Chris Cross (Showtime)

Children's Educational or Informational Special or Series
The Incredible Voyage of Bill Pinckney
    (Disney Channel)

Animated Programming Special or Series
The Tale of Tom Kitten and Jemima Puddle-Duck
    (Family Channel)

International Children's Programming or Series
The Borrowers (TNT)

Writing a Children's Special or Series
Ken Sagoes, *On Promised Land*

Dramatic Series
Avonlea (Disney Channel)

Actor in a Dramatic Series
David Packer, *Big Al*

Actress in a Dramatic Series
Glenda Jackson, *The South Bank Show:*
    "The Secret Life of Arnold Bax"

Directing a Dramatic Series
Gary Fleder, *Tales From the Crypt:* "Forever
    Ambergris"

Writing a Dramatic Series
Heather Conkie, *Avonlea:* "Memento Mori"

**Direction of Photography and/or Lighting
Direction in a Comedy or Dramatic Series**
Rick Bota, *Tales From the Crypt*

Dramatic or Theatrical Special
A Life in the Theatre (TNT)

Music Special
Jackson Brown: Going Home (Disney Channel)

Music Series
MTV Unplugged (MTV)

Performance in a Music Special or Series
Barbra Streisand, *Barbra Streisand: The Concert*

**Direction of Photography and/or Lighting Direction
in a Comedy or Music Special**
Chas Herington, Peter Morse, Tim Phelps and Toby
    Phillips, *Madonna — Live Down Under: The
    Girlie Show*

Directing a Music Special or Series
Dwight Hemion and Barbra Streisand, *Barbra
    Streisand: The Concert*

MADMAN OF THE PEOPLE
NBC
Fall Debut
Thursday 9:30–10:00 P.M.; on hiatus spring season
Cast: Dabney Coleman, Cynthia Gibb, Concetta
Tomei, John Ales, Craig Bierko and Sasha Danziger
Satirical magazine columnist Jack Buckman
(Coleman) has a hard time answering to the new
publisher of his magazine, who happens to be
his daughter (Gibb).

M.A.N.T.I.S.
Fox
Fall Debut; on hiatus spring season
Friday 8:00–9:00 P.M.
Cast: Carl Lumbly, Roger Rees, Christopher Gartin
and Galyn Gorg
A paraplegic biophysicist (Lumbly) invents a
high-tech device, the exoskeleton, that gives
him the strength and agility to become Mantis, a
crime-fighting hero.

MARKER
UPN
Spring Debut
Tuesday 8:00–9:00 P.M.;
moved to Tuesday 9:00–10:00 P.M.
Cast: Richard Grieco, Gates McFadden, Andy
Bumatai and Keone Young
Richard DeMorra (Grieco) discovers that before
his estranged father died, he gave his friends
markers, which are promises to help them when-
ever in trouble. DeMorra moves to Hawaii and
begins to fulfill his father's commitments.

THE MARSHAL
ABC
Spring Debut
Saturday 10:00–11:00 P.M.
Cast: Jeff Fahey, Don S. Davis, Alan C. Peterson,
Duncan Fraser, Frank C. Turner, Nicholas Lea, Oliver
Becker, William MacDonald, Jennifer Clement and
Patricia Harras
U.S. Marshal Winston MacBride (Fahey) uses his
investigative skills, intelligence and intuition to
capture fugitives. His assignments require that
the devoted family man travel all over the coun-
try in pursuit of his quarry.

THE MARTIN SHORT SHOW
NBC
Fall Debut
Tuesday 8:30–9:00 P.M.; canceled fall season
Cast: Martin Short, Jan Hooks, Andrea Martin,
Noley Thornton and Zack Duhame
This television show-within-a-show starred Short,
a husband and father who stars in his own
comedy/variety series.

McKenna

ABC
Fall Debut
Thursday 9:00–10:00 P.M.; canceled fall season after three episodes
Cast: Chad Everett, Eric Close, Shawn Duff and Vinessa Shaw

Brick McKenna (Close) returns home after a two-year absence to help revitalize his demanding father's outdoor-tour business, which suffered when Brick's brother Guy was killed while leading a tour.

Me and the Boys

ABC
Fall Debut
Tuesday 8:30–9:00 P.M.; on hiatus spring season
Cast: Steve Harvey, Chaz Lamar Shepard, Wayne Collins, Benjamin LeVert and Madge Sinclair

A widower (Harvey), intent on keeping his three sons on the right track, uses his own unorthodox approach in raising them. His mother-in-law provides a tender and nurturing touch to the all-male household.

Medicine Ball

Fox
Spring Mid-Season Debut
Monday 9:00–10:00 P.M.
Cast: Jensen Daggett, Darryl Fong, Donal Logue, Harrison Pruett, Jeffrey D. Sams, Kai Soremekun, Vincent Ventresca and Sam McMurray

Five first-year residents bond as they struggle through long hours, stretches of sleepless days, high stress levels and junk-food diets. The senior residents hinder as much as they help the neophyte doctors.

Models Inc.

Fox
Fall Debut
Wednesday 9:00–10:00 P.M.; moved to Monday 9:00–10:00 P.M. spring season; on hiatus spring mid-season
Cast: Linda Gray, Kylie Travis, Cassidy Rae, Teresa Hill, Carrie Anne-Moss, Stephanie Romanov, Garcelle Beauvais, Cameron Daddo, Brian Gaskill and David Goldsmith

A spinoff of *Melrose Place*
Careers are made and hopes dashed in the cut-throat modeling industry, but the competition is even more fierce for the beautiful young women and men in Hillary Michaels's (Gray) Los Angeles Models Inc. agency.

Muscle

WB
Spring Debut
Wednesday 9:30–10:00 P.M.
Cast: Wendy Benson, Michael Boatman, Nestor Carbonell, Dan Gauthier, Stephen Henneberry, Shannon Kenny, Jerry Levine, Amy Pietz, Alan Ruck, T.E. Russell, Michole White, Adam West, Maree Cheatam, Jack Wallace, Brent Hinkley, Valorie Armstrong, Myra Turley, Lisa Coles and Alexander Polinsky

The stories and secrets of the vain and brawny

Original Song
Alan Bergman, Marilyn Bergman and Marvin Hamlisch, "Ordinary Miracle," *Barbra Streisand: The Concert*

Original Score
Patrick Williams, *Geronimo*

Entertainment/Cultural Documentary or Informational Special
All About Bette (TNT)

Environmental/Nature Documentary Special
National Geographic Explorer: "Antarctica: Life in the Freezer" (TBS)

Documentary Special
Gang War: Bangin' in Little Rock: America Undercover (HBO)

Documentary Series
Biography (A&E Network)

International Documentary Special
A Kid Called Troy (HBO)

International Documentary Series
Science Frontiers (The Learning Channel)

Informational or Documentary Host
Ed Feldman and Joe L'Erario, *Furniture to Go*

Directing a Documentary Special
Eitan Weinreich, *National Geographic Explorer:* "Life on the Line"

Writing a Documentary Special
Christopher Olgiati, *Southern Justice: The Murder of Medgar Evers: America Undercover*

Editing a Documentary Special or Series
Brian P. Forti, John Holtzman, Kevin C. Layne and Dana L. Perri, *Gloria Estefan: Mi Tierra — My Homeland*

News Special or Series
CNN Presents . . . Terror Nation? U.S. Creation? (CNN)

Extended News or Public Affairs Coverage
CNN's Coverage of the Los Angeles Earthquake (CNN)

Newscaster
Judy Woodruff, *Prime News*

Magazine Show Special or Series
National Geographic Explorer (TBS)

Magazine Host
Chuck Henry, *End of the Road*

Public Affairs Special or Series
Erase the Hate (USA)

International Informational Special or Series
Deadly Currents (Discovery Channel)

CONTINUED ON NEXT PAGE ▶

Business or Consumer Programming Special or Series
Investigative Reports: "Thalidomide: The Drug that Came Back" (A&E Network)

Educational or Instructional Special or Series
Southern Justice: The Murder of Medgar Evers: America Undercover (HBO)

Talk Show Series
Politically Incorrect (HBO)

Program Interviewer
Patrick Buchanan, Michael Kinsley and John Sununu, *Crossfire*

Cultural or Performing Arts Special or Series
The South Bank Show: "Sylvie Guillem" (BRAVO)

International Cultural, Performing Arts, Theatrical or Music Special or Series
Linda McCartney: Behind the Lens (A&E Network)

Variety Special or Series
Comic Relief VI (HBO)

Short-Form Programming Special
The Misery Trade (CNN)

Short-Form Programming Series
Dr. Katz (Comedy Central)

Recreation and Leisure Special or Series
Blue Angels: Around the World at the Speed of Sound (A&E Network)

Game Show Special or Series
Legends of the Hidden Temple (Nickelodeon)

Governor's Award
Dr. John C. Malone, president and chief executive officer of Tele-Communications, Inc.

Golden CableACE Award
The C-Span School Bus (C-Span)

Creators Award
Ready, Set, Learn! (The Learning Channel)

unfold and intersect in New York's trendy Survival Gym. *Muscle* covers many topics — homosexuality, guilt, greed, sexism and relationships — but none of them well.

MY SO-CALLED LIFE
ABC
Fall Debut
Thursday 8:00–9:00 P.M.; on hiatus spring season
MTV picked up reruns spring mid-season
Cast: Claire Danes, Bess Armstrong, Wilson Cruz, Devon Gummersall, A.J. Langer, Jared Leto, Devon Odessa, Lisa Wilhoit and Tom Irwin
In this critically acclaimed series (but still shelved by the network) Angela Chase (Danes), a 15-year-old angst-ridden, high-school student, chronicles the constantly changing experiences of a teenager and questions contemporary life and family values.

NEWSRADIO
NBC
Spring Mid-Season Debut
Tuesday 8:30–9:00 P.M.
Cast: David Foley, Stephen Root, Andy Dick, Maura Tierney, Vicki Lewis, Ella Joyce, Phil Hartman, Kurt Fuller, Greg Lee, Wallace Langham, Beau Billingslea and Khandi Alexander
The neurotic radio news staff of New York's WNYX spends long, chaotic days preparing for each broadcast. Despite behind-the-scenes disasters, they always seem to pull off each show, but quality programming is often comprised.

NEW YORK UNDERCOVER
Fox
Fall Debut
Thursdays 9:00–10:00 P.M.
Cast: Malik Yoba, Michael DeLorenzo, Fatima Faloye, Michael Michele and Patti D'Arbanville-Quinn
Two New York City police detectives (Yoba and DeLorenzo) work to clean the streets of criminals and attempt to make sense of their often confused personal lives.

THE OFFICE
CBS
Spring Mid-Season Debut
Saturday 9:00–9:30 P.M.
Cast: Valerie Harper, Kristin Datillo-Hayward, Andrea Abbate, Debra Jo Rupp, Gary Dourdan, Dakin Matthews, Lisa Darr and Kevin Conroy
Career secretary Rita Stone (Harper) has devoted her life to her office, comprised of stereotypical male bosses and female secretaries, and to her co-workers' problems. The one woman executive (Darr) struggles to maintain her place in the boys club.

ON OUR OWN
ABC
Fall Debut
Sunday 7:30–8:00 P.M.; on hiatus spring season
Cast: Ralph Louis Harris, JoJo Smollett, Jazz Smollett, Jussie Smollett, Jurnee Smollett, Jake Smollett, Jacqui Smollett, Kimberley Kates and Roger Aaron Brown
The seven orphaned Jerrico children (six of them real-life siblings), ranging in age from 18 months to 20 years, work and scheme together to convince social workers that they should remain a family.

THE PARENT 'HOOD
WB
Spring Debut
Wednesday 8:30–9:00 P.M.
Cast: Robert Townsend, Suzzanne Douglas, Kenny Blank, Reagan Gomez-Preston, Curtis Williams, Ashli Adams, Bobby McGee, Carol Woods, Faizon Love and Doug Kruze
Baby-boomer parents Robert (Townsend) and Jerri (Douglas) Peterson confront issues of the 1990s such as gangs, drugs, gangsta rap and guns while raising their four children using their own unconventional methods.

PARTY OF FIVE
Fox
Fall Debut
Monday 9:00–10:00 P.M.; moved to Wednesday 9:00–10:00 P.M. spring season
Cast: Matthew Fox, Scott Wolf, Neve Campbell and Lacey Chabert

Five siblings, ranging in age from 11 months to 24 years, struggle to hold the family together, financially and emotionally, after their parents are killed in a car accident.

PIG STY
UPN
Spring Debut
Monday 9:30–10:00 P.M.; moved to Monday 9:00–9:30 P.M. spring mid-season
Cast: David Arnott, Matt Borlenghi, Timothy Fall, Brian McNamara, Sean O'Bryan and Liz Vassey
Five men, from an assistant district attorney to a bohemian folk singer, live together in a cramped, two-bedroom apartment in New York, which, of course, is managed by a beautiful superintendent.

PLATYPUS MAN
UPN
Spring Debut
Monday 9:00–9:30 P.M.; moved to 9:30–10:00 P.M. spring mid-season
Cast: Richard Jeni, Ron Orbach, Denise Miller and David Dundara
Richard Jeni (playing himself), host of a New York cooking show targeted at bachelors, is always pursuing potential mates but seems to spend most of his time alone or in the company of his best friend and executive producer Lou (Orbach).

PRIDE & JOY
NBC
Spring Mid-Season Debut
Tuesday 9:30–10:00 P.M.
Cast: Julie Warner, Craig Bierko, Jeremy Piven and Caroline Rhea
Two thirtysomething couples living in New York try to manage their children, careers and marriages. Their similar situations — they are neighbors, both have toddlers, the husbands are at home and the wives work together — prompt them to look to each other for support and advice.

SISTER, SISTER
ABC
Fall Mid-Season Debut
Wednesday 8:00–8:30 P.M.; on hiatus spring mid-season
Cast: Tia Mowry, Tamera Mowry, Jackee Harry, Tim Reid and Marques Houston
Identical twins who were separated at birth are unexpectedly reunited when they meet in a clothing store. Their single parents move in together to keep the girls under one roof, (not for romantic reasons).

SLIDERS
Fox
Spring Mid-Season Debut
Wednesday 9:00–10:00 P.M.
Cast: Jerry O'Connell, John Rhys-Davies, Sabrina Lloyd and Cleavant Derricks
Quinn Mallory (O'Connell), a crack physics student, accidentally creates a wormhole that transports him and three friends to alternate versions of Earth. Their visits include an Earth where Elvis is still the king and another where the Communists won the Cold War.

SOMETHING WILDER
NBC
Fall Debut
Saturdays 8:00–8:30 P.M.; moved to Tuesday 8:30–9:00 P.M. fall season; on hiatus spring season
Cast: Gene Wilder, Hillary B. Smith, Ian Bottiglieri and Carl Michael Lindner
A working couple and their four-year-old twins leave fast-paced New York City for the rural Berkshires, but they unexpectedly find chaos in the small town.

STAR TREK: VOYAGER

UPN
Spring Debut
Monday 8:00–9:00 P.M.
Cast: Kate Mulgrew,
Robert Beltran,
Roxann Biggs-
Dawson, Jennifer
Lien, Robert Duncan
McNeill, Ethan

Phillips, Robert Picardo, Tim Russ, Garrett Wang, Basil
Langton, Gavan O'Herlihy, Angela Paton and Armin
Shimerman
The crew of the U.S.S. *Voyager*, commanded for
the first time by a woman (Mulgrew), is thrust
into a distant galaxy. They must team up with
their former enemy, the Maquis, to make their
way back to Federation space.

SWEET JUSTICE

NBC
Fall Debut
Saturday 9:00–10:00 P.M.
Cast: Melissa Gilbert, Cicely Tyson, Cree Summer,
Greg Germann, Jim Antonio and Jason Gedrick
A young attorney leaves her lucrative Wall Street
job for a position in a maverick firm in her south-
ern hometown, which is also the archrival of her
father's conservative firm.

TOUCHED BY AN ANGEL

CBS
Fall Debut
Wednesday 9:00–10:00 P.M.; on hiatus spring season
Cast: Roma Downey and Della Reese
An angel (Reese), sent from heaven to inspire
people at crossroads in their lives, works through
her secret agent Monica (Downey). Monica
involves herself in the lives of the most needy,
whether they know it or not, and creates opportunities for miracles to happen.

UNDER ONE ROOF

CBS
Spring Mid-Season
Debut
Tuesday 8:00–9:00
P.M.
Cast: James Earl
Jones, Joe Morton,
Vanessa Bell
Calloway, Essence
Atkins, Marlin
Santana, Monique

Ridge, Ronald Joshua Scott and Terrence Knox
The African-American Langston family lives in a
two-family house headed by patriarch Ned
(Jones). Ned's wife died a year ago and he looks to
his children and grandchildren for support, and
they look to him for guidance.

UNDER SUSPICION

CBS
Fall Debut
Friday 9:00–10:00 P.M.; on hiatus spring mid-season
Cast: Karen Sillas, Seymour Cassel and Philip Casnoff
As the lone woman detective in the squad room,
Rose "Phil" Phillips (Sillas) realizes that although
she tries to play the game, she's not one of the
boys. The mysterious disappearance of her partner — and best friend — further complicates her
situation as she becomes responsible for the case
and his family.

UNHAPPILY EVER AFTER

WB
Spring Debut
Wednesday 9:00–9:30 P.M.
Cast: Geoff Pierson, Stephanie Hodge, Kevin Connolly,
Nikki Cox, Justin Berfield, Joyce Van Patten and
Bobcat Goldthwait
While dysfunctional couple Jennie (Hodge) and
Jack (Pierson) Malloy are going through a bitter
divorce, they find that though they can't live with
each other, they can't live without each other either.

V.R. 5

Fox
Spring Debut
Friday 8:00–9:00 P.M.
Cast: Lori Singer, David McCallum, Louise Fletcher,
Anthony Head and Michael Easton
Sydney Bloom (Singer), a telephone linewoman
by day and a computer hacker by night, inadver-
tently discovers that by tapping another person's
telephone, she can time-travel to another dimen-
sion — the fifth level of virtual reality.

THE WATCHER

UPN
Spring Debut
Tuesday 9:00–10:00 P.M.; on hiatus mid-season
Cast: Sir Mix-A-Lot
The Watcher (Sir Mix-A-Lot) uses hidden cameras
to spy on gamblers in a Las Vegas casino. He
watches firsthand as dreams are realized and
even more are shattered.

THE WAYANS BROS.

WB
Spring Debut
Wednesday 8:00–8:30 P.M.
Cast: Shawn Wayans, Marlon Wayans, Lela Rochon
and John Witherspoon
Shawn and Marlon Williams (the Wayans respec-
tively) are always looking for a get-rich-quick
scheme but most often end up in trouble. Shawn's
strait-laced girlfriend Lisa (Rochon) tries to keep
them somewhat in line.

A Whole New Ballgame

ABC
Spring Debut
Monday 8:30–9:00 P.M.; on hiatus mid-season
Cast: Corbin Bernsen, Julia Campbell, Stephen Tobolowsky, Richard Kind and John O'Hurley
Milwaukee television station manager Meg O'Donnell (Campbell) hires the womanizing, striking baseball player Brett Sooner (Bernsen). As a sportscaster, Sooner is arrogant yet embarrassingly incompetent.

Wild Oats

Fox
Fall Debut
Sunday 9:30–10:00 P.M.; canceled fall season
Cast: Tim Conlon, Jana Marie Hupp, Paula Marshall and Paul Stephen Rudd
A group of wild, out-all-night twentysomethings living in Chicago look for love and friendship in their chaotic lives, which intersect at every turn.

Women of the House

CBS
Spring Debut
Wednesday 8:00–8:30 P.M.; on hiatus mid-season
Cast: Delta Burke, Teri Garr, Patricia Heaton, Valerie Mahaffey, Jonathan Banks and Brittany Parkyn
Former southern beauty queen Suzanne Sugarbaker (Burke) inherits her late husband's seat in the U.S. House of Representatives and brings with her to Washington an unlikely, all-female staff.

The Wright Verdicts

CBS
Spring Mid-Season Debut
Friday 9:00–10:00 P.M.
Cast: Tom Conti, Margaret Colin and Aida Turturro
Wright (Conti) uses his charm, British wit and sly grin to help him win his cases. *The Wright Verdicts* follows a familiar format: someone commits a crime, Wright investigates and successfully argues his cases in a climactic courtroom scene.

All times are Eastern Standard Time.

1994 Alfred I. duPont — Columbia University Awards in Television and Radio Journalism

The Alfred I. duPont Awards, administered by Columbia University, recognize excellence in television and radio broadcasting.

GOLD BATON
ABC News

For the depth and range of its coverage, producing, in a single year, outstanding television journalism in various programs and in all forms.

Entries cited:

Coverage of Haiti by Linda Pattillo

World News Tonight: "American Agenda: Women's Health Week"

Day One: "Smokescreen"

Turning Point: "Inside the Struggle — The Amy Biehl Story"

Peter Jennings Reporting: While America Watched — The Bosnia Tragedy

SILVER BATONS
TELEVISION AWARDS
Charles Kuralt, *CBS News*

60 Minutes: "Semipalatinsk" (CBS)

CNN, coverage of the Moscow uprising

Frontline: "Innocence Lost: The Verdict" (PBS)

Frontline: "Romeo and Juliet in Sarajevo" (PBS)

Major Market Television
The Last Hit: Children and Violence (WTVS-TV, Detroit, MI)

Medium Market Television
Missing the Beat (WCCO-TV, Minneapolis, MN)

Small Market Television
My Promised Land: Bernice Cooper's Story (Wisconsin Public Television)

Independent Television Production
The Great Depression (PBS)

Cable Television
I Am a Promise: The Children of Stanton Elementary School (HBO)

RADIO AWARDS
Michael Skoler, coverage of Rwanda (NPR)

Coverage of South Africa (NPR)

Fall 1994 Season

Friends

Earth 2

All American Girl

Day	Network	8:00-8:30
M	ABC	Coach
	CBS	The Nanny
	NBC	Fresh Prince
	FOX	Melrose Place ———————
T	ABC	Full House
	CBS	Rescue 911 ———————
	NBC	Wings
	FOX	Tuesday Movie ———————
W	ABC	Thunder Alley; Sister, Sister
	CBS	The Boys Are Back
	NBC	The Cosby Mysteries ———————
	FOX	Beverly Hills 90210 ———————
Th	ABC	My So-Called Life ———————
	CBS	Due South ———————
	NBC	Mad About You
	FOX	Martin
F	ABC	Family Matters
	CBS	Diagnosis Murder ———————
	NBC	Unsolved Mysteries ———————
	FOX	M.A.N.T.I.S. ———————
Sat	ABC	Saturday Movie ———————
	CBS	Dr. Quinn, Medicine Woman ———————
	NBC	Something Wilder - *moved late fall season, no permanent replacement*
	FOX	Cops

Day	Network	7:00-7:30	7:30-8:00	
Sun	ABC	America's Funniest Home Videos	On Our Own	Lois & Clark ———————
	CBS	60 Minutes ——————→		Murder, She Wrote ———————
	NBC	Earth 2 ——————→		Seaquest DSV ———————
	FOX	Fortune Hunter - *canceled, no permanent replacement* ——————→		The Simpsons

8:30-9:00	9:00-9:30	9:30-10:00	10:00-11:00
Blue Skies - *on hiatus, no permanent replacement*	Monday Night Football ———————————————————>		
Dave's World	Murphy Brown	Love and War	Northern Exposure
Blossom	Monday Night Movie ———————————————————————————————————————>		
——————————————————> Party of Five ————————————————————————>			
Me and the Boys	Home Improvement	Grace Under Fire	NYPD Blue
——————————————————> Tuesday Night Movie ——————————————————————————————>			
Martin Short Show; Something Wilder	Frasier	John Larroquette Show	Dateline NBC
——>			
All American Girl	Roseanne	Ellen	Turning Point
Daddy's Girls - *canceled, no permanent replacement*	Touched by an Angel ———————————————————————————>		48 Hours
——————————————————> Dateline NBC ——>			Law & Order
——————————————————> Models Inc. ———————————————————————————>			
——————————————————> McKenna - *canceled, no permanent replacement*			PrimeTime Live
——————————————————> Eye to Eye With Connie Chung—————————————————————————>			Chicago Hope
Friends	Seinfeld	Madman of the People ·	ER
Living Single	New York Undercover ————————————————————————>		
Boy Meets World	Step by Step	Hangin' With Mr. Cooper	20/20
——————————————————> Under Suspicion—————————————————————————————————————>			Picket Fences
——————————————————> Dateline NBC ——>			Homicide
——————————————————> The X-Files ———————————————————————————>			
——>			The Commish
——————————————————> The Five Mrs. Buchanans	Hearts Afire		Walker, Texas Ranger
Empty Nest	Sweet Justice———>		Sisters
Cops 2	America's Most Wanted———————————————————————————>		
——————————————————> ABC Sunday Night Movie———>			
——————————————————> CBS Sunday Night Movie———>			
——————————————————> NBC Sunday Night Movie———>			
Hardball - *canceled, no permanent replacement*	Married. . . With Children	Wild Oats; George Carlin	

Spring 1995 Season

Seinfeld

Star Trek: Voyager

Melrose Place

DAY	NETWORK	8:00–8:30
M	ABC	Coach - *moved,* *no permanent replacement*
	CBS	The Nanny
	NBC	Fresh Prince of Bel Air
	FOX	Melrose Place———————
	UPN	Star Trek: Voyager———————
T	ABC	Full House
	CBS	Rescue 911; Under One Roof———
	NBC	Wings
	FOX	Tuesday Movie———————
	UPN	Marker; Legend———————
W	ABC	Sister, Sister; Roseanne*
	CBS	Women of the House; The George Wendt Show
	NBC	Cosby Mysteries———————
	FOX	Beverly Hills 90210———————
	WB	The Wayans Brothers
TH	ABC	Matlock; Extreme———————
	CBS	Due South———————
	NBC	Mad About You
	FOX	Martin
F	ABC	Family Matters
	CBS	Diagnosis Murder———————
	NBC	Unsolved Mysteries———————
	FOX	M.A.N.T.I.S.; V.R. 5———
SAT	ABC	Saturday Movie———————
	CBS	Dr. Quinn, Medicine Woman ———
	NBC	Empty Nest; Amazing Grace———————
	FOX	Cops

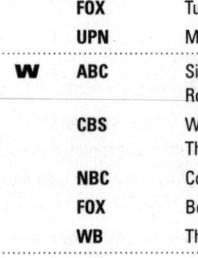

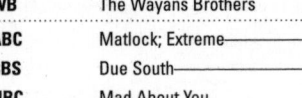

DATE	NETWORK	7:00–7:30	7:30–8:00	
SUN	ABC	America's Funniest Home Videos——————→		Lois & Clark———————
	CBS	60 Minutes———————		→ Murder, She Wrote———————
	NBC	Earth 2———————		→ SeaQuest DSV———————
	FOX	The Simpsons	Get Smart - *on hiatus,* *no permanent replacement*	The Simpsons

* Shows returned to their original time in May

8:30-9:00	9:00-9:30	9:30-10:00	10:00-11:00
A Whole New Ballgame - *on hiatus, no permanent replacement*	Monday Night Movie————————→		
Dave's World	Murphy Brown	Cybill	Chicago Hope
Blossom; In the House	Monday Night Movie————————→		
————————→	Models Inc.; Medicine Ball————→		
————————→	Platypus Man; Pig Sty	Pig Sty; Platypus Man	
Me and the Boys; Thunder Alley	Home Improvement	Grace Under Fire - *moved, no permanent replacement*	NYPD Blue
————————→	Tuesday Night Movie————————————→		
Something Wilder; NewsRadio	Frasier	John Larroquette Show*; Pride and Joy	Dateline NBC
————————→	————————————————————————→		
————————→	The Watcher; Legend————————————→		
All American Girl; Ellen*	Roseanne; Grace Under Fire*	Ellen; Coach*	PrimeTime Live
No permanent programming; Double Rush;	Double Rush; Wednesday Movie————→	Love and War;	Northern Exposure*; ————→
————————→	Dateline NBC————————————————→		Law & Order
————————→	Party of Five; Sliders————————————→		
The Parent 'Hood	Unhappily Ever After	Muscle	
————————→	The Commish————————————————→		Day One
————————→	Eye to Eye With Connie Chung————→		48 Hours
Friends; Hope & Gloria	Seinfeld	Madman of the People; Friends	ER
Living Single	New York Undercover————————————→		
Boy Meets World	Step by Step	Hangin' With Mr. Cooper; On Our Own	20/20
————————→	Under Suspicion; The Wright Verdicts————————————————→		Picket Fences
————————→	Dateline NBC————————————————→		Homicide
————————→	The X-Files————————————————————→		
————————————————————————————————→			The Marshal
————————→	The Boys Are Back; The Office	The Five Mrs. Buchanans	Walker, Texas Ranger
Mommies; ————————→	Sweet Justice————————————————→		Sisters
Cops 2	America's Most Wanted————————————→		
————————→	ABC Sunday Night Movie————————————————————————————————→		
————————→	CBS Sunday Night Movie————————————————————————————————→		
————————→	NBC Sunday Movie————————————————————————————————→		
House of Buggin'; The Critic; House of Buggin'	Married . . . With Children	Dream On	

1995 Prime-Time Broadcast Premieres

ALMOST PERFECT

CBS
Sunday 8:30–9:00 P.M.
Cast: Nancy Travis and Kevin Kilner
Two ambitious crime fighters meet and fall in love, but there's a problem: their hectic schedules don't allow time to pursue a relationship. Kim Cooper (Travis) has just been promoted to executive producer of a hot cop show and district attorney Mike Ryan (Kilner) can barely have a conversation without his beeper interrupting.

AMERICAN GOTHIC

CBS
Friday 10:00–11:00 P.M.
Cast: Gary Cole, Nicholas Searcy, Jake Weber, Paige Turco and Lucas Black

Trinity, South Carolina, seems to be a picture-perfect rural community, but its appearance is deceptive. The demonic Sheriff Lucas Buck's (Cole) corruption threatens the citizens of Trinity. Deputy Healy (Searcy), Dr. Crower (Weber) and Gail Emory (Turco) collaborate to stop their adversary.

BLESS THIS HOUSE

CBS
Wednesday 8:00–8:30 P.M.
Cast: Andrew Clay, Cathy Moriarty, Raegan Kotz, Molly Price, Don Stark and Sam Gifaldi
Working-class couple Burt (Clay) and Alice (Moriarty) Clayton certainly know how to fight — and how to make up. Though they don't agree on much, they do see eye-to-eye when it comes to their children and their dream of buying a house.

BONNIE

CBS
Friday 8:30–9:00 P.M.
Cast: Bonnie Hunt
Bonnie Kelly (Hunt), trying to adjust to her high-profile job as a Chicago broadcast reporter, struggles to put aside her small-town ways in order to succeed in the big city. This comedy combines scripted and improvisational material that is shot in real time without retakes. David Letterman is an executive producer of the show.

BROTHERLY LOVE

NBC
Sunday 7:00–7:30 P.M.
Cast: Joey Lawrence, Matthew Lawrence, Andy Lawrence, Melinda Culea and Mike McShane

After the death of his father, Joe (Joey Lawrence) sacrifices his dream of becoming a Daytona race car driver to provide for his step-brothers (including two of Lawrence's real-life siblings) as a mechanic in the struggling family garage bequeathed to them by their father.

CAN'T HURRY LOVE

CBS
Monday 8:30–9:00 P.M.
Cast: Nancy McKeon, Mariska Hargitay and Louis Mandylor
Annie (McKeon), a placement coordinator at a New York personnel agency, her often crude co-worker Roger (Mandylor) and her best friend (and relationship counselor) Didi (Hargitay) confront the ups and downs of romance while searching for the perfect mate.

CAROLINE IN THE CITY

NBC
Thursday 9:30–10:00 P.M.
Cast: Lea Thompson, Eric Lutes, Malcolm Gets and Amy Pietz
New Yorker Caroline Duffy (Thompson), a cartoonist in a greeting-card company, cannot keep her personal life from turning up in her work. She gets a hand from her social circle, which includes her sometime boyfriend (Lutes), who is also the president of her company, her brooding colorist (Gets) and her best friend Annie (Pietz).

CENTRAL PARK WEST
CBS
Wednesday 9:00–10:00 P.M.

Cast: Mariel Hemingway, Lauren Hutton, Madchen Amick, John Barrowman, Melissa Errico, Justin Lazard, Michael Michele and Tom Verica

From the creators of *Melrose Place* and *Beverly Hills 90210*, this urban drama centers around a group of glamorous young New Yorkers — a stockbroker, a Soho art gallery owner, the editor of a slick monthly magazine, a district attorney and a tabloid journalist — who live their lives with enough intensity to light up the city. And true to nighttime soap format, there's plenty of romance, scandal and backstabbing.

CHARLIE GRACE
ABC
Thursday 8:00–9:00 P.M.

Cast: Mark Harmon, Cindy Katz, Robert Costanzo and Leelee Sobieski

Charlie Grace (Harmon), a street-smart Los Angeles private investigator, has a tough time balancing his work and single parenthood. His 12-year-old daughter Jenny (Sobieski) is the only thing that keeps him going when things get out of hand, as they often do in the detective business.

CLEGHORNE!
WB
Sunday 9:30–10:00 P.M.

Cast: Ellen Cleghorne, Cerita Monet Bickelmann, Garrett Morris, Alaina Reed Hall, Sherri Shepherd and Michael Ralph

Based on the real-life experiences of Saturday Night Live's Cleghorne, the comedy centers on her life as a single mother trying to balance her career and motherhood.

COURTHOUSE
CBS
Wednesday 10:00–11:00 P.M.

Cast: Patricia Wettig, Robin Givens, Brad Johnson, Annabeth Gish, Bob Gunton, Michael Lerner, Jennifer Lewis and Jeffrey Sams

In a world of shrinking budgets, overcrowded calendars, clashing philosophies and passionate attorneys, big-city legal professionals (facing big-city cases) struggle to administer justice in a system on the verge of self-destruction.

THE CREW
Fox
Thursday 8:30–9:00 P.M.

Cast: Rose Jackson, Kristen Bauer, Charles Esten, David Burke, Christine Estabrook and Lane Davies

As they wait hand and foot on the passengers of Imperial Air, four young, sexy flight attendants — Jess (Jackson), Maggie (Bauer), Randy (Esten) and Paul (Burke) — deal with their whiny charges in their own way. Off-duty, their lives are just as harried as they are in the air.

DEADLY GAMES
UPN
Tuesday 8:00–9:00 P.M.

Cast: Cynthia Gibb, Christopher Lloyd, James Calvert and Stephen T. Kay

A young, innovative scientist, Dr. Gus Lloyd, (Calvert) is horrified when the characters in the video game he created come to life after a freak lab accident.

THE DREW CAREY SHOW
ABC
Wednesday 8:30–9:00 P.M.

Cast: Drew Carey, Dietrich Bader, Ryan Stiles and Christa Miller

Friends since high school, Drew (Carey), Oswald (Bader), Lewis (Stiles) and Kate (Miller) share career, romantic and financial troubles in working-class Cleveland and look to each other for laughs and support in the unpredictable 1990s.

DWEEBS
CBS
Friday 8:00–8:30 P.M.

Cast: Farrah Forke, Peter Scolari, Stephen Tobolowsky, Corey Feldman, David Kaufman, Adam Biesk and Holly Fulger

When computer-illiterate Carey (Forke) accepts a job as office manager at Cyberbyte, Inc., run by software legend Warren (Scolari), she is surrounded by a group of brilliant technogeeks. Though she can't talk to them about computers or networks, she can teach them social skills, especially dating basics.

FIRST TIME OUT
WB
Sunday 9:00–9:30 P.M.

Cast: Jackie Guerra, Mia Cottet, Leah Remini and Craig Anton

Three young female roommates living in Los Angeles confront love and life together in the fast-paced city.

THE HOME COURT
NBC
Saturday 9:30–10:00 P.M.
Cast: Pamela Reed, Breckin Meyer, Meghann Haldeman, Robert Gorman, Phillip Glenn Van Dyke, Dennis Arndt and Meagen Fay

As a Chicago family-court judge, Sydney J. Solomon (Reed) intimidates even the toughest prosecuting attorney and the most flagrant offenders, but there's one group upon which she can't exercise full control — her four children. As a single parent, her three teens and one pre-adolescent present her more challenges than she faces on the bench.

HUDSON STREET
ABC
Tuesday 8:30–9:00 P.M.
Cast: Tony Danza, Lori Loughlin, Shareen Mitchell, Frank J. Galasso, Jerry Adler, Christine Dunford and Tom Gallop
Set in a Hoboken, New Jersey, police station, sparks fly between the chauvinistic, hard-line detective Tony Canetti (Danza) and the idealistic, liberal crime reporter Melanie Clifford (Loughlin). Divorced dad Tony shares custody of his 10-year-old son (Galasso) with his ex-wife Lucy (Mitchell) who always seems to be around.

IF NOT FOR YOU
CBS
Monday 9:30–10:00 P.M.
Cast: Elizabeth McGovern and Hank Azaria

Jessie Kent (McGovern) and Craig Schaeffer (Azaria) are engaged to the wrong people. She is betrothed to a depressed architect who is obsessed with fat content in food, and he to a neurotic recording artist. Fate brings them together at a local Chinese restaurant, and they realize that the solution to their disastrous engagements is each other.

JAG
NBC
Saturday 8:00–9:00 P.M.
Cast: David James Elliott, Andrea Parker, Terry O'Quinn, and Kevin Dunn
Assigned as Judge Advocate General (JAG) officer in Navy parlance, Lt. Harmon Rabb, Jr. (Elliott), a Navy lawyer, must investigate the murder of a high-profile female fighter pilot on an aircraft carrier. The investigation hits home for Rabb, as his father's career as a Navy pilot ended after an accident aboard a carrier.

JOHN GRISHAM'S THE CLIENT
CBS
Tuesday 8:00–9:00 P.M.
Cast: JoBeth Williams, John Heard, Ossie Davis, Polly Holliday and Raphael Sbarge
Based on the novel by John Grisham

Reggie Love (Williams), an Atlanta-based attorney and recovering alcoholic, uses her specialty in family law to help kids in trouble and to continue her fight to regain custody of her own children, whom she lost when she was drinking. Love has allies in Mama Love (Holliday), who shelters Reggie's wayward clients, and Judge Roosevelt (Davis), her advocate in the court system.

KIRK
WB
Sunday 8:30–9:00 P.M.
Cast: Kirk Cameron, Chelsea Noble, Debra Mooney, Will Estes, Taylor Fry and Courtland Mead
A 24-year-old aspiring artist (Cameron) suddenly becomes responsible for his three younger siblings and tries to look for a love interest and mind his new charges.

LIVE SHOT
UPN
Tuesday 9:00–10:00 P.M.
Cast: David Birney, Wanda De Jesus, Hill Harper, Spencer Klein, Cheryl Pollak, Rebecca Staab, Michael Watson and Jeff Yagher
This fast-paced drama focuses on the competitive, chaotic environment and frenzied people and personalities in a television newsroom.

MAYBE THIS TIME
ABC
Saturday 8:00–8:30 P.M.
Cast: Marie Osmond, Ashley Johnson and Betty White
One year after her divorce, Julia (Osmond) decides to give up on love and focus her attention on her precocious daughter Gracie (Johnson), her mother Shirley (White) and the family cafe. Julia's daughter and mother work hard to convince her to give romance another chance.

MINOR ADJUSTMENTS

NBC

Sunday 7:30–8:00 P.M.

Cast: Rondell Sheridan, Wendy Raquel Robinson, Bobby E. McAdams II, Camille Winbush, Linda Kash, Mitchell Whitfield and Sara Rue

Despite his special way with children, child psychologist Dr. Ron Aimes (Sheridan) daily discovers that it takes much more to be a good parent than being a good psychologist.

MISERY LOVES COMPANY

Fox

Sunday 9:30–10:00 P.M.

Cast: Dennis Boutsikaris, Julius Carry, Stephen Furst and Lorraine Tessaint

In this comic look at divorce and marriage from the male perspective, four friends with love woes — three in the middle of bitter divorces and one still looking for that perfect woman — carouse and sympathize with each other.

THE MONROES

ABC

Thursday 9:00–10:00 P.M.

Cast: William Devane, Susan Sullivan, David Andrews, Steven Eckholdt, Cecil Hoffmann, Tracy Griffith, Tristan Tait, Darryl Theirse, Lynn Clark and Vince Grant

John Monroe (Devane), patriarch of his rich and powerful family, aspires to be president, but when a scandal foils his political career he quickly makes other plans that involve his children's futures. This larger-than-life family delves into international intrigue, power, money and betrayal.

MURDER ONE

ABC

Thursday 10:00–11:00 P.M.

Cast: Daniel Benzali and Stanley Tucci

Famed Los Angeles attorney Ted Hoffman (Benzali) defends Richard Cross (Tucci), a wealthy entrepreneur implicated in the murder of his mistress's teenage sister, in this behind-the-scenes look at a police investigation and the legal process. Throughout the entire season, *Murder One* follows this one case from beginning to end.

NED AND STACEY

Fox

Monday 9:30–10:00 P.M.

Cast: Thomas Haden Church and Deborah Messing

An ambitious advertising executive (Church) needs the perfect wife for a promotion, and a socially conscious journalist (Messing) needs to get out of her parents' house to remain sane. The perfect solution? A marriage of convenience.

NEW YORK NEWS

CBS

Thursday 9:00–10:00 P.M.

Cast: Mary Tyler Moore, Melina Kanakaredes, Madeline Kahn, Joe Morton and Gregory Harrison

Emotions run high in the newsroom of New York's *Reporter*, which is run by the iron-fisted Louise "The Dragon Lady" Felcott (Moore). Her staff includes Angela Villanova (Kanakaredes), a young reporter who will stop at nothing to get a story, and veteran gossip columnist Nan Chase (Kahn), who has climbed and clawed her way to the top of the trivial industry.

NOWHERE MAN

UPN

Monday 9:00–10:00 P.M.

Cast: Bruce Greenwood, Mary Gregory and Megan Gallagher

Documentary photographer Thomas Veil's (Greenwood) whole life has been erased leaving no trace of his existence. His mother (Gregory), wife (Gallagher) and close friends are involved in the scheme. Veil desperately undertakes a dangerous quest to determine what has happened to his life.

PARTNERS

Fox

Monday 9:00–9:30 P.M.

Cast: Jon Cryer, Tate Donovan and Maria Pitillo

An architect (Donovan) is caught in the middle of a tug-of-war battle between his fiancée (Pitillo) and neurotic best friend (Cryer), who are fighting for his attention.

THE PRESTON EPISODES

Fox

Saturday 8:30–9:00 P.M.

Cast: David Alan Grier

A recently divorced English professor (Grier) harbors high hopes of becoming a Pulitzer Prize-winning journalist. He abandons his academic career for a position as a cub reporter at a less-than-reputable tabloid.

PURSUIT OF HAPPINESS

NBC

Tuesday 9:30–10:00 P.M.

Cast: Tom Amandes, Meredith Scott Lynn, Melinda McGraw, Larry Miller, Brad Garrett and Maxine Stuart

Chicago lawyer Steve Gerard (Amandes) suddenly faces several heavy issues: his careerist wife (McGraw) recently lost her job, his scatterbrained brother-in-law (Miller) is moving in, his grandmother (Stuart) is losing her mind and his partner/best friend (Garrett) has just come out of the closet.

SIMON
WB
Sunday 8:30–9:00 P.M.
Cast: Harland Williams, Jason Bateman, Paxton Whitehead, Clifton Powell, Patrick Breen and Andrea Bendeald
A young, wide-eyed optimist (Williams) loves his job working for a New York "vintage" television network but living with his cynical brother is less than enjoyable.

THE SINGLE GUY
NBC
Thursday 8:30–9:00 P.M.
Cast: Jonathan Silverman, Joey Slotnick, Ming-Na Wen, Jessica Hecht, Mark Moses and Ernest Borgnine

Jonathan (Silverman) feels as if he's the last bachelor. All of his friends are married and are diligently trying to find him the perfect mate. His matchmaking entourage includes his best friend Sam (Slotnick), Sam's wife Trudy (Wen) and longtime platonic friend Janeane (Hecht).

SISTER, SISTER
WB
Sunday 7:30–8:00 P.M.
The WB network acquired this show from ABC. See page 443 for a description

STEVEN SPIELBERG PRESENTS PINKY AND THE BRAIN
WB
Sunday 7:00–7:30 P.M.
A spinoff of *Steven Spielberg Presents Animaniacs* Pinky and the Brain, two industrious mice from Acme Labs, relentlessly try to take control of the world.

SOMEWHERE IN AMERICA
ABC
Saturday 8:30–9:00 P.M.
Cast: Jeff Foxworthy, Anity Barone, Kelsey Mulrooney and Shawna Duling
Jeff (Foxworthy), full of southern charm and a common-sense perspective (translation: he's a redneck), and his wife Lisa (Barone), who puts Jeff in line when necessary, are the happily married parents of two daughters, Jessica (Mulrooney) and Chloe (Duling). The girls prove to be a handful for the couple.

SPACE: ABOVE AND BEYOND
Fox
Sunday 7:00–8:00 P.M.
Cast: Morgan Weisser, Rodney Rowland, Kristin Cloke, Lanei Chapman, Joel De LaFuente and James Morrison
A Marine cadets corps is unexpectedly dispatched to the frontlines of an intergalactic war after Earth's most elite fighting squadron is decimated in an attack by a previously unknown alien race.

STRANGE LUCK
Fox
Friday 8:00–9:00 P.M.
Cast: D.B. Sweeney, Pamela Gidley and Frances Fisher
Ever since he survived a plane crash as a child, strange luck — both good and bad — has followed this photojournalist (Sweeney). Wherever he goes, something odd occurs, which can be very interesting given his profession.

TOO SOMETHING
Fox
Sunday 8:30–9:00 P.M.
Cast: Eric Schaeffer and Donal Lardner Ward
Based on the film *My Life's in Turnaround*
Two best friends Eric (Schaeffer) and Donny (Ward) work together in the mailroom of an investment bank while pursuing their career dreams: Eric wants to be a writer and Donny is studying in night school to be an astronaut.

WILDE AGAIN
ABC
Wednesday 9:30–10:00 P.M.
Cast: Tea Leone, Jonathan Penner and Holland Taylor
Nora Wilde (Leone) walked away from her media-mogul, philandering husband confident that with hard work, she could regain her former status as a respected photojournalist. She soon finds that her ex-husband has blackballed her from every reputable paper in the country, and she must resort to taking pictures for a trashy tabloid.

What We're Watching

Would you dare show even your best friends your personal TV guide where for every *Nova* there lurked a hidden fascination with *Melrose Place?* Below, the editors of *The Entertainment Almanac* bare their cable tuners. This is what we watched in the fall of 1995. You did, too. Admit it.

	8:00–8:30 P.M.	8:30–9:00 P.M.	9:00–9:30 P.M.	9:30–10:00 P.M.	10:00–10:30 P.M.	10:30–11:00 P.M.
Monday	Melrose Place (Fox) or Star Trek: Voyager (UPN), depending on who gets the clicker first.		**Murphy Brown** (CBS)	Check out the second quarter of **Monday Night Football** (ABC)	Chicago Hope (CBS)	
Tuesday	**Roseanne** (ABC)	Catch the last half of **Nova** (PBS)	**Frasier** (NBC)	**Pursuit of Happiness** (NBC)	**NYPD Blue** (ABC)	
Wednesday	Ellen (ABC)	**The Jetsons** (Cartoon Network)	**Central Park West** (Fox)		**Law & Order** (NBC)	
Thursday	Friends (NBC)	**The Single Guy** (NBC)	Seinfeld (NBC)	**Caroline in the City** (NBC)	ER (NBC)	
Friday	Play MiSTie for Me – Mystery Science Theater 3000 Viewers Choice (Comedy Central)		**The X-Files** (Fox)		**Homicide: Life on the Street** (NBC)	
Saturday	The networks program as if no one is home on a Saturday night. If, however, you are a shut-in or just plain tired, rent a video or search for a classic Hollywood movie.					
Sunday	**The Simpsons** (Fox)	Hope and Gloria (NBC)	Search for a bearable disease-of-the-week movie, a classic Hollywood movie or hope for a quality *Masterpiece Theatre* production.			

Fall 1995 Season

Beverly Hills 90210

The X-Files

Murphy Brown

Day	Network	8:00–8:30
M	ABC	The Marshal————
	CBS	The Nanny
	NBC	Fresh Prince of Bel Air
	FOX	Melrose Place————
	UPN	Star Trek: Voyager————
T	ABC	Roseanne
	CBS	John Grisham's The Client
	NBC	Wings
	FOX	Fox Tuesday Night Movie————
	UPN	Deadly Games————
W	ABC	Ellen
	CBS	Bless This House
	NBC	SeaQuest DSV————
	FOX	Beverly Hills 90210————
	WB	Sister, Sister
Th	ABC	Charlie Grace————
	CBS	Murder, She Wrote
	NBC	Friends
	FOX	Living Single
F	ABC	Family Matters
	CBS	Dweebs
	NBC	Unsolved Mysteries————
	FOX	Strange Luck————
Sat	ABC	Maybe This Time
	CBS	Dr. Quinn, Medicine Woman————
	NBC	JAG————
	FOX	Martin

Day	Network	7:00–7:30	7:30–8:00	
Sun	ABC	America's Funniest Videos Hour————————→		Lois and Clark————
	CBS	60 Minutes————————→		Cybill
	NBC	Brotherly Love	Minor Adjustments	Mad About You
	FOX	Space: Above and Beyond————————→		The Simpsons
	WB	Steven Spielberg presents Pinky and the Brain	Sister, Sister	Kirk

8:30-9:00	9:00-9:30	9:30-10:00	10:00-11:00
	Monday Night Football————————————————————————→		
Can't Hurry Love	Murphy Brown	If Not for You	Chicago Hope
In the House	NBC Monday Night Movie——————————————————————→		
————————————→	Partners	Ned and Stacey	
————————————→	Nowhere Man———————————————————→		
Hudson Street	Home Improvement	Coach	NYPD Blue
————————————→	CBS Tuesday Night Movie————————————————————→		
NewsRadio	Frasier	Pursuit of Happiness	Dateline NBC
————————————→		————————————→	
————————————→	Live Shot——————————————————————→		
The Drew Carey Show	Grace Under Fire	Wilde Again	PrimeTime Live
Dave's World	Central Park West————————————→		Courthouse
————————————→	Dateline NBC——————————————→		Law & Order
————————————→	Party of Five———————————————→		
The Parent 'Hood	The Wayans Brothers	Unhappily Ever After	
————————————→	The Monroes———————————————→		Murder One
————————————→	New York News——————————————→		48 Hours
The Single Guy	Seinfeld	Caroline in the City	ER
The Crew	New York Undercover————————————→		
Boy Meets World	Step by Step	Hangin' With Mr. Cooper	20/20
Bonnie	Picket Fences————————————→		American Gothic
————————————→	Dateline NBC——————————————→		Homicide: Life on the Street
————————————→	The X-Files——————————————→		
Somewhere in America	ABC Saturday Night Movie————————————————————————→		
————————————→	Touched by an Angel————————————→		Walker, Texas Ranger
————————————→	John Larroquette Show	The Home Court	Sisters
The Preston Episodes	Cops	America' s Most Wanted	
————————————→	ABC Sunday Night Movie————————————————————————→		
Almost Perfect	CBS Sunday Night Movie————————————————————————→		
Hope and Gloria	NBC Sunday Night Movie————————————————————————→		
Too Something	Married . . . With Children	Misery Loves Company———————————→	
Simon	First Time Out	Cleghorne!	

1994–1995 Prime-Time Nielsen Ratings

FALL 1994

Home Improvement

Rank	Show	Network	Rating*
1.	Home Improvement	ABC	20.8
2.	Grace Under Fire	ABC	20.0
3.	Seinfeld	NBC	19.7
4.	ER	NBC	18.5
5.	NYPD Blue	ABC	18.1
6.	60 Minutes	CBS	17.9
7.	Monday Night Football	ABC	17.4
8.	Roseanne	ABC	17.3
9.	Murder, She Wrote	CBS	16.2
10.	Ellen	ABC	15.5
11.	Frasier	NBC	15.0
12.	Mad About You	NBC	14.8
13.	Murphy Brown	CBS	14.8
14.	CBS Sunday Night Movie	CBS	14.7
15.	Madman of the People	NBC	14.6
16.	NBC Monday Night Movie	NBC	14.1
17.	Friends	NBC	13.9
18.	Dave's World	CBS	13.8
19.	20/20	ABC	13.7
20.	Me and the Boys	ABC	13.5
21.	Full House	ABC	13.0
22.	Law & Order	NBC	12.9

Rank	Show	Network	Rating
23.	Love and War	CBS	12.8
24.	Northern Exposure	CBS	12.8
25.	The Nanny	CBS	12.8
26.	ABC Sunday Night Movie	ABC	12.8
27.	Wings	NBC	12.6
28.	NBC Sunday Night Movie	NBC	12.0
29.	Beverly Hills 90210	Fox	11.6
30.	Step by Step	ABC	11.7
31.	The Martin Short Show	NBC	11.7
32.	Walker, Texas Ranger	CBS	11.6
33.	Dr. Quinn, Medicine Woman	CBS	11.5
34.	Family Matters	ABC	11.5
35.	Dateline NBC, Tuesday	NBC	11.5
36.	CBS Tuesday Movie	CBS	11.4
37.	Boy Meets World	ABC	11.4
38.	John Larroquette Show	NBC	11.4
39.	Hangin' With Mr. Cooper	ABC	11.3
40.	Turning Point	ABC	11.2
41.	Earth 2	NBC	10.9
42.	Due South	CBS	10.9
43.	Rescue 911	CBS	10.9
44.	Fresh Prince of Bel Air	NBC	10.6
45.	Chicago Hope	CBS	10.7
46.	Blossom	NBC	10.6
47.	All American Girl	ABC	10.5
48.	Diagnosis Murder	CBS	10.5
49.	Cosby Mysteries	NBC	10.5
50.	Picket Fences	CBS	10.3
51.	SeaQuest DSV	NBC	10.2
52.	Dateline NBC, Wednesday	NBC	10.2
53.	Lois and Clark	ABC	10.1
54.	Thunder Alley	ABC	10.0
55.	The Simpsons 2	Fox	10.0
56.	PrimeTime Live	ABC	10.0
57.	Coach	ABC	10.0
58.	Married ... With Children	Fox	9.9

*Each rating point represents 954,000 households using television

Rank	Show	Network	Rating
59.	*Matlock*	ABC	9.8
60.	*The Commish*	ABC	9.6
61.	*Sister, Sister*	ABC	9.6
62.	*48 Hours*	CBS	9.5
63.	*The Simpsons*	Fox	9.5
64.	*Melrose Place*	Fox	9.5
65.	*The Five Mrs. Buchanans*	CBS	9.4
66.	*America's Funniest Home Videos*	ABC	9.4
67.	*Under Suspicion*	CBS	9.3
68.	*The Boys Are Back*	CBS	9.3
69.	*The X-Files*	Fox	9.1
70.	*Sisters*	NBC	9.1
71.	*Dateline NBC, Friday*	NBC	9.0
72.	*Coach 2*	ABC	8.9
73.	*Daddy's Girls*	CBS	8.9
74.	*Touched by An Angel*	CBS	8.8
75.	*Living Single*	Fox	8.8
76.	*Hearts Afire*	CBS	8.7
77.	*Unsolved Mysteries*	NBC	8.7
78.	*Eye to Eye With Connie Chung*	CBS	8.6
79.	*ABC Saturday Night Movie*	ABC	8.4
80.	*Martin*	Fox	8.0
81.	*On Our Own*	ABC	8.0
82.	*Sweet Justice*	NBC	7.9
83.	*Something Wilder*	NBC	7.6
84.	*New York Undercover*	Fox	7.6
85.	*Homicide*	NBC	7.5
86.	*McKenna*	ABC	7.5
87.	*Cops 2*	Fox	7.4
88.	*George Carlin Show*	Fox	7.3
89.	*Blue Skies*	ABC	7.3
90.	*America's Most Wanted*	Fox	7.2
91.	*Models Inc.*	Fox	7.2
92.	*Hardball*	Fox	7.2
93.	*Cops*	Fox	6.9
94.	*My So-Called Life*	ABC	6.8
95.	*Empty Nest*	NBC	6.7
96.	*Fox Tuesday Night Movie*	Fox	6.7
97.	*Wild Oats*	Fox	6.0
98.	*Party of Five*	Fox	5.9
99.	*Encounters*	Fox	5.4
100.	*M.A.N.T.I.S.*	Fox	5.2
101.	*Fortune Hunter*	Fox	5.0

SPRING 1995

Rank	Show	Network	Rating
1.	*ER*	NBC	21.6
2.	*Seinfeld*	NBC	21.5
3.	*Home Improvement*	ABC	19.3
4.	*Friends*	NBC	18.4
5.	*Grace Under Fire*	ABC	17.9
6.	*Madman of the People*	NBC	16.8
6.	*60 Minutes*	CBS	16.8
8.	*NYPD Blue*	ABC	15.8
9.	*Mad About You, Thursday*	NBC	15.6
10.	*Murder, She Wrote*	CBS	15.1
11.	*20/20*	ABC	14.7
12.	*Hope and Gloria*	NBC	14.6
13.	*Roseanne*	ABC	14.3
14.	*Frasier*	NBC	14.1
15.	*Ellen*	ABC	14.0
16.	*Murphy Brown*	CBS	13.9
17.	*PrimeTime Live*	ABC	13.6
18.	*Dave's World*	CBS	13.1
18.	*NBC Monday Night Movie*	NBC	13.1
20.	*CBS Sunday Night Movie*	CBS	13.0
21.	*Chicago Hope*	CBS	12.9
22.	*ABC Sunday Night Movie*	ABC	12.7
22.	*Cybill*	CBS	12.7
24.	*Me and the Boys*	ABC	12.6
24.	*Thunder Alley*	ABC	12.6
26.	*NBC Sunday Night Movie*	NBC	12.4
27.	*America's Funniest Home Videos 2*	ABC	12.3
27.	*The Nanny*	CBS	12.3
29.	*Dateline NBC, Tuesday*	NBC	12.0
29.	*Full House*	ABC	12.0
31.	*Boy Meets World*	ABC	11.8
32.	*Law & Order*	NBC	11.7
33.	*ABC Monday Night Movie*	ABC	11.6
33.	*Family Matters*	ABC	11.6
33.	*Wings*	NBC	11.6

Rank	Show	Network	Rating
36.	Dateline NBC, Wednesday	NBC	11.5
37.	NewsRadio	NBC	11.4
38.	Coach	ABC	11.3
38.	Step by Step	ABC	11.3
40.	Hangin' With Mr. Cooper	ABC	11.0
40.	Walker, Texas Ranger	CBS	11.0
42.	John Larroquette Show	NBC	10.9
43.	Lois and Clark	ABC	10.7
44.	Diagnosis Murder	CBS	10.6
44.	On Our Own	ABC	10.6
44.	Rescue 911	CBS	10.6
47.	In the House	NBC	10.5
47.	Pride and Joy	NBC	10.5
49.	Blossom	NBC	10.4
49.	Matlock	ABC	10.4
51.	All American Girl	ABC	10.3
51.	Sister, Sister	ABC	10.3
53.	Dr. Quinn, Medicine Woman	CBS	10.2
53.	Fresh Prince of Bel Air	NBC	10.2
55.	Beverly Hills 90210	Fox	10.1
55.	Dateline NBC, Friday	NBC	10.1
55.	Melrose Place	Fox	10.1
58.	Something Wilder	NBC	10.0
59.	America's Funniest Home Videos	ABC	9.9
60.	CBS Tuesday Night Movie	CBS	9.6
61.	Women of the House	CBS	9.4
61.	The X-Files	Fox	9.4
63.	Married . . . With Children	Fox	9.3
63.	Northern Exposure	CBS	9.3
63.	The Simpsons	Fox	9.3
66.	Unsolved Mysteries	NBC	9.2
67.	The Cosby Mysteries	NBC	9.1
67.	Due South	CBS	9.1
69.	Sisters	NBC	8.9
70.	Living Single	Fox	8.8
71.	SeaQuest DSV	NBC	8.7
72.	The Commish	ABC	8.6
72.	Day One	ABC	8.6
72.	Homicide: Life on the Street	NBC	8.6
72.	Picket Fences	CBS	8.6
76.	48 Hours	CBS	8.5
77.	Under Suspicion	CBS	8.3
78.	The Boys Are Back	CBS	8.1
78.	Martin	Fox	8.1
80.	CBS Wednesday Night Movie	CBS	8.0
80.	Cops 2	Fox	8.0
80.	Eye to Eye With Connie Chung	CBS	8.0
80.	The Marshal	ABC	8.0
80.	Sliders	Fox	8.0
85.	America's Most Wanted	Fox	7.9
85.	The Five Mrs. Buchanans	CBS	7.9
85.	House of Buggin'	Fox	7.9
85.	NBA Basketball, Game 2	NBC	7.9
89.	A Whole New Ballgame	ABC	7.8
89.	Under One Roof	CBS	7.8
91.	Hearts Afire	CBS	7.7
91.	Star Trek: Voyager	UPN	7.7
93.	ABC Saturday Night Movie	ABC	7.4
93.	Cops	Fox	7.4
93.	The Critic	Fox	7.4
93.	The George Wendt Show	CBS	7.4
93.	New York Undercover	Fox	7.4
98.	Extreme	ABC	7.3
98.	The Wright Verdicts	CBS	7.3
100.	My So-Called Life	ABC	7.2
100.	Sweet Justice	NBC	7.2
102.	Earth 2	NBC	7.1
102.	Mommies	NBC	7.1
104.	Empty Nest	NBC	7.0
104.	Love and War	CBS	7.0
106.	Models Inc.	Fox	6.8
107	Party of Five	Fox	6.7
108.	The Office	CBS	6.6
109.	Double Rush	CBS	6.5
110.	Fox Tuesday Night Movie	Fox	6.4
111.	Amazing Grace	NBC	6.1
112.	Burke's Law	CBS	6.0
112.	Dream On	Fox	6.0
112.	Medicine Ball	Fox	6.0
115.	The Simpsons 2	Fox	5.6
116.	V.R. 5	Fox	5.4
117.	M.A.N.T.I.S.	Fox	5.1
118.	Get Smart	Fox	5.0
119.	Legend	UPN	4.2
120.	Encounters	Fox	4.0
121.	Great Defender	Fox	3.4

RANK	SHOW	NETWORK	RATING
121.	*Marker*	UPN	3.4
123.	*Platypus Man*	UPN	2.6
123.	*The Watcher*	UPN	2.6
125.	*Pig Sty*	UPN	2.4

RANK	SHOW	NETWORK	RATING
126.	*The Wayans Brothers*	WB	2.1
127.	*The Parent 'Hood*	WB	2.0
128.	*Unhappily Ever After*	WB	1.8
129.	*Muscle*	WB	1.5

OVERALL 1994–1995 RATINGS

ER

RANK	SHOW	NETWORK	RATING
1.	*Seinfeld*	NBC	20.5
2.	*ER*	NBC	20.0
3.	*Home Improvement*	ABC	19.9
4.	*Grace Under Fire*	ABC	18.8
5.	*NFL Monday Night Football*	ABC	17.8
6.	*60 Minutes*	CBS	17.1
7.	*NYPD Blue*	ABC	16.5
8.	*Friends*	NBC	16.1
9.	*Roseanne*	ABC	15.6
9.	*Murder, She Wrote*	CBS	15.6
11.	*Mad About You, Thursday*	NBC	15.2
12.	*Madman of the People*	NBC	14.9
13.	*Ellen*	ABC	14.7
14.	*Hope and Gloria*	NBC	14.6
15.	*Frasier*	NBC	14.3
16.	*Murphy Brown*	CBS	14.1
17.	*20/20*	ABC	14.0
18.	*CBS Sunday Night Movie*	CBS	13.7
19.	*NBC Monday Night Movie*	NBC	13.5
20.	*Dave's World*	CBS	13.4
21.	*Me and the Boys*	ABC	13.1

RANK	SHOW	NETWORK	RATING
22	*Cybill*	CBS	12.8
23.	*ABC Sunday Night Movie*	ABC	12.7
24.	*The Nanny*	CBS	12.5
24.	*Full House*	ABC	12.5
26.	*America's Funniest Home Videos 2*	ABC	12.4
27.	*Law & Order*	NBC	12.2
28.	*Chicago Hope*	CBS	12.0
28.	*NBC Sunday Night Movie*	NBC	12.0
30.	*Wings*	NBC	11.9
31.	*PrimeTime Live*	ABC	11.7
31.	*ABC Monday Night Movie*	ABC	11.7
31.	*The Martin Short Show*	NBC	11.7
34.	*Family Matters*	ABC	11.6
34.	*Dateline NBC, Tuesday*	NBC	11.6
36.	*Thunder Alley*	ABC	11.5
36.	*Turning Point*	ABC	11.5
36.	*Boy Meets World*	ABC	11.5
38.	*Step by Step*	ABC	11.4
38.	*NewsRadio*	NBC	11.4
40.	*Hangin' With Mr. Cooper*	ABC	11.2
40.	*Walker, Texas Ranger*	CBS	11.2
40.	*Northern Exposure*	CBS	11.2
43.	*John Larroquette Show*	NBC	11.1
43.	*In the House*	NBC	11.1
45.	*Beverly Hills 90210*	Fox	11.0
46.	*Love and War*	CBS	10.9
47.	*Rescue 911*	CBS	10.8
49.	*Dr. Quinn, Medicine Woman*	CBS	10.7
49.	*Dateline NBC, Wednesday*	NBC	10.7
51.	*All American Girl*	ABC	10.6
51.	*CBS Tuesday Night Movie*	CBS	10.6
53.	*Coach*	ABC	10.5
53.	*Pride and Joy*	NBC	10.5
55.	*Diagnosis Murder*	CBS	10.4
55.	*Fresh Prince of Bel Air*	NBC	10.4
55.	*Blossom*	NBC	10.4

Rank	Show	Network	Rating
58.	*Due South*	CBS	10.2
58.	*Lois & Clark*	ABC	10.2
60.	*Sister, Sister*	ABC	10.1
61.	*Matlock*	ABC	10.0
62.	*The Cosby Mysteries*	NBC	9.9
63.	*Melrose Place*	Fox	9.8
64.	*Picket Fences*	CBS	9.5
64.	*America's Funniest Home Videos*	ABC	9.5
64.	*Married . . . With Children*	Fox	9.5
64.	*SeaQuest DSV*	NBC	9.5
68.	*The Simpsons*	Fox	9.4
68.	*Dateline NBC, Friday*	NBC	9.4
68.	*Women of the House*	CBS	9.4
71.	*The X-Files*	Fox	9.2
72.	*Fox NFL Sunday — Postgame Show*	Fox	9.1
72.	*Something Wilder*	NBC	9.1
72.	*48 Hours*	CBS	9.1
75.	*The Commish*	ABC	9.0
75.	*Unsolved Mysteries*	NBC	9.0
75.	*Sisters*	NBC	9.0
78.	*Under Suspicion*	CBS	8.9
78.	*Earth 2*	NBC	8.9
78.	*Daddy's Girls*	CBS	8.9
78.	*Coach 2*	ABC	8.9
78.	*Touched by an Angel*	CBS	8.9
83.	*On Our Own*	ABC	8.7
83.	*Living Single*	Fox	8.7
85.	*The Five Mrs. Buchanans*	CBS	8.6
85.	*The Boys Are Back*	CBS	8.6
87.	*Day One*	ABC	8.5
88.	*Eye to Eye With Connie Chung*	CBS	8.3
89.	*Homicide: Life on the Street*	NBC	8.2
89.	*Sliders*	Fox	8.2
89.	*Hearts Afire*	CBS	8.2
92.	*Martin*	Fox	8.1
92.	*CBS Wednesday Night Movie*	CBS	8.1
94.	*McKenna*	ABC	8.0
95.	*House of Buggin'*	Fox	7.9
95.	*Under One Roof*	CBS	7.9
95.	*The Marshal*	ABC	7.9
95.	*Star Trek: Voyager*	UPN	7.9
95.	*NBA Basketball Game 2, Sunday*	NBC	7.9
100.	*A Whole New Ballgame*	ABC	7.8
101.	*Cops 2*	Fox	7.7
102.	*Sweet Justice*	NBC	7.6
102.	*America's Most Wanted*	Fox	7.6
104.	*ABC Saturday Family Movie*	ABC	7.5
104.	*Blue Skies*	ABC	7.5
104.	*The Critic*	Fox	7.5
107.	*The Simpsons 2*	Fox	7.4
107.	*The George Wendt Show*	CBS	7.4
107.	*Hardball*	Fox	7.4
107.	*New York Undercover*	Fox	7.4
107.	*Extreme*	ABC	7.4
112.	*The Wright Verdicts*	CBS	7.3
113.	*Cops*	Fox	7.1
113.	*Models Inc.*	Fox	7.1
113.	*Mommies*	NBC	7.1
116.	*My So-Called Life*	ABC	7.0
116.	*George Carlin Show*	Fox	7.0
118.	*Empty Nest*	NBC	6.9
119.	*Fox Tuesday Night Movie*	Fox	6.6
119.	*The Office*	CBS	6.6
121.	*Wild Oats*	Fox	6.5
121.	*Best of The X-Files*	Fox	6.5
121.	*Double Rush*	CBS	6.5
124.	*Amazing Grace*	NBC	6.3
125.	*Party of Five*	Fox	6.2
126.	*Medicine Ball*	Fox	6.1
127.	*Burke's Law*	CBS	6.0
127.	*Dream On*	Fox	6.0
129.	*V.R. 5*	Fox	5.6
130.	*Fortune Hunter*	Fox	5.3
130.	*M.A.N.T.I.S.*	Fox	5.3
132.	*Encounters*	Fox	5.1
133.	*Get Smart*	Fox	5.0
134.	*Marker*	UPN	3.4
134.	*Great Defender*	Fox	3.4
136.	*Platypus Man*	UPN	2.7
137.	*The Watcher*	UPN	2.6
138.	*Pig Sty*	UPN	2.4
139.	*The Wayans Brothers*	WB	2.1
140.	*The Parent 'Hood*	WB	2.0
141.	*Unhappily Ever After*	WB	1.8
142.	*Muscle*	WB	1.6

1994–1995 Emmy Awards

The 47th Annual Emmy Awards were presented in two ceremonies, one untelevised on September 9, 1995, and the other televised on September 10, 1995.

Outstanding Drama Series
NYPD Blue (ABC)

Outstanding Lead Actor in a Drama Series
Mandy Patinkin, *Chicago Hope*

Outstanding Lead Actress in a Drama Series
Kathy Baker, *Picket Fences*

Outstanding Supporting Actor in a Drama Series
Ray Walston, *Picket Fences*

Outstanding Supporting Actress in a Drama Series
Julianna Margulies, *ER*

Outstanding Guest Actor in a Drama Series
Paul Winfield, *Picket Fences*: "Enemy Lines"

Outstanding Guest Actress in a Drama Series
Shirley Knight, *NYPD Blue*: "Large Mouth Bass"

Outstanding Individual Achievement in Directing in a Drama Series
Mimi Leder, *ER*: "Love's Labor Lost"

Outstanding Individual Achievement in Writing in a Drama Series
Lance A. Gentile, *ER*: "Love's Labor Lost"

Outstanding Comedy Series
Frasier (NBC)

Outstanding Lead Actor in a Comedy Series
Kelsey Grammer, *Frasier*

Outstanding Lead Actress in a Comedy Series
Candice Bergen, *Murphy Brown*

Outstanding Supporting Actor in a Comedy Series
David Hyde Pierce, *Frasier*

Outstanding Supporting Actress in a Comedy Series
Christine Baranski, *Cybill*

Outstanding Guest Actor in a Comedy Series
Carl Reiner, *Mad About You*: "The Alan Brady Show"

Outstanding Guest Actress in a Comedy Series
Cyndi Lauper, *Mad About You*: "Money Changes Everything"

Outstanding Individual Achievement in Directing in a Comedy Series
David Lee, *Frasier*: "The Matchmaker"

Outstanding Individual Achievement in Writing in a Comedy Series
Chuck Ranberg and Anne Flett-Giordano, *Frasier*: "An Affair to Remember"

Outstanding Variety, Music or Comedy Series
The Tonight Show With Jay Leno (NBC)

Outstanding Individual Performance in a Variety or Music Program
Barbra Streisand, *Barbra Streisand: The Concert*

Outstanding Individual Achievement in Directing in a Variety or Music Program
Jeff Margolis, *The 67th Annual Academy Awards*

Outstanding Individual Achievement in Writing in a Variety or Music Program
Eddie Feldmann, writing supervisor; Jeff Cesario, Ed Driscoll, David Feldman, Gregory Greenberg, Dennis Miller and Kevin Rooney, writers, *Dennis Miller Live*

Outstanding Variety, Music or Comedy Special
Barbra Streisand: The Concert (HBO)

Outstanding Miniseries
Joseph (TNT)

Outstanding Lead Actor in a Miniseries or Special
Raul Julia, *The Burning Season*

Outstanding Lead Actress in a Miniseries or a Special
Glenn Close, *Serving in Silence: The Margarethe Cammermeyer Story*

Outstanding Supporting Actor in a Miniseries or Special
Donald Sutherland, *Citizen X*

Outstanding Supporting Actress in a Miniseries or a Special (tie)
Judy Davis, *Serving in Silence: The Margarethe Cammermeyer Story*

Shirley Knight, *Indictment: The McMartin Trial*

Outstanding Individual Achievement in Directing in a Miniseries or a Special
John Frankenheimer, *The Burning Season*

Outstanding Individual Achievement in Writing in a Miniseries or a Special
Alison Cross, writer, *Serving in Silence: The Margarethe Cammermeyer Story*

Outstanding Made for Television Movie
Indictment: The McMartin Trial (HBO)

Outstanding Informational Series (tie)
Baseball (PBS)

TV Nation (NBC)

Outstanding Information Special
Taxicab Confessions (HBO)

Outstanding Cultural Program
Verdi's La Traviata — With the New York City Opera (PBS)

Outstanding Children's Program (Prime Time)
The World Wildlife Fund Presents — Going, Going, Almost Gone! Animals in Danger (HBO)

Outstanding Animated Program (for Programming One Hour or Less)
The Simpsons (Fox)

Planned Cable Channels

Here's a glimpse at the cable future. If the telecommunications bill being debated at publication date becomes law, look for cable systems to add new channels and networks such as these, which have been on the drawing boards but are as yet unlaunched, to debut on your local system.

Action America
Audience participation programming

America's Collectibles Network
Home shopping for gems, coins and jewelry

America's Health Network
Home shopping and live call-in medical advice

Animal Planet
Nature and wildlife programming

Applause!
Drama and variety shows from the 1950s and 1960s, and alternative films and videos from independent producers

Arts and Craft Network
Arts-and-crafts-oriented home-shopping

Arts and Antiques Network
Arts, antiques and historic preservation programming with live interactive auctions

The Auto Channel
Motor sports and information with interactive elements

Automotive Television Network/ATN
Motor sports and automobile information

BBC World Channel
International news and documentary programming

The Benefit Network
Education and entertainment programming to benefit worthy causes

BET on Jazz
Jazz video, performance and feature programming

Black Shopping Network
Home shopping channel with products targeted to African Americans

Booknet
Home shopping and discussions, movies and documentaries related to books

Career and Education Opportunity Network
Programs that provide information about career and education opportunities

The CEO Channel
Programs of interest to corporate leaders

Channel 500
Nonfiction and documentary programming

Children's Cable Network
Entertainment and education programming for children

Children's Television Workshop
Entertainment and education programming for children

CHOP TV
Martial arts-related programming

Classics Arts Showcase
Performing arts clips shown to sell full-length videos

Classics Music Channel
Classic videos of various music genres

c/NET: The Computer Network
Computer, on-line and interactive programming

Collectors Channel
Interactive service of interest to merchandise and memorabilia collectors

Conservative Television Network
News, information and entertainment geared toward viewers of conservative political orientation

Consumer Resource Network
New consumer products and services information channel

Davinci Time and Space
Children's education and entertainment programming with interactive elements

The Ecology Channel
Environmental issues programming

The Enrichment Channel
Global perspectives of human potential, self-help and news

Entertainment Prosperity Insight Channel
Information programming about money, sex and power

Fashion and Design Television
Fashion, design, travel and entertainment programming

Fashion and Style Network
Fashion information programming

Gaming Entertainment Television
Live coverage of worldwide gaming with interactive elements

Global Village Network
International business and culture programming

Golden American Network
Talk shows, news, interactive games shows and information services for senior citizens

The Gospel Network
Entertainment and gospel music programming

The Health Channel
Health, medical and personal care services

Hip-Hop Television
Sitcoms, music videos, arts and poetry programming targeted to young African Americans

Hobby Craft Network
Demonstrations of various hobbies and crafts by artisans

Horizons Cable
National cultural and intellectual events programming

International Channel Multiplex
Separate pay channels in many different languages including Mandarin, Polish and Tagalog

The Jackpot Channel
Entertainment programming featuring the game industry

Jones Health Network
Health information programming

Jones Language Network
Language-education programming

Las Vegas Television Network
Las Vegas lifestyle and entertainment programming

Lightspan
Interactive education for children

Living
Home-living programs such as cooking and how-to shows

The Lottery Channel
State lottery information and entertainment programming

The Love Network
Programs concerning self-esteem, self-improvement and relationships

The MBC Movie Network
Movie channel targeted to African Americans

Music Video Service
Music-video programming

National Health Network
Health-care information programming

New Culture Network
Independent, student and foreign films aimed at twentysomethings

New Science Network
News and information of developments in science

Newsworld International
Global news and documentaries

Ovation — The Fine Arts Channel
Performance and visual arts programming

Parents Channel
Child development information and instruction channel

Parent Television
Parenting, family life and prenatal care issues

Parenting Satellite Television Network
Home shopping and programs for parents of children and teens

The Pet Television Network
Programs of interest to pet owners and animal lovers

Planet Central Television
Human development and national and global events from an ecological perspective

Play and Win Channel
Interactive, trivia-oriented programming

Premiere Horse Network
Equestrian, rodeo and related events coverage

Prime Life Network
Programming for senior citizens

Product Viewpoint
Video catalogs, brochures and magazines with interactive format

Quark!
Science and technology programming with focus on the information superhighway

The Real Estate Network
Homes, home improvement, architecture and real estate investment information and an interactive home browsing service

Recoverynet/The Wellness Channel
Self-help programming for people with problems such as drug addiction and sexual abuse

Romance Classics
Romantic classic movies and original programming

The Seminar Channel
Health-education programming

Sewing and Needle Arts Network
Sewing and crafts information, instruction and entertainment

Share TV
Multi-niche programming covering pets, weddings and books

The Singles Network
Singles' lifestyle programming

Singlevision
Lifestyle, travel and local dating service

Speedvision
Automotive, aviation and marine information

The Success Channel
Education and motivational programming

Sundance Film Channel
Independent film programming

Talk TV Network
All-talk programming

TCI/Microsoft Channel
Personal computer developments, multimedia and home shopping

The Technology Channel
Technological developments information programming

Telecompras Shopping Network
Home shopping for Spanish-speaking viewers

Time Traveler
Historical documentaries

Trax: High Performance Television
Home-shopping and motor-sports programming

Trio
Family entertainment and non-fiction programming

TSM
Home-shopping programming

TV5
French-language channel

WFIT/The Health and Fitness Network
Health and lifestyle information

Women's Sports Network
News coverage and information on women's sports

Women's Sports Service
Coverage and news of women's sporting events

World African Network
Programming of interest to people of African descent

WorldJazz
Jazz programming

XTV
Independent and student films of interest to Generation X

Public Radio at the Crossroads

■ BY ROBERT SIEGEL

Robert Siegel hosts NPR's _All Things Considered_.

BY ANY CONVENTIONAL STANDARD, 1994 and 1995 were banner years for National Public Radio. The network's coverage of Africa won two duPont-Columbia University Awards (to Michael Skolar for his reporting on the flight of Rwandan refugees, and to NPR News for coverage of the South African election, particularly on the afternoon _Talk of the Nation_). Two equally prestigious Peabody Awards went to NPR, one for _Wade in the Water,_ a series on religious music, and the other to NPR science reporters for their stories on the tobacco industry's knowledge of the dangers of nicotine.

RADIO

The system's success was measured in quantity as well as quality. By 1995, NPR comprised 227 full-service member radio stations, as well as another 250 stations enjoying lesser forms of membership. Stations typically offered either news and information programming, classical music, jazz or a mix of all of the above. NPR's most listened to programs nationwide were the newsmagazines _Morning Edition, All Things Considered_ and _Weekend Edition_, as well as programs distributed by NPR, but produced independently: _Fresh Air With Terry Gross,_ an hourlong interview program from WHYY, Philadelphia and _Cartalk,_ Tom and Ray Magliozzi's authoritative and hilarious program of automotive advice. Many NPR member stations affiliated as well to Public Radio International (PRI), the renamed American Public Radio. Its most popular programs included _A Prairie Home Companion With Garrison Keillor,_ successfully repatriated to the Twin Cities after a New York City sojourn in the late 1980s, and _Marketplace,_ a weekday afternoon business program produced in Los Angeles.

From the standpoint of NPR's Washington D.C. headquarters in the renovated bank building it purchased and occupied in February 1994, the future was relatively rosy for the ever-perilous non-profit sector. NPR News and Information was a rarity: a network

Newt Gingrich

466

news division that provided the core of the network's audience. According to Arbitron, just under 10 million Americans heard at least one NPR news broadcast every week. The most troubling prospect for NPR News executives was a plan for a beefed-up competitor from PRI, a weekday hourlong news program, concentrating on international affairs, produced in partnership with the British Broadcasting Corporation. It was intended to offer public radio stations what All Things Considered had not, programming for the hour from 4:00 p.m. Eastern Time until 5:00 p.m., an hour deemed rich in potential public radio listeners. In response to the challenge from PRI, and to long-standing requests from its member stations, NPR adopted a plan to shift All Things Considered to 4:00 p.m. and expand it from 90 minutes to two hours — the most ambitious program expansion the network had undertaken since the launch of its two Weekend Edition programs in the mid-1980s.

By mid-1995, the outlook for NPR, and for all public radio was far less sanguine. Among the many questions about the role and limits of national government and federal funding raised by the 1994 congressional election was the question of public broadcasting: should public radio stations and national producers (primarily NPR) enjoy the benefits of public subsidy? Cutting federal funding was not a provision of the Republican Contract With America, but within days of the Republican victory, its main author, Speaker-designate of the House of Representatives Newt Gingrich, indicated his desire to eliminate federal funding altogether. In the congressional hearings, grassroots campaigns and dozens of op-ed articles and editorials that followed, the American public was asked to reconsider taxpayer support for public radio and television. Public broadcasters urged Congress to maintain federal funding, speaking in unison at the outset of the debate, but dividing into two distinct camps.

Critics marshaled several arguments against federal funding for public broadcasting. First, and least specific to the case of broadcasting,

What Do They Look Like?

The voices of NPR have inspired, informed and charmed many of us, becoming as welcome and reassuring as family members. Now you have a face to go with the voice.

Robert Siegel, Linda Wertheimer and **Noah Adams**
Hosts, *All Things Considered*

George Collinet
Host, *Afropop Worldwide*

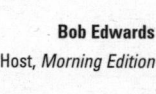

Bob Edwards
Host, *Morning Edition*

Liane Hansen
Host, *Weekend Edition*

Terry Gross
Host, *Fresh Air*

Cokie Roberts
Senior News Analyst

Scott Simon
Host, *Weekend Edition*

was a simple fiscal argument: the federal deficit is enormous and expanding; all expenditures should be reduced or eliminated; and public radio is no different from farm subsidies or the U.S. Department of Commerce. In addition, there were questions posed specifically to public broadcasters: Why should taxpayers support radio stations they choose not to listen to? Why support public television in the age of cable? Conservative media critics assailed public radio as a liberal bastion, whose programs subverted Christianity, Judaism and the values of the American family.

Speaker Gingrich summed up his position in a February 1995 speech to former Republican congressional staffers. "I will not recognize a proposal that will appropriate money for the CPB [Corporation for Public Broadcasting]." He added: "I don't understand why they call it public broadcasting. As far as I'm concerned, there's nothing public about it. It's an elitist enterprise. Rush Limbaugh is public broadcasting."

Later in the winter, in an unprecedented White House salute to National Public Radio, President Clinton pronounced himself "an NPR kind of president." More important was an outpouring of listener support for continued federal funding, encouraged by stations. Several arguments were made on public radio's behalf: its cost was barely thirty cents per citizen per year in tax dollars; unlike public television, it did not share the dial with cable channels providing similar programming; it provided unique service to rural areas too small to support commercial radio stations.

At stake in this debate was the financial health, perhaps the survival, of public radio in both the short and long term. Of the money appropriated to the CPB, most went to television, but its payments to qualified radio stations accounted on average for one sixth of their total financial resources. The typical NPR member station spent roughly one tenth of its budget to pay for NPR programming. A deep cut in CPB funding, it was feared, would put some small, highly CPB-dependent stations out of business. Deprived of their dues, NPR would be forced to cut service, reducing its value to larger stations. A downward spiral to insignificance was reasonably feared as the consequence of a rapid federal pull-out.

By the spring, a rapid pull-out appeared unlikely. Confronted with strong listener objections, Republican congressmen spoke of recisions in the previously appropriated budgets for fiscal years 1996 and 1997 on the order of 15 percent the first year and 30 percent the following year. Furthermore, the key congressional sub-committee chairman, Rep. John Porter (R-Illinois) and Rep. Jack Fields (R-Texas) asked public broadcasters to present new ideas on economies and new funding sources. Here the united front of public broadcasting cracked apart. Persuaded that there were no economies, or proprietary ventures that could replace federal dollars, NPR and PBS proposed a trust fund to be created with revenues from spectrum use and transfer charges.

The CPB, the only public broadcasting body that actually receives an appropriation from Congress, demurred and called only for a program of cost-cutting and revenue enhancement. In short, the CPB accepted what its beneficiaries did not: its extinction as a recipient of federal funds.

As the Congress moved toward rescinding some of public broadcasting's funds, much was unclear, but many issues were settled: public radio stations, despite very successful fundraising in the spring of 1995, foresaw cuts in their budgets, staffs and program offerings; NPR appeared guaranteed to survive two or three years of reduced funding; *All Things Considered*'s expansion, which might well have been a casualty of the cuts, was produced on schedule. The public radio system would be able to lean more heavily on its most successful national programs, but whether that support could substitute for lost federal funding three years down the road was the great question hovering over all of public radio. ∎

Susan Stamberg
Special Correspondent

Ray Suarez
Host, *Talk of the Nation*

Nina Totenberg
Legal Affairs
Correspondent

Daniel Zwerdling
Weekend Host,
All Things Considered

Radio Formats and Audiences

The following charts indicate percentages of the radio audience listening to a particular program format at a particular time of day. Note the changes in these format shares between audiences of different ages.

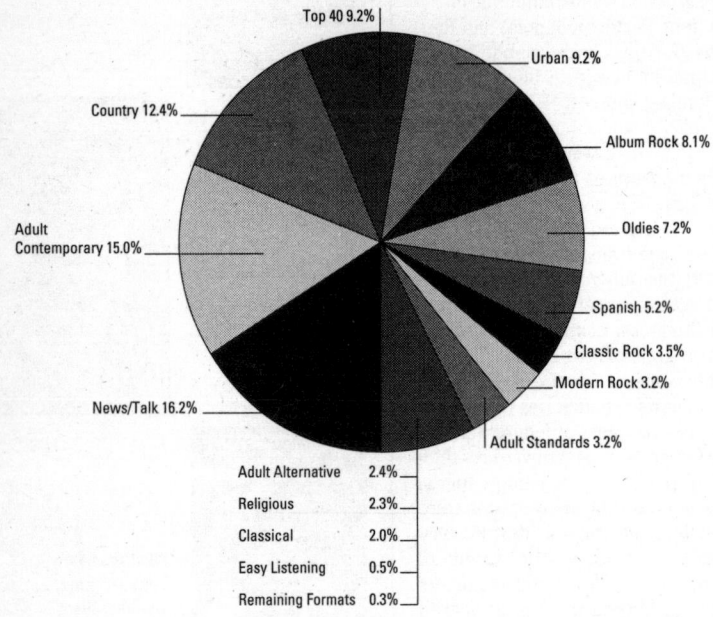

Top 40 9.2%
Urban 9.2%
Country 12.4%
Album Rock 8.1%
Adult Contemporary 15.0%
Oldies 7.2%
Spanish 5.2%
Classic Rock 3.5%
Modern Rock 3.2%
News/Talk 16.2%
Adult Standards 3.2%

Adult Alternative	2.4%
Religious	2.3%
Classical	2.0%
Easy Listening	0.5%
Remaining Formats	0.3%

SHARE OF LISTENING BY RADIO FORMATS
PERSONS 12+
FOR ALL MARKETS
MONDAY–SUNDAY, 6 A.M.–MIDNIGHT

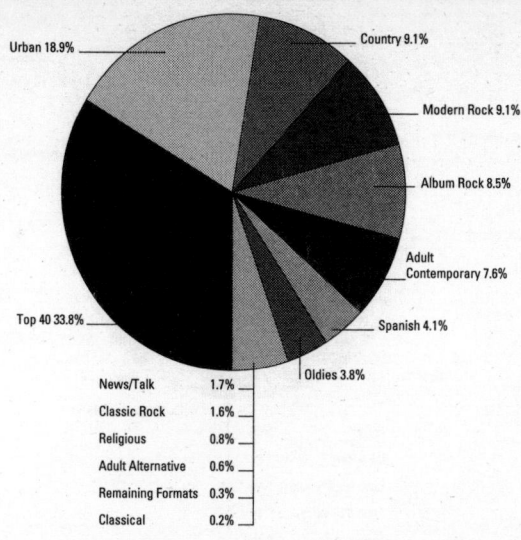

Urban 18.9%

Country 9.1%

Modern Rock 9.1%

Album Rock 8.5%

Adult Contemporary 7.6%

Spanish 4.1%

Oldies 3.8%

Top 40 33.8%

News/Talk 1.7%
Classic Rock 1.6%
Religious 0.8%
Adult Alternative 0.6%
Remaining Formats 0.3%
Classical 0.2%

**SHARE OF LISTENING BY RADIO FORMATS
PERSONS 12-17
FOR ALL MARKETS
MONDAY-SUNDAY, 6 A.M.-MIDNIGHT**

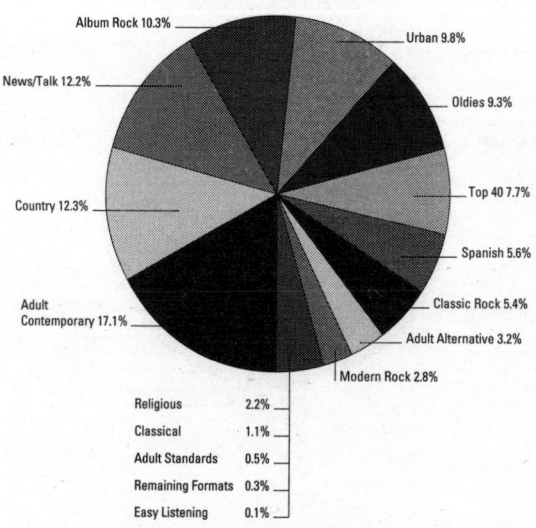

Album Rock 10.3%

Urban 9.8%

News/Talk 12.2%

Oldies 9.3%

Top 40 7.7%

Country 12.3%

Spanish 5.6%

Classic Rock 5.4%

Adult Alternative 3.2%

Adult Contemporary 17.1%

Modern Rock 2.8%

Religious 2.2%
Classical 1.1%
Adult Standards 0.5%
Remaining Formats 0.3%
Easy Listening 0.1%

**SHARE OF LISTENING BY RADIO FORMATS
PERSONS 25-49
FOR ALL MARKETS
MONDAY-SUNDAY, 6 A.M.-MIDNIGHT**

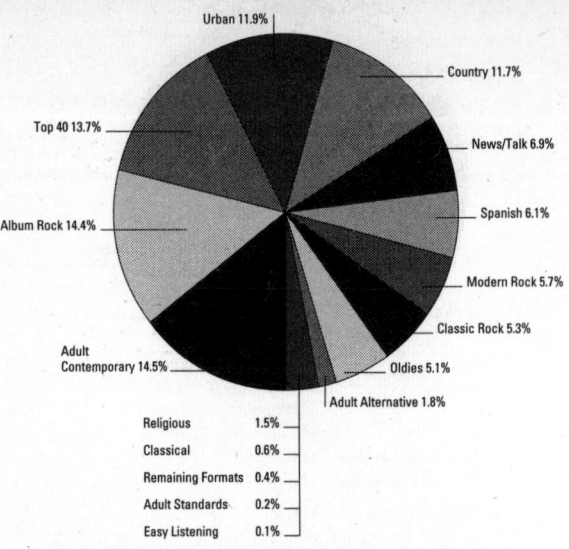

Urban 11.9%

Country 11.7%

Top 40 13.7%

News/Talk 6.9%

Album Rock 14.4%

Spanish 6.1%

Modern Rock 5.7%

Classic Rock 5.3%

Adult
Contemporary 14.5%

Oldies 5.1%

Adult Alternative 1.8%

Religious   1.5%
Classical   0.6%
Remaining Formats 0.4%
Adult Standards   0.2%
Easy Listening   0.1%

**SHARE OF LISTENING BY RADIO FORMATS
PERSONS 18–34
FOR ALL MARKETS
MONDAY–SUNDAY, 6 A.M.–MIDNIGHT**

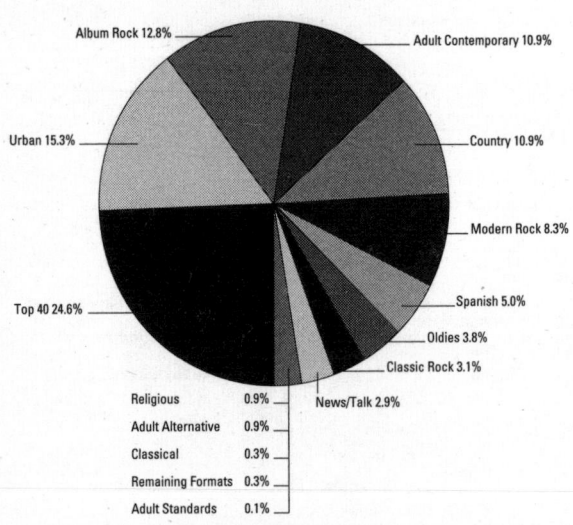

Album Rock 12.8%

Adult Contemporary 10.9%

Urban 15.3%

Country 10.9%

Modern Rock 8.3%

Spanish 5.0%

Oldies 3.8%

Classic Rock 3.1%

Top 40 24.6%

News/Talk 2.9%

Religious   0.9%
Adult Alternative 0.9%
Classical   0.3%
Remaining Formats 0.3%
Adult Standards   0.1%

**SHARE OF LISTENING BY RADIO FORMATS
PERSONS 12 – 24
FOR ALL MARKETS
MONDAY–SUNDAY, 6 A.M.–MIDNIGHT**

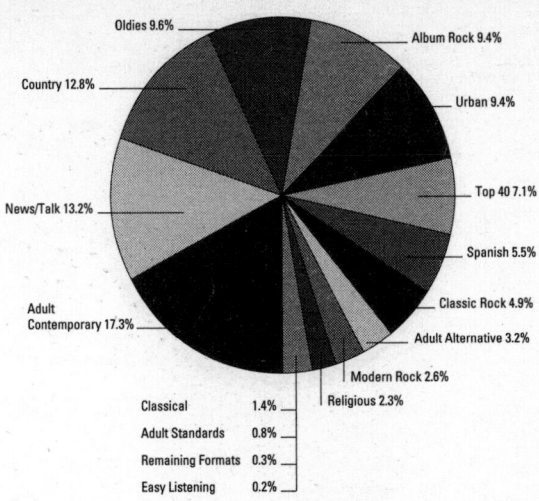

SHARE OF LISTENING BY RADIO FORMATS
PERSONS 25 – 54
FOR ALL MARKETS
MONDAY-SUNDAY, 6 A.M.-MIDNIGHT

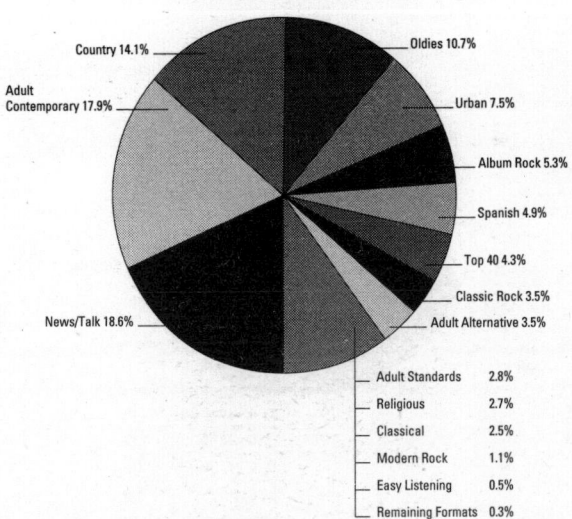

SHARE OF LISTENING BY RADIO FORMATS
PERSONS 35 – 64
FOR ALL MARKETS
MONDAY-SUNDAY, 6 A.M.-MIDNIGHT

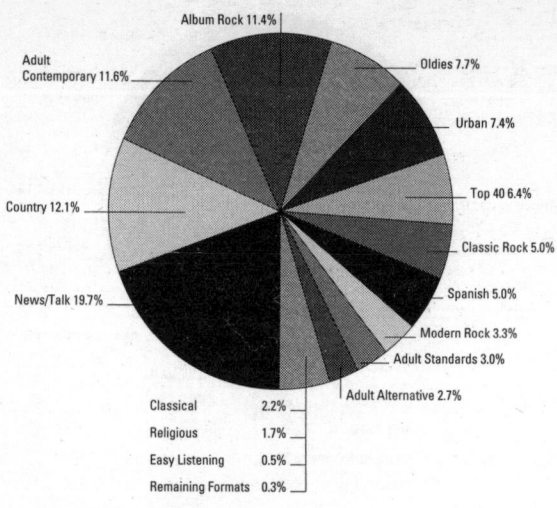

Album Rock 11.4%

Adult Contemporary 11.6%

Oldies 7.7%

Urban 7.4%

Top 40 6.4%

Country 12.1%

Classic Rock 5.0%

Spanish 5.0%

News/Talk 19.7%

Modern Rock 3.3%

Adult Standards 3.0%

Adult Alternative 2.7%

Classical 2.2%
Religious 1.7%
Easy Listening 0.5%
Remaining Formats 0.3%

SHARE OF LISTENING BY RADIO FORMATS
MEN 18+
FOR ALL MARKETS
MONDAY–SUNDAY, 6 A.M.–MIDNIGHT

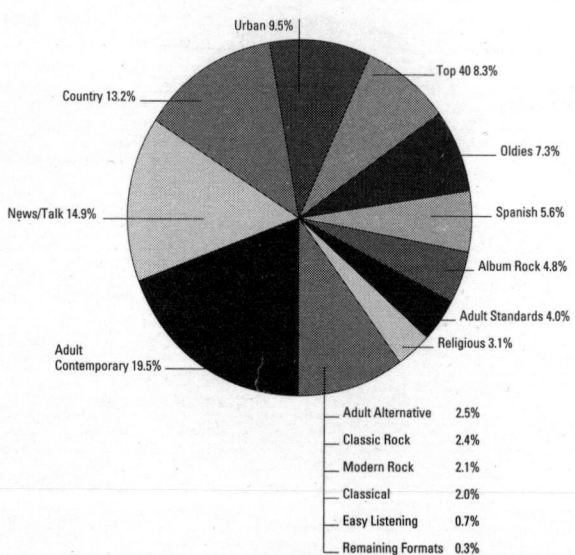

Urban 9.5%

Top 40 8.3%

Country 13.2%

Oldies 7.3%

News/Talk 14.9%

Spanish 5.6%

Album Rock 4.8%

Adult Standards 4.0%

Religious 3.1%

Adult Contemporary 19.5%

Adult Alternative 2.5%
Classic Rock 2.4%
Modern Rock 2.1%
Classical 2.0%
Easy Listening 0.7%
Remaining Formats 0.3%

SHARE OF LISTENING BY RADIO FORMATS
WOMEN 18+
FOR ALL MARKETS
MONDAY–SUNDAY, 6 A.M.–MIDNIGHT

Source: Arbitron Co.

Radio Audiences

The Arbitron Company measures radio listenership to determine audience size and help determine how much to charge advertisers for commercial time. The audience is measured in average quarter hour (AQH) segments.

TOP 100 STATIONS BY TOTAL AUDIENCE

These are the nation's largest stations defined by average quarter (AQH) statistics for the number of listeners 12 years old and up from Monday–Sunday, 6 a.m.– midnight.

FALL 1994

	Station	Frequency	Market	Format	AQH
1.	WCBS-FM	101.1	New York	Oldies	126,600
2.	WQHT	97.1	New York	R&B	124,900
3.	WABC	770	New York	Talk	119,900
4.	WLTW	106.7	New York	Soft Adult Contemporary	114,600
5.	WHTZ	100.3	New York	Contemporary Hits Radio/New Rock	108,400
6.	WSKQ-FM	97.9	New York	Spanish Classic Hits Radio	108,100
7.	WQCD	101.9	New York	Jazz	101,500
8.	WPLJ	95.5	New York	Adult Hits	99,000
9.	WBLS	107.5	New York	R&B	98,600
10.	WRKS	98.7	New York	R&B Oldies	97,400
11.	KLAX-FM	97.9	Los Angeles	Spanish/ Regional Mexican	95,800
12.	KPWR	105.9	Los Angeles	Dance/CHR	93,700
13.	WINS	1010	New York	News	92,700
14.	WCBS	880	New York	News	89,700
15.	WMXV	105.1	New York	Adult Contemporary	85,800
16.	WOR	710	New York	Talk	85,300
17.	WXRK	92.3	New York	Classic Rock	84,700
18.	WGN	720	Chicago	Talk	83,700
19.	KFI	640	Los Angeles	Talk	78,600
20.	WGCI-FM	107.5	Chicago	R&B	76,900
21.	KROQ-FM	106.7	Los Angeles	New Rock	76,200
22.	WFAN	660	New York	Sports	70,900
23.	WQXR-FM	96.3	New York	Classical	69,400
24.	KIIS-FM	102.7	Los Angeles	CHR	69,100
25.	KGO	810	San Francisco/Oakland	News/Talk	68,500
26.	KOST	103.5	Los Angeles	AC	67,600
27.	KRTH	101.1	Los Angeles	Oldies	65,100
28.	KKBT	92.3	Los Angeles	R&B	65,100
29.	WPAT-FM	93.1	New York	Soft AC	62,400
30.	KBIG	104.3	Los Angeles	AC	61,400
31.	WNEW	102.7	New York	Rock	58,700
32.	KABC	790	Los Angeles	News/Talk	55,300
33.	WJLB	97.9	Detroit	R&B	55,100

	Station	Frequency	Market	Format	AQH
34.	KMOX	1120	St. Louis	News/Talk	53,800
35.	KYW	1060	Philadelphia	News	53,300
36.	WPGC-FM	95.5	Washington	R&B	52,600
37.	WBBM-FM	96.3	Chicago	Dance/CHR	52,200
38.	WVAZ	102.7	Chicago	Urban AC	52,000
39.	KLVE	107.5	Los Angeles	Spanish/Tropical	51,600
40.	WVEE	103.3	Atlanta	R&B	50,700
41.	WUSN	99.5	Chicago	Country	50,100
42.	WLIT-FM	93.9	Chicago	Soft AC	50,000
43.	WJR	760	Detroit	News/Talk	48,400
44.	WBBM	780	Chicago	News	47,700
45.	WYNY	103.5	New York	Country	47,200
46.	KLOS	95.5	Los Angeles	Rock	46,700
47.	WAXQ	104.3	New York	Rock	45,700
48.	KDKA	1020	Pittsburgh	News/Talk	45,700
49.	WKHX-FM	101.5	Atlanta	Country	44,600
50.	WKQX	101.1	Chicago	New Rock	44,200
51.	WBZ	1030	Boston	News/Talk	44,100
52.	WADO	1280	New York	Spanish-News/Talk	43,800
53.	KYSR	98.7	Los Angeles	Adult Hits	43,600
54.	KFWB	980	Los Angeles	News	43,500
55.	KTWV	94.7	Los Angeles	Jazz	43,200
56.	WPEN	950	Philadelphia	Adult Standards	43,100
57.	WLS	890	Chicago	Talk	42,900
58.	KQRS-FM	92.5	Minneapolis/St. Paul	Rock	42,900
59.	WNUA	95.5	Chicago	Jazz	42,700
60.	WRKO	680	Boston	Talk	41,200
61.	KLSX	97.1	Los Angeles	Classic Rock/Talk	41,200
62.	WUSL	98.9	Philadelphia	R&B	41,200
63.	KCBS	740	San Francisco/Oakland	News	41,100
64.	WPOC	93.1	Baltimore	Country	41,000
65.	WLUP-FM	97.9	Chicago	Talk/Rock	40,700
66.	KCBS-FM	93.1	Los Angeles	Classic Rock	40,600
67.	KSCS	96.3	Dallas/Fort Worth	Country	39,700
68.	KZLA-FM	93.9	Los Angeles	Country	39,500
69.	WCCO	830	Minneapolis/St. Paul	Talk/Sports	39,500
70.	WDAS-FM	105.3	Philadelphia	Urban AC	38,800
71.	WDVE	102.5	Pittsburgh	Rock	38,400
72.	WRCX	103.5	Chicago	Rock	38,200
73.	KNX	1070	Los Angeles	News	38,000
74.	WWJ	950	Detroit	News	37,700
75.	WJMK	104.3	Chicago	Oldies	37,600
76.	KXED	1540	Los Angeles	Spanish	37,500
77.	WMZQ-FM	98.7	Washington	Country	36,900
78.	KNBR	680	San Francisco/Oakland	Sports/Talk	36,600
79.	WBAP	820	Dallas/Fort Worth	Talk/Country overnight	36,500
80.	KODA	99.1	Houston/Galveston	Soft AC	36,100
81.	KMEL	106.1	San Francisco/Oakland	R&B	36,100
82.	WYSP	94.1	Philadelphia	Classic Rock	35,700
83.	WWDB	96.5	Philadelphia	Talk	35,500

	Station	Frequency	Market	Format	AQH
84.	KILT-FM	100.3	Houston/Galveston	Country	35,400
85.	WOGL-FM	98.1	Philadelphia	Oldies	35,100
86.	WMMR	93.3	Philadelphia	Rock	34,100
87.	WQEW	1560	New York	Adult Standards	33,900
88.	WXKS-FM	107.9	Boston	CHR	33,400
89.	WOJO	105.1	Chicago	Spanish/Reg. Mex.	33,400
90.	WXRT	93.1	Chicago	Alternative	32,900
91.	WPCH	94.9	Atlanta	Soft AC	32,700
92.	KOIT-FM	96.5	San Francisco/Oakland	Soft AC	32,700
93.	WMXD	92.3	Detroit	Urban AC	32,500
94.	WEDR	99.1	Miami/Fort Lauderdale	R&B	32,500
95.	KHKS	106.1	Dallas/Fort Worth	CHR	32,400
96.	WGAR-FM	99.5	Cleveland	Country	32,300
97.	KXEZ	100.3	Los Angeles	Soft AC	32,300
98.	WLYF	101.5	Miami/Fort Lauderdale	Soft AC	32,000
99.	WIP	610	Philadelphia	Sports	32,000
100.	WBEB-FM	101.1	Philadelphia	AC	31,700

WINTER 1995

	Station	Frequency	Market	Format	AQH
1.	WRKS	98.7	New York	Urban AC	196,000
2.	WQHT	97.1	New York	R&B	144,100
3.	WCBS-FM	101.1	New York	Oldies	123,600
4.	WHTZ	100.3	New York	CHR/New Rock	118,400
5.	WSKQ-FM	97.9	New York	Spanish CHR	117,100
6.	WLTW	106.7	New York	Soft AC	109,300
7.	WABC	770	New York	Talk	108,700
8.	WINS	1010	New York	News	107,700
9.	WPLJ	95.5	New York	Adult Hits/'70s Oldies	92,900
10.	WCBS	880	New York	News	92,700
11.	KLVE	107.5	Los Angeles	Spanish/Tropical	88,900
12.	WGN	720	Chicago	Talk	88,200
13.	WQCD	101.9	New York	Jazz	87,300
14.	WXRK	92.3	New York	Classic Rock	86,600
15.	KPWR	105.9	Los Angeles	Dance/CHR	85,200
16	WOR	710	New York	Talk	79,900
17.	WGCI-FM	107.5	Chicago	R&B	78,400
18.	KLAX-FM	97.9	Los Angeles	Spanish/Reg. Mex.	76,000
19.	KROQ-FM	106.7	Los Angeles	New Rock	74,600
20.	WQXR-FM	96.3	New York	Classical	73,900
21.	WBLS	107.5	New York	Urban AC	73,000
22.	WYNY	103.5	New York	Country	72,900
23.	WMXV	105.1	New York	AC	71,200
24.	KIIS-FM	102.7	Los Angeles	CHR	70,900
25.	KOST	103.5	Los Angeles	AC	70,700
26.	KKBT	92.3	Los Angeles	R&B	67,900
27.	KNX	1070	Los Angeles	News	63,400
28.	KGO	810	San Francisco/Oakland	News/Talk	62,400
29.	WFAN	660	New York	Sports	59,900

Station		Frequency	Market Name	Format	AQH
30.	KYW	1060	Philadelphia	News	59,100
31.	KFI	640	Los Angeles	Talk	57,800
32.	WJLB	97.9	Detroit	R&B	57,100
33.	WADO	1280	New York	Spanish-News/Talk	56,400
34.	WNEW	102.7	New York	Rock	56,100
35.	WAXQ	104.3	New York	Rock	55,400
36.	WVEE	103.3	Atlanta	R&B	55,400
37.	KRTH	101.1	Los Angeles	Oldies	55,200
38.	WJR	760	Detroit	News/Talk	55,000
39.	KBIG	104.3	Los Angeles	AC	53,900
40.	WUSN	99.5	Chicago	Country	52,700
41.	WPGC-FM	95.5	Washington	R&B	51,700
42.	WLIT-FM	93.9	Chicago	Soft AC	51,100
43.	KDKA	1020	Pittsburgh	News/Talk	50,400
44.	WPAT-FM	93.1	New York	Soft AC	50,100
45.	KMOX	1120	St. Louis	News/Talk	49,800
46.	WBBM-FM	96.3	Chicago	Dance/CHR	49,800
47.	WBZ	1030	Boston	News/Talk	49,100
48.	WKHX-FM	101.5	Atlanta	Country	48,100
49.	WVAZ	102.7	Chicago	Urban AC	48,000
50.	KZLA-FM	93.9	Los Angeles	Country	47,600
51.	WQEW	1560	New York	Adult Standards	46,800
52.	WCCO	830	Minneapolis/St. Paul	Talk/Sports	46,600
53.	KQRS-FM	92.5	Minneapolis/St. Paul	Rock	46,200
54.	WKQX	101.1	Chicago	New Rock	45,900
55.	WUSL	98.9	Philadelphia	R&B	45,100
56.	KABC	790	Los Angeles	News/Talk	44,800
57.	WMAQ	670	Chicago	News/Sports	44,300
58.	KTWV	94.7	Los Angeles	Jazz	43,900
59.	KYSR	98.7	Los Angeles	Adult Hits	42,900
60.	KCBS	740	San Francisco/Oakland	News	42,800
61.	KFWB	980	Los Angeles	News	42,800
62.	WBBM	780	Chicago	News	42,500
63.	WBEB	101.1	Philadelphia	AC	41,700
64.	WPEN	950	Philadelphia	Adult Standards	41,600
65.	WJMK	104.3	Chicago	Oldies	41,500
66.	WWDB	96.5	Philadelphia	Talk	41,400
67.	KCBS-FM	93.1	Los Angeles	Classic Rock	41,000
68.	WNUA	95.5	Chicago	Jazz	40,000
69.	WLUP-FM	97.9	Chicago	Talk/Rock	39,400
70.	WDAS-FM	105.3	Philadelphia	Urban AC	39,300
71.	WRKO	680	Boston	Talk	38,700
72.	KLOS	95.5	Los Angeles	Rock	38,400
73.	KMEL	106.1	San Francisco/Oakland	R&B	37,500
74.	KODA	99.1	Houston/Galveston	Soft AC	37,300
75.	WOGL-FM	98.1	Philadelphia	Oldies	37,200
76.	KKHJ	930	Los Angeles	Spanish/Reg. Mex.	36,800
77.	WXTU	92.5	Philadelphia	Country	36,800
78.	WMMR	93.3	Philadelphia	Rock	36,600
79.	KLSX	97.1	Los Angeles	Classic Rock/Talk	36,500

Station	Frequency	Market	Format	AQH
80. WRCX	103.5	Chicago	Rock	36,500
81. KXEZ	100.3	Los Angeles	Soft AC	36,400
82. WDVE	102.5	Pittsburgh	Rock	36,300
83. WLS	890	Chicago	Talk	35,600
84. KBXX	97.9	Houston/Galveston	R&B	35,500
85. WMZQ-FM	98.7	Washington	Country	35,200
86. WYSP	94.1	Philadelphia	Classic Rock	35,200
87. KNBR	680	San Francisco/Oakland	Sports/Talk	35,100
88. WXRT	93.1	Chicago	Alternative	35,000
89. WEDR	99.1	Miami/Fort Lauderdale	R&B	34,700
90. WIP	610	Philadelphia	Sports	34,200
91. WOJO	105.1	Chicago	Spanish/Reg. Mex.	33,700
92. WWJ	950	Detroit	News	33,400
93. KSCS	96.3	Dallas/Fort Worth	Country	33,300
94. KILT-FM	100.3	Houston/Galveston	Country	33,100
95. KVIL-FM	103.7	Dallas/Fort Worth	AC	33,000
96. WYXR	104.5	Philadelphia	Adult Hits	33,000
97. WNIC	100.3	Detroit	AC	32,700
98. WIL-FM	92.3	St. Louis	Country	32,100
99. WWWW-FM	106.7	Detroit	Country	32,100
100. WPLY	100.3	Philadelphia	CHR/New Rock	32,000

TOP 100 STATIONS BY SHARE OF AUDIENCE

These are the most successful radio stations in the nation as measured by the percent of total audience listening during the AQH.

FALL 1994

Station	Frequency	Market	Format	Share
1. WXBQ-FM	96.9	Johnson City/Kingsport, TN	Country	33.2
2. WQBE-FM	97.5	Charleston, SC	Country	31.9
3. WIVK-FM	107.7	Knoxville, TN	Country	28.3
4. WDRM-FM	102.1	Huntsville, AL	Country	27.2
5. KCTR-FM	102.9	Billings, MT	Country	26.1
6. WTCR-FM	103.3	Huntington, WV	Country	25.7
7. KEAN-FM	105.1	Abilene, TX	Country	25.6
8. KKIX	103.9	Fayetteville, AR	Country	23.7
9. WTVY	95.5	Dothan, AL	Country	21.8
10. WVLK-FM	92.9	Lexington, KY	County	21.6
11. WPCV	97.5	Lakeland, FL	Country	21.1
12. WUSY	100.7	Chattanooga, TN	Country	20.5
13. KLLL-FM	96.3	Lubbock, TX	Country	20.4
14. WZID	95.7	Manchester/Nashua, NH	AC	20.3
15. WZFX	99.1	Fayetteville, AR	R&B	19.9
16. WHWK	98.1	Binghamton, NY	Country	19.5
17. WDEN-FM	105.3	Macon, GA	Country	19.3
18. WRFY-FM	102.5	Reading, PA	Rock/CHR	18.7
19. WLWI-FM	92.3	Montgomery, AL	Country	18.6
20. WKDQ	99.5	Evansville, IN	Country	18.5
21. WXCL	104.9	Peoria, IL	Country	18.3
22. WSSL-FM	100.5	Greenville/Spartanburg, SC	Country	17.9

Station		Frequency	Market	Format	Share
23.	WRNS-FM	95.1	New Bern/Morehead City, NC	Country	17.9
24.	WFRG-FM	104.3	Utica/Rome, NY	Country	17.8
25.	WLLR-FM	101.3	Davenport (Quad Cities), IA	Country	17.7
26.	WOKO	98.9	Burlington/Plattsburgh, VT	Country	17.6
27.	WZHT	105.7	Montgomery, AL	R&B	17.2
28.	WXRX	104.9	Rockford, IL	Rock	17.1
29.	KUZZ-FM	107.9	Bakersfield, CA	Country	16.7
30.	KATM	103.3	Modesto, CA	Country	16.7
31.	KRKX	94.1	Billings, MT	Rock	16.4
32.	WWDM	101.3	Columbia, SC	R&B	16.4
33.	WKHY	93.5	Lafayette, IN	Classic Rock	16.4
34.	WITL-FM	100.7	Lansing, MI	Country	16.4
35.	KRMD-FM	101.1	Shreveport, LA	Country	16.3
36.	WKML	95.7	Fayetteville, AR	Country	16.2
37.	WAYZ-FM	101.5	Hagerstown, MD	Country	16.2
38.	WMSI	102.9	Jackson, MS	Country	16.2
39.	WSIX-FM	97.9	Nashville, TN	Country	15.9
40.	WAMZ	97.5	Louisville, KY	Country	15.8
41.	KQMS	1400	Redding, CA	News/Talk	15.7
42.	WIZN	106.7	Burlington/Plattsburgh, VT	Rock	15.6
43.	WMTZ	96.5	Johnstown, PA	Country	15.5
44.	KSSN	95.7	Little Rock, AR	Country	15.3
45.	KXXY-FM	96.1	Oklahoma City, OK	Country	15.3
46.	WZZK-FM	104.7	Birmingham, AL	Country	15.0
47.	WIKY-FM	104.1	Evansville, IN	Soft AC	14.9
48.	WXBM-FM	102.7	Pensacola, FL	Country	14.9
49.	KMOX	1120	St. Louis, MO	News/Talk	14.9
50.	WXLP	96.9	Davenport (Quad Cities), IA	Rock	14.8
51.	WHO	1040	Des Moines, IA	News/Talk	14.8
52.	KQXL	106.5	Baton Rouge, LA	R&B	14.7
53.	WXTA	97.9	Erie, PA	Country	14.7
54.	KMJ	580	Fresno, CA	News/Talk	14.7
55.	WLZW	98.7	Utica/Rome, NY	AC	14.6
56.	WPOR-FM	101.9	Portland/Lewiston, ME	Country	14.4
57.	WJMI	99.7	Jackson, MS	R&B	14.3
58.	WTQR	104.1	Greensboro/Winston-Salem, NC	Country	14.2
59.	KHTN	104.7	Merced, CA	Dance/CHR	14.1
60.	WPXC	102.9	Cape Cod, MA	Rock	14.0
61.	KGGO	94.9	Des Moines, IA	Rock	14.0
62.	KIIM-FM	99.5	Tucson, AZ	Country	14.0
63.	WNNK-FM	104.1	Harrisburg, PA	CHR	13.9
64.	KFBK	1530	Sacramento, CA	News/Talk	13.9
65.	KRYS-FM	99.1	Corpus Christi, TX	Country	13.8
66.	WKOA	105.3	Lafayette, IN	Country	13.8
67.	KPSI-FM	100.5	Palm Springs/Indio, CA	CHR	13.8
68.	WEEU	850	Reading, PA	AC/Talk	13.8
69.	KASE	100.7	Austin, TX	Country	13.7
70.	WWWZ	93.3	Charleston, SC	R&B	13.7
71.	WNBF	1290	Binghamton, AL	News/Talk	13.6
72.	WXXX	95.3	Burlington/Plattsburgh, VT	CHR	13.6

	Station	Frequency	Market	Format	Share
73.	WYNG-FM	105.3	Evansville, IN	Country	13.6
74.	WCRZ	107.9	Flint, MI	Gold-Based AC	13.6
75.	WIOV-FM	105.1	Lancaster, PA	Country	13.6
76.	WQUE-FM	93.3	New Orleans, LA	R&B	13.6
77.	WYNK-FM	101.5	Baton Rouge, LA	Country	13.5
78.	WHBC	1480	Canton, OH	Soft AC/Talk	13.5
79.	KXKC	99.1	Lafayette, LA	Country	13.5
80.	WHAS	840	Louisville, KY	Talk/Oldies	13.5
81.	WBLX-FM	92.9	Mobile, AL	R&B	13.5
82.	KQKQ-FM	98.5	Omaha, NE	CHR	13.5
83.	WHAM	1180	Rochester, NY	News/Talk	13.5
84.	WSRS	96.1	Worcester, MA	Soft AC	13.4
85.	WQXK	105.1	Youngstown, OH	Country	13.4
86.	WIKS	101.9	New Bern/Morehead City, NC	R&B	13.3
87.	KGEE	99.9	Odessa/Midland, TX	Country	13.3
88.	WSYR	570	Syracuse, NY	Talk	13.2
89.	WKXC-FM	99.5	Augusta, GA	Country	13.1
90.	WCOS-FM	97.5	Columbia, SC	Country	13.1
91.	KPRR	102.1	El Paso/Cuidad Juarez, TX	Dance/CHR	13.1
92.	KDKA	1020	Pittsburgh, PA	News/Talk	13.1
93.	KZFM	95.5	Corpus Christi, TX	Dance/CHR	13.0
94.	WDAQ	98.3	Danbury, CT	AC	12.9
95.	KMJJ-FM	99.7	Shreveport, LA	R&B	12.9
96.	WICC	600	Bridgeport, CT	AC/Talk	12.8
97.	WKKO	99.9	Toledo, OH	Country	12.8
98.	KWEN	95.5	Tulsa, OK	Country	12.8
99.	WTFM	98.5	Johnson City/Kingsport, TN	AC	12.6
100.	KAYD	97.5	Beaumont, TX	Country	12.5
101.	WAZY	96.5	Lafayette, AR	CHR	12.5
102.	KZII	102.5	Lubbock, TX	CHR	12.5

WINTER 1995

	Station	Frequency	Market	Format	Share
1.	WIVK-FM	107.7	Knoxville, TN	Country	27.0
2.	WDRM-FM	102.1	Huntsville, AL	Country	24.6
3.	WUSY	100.7	Chattanooga, TN	Country	22.9
4.	WRNS-FM	95.1	New Bern/Morehead City, NC	Country	18.3
5.	WWDM	101.3	Columbia, SC	R&B	17.5
6.	KRMD-FM	101.1	Shreveport, LA	Country	15.7
7.	WSSL-FM	100.5	Greenville/Spartanburg, SC	Country	15.7
8.	WIKS	101.9	New Bern/Morehead City, NC	R&B	15.6
9.	KSSN	95.7	Little Rock, AR	Country	15.3
10.	WSIX-FM	97.9	Nashville, TN	Country	14.7
11.	WYNK-FM	101.5	Baton Rouge, LA	Country	14.6
12.	KDKA	1020	Pittsburgh, PA	News/Talk	14.3
13.	WTQR	104.1	Greensboro/Winston-Salem, NC	Country	14.2
14.	KASE	100.7	Austin, TX	Country	14.1
15.	WITL-FM	100.7	Lansing, MI	Country	13.9
16.	KMOX	1120	St. Louis, MO	News/Talk	13.8
17.	WAMZ	97.5	Louisville, KY	Country	13.8

	Station	Frequency	Market	Format	Share
18.	WHO	1040	Des Moines, IA	News/Talk	13.8
19.	KMJJ-FM	99.7	Shreveport, LA	R&B	13.7
20.	WJMI	99.7	Jackson, MS	R&B	13.7
21.	WNNK-FM	104.1	Harrisburg, PA	CHR	13.7
22.	KGGO	94.9	Des Moines, IA	Rock	13.6
23.	KIIM-FM	99.5	Tucson, AZ	Country	13.5
24.	WZZK-FM	104.7	Birmingham, AL	Country	13.5
25.	WKKO	99.9	Toledo, OH	Country	13.4
26.	WBLX-FM	92.9	Mobile, AL	R&B	13.3
27.	KPRR	102.1	El Paso/Ciudad Juarez, TX	Dance/CHR	13.2
28.	WAEB-FM	104.1	Allentown/Bethlehem, PA	CHR	13.1
29.	WSM-FM	95.5	Nashville, TN	Country	13.1
30.	WCOS-FM	97.5	Columbia, SC	Country	13.0
31.	WQUE-FM	93.3	New Orleans, LA	R&B	13.0
32.	KJJY-FM	92.5	Des Moines, IA	Country	12.8
33.	KBFM	104.1	McAllen/Brownsville, TX.	Dance/CHR	12.7
34.	WGNA-FM	107.7	Albany/Schenectady/Troy, NY	Country	12.7
35.	KUZZ-FM	107.9	Bakersfield, CA	Country	12.6
36.	WBEE-FM	92.5	Rochester, NY	Country	12.6
37.	WTIC	1080	Hartford, CT.	News/Talk	12.6
38.	KIWW	96.1	McAllen/Brownsville, TX.	Spanish/Tejano	12.4
39.	KWEN	95.5	Tulsa, OK	Country	12.4
40.	WCCO	830	Minneapolis/St. Paul, MN	Talk/Sports	12.4
41.	WHAS	840	Louisville, KY	Talk/Oldies	12.3
42.	KQRS-FM	92.5	Minneapolis/St. Paul, MN	Rock	12.2
43.	KFDI-FM	101.3	Wichita, KS	Country	12.1
44.	WHRK	97.1	Memphis, TN	R&B	12.1
45.	WMSI	102.9	Jackson, MS	Country	12.1
46.	WFBQ	94.7	Indianapolis, IN	Rock	12.0
47.	WVEE	103.3	Atlanta, GA	R&B	11.9
48.	WHAM	1180	Rochester, NY	News/Talk	11.8
49.	KVKI-FM	96.5	Shreveport, LA	AC	11.7
50.	WCMF-FM	96.5	Rochester, NY	Rock	11.7
51.	KRST	92.3	Albuquerque, NM	Country	11.6
52.	WFMS	95.5	Indianapolis, IN	Country	11.6
53.	WWWZ	93.3	Charleston, SC	R&B	11.6
54.	KFBK	1530	Sacramento, CA	News/Talk	11.4
55.	KMJ	580	Fresno, CA.	News/Talk	11.2
56.	WJMZ-FM	107.3	Greenville/Spartanburg, SC.	R&B	11.2
57.	WKCQ	98.1	Saginaw/Bay City/Midland, MI	Country	11.2
58.	KBOS-FM	94.9	Fresno, CA.	Dance/CHR	11.1
59.	WFYV-FM	104.5	Jacksonville, FL	Rock	11.1
60.	WARM-FM	103.3	York, PA	AC	11.0
61.	WENN	107.7	Birmingham, AL	R&B	11.0
62.	WGTY	107.7	York, PA	Country	11.0
63.	KKXX-FM	105.3	Bakersfield, CA.	Dance/CHR	10.9
64.	KTSM-FM	99.9	El Paso/Ciudad Juarez, TX	Soft AC	10.9
65.	WHKO	99.1	Dayton, OH	Country	10.9
66.	WLW	700	Cincinnati, OH	Talk/Country overnight	10.9
67.	KSFI	100.3	Salt Lake City/Ogden, UT	Soft AC	10.8

	Station	Frequency	Market	Format	Share
68.	WSYR	570	Syracuse, NY	Talk	10.8
69.	WYRK	106.5	Buffalo/Niagara Falls, NY	Country	10.8
70.	WLEV	96.1	Allentown/Bethlehem, PA	AC	10.6
71.	WRVA	1140	Richmond, VA	News/Talk/Sports	10.6
72.	WPEG	97.9	Charlotte, NC	R&B	10.5
73.	WQIK-FM	99.1	Jacksonville, FL	Country	10.5
74.	KDKS-FM	103.7	Shreveport, LA	Urban AC	10.4
75.	WKHX-FM	101.5	Atlanta, GA	Country	10.4
76.	WUBE-FM	105.1	Cincinnati, OH	Country	10.4
77.	KJYO	102.7	Oklahoma City, OK	CHR	10.3
78.	WDVE	102.5	Pittsburgh, PA	Rock	10.3
79.	WJXQ	106.1	Lansing, MI	Rock	10.3
80.	WKHK	95.3	Richmond, VA	Country	10.3
81.	WKRZ	98.5	Scranton/Wilkes-Barre, PA	CHR	10.2
82.	WFMZ	100.7	Allentown/Bethlehem, PA	Soft AC	10.1
83.	WTUE	104.7	Dayton, OH	Rock	10.1
84.	KLAQ	95.5	El Paso/Ciudad Juarez, TX	Rock	10.0
85.	WCDX	92.7	Richmond, VA	R&B	10.0
86.	WSOC-FM	103.7	Charlotte, NC	Country	10.0
87.	KKCS-FM	101.9	Colorado Springs, CO	Country	9.9
88.	KSSK-FM	92.3	Honolulu, HI	AC	9.9
89.	KGBT	1530	McAllen/Brownsville, TX	Spanish/Reg. Mex.	9.8
90.	KIPR	92.3	Little Rock, AR	R&B	9.8
91.	KTEX	100.3	McAllen/Brownsville, TX	Country	9.8
92.	WDAF	610	Kansas City, MO	Country	9.8
93.	WDEF-FM	92.3	Chattanooga, TN	Soft AC	9.8
94.	KLPX	96.1	Tucson, AZ	Rock	9.7
95.	KQXL	106.5	Baton Rouge, LA	R&B	9.7
96.	WHYN-FM	93.1	Springfield, MA	Gold-Based AC	9.7
97.	KTAR	620	Phoenix, AZ	News/Talk	9.6
98.	KXXY-FM	96.1	Oklahoma City, OK	Country	9.6
99.	KZZU-FM	92.9	Spokane, WA	CHR	9.6
100.	KFRG	95.1	Riverside/San Bernardino, CA	Country	9.5
100.	KIKI-FM	93.9	Honolulu, HI	Dance/CHR	9.5
100.	KKOR	770.0	Albuquerque, NM	Talk	9.5
100.	KQKQ-FM	98.5	Omaha-Council Bluffs, NE	CHR	9.5
100.	WAHR	99.1	Huntsville, AL	Gold Based AC	9.5
100.	WBCT	93.7	Grand Rapids, MI	Country	9.5
100.	WNTQ	93.1	Syracuse, NY	CHR	9.5

Sources: M Street Radio Directory and the Arbitron Co. © 1995. All rights reserved.

The Emmy Awards

The Emmy Awards, named after Immy, a nickname for the tube used in television image transmission, have evolved along with television's 46-year history. In the 1976–1977 Emmy season, the television academy split into two entities: the Academy of Television Arts and Sciences, which administers the prime-time awards, and the National Academy of Television Arts and Sciences, which presents the daytime awards. The awards are now featured in two ceremonies, prime-time in the fall and daytime in the spring.

1948

Most Popular Television Program
Pantomime Quiz Time (KTLA)

Most Outstanding Television Personality
Shirley Dinsdale and her puppet Judy Splinters

Best Film Made for Television
The Necklace

1949

Best Live Show
Ed Wynn (KTTV)

Most Outstanding Live Personality
Ed Wynn

Best Kinescope Show
Texaco Star Theatre (KNBH, NBC)

Most Outstanding Kinescoped Personality
Milton Berle

Best Film Made for and Viewed on Television in 1949
Life of Riley (KNBH)

Best Public Service, Cultural or Educational Program
Crusade in Europe (KECA-TV, KTTV)

Best Sports Coverage
Wrestling (KTLA)

Best Children's Show
Time for Beany (KTLA)

1950

Best Dramatic Show
Pulitzer Prize Playhouse (KECA-TV)

Best Actor
Alan Young

Best Actress
Gertrude Berg

Most Outstanding Personality
Groucho Marx

Best Variety Show
The Alan Young Show (KTTV, CBS)

Best Game and Audience Participation Show
Truth or Consequences (KTTV, CBS)

Best Public Service
City at Night (KTLA)

Edward R. Murrow

Best News Program
KTLA Newsreel

Best Sports Program
Rams Football (KNBH)

Best Cultural Show
Campus Chorus and Orchestra (KTSL)

Best Educational Show
KFI-TV University (KFI-TV)

Best Children's Show
Time for Beany (KTLA)

1951

Best Dramatic Show
Studio One (CBS)

Best Actor
Sid Caesar

Best Actress
Imogene Coca

Best Comedy Show
Red Skelton Show (NBC)

Best Comedian or Comedienne
Red Skelton

Best Variety Show
Your Show of Shows (NBC)

1952

Best Dramatic Program
Robert Montgomery Presents (NBC)

Best Actor
Thomas Mitchell

Best Actress
Helen Hayes

Most Outstanding Personality
Bishop Fulton J. Sheen

Best Situation Comedy
I Love Lucy (CBS)

Best Comedian
Jimmy Durante

Best Comedienne
Lucille Ball

Best Variety Program
Your Show of Shows (NBC)

Best Mystery, Action or Adventure Program
Dragnet (NBC)

Best Public Affairs Program
See It Now (CBS)

Best Children's Program
Time for Beany (KTLA)

Best Audience Participation, Quiz or Panel Program
What's My Line? (CBS)

1953

Best Dramatic Program
U.S. Steel Hour (ABC)

Best Male Star of a Regular Series
Donald O'Connor, *Colgate Comedy Hour*

Best Female Star of a Regular Series
Eve Arden, *Our Miss Brooks*

Best Series Supporting Actor
Art Carney, *Jackie Gleason Show*

Best Series Supporting Actress
Vivian Vance, *I Love Lucy*

Most Outstanding Personality
Edward R. Murrow

Best New Program (tie)
Make Room for Daddy (ABC)
U.S. Steel Hour (ABC)

Best Situation Comedy
I Love Lucy (CBS)

Best Variety Program
Omnibus (CBS)

Best Mystery, Action or Adventure Program
Dragnet (NBC)

Best Public Affairs Program
Victory at Sea (NBC)

Best Program of News or Sports
See It Now (CBS)

Best Children's Program
Kukla, Fran and Ollie (NBC)

Best Audience Participation, Quiz or Panel Program (tie)
This Is Your Life (NBC)
What's My Line? (CBS)

1954

Best Dramatic Series
U.S. Steel Hour (ABC)

Best Actor Starring in a Regular Series
Danny Thomas, *Make Room for Daddy*

Best Actress Starring in a Regular Series
Loretta Young, *Loretta Young Show*

Best Supporting Actor in a Regular Series
Art Carney, *Jackie Gleason Show*

Best Supporting Actress in a Regular Series
Audrey Meadows, *Jackie Gleason Show*

Best Individual Program of the Year
Operation Undersea (ABC)

Best Actor in a Single Performance
Robert Cummings, *Studio One: Twelve Angry Men*

Best Actress in a Single Performance
Judith Anderson, *Hallmark Hall of Fame: Macbeth*

Best Direction
Franklin Schaffner, *Studio One: Twelve Angry Men*

Best Written Dramatic Material
Reginald Rose, *Twelve Angry Men*

Most Outstanding New Personality
George Gobel

Best Situation Comedy Series
Make Room for Daddy (ABC)

Best Written Comedy Material
James Allardice, Jack Douglas, Hal Kanter and
    Harry Winkler, *George Gobel Show*

Best Variety Series, Including Musical Varieties
Disneyland (ABC)

Best Mystery or Intrigue Series
Dragnet (NBC)

Best Western or Adventure Series
Stories of the Century (Syndicated)

Best Cultural, Religious or Educational Program
Omnibus (CBS)

Best News Reporter or Commentator
John Daly

Best Sports Program
Gillette Cavalcade of Sports (NBC)

Best Children's Program
Lassie (CBS)

Best Audience, Guest Participation or Panel Program
This Is Your Life (NBC)

1955

Best Dramatic Series
Producers' Showcase (NBC)

Best Actor, Continuing Performance
Phil Silvers, *Phil Silvers Show, You'll Never Get Rich*

Best Actress, Continuing Performance
Lucille Ball, *I Love Lucy*

Best Actor in a Supporting Role
Art Carney, *Honeymooners*

Best Actress in a Supporting Role
Nanette Fabray, *Caesar's Hour*

Best Single Program of the Year
Producers' Showcase: Peter Pan (NBC)

Best Actor, Single Performance
Lloyd Nolan, *Ford Star Jubilee: Caine Mutiny Court Martial*

Best Actress, Single Performance
Mary Martin, *Producers' Showcase: Peter Pan*

Best Television Adaptation
Paul Gregory and Franklin Schaffner, *Caine Mutiny Court Martial* by Herman Wouk

Best Director, Film Series
Nat Hiken, *Phil Silvers Show, You'll Never Get Rich*

Best Director, Live Series
Franklin Schaffner, *Caine Mutiny Court Martial*

Best Original Teleplay Writing
Rod Serling, *Kraft TV Theatre: Patterns*

Best Comedy Series
Phil Silvers Show, You'll Never Get Rich (CBS)

Best Comedian
Phil Silvers

Best Comedienne
Nanette Fabray

Best Comedy Writing
Nat Hiken, Barry Blitser, Arnold Auerbach, Harvey Orkin, Vincent Bogert, Arnold Rosen, Coleman Jacoby, Tony Webster and Terry Ryan, *Phil Silvers Show, You'll Never Get Rich*

Best Variety Series
Ed Sullivan Show (CBS)

Best Music Series
Your Hit Parade (NBC)

Best Action or Adventure Series
Disneyland (ABC)

Best Documentary Program, Religious, Informational, Educational or Interview
Omnibus (CBS)

Best News Commentator or Reporter
Edward R. Murrow

Best Children's Series
Lassie (CBS)

Best Audience Participation Series (Quiz, Panel, etc.)
$64,000 Question (CBS)

Best Specialty Act, Single or Group
Marcel Marceau

Best MC or Program Host, Male or Female
Perry Como

1956

Best Series, Half Hour or Less
Phil Silvers Show (CBS)

Best Series, One Hour or More
Caesar's Hour (NBC)

Best Continuing Performance by an Actor in a Dramatic Series
Robert Young, *Father Knows Best*

Best Continuing Performance by an Actress in a Dramatic Series
Loretta Young, *Loretta Young Show*

Best Supporting Performance by an Actor
Carl Reiner, *Caesar's Hour*

Best Supporting Performance by an Actress
Pat Carroll, *Caesar's Hour*

Best Direction, Half Hour or Less
Sheldon Leonard, *Danny Thomas Show:* "Danny's Comeback"

Best Teleplay Writing, Half Hour or Less
James P. Cavanagh, *Alfred Hitchcock Presents:* "Fog Closing In"

Best Direction, One Hour or More
Ralph Nelson, *Playhouse 90: Requiem for a Heavyweight*

Best Teleplay Writing, One Hour or More
Rod Serling, *Playhouse 90: Requiem for a Heavyweight*

Best Male Personality, Continuing Performance
Perry Como

Best Female Personality, Continuing Performance
Dinah Shore

Best New Program Series
Playhouse 90 (CBS)

Best Single Program of the Year
Playhouse 90: Requiem for a Heavyweight (CBS)

Best Single Performance by an Actor
Jack Palance, *Playhouse 90: Requiem for a Heavyweight*

Best Single Performance by an Actress
Claire Trevor, *Producers' Showcase: Dodsworth*

Best Continuing Performance by a Comedian in a Series
Sid Caesar, *Caesar's Hour*

Best Continuing Performance by a Comedienne in a Series
Nanette Fabray, *Caesar's Hour*

Best Comedy Writing, Variety or Situation Comedy
Nat Hiken, Billy Friedberg, Tony Webster, Leonard Stern, Arnold Rosen and Coleman Jacoby, *Phil Silvers Show*

Best Public Service Series
See It Now (CBS)

Best News Commentator
Edward R. Murrow

1957

Best Dramatic Series With Continuing Characters
Gunsmoke (CBS)

Best Dramatic Anthology Series
Playhouse 90 (CBS)

Actor, Best Single Performance, Lead or Support
Peter Ustinov, *Omnibus: The Life of Samuel Johnson*

Actress, Best Single Performance, Lead or Support
Polly Bergen, *Playhouse 90: Helen Morgan Story*

Best Single Program of the Year
Playhouse 90: The Comedian (CBS)

Best New Program Series of the Year
Seven Lively Arts (CBS)

Best Comedy Series
Phil Silvers Show (CBS)

Best Continuing Performance by an Actor in a Leading Role in a Dramatic or Comedy Series
Robert Young, *Father Knows Best*

Best Continuing Performance by an Actress in a Leading Role in a Dramatic or Comedy Series
Jane Wyatt, *Father Knows Best*

Best Continuing Supporting Performance by an Actor in a Dramatic or Comedy Series
Carl Reiner, *Caesar's Hour*

Best Continuing Supporting Performance by an Actress in a Dramatic or Comedy Series
Ann B. Davis, *Bob Cummings Show*

Best Comedy Writing
Nat Hiken, Billy Friedberg, Phil Sharp, Terry Ryan, Coleman Jacoby, Arnold Rosen, Sidney Zelinka, A.J. Russell and Tony Webster, *Phil Silvers Show*

Best Musical, Variety, Audience Participation or Quiz Series
Dinah Shore Chevy Show (NBC)

Best Continuing Performance (Male) in a Series by a Comedian, Singer, Host, Dancer, MC, Announcer, Narrator, Panelist or Any Person Who Essentially Plays Himself
Jack Benny, *Jack Benny Show*

Best Continuing Performance (Female) in a Series by a Comedienne, Singer, Hostess, Dancer, MC, Announcer, Narrator, Panelist or Any Person Who Essentially Plays Herself
Dinah Shore, *Dinah Shore Chevy Show*

Best Direction, Half Hour or Less
Robert Stevens, *Alfred Hitchcock Presents:* "The Glass Eye"

Best Teleplay Writing, Half Hour or Less
Paul Monash, *Schlitz Playhouse of Stars:* "The Lonely Wizard"

Best Direction, One Hour or More
Bob Banner, *Dinah Shore Chevy Show*

Best Teleplay Writing, One Hour or More
Rod Serling, *Playhouse 90: The Comedian*

Best Public Service Program or Series
Omnibus (ABC, NBC)

Best News Commentary
Edward R. Murrow

1958–1959

Best Dramatic Series, Less Than One Hour
Alcoa-Goodyear Theatre (NBC)

Best Dramatic Series, One Hour or Longer
Playhouse 90 (CBS)

Best Actor in a Leading Role (Continuing Character) in a Dramatic Series
Raymond Burr, *Perry Mason*

Best Actress in a Leading Role (Continuing Character) in a Dramatic Series
Loretta Young, *Loretta Young Show*

Best Supporting Actor (Continuing Character) in a Dramatic Series
Dennis Weaver, *Gunsmoke*

Best Supporting Actress (Continuing Character) in a Dramatic Series
Barbara Hale, *Perry Mason*

Best Direction of a Single Program of a Dramatic Series, Less Than One Hour
Jack Smight, *Alcoa-Goodyear Theatre:* "Eddie"

Best Writing of a Single Program of a Dramatic Series, Less Than One Hour
Alfred Brenner and Ken Hughes, *Alcoa-Goodyear Theatre:* "Eddie"

Best Special Dramatic Program, One Hour or Longer
Hallmark Hall of Fame: Little Moon of Alban (NBC)

Best Direction of a Single Dramatic Program, One Hour or Longer
George Schaefer, *Hallmark Hall of Fame:* Little Moon of Alban

Best Writing of a Single Dramatic Program, One Hour or Longer
James Costigan, *Hallmark Hall of Fame:* Little Moon of Alban

Most Outstanding Single Program of the Year
An Evening With Fred Astaire (NBC)

Best Single Performance by an Actor
Fred Astaire, *An Evening With Fred Astaire*

Best Single Performance by an Actress
Julie Harris, *Hallmark Hall of Fame:* Little Moon of Alban

Best Comedy Series
Jack Benny Show (CBS)

Best Actor in a Leading Role (Continuing Character) in a Comedy Series
Jack Benny, *Jack Benny Show*

Best Actress in a Leading Role (Continuing Character) in a Comedy Series
Jane Wyatt, *Father Knows Best*

Best Supporting Actor (Continuing Character) in a Comedy Series
Tom Poston, *Steve Allen Show*

Best Supporting Actress (Continuing Character) in a Comedy Series
Ann B. Davis, *Bob Cummings Show*

Best Direction of a Single Program of a Comedy Series
Peter Tewksbury, *Father Knows Best:* "Medal for Margaret"

Best Writing of a Single Program of a Comedy Series
Sam Perrin, George Balzer, Hal Goldman and Al Gordon, *Jack Benny Show:* "Jack Benny Show With Ernie Kovacs"

Best Musical or Variety Series
Dinah Shore Chevy Show (NBC)

Best Performance by an Actor (Continuing Character) in a Musical or Variety Series
Perry Como, *Perry Como Show*

Best Performance by an Actress (Continuing Character) in a Musical or Variety Series
Dinah Shore, *Dinah Shore Chevy Show*

Best Special Musical or Variety Program, One Hour or Longer
An Evening With Fred Astaire (NBC)

Loretta Young, *Loretta Young Show*

Jack Benny Show

Best Direction of a Single Musical or Variety Program
Bud Yorkin, *An Evening With Fred Astaire*

Best Writing of a Single Musical or Variety Program
Bud Yorkin and Herbert Baker, *An Evening With Fred Astaire*

Best Western Series
Maverick (ABC)

Best Public Service Program or Series
Omnibus (NBC)

Best News Reporting Series
Huntley-Brinkley Report (NBC)

Best Special News Program
Face of Red China (CBS)

Best News Commentator or Analyst
Edward R. Murrow

Best Panel, Quiz or Audience Participation Series
What's My Line? (CBS)

1959—1960

Outstanding Program Achievement in the Field of Drama
Playhouse 90 (CBS)

Outstanding Performance by an Actor in a Series (Lead or Support)
Robert Stack, *The Untouchables*

Outstanding Performance by an Actress in a Series (Lead or Support)
Jane Wyatt, *Father Knows Best*

Outstanding Directorial Achievement in Drama
Robert Mulligan, *The Moon and Sixpence*

Outstanding Writing Achievement in Drama
Rod Serling, *Twilight Zone*

Outstanding Single Performance by an Actor (Lead or Support)
Laurence Olivier, *The Moon and Sixpence*

Outstanding Single Performance by an Actress (Lead or Support)
Ingrid Bergman, *Ford Startime: The Turn of the Screw*

Outstanding Program Achievement in the Field of Humor
Art Carney Special (NBC)

Outstanding Directorial Achievement in Comedy
Ralph Levy and Bud Yorkin, *Jack Benny* specials

Outstanding Writing Achievement in Comedy
Sam Perrin, George Balzer, Al Gordon and Hal Goldman, *Jack Benny Show*

Outstanding Program Achievement in the Field of Variety
Fabulous Fifties (CBS)

Outstanding Performance in a Variety or Musical Program or Series
Harry Belafonte, *Revlon Revue: Tonight With Belafonte*

Outstanding Achievement in the Field of Music
Leonard Bernstein and the New York Philharmonic (CBS)

Outstanding Program Achievement in the Field of Public Affairs and Education
Twentieth Century (CBS)

Outstanding Program Achievement in the Field of News
Huntley-Brinkley Report (NBC)

Outstanding Writing Achievement in the Documentary Field
Howard K. Smith and Av Westin, *The Population Explosion*

Outstanding Achievement in the Field of Children's Programming
Huckleberry Hound (Syndicated)

1960—1961

Outstanding Program Achievement in the Field of Drama
Hallmark Hall of Fame: Macbeth (NBC)

Outstanding Performance by an Actor in a Series (Lead)
Raymond Burr, *Perry Mason*

Outstanding Performance by an Actress in a Series (Lead)
Barbara Stanwyck, *Barbara Stanwyck Show*

Outstanding Performance in a Supporting Role by an Actor or Actress in a Series
Don Knotts, *The Andy Griffith Show*

Outstanding Directorial Achievement in Drama
George Schaefer, *Hallmark Hall of Fame: Macbeth*

Outstanding Writing Achievement in Drama
Rod Serling, *The Twilight Zone*

The Program of the Year
Hallmark Hall of Fame: Macbeth (NBC)

Outstanding Single Performance by an Actor in a Leading Role
Maurice Evans, *Hallmark Hall of Fame: Macbeth*

Outstanding Single Performance by an Actress in a Leading Role
Judith Anderson, *Hallmark Hall of Fame: Macbeth*

Outstanding Performance in a Supporting Role by an Actor or Actress in a Single Program
Roddy McDowall, *Equitable's American Heritage: Not Without Honor*

Outstanding Program Achievement in the Field of Humor
Jack Benny Show (CBS)

Outstanding Directorial Achievement in Comedy
Sheldon Leonard, *The Danny Thomas Show*

Outstanding Writing Achievement in Comedy
Sherwood Schwartz, Dave O'Brien, Al Schwartz, Martin Ragaway and Red Skelton, *Red Skelton Show*

Outstanding Program Achievement in the Field of Variety
Astaire Time (NBC)

Outstanding Performance in a Variety or Musical Program or Series
Fred Astaire, *Astaire Time*

Outstanding Program Achievement in the Field of Public Affairs and Education
The Twentieth Century (CBS)

Outstanding Program Achievement in the Field of News
Huntley-Brinkley Report (NBC)

Outstanding Writing Achievement in the Documentary Field
Victor Wolfson, *Winston Churchill, The Valiant Years*

Outstanding Achievement in the Field of Children's Programming
Young People's Concert: Aaron Copland's Birthday Party (CBS)

1961–1962

Outstanding Program Achievement in the Field of Drama
The Defenders (CBS)

Outstanding Continued Performance by an Actor in a Series (Lead)
E.G. Marshall, *The Defenders*

Outstanding Continued Performance by an Actress in a Series (Lead)
Shirley Booth, *Hazel*

Outstanding Performance in a Supporting Role by an Actor
Don Knotts, *The Andy Griffith Show*

Outstanding Performance in a Supporting Role by an Actress
Pamela Brown, *Hallmark Hall of Fame: Victoria Regina*

Outstanding Directorial Achievement in Drama
Franklin Schaffner, *The Defenders:* various episodes

Outstanding Writing Achievement in Drama
Reginald Rose, *The Defenders:* various episodes

The Program of the Year
Hallmark Hall of Fame: Victoria Regina (NBC)

Outstanding Single Performance by an Actor in a Leading Role
Peter Falk, *Dick Powell Show:* "The Price of Tomatoes"

Outstanding Single Performance by an Actress in a Leading Role
Julie Harris, *Hallmark Hall of Fame: Victoria Regina*

Outstanding Program Achievement in the Field of Humor
Bob Newhart Show (NBC)

Outstanding Directorial Achievement in Comedy
Nat Hiken, *Car 54, Where Are You?*

Outstanding Writing Achievement in Comedy
Carl Reiner, *Dick Van Dyke Show*

Outstanding Program Achievements in the Fields of Variety and Music
VARIETY
Garry Moore Show (CBS)
MUSIC
Leonard Bernstein and the New York Philharmonic in Japan (CBS)

Outstanding Performance in a Variety or Musical Program or Series
Carol Burnett, *Garry Moore Show*

Outstanding Program Achievement in the Field of Educational and Public Affairs Programming
David Brinkley's Journal (NBC)

Outstanding Program Achievement in the Field of News
Huntley-Brinkley Report (NBC)

Outstanding Writing Achievement in the Documentary Field
Lou Hazam, *Vincent Van Gogh: A Self Portrait*

Outstanding Program Achievement in the Field of Children's Programming
New York Philharmonic Young People's Concerts With Leonard Bernstein (CBS)

1962–1963

Outstanding Program Achievement in the Field of Drama
The Defenders (CBS)

Outstanding Continued Performance by an Actor in a Series (Lead)
E.G. Marshall, *The Defenders*

Outstanding Continued Performance by an Actress in a Series (Lead)
Shirley Booth, *Hazel*

Outstanding Performance in a Supporting Role by an Actor
Don Knotts, *The Andy Griffith Show*

Outstanding Performance in a Supporting Role by an Actress
Glenda Farrell, *Ben Casey:* "A Cardinal Act of Mercy"

Outstanding Directorial Achievement in Drama
Stuart Rosenberg, *The Defenders:* "The Madman"

Outstanding Writing Achievement in Drama
Robert Thom and Reginald Rose, *The Defenders:* "The Madman"

The Program of the Year
The Tunnel (NBC)

Outstanding Single Performance by an Actor in a Leading Role
Trevor Howard, *Hallmark Hall of Fame: The Invincible Mr. Disraeli*

Outstanding Single Performance by an Actress in a Leading Role
Kim Stanley, *Ben Casey:* "A Cardinal Act of Mercy"

Outstanding Program Achievement in the Field of Humor
The Dick Van Dyke Show (CBS)

Outstanding Directorial Achievement in Comedy
John Rich, *The Dick Van Dyke Show*

Outstanding Writing Achievement in Comedy
Carl Reiner, *The Dick Van Dyke Show*

Outstanding Program Achievement in the Field of Variety
The Andy Williams Show (NBC)

Outstanding Program Achievement in the Field of Music
Julie and Carol at Carnegie Hall (CBS)

Outstanding Performance in a Variety or Musical Program or Series
Carol Burnett, *Julie and Carol at Carnegie Hall*

Outstanding Program Achievement in the Field of News Commentary or Public Affairs
David Brinkley's Journal (NBC)

Outstanding Program Achievement in the Field of News
Huntley-Brinkley Report (NBC)

Outstanding Achievement in the Field of Documentary Programs
The Tunnel (NBC)

Outstanding Program Achievement in the Field of Children's Programming
Walt Disney's Wonderful World of Color (NBC)

Outstanding Program Achievement in the Field of Panel, Quiz or Audience Participation
G-E College Bowl (CBS)

1963–1964

Outstanding Program Achievement in the Field of Drama
The Defenders (CBS)

Outstanding Continued Performance by an Actor in a Series (Lead)
Dick Van Dyke, *The Dick Van Dyke Show*

Outstanding Continued Performance by an Actress in a Series (Lead)
Mary Tyler Moore, *The Dick Van Dyke Show*

Outstanding Performance in a Supporting Role by an Actor
Albert Paulsen, *Bob Hope Presents the Chrysler Theatre: One Day in the Life of Ivan Denisovich*

Outstanding Performance in a Supporting Role by an Actress
Ruth White, *Hallmark Hall of Fame: Little Moon of Alban*

Outstanding Directorial Achievement in Drama
Tom Gries, *East Side/West Side:* "Who Do You Kill?"

Outstanding Writing Achievement in Drama, Original
Ernest Kinoy, *The Defenders:* "Blacklist"

Outstanding Writing Achievement in Drama, Adaptation
Rod Serling, *Bob Hope Presents the Chrysler Theatre: It's Mental Work,* from the story by John O'Hara

The Program of the Year
The Making of the President 1960 (ABC)

Outstanding Single Performance by an Actor in a Leading Role
Jack Klugman, *The Defenders:* "Blacklist"

Outstanding Single Performance by an Actress in a Leading Role
Shelley Winters, *Bob Hope Presents the Chrysler Theatre: Two Is the Number*

Outstanding Program Achievement in the Field of Comedy
The Dick Van Dyke Show (CBS)

Outstanding Directorial Achievement in Comedy
Jerry Paris, *The Dick Van Dyke Show*

Outstanding Writing Achievement in Comedy or Variety
Carl Reiner, Sam Denoff and Bill Persky, *The Dick Van Dyke Show:* various episodes

Outstanding Program Achievement in the Field of Variety
The Danny Kaye Show (CBS)

Outstanding Program Achievement in the Field of Music
Bell Telephone Hour (NBC)

Outstanding Performance in a Variety or Musical Program or Series
Danny Kaye, *The Danny Kaye Show*

Outstanding Directorial Achievement in Variety or Music
Robert Scheerer, *The Danny Kaye Show*

Outstanding Program Achievement in the Field of News Commentary or Public Affairs
Cuba, parts I and II — *The Bay of Pigs* and *The Missile Crisis* (NBC)

Outstanding Program Achievement in the Field of News Reports
Huntley-Brinkley Report (NBC)

Outstanding Achievement in the Field of Documentary Programs
The Making of the President 1960 (ABC)

Outstanding Program Achievement in the Field of Children's Programming
Discovery '63–'64 (ABC)

1964–1965

Outstanding Program Achievements in Entertainment
The Dick Van Dyke Show (CBS)
Hallmark Hall of Fame: The Magnificent Yankee (NBC)
My Name is Barbra (CBS)
New York Philharmonic Young People's Concerts With Leonard Bernstein: "What Is Sonata Form?" (CBS)

Outstanding Individual Achievements in Entertainment
ACTORS AND PERFORMERS
Leonard Bernstein, *New York Philharmonic Young People's Concerts With Leonard Bernstein*
Lynn Fontanne, *Hallmark Hall of Fame: The Magnificent Yankee*
Alfred Lunt, *Hallmark Hall of Fame: The Magnificent Yankee*
Barbra Streisand, *My Name is Barbra*
Dick Van Dyke, *The Dick Van Dyke Show*
DIRECTOR
Paul Bogart, *The Defenders:* "The 700-Year-Old Gang"
WRITER
David Karp, *The Defenders:* "The 700-Year-Old Gang"

Outstanding Program Achievements in News, Documentaries, Information and Sports
Saga of Western Man: I, Leonardo Da Vinci (ABC)
The Louvre (NBC)

Outstanding Individual Achievements in News, Documentaries, Information and Sports
NARRATORS
Richard Basehart, *Let My People Go*
Charles Boyer, *The Louvre*
DIRECTOR
John J. Sughrue, *The Louvre*
WRITER
Sidney Carroll, *The Louvre*

1965–1966

Outstanding Dramatic Series
The Fugitive (ABC)

Outstanding Continued Performance by an Actor in a Leading Role in a Dramatic Series
Bill Cosby, *I Spy*

The Dick Van Dyke Show

Outstanding Continued Performance by an Actress in a Leading Role in a Dramatic Series
Barbara Stanwyck, *The Big Valley*

Outstanding Performance by an Actor in a Supporting Role in a Drama
James Daly, *Hallmark Hall of Fame: Eagle in a Cage*

Outstanding Performance by an Actress in a Supporting Role in a Drama
Lee Grant, *Peyton Place*

Outstanding Directorial Achievement in Drama
Sidney Pollack, *Bob Hope Presents the Chrysler Theatre: The Game*

Outstanding Writing Achievement in Drama
Millard Lampell, *Hallmark Hall of Fame: Eagle in a Cage*

Outstanding Dramatic Program
Ages of Man (CBS)

Outstanding Single Performance by an Actor in a Leading Role in a Drama
Cliff Robertson, *Bob Hope Presents the Chrysler Theatre: The Game*

Outstanding Single Performance by an Actress in a Leading Role in a Drama
Simone Signoret, *Bob Hope Presents the Chrysler Theatre: A Small Rebellion*

Outstanding Comedy Series
The Dick Van Dyke Show (CBS)

Outstanding Continued Performance by an Actor in a Leading Role in a Comedy Series
Dick Van Dyke, *The Dick Van Dyke Show*

Outstanding Continued Performance by an Actress in a Leading Role in a Comedy Series
Mary Tyler Moore, *The Dick Van Dyke Show*

Outstanding Performance by an Actor in a Supporting Role in a Comedy
Don Knotts, *The Andy Griffith Show:* "The Return of Barney Fife"

Outstanding Performance by an Actress in a Supporting Role in a Comedy
Alice Pearce, *Bewitched*

Outstanding Directorial Achievement in Comedy
William Asher, *Bewitched*

Outstanding Writing Achievement in Comedy
Bill Persky and Sam Denoff, *The Dick Van Dyke Show:* "Coast to Coast Big Mouth"

Outstanding Variety Series
The Andy Williams Show (NBC)

Outstanding Variety Special
Chrysler Presents the Bob Hope Christmas Special (NBC)

Outstanding Musical Program
Frank Sinatra: A Man and His Music (NBC)

Outstanding Directorial Achievement in Variety or Music
Alan Handley, *The Julie Andrews Show*

Outstanding Writing Achievement in Variety
Al Gordon, Hal Goldman and Sheldon Keller, *An Evening With Carol Channing*

Program Achievements in News and Documentaries
American White Paper: United States Foreign Policy (NBC)

CBS Reports: KKK — The Invisible Empire (CBS)

Senate Hearings on Vietnam (NBC)

Program Achievements in Sports
ABC Wide World of Sports (ABC)

CBS Golf Classic (CBS)

Shell's Wonderful World of Golf (NBC)

Outstanding Children's Program
A Charlie Brown Christmas (CBS)

1966—1967

Outstanding Dramatic Series
Mission: Impossible (CBS)

Outstanding Continued Performance by an Actor in a Leading Role in a Dramatic Series
Bill Cosby, *I Spy*

Outstanding Continued Performance by an Actress in a Leading Role in a Dramatic Series
Barbara Bain, *Mission: Impossible*

Outstanding Performance by an Actor in a Supporting Role in a Drama
Eli Wallach, *Xerox Special: The Poppy Is Also a Flower*

Outstanding Performance by an Actress in a Supporting Role in a Drama
Agnes Moorehead, *Wild, Wild West:* "Night of the Vicious Valentine"

Outstanding Directorial Achievement in Drama
Alex Segal, *Death of a Salesman*

Outstanding Writing Achievement in Drama
Bruce Geller, *Mission: Impossible*

Outstanding Dramatic Program
Death of a Salesman (CBS)

Outstanding Single Performance by an Actor in a Leading Role in a Drama
Peter Ustinov, *Hallmark Hall of Fame: Barefoot in Athens*

Outstanding Single Performance by an Actress in a Leading Role in a Drama
Geraldine Page, *ABC Stage 67: A Christmas Memory*

Outstanding Comedy Series
The Monkees (NBC)

Outstanding Continued Performance by an Actor in a Leading Role in a Comedy Series
Don Adams, *Get Smart!*

Outstanding Continued Performance by an Actress in a Leading Role in a Comedy Series
Lucille Ball, *The Lucy Show*

Outstanding Performance by an Actor in a Supporting Role in a Comedy
Don Knotts, *The Andy Griffith Show:* "Barney Comes to Mayberry"

Outstanding Performance by an Actress in a Supporting Role in a Comedy
Frances Bavier, *The Andy Griffith Show*

The Monkees

Outstanding Directorial Achievement in Comedy
James Frawley, *The Monkees:* "Royal Flush"

Outstanding Writing Achievement in Comedy
Buck Henry and Leonard Stern, *Get Smart!:* "Ship of Spies"

Outstanding Variety Series
The Andy Williams Show (NBC)

Outstanding Variety Special
The Sid Caesar, Imogene Coca, Carl Reiner and Howard Morris Special (CBS)

Outstanding Musical Program
Brigadoon (ABC)

Outstanding Directorial Achievement in Variety or Music
Fielder Cook, *Brigadoon*

Outstanding Writing Achievement in Variety
Mel Brooks, Sam Denoff, Bill Persky, Carl Reiner and Mel Tolkin, *The Sid Caesar, Imogene Coca, Carl Reiner and Howard Morris Special*

Program Achievements in News and Documentaries
China: The Roots of Madness (Syndicated)

Hall of Kings (ABC)

The Italians (CBS)

Program Achievement in Sports
ABC's Wide World of Sports (ABC)

Outstanding Children's Program
Jack and the Beanstalk (NBC)

1967–1968

Outstanding Dramatic Series
Mission: Impossible (CBS)

Outstanding Continued Performance by an Actor in a Leading Role in a Dramatic Series
Bill Cosby, *I Spy*

Outstanding Continued Performance by an Actress in a Leading Role in a Dramatic Series
Barbara Bain, *Mission: Impossible*

Outstanding Performance by an Actor in a Supporting Role in a Drama
Milburn Stone, *Gunsmoke*

Outstanding Performance by an Actress in a Supporting Role in a Drama
Barbara Anderson, *Ironside*

Outstanding Directorial Achievement in Drama
Paul Bogart, *CBS Playhouse: Dear Friends*

Outstanding Writing Achievement in Drama
Loring Mandel, *CBS Playhouse: Do Not Go Gentle Into That Good Night*

Outstanding Dramatic Program
Hallmark Hall of Fame: Elizabeth the Queen (NBC)

Outstanding Single Performance by an Actor in a Leading Role in a Drama
Melvyn Douglas, *CBS Playhouse: Do Not Go Gentle Into That Good Night*

Outstanding Single Performance by an Actress in a Leading Role in a Drama
Maureen Stapleton, *Among the Paths to Eden*

Outstanding Comedy Series
Get Smart! (NBC)

Outstanding Continued Performance by an Actor in a Leading Role in a Comedy Series
Don Adams, *Get Smart!*

Outstanding Continued Performance by an Actress in a Leading Role in a Comedy Series
Lucille Ball, *The Lucy Show*

Outstanding Performance by an Actor in a Supporting Role in a Comedy
Werner Klemperer, *Hogan's Heroes*

Outstanding Performance by an Actress in a Supporting Role in a Comedy
Marion Lorne, *Bewitched*

Outstanding Directorial Achievement in Comedy
Bruce Bilson, *Get Smart!:* "Maxwell Smart, Private Eye"

Outstanding Writing Achievement in Comedy
Allan Burns and Chris Hayward, *He and She:* "The Coming Out Party"

Outstanding Musical or Variety Series
Rowan and Martin's Laugh-In (NBC)

Outstanding Musical or Variety Program
Rowan and Martin's Laugh-In Special (NBC)

Outstanding Directorial Achievement in Music or Variety
Jack Haley, Jr., *Movin' With Nancy*

Outstanding Writing Achievement in Music or Variety
Chris Beard, Phil Hahn, Jack Hanrahan, Coslough Johnson, Paul Keyes, Marc London, Allan Manings, David Panich, Hugh Wedlock and Digby Wolfe, *Rowan and Martin's Laugh-In*

Outstanding Program Achievement Within Regularly Scheduled News Programs
Public Broadcast Laboratory: Crisis in the Cities (NET)

Outstanding Program Achievements in News Documentaries
Africa (ABC)

Summer '67: What We Learned (NBC)

Other News and Documentary Program Achievements
The 21st Century (CBS)

CBS News Special: Science and Religion: Who Will Play God? (CBS)

Outstanding Program Achievements in Cultural Documentaries
CBS News Special: Eric Hoffer: The Passionate State of Mind (CBS)

CBS News Special: Gauguin in Tahiti: The Search for Paradise (CBS)

John Steinbeck's America and Americans (NBC)

NET Festival: Dylan Thomas: The World I Breathe (NET)

Outstanding Achievement in Sports Programming
ABC's Wide World of Sports (ABC)

Outstanding Achievements in Children's Programming
He's Your Dog Charlie Brown (CBS)

Mister Rogers's Neighborhood (NET)

You're in Love, Charlie Brown (CBS)

1968–1969

Outstanding Dramatic Series
NET Playhouse (NET)

Outstanding Continued Performance by an Actor in a Leading Role in a Dramatic Series
Carl Betz, *Judd for the Defense*

Outstanding Continued Performance by an Actress in a Leading Role in a Dramatic Series
Barbara Bain, *Mission: Impossible*

Outstanding Continued Performance by an Actor in a Supporting Role in a Series
Werner Klemperer, *Hogan's Heroes*

Outstanding Continued Performance by an Actress in a Supporting Role in a Series
Susan Saint James, *The Name of the Game*

Outstanding Directorial Achievement in Drama
David Green, *CBS Playhouse: The People Next Door*

Outstanding Writing Achievement in Drama
JP Miller, *CBS Playhouse: The People Next Door*

Outstanding Dramatic Program
Hallmark Hall of Fame: Teacher, Teacher (NBC)

Outstanding Single Performance by an Actor in a Leading Role
Paul Scofield, *Prudential's on Stage: Male of the Species*

Outstanding Single Performance by an Actress in a Leading Role
Geraldine Page, *The Thanksgiving Visitor*

Outstanding Single Performance by an Actor in a Supporting Role
No award presented

Outstanding Single Performance by an Actress in a Supporting Role
Anna Calder-Marshall, *Prudential's on Stage: Male of the Species*

Outstanding Comedy Series
Get Smart! (NBC)

Outstanding Continued Performance by an Actor in a Leading Role in a Comedy Series
Don Adams, *Get Smart!*

Outstanding Continued Performance by an Actress in a Leading Role in a Comedy Series
Hope Lange, *The Ghost and Mrs. Muir*

Outstanding Variety or Musical Series
Rowan and Martin's Laugh-In (NBC)

Outstanding Variety or Musical Program
The Bill Cosby Special (NBC)

Outstanding Directorial Achievement in Comedy, Variety or Music
No award presented

Outstanding Writing Achievement in Comedy, Variety or Music
Allan Blye, Bob Einstein, Murray Roman, Carl Gottlieb, Jerry Music, Steve Martin, Cecil Tuck, Paul Wayne, Cy Howard and Mason Williams, *The Smothers Brothers Comedy Hour*

Outstanding Achievement Within Regularly Scheduled News Programs
The Huntley-Brinkley Report: "Coverage of Hunger in the United States" (NBC)

Outstanding News Documentary Program Achievements
CBS News Hour: "Hunger in America" (CBS)

Public Broadcast Laboratory: Law and Order (NET)

Outstanding Cultural Documentary and "Magazine-Type" Program or Series Achievements
CBS News Hour: "Don't Count the Candles" (CBS)

CBS News Hour: "Justice Black and the Bill of Rights" (CBS)

Bell Telephone Hour: "Man Who Dances: Edward Villella" (NBC)

CBS News Hour: "The Great American Novel" (CBS)

Outstanding Achievement in Sports Programming
19th Summer Olympics Games (ABC)

Outstanding Achievement in Children's Programming
Mister Rogers's Neighborhood (NET)

1969–1970

Outstanding Dramatic Series
Marcus Welby, M.D. (ABC)

Outstanding Continued Performance by an Actor in a Leading Role in a Dramatic Series
Robert Young, *Marcus Welby, M.D.*

Outstanding Continued Performance by an Actress in a Leading Role in a Dramatic Series
Susan Hampshire, *The Forsyte Saga*

Outstanding Performance by an Actor in a Supporting Role in Drama
James Brolin, *Marcus Welby, M.D.*

Outstanding Performance by an Actress in a Supporting Role in Drama
Gail Fisher, *Mannix*

Outstanding Directorial Achievement in Drama
Paul Bogart, *CBS Playhouse: Shadow Game*

Outstanding Writing Achievement in Drama
Richard Levinson and William Link, *My Sweet Charlie*

Outstanding Dramatic Program
Hallmark Hall of Fame: A Storm in Summer (NBC)

Outstanding Single Performance by an Actor in a Leading Role
Peter Ustinov, *Hallmark Hall of Fame: A Storm in Summer*

Outstanding Single Performance by an Actress in a Leading Role
Patty Duke, *My Sweet Charlie*

Outstanding New Series
Room 222 (ABC)

Outstanding Comedy Series
My World and Welcome to It (NBC)

Outstanding Continued Performance by an Actor in a Leading Role in a Comedy Series
William Windom, *My World and Welcome to It*

Outstanding Continued Performance by an Actress in a Leading Role in a Comedy Series
Hope Lange, *The Ghost and Mrs. Muir*

Outstanding Performance by an Actor in a Supporting Role in Comedy
Michael Constantine, *Room 222*

Outstanding Performance by an Actress in a Supporting Role in Comedy
Karen Valentine, *Room 222*

Outstanding Variety or Musical Series
The David Frost Show (Syndicated)

Outstanding Variety or Musical Program
Variety and Popular Music
Annie, The Women in the Life of a Man (CBS)

Classical Music
NET Festival: Cinderella, National Ballet of Canada (NET)

Outstanding Directorial Achievement in Comedy, Variety or Music
Dwight A. Hemion, *Kraft Music Hall: The Sound of Burt Bacharach* (NBC)

Outstanding Writing Achievement in Comedy, Variety or Music
Gary Belkin, Peter Bellwood, Herb Sargent, Thomas Meehan and Judith Viorst, *Annie, The Women in the Life of a Man*

Outstanding Achievements Within Regularly Scheduled News Programs
The Huntley-Brinkley Report: "An Investigation of Teenage Drug Addiction — Odyssey House" (NBC)

CBS Evening News With Walter Cronkite: "Can the World Be Saved?" (CBS)

Outstanding Achievement in News Documentary Programming
NET Journal: "Hospital" (NET)

Outstanding Achievement in Magazine-Type Programming
Black Journal (NET)

Outstanding Achievements in Cultural Documentary Programming
Artur Rubinstein (NBC)

CBS News Hour: "Fathers and Sons" (CBS)

CBS News Hour: "The Japanese" (CBS)

Outstanding Achievement in Sports Programming
The NFL Games (CBS)

Outstanding Achievement in Children's Programming
Sesame Street (NET)

1970–1971

Outstanding Series, Drama
The Bold Ones: The Senator (NBC)

Outstanding Continued Performance by an Actor in a Leading Role in a Dramatic Series
Hal Holbrook, *The Bold Ones: The Senator*

Outstanding Continued Performance by an Actress in a Leading Role in a Dramatic Series
Susan Hampshire, *Masterpiece Theatre: The First Churchills*

Outstanding Performance by an Actor in a Supporting Role in Drama
David Burns, *Hallmark Hall of Fame: The Price*

Outstanding Performance by an Actress in a Supporting Role in Drama
Margaret Leighton, *Hallmark Hall of Fame: Hamlet*

Outstanding Directorial Achievement in Drama (Single Program of a Series)
Daryl Duke, *The Bold Ones: The Senator:* "The Day the Lion Died"

Outstanding Writing Achievement in Drama (Single Program of a Series)
Joel Oliansky, *The Bold Ones: The Senator:* "To Taste of Death but Once"

Outstanding Single Program, Drama or Comedy
Hollywood Television Theatre: The Andersonville Trial (PBS)

Outstanding Single Performance by an Actor in a Leading Role
George C. Scott, *Hallmark Hall of Fame: The Price*

Outstanding Single Performance by an Actress in a Leading Role
Lee Grant, *NBC Monday Night at the Movies: The Neon Ceiling*

Outstanding Directorial Achievement in Drama (Single Program)
Fielder Cook, *Hallmark Hall of Fame: The Price*

Outstanding Writing Achievement in Drama, Original Teleplay
Tracy Keenan Wynn and Marvin Schwartz, *Movie of the Week on ABC: Tribes*

Outstanding Writing Achievement in Drama, Adaptation
Saul Levitt, *Hollywood Television Theatre: The Andersonville Trial*

Outstanding New Series
All in the Family (CBS)

Outstanding Series, Comedy
All in the Family (CBS)

Outstanding Continued Performance by an Actor in a Leading Role in a Comedy Series
Jack Klugman, *The Odd Couple*

Outstanding Continued Performance by an Actress in a Leading Role in a Comedy Series
Jean Stapleton, *All in the Family*

Outstanding Performance by an Actor in a Supporting Role in Comedy
Edward Asner, *The Mary Tyler Moore Show*

Outstanding Performance by an Actress in a Supporting Role in Comedy
Valerie Harper, *The Mary Tyler Moore Show*

Outstanding Directorial Achievement in Comedy
Jay Sandrich, *The Mary Tyler Moore Show:* "Toulouse Lautrec Is One of My Favorite Artists"

Outstanding Writing Achievement in Comedy
James L. Brooks and Allan Burns, *The Mary Tyler Moore Show:* "Support Your Local Mother"

Outstanding Variety Series, Musical
The Flip Wilson Show (NBC)

Outstanding Variety Series, Talk
The David Frost Show (Syndicated)

Outstanding Directorial Achievement in Variety or Music
Mark Warren, *Rowan and Martin's Laugh-In* (with Orson Welles)

Outstanding Writing Achievement in Variety or Music
Herbert Baker, Hal Goodman, Larry Klein, Bob Weiskopf, Bob Schiller, Norman Steinberg and Flip Wilson, *The Flip Wilson Show* (with Lena Horne and Tony Randall)

Outstanding Single Program, Variety or Musical Variety and Popular Music
Singer Presents Burt Bacharach (CBS)

Classical Music
NET Festival: Leopold Stokowski (PBS)

Outstanding Directorial Achievement in Comedy, Variety or Music (Single Program)
Sterling Johnson, *Timex Presents Peggy Fleming at Sun Valley*

Outstanding Writing Achievement in Comedy, Variety or Music (Single Program)
Bob Ellison and Marty Farrell, *Singer Presents Burt Bacharach*

Outstanding Achievement Within Regularly Scheduled News Programs
NBC Nightly News: "Five Part Investigation of Welfare" (NBC)

All in the Family

Outstanding Achievements in News Documentary Programming
CBS News: "The Selling of the Pentagon" (CBS)

CBS News: "The World of Charlie Company" (CBS)

NBC News: NBC White Paper: Pollution is a Matter of Choice (NBC)

Outstanding Achievements in Magazine-Type Programming
60 Minutes: "Gulf of Tonkin Segment" (CBS)

The Great American Dream Machine (PBS)

Outstanding Achievements in Cultural Documentary Programming
NBC News: The Everglades (NBC)

The Making of Butch Cassidy and the Sundance Kid (NBC)

Arthur Penn, 1922–: Themes and Variants (PBS)

Outstanding Achievement in Sports Programming
ABC's Wide World of Sports (ABC)

Outstanding Achievement in Children's Programming
Sesame Street (PBS)

1971–1972

Outstanding Series, Drama
Masterpiece Theatre: Elizabeth R (PBS)

Outstanding Continued Performance by an Actor in a Leading Role in a Dramatic Series
Peter Falk, *NBC Mystery Movie: Columbo*

Outstanding Continued Performance by an Actress in a Leading Role in a Dramatic Series
Glenda Jackson, *Masterpiece Theatre: Elizabeth R*

Outstanding Performance by an Actor in a Supporting Role in Drama
Jack Warden, *Movie of the Week: Brian's Song*

Outstanding Performance by an Actress in a Supporting Role in Drama
Jenny Agutter, *Hallmark Hall of Fame: The Snow Goose*

Outstanding Directorial Achievement in Drama (Single Program of a Series)
Alexander Singer, *The Bold Ones: The Lawyers:* "The Invasion of Kevin Ireland"

Outstanding Writing Achievement in Drama (Single Program of a Series)
Richard L. Levinson and William Link, *NBC Mystery Movie: Colombo: Death Lends a Hand*

Outstanding Single Program, Drama or Comedy
Movie of the Week: Brian's Song (ABC)

Outstanding Single Performance by an Actor in a Leading Role
Keith Michell, *The Six Wives of Henry VIII: Catherine Howard*

Outstanding Single Performance by an Actress in a Leading Role
Glenda Jackson, *Masterpiece Theatre: Elizabeth R:* "Shadow in the Sun"

Outstanding Directorial Achievement in Drama (Single Program)
Tom Gries, *The New CBS Friday Night Movies: The Glass House*

Outstanding Writing Achievement in Drama, Original Teleplay
Allan Sloane, *To All My Friends on Shore*

Outstanding Writing Achievement in Drama, Adaptation
William Blinn, *Movie of the Week: Brian's Song*

Outstanding New Series
Masterpiece Theatre: Elizabeth R (PBS)

The Carol Burnett Show

Outstanding Series, Comedy
All in the Family (CBS)

Outstanding Continued Performance by an Actor in a Leading Role in a Comedy Series
Carroll O'Connor, *All in the Family*

Outstanding Continued Performance by an Actress in a Leading Role in a Comedy Series
Jean Stapleton, *All in the Family*

Outstanding Performance by an Actor in a Supporting Role in Comedy
Edward Asner, *The Mary Tyler Moore Show*

Outstanding Performance by an Actress in a Supporting Role in a Comedy (tie)
Valerie Harper, *The Mary Tyler Moore Show*

Sally Struthers, *All in the Family*

Outstanding Directorial Achievement in Comedy
John Rich, *All in the Family:* "Sammy's Visit"

Outstanding Writing Achievement in Comedy
Burt Styler, *All in the Family:* "Edith's Problem"

Outstanding Variety Series, Musical
The Carol Burnett Show (CBS)

Outstanding Variety Series, Talk
The Dick Cavett Show (ABC)

Outstanding Achievement by a Performer in Music or Variety
Harvey Korman, *The Carol Burnett Show*

Outstanding Directorial Achievement in Variety or Music
Art Fisher, *The Sonny and Cher Comedy Hour* (with Tony Randall)

Outstanding Writing Achievement in Variety or Music
Don Hinkley, Stan Hart, Larry Siegel, Woody Kling, Roger Beatty, Art Baer, Ben Joelson, Stan Burns, Mike Marmer and Arnie Rosen, *The Carol Burnett Show* (with Tim Conway and Ray Charles)

Outstanding Single Program, Variety or Musical
VARIETY AND POPULAR MUSIC
Bell System Family Theatre: Jack Lemmon in 'S Wonderful, 'S Marvelous, 'S Gershwin (NBC)

CLASSICAL MUSIC
Beethoven's Birthday: A Celebration in Vienna With Leonard Bernstein (CBS)

Outstanding Directorial Achievement in Comedy, Variety or Music (Special Program)
Walter C. Miller and Martin Charnin, *Bell System Family Theatre: Jack Lemmon in 'S Wonderful, 'S Marvelous, 'S Gershwin*

Outstanding Writing Achievement in Comedy, Variety or Music (Special Program)
Anne Howard Bailey, *NET Opera Theatre: The Trial of Mary Lincoln*

Outstanding Achievement Within Regularly Scheduled News Programs
NBC Nightly News: "Defeat of Dacca" (NBC)

Outstanding Achievements for Regularly Scheduled Magazine-Type Programs
Chronolog (NBC)

The Great American Dream Machine (PBS)

Outstanding Documentary Program Achievements
CURRENT SIGNIFICANCE
CBS Reports: "A Night in Jail, A Day in Court" (CBS)

This Child Is Rated X: An NBC News White Paper on Juvenile Justice (NBC)

CULTURAL
The Monday Night Special: Hollywood: The Dream Factory (ABC)

The Undersea World of Jacques Cousteau: A Sound of Dolphins (ABC)

The Undersea World of Jacques Cousteau: The Unsinkable Sea Otter (ABC)

Outstanding Achievement in Sports Programming
ABC's Wide World of Sports (ABC)

Outstanding Achievement in Children's Programming
Sesame Street (PBS)

Special Classification of Outstanding Program Achievement
General Programming
PBS Special: The Pentagon Papers (PBS)

Docu-Drama
The Search for the Nile, parts I–VI (NBC)

1972–1973

Outstanding Drama Series, Continuing
The Waltons (CBS)

Outstanding Continued Performance by an Actor in a Leading Role in a Drama
Richard Thomas, *The Waltons* (CBS)

Outstanding Continued Performance by an Actress in a Leading Role in a Drama
Michael Learned, *The Waltons* (CBS)

Outstanding Performance by an Actor in a Supporting Role in Drama
Scott Jacoby, *Wednesday Movie of the Week: That Certain Summer*

Outstanding Performance by an Actress in a Supporting Role in Drama
Ellen Corby, *The Waltons*

Outstanding Directorial Achievement in Drama (Single Program of a Series)
Jerry Thorpe, *Kung Fu:* "An Eye for an Eye"

Outstanding Writing Achievement in Drama (Single Program of a Series)
John McGreevey, *The Waltons:* "The Scholar"

Outstanding Single Program, Drama or Comedy
The New CBS Tuesday Night Movies: A War of Children (CBS)

Outstanding Single Performance by an Actor in a Leading Role
Laurence Olivier, *Long Day's Journey Into Night* (ABC)

Outstanding Single Performance by an Actress in a Leading Role
Cloris Leachman, *Tuesday Movie of the Week: A Brand New Life* (ABC)

Outstanding Directorial Achievement in Drama (Single Program)
Joseph Sargent, *The CBS Thursday Night Movies: The Marcus-Nelson Murders*

Outstanding Writing Achievement in Drama, Original Teleplay
Abby Mann, *The CBS Thursday Night Movies: The Marcus-Nelson Murders*

Outstanding Writing Achievement in Drama, Adaptation
Eleanor Perry, *The House Without a Christmas Tree*

Outstanding New Series
America (NBC)

Outstanding Comedy Series
All in the Family (CBS)

Outstanding Continued Performance by an Actor in a Leading Role in a Comedy Series
Jack Klugman, *The Odd Couple*

Outstanding Continued Performance by an Actress in a Leading Role in a Comedy Series
Mary Tyler Moore, *The Mary Tyler Moore Show*

Outstanding Performance by an Actor in a Supporting Role in Comedy
Ted Knight, *The Mary Tyler Moore Show*

Outstanding Performance by an Actress in a Supporting Role in Comedy
Valerie Harper, *The Mary Tyler Moore Show*

Outstanding Directorial Achievement in Comedy
Jay Sandrich, *The Mary Tyler Moore Show:* "It's Whether You Win or Lose"

Outstanding Writing Achievement in Comedy
Michael Ross, Bernie West and Lee Kalcheim, *All in the Family:* "The Bunkers and the Swingers"

Outstanding Variety Musical Series
The Julie Andrews Hour (ABC)

Outstanding Achievement by a Supporting Performer in Music or Variety
Tim Conway, *The Carol Burnett Show*

Outstanding Directorial Achievement in Variety or Music
Bill Davis, *The Julie Andrews Hour* (with "Liza Doolittle" and "Mary Poppins")

Outstanding Writing Achievement in Variety or Music
Stan Hart, Larry Siegel, Gail Parent, Woody Kling, Roger Beatty, Tom Patchett, Jay Tarses, Robert Hilliard, Arnie Kogen, Bill Angelos and Buz Kohan, *The Carol Burnett Show* (with Steve Lawrence and Lili Tomlin)

Outstanding Single Program, Variety and Popular Music
Singer Presents Liza With a 'Z' (NBC)

Outstanding Single Program, Classical Music
The Sleeping Beauty (PBS)

Outstanding Directorial Achievement in Comedy, Variety or Music (Special Program)
Bob Fosse, *Singer Presents Liza With a 'Z'*

Outstanding Writing Achievement in Comedy, Variety or Music (Special Program)
Renée Taylor and Joseph Bologna, *Acts of Love — And Other Comedies*

Outstanding Drama/Comedy, Limited Episodes
Masterpiece Theatre: Tom Brown's Schooldays, parts I–V (PBS)

Outstanding Continued Performance by an Actor in a Leading Role in a Drama or Comedy, Limited Episodes
Anthony Murphy, *Masterpiece Theatre: Tom Brown's Schooldays,* parts I–V (PBS)

Outstanding Continued Performance by an Actress in a Leading Role in a Drama or Comedy, Limited Episodes
Susan Hampshire, *Masterpiece Theatre: Vanity Fair,* parts I–V

Outstanding Achievement Within Regularly Scheduled News Programs
CBS Evening News With Walter Cronkite: "The US/Soviet Wheat Deal: Is There a Scandal?" (CBS)

Outstanding Achievements for Regularly Scheduled Magazine-Type Programs
60 Minutes: "The Poppy Fields of Turkey — The Heroin Labs of Marseilles — The N.Y. Connection" (CBS)

60 Minutes: "The Selling of Colonel Herbert" (CBS)

60 Minutes (CBS)

Outstanding Documentary Program Achievements
CURRENT SIGNIFICANCE
NBC News White Paper: The Blue Collar Trap (NBC)

CBS Reports: "The Mexican Connection" (CBS)

NBC Reports: "One Billion Dollar Weapon and Now the War Is Over: The American Military in the 70's" (NBC)

CULTURAL
America (NBC)

Jane Goodall and the World of Animal Behavior: The Wild Dogs of Africa (ABC)

Outstanding Achievements in Sports Programming
ABC's Wide World of Sports (ABC)

1972 Summer Olympic Games (ABC)

Outstanding Achievements in Children's Programming
ENTERTAINMENT/FICTIONAL
Sesame Street (PBS)

Zoom (PBS)

INFORMATION/FACTUAL
The ABC Afterschool Special: Last of the Curlews (ABC)

Special Classification of Outstanding Program Achievements
The Advocates (PBS)

Special of the Week: "VD Blues" (PBS)

1973–1974

Actor of the Year, Series
Alan Alda, *M*A*S*H*

Actress of the Year, Series
Mary Tyler Moore, *The Mary Tyler Moore Show*

Supporting Actor of the Year
Michael Moriarty, *The Glass Menagerie*

Supporting Actress of the Year
Joanna Miles, *The Glass Menagerie*

Director of the Year, Series
Robert Butler, *The Blue Knight, Part III*

Writer of the Year, Series
Treva Silverman, *The Mary Tyler Moore Show:* "The Lou and Edie Story"

Actor of the Year, Special
Hal Holbrook, *ABC Theatre: Pueblo*

Actress of the Year, Special
Cicely Tyson, *The Autobiography of Miss Jane Pittman*

Director of the Year, Special
Dwight Hemion, *Barbra Streisand . . . And Other Musical Instruments*

Writer of the Year, Special
Fay Kanin, *GE Theater: Tell Me Where It Hurts*

Outstanding Drama Series
Masterpiece Theatre: Upstairs, Downstairs (PBS)

Best Lead Actor in a Drama Series
Telly Savalas, *Kojak*

Best Lead Actress in a Drama Series
Michael Learned, *The Waltons*

Best Lead Actor in a Drama (for a Special Program, Comedy or Drama or a Single Appearance in a Drama or Comedy Series)
Hal Holbrook, *ABC Theatre: Pueblo*

Best Lead Actress in a Drama (for a Special Program, Comedy or Drama or a Single Appearance in a Drama or Comedy Series)
Cicely Tyson, *The Autobiography of Miss Jane Pittman*

Best Supporting Actor in Drama (for a Special Program, a One-Time Appearance in a Series or a Continuing Role)
Michael Moriarty, *The Glass Menagerie*

Best Supporting Actress in Drama (for a Special Program, a One-Time Appearance in a Series or a Continuing Role)
Joanna Miles, *The Glass Menagerie*

Best Directing in a Drama (Single Program of a Series)
Robert Butler, *The Blue Knight, Part III*

Best Writing in Drama (Single Program of a Series)
Joanna Lee, *The Waltons:* "The Thanksgiving Story"

Best Writing in Drama, Original Teleplay
Fay Kanin, *GE Theater: Tell Me Where It Hurts*

Best Writing in Drama, Adaptation
Tracy Keenan Wynn, *The Autobiography of Miss Jane Pittman*

Outstanding Special, Comedy or Drama
The Autobiography of Miss Jane Pittman (CBS)

Best Directing in Drama (Single Program, Comedy or Drama)
John Korty, *The Autobiography of Miss Jane Pittman*

Outstanding Comedy Series
*M*A*S*H* (CBS)

Best Lead Actor in a Comedy Series
Alan Alda, *M*A*S*H*

Best Lead Actress in a Comedy Series
Mary Tyler Moore, *The Mary Tyler Moore Show*

Best Supporting Actor in Comedy
Rob Reiner, *All in the Family*

Alan Alda, *M*A*S*H*

Best Supporting Actress in Comedy
Cloris Leachman, *The Mary Tyler Moore Show*: "The Lars Affair"

Best Directing in Comedy
Jack Cooper, *M*A*S*H*: "Carry On, Hawkeye"

Best Writing in Comedy
Treva Silverman, *The Mary Tyler Moore Show*: "The Lou and Edie Story"

Outstanding Music-Variety Series
The Carol Burnett Show (CBS)

Best Supporting Actor in Comedy-Variety, Variety or Music
Harvey Korman, *The Carol Burnett Show*

Best Supporting Actress in Comedy-Variety, Variety or Music
Brenda Vaccaro, *The Shape of Things*

Best Directing in Variety or Music
Dave Powers, *The Carol Burnett Show*: "The Australia Show"

Best Writing in Variety or Music
Ed Simmons, Gary Belkin, Roger Beatty, Arnie Kogen, Bill Richmond, Gene Perret, Rudy DeLuca, Barry Levinson, Dick Clair, Jenna McMahon and Barry Harman, *The Carol Burnett Show* (with Tim Conway and Bernadette Peters)

Outstanding Comedy-Variety, Variety or Music Special
Lily (CBS)

Best Directing in Comedy-Variety, Variety or Music (Special Program)
Dwight Hemion, *Barbra Streisand . . . And Other Musical Instruments*

Best Writing in Comedy-Variety, Variety or Music (Special Program)
Herb Sargent, Rosalyn Drexler, Lorne Michaels, Richard Pryor, Jim Rusk, James R. Stein, Robert Illes, Lily Tomlin, George Yanok, Jane Wagner, Rod Warren, Ann Elder and Karyl Geld, *Lily*

Outstanding Limited Series
NBC Sunday Mystery Movie: Columbo (NBC)

Best Lead Actor in a Limited Series
William Holden, *The Blue Knight*

Best Lead Actress in a Limited Series
Mildred Natwick, *NBC Tuesday Mystery Movie: The Snoop Sisters*

Outstanding Achievements Within Regularly Scheduled News Programs
CBS Evening News With Walter Cronkite: "Coverage of the October War From Israel's Northern Front" (CBS)
CBS Evening News With Walter Cronkite: "The Agnew Resignation" (CBS)
CBS Evening News With Walter Cronkite: "The Key Biscayne Bank Charter Struggle" (CBS)
NBC Nightly News: "Reports on World Hunger" (NBC)

Outstanding Television News Broadcaster (tie)
Harry Reasoner, *ABC News*
Bill Moyers, *Bill Moyers' Journal*: "Essay on Watergate"

Outstanding Achievements for Regularly Scheduled Magazine-Type Programs
First Tuesday: "America's Nerve Gas Arsenal" (NBC)
Behind the Lines: "The Adversaries" (PBS)
Bill Moyers' Journal: "A Question of Impeachment" (PBS)

Outstanding Interview Program (tie)
CBS News Special: "Solzhenitsyn" (CBS)
Bill Moyers' Journal: "Henry Steele Commager" (PBS)

Star Trek

Outstanding Documentary Program Achievements
CURRENT SIGNIFICANCE
ABC News Close Up: Fire! (ABC)
CBS News Special Report: The Senate and the Watergate Affair (CBS)
CULTURAL
Journey to the Outer Limits (ABC)
The World at War (Syndicated)
CBS Reports: The Rockefellers (CBS)

Outstanding Achievement in News and Documentary Directing
ABC News Close-up: Fire! (ABC)

Outstanding Children's Special
Marlo Thomas and Friends in Free to Be . . . You and Me (ABC)

Outstanding Informational Children's Series (Prime Time)
Make a Wish (ABC)

Outstanding Informational Children's Special (Prime Time)
The Runaways (ABC)

Outstanding Children's Entertainment Series (Daytime)
Zoom (PBS)

Outstanding Children's Entertainment Special (Daytime)
The ABC Afterschool Special: Rookie of the Year (ABC)

Outstanding Instructional Children's Programming
Inside/Out (Syndicated)

Outstanding Game Show
Password (ABC)

Outstanding Talk, Service or Variety Series
The Merv Griffin Show (Syndicated)

1974–1975

Outstanding Drama Series
Masterpiece Theatre: Upstairs, Downstairs (PBS)

Outstanding Lead Actor in a Drama Series
Robert Blake, *Baretta* (ABC)

Outstanding Lead Actress in a Drama Series
Jean Marsh, *Masterpiece Theatre: Upstairs, Downstairs*

Outstanding Continuing Performance by a Supporting Actor in a Drama Series
Will Geer, *The Waltons*

Outstanding Continuing Performance by a Supporting Actress in a Drama Series
Ellen Corby, *The Waltons*

Outstanding Single Performance by a Supporting Actor in a Comedy or Drama Series
Patrick McGoohan, *NBC Sunday Mystery Movie: Columbo: By Dawn's Early Light*

Outstanding Single Performance by a Supporting Actress in a Comedy or Drama Series (tie)
Cloris Leachman, *The Mary Tyler Moore Show: "Phyllis Whips Inflation"*

Zohra Lampert, *Kojak: "Queen of the Gypsies"*

Outstanding Directing in a Drama Series
Bill Bain, *Masterpiece Theatre: Upstairs, Downstairs: "A Sudden Storm"*

Outstanding Writing in a Drama Series
Howard Fast, *Benjamin Franklin: "The Ambassador"*

Outstanding Special, Drama or Comedy
The Law (NBC)

Outstanding Lead Actor in a Special Program, Drama or Comedy
Laurence Olivier, *ABC Theatre: Love Among the Ruins*

Outstanding Lead Actress in a Special Program, Drama or Comedy
Katharine Hepburn, *ABC Theatre: Love Among the Ruins*

Outstanding Single Performance by a Supporting Actor in a Comedy or Drama Special
Anthony Quale, *ABC Movie Special: QB VII, parts 1 and 2*

Outstanding Single Performance by a Supporting Actress in a Comedy or Drama Special
Juliet Mills, *ABC Movie Special: QB VII, parts 1 and 2*

Outstanding Directing in a Special Program, Drama or Comedy
George Cukor, *ABC Theatre: Love Among the Ruins*

Outstanding Writing in a Special Program, Drama or Comedy, Original Teleplay
James Costigan, *ABC Theatre: Love Among the Ruins*

Outstanding Writing in a Special Program, Drama or Comedy, Adaptation
David W. Rintels, *IBM Presents Clarence Darrow*

Outstanding Comedy Series
The Mary Tyler Moore Show (CBS)

Outstanding Lead Actor in a Comedy Series
Tony Randall, *The Odd Couple*

Outstanding Lead Actress in a Comedy Series
Valerie Harper, *Rhoda*

Outstanding Continuing Performance by a Supporting Actor in a Comedy Series
Ed Asner, *The Mary Tyler Moore Show*

Outstanding Continuing Performance by a Supporting Actress in a Comedy Series
Betty White, *The Mary Tyler Moore Show*

Outstanding Directing in a Comedy Series
Gene Reynolds, *M*A*S*H*

Outstanding Writing in a Comedy Series
Ed Weinberger and Stan Daniels, *The Mary Tyler Moore Show: "Mary Richards Goes to Jail"*

Outstanding Comedy-Variety or Music Series
The Carol Burnett Show (CBS)

Outstanding Continuing or Single Performance by a Supporting Actor in Variety or Music
Jack Albertson, *Cher*

Outstanding Continuing or Single Performance by a Supporting Actress in Variety or Music
Cloris Leachman, *Cher*

Outstanding Directing in a Comedy-Variety or Music Series
Dave Powers, *The Carol Burnett Show* (with Alan Alda)

Outstanding Writing in a Comedy-Variety or Music Series
Ed Simmons, Gary Belkin, Roger Beatty, Arnie Kogen, Bill Richmond, Gene Perret, Rudy DeLuca, Barry Levinson, Dick Clair and Jenna McMahon, *The Carol Burnett Show* (with Alan Alda)

Outstanding Special, Comedy-Variety or Music
An Evening With John Denver (ABC)

Outstanding Directing in a Comedy-Variety or Music Special
Bill Davis, *An Evening With John Denver*

Outstanding Writing in a Comedy-Variety or Music Special
Bob Wells, John Bradford and Cy Coleman, *Shirley MacLaine: If They Could See Me Now*

Outstanding Limited Series
Benjamin Franklin (CBS)

Outstanding Lead Actor in a Limited Series
Peter Falk, *NBC Sunday Night Mystery Movie: Columbo*

Outstanding Lead Actress in a Limited Series
Jessica Walter, *NBC Sunday Mystery Movie: Amy Prentiss*

Outstanding Sports Program
Wide World of Sports (ABC)

Outstanding Children's Special (Prime Time)
Yes, Virginia, There Is a Santa Claus (ABC)

Outstanding Entertainment Children's Series (Daytime)
Star Trek (NBC)

Outstanding Entertainment Children's Special (Daytime)
The CBS Festival of Lively Arts for Young People: Harlequin (CBS)

Outstanding Game or Audience Participation Show
Hollywood Squares (NBC)

Outstanding Talk, Service or Variety Series
Dinah! (Syndicated)

Special Classification of Outstanding Program Achievement
The American Film Institute Salute to James Cagney (CBS)

1975–1976

Outstanding Drama Series
Police Story (NBC)

Outstanding Lead Actor in a Drama Series
Peter Falk, *NBC Sunday Mystery Movie: Columbo*

Outstanding Lead Actress in a Drama Series
Michael Learned, *The Waltons*

Outstanding Continuing Performance by a Supporting Actor in a Drama Series
Anthony Zerbe, *Harry O*

Outstanding Continuing Performance by a Supporting Actress in a Drama Series
Ellen Corby, *The Waltons*

Outstanding Lead Actor for a Single Appearance in a Drama or Comedy Series
Edward Asner, *Rich Man, Poor Man*

Outstanding Lead Actress for a Single Appearance in a Drama or Comedy Series
Kathryn Walker, *The Adams Chronicles:* "John Adams, Lawyer"

Outstanding Single Performance by a Supporting Actor in a Comedy or Drama Series
Gordon Jackson, *Masterpiece Theatre: Upstairs, Downstairs:* "The Beastly Hun"

Outstanding Single Performance by a Supporting Actress in a Comedy or Drama Series
Fionnuala Flanagan, *Rich Man, Poor Man*

Outstanding Directing in a Drama Series
David Greene, *Rich Man, Poor Man,* Episode 8

Outstanding Writing in a Drama Series
Sherman Yellen, *The Adams Chronicles:* "John Adams, Lawyer"

Outstanding Special, Drama or Comedy
ABC Theatre: Eleanor and Franklin (ABC)

Outstanding Lead Actor in a Drama or Comedy Special
Anthony Hopkins, *The Lindbergh Kidnapping Case*

Outstanding Lead Actress in a Drama or Comedy Special
Susan Clark, *Babe*

Outstanding Single Performance by a Supporting Actor in a Comedy or Drama Special
Ed Flanders, *ABC Theatre: A Moon for the Misbegotten*

Outstanding Single Performance by a Supporting Actress in a Comedy or Drama Special
Rosemary Murphy, *ABC Theatre: Eleanor and Franklin*

Outstanding Directing in a Special Program, Drama or Comedy
Daniel Petrie, *ABC Theatre: Eleanor and Franklin*

Outstanding Writing in a Special Program, Drama or Comedy, Original Teleplay
James Costigan, *ABC Theatre: Eleanor and Franklin*

Outstanding Writing in a Special Program, Drama or Comedy, Adaptation
David W. Rintels, *Fear on Trial*

Outstanding Comedy Series
The Mary Tyler Moore Show (CBS)

Outstanding Lead Actor in a Comedy Series
Jack Albertson, *Chico and the Man*

James Garner, *The Rockford Files*

Outstanding Lead Actress in a Comedy Series
Mary Tyler Moore, *The Mary Tyler Moore Show*

Outstanding Continuing Performance by a Supporting Actor in a Comedy Series
Ted Knight, *The Mary Tyler Moore Show*

Outstanding Continuing Performance by a Supporting Actress in a Comedy Series
Betty White, *The Mary Tyler Moore Show*

Outstanding Directing in a Comedy Series
Gene Reynolds, *M*A*S*H:* "Welcome to Korea"

Outstanding Writing in a Comedy Series
David Lloyd, *The Mary Tyler Moore Show:* "Chuckles Bites the Dust"

Outstanding Comedy-Variety or Music Series
NBC's Saturday Night (NBC)

Outstanding Continuing or Single Performance by a Supporting Actor in Variety or Music
Chevy Chase, *NBC's Saturday Night*

Outstanding Continuing or Single Performance by a Supporting Actress in Variety or Music
Vicki Lawrence, *The Carol Burnett Show*

Outstanding Directing in a Comedy-Variety or Music Series
Dave Wilson, *NBC's Saturday Night* (with Paul Simon)

Outstanding Writing in a Comedy-Variety or Music Series
Anne Beatts, Chevy Chase, Al Franken, Tom Davis, Lorne Michaels, Marilyn Suzanne Miller, Michael O'Donoghue, Herb Sargent, Tom Schiller, Rosie Shuster and Alan Zweibel, *NBC's Saturday Night* (with Elliott Gould)

Outstanding Special, Comedy-Variety or Music
Gypsy in My Soul (CBS)

Outstanding Directing in a Comedy-Variety or Music Special
Dwight Hemion, *Steve and Eydie: Our Love Is Here to Stay*

Outstanding Writing in a Comedy-Variety or Music Special
Jane Wagner, Lorne Michaels, Ann Elder, Christopher Guest, Earl Pomerantz, Jim Rusk, Lily Tomlin, Rod Warren and George Yanok, *Lily Tomlin*

Outstanding Limited Series
Masterpiece Theatre: Upstairs, Downstairs (PBS)

Outstanding Lead Actor in a Limited Series
Hal Holbrook, *Sandburg's Lincoln*

Outstanding Lead Actress in a Limited Series
Rosemary Harris, *Masterpiece Theatre: Notorious Woman*

Outstanding Live Sports Series
NFL Monday Night Football (ABC)

Outstanding Live Sports Special
1975 World Series (NBC)

Outstanding Edited Sports Series
ABC's Wide World of Sports (ABC)

Outstanding Edited Sports Special
XII Winter Olympic Games (ABC)

Outstanding Children's Special (Prime Time) (tie)
You're a Good Sport, Charlie Brown (CBS)
Huckleberry Finn (ABC)
Triumph and Tragedy . . . The Olympic Experience (ABC)

Outstanding Entertainment Children's Series (Daytime)
Big Blue Marble (Syndicated)

Outstanding Entertainment Children's Special (Daytime)
The CBS Festival of Lively Arts for Young People: Danny Kaye's Look-In at the Metropolitan Opera (CBS)

Outstanding Informational Children's Series (Daytime)
Go (NBC)

Outstanding Informational Children's Special (Daytime)
Happy Anniversary, Charlie Brown (CBS)

Outstanding Instructional Children's Programming, Series and Specials (Daytime)
Grammar Rock (ABC)

Outstanding Daytime Game or Audience Participation Show
The $20,000 Pyramid (ABC)

Outstanding Daytime Talk, Service or Variety Series
Dinah! (Syndicated)

Special Classification of Outstanding Program Achievement (tie)
Bicentennial Minutes (CBS)

The Tonight Show Starring Johnny Carson (NBC)

1976–1977

Outstanding Drama Series
Masterpiece Theatre: Upstairs, Downstairs (PBS)

Outstanding Lead Actor in a Drama Series
James Garner, *The Rockford Files*

Outstanding Lead Actress in a Drama Series
Lindsay Wagner, *The Bionic Woman*

Outstanding Continuing Performance by a Supporting Actor in a Drama Series
Gary Frank, *Family*

Outstanding Continuing Performance by a Supporting Actress in a Drama Series
Kristy McNichol, *Family*

Outstanding Lead Actor for a Single Appearance in a Drama or Comedy Series
Louis Gossett, Jr., *Roots, Part 2*

Outstanding Lead Actress for a Single Appearance in a Drama or Comedy Series
Beulah Bondi, *The Waltons:* "The Pony Cart"

Outstanding Single Performance by a Supporting Actor in a Comedy or Drama Series
Edward Asner, *Roots, Part 1*

Outstanding Single Performance by a Supporting Actress in a Comedy or Drama Series
Olivia Cole, *Roots, Part 8*

Outstanding Directing in a Drama Series
David Greene, *Roots, Part 1*

Outstanding Writing in a Drama Series
Ernest Kinoy and William Blinn, *Roots, Part 2*

Outstanding Special, Drama or Comedy
ABC Theatre: Eleanor and Franklin: The White House Years (ABC)

Outstanding Lead Actor in a Drama or Comedy Special
Ed Flanders, *Harry S. Truman: Plain Speaking*

Outstanding Lead Actress in a Drama or Comedy Special
Sally Field, *Sybil*

Outstanding Performance by a Supporting Actor in a Comedy or Drama Special
Burgess Meredith, *Tail Gunner Joe*

Outstanding Performance by a Supporting Actress in a Comedy or Drama Special
Diana Hyland, *The ABC Friday Night Movie: The Boy in the Plastic Bubble*

Outstanding Directing in a Special Program, Drama or Comedy
Daniel Petrie, *ABC Theatre: Eleanor and Franklin: The White House Years*

Outstanding Writing in a Special Program, Drama or Comedy, Original Teleplay
Lane Slate, *Tail Gunner Joe*

Outstanding Writing in a Special Program, Drama or Comedy, Adaptation
Stewart Stern, *Sybil*

Sally Field, *Sybil*

Outstanding Comedy Series
The Mary Tyler Moore Show (CBS)

Outstanding Lead Actor in a Comedy Series
Carroll O'Connor, *All in the Family*

Outstanding Lead Actress in a Comedy Series
Beatrice Arthur, *Maude*

Outstanding Continuing Performance by a Supporting Actor in a Comedy Series
Gary Burghoff, *M*A*S*H*

Outstanding Continuing Performance by a Supporting Actress in a Comedy Series
Mary Kay Place, *Mary Hartman, Mary Hartman*

Outstanding Directing in a Comedy Series
Alan Alda, *M*A*S*H:* "Dear Sigmund"

Outstanding Writing in a Comedy Series
Allan Burns, James L. Brooks, Ed Weinberger, Stan Daniels, David Lloyd and Bob Ellison, *The Mary Tyler Moore Show:* "The Last Show"

Outstanding Comedy-Variety or Music Series
Van Dyke and Company (NBC)

Outstanding Continuing or Single Performance by a Supporting Actor in Variety or Music
Tim Conway, *The Carol Burnett Show,* entire series

Outstanding Continuing or Single Performance by a Supporting Actress in Variety or Music
Rita Moreno, *The Muppet Show*

Outstanding Directing in a Comedy-Variety or Music Series
Dave Powers, *The Carol Burnett Show* (with Eydie Gormé)

Outstanding Writing in a Comedy-Variety or Music Series
Anne Beatts, Dan Aykroyd, Al Franken, Tom Davis, James Downey, Lorne Michaels, Marilyn Suzanne Miller, Michael O'Donoghue, Herb Sargent, Tom Schiller, Rosie Shuster, Alan Zweibel, John Belushi and Bill Murray, *NBC's Saturday Night* (with Sissy Spacek)

Outstanding Special, Comedy-Variety or Music
The Barry Manilow Special (ABC)

Outstanding Directing in a Comedy-Variety or Music Special
Dwight Hemion, *America Salutes Richard Rodgers: The Sound of His Music*

Outstanding Writing in a Comedy-Variety or Music Special
Alan Buz Kohan and Ted Strauss, *America Salutes Richard Rodgers: The Sound of His Music*

Outstanding Limited Series
ABC Novel for Television: Roots (ABC)

Outstanding Lead Actor in a Limited Series
Christopher Plummer, *NBC World Premiere: The Moneychangers*

Outstanding Lead Actress in a Limited Series
Patty Duke Astin, *NBC's Best Seller: Captains and the Kings*

Outstanding Children's Special (Prime Time)
Piccadilly Circus: Ballet Shoes (PBS)

Outstanding Children's Entertainment Series (Daytime)
Zoom (PBS)

Outstanding Children's Entertainment Special (Daytime)
Special Treat: Big Henry and the Polka Dot Kid (NBC)

Outstanding Children's Informational Series (Daytime)
The Electric Company (PBS)

Outstanding Children's Informational Special (Daytime)
ABC Afterschool Special: My Mom's Having a Baby (ABC)

Outstanding Children's Instructional Programming, Series and Specials (Daytime)
Sesame Street (PBS)

Outstanding Game or Audience Participation Show (Daytime or Prime Time)
Family Feud (ABC)

Outstanding Daytime Talk, Service or Variety Series
The Merv Griffin Show (Syndicated)

Special Classification of Outstanding Program Achievement
The Tonight Show Starring Johnny Carson (NBC)

1977–1978

Outstanding Drama Series
The Rockford Files (NBC)

Outstanding Lead Actor in a Drama Series
Edward Asner, *Lou Grant*

Outstanding Lead Actress in a Drama Series
Sada Thompson, *Family*

Outstanding Continuing Performance by a Supporting Actor in a Drama Series
Robert Vaughn, *Washington: Behind Closed Doors*

Outstanding Continuing Performance by a Supporting Actress in a Drama Series
Nancy Marchand, *Lou Grant*

Outstanding Lead Actor for a Single Appearance in a Drama or Comedy Series
Barnard Hughes, *Lou Grant*

Outstanding Lead Actress for a Single Appearance in a Drama or Comedy Series
Rita Moreno, *The Rockford Files:* "The Paper Palace"

Outstanding Single Performance by a Supporting Actor in a Comedy or Drama Series
Ricardo Montalban, *How the West Was Won, Part II*

Outstanding Single Performance by a Supporting Actress in a Comedy or Drama Series
Blanche Baker, *Holocaust, Part I*

Outstanding Directing in a Drama Series
Marvin J. Chomsky, *Holocaust,* entire series

Outstanding Writing in a Drama Series
Gerald Green, *Holocaust,* entire series

Outstanding Special, Drama or Comedy
The Gathering (ABC)

Outstanding Lead Actor in a Drama or Comedy Special
Fred Astaire, *A Family Upside Down*

Outstanding Lead Actress in a Drama or Comedy Special
Joanne Woodward, *GE Theater: See How She Runs*

Outstanding Performance by a Supporting Actor in a Comedy or Drama Special
Howard Da Silva, *Great Performances: Verna: USO Girl*

Outstanding Performance by a Supporting Actress in a Drama or Comedy Special
Eva LeGallienne, *The Royal Family*

Outstanding Directing in a Special Program, Drama or Comedy
David Lowell Rich, *The Defection of Simas Kudirka*

Outstanding Writing in a Special Program, Drama or Comedy, Original Teleplay
George Rubino, *The Last Tenant*

Outstanding Writing in a Special Program, Drama or Comedy, Adaptation
Caryl Ledner, *Mary White*

Outstanding Comedy Series
All in the Family (CBS)

Outstanding Lead Actor in a Comedy Series
Carroll O'Connor, *All in the Family*

Outstanding Lead Actress in a Comedy Series
Jean Stapleton, *All in the Family*

Outstanding Continuing Performance by a Supporting Actor in a Comedy Series
Rob Reiner, *All in the Family*

Outstanding Continuing Performance by a Supporting Actress in a Comedy Series
Julie Kavner, *Rhoda*

Outstanding Directing in a Comedy Series
Paul Bogart, *All in the Family:* "Edith's 50th Birthday"

Outstanding Writing in a Comedy Series
Bob Weiskopf and Bob Schiller, *Teleplay*

Outstanding Comedy-Variety or Music Series
The Muppet Show (Syndicated)

Outstanding Continuing or Single Performance by a Supporting Actor in Variety or Music
Tim Conway, *The Carol Burnett Show*

Outstanding Continuing or Single Performance by a Supporting Actress in Variety or Music
Gilda Radner, *NBC's Saturday Night Live*

Outstanding Directing in a Comedy-Variety or Music Series
Dave Powers, *The Carol Burnett Show* (with Steve Martin and Betty White)

The Tonight Show Starring Johnny Carson

Outstanding Writing in a Comedy-Variety or Music Series
Ed Simmons, Roger Beatty, Rick Hawkins, Liz Sage,
  Robert Illes, James Stein, Franelle Silver
  Larry Siegel, Tim Conway, Bill Richmond,
  Gene Perret, Dick Clair and Jenna McMahon,
  The Carol Burnett Show (with Steve Martin
  and Betty White)

Outstanding Special, Comedy-Variety or Music
Bette Midler — Ol' Red Hair Is Back (NBC)

Outstanding Directing in a Comedy-Variety or Music Special
Dwight Hemion, *The Sentry Collection Presents
  Ben Vereen — His Roots*

Outstanding Writing in a Comedy-Variety or Music Special
Lorne Michaels, Paul Simon, Chevy Chase, Tom Davis,
  Al Franken, Charles Grodin, Lily Tomlin and
  Alan Zweibel, *The Paul Simon Special*

Outstanding Limited Series
Holocaust (NBC)

Outstanding Lead Actor in a Limited Series
Michael Moriarty, *Holocaust*

Outstanding Lead Actress in a Limited Series
Meryl Streep, *Holocaust*

Outstanding Informational Series
The Body Human (CBS)

Outstanding Informational Special
National Geographic: The Great Whales (PBS)

Outstanding Children's Special (Prime Time)
Halloween Is Grinch Night (ABC)

Outstanding Children's Entertainment Series (Daytime)
Captain Kangaroo (CBS)

Outstanding Children's Entertainment Special (Daytime)
ABC Afterschool Special: Hewitt's Just Different (ABC)

Outstanding Children's Informational Series (Daytime)
Animals Animals Animals (ABC)

Outstanding Children's Informational Special (Daytime)
ABC Afterschool Special: Very Good Friends (ABC)

Outstanding Children's Instructional Series (Daytime)
Schoolhouse Rock (ABC)

Outstanding Game or Audience Participation Show
The Hollywood Squares (NBC)

Outstanding Talk, Service or Variety Series
Donahue (Syndicated)

Special Classification of Outstanding Program Achievement
The Tonight Show Starring Johnny Carson (NBC)

1978–1979

Outstanding Drama Series
Lou Grant (CBS)

Outstanding Lead Actor in a Drama Series
Ron Leibman, *Kaz*

Outstanding Lead Actress in a Drama Series
Mariette Hartley, *The Incredible Hulk*: "Married"

Outstanding Supporting Actor in a Drama Series
Stuart Margolin, *The Rockford Files*

Outstanding Supporting Actress in a Drama Series
Kristy McNichol, *Family*

Outstanding Directing in a Drama Series
Jackie Cooper, *The White Shadow*: Pilot

Outstanding Writing in a Drama Series
Michele Gallery, *Lou Grant*: "Dying"

Outstanding Drama or Comedy Special
Friendly Fire (ABC)

Outstanding Comedy Series
Taxi (ABC)

Outstanding Lead Actor in a Comedy Series
Carroll O'Connor, *All in the Family*

Outstanding Lead Actress in a Comedy Series
Ruth Gordon, *Taxi*: "Sugar Mama"

**Outstanding Supporting Actor in a Comedy or Comedy-Variety
or Music Series**
Robert Guillaume, *Soap*

**Outstanding Supporting Actress in a Comedy or Comedy-
Variety or Music Series**
Sally Struthers, *All in the Family*: "California Here We Are"

**Outstanding Directing in a Comedy or Comedy-Variety or
Music Series**
Noam Pitlik, *Barney Miller*: "The Harris Incident"

**Outstanding Writing in a Comedy or Comedy-Variety or Music
Series**
Alan Alda, *M*A*S*H*: "Inga"

Outstanding Comedy-Variety or Music Program
Steve and Eydie Celebrate Irving Berlin (NBC)

Outstanding Limited Series
Roots: The Next Generations (ABC)

Outstanding Lead Actor in a Limited Series or a Special
Peter Strauss, *The Jericho Mile*

Outstanding Lead Actress in a Limited Series or a Special
Bette Davis, *Strangers: The Story of a Mother and Daughter*

Outstanding Supporting Actor in a Limited Series or a Special
Marlon Brando, *Roots: The Next Generations,* Episode Seven

Outstanding Supporting Actress in a Limited Series or a Special
Esther Rolle, *Summer of My German Soldier*

Outstanding Directing in a Limited Series or a Special
David Greene, *Friendly Fire*

Outstanding Writing in a Limited Series or a Special
Patrick Nolan and Michael Mann, *The Jericho Mile*

Outstanding Informational Program
Scared Straight! (Syndicated)

Outstanding Children's Program (Prime Time)
Christmas Eve on Sesame Street (PBS)

Outstanding Children's Entertainment Series (Daytime)
Kids Are People Too (ABC)

Outstanding Children's Entertainment Special (Daytime)
The Tap Dance Kid (NBC)

Outstanding Children's Informational Series (Daytime)
Big Blue Marble (Syndicated)

Outstanding Children's Informational Special (Daytime)
Razzmatazz (CBS)

Outstanding Children's Instructional Series (Daytime)
Science Rock (ABC)

Outstanding Animated Program
The Lion, the Witch and the Wardrobe (CBS)

Outstanding Game or Audience Participation Program
The Hollywood Squares (NBC)

Outstanding Talk, Service or Variety Series
Donahue (Syndicated)

Outstanding Program Achievement, Special Class
The Tonight Show Starring Johnny Carson (NBC)

1979–1980

Outstanding Drama Series
Lou Grant (CBS)

Outstanding Lead Actor in a Drama Series
Ed Asner, *Lou Grant*

Outstanding Lead Actress in a Drama Series
Barbara Bel Geddes, *Dallas*

Outstanding Supporting Actor in a Drama Series
Stuart Margolin, *The Rockford Files*

Outstanding Supporting Actress in a Drama Series
Nancy Marchand, *Lou Grant*

Outstanding Directing in a Drama Series
Roger Young, *Lou Grant*: "Cop"

Outstanding Writing in a Drama Series
Seth Freeman, *Lou Grant*: "Cop"

Outstanding Drama or Comedy Special
The Miracle Worker (NBC)

Outstanding Comedy Series
Taxi (ABC)

Outstanding Lead Actor in a Comedy Series
Richard Mulligan, *Soap*

Outstanding Lead Actress in a Comedy Series
Cathryn Damon, *Soap*

Outstanding Supporting Actor in a Comedy or Variety or Music Series
Harry Morgan, *M*A*S*H*

Outstanding Supporting Actress in a Comedy or Variety or Music Series
Loretta Swit, *M*A*S*H*

Outstanding Directing in a Comedy Series
James Burrows, *Taxi*: "Louie and the Nice Girl"

Outstanding Writing in a Comedy Series
Bob Colleary, *Barney Miller*: "Photographer"

Shogun

Outstanding Variety or Music Program
IBM Presents Baryshnikov on Broadway (ABC)

Outstanding Writing in a Variety or Music Program
Buz Kohan, *Shirley MacLaine . . . 'Every Little Movement'*

Outstanding Directing in a Variety or Music Program
Dwight Hemion, *IBM Presents Baryshnikov on Broadway*

Outstanding Limited Series
Edward and Mrs. Simpson (Syndicated)

Outstanding Lead Actor in a Limited Series or a Special
Powers Booth, *Guyana Tragedy: The Story of Jim Jones*

Outstanding Lead Actress in a Limited Series or a Special
Patty Duke Astin, *The Miracle Worker*

Outstanding Supporting Actor in a Limited Series or a Special
George Grizzard, *The Oldest Living Graduate*

Outstanding Supporting Actress in a Limited Series or a Special
Mare Winningham, *Amber Waves*

Outstanding Directing in a Limited Series or a Special
Marvin J. Chomsky, *Attica*

Outstanding Writing in a Limited Series or a Special
David Chase, *Off the Minnesota Strip*

Outstanding Informational Program
The Body Human: The Magic Sense (CBS)

Outstanding Children's Program (Prime Time)
Benji at Work (ABC)

Outstanding Children's Entertainment Series (Daytime)
Hot Hero Sandwich (NBC)

Outstanding Children's Entertainment Special (Daytime)
ABC Afterschool Special: The Late Great Me: Story of a Teenage Alcoholic (ABC)

Outstanding Children's Anthology/Dramatic Programming (Daytime) (tie)
CBS Library: Animal Talk (CBS)

ABC Weekend Special: The Gold Bug (ABC)

Once Upon a Classic: Leatherstocking Tales (PBS)

CBS Library: Once Upon a Midnight Dreary (CBS)

Outstanding Children's Informational Instructional Series/Specials (Daytime) (tie)
Sesame Street (PBS)

30 Minutes (CBS)

CBS Festival of Lively Arts for Young People: Why a Conductor? (CBS)

Outstanding Children's Informational/Instructional Programming, Short Format (Daytime) (tie)
Schoolhouse Rock (ABC)

Dr. Henry's Emergency Lessons for People (ABC)

In the News (CBS)

Outstanding Animated Program
Carlton Your Doorman (CBS)

Outstanding Game or Audience Participation Show (tie)
The Hollywood Squares (NBC)

The $20,000 Pyramid (ABC)

Outstanding Talk, Service or Variety Series
Donahue (Syndicated)

Outstanding Program Achievement, Special Class
Fred Astaire: Change Partners and Dance (PBS)

1980–1981

Outstanding Drama Series
Hill Street Blues (NBC)

Outstanding Lead Actor in a Drama Series
Daniel J. Travanti, *Hill Street Blues*

Outstanding Lead Actress in a Drama Series
Barbara Babcock, *Hill Street Blues:* "Fecund Hand Rose"

Outstanding Supporting Actor in a Drama Series
Michael Conrad, *Hill Street Blues*

Outstanding Supporting Actress in a Drama Series
Nancy Marchand, *Lou Grant*

Outstanding Directing in a Drama Series
Robert Butler, *Hill Street Blues:* "Hill Street Station"

Outstanding Writing in a Drama Series
Michael Kozoll and Steven Bochco, *Hill Street Blues*

Outstanding Drama Special
Playing for Time (CBS)

Outstanding Comedy Series
Taxi (ABC)

Outstanding Lead Actor in a Comedy Series
Judd Hirsch, *Taxi*

Outstanding Lead Actress in a Comedy Series
Isabel Sanford, *The Jeffersons*

Outstanding Supporting Actor in a Comedy or Variety or Music Series
Danny DeVito, *Taxi*

Outstanding Supporting Actress in a Comedy or Variety or Music Series
Eileen Brennan, *Private Benjamin*

Outstanding Directing in a Comedy Series
James Burrows, *Taxi:* "Elaine's Strange Triangle"

Outstanding Writing in a Comedy Series
Michael Leeson, *Taxi:* "Tony's Sister and Jim"

Outstanding Variety, Music or Comedy Program
Lily: Sold Out (CBS)

Outstanding Writing in a Variety, Music or Comedy Program
Jerry Juhl, David Odell and Chris Langham, *The Muppet Show* (with Carol Burnett)

Outstanding Directing in a Variety, Music or Comedy Program
Don Mischer, *The Kennedy Center Honors: A National Celebration of the Performing Arts*

Outstanding Limited Series
Shogun (NBC)

Outstanding Lead Actor in a Limited Series or a Special
Anthony Hopkins, *The Bunker*

Outstanding Lead Actress in a Limited Series or a Special
Vanessa Redgrave, *Playing for Time*

Outstanding Supporting Actor in a Limited Series or a Special
David Warner, *Masada*

Outstanding Supporting Actress in a Limited Series or a Special
Jane Alexander, *Playing for Time*

Outstanding Directing in a Limited Series or a Special
James Goldstone, *Kent State*

Outstanding Writing in a Limited Series or a Special
Arthur Miller, *Playing for Time*

Outstanding Informational Series
Steve Allen's Meeting of Minds (PBS)

Outstanding Informational Special
The Body Human: The Bionic Breakthrough (CBS)

Outstanding Children's Program (Prime Time)
Donahue and Kids: Project Peacock (NBC)

Outstanding Children's Entertainment Series (Daytime) (tie)
Captain Kangaroo (CBS)

Once Upon a Classic: A Tale of Two Cities (PBS)

Outstanding Children's Entertainment Special (Daytime)
ABC Afterschool Special: A Matter of Time (ABC)

Outstanding Children's Informational/Instructional Series (Daytime)
30 Minutes (CBS)

Outstanding Children's Informational/Instructional Special (Daytime)
The CBS Festival of Lively Arts for Young People: Julie Andrews' Invitation to the Dance With Rudolf Nureyev (CBS)

Outstanding Animated Program
Life is a Circus, Charlie Brown (CBS)

Outstanding Game or Audience Participation Show
The $20,000 Pyramid (ABC)

Outstanding Talk/Service Series
Donahue (Syndicated)

1981–1982

Outstanding Drama Series
Hill Street Blues (NBC)

Outstanding Lead Actor in a Drama Series
Daniel J. Travanti, *Hill Street Blues*

Outstanding Lead Actress in a Drama Series
Michael Learned, *Nurse*

Outstanding Supporting Actor in a Drama Series
Michael Conrad, *Hill Street Blues*

Outstanding Supporting Actress in a Drama Series
Nancy Marchand, *Lou Grant*

Outstanding Directing in a Drama Series
Harry Harris, *Fame:* "To Soar and Never Falter"

Outstanding Writing in a Drama Series
Steven Bochco, Anthony Yerkovich, Jeffrey Lewis and Michael Wagner, teleplay; Michael Kozoll and Steven Bochco, story, *Hill Street Blues:* "Freedom's Last Stand"

Outstanding Drama Special
A Woman Called Golda (Syndicated)

Outstanding Comedy Series
Barney Miller (ABC)

Outstanding Lead Actor in a Comedy Series
Alan Alda, *M*A*S*H*

Outstanding Lead Actress in a Comedy Series
Carol Kane, *Taxi:* "Simka Returns"

Outstanding Supporting Actor in a Comedy or Variety or Music Series
Christopher Lloyd, *Taxi*

Outstanding Supporting Actress in a Comedy or Variety or Music Series
Loretta Swit, *M*A*S*H*

Outstanding Directing in a Comedy Series
Alan Rafkin, *One Day at a Time:* "Barbara's Crisis"

Outstanding Writing in a Comedy Series
Ken Estin, *Taxi:* "Elegant Iggy"

Outstanding Variety, Music or Comedy Program
Night of 100 Stars (ABC)

Outstanding Directing in a Variety or Music Program
Dwight Hemion, *Goldie and Kids . . . Listen to Us*

Outstanding Writing in a Variety or Music Program
John Candy, Joe Flaherty, Eugene Levy, Andrea Martin, Rick Moranis, Catherine O'Hara, Dave Thomas, Dick Blasucci, Paul Flaherty, Bob Dolman, John McAndrew, Doug Steckler, Mert Rich, Jeffrey Barron, Michael Short, Chris Cluess, Stuart Kreisman and Brian McConnachie, *SCTV Network: Moral Majority Show*

Outstanding Limited Series
Marco Polo (NBC)

Outstanding Lead Actor in a Limited Series or a Special
Mickey Rooney, *Bill*

Outstanding Lead Actress in a Limited Series or a Special
Ingrid Bergman, *A Woman Called Golda*

Outstanding Supporting Actor in a Limited Series or a Special
Laurence Olivier, *Brideshead Revisited*

Outstanding Supporting Actress in a Limited Series or a Special
Penny Fuller, *The Elephant Man*

Outstanding Directing in a Limited Series or a Special
Marvin J. Chomsky, *Inside the Third Reich*

Outstanding Writing in a Limited Series or a Special
Corey Blechman, teleplay; Barry Morrow, story, *Bill*

Outstanding Informational Series
Creativity with Bill Moyers (PBS)

Outstanding Informational Special
Making of Raiders of the Lost Ark (PBS)

Outstanding Children's Program (Prime Time)
The Wave (ABC)

Outstanding Children's Entertainment Series (Daytime)
Captain Kangaroo (CBS)

Outstanding Children's Entertainment Special (Daytime)
ABC Afterschool Special: Starstruck (ABC)

Outstanding Children's Informational/Instructional Series (Daytime)
30 Minutes (CBS)

Outstanding Informational/Instructional Programming, Short Format
In the News (CBS)

Outstanding Children's Informational/Instructional Special (Daytime)
Kathy (PBS)

Outstanding Animated Program
The Grinch Grinches the Cat in the Hat (ABC)

Outstanding Game or Audience Participation Show
Password Plus (NBC)

Outstanding Talk or Service Series
The Richard Simmons Show (Syndicated)

1982–1983

Outstanding Drama Series
Hill Street Blues (NBC)

Outstanding Lead Actor in a Drama Series
Ed Flanders, *St. Elsewhere*

Outstanding Lead Actress in a Drama Series
Tyne Daly, *Cagney and Lacey*

Outstanding Supporting Actor in a Drama Series
James Coco, *St. Elsewhere:* "Cora and Arnie"

Outstanding Supporting Actress in a Drama Series
Doris Roberts, *St. Elsewhere:* "Cora and Arnie"

Outstanding Directing in a Drama Series
Jeff Bleckner, *Hill Street Blues:* "Life in the Minors"

Outstanding Writing in a Drama Series
David Milch, *Hill Street Blues:* "Trial by Fury"

Outstanding Drama Special
Special Bulletin (NBC)

Outstanding Comedy Series
Cheers (NBC)

Outstanding Lead Actor in a Comedy Series
Judd Hirsch, *Taxi*

Outstanding Lead Actress in a Comedy Series
Shelley Long, *Cheers*

Outstanding Supporting Actor in a Comedy, Variety or Music Series
Christopher Lloyd, *Taxi*

Outstanding Supporting Actress in a Comedy, Variety or Music Series
Carol Kane, *Taxi*

Outstanding Directing in a Comedy Series
James Burrows, *Cheers:* "Showdown, Part 2"

Outstanding Writing in a Comedy Series
Glen Charles and Les Charles, *Cheers:* "Give Me a Ring Sometime"

Outstanding Variety, Music or Comedy Program
Motown 25: Yesterday, Today, Forever (NBC)

Outstanding Directing in a Variety or Music Program
Dwight Hemion, *Sheena Easton . . . Act One*

Outstanding Writing in a Variety or Music Program
John Candy, Joe Flaherty, Eugene Levy, Andrea Martin, Martin Short, Dick Blasucci, Paul Flaherty, John McAndrew, Doug Steckler, Bob Dolman, Michael Short and Mary Charlotte Wilcox, *SCTV Network: The Energy Ball/Sweeps Week*

Outstanding Individual Performance in a Variety or Music Program
Leontyne Price, *Live From Lincoln Center, Leontyne Price, Zubin Mehta and the New York Philharmonic*

Outstanding Limited Series
Nicholas Nickleby (Syndicated)

Outstanding Lead Actor in a Limited Series or a Special
Tommy Lee Jones, *The Executioner's Song*

Outstanding Lead Actress in a Limited Series or a Special
Barbara Stanwyck, *The Thorn Birds, Part 1*

Outstanding Supporting Actor in a Limited Series or a Special
Richard Kiley, *The Thorn Birds, Part 1*

Outstanding Supporting Actress in a Limited Series or a Special
Jean Simmons, *The Thorn Birds*

Outstanding Directing in a Limited Series or a Special
John Erman, *Who Will Love My Children?*

Outstanding Writing in a Limited Series or a Special
Marshall Herskovitz, teleplay; Edward Zwick and Marshall Herskovitz, story, *Special Bulletin*

Outstanding Informational Series
The Barbara Walters Specials (ABC)

Outstanding Informational Special
The Body Human: The Living Code (CBS)

Outstanding Children's Program (Prime Time)
Big Bird in China (NBC)

Outstanding Children's Entertainment Series (Daytime)
Smurfs (NBC)

Outstanding Children's Entertainment Special (Daytime)
ABC Afterschool Special: The Woman Who Willed a Miracle (ABC)

Outstanding Children's Informational/Instructional Series (Daytime)
Sesame Street (PBS)

Outstanding Children's Informational/Instructional Special (Daytime)
Winners (Syndicated)

Outstanding Informational/Instructional Programming, Short Form (Daytime)
In the News (CBS)

Cheers

Outstanding Animated Program
Ziggy's Gift (ABC)

Outstanding Game or Audience Participation Show
The New $25,000 Pyramid (CBS)

Outstanding Talk/Service Series
This Old House (PBS)

1983–1984

Outstanding Drama Series
Hill Street Blues (NBC)

Outstanding Lead Actor in a Drama Series
Tom Selleck, *Magnum, P.I.*

Outstanding Lead Actress in a Drama Series
Tyne Daly, *Cagney and Lacey*

Outstanding Supporting Actor in a Drama Series
Bruce Weitz, *Hill Street Blues*

Outstanding Supporting Actress in a Drama Series
Alfre Woodard, *Hill Street Blues:* "Doris in Wonderland"

Outstanding Directing in a Drama Series
Corey Allen, *Hill Street Blues:* "Goodbye, Mr. Scripps"

Outstanding Writing in a Drama Series
John Ford Noonan, teleplay; John Masius and Tom Fontana,
story, *St. Elsewhere:* "The Women"

Outstanding Drama/Comedy Special
An ABC Theatre Presentation: Something About Amelia (ABC)

Outstanding Comedy Series
Cheers (NBC)

Outstanding Lead Actor in a Comedy Series
John Ritter, *Three's Company*

Outstanding Lead Actress in a Comedy Series
Jane Curtin, *Kate and Allie*

Outstanding Supporting Actor in a Comedy Series
Pat Harrington, Jr., *One Day at a Time*

Outstanding Supporting Actress in a Comedy Series
Rhea Perlman, *Cheers*

Outstanding Directing in a Comedy Series
Bill Persky, *Kate and Allie:* "A Very Loud Family"

Outstanding Writing in a Comedy Series
David Angell, *Cheers:* "Old Flames"

Outstanding Variety, Music or Comedy Program
*The 6th Annual Kennedy Center Honors: A Celebration
of the Performing Arts* (CBS)

**Outstanding Individual Performance in a Variety or Music
Program**
Cloris Leachman, *Screen Actors Guild 50th
Anniversary Celebration*

Outstanding Directing in a Variety or Music Program
Dwight Hemion, *Here's Television Entertainment*

Outstanding Writing in a Variety or Music Program
Steve O'Donnell, Gerard Mulligan, Sanford Frank,
Joseph E. Toplyn, Christopher Elliott, Matt Wickline,
Jeff Martin, Ted Greenberg, David Yazbek, Merrill
Markoe and David Letterman, *Late Night With David
Letterman, Show #312*

Outstanding Limited Series
American Playhouse: Concealed Enemies (PBS)

Outstanding Lead Actor in a Limited Series or a Special
Laurence Olivier, *Laurence Olivier's King Lear*

Outstanding Lead Actress in a Limited Series or a Special
Jane Fonda, *An ABC Theatre Presentation: The Dollmaker*

Outstanding Supporting Actor in a Limited Series or a Special
Art Carney, *An ITT Theatre Special: Terrible Joe Moran*

**Outstanding Supporting Actress in a Limited Series or
Special**
Roxana Zal, *An ABC Theatre Presentation: Something About
Amelia*

Outstanding Directing in a Limited Series or a Special
Jeff Bleckner, *American Playhouse: Concealed Enemies, Part
3: Investigation*

Outstanding Writing in a Limited Series or a Special
William Hanley, *An ABC Theatre Presentation: Something
About Amelia*

Outstanding Informational Series
A Walk Through the 20th Century With Bill Moyers (PBS)

Outstanding Informational Special
America Remembers John F. Kennedy (Syndicated)

Outstanding Children's Program (Prime Time)
He Makes Me Feel Like Dancin' (NBC)

Outstanding Children's Entertainment Series (Daytime)
Captain Kangaroo (CBS)

Outstanding Children's Entertainment Specials
ABC Afterschool Special: The Great Love Experiment (ABC)

Outstanding Children's Informational/Instructional Special
Dead Wrong: The John Evans Story (CBS)

**Outstanding Children's Informational/Instructional
Programming, Short Form**
Just Another Stupid Kid (Syndicated)

**Outstanding Children's Informational/Instructional
Programming**
The ABC Weekend Special (ABC)

Outstanding Animated Program (Prime Time)
Garfield on the Town (CBS)

Outstanding Game or Audience Participation Show
The $25,000 Pyramid (CBS)

Outstanding Talk or Service Series
Woman to Woman (Syndicated)

1984–1985

Outstanding Drama Series
Cagney and Lacey (CBS)

Outstanding Lead Actor in a Drama Series
William Daniels, *St. Elsewhere*

Outstanding Lead Actress in a Drama Series
Tyne Daly, *Cagney and Lacey*

Outstanding Supporting Actor in a Drama Series
Edward James Olmos, *Miami Vice*

Outstanding Supporting Actress in a Drama Series
Betty Thomas, *Hill Street Blues*

Outstanding Directing in a Drama Series
Karen Arthur, *Cagney and Lacey:* "Heat"

Outstanding Writing in a Drama Series
Patricia Green, *Cagney and Lacey:* "Who Said It's Fair, Part II"

Outstanding Drama/Comedy Special
Do You Remember Love (CBS)

Outstanding Comedy Series
The Cosby Show (NBC)

Outstanding Lead Actor in a Comedy Series
Robert Guillaume, *Benson*

Outstanding Lead Actress in a Comedy Series
Jane Curtin, *Kate and Allie*

Outstanding Supporting Actor in a Comedy Series
John Larroquette, *Night Court*

Outstanding Supporting Actress in a Comedy Series
Rhea Perlman, *Cheers*

Outstanding Directing in a Comedy Series
Jay Sandrich, *The Cosby Show:* "The Younger Woman"

Outstanding Writing in a Comedy Series
Ed Weinberger and Michael Leeson, *The Cosby Show:* Premiere
  Episode

**Outstanding Individual Performance in a Variety or Music
Program**
George Hearn, *Great Performances: Sweeney Todd*

Outstanding Variety, Music or Comedy Program
Motown Returns to the Apollo (NBC)

Outstanding Directing in a Variety or Music Program
Terry Hughes, *Great Performances: Sweeney Todd*

Outstanding Writing in a Variety or Music Program
Gerard Mulligan, Sandy Frank, Joe Toplyn, Chris Elliott, Matt
  Wickline, Jeff Martin, Eddie Gorodetsky, Randy Cohen,
  Larry Jacobson, Kevin Curran, Fred Graver, Merrill
  Markoe and David Letterman, *Late Night With David
  Letterman:* "Christmas With the Lettermans"

Outstanding Limited Series
Masterpiece Theatre: The Jewel in the Crown (PBS)

Outstanding Lead Actor in a Limited Series or a Special
Richard Crenna, *An ABC Theater Presentation: The Rape of
  Richard Beck*

Outstanding Lead Actress in a Limited Series or a Special
Joanne Woodward, *Do You Remember Love*

Outstanding Supporting Actor in a Limited Series or a Special
Karl Malden, *Fatal Vision*

**Outstanding Supporting Actress in a Limited Series or a
Special**
Kim Stanley, *American Playhouse: Cat on a Hot Tin Roof*

Outstanding Directing in a Limited Series or a Special
Lamont Johnson, *Wallenberg: A Hero's Story*

Outstanding Writing in a Limited Series or a Special
Vickie Patik, *Do You Remember Love*

Outstanding Informational Series
The Living Planet: A Portrait of the Earth (PBS)

Outstanding Informational Special
Cousteau: Mississippi (Syndicated)

Outstanding Children's Program (Prime Time)
American Playhouse: Displaced Person (PBS)

Outstanding Children's Series (Daytime)
Sesame Street (PBS)

Outstanding Children's Special (Daytime)
All the Kids Do It (CBS)

Outstanding Animated Program (Daytime)
Jim Henson's Muppet Babies (CBS)

Outstanding Animated Program (Prime Time)
Garfield in the Rough (CBS)

Outstanding Game/Audience Participation Show
The $25,000 Pyramid (CBS)

Outstanding Talk or Service Series
Donahue (Syndicated)

1985–1986

Outstanding Drama Series
Cagney and Lacey (CBS)

Outstanding Lead Actor in a Drama Series
William Daniels, *St. Elsewhere*

Outstanding Lead Actress in a Drama Series
Sharon Gless, *Cagney and Lacey*

Outstanding Supporting Actor in a Drama Series
John Karlen, *Cagney and Lacey*

Outstanding Supporting Actress in a Drama Series
Bonnie Bartlett, *St. Elsewhere*

Outstanding Guest Performer in a Drama Series
John Lithgow, *Amazing Stories:* "The Doll"

Outstanding Directing in a Drama Series
George Stanford Brown, *Cagney and Lacy:* "Parting Shots"

Outstanding Writing in a Drama Series
Tom Fontana, John Tinker and John Masius, *St. Elsewhere:*
  "Time Heals"

Outstanding Drama/Comedy Special
Hallmark Hall of Fame: Love Is Never Silent (NBC)

Outstanding Comedy Series
The Golden Girls (NBC)

Outstanding Lead Actor in a Comedy Series
Michael J. Fox, *Family Ties*

Outstanding Lead Actress in a Comedy Series
Betty White, *The Golden Girls*

Outstanding Supporting Actress in a Comedy Series
Rhea Perlman, *Cheers*

Outstanding Supporting Actor in a Comedy Series
John Larroquette, *Night Court*

Outstanding Guest Performer in a Comedy Series
Roscoe Lee Browne, *The Cosby Show:* "The Card Game"

The Golden Girls

Outstanding Directing in a Comedy Series
Jay Sandrich, *The Cosby Show:* "Denise's Friend"

Outstanding Writing in a Comedy Series
Barry Fanaro and Mort Nathan, *The Golden Girls:* "A Little Romance"

Outstanding Variety, Music or Comedy Program
The Kennedy Center Honors: A Celebration of the Performing Arts (CBS)

Outstanding Individual Performance in a Variety or Music Program
Whitney Houston, *The 28th Annual Grammy Awards*

Outstanding Directing in a Variety or Music Program
Waris Hussein, *Copacabana*

Outstanding Writing in a Variety or Music Program
David Letterman, Steve O'Donnell, Sandy Frank, Joe Toplyn, Chris Elliott, Matt Wickline, Jeff Martin, Gerard Mulligan, Randy Cohen, Larry Jacobson, Kevin Curran, Fred Graver and Merrill Markoe, *Late Night With David Letterman, Fourth Anniversary Special*

Outstanding Miniseries
Peter the Great (NBC)

Outstanding Lead Actor in a Miniseries or a Special
Dustin Hoffman, *Death of a Salesman*

Outstanding Lead Actress in a Miniseries or a Special
Marlo Thomas, *Nobody's Child*

Outstanding Supporting Actor in a Miniseries or a Special
John Malkovich, *Death of a Salesman*

Outstanding Supporting Actress in a Miniseries or a Special
Colleen Dewhurst, *Between Two Women*

Outstanding Directing in a Miniseries or a Special
Joseph Sargent, *Hallmark Hall of Fame: Love Is Never Silent*

Outstanding Writing in a Miniseries or a Special
Ron Cowen and Daniel Lipman, teleplay; Sherman Yellen, story, *An Early Frost*

Outstanding Informational Series (tie)
Great Performances: Laurence Olivier — A Life (PBS)

Planet Earth (PBS)

Outstanding Informational Special
W. C. Fields Straight Up (PBS)

Outstanding Children's Program (Prime Time)
Anne of Green Gables (PBS)

Outstanding Children's Series (Daytime)
Sesame Street (PBS)

Outstanding Children's Special (Daytime)
CBS Schoolbreak Special: The War Between the Classes (CBS)

Outstanding Animated Program (Daytime)
Jim Henson's Muppet Babies (CBS)

Outstanding Animated Program (Prime Time)
Garfield's Halloween Adventure (CBS)

Outstanding Game/Audience Participation Show
The $25,000 Pyramid (CBS)

Outstanding Talk/Service Program
Donahue (Syndicated)

1986–1987

Outstanding Drama Series
L.A. Law (NBC)

Outstanding Lead Actor in a Drama Series
Bruce Willis, *Moonlighting*

Outstanding Lead Actress in a Drama Series
Sharon Gless, *Cagney and Lacey*

Outstanding Supporting Actor in a Drama Series
John Hillerman, *Magnum, P.I.*

Outstanding Supporting Actress in a Drama Series
Bonnie Bartlett, *St. Elsewhere*

Outstanding Guest Performer in a Drama Series
Alfre Woodard, *L.A. Law:* Pilot

Outstanding Directing in a Drama Series
Gregory Hoblit, *L.A. Law:* Pilot

Outstanding Writing in a Drama Series
Steven Bochco and Terry Louise Fisher, *L.A. Law:* "Venus Butterfly"

Outstanding Drama/Comedy Special
Hallmark Hall of Fame: Promise (CBS)

Outstanding Comedy Series
The Golden Girls (NBC)

Outstanding Lead Actor in a Comedy Series
Michael J. Fox, *Family Ties*

Outstanding Lead Actress in a Comedy Series
Rue McClanahan, *The Golden Girls*

Outstanding Supporting Actor in a Comedy Series
John Larroquette, *Night Court*

Outstanding Supporting Actress in a Comedy Series
Jackee Harry, *227*

Outstanding Guest Performer in a Comedy Series
John Cleese, *Cheers:* "Simon Says"

Outstanding Directing in a Comedy Series
Terry Hughes, *The Golden Girls:* "Isn't It Romantic"

Outstanding Writing in a Comedy Series
Gary David Goldberg and Alan Uger, *Family Ties:* " 'A,' My Name Is Alex"

Outstanding Variety, Music or Comedy Program
The 1987 Tony Awards (CBS)

Outstanding Individual Performance in a Variety or Music Program
Robin Williams, *A Carol Burnett Special: Carol, Carl, Whoopi and Robin*

Outstanding Directing in a Variety or Music Program
Don Mischer, *The Kennedy Center Honors: A Celebration of the Performing Arts*

Outstanding Writing in a Variety or Music Program
Steve O'Donnell, Sandy Frank, Joe Toplyn, Chris Elliott, Matt Wickline, Jeff Martin, Gerard Mulligan, Randy Cohen, Larry Jacobson, Kevin Curran, Fred Graver, Adam Resnick and David Letterman, *Late Night With David Letterman: Fifth Anniversary Special*

Outstanding Miniseries
A Year in the Life (NBC)

Outstanding Lead Actor in a Miniseries or Special
James Woods, *Hallmark Hall of Fame: Promise*

Outstanding Lead Actress in Miniseries or a Special
Gena Rowlands, *The Betty Ford Story*

Outstanding Supporting Actor in a Miniseries or a Special
Dabney Coleman, *Sworn to Silence*

Outstanding Supporting Actress in a Miniseries or a Special
Piper Laurie, *Hallmark Hall of Fame: Promise*

Outstanding Directing in a Miniseries or a Special
Glenn Jordan, *Hallmark Hall of Fame: Promise*

Outstanding Writing in a Miniseries or a Special
Richard Friedenberg, teleplay; Kenneth Blackwell, Tennyson Flowers and Richard Friedenberg, story, *Hallmark Hall of Fame: Promise*

Outstanding Informational Series (tie)
Smithsonian World (PBS)

American Masters: Unknown Chaplin (PBS)

Outstanding Informational Special
Great Performances: Dance in America: Agnes, the Indomitable DeMille (PBS)

Outstanding Children's Program (Prime Time)
Jim Henson's the Story Teller: Hans My Hedgehog (NBC)

Outstanding Children's Series (Daytime)
Sesame Street (PBS)

Outstanding Children's Special (Daytime)
ABC Afterschool Special: Wanted: The Perfect Guy (ABC)

Outstanding Animated Program (Daytime)
Jim Henson's Muppet Babies (CBS)

Outstanding Animated Program (Prime Time)
Cathy (CBS)

Outstanding Game/Audience Participation Show
The $25,000 Pyramid (CBS)

Outstanding Talk/Service Show
The Oprah Winfrey Show (Syndicated)

1987–1988

Outstanding Drama Series
thirtysomething (ABC)

Outstanding Lead Actor in a Drama Series
Richard Kiley, *A Year in the Life*

Outstanding Lead Actress in a Drama Series
Tyne Daly, *Cagney and Lacey*

Outstanding Supporting Actor in a Drama Series
Larry Drake, *L.A. Law*

Outstanding Supporting Actress in a Drama Series
Patricia Wettig, *thirtysomething*

Outstanding Guest Performer in a Drama Series
Shirley Knight, *thirtysomething:* "The Parents Are Coming"

Outstanding Directing in a Drama Series
Mark Tinker, *St. Elsewhere:* "Weigh In, Way Out"

Outstanding Writing in a Drama Series
Paul Haggis and Marshall Herskovitz, *thirtysomething:* "Business as Usual" ("Michael's Father's Death")

Outstanding Drama/Comedy Special
AT&T Presents: Inherit the Wind (NBC)

Outstanding Comedy Series
The Wonder Years (ABC)

Outstanding Lead Actor in a Comedy Series
Michael J. Fox, *Family Ties*

Outstanding Lead Actress in a Comedy Series
Beatrice Arthur, *The Golden Girls*

Outstanding Supporting Actor in a Comedy Series
John Larroquette, *Night Court*

Outstanding Supporting Actress in a Comedy Series
Estelle Getty, *The Golden Girls*

Outstanding Guest Performer in a Comedy Series
Beah Richards, *Frank's Place:* "The Bridge"

Outstanding Directing in a Comedy Series
Gregory Hoblit, *Hooperman:* Pilot

Outstanding Writing in a Comedy Series
Hugh Wilson, *Frank's Place:* "The Bridge"

Outstanding Variety, Music or Comedy Program
Irving Berlin's 100th Birthday Celebration (CBS)

Outstanding Individual Performance in a Variety or Music Program
Robin Williams, *ABC Presents a Royal Gala*

thirtysomething

Outstanding Directing in a Variety or Music Program
Patricia Birch and Humphrey Burton, *Great Performances: Celebrating Gershwin*

Outstanding Writing in a Variety or Music Program
Jackie Mason, *Jackie Mason on Broadway*

Outstanding Miniseries
The Murder of Mary Phagan (NBC)

Outstanding Lead Actor in a Miniseries or a Special
Jason Robards, *AT&T Presents: Inherit the Wind*

Outstanding Lead Actress in a Miniseries or a Special
Jessica Tandy, *Hallmark Hall of Fame: Foxfire*

Outstanding Supporting Actor in a Miniseries or a Special
John Shea, *An ABC Circle Film: Baby M*

Outstanding Supporting Actress in a Miniseries or a Special
Jane Seymour, *Onassis: The Richest Man in the World*

Outstanding Directing in a Miniseries or a Special
Lamont Johnson, *Gore Vidal's Lincoln*

Outstanding Writing in a Miniseries or a Special
William Hanley, *General Foods Golden Showcase: The Attic: The Hiding of Anne Frank*

Outstanding Informational Series
American Masters: Buster Keaton: A Hard Act to Follow (PBS)

Outstanding Informational Special
Dear America: Letters Home From Vietnam (HBO)

Outstanding Children's Program (Prime Time)
Hallmark Hall of Fame: The Secret Garden (CBS)

Outstanding Children's Series (Daytime)
Sesame Street (PBS)

Outstanding Children's Special (Daytime)
CBS Schoolbreak Special: Never Say Goodbye (CBS)

Oustanding Animated Program (Daytime)
Jim Henson's Muppet Babies (CBS)

Outstanding Animated Program (Prime Time)
A Claymation Christmas Celebration (CBS)

Outstanding Game/Audience Participation Show
The Price Is Right (CBS)

Outstanding Talk/Service Show
The Oprah Winfrey Show (Syndicated)

1988–1989

Outstanding Drama Series
L.A. Law (NBC)

Outstanding Lead Actor in a Drama Series
Carroll O'Connor, *In the Heat of the Night*

Outstanding Lead Actress in a Drama Series
Dana Delany, *China Beach*

Outstanding Supporting Actor in a Drama Series
Larry Drake, *L.A. Law*

Outstanding Supporting Actress in a Drama Series
Melanie Mayron, *thirtysomething*

Outstanding Guest Actor in a Drama Series
Joe Spano, *Midnight Caller*: "The Execution
of John Saringo"

Outstanding Guest Actress in a Drama Series
Kay Lenz, *Midnight Caller*: "After It Happened . . ."

Outstanding Directing in a Drama Series
Robert Altman, *Tanner '88*: "The Boiler Room"

Outstanding Writing in a Drama Series
Joseph Dougherty, *thirtysomething*: "First Day/Last Day"

Outstanding Drama/Comedy Special
AT&T Presents: Day One (CBS)

Outstanding Comedy Series
Cheers (NBC)

Outstanding Lead Actor in a Comedy Series
Richard Mulligan, *Empty Nest*

Outstanding Lead Actress in a Comedy Series
Candice Bergen, *Murphy Brown*

Outstanding Supporting Actor in a Comedy Series
Woody Harrelson, *Cheers*

Outstanding Supporting Actress in a Comedy Series
Rhea Perlman, *Cheers*

Outstanding Guest Actor in a Comedy Series
Cleavon Little, *Stand By Your Man*

Outstanding Guest Actress in a Comedy Series
Colleen Dewhurst, *Murphy Brown*: "Mama Said"

Outstanding Directing in a Comedy Series
Peter Baldwin, *The Wonder Years*: "Our Miss White"

Outstanding Writing in a Comedy Series
Diane English, *Murphy Brown*: "Respect"

Outstanding Variety, Music or Comedy Program
The Tracey Ullman Show (Fox)

Outstanding Individual Performance in a Variety or Music Program
Linda Ronstadt, *Great Performances: Canciones de Mi Padre*

Outstanding Directing in a Variety or Music Program
Jim Henson, *The Jim Henson Hour*: "Dog City"

Outstanding Writing in a Variety or Music Program
James Downey, head writer; John Bowman, A. Whitney
Brown, Gregory Daniels, Tom Davis, Al Franken,
Shannon Gaughan, Jack Handey, Phil Hartman,
Lorne Michaels, Mike Myers, Conan O'Brien,
Bob Odenkirk, Herb Sargent, Tom Schiller,
Robert Smigel, Bonnie Turner, Terry Turner and
Christine Zander, writers; George Meyer,
additional sketches, *Saturday Night Live*

Outstanding Miniseries
War and Remembrance (NBC)

Outstanding Lead Actor in a Miniseries or Special
James Woods, *Hallmark Hall of Fame: My Name Is Bill W.*

Outstanding Lead Actress in a Miniseries or a Special
Holly Hunter, *Roe vs. Wade*

Outstanding Supporting Actor in a Miniseries or Special
Derek Jacobi, *Hallmark Hall of Fame: The Tenth Man*

Outstanding Supporting Actress in a Miniseries or Special
Colleen Dewhurst, *Those She Left Behind*

Outstanding Directing in a Miniseries or a Special
Simon Wincer, *Lonesome Dove*

Outstanding Writing in a Miniseries or a Special
Abby Mann, Robin Vote and Ron Hutchinson, *Murderers
Among Us: The Simon Wiesenthal Story*

Outstanding Informational Series
Nature (PBS)

Outstanding Informational Special
American Masters: Lillian Gish: The Actor's Life for Me (PBS)

Outstanding Performance in Informational Programming
Hal Holbrook, *Portrait of America: Alaska*

Outstanding Directing in Informational Programming
Linda Otto, *Destined To Live*

Outstanding Writing in Informational Programming
John Heminway, *The Mind*

Outstanding Children's Program (Prime Time)
Free to Be . . . a Family (ABC)

Outstanding Children's Series (Daytime)
Newton's Apple (PBS)

Outstanding Children's Special (Daytime)
ABC Afterschool Special: Taking a Stand (ABC)

Outstanding Animated Program (Daytime)
The New Adventures of Winnie the Pooh (ABC)

**Outstanding Animated Program (Prime Time, for Programming
Less Than One Hour)**
Garfield: Babes and Bullets (CBS)

**Outstanding Animated Program (Prime Time, for Programming
More Than One Hour)**
Disney's Ducktales: Super Ducktales (NBC)

Outstanding Game/Audience Participation Show
The $25,000 Pyramid (CBS)

Outstanding Talk/Service Program
The Oprah Winfrey Show (Syndicated)

1989—1990

Outstanding Drama Series
L.A. Law (NBC)

Outstanding Lead Actor in a Drama Series
Peter Falk, *Columbo*

Outstanding Lead Actress in a Drama Series
Patricia Wettig, *thirtysomething*

Outstanding Supporting Actor in a Drama Series
Jimmy Smits, *L.A. Law*

Outstanding Supporting Actress in a Drama Series
Marg Helgenberger, *China Beach*

Outstanding Guest Actor in a Drama Series
Patrick McGoohan, *Columbo*: "Agenda for Murder"

Outstanding Guest Actress in a Drama Series
Viveca Lindfors, *Life Goes On*: "Save the Last Dance for Me"

Outstanding Directing in a Drama Series
Thomas Carter, *Equal Justice*: "Promises to Keep"

Outstanding Writing in a Drama Series
David E. Kelley, *L.A. Law*: "Blood, Sweat and Fears"

Outstanding Drama/Comedy Special
Hallmark Hall of Fame: Caroline? (CBS)

Outstanding Comedy Series
Murphy Brown (CBS)

Outstanding Lead Actor in a Comedy Series
Ten Danson, *Cheers*

Outstanding Lead Actress in a Comedy Series
Candice Bergen, *Murphy Brown*

Outstanding Supporting Actor in a Comedy Series
Alex Rocco, *The Famous Teddy Z*

Outstanding Supporting Actress in a Comedy Series
Bebe Neuwirth, *Cheers*

The Simpsons

Outstanding Guest Actor in a Comedy Series
Jay Thomas, *Murphy Brown:* "Heart of Gold"

Outstanding Guest Actress in a Comedy Series
Swoosie Kurtz, *Carol and Company:* "Reunion"

Outstanding Directing in a Comedy Series
Michael Dinner, *The Wonder Years:* "Good-Bye"

Outstanding Writing in a Comedy Series
Bob Brush, *The Wonder Years:* "Good-Bye"

Outstanding Variety, Music or Comedy Series
In Living Color (Fox)

Outstanding Variety, Music or Comedy Special
Sammy Davis, Jr.'s 60th Anniversary Celebration (ABC)

Outstanding Individual Performance in a Variety or Music Program
Tracey Ullman, *The Best of the Tracey Ullman Show*

Outstanding Directing in a Variety or Music Program
Dwight Hemion, *The Kennedy Center Honors: A Celebration of the Performing Arts*

Outstanding Writing in a Variety or Music Program
Billy Crystal, *Billy Crystal: Midnight Train to Moscow*

Outstanding Miniseries
Drug Wars: The Camarena Story (NBC)

Outstanding Lead Actor in a Miniseries or a Special
Hume Cronyn, *Age-Old Friends*

Outstanding Lead Actress in a Miniseries or a Special
Barbara Hershey, *A Killing in a Small Town*

Outstanding Supporting Actor in a Miniseries or a Special
Vincent Gardenia, *Age-Old Friends*

Outstanding Supporting Actress in a Miniseries or a Special
Eva Marie Saint, *People Like Us*

Outstanding Directing in a Miniseries or a Special
Joseph Sargent, *Hallmark Hall of Fame: Caroline?*

Outstanding Writing in a Miniseries or a Special
Terrence McNally, *American Playhouse: Andre's Mother*

Outstanding Informational Series
Smithsonian World (PBS)

Outstanding Informational Special
Great Performances: Dance in America: Bob Fosse Steam Heat (PBS)

Outstanding Performance in Informational Programming
George Burns, *A Conversation With . . .*

Outstanding Directing in Informational Programming
Gene Lasko, *American Masters: Photography Made Difficult*

Outstanding Writing in Informational Programming
Steve Lawson, *American Masters: Broadway's Dreamers: The Legacy of the Group Theatre*

Outstanding Children's Program (Prime Time)
The Magical World of Disney: A Mother's Courage: The Mary Thomas Story (NBC)

Outstanding Children's Series (Daytime)
Reading Rainbow (PBS)

Outstanding Children's Special (Daytime)
CBS Schoolbreak Special: A Matter of Conscience (CBS)

Outstanding Animated Program (Daytime) (tie)
Beetlejuice (ABC)
The New Adventures of Winnie the Pooh (ABC)

Outstanding Animated Program (Prime Time, for Programming One Hour or Less)
The Simpsons (Fox)

Outstanding Game/Audience Participation Show
Jeopardy! (Syndicated)

Outstanding Talk/Service Show
Sally Jessy Raphael (Syndicated)

1990–1991

Outstanding Drama Series
L.A. Law (NBC)

Outstanding Lead Actor in a Drama Series
James Earl Jones, *Gabriel's Fire*

Outstanding Lead Actress in a Drama Series
Patricia Wettig, *thirtysomething*

Outstanding Supporting Actor in a Drama Series
Timothy Busfield, *thirtysomething*

Outstanding Supporting Actress in a Drama Series
Madge Sinclair, *Gabriel's Fire*

Outstanding Guest Actor in a Drama Series
David Opatoshu, *Gabriel's Fire:* "A Prayer for the Goldsteins"

Outstanding Guest Actress in a Drama Series
Peggy McCay, *The Trials of Rosie O'Neill:* "State of Mind"

Outstanding Directing in a Drama Series
Thomas Carter, *Equal Justice:* "In Confidence"

Outstanding Writing in a Drama Series
David E. Kelley, *L.A. Law:* "On the Toad Again"

Outstanding Comedy Series
Cheers (NBC)

Outstanding Lead Actor in a Comedy Series
Burt Reynolds, *Evening Shade*

Outstanding Lead Actress in a Comedy Series
Kirstie Alley, *Cheers*

Outstanding Supporting Actor in a Comedy Series
Jonathan Winters, *Davis Rules*

Outstanding Supporting Actress in a Comedy Series
Bebe Neuwirth, *Cheers*

Outstanding Guest Actor in a Comedy Series
Jay Thomas, *Murphy Brown:* "Gold Rush"

Outstanding Guest Actress in a Comedy Series
Colleen Dewhurst, *Murphy Brown:* "Bob and Murphy and Ted and Avery"

Outstanding Directing in a Comedy Series
James Burrows, *Cheers*

Outstanding Writing in a Comedy Series
Gary Dontzig and Steven Peterman, *Murphy Brown:* "Jingle Hell, Jingle Hell, Jingle All the Way"

Outstanding Variety, Music or Comedy Program
The 63rd Annual Academy Awards (ABC)

Outstanding Individual Performance in a Variety or Music Program
Billy Crystal, *The 63rd Annual Academy Awards*

Outstanding Directing in a Variety or Music Program
Hal Gurnee, *Late Night With David Letterman, Show #1425*

Outstanding Writing in a Variety or Music Program
Hal Kanter and Buz Kohan, writers; Billy Crystal, David
    Steinberg, Bruce Vilanch and Robert Wuhl, special
    material, *The 63rd Annual Academy Awards*

Outstanding Drama/Comedy Special and Miniseries
*A General Motors Mark of Excellence Presentation:
    Separate but Equal* (ABC)

Outstanding Lead Actor in a Miniseries or a Special
John Gielgud, *Masterpiece Theatre: Summer's Lease*

Outstanding Lead Actress in a Miniseries or a Special
Lynn Whitfield, *The Josephine Baker Story*

Outstanding Supporting Actor in a Miniseries or a Special
James Earl Jones, *Heat Wave*

Outstanding Supporting Actress in a Miniseries or a Special
Ruby Dee, *Hallmark Hall of Fame: Decoration Day*

Outstanding Directing in a Miniseries or a Special
Brian Gibson, *The Josephine Baker Story*

Outstanding Writing in a Miniseries or a Special
Andrew Davies, *Masterpiece Theatre: House of Cards*

Outstanding Informational Series
*A General Motors Mark of Excellence Presentation:
    The Civil War* (PBS)

Outstanding Informational Special
Edward R. Murrow, *American Masters: This Reporter*

Outstanding Directing in Informational Programming
Peter Gelb, Susan Froemke, Albert Maysles and Bob Eisenhardt,
    Soldiers of Music: Rostropovich Returns to Russia

Outstanding Writing in Informational Programming
Geoffrey C. Ward, Ric Burns and Ken Burns,
    *A General Motors Mark of Excellence
    Presentation: The Civil War*

Outstanding Children's Program (Prime Time)
A 3-2-1 Contact Extra: You Can't Grow Home Again (PBS)

Outstanding Children's Series (Daytime)
Sesame Street (PBS)

Outstanding Children's Special (Daytime)
Lost in the Barrens (Disney Channel)

Outstanding Animated Program (Daytime)
Tiny Toon Adventures (Syndicated)

**Outstanding Animated Program (Prime Time, for Programming
One Hour or Less)**
The Simpsons (Fox)

**Outstanding Animated Program (Prime Time for Programming
One Hour or More)**
Disney's Tale Spin: Plunder and Lightning (Syndicated)

Outstanding Game/Audience Participation Show
Jeopardy! (Syndicated)

Outstanding Talk/Service Show
The Oprah Winfrey Show (Syndicated)

1991–1992

Outstanding Drama Series
Northern Exposure (CBS)

Outstanding Lead Actor in a Drama Series
Christopher Lloyd, *Avonlea*

Outstanding Lead Actress in a Drama Series
Dana Delany, *China Beach*

Outstanding Supporting Actor in a Drama Series
Richard Dysart, *L.A. Law*

Outstanding Supporting Actress in a Drama Series
Valerie Mahaffey, *Northern Exposure*

**Outstanding Individual Achievement in Directing in a Drama
Series**
Eric Laneuville, *I'll Fly Away:* "All God's Children"

**Outstanding Individual Achievement in Writing in a Drama
Series**
Andrew Schneider, *Northern Exposure:* "Seoul Mates"

Outstanding Comedy Series
Murphy Brown (CBS)

Outstanding Lead Actor in a Comedy Series
Craig T. Nelson, *Coach*

Outstanding Lead Actress in a Comedy Series
Candice Bergen, *Murphy Brown*

Outstanding Supporting Actor in a Comedy Series
Michael Jeter, *Evening Shade*

Outstanding Supporting Actress in a Comedy Series
Laurie Metcalf, *Roseanne*

**Outstanding Individual Achievement in Directing in a Comedy
Series**
Barnet Kellman, *Murphy Brown:* "Birth 101"

**Outstanding Individual Achievement in Writing in a Comedy
Series**
Elaine Pope, *Seinfeld:* "The Fix Up"

Outstanding Variety, Music or Comedy Program (Series)
The Tonight Show Starring Johnny Carson (NBC)

Outstanding Variety, Music or Comedy Program (Special)
Cirque du Soleil II: A New Experience (HBO)

**Outstanding Individual Performance in a Variety or Music
Program**
Bette Midler, *The Tonight Show Starring Johnny Carson*

**Outstanding Individual Achievement in Directing in a Variety
or Music Program**
Patricia Birch, *Great Performances: Unforgettable, With Love:
    Natalie Cole Sings the Songs of Nat King Cole*

**Outstanding Individual Achievement in Writing in a Variety or
Music Program**
Hal Kanter and Buz Kohan, writers; Billy Crystal, Marc Shaiman,
    David Steinberg, Robert Wuhl and Bruce Vilanch, special
    material, *The 64th Annual Academy Awards*

Outstanding Miniseries
A Woman Named Jackie (NBC)

Outstanding Lead Actor in a Miniseries or Special
Beau Bridges, *Without Warning: The James Brady Story*

Outstanding Lead Actress in a Miniseries or a Special
Gena Rowlands, *Face of a Stranger*

Outstanding Supporting Actor in a Miniseries or Special
Hume Cronyn, *Neil Simon's Broadway Bound*

Outstanding Supporting Actress in a Miniseries or Special
Amanda Plummer, *Hallmark Hall of Fame: Miss Rose White*

**Outstanding Individual Achievement in Directing for a
Miniseries or a Special**
Daniel Petrie, *Mark Twain and Me*

**Outstanding Individual Achievement in Writing in a
Miniseries or a Special**
John Falsey and Joshua Brand, *I'll Fly Away:* Pilot

Outstanding Made for Television Movie
Hallmark Hall of Fame: Miss Rose White (NBC)

Outstanding Informational Series
MGM: When the Lion Roars (TNT)

Outstanding Informational Special
Abortion: Desperate Choices (HBO)

Outstanding Individual Achievement in Informational Programming, Directing
George Hickenlooper, Fax Bahr and Eleanor Coppola, *Hearts of Darkness: A Filmmaker's Apocalypse*

Outstanding Individual Achievement in Informational Programming, Writing
Fax Bahr and George Hickenlooper, *Hearts of Darkness: A Filmmaker's Apocalypse*

Outstanding Children's Program (Prime Time)
Mark Twain and Me (Disney Channel)

Outstanding Children's Series (Daytime)
Sesame Street (Syndicated)

Outstanding Children's Special (Daytime)
Vincent and Me (Disney Channel)

Outstanding Animated Program (Daytime)
Rugrats (Nickelodeon)

Outstanding Animated Program (Prime Time, for Programming One Hour or Less)
A Claymation Easter (CBS)

Outstanding Game/Audience Participation Show
Jeopardy! (Syndicated)

Outstanding Talk/Service Show
The Oprah Winfrey Show (Syndicated)

1992–1993

Outstanding Drama Series
Picket Fences (CBS)

Outstanding Lead Actor in a Drama Series
Tom Skerritt, *Picket Fences*

Outstanding Lead Actress in a Drama Series
Kathy Baker, *Picket Fences*

Outstanding Supporting Actor in a Drama Series
Chad Lowe, *Life Goes On*

Outstanding Supporting Actress in a Drama Series
Mary Alice, *I'll Fly Away*

Outstanding Guest Actor in a Drama Series
Laurence Fishburne, *Tribeca:* "The Box"

Outstanding Guest Actress in a Drama Series
Elaine Stritch, *Law & Order:* "Point of View"

Outstanding Individual Achievement in Directing in a Drama Series
Barry Levinson, *Homicide: Life on the Street:* "Gone for Goode"

Outstanding Individual Achievement in Writing in a Drama Series
Tom Fontana, *Homicide: Life on the Street:* "Three Men and Adena"

Michael Richards, *Seinfeld*

Outstanding Comedy Series
Seinfeld (NBC)

Outstanding Lead Actor in a Comedy Series
Ted Danson, *Cheers*

Outstanding Lead Actress in a Comedy Series
Roseanne Arnold, *Roseanne*

Outstanding Supporting Actor in a Comedy Series
Michael Richards, *Seinfeld*

Outstanding Supporting Actress in a Comedy Series
Laurie Metcalf, *Roseanne*

Outstanding Guest Actor in a Comedy Series
David Clennon, *Dream On:* "For Peter's Sake"

Outstanding Guest Actress in a Comedy Series
Tracey Ullman, *Love and War:* "The Prima Dava"

Outstanding Individual Achievement in Directing in a Comedy Series
Betty Thomas, *Dream On:* "For Peter's Sake"

Outstanding Individual Achievement in Writing in a Comedy Series
Larry David, *Seinfeld:* "The Contest"

Outstanding Variety, Music or Comedy Series
Saturday Night Live (NBC)

Outstanding Individual Performance in a Variety or Music Program
Dana Carvey, *Saturday Night Live: Saturday Night Live's Presidential Bash*

Outstanding Individual Achievement in Directing in a Variety or Music Program
Walter C. Miller, *The 1992 Tony Awards*

Outstanding Individual Achievement in Writing in a Variety or Music Program
Judd Apatow, Robert Cohen, David Cross, Brent Forrester, Jeff Kahn, Bruce Kirschbaum, Bob Odenkirk, Sultan Pepper, Dino Stamatopoulos and Ben Stiller, *The Ben Stiller Show*

Outstanding Variety, Music or Comedy Special
Bob Hope: The First 90 Years (NBC)

Outstanding Miniseries
Mystery: Prime Suspect 2 (PBS)

Outstanding Lead Actor in a Miniseries or Special
Robert Morse, *American Playhouse: Tru*

Outstanding Lead Actress in a Miniseries or a Special
Holly Hunter, *The Positively True Adventures of the Alleged Texas Cheerleader-Murdering Mom*

Outstanding Supporting Actor in a Miniseries or a Special
Beau Bridges, *The Positively True Adventures of the Alleged Texas Cheerleader-Murdering Mom*

Outstanding Supporting Actress in a Miniseries or Special
Mary Tyler Moore, *Stolen Babies*

Outstanding Individual Achievement in Directing for a Miniseries or a Special
James Sadwith, *Sinatra*

Outstanding Individual Achievement in Writing in a Miniseries or a Special
Jane Anderson, *The Positively True Adventures of the Alleged Texas Cheerleader-Murdering Mom*

Outstanding Made for Television Movie
Barbarians at the Gate (HBO)

Outstanding Informational Series
Healing and the Mind With Bill Moyers (PBS)

Outstanding Informational Special
Lucy and Desi: A Home Movie (NBC)

Outstanding Children's Program (Prime Time)
Avonlea (Disney Channel)

Outstanding Children's Series (Daytime)
Reading Rainbow (PBS)

Outstanding Children's Special (Daytime)
ABC Afterschool Special: Shades of a Single Protein (ABC)

Outstanding Animated Program (Daytime)
Tiny Toon Adventures (Fox)

Outstanding Animated Program (Prime Time, for Programming One Hour or Less)
Batman: The Series (Fox)

Outstanding Game/Audience Participation Show
Jeopardy! (Syndicated)

Outstanding Talk/Service Show
Good Morning America (ABC)

1993–1994

Outstanding Drama Series
Picket Fences (CBS)

Outstanding Lead Actor in a Drama Series
Dennis Franz, *NYPD Blue*

Outstanding Lead Actress in a Drama Series
Sela Ward, *Sisters*

Outstanding Supporting Actor in a Drama Series
Fyvush Finkel, *Picket Fences*

Outstanding Supporting Actress in a Drama Series
Leigh Taylor-Young, *Picket Fences*

Outstanding Guest Actor in a Drama Series
Richard Kiley, *Picket Fences:* "Buried Alive"

Outstanding Guest Actress in a Drama Series
Faye Dunaway, *Columbo:* "It's All in the Game"

Outstanding Individual Achievement in Directing in a Drama Series
Daniel Sackheim, *NYPD Blue:* "Tempest in a C-Cup"

Outstanding Individual Achievement in Writing in a Drama Series
Ann Biderman, teleplay/story, *NYPD Blue:* "Steroid Roy"

Outstanding Comedy Series
Frasier (NBC)

Outstanding Lead Actor in a Comedy Series
Kelsey Grammer, *Frasier*

Outstanding Lead Actress in a Comedy Series
Candice Bergen, *Murphy Brown*

Outstanding Supporting Actor in a Comedy Series
Michael Richards, *Seinfeld*

Outstanding Supporting Actress in a Comedy Series
Laurie Metcalf, *Roseanne*

Outstanding Guest Actor in a Comedy Series
Martin Sheen, *Murphy Brown:* "Angst for the Memories"

Outstanding Guest Actress in a Comedy Series
Eileen Heckart, *Love and War:* "You Make Me Feel So Young"

Outstanding Individual Achievement in Directing in a Comedy Series
James Burrows, *Frasier:* "The Good Son"

Kelsey Grammer,
Frasier

Outstanding Individual Achievement in Writing in a Comedy Series
David Angell, *Frasier:* "The Good Son"

Outstanding Variety, Music or Comedy Series
Late Show With David Letterman (CBS)

Outstanding Individual Performance in a Variety or Music Program
Tracey Ullman, *Tracey Ullman — Takes on New York*

Outstanding Individual Achievement in Directing in a Variety or Music Program
Walter C. Miller, *The Tony Awards*

Outstanding Individual Achievement in Writing in a Variety or Music Program
Jeff Cesario, Mike Dugan, Eddie Feldmann, Gregory Greenberg, Dennis Miller and Kevin Rooney, *Dennis Miller Live*

Outstanding Variety, Music or Comedy Special
The Kennedy Center Honors (CBS)

Outstanding Miniseries
Mystery: Prime Suspect 3 (PBS)

Outstanding Lead Actor in a Miniseries or Special
Hume Cronyn, *Hallmark Hall of Fame: To Dance With the White Dog*

Outstanding Lead Actress in a Miniseries or a Special
Kirstie Alley, *David's Mother*

Outstanding Supporting Actor in a Miniseries or Special
Michael Goorjian, *David's Mother*

Outstanding Supporting Actress in a Miniseries or a Special
Cicely Tyson, *Oldest Living Confederate Widow Tells All,* parts 1 and 2

Outstanding Individual Achievement in Directing for a Miniseries or a Special
John Frankenheimer, *Against the Wall*

Outstanding Individual Achievement in Writing in a Miniseries or a Special
Bob Randall, *David's Mother*

Outstanding Made for Television Movie
And the Band Played On (HBO)

Outstanding Informational Series
Later With Bob Costas (NBC)

Outstanding Information Special
I Am a Promise: The Children of Stanton Street Elementary School (HBO)

Outstanding Cultural Program
Vladimir Horowitz: A Reminiscence (PBS)

Outstanding Children's Program (Prime Time)
Kids Killing Kids/Kids Saving Kids (CBS, Fox)

Outstanding Children's Series (Daytime)
Sesame Street (PBS)

Outstanding Children's Special (Daytime)
Dead Drunk: The Kevin Tunell Story (HBO)

Outstanding Animated Children's Program (Daytime)
Rugrats (Nickelodeon)

Outstanding Animated Program (Prime Time, for Programming One Hour or Less)
The Roman City (PBS)

Outstanding Game/Audience Participation Show
Jeopardy! (Syndicated)

Outstanding Service Show
This Old House (PBS)

Outstanding Talk Show
The Oprah Winfrey Show (Syndicated)

What We Watched

Nielsen Media Research tracks the shows we watch each television season. The networks use the ratings to plan programming strategy and to determine how much to charge advertisers for commercials. Here are the most popular television programs since 1950.

October 1950 – April 1951

1. *The Texaco Star Theater* . . . . NBC
2. *Fireside Theatre* . . . . NBC
3. *Your Show of Shows* . . . . NBC
4. *Philco Television Playhouse* . . . . NBC
5. *The Colgate Comedy Hour* . . . . NBC
6. *Gillette Cavalcade of Sports* . . . . NBC
7. *Arthur Godfrey's Talent Scouts* . . . . CBS
8. *Mama* . . . . CBS
9. *Robert Montgomery Presents* . . . . NBC
10. *Martin Kane, Private Eye* . . . . NBC
11. *Man Against Crime* . . . . CBS
12. *Somerset Maugham Playhouse* . . . . NBC
13. *Kraft Television Theatre* . . . . NBC
14. *The Toast of the Town* . . . . CBS
15. *The Aldrich Family* . . . . NBC
16. *Your Bet Your Life* . . . . NBC
17. *Armstrong Circle Theatre* . . . . NBC
18. *Big Town* . . . . CBS
19. *Lights Out* . . . . NBC
20. *The Alan Young Show* . . . . CBS

October 1951 – April 1952

1. *Arthur Godfrey's Talent Scouts* . . . . CBS
2. *The Texaco Star Theater* . . . . NBC
3. *I Love Lucy* . . . . CBS
4. *The Red Skelton Show* . . . . NBC
5. *The Colgate Comedy Hour* . . . . NBC
6. *Fireside Theatre* . . . . NBC

I Love Lucy

7. *The Jack Benny Program* . . . . CBS
8. *Your Show of Shows* . . . . NBC
9. *You Bet Your Life* . . . . NBC
10. *Arthur Godfrey and His Friends* . . . . CBS
11. *Mama* . . . . CBS
12. *Philco Television Playhouse* . . . . NBC
13. *Amos 'n Andy* . . . . CBS
14. *Big Town* . . . . CBS
15. *Pabst Blue Ribbon Bouts* . . . . CBS
16. *Gillette Cavalcade of Sports* . . . . NBC
17. *The Alan Young Show* . . . . CBS
18. *The All Star Revue* . . . . NBC
19. *Dragnet* . . . . NBC
20. *Kraft Television Theatre* . . . . NBC

October 1952 – April 1953

1. *I Love Lucy* . . . . CBS
2. *Arthur Godfrey's Talent Scouts* . . . . CBS
3. *Arthur Godfrey and His Friends* . . . . CBS
4. *Dragnet* . . . . NBC
5. *The Texaco Star Theater* . . . . NBC
6. *The Buick Circus Hour* . . . . NBC
7. *The Colgate Comedy Hour* . . . . NBC
8. *Gangbusters* . . . . NBC
9. *You Bet Your Life* . . . . NBC
10. *Fireside Theatre* . . . . NBC
11. *The Red Buttons Show* . . . . CBS
12. *The Jack Benny Show* . . . . CBS
13. *Life With Luigi* . . . . CBS
14. *Pabst Blue Ribbon Bouts* . . . . CBS
15. *Goodyear Playhouse* . . . . NBC

October 1953 – April 1954

1. *I Love Lucy* . . . . CBS
2. *Dragnet* . . . . NBC
3. *Arthur Godfrey's Talent Scouts* . . . . CBS
4. *You Bet Your Life* . . . . NBC
5. *The Bob Hope Show* . . . . NBC
6. *The Milton Berle Show* . . . . NBC
7. *Arthur Godfrey and His Friends* . . . . CBS
8. *The Ford Show* . . . . NBC
9. *The Jackie Gleason Show* . . . . CBS
10. *Fireside Theatre* . . . . NBC
11. *The Colgate Comedy Hour* . . . . NBC
12. *This Is Your Life* . . . . NBC
13. *The Red Buttons Show* . . . . CBS
14. *The Life of Riley* . . . . NBC
15. *Our Miss Brooks* . . . . CBS

October 1954 – April 1955

1.	*I Love Lucy*	CBS
2.	*The Jackie Gleason Show*	CBS
3.	*Dragnet*	NBC
4.	*You Bet Your Life*	NBC
5.	*Toast of the Town*	CBS
6.	*Disneyland*	ABC
7.	*The Bob Hope Show*	NBC
8.	*The Jack Benny Show*	CBS
9.	*The Martha Raye Show*	NBC
10.	*The George Gobel Show*	NBC
11.	*Ford Theatre*	NBC
12.	*December Bride*	CBS
13.	*The Buick-Berle Show*	NBC
14.	*This Is Your Life*	NBC
15.	*I've Got a Secret*	CBS
16.	*Two for the Money*	CBS
17.	*Your Hit Parade*	NBC
18.	*The Millionaire*	CBS
19.	*General Electric Theater*	CBS
20.	*Arthur Godfrey's Talent Scouts*	CBS

October 1955 – April 1956

1.	*The $64,000 Question*	CBS
2.	*I Love Lucy*	CBS
3.	*The Ed Sullivan Show*	CBS
4.	*Disneyland*	ABC
5.	*The Jack Benny Show*	CBS
6.	*December Bride*	CBS
7.	*You Bet Your Life*	NBC
8.	*Dragnet*	NBC
9.	*I've Got a Secret*	CBS
10.	*General Electric Theater*	CBS
11.	*Private Secretary*	CBS
	Ford Theatre	NBC
13.	*The Red Skelton Show*	CBS
14.	*The George Gobel Show*	NBC
15.	*The $64,000 Challenge*	CBS

October 1956 – April 1957

1.	*I Love Lucy*	CBS
2.	*The Ed Sullivan Show*	CBS
3.	*General Electric Theater*	CBS
4.	*The $64,000 Question*	CBS
5.	*December Bride*	CBS
6.	*Alfred Hitchcock Presents*	CBS
7.	*I've Got a Secret*	CBS
	Gunsmoke	CBS
9.	*The Perry Como Show*	NBC
10.	*The Jack Benny Show*	CBS
11.	*Dragnet*	NBC
12.	*Arthur Godfrey's Talent Scouts*	CBS
13.	*The Millionaire*	CBS
	Disneyland	ABC
15.	*Shower of Stars*	CBS

October 1957 – April 1958

1.	*Gunsmoke*	CBS
2.	*The Danny Thomas Show*	CBS
3.	*Tales of Wells Fargo*	NBC
4.	*Have Gun, Will Travel*	CBS
5.	*I've Got a Secret*	CBS
6.	*The Life and Legend of Wyatt Earp*	ABC
7.	*General Electric Theater*	CBS
8.	*The Restless Gun*	NBC
9.	*December Bride*	CBS
10.	*You Bet Your Life*	NBC
11.	*Alfred Hitchcock Presents*	CBS
	Cheyenne	ABC
13.	*The Ford Show*	NBC
14.	*The Red Skelton Show*	CBS
15.	*Wagon Train*	NBC
	Sugarfoot	ABC
	Father Knows Best	CBS
18.	*Twenty-One*	NBC

October 1958 – April 1959

1.	*Gunsmoke*	CBS
2.	*Wagon Train*	NBC
3.	*Have Gun, Will Travel*	CBS
4.	*The Rifleman*	ABC
5.	*The Danny Thomas Show*	CBS
6.	*Maverick*	ABC
7.	*Wells Fargo*	NBC
8.	*The Real McCoys*	ABC
9.	*I've Got a Secret*	CBS
10.	*The Life and Legend of Wyatt Earp*	ABC
11.	*The Price Is Right*	NBC
12.	*The Red Skelton Show*	CBS
13.	*Zane Grey Theater*	CBS
	Father Knows Best	CBS
15.	*The Texan*	CBS
16.	*Wanted: Dead or Alive*	CBS
	Peter Gunn	NBC
18.	*Cheyenne*	ABC
19.	*Perry Mason*	CBS
20.	*The Tennessee Ernie Ford Show*	NBC

October 1959 – April 1960

1.	*Gunsmoke*	CBS
2.	*Wagon Train*	NBC
3.	*Have Gun, Will Travel*	CBS
4.	*The Danny Thomas Show*	CBS
5.	*The Red Skelton Show*	CBS
6.	*Father Knows Best*	CBS
	77 Sunset Strip	ABC
8.	*The Price Is Right*	NBC
9.	*Wanted: Dead or Alive*	CBS
10.	*Perry Mason*	CBS
11.	*The Real McCoys*	ABC
12.	*The Ed Sullivan Show*	CBS
13.	*The Bing Crosby Show*	ABC
14.	*Rifleman*	ABC

15.	The Ford Show	NBC
16.	The Lawman	ABC
17.	Dennis the Menace	CBS
18.	Cheyenne	ABC
19.	Rawhide	CBS
20.	Maverick	ABC

October 1960 – April 1961

1.	Gunsmoke	CBS
2.	Wagon Train	NBC
3.	Have Gun, Will Travel	CBS
4.	The Andy Griffith Show	CBS
5.	The Real McCoys	ABC
6.	Rawhide	CBS
7.	Candid Camera	CBS
8.	The Untouchables	ABC
	The Price Is Right	NBC
10.	The Jack Benny Show	CBS
11.	Dennis the Menace	CBS
12.	The Danny Thomas Show	CBS
13.	My Three Sons	ABC
	77 Sunset Strip	ABC
15.	The Ed Sullivan Show	CBS
16.	Perry Mason	CBS
17.	Bonanza	NBC
18.	The Flintstones	ABC
19.	The Red Skelton Show	CBS
20.	Alfred Hitchcock Presents	CBS

October 1961 – April 1962

1.	Wagon Train	NBC
2.	Bonanza	NBC
3.	Gunsmoke	CBS
4.	Hazel	NBC
5.	Perry Mason	CBS
6.	The Red Skelton Show	CBS
7.	The Andy Griffith Show	CBS
8.	The Danny Thomas Show	CBS
9.	Dr. Kildare	NBC
10.	Candid Camera	CBS
11.	My Three Sons	ABC
12.	The Garry Moore Show	CBS
13.	Rawhide	CBS
14.	The Real McCoys	ABC
15.	Lassie	CBS
16.	Sing Along With Mitch	NBC
17.	Dennis the Menace	CBS
	Gunsmoke	CBS
19.	Ben Casey	ABC
20.	The Ed Sullivan Show	CBS

October 1962 – April 1963

1.	The Beverly Hillbillies	CBS
2.	Candid Camera	CBS
	The Red Skelton Show	CBS
4.	Bonanza	NBC
	The Lucy Show	CBS

6.	The Andy Griffith Show	CBS
7.	Ben Casey	ABC
	The Danny Thomas Show	CBS
9.	The Dick Van Dyke Show	CBS
10.	Gunsmoke	CBS
11.	Dr. Kildare	NBC
	The Jack Benny Show	CBS
13.	What's My Line	CBS
	The Ed Sullivan Show	CBS
15.	Hazel	NBC
16.	I've Got a Secret	CBS
17.	The Jackie Gleason Show	CBS
19.	The Defenders	CBS
	The Garry Moore Show	CBS
20.	To Tell the Truth	CBS

October 1963 – April 1964

1.	The Beverly Hillbillies	CBS
2.	Bonanza	NBC
3.	The Dick Van Dyke Show	CBS
4.	Petticoat Junction	CBS
5.	The Andy Griffith Show	CBS
6.	The Lucy Show	CBS
7.	Candid Camera	CBS
8.	The Ed Sullivan Show	CBS
9.	The Danny Thomas Show	CBS
10.	My Favorite Martian	CBS
11.	The Red Skelton Show	CBS
12.	I've Got a Secret	CBS
	Lassie	CBS
	The Jack Benny Show	CBS
15.	The Jackie Gleason Show	CBS
16.	The Donna Reed Show	ABC
17.	The Virginian	NBC
18.	The Patty Duke Show	ABC
19.	Dr. Kildare	NBC
20.	Gunsmoke	CBS

October 1964 – April 1965

1.	Bonanza	NBC
2.	Bewitched	ABC
3.	Gomer Pyle, U.S.M.C.	CBS
4.	The Andy Griffith Show	CBS
5.	The Fugitive	ABC
6.	The Red Skelton Hour	CBS
7.	The Dick Van Dyke Show	CBS
8.	The Lucy Show	CBS
9.	Peyton Place (II)	ABC
10.	Combat	ABC
11.	Walt Disney's Wonderful World of Color	NBC
12.	The Beverly Hillbillies	CBS
13.	My Three Sons	ABC
14.	Branded	NBC
15.	Petticoat Junction	CBS
16.	The Ed Sullivan Show	CBS
17.	Lassie	CBS

Rowan and Martin's Laugh-In

18.	The Munsters	CBS
19.	Gilligan's Island	CBS
20.	Peyton Place (V)	ABC

October 1965 – April 1966

1.	Bonanza	NBC
2.	Gomer Pyle, U.S.M.C.	CBS
3.	The Lucy Show	CBS
4.	The Red Skelton Hour	CBS
5.	Batman (Thursday)	ABC
6.	The Andy Griffith Show	CBS
7.	Bewitched	ABC
8.	The Beverly Hillbillies	CBS
9.	Hogan's Heroes	CBS
10.	Batman (Wednesday)	ABC
11.	Green Acres	CBS
12.	Get Smart	NBC
13.	The Man From U.N.C.L.E.	NBC
14.	Daktari	CBS
15.	My Three Sons	CBS
16.	The Dick Van Dyke Show	CBS
17.	Walt Disney's Wonderful World of Color	NBC
18.	The Ed Sullivan Show	CBS
19.	The Lawrence Welk Show	ABC
20.	I've Got a Secret	CBS

October 1966 – April 1967

1.	Bonanza	NBC
2.	The Red Skelton Hour	CBS
3.	The Andy Griffith Show	CBS
4.	The Lucy Show	CBS
5.	The Jackie Gleason Show	CBS
6.	Green Acres	CBS
7.	Daktari	CBS
8.	Bewitched	ABC
9.	The Beverly Hillbillies	CBS
10.	Gomer Pyle, U.S.M.C.	CBS
11.	The Virginian	NBC
12.	The Lawrence Welk Show	ABC
13.	The Ed Sullivan Show	CBS
14.	The Dean Martin Show	CBS
15.	Family Affair	CBS
16.	The Smothers Brothers Comedy Hour	CBS
17.	The CBS Friday Night Movie	CBS
18.	Hogan's Heroes	CBS
19.	Walt Disney's Wonderful World of Color	NBC
20.	Saturday Night at the Movies	NBC

October 1967 – April 1968

1.	The Andy Griffith Show	CBS
2.	The Lucy Show	CBS
3.	Gomer Pyle, U.S.M.C.	CBS
4.	Gunsmoke	CBS
5.	Family Affair	CBS
6.	Bonanza	NBC
7.	The Red Skelton Show	CBS
8.	The Dean Martin Show	NBC
9.	The Jackie Gleason Show	CBS
10.	Saturday Night at the Movies	NBC
11.	Bewitched	ABC
12.	The Beverly Hillbillies	CBS
13.	The Ed Sullivan Show	CBS
14.	The Virginian	NBC
15.	The CBS Friday Night Movie	CBS
16.	Green Acres	CBS
17.	Lawrence Welk	ABC
18.	The Smothers Brothers Show	CBS
19.	Gentle Ben	CBS
20.	Tuesday Night at the Movies	NBC

October 1968 – April 1969

1.	Rowan and Martin's Laugh-In	NBC
2.	Gomer Pyle, U.S.M.C.	CBS
3.	Bonanza	NBC
4.	Mayberry R.F.D.	CBS
5.	Family Affair	CBS
6.	Gunsmoke	CBS
7.	Julia	NBC
8.	The Dean Martin Show	NBC
9.	Here's Lucy	CBS
10.	The Beverly Hillbillies	CBS
11.	Mission: Impossible	CBS
12.	Bewitched	ABC
13.	The Red Skelton Hour	CBS
14.	My Three Sons	CBS
15.	The Glen Campbell Goodtime Hour	CBS
16.	Ironside	NBC
17.	The Virginian	NBC
18.	The F.B.I.	ABC
19.	Green Acres	CBS
20.	Dragnet	NBC

October 1969 – April 1970

1.	Rowan and Martin's Laugh-In	NBC
2.	Gunsmoke	CBS
3.	Bonanza	NBC
4.	Mayberry R.F.D.	CBS
5.	Family Affair	CBS
6.	Here's Lucy	CBS
7.	The Red Skelton Hour	CBS
8.	Marcus Welby, M.D.	ABC
9.	The Wonderful World of Disney	NBC
10.	The Doris Day Show	CBS
11.	The Bill Cosby Show	NBC
12.	The Jim Nabors Hour	CBS
13.	The Carol Burnett Show	CBS
14.	The Dean Martin Show	NBC
15.	My Three Sons	CBS
	Ironside	NBC
	The Johnny Cash Show	ABC
18.	The Beverly Hillbillies	CBS
19.	Hawaii Five-O	CBS
20.	The Glen Campbell Goodtime Hour	CBS

October 1970 – April 1971

1.	Marcus Welby, M.D.	ABC
2.	The Flip Wilson Show	NBC
3.	Here's Lucy	CBS
4.	Ironside	NBC
5.	Gunsmoke	CBS
6.	ABC Movie of the Week	ABC
7.	Hawaii Five-O	CBS
8.	Medical Center	CBS
9.	Bonanza	NBC
10.	The F.B.I.	ABC
11.	The Mod Squad	ABC
12.	Adam-12	NBC
13.	Rowan and Martin's Laugh-In	NBC
	The Wonderful World of Disney	NBC
15.	Mayberry R.F.D.	CBS
16.	Hee Haw	CBS
17.	Mannix	CBS
18.	The Men From Shiloh	NBC
19.	My Three Sons	CBS
20.	The Doris Day Show	CBS

October 1971 – April 1972

1.	All in the Family	CBS
2.	The Flip Wilson Show	NBC
3.	Marcus Welby, M.D.	ABC
4.	Gunsmoke	CBS
5.	ABC Movie of the Week	ABC
6.	Sanford and Son	NBC
7.	Mannix	CBS
8.	Funny Face	CBS
	Adam-12	NBC
10.	The Mary Tyler Moore Show	CBS
11.	Here's Lucy	CBS
12.	Hawaii Five-O	CBS

13.	Medical Center	CBS
14.	NBC Mystery Movie	NBC
15.	Ironside	NBC
16.	The Partridge Family	ABC
17.	The F.B.I.	ABC
18.	The New Dick Van Dyke Show	CBS
19.	The Wonderful World of Disney	NBC
20.	Bonanza	NBC

October 1972 – April 1973

1.	All in the Family	CBS
2.	Sanford and Son	NBC
3.	Hawaii Five-O	CBS
4.	Maude	CBS
5.	Bridget Loves Bernie	CBS
	Sunday Mystery Movie	NBC
7.	The Mary Tyler Moore Show	CBS
	Gunsmoke	CBS
9.	The Wonderful World of Disney	NBC
10.	Ironside	NBC
	Adam-12	NBC
12.	The Flip Wilson Show	NBC
13.	Marcus Welby, M.D.	ABC
14.	Cannon	CBS
15.	Here's Lucy	CBS
16.	The Bob Newhart Show	CBS
17.	Tuesday Movie of the Week	ABC
18.	ABC NFL Football	ABC
19.	The Partridge Family	ABC
	The Waltons	CBS

September 1973 – April 1974

1.	All in the Family	CBS
2.	The Waltons	CBS
3.	Sanford and Son	NBC
4.	M*A*S*H	CBS
5.	Hawaii Five-O	CBS

All in the Family

6.	Maude	CBS
7.	Kojak	CBS
	The Sonny and Cher Comedy Hour	CBS
9.	The Mary Tyler Moore Show	CBS
	Cannon	CBS
11.	The Six Million Dollar Man	ABC
12.	The Bob Newhart Show	CBS
	The Wonderful World of Disney	NBC
14.	NBC Sunday Mystery Movie	NBC
15.	Gunsmoke	CBS
16.	Happy Days	ABC
17.	Good Times	CBS
	Barnaby Jones	CBS
19.	ABC Monday Night Football	ABC
	CBS Friday Night Movie	CBS

September 1974 – April 1975

1.	All in the Family	CBS
2.	Sanford and Son	NBC
3.	Chico and the Man	NBC
4.	The Jeffersons	CBS
5.	M*A*S*H	CBS
6.	Rhoda	CBS
7.	Good Times	CBS
8.	The Waltons	CBS
9.	Maude	CBS
10.	Hawaii Five-O	CBS
11.	The Mary Tyler Moore Show	CBS
12.	The Rockford Files	NBC
13.	Little House on the Prairie	NBC
14.	Kojak	CBS
15.	Police Woman	NBC
16.	S.W.A.T.	ABC
17.	The Bob Newhart Show	CBS
18.	The Wonderful World of Disney	NBC
	The Rookies	ABC
20.	Mannix	CBS
	Cannon	CBS

September 1975 – April 1976

1.	All in the Family	CBS
2.	Rich Man, Poor Man	ABC
3.	Laverne and Shirley	ABC
4.	Maude	CBS
5.	The Bionic Woman	ABC
6.	Phyllis	CBS
7.	Sanford and Son	NBC
	Rhoda	CBS
9.	The Six Million Dollar Man	ABC
10.	ABC Monday Night Movie	ABC
11.	Happy Days	ABC
12.	One Day at a Time	CBS
13.	ABC Sunday Night Movie	ABC
14.	The Waltons	CBS
	M*A*S*H	CBS
16.	Starsky and Hutch	ABC

	Good Heavens	ABC
18.	Welcome Back, Kotter	ABC
19.	The Mary Tyler Moore Show	CBS
20.	Kojak	CBS

September 1976 – April 1977

1.	Happy Days	ABC
2.	Laverne and Shirley	ABC
3.	ABC Monday Night Movie	ABC
4.	M*A*S*H	CBS
5.	Charlie's Angels	ABC
6.	The Big Event	NBC
7.	The Six Million Dollar Man	ABC
8.	ABC Sunday Night Movie	ABC
	Baretta	ABC
	One Day at a Time	CBS
11.	Three's Company	ABC
12.	All in the Family	CBS
13.	Welcome Back, Kotter	ABC
14.	The Bionic Woman	ABC
15.	The Waltons	CBS
	Little House on the Prairie	NBC
17.	Barney Miller	ABC
18.	60 Minutes	CBS
	Hawaii Five-O	CBS
20.	NBC Monday Night Movie	NBC

September 1977 – April 1978

1.	Laverne and Shirley	ABC
2.	Happy Days	ABC
3.	Three's Company	ABC
4.	60 Minutes	CBS
	Charlie's Angels	ABC
	All in the Family	CBS
7.	Little House on the Prairie	NBC
8.	Alice	CBS
	M*A*S*H	CBS
10.	One Day at a Time	CBS
11.	How the West Was Won	ABC
12.	Eight Is Enough	ABC
13.	Soap	ABC
14.	The Love Boat	ABC
15.	NBC Monday Night Movie	NBC
16.	Monday Night Football	ABC
17.	Fantasy Island	ABC
	Barney Miller	ABC
19.	The Amazing Spider-Man	CBS
	Project U.F.O.	NBC

September 1978 – April 1979

1.	All in the Family	CBS
2.	Three's Company	ABC
3.	Happy Days	ABC
4.	Mork and Mindy	ABC
5.	Angie	ABC
6.	M*A*S*H	CBS

7.	60 Minutes	CBS
8.	All in the Family	CBS
9.	The Ropers	ABC
10.	Taxi	ABC
11.	Charlie's Angels	ABC
12.	Eight Is Enough	ABC
13.	Alice (8:30)	CBS
14.	What's Happening (Thursday)	ABC
15.	One Day at a Time (Monday)	CBS
16.	One Day at a Time	CBS
17.	Little House on the Prairie	NBC
18.	ABC Sunday Night Movie	ABC
	Barney Miller	ABC
20.	Alice	CBS

September 1979 – April 1980

1.	60 Minutes	CBS
2.	Three's Company	ABC
3.	That's Incredible	ABC
4.	M*A*S*H	CBS
5.	Alice	CBS
6.	Dallas	CBS
7.	Flo	CBS
8.	The Jeffersons	CBS
9.	The Dukes of Hazzard	CBS
10.	One Day at a Time	CBS
11.	WKRP in Cincinnati (9:30)	CBS
12.	Goodtime Girls (Tuesday)	ABC
13.	Archie Bunker's Place	CBS
14.	Taxi	ABC
15.	Eight Is Enough	ABC
16.	Little House on the Prairie	NBC
17.	House Calls	CBS
18.	Real People	NBC
19.	CHiPs (Saturday)	NBC
20.	Happy Days	ABC

September 1980 – April 1981

1.	Dallas	CBS
2.	60 Minutes	CBS
3.	The Dukes of Hazzard	CBS
4.	Private Benjamin	CBS
5.	M*A*S*H	CBS
6.	The Love Boat	ABC
7.	The NBC Tuesday Night Movie	NBC
8.	House Calls	CBS
9.	The Jeffersons	CBS
	Little House on the Prairie	NBC
11.	The Two of Us	CBS
12.	Alice	CBS
13.	Three's Company	ABC
	Real People	NBC
15.	One Day at a Time	CBS
	The NBC Movie of the Week	NBC
17.	Too Close for Comfort	ABC
	Magnum, P.I.	CBS

19.	NFL Monday Night Football	ABC
	Diff'rent Strokes	NBC

September 1981 – April 1982

1.	Dallas	CBS
2.	Dallas (10:00)	CBS
3.	60 Minutes	CBS
4.	Three's Company	ABC
	CBS NFL Football Post 2	CBS
6.	The Jeffersons	CBS
7.	Joanie Loves Chachi	ABC
8.	The Dukes of Hazzard (9:00)	CBS
9.	Alice	CBS
	The Dukes of Hazzard	CBS
11.	The ABC Monday Night Movie	ABC
	Too Close for Comfort	ABC
13.	M*A*S*H	CBS
14.	One Day at a Time	CBS
15.	NFL Monday Night Football	ABC
16.	Falcon Crest	CBS
17.	Archie Bunker's Place	CBS
	The Love Boat	ABC
19.	Hart to Hart	ABC
20.	Trapper John, M.D.	CBS

September 1982 – April 1983

1.	60 Minutes	CBS
2.	Dallas	CBS
3.	M*A*S*H	CBS
	Magnum, P.I.	CBS
5.	Dynasty	ABC
6.	Three's Company	ABC
7.	Simon and Simon	CBS
8.	Falcon Crest	CBS
9.	NFL Monday Night Football	ABC
10.	The Love Boat	ABC
11.	One Day at a Time (Sunday)	CBS
12.	Newhart (Monday)	CBS
13.	The A-Team	NBC
	The Jeffersons	CBS
15.	The Fall Guy (9:00)	ABC
16.	Newhart (9:30)	CBS
17.	The Mississippi	CBS
18.	9 to 5	ABC
19.	The Fall Guy	ABC
20.	The ABC Monday Night Movie	ABC

September 1983 – April 1984

1.	Dallas	CBS
2.	Dynasty	ABC
3.	The A-Team	NBC
4.	60 Minutes	CBS
5.	Simon and Simon	CBS
6.	Magnum, P.I.	CBS
7.	Falcon Crest	CBS
8.	Kate and Allie	CBS
9.	Hotel	ABC

The Bill Cosby Show

10.	Cagney and Lacey	CBS
11.	Knots Landing	CBS
12.	The ABC Sunday Night Movie	ABC
	The ABC Monday Night Movie	ABC
14.	TV's Bloopers and Practical Jokes	NBC
15.	AfterMASH	CBS
16.	The Fall Guy	ABC
17.	Four Seasons (8:00)	CBS
18.	The Love Boat	ABC
19.	Riptide	NBC
20.	The Jeffersons	CBS

September 1984 – April 1985

1.	Dynasty	ABC
2.	Dallas	CBS
3.	The Bill Cosby Show	NBC
4.	60 Minutes	CBS
	Family Ties	NBC
6.	Simon and Simon	CBS
	The A-Team	NBC
8.	Knots Landing	CBS
	Murder, She Wrote	CBS
10.	Crazy Like a Fox	CBS
	Falcon Crest	CBS
12.	Hotel	ABC
13.	Cheers	NBC
14.	Who's the Boss?	ABC
	Riptide	NBC
16.	Magnum, P.I.	CBS
17.	Hail to the Chief	ABC
18.	Newhart	CBS
19.	Kate and Allie	CBS
20.	NBC Monday Night Movies	NBC

September 1985 – April 1986

1.	The Bill Cosby Show	NBC
2.	Family Ties	NBC
3.	Murder, She Wrote	CBS
4.	60 Minutes	CBS
5.	Cheers	NBC
6.	Dallas	CBS
	Dynasty	ABC
	The Golden Girls	NBC
9.	Miami Vice	NBC
10.	Who's the Boss?	ABC
11.	Perfect Strangers	ABC
12.	Night Court	NBC
13.	The CBS Sunday Night Movie	CBS
14.	Highway to Heaven	NBC
	Kate and Allie	CBS
16.	NFL Monday Night Football	ABC
17.	Newhart	CBS
18.	Knots Landing	CBS
	Growing Pains	ABC
20.	227	NBC

September 1986 – April 1987

1.	The Bill Cosby Show	NBC
2.	Family Ties	NBC
3.	Cheers	NBC
4.	Murder, She Wrote	CBS
5.	Night Court (Thursday)	NBC
6.	The Golden Girls	NBC
7.	60 Minutes	CBS
8.	Growing Pains	ABC
9	Moonlighting	ABC
10.	Who's the Boss?	ABC
11.	Dallas	CBS
12.	Nothing in Common	NBC
13.	Newhart	CBS
14.	Amen	NBC
15.	227	NBC
16.	The CBS Sunday Movie	CBS
	Matlock	NBC
	NBC Monday Night Movies	NBC
19.	Kate and Allie	CBS
	NFL Monday Night Football	ABC

September 1987 – April 1988

1.	The Bill Cosby Show	NBC
2.	A Different World	NBC
3.	Cheers	NBC
4.	Growing Pains (Tuesday)	ABC
5.	Night Court (Thursday)	NBC
6.	The Golden Girls	NBC
7.	Who's the Boss?	ABC
8.	60 Minutes	CBS
9.	Murder, She Wrote	CBS
10.	The Wonder Years	ABC
11.	Alf	NBC
12.	Moonlighting	ABC
	L.A. Law	NBC
14.	NFL Monday Night Football	ABC
15.	Matlock	NBC

	Growing Pains (Wednesday)	ABC
17.	*Amen*	NBC
18.	*Family Ties*	NBC
19.	*Hunter* (Saturday)	NBC
20.	*The CBS Sunday Night Movie*	CBS

September 1988 – April 1989

1.	*Roseanne*	ABC
	The Bill Cosby Show	NBC
3.	*A Different World*	NBC
	Roseanne (8:30)	ABC
5.	*Cheers*	NBC
6.	*60 Minutes*	CBS
7.	*The Golden Girls*	NBC
8.	*Who's the Boss?*	ABC
9.	*The Wonder Years*	ABC
10.	*Murder, She Wrote*	CBS
11.	*Empty Nest*	NBC
12.	*Anything but Love*	ABC
13.	*Dear John*	NBC
14.	*Growing Pains*	ABC
15.	*Alf*	NBC
	L.A. Law	NBC
17.	*Matlock*	NBC
18.	*Hunter*	NBC
	Unsolved Mysteries	NBC
20.	*In the Heat of the Night*	NBC

September 1989 – April 1990

1.	*Roseanne*	ABC
2.	*The Bill Cosby Show*	NBC
3.	*Cheers*	NBC
4.	*A Different World*	NBC
5.	*America's Funniest Home Videos*	ABC
6.	*The Golden Girls*	NBC
7.	*60 Minutes*	CBS
8.	*The Wonder Years*	ABC
9.	*Empty Nest*	NBC
10.	*Chicken Soup*	ABC

Roseanne

11.	*NFL Monday Night Football*	ABC
12.	*Unsolved Mysteries*	NBC
13.	*Who's the Boss?*	ABC
14.	*L.A. Law*	NBC
	Murder, She Wrote	CBS
16.	*Grand*	NBC
17.	*In the Heat of the Night*	NBC
18.	*Dear John*	NBC
19.	*Coach*	ABC
20.	*Matlock*	NBC

September 1990 – April 1991

1.	*Cheers*	NBC
2.	*60 Minutes*	CBS
3.	*Roseanne*	ABC
4.	*A Different World*	NBC
5.	*The Bill Cosby Show*	NBC
6.	*NFL Monday Night Football*	ABC
7.	*America's Funniest Home Videos*	ABC
8.	*Murphy Brown*	CBS
9.	*America's Funniest People*	ABC
	Designing Women	CBS
	Empty Nest	NBC
12.	*The Golden Girls*	NBC
13.	*Murder, She Wrote*	CBS
14.	*Unsolved Mysteries*	NBC
15.	*Full House*	ABC
16.	*Family Matters*	ABC
17.	*Coach*	ABC
	Matlock	NBC
19.	*In the Heat of the Night*	NBC
20.	*Major Dad*	CBS

September 1991 – April 1992

1.	*60 Minutes*	CBS
2.	*Roseanne*	ABC
3.	*Murphy Brown*	CBS
4.	*Cheers*	NBC
5.	*Home Improvement*	ABC
6.	*Designing Women*	CBS
7.	*Coach*	ABC
8.	*Full House*	ABC
9.	*Murder, She Wrote*	CBS
10.	*Unsolved Mysteries*	NBC
11.	*Major Dad*	CBS
	NFL Monday Night Football	ABC
13.	*Room for Two*	ABC
14.	*The CBS Sunday Night Movie*	CBS
15.	*Evening Shade*	CBS
16.	*Northern Exposure*	CBS
17.	*A Different World*	NBC
18.	*The Bill Cosby Show*	NBC
19.	*Wings*	NBC
20.	*America's Funniest Home Videos*	ABC
	Fresh Prince of Bel Air	NBC

September 1992 – April 1993

1. *60 Minutes* .... CBS
2. *Roseanne* .... ABC
3. *Home Improvement* .... ABC
4. *Murphy Brown* .... CBS
5. *Murder, She Wrote* .... CBS
6. *Coach* .... ABC
7. *NFL Monday Night Football* .... ABC
8. *The CBS Sunday Night Movie* .... CBS
   Cheers .... NBC
10. *Full House* .... ABC
11. *Northern Exposure* .... CBS
12. *Rescue 911* .... CBS
13. *20/20* .... ABC
14. *The CBS Tuesday Night Movie* .... CBS
    Love and War .... CBS
16. *Fresh Prince of Bel Air* .... NBC
    Hangin' With Mr. Cooper .... ABC
    The Jackie Thomas Show .... ABC
19. *Evening Shade* .... CBS
20. *Hearts Afire* .... CBS
    Unsolved Mysteries .... NBC

September 1993 – April 1994

1. *Home Improvement* .... ABC
2. *60 Minutes* .... CBS
3. *Seinfeld* .... NBC
4. *Roseanne* .... ABC
5. *Ellen* .... ABC
6. *Grace Under Fire* .... ABC
7. *Frasier* .... NBC
8. *Coach* .... ABC
9. *Murder, She Wrote* .... CBS
10. *NFL Monday Night Football* .... ABC
11. *Murphy Brown* .... CBS
12. *The CBS Sunday Movie* .... CBS
13. *Thunder Alley* .... ABC
14. *20/20* .... ABC
15. *Love and War* .... CBS
16. *Northern Exposure* .... CBS
17. *Wings* .... NBC
18. *Full House* .... ABC
    PrimeTime Live .... ABC
20. *Dave's World* .... CBS

Broadcast Television Networks

ABC
Capital Cities/ABC Inc.
77 W. 66th St.
New York, NY 10023-6298
(212) 456-7777

CBS Inc.
51 W. 52nd St.
New York, NY 10019
(212) 975-4321

Fox Broadcasting Company
10201 W. Pico Blvd.
Los Angeles, CA 90035
(213) 203-3266

NBC
30 Rockefeller Plaza
New York, NY 10112
(212) 664-4444

Public Broadcasting Service
1320 Braddock Place
Alexandria, VA 22314-1698
(703) 739-5000

Telemundo Group Inc.
1740 Broadway
New York, NY 10019
(212) 492-5500

UPN (United Paramount Network)
5555 Melrose, MOB 1200
Los Angeles, CA 90038
(213) 956-5000

Univision
605 Third Ave., 12th Floor
New York, NY 10158-0180
(212) 455-5200

WB (Warner Bros. Television Network)
4000 Warner Blvd.
Building 34R
Burbank, CA 91522
(818) 954-2884

BROADCASTING TIME LINE

1897
K. F. Braun invents the cathode-ray tube.

1920
KDKA, a Westinghouse station, transmits the first commercial radio broadcast.

1926
RCA, General Electric and Westinghouse found NBC, which operates two national radio networks.

1928
John Baird beams a television image from England to the U.S. GE introduces a television set with a 3" x 4" screen. The first TV sold is a Daven; price: $75.

1936
The British Broadcasting Corporation (BBC) debuts the world's first television service, with three hours of programming a day.

1937
Eleven stations receive experimental broadcast licenses. One of the first demonstrations is a production of the Sherlock Holmes mystery, *The Three Garridebs*.

Cable Television Networks

American Movie Classics (AMC)
150 Crossways Park W.
Woodbury, NY 11797
(516) 364-2222
Uninterrupted classic movies from
Hollywood's golden age and original
classic-movie-related programming

America's Talking
2200 Fletcher Ave.
Ft. Lee, NJ 07024
(201) 585-2622
Around-the-clock talk on national issues

**A&E Network (formerly Arts &
Entertainment Network)**
235 E. 45th St.
New York, NY 10017
(212) 210-1328
Comedy, drama, documentaries and
performing-arts programming

Black Entertainment Television (BET)
1232 31st St. N.W.
Washington D.C. 20007
(202) 337-5260
African-American family programming,
including music, sports, children's
entertainment, news, public affairs and
specials

The Box
12000 Biscayne Blvd.
Miami, FL 33181
(305) 674-5000
Interactive music television programmed
by viewers

Bravo
150 Crossways Park W.
Woodbury, NY 11797
(516) 364-2222
Foreign and independent films and performing-arts programming

Cable Health Club
2877 Guardian Lane
Virginia Beach, VA 23452
(804) 459-6000
Exercise programs and tips for healthy
living

Canal de Noticias NBC
NBC News Channel
925 Wood Ridge Center Drive
Charlotte, NC 28217
(704) 329-8706
Spanish-language news service

Cartoon Network
Box 105264
1050 Techwood Drive N.W.
Atlanta, GA 30318
(404) 827-1717
Colorful animated entertainment from
the Turner Entertainment Co. and
Hanna-Barbera cartoon libraries

Cinemax
1100 Ave. of the Americas
New York, NY 10036
(212) 512-1000
Films and movie-based original programming (pay service)

Classic Sports Network
35 E. 21st St.
New York, NY 10010
(212) 529-8000
Great moments in sports history and
original programming

CMT: Country Music Television
Group W Satellite Communications
250 Harbor Drive, Box 10210
Stamford, CT 06904
(203) 965-6000
Country-music videos, interviews and
specials

CNBC
2200 Fletcher Ave.
Fort Lee, NJ 07024
(201) 585-2622
Fast-breaking business and market news,
consumer information and talk shows

CNN (Cable News Network)
P.O. Box 105366
One CNN Center
Atlanta, GA 30348-5366
(404) 827-1500
News and information programming

Comedy Central
1775 Broadway
New York, NY 10019
(212) 767-8600
Stand-up routines, movies, talk shows,
sitcoms, specials and classic series

Courtroom Television Network
600 Third Ave., 2nd Floor
New York, NY 10016
(212) 973-2800
Legal news, live and taped coverage of
trials and commentary

**C-SPAN/C-SPAN 2 (Cable Satellite
Public Affairs Network)**
400 N. Capitol St. N.W., Suite 650
Washington D.C. 20001
(202) 737-3220
Live gavel-to-gavel coverage of the U.S.
House of Representatives (C-SPAN) and
Senate (C-SPAN 2)

The Discovery Channel
7700 Wisconsin Ave.
Bethesda, MD 20814
(301) 986-1999
Nonfiction programming in science,
nature, history, adventure and world
exploration

1940
Color television is
demonstrated in New
York by CBS.

1941
The first commercial
broadcast station in
New York is WNBT. The
first sponsored quiz pro-
gram is *Uncle Jim's
Question Bee.*

1944
The first network censor-
ship occurs. The sound is
cut off on the Eddie
Cantor and Nora Martin
duet, "We're Having a
Baby, My Baby and Me."
The DuMont network
goes on the air.
Paramount Pictures
backs the start-up
enterprise, but its lack of
affiliated radio networks

leads to its early demise
in 1956.

1945
The Orthicon Tube,
developed by RCA,
improves light sensitivi-
ty by 100 times. The FCC
creates the commercial
broadcasting spectrum
of 13 channels. 130 applications for broadcast
licenses follow.

1950
Saturday morning
children's programming
begins.

1951
Phonevision, the first
pay-per-view service
debuts.

Disney Channel
3800 W. Alameda Ave.
Burbank, CA 91505
(818) 569-7500
Family entertainment, including movies
and specials (pay service)

E! Entertainment Television
5670 Wilshire Blvd.
Los Angeles, CA 90036-3709
(213) 954-2400
Interviews, news and media-savvy features from the entertainment world

Encore!
4700 S. Syracuse Parkway, Suite 1000
Denver, CO 80237-2721
(303) 771-7700
Uncut, unedited movies from 1960 to
1980 (pay service)

ESPN/ESPN 2
ESPN Plaza
Bristol, CT 06010
(203) 585-2000
Sports events, news and information

Eternal Word Television Network
5817 Old Leeds Road
Birmingham, AL 35210
(205) 965-0328
Catholic programming with talk shows,
television series and documentaries

Faith and Values Channel
305 Madison Ave.
New York, NY 10165
(212) 599-2760
Family and interfaith programming
including dramas, documentaries and
children's shows

Family Channel
1000 Centerville Turnpike
Virginia Beach, VA 23463
(804) 523-7301
Family fare including original films, dramatic and comedy series, classic westerns and inspirational programs

f/X
10201 W. Pico
Los Angeles, CA 90035
(310) 203-3474
Movies, television series and original
programming from Fox Broadcasting
and Twentieth Century-Fox

Galavision
6701 Center Drive W., 6th Floor
Los Angeles, CA 90045
(3001) 348-3640
Spanish-language programming including serials, music, movies and sports

Game Show Channel
3801 S. Sheridan
Tulsa, OK 74145
(918) 665-6690
Game shows and interactive games

The Golf Channel
7580 Commerce Center Drive
Orlando, FL 32819
(407) 363-4653
Live tournament coverage, instructional
programs, news and classic tournaments

HBO (Home Box Office)
1100 Ave. of the Americas
New York, NY 10036
(212) 512-1000
Movies, comedy specials, documentaries, sports, original movies and comedy series (pay service)

Headline News
One CNN Center
Atlanta, GA 30348
(404) 827-1500
News and information programming in
half-hour intervals

The History Channel
235 E. 45th St.
New York, NY 10017
(212) 661-4500
Documentaries, movies and original
programming highlighting historical
American events

Home and Garden Television
P.O. Box 50970
Knoxville, TN 37950
(615) 694-2700
Tips and how-to advice for the home
and garden

Home Shopping Network
Box 9090
Clearwater, FL 34618-9090
(813) 572-8585
Televised shopping

Independent Film Channel
150 Crossways Park W.
Woodbury, NY 11797
(516) 364-2222
Films produced outside the Hollywood
studio system

INSP — The Inspirational Network
9700 Southern Pine Blvd.
Charlotte, NC 28273
(704) 525-9800
Movies, talk shows, music programs and
children's shows for those who embrace
family and Judeo-Christian values

International Channel
12401 West Olympic Blvd.
Los Angeles, CA 90064
(310) 826-2429
Foreign-language news, sports, drama
and comedy from around the world

Jones Computer Network
9697 E. Mineral Ave.
Englewood, CO 80112
(303) 792-3111
Original programming related to hardware, software, interactive media, multimedia and on-line services

Kaleidoscope Television
1777 N.E. Loop 410, Suite 301
San Antonio, TX 78217
(210) 824-7446
Programming for people with disabilities

The Learning Channel
7700 Wisconsin Ave.
Bethesda, MD 20814-3539
(301) 986-1999
Adult learning and enrichment programs,
documentaries and educational series

1952

**Leonard Nimoy appears
in a science fiction
series. No, not that one.**
In *Zombies of the
Stratosphere,* Nimoy por-
trays the Martian, Narab.

1953

**Loretta Young abandons
Hollywood for her
stylish debut on the
small screen.**

**The first issue of *TV
Guide* magazine hits the
stands.** The perennial circulation chart topper
debuts on April 3rd in 10
cities with a circulation of
1,560,000. The average TV
household received 3.8
channels.
Lucy has a baby. One of
the most watched events
in TV history is the debut
of Little Ricky on the

I Love Lucy episode of
January 19th.

1954

**The revenues for televi-
sion broadcasters final-
ly surpass those of
radio broadcasters.**
Gross revenues for tele-
vision are $593 million.

1955

**Color television is avail-
able every night.**
NBC broadcasts the
World Series in color for
the first time.
The first watch is tested
for durability on camera.
And it is a Bulova, not a
Timex. The timepiece is
attached to a ball and
hurled over Niagara
Falls.

Lifetime
Lifetime Astoria Studios
36–12 35th Ave.
Astoria, NY 11106
(718) 482-4000
Contemporary programming of interest
to women

The Military Channel
1230 Liberty Bank Lane, Suite 320
Louisville, KY 40222
(502) 425-8161
Military-related movies, documentaries
and home shopping

Mind Extension University (ME/U)
9697 E. Mineral Ave.
Englewood, CO 80155
(303) 792-5808
Innovative use of interactive distance-
learning for college- and graduate-level
education

MOR Music
11500 Ninth St. N.
St. Petersburg, FL 33716
(813) 579-4600
Videos and music shopping

The Movie Channel (TMC)
1633 Broadway, 37th Floor
New York, NY 10019
(212) 708-1600
Movies and movie-related programming
(pay service)

MTV
1515 Broadway
New York, NY 10036
(212) 258-7800
Music videos, music news, interviews
and original programming

Much Music
150 Crossways Park W.
Woodbury, NY 11797
(516) 364-2222
Music videos and more

NASA Select Television
400 Maryland Ave. S.W.
Washington D.C. 20546
(202) 453-8425
Lift-off-to-landing coverage of NASA
missions, plus press conferences and
public-affairs programming

NewSport
150 Crossways Park W.
Woodbury, NY 11797
(516) 364-2222
News and talk shows covering regional
and national sports with continuous
boxscores

NewsTalk Television
303 W. 34th St., 12th Floor
New York, NY 10001
(212) 634-2200
Interactive talk shows covering current
events

Nickelodeon/Nick at Night
1515 Broadway
New York, NY 10036
(212) 258-8000
Programming for children during the
day and classic television at night

Nostalgia Television
650 Massachusetts Ave. N.W.
Washington D.C. 20001
(202) 289-6633
Classic movies and television series

Playboy Channel
9242 Beverly Blvd.
Beverly Hills, CA 90210
(310) 246-4000
Adult entertainment especially for men
(pay service)

Popcorn Channel
TriBeCa Film Center
375 Greenwich St.
New York, NY 10013
(212) 941-2419
Full-length trailers for current and upcoming movies and local theater listings

Prevue Networks
3801 S. Sheridan
Tulsa, OK 74145
(918) 664-5566
Listing of basic, pay and pay-per-view
programming

Prime Sports Channel Networks
150 Crossways Park W.
Woodbury, NY 11797
(516) 364-2222
National cable service that distributes
sports programming to regional networks

QVC Network
Goshen Corporate Park
1365 Enterprise Drive
West Chester, PA 19380
(215) 430-1000
Televised shopping

Sci-Fi Channel
1230 Ave. of the Americas
New York, NY 10020
(212) 408-9100
Science-fiction, fantasy and horror
programming

The Sega Channel
1633 Broadway, 40th Floor
New York, NY 10019
(212) 767-4600
Video games on demand (pay service)

Showtime
1633 Broadway, 37th Floor
New York, NY 10019
(212) 708-1600
Movies, variety and comedy series,
sports and original movies and specials
(pay service)

SportsChannel
150 Crossways Park W.
Woodbury, NY 11797
(516) 364-2222
Sports programming. Regional networks
feature local teams

TBS (Turner Broadcasting System)
P.O. Box 105366
One CNN Center
Atlanta, GA 30348-1947
(404) 827-1700
Original documentaries, exclusive sports,
specials, comedy series and movies

TCM (Turner Classic Movies)
P.O. Box 105366
One CNN Center
Atlanta, GA 30348-1947
(404) 827-1700
Classic movies from the MGM/United
Artists library

1956
Gone With the Wind is
broadcast on TV for the
first time. Fifty-two percent of TV households
watch.

1959
Rumors of cheating on
quiz shows erupt into a
national scandal.

1962
The first transatlantic
television transmission
occurs via the Telestar
Satellite, making world-
wide TV and cable net-
works a reality.

1963
Viewers of NBC-TV wit-
ness Jack Ruby shoot
Lee Harvey Oswald live
on TV — the first live
telecast of a murder.

1966
The first *Star Trek*
episode is broadcast.
"The Man Trap" is pre-
sented as a preview on
September 8. The plot
concerns concerned a
creature that sucks salt
from human bodies.

1967
PBS is formed.

1969
The FCC bans all ciga-
rette advertising on TV
and radio.

1970
FCC regulations require
separate ownership of
the TV networks and
studios.

Telemundo Group Inc.
1740 Broadway
New York, NY 10019
(212) 492-5500
Spanish-language programming featuring movies, novellas, sports and news

Television Food Network
1177 Ave. of the Americas, 31st Floor
New York, NY 10036
(212) 398-8836
Food and food-related programming including nutrition, health and fitness

TNN: The Nashville Network
Box 10210
250 Harbor Plaza Drive
Stamford, CT 06904-2210
(203) 965-6000
Country music entertainment, auto and outdoor sports, news and country-lifestyle programming

TNT: Turner Network Television
1050 Techwood Drive N.W.
Atlanta, GA 30318
(404) 885-2402
Classic movies, original movies and mini-series, sports and children's programming

Travel Channel
2690 Cumberland Parkway, Suite 500
Atlanta, GA 30339
(404) 801-2400
A look at worldwide destinations and travel news

Trinity Broadcasting Network (TBN)
2528 US 31 S.
Greenwood, IN 46143
(317) 535-5542
Around-the-clock religious and inspirational programming

Univision
605 Third Ave.
New York, NY 10158
(212) 455-5200
Spanish-language programming featuring movies, novellas, sports and news

USA Network
1230 Ave. of the Americas
New York, NY 10020
(212) 408-9100
Movies and television series, teen and children's programming and sports specials

VH1
1515 Broadway
New York, NY 10036
(212) 258-7860
Music videos, entertainment news and specials

Video Jukebox
12000 Biscayne Blvd.
Miami, FL 33181
(305) 899-9000
Music videos programmed by local viewers

Weather Channel
2600 Cumberland Parkway
Atlanta, GA 30339
(404) 434-6800
Around-the-clock updates on local, national and worldwide weather conditions

WGN
3801 S. Sheridan Blvd.
Tulsa, OK 74145
(918) 665-6690
Chicago superstation with sports, movies and television series

WPIX
3801 S. Sheridan Blvd.
Tulsa, OK 74145
(918) 665-6690
New York superstation with sports, movies and television series

WWOR/EMI Communications Corp.
P.O. Box 4872
Syracuse, NY 13221
(315) 433-0022
Programming from the 1960s and 1970s and coverage of the New York Mets

ZTV Music Network
15 E. Ohio Ave.
Lake Helen, FL 32744
(904) 228-1000
Christian music videos

National Public Radio Suppliers

National Public Radio
635 Massachusetts Ave. N.W.
Washington D.C. 20001-3753
(202) 414-2000

Pacifica
702 H St. N.W.
Washington D.C. 20001
(202) 783-3100

Public Radio International
100 N. Sixth St., Suite 900A
Minneapolis, MN 55403
(612) 338-5000

1972
Time Inc. transmits over satellite HBO, the first pay cable network.

1974
Ted Turner begins his foray into television when he buys a foundering Atlanta TV station and parlays it into a cable empire.

1975
ABC, CBS and NBC agree to create a "family hour," an early evening time slot that is free of violence and sex.

1986
Barry Diller, then of News Corp., creates Fox, the fourth television network. Fox offers 10 hours of prime-time programming a week.

1992
There are 900 million television sets in use around the world. 201 million are in the U.S.

1995
The price for television commercial time hits an all-time high. Advertisers pays an average of $1 million for a 30-second spot during the broadcast of Superbowl XXIX. Congress is on the verge of passing legislation that will significantly deregulate telecommunications, creating almost limitless opportunities for broadcasters and cable companies.

National Public Radio U.S. Member Stations

STATION	CITY	FREQUENCY
ALABAMA		
WBHM-FM	Birmingham	90.3
WRWA-FM	Dothan	88.7
WSGN-FM	Gadsden	91.5
WLRH-FM	Huntsville	89.3
WLJS-FM	Jacksonville	91.9
WTSU-FM	Montgomery/Troy	89.9
WQPR-FM	Muscle Shoals	88.7
WJAB-FM	Normal	90.9
WUAL-FM	Tuscaloosa	91.5
ALASKA		
KSKA-FM	Anchorage	91.1
KBRW-AM	Barrow	680
KYUK-AM	Bethel	640
KUAC-FM	Fairbanks	104.7
KIYU-AM	Galena	910
KHNS-FM	Haines	102.3
KBBI-AM	Homer	890
KTOO-FM	Juneau	104.3
KCZP-FM	Kenai	91.9
KRBD-FM	Ketchikan	105.9
KMXT-FM	Kodiak	100.1
KFSK-FM	Petersburg	100.9
KCAW-FM	Sitka	104.7
KTNA-FM	Talkeetna	88.5
KCHU-AM	Valdez	770
ARIZONA		
KNAU-FM	Flagstaff	88.7
KJZZ-FM	Phoenix	91.5
KBAQ-FM	Mesa	89.5
KGHR-FM	Tuba City	91.5
KUAT-AM	Tucson	1550
KUAZ-FM	Tucson	89.1
KAWC-AM	Yuma	1320
KAWC-FM	Yuma	88.9
ARKANSAS		
KBSA-FM	El Dorado	90.9
KUAF-FM	Fayetteville	91.3
KUAR-FM	Little Rock	89.1
KLRE-FM	Little Rock	90.5
KASU-FM	State University	91.9
CALIFORNIA		
KHSU-FM	Arcata	90.5
KPRX-FM	Bakersfield	89.1
KNCA-FM	Burney	89.7
KCHO-FM	Chico	91.7
KUBO-FM	Fresno	88.7
KVPR-FM	Fresno	89.3
KXSR-FM	Groveland	91.7

STATION	CITY	FREQUENCY
KCRY-FM	Indio	89.3
KNSQ-FM	Mt. Shasta	88.1
KCRU-FM	Oxnard	89.1
KPCC-FM	Pasadena	89.3
KZYX-FM	Philo	90.7
KFPR-FM	Redding	88.9
KXPR-FM	Sacramento	90.9
KXJZ-FM	Sacramento	88.9
KVCR-FM	San Bernardino	91.9
KPBS-FM	San Diego	89.5
KALW-FM	San Francisco	91.7
KQED-FM	San Francisco	88.5
KCBX-FM	San Luis Obispo	90.1
KUSP-FM	Santa Cruz	88.9
KCRW-FM	Santa Monica	89.9
KUOP-FM	Stockton	91.3
COLORADO		
KRZA-FM	Alamosa	88.7
KAJX-FM	Aspen	91.5
KGNU-FM	Boulder	88.5
KDNK-FM	Carbondale	90.5
KRCC-FM	Colorado Springs	91.5
KSJD-FM	Cortez	91.5
KBUT-FM	Crested Butte	90.3
KUVO-FM	Denver	89.3
KCFR-FM	Denver	90.1
KPRN-FM	Grand Junction	89.5
KUNC-FM	Greeley	91.5
KSUT-FM	Ignacio	91.3
KVNF-FM	Paonia	90.9
KOTO-FM	Telluride	91.7
CONNECTICUT		
WSHU-FM	Fairfield	91.1
WPKT-FM	Hartford	90.5
WNPR-FM	Norwich	89.1
WEDW-FM	Stamford	88.5
WECS-FM	Willimantic	90.1
DISTRICT OF COLUMBIA		
WAMU-FM	Washington	88.5
WDCU-FM	Washington	90.1
WETA-FM	Arlington, VA	90.9
FLORIDA		
WSFP-FM	Fort Myers	90.1
WQCS-FM	Fort Pierce	88.9
WUFT-FM	Gainesville	89.1
WJCT-FM	Jacksonville	89.9
WLRN-FM	Miami	91.3
WUCF-FM	Orlando	89.9
WMFE-FM	Orlando	90.7
WKGC-FM	Panama City	90.7
WKGC-AM	Panama City	1480

STATION	CITY	FREQUENCY
WUWF-FM	Pensacola	88.1
WFSU-FM	Tallahassee	88.9
WFSQ-FM	Tallahassee	91.5
WUSF-FM	Tampa	89.7
WXEL-FM	West Palm Beach	90.7

GEORGIA

STATION	CITY	FREQUENCY
WUNV-FM	Albany	91.7
WUGA-FM	Athens	91.7
WCLK-FM	Atlanta	91.9
WABE-FM	Atlanta	90.1
WJSP-FM	Atlanta	88.1
WACG-FM	Augusta	90.7
WWIO-FM	Brunswick	89.1
WTJB-FM	Columbus	91.7
WJWV-FM	Ft. Gaines	90.9
WDCO-FM	Macon	89.7
WSVH-FM	Savannah	91.1
WABR-FM	Tifton	91.1
WWET-FM	Valdosta	91.7
WXVS-FM	Waycross	90.1

HAWAII

STATION	CITY	FREQUENCY
KHPR-FM	Honolulu	88.1
KIPO-FM	Honolulu	89.3
KIFO-AM	Pearl City	1380
KKUA-FM	Wailuku	90.7

IDAHO

STATION	CITY	FREQUENCY
KBSU-FM	Boise	90.3
KBSU-AM	Boise	730
KBSX-FM	Boise	91.5
KNWO-FM	Cottonwood	90.1
KBSM-FM	McCall	91.7
KRFA-FM	Moscow	91.7
KRIC-FM	Rexburg	100.5
KBSW-FM	Twin Falls	91.7

ILLINOIS

STATION	CITY	FREQUENCY
WSIU-FM	Carbondale	91.9
WBEZ-FM	Chicago	91.5
WNIU-FM	DeKalb	89.5
WSIE-FM	Edwardsville	88.7
WIUM-FM	Macomb	91.3
WGLT-FM	Normal	89.1
WUSI-FM	Olney	90.3
WCBU-FM	Peoria	89.9
WIPA-FM	Pittsfield	89.3
WQUB-FM	Quincy	90.3
WVIK-FM	Rock Island	90.3
WNIJ-FM	Rockford	90.5
WSSU-FM	Springfield	91.9
WILL-FM	Urbana	90.9
WILL-AM	Urbana	580

INDIANA

STATION	CITY	FREQUENCY
WFIU-FM	Bloomington	103.7
WVPE-FM	Elkhart	88.1
WNIN-FM	Evansville	88.3
WBNI-FM	Fort Wayne	89.1
WFYI-FM	Indianapolis	90.1
WBST-FM	Muncie	92.1
WBKE-FM	North Manchester	89.5
WVXR-FM	Richmond	89.3

IOWA

STATION	CITY	FREQUENCY
WOI-FM	Ames	90.1
WOI-AM	Ames	640
KUNI-FM	Cedar Falls	90.9
KCCK-FM	Cedar Rapids	88.3
KIWR-FM	Council Bluffs	89.7
KLNI-FM	Decorah	88.7
KTPR-FM	Fort Dodge	91.1
WSUI-AM	Iowa City	910
KUNY-FM	Mason City	91.5
KWIT-FM	Sioux City	90.3

KANSAS

STATION	CITY	FREQUENCY
KANZ-FM	Garden City	91.1
KHCT-FM	Great Bend	90.9
KZNA-FM	Hill City	90.5
KHCC-FM	Hutchinson	90.1
KANU-FM	Lawrence	91.5
KRPS-FM	Pittsburg	89.9
KHCD-FM	Salina	89.5
KMUW-FM	Wichita	89.1

KENTUCKY

STATION	CITY	FREQUENCY
WKYU-FM	Bowling Green	88.9
WKUE-FM	Elisabethtown	90.9
WEKH-FM	Hazard	90.9
WKPB-FM	Henderson	89.5
WNKU-FM	Highland Heights	89.7
WUKY-FM	Lexington	91.3
WFPL-FM	Louisville	89.3
WMKY-FM	Morehead	90.3
WKMS-FM	Murray	91.3
WEKU-FM	Richmond	88.9
WDCL-FM	Somerset	89.7

LOUISIANA

STATION	CITY	FREQUENCY
KLSA-FM	Alexandria	90.7
WBRH-FM	Baton Rouge	90.3
WRKF-FM	Baton Rouge	89.3
KRVS-FM	Lafayette	88.7
KEDM-FM	Monroe	90.3
WWNO-FM	New Orleans	89.9
KDAQ-FM	Shreveport	89.9

MAINE

STATION	CITY	FREQUENCY
WMEH-FM	Bangor	90.9
WMED-FM	Calais	89.7
WMEA-FM	Portland	90.1
WMEM-FM	Presque Isle	106.1
WMEW-FM	Waterville	91.3

MARYLAND

STATION	CITY	FREQUENCY
WEAA-FM	Baltimore	88.9
WJHU-FM	Baltimore	88.1
WETH-FM	Hagerstown	89.1

STATION	CITY	FREQUENCY
WESM-FM	Princess Anne	91.3
WSCL-FM	Salisbury	89.5

MASSACHUSETTS

STATION	CITY	FREQUENCY
WFCR-FM	Amherst	88.5
WKKL-FM	Barnstable	90.7
WGBH-FM	Boston	89.7
WBUR-FM	Boston	90.9
WAMQ-FM	Gt. Barrington	105.1
WCCT-FM	Harwich	90.3
WSDH-FM	Sandwich	91.5
WICN-FM	Worcester	90.5

MICHIGAN

STATION	CITY	FREQUENCY
WCML-FM	Alpena	91.7
WUOM-FM	Ann Arbor	91.7
WUCX-FM	Bay City	90.1
WDET-FM	Detroit	101.9
WIZY-FM	East Jordan	100.9
WKAR-AM	East Lansing	870
WKAR-FM	East Lansing	90.5
WFUM-FM	Flint	91.1
WGVU-AM	Grand Rapids	1480
WGVU-FM	Grand Rapids	88.5
WVGR-FM	Grand Rapids	104.1
WGGL-FM	Houghton	91.1
WCMW-FM	Harbor Springs	103.9
WIAA-FM	Interlochen	88.7
WMUK-FM	Kalamazoo	102.1
WNMU-FM	Marquette	90.1
WCMU-FM	Mount Pleasant	89.5
WCMZ-FM	Sault Sainte Marie	98.3
WBLV-FM	Twin Lake	90.3
WEMU-FM	Ypsilanti	89.1

MINNESOTA

STATION	CITY	FREQUENCY
KRSU-FM	Appleton	91.3
KMSK-FM	Austin	91.3
KCRB-FM	Bimidji	88.5
KBPR-FM	Brainerd	90.7
WIRR-FM	Buhl	90.9
KNSR-FM	Collegeville	88.9
WSCN-FM	Duluth	100.9
KAXE-FM	Grand Rapids	91.7
KXLC-FM	La Crescent	91.1
KMSU-FM	Mankato	89.7
KNOW-FM	Minneapolis/St. Paul	91.1
WCAL-FM	Minneapolis/St. Paul	89.3
KCCD-FM	Moorhead	90.3
KZSE-FM	Rochester	90.7
KNGA-FM	St. Peter	91.5
KNTN-FM	Thief River Falls	102.7
KRSW-FM	Worthington	91.7

MISSISSIPPI

STATION	CITY	FREQUENCY
WMAH-FM	Biloxi	90.3
WMAE-FM	Booneville	89.5
WMAU-FM	Bude	88.9
WMAO-FM	Greenwood	90.9
WURC-FM	Holly Springs	88.1
WJSU-FM	Jackson	88.5
WMPN-FM	Jackson	91.3
WPRL-FM	Lorman	91.7
WMAW-FM	Meridian	88.1
WMAB-FM	Mississippi State	89.9
WMAV-FM	Oxford	90.3
WNJC-FM	Senatobia	88.9

MISSOURI

STATION	CITY	FREQUENCY
KRCU-FM	Cape Girardeau	90.9
KBIA-FM	Columbia	91.3
KCUR-FM	Kansas City	89.3
KXCV-FM	Maryville	90.5
KCOZ-FM	Pt. Lookout	90.5
KUMR-FM	Rolla	88.5
KSMU-FM	Springfield	91.1
KWMU-FM	St. Louis	90.7
KCMW-FM	Warrensburg	90.9

MONTANA

STATION	CITY	FREQUENCY
KEMC-FM	Billings	91.7
KBMC-FM	Bozeman	102.1
KGPR-FM	Great Falls	89.9
KNMC-FM	Havre	90.1
KECC-FM	Miles City	90.7
KUFM-FM	Missoula	89.1

NEBRASKA

STATION	CITY	FREQUENCY
KTNE-FM	Alliance	91.1
KMNE-FM	Bassett	90.3
KCNE-FM	Chadron	91.9
KHNE-FM	Hastings	89.1
KLNE-FM	Lexington	88.7
KUCV-FM	Lincoln	90.9
KRNE-FM	Merriman	91.5
KXNE-FM	Norfolk	89.3
KPNE-FM	North Platte	91.7
KIOS-FM	Omaha	91.5

NEVADA

STATION	CITY	FREQUENCY
KNCC-FM	Elko	91.5
KNPR-FM	Las Vegas	89.5
KCEP-FM	Las Vegas	88.1
KLNR-FM	Panaca	91.7
KUNR-FM	Reno	88.7
KTPH-FM	Tonopah	91.7

NEW HAMPSHIRE

STATION	CITY	FREQUENCY
WEVO-FM	Concord	89.1
WEVH-FM	Hanover	91.3

NEW JERSEY

STATION	CITY	FREQUENCY
WBGO-FM	Newark	88.3

NEW MEXICO

STATION	CITY	FREQUENCY
KUNM-FM	Albuquerque	89.9
KGLP-FM	Gallup	91.7
KRWG-FM	Las Cruces	90.7
KMTH-FM	Maljamar	98.7

STATION	CITY	FREQUENCY
KTDB-FM	Pine Hill	89.7
KENW-FM	Portales	89.5

NEW YORK

STATION	CITY	FREQUENCY
WAMC-FM	Albany	90.3
WALF-FM	Alfred	89.7
WSKG-FM	Binghamton	89.3
WXLH-FM	Blue Mountain Lake	89.9
WNED-AM	Buffalo	970
WBFO-FM	Buffalo	88.7
WOLN-FM	Buffalo	91.3
WCAN-FM	Canajoharie	93.3
WSLU-FM	Canton	89.5
WEOS-FM	Geneva	89.7
WSQG-FM	Ithaca	90.9
WJFF-FM	Jeffersonville	90.5
WAMK-FM	Kingston	90.9
WSLO-FM	Malone	90.9
WOSR-FM	Middletown	91.7
WNYC-AM	New York	820
WNYC-FM	New York	93.9
WSQC-FM	Oneonta	91.7
WRVO-FM	Oswego	89.9
WXLU-FM	Peru	88.3
WCFE-FM	Plattsburgh	91.9
WRHV-FM	Poughkeepsie	88.7
WXXI-AM	Rochester	1370
WSLL-FM	Saranac Lake	90.5
WMHT-FM	Schenectady	89.1
WCNY-FM	Syracuse	91.3
WAER-FM	Syracuse	88.3
WANC-FM	Ticonderoga	103.9
WRVN-FM	Utica	91.9
WUNY-FM	Utica	89.5
WJNY-FM	Watertown	90.9
WRVJ-FM	Watertown	91.7
WSLJ-FM	Watertown	88.5

NORTH CAROLINA

STATION	CITY	FREQUENCY
WCQS-FM	Asheville	88.1
WUNC-FM	Chapel Hill	91.5
WFAE-FM	Charlotte	90.7
WFSS-FM	Fayetteville	89.1
WFQS-FM	Franklin	91.3
WTEB-FM	New Bern	89.3
WESQ-FM	Rocky Mount	90.9
WNCW-FM	Spindale	88.7
WHQR-FM	Wilmington	91.3
WFDD-FM	Winston-Salem	88.5

NORTH DAKOTA

STATION	CITY	FREQUENCY
KEYA-FM	Belcourt	88.5
KCND-FM	Bismarck	90.5
KDPR-FM	Dickinson	89.9
KDSU-FM	Fargo	91.9
KFJM-FM	Grand Forks	89.3
KFJM-AM	Grand Forks	1370
KMPR-FM	Minot	88.9
KPPR-FM	Williston	89.5
KPRJ-FM	Ypsilanti	93.5

OHIO

STATION	CITY	FREQUENCY
WOUB-FM	Athens	91.3
WOUB-AM	Athens	1340
WOUC-FM	Cambridge	89.1
WOUH-FM	Chillicothe	91.9
WVXC-FM	Chillicothe	89.3
WVXU-FM	Cincinnati	91.7
WGUC-FM	Cincinnati	90.9
WCPN-FM	Cleveland	90.3
WOSU-AM	Columbus	820
WCBE-FM	Columbus	90.5
WOUL-FM	Ironton	89.1
WKSU-FM	Kent	89.7
WGLE-FM	Lima	90.7
WMUB-FM	Oxford	88.5
WGTE-FM	Toledo	91.3
WVXM-FM	West Union	89.5
WKRW-FM	Wooster	89.3
WYSO-FM	Yellow Springs	91.3
WYSU-FM	Youngstown	88.5
WOUZ-FM	Zanesville	90.1

OKLAHOMA

STATION	CITY	FREQUENCY
KCCU-FM	Lawton	89.3
KGOU-FM	Norman	106.3
KROU-FM	Oklahoma City	105.7
KOSU-FM	Stillwater	91.7
KWGS-FM	Tulsa	89.5

OREGON

STATION	CITY	FREQUENCY
KSMF-FM	Ashland	89.1
KSOR-FM	Ashland	90.1
KMUN-FM	Astoria	91.9
KOAB-FM	Bend	91.3
KSBA-FM	Coos Bay	88.5
KLCC-FM	Eugene	89.7
KAGI-AM	Grants Pass	930
KSKF-FM	Klamath Falls	90.9
KLCO-FM	Newport	90.5
KRBM-FM	Pendleton	90.9
KOAC-AM	Portland	550
KOPB-FM	Portland	91.5
KBPS-AM	Portland	1450
KSRS-FM	Roseburg	91.5

PENNSYLVANIA

STATION	CITY	FREQUENCY
WQLN-FM	Erie	91.3
WITF-FM	Harrisburg	89.5
WJAZ-FM	Harrisburg	91.7
WRTY-FM	Mt. Pocono	91.1
WRTI-FM	Philadelphia	90.1
WHYY-FM	Philadelphia	90.9
WDUQ-FM	Pittsburgh	90.5
WVIA-FM	Scranton	89.9
WPSU-FM	State College	91.9

SOUTH CAROLINA

STATION	CITY	FREQUENCY
WLJK-FM	Aiken	89.1
WJWJ-FM	Beaufort	89.9
WSCI-FM	Charleston	89.3
WLTR-FM	Columbia	91.3

STATION	CITY	FREQUENCY
WHMC-FM	Conway	90.1
WEPR-FM	Greenville/Clemson	90.1
WSSB-FM	Orangeburg	90.3
WNSC-FM	Rock Hill	88.9
WRJA-FM	Sumter	88.1

SOUTH DAKOTA

STATION	CITY	FREQUENCY
KESD-FM	Brookings	88.3
KPSD-FM	Faith	97.1
KQSD-FM	Lowry	91.9
KZSD-FM	Martin	102.5
KDSD-FM	Pierpont	90.9
KBHE-FM	Rapid City	89.3
KTSD-FM	Reliance	91.1
KRSD-FM	Sioux Falls	88.1
KCSD-FM	Sioux Falls	90.9
KUSD-AM	Vermillion	690
KUSD-FM	Vermillion	89.7

TENNESSEE

STATION	CITY	FREQUENCY
WUTC-FM	Chattanooga	88.1
WSMC-FM	Collegedale	90.5
WKNQ-FM	Dyersberg	90.7
WKNP-FM	Jackson	90.1
WETS-FM	Johnson City	89.5
WUOT-FM	Knoxville	91.9
WKNO-FM	Memphis	91.1
WMOT-FM	Murfreesboro	89.5
WPLN-FM	Nashville	90.3

TEXAS

STATION	CITY	FREQUENCY
KACU-FM	Abilene	89.7
KUT-FM	Austin	90.5
KVLU-FM	Beaumont	91.3
KAMU-FM	College Station	90.9
KEDT-FM	Corpus Christi	90.3
KERA-FM	Dallas	90.1
KTEP-FM	El Paso	88.5
KMBH-FM	Harlingen	88.9
KUHF-FM	Houston	88.7
KOHM-FM	Lubbock	89.1
KHID-FM	McAllen	88.1
KOCV-FM	Odessa	91.3
KLDN-FM	Redland	88.9
KSTX-FM	San Antonio	89.1
KTXK-FM	Texarkana	91.5

UTAH

STATION	CITY	FREQUENCY
KUSU-FM	Logan	91.5
KPCW-FM	Park City	91.9
KBYU-FM	Provo	89.1
KUER-FM	Salt Lake City	90.1
KCPW-FM	Salt Lake City	88.3

VERMONT

STATION	CITY	FREQUENCY
WVPS-FM	Burlington	107.9
WRVT-FM	Rutland	88.7
WVPR-FM	Colchester	89.5

VIRGINIA

STATION	CITY	FREQUENCY
WVTU-FM	Charlottesville	89.3
WMRA-FM	Harrisonburg	90.7
WMRL-FM	Lexington	89.9
WVTR-FM	Marion	91.9
WHRV-FM	Norfolk	89.5
WHRO-FM	Norfolk	90.3
WCVE-FM	Richmond	88.9
WVTF-FM	Roanoke	89.1

WASHINGTON

STATION	CITY	FREQUENCY
KZAZ-FM	Bellingham	91.7
KNWR-FM	Ellensburg	90.7
KWSU-AM	Pullman	1250
KFAE-FM	Richland	89.1
KUOW-FM	Seattle	94.9
KPBX-FM	Spokane	91.1
KPLU-FM	Tacoma	88.5
KNWY-FM	Yakima	90.3

WEST VIRGINIA

STATION	CITY	FREQUENCY
WVPB-FM	Beckley	91.7
WVPW-FM	Buckhannon	88.9
WVPN-FM	Charleston	88.5
WVWV-FM	Huntington	89.9
WVEP-FM	Martinsburg	88.9
WVPM-FM	Morgantown	90.9
WVPG-FM	Parkersburg	90.3
WVNP-FM	Wheeling	89.9

WISCONSIN

STATION	CITY	FREQUENCY
WLFM-FM	Appleton	91.1
WLBL-AM	Auburndale	930
WHSA-FM	Brule	89.9
WHAD-FM	Delafield	90.7
WUEC-FM	Eau Claire	89.7
WGBW-FM	Green Bay	91.5
WPNE-FM	Green Bay	89.3
WOJB-FM	Hayward	88.9
WHHI-FM	Highland	91.3
WGTD-FM	Kenosha	91.1
WLSU-FM	La Crosse	88.9
WHLA-FM	La Crosse	90.3
WHA-AM	Madison	970
WERN-FM	Madison	88.7
WHWC-FM	Menomonee	88.3
WVSS-FM	Menomonee	90.7
WUWM-FM	Milwaukee	89.7
WRST-FM	Oshkosh	90.3
WHBM-FM	Park Falls	90.3
WXPR-FM	Rhinelander	91.7
KUWS-FM	Superior	91.3
WHRM-FM	Wausau	90.9

WYOMING

STATION	CITY	FREQUENCY
KUWJ-FM	Jackson	90.3
KUWR-FM	Laramie	91.9

National Radio Networks

ABC
Capital Cities/ABC Inc.
77 W. 66th St.
New York, NY 10023-6298
(212) 456-7777

ABC Radio Network
13725 Montfort Drive
Dallas, TX 75240
(214) 991-9200
(800) 527-4892

American Urban Radio Networks
463 Seventh Ave.
New York, NY 10018
(212) 714-1000

Associated Press Network News
Associated Press Broadcast Division
1825 K St. N.W.
Washington D.C. 20006-1253
(800) 821-4747
(202) 736-1100

Bloomberg Business News Radio Network
499 Park Ave.
New York, NY 10022
(800) 448-5678

Business Radio
5025 Centennial Blvd.
Colorado Springs, CO 80919
(719) 528-7040

CBS Radio Network
51 W. 52nd St.
New York, NY 10019
(212) 975-4468

CNN Radio Network
One CNN Center
Box 105366
Atlanta, GA 30348-5366
(404) 827-2750

United Press International
1400 Eye St. N.W.
Washington D.C. 20005
(202) 898-8000
(800) 492-6924

USA Radio Network
2290 Springlake Road, Suite 107
Dallas, TX 75234
(214) 484-3900
(800) 829-8111

Wall Street Journal Radio Network/Dow Jones Radio Network
World Financial Center
200 Liberty St., 12th Floor
New York, NY 10281
(212) 416-2116

Westwood One
9540 Washington Blvd.
Culver City, CA 90232
(310) 204-5000

Television and Radio Magazines and Journals

A&E Monthly
235 E. 45th St.
New York, NY 10019
(212) 210-9722

American Movie Classics Magazine
Working Media, Inc.
18 Shawmut St.
Boston, MA 02116
(800) 669-1002

Billboard
Billboard Publications, Inc.
1515 Broadway, 15th Floor
New York, NY 10036
(212) 764-7300

Broadcasting and Cable Yearbook
R.R. Bowker
121 Chanlon Road
New Providence, NJ 07974-1541
(908) 665-2823

The Cable Guide
(Cable Today/The Cable Guide)
TVSM
309 Lakeside Drive
Horsham, PA 19044-2313
(215) 443-9300

Daytime T.V.
Sterling's Magazines, Inc.
233 Park Ave. S.
New York, NY 10003
(212) 780-3500

Destination Discovery
(TDC Magazine)
Discovery Communications Inc.
7700 Wisconsin Ave.
Bethesda, MD 20814-3578
(800) 769-5908

Disney Channel Magazine
3800 W. Alameda Ave.
Burbank, CA 91505-4398
(818) 569-7797

Entertainment Weekly
1675 Broadway
New York, NY 10019
(212) 522-5600

Multichannel News
Capital Cities/ABC Inc.
825 Seventh Ave.
New York, NY 10022
(212) 887-8387

Radio and Records
10100 Santa Monica Blvd., 5th Floor
Los Angeles, CA 90067
(310) 553-4330

Satellite Orbit
(Satellite Direct)
Commtek Communications Corp.
8330 Boone Blvd., Suite 600
Vienna, VA 22182-2624
(703) 827-0511

Satellite TV Week
Fortuna Communications
140 S. Fortuna Blvd.
Fortuna, CA 95540
(707) 725-6951

Sci-Fi Entertainment
Sovereign Media Company
457 Carlisle Drive
Herndon, VA 22070
(800) 933-6407

Soap Opera Digest
K-III Communications
745 Fifth Ave., 23rd Floor
New York, NY 10151
(212) 645-2100

Soap Opera Weekly
K-III Communications
745 Fifth Ave., 23rd Floor
New York, NY 10151
(212) 645-2100

Total TV
TVSM
309 Lakeside Drive
Horsham, PA 19044-2313
(215) 443-9300

TV Guide
News America Publications
100 Matson Ford Road
Radnor, PA 19088
(800) 866-1400

Variety
5700 Wilshire Blvd., Suite 120
Los Angeles, CA 90036
(213) 857-6600

Video Magazine
Hachette Filipacchi Magazines, Inc.
1633 Broadway
New York, NY 10019
(212) 767-6000

Broadcasting Glossary

A.C. Nielsen Company The audience research conducted by Nielsen Media Research at the A.C. Nielsen Co. provides the most widely accepted measure of television viewership. These program ratings determine what the networks and cable channels charge advertisers for commercials. A combination of viewing diaries and people meters in television sets measure the ratings. The company was founded in 1923 to provide measurements of radio audiences for advertisers.

addressable converter A cable television box that can be individually supplied with programming by a cable system, providing pay-per-view events. In the future, the box may offer interactive television.

blanking The brief period in the television scanning process when the electron beam returns from right to left or from bottom to top of the screen, rendering the video signal invisible. It is during the blanking interval that closed-captioning and teletext occurs.

channel surfing The practice of scanning a series of television channels looking for something that catches the eye or to avoid commercials. Made possible by the remote control, it now occupies some viewers for entire evenings, wreaking havoc on advertisers and programmers. Surfing is one reason programming practices such as seamless transitions from one show to the next and splitting commercials into two 15-second halves have become prevalent.

closed-captioned A program that is broadcast with captions seen only on a specially equipped receiver.

DBS (Direct Broadcast Satellite) Programming services available to home satellite dish owners. Includes RCA's DSS small-dish service, Primestar and Full View TV.

double pumping The programming tactic of presenting the same program twice in one night or in one week.

fin-syn regulations Because of the networks' early de facto monopoly status, the Federal Communications Commission limited the networks' ownership of the programming they broadcast, both from acquiring a financial interest in the program producers and from distributing the programs in syndication, except overseas. The regulations have recently

been repealed because of increased competition from cable and other forms of home entertainment. The repeal has led to the phenomenon of one network producing programming that appears on another network.

hammock The programming slot between two hit shows, often used to launch a new program.

HDTV (high definition television) The broadcast standard that offers greater resolution by increasing the number of scan lines. Currently available in Japan, the format is the object of contention between competing groups of hardware manufacturers.

HUTs and **PUTs** Two measures of statistics used by analysts of Nielsen Media Research to denote houses using television and people using television.

letterbox A technique for showing widescreen movies on television that preserves the original aspect ratio by filling the top and bottom parts of the screen with black bars.

newsmagazine The genre of television programming that covers current events and topical issues.

NTSC (National Television Standards Committee) The governing body that sets the broadcast standard for North America and Japan.

PAL (phase alteration by line) A broadcast transmission standard predominantly found in Europe. It is considered superior to NTSC but incompatible with the North American broadcast standards.

Q rating A measure by TVQ/Marketing Evaluations Co. that attempts to determine the familiarity of performers, products, athletes and other public figures. The recognizability of these personalities influences casting decisions and product endorsements.

Simmons research Studies conducted by the Simmons Marketing Bureau that develop audience composition data which provide demographic and product usage information.

stunt A programming maneuver that moves a show from its usual time slot to a more advantageous slot or to multiple time periods in order to boost ratings or introduce a new program. It also refers to unusual or sensational programming designed to grab attention during sweeps periods. See **hammock** and **double pumping**.

sweeps The monthlong periods, usually February, May, July and November, when Nielsen Media Research measures audiences in all television markets. These periods are important to local stations because they provide comparative ratings across the nation, and important to networks because they provide a large-scale, in-depth view of their audience. Advertising sales for the upcoming programming season are heavily effected by the outcome of the sweeps weeks.

tabloid TV The genre of television programming, including syndicated "news" programs such as *Hard Copy, A Current Affair* or *Inside Edition*, that deals in scandal and celebrity much like its newsstand counterparts.

teletext An electronic communications system in which printed text is broadcast by television signal to sets equipped with decoders.

tent pole A hit program of such strength that its audience will stay with the network for the rest of the evening, maintaining the ratings of the other programs on the schedule.

transponder The device in a communications satellite that receives signals from an uplink on earth and transmits it back to earth (downlink). It is used by cable programmers to deliver signal to local cable systems.

Video & New Media

Interview With The Vampire

Where in the World Is Carmen Sandiego?

The Lion King

Bits & Atoms

■ BY NICHOLAS NEGROPONTE

Nicholas Negroponte is the founder of the Media Lab at MIT. He is also a columnist for *Wired* magazine. His collection of essays, *Being Digital* (Knopf), was published in 1995.

MOST EQUIPMENT AND NETWORK PROVIDERS believe that entertainment will finance the [information] superhighway and that video-on-demand, VOD, is the driving force or killer app of our wired future. I do not disagree with this view, but I marvel at the short-sighted, incomplete, and outright misleading conclusion drawn from it. The case for VOD goes as follows: Let's say a videocassette-rental store has a selection of 2,000 tapes. Suppose it finds that 5 percent of those tapes result in 90 percent of all rentals. Most likely, a good portion of that 5 percent would be new releases and would represent an even larger proportion of the store's rentals if the available number of copies were larger.

Videocassette-rental stores will go out of business within a decade. (It makes no sense to ship atoms when you can ship bits.) The easy conclusion is that the way to build an electronic Blockbuster is to offer only those top 5 percent, those primarily new releases. Not only would this be convenient, it would provide tangible and convincing evidence for what some still consider an experiment. It would take too much time and money to digitize all 29,000 movies made in America by 1990. It would take even more time to digitize the 30,000 TV programs stored in the Museum of Television and Radio in New York, and I'm not even considering the movies made in Europe, the tens of thousands from India, or the 12,000 hours per year of soaps made in Mexico by Televisa.

GETTING WIRED

The question remains: Do most of us really want to see just that top 5 percent? Or, is this herd phenomenon driven by the old technologies of distribution?

Some of the world's senior cellular telephone executives recite this jingle: "anything, anywhere, anytime." These three A's are a sign of being modern and being wired (and wireless, actually). When I hear this mantra I try not to choke, because my goal is to have "nothing, nowhere, never" unless it is timely, important, amusing, relevant or capable of engaging my imagination. AAA stinks as a paradigm for human communication — agents are much better. But AAA is a beautiful way to think about TV.

We hear a great deal of talk about 1,000 channels of TV. Allow me to point out that, even without satellite, more than 1,000 programs are delivered to your home each day! Admittedly, they are sent at all — and odd — hours. The 150-plus channels of TV listed in *Satellite TV Week* add another 2,700 or more programs available per day. If your TV could store every program transmitted, you would already have five times the selectivity offered in the superhighway's broad-brush style of thinking. But, instead of keeping them all, have your agent-TV grab the one or two in which you might have interest, for you to see anywhere and anytime.

Let AAATV expand to a global infrastructure: the quantitative and qualitative changes become interesting. Some people might listen to French television to perfect their French, others might follow Swiss Cable's Channel 11 to see unedited German nudity (5 P.M. New York time) and the 2 million Greek Americans might catch any one of the three national or seven regional channels of Greece. The British devote 75 hours per year to the coverage of chess championships and the French commit 80 hours of broadcasting to the Tour de

Wired Vice President Al Gore

France. Surely American chess and bicycle enthusiasts would enjoy access to these events — anytime, anywhere.

My point is simple: the broadcast model is what is failing. "On-demand" is a much bigger concept than not-walking-out-in-the-rain or not-forgetting-a-rented-cassette-under-the-sofa-for-a-month. It's consumer pull versus media push, my time — the receiver's time — versus the transmitter's time.

Beyond recalling an existing movie or playing any of today's (or yesterday's) TV around the world (roughly 15,000 concurrent channels), VOD could provide a new life for documentary films, even the dreaded infomercial. The hairs of documentary filmmakers will stand on end when they hear this. But it is possible to have TV agents edit movies on the fly, much like a professor assembling an anthology using chapters from different books.

If I were contemplating a visit to the southern coast of Turkey, I might not find a documentary on Bodrum, but I could find sections from movies about wooden-ship building, night-time fishing, underwater antiquities and Oriental carpets. These all could be woven together to suit my purpose. The result would not be an "A+" in Introductory Filmmaking. But one doesn't expect an anthology to be Shakespeare. In fact, one judges production values through the eyes of the beholder. It would help to thread chunks made by great organizations such as National Geographic, PBS or BBC, but the result would have meaning only to me.

Finally, the 3.1 million camcorders sold in the United States last year cannot be ignored. If the broadcast model is colliding with the Internet model, as I firmly believe it is, then each person can be an unlicensed TV station. Yes, Mr. Vice President, this is what you said in L.A. Even before we understand how the Internet will function as a commercial enterprise, we must reckon with uncountable hours of video.

I am not suggesting we consider every home movie to be a prime-time experience. What I am saying is that we can now think of TV as a great deal more than high-production-value mass media when the content strikes home, so to speak. Most telecommunications executives understand the need for broadband into the home. (Broadband, for me, is 1.5 to 6 Mbits per household member, not Gbits.) What they cannot fathom is the need for a back channel of similar capacity.

The video back channel is already accepted in teleconferencing and is a particularly fashionable medium in divorced families for the parent who does not have custody of the children. That's live video. Consider "dead" video. In the near future, individuals will be able to run video servers in the same way that 57,000 Americans run computer bulletin boards today. That's a television landscape of the future which looks like the Internet. Point to multipoint may swing dramatically toward multipoint to multipoint, on my time.

When returning from abroad, you must complete a customs declaration form. But have you ever declared the value of the bits you acquired while traveling? Have customs officers inquired whether you have a diskette that is worth hundreds of thousands of dollars? No. To them, the value of any diskette is the same — full or empty — only a few dollars, or the value of the atoms.

I recently visited the headquarters of one of the United States' top five integrated-circuit manufacturers. I was asked to sign in and, in the process, was asked whether I had a laptop computer with me. Of course I did. The receptionist asked for the model, serial number, and the computer's value. "Roughly $1 to $2 million," I said. "Oh, that cannot be, sir" she replied. "What do you mean? Let me see it."

I showed her my old Powerbook (whose PowerPlate makes it an impressive 4 inches thick), and she estimated its value at $2,000. She wrote down that amount and I was allowed to enter.

Our mind set about value is driven by atoms. The General Agreement on Tariffs and Trade is about atoms. Even new movies and music are shipped as atoms. Companies declare their atoms on a balance sheet and depreciate them according to rigorous schedules. But their bits, often far more valuable, do not appear. Strange.

When Judge Harold Greene broke up AT&T in 1983, he told the newly created regional Bell operating companies that they could not be in the information business. Who did he think he was fooling? The seven sisters were already in the information business and doing just fine, thank you. Their largest margins were (and still are) from the Yellow Pages, which they have sold at great profit. Judge Greene, sir, the companies are and always have been in the information industry. What are you talking about?

What the judge is saying is that the companies have every right to kill thousands of trees, to litter our homes and to fill garbage sites with their information business, as long as this information is in the form of atoms — paper hurled over the transom. But as soon as the companies deliver the exact same information with no-deposit, no-return, environmentally friendly bits, they have broken the law.

Doesn't that sound screwy? Was anyone thinking about the meaning of "Being Digital" during the time that AT&T was being disassembled? I fear not.

During a speech I gave at a recent meeting of shopping center owners, I tried to explain that a company's move into the digital future would be at a speed proportionate to the conversion of its atoms to bits. I used videocassette rental as an example, since these atoms could become bits very easily. It happened that Wayne Huizenga, Blockbuster's former chairman, was the lunch speaker. He defended his stock by saying, "Professor Negroponte is wrong." His argument was based largely on the fact that pay-per-view TV has not worked because it commands such a small piece of the market. By contrast, Blockbuster can pull Hollywood around by the nose, because video stores provide 50 percent of Hollywood's revenues and 60 percent of its profits.

I thought about Huizenga's remark and realized that this extraordinary entrepreneur did not understand the difference between bits and atoms. His atoms — videocassettes — prove that video-on-demand will work. Videocassettes are pay-per-view TV. The only difference is that in his business, he can draw as much as one-third of the profits from late fees.

Thomas Jefferson introduced public libraries as a fundamental American right. What this forefather never considered was that every citizen could enter every library and borrow every book simultaneously, with a keystroke, not a hike. All of a sudden, those library atoms become library bits and are potentially accessible to anyone on the Net. This is not

Thomas Jefferson

what Jefferson imagined. This is not what authors imagine. Worst of all, this is not what publishers imagine.

The problem is simple. When information is embodied in atoms, there is a need for all sorts of industrial-age means and huge corporations for delivery. But suddenly, when the focus shifts to bits, the traditional big guys are no longer needed. Do-it-yourself publishing on the Internet makes sense. It does not for paper copy.

It was through the *New York Times* that I came to know and enjoy the writing of computer and communications business reporter John Markoff. Without the *New York Times*, I probably would not have been introduced to him. However, now it would be far easier for me to collect his new stories automatically and drop them into my personal newspaper or suggested reading file. I would be willing to pay Markoff five cents for each of his new pieces.

If one-fiftieth of the 1995 Internet population subscribed to this idea, and Markoff wrote 20 stories a year, he would earn $1 million, which I am prepared to guess is more than the *New York Times* pays him. If you think one-fiftieth is too large a percentage, then wait awhile. Once someone is established, the added value of a distributor becomes less and less in a digital world.

The distribution and movement of bits is much easier than atoms. But delivery is only part of the issue. A media company is, among other things, a talent scout, and its distribution channels, bits or atoms, provide a test bed for public opinion. But after a certain point, the author may not need this forum. In the digital age, *Wired* authors can sell their stories direct and make more money once they are discovered.

While this does not work today, it will work very well, very soon — when "being digital" becomes the norm. ∎

Adapted from Negroponte's monthly columns in Wired *magazine.*

1994 HOME ENTERTAINMENT PROFILE

WHO'S WIRED

Number of Computer Households
31.1 million

Number of CD-ROM Households
6.7 million

Spending on Reference Software
$156 million

Spending on Educational Software
$522 million

Spending on Video Game Software
$2.3 billion

On-Line Households
4.5 million

WHO'S COUCHBOUND

Number of Television Households
94.2 million

Number of VCR Households
76.9 million

Spending on Video Rentals
$9.39 billion
(based on an average rental price of $2.37)

Spending on Video Sales
$4.64 billion (based on an average price of $13.80)

Source: Veronis, Suhler & Associates

MAJOR ON-LINE SERVICES

America Online (AOL)
(800) 827-6364

CompuServe
(800) 609-1674

Delphi
(800) 695-4005

eWorld
(800) 775-4556

Microsoft Network
(800) 386-5550

Prodigy
(800) PRODIGY

IPEA Picks Significant Video Releases of 1994–1995

From feature films to instructional, kids to music, here are the home-video releases from October 1994 through the summer of 1995 that caught our eye. Look for foreign and classic films on pages 553 and 551. "Rental pricing" means higher than you're willing to pay; wait for the "previously viewed" sale at your video store or just rent.

ALI McGRAW'S YOGA MIND AND BODY
Warner Home Video; $19.98
Instructional
A holistic, updated approach to using ancient yoga techniques for relaxation, to improve concentration and to tone, illustrated by actress Ali McGraw.

AMERICA THE BEAUTIFUL
Reader's Digest Video; $36.96
Documentary
A generous look at the natural beauty and variety of landscape across America through the seasons. The lack of narration allows the viewer to experience the visual splendor without unnecessary interpretation.

ANGELS IN THE OUTFIELD
Walt Disney; $19.99
Feature
Director: William Dear
Rated PG
Cast: Danny Glover, Christopher Lloyd and Milton Davis, Jr.
A big winner in the kids' video market, *Angels* is the story of boy who asks for heavenly intercession for his team, the California Angels, and receives it. You never know, it could happen.

ANTONIO CARLOS JOBIM: AN ALL-STAR TRIBUTE
V.I.E.W. Video; $19.98
Music/Documentary
The late Brazilian composer was captured on video at his last performance, which just happened to include some of the biggest names in jazz, including Shirley Horn, Gal Costa and Elvin Jones.

BARBRA — THE CONCERT
CMV; $24.95
Music
No one needed the last name in the billing for this most renowned concert tour in recent memory. Because she hadn't performed before an audience in years, Streisand gathered record audiences (who paid record prices) in concert, on pay-per-view, on free TV and now for your perpetual video viewing. The show itself was a glamorous overview of a glamorous career, and Streisand was in good voice. We could use a little less psychoanalysis, but, hey, that's part of the deal.

BARCELONA
New Line; rental pricing
Feature
Director: Whit Stillman
Rated PG-13
Cast: Taylor Nichols, Chris Eigeman, Tushka Bergen and Mira Sorvino

Stillman's *Metropolitan* had the feel of fictional anthropology, an excursion into the world of the privileged Eastern establishment with wonderfully witty dialogue. Here the inhabitants of that realm are exposed to the sunny Mediterranean with comic and troubling results. Another great script thoughtfully performed.

BARNEY SAFETY VIDEO
The Lyons Group; $14.98
Children's/Instructional
Even those who cringe at the sight of the Purple One may want to check out the solid lessons in crossing the street, riding bicycles and other travails of tots.

Before Sunrise
Columbia TriStar Home Video; rental pricing
Feature
Director: Richard Linklater
Rated R
Cast: Ethan Hawke and July Delpy
See page 24

The Best of Liquid Television
MTV Home Video/Sony Wonder; $12.98
Animation
The television home of cutting-edge animation art brings a compilation to the small screen. Check this out for an update on modern culture; one of the serials, *Aeon Flux*, even became a book.

Blue Sky
Orion; rental pricing
Feature
Director: Tony Richardson
Rated PG-13
Cast: Jessica Lange and Tommy Lee Jones
Lange won the 1994 Best Actress Oscar for her role as a seductive, troubled army wife who causes problems for her officer husband.

Boys on the Side
Warner Home Video; rental pricing
Feature
Director: Herbert Ross
Rated R
Cast: Drew Barrymore, Whoopi Goldberg and Mary-Louise Parker
See page 25

Bullets Over Broadway
Miramax; rental pricing
Feature
Director: Woody Allen
Rated PG
Cast: John Cusack, Dianne Wiest, Jennifer Tilly and Chazz Palminteri
See page 27

Clerks
Miramax; rental pricing
Feature
Director: Kevin Smith
Rated R
Cast: Brian O'Halloran and Jeff Anderson
See page 29

The Client
Warner Home Video; rental pricing
Director: Joel Schumacher
Rated PG-13
Cast: Susan Sarandon, Tommy Lee Jones, Mary-Louise Parker, Brad Renfro and Anthony LaPaglia
Based on John Grisham's novel
When an 11-year-old boy intervenes as an attorney is about to commit suicide, he puts his own life in jeopardy. He hires his own attorney for a dollar, and the two stay a step ahead of the mob and an overly zealous district attorney.

Corinna, Corinna
New Line; rental pricing
Feature
Director: Jessie Nelson
Rated PG
Cast: Whoopi Goldberg, Ray Liotta and Tina Majorino
A winner as a rental, *Corinna, Corinna* plays better on the small screen. This is the treacly tale of a father and daughter who lose wife and mother and gain an endearing, witty housekeeper.

Ed Wood . . . Look Back in Angora
Jailbait
Plan 9 From Outer Space
Rhino Home Video; $19.95 for documentary, $9.95 for features
Feature/Documentary
Director: Who else?
Not Rated
Casts of dozens
Woodmania! Ed Wood, Jr., gets another *That's Entertainment* treatment along with the release of new cuts of two sub-classic Wood favorites. The documentary is sad and funny; *Jailbait* is actually a seldom-seen revelation; and nothing further needs to be said about *Plan 9*.

The Ed Wood Story: The Plan 9 Companion
MPI Home Video; $19.98
Documentary

This video contains interviews with those who helped create the vision of the man called the worst filmmaker of all time and outtakes from his work. It makes for a splendidly silly companion to Tim Burton's *Ed Wood*.

Billboard compiles weekly statistics based on SoundScan sales data and awards points to titles for each week spent on the charts. The following charts reflect the accumulation of points each title received during the eligibility period of December 4, 1993–November 26, 1994.

TOP 20 VIDEO RENTALS

1. *Sleepless in Seattle*
   (Columbia TriStar Home Video)
2. *Philadelphia*
   (Columbia TriStar Home Video)
3. *In the Line of Fire*
   (Columbia TriStar Home Video)
4. *The Pelican Brief*
   (Warner Home Video)
5. *The Fugitive*
   (Warner Home Video)
6. *The Firm*
   (Paramount Home Video)
7. *Carlito's Way*
   (MCA/Universal Home Video)
8. *Sliver*
   (Paramount
   Home Video)
9. *Ace Ventura: Pet Detective*
   (Warner Home Video)
10. *Mrs. Doubtfire*
    (FoxVideo)
11. *Grumpy Old Men*
    (Warner Home Video)
12. *Rising Sun*
    (FoxVideo)
13. *Cliffhanger*
    (Columbia TriStar Home Video)
14. *Tombstone*
    (Hollywood Home Video)
15. *A Perfect World*
    (Warner Home Video)
16. *Malice*
    (Columbia TriStar Home Video)
17. *Cool Runnings*
    (Walt Disney Home Video)
18. *The Joy Luck Club*
    (Hollywood Home Video)

ELVIS '56 . . . IN THE BEGINNING
Lightyear Entertainment; $19.98
Music/Documentary
The 21-year-old Elvis was poised at the brink of what would become unimaginable stardom in 1956. Rare photos and concert footage of Elvis's prime (and narration by gruff Levon Helm) make this worthwhile.

THE ENDLESS SUMMER II
New Line; rental pricing
Documentary/Sports

The 1966 original brought the surfing phenomenon to America's theaters and made even the land-locked long to hang 10. This updating of the original formula of two California dudes on the prowl for excellent surf travels around the world in pursuit of the tubular. Underwater camera technology has vastly improved since 1966, and the footage is truly awesome.

THE FLINTSTONES
MCA Universal Home Video; $19.98
Feature/Animation
Director: Brian Levant
Rated PG
Cast: John Goodman, Rick Moranis, Elizabeth Perkins and Rosie O'Donnell
The Flintstone and Rubble families make a comeback in this re-creation of the classic after school cartoon *The Flintstones*. Bedrock turns chaotic when Fred gets promoted over best buddy Barney, the two families move in together and Fred's mother-in-law visits.

FLOUNDERING
A-Pix; rental pricing
Feature
Director: Peter McCarthy
Rated R
Cast: James LeGros, John Cusack, Ethan Hawke and Steve Buscemi
The producer of *Repo Man* and *Sid and Nancy* takes the director's helm for a Gen-X story of a twentysomething's search for love and redemption in LA. Included are cameos by rockers Exene Cervenka and David Navarro.

FOUR WEDDINGS AND A FUNERAL
PolyGram; rental pricing
Director: Mike Newell
Rated R
Cast: Hugh Grant and Andie McDowell

The film that propelled Grant's career focuses on the bumbling Englishman who can't commit and watches as his friends do. He does hit it off with a beautiful American woman who happens to attend the same weddings.

GOLF: HEROES OF THE GAME

Warner Home Video; $24.95 for each,
$69.95 for three
Sports
This three-video set takes a fond, well-produced look at the history of the game, from modern heroes such as Nicklaus and Palmer, to earlier legends such as Hogan and Sneed, to golf's greatest women.

GUARDING TESS

Columbia TriStar; rental pricing
Feature
Director: Hugh Wilson
Rated PG-13
Cast: Shirley MacLaine and Nicholas Cage
Four decades into her career, MacLaine brings a well-earned wisdom and comic timing to her roles. The miserable, widowed former first lady drives her Secret Service agent nuts, but behind their scorn for each other is a true bond.

THE HISTORY OF ROCK 'N' ROLL

Time-Life; $13.48 for volume one, $23.48 for volumes 2–10
Documentary/Music
Is there enough material to warrant a 10-volume set of rock history? You'll be surprised at how quickly this well-reviewed series flies through the decades. This overview of the most extensively documented music in history begins in the late 1950s and blazes through the decades to a somewhat truncated view of the current state of rock. It includes many, many interviews and priceless archival footage.

THE HUDSUCKER PROXY

Warner; rental pricing
Feature
Directors: Joel and Ethan Cohen
Rated PG
Cast: Tim Robbins, Paul Newman and Jennifer Jason Leigh
This is truly a big-time comic book of a movie. A poor country boy moves to the big city and dreams of making it big in a heartless mega-corporation. Cigar-chomping Paul Newman almost keeps the film grounded in reality, but this is a flight of fancy that has as much to do with bravura filmmaking as with narrative sense.

19. **Indecent Proposal**
    (Paramount Home Video)

20. **Dave**
    (Warner Home Video)

TOP 20 VIDEO SALES

1. **Aladdin**
   (Walt Disney Home Video)

2. **Playboy Celebrity Centerfold: Dian Parkinson**
   (United Distribution Corp.)

3. **Yanni: Live at the Acropolis**
   (BMG Video)

4. **Free Willy**
   (Warner Home Video)

5. **Mrs. Doubtfire**
   (FoxVideo)

6. **The Fugitive**
   (Warner Home Video)

7. **The Return of Jafar**
   (Walt Disney Home Video)

8. **The Fox and the Hound**
   (Walt Disney Home Video)

9. **Ace Ventura: Pet Detective**
   (Warner Home Video)

10. **Beauty and the Beast**
    (Walt Disney Home Video)

11. **Playboy: 1994 Playmate of the Year**
    (United Distribution Corp.)

12. **The Bodyguard**
    (Warner Home Video)

13. **Playboy 1994 Video Playmate Calendar**
    (United Distribution Corp.)

14. **Beethoven's 2nd**
    (MCA/Universal Home Video)

15. **Homeward Bound: The Incredible Journey**
    (Walt Disney Home Video)

16. **Dennis the Menace**
    (Warner Home Video)

17. **The Secret Garden**
    (Warner Home Video)

18. **Pinocchio**
    (Walt Disney Home Video)

19. **Penthouse: 25th Anniversary Swimsuit Video**
    (A*Vision Entertainment)

20. **The Three Tenors in Concert 1994**
    (A*Vision Entertainment)

CONTINUED ON NEXT PAGE ▶

1994 TOP 20 LASERDISC SALES

1. *Terminator 2: Judgment Day — Special Edition*
    (Pioneer LDCA, Inc.)

2. *The Fugitive*
    (Warner Home Video)

3. *Tombstone*
    (Image Entertainment)

4. *Cliffhanger*
    (Columbia TriStar Home Video)

5. *Mrs. Doubtfire*
    (Image Entertainment)

6. *Rising Sun*
    (Image Entertainment)

7. *In the Line of Fire*
    (Columbia TriStar Home Video)

8. *Demolition Man*
    (Warner Home Video)

9. *Star Wars Trilogy: The Definitive Collection*
    (Image Entertainment)

10. *Philadelphia*
    (Columbia TriStar Home Video)

11. *True Romance*
    (Warner Home Video)

12. *Ace Ventura: Pet Detective*
    (Warner Home Video)

13. *Beauty and the Beast*
    (Image Entertainment)

14. *The Pelican Brief*
    (Warner Home Video)

15. *Free Willy*
    (Warner Home Video)

16. *Hard Target*
    (MCA/Universal Home Video)

17. *The Piano*
    (Pioneer LDCA, Inc.)

18. *In the Name of the Father*
    (MCA/Universal Home Video)

19. *Grumpy Old Men*
    (Warner Home Video)

20. *Sleepless in Seattle*
    (Columbia TriStar Home Video)

Source: Billboard

THE INCREDIBLE VOYAGE OF BILL PINCKNEY

MPI Home Video; $19.98
Documentary

Bill Pinckney, the first African American to sail solo around the world and only the third American to sail under all five capes, captured his thoughts and his breathtaking experience on audio and video diaries, which are the basis for this video. Bill Cosby narrates Pinckney's instructional and inspirational story.

THE INTERNET SHOW

PBS Home Video; $14.98
Instructional

The author of *The Internet for Dummies* brings to the home screen his simplified method for maximizing time spent cruising the information superhighway. He explains in clear language all the geek talk and the easiest way to navigate cyberspace.

INTERVIEW WITH THE VAMPIRE

Warner Home Video; rental pricing
Feature
Director: Neil Jordan
Rated R
Cast: Tom Cruise, Brad Pitt and Kirsten Dunst
See page 43

JAMMIN'

Hal Leonard Corp.; $14.95
Instructional/Music

Closet ax-wielders grab your guitars! These two tapes, *Metal Guitar* and *Blues Guitar*, allow the home-alone guitar hero to play in a "live" situation with a studio session band. Accompanying diagrams show proper fingerings.

JURASSIC PARK

MCA Universal Home Video;
rental pricing
Feature
Director: Steven Spielberg
Rated PG-13
Cast: Sam Neill, Laura Dern, Jeff Goldblum and Richard Attenborough

It's not the same watching this on a small screen — the sound doesn't compare and the genetically-engineered dinosaurs don't look nearly as frightening — but it's still a fun at-home watch.

KATHY IRELAND TOTAL FITNESS WORKOUT
UAV; $19.99
Instructional
Swimsuit model Ireland faced the task of losing 40 pounds after pregnancy and developed a training and diet regimen to accomplish her goal. She became a certified aerobics instructor in the process, and Ireland shares her routines on this tape.

KEN BURNS'S BASEBALL
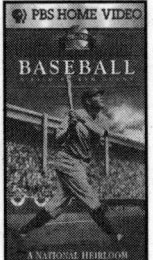
PBS Home Video; $179.98
Documentary
Director: Ken Burns
This nine-part documentary that was first shown on PBS chronicles America's pastime from its inception to the days of Chicago's Black Sox to the Red Sox catastrophic 1986 World Series.

KILLING ZOE
LIVE Home Video; rental pricing
Feature
Director: Roger Avary
Rated R
Cast: Eric Stoltz and Julie Delpy
This is an angst-ridden, corpse-strewn account of a listless safecracker who arrives in Paris and consorts with fellow criminals in a disastrous robbery.

THE LAST SEDUCTION
PolyGram Video; rental pricing
Feature
Director: John Dahl
Rated R
Cast: Linda Fiorentino, Bill Pullman and Peter Berg
See page 46

THE LITTLE RASCALS
MCA Universal Home Video; $24.98
Feature
Director: Penelope Spheeris
Rated PG
Cast: Travis Tedford, Bug Hall, Brittany Holmes, Kevin Woods and Zachary Mabry
In this re-creation of the Saturday morning serial, Porky, Buckwheat, Spanky, Alfalfa, Waldo and Darla continue to find creative solutions to their many humorous predicaments and troubling situations.

THE LION KING
Walt Disney; $26.99
Feature
Rated G
Voices of: Jeremy Irons, Rowan Atkinson, Whoopi Goldberg and Nathan Lane

One of the most popular films of all time, and a favorite of kids that offers entertainment for parents, this is probably a top choice to add to your home collection.

MANUFACTURING CONSENT: NOAM CHOMSKY AND THE MEDIA
Zeitgeist; $59.95
Documentary
MIT professor Chomsky is as well-known as a cultural critic and political lone wolf of dissent as he as a linguist. This three-hour exploration of his life is far from dry — Chomsky sees to that.

THE MASK
New Line Home Video; rental pricing
Feature
Director: Charles Russell
Rated PG-13
Cast: Jim Carrey
When a dull banker dons the ancient mask he found in a river, he becomes an insurmountable superhero who finally gets the girl. The special effects, Carrey's physical humor and the dog make this a worthwhile rent.

MI VIDA LOCA
HBO; rental pricing
Feature
Director: Allison Anders
Rated R
Cast: Angel Aviles, Seidy Lopez and Jacob Vargas
The tough girls that hang out in the gangs in LA's Echo Park area endure harsh street life filled with lots of drugs and crime, but *Mi Vida Loca* reveals the sensitive yet resilient side of the young women.

MURDER WAS THE CASE: THE MOVIE
A*Vision; $16.98
Feature/Music
Director: Dr. Dre
Cast: Snoop Doggy Dog
The G-funk makes it to the big screen as Snoop takes a hot shot but gets levitated by a white devil. The 15-minute main attraction gets support from Snoop's videos and interviews.

NAKED IN NEW YORK
Columbia TriStar; rental pricing
Feature
Director: Dan Algrant
Rated R
Cast: Eric Stoltz, Mary-Louise Parker, Jill Clayburgh, Tony Curtis and Eric Bogosian
This first film by Algrant (produced by Martin Scorsese) follows a young playwright as he works out details of his dramatic work and his romantic life.

NATURAL BORN KILLERS
Warner; rental pricing
Feature
Director: Oliver Stone
Rated R
Cast: Woody Harrelson and Juliette Lewis
A truly great movie for television, as it warps the style (and lack of substance?) of tabloid TV into an dazzlingly visual indictment of the medium.

THE NEW AGE
Warner; rental pricing
Feature
Director: Michael Tolkin
Rated R
Cast: Judy Davis and Peter Weller
Those who found *The Rapture* a compelling meditation on modern morality will find equal sustenance in Tolkin's portrait of a modern marriage saved from irrelevance by the magic of telemarketing.

NIRVANA—LIVE! TONIGHT! SOLD OUT!
Geffen Home Video; $24.99
Music/Documentary
While much attention has been paid to the startlingly revealing Nirvana *Unplugged* session, this concert document of the band's 1991 *Nevermind* tour reminds us how thrilling the band could be with the amps cranked up.

NONESUCH DANCE COLLECTION'S BALANCHINE LIBRARY
Nonesuch; price N/A
Dance/Documentary
This five-tape set includes three tapes of the ballet master's choreography, one of ballerinas telling stories of their experiences dancing for him and one of New York City Ballet's dancers demonstrating his signature techniques.

PIECES OF TIME: DWIGHT YOAKAM
Warner/Reprise; $16.98
Music
Everyone who has seen Yoakam tear up an audience in concert may wish for live footage, but credit the new traditionalist crooner for bigger ambitions than the average big-hat country star. This video collection is strikingly composed and a good overview of recent work.

RAPA NUI
Warner; rental pricing
Feature
Director: Kevin Reynolds
Rated R
Cast: Jason Scott Lee and Esai Morales
The mystery of Easter Island gets a fictional treatment that adds romance and a tribal competition. Shot on location, it also yields a look at one of the most remote places on earth. A classic rental.

THE ROAD TO WELLVILLE
Columbia TriStar Home Video; rental pricing
Feature
Director: Alan Parker
Rated R
Cast: Anthony Hopkins, John Cusack, Bridget Fonda and Matthew Broderick
See page 62

SCHINDLER'S LIST
MCA Universal Home Video; rental pricing
Director: Steven Spielberg
Rated R
Cast: Liam Neeson, Ben Kingsley and Ralph Fiennes
In this true story, WWII profiteer Oskar Schindler saved thousands of Jews by employing them in his factory that manufactured earthenware for the German Army. It won seven Oscars, including Best Picture and Best Director. The film was shot in black-and-white in Poland, adding to its authenticity.

SHAWSHANK REDEMPTION
Columbia TriStar Home Video; rental pricing
Feature
Director: Frank Darabont
Rated R
Cast: Tim Robbins and Morgan Freeman
A bank executive, jailed for allegedly murdering his wife and her lover, experiences the horrors of imprisonment and learns invaluable lessons in patience and understanding from a jail veteran.

SNOW WHITE AND THE SEVEN DWARFS
Buena Vista Home Video; $26.99
Feature/Animation
Director: David Hand
Rated G
Voices of: Adriana Caselotti, Harry Stockwell and Lucille LaVerne

The digitally cleaned and remixed 1937 classic is even more enjoyable in its restored form. It's interesting to see how far animation has come since Disney broke new ground with the first animated feature film.

SPANKING THE MONKEY

New Line; rental pricing
Feature
Director: David O. Russell
Not Rated
Cast: Jeremy Davies and Alberta Watson
Yes, this is the incest movie that had the audiences agog at the Sundance Festival. Premed student Davies shares a tender moment with incapacitated mom Watson, but all the post-adolescent angst is truly funny in a warped sort of way.

SPEED

FoxVideo; rental pricing
Feature
Director: Jan DeBont
Rated R
Keanu Reeves, Sandra Bullock and Dennis Hopper

Speed offers surprisingly gripping suspense despite its less-than-gripping premise, the rigging of a city bus to explode as an extortion device. There's more to it than that, but barely. It was the world's introduction to Bullock.

STAR TREK: THE BEGINNINGS

Paramount; three-cassette boxed set; price NA
From the television series
Though it seems to have be around since the dawn of time, there was actually a beginning to the *Star Trek* madness. The first cassette of this three-tape box contains the original series' two pilots, "The Cage" and "Where No Man Has Gone Before." The other tapes feature the first episodes from the follow-up series *The Next Generation* and *Deep Space Nine*.

THAT'S ENTERTAINMENT III

MGM/UA; $14.95
Documentary
As with the previous editions in this rummage through the song-and-dance stacks at MGM, the scenes from the musicals are dazzling. This installment makes a departure by taking a behind-the-scenes approach with outtakes and explanations of how some production numbers were staged.

THE THREE TENORS 1994

A*Vision; $29.98
Music
This memorable performance features the three great vocalists of classical music — Carreras, Domingo and Pavoratti — and it builds on the phenomenal success of the original concert video and recording. Zubin Mehta conducts the Orchestra del Maggio Musicale Fiorentino and Orchestra del Teatro dell' Opera di Roma.

TIM BURTON'S THE NIGHTMARE BEFORE CHRISTMAS

Touchstone Home Video; rental pricing
Feature/Animation
Director: Henry Selick
Rated PG
Voices of: Danny Elfman, Chris Sarandon and Catherine O'Hara
In an amazing example of stop-motion animation, Jack Skellington, the Pumpkin of Halloween, tires of the October holiday and tries to move in on Christmas.

TONY BENNETT: MTV UNPLUGGED

SMV; $19.95
Music
Surely one of the strangest comebacks in pop music history — not because of lack of talent, but because of the young audience for the resurgence — is played out here, with Bennett swinging the standards. Guests include Elvis Costello and k.d. lang.

TRUE LIES

Fox Home Video; rental pricing
Feature
Director: James Cameron
Rated R
Cast: Jamie Lee Curtis, Arnold Schwarzenegger and Tom Arnold
For once, Arnold steals the show. A legal secretary thinks her husband is a computer salesman, but he is really a high-level government spy who, of course, has superhero power.

UPSTAIRS, DOWNSTAIRS

Arts & Entertainment Home Video; seven-cassette set $149.95
From the A&E television series
Those who doted on the trials and tribulations of the aristocratic British family and their faithful family retainers will be delighted to know that A&E has released all 14 episodes in a boxed set.

VIDEO BABY

Quality Video; price
Instructional
A 30-minute baby experience for those just too darn busy to conceive. Lots of crawling, playing, cooing and so forth, with none of the messy clean-up.

When a Man Loves a Woman

Touchstone Home Video; rental pricing
Feature
Director: Luis Mandoki
Rated R
Cast: Andy Garcia and Meg Ryan
What could have descended to emotional hogwash is redeemed by the intriguing casting of always perky Ryan as an alcoholic whose problem threatens her marriage. The script (by Ron Bass and Al Franken) is frank and sharp-tongued.

Widow's Peak

New Line; rental pricing
Feature
Director: John Irvin
Rated PG
Cast: Mia Farrow, Natasha Richardson and Joan Plowright
The titular Irish town only accepts widows as residents with the exceptions spinster teacher and of the mayor's son. When a newly minted widow looking for action arrives in town, intrigue ensues. Wickedly funny.

Wolf

Columbia TriStar; rental pricing
Feature
Director: Mike Nichols
Rated R
Cast: Jack Nicholson, Michelle Pfeiffer and James Spader
In this updating of the hoary werewolf saga with a wickedly toothy grin, Nicholson still appeals as the hirsute hero. The setting in the scary world of publishing gives us a chuckle, too.

The Wonderful, Horrible Life of Leni Riefenstahl

Kino; rental pricing
Documentary
Had Riefenstahl not been the house diarist of the Third Reich, we may have celebrated her work as an actress, a filmmaker and a photographer. The cloud of Nazi ties makes it harder to see clearly what this film reveals to be an undeniably intriguing life.

Woodstock '94

Polygram Video; $24.95
Music/Documentary
Those who thought the 25th anniversary of the '60s watershed music event would be solely an exercise in nostalgia got a surprise in the compelling, career-making performances of Green Day, The Rollins Band and Nine Inch Nails. The video also features one of the better Dylan sets in some time.

The Year in Rock

MTV Video/Sony Wonder; $14.98
Documentary
Everything from high schoolers' battle for the first amendment to fashion roundups and other trends add to the expected survey of the high points of a year in MTV-generation rock.

You Can't Do That: The Making of A Hard Day's Night

MPI Home Video; $19.98
Music/Documentary
Phil Collins hosts this behind-the-scenes look at The Beatles's first fab film, which celebrated its 30th anniversary in 1994. Interviews with director Richard Lester, his writers and crew complement the relaxed, candid footage.

Neil Young and Crazy Horse: The Complex Sessions

Warner Reprise Video; $16.98
Music
Director Jonathan Demme, who demonstrated his musical taste with the Talking Heads concert film *Stop Making Sense*, here finds Young and Crazy Horse in a recording studio jamming on songs from their *Sleeps With Angels* disk. The recordings are not available in any other format.

Your Personal Best Workout With Elle McPherson

Buena Vista; $19.99
Instructional
Big sales winner with challenging routines and Elle's charming smile. We can't help wondering if most of the buyers are men who never get off the couch.

IPEA Picks Classic Movies on Video

Home video distributors are emptying the movie archives to supply a seemingly endless demand for movie videos. It gives home audiences the chance to see some of the timeless work of cinema's first century. Here are some of the classic movie tapes released between October 1994 and August 1995 that we enjoyed this year. "Rental pricing" means higher than you're willing to pay; wait for the "previously viewed" sale at your video store or just rent.

LEAVE HER TO HEAVEN (1945)
FoxVideo: $19.98
Director: John Stahl
Not Rated
Cast: Gene Tierney and Cornel Wilde
Has there ever been a star as regally beautiful as Tierney? What a perfect face to portray a woman so twisted inside that she would resort to murder to keep her husband.

THAT OBSCURE OBJECT OF DESIRE (1977)
Home Vision; $29.95
Director: Luis Buñuel
Not Rated
Cast: Carole Bouquet, Fernando Rey and Angela Molina
Spain-France
With *Belle de Jour* in the theaters and the release of this tape, 1995 was certainly the year to rediscover Buñuel. It took two actresses to convey the duality and maddening appeal of Buñuel's heroine. The master of cinematic absurdity puts his frustrated hero through some startling trials as he attempts to grasp the nature of the woman he relentlessly pursues. This is a new edition in letterbox format.

LANCELOT OF THE LAKE (1975)
New Yorker; rental pricing
Director: Robert Bresson
Not Rated
Cast: Luc Simon
France
This is a haunting, elegiac telling of the Lancelot/Guinevere romance with the gritty clash of armor and spilling of blood intruding on Camelot fantasies. Bresson's stately pace and characteristic framing make *Lancelot of the Lake* beautiful and troubling at once.

THE RAZOR'S EDGE (1946)
FoxVideo; $19.98
Director: Edmund Goulding
Not Rated
Cast: Tyrone Power, Gene Tierney, Clifton Webb and Anne Baxter
Maugham's tale of the quest for a spiritual life finds an unlikely but effective personification in Power. The conflict between his stony good looks and the internal struggle in the narrative makes for an interesting drama. A sumptuous production.

THE ART OF BUSTER KEATON (1920-1927)
Kino; $29.95 each, $79.95 for three-tape set, $109.95 for four-tape set
Director: Buster Keaton
Not Rated
The release of this collection of Keaton silents was the highlight of 1995 for many classic-movie fans. As the archival prints in the three boxed sets reveal, Keaton was a master actor, director, stunt man, special-effects wizard and writer. Familiar to most movie fans from his iconic stone-face, these 11 features and 19 shorts on 10 tapes reveal not only the multifaceted talent that was Keaton's, but his essential humanity.

SYMPATHY FOR THE DEVIL (1970)
ABKCO; $29.95
Director: Jean-Luc Godard
Not Rated
Cast: The Rolling Stones
France
Known also in the director's cut as *One Plus One*, you might not consider this look at The Rolling Stones a film classic. But it captures Godard's revolutionary concerns of the time, and the vehicle of one of the world's most famous rock bands, known more for hedonism than being exemplars of the Marxist dialectic, makes for a

challenging argument. But the main reason to give this a look is the portrait of the Stones at the peak of their prowess.

ALEXANDER NEVSKY (1938)
BMG Classics; $24.98
Director: Sergei Eisenstein
Not Rated
Cast: Nikolai Cherkassov and Nikolai Okhlophov
Russia

A restored print and new rendition of Prokfiev's stirring score make this a must-see. The composition of the famous battle sequences highlights the story of the leader who repelled a German invasion during the middle ages.

IN A YEAR OF 13 MOONS (1979)
New Yorker; rental pricing
Director: Rainer Werner Fassbinder
Not Rated
Cast: Volker Spengler, Ingrid Craven and Gottfried John
Germany

Fassbinder was unequaled at depictions of rejection, loneliness and existential despair. That his favored milieu was the domestic melodrama typified by Douglas Sirk makes the subject matter both easier to emotionally register, sometimes campy and somehow even sadder. Here a transsexual, abandoned as a child, loses the man for whom he made the gender change. Satirical, pathetic and disturbing.

MY FAIR LADY (1964)

CBS Home Video; $24.98
Director: George Cukor
Not Rated
Cast: Audrey Hepburn, Rex Harrison and Stanley Holloway
The 30th anniversary of one of the most beloved film musicals brings with it a collector's edition video with restored color and clarity. *My Fair Lady* earned eight Oscars including Best Picture, Actor, Director, Cinematography and Art Direction.

INTRODUCING...

A CUPPA JOE, A SINKER AND A CD-ROM
Before you know it, your neighborhood greasy spoon may sprout a monitor next to the sugar bowl. The combination of computers, coffee and Web access has created a whole new entertainment destination — the cyber cafe. Led by the Icon Byte Bar and Grill in San Francisco's SOMA and Cybersmith in Cambridge, Massachusetts, the typical cyber cafe mixes computer games, internet access, magazines, books, software and latte.

MAYBE A LITTLE LATE, BUT AT&T CATCHES ON
The telecommunications giant will start providing Internet access, including business transactions, electronic mail, video conferencing and wireless access via its telephone lines. AT&T has leased Netscape browser software, the wildly popular Internet navigation program, to help users surf with ease.

SHINY, ROUND MAGAZINES
The color, the browsability, the ads . . . everything a magazine does, new CD-ROM magazines do, and more. *Launch,* for example, a product of Santa Monica, California's 2Way Media and Commotion, features Quicktime interviews with rock bands, samples of new recordings, a movie preview section from *Premiere* magazine, cool animations, video game reviews and samples and yes, ads, but ads that are designed to be as interactive as the format. The best CD-ROM magazines aren't simply print products retrofitted for the new format, but new creations that allow you to navigate through a four-color world full of sound and vision. Just don't take it to the beach.

IPEA Picks Foreign Films on Video

Home video releases let us see some of the foreign films that get a limited release in this country. Here's what got our attention between October 1994 and August 1995.

THE ADVENTURES OF PRISCILLA, QUEEN OF THE DESERT

PolyGram; rental pricing
Director: Stephan Elliot
Cast: Terence Stamp, Hugo Weaving and Guy Pearce
Rated R
Australia

Stamp's performance as the transsexual Bernadette lifts a story of friendship among three drag queens as they cross the Australian outback in Priscilla, their garishly painted bus.

BELLE ÉPOQUE

Columbia TriStar; rental pricing
Director: Fernando Tueba
Rated R
Cast: Jorge Sanz, Fernando Fernan Gomez and Ariadna Gil
Spain

This caught some by surprise when it won 1994's Best Foreign Language Oscar because politically laced sex comedies don't usually appeal to the Academy's voters. A painter's four beautiftul daughters seduce a deserter from the Spanish Civil War.

HEAVENLY CREATURES

Miramax; rental pricing
Director: Peter Jackson
Rated R
Cast: Kate Winslet and Melanie Lynskey
New Zealand
See page 41

KIKA

Vidmark; rental pricing
Director: Pedro Almodovar
Not Rated
Cast: Veronique Forque, Peter Coyote and Alex Casanovas
Spain

Anything by stylish director Almodovar is worth a look, but this slight work is probably best suited for whiling away time at home. The labyrinthian plot having to do with a make-up artist and her affairs gives Almodovar opportunities to try for shock, but his efforts are becoming more rote and less eye-raising.

THE SCENT OF GREEN PAPAYA

Columbia TriStar; rental pricing
Director: Hung Tran Anh
Not Rated
Cast: Tran Nu Yen-Kho and Troung Thi Loc
Vietnam

A romance between the classes set in 1950s and 1960s Saigon gets a lush, sensual treatment to which art house habitués responded and garnered it a 1994 Academy Award nomination.

SUNDAY'S CHILDREN

First Run; rental pricing
Director: Daniel Bergman
Not Rated
Cast: Henrik Linnros and Thommy Berggren
Sweden

Ingmar Bergman wrote this recollection of his childhood with the same autumnal sense of bittersweet wonder that he brought to films such as *Fanny & Alexander*. His son Daniel directs in the same masterful manner that made the elder Bergman famous.

THIRTY-TWO SHORT FILMS ABOUT GLENN GOULD

Columbia TriStar; rental pricing
Director: François Girard
Not Rated
Cast: Colm Feore
Canada

Girard may have sacrificed some pianistic quality when he decided to only use Feore to portray the reclusive pianist's life rather than including documentary footage of Gould in interviews and recording sessions. But the film, which takes its format from Bach's *Goldberg Variations*, is a fascinating look at Gould's bizarre life and habits.

IPEA Picks Laserdiscs

With greater image and audio fidelity and the addition of scenes, directors' cuts and behind-the-scenes footage, laserdiscs are fast becoming the cinephile's choice of home-theater format. These are some of the laserdiscs that we noticed released between October 1994 and August 1995.

ALADDIN (1992)

Disney; $49.99
Animation
Voices of: Scott Weinger, Robin Williams Linda Larkin and Jonathon Freeman
Rated G

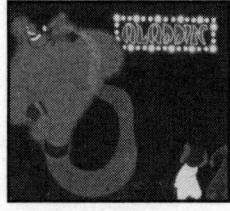

Now that *The Lion King* has overtaken *Aladdin* as the best-selling tape in history, the laserdisc version of *Aladdin* appears and reminds us how much more fun the first film was. The color rendition and sharpness make it obviously superior to the tapes.

THE ASTAIRE AND ROGERS COLLECTION (1934–1937)

Image; $124.99
Director: Various
Not Rated
Cast: Fred Astaire and Ginger Rogers

Four of the highlights of the most renowned song-and-dance collaboration in film make for a stellar four-box set. The titles — *Top Hat, The Gay Divorcee, Follow the Fleet* and *Shall We Dance* — exhibit the grace and finesse that became one of the hallmarks of 1930s Hollywood cinema.

BRIEF ENCOUNTER (1945)

Voyager; $49.95
Director: David Lean
Not Rated
Cast: Trevor Howard, Celia Johnson and Stanley Holloway
U.K.

A chance meeting at a train station leads to the exaltation and regret of illicit romance for two married strangers. Based on a Noel Coward play, the movie has been lauded for its emotional nuance. This is a restored, wide-screen edition.

BUTCH CASSIDY AND THE SUNDANCE KID (1969)

Fox/Image; $99.98
Director: George Roy Hill
Rated PG
Cast: Paul Newman, Robert Redford and Katharine Ross

The sunny Western that started the craze for buddy movies includes a making-of documentary that is better than most, along with commentary by Hill and Oscar-winning cinematographer Conrad Hall. The movie itself, in wonderfully restored wide screen, looks remarkably innocent and good-natured.

DANCES WITH WOLVES

Director: Kevin Costner
Rated PG-13
Cast: Kevin Costner, Mary McDonnell and Graham Greene

The wide-screen version of Costner's popular frontier saga comes with an hour of footage restored from the already longish theaterical release.

THE GENE KELLY COLLECTION (1949–1955)

MGM/UA; price NA
Director: Various
Not Rated

From *Brigadoon* (1954), Lerner and Loewe's (and director Vincente Minnelli's) magical musical of an enchanted Scottish village, to Kelly and Stanley Donen's jubilant *On the Town* (1949), co-starring Frank Sinatra, to a less well-known, but interestingly dark, Kelly and Donen-directed vehicle *It's Always Fair Weather* (1955), this set gives a wonderful overview of Kelly's contribution to film musicals.

HARD BOILED (1993)

Criterion; $124.95
Director: John Woo
Not Rated
Cast: Chow Yun-Fat and Tony Leung
Hong Kong

Woo, the acknowledged master of chop socky — the ultraviolent Hong Kong regurgitation of Hollywood action films — made this just before departing for America. Laserdisc is the way to fully appreciate Woo's kinetic action sequences and perverse sense of humor.

I KNOW WHERE I'M GOING (1945)

Criterion; $69.95
Directors: Michael Powell and Emeric Pressburger
Not Rated
Cast: Wendy Hiller, Roger Livesey and Pamela Brown
U.K.

Another in this year's exploration of Powell and Pressburger, with a new volume of Powell's memoirs and the rerelease of less-well-known material such as this. Though known mostly for mastery of fantastic epics, this intimate story of a woman losing her romantic resolve is just as satisfying. The laserdisc also includes a look at the Scottish setting today.

OKLAHOMA! (1955)

CLV; $59.98
Director: Fred Zinneman
Not Rated
Cast: Shirley Jones, Rod Steiger, Gordon MacRae and Gloria Grahame

The big story here is that the laserdisc (and a new video edition) has been made from the fabled Todd A-O print that until now has been untransferable. The movie was actually shot twice, once in the 65mm process and once in 35mm CinemaScope. The larger negative provided sharper grain, better color, and, because the Todd A-O version was shot first, better performances. An interesting anomaly in film history and a great rediscovery.

PLATOON (1986)

Pioneer; $129.98
Director: Oliver Stone
Cast: Charlie Sheen, Willem Dafoe, Tom Berenger and Forest Whitaker
Rated R

Director Stone has made a career of plumbing the experience — both his own and society at large — of the tumultuous 1960s. The visceral impact of Vietnam, made even more vivid on laserdisc, could only have been rendered by a man who had been there, as his commentary reveals. Interviews with cast and crew reveal the hardships of the shoot.

THE RED SHOES (1948)

Voyager; $124.95
Directors: Michael Powell and Emeric Pressburger
Not Rated
Cast: Moira Shearer, Marius Goring and Anton Walbrook
U.K.

This is why you bought a laserdisc player. Few other directors engage all the senses as the team of Powell and Pressburger do, and the crisp Technicolor of this transfer to laserdisc makes their artistry even more apparent. The backstage glimpse at the ballet is perhaps their most famous effort, and, in addition, the laserdisc yields Martin Scorsese discussing the work of the directors, clips from their other films, interviews and Jeremy Irons reading from a novelization of the story.

REPULSION (1965)

Voyager; $99.95
Director: Roman Polanski
Not Rated
Cast: Catherine Deneuve, Ian Hendry and John Fraser
U.K.

A new letterbox edition from a better-than-average print brings the psychological terror that Polanski perfected into sharp focus. Both the director and Deneuve discuss Polanski's first English-language film on the second audio track.

SCHINDLER'S LIST

MCA/Universal; $134.95
Director: Steven Spielberg
Rated PG-13
Cast: Liam Neeson, Ben Kingsley and Ralph Fiennes

The collector's edition of Spielberg's universally hailed story of the man who saved thousands of Jews from the Holocaust comes with Thomas Kenealy's book, an audio CD of John Williams's score and a picture book with an introduction by Spielberg.

SID AND NANCY (1986)

Voyager; $99.95
Director: Alex Cox
Rated R
Cast: Gary Oldman and Chloe Webb

Cox had to reach for some pretty compelling, but off-the-wall visuals to encompass the black humor and tragedy of Sex Pistols's bassist Sid Vicious and his junkie girlfriend Nancy Spungeon. The punk-rock Romeo and Juliet story is accompanied by candid footage of the real Sid and Nancy, interviews and commentary from the band and hangers-on.

THE SOUND OF MUSIC (1965)

Image; $54.95
Director: Robert Wise
Cast: Julie Andrews, Christopher Plummer and Eleanor Parker
Rated G

The Rodgers and Hammerstein musical based on

the life of the singing Von Trapp family's flight from Nazi-occupied Austria has to be one of the most widely seen and admired of all movie musicals. For its 30th birthday, *The Sound of Music* has been rereleased on laserdisc in a THX, wide screen version. The set also includes a remastered audio CD.

SWING, SWING, SWING: CLASSIC BIG BAND AND JAZZ SHORTS
MGM/UA; $124.98
Director: Various
Not Rated

Jazz fans are thankful that an oddity known as the Vitaphone music short flourished in the 1930s and 1940s. The musical interludes that entertained audiences in movie theaters are now one of the best documents we have of the top bands of the time. This five-disc set includes 45 of the performances, ranging from Artie Shaw to Eubie Blake to Cab Calloway.

TIM BURTON'S THE NIGHTMARE BEFORE CHRISTMAS (1993)
Touchstone; $99.99
Director: Henry Selick
Animation
Rated PG

Three laserdiscs give the viewer plenty of opportunity to marvel at both the inventive animation (with freeze-frame available) and the witty story. The set includes two early animations from producer Burton, *Frankenweenie* and *Vincent*, and plenty of commentary and documentation.

THE VAL LEWTON COLLECTION (1942–1946)
Image; nine film compilation; $179.95
Not Rated

Lewton was the producer who masterminded a flurry of low-budget horror classics at Universal

Studios. This collection brings together in pristine transfers nine of his cult favorites, including *Cat People* and *The Body Snatcher.*

U2: RATTLE AND HUM (1988)
Paramount; $34.95
Director: Phil Joanou
U2
Not Rated

The documentary of U2's rambles around America supporting their *Joshua Tree* album and their contact with local musicians and styles gets a stylish treatment and a remastered soundtrack in this laserdisc reissue.

THE WAVELETS OF THE FUTURE
A compression technology that can produce real-time video on computers may be in the future. The near future, as in, this year. Most current technology displays images at eight frames per second, yielding a jerky, fuzzy picture. The Houston Advanced Research Center has developed a compression technology based on the wavelet theory of mathematics that reduces the need for wide bandwidth or huge storage to transmit full-motion video. You'll be able to catch the wavelet online, in movies on CD-ROM and in computer games.

ENHANCED CD's
Fewer recording artists are satisfied these days with simply recording music onto tape, and the industry is catching up with their multimedia ambitions. Watch for CD-ROMs to include videos, games, screen savers and video wallpaper. A new company, nu.millenia Entertainment, will license material from major labels in order to create interactive, enhanced CDs. One product will be the Super45 that contains one song and one screen saver for $5.95. EPs containing 3–4 songs are expected to sell for $9.95, and full albums will be $19.95.

Leisure-Time Online

■ BY CHRISTINE A. DePEDRO AND NEIL McMANUS

OKAY, IT'S A FRIDAY, 2020, AND JUST 15 MORE MINUTES OF AUTO-ELECTRONIC RESEARCH and you can call it a night. Once you've E-mailed your report to headquarters in Denver, it's time to kick back, relax and . . . dial up a chat line. You've made your usual Friday night date with Odette-Online in the Spank and Tickle forum and don't want to be late. She gets huffy if you keep her waiting. The day's download of top news stories, QuickTime previews of Hollywood summer movies and that family update from mom will have to wait. For the next couple of hours, you'll be in a virtual tête-à-tête.

CYBERTAINMENT

Wait a minute. What was the date again? How about 1995? Yes, it's true. All this (and more) are available to you as we, uh, speak. People are spending their leisure time online — as much as on movies, books, videos or even that less-interactive third-cousin, television. Ask your coworker how he spent the idle hours after quitting time and he may tell you about a furious debate with some hothead in Dallas over the upcoming elections, or how he listened to this week's British Top 40 hits, in real time, from Top of the Pops in London.

With personal computers projected to become as prevalent as telephones, America Online playing on-line host to most of the known world and World Wide Web pages multiplying like bunnies, there is a dramatic shift underway in how we spend our off hours.

What will it take for online services and the Internet to be considered popular entertainment? There are probably hundreds of answers to this question but we're guessing that people will think of on-line surfing as entertainment as soon as getting online becomes absolutely effortless.

In a 1995 Gallup poll, commissioned by MCI, 49 percent of the respondents categorized themselves as resistant to new technology. In the survey, 35 percent of respondents said they fear technology because it forces them to continually learn new skills. These people aren't cyberphobic or technophobic. They just have better things to do than to constantly figure out how to get their computers to work. And the number of non-computer-geek users of the Web is increasing. According to an on-line survey conducted in the fall of 1994 by a University of Michigan professor, 44 percent of his respondents contacted the Web through powerful Unix workstations. By the time of his follow-up survey in the spring of 1995, that share was down to 8.8 percent, and the share of respondents using PCs increased to 52 percent. The number of casual users is increasing rapidly.

Imagine if turning on a television took the same amount of work as going online. Instead of tapping the power and channel buttons on the TV remote, you would have

Netscape

BEST-SELLING SOFTWARE OF 1994

CD-ROM TITLES

1. **Myst,** multimedia PC and Macintosh (Brøderbund)
2. **Doom II,** MS-DOS (GT Interactive)
3. **5 Ft. 10 Pack Volume I,** MS-DOS (Sirius)
4. **Star Wars Rebel Assault,** MS-DOS and Macintosh (LucasArts)
5. **7th Guest,** multimedia PC and Macintosh (Virgin)
6. **Microsoft Encarta,** multimedia PC and Macintosh (Microsoft)
7. **Lion King Story Book,** multimedia PC (Disney)
8. **Print Shop Deluxe CD Ensemble,** Windows and Macintosh (Brøderbund)
9. **Quicken CD-ROM Deluxe,** Windows (Intuit)
10. **Corel Gallery,** Windows and Macintosh (Corel)
11. **5 Ft. 10 Pack Volume 2,** MS-DOS (Sirius)
12. **Microsoft Bookshelf,** multimedia PC and Macintosh (Microsoft)
13. **Outpost,** multimedia PC (Sierra On-line)
14. **Street Atlas USA,** multimedia PC and Macintosh (DeLorme)

Myst

15. **Just Grandma and Me,** multimedia PC and Macintosh (Living Books)
16. **King's Quest VII: The Princeless Bride,** multimedia PC and Macintosh (Sierra On-line)
17. **Where in the World Is Carmen Sandiego?,** multimedia PC and Macintosh (Brøderbund)
18. **Wing Commander III,** multimedia PC (Origin)

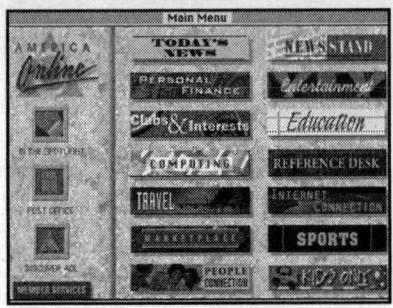

America Online

to turn on the cable box. Turn on the television. Wait for your TV operating system to load up. Open a communications program. Configure the program to initialize the cable box. Set the program to connect your TV to a local cable provider. Type in a password, and, once connected, navigate to the TV program you want by poking through menus, clicking on icons and typing strange command sequences. If TV were that hard, people might venture outdoors more often.

Prodigy, America Online, CompuServe, e-World and the other commercial on-line services cannot expect an avalanche of subscribers until they become brainlessly easy to use. And that ease of use extends beyond how you hook up and navigate the service into how you budget for your monthly bill. Subscribers will flock to whichever on-line services can make themselves push-button easy and make the often-cryptic Internet seem warm, fuzzy and fun.

Assuming that America Online has tapped into Middle America's mindset of point-and-click, with their push-button graphics and folders-within-folders, why haven't the masses jumped on the cyberspace bandwagon? Ya gotta pay to play. While it is true that you don't need the newest, most powerful and most expensive set-up to access most services, having a fast connection (9600 bps or more) certainly adds to the fun and convenience. Waiting 20 minutes for a graphic-laden Web page to download can discourage anyone trying to surf the Net. A peek at your log-in access charge could also prompt a DISCONNECT faster than you can say "MCI Friends and Family."

Of course, none of this has impeded the hard-core cyberjunkies who make on-line connections a way of life. In the digital pharmacopeia, a daily fix of E-mail from family, long-distance friends and even virtual pen pals is a necessity, as vital to one's life as the morning cuppa joe. The day must end with a stopover in the local bulletin board service (BBS) to chat with your favorite columnist from the weekly arts paper or to post a response to the movie reviewer who panned your favorite film. Insomniacs are no longer doomed to B-grade movies and infomercials in the wee hours. Instead, they can while away the hours building a virtual world.

This is all well and good for kids who were brought up sucking on a SIMM chip, but is there anything out in the vast reaches of space for us plain ol' analog-raised folks? Well, yes. There is stuff out there, and more and more of it every day. Traditional methods of information and communication are expanding to include electronic "extras," making on-line browsing more fun. For example, services like AOL and Prodigy host literally hundreds of electronic versions of newsstand magazines. Michael Rogers, managing editor of *Newsweek*'s popular Prodigy site, said his staff relies on editorial savvy, graphical layouts, hyperlinks and audio to raise the high watermark for on-line magazines. "We were waiting for [on-line] technology to catch up to where we could deliver something with real added value and had the characteristics and personality of *Newsweek*, that went beyond *Newsweek* on the page. We certainly applaud *Time* and *US News* [*and World Report*] and all the other 200 magazines that have gone online, but stripping all the typesetting commands from your copy and dropping it into ASCII text to us is not adding value," he said.

Today's on-line providers have a more realistic, as opposed to futuristic, outlook on navigation. Ted Leonsis, president of America Online Services, turned to an unlikely source for inspiration on how AOL would help its members cruise the Web. "I see us becoming the Carnival cruise line of this business," Leonsis said. "Carnival [gives

19. **Commanche Maximum Overkill**, MS-DOS (Nova Logic)

20. **Tortoise and the Hare**, multimedia PC and Macintosh (Living Books)

HOME EDUCATION TITLES FOR MS-DOS/WINDOWS

The following titles are on floppy disk unless otherwise noted.

1. **Microsoft Encarta**, CD-ROM (Microsoft)

2. **Where in the World Is Carmen Sandiego?** (Brøderbund)

3. **Lion King Story Book**, CD-ROM (Disney)

4. **Mavis Beacon Teaches Typing** (Software Toolworks)

The Lion King Storybook

5. **Oregon Trail** (MECC)

6. **Reader Rabbit 1** (Learning Company)

7. **Where in the USA Is Carmen Sandiego?** (Brøderbund)

8. **Microsoft Bookshelf**, CD-ROM (Microsoft)

9. **Grolier's Encyclopedia**, CD-ROM (Grolier)

10. **Reader Rabbit 2** (Learning Company)

HOME EDUCATION TITLES FOR MACINTOSH

The following titles are on floppy disk unless otherwise noted.

1. **Grolier's Encyclopedia** (Grolier)

2. **Where in the World Is Carmen Sandiego?** CD-ROM (Brøderbund)

3. **Mavis Beacon Teaches Typing** (Software Toolworks)

4. **Mario Teaches Typing** (Interplay)

5. **New Math Blaster Plus** (Davidson)

6. **Oregon Trail** (MECC)

7. **Microsoft Encarta**, CD-ROM (Microsoft)

8. **Reader Rabbit 1** (Learning Company)

9. **Just Grandma and Me**, CD-ROM (Living Books)

10. **Where in the USA Is Carmen Sandiego?** (Brøderbund)

The Oregon Trail

Sim City 2000

PC GAMES FOR MS-DOS/WINDOWS

The following titles are on floppy disk unless otherwise noted.

1. **Doom II,** CD-ROM and MS-DOS (GT Interactive)
2. **Myst,** CD-ROM (Broderbund)
3. **Sim City 2000** (Maxis)
4. **5 Ft. 10 Pack Volume 1,** CD-ROM (Sirius)
5. **Microsoft Flight Simulator** (Microsoft)
6. **Tie Fighter** (LucasArts)
7. **Star Wars Rebel Assault,** CD-ROM (LuscasArts)
8. **7th Guest,** CD-ROM (Virgin)
9. **Sim City** (Maxis)
10. **Outpost,** CD-ROM and Windows (Sierra On-line)

MACINTOSH GAMES

The following titles are on floppy disk unless otherwise noted.

1. **Myst,** CD-ROM (Brøderbund)
2. **Sim City 2000** (Maxis)
3. **Chessmaster 3000** (Software Toolworks)
4. **Sim City** (Maxis)
5. **FA-18 Hornet** (Graphic Simulations)
6. **Star Wars Rebel Assault,** CD-ROM (LucasArts)
7. **7th Guest,** CD-ROM (Virgin)
8. **Pathways Into Darkness** (Bungee)
9. **Links Pro** (Access)
10. **Jeopardy With Alex Trebeck** (Gametek)

Source: PC Data

you] predictable pricing: Your fare, your activities on the boat, all of your meals are included. No surprises. Your berth is going to be clean, and it's going to be safe."

Consumers have a decision to make after dinner. According to CNN's interactive specialist Chet Burgess, "Every hour that someone spends on a PC going out and selecting his own information online is an hour he's not available to watch CNN." Leonsis also backs up this notion. "I'm more afraid of Jerry Seinfeld than I am of Bill Gates. You'll be seeing on-line services program like TV networks. . . . We're a prime-time network. We're trying to reach people with families."

Being online has taught people that they can find entertainment for themselves. They do not have to sit and wait for a CNN or HBO producer to put the news story or the movie that they're most interested in on television. And even though people are probably not familiar with all the buzzwords, they are learning that nonlinear systems exist and they can manipulate those systems themselves. The consumers are bypassing the gatekeepers. And the power to control may be the killer app that makes on-line entertainment a common household phrase. ∎

Christine DePedro writes reviews of Unix-Graphics software for several national magazines. She spends most of her days and nights surfing the Void and would really love a new SGI INDY. She can be reached at Xine@sirius.com.

Neil McManus is the executive editor of Digital Media *in San Francisco. He produces CD-ROM titles and World Wide Web home pages, and consults with television networks and print publishers on moving to digital production. His E-mail address is NeilM@netcom.com.*

The IPEA's 20 Must-Have CD-ROMS

BEST OF MICROSOFT ENTERTAINMENT PACK
Microsoft

Tetris, Pipe Dream, Taipei, Tut's Tomb. This popular software from Microsoft combines your favorite games in one package. Test your card skills and luck at the classic game, Dr. Black Jack. Challenge yourself with JazzBall, the lightening fast arcade-style game in which you have to trap the balls and beat the clock. This package includes only the best and is sure to please even the most devout computer-game addicts.

CHESSMASTER 3000
Software Toolworks

Chess players of all levels will love this interactive chess tutorial that offers plenty of options including a replay and analysis of 150 classic chess games and an extensive opening move library. *Chessmaster 3000* not only has unlimited levels of play, it also rates your playing and gives you advice on how to make wiser moves. An interactive correspondence feature allows you to play against opponents in the same room or across the country. Chess notations are in coordinate, algebraic, long algebraic and English descriptions.

DOOM II
GT Interactive

In this lightning-fast, ultraviolent game, it's up to you, the superhero, to save the earth from flesh-eating mutants, monsters and demons of Hell. Like its predecessor, *Doom II* takes you through a labyrinth of corridors — a perfect opportunity to use your arsenal to blow away everything in your path. You can play this game solo or network with a friend or friends.

5 FT. 10 PACK VOLUMES 1 AND 2
Sirius

VOLUME 1

Sirius Publishing packages 10 multimedia titles from several publishers in one bundle. The bundle includes the following games, educational titles and reference products: *Time, Man of the Year; Stellar 7; Doom: Episode I Knee Deep in the Dead; King's Quest V; World Vista Atlas; CD-ROM of CD-ROM's; PC Animation Festival; World Factbook; Best of Media Clips* and *PC Karaoke – Classic Oldies.*

VOLUME 2

Only six months after the commercial success of *5 Ft. 10 Pak Volume I,* Sirius Publishing released Volume II, which includes the following assortment of CDs: *Multimedia Jumpstart; Battle Chess Enhanced; Home Medical Advisor v3.0; Rock, Rap 'N Roll; Movie Select; Space Quest IV; 2000 Fonts; Arts & Letters War Birds* and *PC Karaoke — Family Fun.*

JUST GRANDMA & ME
Brøderbund
Based on the book by Mercer Mayer

While on their way to the beach, Little Critter and his grandma experience a series of adventures ranging from a ride on a wind-blown umbrella to receiving a kiss from a fish. Talking creatures, lively animation, narration and music work together on this CD-ROM to enhance reading and storytelling skills.

MICROSOFT ENCARTA
Microsoft

A must-have reference resource, *Microsoft Encarta* combines 25,000 up-to-date, full-text articles from *Funk & Wagnall's* 29-volume encyclopedia with eight hours of digital sound, thousands of photos, videos, charts, maps and an illustrated time line from 15 million B.C. to the present. More than 250,000 hypertext links exist to facilitate switching from one topic to another.

MICROSOFT FLIGHT SIMULATOR
Microsoft

Experience the thrills of flying as you maneuver your way across the world with the highly realistic *Microsoft Flight Simulator.* You can visit farmlands, cities and towns, mountains and coastlines — all rendered in full color graphics and seasonal colors. This program includes special nighttime effects, changeable weather conditions and the look and sounds of a real cockpit and control panel.

THE MOTION PICTURE GUIDE
Delphi/Fox; distributed by Ransom Interactive

This comprehensive guide offers information on just about everything you want to know about sound film released in the United States from 1927 to 1994. *The Guide* includes 35,000 movie titles and allows you to search by title, cast

and crew member, year of release, keyword and other criteria. A hypertext feature allows you to

Using PC Data's monthly lists of best-selling software and CD-ROMS, we compiled our own list of software hits for the first half of 1995.

CD-ROM TITLES

1. **Myst,** multimedia PC and Macintosh (Brøderbund)
2. **Dark Forces,** multimedia PC (LucasArts)
3. **Doom II,** multimedia PC (GT Interactive)
4. **Print Shop Deluxe CD Ensemble,** Windows (Brøderbund)
5. **D!Zone Collector's Edition,** MS-DOS (Wizard Works)
6. **Quicken CD-ROM Deluxe,** Windows (Intuit)
7. **Street Atlas USA,** multimedia PC and Macintosh (DeLorme)
8. **Lion King Storybook,** multimedia PC (Disney)
9. **7th Guest,** multimedia PC and Macintosh (Virgin)
10. **One Stop CD Shop,** multimedia PC (Softkey)

HOME EDUCATION TITLES FOR MS-DOS/WINDOWS

The following titles are on floppy disk unless otherwise noted.

1. **Lion King Story Book,** CD-ROM (Disney)
2. **Aladdin Activity Center,** CD-ROM (Disney)
3. **Where in the World Is Carmen Sandiego?** (Brøderbund)
4. **Oregon Trail** (MECC)
5. **Math Blaster: In Search of Spot** (Davidson)

HOME EDUCATION TITLES FOR MACINTOSH

The following titles are on floppy disk unless otherwise noted.

1. **Aladdin Activity Center,** CD-ROM (Disney)
2. **Where in the World Is Carmen Sandiego?** (Brøderbund)
3. **Mavis Beacon Teaches Typing** (Mindscape)
4. **Mario Teaches Typing** (Interplay)
5. **Oregon Trail** (MECC)

move from one film to another by a simple click and also compiles filmographies with another click. Each film is summarized and amusing anecdotes and background information are provided.

MYST
Brøderbund

Open the dusty book at your feet and begin to read. Suddenly you are on Myst, an island in another reality. Using clues hidden on the is-land, you solve mind-bending puzzles to unravel the age-old, family-tragedy mystery. Sure to be a classic, it will be tough to surpass Myst's pioneering intrigue.

OREGON TRAIL
MECC

Journey through the rugged terrain of the Old West along trails carved by 19th-century pioneers. Explore the wilderness from Independence, Missouri, to Willamette Valley, Oregon, where you will ford treacherous rivers and face dangers such as broken wagon wheels and disease. Your food supply is limited so you must learn to hunt for survival and trade with Native Americans. As this historical adventure escorts you through our nation's past, you will appreciate the lives of the early settlers and the hardships they endured.

PRINT SHOP DELUXE CD ENSEMBLE
Brøderbund

Get the message out yourself, and enjoy doing it. That's the idea behind this useful ensemble of five Print Shop programs for creating banners, calendars, cards, envelopes, letterhead and more. Intuitive click-and-drag commands make it easy to link up a wide selection of layouts with more than 1,600 graphics and 73 scalable fonts.

QUICKEN CD-ROM DELUXE
Intuit

The world's best-selling personal finance software combines the personal finance management tools introduced in earlier versions with added features. The new features are organized in a three-room suite: a conference room where business experts offer advice to help users make better financial decisions, a home office containing several organizational tools and a library that includes a mutual fund selector, a tax guidebook and a stock guide.

THE RESIDENTS' FREAK SHOW
Voyager

Meet Tex the Barker, Harry the Head, Wanda the Worm, Herman the Human Mole and other freaks when you secretly go behind the circus tent and into the trailers of *The Residents' Freak Show*. Witness rituals and tragic secrets of the bizarre backstage world while you discover members' fetishes as well as fantasies through interactive stories, music videos and digital art. Also included is a selection of notorious underground movies.

7TH GUEST
Virgin

Crazed toy maker Henry Stauf has invited six guests to his mansion for a dark and mysterious visit. You, the seventh guest, explore the mansion solving puzzles and seeking clues to determine the fate of the other six guests.

SIM CITY 2000
Maxis

Imagine a world where you can design and build your own city without making any structural and aesthetic compromises. *Sim City 2000* allows you to create the city of your dreams — complete with an underground layer that includes subways and utilities. Mix and match different buildings in an unlimited number of graphic sets and then show off your work in color or black-and-white printouts.

STAR WARS REBEL ASSAULT
LucasArts

As a rebel fighter pilot named Rookie One, you are immersed in a *Star Wars* universe with video footage, original score and sound effects from the movies. After you master your flight and combat skills, you engage in deep-space battles to defend Tatoome from Imperial attack.

PC GAMES FOR MS-DOS/WINDOWS

The following titles are on floppy disk unless otherwise noted.

1. **Doom II,** CD-ROM and MS-DOS (GT Interactive)
2. **Dark Forces,** CD-ROM (LucasArts)
3. **Myst,** CD-ROM (Brøderbund)
4. **D!Zone Collector's Edition** (Wizard Works)
5. **Descent,** CD-ROM (Interplay)
6. **Sim City 2000,** MS-DOS and Windows (Maxis)
7. **Microsoft Flight Simulator** (Microsoft)
8. **NASCAR Racing,** CD-ROM (Virgin)
9. **Best of Microsoft Entertainment Pack** (Microsoft)
10. **7th Guest,** CD-ROM (Virgin)

MACINTOSH GAMES

The following titles are on floppy disk unless otherwise noted.

1. **Myst,** CD-ROM (Brøderbund)
2. **Marathon,** CD-ROM (Bungee)
3. **Wolfenstein 3D** (Interplay)
4. **Sim City 2000** (Maxis)
5. **Mindscape CD Mac Pack,** CD-ROM (Interplay)
6. **Star Wars Rebel Assault,** CD-ROM (LucasArts)
7. **Links Pro** (Access)
8. **Chessmaster 3000** (Mindscape)
9. **Mac 4 Pack,** CD-ROM (Interplay)
10. **FA-18 Hornet** (Graphic Simulations)

WHIZ KID ON CD-ROM GAMES

BY SO-CHUNG SHINN

Marco Cekic, a 16-year-old whiz kid from Austin, Texas, faces excruciating death at least three times a week. When he isn't hanging out with his buddies or practicing the electric guitar, he plays computer games and challenges the most treacherous, repulsive enemies in bloody battles of survival. After exhausting the courses at his high school a year ago, he takes classes at the University of Texas — Austin, but still finds time for **Doom II** and **Demolition Man**. We spent a few minutes with him to chat about computer games.

What makes a good computer game?
Games can't be too hard because the player will always lose and no one wants to be a chronic loser. Conversely, games shouldn't be too easy, because there is no challenge and the game gets old *fast*. "Games should involve *some* brainwork. **Street Fighter** has excellent graphics but graphics alone don't make a good game. **Gadget** is terrible because you can't screw up. What a waste of time." Apparently, game storylines also contribute to the entertainment factor. Without a coherent storyline, the game is just "dull and mindless." When asked about the explicit violence in today's popular games, he said, "You have to have violence. Violence and plenty of action. The bloodier, the better."

Game strategies
Marco doesn't employ any particular strategies. He just likes to sit down and play. He admits to using the instruction book once in a while for hints, but for the most part, learns by trial and error. And understandably, "the more you play, the better you get."

What Marco likes
He recommends **Rise of the Triad** and **Demolition Man** because they are entertaining and both have adjustable violence levels so they can get pretty gruesome. **Shadow Warrior** is "ridiculously hard" but also an excellent game. **The Daedalus Encounter** has awesome graphics. He highly recommends the entire 3DO system because it generally has high quality games and visual effects. Other games on his top 10 list are **Tie Fighter Wars**, **Full Throttle**, **Siv Net**, **Marathon for the Mac** and **Mortal Kombat III**.

What Marco doesn't like
When asked about his top 10 worst games list, he didn't have many titles to offer. "When you play a game that you don't like, you generally don't play it again. Those games are not worth remembering." He finds **7th Guest** somewhat irritating because it has a lengthy 10 minute introduction that can't be bypassed. "**Censory Overload** sucks. It just sucks." Other huge disappointments include the **Sega Saturn** and the **32X Genesis system**. ∎

STRAVINSKY'S THE RITE OF SPRING
Voyager
Robert Winter chronicles the life and times of Igor Stravinsky. Winter offers a running commentary concerning the controversy of the premiere of "Rite of Spring" and a detailed discussion of the original production. The Montreal Symphony performs the piece, and the user can study the performance bar by bar or listen to the piece as a whole. A Questions and Answers game segment lets you test your knowledge against friends and family.

STREET ATLAS USA
DeLorme
Street Atlas USA provides a complete, up-to-date searchable road map of the entire United States from the largest interstates down to the tiniest back roads. The database provides access to more than one million lakes, ponds, rivers, railroads and monuments. Users can search for data by place name, ZIP code or telephone number.

WHERE IN THE WORLD IS CARMEN SANDIEGO?
Brøderbund
This worldwide chase takes you to exotic sites as you gather evidence to unravel mysteries, identify crooks and discover their whereabouts. Digital sound, original score, *National Geographic* location photographs and hilarious animation provide hours of educational entertainment.

WOLFENSTEIN 3D
Formgen
In this early 3-D CD-ROM game, which is still a favorite of many, you must find your way out of the labyrinthine Nazi headquarters where you are being held captive. It's not an easy escape, though, as the Nazis are heavily armed and many in number. By finding hidden rooms loaded with treasure and ammunition (and for experts, a hidden floor), you can increase your fire power and escape to the roof of the building.

SOMA City: Life Behind the Curtain in Multimedia Gulch

■ BY CHRISTINE A. DEPEDRO

A FTER MOVING TO SAN FRANCISCO FOUR YEARS AGO, I SPENT A SUNNY AFTERNOON deciphering the SF Muni system, finding my way to ground zero of San Francisco's art community. As the double bus snaked its way south of Market, known as SOMA, it passed warehouses and factory outlets, deserted streets farther and farther from downtown high-rises and lunch-time crowds. Where the hell was I? I noticed a small oval of green as I walked up Third toward Market. Dotting the grass were nine-to-fivers eating from their brown bags and catching rays. I couldn't imagine where any of these people would work.

Months later, when I finally landed a job, I was dismayed to discover that my new office was exactly one block east of the little picnic area, known as South Park. Yeow, stuck in the middle of deadsville. It wasn't what I envisioned, and a visiting friend echoed my impression: "It must be a bummer to spend most of your waking hours in a graveyard."

Imagine my surprise when I opened the local paper to a front-page article on the new entertainment hotbed: SOMA, Multimedia Gulch. Defined roughly as the area bound by First, Fourth,

CYBERLIFE

Howard and Townsend streets, with South Park as its shimmering nucleus, Multimedia Gulch was described in the article, and in many others since, as a thriving, pulsing cauldron of creativity. Ignited by the launch of *Wired* magazine, one of the most successful new magazines in recent history, forecasters and investors were scrambling to define this new frontier. Give it a name and a place, throw in some spicy marketing jargon and — voilà! — a new media destination, ready to be packaged and sold. This place was now known for housing the best and brightest, the real pioneers, so with it that whatever they did defined wired and tired for the rest of us.

Needless to say, an industry/trend — or, more accurately trend/industry — defined by an over-hyped magazine should be viewed with a jaundiced eye at best. As the media crowed, my fellow worker-bees and I were ignorant of the phenomenon in our midst. We were still trying to get up to Market Street before dark to avoid the muggers that were conveniently left off the Multimedia Gulch maps. And while *Wired* initially boasted of its spacious old warehouse office, they moved out pretty quickly to more palatial digs after what I assume was a mighty nippy winter in that drafty lodge.

Even now, *Wired* positions itself — and seems to have the whole media boat following in its wake — on the cutting edge. With the recent expansion of the World Wide Web, HotWired, *Wired*'s on-line site, has placed itself on the forefront of a movement that no one else seems to know existed until they brought it to our attention.

Wired

IPEA's Recommended Internet Sites

Here is a selection of Web sites the editors of *The Entertainment Almanac* came across while surfing on the Web.

Alfred Hitchcock's WWW
http://nextdch.mty.itesm.mx/~plopezg/kaplan/Hitchcock.html
An overview of Hitchcock's life and films, this site offers fans a resource for Hitchcock's filmography, classic cameos, a list of the director's best quotes and other valuable information.

American Memory
http://rs6.loc.gov/amhom.html
Relive U.S. history through the Library of Congress's extensive collection of primary sources and archival material covering America's culture and history.

BookWire
http://www.bookwire.com
For surfers who love to read, BookWire provides a comprehensive guide to book-related sources on the Internet including bestseller lists, book reviews and a calendar of events.

Broadway World Wide
http://.www.webcom./~broadway/welcome.html
Get up-to-date Broadway, Off-Broadway and national tour listings and show summaries from this site. Also included is information on London's West End theater district and links to other performing arts sites.

c/net: The Computer Network
http://www.cnet.com/
Based on the c/net cable TV channel, this site keeps you up-to-date on the latest Internet technology and products.

Cool Site of the Day
http://www.infi.net/sounds/cool.au
Users are provided daily with a new link to the coolest sites on the web.

CRAYON
http://sun.bucknell.edu/~boulter/crayon/
With CReAte Your Own Newspaper, a customized newspaper program, users can order a personalized paper that contains only the sections that they want to read.

Creative Labs, Inc.
http://www.creaf.com
Discover exciting new multimedia products from Creative Labs, Inc., a developer and manufacturer of multimedia sound and video products and multimedia kits for entertainment and education.

If this is the hipper-than-thou crowd, things must be pretty slow out in suit-and-tie land. A peek behind the curtain reveals that Multimedia Gulch isn't so much a place as a state of mind. The people who do the actual work are the stuff of myth and they define the reality. And work they do. That's the secret behind the hype. Saunter into Cafe Centro, order a cappuccino and sit down next to the guy in Armani and the *Melrose Place* wannabe. If you lean back and wait to overhear the hatching of the next big thing, you'll be waiting long after the foam has settled to the bottom of the cup. The after-work flute of champagne at Cava 555 may be exciting to sip, perched next to someone who might be important, but posers will be posers, and anybody brandishing a business card reading "multimedia guru" can be counted on to be nothing of the sort. The real movers and shakers will be hunched over a keyboard, the blue glare of the monitor flickering off their faces as they try — just one more time — to get that last code sequence to run without crashing the system. They will still be there as the clock creeps toward prime time, as the networks sign off, and even as the club kids roll out of bed at noon. The defining feature of those-who-must-be-cool would probably be the red rims lining their puffy eyes.

That's what it takes to be a real part of the scene, logging those digital hours. While cramming in two hefty projects before a well-deserved vacation, I spent many late nights and weekends staring at my own 21-inch Radius monitor. During the entire period of leaving in the middle of the night and arriving weekends at the crack of 10 A.M., not once were the lights off at PF Magic, a CD-ROM game publisher down the hall. A fluke? Don't believe it. Hours are long and hard, but not necessarily spent in a drafty SOMA warehouse. As the info superhighway has sprouted more exits and on-ramps, home systems supplement or replace the tony Gulch address. Multimedia life as we know it is being born all over San Francisco — and the U.S. — in basements and bedrooms.

With the curtain pulled back, there's a different perspective on finding digital nirvana located just off South Park. You can go to the dead-zone mapped out by the media, but what would you find there? Chances are, if it's easily found, it's a facade. One of the first businesses in San Francisco to cash in on the scene was the Icon Byte Bar and Grill, a trendy bar/restaurant at Ninth and Folsom with its hook being direct Internet access at terminals placed among the tables so you can surf the Net while you slurp the suds. Out-of-towners who trek down to see and be seen and jostle for a spot on the Internet queue are exposed as "newbies," people new to the Internet community. No dedicated line? No zippy personal net address? Puhleese. Back to the boonies. "Where's your domain?" is the pick-up line of the Net-linked '90s.

All in all, getting a piece of the multimedia swirl in the 1990s is even harder than pulling up a chair for lunch at the Algonquin round table in the 1920s. Without a place of your own, there just isn't any there there. And the rules keep changing every day. Two years ago, WWW if mentioned at all, would not be in the same sentence as multimedia. Today, the Web spins its own tales of fortune, and, much to the relief of the big corporations, anyone, anywhere can check in. The multimedia world steams ahead with no one at the helm. Most of us aren't even in the same ship: sloops bob along side tugs, junks and kayaks vie for space, and everyone's looking for the flagship to lead the way. Perhaps that's why the Gulch was created in the first place. If you can't define *what* is happening, try to pin down *where* it's happening. And as the Gulch fades into the distance as a buzzword which has lost it's buzz, the world looks for another hook. To many, that still means *Wired*, the original denizens of the Gulch and perhaps the Algonquin round table of today. *Wired* creates a world unto itself, writing on a trend that becomes a marketing buzzword that moves into the system on which *Wired* reports, that starts a trend, and so on. The point? Sorry Dorothy, there is no Oz. If you're interested in plugging in, remember: there's no place like home. ∎

Dia Center for the Arts
http://www.diacenter.org/
Check out the extraordinary happenings at the Dia Center for the Arts, a multidisciplinary contemporary-arts organization. This site provides highlights of exhibitions, programs, a calendar of events, publications and poetry.

ESPNet SportsZone
http://espnet.sportszone.com/
The world of sports is finally at your fingertips. ESPN brings the latest sports news, live chats, scoreboards and sports entertainment information right to your computer.

Gilbert and Sullivan Archive
http://diamond.idbsu.edu/gas/GaS.html
This comprehensive archive contains a variety of G&S items such as librettos, song scores and articles. It also includes an extensive opera schedule guide of performances worldwide.

The Gutter Voice
http://www.io.org:80/~gutter/voice.html
Read compelling short works and poetry from novelists and in literary publications such as Gordon Lish's *Quarterly* and Toronto's alternative newspaper the *Eye*.

Internet Movie Database
http://www.cm.cf.ac.uk/Movies
The Internet Movie Database includes thousands of movies, each with reviews, summaries, ratings and credits. Users can search by title, genre, year, cast and crew members.

Macromedia
http://www.macromedia.com/
Explore the multimedia and design industry using this informational source for multimedia and design news, resources and services. Technical support, training and consulting are available on this site.

Mr. Showbiz
http://web3.starwave.com/showbiz/
Everything you ever wanted to know about the biggest celebrities is now on the Web. Read the latest gossip, chat with other surfers or see what albums made the latest *Billboard* top 100.

Money and Investing Update
http://update.wsj.com/
Whether you are reviewing the latest European stock market activity or skimming through business news, this Internet-based publication of the *Wall Street Journal* provides the latest U.S. and global financial news and analysis reports.

CONTINUED ON PAGE 569 ▶

1994 Best of the Web Awards

Web surfers nominated sites over a two-month period and voted for finalists over a two-week period on the Best of the Web Award site (http://wings.buffa-lo.edu/contest/awards). The awards were announced at the International World Wide Web Conference on May 26, 1994 in Geneva. Both the site name and its Uniform Resource Locater (URL) are listed.

Best Overall Site
National Center for Supercomputing Applications
    http://www.ncsa.uiuc.edu

Honorable Mention
World Wide Web Home
    http://info.cern.ch

CMU Computer Science Dept. — Carnegie Mellon University
        http://www.cs.cmu.edu:8001/Web/
        FrontDoor.html

Global Network Navigator
    http://nearnet.gnn.com/gnn/gnn.html

Best Navigational Aid
World Wide Web Worm
    http://wws.cs.colorado.edu/home/
    mcbryan/www.html

Honorable Mention
Internet Meta-Index
    http://cui_www.unige.cn/meta-index.html

DA-CLOD
    http://schiller.wustl.edu/DACLOD/daclod

Galaxy
    http://galaxy.einet.net/galaxy.html

Best Entertainment Service
Sports Information Service
    http://www.mit.edu:8001/services/sis/sports.html

Honorable Mention
Movie Database (Original is located in Wales)
    http://www.cm.cf.ac.uk/Movies/

Mirror of the Movie Database in the United States
    http://www.msstate.edu/Movies/

Doctor Fun
    http://sunsite.unc.edu/Dave/drfun.html

MTV
    http://www.mtv.com

Best Use of Interaction
Xerox Map Server
    http://pubweb.parc.xerox.com/map

Honorable Mention
DA-CLOD
    http://schiller.wustl.edu/DACLOD/daclod

Geometry Applications Gallery
    http://www.geom.umn.edu/apps/gallery.html

Weather Map Requestor
    http://rs560.cl.msu.edu/weather/getmegif.html

Best Use of Multiple Media
Le Louvre
    http://mistral.enst.fr/~pioch/louvre/

Honorable Mention
ArtServe
    http://rubens.anu.edu.au

Coherent Structure in Turbulent Fluid Flow
    http://www.ucar.edu/Restemp.html

Expo
    http://sunsite.unc.edu/expo/ticket_office.html

TNS Technology Demos - MIT Telemedia Networks
    and Systems Group
    http://tns-www.lcs.mit.edu/vs/demos.html

Most Important Service Concept
What's New on the WWW
        http://www.ncsa.uiuc.edu/SDG/Software
        /Mosaic/Docs/old-whats-new-0693

Honorable Mention
Web Magazines: The Global Network Navigator
    http://nearnet.gnn.com/gnn/gnn.html

Distance Learning: The Globewide Network
    Academy
    http://uu-gna.mit.edu:8001/uu-gna

Virtual Museums: Honolulu C.C. Dinosaur Exhibit
    http://www.hcc.hawaii.edu/dinos/dinos1.html

Best Document Design
Travels With Samantha
        http://www-swiss.ai.mit.edu/samantha/travels-
        with-samantha.html

Honorable Mention
Principia Cybernetica Web
    http://pespmc1.vub.ac.be

Telektronikk
    http://www.nta.no/telektronikk/4.93.html

Wired magazine
    http://www.wired.com

Best Campuswide Information Service
Globewide Network Academy

http://uu-gna.mit.edu:8001/uu-gna

Honorable Mention
Rensselaer Polytechnic Institute: RPINFO

http://www.rpi.edu/

St. Olaf College

http://www.stolaf.edu/

University of Kansas: KUFacts

http://kufacts.cc.ukans.edu/cwis/
kufacts_start.html

University of Texas: Austin

http://wwwhost.cc.utexas.edu

Best Educational Service
Introduction to Object-Oriented Programming
Using C++

http://info.desy.de/gna/html/cc/index.html

Honorable Mention
ArtServe

http://rubens.anu.edu.au

Expo

http://sunsite.unc.edu/expo/ticket_office.html

Museum of Paleontology

http://ucmp1.berkeley.edu

Views of the Solar System

http://www.c3.lanl.gov:1331/c3/people/calvin/
homepage.html

Best Professional Service
OncoLink

http://cancer.med.upenn.edu

Honorable Mention
BioInformatics Server

http://www.gdb.org/hopkins.html

Explorer

http://unite.tisl.ukans.edu/xmintro.html

Unified CS Technical Report Index

http://cs.indiana.edu/cstr/search

Climate Data Catalog

http://rainbow.ldgo.columbia.edu/datacatalog.html

Best Commercial Site
O'Reilly and Associates

http://gnn.com/ora

Honorable Mention
Hewlitt-Packard

http://www.hp.com

Novell, Inc.

http://www.novell.com

Sun Microsystems, Inc.

http://www.sun.com

CONTINUED FROM PAGE 567

Online BookStore
http://marketplace.com/obs/top.htm
Use the Online BookStore to order any imprint book
in the world in any of 269 languages offered.

Onsale
http://www.onsale.com/
Find out what's on sale at this interactive retail auction of unique collectibles, limited quantity goods
and close-outs. Prices and availability vary according to customer response.

Paul Phillips's Useless Web Sites
http://www.primus.com/
Entertain yourself with this popular list of 500–600
truly "worthless" web creations compiled by
Internet consultant Paul Phillips.

SportsLine
http://www.sportsline.com/
This on-line service provides access to the latest
sports information and merchandise.

The Spot
http://www.thespot.com
A hybrid of *Melrose Place* and *The Real World, The
Spot* is the first interactive sitcom written and produced for the Internet.

Subway navigator
http://metro.jussieu.fr:10001/bin/cities/english
Get from Cassina De' Pecchi to Bisceglie in the
Milano subway using the Subway navigator. This
site provides users with specific instructions on
how to get from point A to B using subway systems
in numerous cities around the world.

United States Central Intelligence Agency
http://www.odci.gov/
Users now have quick and easy access to intelligence information collected and analyzed by the
CIA concerning developments in foreign countries.

The Utne Lens
http://www.utne.com
This biweekly Web publication provides articles and
discussions on topics such as community, culture,
travel and technology. Also included are highlights
from the its print mothership, *Utne Reader*.

VC InterActive
http://www.ppv.com/
VC InterActive provides information concerning
movies, ratings, sports, events and up-to-the-minute
scheduling from *Viewer's Choice*.

ZD Net
http://www.zdnet.com
Read the latest news, articles, advertisements and
conversation in talk radio format concerning computer matters.

IPEA's Home-Video Library

The ongoing transfer of 100 years of film history to videocassette and laserdisc means that it is possible to treat cinema as we do books. We see current releases in the theater, wait for cable or rental for less-certain bets, and keep a library of those favorite movies that we know we'll want to see at least once a year. This alphabetical list is meant to suggest time periods, genres, actors and directors that you should consider for a home-video library. Your list of meaningful movies, just like your library of books, will represent your own taste, but these titles may be a helpful guide or at least a rental reminder if you've missed any of these classics.

ANNIE HALL (1977)

Director: Woody Allen
Cast: Woody Allen, Diane Keaton and Tony Roberts

Allen's bittersweet chronicle of a love affair makes sharp observations of mid-1970s culture, and is a once-a-year must-see for those with a romantic streak.

THE ART OF BUSTER KEATON (1920–1927)

Director: Buster Keaton
Cast: Various
See page 551

BEAUTY AND THE BEAST (1991)

Directors: Gary Trousdale and Kirk Wise
Voices of: Paige O'Hara, Robby Benson, Jerry Orbach, Angela Lansbury, Richard White and David Ogden Stiers

The first animated feature nominated for a Best Picture Oscar captures the dazzling details of the original masterpiece. Here, the bookish Belle and the Beast fall in love while the Beast holds the beauty captive in his deserted castle.

THE BEST YEARS OF OUR LIVES (1946)

Director: William Wyler
Cast: Fredric March, Myrna Loy, Teresa Wright, Dana Andrews and Harold Russell
Upon returning home from WWII, servicemen face an uncertain future. A fine depiction of its moment in time, it set the stage for the postwar cinema of anxiety.

BREATHLESS (1959)

Director: Jean-Luc Godard
Cast: Jean-Paul Belmondo and Jean Seberg
A typical tale of a cheap gangster on the run (with a weakness for an American girl), *Breathless* became a cornerstone of New Wave film in the hands of Godard.

BRINGING UP BABY (1938)

Director: Howard Hawks
Cast: Cary Grant, Katharine Hepburn, Charlie Ruggles and May Robson
The very definition of screwball comedy, this lightning-fast farce exhibits the characteristic absent-minded hero, madcap heiress and frantic chases, romantic and otherwise.

CITIZEN KANE (1941)

Director: Orson Welles
Cast: Orson Welles, Joseph Cotten, Agnes Moorehead and Everett Sloane

Considered by many to be the finest film of all time, the narrative complexity of Kane's story and the richness of the film technique make it a must for the shelf.

THE CONFORMIST (1970)

Director: Bernardo Bertolucci
Cast: Jean-Louis Trintignant, Stefania Sandrelli, Dominique Sanda and Pierre Clementi
With its stylish blend of social criticism and suspense/chase movie, the film's fluid structure made its mark in 1970s cinema.

DRACULA (1931)

Director: Tod Browning
Cast: Bela Lugosi, David Manners and Dwight Frye

FRANKENSTEIN (1931)

Director: James Whale
Cast: Boris Karloff, Colin Clive, Mae Clarke and Dwight Frye

How does one choose between Universal's twin pillars of fright? Don't bother trying, both are essential atmosphere for Halloween.

FANNY & ALEXANDER (1982)
Director: Ingmar Bergman
Cast: Pernilla Allwin, Bertil Guve, Erland Josephson and Harriet Andersson
Not the dark ruminations on failed love and impending death associated with Bergman's earlier films, this saga of family has a valedictory feel that brings the many threads of Bergman's work together in one fulfilling film.

THE GODFATHER (1972)
THE GODFATHER PART II (1974)
THE GODFATHER PART III (1990)
Director: Francis Ford Coppola
Cast: Al Pacino, Robert De Niro, Robert Duvall, Marlon Brando, Diane Keaton, James Caan and Talia Shire

The story of a gangland family extended over three feature films aptly portrays the 20th-century American experience. The three features are available as a set. Re-evaluate the controversial third chapter after seeing the reassembled cut available on video.

GRAND ILLUSION (1937)
Director: Jean Renoir
Cast: Jean Gabin, Pierre Fresnay, Eric von Stroheim and Marcel Dalio
Renoir's examination of the waning influence of the aristocracy is set as a WWI prisoner-of-war drama. It earned international recognition as a movie milestone as well as a powerful story.

INTOLERANCE (1916)
Director: D.W. Griffith
Cast: Lillian Gish, Mae Marsh and Constance Talmadge
Griffith responded to the outcry over *The Birth of a Nation* with *Intolerance,* and in the process created one of the most ambitious epics of the silent era.

KISS ME DEADLY (1955)
Director: Robert Aldrich
Cast: Ralph Meeker, Albert Dekker and Cloris Leachman
This wild, skittish blend of paranoia, brutality and intrigue makes just the right mix for a darkly cynical film noir.

LA DOLCE VITA (1960)
Director: Federico Fellini
Cast: Marcello Mastroianni, Anita Ekberg and Anouk Aimée
Fellini's masterpiece has endured as one of the icons of the 1960s both in the cinema and in the way it captured the existential ennui of the time — but a fun watch as well.

THE LADY EVE (1941)
Director: Preston Sturges
Cast: Henry Fonda, Barbara Stanwyck, Charles Coburn and Eugene Pallette
Sturges's observations on the romantic clash of men and women improves most with age, with Fonda succumbing not once, but twice to a wily Stanwyck.

L'ECLISSE (1962)
Director: Michaelangelo Antonioni
Cast: Monica Vitti and Alain Delon
The aimless drift of romantic attachment, the inevitability of missed connections, the emptiness of life: brooding 1960s existentialism perhaps, but it manages to be as magnificent as it is despairing.

McCABE AND MRS. MILLER (1971)
Director: Robert Altman
Cast: Warren Beatty, Julie Christie, Rene Auberjonois, Keith Carradine and Shelley Duvall
Some might opt for the more popular *M*A*S*H* or sprawling *Nashville,* but *McCabe* set the tone for much of what was to follow in a beautifully rendered, de-glamorized version of the West.

METROPOLIS (1926)
Director: Fritz Lang
Cast: Brigitte Helm and Alfred Abel
The ageless vision of a dehumanized future is still a relevant theme and great fun to look at. Be sure to avoid the color tinted 1984 edition with its execrable score.

MODERN TIMES (1936)
Director: Charlie Chaplin
Cast: Charlie Chaplin and Paulette Goddard
Another film centered on fear of a mechanized world but with Chaplin's winning humanity.

MONKEY BUSINESS (1931)
Director: Norman Z. MacLeod
Cast: The Marx Brothers and Thelma Todd
The first Marx Brothers vehicle written for the movies (co-scripted by S.J. Perelman) features the boys on a luxury liner. In one of the most memorable scenes, the brothers all pretend to be Maurice Chevalier to get off the ship.

MR. HULOT'S HOLIDAY (1953)
Director: Jacques Tati
Cast: Jacques Tati and Nathalie Pascaud
Silent but for sound effects, Tati's *Mr. Hulot* is an inimitable comic creation and a crowd-pleaser on the order of Chaplin. The intricate gags never go stale.

MY DARLING CLEMENTINE (1946)
Director: John Ford
Cast: Henry Fonda, Linda Darnell, Victor Mature, Walter Brennan and Ward Bond
Though Ford's *Stagecoach* (1939) redefined the screen Western, this contemplative consideration of frontier life (with the O.K. Corrall shootout hovering menacingly in the background) continues to reward repeated viewing.

OUT OF THE PAST (1947)
Director: Jacques Tourneur
Cast: Robert Mitchum, Kirk Douglas, Jane Greer and Rhonda Fleming
The classic example of film noir. Though reference to noir seems to be considered *de rigeur* among today's young filmmakers, a glance at this corrosive film reveals the genuine article. Avoid the colorized version.

THE PHILADELPHIA STORY (1940)
Director: George Cukor
Cast: James Stewart, Cary Grant and Katharine Hepburn

Three of the greatest screen performers of all time at the peak of their power and appeal in this classic that touches on divorce, class distinctions and the durability of true love.

RAGING BULL (1980)
Director: Martin Scorsese
Cast: Robert De Niro, Cathy Moriarty and Joe Pesci
Formal brilliance and heart-stopping performances made this one of the finest works of a director with many memorable films.

REAR WINDOW (1954)
Director: Alfred Hitchcock
Cast: James Stewart, Grace Kelly, Wendell Corey and Thelma Ritter
This may seem an idiosyncratic choice from Hitchcock's work, but many film lovers respond to the metaphor of voyeurism in this story of murder observed. And it features a stylish, luminescent Kelly.

SINGIN' IN THE RAIN (1952)
Directors: Gene Kelly and Stanley Donen
Cast: Gene Kelly, Debbie Reynolds, Donald O'Connor and Cyd Charisse
One of the most innovative of film musicals — and among the cheeriest — this is a treat for eyes and ears.

STAIRWAY TO HEAVEN (1946)
Directors: Michael Powell and Emeric Pressburger
Cast: David Niven, Kim Hunter, Raymond Massey and Roger Livesy
Probably not the first choice of many to represent the work of Powell and Pressburger, best known for *The Red Shoes*, but this meditation on the line between life and death is a beguiling mix of fantasy and reality, a specialty of Powell and Pressburger.

SUNRISE (1927)
Director: F.W. Murnau
Cast: George O'Brien, Janet Gaynor and Margaret Livingston
The story of a farmer planning to murder his wife for another woman, though a simple story, is a fine example of the influence of German Expressionism on Hollywood and one of the greatest cinematic love stories.

THE THIN MAN (1934)
Director: W.S. Van Dyke
Cast: William Powell, Myrna Loy and Maureen O'Sullivan
Powell and Loy define screen chemistry in the best example of romantic comedy/mystery.

THRONE OF BLOOD (1957)
Director: Akira Kurosawa
Cast: Toshiro Mifune and Isuzu Yamada
Set in the milieu of a samurai film, this is arguably one of the greatest movie settings of *Macbeth*.

TO KILL A MOCKINGBIRD (1962)
Director: Robert Mulligan
Cast: Gregory Peck, Mary Badham and Robert Duvall
Purely a sentimental pick as it is that rare commodity, this is a film parents will want to show their children both for its moral sense and because it so lovingly captures a child's point of view.

TOP HAT (1935)
Director: Mark Sandrich
Cast: Fred Astaire, Ginger Rogers, Edward Everett Horton and Eric Blore
Though it's difficult to select one Astaire/Rogers song-and-dance masterpiece, this one features the lovely "Cheek to Cheek."

THE WIZARD OF OZ (1939)
Director: Victor Fleming
Cast: Judy Garland, Ray Bolger, Jack Haley, Bert Lahr, Margaret Hamilton and Billie Burke
You must have one of MGM's (and Fleming's!) color colossi of 1939, and this is the one, rather than *Gone With the Wind*, that remains fresh and continues to appeal to audiences young and old.

Billboard All-Time Video and Laserdisc Charts

These charts appeared in *Billboard*'s 100th Anniversary issue.

Top Video Rentals (with Lead Actor)

FEBRUARY 6, 1982 TO JUNE 25, 1994

1. *Star Wars*
   Mark Hamill
2. *On Golden Pond*
   Katharine Hepburn
3. *48 Hrs.*
   Nick Nolte
4. *The Karate Kid*
   Ralph Macchio
5. *Romancing the Stone*
   Michael Douglas
6. *An Officer and a Gentleman*
   Richard Gere
7. *Flashdance*
   Jennifer Beals
8. *Back to the Future*
   Michael J. Fox
9. *Beverly Hills Cop*
   Eddie Murphy
10. *First Blood*
    Sylvester Stallone
11. *The Terminator*
    Arnold Schwarzenegger
12. *Lethal Weapon*
    Mel Gibson

Star Wars

13. *Dirty Dancing*
    Patrick Swayze
14. *Raiders of the Lost Ark*
    Harrison Ford
15. *Police Academy*
    Steve Guttenberg
16. *Poltergeist*
    Jobeth Williams
17. *Terms of Endearment*
    Shirley MacLaine
18. *Ghost*
    Patrick Swayze
19. *Fort Apache, the Bronx*
    Paul Newman
20. *Arthur*
    Dudley Moore

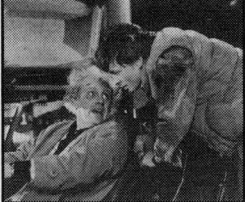

Back to the Future

Top Video Sales (with Lead Actor)

NOVEMBER 17, 1979 TO JUNE 25, 1994

1. *Jane Fonda's Workout*
   Jane Fonda
2. *Jane Fonda's New Workout*
   Jane Fonda
3. *Callanetics*
   Callan Pinckney
4. *Jane Fonda's Low-Impact Aerobics*
   Jane Fonda
5. *Pinocchio*
   Animated
6. *Lady and the Tramp*
   Animated
7. *Raiders of the Lost Ark*
   Harrison Ford
8. *The Sound of Music*
   Julie Andrews
9. *Beauty and the Beast*
   Animated
10. *Alien*
    Sigourney Weaver

Top Laserdisc Sales (with Lead Actor)

OCTOBER 8, 1983 TO JUNE 25, 1994

1. *Back to the Future*
   Michael J. Fox
2. *Top Gun*
   Tom Cruise
3. *Raiders of the Lost Ark*
   Harrison Ford
4. *Dirty Dancing*
   Patrick Swayze
5. *The Karate Kid*
   Ralph Macchio
6. *Terminator 2: Judgment Day — Special Edition*
   Arnold Schwarzenegger
7. *RoboCop*
   Peter Weller
8. *The Untouchables*
   Kevin Costner
9. *Ghost*
   Patrick Swayze
10. *Die Hard*
    Bruce Willis

The IPEA's All-Time Software and CD-ROM Bestsellers

We compiled this list using PC Data's 1993–1995 bestseller charts and our own evaluation based on sales and product reviews.

CD-ROM TITLES

1. **Myst**
   (Brøderbund)

2. **Doom**
   (GT Interactive)

3. **7th Guest**
   (Virgin)

4. **Doom II**
   (GT Interactive)

5. **Star Wars Rebel Assault**
   (LucasArts)

6. **Microsoft Encarta**
   (Microsoft)

7. **Print Shop Deluxe CD Ensemble**
   (Brøderbund)

8. **Quicken CD-ROM Deluxe**
   (Intuit)

9. **Lion King Story Book**
   (Disney)

10. **Street Atlas USA**
    (DeLorme)

HOME EDUCATION TITLES FOR MS-DOS/WINDOWS

The following titles are on floppy disk unless otherwise noted.

1. **Where in the World Is Carmen Sandiego?**
   (Brøderbund)

2. **Mavis Beacon Teaches Typing**
   (Software Toolworks)

3. **Oregon Trail**
   (MECC)

4. **Reader Rabbit 1**
   (Learning Company)

5. **Lion King Story Book**, CD-ROM
   (Disney)

HOME EDUCATION TITLES FOR MACINTOSH

The following titles are on floppy disk unless otherwise noted.

1. **Where in the World Is Carmen Sandiego?**, CD-ROM
   (Brøderbund)

2. **Mavis Beacon Teaches Typing**
   (Software Toolworks)

3. **New Math Blaster Plus**
   (Davidson)

4. **Oregon Trail**
   (MECC)

5. **Just Grandma & Me**, CD-ROM
   (Brøderbund)

PC GAMES FOR MS-DOS/WINDOWS

The following titles are on floppy disk unless otherwise noted.

1. **Myst**, CD-ROM
   (Brøderbund)

2. **Doom**, CD-ROM and MS-DOS
   (GT Interactive)

3. **7th Guest**, CD-ROM
   (Virgin)

4. **Doom II**, CD-ROM and MS-DOS
   (GT Interactive)

5. **Microsoft Flight Simulator**
   (Microsoft)

6. **Sim City 2000**
   (Maxis)

7. **Sim City**
   (Maxis)

8. **Star Wars Rebel Assault**, CD-ROM
   (LucasArts)

9. **Best of Microsoft Entertainment Pack**
   (Microsoft)

10. **Wolfenstein 3D**
    (Formgen)

MACINTOSH GAMES

The following titles are on floppy disk unless otherwise noted.

1. **Myst**, CD-ROM
   (Brøderbund)

2. **Sim City 2000**
   (Maxis)

3. **Sim City**
   (Maxis)

4. **Chessmaster 3000**
   (Software Toolworks)

5. **Star Wars Rebel Assault**, CD-ROM
   (LucasArts)

6. **7th Guest**, CD-ROM
   (Virgin)

7. **FA-18 Hornet**
   (Graphic Simulations)

8. **Links Pro**
   (Access)

9. **Kings Quest V: Red Baron Bundle**
   (Sierra On-Line)

10. **Wolfenstein 3D**
    (Formgen)

MULTIMEDIA TIME LINE

1951
Bing Crosby finances the first use of magnetic tape in television with the Longitudinal Videotape Recording Machine (LVR).

1956
Ampex Corporation demonstrates the Quadruplex videotape recorder, the first black-and-white recorder/playback device.

1957
Douglas Edward With the News is videotaped

for the West Coast. Videotaping shows rather than live broadcast becomes commonplace.

1962
Ivan Sutherland, a graduate student at Massachusetts Institute of Technology, creates the science of computer graphics.

1968
Ivan Sutherland develops the HMD (Head Mounted Display), a virtual reality device that tracks the viewer's head position.

1969
CompuServe, an on-line information database, is

Video, Games and New Media Magazines and Journals

CD-ROM Multimedia Magazine
100 Ballantyne S.
Montreal West, Quebec
Canada H4X ZB3
(800) 565-4623

CD-ROM Today
Imagine Publishing
1350 Old Bayshore Highway, Suite 210
Burlingame, CA 94010
(415) 696-1688

Computer Gaming World
P.O. Box 57166
Boulder, CO 80322-7166
(800) 827-4450

Computer Gaming Review
Sendai Publishing Group, Inc.
1920 Highland Ave., Suite 222
Lombard, IL 60148
(708) 268-2498

Cyber Surfer
475 Park Ave. S.
New York, NY 10016
(212) 689-2830

Electronic Gaming Monthly
Sendai Publishing Group, Inc.
1920 Highland Ave., Suite 222
Lombard, IL 60148
(708) 268-2498

Entertainment Weekly
1675 Broadway
New York, NY 10019
(212) 522-5600

Facets Video
1517 W. Fullerton Ave.
Chicago, IL 60614
(312) 281-9075

Fusion
Sendai Publishing Group, Inc.
1920 Highland Ave., Suite 222
Lombard, IL 60148
(708) 268-2498

Game Players Sega-Nintendo
Imagine Publishing
1350 Old Bayshore Highway, Suite 210
Burlingame, CA 94010
(415) 696-1688

GamePro
Infotainment World, Inc.
951 Mariner's Island Blvd., Suite 700
San Mateo, CA 94404
(800) 879-0499

Internet World
P.O. Box 713
Mt. Morris, IL 61054
(800) 573-3062

Multimedia
Redgate Communications Corp.
660 Beachland Blvd.
Vero Beach, FL 32963
(407) 231-6904

Multimedia World
International Data Group
501 Second St.
San Francisco, CA 94107
(800) 766-3294

The Net
Imagine Publishing
1350 Old Bayshore Highway, Suite 210
Burlingame, CA 94010
(415) 696-1688

Net Guide
CMP Publications
600 Community Drive
Manhasset, NY 11030
(516) 562-5000

NewMedia
Hypermedia Communications, Inc.
P.O. Box 1771
Riverton, NJ 08077-7371
(609) 786-4430

---

introduced by the
Columbus, Ohio company.

1971

Sony introduces the first
practical VCR for corporate markets.

1974

Atari releases *Pong,* the
first electronic video

game in the United
States.

1975

Sony introduces the
Beta format VCR for
consumer use.

1976

Future World debuts the
first use of computer

graphics in film. JVC
develops the Video Home
System (VHS), and dominates the home market.

1979

Atari, Midway, Mattel,
Cinematronics and Sega
introduce games such
as *Pac-Man* and *Space
Invaders,* setting the

stage for the first U.S.
boom in home video
games. Philips-MCA
introduces the Laser
VideoDisc system.

1980

The Sony Corporation
introduces the camcorder.

Online Access
5615 W. Cermak Road
Cicero, IL 60650-2290
(800) 291-6219

PC Gamer
Imagine Publishing
1350 Old Bayshore Highway, Suite 210
Burlingame, CA 94010
(415) 696-1688

PIX-Elation
P.O. Box 4139
Highland Park, NJ 08904
(908) 463-8787

Video Event
Connell Communications, Inc.
86 Elm St.
Peterborough, NH 03458
(603) 924-7013

Video Magazine
Hachette Filipacchi Magazines, Inc.
1633 Broadway, 43rd Floor
New York, NY 10019
(800) 601-8345

Videomaker
Box 4591
Chico, CA 95927-4591
(916) 891-8410

Virtual Reality
Miller Freeman, Inc.
600 Harrison St.
San Francisco, CA 94107
(415) 905-2200

VR World
P.O. Box 3000
Denville, NJ 07834-9975
(800) 783-4903

Wired
530 Third St., 4th Fl.
San Francisco, CA 94107-1427
(800) 769-4733

Glossary

camcorder A self-contained, hand-held unit made up of a video camera and VCR.

CCD (charge coupled device) An electronic chip that replaced the vacuum tube in video cameras. CCDs are more durable, smaller and less expensive than tubes and are responsible for the miniaturization and price decrease of home video equipment.

CD-V A 5-inch audio compact disk that contains up to 20 minutes of audio information and up to five minutes of video information, usually a music video, viewable on a laserdisk system.

Dolby Pro Logic A trademark for an encoding and decoding system that takes audio information on laserdisk or video and divides it into four channels, left, right, center and surround, to give an in-theater feel to home viewing.

dropout The black or white spots or lines that appear on screen when the playback head of a VCR passes over a dirty or bare spot on a videotape.

dubbing To replace either the audio or video tracks on a videotape without disturbing the other tracks. This process is conducted during editing.

DVD (digital videodisk) An audio compact disk-sized video disk format currently under development by two competing factions (with two non-compatible formats) that will likely replace VCRs.

flying erase head The extra head on a VCR that allows for imperceptible cuts in editing.

home theater The combination of a large-screen television, surround-sound receiver, a hi-fi VCR or laserdisk player and a multi-point speaker system set up in one's home to achieve optimal audio and video quality.

jog/shuttle The VCR control that allows the user to quickly rewind or fast forward to a particular frame. Useful for editing.

laserdisc The video playback system that employs a laser to read encoded disks, similar to audio compact disks or CD-ROMs. Laserdiscs are considered by video enthusiasts to have greater image fidelity. Many "director's cut" and special edition movies with interviews and restored scenes are available only on laserdisc.

resolution The fineness of detail that can be seen in an image on a television screen. Measured in horizontal lines per screen.

S-VHS A high-resolution VHS video recording standard that provides more than 400 lines of resolution as opposed to 240 lines of resolution from a regular VHS VCR.

tracking The alignment of playback and record heads on a VCR with the tracks recorded on the videotape. The tracking control on a VCR compensates for the slight differences in head alignment from machine to machine.

1981
IBM introduces the first personal computer.

1984
The first Macintosh computers are introduced with their built-in graphical interface.

1985
Philips and Sony intro- duce the CD-ROM as a **consumer product. America Online is offered to the public.** One of the earliest multimedia computers, the Commodore Amiga, is developed and features built-in chips dedicated to processing graphics and sound. Nintendo arrives in the U.S. home

video game market.

1989
One out of every five homes in America has a Nintendo system. VCRs are found in 62% of homes in the United States.

1992
The reduction of hard- ware costs drives the **sudden growth of multimedia systems.**

1993
The National Center for Super Computing Applications introduces Mosaic and contributes to the tremendous growth of the World Wide Web.

Perform-ing Arts

Der Rosenkavalier

Rake's Progress

How To Succeed In Business Without Really Trying

Dance In Love

A Regional Accent

■ BY CHRISTINE DOLEN

ONCE, AND FOR A VERY LONG TIME, Broadway was American theater's pinnacle. It was the place that inspired the dreams of aspiring actors, playwrights, directors and designers. The place that conferred artistic legitimacy and, for the very lucky, fame and wealth.

Not anymore.

These days, the plays and musicals that create a buzz are being launched from America's own version of national theater, the more than 430 not-for-profit regional theaters. Some of those productions are clearly using their regional breeding ground as the contemporary version of Philadelphia or New Haven: They make a planned leap to Broadway, where a few become hits, buying them a more lucrative life around the country as touring Broadway fare. (This new route to Broadway isn't without its detractors: Peter Zeisler, the retiring head of the Theater Communications Group, calls this "the Russian roulette of Broadway," and Stephen Richard of Washington D.C.'s Arena Stage said regionals bent on taking shows to Broadway are ". . . risking prostitution, if not artistic suicide.")

Other regionally-spawned plays bypass Broadway altogether — Jane Martin's *Keely and Du* and Jose Rivera's *Marisol* are two recent examples — yet go on to their own kind of success in numerous productions all over the United States. Hartford Stage's Mark Lamos

THEATER

> Christine Dolen has been theater critic of the *Miami Herald* since 1979.

Chris Bennion

London Suite

Robert C. Ragsdale

Show Boat

Sunset Boulevard

observes: "We have thriving theater communities and avid audiences all around the country. . . . The regional theater doesn't have hits and flops. A failure will close, but a boffo hit will also close in four weeks. There's always the next play."

The hot shows are now coming from Seattle (Wendy Wasserstein's *The Sisters Rosensweig* and Herb Gardner's *Conversations With My Father* both began at Seattle Repertory Theatre), from Los Angeles (Tony Kushner's *Angels in America* and Anna Deveare Smith's *Twilight: Los Angeles 1992* bowed at the Mark Taper Forum), from Chicago (August Wilson's latest, *Seven Guitars*, premiered at the Goodman during the 1994–1995 season), from Louisville (where the 1995 Humana Festival at Actors' Theater featured new works by Marsha Norman, Donald Margulies, Jose Rivera and Jane Martin) and from La Jolla (both *The Who's Tommy* and the hit revival of *How to Succeed in Business Without Really Trying* started there).

Even in New York, more and more important playwrights take a look at Broadway — with its ever escalating costs (the tab for *Sunset Boulevard* was $13 million) and huge financial risks, as well as its love affair with the jaw-dropping musical spectacle, and simply opt out.

During the 1994–1995 season, David Mamet (*The Cryptogram* and *An Interview*, part of the triple bill *Death Defying Acts*), Woody Allen (*Central Park West*, also part of *Death Defying Acts*), Sam Shepard (*Simpatico*) and, most startlingly, Broadway god Neil Simon (whose *London Suite* broke a string of 23 Broadway productions since 1961's *Come Blow Your Horn*) all snubbed Broadway for the more cost-efficient Off-Broadway.

Tom Stoppard had one play done at Lincoln Center's Broadway-sized house (*Arcadia* in the Vivian Beaumont) but put another (*Hapgood*) in the complex's Off-Broadway Mitzi Newhouse. Eileen Atkins acted on Broadway in *Indiscretions*, but took her own play, *Vita and Virginia*, starring herself and Vanessa Redgrave, to enormous success Off-Broadway.

Tom Stoppard

Horton Foote premiered *The Young Man From Atlanta* at Off-Off-Broadway's Signature Theatre Company and won the 1995 Pulitzer Prize for Drama. Similarly, Edward Albee launched *Three Tall Women* Off-Off-Broadway a season earlier, garnered his third Pulitzer for it and saw it settle into a long, lucrative run after an Off-Broadway transfer.

To be sure, Broadway is still high-profile and big business, particularly for such musical moguls as Andrew Lloyd Webber, Cameron Mackintosh and Harold Prince. It's what the tourists want to see — just like the Empire State Building and the Statue of Liberty — when they go to New York.

THE 1995 TONY AWARDS

The Tony Awards, honoring distinguished achievement in Broadway theater, were presented Sunday June 4, 1995 at Manhattan's Minskoff Theatre.

Catherine Ashmore

Show Boat

Play
  Love! Valour! Compassion!

Musical
  Sunset Boulevard

Revival — Play
  The Heiress

Revival — Musical
  Show Boat

Actor — Play
  Ralph Fiennes, *Hamlet*

Actress — Play
  Cherry Jones, *The Heiress*

Actor — Musical
  Matthew Broderick, *How to Succeed in Business Without Really Trying*

Actress — Musical
  Glenn Close, *Sunset Boulevard*

Featured Actor — Play
  John Glover, *Love! Valour! Compassion!*

Featured Actress — Play
  Frances Sternhagen, *The Heiress*

Featured Actor — Musical
  George Hearn, *Sunset Boulevard*

Featured Actress — Musical
  Gretha Boston, *Show Boat*

T. Charles Erickson

The Heiress

According to statistics compiled by the League of American Theatres and Producers, more than 9 million theatergoers chose Broadway in 1994–1995, the highest attendance level in a dozen years. Ticket sales of more than $406 million set a record with an average price of nearly $45 a ticket (though the best seats to Broadway's biggest hits run $75). An enormous 82 percent of those tickets are for musicals, many of them long-running hits such as *Cats, The Phantom of the Opera, Les Misérables* and *Miss Saigon.*

Numbers, of course, don't tell the whole story.

Though box office and attendance climbed, the number of new productions fell from 37 in 1993–1994 to 28 in 1994–1995. Of those 28 shows, half were revivals, and even the "new" fare, such as Lloyd Webber's hyped-to-the-hilt *Sunset Boulevard* and the deep-sixed flop *On the Waterfront* were built upon the bones of pretested film classics (as this fall's *Victor/Victoria* will be). The season reinforced Broadway's new image as a lavish, living theater museum. Or, if you look at Broadway's love affair with breathtaking effects and the Disney Company's plans for a family-friendly revitalization of the theater district's seedy 42nd Street, as a theatrical theme park.

They did give out Tony Awards in June, though the competition among the "new" musicals was so scant (it was *Sunset Boulevard* vs. *Smokey Joe's Cafe,* a lively revue of songs by Jerry Lieber and Mike Stoller) that *Sunset* got the Tonys for best score and best book on the day that nominations were announced.

Sunset dominated the awards, taking seven Tonys, including the best actress in a musical honor for Glenn Close, whose star turn as silent-screen has-been Norma Desmond was so flamboyantly out there that the musical could have been subtitled *Glenn Close Descending a Staircase.* Another leading lady, Cherry Jones, won the Tony as best actress in a play (after years of acclaimed work in the regionals) for her emotionally riveting performance in Lincoln Center Theater's much-praised Tony-winning revival of *The Heiress.* Hal Prince's rethought revival of Jerome Kern and

Cherry Jones

Oscar Hammerstein's 1927 classic *Show Boat* won the best musical revival Tony. And Terrence McNally's exuberant gay play *Love! Valour! Compassion!*, a transfer from the Manhattan Theatre Club under the cost-cutting Broadway Alliance, was chosen best play.

Off-Broadway's 40th annual Obie Awards celebrated *Love! Valour! Compassion!* even more, giving honors to McNally, director Joe Mantello and all seven original Manhattan Theatre Club cast members (including Nathan Lane, who made the move to Broadway, only to be snubbed by Tony nominators to widespread outrage in the theater community). Other Obie winners included Mamet, whose *Cryptogram* was chosen best new American play, and Tony Kushner, fresh off a Pulitzer and a pair of Tonys for *Angels in America* and *Slavs!*

Among other notable aspects and events of the 1994–1995 season:

• George C. Wolfe put a bold, multicultural stamp on New York's Joseph Papp Public Theater, presenting new works from Hispanic and African-American playwrights while luring such theater veterans as Hal Prince, Sam Shepard and Ron Liebman to the building. However, more than a few of the Public's shows (many of

Director — Play
Gerald Gutierrez, *The Heiress*

Director — Musical
Harold Prince, *Show Boat*

Book — Musical
Sunset Boulevard, Christopher Hampton and Don Black

Score — Musical
Sunset Boulevard, Andrew Lloyd Webber, music; Christopher Hampton and Don Black, lyrics

Scenic Designer
John Napier, *Sunset Boulevard*

Costume Designer
Florence Klotz, *Show Boat*

Choreographer
Susan Stroman, *Show Boat*

Lighting Designer
Andrew Bridge, *Sunset Boulevard*

Special Tony Awards
Carol Channing, lifetime achievement
Harvey Sabinson, executive director of the League of American Theatres and Producers, lifetime achievement
Goodspeed Opera House
National Endowment for the Arts

INTRODUCING...

STRANGE BEDFELLOWS
Steven Spielberg's Amblin Entertainment commissioned new plays from Off-Broadway's Playwrights Horizons that the company hopes will translate to the big screen and big bucks. The writers who received the $10,000 grant, Neena Beber, Neal Bell, Nicky Silver and playwrights/composers Mark St. Germain and Randy Courts, will be producing partners if Amblin decides to make screen adaptations from the plays. A similiar deal has been brokered between Vanguard Films and London's Hampstead and Bush theaters. Vanguard has agreed to pay the theaters $10,000 each annually for script and writer information.

These productions mounted major national tours during the 1994–1995 theater season.

Angels in America

Blood Brothers

Buskers

Family Secrets

Fiddler on the Roof

Godspell

Grease!

Hello, Dolly!

Jelly's Last Jam

Joseph and the Amazing Technicolor Dreamcoat

Just for Laughs

Kiss of the Spiderwoman

Laughter on the 23rd Floor

Miss Saigon 2

Rodgers and Hammerstein's A Grand Night for Singing

She Loves Me

Source: League of American Theatres and Producers

1994–1995 BROADWAY SEASON STATISTICS

Ticket Sales

Musical	$349,834,240
Straight Play	49,950,495
Special Attraction	6,364,001
Total	**$406,148,736**

Attendance

Musical	7,390,006
Straight Play	1,451,355
Special Attraction	197,616
Total	**9,038,977**

Average paid admission	**$44.93**

Source: League of American Theatres and Producers

George Abbott

which had minuscule runs) got hammered by the critics.

•The *New York Times*'s David Richards abruptly left the chief theater critic's position he had held for just a year to go back to the *Washington Post*. He was replaced by 70-year-old Vincent Canby, the paper's veteran film critic and most recently its Sunday theater critic. Canby was replaced by Margo Jefferson, who promptly won the Pulitzer Prize for criticism for her *Times* reviews.

•Raul Julia, who built a grand career at Papp's Shakespeare Festival, on Broadway and in movies, died at 54 of cancer.

•Broadway's longest-shining light, George Abbott, the director and playwright who *was* Broadway to the generations of actors, choreographers, composers and others whose careers he fostered, was extinguished when he died at the age of 107. Mr. Abbott (he was always "Mr. Abbott") began his unparalleled career as a Broadway actor in 1913. His last Broadway venture was 1994's hit revival of his 1955 smash, *Damn Yankees*. In between were some 125 shows, including *Three Men on a Horse, Broadway, Pal Joey, Call Me Madam, On the Town, Wonderful Town, The Pajama Game, Fiorello!* and *A Funny Thing Happened on the Way to the Forum*. In gracing classic musicals with what came to be known as The Abbott Touch, Mr. Abbott gave audiences the kind of snappy, polished, emotionally knowing theater they came to equate with Broadway at its best. ■

1994–1995 Broadway Premieres

This year, a record low number of shows premiered on Broadway, and several with high expectations closed after running only days. This alphabetical list presents Broadway shows that opened between October 1994 and August 1995.

Joan Marcus

Arcadia

ARCADIA
By: Tom Stoppard; **Director:** Trevor Nunn; **Sets and Costumes:** Mark Thompson; **Lighting:** Paul Pyant; **Original Music:** Jeremy Sams; **Artistic Director:** Andre Bishop
Opening: 3/95 at the Vivian Beaumont Theatre
Cast: Blair Brown, Victor Garber, Robert Sean Leonard, Billy Crudup, Jennifer Dundas, Paul Giamatti, Peter Maloney, Lisa Banes and Haviland Morris
Present and past spin complex webs around each other when arrogant academic Bernard (Garber) and enigmatic landscape historian Hannah (Brown) muddle through 19th-century mysteries that unfold in Derbyshire's Sidley Park. Did Lord Byron duel with and kill a failed poet there? Who was the hermit in the garden? To reveal the truth in its many facets, *Arcadia* alternates scenes between the estate's 19th-century inhabitants: math prodigy Thomasina (Dundas), her tutor Septimus (Crudup), poet Chater (Giamatti) and landscape architect Noakes (Maloney) and current owners: mathematician Valentine (Leonard) and his sister. Love and lust, landscape and language, mathematics and metaphysics intersect in fascinating and playful ways.

A CHRISTMAS CAROL — THE PLAY
By: Charles Dickens, adapted by Patrick Stewart; **Director:** Patrick Stewart; **Executive Producer:** Kate Elliott; **Lighting:** Fred Allen

Opening: 12/94 at the Richard Rodgers Theatre
Cast: Patrick Stewart
Dickens's language replaces melodrama as the core of this exceptional one-person staging of the perennial Christmas tale. Stewart, whose repertoire ranges from Shakespeare to *Star Trek: The Next Generation*, uses his renowned vocal range to impart intense emotion and life into each character, from somber Scrooge, to frail Tiny Tim, the child who eventually softens the miser's stingy heart. Spare staging and effective lighting emphasize the gamut of emotions portrayed, from stark despair to seasonal cheer.

COMEDY TONIGHT
Director: Alexander H. Cohen; **Musical Staging:** Albert Stephenson; **Musical Director:** Peter Howard; **Sets:** Ray Klausen; **Costumes:** Alvin Colt; **Lighting:** Richard Nelson
Opening: 12/94 at the Lunt-Fontanne Theatre
Cast: Joy Behar, Michael Davis, Dorothy Loudon and Mort Sahl
Each performer plies his or her trade in 30-minute segments. Behar's stand-up routine focuses on Brooklyn Jews and Italians. Davis's juggling act includes tossing objects such as helium balloons and bowling balls. Singer Loudon does her best with a poor script, including belting out Alan and Marilyn Bergman's "Fifty Percent" from the 1978 play *Ballroom*. Political satirist Sahl's performance is off target, missing more jokes than he hits.

DEFENDING THE CAVEMAN
By: Rob Becker; **Production Stage Manager:** Jason Lindhorst
Opening: 3/95 at the Helen Hayes Theatre
Cast: Rob Becker
Men can breathe a sigh of relief: They are not contemptible people, they are just different from women. That's Becker's explanation of common male idiosyncracies. Becker's one-man show laughs at men for their endless channel surfing, for being too proud to ask directions (even when they are hopelessly lost) and for being slobs. Though his stereotypical women are neater and more patient than men and obsessed with shopping, Becker concludes that the two sexes mesh well together. As the title suggests, this is stand-up humor, enjoyable but not particularly subtle.

THE FLYING KARAMAZOV BROTHERS DO THE IMPOSSIBLE!

Musical Director: Doug Wieselman
Cast: Paul Magid, Howard Jay Patterson, Michael Preston and Sam Williams
Opening: 11/94 at the Helen Hayes Theatre

Has anyone ever successfully juggled a filleted trout, a plate of Chinese food and a plastic slinky? Ivan Karamazov (Patterson) got a pie in the face for failing. Regardless of the challenge, he attempts to juggle whatever three objects the audience chooses in "The Gamble," a routine highlighted in the fourth Brothers' production. Other feats by this ensemble of four distinctive performers include a ballet impersonation and a virtuoso juggling episode. A brass-and-drum band, the Kamikaze Ground Crew, accompanies the act.

GENTLEMEN PREFER BLONDES

Adapted from the novel by Anita Loos; **Music:** Jule Styne; **Lyrics:** Leo Robin; **Book:** Anita Loos and Joseph Fields; **Director:** Charles Repole; **Choreographer:** Michael Lichtefeld; **Music Director:** Andrew Wilder; **Sets and Costumes:** Eduardo Sicangco; **Lighting:** Kirk Bookman
Opening: 4/95 at the Lyceum Theatre
Cast: K. T. Sullivan, Karen Prunzik, Allen Fitzpatrick, David Ponting, Jamie Ross, Susan Rush, Carol Swarbrick, George Dvorsky, Dick Decareau, Craig Waletzko, Ken Nagy, Joe Bowerman and John Hoshko

The story of a "dumb blond" chorine from the Roaring Twenties does not deliver the same dazzle in the 1990s as it did in the 1949 original production. Lorelei Lee (Sullivan), the dim-witted bombshell, and her friend (Prunzik) travel to Paris to capture the fancy of potential mates. Lee steals the heart of a button magnate (Fitzpatrick) about to lose his kingdom to the zipper.

THE GLASS MENAGERIE

By: Tennessee Williams; **Director:** Frank Galati; **Set:** Loy Arcenas; **Lighting:** Mimi Jordan Sherin; **Costumes:** Noel Taylor
Cast: Julie Harris, Calista Flockhart, Zeljko Ivanek and Kevin Kilner
Opening: 11/94 at Criterion Center Stage Right

The 50th anniversary production of the 1945 classic One of the most popular theater revivals, this production of *The Glass Menagerie* had special significance as it celebrated the 50th anniversary of Williams's play, and the actors preserved the emotion of the original. Amanda (Harris) a former southern belle now frumpy middle-aged mother, seeks a suitor for her introverted, disabled daughter Laura (Flockhart), who would rather hide in her room with her collection of glass animals than date. Amanda persuades her son Tom (Ivanek), who slaves away in a warehouse to support the family, to bring home a coworker for Laura. Jim (Kilner) takes Laura on a date, and though they don't become a couple, he instills in Laura confidence and hope.

Ivan Kyncl

Hamlet

HAMLET

By: William Shakespeare; **Director:** Jonathan Kent; **Sets:** Peter J. Davison; **Costumes:** James Acheson; **Lighting:** Mark Henderson; **Music:** Jonathan Dove
Opening: 5/95 at the Belasco Theatre
Cast: Ralph Fiennes, Francesca Annis, Terence Rigby, Tara FitzGerald, James Laurenson, Peter Eyre, Damian Lewis, Paterson Joseph, James Wallace, Nicholas Rowe, Rupert-Penry Jones and Terry McGinity

Curiosity about this London-import production centered on the Broadway debut of its star, film idol Fiennes, who adds Hamlet to his repertoire of morally tormented characters. As the Danish prince who discovers with horror that his mother, Queen Gertrude (Annis), has betrayed her husband, Fiennes gives an intensely physical performance that anchors this rapid-fire production. While this version offers no new reading of *Hamlet*, it does hold some revelations, chiefly in Annis's unusually sympathetic portrayal of a Gertrude at the mercy of her despotic husband, whose ghost is played with equal power by Rigby.

HAVING OUR SAY

By: Emily Mann, adapted from *Having Our Say; The Delany Sisters' First 100 Years,* by Sarah L. Delany and A. Elizabeth Delany, with Amy Hill Hearth;

T. Charles Erickson

Having Our Say

Director: Emily Mann; **Sets:** Thomas Lynch;
Costumes: Judy Dearing; **Lighting:** Allen Lee Hughes;
Projections: Wendall K. Harrington, Sage Marie
Carter; **Original Music:** Baikida Carroll
Opening: 4/95 at the Booth Theatre
Cast: Gloria Foster and Mary Alice

Centenarian sisters Sadie (Foster) and Bessie (Alice) Delany, daughters of a former slave who became the first black Episcopal bishop, guide the audience on a trip down the often rocky road of African-American life. Raised in a middle-class North Carolina family, both Columbia University graduates became pioneers — diplomatic Sadie as a high school home economics teacher in New York City and outspoken Bessie as one of the first two black woman dentists in New York. The sisters play off each other as they conjure up characters and incidents from the past, while still photographs of actual persons involved are projected around them.

THE HEIRESS

Adapted by: Ruth and Augustus Goetz from
Washington Square by Henry James; **Director:**
Gerald Gutierrez; **Sets:** John Lee Beatty; **Costumes:**
Jane Greenwood; **Lighting:** Beverly Emmons;
Original Music: Robert Waldman; **Artistic Director:**
Andre Bishop
Opening: 3/95 at the Cort Theatre
Cast: Philip Bosco, Frances Sternhagen, Cherry
Jones, Jon Tenney, Patricia Conolly, Katie Finneran,
Karl Kenzler, Michelle O'Neill and Lizbeth Mackay

Material riches and emotional poverty drive this revival of the 1947 psychological drama. Plain, shy heiress Catherine (Jones), blamed by her domineering, unloving father (Bosco) for her mother's death in childbirth, is destined for spinsterhood until she meets the penniless, but charming, fortune hunter Morris Townsend (Tenney). She blossoms under his attention, but is crushed when her father cruelly informs her that Townsend is only attracted to her money. Catherine reemerges, however, and exacts revenge.

HOW TO SUCCEED IN BUSINESS WITHOUT REALLY TRYING

Music and Lyrics: Frank Loesser; **Book:** Abe
Burrows, Jack Weinstock and Willie Gilbert, based on
the novel by Shepherd Mead; **Director:** Des McAnuff;
Choreography: Wayne Cilento; **Music direction and
vocal arrangements:** Ted Sperling; **Sets:** John Arnone;
Costumes: Susan Hilferty; **Lighting:** Howell Binkley;
Orchestrations by Danny Troob
Opening: 3/95 at the Richard Rodgers Theatre
Cast: Matthew Broderick, Jonathan Freeman, Ronn
Carroll, Megan Mullally, Victoria Clark, Jeff
Blumenkrantz, Lillias White, Gerry Vichi, Luba Mason
and Walter Cronkite

Corporate success has always required a special touch, but it hasn't always been as much fun as in this 1961 tongue-in-cheek classic. World Wide Wicket Company window-washer J. Pierrepont

Finch (Broderick) may appear wide-eyed, but he knows how to scheme his way to the top of the corporate ladder. Des McAnuff's direction successfully re-creates the wacky free-for-all ambition of the original production, and the songs are fully and faithfully rendered by various secretaries, mail-room attendants, business rivals and others in the cast of corporate characters.

INDISCRETIONS

By: Jean Cocteau, adapted and translated by
Jeremy Sams; **Director:** Sean Mathias; **Sets and
Costumes:** Stephen Brimson Lewis; **Lighting:** Mark
Henderson; **Music:** Jason Carr
Opening: 4/95 at the Ethel Barrymore Theatre
Cast: Kathleen Turner, Eileen Atkins, Roger Rees,
Jude Law and Cynthia Nixon

Joan Marcus

Indiscretions

They live in 1938 Paris, but the comfortably bourgeois family members in *Indiscretions* are too preoccupied with their own foibles to see World War II lurking. Yvonne (Turner), a bedridden diabetic, has eyes only for her beautiful son (Law), who falls in love with innocent bookbinder Madeleine (Nixon), who in turn, is secretly being kept by Yvonne's husband, the ineffectual underwater machine-gun inventor George (Rees). Slightly apart from the rest stands Yvonne's sensible, personable sister Léonie (Atkins), who is bound to the family by unrequited love for George. Passions erupt when George realizes that he and his son are involved with the same woman.

LOVE! VALOUR! COMPASSION!

By: Terrence McNally; **Director:** Joe Mantello; **Sets:**
Loy Arcenas; **Costumes:** Jess Goldstein; **Lighting:**
Brian MacDevitt; **Choreography:** John Carrafa
Opening: 2/95 at the Walter Kerr Theatre
Cast: Nathan Lane, John Glover, Stephen Bogardus,
Anthony Heald, Randy Becker, John Benjamin
Hickey and Justin Kirk
Originally appeared Off-Broadway

Eight upper-middle-class gay men gather for three summer weekends at a New York farmhouse to relax, reflect and plan for their survival

The 45th annual Outer Critics Circle Awards were presented on May 26, 1995 at New York's venerable Sardi's restaurant. The Outer Critcs Circle includes theater writers who review New York theater productions for out-of-town publications.

Ken Howard

How to Succeed in Business Without Really Trying

Outstanding Broadway Play
Love! Valour! Compassion!

Outstanding Broadway Musical
Sunset Boulevard

Outstanding Revival — Play
The Heiress

Outstanding Revival — Musical
Show Boat

Outstanding Off-Broadway Play
Camping With Henry and Tom

Outstanding Off-Broadway Musical
Jelly Roll!

Outstanding Performance by an Actor
Nathan Lane, *Love! Valour! Compassion!*

Outstanding Performance by an Actress
Cherry Jones, *The Heiress*

Outstanding Actor in a Musical
Matthew Broderick, *How to Succeed in Business Without Really Trying*

Outstanding Actress in a Musical
Glenn Close, *Sunset Boulevard*

Outstanding Solo Performance
James Lecesne, *James Lecesne's Word of Mouth*

Martha Swope

Love! Valour! Compassion!

in the time of AIDS. Aging choreographer Gregory Mitchell (Bogardus) and his blind lover Bobby Brahms (Kirk) host the outings, which are attended by accountant Arthur Pape (Hickey) and lawyer Perry Sellars (Heald); John Jeckyll (Glover), author of a musical flop, and his current boy toy Ramon Fornos (Becker), a Puerto Rican dancer; Jeckyll's twin brother James (also Glover); and AIDS sufferer Buzz Hauser (Lane). Hauser's comic response to his condition lightens a serious comedy about love and death.

THE MOLIÈRE COMEDIES
By: Molière, translated by Richard Wilbur; **Director:** Michael Langham; **Sets:** Douglas Stein; **Costumes:** Ann Hould-Ward; **Lighting:** Richard Nelson; **Artististic Director:** Todd Haimes
Opening: 2/95 at the Criterion Center Stage Right
Cast: Brian Bedford, Remak Ramsay, Suzanne Bertish, Patricia Dunnok, Cheryl Gaysunas, Malcolm Gets, David Aaron Baker, Reg Rogers, Denis Holmes and Jeff Stafford
Double bill including *The School for Husbands* and *The Imaginary Cuckold*
Once a cuckold, always a cuckold, and Molière's Sganarelle (Bedford) hasn't gotten any smarter in the 300-odd years since he made his first appearance. As the unwitting courier between his ward/intended wife and her true love in *The School for Husbands*, he's blissfully self-satisfied with his every bourgeois blunder. Deceived again as a gawky provincial husband in *The Imaginary Cuckold*, he vaunts his cowardice as the height of good sense. Wilbur's translations capture the fun of the original verses without turning them into rhymed doggerel, and cast members are solid in their dual roles.

A MONTH IN THE COUNTRY
By: Ivan Turgenev, translated by Richard Freeborn; **Director:** Scott Ellis; **Sets:** Santo Loquasto; **Costumes:** Jane Greenwood; **Lighting:** Brian Nason
Opening: 4/95 at the Criterion Center Stage Right

Cast: Helen Mirren, Ron Rifkin, F. Murray Abraham, Kathryn Erbe, John Christopher Jones, Alessandro Nivola and Gail Grate

A summer idyll on a country estate breeds boredom and romantic intrigue when Natalya Petrovna (Mirren) discovers a passion for her son's tutor Belyaev (Nivola), disappointing her own admirer Rakitin (Rifkin) and ruining the hopes of her ward (Erbe). Comic relief comes from a bumbling doctor and would-be anarchist Shpigelsky (Abraham), who courts the family governess (Grate) and from self-important landowner Bolshintsov (Jones), who eventually marries the unhappy Vera.

MY THING OF LOVE

By: Alexandra Gersten; **Director:** Michael Maggio; **Sets:** John Lee Beatty; **Costumes:** Erin Quigley; **Lighting:** Howell Binkley; **Music:** Rob Milburn and Michael Bodeen
Opening: 5/95 at the Martin Beck Theatre
Cast: Laurie Metcalf, Tom Irwin, Jane Fleiss and Mark Blum

Roseanne stalwart Metcalf is the linchpin of this production in her role as wife and mother Elly, who discovers that her husband of 11 years, Jack (Irwin), is having an affair with a younger woman (Fleiss). The already bad situation further erodes when Jack breaks his promise to end the affair, one of their daughters causes trouble at school and misery engulfs the family. Despite their problems, the couple cannot make a clean break, and issues are thrashed out with no decisive conclusion. *My Thing of Love* survived an unstable pre-production period before seeing the stage, but enjoyed only a short Broadway run before being pulled.

Carol Rosegg

On the Waterfront

ON THE WATERFRONT

By: Budd Schulberg, adapted from the 1954 film by Elia Kazan; **Director:** Adrian Hall; **Sets:** Eugene Lee; **Costumes:** Ann Hould-Ward; **Lighting:** Peter Kaczorowski; **Music:** David Amram
Opening: 5/95 at the Brooks Atkinson Theatre
Cast: Ron Eldard, David Morse, Penelope Ann Miller, Kevin Conway, Michael Harney, Brad Sullivan and George N. Martin

Outstanding Debut of an Actor
Billy Crudup, *Arcadia*

Outstanding Debut of an Actress
Helen Mirren, *A Month in the Country*

John Gassner Playwriting Award
Anne Meara, *After-Play*

Outstanding Director of a Play
Joe Mantello, *Love! Valour! Compassion!*

Outstanding Director of a Musical
Harold Prince, *Show Boat*

Outstanding Choreography
Susan Stroman, *A Christmas Carol* and *Show Boat*

Outstanding Design
Eugene Lee, production design; Florence Klotz, costume design; Richard Pilbrow, lighting design, *Show Boat*

Special Achievement Awards
Jerry Lewis, "Dazzling the Great White Way," *Damn Yankees*

The Horton Foote Plays: *Night Seasons, Taking Pictures, The Young Man From Atlanta* and *Laura Dennis* at the Signature Theatre

Encores! Great American Musicals in Concert at City Center

The cast of *Travels With My Aunt* for outstanding ensemble performance

....

1994 NEW YORK DRAMA CRITICS' CIRCLE AWARDS

The New York Drama Critics' Circle announced 1994's winners on May 9, 1995. The 17-member group includes critics from all New York City's newspapers, magazines and wire services except the *New York Times*.

Best New Play
Arcadia

Best New American Play
Love! Valour! Compassion!

Best Musical
No award given

Outstanding Achievement Award
Signature Theatre Company, which dedicated its season to the works by Horton Foote

The 1995 Los Angeles Drama Critics Circle Awards were presented March 20, 1995 at Studio City's Sportsmen's Lodge.

Productions
Counsellor at Law
The Seagull
The Visit

Lead Performances
Nancy Linehan Charles, *The Visit*
Pat Destro, *Dylan*
Marilyn Fox, *Awake and Sing*
Dave Higgins, *Dylan*
John Rubinstein, *Counsellor at Law*

Featured Performances
Mary Carver, *Counsellor at Law*
Jane Lanier, *Counsellor at Law*
Marilyn McIntyre, *Counsellor at Law*

Creation Performance
Colin Martin, *Virgins and Other Myths*

Writing
Scott McPherson, *Marvin's Room*

Direction
Alan Johnson, *1940's Radio Hour*
Milton Katselas, *The Seagull*
John Rubinstein and Anita Khanzadian, *Counsellor at Law*
Stephanie Shroyer, *The Visit*

Musical Direction
Brian Miller, *1940's Radio Hour*
Louis St. Louis, *Smokey Joe's Cafe*

Choreography
Wayne Cilento, *The Who's Tommy*

Music And Lyrics
Stephen Sondheim, *Assassins*

Original Music
Tom Gerou, *The Visit*

Scenic Design
John Arnone, *The Who's Tommy*
Matthew C. Jacobs, *The Visit*
Bradley Kaye, *Counsellor at Law*

Hoping to successfully spin off the 1954 classic film, *On the Waterfront* quickly gained notoriety as the biggest non-musical money-loser in history when it closed after only eight regular performances. Stormy events surrounding the production, including last-minute changes of directors, the hushed-up departure of a lead actor and a cast member's heart attack during a performance, rivaled the on-stage drama of former small-time boxer and longshoreman Terry Malloy (Eldard), forced to grapple with his conscience when called to testify about corruption on the New York docks. Overwhelmed by a crowded cityscape set and shortchanged by a script too much like a screenplay, the actors performed valiantly, even managing to extract the play's characters from their indelibly etched movie models.

THE PLAY'S THE THING
By: Ferenc Molnar, adapted by P. G. Wodehouse; **Director:** Gloria Muzio; **Sets:** Stephan Olson; **Costumes:** Jess Goldstein; **Lighting:** Peter Kaczorowski; **Production Stage Manager:** Denise Yaney
Opening: 7/95 at the Criterion Center Stage Right
Cast: Joe Grifasi, Peter Frechette, Jay Goede, Paul Benedict, J. Smith-Cameron, Jeff Weiss and Keith Reddin

The miscast actors struggle to pull off this potentially hilarious production, and while they do succeed at times, they barely skate by in others. Sandor Turai (Frechette), a successful playwright, his collaborator Mansky (Grifasi) and their protégé Albert Adam (Goede) arrive at an Italian castle planning to surprise Ilona (Smith-Cameron), an opera singer who is to perform Adam's operetta. Adam, who is madly in love with Ilona, is shattered when he overhears her having sex with her voice teacher Almady (Weiss). He threatens to scrap his work, but Turai convinces him to do otherwise. Turai inserts a scene in the play that has Ilona and Almady having sex, and tries to convince Adam that the pair were simply rehearsing.

Carol Rosegg

The Play's the Thing

THE ROSE TATTOO

By: Tennessee Williams; **Director:** Robert Falls; **Sets:** Santo Loquasto; **Costumes:** Catherine Zuber; **Lighting:** Kenneth Posner
Opening: 4/95 at the Circle in the Square Theatre
Cast: Mercedes Ruehl, Anthony LaPaglia, Antonia Rey, Cara Buono, Deborah Jolly, Irma St. Paule, Dominic Chianese, Philip LeStrange, Ellen Tobie, Catherine Campbell, Kay Walbye and Dylan Chalfy
Strong-willed Italian seamstress Serafina (Ruehl) lives on the Gulf Coast in a steamy dream world, caring for her daughter Rosa (Buono) and lost in erotic memories of her late husband. When truck driver Alvaro (LaPaglia) appears, Serafina's earthy desires find a new object, and she gradually emerges from her fantasies to find happiness. While other Williams plays end in disappointment, *The Rose Tattoo* allows its characters to fulfill their hopes and celebrate the joys of life and love in highly musical language.

THE SHADOW BOX

By: Michael Cristofer; **Director:** Jack Hofsiss; **Set:** David Jenkins; **Costumes:** Carrie Robbins; **Lighting:** Richard Nelson; **Artistic Directors:** Ted Mann and Josephine R. Abady
Opening: 11/94 at the Circle in the Square Theatre
Cast: Mary Alice, Mercedes Ruehl, Marlo Thomas, Ron Frazier, Frankie R. Faison, Sean Nelson, Jamey Sheridan, Raphael Sbarge and Estelle Parsons
The prospect of death and dying seems an unlikely agent of rebirth, but this revival of the 1977 Pulitzer- and Tony-winning drama of three terminally ill patients in a California hospice brings new life to both the play and the Circle in the Square Theatre. Counseled in separate cottages by the same unseen psychiatrist, a working-class family (Faison, Alice and Nelson), a writer, his lover and his ex-wife (Sheridan, Sbarge and Ruehl) and an older women and her daughter (Parsons and Thomas) do the best they can with the time left. The current production was inspired by Ruehl and Parsons, participants in a reading staged to protest the firing of a high-school drama teacher whose students had performed the play.

SHOW BOAT

By: Jerome Kern, based on the book by Edna Ferber; **Lyrics:** Oscar Hammerstein II; **Director:** Hal Prince; **Choreographer:** Susan Stroman; **Sets:** Eugene Lee
Opening: 10/94 at the Gershwin Theatre
Cast: John McMartin, Elaine Stritch, Dorothy Stanley, Joel Blum, Rebecca Luker, Lonette McKee, Gretha Boston and Michel Bell
Ol' Man River has been rollin' on since 1927, when this full-blooded re-creation of life on a Mississippi showboat was first performed. Essentially a love story, the show surprised early audiences by depicting life's seamier sides — alcoholism, racial prejudice and marital problems. Although these are now familiar dramatic

Lighting Design
  Deena Lynn Mullen, *The Visit*
  Chris Parry, *The Who's Tommy*

Costume Design
  Jonathan Bixby, *Sayonara*
  Cara Varnett, *The Visit*

Sound Design
  Alan Faulkner, *1940's Radio Hour*

Ted Schmitt Award
  Justin Tanner, *Pot Mom*

Angstrom Lighting Award
  Ken Booth

Margaret Harford Award
  Theatre 40

Lifetime Achievement Award
  Betty Garrett

Special Award
  CAST Theatre, *The Justin Tanner Festival*

Special Awards
  Tim Miller and Highways
  Timothy M. Gray

 **INTRODUCING...**

ANGEL CORELLA
The 19-year-old Spanish ballet dancer, after only months in the United States, is considered the type of dancer who can turn a performance into a major event. During the 1995 summer season, he danced with the American Ballet Theatre at The Met, performing the *Bronze Idol* in *La Bayadère*, considered one of the most virtuosic solos in classical ballet.

THE WIRED MET
James Levine, artistic director of The Metropolitan Opera House, once declared that The Met would use titles "over my dead body," but Levine is still alive and kicking and the 1995–1996 season will premiere the $2 million system that transmits lyrics in English onto mini-screens on the back of each seat. Traditionalists can turn off the device, but the screens on other seats will still be visible.

elements, the show is dated by its clichéd and sentimentalized black characters. The current production thankfully downplays this stereotyping to appeal to contemporary taste, although it loses some of the original's flavorful dialect in the process.

Smokey Joe's Cafe

SMOKEY JOE'S CAFE
Words and Music: Jerry Leiber and Mike Stoller; **Original Concept:** Stephen Helper and Jack Viertel, with Otis Sallid; **Director:** Jerry Zaks; **Musical Staging:** Joey McKneely; **Sets:** Heidi Landesman; **Costumes:** William Ivey Long; **Lighting:** Timothy Hunter; **Orchestrations:** Steve Margoshes
Opening: 3/95 at the Virginia Theatre
Cast: Ken Ard, Adrian Bailey, Brenda Baxton, Victor Trent Cook, B. J. Crosby, Pattie Darcy Jones, DeLee Lively, Frederick B. Owens and Michael Park
On a fire-escape set covered with '50s and '60s memorabilia, nine singers perform 39 catchy, familiar songs by the writers who bridged the gap between Tin Pan Alley and rock with songs including "Hound Dog," "Fools Fall in Love," "Keep on Rollin'," "On Broadway" and "Spanish Harlem." Performances in the two-hour special range from good to compelling, though the show itself has been compared to a late-night, golden oldies television spot.

SUNSET BOULEVARD
Music: Andrew Lloyd Webber; **Book and lyrics:** Don Black and Christopher Hampton; **Director:** Trevor Nunn; **Costumes:** Anthony Powell; **Lighting:** Andrew Bridge
Opening: 11/94
Based on Billy Wilder's 1950 film
Cast: Glenn Close (Betty Buckley replaced Close in July), Alan Campbell, George Hearn, Alice Ripley, Alan Oppenenheimer and Vincent Tumeo
The most anticipated and publicized Broadway production of the 1994–1995 season did not disappoint. Controversy and hype followed *Sunset*, beginning when the play opened in Los Angeles rather than New York, followed by the Faye Dunaway incident in which Webber fired her and she in turn sued. Then Close threatened to quit when an insider fudged ticket sales figures when she did not perform. But *Sunset* prevailed, and it was *big. Sunset* chronicles the relationship between formerly famous movie star but now reclusive Norma Desmond (Close and Buckley) and an unsuccessful screenwriter Joe Gillis (Campbell). Gillis, on the run from a repo man, takes refuge in Desmond's mansion and stays on as a kept man, helping her write a script for *Salome*, which she thinks will put her back in the limelight.

TRANSLATIONS
By: Brian Friel; **Director:** Howard Davies; **Sets:** Ashley Martin-Davis; **Lighting:** Chris Parry; **Costumes:** Joan Bergin
Opening: 3/95 at the Plymouth Theatre
Cast: Brian Dennehy, Dana Delany, Donal Donnelly, Rufus Sewell, Rob Campbell, Amelia Campbell, David Herlihy, Miriam Healy-Louie, Geoffrey Wade, Michael Cumpsty and Hugh O'Gorman
Words can be translated, but the culture they embody dies with the original. Even today, the struggle persists to preserve Gaelic in Ireland, mainly in the rugged west coast areas of the Gaeltacht, where *Translations* takes place. British army engineers have arrived in 1833 Baile Beag to map the territory and Anglicize local place names (Baile Beag became Ballybeg). Multilingual "hedge school" master Hugh (Dennehy) teaches both English and Irish but lives in the past, convincing himself that a drunken escapade was a brave stand against the British. Reality intrudes when his son Owen (Sewell) arrives as a translator for the army, and the two worlds clash when English officer Yol-land (Cumpsty) and Irish beauty Maire (Delany) fall in love.

Sunset Boulevard

A Tuna Christmas

Writers: Jason Williams, Joe Sears and Ed Howard; **Director:** Ed Howard; **Sets:** Loren Sherman; **Costumes:** Linda Fisher; **Lighting:** Judy Rasmuson

Opening: 12/94 at the Booth Theatre

Cast: Joe Sears and Jaston Williams

Tuna may be the third-smallest town in Texas, but that doesn't guarantee a merry little Christmas. Smut Snatchers are busy banning "Silent Night," the electric company may pull the plug on "A Christmas Carol" and a Christmas Phantom has it in for station OKKK's annual lawn-display contest. Action is frantic on- and off-stage, as Williams and Sears each portray 11 townspeople, from gun store owner to animal rescuer, complete with appropriate costume changes and telling mannerisms. Underlying the manic cleverness is the desolation of a desert Christmas, lacking genuine cheer but never entirely without hope.

Uncle Vanya

By: Anton Chekhov, translated by Jean-Claude van Itallie; **Director:** Braham Murray; **Set:** Loren Sherman; **Costumes:** Mimi Maxmen; **Lighting:** Tharon Musser

Opening: 2/95 at the Circle in the Square Theatre

Cast: Tom Courtenay, James Fox, Amanda Donohoe, Werner Klemperer, Gerry Bamman, Elizabeth Franz and Kate Skinner

Inert Vanya (Courtenay) and his loyal niece Sonya (Franz) are misused by Serebryakov (Klemperer), the fraudulent academic they have supported for years. The two are also thwarted in love, Vanya by Serebryakov's lovely wife Yelena (Donohoe), and Sonya by eccentric environmentalist Astrov (Fox), who is in love with Yelena. Seismic emotional shifts produce no actual change, and all must live on with unfulfilled desires.

What's Wrong With This Picture?

By: Donald Margulies; **Director:** Joe Mantello; **Sets:** Derek McLane; **Costumes:** Ann Roth; **Lighting:** Brian MacDevitt; **Music:** Mel Marvin

Opening: 12/94 at the Brooks Atkinson Theatre

Cast: Faith Prince, Alan Rosenberg, Jerry Stiller, David Moscow, Marcell Rosenblatt and Florence Stanley

Middle-class Jewish housewife Shirley (Prince) has choked to death on moo-shu pork, and is being mourned by son Artie (Moscow) and husband Mort (Rosenberg) when she suddenly materializes to do some final housecleaning. But it's unclear exactly what messes she left behind. Was she unfaithful? Did she play cruel tricks on her son? What begins as manic shtick on the incongruities of life and death loses momentum and focus as it fails to bridge the gap between throwaway comedy and serious comment.

1995 Drama Desk Awards

The Drama Desk, a group of 150 drama critics and reporters, announced the 1995 award winners on May 21, 1995.

Outstanding Play
Love! Valour! Compassion!

Outstanding Musical
Show Boat

Outstanding Revival
The Heiress

Outstanding One-Person Show
James Lescene's Word of Mouth

Unique Theatrical Experience
Travels With My Aunt

Best Actor in a Play
Ralph Fiennes, Hamlet

Best Actress in a Play
Cherry Jones, The Heiress

Best Featured Actor in a Play
Nathan Lane, Love! Valour! Compassion!

Best Featured Actress in a Play (tie)
Tara FitzGerald, Hamlet

Hallie Foote for roles in several Horton Foote plays

Best Actor in a Musical
Matthew Broderick, How to Succeed in Business Without Really Trying

Best Actress in a Musical
Glenn Close, Sunset Boulevard

Best Director
Harold Prince, Show Boat

Best Director of a Play
Gerald Gutierrez, The Heiress

Set Design
Eugene Lee, Show Boat

Lighting
Richard Pilbrow, Show Boat

Costumes
Florence Klotz, Show Boat

Honorary Awards
Eileen Atkins, Vita and Virginia and Indiscretions

Otis Guernsey, editor of Best Plays

Non-Traditional Casting Project

Barrow Group

1994–1995 Major Off-Broadway and Off-Off Broadway Productions

Henry Horenstein/Courtesy of American Repertory Theatre

Cryptogram

Acts of Desire by Nina Beber
Presented by the Watermark Theater
Opening: 5/95

After-Play by Anne Meara
Presented by Manhattan Theatre Club
Opening: 1/95 at City Center Stage II

All About Steve: Musings of an Ebony Queer by Stephen Patterson
Presented by Ditto Productions
Opening: 4/95 at Grove Street Playhouse

Amphitryon by Eric Overmyer
Presented by Classic Stage Company
Opening: 4/95

Around the World in 80 Days by Allan Knee;
based on the novel by Jules Verne
Presented by Theaterworks/USA
Opening: 7/95 at the Promenade Theater

As You Like It by William Shakespeare
Presented by the Brooklyn Academy of Music
Opening: 10/94 at the Brooklyn Academy of Music Majestic Theater

The Ballad of Little Jo and Camila
Double Bill: **The Ballad of Little Jo** by Sarah Schlesinger; **Camila** by Rod Koats
Presented by The Director's Company
Opening 6/95 at the Theater at St. Peter's Church

Camping With Henry and Tom by Mark St. Germain
Presented by Daryl Roth, Wind Dancer Theater
Opening: 2/95 at the Lucille Lortel Theater

Carmen by Everett Quinton
Presented by Ridiculous Theatrical Company
Opening: 1/95 at Charles Ludlam Theater

A Cheever Evening by A. R. Gurney;
based on stories by John Cheever
Presented by Playwrights Horizons
Opening: 10/94

Chronicle of a Death Foretold based on the novel by Gabriel García Márquez; adapted by Graciela Daniele and Jim Lewis
Presented by Lincoln Center Theater
Opening: 6/95 at the Plymouth Theater

Circus Life by Murray Schisgal
Presented by Martin R. Kaufman
Opening: 2/95 at the Martin Kaufman Theater

Coming Through adapted and written by Wynn Handman
Presented by the American Place Theater
Opening: 5/95

The Compleat Works of Willm Shkspr (Abridged)
by Adam Long, Daniel Singer and Jess Winfield
Presented by Jeffrey Richards, Richard Gross and Jamie deRoy
Opening: 2/95 at the Westside Theater

Crumbs From the Table of Joy by Lynn Nottage
Presented by the Second Stage Theater
Opening: 6/95 at the McGinn/Cazale Theater

Cryptogram by David Mamet
Presented by Frederick Zollo, Nicholas Paleologos, Gregory Mosher and Jujamcyn Theaters in association with Herb Alpert and Margo Lino
Opening: 4/95 at the Westside Theater Upstairs

Dancing on Moonlight by Keith Glover
Presented by the New York Shakespeare Festival
Opening: 4/95 at the Joseph Papp Public Theater

Dates and Nuts by Gary Lennon
Presented by the Wiessberger Group
Opening: 5/95 at Theater Off Park

Death Defying Acts by David Mamet, Woody Allen and Elaine May
Presented by Richard Frankel Productions
Opening: 3/95 at the Variety Arts Theater

The Diva Is Dismissed by Lewis and Charles Randolph-Wright
Presented by the New York Shakespeare Festival
Opening: 12/94 at the Joseph Papp Public Theater

Dog Opera by Constance Congdon
Presented by the New York Shakespeare Festival
Opening: 5/95 at the Joseph Papp Public Theater

A Doll's House by Henrik Ibsen
Presented by The Acting Company
Opening: 3/95 at the TriBeCa Performing Arts Center

A Doll's Life book and lyrics by Betty Comden
and Adolph Green
Presented by the York Theater Company
Opening: 12/94 at Citicorp Center

Ecstasy by Mike Leigh
Presented by the New Group
Opening: 4/95 at the John Houseman Theater Center

Extraordinary Measures by Eve Ensler
Presented by Music-Theater Group and Home for
Contemporary Theater and Art
Opening: 5/95

The Family Business by Ain Gordon and Dave Gordon
Presented by New York Theater Workshop
Opening: 4/95

**For Colored Girls Who Have Considered Suicide
When the Rainbow Is Enuf** by Ntozake Shange
Presented by the New Federal Theater
Opening: 6/95 at Harry De Jur Playhouse

Ghost Sonata by August Strindberg
Presented by the Irondale Ensemble Project
Opening: 5/95 at the White Street Theater

Girl Gone by Jacquelyn Reingold
Presented by A Manhattan Class Company
Opening: 12/94

Goose and Tomtom by David Rabe
Presented by the Willow Cabin Theater Company
Opening: 4/95 at the 28th Street Theater

Gorodish by Hillel Mittelpunkt
Presented by the Brooklyn Academy of Music
Opening: 4/95 at the Carey Playhouse

Grandma Sylvia's Funeral by Glenn Wein
and Amy Lord
Presented by Dana Matthow
Opening: 10/94 at the Playhouse on Van Dam

Hapgood by Tom Stoppard
Presented by Lincoln Center Theater
Opening: 12/94 at the Mitzi E. Newhouse Theater

The Heart Is a Lonely Hunter by Carson McCullers
Presented by Theater for the New City
Opening: 8/95

Henry VI by William Shakespeare
Presented by the Theater for a New Audience
Opening: 3/95 at the Theater at St. Clement's

Him by Christopher Walken
Presented by the New York Shakespeare Festival
Opening: 1/95 at the Joseph Papp Public Theater

Holiday Heart by Cheryl L. West
Presented by Manhattan Theatre Club
Opening: 2/95 at City Center, Stage I

Hundreds of Hats by Howard Ashman
Presented by the WPA Theater
Opening: 6/95

Incommunicado by Tom Dulack
Presented by Maxemmus Theater
Opening: 3/95 at the Judith Anderson Theater

I've Got the Shakes by Richard Foreman
Presented by Ontological-Hysteric Theater
Opening: 1/95

Jack's Holiday music and lyrics by Randy Courts;
book and lyrics by Mark St. Germain
Presented by Playwrights Horizons
Opening: 3/95

Jesus Christ Superstar
music by Andrew Lloyd Webber; lyrics by Tim Rice
Presented by Landmark Entertainment Group
Opening: 1/95 at the Paramount

john & jen music by Andrew Lippa; lyrics by Tom
Greenwald; book by Andrew Lippa and Tom
Greenwald
Presented by the Lamb Theater Company and
Carolyn Rossi Copeland
Opening: 6/95 at the Lamb's Little Theater

J. P. Morgan Saves the Nation book and lyrics by
Jeffrey M. Jones; music by Johnathan Larson
Presented by En Garde Arts
Opening: 6/95 at the Corner of Wall and Broad streets

Lady-like by Laura Shamas
Presented by The Glines
Opening: 6/95 at the Grove Street Playhouse

A Language of Their Own by Chay Yew
Presented by the New York Shakespeare Festival
Opening: 4/95 at the Joseph Papp Public Theater

Laura Dennis by Horton Foote
Presented by the Signature Theatre Company
Opening: 3/95 at Kampo Cultural Center

The Little Book of Professor Enigma by Harry
Kondoleon
Presented by Theater for New York City
Opening: 12/94

London Suite by Neil Simon
Presented by Emanuel Azenberg and Leonard
Soloway
Opening: 4/95 at the Union Square Theater

Lonely Planet by Steven Dietz
Presented by Circle Repertory Company
Opening: 6/95

Luck, Pluck and Virtue by James Lapine
Presented by the Atlantic Theater Company
Opening: 4/95

Madame de Sade by Yukio Mishima
Presented by Brooklyn Academy of Music
Opening: 6/95 at the Opera House of the Brooklyn
Academy of Music

Marathon '95 by David Mamet
Presented by Ensemble Studio Theater
Opening: 6/95

The Merchant of Venice by William Shakespeare
Presented by the New York Shakespeare Festival
Opening: 2/95 at the Joseph Papp Public Theater

A Midsummer Night's Dream by William
Shakespeare
Presented by the Ridiculous Theatrical Company
Opening: 10/95 at the Charles Ludlam Theater

Missing Persons by Craig Lucas
Presented by the Atlantic Theater Company
Opening: 2/95

The Mountain of Giants by Luigi Pirandello
Presented by the Brooklyn Academy of Music
Opening: 4/95 at the Opera House of Brooklyn
Academy of Music

Mrs. Warren's Profession by Bernard Shaw
Presented by the Pearl Theater Company
Opening: 4/95

Night and Her Stars by Richard Greenberg
Presented by Manhattan Theatre Club
Opening: 5/95 at the American Palace Theater

The Old Lady's Guide to Survival by Mayo Simon
Presented by Daniel Mayer Selznick
Opening: 2/95 at the Lamb's Theater

One Woman Shoe by the Talent Family
Presented by La Mama E.T.C.
Opening: 1/95 at the Club at La Mama

The Only Thing Worse You Could Have Told Me . . .
by Dan Butler
Presented by Scott Allyn
Opening: 4/95 at the Actor's Playhouse

Othello by William Shakespeare
Presented by The Acting Company
Opening: 3/95 at the TriBeCa Performing Arts Center

The Petrified Prince Book by Edward Gallardo;
music and lyrics by Michael John LaChiusa, based
on a screenplay by Ingmar Bergen
Presented by the New York Shakespeare Festival
Opening: 12/94 at the Joseph Papp Public Theater

Police Boys by Marion McClinton
Presented by Playwrights Horizons
Opening: 5/95

Prisoner of Love by Jean Genêt; translated by
Barbara Bray; adapted by JoAnne Akalaitis, Ruth
Maleczech and Chiori Miyagawa
Presented by New York Theater Workshop
Opening: 6/95

The Professional by Dusan Kovacevic; translated
and adapted by Bob Kjurdjevic
Presented by Circle Repertory Company
Opening: 5/95

The Radical Mystique by Arthur Laurents
Presented by the New Theater Workshop
Opening: 6/95 at the Manhattan Theatre Club

Rush Limbaugh in Night School by Charles Varon
Presented by Second Stage Theater
Opening: 3/95

Silence, Cunning, Exile by Stuart Greenman
Presented by the New York Shakespeare Festival
Opening: 2/95 at the Joseph Papp Public Theater

Slavs! by Tony Kushner
Presented by the New York Theater Workshop
Opening: 12/94

Small Lives/Big Dreams based on the five major plays
by Anton Chekhov, conceived by Anne Bogart
Presented by Performance Space 122
Opening: 2/95

Some People by Danny Hoch
Presented by the New York Shakespeare Festival
Opening: 12/94 at the Joseph Papp Public Theater

The Springhill Singing Disaster by Karen Trott
Presented by Playwrights Horizons
Opening: 6/95

Swingtime Canteen by Steve Brustein
Presented by Miranda Theater Company
Opening: 2/95 at the Blue Angel

Sylvia by A. R. Gurney
Presented by Manhattan Theatre Club
Opening: 5/95 at City Center, Stage I

Talking Pictures by Horton Foote
Presented by the Signature Theatre Company
Opening: 10/94 at the Kampo Cultural Center

The Tempest by William Shakespeare
Presented by the New York Shakespeare
Festival/Joseph Papp Public Theater
Opening: 7/95 at the Delacorte Theater

Three Viewings by Jeffrey Hatcher
Presented by Manhattan Theatre Club
Opening: 4/95 at City Center, Stage 2

Travels With My Aunt by Graham Greene; adapted
by Giles Havergal
Presented by Bill Kenwright
Opening: 4/95 at the Minetta Lane Theater

The Truth-Teller by Joyce Carol Oates
Presented by Circle Repertory
Opening: 1/95

Twelve Dreams by James Lapine
Presented by Lincoln Center Theater
Opening: 6/95 at the Mitzi E. Newhouse Theater

Two Boys in a Bed on a Cold Winter's Night by
James Edwin Parker
Presented by Rattlestick Productions and Theater
Off Park
Opening: 7/95 at Theater Off Park

2: Goring at Nuremburg by Romulus Linney
Presented by Primary Stages
Opening: 5/19

Two Johns Kissing Leslie
Presented by the Chicago City Limits
Improvisational Theater
Opening: 7/95 at Chicago City Limits

Uncle Bob by Austin Pendleton
Presented by the Mint Theater Company
Opening: 2/95

Unexpected Tenderness by Israel Horovitz
Presented by WPA Theater
Opening: 10/94

Uncommon Women and Others by Wendy
Wasserstein
Presented by the Second Stage Theater
Opening: 10/94 at the Lucile Lortel Theater

The Venetian Twins by Carlo Goldini; translated by
Michael Feingold
Presented by the Pearl Theater Company
Opening: 12/94 at Theater 80

Vita and Virginia Adapted by Eileen Atkins from the
correspondence between Vita Sackville-West and
Virginia Woolf
Presented by Lewis Allen, Robert Fox, Ltd. and
Julian Schlossberg
Opening: 12/94 at the Union Square Theater

The Winter's Tale by William Shakespeare
Presented by the Brooklyn Academy of Music
Opening: 6/95 at the Brooklyn Academy of Music
Opera House

The Young Man From Atlanta by Horton Foote
Presented by the Signature Theatre Company
Opening: 1/95 at the Kampo Cultural Center

1995 OBIE AWARDS

The 1995 Obie Awards, honoring distinguished
achievement in Off-Broadway and Off-Off-
Broadway productions, were presented May 22,
1995 at New York's Manhattan Center.

Best Play
David Mamet, *Cryptogram*

Playwriting
David Hancock, *The Convention of Cartography*
Tony Kushner, *Slavs!*
Terrence McNally, *Love! Valour! Compassion!*
Susan Miller, *My Left Breast*

Direction
Robert Falls, *SubUrbia*
Don Scardino, *A Cheever Evening*
Susan Shulman, *Merrily We Roll Along*

Performances
Joanna Adler, *The Boys in the Basement*
Eileen Atkins and Vanessa Redgrave, *Vita and
Virginia*
Paul Calderon, *Blade to the Heart*
Malcolm Gets, *Merrily We Roll Along* and *Two
Gentlemen of Verona*
Felicity Huffman, *Cryptogram*
Linda Lavin, *Death Defying Acts*
Ron Leibman, *The Merchant of Venice*
Camryn Manheim, *Missing Persons*
Joe Mantello, director; entire cast, *Love!
Valour! Compassion!*
Kristine Nielsen, *Dog Opera*
Mary Beth Peil, *The Naked Truth, Missing
Persons* and *A Cheever Evening*
Barbara Eda Young, *Slavs!*

Design
Wendall K. Harrington, sustained excellence of
projection
Jennifer von Mayrhauser, sustained excellence
of costume design

Sustained Achievement
Ming Cho Lee

1994–1995 Major Regional Theater Productions

ACTORS THEATRE OF LOUISVILLE
316 W. Main St.
Louisville, KY 40202-4218
(502) 584-1205

MAINSTAGE SERIES
I Hate Hamlet by Paul Rudnick
10/26/94–11/19/94

The Adding Machine by Elmer Rice
1/4/95–1/28/95

Corpse by Gerald Moon
2/1/95–3/4/95

Humana Festival of New American Plays
3/8/95–4/8/95

From the Mississippi Delta by Endesha Ida Mae Holland
4/11/95–6/4/95

The Strange Case of Dr. Jekyll and Mr. Hyde by David Edgar
5/10/95–6/11/95

Sleuth by Anthony Shaffer
9/20/95–10/21/95

OFF-BROADWAY SERIES
Someone Who'll Watch Over Me by Frank McGuinness
10/4/94–10/23/94

Small Lives/Big Dreams
based on the text by Anton Chekhov
1/17/95–1/28/95

Humana Festival of New American Plays
2/28/95–4/2/95

Flying Solo and Friends
9/5/95–9/24/95

SPECIAL PERFORMANCES
Flying Solo and Friends
A festival showcasing avant-garde performers
11/1/94–11/13/94

A Christmas Carol by Charles Dickens; adapted by Jon Jory and Marcia Dixcy
11/24/94–12/29/94

The Gift of the Magi by O. Henry; adapted by Peter Ekstrom
12/6/94–12/23/94

The Medium
1/26/95–1/29/95

Rock 'n' Roles From William Shakespeare by Jim Luigs
4/24/95–4/28/95

SUMMER MUSICAL SERIES
Forever Plaid by Stuart Ross and James Raitt
7/18/95–8/27/95

AMERICAN CONSERVATORY THEATER
30 Grant Ave., 6th Floor
San Francisco, CA 94108-5800
(415) 834-3218

Angels in America — Part I: Millennium Approaches by Tony Kushner
10/12/94–2/5/95

Angels in America — Part II: Perestroika by Tony Kushner
10/19/94–2/5/95

Home by David Storey
10/26/94–12/4/94

Rosencrantz and Guildenstern Are Dead by Tom Stoppard
12/21/94–2/5/95

The Play's the Thing by Ferenc Molnar; adapted by P.G. Wodehouse
2/22/95–4/2/95

Hecuba by Euripides; adapted by Timberlake Wertenbaker
5/3/95–6/4/95

Othello by William Shakespeare
5/19/95–6/4/95

AMERICAN REPERTORY THEATRE
64 Brattle St.
Cambridge, MA 02138
(617) 547-8300

Waiting for Godot by Samuel Beckett
1/13/95–2/12/95

The Cryptogram by David Mamet
2/2/95–2/19/95

Henry V by William Shakespeare
2/19/95–3/25/95

Demons by Robert Brustein
3/30/95–5/5/95

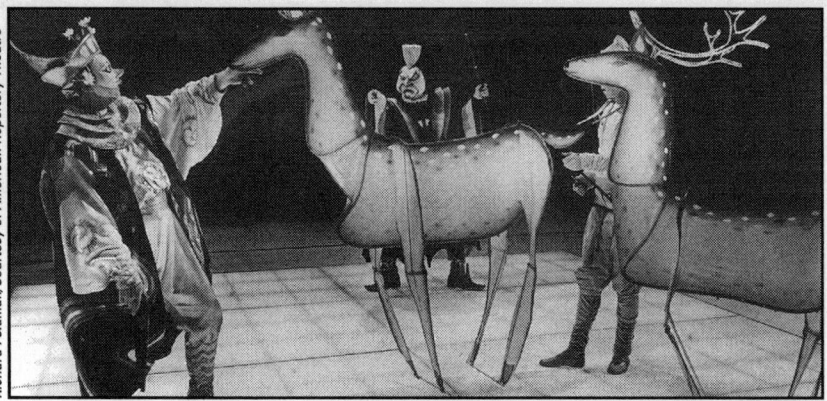

The King Stag

The Accident by Carol K. Mack
4/6/95–5/7/95

**The Reduced Shakespeare Company:
The Bible: The Complete Word of God
(Abridged)**
4/18/95–5/7/95

The Threepenny Opera by Bertolt Brecht
and Kurt Weill
5/12/95–7/24/95

Ubu Rock
6/2/95–7/16/95

Fall Festival '95
9/19/95–10/7/95

SUMMER SERIES
The King Stag based on a fable by Carlo Gozzi
7/27/95–8/26/95

DENVER CENTER THEATRE COMPANY
1245 Champa St.
Denver, CO 80204-2154
(303) 893-4000

Oleanna by David Mamet
11/17/94–12/24/95

A Christmas Carol by Charles Dickens; adapted by
Dennis Powers and Laird Williamson
11/25/94–12/24/94

Coming of the Hurricane by Keith Glover
1/6/95–2/11/95

The Quick-Change Room by Nagic Jackson
1/13/95–2/11/95

Taming of the Shrew by William Shakespeare
1/20/95–2/25/95

The Education of Walter Kaufmann by Kevin Kling
3/3/95–4/11/95

The Imaginary Invalid by Molière
3/10/95–4/15/95

Someone Who'll Watch Over Me by Frank
McGuinness
3/17/95–4/22/95

Marisol by José Rivera
4/21/95–5/20/95

Man of the Moment by Alan Ayckbourn
5/5/95–6/10/95

Romeo and Juliet by William Shakespeare
9/28/95–11/11/95

THE GUTHRIE THEATER
725 Vineland Place
Minneapolis, MN 55403
(612) 377-2224

A Christmas Carol by Charles Dickens;
adapted by Barbara Field
11/25/94–12/30/94

Macbeth by William Shakespeare
1/13/95–2/5/95

King Lear by William Shakespeare
7/5/95–7/21/95 and 9/19/95–11/18/95

The Royal Family
by George S. Kaufman and Edna Ferber
7/7/95–9/9/95

A Program of Short Plays
7/14/95–9/9/95

The Firebugs by Max Frisch
8/4/95–9/9/95

Old Times by Harold Pinter
8/18/95–9/10/95

Big White Fog by Theodore Ward
9/22/95–11/4/95

K: Impressions of Kafka's The Trial by Garland
White
9/26/95–11/5/95

LONG WHARF THEATRE
222 Sargent Drive
New Haven, CT 06511
(203) 787-4284

NEWTON SCHENCK STAGE
Saturday, Sunday, Monday by Eduardo de Filippo
11/8/94–12/11/94

Arsenic and Old Lace by Joseph Kesseiring
1/17/95–2/26/95

Ceremonies in Dark Old Men by Lonne Elder III
3/7/95–4/9/95

Banjo Dancing by Stephen Wade
4/19/95–4/30/95

The Entertainer by John Osborne
5/23/95–6/25/95

STAGE II
Travels With My Aunt by Graham Greene
11/14/94–12/20/94

In the Heart of America by Naomi Wallace
11/29/94–12/11/94

A Swell Party
2/14/95–3/19/95

Ruler of My Destiny by Jocelyn Meinhardt
3/21/95–4/2/95

Some People by Danny Hoch
5/17/95–5/21/95

MARK TAPER FORUM
Los Angeles Music Center
135 N. Grand Ave.
Los Angeles, CA 90012
(213) 972-0700

Floating Islands by Eduardo Machado
10/5/94–12/11/94

Black Elk Speaks by John G. Neihardt; adapted by
Christopher Sergel
1/12/95–2/26/95

Three Hotels by Jon Robin Baitz
3/23/95–4/30/95

Master Class by Terrence McNally
5/18/95–7/1/95

Hysteria by Terry Johnson
7/27/95–9/3/95

SEATTLE REPERTORY THEATRE
155 Mercer St.
Seattle, WA 98109
(206) 443-2202

London Suite by Neil Simon
10/12/94–11/5/95

The Real Inspector Hound by Tom Stoppard
10/26/94–11/13/95

The Sisters Rosensweig by Wendy Wasserstein
11/16/94–12/17/94

In the Heart of the Wood by Todd Jefferson Moore
11/30/94–12/18/94

Dancing at Lughnasa by Brian Friel
1/4/95–1/28/95

Jolson Sings Again by Arthur Laurenis
2/8/95–3/4/95

Voir Dire by Joe Sutton
2/22/95–3/12/95

SOUTH COAST REPERTORY
655 Town Center Drive
Costa Mesa, CA 92626
(714) 957-2602

MAINSTAGE
Green Icebergs by Cecilia Fannon
10/14/94–11/20/95

A Christmas Carol by Charles Dickens; adapted
by Jerry Patch
11/29/94–12/24/94

The Misanthrope by Moliére
1/6/95–2/12/95

Ghost in the Machine by David Gilman
2/24/95–4/2/95

Blithe Spirit by Noel Coward
4/7/95–5/14/95

The Cherry Orchard by Anton Chekhov
5/26/95–7/2/95

She Stoops to Folly by Tom Murphy
9/8/95–10/8/95

SECOND STAGE
Jar the Floor by Cheryl L. West
11/1/94–12/4/94

La Posada Magic by Octavio Solis
12/9/94–12/24/94

Chris Bennion

London Suite

Playland

Wit by Margaret Edson
1/24/95–2/26/95

Pterodactyls by Nicky Silver
3/14/95–4/16/95

Faith Healer by Brian Friel
4/25/95–5/28/95

STEPPENWOLF THEATRE COMPANY
1650 N. Halstead St.
Chicago, IL 60614
(312) 335-1888

Playland by Athol Fugard
12/11/94–1/22/95

Time of My Life by Alan Ayckbourn
2/12/95–3/19/95

Nomathemba by Ntozake Shange, Joseph Shabalala and Eric Simonson
4/9/95–6/4/95

As I Lay Dying by William Faulkner; adapted by Frank Galati
7/9/95–8/13/95

TRINITY REPERTORY COMPANY
201 Washington St.
Providence, RI 02903
(401) 521-1100

The Waiting Room by Lisa Loomer
10/25/94–12/4/94

A Christmas Carol by Charles Dickens; adapted by Hall and Cumming
11/22/94–12/24/94

From the Mississippi Delta by Endesha Ida Mae Holland
12/30/94–2/12/95

The Illusion by Pierre Corneille; adapted by Tony Kushner
2/3/95–3/12/95

Slavs! by Tony Kushner
3/10/95–4/16/95

God's Heart by Craig Luca
5/5/95–6/11/95

Once in a Lifetime by George S. Kaufman and Moss Hart
9/15/95–10/22/95

YALE REPERTORY THEATRE
222 York St.
New Haven, CT 06520
(203) 432-1515

Antigone in New York by Janusz Glowacki
10/20/94–11/12/94

The Three Sisters by Anton Chekhov
10/25/94–10/29/94

Figaro Gets a Divorce by Ödön von Horváth; adapted by Eric Overmyer
12/1/94–12/17/94

The Marriage of Figaro by Pierre de Beaumarchais
12/1/94–12/17/94

The Good Person of Szechwan by Bertolt Brecht
12/2/94–12/10/94

Twelfth Night by William Shakespeare
1/26/95–2/18/95

Slavs! by Tony Kushner
2/24/95–3/18/95

Waiting for Godot by Samuel Beckett
3/7/95–3/11/95

Uncle Vanya by Anton Chekhov
3/30/95–4/15/95

Le Bourgeois Avant-Garde by Charles Ludlam
4/27/95–5/20/95

Imperceptible Mutabilities in the Third Kingdom by Suzan-Lori Parks
5/9/95–5/13/95

SUMMER SERIES
The Rats by Agatha Christie
6/21/95–7/1/95

Wooed and Viewed by Georges Feydeau
6/21/95–7/1/95

The Tempest by William Shakespeare
7/4/95–7/15/95

How He Lied to Her Husband by George Bernard Shaw
7/18/95–7/29/95

Overruled by George Bernard Shaw
7/18/95–7/29/95

The Fattest Man in the World Lives Upstairs by Janet Allard
8/1/95–8/12/95

1994–1995 Major West End Premieres

London's West End theater district is considered the Broadway of London. Each year several productions that originate in London eventually appear on the Great White Way. Here is a list of major West End productions of the 1994–1995 season.

After Easter
Opening: 4/95 at The Pit

Ain't Misbehavin'
Opening: 3/95 at the Lyric

Alice's Adventures Under Ground
Opening: 11/94 at the Cottesloe Theatre

Bingo
Opening: 6/95 at The Young Vic

Burning Blue
Opening: 7/95 at Haymarket

Cavalcade
Opening: 8/95 at Sadler's Wells

A Christmas Carol
Opening: 12/94 at Barbican Centre

Communicating Doors
Opening: 1/95 at the Gielgud

Dead Funny
Opening: 9/95 at the Savoy

Dead Guilty
Opening: 7/95 at the Apollo

Dealer's Choice
Opening: 2/95 at the Vaudeville

Editing Process
Opening: 11/94 at the Royal Court

Fame
Opening: 6/95 at the Cambridge

Five Guys Named Moe
Opening: 5/95 at the Albery

The Glass Menagerie
Opening: 9/95 at Donmar Warehouse

Hamlet
Opening: 11/94 at the Gielgud

Hot Mikado
Opening: 5/95 at the Queens

The Importance of Being Earnest
Opening: 7/95 at The Old Vic

Indian Ink
Opening: 2/95 at the Adelphi

Insignificance
Opening: 6/95 at Donmar Warehouse

Ion
Opening: 10/94 at The Pit

La Grande Magia
Opening: 7/95 at the Lyttelton Theatre

Landscape
Opening: 11/94 at the Cottesloe Theatre

The Libertine
Opening: 12/94 at the Royal Court

Mama, I Want to Sing
Opening: 2/95 at the Gielgud

The Man of Mode
Opening: 12/94 at the Royal Court

Measure for Measure
Opening: 6/95 at Barbican Centre

The Merchant of Venice
Opening: 11/94 at Barbican Centre

The Merry Wives of Windsor
Opening: 1/95 at the Olivier Theater

A Midsummer Night's Dream
Opening: 4/95 at Barbican Centre

A Midsummer Night's Dream
Opening: 5/95 at Open Air

A Midsummer's Night Dream
Opening: 11/94 at The Pit

Mojo
Opening: 7/95 at the Royal Court

Moscow Stations
Opening: 10/94 at the Garrick

My Night With Reg
Opening: 11/94 at the Criterion

Neville's Island
Opening: 10/94 at the Apollo

New England
Opening: 11/94 at The Pit

Old Times
Opening: 7/95 at Wyndham's

BRITISH THEATER 1993-1995

	7/10/95	7/11/94	7/12/93
Theaters open	45	40	41
Theaters dark	4	5	6
Straight plays	7	6	7
Comedies	4	5	8
Musicals	20	17	15
Thrillers	3	2	2
Theater repertory seasons	7	7	6
Separate productions (including repertories)	54	48	51

Source: The Society of London Theatre

Oliver!
Opening: 12/94 at the London Palladium

On Approval
Opening: 10/94 at the Playhouse

Only the Lonely
Opening: 10/94 at the Piccadilly

Out of a House Walked A Man . . .
Opening: 12/94 at the Lyttelton Theater

Out of the Blue
Opening: 11/94 at the Shaftesbury

A Passionate Woman
Opening: 11/94 at the Comedy

Pentecost
Opening: 6/95 at The Young Vic

The Prime of Miss Jean Brodie
Opening: 10/94 at the Strand

Richard II
Opening: 6/95 at the Cottesloe Theatre

Richard III
Opening: 5/95 at the Open Air

The Rocky Horror Show
Opening: 5/95 at Duke of York's

Romeo and Juliet
Opening: 11/94 at The Pit

Skylight
Opening: 5/95 at the Cottesloe Theatre

The Stewart of Christendom
Opening: 9/95 at the Royal Court

Street of Crocodiles
Opening: 10/94 at the Whitehall

Taking Sides
Opening: 7/95 at the Criterion

The Tale of Lear
Opening: 11/94 at Barbican Centre

The Tempest
Opening: 6/95 at The Young Vic

Tho Broken Heart
Opening: 5/95 at The Pit

Three Tall Women
Opening: 11/94 at Wyndham's

The Threepenny Opera
Opening: 12/94 at the Donmar Warehouse

True West
Opening: 11/94 at the Donmar Warehouse

Twelfth Night
Opening: 4/95 at Barbican Centre

Under Milk Wood
Opening: 4/95 at the Olivier Theater

Unforgettable
Opening: 6/95 at the Garrick

The Wives' Excuse
Opening: 4/95 at The Pit

Source: The Society of London Theatre

Balanced on the Edge

■ BY ANNA KISSELGOFF

Anna Kisselgoff
is a dance critic
for the *New
York Times*.

SMALL DETAILS CAN OFTEN SYMBOLIZE BIG CHANGES. The San Francisco Ballet, for instance, will leave the War Memorial Opera House in January 1996 for 18 months so that its home theater can undergo "seismic upgrading." But after damage from the 1989 earthquake is repaired and the state-of-the-art renovation is complete, one of the opera house's old amenities is likely to be missing: the metal holder for top hats that architect Arthur Brown had placed under every orchestra section seat in 1932.

Gone with the top hats is the idea that a gala opening is a social occasion. Nowadays, a gala means the ubiquitous fund-raising benefit necessary to every dance company's survival.

The past decade has found American dance in a state of transition and the 1994–1995 season was no exception. The artistic side was encouraging enough: Technique among dancers was of the highest standard and creativity poured out from established figures such as Merce Cunningham, Jerome Robbins and Paul Taylor, as well as young choreographers at all levels.

Nonetheless, aesthetics were in flux and artistic policies of ballet and modern dance troupes were threatened by rising costs, funding cuts and reduced touring. The dance world did not have to wait for the potential demise of the National Endowment for the Arts to face a clouded future.

Clearly, dance companies were scrambling to find new solutions.

In July 1995, the Joffrey Ballet announced that it was moving its base from New York City, where it could no longer afford an annual season, to Chicago, where it was promised stronger support. But two aspects of this announcement came as a surprise: A proposed merger with Ballet Chicago did not take place and the Joffrey renamed itself the Arpino Ballet after its current director, Gerald Arpino, in order to secure financing on a new legal footing.

Less startling, but more typical, was the merger announced by two small ballet companies in New Jersey, the Garden State Ballet and the American Repertory Ballet Company (formerly the Princeton Ballet).

Cost-sharing, a persistent theme among dance administrators, expanded in other ways. It was common to see a list of not-for-profit producers (known as "presenters") around the country credited with the commission of one premiere, as in the case of *Still/Here*, a modern-dance piece by Bill T. Jones.

The Kennedy Center for the Performing Arts in Washington D.C., on the other hand, acted as a single producer when it shared grant money among seven ballet companies, each of which performed a premiere commissioned by the Center. The proviso in this project, which began in 1991, was that the seven choreographers allow their new works to be performed by all the companies. In 1995, the Center announced that three more ballets

American Ballet Theatre

would be commissioned for the American Ballet Theatre, Dance Theater of Harlem and the Joffrey.

In addition to pooling resources, companies everywhere went in search of new audiences. It was rare to find a modern-dance or ballet troupe that did not participate in a "community outreach" program either through performances for schoolchildren or extended residencies that involved the public in auxiliary activities (backstage visits, lectures, rehearsals, dance classes). Marketing brochures this season were increasingly designed to lure newcomers to dance at a time when the core audience was either shifting allegiances or finding increased ticket prices too high for the repeated attendance that was traditional to dancegoers.

For fans who lived through the dance boom that lasted from the 1960s through the 1980s, the 1990s have been less than a golden age. The deaths, since 1983, of George Balanchine, Martha Graham, Anthony Tudor and, in England, Sir Frederick Ashton, have robbed choreography of its mold-breaking geniuses, choreographers whose pioneering work since the 1930s virtually re-created theatrical dance in the 20th century.

The recent era of the ballet superstar has also drawn to a close. Although Mikhail Baryshnikov continues, at the age of 47, to tour with the White Oak Dance Project, his small troupe of modern dancers, his reputation is based on his career as a classical dancer. With Baryshnikov, Rudolf Nureyev, Margot Fonteyn and Erik Bruhn no longer on the ballet scene, the public has been in search of fresh idols.

Yet the truth is that any art form is larger than any individual and vitality is sure to be regained. One need only recall the lament of critics who surveyed the state of American dance in the early 1960s and concluded that modern dance had run its course while ballet was in decline. Instead, the 1960s ushered in an unprecedented era of innovation and popularity for dance.

It was true that the future for ballet companies looked bleak after the Ballet Russe de Monte Carlo, based in New York, closed down in 1962 and the American Ballet Theatre, which had disbanded several times, appeared on the verge of distinction. Yet the Ballet Theatre was saved in 1965 by the then recently established National Endowment for the Arts.

And the New York City Ballet, which had struggled to win audiences with Balanchine's contemporary plotless ballets rather than a conventional repertory with stars and 19th-century classics, suddenly acquired Establishment status. The company moved to New York's newly built Lincoln Center in 1964 and Balanchine's pure-dance aesthetic, reaching a better-educated public after 30 years of effort, gained the recognition it deserved.

At the same time, ballet found wider acceptance through Rudolph Nureyev's charisma. After Nureyev and Fonteyn appeared regularly in America with Britain's Royal Ballet in the 1960s, they reached millions of viewers beyond the traditional ballet public.

Meanwhile, modern dance, always a form of individual expression, reinvented itself in the 1960s. Rejecting the psychological dance drama of earlier years, Merce Cunningham, Alwin Nikolais and Erick Hawkins promoted pure movement in their choreography. The avant-garde Judson Dance Theater, from 1962 to 1964, spawned the rebels who incorporated even non-dance movement in their works. Dance, in effect, was redefined. Like Twyla Tharp, who began choreographing in this period, several charter members of the Judson group — Trisha Brown, Lucinda Childs, Meredith Monk — are active today as leaders in experimental dance.

By the 1970s, American dance could embrace the trend toward abstraction or formalism epitomized by Cunningham and Balanchine; the renewed vigor of Martha Graham; the eclecticism of new companies such as Dance Theater of Harlem, Eliot Feld's troupe and Ballet Theater; and the social concerns of Alvin Ailey and the younger African-American choreographers who followed him.

In this context, the lesson of the 1960s is a cautionary tale for the 1990s. Giants like Graham and Balanchine who leave their stamp on the entire history of an art form are unlikely to emerge more than a few times in a century. But what seems like the end can, in fact, lead to a new beginning. Change is already in the air. New choreography was uneven this season, but it was diverse and did not have the homogenized look of recent years.

Young dancers with star appeal also burst upon the ballet stage. At the American Ballet Theatre, the virtuoso Julio Bocca and the teenage prodigy Paloma Herrera were joined by the exciting newcomers Angel Corella and Vladimir Malakhov. At the City Ballet, Darcey Bussell of the Royal Ballet drew packed houses in her third year of guest appearances amid a strong male contingent led by Ethan Stiefel, Damian Woetzel, Peter Boal and Nikolaj Hubbe.

Twelve years after Balanchine's death, however, ballet was still in search of a major new classical choreographer. The return of Jerome Robbins to the New York City Ballet in 1994 after six years away from dancemaking, highlighted the gap between creative genius and the serviceability that, with a few exceptions, marks the contemporary ballet premieres.

Robbins, widely known for his Broadway musicals, is also one of 20th-century ballet's greatest choreographers. Nonetheless, his reentry on the scene was as cautious as it was stunning. It was only after his new Bach ballet, *Two- and Three-Part Inventions*, enjoyed a huge success with City Ballet's School of American Ballet that Robbins staged it for the Company in 1995. In both instances, he knew how to translate Bach's counterpoint and canons into an ingenious blend of complexity and simplicity.

In the spring, Robbins gave the City Ballet a box-office smash with *West Side Story Suite*. Here, he excerpted six dance numbers from his 1957 musical and added a new solo, set to the song "Something's Coming." Rather than looking like a disconnected series of dances, the *Suite* worked marvelously as a distillation of the original show.

Peter Martins, the City Ballet's artistic director, continued to choreograph as the best of Balanchine's disciples with *Adams Violin Concerto*. The acclaimed score by the post-minimalist composer John Adams was commissioned by an unusual mix of organizations: the City Ballet as well as the London Symphony Orchestra and the Minnesota Orchestra. Martin's intricate partnering and speed were rendered by a brilliant cast: Darci Kistler, Wendy Whelan, Jack Soto, Nilas Martins and Nikolaj Hubbe.

Although Martins is sometimes criticized for choreographing with his brain rather than his heart, he has an encyclopedic knowledge of the classical idiom, and *Untitled*, his new duet for Peter Boal and Margaret Tracey, had a lyric edge. Other premieres for the Company were Richard Tanner's *Operetta Affezionata*, a confused mock pastorale, and Kevin O'Day's *Huoah*, a facile but refreshing mix of vernacular gestures and ballet technique.

American Ballet Theatre's new productions moved away from the Balanchine model of dance for dance's sake and hinted at dramatic subtexts. Movement always expresses emotion for James Kudelka. *Cruel World*, his hit for the company in 1994, offered a turbulent study of relationships. *States of Grace*, his latest work, was too preoccupied with experiments in partnering to make its theme clear. Nonetheless, Kudelka seemed concerned with an antiwar motif that may have been inspired by Hindemith's musings on a 16th-century peasant revolt in his *Mathis de Maler* symphony.

Ballet Theatre's other premieres were by leading modern-dance choreographers: Both Twyla Tharp and Lar Lubovitch have worked with ballet troupes and fuse ballet technique with their personal idioms.

Lubovitch, although more conventional, was more successful with *A Brahms Symphony* and the company's dancers captured its surge and passion. Tharp was less neat but more daring in her ambitious work to Benjamin Britten's music: *So Near Heaven* was burdened with an allegory about duality and an ideal whole but its choreography was full of rich detail. Tharp also created two minor ballets for the company, *Americans We* and *Jump Start*, set to a new score by Wynton Marsalis.

Feld Ballets/NY had four new works by Eliot Feld. *Gnossiennes*, *Ogive*, *Chi* and *Ludwig Gambits* continued the choreographer's fascination with either repetitive structures or imagery from Diaghilev's Ballets Russes. But Feld broke loose with a more happily inspired solo for Mikhail Baryshnikov, who appeared as a guest. *Tongue and Groove* captured the superstar's range of moods with its sassy collage of grimaces and fast footwork.

Elsewhere, Dance Theater of Harlem gave its dancers a good workout with two disparate pieces, Alonzo King's *Signs and Wonders* and Robert Garland's *Joplin Dances*. A major ballet event was the United We

Dance festival presented by the San Francisco Ballet in tribute to the 50th anniversary of the United Nations. The dancing from 13 countries was outstanding but most of the choreography was mediocre — with three exceptions. These included two premieres with a peace-making theme, *Meeting Point* by Christopher Bruce for Britain's Rambert Dance Company, and *Pacific* by Mark Morris for the San Francisco Ballet. Stanton Welch's *Corroboree* for the Australian Ballet also impressed with its mix of toe work and fervor.

The distinct voices in this ballet festival were presaged in modern dance, where no dominant aesthetic now holds sway.

Strict formalists descended from Merce Cunningham are still active. Trisha Brown continues to strip gesture of narrative connotation, as she showed again in the complex structures of *M.O.* Brown, who often uses silence, turned for the first time to Bach as a springboard. Baryshnikov, in contrast, essayed a long solo to silence when Dana Reitz, once regarded as a minimalist, created *Unspoken Territory* for him.

Increasingly, however, modern dance has reverted to emotional expression and social concerns, as seen in Susan Marshall's *Fields of View* and *Spectators at an Event*. Bill T. Jones's *Still/Here* was the most ambitious work of the genre and began when volunteers in 10 cities spoke to Jones about their life-threatening illnesses. In the finished work, however, no ill persons were on stage and the highly formal choreography was performed by the professional dancers of the Bill T. Jones/Arnie Zane Dance Company. Some of the interviews were used in lyrics for the original score, and the mixed-media piece used anonymous images of the volunteers. Rather than exploit public sympathy, *Still/Here* transformed its raw material into an abstract work of art with an emotional resonance. Audiences were highly receptive and *Still/Here* was scheduled to tour through 1996.

Paul Taylor and Merce Cunningham, the two reigning masters of modern dance, remained true to form. Cunningham's *Ground Level Overlay* was a visually striking example of his interest in movement for its own sake. Taylor's premieres were wide-ranging comments on music. *Moonbine,* set to Debussy, pitted two death figures against an energetic group. In his hilarious *Funny Papers,* Taylor enhanced the silliest of 1960s pop songs with witty, kinetic images.

Lar Lubovitch offered a grotesque take on Cole Porter in *So in Love.* Mark Morris, who also treats popular music with irony, revived his 1988 Handel work *L'Allegro il Penseroso ed il Moderato* before preparing a season schedule for the 1995 Next Wave Festival at the Brooklyn Academy of Music.

The 1994 Next Wave had opened with the Martha Graham Dance Company's spectacularly danced Radical Graham retrospective. Graham, who died in 1991, is increasingly revealed as a forerunner of many of today's choreographers. Two rare revivals included the witty 1932 solo *Satyric Festival Song* and abstract segments from *Chronicle,* a 1936 social protest piece.

Companies visiting from abroad favored a return to more overt expressionism, as seen in German Pina Bausch's *Two Cigarettes in the Dark,* Saburo Teshigawara's *Noiject* from Japan and Jiri Kylian's works for three companies known as the Netherlands Dance Theater. Unlike the high-energy pieces that won him acclaim in 1970s, Kylian's current choreography is gloomy and unduly restricted. Nonetheless, he offered an impressively haunting duet, *No Sleep Till Dawn of Day* for Netherlands Dance Theater 3, the troupe established for mature dancers over 40 years of age.

Visiting ballet troupes included France's Lyon Opera Ballet, which showed off its *Romeo and Juliet,* set by the choreographer in a totalitarian state. Angelin Preljocaj's unpredictable, imaginative ideas were also visible in his erotic version of *Le Spectre de la Rose* at the American Dance Festival in Durham, North Carolina. In New York and on tour, Russia's Kirov Ballet presented dramatically incoherent versions of *Swan Lake* and *Cinderella* by its director Oleg Vinogradov and more visually dazzling stagings of *The Firebird* and *Scheherazade.* While still boasting a strong female corps, the Kirov looked like a shadow of its former self.

Cinderella was ubiquitous in the repertoires of regional American ballet companies and was performed in various versions by the Houston Ballet, the Pennsylvania Ballet, the Cincinnati Ballet and Pacific Northwest Ballet in Seattle. A ballet landscape dotted with productions of *Cinderella* was hardly indicative of adventurous programming. Artistic directors were obviously choreographing with an eye to the box office.

Such pressures were bound to increase but a look at the 1995–1996 season does not yet impose any kind of pattern. At the Kennedy Center, Suzanne Farrell, formerly of the New York City Ballet, organized a one-week presentation of Balanchine ballets. The Center's new America Dancing series launched a five-year retrospective of modern dance beginning with revivals of works by Isadora Duncan. Robert Wilson, known for his theater of images, agreed to create a work for Martha Graham's troupe in connection with the series.

The eagerly awaited reconstruction of Bronislava Nijinska's 1928 *Bolero* for which Ravel wrote the famous score is on the Oakland Ballet's 1995–1996 production calendar. Ethnic dance, always popular, will be represented in 1995–1996 by tours of several troupes from Africa, the National Ballet of Spain, the Cuban National Folklore Ensemble and Bale Foclorico da Bahia, a vibrant Afro-Brazilian company.

Highlights of 1995–1996 will include the return of the Central Ballet of China from Beijing for the first time in nearly a decade and the Paris Opera Ballet's season in New York. The company's superb dancers will be seen in Nureyev's staging of *La Bayadere* and in *Le Parc*, a contemporary piece by Preljocaj.

A new summer festival at Lincoln Center in 1996 will include plans to produce *Ocean*, which Merce Cunningham staged in the round with 112 musicians in Brussels in 1994. Cunningham's fragmented, nonlinear choreography has taught audiences to look at dance in a revolutionary new way. Cunningham sees the same lack of continuity in both life and art. This discontinuity can also serve as a metaphor for the state of dance today: the certainties of the past are juxtaposed, but not connected with, new aesthetics still to be defined. ∎

Summer Music and Dance Festivals

ARKANSAS

Opera in the Ozarks at Inspiration Point
Inspiration Point Theater
Eureka Springs, AR
(501) 253-8595

Opera Theatre at Wildwood
Wildwood Park for the Performing Arts
Little Rock, AR
(501) 821-7281

CALIFORNIA

Cabrillo Music Festival
Santa Cruz, CA
(408) 429-3444

Carmel Bach Festival
Sunset Theater
Carmel, CA
(408) 624-2046

Festival Opera in Walnut Creek
Walnut Creek, CA
(510) 944-9610

Hollywood Bowl Summer Festival
Los Angeles, CA
(213) 850-2000

Lamplighters Music Theatre
Presentation Theater
San Francisco, CA
(415) 227-0331

Los Angeles Music Center Opera
Chandler Pavilion
Los Angeles, CA
(213) 972-7211

Music From Bear Valley
Bear Valley, CA
(209) 753-2574

Ojai Music Festival
Ojai, CA
(805) 646-2094

San Francisco Ethnic Dance Festival
Palace of Fine Arts
San Francisco, CA
(415) 474-3914

CONTINUED ON PAGE 611 ▶

1994—1995 Major Dance Events

**Paloma Herrera,
American Ballet Theatre**

THE ALVIN AILEY AMERICAN DANCE THEATER

Program included the premieres of *Mnemonic Verse* and *Scissors Paper Stone*
Choreographers: Elisa Monte and Brenda Way; **Music:** Jon Hassell's "Pano da Costa," John "Mighty Mouth" Moschitta, John Lee Hooker, Loudon Wainwright III and Jimi Hendrix; **Costumes:** Barbara Forbes and Eleanor Coppola; **Set Design:** Offer Zaks and Maria Barrios; **Lighting:** Mark Mongold and Alex Nichols
Opening: 12/94 at New York City's City Center
As always, The Alvin Ailey American Dance Theater delivered. While the dances themselves were uneven, the dancers were not. The troupe commanded the stage with its powerful grace and spiritual exuberance. The program featured an exciting revival of choreographer John Butler's 1959 ballet to *Carmina Burana*, the reworking of medieval monks' secular pleasures, and notable premieres. *Mnemonic Verses* harkened back to a utopian gynecocentric time, chronicling how sensuality and freedom come to ruin with the invasion of men. In *Scissors Paper Stone*, choreographer Brenda Way offered an animated romp about breaking up and making up. Speedy and witty, the piece had a cartoon quality that delights the senses, although its larger meaning failed to establish itself.

AMERICAN BALLET THEATRE

First program included *Les Sylphides*; **Soloists:** Wes Chapman, Cynthia Harvey, Paloma Herrera and Marianna Tcherkassky; **Music:** Chopin's *Les Sylphides*

Costumes: Lucinda Ballard; **Lighting:** Jean Rosenthal and Nananne Porcher
Opening: 5/95 at New York City's Metropolitan Opera House
Second program included premiere of *How Near Heaven*
Soloists: Charles Askegard, Gil Boggs, Guillaume Graffin, Cynthia Harvey, Paloma Herrera and Kathleen Moore
Choreographer: Twyla Tharp; **Music:** Benjamin Britten's *Variations on a Theme of Frank Bridge;*
Costumes: Gianni Versace; **Lighting:** Jennifer Tipton
Opening: 3/95 at New York City's Kennedy Center Opera House
In one glorious day at the Met, American Ballet Theatre's prodigious Paloma Herrera, who in 1995 at age 19 was promoted to principal dancer, delivered a gifted performance of the waltz solo in *Les Sylphides* and a powerful New York debut of Twyla Tharp's bold *How Near Heaven.* Her superb skills were showcased in Tharp's powerful fusion of classical ballet and modern dance, as well as waltz, disco and voguing into a work that addressed eternal grace and repose. Tharp's piece ultimately raised many questions about the nature of heaven, the kind of dancing that would happen there (old or new? peaceful or hopeful?) and whether Gianni Versace's dresses allowed the dancers full mobility.

TRISHA BROWN COMPANY

Program included the American premiere of *M.O.*
Music: Bach's *The Musical Offering*, directed by Kenneth Weiss; **Costumes:** Irié; **Lighting:** Jennifer Tipton
Opening: 7/95 at New York City's Lincoln Center during the Serious Fun! Festival
In May 1995, the modern-dance pioneer Trisha Brown, a 1991 MacArthur Foundation Fellowship "genius" grant recipient, premiered her hourlong work, the magisterial *M.O.*, to great acclaim in Brussels. Over the past decade, Brown has been uniformly praised overseas, where dance approaches are more in keeping with her own avant-garde sensibility. Ironically, continental critics appreciate what they see as her typically American approach. *M.O.* was set to Bach's *The Musical Offering*, which was interesting in and of itself, due to Brown's long-standing vow of silence. Before 1981, she refused to choreograph to music, and when she finally decided to use music, she only used modern music. In the United States, Brown premiered *M.O.* at the Serious Fun! Festival at Lincoln Center and performed it again at Jacob's Pillow Dance Festival in western Massachusetts. Audiences reacted enthusiastically to her contrapuntal setting of geometric

movements to the complexities of Bach's rich score. With increasing domestic acclaim and the reworking of her solo, "If You Couldn't See Me," into a high-profile duet, "You Can See Us," for herself and powerhouse choreographer Bill T. Jones, Brown may soon be able to count the hometown audience among her biggest fans.

JANE COMFORT AND COMPANY

Program included the premiere of *S/He*
Music: Mio Morales; **Costumes:** Liz Prince; **Lighting:** David Ferri
Opening: 1/95 at New York City's The Joyce Theater during The Altogether Different Festival
Accompanied by taped excerpts from the Anita Hill/Clarence Thomas senate hearings, choreographer Jane Comfort put sexual and racial relations on the stand in her new work, *S/He*. She wittily reversed the situation by casting a white male as Hill, a white female as Thomas and black female senators. Comfort's dance-theater oozes a hip, street-smart, downtown attitude — an altogether cool approach appreciated by audiences at the Altogether Different Festival.

MERCE CUNNINGHAM DANCE COMPANY

Ground Level Overlay
Music: Stuart Dempster; **Set:** Leonardo Drew; **Costumes:** Suzanne Gallo; **Lighting:** Aaron Copp
Opening: 3/95 at New York City's City Center
Who else but Merce Cunningham would blaze the terpsichorean trail through computer land? Cunningham has made a career of going where no choreographer has gone before, much of the time joined by his late collaborator, John Cage, who shared his fascination with non-Western approaches to composition. The 75-year-old master's latest offering was a revolutionary, deeply imaginative work created with the help of

a new software program, LifeForms. The result was a fast-moving, energetic piece about gravity, reflected in the coming-togethers and pulling-aparts of the dancers. With elegance and energy, the dancers broke into and out of couples, at times in exuberance, at times in despair. For its remarkable score, after which the piece is titled, composer Stuart Dempster recorded a symphony of trombones in an underwater tank.

GARTH FAGAN DANCE

Postcards, Pressures and Possibilities
Music: David N. Baker; **Costumes:** Garth Fagan and Zinda Williams; **Lighting:** C. T. Oakes
Opening: 11/94 at New York City's The Joyce Theater
The always unpredictable Garth Fagan and his company tackled an ambitious subject in this intriguing look at arrivals and departures. In a series of sketches, each taking its title from a postcard-like greeting, Fagan created a powerful montage of emotions abroad. Sometimes, as in the first scene, when dancer Chris Morrison moved his long legs alternately in a tick-tock-like angular motion, the piece detailed the fears and anxieties of leaving home. At other moments, as when dancer Sharon Skepple, portraying a tourist, sashayed her hips to the steel-drums of her Caribbean sun-and-fun vacation, the work celebrated the joys of getting away from it all.

FELD BALLETS/NY

Program included *Gnossiennes, Ogive* and *Aurora II*
Music: Erik Satie's "Ludwig Gambits," Beethoven's *Fourth Symphony,* and Steve Reich; **Performed by:** Howard Klein; Peter Longiaru, pianist; **Costumes:** Martin Pakledinaz; **Set Design:** Mark Mongold and Eliot Feld
Opening: 3/95 at New York City's The Joyce Theater
Featuring guest artists Mikhail Baryshnikov, Gregory Hines and 100 children from New York's New Ballet School, the Feld Ballets's opening night was one of the spectacles of the spring season. Company choreographer Eliot Feld premiered four works, including the standouts *Ogive,* set to Satie's atmospheric music, and Reich's *Aurora II,* and resurrected six revivals. *Ogive*'s title refers to a diagonal rib in a Gothic vault. Throughout the piece, five dancers moved in gymnastic and architectonic configurations; in one scene, four women lifted dancer Darren Gibson to the sky, serving as the underpinning structure for his on-high position. The work lyrically demonstrated an analogy: bodies in space are to dance as structure in space is to architecture. The impressive *Aurora II* was a spirited ode to movement that took place on an inclined stage. The dancers, who wore running shoes, raced up and slid down a hilly slope with riveting, kinetic results.

Lois Greenfield/Courtesy Feld Ballets/NY

Feld Ballets/NY

Martha Graham

MARTHA GRAHAM DANCE COMPANY

Music: The Brooklyn Philharmonic, conducted by Stanley Sussman
Opening: 10/94 at New York's Brooklyn Academy of Music Opera House

For many, it all began with Martha Graham. With one foot in the future and the other in the ritualistic roots of our ancestors, the pioneer devoured the stage and stunned audiences with her mythic, vibrant, emotional approach to movement. She remained an iconoclast until her death in 1991, but her troupe endures, and in a brilliant stroke of marketing, presented the revival program *Radical Graham*. The show provided younger audiences the opportunity to see for the first time the choreographer's once-radical work — still riveting and relevant.

ERICK HAWKINS DANCE COMPANY

Program included *Cantilever Two*, *Early Floating* and *Heyoka*
Music: Lucia Dlugoszewski and Ross Lee Finney, performed by: The Hawkins Theater Orchestra, conducted by David Briskin; **Sculpture:** Ralph Dorazio
Opening: 2/95 at New York City's The Joyce Theater

When veteran dancer/choreographer Erick Hawkins died suddenly in November 1994 at age 85, modern dance lost one of its pioneers and one of the first male dancers in the field. An original member of Martha Graham's company, he went on to establish his own company to great acclaim. Hawkins's fluidity and spiritually uplifting purity of movement was celebrated by his 13-member company. His works were accompanied, as always, by the at-times frenzied, at-times meditative music of his wife, Lucia Dlugoszewski. Although the couple were longtime collaborators, their actual relationship was only revealed after Hawkins's death. The two kept their three-decade marriage a secret for "professional reasons," Dlugoszewski revealed.

HUBBARD STREET DANCE CHICAGO

Program included the New York premiere of *Heroes*
Choreographer: James Kudelka; **Music:** John Adams's *The Chairman Dances;* **Costumes:** Santo Loquasto; **Lighting:** David A. Finn
Opening: 10/94 at New York City's The Joyce Theater

Great fanfare greeted this Windy City dance company's Manhattan debut, as much for its dazzling, surefire dancers as for its four rarely seen Twyla Tharp works. The group's trademark, razor-sharp technique and open staging were in full evidence in the New York premiere of *Heroes*, by James Kudelka, who seems to be everyone's favorite up-and-coming choreographer. The Tharp dances offered audiences a special treat since they had never been performed by a company other than Tharp's. In *Sue's Leg*, diminutive dancer Sandi J. Cooksey astounded with her revealing interpretation of the role Tharp designed for herself, while remaining true to the piece's original intentions. Hubbard Street Dance Chicago did equally well with the lyrical and witty *Baker's Dozen*, as well as captured the emotion and the glitz of *Nine Sinatra Songs* and delivered on the high-energy, over-the-top *The Golden Section*.

JAZZDANCE BY DANNY BURACZESKI

Program included the premieres of *Swing Concerto*, *On My Way* and *Fuerza Viva*
Music: Brave Old World, Artie Shaw, Benny Goodman, Mahalia Jackson, Celia Cruz and *The Mambo Kings* soundtrack; **Sets:** Susan Weil;
Lighting: Barry Browning
Opening: 2/95 at New York City's The Joyce Theater

These surprisingly austere, abstract works served as both an ode to the swing dance days and as proof that theatrical dance forms have a place in modern dance. Minneapolis-based choreographer Buraczeski exuberantly rallied his dancers toward an infectious vision of big band, spiritual and Latin rhythms, without cliché or disrespect to the tradition. Many companies are loathe to use the "j" word, but Buraczeski ably showed that jazz dance is still compelling and, well, fun.

BILL T. JONES AND ARNIE ZANE DANCE COMPANY

Still/Here
Music: *Still:* Odetta performed original music by Kenneth Frazell; *Here:* original music by Vernon Reid;
Visual Concept and Media Environment: Gretchen Bender; **Costumes:** Liz Prince; **Lighting:** Robert Wierzel
Opening: 10/94 at Iowa City's Hancher Auditorium

The dance brouhaha of the year. In November, Bill T. Jones put dance in the news when his company performed *Still/Here* at the Brooklyn Academy of Music. Everyone in New York went, except *The New Yorker* critic Arlene Croce, who panned it sight unseen, condemning it as as "victim art." Dance critics had their 15 minutes of media attention, and the house sold out as audiences flocked to the production. Jones, who is HIV-positive, choreographed the piece in "survival workshops" with the input of terminally ill participants. The spiritual, energetic *Still/Here* is both a meditation on death and a celebration of the living. Company members interacted with Gretchen Bender's video installations of the survival workshops. Upon viewing, the piece seemed strongest in smaller, moment-by-moment miracles of movement rather than as the definitive epic it attempted to be. What emerged clearly at the end of the night is that Bill T. Jones has a lot more to say.

This has been a busy year for Jones. He collaborated with author Toni Morrison and jazz great Max Roach for Lincoln Center's Serious Fun! Festival, where he also performed a duet with Trisha Brown. Pantheon published his autobiography, *Last Night on Earth*, and Bill Moyers hosted a special on the making of *Still/Here*, which might stir the controversy all over again.

PAULA JOSA-JONES/
PERFORMANCE WORKS
Wonderland
Music: Dierdre Broderick, Vangelis/Skellern and John Zorn; **Costumes:** Christine Joly de Lotbinniere; **Lighting:** Blu; **Set Design:** Mark Nayden
Opening: 7/95 at Becket, Massachusetts's Ted Shawn Theatre, Jacob's Pillow
Boston-based Paula Josa-Jones took audiences back to the future when she melded the two worlds of *Alice in Wonderland* and *Blade Runner* in her new, full-length work. East met West and dance met theater as Josa-Jones's company sought to fuse "expressionistic dynamism with the powerful and mysterious physical transformations of contemporary Asian dance." *Wonderland* offered an imaginative window into the topsy-turvy travels and travails of Alice, the

Pam White/Courtesy Paula Josa-Jones/Performance Works

Paula Josa-Jones/Performance Works, *Wonderland*

MUSIC AND DANCE FESTIVALS
CONTINUED FROM PAGE 607

The Art Commission/San Francisco Symphony Summer Pops Series
San Francisco, CA
(415) 431-5400

Summer Nights at the Ford
Ford Amphitheatre
Los Angeles, CA
(213) 466-1767

COLORADO

Aspen Music Festival
Aspen Festival Tent
Aspen, CO
(303) 925-5482
(303) 925-9042

Breckenridge Music Festival
Riverwalk Center
Breckenridge, CO
(303) 453-2120

Central City Opera Summer Series
Central City Opera House
Central City, CO
(303) 292-6700

Colorado Dance Festival
Boulder, CO
(303) 442-7666

Colorado Music Festival
Boulder, CO
(303) 449-1397

Colorado Opera Festival
Pikes Peak Center
Colorado Springs, CO
(719) 520-7469

CONNECTICUT

Connecticut Early Music Festival
Harkness Chapel
Connecticut College
New London, CT
(203) 444-2419

Norfolk Chamber Music Festival
Norfolk, CT
(203) 542-3000

Opera Theater of Connecticut Summer Production
Andrews Memorial Theatre
Clinton, CT
(203) 669-8999

CONTINUED ON PAGE 613

Red Queen, the Mad Hatter and the gang. Set in an apocalyptic, futuristic world, the dancers strove for survival in a world that doesn't indulge fear of change or innocence. Madness was the norm and the characters discovered, through their relationships with themselves and each other, how to create sanity. In certain sections, the overflow of ideas tended to weigh the piece down, but the audience gave Jones and company a standing ovation for the sheer ingenuity of what they had just seen.

LIZ LERMAN DANCE EXCHANGE

Program included *Flying Into the Middle*
Music: Tchaikovsky's *Piano Trio, op. 50;* **Costumes:** Teri Hume Prell; **Lighting:** David Rosenburg
Opening: 1/95 at New York City's The Joyce Theater during The Altogether Different Festival

Everyone can dance, argues choreographer Liz Lerman, who doesn't buy into the notion that dancers must be young, thin or built like Greek gods. The nine members of her company typically spanned the generations, races and body types. In *Flying Into the Middle*, Lerman, 47, offered a whimsical look at middle age. In her warmhearted piece, young and old dancers cavorted, jumped and fell as they moved together across the stage and through their lives. Middle age is no midlife crisis, Lerman suggested, but simply another stage in the march of time.

LAR LUBOVITCH DANCE COMPANY

Program included the premiere of *So in Love*
Music: Cole Porter: "It's All Right With Me," performed by Tom Waits; "From This Moment On," performed by Jimmy Somerville; "In the Still of the Night," performed by the Neville Brothers; "Ev'ry Time We Say Goodbye," performed by Annie Lennox; and "So in Love," performed by k.d. lang; **Lighting:** Clifton Taylor
Opening: 11/94 at New York City's The Joyce Theater

The nihilistic '90s met the gay '20s when choreographer Lar Lubovitch brought pop culture to *So in Love*, his revisionist take on five Cole Porter tunes. The dark intonations of singers such as Tom Waits and k.d. lang and the jerky, hip moves of street dancing both enriched and undercut Porter's sophisticated melodies. From minimalism to ragtime to balletic pas de deux, Lubovitch's company, celebrating its 25th anniversary season, delivered a joyous, kick-up-your heels performance.

SUSAN MARSHALL & COMPANY

Spectators at an Event
Music: Henryk Górecki; **Costumes:** Kasia Walicka-Maimone; **Projected Images:** Christopher Kondek; **Lighting:** Mark Stanley
Opening: 11/94 at New York's Brooklyn Academy of Music Majestic Theater

Who's watching whom? Susan Marshall's premiere at BAM, *Spectators at an Event*, raised compelling questions about seeing, being seen and the fine line where the two meet. Marshall's choreography was typically athletic and intense, reflecting contemporary storylines and concerns, and this proved no exception. At one moment, a dancer looked out at the audience, and at another, fell to the ground, trapped by the unrelenting spotlight's glare. The dancers' steps were simple but elegant, as they prodded and poked audiences into considering the many levels of meaning associated with being a spectator. Hovering over the dancers were projected stills by Weegee, the photographer who often turned his camera on bystanders.

ELISA MONTE DANCE COMPANY

Program included the premieres of *New York Moonglow* and *Labess*
Music: Barbara Kolb and Zap Mama; **Musicians:** Lew Tabackin, Erik Charleston, Alan Dean, Lois Martin, Lanny Paykin and Al Regni; **Costumes:** David Brown, Barbara Forbes and Elisa Monte; **Lighting:** Mark Mongold
Opening: 4/95 at New York City's The Joyce Theater

Former Martha Graham principal Elisa Monte delivered an impressive two-week run that included a new work, *New York Moonglow*. The piece, in which seven of her dancers weave in and out of twos and threes, culminated, according to the *New York Times* critic Jennifer Dunning, in "a sort of pointillism in which each dancer [was] an atom bursting with controlled energy." The evening included several of her oldies but goodies, including the acrobatic duet *Vejle/Border Crossing*. The dancers shone individually in a program that delivered bright, gutsy and just-plain-fun performances.

MARK MORRIS DANCE GROUP

Program included the premiere of *Somebody's Coming to See Me Tonight*
Music: Stephen Foster; **Costumes:** Susan Ruddie; **Lighting:** Michael Chybowski
Opening: 5/95 at Boston's Emerson Majestic Theater, commissioned and produced by Dance Umbrella

Mark Morris is arguably *the* dancemaker of our time, the destroyer of what came before and the Prometheus who delivers the new. In his hands, dance has been transformed into a new language that speaks to both aficionados and mainstream audiences. As his company moves through the steps, they remain ever elegant, ever irreverent in the seemingly impossible combination that makes Morris's work so delicious. Audiences love Morris because he's part James Dean, part art snob.

In 1995, Morris was hard at work making dances for such prestigious companies as the

Tom Brazil/Courtesy of Mark Morris Dance Group

Mark Morris Dance Group

White Oak Dance Project and the San Francisco Ballet. In fact, commissions kept Morris so busy that his sole company premiere was the plucky *Somebody's Coming to See Me Tonight.* The lovely strains of Stephen Foster's songs evoked an America long gone, but Morris is never one to sink to sappiness. His dancers may have worn 19th-century-inspired long gowns and ruffles, but the themes of the piece were timeless. Humor and innocence abounded as the company danced and romanced its way through such classics as "Beautiful Dreamer." Morris seems to be just as happy choreographing to campy country two-step, baroque oratorio or terrifying silence. He listens to the music and follows its directives; from the sound comes the motion and the results are ravishing.

NEW YORK CITY BALLET
West Side Story Suite
Choreographer: Jerome Robbins; **Music:** Leonard Bernstein; **Conductor:** Paul Gemignani; **Lyrics:** Stephen Sondheim; **Set Design:** Oliver Smith; **Costumes:** Irene Sharaff; **Lighting:** Jennifer Tipton
Opening: 5/95 at the New York State Theater, Lincoln Center during the 1995 Spring Gala
Ever since George Balanchine died in 1983, N.Y.C.B. ballet master-in-chief Peter Martins has faced the challenge of providing the vision and leadership to guide the N.Y.C.B. into the 21st century — a daunting task considering ballet's masterpieces are aging and the dance world still has not anointed the next Balanchine. Martins has solved his dilemma by demanding a new level of performance from his dancers, complementing the company's trademark energy with a newfound visual clarity and by commissioning new works. The result is a brilliant troupe that performs pieces that are hit or miss. One sure-

◀ MUSIC AND DANCE FESTIVALS
CONTINUED FROM PAGE 611

DISTRICT OF COLUMBIA

DanceAfrica, D.C. Festival
Washington D.C.
(202) 269-1600

Summer Opera Theatre Co.
Hartke Theatre
Catholic University
Washington D.C.
(202) 526-1669

GEORGIA

Atlanta Opera
Fox Theatre
Atlanta, GA
(404) 355-3311

ILLINOIS

Chicago Opera Theater Spring Fest
Athenaeum Theatre
Chicago, IL
(312) 292-7578

Grant Park Music Festival
Petrillo Band Shell
Grant Park
Chicago, IL
(312) 294-2420, (312) 819-0614
(800) 588-4443

Ravinia Festival
Pavilion, IL
(312) 728-4642

IOWA

Des Moines Metro Opera Summer Festival
Blank Performing Arts Center
Indianola, IA
(515) 961-6221

Dorian Opera Theatre
Center for Faith and Life
Luther College
Decorah, IA
(319) 387-1036

35th Annual National Choreography Conference
Iowa City, IA
(713) 496-4670

MAINE

Bowdoin Summer Music Festival
Brunswick, ME
(207) 725-3322

CONTINUED ON PAGE 619 ▶

fire hit was the virtuoso premiere of Jerome Robbins' *West Side Story Suite*. Based on the Tony Award-winning show, the evening was no slick, greatest-hits repackaging effort. Rather, Robbins found the numbers' essence and reinterpreted them for N.Y.C.B. The high-energy music-theater spectacle was a masterpiece, and Robbins is to be congratulated for his guts and vision.

PILOBOLUS DANCE THEATER

Programs included the premieres of *Masters of Ceremony* and *The Doubling Cube*
Choreographers: Robby Barnett, Alison Chase, Michael Tracy and Jonathan Wolken; **Music:** Paul Sullivan and Jane Ira Bloom; **Lighting:** Neil Peter Jampolis and Jane Reisman
Opening: 7/95 at New York City's The Joyce Theater
For a quarter century, Pilobolus has been astonishing audiences with its collectively created, body-and-mind bending movements. The troupe's themes are cosmic and childlike, its gyrations gymnastic and kinetic. The universal nature and loftiness of the dances' subjects (for example, *Shizen* examined the creation of human life), however, does not preclude humor from taking its usual centerstage spot on the Pilobolus program. The successful 1995 season at the The Joyce showcased the Pils's strengths. *Master of Ceremonies* opened to a scene of a sleeping figure in a chair, holding a rope that was tied to the ankle of a man groveling on the floor. These two could only be Pozzo and Lucky, the master and slave in *Waiting for Godot*. Throughout the piece, the tensions of their relationship were played out with jokey asides and kinetic precision until the oppressor and the oppressed achieved a common understanding at the end. The style of *The Doubling Cube* was more in keeping with the group's collectively created themes and approaches. Emphasizing the group's acrobatic physicality, the premiere addressed issues of

Pilobolus

gravity, time and space as six dancers were pulled together and apart by a sprawling, powerful force. For 25 years, Pilobolus has been the troupe that wasn't afraid to ask childish questions and share their answers. Their fans love them for it.

SAN FRANCISCO BALLET

The Dance House
Choreographer: David Bintley; **Set and Costume Design:** Robert Heindel; **Lighting:** Lisa J. Pinkham; **Music:** Dimitri Shostakovich's *Piano Concerto No. 1, Op. 35*
Opening: 2/95 San Francisco's War Memorial Opera House
Terra Firma
Choreographer: James Kudelka; **Music:** Michael Torke's "Ash," "Purple" and "Bright Blue Music;" **Costumes:** Denis Lavoie and Carmen Alie; **Lighting:** David A. Finn
Opening: 2/95 at San Francisco's War Memorial Opera House
David Bintley's full-length abstract ballet *The Dance House* was a funereal lament for a friend who died of AIDS. At its conclusion, a haunting Death figure stalked 19 dancers marked by red gash-like bands from throat to groin. They fell to the floor and Death leaped over the barre at the center of the stage in a manic frenzy. Bintley, director of England's Birmingham Royal Ballet, offered audiences a glimpse of hope for those seeking solace in the age of AIDS. In *Terra Firma*, the San Francisco Ballet unveiled the rapidly rising Canadian choreographer James Kudelka's new abstract-expressive ballet, which was firmly rooted in the classics, yet arched forward to offer a vision of the present. The work married transcendently simple and idiosyncratic gestures to Michael Torke's compositions, which translated impressions of color to music.

ANNA SOKOLOW 85TH BIRTHDAY CELEBRATION

Opening: 2/95 at New York City's Sylvia and Danny Kaye Playhouse
Luminaries from the dance and theater worlds turned out for the celebration of legendary choreographer Anna Sokolow. A dance pioneer who worked with Martha Graham in the 1920s, she later trained many of today's top dancers and actors and many of them attended to thank her. The emotional retrospective featured film clips and performances by her company, the Players Project, as well as tributes by Jerome Robbins, Paul Taylor and Uta Hagen. The works performed ranged from the modern *Rooms*, a piece that began much like Mark Morris's *The Office*, with dancers sitting in separate, lonely, waiting-room-like chairs, to *Tiger Rag*, a jazzy ode to flappers, to the elegant and spare *Scenes From the Music of Charles Ives*.

TANZTHEATER WUPPERTAL
Two Cigarettes in the Dark
Choreographer: Pina Bausch in collaboration with
Matthias Bruckert; **Music:** Brahms, Beethoven,
Bach, Alberta Hunter, Monteverdi, Purcell, Ben
Webster, Wolf and medieval music; **Set:** Peter Pabst;
Costumes: Marion Cito
Opening: 11/94 at New York's Brooklyn Academy of
Music Opera House

German choreographer Pina Bausch creates difficult avant-garde works with haunting theatrical
elements. Her appearance at BAM promised to
present her most accessible and "funniest" work.
It wasn't, but that's beside the point; "funny" isn't
why we like Bausch, anyway. We liked *Two
Cigarettes* because of the way her harsh yet soothing images resonated with memories we didn't
know we had. In *Two Cigarettes*, five men and six
women came and went within the vast expanse of
a stark, white stage, which was flanked by three
walls. Each wall was dominated by a picture window filled with the materials of an ecosystem:
water and live fish, a cacti-filled sand box and a
lush jungle landscape. At times jokey, at times
bleak, the evening's dramatic highlights included
a stuffed cow and vampish dancing down the
aisle, as well as grieving lunges at the walls.

PAUL TAYLOR DANCE COMPANY
Funny Papers
Music: Novelty tunes; **Costumes:** Santo Loquasto;
Lighting: Jennifer Tipton
Opening: 10/94 at New York City's City Center

Life is just beginning at 40 for the Paul Taylor
Dance Company, which continues to be one of the
most imaginative, fun-loving troupes in the field. A
former soloist with Martha Graham, Taylor is one
of a handful of modern dance masters who has
successfully translated his vision to mainstream
audiences. In *Funny Papers*, Taylor lampoons and
celebrates pop culture. Set to such happy-go-lucky
looney tunes as "Does Your Chewing Gum Lose Its
Flavor (on the Bedpost Overnight)" and "I Like
Bananas Because They Have No Bones," the piece
was a mix of one part athleticism, one part wacki-
ness and one part gravity (offering a dead-serious
celebration of the rich and complex role humor
plays in America). In the program notes, Taylor
dedicated the work to "all those who, before reading the front-page news, turn to the funnies first."

TWYLA THARP
Twyla Tharp Red White & Blues
Music: Bela Bartok, Drummers of Burundi, The Five
Satins, Gluck, Ellington, Marsalis and Ken Burns's
The Civil Wars Original Soundtrack
Opening: 1/95 at New York's Brooklyn Academy of
Music Opera House

The patriotic title of this American iconoclast's
latest seemed to be the suggestive rather than
definitive aspect of her work in progress. Audiences were treated to a glimpse of her rich, intelligent approach minus lighting and costumes,
but the effect was powerful and dramatic.

Between choreographing work for such prominent companies as the American Ballet Theatre
and high-profile festivals, Tharp remains one of
our most prominent choreographers.

WHITE OAK DANCE PROJECT
Program included the premieres of *Three Russian
Preludes, Unspoken Territory* and *Make Like a Tree*
Choreographers: Mark Morris, Dana Reitz and Kraig
Patterson; **Music:** Dimitri Shostakovich and Alberto
Ginastera; **Costumes:** Isaac Mizrahi, Santo Loquasto
and Pietro Luigi Roncalli; **Lighting:** Michael
Tchybowski, Jennifer Tipton and David Finn
Opening: 6/95 Becket, Massachusetts's Ted Shawn
Theatre, Jacob's Pillow

They came to see the legendary Mikhail Baryshnikov, but they stayed for the ensemble's riveting
new-works program and top-flight dancing. This
year, White Oak kicked off the Jacobs Pillow's summer season with a glamorous opening-night gala —
a sign of the company's undisputed position at the
top. Six years ago, in a red-letter day for the dance
world, classical and modern were joined thanks to
a partnership between the world-famous master,
Baryshnikov, and the genius iconoclast, Mark
Morris. The result was the White Oak project,
which promised to handpick the country's best
modern dancers and choreographers. Individuality
— of the performers' styles and the works themselves — is the group's strength. This year, White
Oak presented three premieres, including Mark
Morris's elegant *Three Russian Preludes*. Created as
a solo for a Russian using music by a Russian, the
piece matched the talents of Baryshnikov and
Shostakovich in a coup that showcased the choreographer's roundly hailed skills at combining the
most disparate of dance forms into a work that is
both lyrical and playful. The company remains eloquent even when silent, as White Oak ably demonstrated in Dana Reitz's musicless *Unspoken Territory*.
As it continues to commission works from the
world's top choreographers — from veterans such
as Jerome Robbins to newcomers such as Kevin
O'Day — White Oak will be a continuing source of
vision and excellence.

Courtesy White Oak Dance Project

White Oak Dance Project

Vox Populi

Lawrence
O'Toole is a
freelance
writer for
publications
including the
*New York
Times* and
*Entertainment
Weekly.*

■ BY LAWRENCE O'TOOLE

NO PRODUCTION OR PERFORMANCE DOMINATED discussion of opera in 1995 as did a technical application: surtitles finally arrived at The Metropolitan Opera. Surtitles — projected translation of a libretto's text above the stage action — have been in use for over a decade and up until this year every other major opera company in the country employed them to attract a larger and more diversified audience into the opera house, traditionally the province of the monied, privileged and socially connected.

The Met has been the last hold-out on becoming "opera-friendly." Music director James Levine vowed that surtitles would arrive there over his dead body. It proved an empty promise. (The actual surtitles at The Met are, however, different: they are "televised" to monitors on the backs of individual seats. How successful this new technique will be literally remains to be seen.)

The Met, dragged kicking and screaming into the present, has had to give way to the changing tide in opera and the need, in this art form, to make itself more accessible to the general public which, as the monster concerts of the Three Tenors prove, is clamoring for the stuff. Even those who don't know a mezzo from a matzoh are familiar with the names of Pavarotti, Domingo and Carreras.

OPERA

As well as seducing the masses, opera has become more democratic in both its substance and style. One of 1995's operatic highlights was Stewart Wallace's *Harvey Milk,* originating at the Houston Grand Opera and later produced at the New York City Opera. The

story of the first openly gay San Francisco elected politician, whose assassination caused riots in that city would, a couple of decades ago, have been unheard of as a subject for an opera. Not only has society relaxed towards gay subject matter, but opera has cast its net wider than ever before for subjects to pursue.

This was also the year that The Metropolitan Opera brought back its "new" hit from a couple of years back, John Corgliano's *The Ghosts of Versailles,* which was also performed in 1995 by the Chicago Lyric Opera. (Normally, new works at major opera houses don't have an afterlife,

Carol Rosegg/Courtesy of New York City Opera

Harvey Milk

The Ghosts of Versailles

but that is clearly changing.) Dario Argento's *The Dream of Valentino,* which took the life and death of the silent film star for its focus, was given an encore performance in Dallas after premiering in Washington. And the San Francisco Opera premiered Conrad Susa's *The Dangerous Liaisons,* made popular both on Broadway and in film.

"That opera holds any place at all when people can get 68 different channels is extraordinary," says mezzo-soprano Frederica von Stade, who sang Madame de Merteuil in *The Dangerous Liaisons*. Indeed, more and more people are going to the opera. The latest figures available from Opera America (for the 1992–1993 season) show that opera attendance in this country is up to slightly more than six million, box-office receipts were up to almost $190,000,000 and the number of opera companies posting deficits declined.

The 1994–1995 season had more than its share of *Carmens, Aïdas* and *La Bohemes*. Consumptive courtesans, pious virgins, vengeful courtiers and their ilk still populate both big and small opera houses around the country. Now a new audience is discovering those old chestnuts for the first time. Because of opera's scope and sweep — its ability to deal dramatically, musically and visually with large subjects all at once — it has attracted an increasing number of artists from other disciplines, whether poets (Alice Goodman, *Nixon in China,* William Hoffmann, *The Ghosts of Versailles*), stage and film directors (Peter Sellars, Frank Galati, Herbert Ross, Nicholas Hytner and Robert Altman) and costume designers (Bob Mackie, Gianni Versace and Willa Kim). The glamor that was once found in the movies, but has been somewhat reduced by the video revolution, and in the legitimate theater, dissipated by the slow demise of Broadway, has now found its way into opera.

Perhaps a little history is in order:

It all began, more or less, in 1975 when Robert Wilson and Philip Glass brought their *Einstein on the Beach* to The Metropolitan Opera. Not only did *Einstein* change the face of the form, it also changed its audience. The postmodern fusion of visual, choreographic and

Pelléas et Mélisande

musical design brought out the hip, bohemian dressed-all-in-black rather than black-tie audience. Curious about the stir *Einstein* created, opera companies presented other works by Glass such as *Satyagraha* and *Akhnaten,* which proved to be big hits. Glass's minimalist work, which heralded the New Age movement in popular music, has proved durable, and he has become a regular at the opera, most recently his take on Jean Cocteau's *La Belle et la Bête* at the Brooklyn Academy of Music.

The next operatic event of seismic proportion was John Adams's unlikely operatic subject, *Nixon in China,* directed by Harvard theater *wunderkind* Peter Sellars who gave it the same immediacy and directness as the nightly news. Later the two collaborated in *The Death of Klinghoffer,* an opera (once again unlikely) about the hijacking of the Italian cruise ship *Achille Lauro.* For his own part, Sellars went further by creating eccentric and anarchic redressings of Mozart's Holy Trinity — *Cosi Fan Tutte, The Marriage of Figaro* and *Don Giovanni* — by setting them in a diner, at Trump Tower and on the mean streets of Manhattan. And Sellars was at it again in 1995 with his post-modern Los Angeles version of Debussy's *Pelleas and Melisande,* usually found in a kind of dark fairy-tale setting — a castle in a forest.

By creating a new public consciousness for opera in which anything is possible, Glass, Wilson, Adams and Sellars opened the field to practically everything and everyone. The rush began and has not abated much. Among those who have composed or are currently composing operas are popular artists such as Stewart Copeland (of the Police), Carly Simon and Bobby McFerrin (whose *Gethsemane* is in preparation for San Francisco).

Visual artists, too, have joined the fray. The most prominent, perhaps, is David Hockney whose designs for Mozart's *The Magic Flute* and Puccini's *Turandot,* among others, can now be seen each year, including the 1995 season, on various opera stages. Projection designer Jerome Sirlin, whose innovative projections have served Madonna and Paul Simon well, and whose work can be seen currently on Broadway in *Kiss of the Spider Woman*, is just one of the crop of visual artists drawn to the possibilities — and freedom — of the opera stage.

Sirlin has designed for Philip Glass (*Hydrogen Jukebox, 1,000 Airplanes on the Roof*) and the New York City Opera (Lukas Foss's *Griffelkin* and Ezra Ladermann's *Marilyn*, based on the movie queen's sad tale). Sirlin believes there's more opportunity for conceptual exploration in opera than the legitimate theater, explaining that, for example, through tricks of lighting and perspective, even Frank Lloyd Wright's dream of a mile-high building could exist on the opera stage. (The revered architect himself showed up in Daron Aric Hagen's *Shining Brow* at the Madison Opera during the 1993 season.)

These visual artists are drawn, as well, to the cachet opera now has. When the Seattle Opera put on a new *Pelleas and Melisande* in 1993, it asked glass designer Dale Chihuly to create it for them. The result was an explosion of striking neon colors. Like other artists from disciplines outside opera, Chihuly has admitted being attracted to the notion of holding an audience of thousands hostage for a few hours. The most memorable moment for him came when he went out to the parking lot to his pink pickup truck after a performance of *Pelleas*. "About 20 people were left waiting on the sidewalk," he recalled. "Someone recognized me and began to clap. Then another clapped. Soon, all 20 people or so were clapping. It's just not like that in the art world."

All kinds of culture are now being represented on the operatic stage. At the Santa Fe Opera in 1995, the company's "new" production (it includes a new, contemporary, and/or "difficult" opera each year) was *Modern Painters* by David Lang, with a libretto by opera critic Manuela Hoelterhoff, which tells the story of art critic John Ruskin and his tortured relationships with women, primarily his mother and his wife, and finally his obsession with a 13-year-old girl.

That's a far cry indeed from *The Woman at Otowi Crossing*, a world premiere

◀ MUSIC AND DANCE FESTIVALS
CONTINUED FROM PAGE 613

MASSACHUSETTS

Amherst Early Music Festival
Amherst, MA
(413) 542-3236
(212) 222-3351

Berkshire Opera Co.
Monument Mountain High School Theater
Great Barrington, MA
(413) 243-1343

College Light Opera Co.
Highfield Theatre
Falmouth, MA
(508) 548-0668

Harvard Summer Dance Series
Cambridge, MA
(617) 495-5535

Jacob's Pillow Dance Festival
Ted Shawn Theater
Becket, MA
(413) 243-0745

Musicordia Festival
South Hadley, MA
(413) 538-2590

Tanglewood Festival
Lenox, MA
(617) 266-1492
(413) 637-1940

MICHIGAN

Interlochen Arts Festival
Interlochen, MI
(616) 276-6230

Pine Mountain Music Festival
Calumet, Escanaba, Houghton and
Iron Mountain, MI
(906) 487-2844

MINNESOTA

Minnesota Orchestra Viennese Sommerfest
Orchestra Hall
Minneapolis, MN
(612) 371-5656

MISSOURI

Summerfest St. Louis
St. Louis, MO
(314) 534-1700

CONTINUED ON PAGE 621 ▶

for Opera Theatre of St. Louis's 20th anniversary season. The title character is a quiet Philadelphia woman named Edith Warner, who befriended New Mexico's Indians, whose beliefs in the natural world she cherished, *and* the scientists of the Manhattan Project. She then experiences a terrifying vision of the consequences of nuclear experimentation.

"The whole opera field has had a wake-up call," Charles Mackay, Opera Theatre of St. Louis's general director declared. "Unless we do something proactive to ensure there's a future audience, we're in for a shock." The word is out: the way to get newcomers to see *Madama Butterfly* is to first attract them by

John Adams, June Jordan and Peter Sellars

accessible — usually, relatively contemporary — subject matter.

Opera companies also have become much more savvy about selling their product. When, for example, Houston produced *Harvey Milk,* they hosted panel discussions ("Is Houston Ready for *Harvey Milk?*") and an AIDS benefit. When Seattle Opera presented Richard Wagner's massive tetralogy, *The Ring of the Nibelungen,* an opera-going event that couldn't be *more* traditional, it cleverly involved the whole city in a six-week "ring" hunt, celebrated Wagner's birthday in downtown Westlake Plaza with a giant birthday cake shaped in the bust of the composer and offered opera patrons ($5,000-plus donors) the opportunity to ride 22 feet above the ground on the magic Ring horses before the production was retired. This is no longer the kind of pearls-and-lorgnette opera-going the Marx Brothers lampooned in *A Night at the Opera.*

In fact, nights at the musical theater during the last decade or so have come to resemble those at the opera. What is *Sunset Boulevard* if not an operatic experience? The big musical-theater war horses of our generation — *The Phantom of the Opera, Miss Saigon* — are operatic by nature, with little room for actual dialogue. Actually, there's more dialogue in Beethoven's *Fidelio* and Mozart's *The Magic Flute* than in these last two and *Les Misérables* is almost entirely sung. Heavy-duty, expensive musical theater may well be, as San Francisco Opera's general director Lotfi Mansouri describes it, "opera with third-rate music." One of Broadway's current long-running hits is, yes, an opera: *The Who's Tommy.*

By the same token, musical theater has found its way onto the opera stage. Andrew Lloyd Webber, the Crown Prince of the musical theater, has made his way there: Opera

Omaha performed his *Requiem Variations*. Throughout the country during the 1994–1995 season, here are some of the other titles the opera-going public has seen: *Side by Side With Sondheim, The Secret Garden, The Most Happy Fella, A Little Night Music, Kismet, Brigadoon* and *Carousel*.

According to Christopher Keene, general director of the New York City Opera, "In the middle of the 1950s putting a musical like *Show Boat* on the operatic stage was pure heresy, but here we've broken down the boundaries between opera and musicals. Our *A Little Night Music* was the first production in New York in 20 years. *One Hundred-Ten in the Shade* was practically unknown." And the company's production of Rodgers and Hammerstein's *Cinderella* was the first time that work was seen on the New York stage.

Opera now owns the glamour ballet had in the 1970s, but it also seems to be much more than flavor of the decade. "Nobody knows the Traubels I've seen," moaned The Met's general manager Rudolf Bing in the 1950s, referring to Wagnerian soprano Helen Traubel's predilection for swinging low in jazz clubs. Today there isn't an opera star who doesn't have some kind of crossover disk on the market.

An opera-goer from, say, the early part of this century probably wouldn't believe his or her eyes — or ears — today. The boundaries between what is opera and what is theater have, since the 1970s, become increasingly tenuous. One of the major "opera" productions of the 1994–1995 season might be counted by some as not an opera at all: *I Was Looking at the Ceiling and Then I Saw the Sky*, a collaboration between director Peter Sellars, poet June Jordan and composer John Adams. Adams and Sellars were the team that gave us *Nixon in China* and *The Death of Klinghoffer*. The piece, which was first performed in Berkeley and later in New York, used an eight-piece rock band to tell the story of seven Los Angeles characters.

Others, of course, would argue fiercely that yes, indeed, it *is* opera: a series of songs, dramatically presented, expressing

MUSIC AND DANCE FESTIVALS CONTINUED FROM PAGE 619

NEW HAMPSHIRE

Monadnock Music Festival
Pine Hill Waldorf Auditorium
Wilton, NH
(603) 924-7610

NEW JERSEY

New Jersey State Opera Summer Sounds
Garden State Arts Center
Holmdel, NJ
(908) 442-9200

Opera Festival of New Jersey
Kirby Arts Center
Lawrenceville, NJ
(609) 936-1500

NEW MEXICO

Santa Fe Chamber Music Festival
Santa Fe, NM
(505) 983-2075

NEW YORK

Artpark/Artpark at the Church
Art Theater
Lewiston, NY
(716) 754-4375

Aston Magna at Bard
Annandale-on-Hudson, NY
(914) 758-3226

Bach Aria Festival & Institute
Stony Brook, NY
(516) 632-7239

Bridgehampton Chamber Music Fesival
Bridgehampton, NY
(212) 750-5776

Caramoor International Music Festival
Katonah, NY
(914) 232-1252
(800) 848-2742

Chautauqua Institution
Chautauqua, NY
(800) 249-1441

Dance Theater Workshop
New York, NY
(212) 691-6500

Glimmerglass Opera Festival
Alice Busch Opera Theater
Cooperstown, NY
(607) 547-2255

CONTINUED ON PAGE 625

1994—1995 Opera Premieres and New Productions

Courtesy of The Minnesota Opera

Bok Choy Variations

AÏDA
Pittsburgh Opera
Composer: Giuseppe Verdi; **Libretto:** Antonio Ghislanzoni; **Conductor:** Anton Guadagno; **Stage Director:** Bernard Uzan; **Set Designers:** Claude Girard and Bernard Uzan; **Costume Designer:** Claude Girard
Opening: 10/95 at Benedum Center
Verdi's awe-inspiring opera is set in the temples of ancient Egypt. Aïda, the beautiful Ethiopian princess, is taken captive and forced to serve the Egyptian princess, Amneris. Torn between patriotism to her country and passion for Radames, Egyptian captain of the guard, she is tormented by her conflicting desires. Amneris, who also loves Radames, constantly battles jealousy and love, as Radames has sworn his love to Aïda. The mighty Ethiopian ruler is enslaved after an Egyptian victory and Aïda's romance turns to tragedy as he commands his daughter's loyalty, forcing her to choose between love and her country.

THE BARBER OF SEVILLE
The Minnesota Opera
Composer: Gioacchino Rossini; **Libretto:** Cesare Sterbini; **Conductor:** George Manahan; **Stage Director:** Christopher Mattaliano; **Set Designer:** Allen Moyer; **Costume Designer:** James Scott; **Lighting Designer:** Paul Palazzo
Opening: 3/95 at the Ordway Music Theatre
Based on the comedy *Le Barbier de Séville* by Pierre de Beaumarchais
Rossini's comedy unfolds amid pranks, confusion and all-around mayhem, as the handsome Count Almaviva falls in love with the beautiful young Rosina, ward of the cantakerous old Dr. Bartolo. The Count employs the help of Figaro, jack-of-all-trades, in order to win Rosina away from her guardian, but the scheming doctor is determined to marry Rosina himself and keeps her under close scrutiny. A series of close escapes and escapades follows as Figaro creates several disguises for the enterprising Count. Ultimately, Figaro's master plan prevails — just another day's work for the busiest barber of Seville.

LA BOHÈME
Virginia Opera
Composer: Giacomo Puccini; **Libretto:** Giuseppe Giacosa and Luigi Illica; **Conductor:** Jerome Shannon; **Stage Director:** Johnathon Pape; **Set and Costume Designer:** Allen Charles Klein; **Lighting Designer:** David Latham
Opening: 3/95 at the the Harrison Opera House
Based on the novel *Scène de la Vie de Bohème* by Henri Murger
Puccini's heartbreaking story of tender young love centers on a struggling group of artists living in Paris's Latin Quarter. Rudolfo, a poet, falls in love with the ailing seamstress Mimi. The painter Marcello loves Mimi's flamboyant, coquettish friend, Musetta. Love conquers all but death in this tale that begins ecstatically on a moonlit Christmas Eve and ends tragically when Mimi dies of consumption.

BOK CHOY VARIATIONS
The Minnesota Opera
Composer: Evan Chen; **Libretto:** Fifi Servoss; **Conductor:** Jeffrey Lewis; **Stage Director:** Eric Simonson; **Chorus Master:** Janice Kimes; **Set Designer:** Robert Brill; **Costume Designer:** Allison Reeds; **Lighting Designer:** Kevin Ramach; **Choreographer:** Joseph Chvala
Opening: 6/95 at the Ordway Music Theatre
Bok Choy Variations, a semi-autobiographical story of the composer Evan Chen, chronicles the life of an aspiring composer in Maoist China. Opportunities are limited for the boy because his father is a political dissident, so Da Wei journeys to America in search of political and artistic freedom. Disillusioned and alienated, he struggles to juggle work, school and art endeavors while coping with culture shock. After arduously gaining acceptance into the community, Da Wei turns to his artistic expression for comfort.

CANDIDE
Lyric Opera of Chicago
Composer: Leonard Bernstein; **Libretto:** Richard Wilbur, Leonard Bernstein, Stephen Sondheim and John LaTouche; **Conductor:** George Manahan; **Stage Director:** Harold Prince; **Chorus Master:** Donald Palumbo; **Set Designer:** Clarke Dunham; **Costume Designer:** Judith Dolan; **Lighting Designer:** Ken Billington
Opening: 11/94 at the Civic Opera House
Based on Voltaire's Candide

Candide, an illegitimate cousin of the Baron of Thunder-Ten-Tronck, loves the Baron's nubile daughter, Cunegonde, but because of the irregularity of his birth, Candide is deemed ineligible as a husband and banned from the Baron's castle, where he lives. He and his cohorts journey from one adventure to the next, and neither plague, plunder nor gloom of the Spanish Inquisition dims their adventurous spirits.

CAPRICCIO
Lyric Opera of Chicago
Composer: Richard Strauss; **Libretto:** Clemens Krauss and Richard Strauss; **Conductor:** Andrew Davis; **Stage Director:** John Cox; **Set Designer:** Mauro Pagano; **Costume Designer:** Costumes from Glyndebourne Festival; **Lighting Designer:** Duane Schuler
Opening: 11/94 at the Civic Opera House
Based on the short opera by Antonio Salieri and Giovanni Battista Casti

This sophisticated opera takes place during a single afternoon and cleverly asks the characters: What is more important in opera — words or music? A passionate poet and an equally ardent musician each discover that they both love a countess. They compose an opera for her in honor of her birthday and ask her to choose between the art and the artists, a topic that is discussed throughout the afternoon.

CARMEN
Opera Pacific
Composer: Georges Bizet; **Libretto:** Henri Meilhae and Ludovic Halévy; **Conductor:** Mark Gibson; **Stage Director:** Dejan Miladinovic; **Set and Costume Designer:** The Washington Opera
Opening: 9/95 at the Orange County Performing Arts Center

The Washington Opera
Composer: Georges Bizet; **Libretto:** Henri Meilhae and Ludovic Halévy; **Conductor:** Cal Stewart Kellogg; **Stage Director:** Ann-Margret Pettersson; **Chorus Master:** Alan Nathan; **Set and Costume Designer:** Lennart Mörk; **Lighting Designer:** Joan Sullivan; **Choreographer:** Brad Waller
Opening: 3/95 at the Kennedy Center Opera House
Based on Carmen by Posper Mérimée

One of the universal favorites of the opera stage, Carmen rings true to Spanish temperament and atmosphere through Bizet's vivid musical characterization, brilliant orchestration and dramatic flair. A story of violent emotion and explosive sexuality, the fatalistic gypsy Carmen lives by her own rules, yet understands that everyone must eventually yield to fate. She flaunts her mesmerizing power over the vulnerable Don José, a young army corporal with a dangerous past, only to throw him to the toreador Escamillo, knowing his fate will inevitably lead to death.

LA CENERENTOLA (CINDERELLA)
Opera Colorado
Composer: Gioacchino Rossini; **Libretto:** Jacopo Ferretti; **Conductor:** Richard Bonynge; **Stage Director:** Nathaniel Merrill; **Set Designer:** Jean Robertson; **Costume Designer:** Malabar Company; **Lighting Designer:** James Sale
Opening: 5/95 at Boettcher Hall

The course of true love unfolds in this classic fairy tale as Prince Ramiro frantically searches for the mysterious and beautiful woman who disappeared after a ball at his palace. Disguised as a valet, the prince's search for a bride leads him to Don Magnifico's kitchen maid, Cinderella. Despite the omission of the slippers, the pumpkin turning into a carriage and Cinderella's magical transformation at midnight, the legend's charm is retained through Rossini's melodious and enchanting score.

Carol Pratt/Courtesy of The Washington Opera

Carmen

THE CUNNING LITTLE VIXEN
Seattle Opera

Composer and Libretto: Leos Janácek; **Conductor:** Gerard Schwarz; **Stage Director and Set Designer:** Neil Peter Jampolis; **Costume Designer:** Steven Feldman; **Lighting Designer:** Neil Peter Jampolis; **Choreographer:** Peggy Hickey

Opening: 10/94 at Seattle Center Opera House

Based on the novelette *Lidové Noviny* by Rudolf Tesnohlidek

Janácek's *The Cunning Little Vixen* is pastoral, simple, full of quiet moments, little talk and much choeographed movement. Set in a timeless world where fantasy is fused with reality, nature teaches a lesson of life, aging and death: that man like the animals, is part of nature and should accept his place in nature's cycle of youth, maturity, death and renewal.

THE DAUGHTER OF THE REGIMENT
Michigan Opera Theater

Composer: Gaetano Donizetti; **Libretto:** Jules Henri Vernoy de Saint-Georges and Jean Francois Bayard; **Conductor:** Suzanne Acton; **Stage Director:** Dorothy Danner; **Chorus Master:** Suzanne Acton; **Set Designer:** Peter Dean Beck **Costume Designer:** John Lehmeyer; **Lighting Designer:** Kendall Smith

Opening: 11/94 at the Fisher Theatre

In this opera comique, Marie, the spoiled darling of a regiment of fathers who found her on the battlefield as a child, campaigns to marry whom she chooses, but the soldiers insist that she marry one of their own. They never come to an agreement as she is reclaimed by her long-lost noble family that desperately tries to transform her into a proper young lady.

DER ROSENKAVALIER (THE ROSE BEARER)
Houston Grand Opera

Composer: Richard Strauss; **Libretto:** Hugo von Hofmannsthal; **Conductor:** Christoph Eschenbach; **Stage Director:** Jonathan Miller; **Set Designer:** Peter Davison; **Costume Designer:** Sue Blane; **Lighting Designer:** Noele Stollmack

Opening: 4/95 at Wortham Center's Brown Theater

In this poignant story of tangled relationships, the Marschallin, a married noblewoman of Vienna, is having an affair with her zealous young 17-year-old cousin Octavian. What follows is a complicated web of intrigue, cross-dressing, gender reversal and sexual ambiguity, all brilliantly characterized in some of the composer's wittiest and most ingratiating melodies.

Jim Caldwell/Courtesy of Houston Grand Opera

Der Rosenkavalier

DIDO AND AENEAS
Houston Grand Opera

Composer: Sir Henry Purcell; **Libretto:** Nahum Tate; **Conductor:** Marc Minkowski; **Stage Director:** Marshall Pynkoski; **Set Designer:** William Schmuck; **Costume Designer:** Dora Rust D'Eye; **Lighting Designer:** Kevin Fraser; **Choreographer:** Jeannette Zingg

Opening: 2/95 at Wortham Center's Cullen Theater

Based on Virgil's *Aeneid*

In this tale of the fated love between Dido, Queen of Carthage, and Aeneas, a noble refugee from Troy, Dido gives refuge to Aeneas after he flees Troy during the Trojan War. They fall in love only to become victims of a conspiracy conceived by a malevolent sorceress and her witches. An evil spirit employed by the sorceress falsely informs Aeneas that Jove has commanded him to sail to Italy. Aeneas reluctantly obeys and leaves Carthage, whereupon Dido stabs herself, believing Aeneas deserted her.

DIE MEISTERSINGER
Cleveland Opera

Composer and Libretto: Richard Wagner; **Conductor:** Imre Pallo; **Stage Director:** Francois Rochaix; **Chorus Master:** David Gooding; **Set and Costume Designer:** Jean-Claude Maret; **Lighting Designer:** Joan Sullivan

Opening: 5/95 at Playhouse Square Center State Theatre

The story of *Die Meistersinger* centers around the traditional song competitions held in Germany by the medieval guilds. The winner of the competition receives Eva's hand in marriage, though she desperately wants to marry Walther. Despite his lack of vocal training, Walther enters the contest and is challenged by the talented mastersingers of Nürnberg. The dignity of Hans Sachs, one of the most distinguished mastersingers, and the love of Eva and Walter are highlighted in the dominant themes of Wagner's magnificent opera.

DIE FLIEGENDE HOLLÄNDER (THE FLYING DUTCHMAN)

Los Angeles Opera

Composer and Libretto: Richard Wagner; **Conductor:** Asher Fisch; **Stage Director:** Julie Taymor; **Set Designer:** George Tsypin; **Costume Designer:** Constance Hoffman; **Lighting Designer:** Paul Pyant
Opening: 9/95 at Dorothy Chandler Pavilion

One of Wagner's most popular operas, *The Flying Dutchman* is a dramatic retelling of an ancient legend about a Dutch seafarer who tried to round the Cape of Good Hope in a furious storm. Swearing that he would succeed even if he had to sail forever, the devil condemned him to sail the seas until he found a woman who would faithfully and eternally love him. Once every seven years he is permitted to dock his ghostly vessel and search for his beloved.

THE GHOSTS OF VERSAILLES

The Metropolitan Opera

Composer: John Corigliano; **Libretto:** William M. Hoffman; **Conductor:** James Levine; **Stage Director:** Colin Graham; **Set and Costume Designer:** John Conklin; **Lighting Designer:** Gil Wechsler; **Choreographer:** Debra Brown
Opening: 4/95 at The Metropolitan Opera

Corigliano's first opera, *The Ghosts of Versailles* concerns a blossoming love affair between the ghosts of Marie Antoinette and Pierre de Beaumarchais. Beaumarchais, the playwright whose Figaro plays are the basis of operas by Mozart and Rossini, turns back the clock and conjures an opera-within-an-opera for the queen in hope of saving her life and in turn winning her affections. Figaro, Susanna, Count Almaviva and a host of other characters from the Almaviva household also take part in the action.

Winnie Klotz/Courtesy of The Metropolitan Opera

The Ghosts of Versailles

MUSIC AND DANCE FESTIVALS
CONTINUED FROM PAGE 621

Huntington Summer Arts Festival
Huntington, NY
(516) 271-8442

Lake George Opera Festival
Queensbury High School Auditorium
Queensbury, NY
(518) 793-3859

Lincoln Center Out-of-Doors
New York, NY
(212) 875-5108

Lincoln Center Summer Festival
New York, NY
(212) 721-6500

Maverick Concerts
Woodstock, NY
(914) 679-8217

Mohonk Music Week and Festival of the Arts
New Paltz, NY
(800) 772-6646

Mostly Mozart Festival
New York, NY
(212) 721-6500

New York Grand Opera
Rumsey Field
Central Park
New York, NY
(212) 245-8837

New York Philharmonic Parks Concerts
New York, NY
(212) 875-5709

Serious Fun! Festival
Lincoln Center
New York, NY
(212) 721-6500

NORTH CAROLINA

American Dance Festival
Durham, NC
(919) 684-6402

Brevard Music Festival
Brevard Music Center
Whittington Pfohl Auditorium
Brevard, NC
(704) 884-2019

OHIO

Cincinnati Opera Summer Festival
Music Hall
Cincinnati, OH
(513) 241-2742

CONTINUED ON PAGE 627

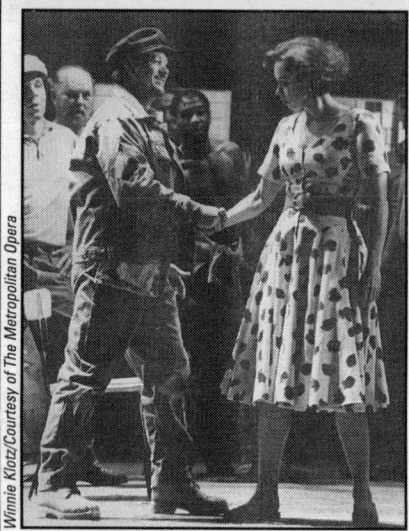

Lady MacBeth of Mtsensk

HARVEY MILK
New York City Opera
Composer: Stewart Wallace; **Libretto:** Michael Korie; **Conductor:** Christopher Keene; **Stage Director:** Christopher Alden; **Set Designer:** Paul Steinberg; **Costume Designer:** Gabriel Berry; **Lighting Designer:** Jeff Davis
Opening: 4/95 at the New York State Theater

Houston Grand Opera
Composer: Stewart Wallace; **Libretto:** Michael Korie; **Conductor:** Ward Holmquist; **Stage Director:** Christopher Alden; **Set Designer:** Paul Steinberg; **Costume Designer:** Gabriel Berry; **Lighting Designer:** Noele Stollmack
Opening: 1/95 at Wortham Center's Brown Theater
This story of grassroots activism, dirty politics, murder and riot was inspired by the life of San Francisco's first openly gay elected public official, Mayor Harvey Milk. As America's gay movement emerged in the 1970s, Milk became a leader in the community. He succeeded in city politics as he drew together coalitions from the minority communities and other marginalized citizens. This portrait of Milk, who was assassinated, brings to life the drama of his triumph and tragedy and his ideals of individual freedom.

LADY MACBETH OF MTSENSK
The Metropolitan Opera
Composer: Dmitri Shostakovich; **Libretto:** Dmitri Shostakovich and Alexander Preis; **Conductor:** James Conlon; **Stage Director:** Graham Vick; **Set and Costume Designer:** Paul Brown; **Lighting Designer:** Nick Chelton; **Choreographer:** Ron Howell
Opening: 11/94 at The Metropolitan Opera

Lady Macbeth of Mtsensk recounts the gradual corruption and death of Katerina Ismailova, a lonely woman bound in a loveless marriage. Her disagreeable father-in-law, aware that she wants to take a lover, watches her with strict scrutiny. When her husband leaves the property, she falls prey to the advances of the handsome new laborer Sergei, who is quick to perceive Katerina's desire and seduces her. When the couple decides to marry, they murder Katerina's husband and hide his corpse in the cellar, but a drunken peasant soon discovers the body. Shackled and held prisoner, the faithless Sergei blames Katerina for his current plight and seduces another convict, Sonyetka. As the women confront each other near a bridge they fall into the swift-flowing river and drown.

MACBETH
San Diego Opera
Composer: Giuseppe Verdi; **Libretto:** Francesco Maria Piave; **Conductor:** Edoardo Miller; **Stage Director:** Wolfgang Weber; **Set Designer:** Davis West; **Costume Designer:** Suzanne Mess; **Lighting Designer:** Gregory Allen Hirsch
Opening: 3/95 at the Civic Theatre
Based on William Shakespeare's tragedy *Macbeth*
An intensely brooding story of the supernatural, Verdi's *Macbeth* is filled with prophecies, witches, ghosts, unbridled ambition and regicide, all mixed together in a magical musical cauldron. After encountering a coven of witches on a barren Scottish heath, Macbeth learns that he will become King of Scotland. Not satisfied to let events run their course, Macbeth's wife convinces him to murder King Duncan, a bloody deed that results in Macbeth's own demise.

MADAMA BUTTERFLY
The Metropolitan Opera
Composer: Giacomo Puccini; **Libretto:** Giuseppe Giacos and Luigi Illica; **Conductor:** Daniele Gatti; **Stage Director:** Giancarlo del Monaco; **Set Designer:** Michael Scott; **Costume Designer:** Michael Scott; **Lighting Designer:** Gil Wechsler
Opening: 12/94 at The Metropolitan Opera
Based on David Belasco's play
This Puccini masterpiece evokes the atmosphere of 19th-century Japan as the setting for tragic love and colliding cultures. In one of opera's most heartbreaking tragedies, a beautiful young Japanese woman, Cio-Cio San, is betrayed by her husband, an American naval officer. She decides to die with honor rather than live with disgrace and kills herself with the same dagger that her father used to commit suicide. Through Puccini's compassionate and poignant score, Cio-Cio San's final sacrifice becomes an unforgettable emotional experience.

THE MERRY WIDOW
New York City Opera

Composer: Franz Lehár; **Libretto:** Victor Leon and Leo Stein; **Conductor:** Eric Stern; **Stage Director:** Robert Johanson; **Chorus Master:** Joseph Colaneri; **Set Designer:** Michael Anania; **Costume Designer:** Gregg Barnes; **Lighting Designer:** Mark W. Stanley; **Choreographer:** Sharon Halley
Opening: 3/95 at the New York State Theatre

Waltz-like rhythms and soft, dreamy melodies abound in Lehár's ravishing score. Through society balls, dinner at Maxim's, a cast of elegant ladies and a coterie of eligible bachelors, this comic operetta epitomizes the intoxicating glamor of 19th-century Parisian society. The fabulously wealthy and recently widowed Hanna Glawari must marry a Marsovian national to keep her fortune. Her former lover, Danilo, is assigned to watch over her. Not wanting to appear to be after her money, he does not reveal that he still loves her, but she suspects his true feelings. After numerous games and tests, Hanna is convinced of his love.

PELLÉAS ET MÉLISANDE
The Metropolitan Opera

Composer: Claude Debussy; **Libretto:** Maurice Maeterlinck; **Conductor:** James Levine; **Stage Director:** Jonathan Miller; **Set Designer:** John Conklin; **Costume Designer:** Clare Mitchell; **Lighting Designer:** Duane Schuler
Opening: 3/95 at The Metropolitan Opera

Set in the legendary kingdom of Allemonde, *Pelléas et Mélisande* illustrates a tragic tale of suppressed love and unfounded jealousy. Golaud, widower and son of King Arkel, is married to Mélisande, a mysterious child-like maiden whom he found while lost in the forest. Though the young girl loves Golaud's younger brother Pelléas, she remains faithful to her husband and keeps her love secret. Despite her loyalty, Golaud's jealousy is sparked at the slightest incident and he handles Mélisande so violently that King Arkel must intervene. When Mélisande finally confesses her feelings to Pelléas, Golaud murders his brother in a fit of rage. After giving birth to a child, Mélisande becomes ill and it is then that Golaud realizes his wife's innocence. Her strength failing, she forgives Golaud with her last breath.

PORGY AND BESS
A co-production of the following four opera companies:

Cleveland Opera
Opening: 4/95 at the Playhouse Square Center State Theater
Composer: George Gershwin; **Libretto:** Du Bose Heyward; **Conductor:** John DeMain; **Stage Director:** Hope Clarke; **Set Designer:** Ken Foy; **Costume Designer:** Judy Dearing; **Lighting Designer:** Ken Billington; **Choreographer:** Hope Clarke

MUSIC AND DANCE FESTIVALS
CONTINUED FROM PAGE 625

Lyric Opera Cleveland Summer Festival
Kulas Hall, Cleveland Institute of Music
Cleveland, OH
(216) 231-2910

Ohio Ballet Summer Festival
Akron, OH
(216) 972-7900

Ohio Light Opera
Freedlander Theatre
Wooster, OH
(216) 263-2345

OKLAHOMA

Opera Festival of Oklahoma
Hardemann Auditorium
Oklahoma City, OK
(405) 297-3000

OREGON

Chamber Music Northwest
Portland, OR
(503) 294-6400

Oregon Bach Festival
Eugene, OR
(800) 457-1486

PENNSYLVANIA

American Music Theater Festival
Plays & Players Theater
Philadelphia, PA
(215) 893-1145

Mann Music Center Summer Festival
West Fairmount Park
Philadelphia, PA
(215) 878-7707

RHODE ISLAND

Newport Music Festival
Newport, RI
(401) 846-1133

SOUTH CAROLINA

Spoleto Festival U.S.A.
Dock Street Theatre
Charleston, SC
(803) 577-4500

CONTINUED ON PAGE 629

Jim Caldwell/Courtesy of Houston Grand Opera

Porgy and Bess

Based on the play *Porgy* by Du Bose and Dorothy Heyward

Houston Grand Opera
Opening: 1/95 at Wortham Center's Brown Theater

San Diego Opera
Opening: 3/95 at the Civic Theatre

Seattle Opera
Opening: 3/95 at the Seattle Center Opera House

Founded on the jazz rhythms of the 1920s, Gershwin's *Porgy and Bess* is recognized as the first truly American opera. Bess's boyfriend Crown, tells her to wait for him while he kills Robbins over a squabble at a crap game. Sportin' Life, a dope peddler, offers Bess refuge, but she opts to hide in Porgy's room. Porgy, a disabled begger, becomes Bess' protector and they fall in love, but their brief bliss is disrupted by Crown's return, who attempts to reclaim Bess with force and seduction. Porgy kills Crown, and while Porgy is at the police station, Sportin' Life steps in to claim Bess.

The Rake's Progress

Lyric Opera of Chicago
Composer: Igor Stravinsky; **Libretto:** W.H. Auden and Chester Kallman; **Conductor:** Dennis Russel Davies; **Stage Director:** Graham Vick; **Chorus Master:** Donald Palumbo; **Set Designer:** Richard Hudson; **Costume Designer:** Richard Hudson; **Lighting Designer:** Duane Schuler
Opening: 10/94 at the Civic Opera House

"For idle hands and hearts, the devil finds work to do" moralizes Stravinsky's *A Rake's Progress.* Inspired by William Hogarth's paintings, this Faustian legend features a callow, country youth who sells his soul to the devil in exchange for wealth. His naiveté comes at the expense of his beloved, whom he rejects for a life of drink and whores. Ultimately, the devil fails to collect his fee when the youth is redeemed by his beloved's faith and intervention.

Rigoletto

Houston Grand Opera
Composer: Giuseppe Verdi; **Libretto:** Francesco Maria Piave; **Conductor:** Vjekoslav Sutej; **Stage Director:** Harry Silverstein; **Set Designer:** Michael Yeargan; **Costume Designer:** Peter J. Hall; **Lighting Designer:** Noele Stollmack
Opening: 10/94 at Wortham Center's Brown Theater
Based on *Le Roi s'Amuse* by Victor Hugo

An exquisite and moving human tragedy, Verdi's powerful opera recounts the story of the Duke of Mantua's hunchbacked court jester, Rigoletto. Though publicly caustic and bitter, Rigoletto's acid-tongued, venomous behavior at court is a stark contrast to the loving demeanor he displays at home to his treasured daughter, Gilda. When the lecherous Duke turns his attentions to Gilda and ultimately dishonors her, Rigoletto swears vengeance on the Duke, but his ill-fated vendetta costs his beloved Gilda her life.

Salome

Virginia Opera
Composer: Richard Strauss; **Libretto:** Hedwig Lachmann; **Conductor:** Peter Mark; **Stage Director:** Sergio Vela; **Set Designer:** Hugh Landwehr; **Costume Designer:** Donna Zakowska; **Lighting Designer:** Sergio Vela
Opening: 11/94 at the Harrison Opera House
Based on Oscar Wilde's play

Infatuated with Jokanaan's voice, Salome seduces the captain of the guard and he frees Jokanaan, who is a prisoner in her stepfather's underground cistern. Rejected by him, she seeks revenge by asking for his head on a silver platter in return for dancing for King Herod. Herod desperately tries to dissuade her from this gruesome request, but ultimately complies and orders the execution. Salome eagerly seizes the head and pours forth her repressed desire for the dead Jokanaan. Herod, horrified by Salome's actions, orders her death.

Samson et Dalila

Baltimore Opera Company
Composer: Camille Saint-Saëns; **Libretto:** Ferdinand Lemaire; **Conductor:** Alexander Sander; **Stage Director and Set Designer:** Roberto Oswald; **Costume Designer:** Anibal Lapiz; **Lighting Designer:** Roberto Oswald; **Choreographer:** Peter Pucci
Opening: 3/95 at the Lyric Opera House
Based on the Bible's book of *Judges*

A faithful servant of God, Samson rebukes the Philistines for their lack of faith and warns them that God's vengeance will strike them down. The high priest and the Philistine princess Dalila, who hate Samson equally, plot to destroy him by discovering the secret of his strength. Ignoring an old Hebrew's warning, Samson is powerfully stirred by the sensuous princess and surrenders his secret, only to be betrayed by Dalila and left at the mercy of the Philistines. Samson cries out to God for one final burst of strength and destroys the pagan temple in which he is held captive, bringing down the temple upon himself and his enemies.

SIEGFRIED
Lyric Opera of Chicago
Composer and Libretto: Richard Wagner; **Conductor:** Zubin Mehta; **Stage Director:** August Everding; **Set Designer:** John Conklin; **Costume Designer:** John Conklin; **Lighting Designer:** Duane Schuler
Opening: 1/95 at the Civic Opera House
Siegfried introduces the central character of Wagner's monumental *Ring* cycle, an ambitious four-opera production created to be performed over the course of a week. In this tale inspired by Norse mythology, Siegfried slays a terrible dragon and gains possession of the coveted ring that enables its possessor to rule the world. Siegfried, as "supreme hero," is destined to triumph because he is oblivious to fear and learns the lesson of passionate love.

Dan Rest/Courtesy of Lyric Opera of Chicago

Siegfried

SIMON BOCCANEGRA
The Metropolitan Opera
Composer: Giuseppe Verdi; **Libretto:** Francesco Maria Piave and Arrigo Boito; **Conductor:** James Levine; **Stage Director:** Giancarlo del Monaco; **Set Designer:** Michael Scott; **Costume Designer:** Michael Scott; **Lighting Designer:** Gil Wechsler
Opening: 1/95 at The Metropolitan Opera
Based on the drama by Antonio Garcia Gutiérrez
Verdi's riveting masterpiece recounts Simon Boccanegra's rise to power and his final con-

MUSIC AND DANCE FESTIVALS
CONTINUED FROM PAGE 627

TEXAS
International Summer Music Festival
Dallas, TX
(214) 692-0203

Round Top Festival
Round Top, TX
(409) 249-3129

UTAH
Moab Music Festival
Moab, UT
(801) 259-8431

Utah Festival Opera Co.
Ellen Eccles Theatre
Logan, UT
(800) 830-6088

VERMONT
Manchester Music Festival
P.O. Box 1165
Manchester Center, VT 05255-1165
(802) 362-1956
(800) 639-5868

Marlboro Music Festival
P.O. Box K
Marlboro, VT 05344
(215) 569-4690
(802) 254-2394

VIRGINIA
Ash Lawn — Highland Summer Festival
Boxwood Gardens
Charlottesville, VA
(804) 293-4500

WASHINGTON
Seattle Chamber Music Festival
Seattle, WA
(206) 328-1425

Seattle International Music Festival
Seattle, WA
(206) 233-0993

WYOMING
Grand Teton Music Festival
Teton Village
(307) 733-1128

■

Carol Rosegg/Courtesy of New York City Opera

La Traviata

frontation with his mortal enemy, Fiesco, a wealthy nobleman and grandfather of his illegitimate daughter. Boccanegra is elected to power by two corrupt citizens of Genoa, and, with their aid, becomes a tyrant. Fearing for his safety, Fiesco flees and assumes a new name. Unknown to Fiesco and Boccanegra, Fiesco's adopted daughter is his true granddaugher, the child of Boccanegra. Violence, venom and a plea for peace envelop 14th century Genoa — and the power of love is victorious.

SIMON BOLIVAR
Virginia Opera
Composer and Libretto: Thea Musgrave; **Conductor:** Peter Mark; **Stage Director:** Lillian Garrett-Groag; **Set Designer:** John Conklin; **Costume Designer:** David Murin; **Lighting Designer:** Mark Stanley
Opening: 1/95 at the Harrison Opera House
Based on historical events and writings of Símon Bolívar

Set in northwest South America during the early 19th century, *Simon Bolivar* moves through a series of short connected scenes to the climax of the liberation of South America from Spanish rule. Exiled, dying in poverty and seemingly forgotten after his idealistic union of states fails to hold together, Bolivar's songs, heard as the story telescopes into the 20th century, invoke the ideal of freedom and the heavy demands it places on those who seek it.

TALES OF HOFFMAN
Portland Opera
Composer: Jacques Offenbach; **Libretto:** Jules Barbier and Michel Carré; **Conductor:** Marc Trautmann; **Stage Director:** Robert Bailey; **Set Designer:** Loy Arcenas; **Costume Designer:** Claudia Stephens; **Lighting Designer:** Peter Maradudin
Opening: 3/95 at the Civic Auditorium
Based on the writings of Ernst Theodor Wilhelm Hoffman

Three fantastic, magical stories from the endless imagination of Hoffman are brought to life in *Tales of Hoffman.* The poet Hoffman falls recklessly in love with a mechanical dancing doll, a woman is drawn to sing by her mother's portrait and a seductress steals men's souls. An intriguing opera about love, this vivid blend of eccentric magic and bizarre fantasy illustrates Hoffman's three great romances and the bitter struggle between human love and an artist's dedication to his work.

TIEFLAND
The Washington Opera
Composer: Eugen d'Albert; **Libretto:** Rudolf Lothar; **Conductor:** Heinz Fricke; **Stage Director:** Roman Terleckyj; **Chorus Master:** Alan Nathan; **Set Designer:** Zack Brown; **Costume Designer:** Zack Brown; **Lighting Designer:** Joan Sullivan
Opening: 3/95 at the Kennedy Center Opera House
D'Albert's *Tiefland* evokes the long tradition of pastoral European culture and juxtaposes two worlds, the simple country life of the shepherd and the world of commerce. Pedro, a shepherd on the slopes of the Pyrenees, is offered Marta's hand in marriage and a position at the mill by her master and landowner Sebastiano. An innocent pawn in Sebastiano's scheme, Pedro accepts and eagerly sets off for the lowlands. Disenchanted by his new lifestyle, Pedro returns to his ethical values of the pastoral world and rejects those of the urban milieu. Brooding, melancholy, romantic and stormy, D'Albert's music propels and underscores the story.

LA TRAVIATA
New York City Opera
Composer: Giuseppe Verdi; **Libretto:** Francesco Maria Piave; **Conductor:** Yves Abel; **Stage Director:** Renata Scotto; **Set Designer:** Thierry Bosquet; **Costume Designer:** Thierry Bosquet; **Lighting Designer:** Jeff Davis; **Opening:** 3/95 at the New York State Theater

Pittsburgh Opera
Composer: Giuseppe Verdi; **Libretto:** Francesco Maria Piave; **Conductor:** Lorin Maazel; **Stage Director:** Tito Capobianco; **Set Designer:** Albert Filoni; **Costume Designer:** Susan O'Neill; **Lighting Designer:** James Latzel; **Choreographer:** Gigi Elena
Opening: 10/94 at the Benedum Center for the Performing Arts

Vanessa

Based on the play *La Dame Aux Camelias* (Camille) by Alexandre Dumas

A favorite of opera lovers worldwide, Verdi's heartwrenching story is set in the glamour and frivolity of 19th-century Parisian society. Violetta Valéry gives up her courtesan life of merry dinner parties and wealth for Alfredo Germont's love. She sells her possessions to finance their life together but is soon asked by Alfredo's father to leave him, as Alfredo's sister's forthcoming marriage is threatened by the scandal of Alfredo's liaison with Violetta. Violetta complies, but Alfredo, unaware of the true reason behind her departure, shuns and humiliates her in public. When finally told of her sacrifice, he returns to Violetta to ask for forgiveness. Weakened by an ongoing illness, she has just enough strength to proclaim her love for him and collapses dead.

TURANDOT
The Minnesota Opera

Composer: Giacomo Puccini; **Libretto:** Giuseppe Adami and Renato Simoni; **Conductor:** George Manahan; **Stage Director:** James Robinson; **Chorus Master:** Janice Kimes; **Set Designer:** Anita Stewart; **Costume Designer:** Anna Oliver; **Lighting Designer:** Marcus Dilliard
Opening: 1/95 at the Ordway Music Theater
Based on Schiller's version of the story by Count Carlo Gozzi

Turandot, Puccini's last, and arguably, greatest opera is one of the most monumental and boldest works ever staged. Puccini died before he could complete this preeminent masterpiece, and the score was finished by his friend, Franco Alfano, who worked from sketches left by the composer. An epic love story told through opulent music of unprecedented passion and power, *Turandot* tells of a Chinese princess whose fear of love and being loved compels her to sentence her many suitors to death if they cannot correctly answer three riddles.

VANESSA
The Washington Opera with The Dallas Opera

Composer: Samuel Barber; **Libretto:** Gian Carlo Menotti; **Conductor:** Anne Manson; **Stage Director:** Michael Kahn; **Chorus Master:** Alan Nathan; **Set Designer:** Michael Yeargan; **Costume Designer:** Marin Pakledinaz; **Lighting Designer:** Joan Sullivan; **Choreographer:** Karma Camp
Opening: 1/95 at the Kennedy Center Opera House
Set in a Scandinavian country during the early 21st century, the beautiful Vanessa has waited for the return of her lover, Anatol, for 20 years. Attempting to stop time, Vanessa veiled all the mirrors and portraits in the house. After the arrival of the son and namesake of Vanessa's late beloved, the young Anatol wastes no time in seducing both Vanessa and Erika, Vanessa's niece. After Vanessa and Anatol's marriage, Erika, now pregnant with Anatol's child, causes a miscarriage by running away into the chilly night. When Vanessa and Anatol leave for Paris, it is Erika's turn to cover the mirrors and wait.

WONDERFUL TOWN
New York City Opera

Composer: Leonard Bernstein; **Libretto:** Betty Comden and Adolph Green; **Conductor:** Eric Stern; **Stage Director:** Richard Sabellico; **Chorus Master:** Joseph Colaneri; **Set Designer:** Michael Anania; **Costume Designer:** Gail Baldoni; **Lighting Designer:** Jeff Davis; **Choreographer:** Tina Paul
Based on Ruth McKenney's *My Sister Eileen*
Opening: 11/94 at the New York State Theater
Bernstein's *Wonderful Town* first opened at Manahattan's Winter Garden Theater in 1953 and was immediately a smash hit. Based on the successful adaptation of McKenny's *My Sister Eileen*, this tuneful panorama of New York in the 1930s, 1940s and 1950s tells of two sisters from Columbus, Ohio, who have an uncanny ability to create zany hilarity and thwart convention. Living in a subterranean Greenwhich Village apartment, Ruth and Eileen face a different adventure every day.

The Tony Awards

The Antoinette Perry (Tony®) Awards, presented each June by the American Theatre Wing and the League of American Theatres and Producers, honor distinguished achievement in Broadway theater.

1947

ACTORS — PLAY
José Ferrer, *Cyrano de Bergerac*
Fredric March, *Years Ago*

ACTRESSES — PLAY
Ingrid Bergman, *Joan of Lorraine*
Helen Hayes, *Happy Birthday*

SUPPORTING OR FEATURED ACTRESS — PLAY
Patricia Neal, *Another Part of the Forest*

SUPPORTING OR FEATURED ACTOR — MUSICAL
David Wayne, *Finian's Rainbow*

DIRECTOR
Elia Kazan, *All My Sons*

COSTUME DESIGNER
Lucinda Ballard, *Happy Birthday, Another Part of the Forest, Street Scene, John Loves Mary* and *The Chocolate Soldier*

CHOREOGRAPHERS
Agnes De Mille, *Brigadoon*
Michael Kidd, *Finian's Rainbow*

SPECIAL AWARDS
Dora Chamberlain
Mr. and Mrs. Ira Katzenberg
Jules Leventhal
P.A. MacDonald
Burns Mantle
Arthur Miller
Vincent Sardi, Sr.
Kurt Weill

1948

PLAY
Mister Roberts, Thomas Heggen and Joshua Logan
(based on the Thomas Heggen novel)

ACTORS — PLAY
Henry Fonda, *Mister Roberts*
Paul Kelly, *Command Decision*
Basil Rathbone, *The Heiress*

ACTRESSES — PLAY
Judith Anderson, *Medea*
Katharine Cornell, *Antony and Cleopatra*
Jessica Tandy, *A Streetcar Named Desire*

ACTOR — MUSICAL
Paul Hartman, *Angel in the Wings*

Henry Fonda

ACTRESS — MUSICAL
Grace Hartman, *Angel in the Wings*

AUTHORS
Thomas Heggen and Joshua Logan, *Mister Roberts*

PRODUCER
Leland Hayward, *Mister Roberts*

SCENIC DESIGNER
Horace Armistead, *The Medium*

COSTUME DESIGNER
Mary Percy Schenck, *The Heiress*

CHOREOGRAPHER
Jerome Robbins, *High Button Shoes*

STAGE TECHNICIANS
George Gebhardt
George Pierce

SPECIAL AWARDS
Vera Allen
Paul Beisman
Joe E. Brown
Robert Dowling
Experimental Theatre, Inc.
Rosamond Gilder
June Lockhart
Mary Martin
Robert Porterfield
James Whitmore

1949

PLAY
Death of a Salesman, Arthur Miller

MUSICAL
Kiss Me Kate, Cole Porter, music and lyrics; Bella and Samuel Spewack, book

ACTOR — PLAY
Rex Harrison, *Anne of the Thousand Days*

ACTRESS — PLAY
Martita Hunt, *The Madwoman of Chaillot*

SUPPORTING OR FEATURED ACTOR — PLAY
Arthur Kennedy, *Death of a Salesman*

SUPPORTING OR FEATURED ACTRESS — PLAY
Shirley Booth, *Goodbye, My Fancy*

ACTOR — MUSICAL
Ray Bolger, *Where's Charley?*

ACTRESS — MUSICAL
Nanette Fabray, *Love Life*

AUTHOR — PLAY
Arthur Miller, *Death of a Salesman*

AUTHOR — MUSICAL
Bella and Samuel Spewack, *Kiss Me Kate*

DIRECTOR
Elia Kazan, *Death of a Salesman*

PRODUCERS — PLAY
Kermit Bloomgarden and Walter Fried, *Death of a Salesman*

PRODUCERS — MUSICAL
Saint-Subber and Lemuel Ayers, *Kiss Me Kate*

COMPOSER AND LYRICIST
Cole Porter, *Kiss Me Kate*

SCENIC DESIGNER
Jo Mielziner, *Sleepy Hollow, Summer and Smoke, Anne of the Thousand Days, Death of a Salesman* and *South Pacific*

COSTUME DESIGNER
Lemuel Ayers, *Kiss Me Kate*

CHOREOGRAPHER
Gower Champion, *Lend an Ear*

CONDUCTOR AND MUSICAL DIRECTOR
Max Meth, *As the Girls Go*

1950

PLAY
The Cocktail Party, T. S. Eliot

MUSICAL
South Pacific, Richard Rodgers, music; Oscar Hammerstein II, lyrics; Oscar Hammerstein II and Joshua Logan, book

ACTOR — PLAY
Sidney Blackmer, *Come Back, Little Sheba*

ACTRESS — PLAY
Shirley Booth, *Come Back, Little Sheba*

ACTOR — MUSICAL
Ezio Pinza, *South Pacific*

ACTRESS — MUSICAL
Mary Martin, *South Pacific*

SUPPORTING OR FEATURED ACTOR — MUSICAL
Myron McCormick, *South Pacific*

SUPPORTING OR FEATURED ACTRESS — MUSICAL
Juanita Hall, *South Pacific*

AUTHOR — PLAY
T. S. Eliot, *The Cocktail Party*

AUTHORS — MUSICAL
Oscar Hammerstein II and Joshua Logan, *South Pacific*

DIRECTOR
Joshua Logan, *South Pacific*

PRODUCER — PLAY
Gilbert Miller, *The Cocktail Party*

PRODUCERS — MUSICAL
Richard Rodgers, Oscar Hammerstein II, Leland Hayward and Joshua Logan, *South Pacific*

COMPOSER
Richard Rodgers, *South Pacific*

SCENIC DESIGNER
Jo Mielziner, *The Innocents*

COSTUME DESIGNER
Aline Bernstein, *Regina*

CHOREOGRAPHER
Helen Tamiris, *Touch and Go*

CONDUCTOR AND MUSICAL DIRECTOR
Maurice Abravanel, *Regina*

STAGE TECHNICIAN
Joe Lynn, *Miss Liberty*

SPECIAL AWARDS
Maurice Evans

Mrs. Eleanor Roosevelt presented a special award to a volunteer worker of the American Theatre Wing's hospital program

1951

PLAY
The Rose Tattoo, Tennessee Williams

MUSICAL
Guys and Dolls, Frank Loesser, music and lyrics; Jo Swerling and Abe Burrows, book

ACTOR — PLAY
Claude Rains, *Darkness at Noon*

ACTRESS — PLAY
Uta Hagen, *The Country Girl*

SUPPORTING OR FEATURED ACTOR — PLAY
Eli Wallach, *The Rose Tattoo*

SUPPORTING OR FEATURED ACTRESS — PLAY
Maureen Stapleton, *The Rose Tattoo*

ACTOR — MUSICAL
Robert Alda, *Guys and Dolls*

ACTRESS — MUSICAL
Ethel Merman, *Call Me Madam*

SUPPORTING OR FEATURED ACTOR — MUSICAL
Russell Nype, *Call Me Madam*

SUPPORTING OR FEATURED ACTRESS — MUSICAL
Isabel Bigley, *Guys and Dolls*

AUTHOR — PLAY
Tennessee Williams, *The Rose Tattoo*

AUTHORS — MUSICAL
Jo Swerling and Abe Burrows, *Guys and Dolls*

DIRECTOR
George S. Kaufman, *Guys and Dolls*

PRODUCER — PLAY
Cheryl Crawford, *The Rose Tattoo*

PRODUCERS — MUSICAL
Cy Feuer and Ernest H. Martin, *Guys and Dolls*

COMPOSER AND LYRICIST
Frank Loesser, *Guys and Dolls*

SCENIC DESIGNER
Boris Aronson, *The Rose Tattoo, The Country Girl* and *Season in the Sun*

COSTUME DESIGNER
Miles White, *Bless You All*

CHOREOGRAPHER
Michael Kidd, *Guys and Dolls*

CONDUCTOR AND MUSICAL DIRECTOR
Lehman Engel, *The Consul*

STAGE TECHNICIAN
Richard Raven, *The Autumn Garden*

SPECIAL AWARD
Ruth Green

1952

PLAY
The Fourposter, Jan de Hartog

MUSICAL
The King and I, Oscar Hammerstein II, book and lyrics; Richard Rodgers, music

ACTOR — PLAY
José Ferrer, *The Shrike*

ACTRESS — PLAY
Julie Harris, *I Am a Camera*

SUPPORTING OR FEATURED ACTOR — PLAY
John Cromwell, *Point of No Return*

SUPPORTING OR FEATURED ACTRESS — PLAY
Marian Winters, *I Am a Camera*

ACTOR — MUSICAL
Phil Silvers, *Top Banana*

ACTRESS — MUSICAL
Gertrude Lawrence, *The King and I*

SUPPORTING OR FEATURED ACTOR — MUSICAL
Yul Brynner, *The King and I*

SUPPORTING OR FEATURED ACTRESS — MUSICAL
Helen Gallagher, *Pal Joey*

DIRECTOR
José Ferrer, *The Shrike, The Fourposter* and *Stalag 17*

SCENIC DESIGNER
Jo Mielziner, *The King and I*

The King and I

COSTUME DESIGNER
Irene Sharaff, *The King and I*

CHOREOGRAPHER
Robert Alton, *Pal Joey*

CONDUCTOR AND MUSICAL DIRECTOR
Max Meth, *Pal Joey*

STAGE TECHNICIAN
Peter Feller, *Call Me Madam*

SPECIAL AWARDS
Edward Kook

Judy Garland

Charles Boyer

1953

PLAY
The Crucible, Arthur Miller

MUSICAL
Wonderful Town, Joseph Fields and Jerome Chodorov, book; Leonard Bernstein, music; Betty Comden and Adolph Green, lyrics

ACTOR — PLAY
Tom Ewell, *The Seven Year Itch*

ACTRESS — PLAY
Shirley Booth, *Time of the Cuckoo*

SUPPORTING OR FEATURED ACTOR — PLAY
John Williams, *Dial M for Murder*

SUPPORTING OR FEATURED ACTRESS — PLAY
Beatrice Straight, *The Crucible*

ACTOR — MUSICAL
Thomas Mitchell, *Hazel Flagg*

ACTRESS — MUSICAL
Rosalind Russell, *Wonderful Town*

SUPPORTING OR FEATURED ACTOR — MUSICAL
Hiram Sherman, *Two's Company*

SUPPORTING OR FEATURED ACTRESS — MUSICAL
Sheila Bond, *Wish You Were Here*

AUTHOR — PLAY
Arthur Miller, *The Crucible*

AUTHORS — MUSICAL
Joseph Fields and Jerome Chodorov, *Wonderful Town*

DIRECTOR
Joshua Logan, *Picnic*

PRODUCER — PLAY
Kermit Bloomgarden, *The Crucible*

PRODUCER — MUSICAL
Robert Fryer, *Wonderful Town*

COMPOSER
Leonard Bernstein, *Wonderful Town*

SCENIC DESIGNER
Raoul Pène Du Bois, *Wonderful Town*

COSTUME DESIGNER
Miles White, *Hazel Flagg*

CHOREOGRAPHER
Donald Saddler, *Wonderful Town*

CONDUCTOR AND MUSICAL DIRECTOR
Lehman Engel, *Wonderful Town* and Gilbert and Sullivan
    season

STAGE TECHNICIAN
Abe Kurnit, *Wish You Were Here*

SPECIAL AWARDS
Beatrice Lillie

Danny Kaye

Equity Community Theatre

1954

PLAY
The Teahouse of the August Moon, John Patrick

MUSICAL
Kismet, Charles Lederer and Luther Davis, book; Alexander
    Borodin, music; Robert Wright and George Forrest,
    adaptation and lyrics

ACTOR — PLAY
David Wayne, *The Teahouse of the August Moon*

ACTRESS — PLAY
Audrey Hepburn, *Ondine*

SUPPORTING OR FEATURED ACTOR — PLAY
John Kerr, *Tea and Sympathy*

SUPPORTING OR FEATURED ACTRESS — PLAY
Jo Van Fleet, *The Trip to Bountiful*

ACTOR — MUSICAL
Alfred Drake, *Kismet*

ACTRESS — MUSICAL
Dolores Gray, *Carnival in Flanders*

SUPPORTING OR FEATURED ACTOR — MUSICAL
Harry Belafonte, *John Murray Anderson's Almanac*

SUPPORTING OR FEATURED ACTRESS — MUSICAL
Gwen Verdon, *Can-Can*

AUTHOR — PLAY
John Patrick, *The Teahouse of the August Moon*

AUTHORS — MUSICAL
Charles Lederer and Luther Davis, *Kismet*

DIRECTOR
Alfred Lunt, *Ondine*

PRODUCERS — PLAY
Maurice Evans and George Schaefer, *The Teahouse of the
    August Moon*

PRODUCER — MUSICAL
Charles Lederer, *Kismet*

COMPOSER
Alexander Borodin, *Kismet*

SCENIC DESIGNER
Peter Larkin, *Ondine* and *The Teahouse of the August Moon*

COSTUME DESIGNER
Richard Whorf, *Ondine*

CHOREOGRAPHER
Michael Kidd, *Can-Can*

MUSICAL CONDUCTOR
Louis Adrian, *Kismet*

STAGE TECHNICIAN
John Davis, *Picnic*

1955

PLAY
The Desperate Hours, Joseph Hayes

MUSICAL
The Pajama Game, George Abbott and Richard Bissell, book;
    Richard Adler and Jerry Ross, music and lyrics

ACTOR — PLAY
Alfred Lunt, *Quadrille*

ACTRESS — PLAY
Nancy Kelly, *The Bad Seed*

SUPPORTING OR FEATURED ACTOR — PLAY
Francis L. Sullivan, *Witness for the Prosecution*

SUPPORTING OR FEATURED ACTRESS — PLAY
Patricia Jessel, *Witness for the Prosecution*

ACTOR — MUSICAL
Walter Slezak, *Fanny*

ACTRESS — MUSICAL
Mary Martin, *Peter Pan*

SUPPORTING OR FEATURED ACTOR — MUSICAL
Cyril Ritchard, *Peter Pan*

SUPPORTING OR FEATURED ACTRESS — MUSICAL
Carol Haney, *The Pajama Game*

AUTHOR — PLAY
Joseph Hayes, *The Desperate Hours*

AUTHORS — MUSICAL
George Abbott and Richard Bissell, *The Pajama Game*

DIRECTOR
Robert Montgomery, *The Desperate Hours*

PRODUCERS — PLAY
Howard Erskine and Joseph Hayes, *The Desperate Hours*

PRODUCERS — MUSICAL
Frederick Brisson, Robert Griffith and Harold S. Prince, *The
    Pajama Game*

COMPOSER AND LYRICIST
Richard Adler and Jerry Ross, *The Pajama Game*

SCENIC DESIGNER
Oliver Messel, *House of Flowers*

COSTUME DESIGNER
Cecil Beaton, *Quadrille*

CHOREOGRAPHER
Bob Fosse, *The Pajama Game*

CONDUCTOR AND MUSICAL DIRECTOR
Thomas Schippers, *The Saint of Bleecker Street*

STAGE TECHNICIAN
Richard Rodda, *Peter Pan*

SPECIAL AWARD
Proscenium Productions

1956

PLAY
The Diary of Anne Frank, Frances Goodrich and Albert Hackett

MUSICAL
Damn Yankees, George Abbott and Douglass Wallop, book;
    Richard Adler and Jerry Ross, music

ACTOR — PLAY
Paul Muni, *Inherit the Wind*

ACTRESS — PLAY
Julie Harris, *The Lark*

SUPPORTING OR FEATURED ACTOR — PLAY
Ed Begley, *Inherit the Wind*

SUPPORTING OR FEATURED ACTRESS — PLAY
Una Merkel, *The Ponder Heart*

ACTOR — MUSICAL
Ray Walston, *Damn Yankees*

ACTRESS — MUSICAL
Gwen Verdon, *Damn Yankees*

SUPPORTING OR FEATURED ACTOR — MUSICAL
Russ Brown, *Damn Yankees*

SUPPORTING OR FEATURED ACTRESS — MUSICAL
Lotte Lenya, *The Threepenny Opera*

AUTHORS — PLAY
Frances Goodrich and Albert Hackett, *The Diary of Anne Frank*

AUTHORS — MUSICAL
George Abbott and Douglass Wallop, *Damn Yankees*

DIRECTOR
Tyrone Guthrie, *The Matchmaker*

PRODUCER — PLAY
Kermit Bloomgarden, *The Diary of Anne Frank*

PRODUCERS — MUSICAL
Frederick Brisson, Robert Griffith and Harold S. Prince in asso-
    ciation with Albert B. Taylor, *Damn Yankees*

COMPOSER AND LYRICIST
Richard Adler and Jerry Ross, *Damn Yankees*

SCENIC DESIGNER
Peter Larkin, *Inherit the Wind* and *No Time for Sergeants*

COSTUME DESIGNER
Alvin Colt, *Pipe Dream*

CHOREOGRAPHER
Bob Fosse, *Damn Yankees*

CONDUCTOR AND MUSICAL DIRECTOR
Hal Hastings, *Damn Yankees*

STAGE TECHNICIAN
Harry Green, *Middle of the Night* and *Damn Yankees*

SPECIAL AWARDS
The Threepenny Opera
The Theatre Collection of the New York Public Library

1957

PLAY
Long Day's Journey Into Night, Eugene O'Neill

MUSICAL
My Fair Lady, Alan Jay Lerner, book and lyrics; Frederick
    Loewe, music

ACTOR — PLAY
Fredric March, *Long Day's Journey Into Night*

ACTRESS — PLAY
Margaret Leighton, *Separate Tables*

SUPPORTING OR FEATURED ACTOR — PLAY
Frank Conroy, *The Potting Shed*

SUPPORTING OR FEATURED ACTRESS — PLAY
Peggy Cass, *Auntie Mame*

ACTOR — MUSICAL
Rex Harrison, *My Fair Lady*

ACTRESS — MUSICAL
Judy Holliday, *Bells Are Ringing*

SUPPORTING OR FEATURED ACTOR — MUSICAL
Sydney Chaplin, *Bells Are Ringing*

SUPPORTING OR FEATURED ACTRESS — MUSICAL
Edith Adams, *Li'l Abner*

AUTHOR — PLAY
Eugene O'Neill, *Long Day's Journey Into Night*

AUTHOR — MUSICAL
Alan Jay Lerner, *My Fair Lady*

DIRECTOR
Moss Hart, *My Fair Lady*

PRODUCERS — PLAY
Leigh Connell, Theodore Mann and José Quintero, *Long Day's
    Journey Into Night*

PRODUCER — MUSICAL
Herman Levin, *My Fair Lady*

COMPOSER
Frederick Loewe, *My Fair Lady*

SCENIC DESIGNER
Oliver Smith, *My Fair Lady*

COSTUME DESIGNER
Cecil Beaton, *My Fair Lady*

CHOREOGRAPHER
Michael Kidd, *Li'l Abner*

CONDUCTOR AND MUSICAL DIRECTOR
Franz Allers, *My Fair Lady*

STAGE TECHNICIAN
Howard McDonald, *Major Barbara*

SPECIAL AWARDS

American Shakespeare Festival

Jean-Louis Barrault — French Repertory

Robert Russell Bennett

William Hammerstein

Paul Shyre

1958

PLAY
Sunrise at Campobello, Dore Schary

MUSICAL
The Music Man, Meredith Willson and Franklin Lacey, book;
Meredith Willson, music and lyrics

ACTOR — PLAY
Ralph Bellamy, *Sunrise at Campobello*

ACTRESS — PLAY
Helen Hayes, *Time Remembered*

SUPPORTING OR FEATURED ACTOR — PLAY
Henry Jones, *Sunrise at Campobello*

SUPPORTING OR FEATURED ACTRESS — PLAY
Anne Bancroft, *Two for the Seesaw*

ACTOR — MUSICAL
Robert Preston, *The Music Man*

ACTRESSES — MUSICAL
Thelma Ritter, *New Girl in Town*
Gwen Verdon, *New Girl in Town*

SUPPORTING OR FEATURED ACTOR — MUSICAL
David Burns, *The Music Man*

SUPPORTING OR FEATURED ACTRESS — MUSICAL
Barbara Cook, *The Music Man*

AUTHOR — PLAY
Dore Schary, *Sunrise at Campobello*

AUTHORS — MUSICAL
Meredith Willson and Franklin Lacey, *The Music Man*

DIRECTOR — PLAY
Vincent J. Donehue, *Sunrise at Campobello*

PRODUCERS — PLAY
Lawrence Langner, Theresa Helburn, Armina Marshall and
Dore Schary, *Sunrise at Campobello*

PRODUCERS — MUSICAL
Kermit Bloomgarden, Herbert Greene and Frank Productions,
The Music Man

COMPOSER AND LYRICIST
Meredith Willson, *The Music Man*

SCENIC DESIGNER
Oliver Smith, *West Side Story*

COSTUME DESIGNER
Motley, *The First Gentleman*

CHOREOGRAPHER
Jerome Robbins, *West Side Story*

CONDUCTOR AND MUSICAL DIRECTOR
Herbert Greene, *The Music Man*

STAGE TECHNICIAN
Harry Romar, *Time Remembered*

Jerome Robbins

SPECIAL AWARDS

New York Shakespeare Festival

Mrs. Martin Beck

1959

PLAY
J. B., Archibald MacLeish

MUSICAL
Redhead, Herbert and Dorothy Fields, Sidney Sheldon and
David Shaw, book; Albert Hague, music; Dorothy Fields,
lyrics

ACTOR — PLAY
Jason Robards, Jr., *The Disenchanted*

ACTRESS — PLAY
Gertrude Berg, *A Majority of One*

SUPPORTING OR FEATURED ACTOR — PLAY
Charlie Ruggles, *The Pleasure of His Company*

SUPPORTING OR FEATURED ACTRESS — PLAY
Julie Newmar, *The Marriage-Go-Round*

ACTOR — MUSICAL
Richard Kiley, *Redhead*

ACTRESS — MUSICAL
Gwen Verdon, *Redhead*

SUPPORTING OR FEATURED ACTORS — MUSICAL
Russell Nype, *Goldilocks*
Cast of *La Plume de Ma Tante*

**SUPPORTING OR FEATURED ACTRESSES —
MUSICAL**
Pat Stanley, *Goldilocks*
Cast of *La Plume de Ma Tante*

AUTHOR — PLAY
Archibald MacLeish, *J. B.*

AUTHORS — MUSICAL
Herbert and Dorothy Fields, Sidney Sheldon and David Shaw,
Redhead

DIRECTOR
Elia Kazan, *J. B.*

PRODUCER — PLAY
Alfred de Liagre, Jr., *J. B.*

PRODUCERS — MUSICAL
Robert Fryer and Lawrence Carr, *Redhead*

COMPOSER
Albert Hague, *Redhead*

SCENIC DESIGNER
Donald Oenslager, *A Majority of One*

COSTUME DESIGNER
Rouben Ter-Arutunian, *Redhead*

CHOREOGRAPHER
Bob Fosse, *Redhead*

CONDUCTOR AND MUSICAL DIRECTOR
Salvatore Dell'Isola, *Flower Drum Song*

STAGE TECHNICIAN
Sam Knapp, *The Music Man*

SPECIAL AWARDS
John Gielgud
Howard Lindsay and Russel Crouse

1960

PLAY
A Raisin in the Sun, Lorraine Hansberry

MUSICALS
Fiorello!, Jerome Weidman and George Abbott, book; Jerry
   Bock, music; Sheldon Harnick, lyrics

The Sound of Music, Howard Lindsay and Russel Crouse,
   book; Richard Rodgers, music; Oscar Hammerstein II,
   lyrics

ACTOR — PLAY
Melvyn Douglas, *The Best Man*

ACTRESS — PLAY
Anne Bancroft, *The Miracle Worker*

SUPPORTING OR FEATURED ACTOR — PLAY
Roddy McDowall, *The Fighting Cock*

SUPPORTING OR FEATURED ACTRESS — PLAY
Anne Revere, *Toys in the Attic*

ACTOR — MUSICAL
Jackie Gleason, *Take Me Along*

ACTRESS — MUSICAL
Mary Martin, *The Sound of Music*

SUPPORTING OR FEATURED ACTOR — MUSICAL
Tom Bosley, *Fiorello!*

SUPPORTING OR FEATURED ACTRESS — MUSICAL
Patricia Neway, *The Sound of Music*

AUTHOR — PLAY
William Gibson, *The Miracle Worker*

AUTHORS — MUSICAL
Jerome Weidman and George Abbott, *Fiorello!*
Howard Lindsay and Russel Crouse, *The Sound of Music*

DIRECTOR — PLAY
Arthur Penn, *The Miracle Worker*

DIRECTOR — MUSICAL
George Abbott, *Fiorello!*

PRODUCER — PLAY
Fred Coe, *The Miracle Worker*

PRODUCERS — MUSICAL
Robert Griffith and Harold Prince, *Fiorello!*
Leland Hayward and Richard Halliday, *The Sound of Music*

COMPOSERS
Jerry Bock, *Fiorello!*
Richard Rodgers, *The Sound of Music*

SCENIC DESIGNER — DRAMATIC
Howard Bay, *Toys in the Attic*

SCENIC DESIGNER — MUSICAL
Oliver Smith, *The Sound of Music*

COSTUME DESIGNER
Cecil Beaton, *Saratoga*

CHOREOGRAPHER
Michael Kidd, *Destry Rides Again*

CONDUCTOR AND MUSICAL DIRECTOR
Frederick Dvonch, *The Sound of Music*

STAGE TECHNICIAN
John Walters, *The Miracle Worker*

SPECIAL AWARDS
John D. Rockefeller III
James Thurber and Burgess Meredith, *A Thurber Carnival*

1961

PLAY
Becket, Jean Anouilh (translated by Lucienne Hill)

MUSICAL
Bye, Bye Birdie, Michael Stewart, book; Charles Strouse,
   music; Lee Adams, lyrics

ACTOR — PLAY
Zero Mostel, *Rhinoceros*

ACTRESS — PLAY
Joan Plowright, *A Taste of Honey*

SUPPORTING OR FEATURED ACTOR — PLAY
Martin Gabel, *Big Fish, Little Fish*

SUPPORTING OR FEATURED ACTRESS — PLAY
Colleen Dewhurst, *All the Way Home*

ACTOR — MUSICAL
Richard Burton, *Camelot*

ACTRESS — MUSICAL
Elizabeth Seal, *Irma la Douce*

SUPPORTING OR FEATURED ACTOR — MUSICAL
Dick Van Dyke, *Bye, Bye Birdie*

SUPPORTING OR FEATURED ACTRESS — MUSICAL
Tammy Grimes, *The Unsinkable Molly Brown*

AUTHOR — PLAY
Jean Anouilh, *Becket*

AUTHOR — MUSICAL
Michael Stewart, *Bye, Bye Birdie*

DIRECTOR — PLAY
Sir John Gielgud, *Big Fish, Little Fish*

Richard Burton, *Camelot*

DIRECTOR — MUSICAL
Gower Champion, *Bye, Bye Birdie*

PRODUCER — PLAY
David Merrick, *Becket*

PRODUCER — MUSICAL
Edward Padula, *Bye, Bye Birdie*

SCENIC DESIGNER — PLAY
Oliver Smith, *Becket*

SCENIC DESIGNER — MUSICAL
Oliver Smith, *Camelot*

COSTUME DESIGNER — PLAY
Motley, *Becket*

COSTUME DESIGNERS — MUSICAL
Adrian and Tony Duquette, *Camelot*

CHOREOGRAPHER
Gower Champion, *Bye, Bye Birdie*

CONDUCTOR AND MUSICAL DIRECTOR
Franz Allers, *Camelot*

STAGE TECHNICIAN
Teddy Van Bemmel, *Becket*

SPECIAL AWARDS
David Merrick
The Theatre Guild

1962

PLAY
A Man for All Seasons, Robert Bolt

MUSICAL
How to Succeed in Business Without Really Trying, Abe Burrows, Jack Weinstock and Willie Gilbert, book; Frank Loesser, music and lyrics

ACTOR — PLAY
Paul Scofield, *A Man for All Seasons*

ACTRESS — PLAY
Margaret Leighton, *Night of the Iguana*

SUPPORTING OR FEATURED ACTOR — PLAY
Walter Matthau, *A Shot in the Dark*

SUPPORTING OR FEATURED ACTRESS — PLAY
Elizabeth Ashley, *Take Her, She's Mine*

ACTOR — MUSICAL
Robert Morse, *How to Succeed in Business Without Really Trying*

ACTRESSES — MUSICAL
Anna Maria Alberghetti, *Carnival*
Diahann Carroll, *No Strings*

SUPPORTING OR FEATURED ACTOR — MUSICAL
Charles Nelson Reilly, *How to Succeed in Business Without Really Trying*

SUPPORTING OR FEATURED ACTRESS — MUSICAL
Phyllis Newman, *Subways Are for Sleeping*

AUTHOR — PLAY
Robert Bolt, *A Man for All Seasons*

AUTHORS — MUSICAL
Abe Burrows, Jack Weinstock and Willie Gilbert, *How to Succeed in Business Without Really Trying*

DIRECTOR — PLAY
Noel Willman, *A Man for All Seasons*

DIRECTOR — MUSICAL
Abe Burrows, *How to Succeed in Business Without Really Trying*

PRODUCERS — PLAY
Robert Whitehead and Roger L. Stevens, *A Man for All Seasons*

PRODUCERS — MUSICAL
Cy Feuer and Ernest Martin, *How to Succeed in Business Without Really Trying*

COMPOSER
Richard Rodgers, *No Strings*

SCENIC DESIGNER
Will Steven Armstrong, *Carnival*

COSTUME DESIGNER
Lucinda Ballard, *The Gay Life*

CHOREOGRAPHERS
Agnes De Mille, *Kwamina*
Joe Layton, *No Strings*

CONDUCTOR AND MUSICAL DIRECTOR
Elliot Lawrence, *How to Succeed in Business Without Really Trying*

STAGE TECHNICIAN
Michael Burns, *A Man for All Seasons*

SPECIAL AWARDS
Brooks Atkinson
Franco Zeffirelli
Richard Rodgers
Richard Rodgers, *No Strings*

1963

PLAY
Who's Afraid of Virginia Woolf?, Edward Albee

MUSICAL
A Funny Thing Happened on the Way to the Forum, Burt Shevelove and Larry Gelbart, book; Stephen Sondheim, music and lyrics

ACTOR — PLAY
Arthur Hill, *Who's Afraid of Virginia Woolf?*

ACTRESS — PLAY
Uta Hagen, *Who's Afraid of Virginia Woolf?*

SUPPORTING OR FEATURED ACTOR — PLAY
Alan Arkin, *Enter Laughing*

SUPPORTING OR FEATURED ACTRESS — PLAY
Sandy Dennis, *A Thousand Clowns*

ACTOR — MUSICAL
Zero Mostel, *A Funny Thing Happened on the Way to the Forum*

ACTRESS — MUSICAL
Vivien Leigh, *Tovarich*

Alec Guinness, *Dylan*

SUPPORTING OR FEATURED ACTOR — MUSICAL
David Burns, *A Funny Thing Happened on the Way to the Forum*

SUPPORTING OR FEATURED ACTRESS — MUSICAL
Anna Quayle, *Stop the World — I Want to Get Off*

AUTHORS — MUSICAL
Burt Shevelove and Larry Gelbart, *A Funny Thing Happened on the Way to the Forum*

DIRECTOR — PLAY
Alan Schneider, *Who's Afraid of Virginia Woolf?*

DIRECTOR — MUSICAL
George Abbott, *A Funny Thing Happened on the Way to the Forum*

PRODUCERS — PLAY
Richard Barr and Clinton Wilder, Theatre 1963, *Who's Afraid of Virginia Woolf?*

PRODUCER — MUSICAL
Harold Prince, *A Funny Thing Happened on the Way to the Forum*

COMPOSER AND LYRICIST
Lionel Bart, *Oliver!*

SCENIC DESIGNER
Sean Kenny, *Oliver!*

COSTUME DESIGNER
Anthony Powell, *The School for Scandal*

CHOREOGRAPHER
Bob Fosse, *Little Me*

CONDUCTOR AND MUSICAL DIRECTOR
Donald Pippin, *Oliver!*

STAGE TECHNICIAN
Solly Pernick, *Mr. President*

SPECIAL AWARDS
W. McNeil Lowry

Irving Berlin

Alan Bennett

Peter Cook

Jonathan Miller

Dudley Moore

1964

PLAY
Luther, John Osborne

MUSICAL
Hello, Dolly!, Michael Stewart, book; Jerry Herman, music and lyrics

ACTOR — PLAY
Alec Guinness, *Dylan*

ACTRESS — PLAY
Sandy Dennis, *Any Wednesday*

SUPPORTING OR FEATURED ACTOR — PLAY
Hume Cronyn, *Hamlet*

SUPPORTING OR FEATURED ACTRESS — PLAY
Barbara Loden, *After the Fall*

ACTOR — MUSICAL
Bert Lahr, *Foxy*

ACTRESS — MUSICAL
Carol Channing, *Hello, Dolly!*

SUPPORTING OR FEATURED ACTOR — MUSICAL
Jack Cassidy, *She Loves Me*

SUPPORTING OR FEATURED ACTRESS — MUSICAL
Tessie O'Shea, *The Girl Who Came to Supper*

AUTHOR — PLAY
John Osborne, *Luther*

AUTHOR — MUSICAL
Michael Stewart, *Hello, Dolly!*

DIRECTOR — PLAY
Mike Nichols, *Barefoot in the Park*

DIRECTOR — MUSICAL
Gower Champion, *Hello, Dolly!*

PRODUCER — PLAY
Herman Shumlin, *The Deputy*

PRODUCER — MUSICAL
David Merrick, *Hello, Dolly!*

COMPOSER AND LYRICIST
Jerry Herman, *Hello, Dolly!*

SCENIC DESIGNER
Oliver Smith, *Hello, Dolly!*

COSTUME DESIGNER
Freddy Wittop, *Hello, Dolly!*

CHOREOGRAPHER
Gower Champion, *Hello, Dolly!*

CONDUCTOR AND MUSICAL DIRECTOR
Shepard Coleman, *Hello, Dolly!*

SPECIAL AWARD
Eva Le Gallienne

1965

PLAY
The Subject Was Roses, Frank Gilroy

MUSICAL
Fiddler on the Roof, Joseph Stein, book; Jerry Bock, music; Sheldon Harnick, lyrics

ACTOR — PLAY
Walter Matthau, *The Odd Couple*

ACTRESS — PLAY
Irene Worth, *Tiny Alice*

SUPPORTING OR FEATURED ACTOR — PLAY
Jack Albertson, *The Subject Was Roses*

SUPPORTING OR FEATURED ACTRESS — PLAY
Alice Ghostley, *The Sign in Sidney Brustein's Window*

ACTOR — MUSICAL
Zero Mostel, *Fiddler on the Roof*

ACTRESS — MUSICAL
Liza Minnelli, *Flora, the Red Menace*

SUPPORTING OR FEATURED ACTOR — MUSICAL
Victor Spinetti, *Oh, What a Lovely War*

SUPPORTING OR FEATURED ACTRESS — MUSICAL
Maria Karnilova, *Fiddler on the Roof*

AUTHOR — PLAY
Neil Simon, *The Odd Couple*

AUTHOR — MUSICAL
Joseph Stein, *Fiddler on the Roof*

DIRECTOR — PLAY
Mike Nichols, *Luv* and *The Odd Couple*

DIRECTOR — MUSICAL
Jerome Robbins, *Fiddler on the Roof*

PRODUCER — PLAY
Claire Nichtern, *Luv*

PRODUCER — MUSICAL
Harold Prince, *Fiddler on the Roof*

COMPOSER AND LYRICIST
Jerry Bock and Sheldon Harnick, *Fiddler on the Roof*

SCENIC DESIGNER
Oliver Smith, *Baker Street*

COSTUME DESIGNER
Patricia Zipprodt, *Fiddler on the Roof*

CHOREOGRAPHER
Jerome Robbins, *Fiddler on the Roof*

SPECIAL AWARDS
Gilbert Miller

Oliver Smith

1966

PLAY
Marat/Sade, Peter Weiss (English version by Geoffrey Skelton)

MUSICAL
Man of La Mancha, Dale Wasserman, book; Mitch Leigh, music; Joe Darion, lyrics

ACTOR — PLAY
Hal Holbrook, *Mark Twain Tonight!*

ACTRESS — PLAY
Rosemary Harris, *The Lion in Winter*

SUPPORTING OR FEATURED ACTOR — PLAY
Patrick Magee, *Marat/Sade*

SUPPORTING OR FEATURED ACTRESS — PLAY
Zoe Caldwell, *Slapstick Tragedy*

ACTOR — MUSICAL
Richard Kiley, *Man of La Mancha*

ACTRESS — MUSICAL
Angela Lansbury, *Mame*

SUPPORTING OR FEATURED ACTOR — MUSICAL
Frankie Michaels, *Mame*

SUPPORTING OR FEATURED ACTRESS — MUSICAL
Beatrice Arthur, *Mame*

DIRECTOR — PLAY
Peter Brook, *Marat/Sade*

DIRECTOR — MUSICAL
Albert Marre, *Man of La Mancha*

COMPOSER AND LYRICIST
Mitch Leigh and Joe Darion, *Man of La Mancha*

SCENIC DESIGNER
Howard Bay, *Man of La Mancha*

COSTUME DESIGNER
Gunilla Palmstierna-Weiss, *Marat/Sade*

CHOREOGRAPHER
Bob Fosse, *Sweet Charity*

SPECIAL AWARD
Helen Menken (posthumous)

1967

PLAY
The Homecoming, Harold Pinter

MUSICAL
Cabaret, Joe Masteroff, book; John Kander, music; Fred Ebb, lyrics

ACTOR — PLAY
Paul Rogers, *The Homecoming*

ACTRESS — PLAY
Beryl Reid, *The Killing of Sister George*

SUPPORTING OR FEATURED ACTOR — PLAY
Ian Holm, *The Homecoming*

SUPPORTING OR FEATURED ACTRESS — PLAY
Marian Seldes, *A Delicate Balance*

ACTOR — MUSICAL
Robert Preston, *I Do! I Do!*

ACTRESS — MUSICAL
Barbara Harris, *The Apple Tree*

SUPPORTING OR FEATURED ACTOR — MUSICAL
Joel Grey, *Cabaret*

SUPPORTING OR FEATURED ACTRESS — MUSICAL
Peg Murray, *Cabaret*

DIRECTOR — PLAY
Peter Hall, *The Homecoming*

DIRECTOR — MUSICAL
Harold Prince, *Cabaret*

COMPOSER AND LYRICIST
John Kander and Fred Ebb, *Cabaret*

SCENIC DESIGNER
Boris Aronson, *Cabaret*

COSTUME DESIGNER
Patricia Zipprodt, *Cabaret*

CHOREOGRAPHER
Ron Field, *Cabaret*

1968

PLAY
Rosencrantz and Guildenstern Are Dead, Tom Stoppard

MUSICAL
Hallelujah, Baby!, Arthur Laurents, book; Jule Styne, music; Betty Comden and Adolph Green, lyrics

ACTOR — PLAY
Martin Balsam, *You Know I Can't Hear You When the Water's Running*

ACTRESS — PLAY
Zoe Caldwell, *The Prime of Miss Jean Brodie*

SUPPORTING OR FEATURED ACTOR — PLAY
James Patterson, *The Birthday Party*

SUPPORTING OR FEATURED ACTRESS — PLAY
Zena Walker, *Joe Egg*

ACTOR — MUSICAL
Robert Goulet, *The Happy Time*

ACTRESSES — MUSICAL
Patricia Routledge, *Darling of the Day*
Leslie Uggams, *Hallelujah, Baby!*

SUPPORTING OR FEATURED ACTOR — MUSICAL
Hiram Sherman, *How Now, Dow Jones*

SUPPORTING OR FEATURED ACTRESS — MUSICAL
Lillian Hayman, *Hallelujah, Baby!*

DIRECTOR — PLAY
Mike Nichols, *Plaza Suite*

DIRECTOR — MUSICAL
Gower Champion, *The Happy Time*

PRODUCER — PLAY
David Merrick Arts Foundation, *Rosencrantz and Guildenstern Are Dead*

PRODUCERS — MUSICAL
Albert Selden, Hal James, Jane C. Nusbaum and Harry Rigby, *Hallelujah, Baby!*

COMPOSER AND LYRICIST
Jule Styne, Betty Comden and Adolph Green, *Hallelujah, Baby!*

SCENIC DESIGNER
Desmond Heeley, *Rosencrantz and Guildenstern Are Dead*

COSTUME DESIGNER
Desmond Heeley, *Rosencrantz and Guildenstern Are Dead*

CHOREOGRAPHER
Gower Champion, *The Happy Time*

SPECIAL
AWARDS
Audrey Hepburn
Carol Channing
Pearl Bailey
David Merrick
Maurice Chevalier
APA-Phoenix Theatre
Marlene Dietrich

1969

PLAY
The Great White Hope, Howard Sackler

MUSICAL
1776, Peter Stone, book; Sherman Edwards, music and lyrics

Angela Lansbury

ACTOR — PLAY
James Earl Jones, *The Great White Hope*

ACTRESS — PLAY
Julie Harris, *Forty Carats*

SUPPORTING OR FEATURED ACTOR — PLAY
Al Pacino, *Does a Tiger Wear a Necktie?*

SUPPORTING OR FEATURED ACTRESS — PLAY
Jane Alexander, *The Great White Hope*

ACTOR — MUSICAL
Jerry Orbach, *Promises, Promises*

ACTRESS — MUSICAL
Angela Lansbury, *Dear World*

SUPPORTING OR FEATURED ACTOR — MUSICAL
Ronald Holgate, *1776*

SUPPORTING OR FEATURED ACTRESS — MUSICAL
Marian Mercer, *Promises, Promises*

DIRECTOR — PLAY
Peter Dews, *Hadrian VII*

DIRECTOR — MUSICAL
Peter Hunt, *1776*

SCENIC DESIGNER
Boris Aronson, *Zorba*

COSTUME DESIGNER
Louden Sainthill, *Canterbury Tales*

CHOREOGRAPHER
Joe Layton, *George M!*

SPECIAL AWARDS
The National Theatre Company of Great Britain
The Negro Ensemble Company
Rex Harrison
Leonard Bernstein
Carol Burnett

1970

PLAY
Borstal Boy, Frank McMahon

MUSICAL
Applause, Betty Comden and Adolph Green, book; Charles
Strouse, music; Lee Adams, lyrics

ACTOR — PLAY
Fritz Weaver, *Child's Play*

ACTRESS — PLAY
Tammy Grimes, *Private Lives* (Revival)

SUPPORTING OR FEATURED ACTOR — PLAY
Ken Howard, *Child's Play*

SUPPORTING OR FEATURED ACTRESS — PLAY
Blythe Danner, *Butterflies Are Free*

ACTOR — MUSICAL
Cleavon Little, *Purlie*

ACTRESS — MUSICAL
Lauren Bacall, *Applause*

SUPPORTING OR FEATURED ACTOR — MUSICAL
René Auberjonois, *Coco*

SUPPORTING OR FEATURED ACTRESS — MUSICAL
Melba Moore, *Purlie*

DIRECTOR — PLAY
Joseph Hardy, *Child's Play*

DIRECTOR — MUSICAL
Ron Field, *Applause*

SCENIC DESIGNER
Jo Mielziner, *Child's Play*

COSTUME DESIGNER
Cecil Beaton, *Coco*

CHOREOGRAPHER
Ron Field, *Applause*

LIGHTING DESIGNER
Jo Mielziner, *Child's Play*

SPECIAL AWARDS
Noel Coward
Alfred Lunt and Lynn Fontanne
New York Shakespeare Festival
Barbra Streisand

1971

PLAY
Sleuth, Anthony Shaffer

MUSICAL
Company

ACTOR — PLAY
Brian Bedford, *The School for Wives*

ACTRESS — PLAY
Maureen Stapleton, *Gingerbread Lady*

SUPPORTING OR FEATURED ACTOR — PLAY
Paul Sand, *Story Theatre*

SUPPORTING OR FEATURED ACTRESS — PLAY
Rae Allen, *And Miss Reardon Drinks a Little*

ACTOR — MUSICAL
Hal Linden, *The Rothschilds*

ACTRESS — MUSICAL
Helen Gallagher, *No, No, Nanette*

SUPPORTING OR FEATURED ACTOR — MUSICAL
Keene Curtis, *The Rothschilds*

SUPPORTING OR FEATURED ACTRESS — MUSICAL
Patsy Kelly, *No, No, Nanette*

DIRECTOR — DRAMATIC
Peter Brook, *A Midsummer Night's Dream*

DIRECTOR — MUSICAL
Harold Prince, *Company*

PRODUCERS — PLAY
Helen Bonfils, Morton Gottlieb and Michael White, *Sleuth*

PRODUCER — MUSICAL
Harold Prince, *Company*

BOOK — MUSICAL
George Furth, *Company*

LYRICS — MUSICAL
Stephen Sondheim, *Company*

SCORE — MUSICAL
Stephen Sondheim, *Company*

SCENIC DESIGNER
Boris Aronson, *Company*

COSTUME DESIGNER
Raoul Pène Du Bois, *No, No, Nanette*

CHOREOGRAPHER
Donald Saddler, *No, No, Nanette*

LIGHTING DESIGNER
H. R. Poindexter, *Story Theatre*

SPECIAL AWARDS
Elliot Norton
Ingram Ash
Playbill
Roger L. Stevens

1972

PLAY
Sticks and Bones, David Rabe

MUSICAL
Two Gentlemen of Verona

ACTOR — PLAY
Cliff Gorman, *Lenny*

ACTRESS — PLAY
Sada Thompson, *Twigs*

SUPPORTING OR FEATURED ACTOR — PLAY
Vincent Gardenia, *The Prisoner of Second Avenue*

SUPPORTING OR FEATURED ACTRESS — PLAY
Elizabeth Wilson, *Sticks and Bones*

ACTOR — MUSICAL
Phil Silvers, *A Funny Thing Happened on the Way to the Forum*

ACTRESS — MUSICAL
Alexis Smith, *Follies*

SUPPORTING OR FEATURED ACTOR — MUSICAL
Larry Blyden, *A Funny Thing Happened on the Way to the Forum*

SUPPORTING OR FEATURED ACTRESS — MUSICAL
Linda Hopkins, *Inner City*

DIRECTOR — PLAY
Mike Nichols, *The Prisoner of Second Avenue*

DIRECTORS — MUSICAL
Harold Prince and Michael Bennett, *Follies*

BOOK — MUSICAL
Two Gentlemen of Verona, John Guare and Mel Shapiro

SCORE — MUSICAL
Follies, Stephen Sondheim, music and lyrics

SCENIC DESIGNER
Boris Aronson, *Follies*

COSTUME DESIGNER
Florence Klotz, *Follies*

CHOREOGRAPHER
Michael Bennett, *Follies*

LIGHTING DESIGNER
Tharon Musser, *Follies*

SPECIAL AWARDS
The Theatre Guild — American Theatre Society
Richard Rodgers
Fiddler on the Roof
Ethel Merman

1973

PLAY
That Championship Season, Jason Miller

MUSICAL
A Little Night Music

ACTOR — PLAY
Alan Bates, *Butley*

ACTRESS — PLAY
Julie Harris, *The Last of Mrs. Lincoln*

SUPPORTING OR FEATURED ACTOR — PLAY
John Lithgow, *The Changing Room*

SUPPORTING OR FEATURED ACTRESS — PLAY
Leora Dana, *The Last of Mrs. Lincoln*

ACTOR — MUSICAL
Ben Vereen, *Pippin*

ACTRESS — MUSICAL
Glynis Johns, *A Little Night Music*

SUPPORTING OR FEATURED ACTOR — MUSICAL
George S. Irving, *Irene*

**Phil Silvers, *A Funny Thing
Happened on the Way to the Forum***

SUPPORTING OR FEATURED ACTRESS — MUSICAL
Patricia Elliot, *A Little Night Music*

DIRECTOR — PLAY
A. J. Antoon, *That Championship Season*

DIRECTOR — MUSICAL
Bob Fosse, *Pippin*

BOOK — MUSICAL
A Little Night Music, Hugh Wheeler

SCORE — MUSICAL
A Little Night Music, Stephen Sondheim, music and lyrics

SCENIC DESIGNER
Tony Walton, *Pippin*

COSTUME DESIGNER
Florence Klotz, *A Little Night Music*

CHOREOGRAPHER
Bob Fosse, *Pippin*

LIGHTING DESIGNER
Jules Fisher, *Pippin*

SPECIAL AWARDS
John Lindsay
Actors' Fund of America
Shubert Organization

1974

PLAY
The River Niger, Joseph A. Walker

MUSICAL
Raisin

ACTOR — PLAY
Michael Moriarty, *Find Your Way Home*

ACTRESS — PLAY
Colleen Dewhurst, *A Moon for the Misbegotten*

SUPPORTING OR FEATURED ACTOR — PLAY
Ed Flanders, *A Moon for the Misbegotten*

SUPPORTING OR FEATURED ACTRESS — PLAY
Frances Sternhagen, *The Good Doctor*

ACTOR — MUSICAL
Christopher Plummer, *Cyrano*

ACTRESS — MUSICAL
Virginia Capers, *Raisin*

SUPPORTING OR FEATURED ACTOR — MUSICAL
Tommy Tune, *Seesaw*

SUPPORTING OR FEATURED ACTRESS — MUSICAL
Janie Sell, *Over Here!*

DIRECTOR — PLAY
José Quintero, *A Moon for the Misbegotten*

DIRECTOR — MUSICAL
Harold Prince, *Candide*

BOOK — MUSICAL
Candide, Hugh Wheeler

SCORE
Gigi, Frederick Loewe, music; Alan Jay Lerner, lyrics

SCENIC DESIGNERS
Franne and Eugene Lee, *Candide*

COSTUME DESIGNER
Franne Lee, *Candide*

CHOREOGRAPHER
Michael Bennett, *Seesaw*

LIGHTING DESIGNER
Jules Fisher, *Ulysses in Nighttown*

SPECIAL AWARDS
Liza Minnelli

Bette Midler

Peter Cook and Dudley Moore, *Good Evening*

A Moon for the Misbegotten

Candide

Actors' Equity Association

Theatre Development Fund

John F. Wharton

Harold Friedlander

1975

PLAY
Equus, Peter Shaffer

MUSICAL
The Wiz

ACTORS — PLAY
John Kani and Winston Ntshona, *Sizwe Banzi Is Dead* and *The Island*

ACTRESS — PLAY
Ellen Burstyn, *Same Time, Next Year*

SUPPORTING OR FEATURED ACTOR — PLAY
Frank Langella, *Seascape*

SUPPORTING OR FEATURED ACTRESS — PLAY
Rita Moreno, *The Ritz*

ACTOR — MUSICAL
John Cullum, *Shenandoah*

ACTRESS — MUSICAL
Angela Lansbury, *Gypsy*

SUPPORTING OR FEATURED ACTOR — MUSICAL
Ted Ross, *The Wiz*

SUPPORTING OR FEATURED ACTRESS — MUSICAL
Dee Dee Bridgewater, *The Wiz*

DIRECTOR — PLAY
John Dexter, *Equus*

DIRECTOR — MUSICAL
Geoffrey Holder, *The Wiz*

BOOK — MUSICAL
Shenandoah, James Lee Barrett, Peter Udell and Philip Rose

SCORE
The Wiz, Charlie Smalls, music and lyrics

SCENIC DESIGNER
Carl Toms, *Sherlock Holmes*

COSTUME DESIGNER
Geoffrey Holder, *The Wiz*

CHOREOGRAPHER
George Faison, *The Wiz*

LIGHTING DESIGNER
Neil Peter Jampolis, *Sherlock Holmes*

SPECIAL AWARDS
Neil Simon

Al Hirschfeld

1976

PLAY
Travesties, Tom Stoppard

MUSICAL
A Chorus Line

ACTOR — PLAY
John Wood, *Travesties*

ACTRESS — PLAY
Irene Worth, *Sweet Bird of Youth*

FEATURED ACTOR — PLAY
Edward Herrmann, *Mrs. Warren's Profession*

FEATURED ACTRESS — PLAY
Shirley Knight, *Kennedy's Children*

ACTOR — MUSICAL
George Rose, *My Fair Lady*

ACTRESS — MUSICAL
Donna McKechnie, *A Chorus Line*

FEATURED ACTOR — MUSICAL
Sammy Williams, *A Chorus Line*

FEATURED ACTRESS — MUSICAL
Carole Bishop, *A Chorus Line*

DIRECTOR — PLAY
Ellis Rabb, *The Royal Family*

DIRECTOR — MUSICAL
Michael Bennett, *A Chorus Line*

BOOK — MUSICAL
A Chorus Line, James Kirkwood and Nicholas Dante

SCORE
A Chorus Line, Marvin Hamlisch, music; Edward Kleban, lyrics

SCENIC DESIGNER
Boris Aronson, *Pacific Overtures*

COSTUME DESIGNER
Florence Klotz, *Pacific Overtures*

CHOREOGRAPHERS
Michael Bennet and Bob Avian, *A Chorus Line*

LIGHTING DESIGNER
Tharon Musser, *A Chorus Line*

SPECIAL AWARDS
Mathilde Pincus, *Circle in the Square*
Thomas H. Fitzgerald, *The Arena Stage*
Richard Burton, *Equus*

1977

PLAY
The Shadow Box, Michael Cristofer

MUSICAL
Annie

ACTOR — PLAY
Al Pacino, *The Basic Training of Pavlo Hummel*

ACTRESS — PLAY
Julie Harris, *The Belle of Amherst*

FEATURED ACTOR — PLAY
Jonathan Pryce, *Comedians*

FEATURED ACTRESS — PLAY
Trazana Beverley, *For Colored Girls Who Have Considered Suicide When the Rainbow is Enuf*

ACTOR — MUSICAL
Barry Bostwick, *The Robber Bridegroom*

ACTRESS — MUSICAL
Dorothy Loudon, *Annie*

FEATURED ACTOR — MUSICAL
Lenny Baker, *I Love My Wife*

FEATURED ACTRESS — MUSICAL
Delores Hall, *Your Arm's Too Short to Box With God*

DIRECTOR — PLAY
Gordon Davidson, *The Shadow Box*

DIRECTOR — MUSICAL
Gene Saks, *I Love My Wife*

BOOK — MUSICAL
Annie, Thomas Meehan

SCORE
Annie, Charles Strouse, music; Martin Charnin, lyrics

SCENIC DESIGNER
David Mitchell, *Annie*

COSTUME DESIGNERS
Theoni V. Aldredge, *Annie*
Santo Loquasto, *The Cherry Orchard*

CHOREOGRAPHER
Peter Gennaro, *Annie*

LIGHTING DESIGNER
Jennifer Tipton, *The Cherry Orchard*

MOST INNOVATIVE PRODUCTION OF A REVIVAL
Porgy and Bess, Sherwin M. Goldman and Houston Grand Opera, producers

SPECIAL AWARDS
Lily Tomlin
Barry Manilow
Diana Ross
National Theatre for the Deaf
Mark Taper Forum
Equity Library Theatre

1978

PLAY
Da, Hugh Leonard

MUSICAL
Ain't Misbehavin'

ACTOR — PLAY
Barnard Hughes, *Da*

Liza Minnelli

ACTRESS — PLAY
Jessica Tandy, *The Gin Game*

FEATURED ACTOR — PLAY
Lester Rawlins, *Da*

FEATURED ACTRESS — PLAY
Ann Wedgeworth, *Chapter Two*

ACTOR — MUSICAL
John Cullum, *On the Twentieth Century*

ACTRESS — MUSICAL
Liza Minnelli, *The Act*

FEATURED ACTOR — MUSICAL
Kevin Kline, *On the Twentieth Century*

FEATURED ACTRESS — MUSICAL
Nell Carter, *Ain't Misbehavin'*

DIRECTOR — PLAY
Melvin Bernhardt, *Da*

DIRECTOR — MUSICAL
Richard Maltby, Jr., *Ain't Misbehavin'*

BOOK — MUSICAL
On the Twentieth Century, Betty Comden and Adolph Green

SCORE
On the Twentieth Century, Cy Coleman, music; Betty Comden and Adolph Green, lyrics

SCENIC DESIGNER
Robin Wagner, *On the Twentieth Century*

COSTUME DESIGNER
Edward Gorey, *Dracula*

CHOREOGRAPHER
Bob Fosse, *Dancin'*

LIGHTING DESIGNER
Jules Fisher, *Dancin'*

MOST INNOVATIVE PRODUCTION OF A REVIVAL
Dracula, Jujamcyn Theatre, Elizabeth I. McCann, John Wulp,
    Victor Lurie, Nelle Nugent and Max Weitzenhoffer, producers

SPECIAL AWARD
The Long Wharf Theatre

1979

PLAY
The Elephant Man, Bernard Pomerance

MUSICAL
Sweeney Todd

ACTOR — PLAY
Tom Conti, *Whose Life Is It Anyway?*

ACTRESSES — PLAY
Constance Cummings, *Wings*
Carole Shelley, *The Elephant Man*

FEATURED ACTOR — PLAY
Michael Gough, *Bedroom Farce*

FEATURED ACTRESS — PLAY
Joan Hickson, *Bedroom Farce*

ACTOR — MUSICAL
Len Cariou, *Sweeney Todd*

ACTRESS — MUSICAL
Angela Lansbury, *Sweeney Todd*

FEATURED ACTOR — MUSICAL
Henderson Forsythe, *The Best Little Whorehouse in Texas*

FEATURED ACTRESS — MUSICAL
Carlin Glynn, *The Best Little Whorehouse in Texas*

DIRECTOR — PLAY
Jack Hofsiss, *The Elephant Man*

DIRECTOR — MUSICAL
Harold Prince, *Sweeney Todd*

BOOK — MUSICAL
Sweeney Todd, Hugh Wheeler

SCORE
Sweeney Todd, Stephen Sondheim, music and lyrics

SCENIC DESIGNER
Eugene Lee, *Sweeney Todd*

COSTUME DESIGNER
Franne Lee, *Sweeney Todd*

CHOREOGRAPHERS
Michael Bennett and Bob Avian, *Ballroom*

LIGHTING DESIGNER
Roger Morgan, *The Crucifer of Blood*

SPECIAL AWARDS
Henry Fonda

Walter F. Diehl
Eugene O'Neill Memorial Theatre Center
American Conservatory Theater

1980

PLAY
Children of a Lesser God, Mark Medoff

MUSICAL
Evita

ACTOR — PLAY
John Rubinstein, *Children of a Lesser God*

ACTRESS — PLAY
Phyllis Frelich, *Children of a Lesser God*

FEATURED ACTOR — PLAY
David Rounds, *Morning's at Seven*

FEATURED ACTRESS — PLAY
Dinah Manoff, *I Ought to Be in Pictures*

ACTOR — MUSICAL
Jim Dale, *Barnum*

ACTRESS — MUSICAL
Patti LuPone, *Evita*

FEATURED ACTOR — MUSICAL
Mandy Patinkin, *Evita*

FEATURED ACTRESS — MUSICAL
Priscilla Lopez, *A Day in Hollywood* and *A Night in the Ukraine*

DIRECTOR — PLAY
Vivian Matalon, *Morning's at Seven*

DIRECTOR — MUSICAL
Harold Prince, *Evita*

BOOK — MUSICAL
Evita, Tim Rice

SCORE
Evita, Andrew Lloyd Webber, music; Tim Rice, lyrics

SCENIC DESIGNERS
John Lee Beatty, *Talley's Folly*
David Mitchell, *Barnum*

COSTUME DESIGNER
Theoni V. Aldredge, *Barnum*

CHOREOGRAPHERS
Tommy Tune and Thommie Walsh, *A Day in Hollywood* and
    A Night in the Ukraine

LIGHTING DESIGNER
David Hersey, *Evita*

REPRODUCTION — PLAY OR MUSICAL
Morning's at Seven

SPECIAL AWARDS
Mary Tyler Moore
Actors Theatre of Louisville
Goodspeed Opera House

Kevin Kline, *The Pirates of Penzance*

1981

PLAY
A Lesson From Aloes, Athol Fugard

MUSICAL
42nd Street

ACTOR — PLAY
Ian McKellen, *Amadeus*

ACTRESS — PLAY
Jane Lapotaire, *Piaf*

FEATURED ACTOR — PLAY
Brian Backer, *The Floating Light Bulb*

FEATURED ACTRESS — PLAY
Swoosie Kurtz, *Fifth of July*

ACTOR — MUSICAL
Kevin Kline, *The Pirates of Penzance*

ACTRESS — MUSICAL
Lauren Bacall, *Woman of the Year*

FEATURED ACTOR — MUSICAL
Hinton Battle, *Sophisticated Ladies*

FEATURED ACTRESS — MUSICAL
Marilyn Cooper, *Woman of the Year*

DIRECTOR — PLAY
Peter Hall, *Amadeus*

DIRECTOR — MUSICAL
Wilford Leach, *The Pirates of Penzance*

BOOK — MUSICAL
Woman of the Year, Peter Stone

SCORE
Woman of the Year, John Kander, music; Fred Ebb, lyrics

SCENIC DESIGNER
John Bury, *Amadeus*

COSTUME DESIGNER
Willa Kim, *Sophisticated Ladies*

CHOREOGRAPHER
Gower Champion, *42nd Street*

LIGHTING DESIGNER
John Bury, *Amadeus*

REPRODUCTION (PLAY OR MUSICAL)
The Pirates of Penzance

SPECIAL AWARDS
Lena Horne

Trinity Square Repertory Company

1982

PLAY
The Life and Adventures of Nicholas Nickleby, David Edgar

MUSICAL
Nine

ACTOR — PLAY
Roger Rees, *The Life and Adventures of Nicholas Nickleby*

ACTRESS — PLAY
Zoe Caldwell, *Medea*

FEATURED ACTOR — PLAY
Zakes Mokae, *'Master Harold' . . . and the Boys*

FEATURED ACTRESS — PLAY
Amanda Plummer, *Agnes of God*

ACTOR — MUSICAL
Ben Harney, *Dreamgirls*

ACTRESS — MUSICAL
Jennifer Holliday, *Dreamgirls*

FEATURED ACTOR — MUSICAL
Cleavant Derricks, *Dreamgirls*

FEATURED ACTRESS — MUSICAL
Liliane Montevecchi, *Nine*

DIRECTORS — PLAY
Trevor Nunn and John Caird, *The Life and Adventures of Nicholas Nickleby*

DIRECTOR — MUSICAL
Tommy Tune, *Nine*

BOOK — MUSICAL
Dreamgirls, Tom Eyen

SCORE
Nine, Maury Yeston, music and lyrics

SCENIC DESIGNERS
John Napier and Dermot Hayes, *The Life and Adventures of Nicholas Nickleby*

COSTUME DESIGNER
William Ivey Long, *Nine*

CHOREOGRAPHERS
Michael Bennett and Michael Peters, *Dreamgirls*

LIGHTING DESIGNER
Tharon Musser, *Dreamgirls*

REPRODUCTION — PLAY OR MUSICAL
Othello

SPECIAL AWARDS
The Guthrie Theatre

The Actors Fund of America

1983

PLAY
Torch Song Trilogy, Harvey Fierstein

MUSICAL
Cats

ACTOR — PLAY
Harvey Fierstein, *Torch Song Trilogy*

ACTRESS — PLAY
Jessica Tandy, *Foxfire*

FEATURED ACTOR — PLAY
Matthew Broderick, *Brighton Beach Memoirs*

FEATURED ACTRESS — PLAY
Judith Ivey, *Steaming*

ACTOR — MUSICAL
Tommy Tune, *My One and Only*

ACTRESS — MUSICAL
Natalia Makarova, *On Your Toes*

FEATURED ACTOR — MUSICAL
Charles "Honi" Coles, *My One and Only*

FEATURED ACTRESS — MUSICAL
Betty Buckley, *Cats*

DIRECTOR — PLAY
Gene Saks, *Brighton Beach Memoirs*

DIRECTOR — MUSICAL
Trevor Nunn, *Cats*

BOOK — MUSICAL
Cats, T. S. Eliot

SCORE
Cats, Andrew Lloyd Webber, music; T. S. Eliot, lyrics

SCENIC DESIGNER
Ming Cho Lee, *K2*

COSTUME DESIGNER
John Napier, *Cats*

CHOREOGRAPHERS
Tommy Tune and Thommie Walsh, *My One and Only*

Matthew Broderick

LIGHTING DESIGNER
David Hersey, *Cats*

REPRODUCTION
On Your Toes

SPECIAL AWARDS
The Theatre Collection, Museum of the City of New York

Shakespearean Festival Association

1984

PLAY
The Real Thing, Tom Stoppard

MUSICAL
La Cage aux Folles

ACTOR — PLAY
Jeremy Irons, *The Real Thing*

ACTRESS — PLAY
Glenn Close, *The Real Thing*

FEATURED ACTOR — PLAY
Joe Mantegna, *Glengarry Glen Ross*

FEATURED ACTRESS — PLAY
Christine Baranski, *The Real Thing*

ACTOR — MUSICAL
George Hearn, *La Cage aux Folles*

ACTRESS — MUSICAL
Chita Rivera, *The Rink*

FEATURED ACTOR — MUSICAL
Hinton Battle, *The Tap Dance Kid*

FEATURED ACTRESS — MUSICAL
Martine Allard, *The Tap Dance Kid*

DIRECTOR — PLAY
Mike Nichols, *The Real Thing*

DIRECTOR — MUSICAL
Arthur Laurents, *La Cage aux Folles*

BOOK — MUSICAL
La Cage aux Folles, Harvey Fierstein

SCORE — MUSICAL
La Cage aux Folles, Jerry Herman, music and lyrics

SCENIC DESIGNER
Tony Straiges, *Sunday in the Park With George*

COSTUME DESIGNER
Theoni V. Aldredge, *La Cage aux Folles*

CHOREOGRAPHER
Danny Daniels, *The Tap Dance Kid*

LIGHTING DESIGNER
Richard Nelson, *Sunday in the Park With George*

REPRODUCTION
Death of a Salesman

SPECIAL AWARDS
San Diego Old Globe Theatre

La Tragedie de Carmen

Al Hirschfeld (Brooks Atkinson Award)

Peter Feller

Yul Brynner

1985

PLAY
Biloxi Blues, Neil Simon

MUSICAL
Big River

ACTOR — PLAY
Derek Jacobi, *Much Ado About Nothing*

ACTRESS — PLAY
Stockard Channing, *Joe Egg*

FEATURED ACTOR — PLAY
Barry Miller, *Biloxi Blues*

FEATURED ACTRESS — PLAY
Judith Ivey, *Hurlyburly*

FEATURED ACTOR — MUSICAL
Ron Richardson, *Big River*

FEATURED ACTRESS — MUSICAL
Leilani Jones, *Grind*

DIRECTOR — PLAY
Gene Saks, *Biloxi Blues*

DIRECTOR — MUSICAL
Des McAnuff, *Big River*

BOOK — MUSICAL
Big River, William Hauptman

SCORE
Big River, Roger Miller

SCENIC DESIGNER
Heidi Landesman, *Big River*

COSTUME DESIGNER
Florence Klotz, *Grind*

LIGHTING DESIGNER
Richard Riddell, *Big River*

REPRODUCTION (PLAY OR MUSICAL)
Joe Egg

SPECIAL AWARDS
Yul Brynner
Edwin Lester
New York State Council on the Arts
Steppenwolf Theatre

1986

PLAY
I'm Not Rappaport, Herb Gardner

MUSICAL
The Mystery of Edwin Drood

ACTOR — PLAY
Judd Hirsch, *I'm Not Rappaport*

ACTRESS — PLAY
Lily Tomlin, *The Search for Signs of Intelligent Life in the Universe*

FEATURED ACTOR — PLAY
John Mahoney, *The House of Blue Leaves*

FEATURED ACTRESS — PLAY
Swoosie Kurtz, *The House of Blue Leaves*

ACTOR — MUSICAL
George Rose, *The Mystery of Edwin Drood*

ACTRESS — MUSICAL
Bernadette Peters, *Song & Dance*

FEATURED ACTOR — MUSICAL
Michael Rupert, *Sweet Charity*

FEATURED ACTRESS — MUSICAL
Bebe Neuwirth, *Sweet Charity*

DIRECTOR — PLAY
Jerry Zaks, *The House of Blue Leaves*

DIRECTOR — MUSICAL
Wilford Leach, *The Mystery of Edwin Drood*

BOOK — MUSICAL
The Mystery of Edwin Drood, Rupert Holmes

SCORE
The Mystery of Edwin Drood, Rupert Holmes

SCENIC DESIGNER
Tony Walton, *The House of Blue Leaves*

COSTUME DESIGNER
Patricia Zipprodt, *Sweet Charity*

CHOREOGRAPHER
Bob Fosse, *Big Deal*

LIGHTING DESIGNER
Pat Collins, *I'm Not Rappaport*

REPRODUCTION (PLAY OR MUSICAL)
Sweet Charity

SPECIAL AWARD
American Repertory Theatre

1987

PLAY
Fences, August Wilson

MUSICAL
Les Misérables

BEST REVIVAL
All My Sons

ACTOR — PLAY
James Earl Jones, *Fences*

ACTRESS — PLAY
Linda Lavin, *Broadway Bound*

FEATURED ACTOR — PLAY
John Randolph, *Broadway Bound*

FEATURED ACTRESS — PLAY
Mary Alice, *Fences*

ACTOR — MUSICAL
Robert Lindsay, *Me and My Girl*

ACTRESS — MUSICAL
Maryann Plunkett, *Me and My Girl*

FEATURED ACTOR — MUSICAL
Michael Maguire, *Les Misérables*

FEATURED ACTRESS — MUSICAL
Frances Ruffelle, *Les Misérables*

DIRECTOR — PLAY
Lloyd Richards, *Fences*

DIRECTORS — MUSICAL
Trevor Nunn and John Caird, *Les Misérables*

BOOK — MUSICAL
Les Misérables, Alain Boublil and Claude-Michel Schönberg

SCORE
Les Misérables, Claude-Michel Schönberg, music; Herbert Kretzmer and Alain Boublil, lyrics

SCENIC DESIGNER
John Napier, *Les Misérables*

COSTUME DESIGNER
John Napier, *Starlight Express*

CHOREOGRAPHER
Gillian Gregory, *Me and My Girl*

LIGHTING DESIGNER
David Hersey, *Les Misérables*

SPECIAL AWARDS
George Abbott
Jackie Mason
San Francisco Mime Troupe

James Earl Jones

1988

PLAY
M. Butterfly, David Henry Hwang

MUSICAL
The Phantom of the Opera

REVIVAL
Anything Goes

ACTOR — PLAY
Ron Silver, *Speed-the-Plow*

ACTRESS — PLAY
Joan Allen, *Burn This*

FEATURED ACTOR — PLAY
B. D. Wong, *M. Butterfly*

FEATURED ACTRESS — PLAY
L. Scott Caldwell, *Joe Turner's Come and Gone*

ACTOR — MUSICAL
Michael Crawford, *The Phantom of the Opera*

ACTRESS — MUSICAL
Joanna Gleason, *Into the Woods*

FEATURED ACTOR — MUSICAL
Bill McCutcheon, *Anything Goes*

FEATURED ACTRESS — MUSICAL
Judy Kaye, *The Phantom of the Opera*

DIRECTOR — PLAY
John Dexter, *M. Butterfly*

DIRECTOR — MUSICAL
Harold Prince, *The Phantom of the Opera*

BOOK — MUSICAL
Into the Woods, James Lapine

SCORE — MUSICAL
Into the Woods, Stephen Sondheim, music and lyrics

SCENIC DESIGNER
Maria Björnson, *The Phantom of the Opera*

COSTUME DESIGNER
Maria Björnson, *The Phantom of the Opera*

CHOREOGRAPHER
Michael Smuin, *Anything Goes*

LIGHTING DESIGNER
Andrew Bridge, *The Phantom of the Opera*

SPECIAL AWARDS
Brooklyn Academy of Music
South Coast Repertory of Costa Mesa, CA

1989

PLAY
The Heidi Chronicles, Wendy Wasserstein

MUSICAL
Jerome Robbins' Broadway

REVIVAL
Our Town

ACTOR — PLAY
Philip Bosco, *Lend Me a Tenor*

ACTRESS — PLAY
Pauline Collins, *Shirley Valentine*

FEATURED ACTOR — PLAY
Boyd Gaines, *The Heidi Chronicles*

FEATURED ACTRESS — PLAY
Christine Baranski, *Rumors*

ACTOR — MUSICAL
Jason Alexander, *Jerome Robbins' Broadway*

ACTRESS — MUSICAL
Ruth Brown, *Black and Blue*

FEATURED ACTOR — MUSICAL
Scott Wise, *Jerome Robbins' Broadway*

FEATURED ACTRESS — MUSICAL
Debbie Shapiro, *Jerome Robbins' Broadway*

DIRECTOR — PLAY
Jerry Zaks, *Lend Me a Tenor*

DIRECTOR — MUSICAL
Jerome Robbins, *Jerome Robbins' Broadway*

SCENIC DESIGNER
Santo Loquasto, *Cafe Crown*

COSTUME DESIGNERS
Claudio Segovia and Hector Orezzoli, *Black and Blue*

CHOREOGRAPHERS
Cholly Atkins, Henry LeTang, Frankie Manning and Fayard Nicholas, *Black and Blue*

LIGHTING DESIGNER
Jennifer Tipton, *Jerome Robbins' Broadway*

SPECIAL AWARD
Hartford Stage Company

1990

PLAY
The Grapes of Wrath, Frank Galati

MUSICAL
City of Angels

Tyne Daly

REVIVAL
Gypsy

ACTOR — PLAY
Robert Morse, *Tru*

ACTRESS — PLAY
Maggie Smith, *Lettice and Lovage*

FEATURED ACTOR — PLAY
Charles Durning, *Cat on a Hot Tin Roof*

FEATURED ACTRESS — PLAY
Margaret Tyzack, *Lettice and Lovage*

ACTOR — MUSICAL
James Naughton, *City of Angels*

ACTRESS — MUSICAL
Tyne Daly, *Gypsy*

FEATURED ACTOR — MUSICAL
Michael Jeter, *Grand Hotel, the Musical*

FEATURED ACTRESS — MUSICAL
Randy Graff, *City of Angels*

DIRECTOR — PLAY
Frank Galati, *The Grapes of Wrath*

DIRECTOR — MUSICAL
Tommy Tune, *Grand Hotel, the Musical*

BOOK — MUSICAL
City of Angels, Larry Gelbart

SCORE
City of Angels, Cy Coleman, music; David Zippel, lyrics

SCENIC DESIGNER
Robin Wagner, *City of Angels*

COSTUME DESIGNER
Santo Loquasto, *Grand Hotel, the Musical*

CHOREOGRAPHER
Tommy Tune, *Grand Hotel, the Musical*

LIGHTING DESIGNER
Jules Fisher, *Grand Hotel, the Musical*

SPECIAL TONY AWARD
Seattle Repertory Theatre

TONY HONOR
Alfred Drake for excellence in the theater

1991

PLAY
Lost in Yonkers, Neil Simon

MUSICAL
Miss Saigon

REVIVAL
Fiddler on the Roof

ACTOR — PLAY
Nigel Hawthorne, *Shadowlands*

ACTRESS — PLAY
Mercedes Ruehl, *Lost in Yonkers*

FEATURED ACTOR — PLAY
Kevin Spacey, *Lost in Yonkers*

FEATURED ACTRESS — PLAY
Irene Worth, *Lost in Yonkers*

Mercedes Ruehl

ACTOR — MUSICAL
Jonathan Pryce, *Miss Saigon*

ACTRESS — MUSICAL
Lea Salonga, *Miss Saigon*

FEATURED ACTOR — MUSICAL
Hinton Battle, *Miss Saigon*

FEATURED ACTRESS — MUSICAL
Daisy Eagan, *The Secret Garden*

DIRECTOR — PLAY
Jerry Zaks, *Six Degrees of Separation*

DIRECTOR — MUSICAL
Tommy Tune, *The Will Rogers Follies*

BOOK — MUSICAL
The Secret Garden, Marsha Norman

SCORE — MUSICAL
Miss Saigon, Claude-Michel Schönberg, music; Richard
  Maltby, Jr. and Alain Boublil, lyrics

SCENIC DESIGNER
Heidi Landesman, *The Secret Garden*

COSTUME DESIGNER
Willa Kim, *The Will Rogers Follies*

CHOREOGRAPHER
Tommy Tune, *The Will Rogers Follies*

LIGHTING DESIGNER
Jules Fisher, *The Will Rogers Follies*

SPECIAL TONY AWARD
Yale Repertory Theatre

TONY HONOR
Father George Moore

1992

PLAY
Dancing at Lughnasa, Brian Friel

MUSICAL
Crazy for You

REVIVAL
Guys and Dolls

ACTOR — PLAY
Judd Hirsch, *Conversations With My Father*

ACTRESS — PLAY
Glenn Close, *Death and the Maiden*

FEATURED ACTOR — PLAY
Larry Fishburne, *Two Trains Running*

FEATURED ACTRESS — PLAY
Brid Brennan, *Dancing at Lughnasa*

ACTOR — MUSICAL
Gregory Hines, *Jelly's Last Jam*

ACTRESS — MUSICAL
Faith Prince, *Guys and Dolls*

FEATURED ACTOR — MUSICAL
Scott Waara, *The Most Happy Fella*

FEATURED ACTRESS — MUSICAL
Tonya Pinkins, *Jelly's Last Jam*

DIRECTOR — PLAY
Patrick Mason, *Dancing at Lughnasa*

DIRECTOR — MUSICAL
Jerry Zaks, *Guys and Dolls*

BOOK — MUSICAL
Falsettos, William Finn and James Lapine

SCORE
Falsettos, William Finn, music and lyrics

SCENIC DESIGNER
Tony Walton, *Guys and Dolls*

COSTUME DESIGNER
William Ivey Long, *Crazy for You*

CHOREOGRAPHER
Susan Stroman, *Crazy for You*

LIGHTING DESIGNER
Jules Fisher, *Jelly's Last Jam*

SPECIAL TONY AWARD
The Goodman Theatre of Chicago

TONY HONOR
The Fantasticks

Gregory Hines

Madeline Kahn

1993

PLAY
Angels in America: Millennium Approaches, Tony Kushner

MUSICAL
Kiss of the Spider Woman — The Musical

REVIVAL
Anna Christie

ACTOR — PLAY
Ron Leibman, *Angels in America: Millennium Approaches*

ACTRESS — PLAY
Madeline Kahn, *The Sisters Rosensweig*

FEATURED ACTOR — PLAY
Stephen Spinella, *Angels in America: Millennium Approaches*

FEATURED ACTRESS — PLAY
Debra Monk, *Redwood Curtain*

ACTOR — MUSICAL
Brent Carver, *Kiss of the Spider Woman — The Musical*

ACTRESS — MUSICAL
Chita Rivera, *Kiss of the Spider Woman — The Musical*

FEATURED ACTOR — MUSICAL
Anthony Crivello, *Kiss of the Spider Woman — The Musical*

FEATURED ACTRESS — MUSICAL
Andrea Martin, *My Favorite Year*

DIRECTOR — PLAY
George C. Wolfe, *Angels in America: Millennium Approaches*

DIRECTOR — MUSICAL
Des McAnuff, *The Who's Tommy*

BOOK — MUSICAL
Kiss of the Spider Woman — The Musical, Terrence McNally

SCORES — MUSICAL
Kiss of the Spider Woman — The Musical, John Kander,
  music; Fred Ebb, lyrics

The Who's Tommy, Pete Townshend, music and lyrics

SCENIC DESIGNER
John Arnone, *The Who's Tommy*

COSTUME DESIGNER
Florence Klotz, *Kiss of the Spider Woman — The Musical*

CHOREOGRAPHER
Wayne Cilento, *The Who's Tommy*

LIGHTING DESIGNER
Chris Parry, *The Who's Tommy*

SPECIAL TONY AWARDS
Oklahoma! — 50th Anniversary
La Jolla Playhouse

TONY HONORS
IATSE
Broadway Cares/Equity Fights AIDS

1994

PLAY
Angels in America: Perestroika, Tony Kushner

MUSICAL
Passion

REVIVAL — PLAY
An Inspector Calls

REVIVAL — MUSICAL
Carousel

ACTOR — PLAY
Stephen Spinella, *Angels in America: Perestroika*

ACTRESS — PLAY
Diana Rigg, *Medea*

FEATURED ACTOR — PLAY
Jeffrey Wright, *Angels in America: Perestroika*

FEATURED ACTRESS — PLAY
Jane Adams, *An Inspector Calls*

ACTOR — MUSICAL
Boyd Gaines, *She Loves Me*

ACTRESS — MUSICAL
Donna Murphy, *Passion*

FEATURED ACTOR — MUSICAL
Jarrod Emick, *Damn Yankees*

FEATURED ACTRESS — MUSICAL
Audra Ann McDonald, *Carousel*

DIRECTOR — PLAY
Stephen Daldry, *An Inspector Calls*

DIRECTOR — MUSICAL
Nicholas Hytner, *Carousel*

BOOK — MUSICAL
Passion, James Lapine

ORIGINAL MUSICAL SCORE
Beauty and the Beast, Alan Menken, music; Howard Ashman
  and Tim Rice, lyrics

SCENIC DESIGNER
Bob Crowley, *Carousel*

COSTUME DESIGNER
Ann Hould-Ward, *Beauty and the Beast*

CHOREOGRAPHER
Sir Kenneth MacMillan, *Carousel*

LIGHTING DESIGNER
Rick Fisher, *An Inspector Calls*

SPECIAL TONY AWARDS
Jessica Tandy and Hume Cronyn, lifetime achievement
McCarter Theatre

The Obie Awards

The Obie Awards, administered by New York's *Village Voice,* recognize distinguished achievement in Off-Broadway and Off-Off-Broadway productions. The Obies honor people and productions, regardless of number, in informally structured award categories.

1955–1956

BEST NEW PLAY
Absalom, Lionel Abel

BEST ALL-AROUND PRODUCTION
Uncle Vanya

BEST MUSICAL
The Threepenny Opera

BEST DIRECTOR
José Quintero, *The Iceman Cometh*

BEST ACTOR (TIE)
Jason Robards, Jr., *The Iceman Cometh*
George Voskevec, *Uncle Vanya*

BEST ACTRESS
Julie Bovasso, *The Maids*

BEST SUPPORTING ACTOR
Gerald Hiken, *The Cherry Orchard* and *Uncle Vanya*

BEST SUPPORTING ACTRESS
Peggy McCay, *Uncle Vanya*

DISTINGUISHED PERFORMANCES (ACTORS)
Alan Ansara, *The Private Life of the Master Race*
Roberts Blossom, *A Village Wooing*
Addison Powell, *The Iceman Cometh*

DISTINGUISHED PERFORMANCES (ACTRESSES)
Shirlee Emmons, *The Mother of Us All*
Frances Sternhagen, *The Admirable Basheville*
Nancy Wickwire, *The Cherry Orchard*

FOR HIGH TECHNICAL ACCOMPLISHMENT IN SETS, LIGHTING AND COSTUMES
Klaus Holm and Alvin Cold (Phoenix Theatre)

1956–1957

BEST NEW PLAY
Louis A. Lippa, *A House Remembered*

BEST ALL-AROUND PRODUCTION
Exiles

BEST DIRECTOR
Gene Frankel, *Volpone*

BEST ACTOR
William Smithers, *The Sea Gull*

BEST ACTRESS
Colleen Dewhurst, *The Taming of the Shrew, The Eagle Has Two Heads* and *Camille*

Arthur Miller

DISTINGUISHED PERFORMANCES (ACTORS)
Thayer David, *Saint Joan* and *Oscar Wilde*
Michael Kane, *Exiles*
Arthur Malet, *Volpone, The Misanthrope* and *The Apollo of Bellac*

DISTINGUISHED PERFORMANCES (ACTRESSES)
Marguerite Lenery, *House of Breath*
Betty Miller, *Exiles*
Jutta Wolf, *Exiles*

1957–1958

BEST PLAY (ADAPTATION)
The Brothers Karamazov, Boris Tumarin and Jack Sydow

BEST REVIVAL
The Crucible, Arthur Miller

BEST ONE-ACT PLAY
Guests of the Nation, Neil McKenzie

BEST COMEDY
Comic Strip, George Panetta

BEST FOREIGN PLAY
Samuel Beckett, *Endgame*

BEST DIRECTOR
Stuart Vaughan, New York Shakespeare Festival

BEST ACTOR
George C. Scott, *Richard III, As You Like It* and *Children of Darkness*

BEST ACTRESS
Anne Meacham, *Garden District*

DISTINGUISHED PERFORMANCES (ACTORS)
Jack Cannon, New York Shakespeare Festival and *Children of Darkness*

Leonardo Cimino, *The Brothers Karamazov*

Robert Geiringer, New York Shakespeare Festival and *Guests of the Nation*

Michael Higgins, *The Crucible*

DISTINGUISHED PERFORMANCES (ACTRESSES)
Tammy Grimes, *Clerambard*

Grania O'Malley, *Guests of the Nation*

Nydia Westman, *Endgame*

1958–1959

BEST NEW PLAY
Brendan Behan, *The Quare Fellow*

BEST ALL-AROUND PRODUCTION
Ivanov

BEST MUSICAL
A Party With Betty Comden and Adolph Green

BEST REVUE
Steven Vinaver, *Diversions*

BEST DIRECTOR (AMERICAN PLAY)
Jack Ragotzy, Arthur Laurents cycle

BEST DIRECTOR (FOREIGN PLAY)
William Ball, *Ivanov*

BEST ACTOR
Alfred Ryder, *I Rise in Flame, Cried the Phoenix*

BEST ACTRESS
Kathleen Maguire, *The Time of the Cuckoo*

DISTINGUISHED PERFORMANCES (ACTORS)
Zero Mostel, *Ulysses in Nighttown*

Lester Rawlins, *The Quare Fellow*

Harold Scott, *Deathwatch*

DISTINGUISHED PERFORMANCES (ACTRESSES)
Rosina Fernhoff, *Fashion* and *The Geranium Hat*

Anne Fielding, *Ivanov*

Nancy Wickwire, *A Clearing in the Woods*

BEST MUSIC
David Amram

BEST OPEN-STAGE SET
David Hays, *The Quare Fellow*

BEST PROSCENIUM SET
Will Stevens Armstrong, *Ivanov*

BEST LIGHTING
Nikola Cernovich

Brendan Behan

1959–1960

BEST NEW PLAY
Jack Gelber, *The Connection*

BEST ALL-AROUND PRODUCTION
The Connection

BEST FOREIGN PLAY
Jean Genet, *The Balcony*

DISTINGUISHED PLAYS
Edward Albee, *The Zoo Story*

Samuel Beckett, *Krapp's Last Tape*

Jack Richardson, *The Prodigal*

BEST DIRECTOR
Gene Frankel, *Machinal*

BEST ACTOR
Warren Finnerty, *The Connection*

BEST ACTRESS
Eileen Brennan, *Little Mary Sunshine*

DISTINGUISHED PERFORMANCES (ACTORS)
William Daniels, *The Zoo Story*

Donald Davis, *Krapp's Last Tape*

Vincent Gardenia, *Machinal*

John Heffernan, *Henry IV, Part 2*

Jock Livingston, *The Balcony*

DISTINGUISHED PERFORMANCES (ACTRESSES)
Patricia Falkenhain, *Peer Gynt* and *Henry IV*

Elisa Loti, *Come Share My House*

Nancy Marchand, *The Balcony*

SETS
David Hays, *The Balcony*

1960–1961

BEST NEW PLAY
Jean Genet, *The Blacks*

BEST OVERALL PRODUCTION
Hedda Gabler

BEST OFF-OFF-BROADWAY PRODUCTION
The Premise

BEST DIRECTOR
Gerald A. Freedman, *The Taming of the Shrew*

BEST ACTOR
Khigh Dhiegh, *In the Jungle of Cities*

BEST ACTRESS
Anne Meacham, *Hedda Gabler*

DISTINGUISHED PERFORMANCES (ACTORS)
Godfrey M. Cambridge, *The Blacks*
James Coco, *The Moon in the Yellow River*
Lester Rawlins, *Hedda Gabler*

DISTINGUISHED PERFORMANCES (ACTRESSES)
Joan Hackett, *Call Me by My Rightful Name*
Gerry Jedd, *She Stoops to Conquer*
Surya Kumari, *The King of the Darn Chamber*

BEST MUSIC
Teiji Ito, *In the Jungle of Cities, Three Modern Japanese Plays* and *Ubu*

1961–1962

BEST AMERICAN PLAY
Frank D. Gilroy, *Who'll Save the Plowboy?*

BEST MUSICAL
Fly Blackbird, C. Jackson, James Hatch and Jerome Eskow

BEST FOREIGN PLAY
Samuel Beckett, *Happy Days* (Walter Kerr abstaining)

BEST ACTORS
James Earl Jones, *Clandestine on the Morning Line, The Apple* and *Moon on a Rainbow Shawl*

BEST ACTRESS
Barbara Harris, *Oh, Dad, Poor Dad, Mamma's Hung You in the Closet and I'm Feelin' So Sad*

DISTINGUISHED PERFORMANCES (ACTORS)
Clayton Corzatte, APA Repertory
Geoff Garland, *The Hostage*
Gerald O'Loughlin, *Who'll Save the Plowboy?*
Paul Roebling, *This Side of Paradise*

DISTINGUISHED PERFORMANCES (ACTRESSES)
Sudie Bond, *Theatre of the Absurd*
Vinnette Carroll, *Moon on a Rainbow Shawl*
Rosemary Harris, APA Repertory
Ruth White, *Happy Days*

BEST SET
Norris Houghton, *Who'll Save the Plowboy?*

1962–1963

BEST PRODUCTION (PLAY)
Luigi Pirandello, *Six Characters in Search of an Author*

BEST PRODUCTION (MUSICAL)
The Boys From Syracuse

BEST DIRECTOR
Alan Schneider, *The Pinter Plays*

BEST ACTOR
George C. Scott, *Desire Under the Elms*

BEST ACTRESS
Colleen Dewhurst, *Desire Under the Elms*

DISTINGUISHED PERFORMANCES
Jacqueline Brookes, *Six Characters in Search of an Author*
Joseph Chaikin, *A Man's a Man*
Olympia Dukakis, *A Man's a Man*
Anne Jackson, *The Typists* and *The Tiger*
Michael O'Sullivan, *Six Characters in Search of an Author*
James Patterson, *The Collection: The Pinter Plays*
Madeleine Sherwood, *Hey You, Light Man!*
Eli Wallach, *The Typists* and *The Tiger*

1963–1964

BEST PLAY
Samuel Beckett, *Play*

BEST AMERICAN PLAY
Le Roi Jones, *Dutchman*

BEST PRODUCTION (PLAY)
The Brig

BEST PRODUCTION (MUSICAL)
What Happened

DISTINGUISHED PLAYS
Rosalyn Drexler, *Home Movies*
Adrienne Kennedy, *Funnyhouse of a Negro*

BEST DIRECTION
Judith Malina, *The Brig*

DISTINGUISHED DIRECTION
Lawrence Kornfeld, *What Happened*

BEST PERFORMANCE
Gloria Foster, *In White America*

DISTINGUISHED PERFORMANCES
Philip Bruns, *Mr. Simian*
Joyce Ebert, *The Trojan Women*
Lee Grant, *The Maids*
David Hurst, *A Month in the Country*
Taylor Mead, *The General Returns From One Place to Another*
Estelle Parsons, *Next Time I'll Sing to You* and *In the Summer House*
Diana Sands, *The Living Premise*
Marian Seldes, *The Ginger Man*
Jack Warden, *Epiphany*
Ronald Weyland, *The Lesson*

BEST MUSIC
Al Carmines, *Home Movies* and *What Happened*

BEST DESIGN
Julian Beck, *The Brig*

1964–1965

BEST AMERICAN PLAY
Robert Lowell, *The Old Glory*

BEST MUSICAL PRODUCTION
The Cradle Will Rock

DISTINGUISHED PLAYS
Maria Irene Fornes, *Promenade* and *The Successful Life of Three*

BEST DIRECTION
Ulu Grosbard, *A View From the Bridge*

BEST PERFORMANCES
Roscoe Lee Browne, Frank Langella and Lester Rawlins, *The Old Glory*

DISTINGUISHED PERFORMANCES
Brian Bedford, *The Knock*

Roberts Blossom, *Do Not Pass Go*

Joseph Chaikin, *Victims of Duty* and *The Exception and the Rule*

Margaret De Priest, *The Place for Chance*

Dean Dittmann, *The Cradle Will Rock*

Robert Duvall, *A View From the Bridge*

Rosemary Harris, APA Repertory

James Earl Jones, *Beal*

Frances Sternhagen, *The Room* and *A Slight Ache*

Sada Thompson, *Tartuffe*

BEST COSTUMES
Willa Kim, *The Old Glory*

1965–1966

BEST AMERICAN PLAY
Ronald Ribman, *The Journey of the Fifth Horse*

DISTINGUISHED PLAYS
Emanuel Peluso, *Good Day*

Sam Shepard, *Chicago, Icarus's Mother* and *Red Cross*

DISTINGUISHED DIRECTION
Remy Charlip, *A Beautiful Day*

Jacques Levy, *You're Only as Old as Your Arteries, Red Cross* and *The Next Thing*

BEST ACTOR
Dustin Hoffman, *The Exhaustion of Our Son's Love*

BEST ACTRESS
Jane White, *Coriolanus* and *Love's Labour's Lost*

DISTINGUISHED PERFORMANCES
Clarice Blackburn, *The Exhaustion of Our Son's Love*

Mari-Claire Charba, *Birdbath*

Gloria Foster, *Medea*

Sharon Gans, *Soon Jack November*

Frank Langella, *Good Day* and *The White Devil*

Michael Lipton, *The Trigon*

Kevin O'Connor, *Chicago*

Jess Osuna, *Bugs* and *Veronica*

Florence Tarlow, *Istanbul, Red Cross* and *A Beautiful Day*

Douglas Turner, *Days of Absence*

SET DESIGN
Lindsey Decker, *Red Cross*

Ed Wittstein, *Serjeant Musgrace's Dance*

1966–1967

DISTINGUISHED PLAYS
Henry Livings, *Eh?*

Rochelle Owens, *Futz*

Sam Shepard, *La Turista*

BEST DIRECTOR
Tom O'Horgan, *Futz*

BEST ACTOR
Seth Allen, *Futz*

DISTINGUISHED PERFORMANCES
Tom Aldredge, *Measure for Measure* and *Stock Up on Pepper Cause Turkey's Going to War*

Robert Bonnard, *The Chairs*

Alvin Epstein, *Dynamite Tonite*

Neil Flanagan, *The Madness of Lady Bright*

Bette Henritze, *Measure for Measure*, the Wilder plays, *The Distinguished Person* and *The Rimers of Eldrich*

Stacy Keach, *MacBird!*

Terry Kiser, *Fortune and Men's Eyes*

Eddie McCarthy, *Kitchenette*

Robert Salvio, *Hemp*

Rip Torn, *The Deer Park*

BEST LIGHTING
John Dodd, *The White W, The Madness of Lady Bright* and *Charles Dickens' "Christmas Carol"*

1967–1968

DISTINGUISHED PLAYS
John Guare, *Muzzeha*

Israel Horovitz, *The Indian Wants the Bronz*

Sam Shepard, *Forensic and the Navigator* and *Melodrama Play*

BEST MUSICAL
In Circles, Gertrude Stein and Al Carmines

BEST FOREIGN PLAY
Vaclav Havel, *The Memorandum*

BEST DIRECTOR
Michael A. Schultz, *Song of the Lusitanian Bogey*

DISTINGUISHED DIRECTION
John Hancock, *A Midsummer Night's Dream*

Rip Torn, *The Beard*

BEST ACTOR
Al Pacino, *The Indian Wants the Bronz*

BEST ACTRESS
Billie Dixon, *The Beard*

DISTINGUISHED PERFORMANCES
John Cazale, *Line* and *The Indian Wants the Bronx*

James Coco, *Fragments*

Jean David, *Istanbul*

Cliff Gorman, *The Boys in the Band*

Mari Gorman, *The Memorandum* and *Walking to Waldheim*

Moses Gunn, The Negro Ensemble Company repertory

Peggy Pope, *Maaamama*

Roy R. Scheider, *Stephen D.*

BEST DESIGN
Robert LaVigne, *A Midsummer Night's Dream* and *Endecott and the Red Circus*

1968–1969

There were no category classifications this year.

Julian Beck, *Antigone*

Julie Bovasso, *Gloria and Esperansa*

Jules Feiffer, *Little Murders*

Nathan George and Ron O'Neal, *No Place to Be Somebody*

Israel Horovitz, *The Honest-to-God Schnozzola*

The Living Theatre, *Frankenstein*

Judith Molina, *Antigone*

OM Theatre, *Riot*

Open Theatre, *The Serpent*

Performance group, *Dionysus in '69*

Arlene Rothlein, *The Poor Little Match Girl*

Ronald Tavel, *The Boy on the Straight Back Chair*

Theatre Genesis, sustained excellence

Jeff Weiss, *The International Wrestling Match*

1969–1970

BEST AMERICAN PLAY
Megan Terry, *Approaching Simone*

Paul Zindel, *The Effect of Gamma Rays on Man-in-the-Moon Marigolds*

BEST MUSICAL
Gretchen Cryer and Nancy Ford, *The Last Sweet Days of Isaac*

Robert Livingston, Gary William Friedman and Will Holt, *The Me Nobody Knows*

BEST FOREIGN PLAY
Joe Orton, *What the Butler Saw*

DISTINGUISHED PLAYS
Vaclav Havel, *The Increased Difficulty of Concentration*

Murray Mednick, *The Deer Kill*

DISTINGUISHED DIRECTION
Alan Arkin, *The White House Murder Case*

Melvin Bernhardt, *The Effect of Gamma Rays on Man-in-the-Moon Marigolds*

Maxine Klein, *Approaching Simone*

Gilbert Moses, *Slave Ship*

BEST PERFORMANCE
Sada Thompson, *The Effect of Gamma Rays on Man-in-the-Moon Marigolds*

Ruby Dee

DISTINGUISHED PERFORMANCES
Beeson Carroll, *The Unseen Hand*

Vincent Gardenia, *Passing Through Exotic Places*

Harold Gould, *The Increased Difficulty of Concentration*

Anthony Holland, *The White House Murder Case*

Lee Kissman, *The Unseen Hand*

Ron Leibman, *Transfers*

Roberta Maxwell, *Whistle in the Dark*

Rue McClanahan, *Who's Happy Now?*

Pamela Payton-Wright, *The Effect of Gamma Rays on Man-in-the-Moon Marigolds*

Austin Pendleton, *The Last Sweet Days of Isaac*

Fredericka Weber, *The Last Sweet Days of Isaac*

1970–1971

BEST AMERICAN PLAY
John Guare, *House of Blue Leaves*

BEST FOREIGN PLAY
Athol Fugard, *Boesman and Lena*

Derek Walcott, *Dream on Monkey Mountain*

Heathcote Williams, *AC/DC*

DISTINGUISHED PLAYS
Ed Bullins, *The Fabulous Miss Maria* and *In New England Winter*

David Rabe, *Basic Training of Pavlo Hummel*

DISTINGUISHED PRODUCTION
The Trial of the Catonsville 9

DISTINGUISHED DIRECTION
John Berry, *Boesman and Lena*

Jeff Bleckner, *Basic Training of Pavlo Hummel*

Gordon Davidson, *The Trial of the Catonsville 9*

John Hirsch, *AC/DC*

Larry Kornfeld, *Dracular Sabbat*

BEST PERFORMANCE BY AN ACTOR
Jack MacGowran, *Beckett*

BEST PERFORMANCE BY AN ACTRESS
Ruby Dee, *Boesman and Lena*

DISTINGUISHED PERFORMANCES
Susan Batson, *AC/DC*
Margaret Braidwood, *Saved*
Hector Elizondo, *Steambath*
Donald Ewer, *Saved*
Sonny Jim, *The Fabulous Miss Marie*
Stacy Keach, *Long Day's Journey Into Night*
Kirk Kirksey, consistent excellence of performance
Harris Laskawy, *Uncle Vanya*
Joan MacIntosh, *Commune*
William Schallert, *The Trial of the Catonsville 9*
James Woods, *Saved*

SET DESIGN
John Scheffler, *AC/DC*

1971–1972

BEST THEATER PIECE
The Open Theatre, *The Mutation Show*

DISTINGUISHED DIRECTION
Wilford Leach and John Braswell, *The Only Jealousy of Emer*
Mel Shapiro, *Two Gentlemen of Verona*
Michael Smith, *Country Music*
Tom Sydorick, *20th Century Tar*

DISTINGUISHED PERFORMANCES
Salome Bey, *Love Me, Love My Children*
Maurice Blanc, *The Celebrations: Joos/Guns/Movies/The Abyss*
Alex Bradford, *Don't Bother Me, I Can't Cope*
Marilyn Chris, *Kaddish*
Ron Faber, *And They Put Handcuffs on Flowers*
Jeanne Hepple, *The Reliquary of Mr. and Mrs. Potterfield*
Danny Sewell, *The Homecoming*
Marilyn Sokol, *The Beggar's Opera*
Kathleen Widdoes, *The Beggar's Opera*
Elizabeth Wilson, *Sticks and Bones*
Ed Zang, *The Reliquary of Mr. and Mrs. Potterfield*

MUSIC AND LYRICS
Micki Grant, *Don't Bother Me, I Can't Cope*

COMPOSER
Liz Swados, *Medea*

VISUAL EFFECTS
Video Free America, *Kaddish*

1972–1973

BEST AMERICAN PLAY
Joseph A. Walker, *The River Niger*
Lanford Wilson, *The Hot L Baltimore*

BEST FOREIGN PLAY
Samuel Beckett, *Not I*
Peter Handke, *Kaspar*

DISTINGUISHED PLAYS
J.E. Gaines, *What if It Had Turned up Heads?*
Sam Shepard, *The Tooth of Crime*
Ronald Tavel, *Big Foot*

DISTINGUISHED DIRECTION
Jack Gelber, *The Kid*
William E. Lathan, *What if It Had Turned up Heads?*
Marshall W. Mason, *The Hot L Baltimore*

DISTINGUISHED PERFORMANCES
Hume Cronyn, *Krapp's Last Tape*
Mari Gorman, *The Hot L Baltimore*
James Hilbrandt, *A Boy Named Dog*
Stacy Keach, *Hamlet*
Christopher Lloyd, *Kaspar*
Charles Ludlam, *Corn* and *Camille*
Lola Pashalinski, *Corn*
Alice Playten, *Lemmings*
Roxie Roker, *The River Niger*
Jessica Tandy, *Not I*
Douglas Turner Ward, *The River Niger*
Sam Waterston, *Much Ado About Nothing*

1973–1974

BEST AMERICAN PLAY
Miguel Pinero, *Short Eyes*

BEST FOREIGN PLAY
David Storey, *The Contractor*

DISTINGUISHED PLAYS
Paul Carter Harrison, *The Great MacDaddy*
Terrence McNally, *Bad Habits*
Mark Medoff, *When You Comin' Back, Red Ryder?*

DISTINGUISHED DIRECTION
Marvin Felix Camillo, *Short Eyes*
Robert Drivas, *Bad Habits*
David Light, *Hard to Be a Jew*
John Pasquin, *Moonchildren*
Harold Prince, *Candide*

DISTINGUISHED PERFORMANCES
Barbara Barrie, *The Killdeer*
Joseph Buloff, *Hard to Be a Jew*
Kevin Conway, *When You Comin' Back, Red Ryder*
Conchata Ferrell, *The Sea Horse*
Loretta Greene, *The Sirens*
Barbara Montgomery, *My Sister, My Sister*
Zipora Spaizman, *Stepemyu*
Elizabeth Sturges, *When You Comin' Back, Red Ryder*

MUSIC
Bill Elliott, *C.O.R.F.A.X.*

COSTUMES
Theoni Aldredge (The Public Theatre)

SET DESIGN
Holmes Easley (The Roundabout Theatre)
Christopher Thomas, *The Lady From the Sea*

1974–1975

BEST NEW AMERICAN PLAY
Leslie Lee, *The First Breeze of Summer*

PLAYWRITING
Ed Bullins, *The Taking of Miss Janie*

Wallace Shawn, *Our Late Night*

Sam Shepard, *Action*

Lanford Wilson, *The Mound Builders*

DIRECTION
Lawrence Kornfeld, *Listen to Me*

Marshall W. Mason, *Battle of Angels* and *The Mound Builders*

Gilbert Moses, *The Talking of Miss Janie*

PERFORMANCES
Tanya Berezin, *The Mound Builders*

Cara Duff-MacCormick, *Craig's Wife*

Tovah Feldshuh, *Yentl the Yeshiva Boy*

Moses Gunn, *The First Breeze of Summer*

Dick Latessa, *Philemon*

Kevin McCarthy, *Harry Outside*

Stephen D. Newman, *Polly*

Reyno, *The First Breeze of Summer*

Priscilla Smith, *Trilogy*

Ian Trigger, *The True History of Squire Jonathan*

Christopher Walken, *Kid Champion*

DESIGN
John Lee Beatty, distinguished set design, *Down by the River . . .*, *Battle of Angels* and *The Mound Builders*

Robert U. Taylor, distinguished set design, *Polly*

SPECIAL 20-YEAR OBIES
Judith Malina and Julian Beck

Ted Mann and the Circle in the Square

Joseph Papp

Ellen Stewart

The Fantasticks

1975–1976

BEST NEW AMERICAN PLAYS
David Mamet, *American Buffalo* and *Sexual Perversity in Chicago*

BEST THEATER PIECE
Richard Foreman, *Rhoda in Potatoland*

DIRECTION
JoAnne Akalaitis, *Cassandra*

Marshall Mason, *Knock Kryla* and *Serenading Louie*

PERFORMANCES
Joyce Aaron, *Academics*

Roberts Blossom, *Ice Age*

Robert Christian, *Blood*

Crystal Field, *Day Old Bread*

June Gable, *Comedy of Errors*

Mike Kellin, *American Buffalo*

Tony Lo Bianco, *Yanks 3 Detroit 0 Top of the Seventh*

Priscilla Lopez, *A Chorus Line*

Kate Manheim, *Rhoda in Potatoland*

T. Miratti, *The Shortchanged Review*

Pamela Payton-Wright, *Jesus and the Bandit Queen*

Priscilla Smith, *Good Woman of Setzuan*

David Warrilow, *The Warrilow* and *The Last Ones*

Sammy Williams, *A Chorus Line*

1976–1977

BEST NEW AMERICAN PLAY
Sam Shepard, *Curse of the Starving Class*

DISTINGUISHED PRODUCTIONS
Eve Merriam, playwright; Tommy Tune, director; Kate Carmel, costume designer; entire cast, *The Club*

Ntozake Shange, poet; Oz Scott, director; entire cast, *For Colored Girls Who Have Considered Suicide When the Rainbow Is Enuf*

Mabou Mines, *Dressed Like an Egg*

PLAYWRITING
David Berry, *G.R. Point*

Maria Irene Fornes, *Fefu and Her Friends*

William Hauptmann, *Domino Courts*

Albert Innaurato, *German* and *The Transfiguration of Benno Blimpie*

David Rudkin, *Ashes*

DIRECTION
Melvin Bernhardt, *Children*

Gordon Davidson, *Savages*

PERFORMANCES
Danny Aiello, *German*

Martin Balsam, *Cold Storage*

Lucinda Childs, *Einstein on the Beach*

James Coco, *The Transfiguration of Benno Blimpie*

Anne DeSalvo, *German*

John Heard, *G.R. Point*

Jo Henderson, *Ladyhouse Blues*

William Hurt, *My Life*

Joseph Maher, *Savages*

Roberta Maxwell, *Ashes*

Brian Murray, *Ashes*

Lola Pashalinski, *Der Ring Gott Farblonjet*

Martin Seldes, *Isadora Duncan Sleeps With the Russian Navy*

Margaret Wright, *A Manoir*

1977–1978

BEST NEW AMERICAN PLAY
Lee Breuer, *Shaggy Dog Animation*

DIRECTION
Robert Allan Ackerman, *Prayer for My Daughter*

Thomas Bullard, *Statements After an Arrest Under the Immorality Act*

Elizabeth Swados, *Runaways*

PERFORMANCES
Richard Bauer, *Landscape of the Body* and *The Dybbuk*
Nell Carter, *Ain't Misbehavin'*
Alma Cuervo, *Uncommon Women*
Swoosie Kurtz, *Uncommon Women*
Kaiulani Lee, *Safe House*
Bruce Myers, *The Dybbuk*
Lee S. Wilkof, *The Present Tense*

DESIGN
Garland Wright and John Arnone, *K*
Robert Yudice, *Museum*

LIFETIME ACHIEVEMENT
Peter Schumann's Bread & Puppet Theatre

1978–1979

BEST NEW AMERICAN PLAY
Michael McClure, *Josephine*

PLAYWRITING
Rosalyn Drexler, *The Writer's Opera*
Susan Miller, *Nasty Rumors* and *Final Remarks*
Richard Nelson, *Vienna Notes*
Bernard Pomerance, *The Elephant Man*
Sam Shepard, *Buried Child*

DIRECTION
Maria Irene Fornes, *Eyes on the Harem*
Jack Holssiss, *The Elephant Man*

PERFORMANCES
Mary Alice, *Nongogo* and *Julius Caesar*
Philip Anglim, *The Elephant Man*
Joseph Buloff, *The Price*
Constance Cummings, *Wings*
Fred Gwynne, *Grand Magic*
Judd Hirsch, *Talley's Folly*
Marcell Rosenblatt, *Vienna Notes*
Elizabeth Wilson, *Taken in Marriage*

DESIGN
Theatre X, set design and lighting design, *A Fierce Longing*
Jennifer Tipton, Public Theatre, set design and lighting design

SUSTAINED ACHIEVEMENT
Al Carmines

1979–1980

PLAYWRITING
Lee Breuer, *A Prelude to Death in Venice*
Christopher Durang, *Sister Mary Ignatius Explains It All for You*
Romulus Linney, *Tennessee*
Roland Muldoon, *Full Confessions of a Socialist*
Jeff Weiss, *That's How the Rent Gets Paid* (Part Three)

DIRECTION
A. J. Antoon, *The Art of Dining*
Edward Cornell, *Johnny on a Spot*
Elizabeth LeCompte, *Point Judith*

Meryl Streep

PERFORMANCES
Michael Burrell, *Hess*
Michael Cristofer, *Chinchilla*
Lindsay Crouse, *Reunion*
Elizabeth Franz, *Sister Mary Ignatius Explains It All for You*
Morgan Freeman, *Mother Courage* and *Coriolanus*
John Heard, *Othello* and *Split*
Michael Higgins, *Reunion*
Madeleine Le Houx, *La Justice*
Jon Polito, performances with Dodger Theatre Company and the BAM Theater Company
Bill Raymond, *A Prelude to Death in Venice*
Dianne Wiest, *The Art of Dining*
Hattie Winston, *Mother Courage* and *The Michigan*

DESIGN
Laura Crow, costume design, *Mary Stuart*
Beverly Emmons, distinguished lighting design
Sally Jacobs, *Conference of the Birds*
Ruth Maleczech and Julie Archer, *Vanishing Pictures*

SUSTAINED ACHIEVEMENT
Sam Shepard

1980–1981

BEST NEW AMERICAN PLAY
David Henry Hwang, *FOB*

BEST PRODUCTION
Emily Mann, *Still Life*

PLAYWRITING
Charles Fuller, *Zooman and the Sign*
Amlin Gray, *How I Got That Story*
Len Jenkin, *Limbo Tales*

DIRECTION
Melvin Bernhardt, *Crimes of the Heart*
Wilford Leach, *The Pirates of Penzance*
Toby Robertson, *Pericles*

PERFORMANCES
Giancarlo Esposito, *Zooman and the Sign*
Bob Gunton, *How I Got That Story*
Mary Beth Hurt, *Crimes of the Heart*
Kevin Kline, *The Pirates of Penzance*
John Lone, *FOB* and *The Dance and the Railroad*
Mary McDonnel, *Still Life*
Timothy Near, *Still Life*
William Sadler, *Limbo Tales*
Michele Shay, *Meetings*
John Spencer, *Still Life*
Meryl Streep, *Alice in Concert*
Christopher Walken, *The Sea Gull*

DESIGN
Bloolips, costume design, *Lust in Space*
Manuel Lutgenhorst and Douglas Ball, *Request Concert*
June Maeda, sustained excellence in set design
Donnie Perichy, sustained excellence in lighting design

SUSTAINED ACHIEVEMENT
Negro Ensemble Company

1981–1982

BEST NEW AMERICAN PLAYS
Metamorphosis in Miniature
Mr. Dead and Mrs. Free

BEST THEATER PIECE
Tadeusz Kantor, *Wielopole, Wielopole*

PLAYWRITING
Robert Auletta, *Stops* and *Virgins*
Caryl Churchill, *Cloud 9*

DIRECTION
Tommy Tune, *Cloud 9*

PERFORMANCES
Kevin Bacon, *Forty Deuce* and *Poor Little Lambs*
James Barbosa, *Soon Jack November*
Ray Dooley, *Peer Gynt*

Kevin Kline, *The Pirates of Penzance*

Christine Estabrook, *Pastorale*
Michael Gross, *No End of Blame*
E. Katherine Karr, *Cloud 9*
Kenneth McMillan, *Weekends Like Other People*
Kevin O'Connor, *Chucky's Hunch*, *Birdbath* and *Crossing the Crab Nebula*
Carole Shelley, *Twelve Dreams*
Josef Sommer, *Lydie Breeze*
Irene Worth, *The Chalk Garden*

DISTINGUISHED ENSEMBLE PERFORMANCES
Lisa Banes, Brenda Currin, Elizabeth McGovern and Beverly May, *My Sister in This House*
Adolph Caesar, Larry Riley and Denzel Washington, *A Soldier's Play*

DESIGN
Jim Clayburgh, sustained excellence in set design
Arden Fingerhut, sustained excellence in lighting design

SUSTAINED ACHIEVEMENT
Maria Irene Fornes

1982–1983

BEST NEW AMERICAN PLAY
Tina Howe, Harry Kondoleon and David Mamet shared the $1,000 prize.

PLAYWRITING
Caryl Churchill, *Top Girls*
Tina Howe, distinguished playwriting
Harry Kondoleon, most promising young playwright
David Mamet, *Edmond*

DIRECTION
Gregory Mosher, *Edmond*
Gary Sinise, *True West*

PERFORMANCES
Ernest Abuba, *Yellow Fever*
Christine Baranski, *A Midsummer Night's Dream*
Glenn Close, *The Singular Life of Albert Nobbs*
Jeff Daniels, *Johnny Got His Gun*
Ruth Maleczech, *Haff*
John Malkovich, *True West*
Donald Moffat, *Painting Churches*
Harry Wise, *The Tooth of Crime*

ENSEMBLE PERFORMANCES
Kenneth Frankel, director; cast, *Quartermaine's Terms*
Max Sufford-Clark, director; Royal Court cast, *Top Girls*
The New York Shakespeare Festival cast, *Top Girls*

DESIGN
Heidi Landesman, *A Midsummer Night's Dream* and *Painting Churches*

SUSTAINED ACHIEVEMENT
Lanford Wilson, Marshall Mason and the Circle Repertory Company

1983–1984

BEST NEW AMERICAN PLAY
Sam Shepard, *Fool for Love*

BEST MUSICAL
Lee Bruer and Bob Telson, *Gospel at Colonus*

PLAYWRITING
Samuel Beckett, *Ohio Impromptu, What Where, Catastrophe* and *Pocket*
Maria Irene Fornes, *The Danube, Sarita* and *Mud*
Vaclav Havel, *A Private View*
Len Jenkin, *Five of Us*
Franz Xaver Kroetz, *Through the Leaves* and *Mensch Meier*
Ted Tally, *Terra Nova*

DIRECTION
JoAnne Akalaitis, *Through the Leaves*
Maria Irene Fornes, *The Danube, Sarita* and *Mud*
Lawrence Sacharow, *Five of Us*
Sam Shepard, *Fool for Love*

PERFORMANCES
F. Murray Abraham, *Uncle Vanya*
Kathy Baker, *Fool for Love*
Sheila Dabney, *Sarita*
Morgan Freeman, *Gospel at Colonus*
George Guidall, *Cinders*
Ed Harris, *Fool for Love*
Frederick Haumann, *Through the Leaves*
Richard Jordan, *A Private View*
Ruth Maleczech, *Through the Leaves*
Stephen McHattie, *Mensch Meier*
Will Patton, *Fool for Love*
Pamela Reed, sustained excellence of performance
Dianne Wiest, *Serenading Louie* and *Other Places*

DESIGN
Adrianne Lobel, set design, *The Vampires* and *All Night Long*
Anne Militello, sustained excellence of lighting design
Bill Stabile, set design, *Spookhouse, Damnee Hanon* and *Sacree Sandre*
Douglas Stein, set design, *Through the Leaves*

SUSTAINED ACHIEVEMENT
Music-Theatre Group/Lenox Arts Center

1984–1985

NEW AMERICAN PLAY
Maria Irene Fornes, *The Conduct of Life*

PLAYWRITING
Rosalyn Drexler, *Transients Welcome*
Christopher Durang, *The Marriage of Bette and Boo*
William M. Hoffman, *As Is*

DIRECTION
John Malkovich, *Balm in Gilead*
Barbara Vann, *Bound to Rise*
Jerry Zaks, *The Foreigner* and *The Marriage of Bette and Boo*

John Malkovich

PERFORMANCES
Dennis Boutsikaris, *The Nest of the Woodgrouse*
Frances Foster, sustained excellence in performance
Jonathan Hadary, *As Is*
Anthony Heald, *Henry V, The Foreigner* and *Digby*
Laurie Metcalf, *Balm in Gilead*
John Turturro, *Danny and the Deep Blue Sea*
Ron Vawter, sustained excellence in performance

ENSEMBLE PERFORMANCES
Charles Ludlam and Everett Quinton, *The Mystery of Irma Vep*
Entire cast, *The Marriage of Bette and Boo*

MUSIC
Peter Gordon, *Otello*
Max Roach, *Shepardsets*

DESIGN
Judy Dearing, costume design
Victor En Yu Tan, lighting design
Loren Sherman, set design

SUSTAINED ACHIEVEMENT
Meredith Monk

1985–1986

DISTINGUISHED PLAYWRITING
Wallace Shawn, *Aunt Dan and Lemon*

PLAYWRITING
Eric Bogosian, *Drinking in America*
Martha Clarke, *Vienna: Lusthaus*
John Jesurun, *Deep Sleep*
Tadeusz Kantor, *Let the Artist Die*
Lee Nagrin, *Bird/Bear*

DIRECTION
Richard Foreman, *Largo Desolato*

BEST PERFORMANCE
Swoosie Kurtz, *The House of Blue Leaves*

PERFORMANCES
Norma Aleandro, *About Love and Other Stories About Love*
Dylan Baker, *Not About Heroes*
Tom Cayler, *A Matter of Life and Death*
Jill Eikenberry, *Lemon Sky* and *Life Under Water*
Farley Granger, *Talley & Son*
Kathryn Posson, *Aunt Dan and Lemon*
Josef Sommer, *Largo Desolato*
Helen Stenborg, *Talley & Son*
Elisabeth Welch, *Time to Start Living*
Elizabeth Wilson, *Anteroom*

SUSTAINED EXCELLENCE IN PERFORMANCE
Edward Herrmann
Kevin Kline

DESIGN
Paul Gallo, lighting design
Edward T. Gianfrancesco, set design
Rita Ryack, costume design

SUSTAINED ACHIEVEMENT
Mabou Mines

1986–1987

BEST NEW AMERICAN PLAY
Richard Foreman, *The Cure* and *Film Is Evil, Radio Is Good*

DIRECTION
Garland Wright, *On the Verge*

PERFORMANCES
Robin Bartlett, *The Early Girl*
Rob Besserer, *The Hunger Artist*
Morgan Freeman, *Driving Miss Daisy*
Laura Hicks, *On the Verge*
Anthony Holland, *The Hunger Artist*
Dana Ivey, *Driving Miss Daisy*
John Kelly, *Pass the Blutwurst* and *Bitte (The Egon Schiele Story)*

Eric Bogosian

Gcina Mhlophe, *Born in the RSA*
Bill Raymond, *Cold Harbor*
Clarice Taylor, *Moms*

SUSTAINED EXCELLENCE OF PERFORMANCE
Blackeyed-Susan
Philip Bosco
Andrew Jackson

DESIGN
Paul Gallo, lighting design, *The Hunger Artist*
James F. Ingalls, sustained excellence of lighting design
Robert Israel, set and costume design, *The Hunger Artist*

SUSTAINED ACHIEVEMENT
Charles Ludlam and the Ridiculous Theatrical Company

1987–1988

BEST NEW AMERICAN PLAY
Caryl Churchill, *Serious Money*
Maria Irene Fornes, *Abingdon Square*

DIRECTION
Anne Bogart, *No Plays No Poetry . . .*
Peter Brook, *The Mahabharata*
Julie Taymor, *Juan Darien*

PERFORMANCES
Kathy Bates, *Frankie & Johnny in the Clair de Lune*
Larry Bazzell, *The Signal Season of Dummy Hoy*
Yvonne Bryceland, *The Road to Mecca*
Victor Garber, *Wenceslas Square*
Amy Irving, *The Road to Mecca*
Erland Josephson, *The Cherry Orchard*
Gordana Rashovich, *A Shayna Maidel*
John Seitz, *Abingdon Square*
Peggy Shaw, *Dress Suits to Hire*
Tina Shepard, *The Three Lives of Lucie Cabrol*
Lauren Tom, *American Notes*

DESIGN
Eva Buchmuller, sustained excellence of stage design
Huck Snyder, sustained excellence of scenic design

SUSTAINED ACHIEVEMENT
Richard Foreman

1988–1989

PLAYWRIGHTING
Intar Hispanic Playwrights-in-Residence Laboratory
The Frank Silva Writers Workshop

DIRECTION
Ingmar Bergman, *Hamlet*
Rene Buch, sustained excellence of direction
Peter Stein, *Falstaff*

PERFORMANCES
Mark Blum, *Gus and Al*
Niall Buggy, *Aristocrats*
William Converse-Roberts, *Love's Labor's Lost*
Fyvush Finkel, *Cafe Crown*

Gloria Foster, *The Forbidden City*

Paul Hecht, *Enrico IV*

Nancy Marchand, *The Cocktail Hour*

Tim McDonnell, *Diary of a Madman*

Kathy Najimy and Mo Gaffney, *The Kathy and Mo Show*

Will Patton, *What Did He See?*

Lonny Price, *The Immigrant*

Everett Quinton, *A Tale of Two Cities*

Rocco Sisto, *The Winter's Tale*

DESIGN
Gabriel Berry, sustained excellence of costume design

Donald Eastman, sustained excellence of set design

SUSTAINED ACHIEVEMENT
Irene Worth

1989–1990

BEST NEW AMERICAN PLAYS
Craig Lucas, *Prelude to a Kiss*

Suzan-Lori Parks, *Imperceptible Mutabilities in the Third Kingdom*

Mac Wellman, *Bad Penny, Crowbar* and *Terminal Hip*

DIRECTION
Liz Diamond, *Imperceptible Mutabilities in the Third Kingdom*

Norman Rene, *Prelude to a Kiss*

Jim Simpson, *Bad Penny*

George C. Wolfe, *Spunk*

PERFORMANCES
Alec Baldwin, *Prelude to a Kiss*

Elzbieta Czyzewska, *Crowbar*

Karen Evans-Kandel, *Lear*

Marcia Jean Kurtz, *The Loman Family Picnic* and *When She Danced*

Ruth Maleczech, *Lear*

Greg Mehrten, *Lear*

Stephen Mellor, *Terminal Hip*

Isabell Monk, *Lear*

Jean Stapleton, *Mountain Language* and *The Birthday Party*

Stockard Channing

Pamela Tyson, *Imperceptible Mutabilities in the Third Kingdom*

Courtney B. Vance, *My Children! My Africa!*

Danitra Vance, *Spunk*

Lillias White, *Romance in Hard Times*

Mary Shultz, sustained excellence in performance

DESIGN
Daniel Moses Schreler, sustained excellence of sound design

George Tsypin, sustained excellence of set design

SUSTAINED ACHIEVEMENT
Money awarded to ACT-UP for the fight against AIDS

1990–1991

BEST NEW AMERICAN PLAY
Wallace Shawn, *The Fever*

PLAYWRITING
John Guare, *Six Degrees of Separation*

Mac Wellma, *Sincerity Forever*

DIRECTION
Michael Grief, *Machinal*

Lisa Peterson, *Light Shining in Buckinghamshire*

PERFORMANCES
Eileen Atkins, *A Room of One's Own*

Stockard Channing, *Six Degrees of Separation*

Joan Copeland, *The American Plan*

Angela Goethals, *The Good Times Are Killing Me*

Tony Goldwyn, *The Sum of Us*

Jan Leslie Harding, *Sincerity Forever*

John Leguizamo, *Mambo Mouth*

Michael Lombard, *What's Wrong With This Picture?*

Jodie Markell, *Machinal*

Anne Pitoniak, *Pygmalion*

Ron Rifkin, *The Substance of Fire*

Kathleen Widdoes, *Tower of Evil*

Betty Bourne, Precious Pearl, Peggy Shaw and Lois Weaver, ensemble performance, *Belle Reprieve*

DESIGN
Frances Aronson, sustained excellence of lighting design

Mark Board, sustained excellence of set design

William Ivey Long, sustained excellence of costume design

John Gromada, sound design, *Machinal*

SUSTAINED ACHIEVEMENT
The Wooster Group

1991–1992

BEST NEW AMERICAN PLAY (TIE)
Donald Margulies, *Sight Unseen*

Robbie McCauley, *Sally's Rape*

Paula Vogel, *The Baltimore Waltz*

PLAYWRITING
Neal Bell, sustained excellence

Romulus Linney, sustained excellence

Edward Albee

DIRECTION
Anne Bogart, *The Baltimore Waltz*
Mark Wing-Davy, *Mad Forest*

PERFORMANCES
Dennis Boutsikaris, *Sight Unseen*
Larry Bryggman, sustained excellence of performance
Randy Danson, sustained excellence of performance
Laura Esterman, *Marvin's Room*
Ofelia Gonzales, sustained excellence of performance
Deborah Hedwall, *Sight Unseen*
Cherry Jones, *The Baltimore Waltz*
Nathan Lane, sustained excellence of performance
James McDaniel, *Before It Hits Home*
S. Epatha Merkerson, *I'm Not Stupid*
Roger Rees, *The End of the Day*
Lynne Thigpen, *Boesman and Lena*

DESIGN
John Arnone, sustained excellence of set design
Marina Dragnici, sets and costumes, *Mad Forest*

SUSTAINED ACHIEVEMENT
Athol Fugard

1992–1993

PLAYWRITING
Harry Kondoleon, *The Houseguests*
Larry Kramer, *The Destiny of Me*
José Rivera, *Marisol*
Paul Rudnick, *Jeffrey*

DIRECTION
Christopher Ashley, *Jeffrey*
Michael Maggio, *Wings*
Frederick Zollo, *Aven' U Boys*

PERFORMANCES
Jane Alexander, *The Sisters Rosensweig*
Miriam Colon, sustained excellence of performance
Frances Conroy, *The Last Yankee*
David Drake, *The Night Larry Kramer Kissed Me*
Giancarlo Esposito, *Distant Fires*
Geoffrey C. Ewing, *Ali*
Hallie Foote, *The Roads to Home*
Edward Hibbert, *Jeffrey*
Bill Irwin, *Texts for Nothing*
John Cameron Mitchell, *The Destiny of Me*
Ellen Parker, sustained achievement of performance
Linda Stephens, *Wings*

DESIGN
Loy Arcenas, sustained excellence of set design
Howard Thies, sustained excellence of lighting design

SUSTAINED ACHIEVEMENT
JoAnne Akalaitis

1993–1994

BEST PLAY
Anna Deavere Smith, *Twilight: Los Angeles, 1992*

PLAYWRITING
Eric Bogosian, *Pounding Nails in the Floor With My Forehead*
Howard Korder, *The Lights*

DIRECTION
Andre Ernotte, *Christina Aberta's Father*
David Warren, *Pterodactyls*

PERFORMANCES
Carolee Carmello, *Hello Again*
Myra Carter, *Three Tall Women*
Gail Grate, *The America Play*
Danny Hoch, *Some People*
Judith Ivey, *The Moonshot Tape*
Peter Francis James, *The Maids*
Jefferson Mays, *Orestes*
Christopher McCann, *The Lights*
Tom Nelis, *The Medium*
Alice Playten, *The First Lady Suite*
Michael Potts, *The America Play*
Robert Stanton, *All in the Timing*

DESIGN
Kyle Chepulis, sustained excellence of set design
Brian MacDevitt, sustained excellence of lighting design

SUSTAINED ACHIEVEMENT
Edward Albee

New York Drama Critics' Circle Awards

1935–1936
Winterset, Maxwell Anderson

1936–1937
High Tor, Maxwell Anderson

1937–1938
Of Mice and Men, John Steinbeck

Citation for Best Foreign Play
Shadow and Substance, Paul Vincent
Carroll

1938–1939
No award

Citation for Best Foreign Play
The White Steed, Paul Vincent Carroll

1939–1940
The Time of Your Life, William Saroyan

1940–1941
Watch on the Rhine, Lillian Hellman

Citation for Best Foreign Play
The Corn Is Green, Emlyn Williams

1941–1942
No award

Citation for Best Foreign Play
Blithe Spirit, Noel Coward

1942–1943
The Patriots, Sidney Kingsley

1943–1944
No award

Citation for Best Foreign Play
Jacobowsky and the Colonel, Franz
Werfel and S. N. Behrman

1944–1945
The Glass Menagerie, Tennessee
Williams

1945–1946
No award

Citation for Best Musical
Carousel, Richard Rodgers and Oscar
Hammerstein II

1946–1947
All My Sons, Arthur Miller

Citation for Best Foreign Play
No Exit, Jean-Paul Sartre

Citation for Best Musical
Brigadoon, Alan Jay Lerner and
Frederick Loewe

Richard Rodgers and Oscar Hammerstein II

1947–1948
A Streetcar Named Desire, Tennessee
Williams

Citation for Best Foreign Play
The Winslow Boy, Terence Rattigan

1948–1949
Death of a Salesman, Arthur Miller

Citation for Best Foreign Play
The Madwoman of Chaillot, Jean
Giraudoux and Maurice Valency

Citation for Best Musical
South Pacific, Richard Rodgers, Oscar
Hammerstein II and Joshua Logan

1949–1950
The Member of the Wedding, Carson
McCullers

Citation for Best Foreign Play
The Cocktail Party, T. S. Eliot

Citation for Best Musical
The Consul, Gian Carlo Menotti

1950–1951
Darkness at Noon, Sidney Kingsley

Citation for Best Foreign Play
The Lady's Not for Burning,
Christopher Fry

Citation for Best Musical
Guys and Dolls, Abe Burrows, Jo
Swerling and Frank Loesser

1951–1952
I Am a Camera, John Van Druten

Citation for Best Foreign Play
Venus Observed, Christopher Fry

Citation for Best Musical
Pal Joey, Richard Rodgers, Lorenz Hart
and John O'Hara

**Distinguished and Original Contribution
to Theater**
Don Juan in Hell, George Bernard Shaw

1952–1953
Picnic, William Inge

Citation for Best Foreign Play
The Love of Four Colonels, by
Peter Ustinov

Citation for Best Musical
Wonderful Town, Joseph Fields, Jerome
Chodorov, Betty Comden, Adolph
Green and Leonard Bernstein

1953–1954
The Teahouse of the August Moon,
John Patrick

Citation for Best Foreign Play
Ondine, Jean Giraudoux

Citation for Best Musical
The Golden Apple, John Latouche and
Jerome Moross

1954–1955
Cat on a Hot Tin Roof, Tennessee
Williams

Citation for Best Foreign Play
Witness for the Prosecution,
Agatha Christie

Citation for Best Musical
The Saint of Bleecker Street, Gian Carlo
    Menotti

1955-1956
The Diary of Anne Frank, Frances
    Goodrich and Albert Hackett

Citation for Best Foreign Play
Tiger at the Gates, Jean Giraudoux and
    Christopher Fry

Citation for Best Musical
My Fair Lady, Frederick Loewe and Alan
    Jay Lerner

1956-1957
Long Day's Journey Into Night,
    Eugene O'Neill

Citation for Best Foreign Play
Waltz of the Toreadors, Jean Anouilh

Citation for Best Musical
The Most Happy Fella, Frank Loesser

1957-1958
Look Homeward, Angel, Ketti Frings

Citation for Best Foreign Play
Look Back in Anger, John Osborne

Citation for Best Musical
The Music Man, Meredith Willson

1958-1959
A Raisin in the Sun, Lorraine Hansberry

Citation for Best Foreign Play
The Visit, Friedrich Duerrenmatt-
    Maurice Valency

Citation for Best Musical
La Plume de ma Tante, Robert Dhery
    and Gerard Calvi

1959-1960
Toys in the Attic, Lillian Hellman

Citation for Best Foreign Play
Five Finger Exercise, Peter Shaffer

Citation for Best Musical
Fiorello!, Jerome Weidman, George
    Abbott, Jerry Bock and Sheldon
    Harnick

1960-1961
All the Way Home, Tad Mosel

Citation for Best Foreign Play
A Taste of Honey, Shelagh Delaney

Citation for Best Musical
Carnival, Michael Stewart

1961-1962
The Night of the Iguana, Tennessee
    Williams

Citation for Best Foreign Play
A Man for All Seasons, Robert Bolt

Citation for Best Musical
*How to Succeed in Business Without
    Really Trying,* Abe Burrows, Jack
    Weinstock, Willie Gilbert and Frank
    Loesser

1962-1963
Who's Afraid of Virginia Woolf?, Edward
    Albee

Special Citation
Beyond the Fringe, Alan Bennett, Peter
    Cook, Jonathan Miller and Dudley
    Moore

1963-1964
Luther, John Osborne

Citation for Best Musical
Hello, Dolly, Michael Stewart and Jerry
    Herman

Special Citation
The Trojan Women, Euripides

1964-1965
The Subject Was Roses, Frank D. Gilroy

Citation for Best Musical
Fiddler on the Roof, Joseph Stein, Jerry
    Bock and Sheldon Harnick

1965-1966
*The Persecution and Assassination of
    Marat as Performed by the
    Inmates of the Asylum of
    Charenton Under the Direction of
    the Marquis de Sade,* Peter Weiss

The Man of La Mancha, Dale
    Wasserman, Mitch Leigh and Joe
    Darion

1966-1967
The Homecoming, Harold Pinter

Citation for Best Musical
Cabaret, Joe Masteroff, John Kander
    and Fred Ebb

1967-1968
*Rosencrantz and Guildenstern Are
    Dead,* Tom Stoppard

Citation for Best Musical
Your Own Thing, Donald Driver, Hal
    Hester and Danny Apolinar

1968-1969
*The Great White
    Hope,* Howard
    Sackler

**Citation for Best
Musical**
1776, Sherman
    Edwards and
    Peter Stone

1969-1970
Borstal Boy, Frank McMahon

Citation for Best American Play
*The Effect of Gamma Rays on Man-in-
    the-Moon Marigolds,* Paul Zindel

Citation for Best Musical
Company, George Furth and Stephen
    Sondheim

1970-1971
Home, David Storey

Citation for Best American Play
The House of Blue Leaves, John Guare

Citation for Best Musical
Follies, James Goldman and Stephen
    Sondheim

1971-1972
That Championship Season, Jason
    Miller

Citation for Best Foreign Play
The Screens, Jean Genet

Citation for Best Musical
Two Gentlemen of Verona, adapted by
    John Guare and Mel Shapiro

1972-1973
The Changing Room, David Storey

Citation for Best American Play
The Hot l Baltimore, Lanford Wilson

Citation for Best Musical
A Little Night Music, Hugh Wheeler and
    Stephen Sondheim

1973-1974
The Contractors, David Storey

Citation for Best American Play
Short Eyes, Miguel Pinero

Citation for Best Musical
Candide, Leonard Bernstein, Hugh
    Wheeler and Richard Wilbur

1974-1975
Equus, Peter Shaffer

Tennessee Williams

Citation for Best American Play
The Taking of Miss Janie, Ed Bullins

Citation for Best Musical
A Chorus Line, James Kirkwood and Nicholas Dante

1975–1976
Travesties, Tom Stoppard

Citation for Best American Play
Streamers, David Rabe

Citation for Best Musical
Pacific Overtures, Stephen Sondheim, John Weidman and Hugh Wheeler

1976–1977
Otherwise Engaged, Simon Gray

Citation for Best American Play
American Buffalo, David Mamet

Citation for Best Musical
Annie, Thomas Meehan, Charles Strouse and Martin Charnin

1977–1978
Da, Hugh Leonard

Citation for Best Musical
Ain't Misbehavin', conceived by Richard Maltby, Jr.

1978–1979
The Elephant Man, Bernard Pomerance

Citation for Best Musical
Sweeney Todd, Hugh Wheeler and Stephen Sondheim

1979–1980
Talley's Folly, Lanford Wilson

Evita, Andrew Lloyd Webber and Tim Rice

Citation for Best Foreign Play
Betrayal, Harold Pinter

1980–1981
A Lesson From Aloes, Athol Fugard

Citation for Best American Play
Crimes of the Heart, Beth Henley

1981–1982
The Life and Adventures of Nicholas Nickleby, adapted by David Edgar

Citation for Best American Play
A Soldier's Play, Charles Fuller

1982–1983
Brighton Beach Memoirs, Neil Simon

Citation for Best Foreign Play
Plenty, David Hare

Citation for Best Musical
Little Shop of Horrors, Alan Menken and Howard Ashman

1983–1984
The Real Thing, Tom Stoppard

Citation for Best American Play
Glengarry Glen Ross, David Mamet

Citation for Best Musical
Sunday in the Park With George, Stephen Sondheim and James Lapine

1984–1985
Ma Rainey's Black Bottom, August Wilson

1985–1986
Lie of the Mind, Sam Shepard

Citation for Best Foreign Play
Benefactors, Michael Frayn

Special Citation
The Search for Signs of Intelligent Life in the Universe, Lily Tomlin and Jane Wagner

1986–1987
Fences, August Wilson

Citation for Best Foreign Play
Les Liaisons Dangereuses, Christopher Hampton

Citation for Best Musical
Les Misérables, Claude-Michel Schönberg and Alain Boublil

1987–1988
Joe Turner's Come and Gone, August Wilson

Citation for Best Foreign Play
The Road to Mecca, Athol Fugard

Citation for Best Musical
Into the Woods, Stephen Sondheim and James Lapine

1988–1989
The Heidi Chronicles, Wendy Wasserstein

Citation for Best Foreign Play
Aristocrats, Brian Friel

Special Citation
Largely New York, Bill Irwin

1989–1990
The Piano Lesson, August Wilson

Citation for Best Foreign Play
Privates on Parade, Peter Nichols

Citation for Best Musical
City of Angels, Larry Gelbart, Cy Coleman and David Zippel

1990–1991
Six Degrees of Separation, John Guare

Citation for Best Foreign Play
Our Country's Good, Timberlake Wertenbaker

Tom Stoppard

Citation for Best Musical
The Will Rogers Follies, Cy Coleman, Peter Stone, Betty Comden and Adolph Green

Special Citation
Eileen Atkins, *A Room of One's Own*

1991–1992
Dancing at Lughnasa, Brian Friel

Citation for Best American Play
Two Trains Running, August Wilson

1992–1993
Angels in America: Millennium Approaches, Tony Kushner

Citation for Best Foreign Play
Someone Who'll Watch Over Me, Frank McGuinness

Citation for Best Musical
Kiss of the Spider Woman, John Kander, Fred Ebb and Terrence McNally

1993–1994
Three Tall Women, Edward Albee

Twilight: Los Angeles, 1992, Anna Deavere Smith, writer/actress, received an award "for unique contribution to theatrical form."

Broadway's Longest-Running Shows

SHOW	DATES	PERFORMANCES
A Chorus Line	10/75–4/90	6,137
Oh, Calcutta!	9/76–8/89	5,962
Cats	10/82–present	5,172
42nd Street	8/80–1/89	3,485
Grease	2/72–4/80	3,388
Les Misérables	3/87–present	3,261
Fiddler on the Roof	9/64–7/72	3,242
Life With Father	11/39–7/47	3,224
Tobacco Road	12/33–5/41	3,182
Phantom of the Opera	1/88–present	2,974
Hello, Dolly!	1/64–12/70	2,844

Oh, Calcutta!

SHOW	DATES	PERFORMANCES
My Fair Lady	3/56–9/62	2,717
Annie	4/77–1/83	2,377
Man of La Mancha	11/65–6/71	2,329
Abies Irish Rose	5/22–10/27	2,327
Oklahoma!	3/43–5/48	2,212
South Pacific	4/49–1/54	1,925
Magic Show	5/74–12/78	1,920
Pippin	10/72–6/77	1,908
Gemini	5/77–9/81	1,819
Deathtrap	2/78–6/82	1,793
Harvey	11/44–1/49	1,775
Dancin'	3/78–6/82	1,774
La Cage Aux Folles	6/83–11/87	1,761
Hair	4/68–7/72	1,742
The Wiz	1/75–1/79	1,672
Born Yesterday	2/46–12/49	1,642
Miss Saigon	4/91–present	1,617
Ain't Misbehavin'	5/78–2/82	1,604
Best Little Whorehouse in Texas	6/78–3/82	1,584

SHOW	DATES	PERFORMANCES
Mary, Mary	3/61–12/64	1,572
Evita	9/79–6/83	1,567
Voice of the Turtle	12/43–1/48	1,557
Barefoot in the Park	10/63–6/64	1,532
Dreamgirls	12/81–7/85	1,521
Mame	5/66–1/70	1,503
Same Time, Next Year	3/76–9/78	1,453
Arsenic and Old Lace	1/41–6/44	1,444
The Sound of Music	11/59–6/63	1,443
How to Succeed in Business Without Really Trying	10/61–3/65	1,417
Hellzapoppin'	9/38–12/41	1,404
The Music Man	12/57–4/61	1,375
Funny Girl	3/64–7/67	1,348
Mummenschantz	3/77–4/80	1,326
Oh, Calcutta!	6/69–8/72	1,314
Brighton Beach Memoirs	3/83–5/86	1,299
Angel Street	12/41–12/44	1,295
Lightnin'	8/18–8/21	1,291
Promises, Promises	12/68–1/72	1,281
Crazy for You	2/92–present	1,262
The King and I	4/51–4/54	1,246
Cactus Flower	12/65–11/68	1,234
Sleuth	11/70–10/73	1,222
Torch Song Trilogy	6/82–5/85	1,222
1776	3/69–2/72	1,217
Equus	10/74–10/77	1,209
Sugar Babies	10/79–8/82	1,208
Guys and Dolls	11/50–6/53	1,200
Cabaret	11/66–9/69	1,166
Amadeus	12/80–9/83	1,161
Mister Roberts	2/48–1/51	1,157
Annie Get Your Gun	5/46–2/49	1,147
Guys and Dolls	4/92–1/95	1,143
The Seven Year Itch	11/52–8/55	1,141
Butterflies Are Free	10/69–7/72	1,128
Pins and Needles	11/37–6/40	1,108
Plaza Suite	2/68–10/70	1,097
They're Playing Our Song	2/79–9/81	1,082
Kiss Me, Kate	12/48–7/51	1,071
Don't Bother Me, I Can't Cope	4/72–11/74	1,065
Pajama Game	5/54–11/56	1,063
Shenandoah	1/75–8/77	1,050
Teahouse of the August Moon	10/53–4/56	1,027
Damn Yankees	5/55–10/57	1,019
Grand Hotel	11/89–4/92	1,018
Never Too Late	11/62–4/65	1,007
Beatlemania	6/77–10/79	1,006

Source: League of American Theatres and Producers

Broadway Season Statistics

Season	Gross (in millions)	Attendance (in millions)	New Productions	Touring Gross (in millions)
1957–1958	$ 38	7.2	56	$ 23
1958–1959	40	7.7	56	23
1959–1960	46	7.9	58	27
1960–1961	44	7.7	48	34
1961–1962	44	6.8	53	39
1962–1963	44	7.4	54	32
1963–1964	40	6.8	63	34
1964–1965	50	8.2	67	36
1965–1966	54	9.6	68	32
1966–1967	55	9.3	69	44
1967–1968	59	9.5	74	45
1968–1969	58	8.6	67	43
1969–1970	53	7.1	62	48
1970–1971	55	7.4	49	50
1971–1972	52	6.5	55	50
1972–1973	45	5.4	55	56
1973–1974	46	5.7	43	46
1974–1975	57	6.6	54	51
1975–1976	71	7.3	55	53
1976–1977	93	8.8	54	83
1977–1978	114	9.8	42	106
1978–1979	134	9.6	50	141
1979–1980	146	9.6	61	181
1980–1981	197	11.0	60	219
1981–1982	223	10.1	48	250
1982–1983	209	8.4	50	184
1983–1984	227	7.9	36	202
1984–1985	213	7.4	33	226
1985–1986	191	6.6	33	236
1986–1987	209	7.05	41	224
1987–1988	253	8.14	32	223
1988–1989	262	7.97	30	256
1989–1990	283	8.03	35	367
1990–1991	267	7.32	28	450
1991–1992	292	7.37	37	503
1992–1993	328	7.86	33	621
1993–1994	356	8.10	37	688

Source: League of American Theatres and Producers

PERFORMING ARTS TIME LINE

534 B.C.
The first formal competitions among playwrights are established in Greece. Thespis wins the first public contest for tragic poets and the term thespian derives from his name.

525–385 B.C.
The Athenian or Classical period introduces a dramatic era of tragic poets that includes Aeschylus (Agamemnon, 458 B.C.), Sophocles (Antigone, 441 B.C.; Oedipus Rex, 430 B.C.) and Euripides (Medea, 431 B.C.).

ca. 350 B.C.
Aristotle (384–322 B.C.) writes The Poetics, an analytical work that provides insight into the theoretical basis of Greek tragedy and comedy.

350–250 B.C.
The Hellenistic or Colonial period marks an era when comedy is preferred over tragedy. Old Comedy, buffoonery and farce that often attacks individuals and portrays the foibles of a social class, evolves into New Comedy, a more polished and refined humor that centers on shortcomings of middle classes. Comic drama moves from politics and philosophy to everyday life.

Broadway Theaters

Thirty-four theaters grace the Great White Way, the Broadway theater district, which lies within 41st to 53rd streets and Sixth to Ninth avenues.

Broadway in the 1920s

Circle in the Square
1633 Broadway
New York, NY 10019
(212) 239-6200

Cort Theatre
138 W. 48th St.
New York, NY 10036
(212) 239-6200

Gershwin Theatre
222 W. 51st St.
New York, NY 10019
(212) 307-4100

John Golden Theatre
252 W. 45th St.
New York, NY 10036
(212) 239-6200

Helen Hayes Theatre
240 W. 44th St.
New York, NY 10036
(212) 307-4100

Imperial Theatre
249 W. 45th St.
New York, NY 10036
(212) 239-6200

Walter Kerr Theatre
219 W. 48th St.
New York, NY 10036
(212) 239-6200

Longacre Theatre
220 W. 48th St.
New York, NY 10036
(212) 239-6200

Lunt-Fontanne Theatre
205 W. 46th St.
New York, NY 10036
(212) 307-4100

Ambassador Theatre
215 W. 49th St.
New York, NY 10019
(212) 239-6200

Brooks Atkinson Theatre
256 W. 47th St.
New York, NY 10036
(212) 307-4100

Ethel Barrymore Theatre
243 W. 47th St.
New York, NY 10036
(212) 239-6200

Martin Beck Theatre
302 W. 45th St.
New York, NY 10036
(212) 239-6200

Belasco Theatre
111 W. 44th St.
New York, NY 10036
(212) 239-6200

Booth Theatre
222 W. 45th St.
New York, NY 10036
(212) 239-6200

Broadhurst Theatre
235 W. 44th St.
New York, NY 10036
(212) 239-6200

Broadway Theatre
1681 Broadway
New York, NY 10019
(212) 239-6200

---

240 B.C.

A former slave, Livius Andronicus, presents performances of his Latin translations of a Greek tragedy and comedy to the Romans, giving them their first taste of Greek drama and literature. Roman theatrical productions begin to flourish.

1425

An anonymous writer composes the finest example in English of a medieval mystery play, *The Second Shephard's Play.* A popular form of medieval drama, mystery plays are dramatizations of incidents in the Old Testament.

1495

Everyman, the best surviving example of a morality play, is written. The morality play touches on large contemporary issues with moral overtones and describes the lives of everyday people facing temptation.

1489

Ballet is performed for the first time at a feast given by the Duke of Milan to celebrate his marriage to Isabella of Aragon.

Broadway in the 1940s

Lyceum Theatre
149 W. 45th St.
New York, NY 10036
(212) 239-6200

Majestic Theatre
245 W. 44th St.
New York, NY 10036
(212) 239-6200

Marquis Theatre
1535 Broadway
New York, NY 10036
(212) 307-4100

Minskoff Theatre
200 W. 45th St.
New York, NY 10036
(212) 307-4100

Music Box Theatre
239 W. 45th St.
New York, NY 10036
(212) 239-6200

Nederlander Theatre
208 W. 41st St.
New York, NY 10036
(212) 307-4100

Eugene O'Neill Theatre
230 W. 49th St.
New York, NY 10036
(212) 239-6200

Palace Theatre
1564 Broadway
New York, NY 10036
(212) 307-4100

Plymouth Theatre
236 W. 45th St.
New York, NY 10036
(212) 239-6200

Richard Rodgers Theatre
226 W. 46th St.
New York, NY 10036
(212) 307-4100

Roundabout Theatre
1530 Broadway
New York, NY 10036
(212) 869-8400

Royale Theatre
242 W. 45th St.
New York, NY 10036
(212) 239-6200

St. James Theatre
246 W. 44th St.
New York, NY 10036
(212) 239-6200

Neil Simon Theatre
250 W. 52nd St.
New York, NY 10019
(212) 307-4100

Shubert Theatre
225 W. 44th St.
New York, NY 10036
(212) 239-6200

Virginia Theatre
245 W. 52nd St.
New York, NY 10036
(212) 239-6200

Winter Garden Theatre
1634 Broadway
New York, NY 10019
(212) 239-6200

Broadway today

1570
Count Giovanni Bardi introduces the Elizabethan masque, an aristocratic form of entertainment that features music, dance and fantastic costuming.

1597
Jacopo Peri's musical fable, *Dafne*, often considered the first opera, is performed at the palace of Jacopo Corsi. Opera becomes the preferred entertainment of the aristocracy.

1598–1608
William Shakespeare writes *Much Ado About Nothing, As You Like It, All's Well That End's Well, Julius Caesar, Hamlet, Othello, King Lear, Macbeth* and *Anthony and Cleopatra*.

1607
Regarded as the first masterpiece in opera history, Claude Monteverdi's *Orfeo*, is performed and revolutionizes music by establishing a tonal system and giving the recitative a more flexible accompaniment.

1637
Venice becomes the home of the first public opera house, the San Cassiano Theater.

1661
Louis XIV officially recognizes dance instruction by establishing the Académie Royale de Danse.

Dance Magazine Awards

The *Dance Magazine* Awards, awarded annually in the spring, honor not only performers, but also choreographers, designers, administrators, historians, musicians and others whose contribution to dance merits special recognition.

1954
Dance on television:

Adventure (CBS)
Tony Charmoli (NBC)
Max Liebman (NBC)
Omnibus (CBS)

1955
Jack Cole
Gene Nelson
Moira Shearer

1956
Agnes De Mille
Martha Graham

1957
Lucia Chase
José Limón
Alicia Markova
Jerome Robbins

1958
Alicia Alonso
Doris Humphrey
Gene Kelly
Igor Youskevitch

1959
Dorothy Alexander
Fred Astaire
George Balanchine

1960
Merce Cunningham
Igor Moiseyev
Maria Tallchief

1961
Melissa Hayden
Anna Sokolow
Gwen Verdon

1962
Isadora Bennett
Margot Fonteyn
Bob Fosse

1963
Gower Champion
Robert Joffrey
Pauline Koner

1964
John Butler
Peter Gennaro
Edward Villella

1965
Edwin Denby
Margaret H'Doubler
Maya Plisetskaya

1966
Carmen de Lavallade
Sol Hurok
Wesleyan University Press

1967
Eugene Loring
Alwin Nikolais
Violette Verdy

1968
Erik Bruhn
Katherine Dunham
Carla Fracci

Martha Graham

1969
Sir Frederick Ashton
Carolyn Brown
Ted Shawn

1970
No Awards

1971
No Awards

1972
Anthony Dowell
Judith Jamison

1665

William Darby's *Ye Bare and Ye Cubb*, reportedly the first English-language play presented in the colonies, is performed in Accomac County, Virginia.

1685

Alessandro Scarlatti founds the Neapolitan School of opera, which establishes the da capo, or three-part aria. Mythological themes in opera are abandoned for historical material.

1689

The young women at Josias Priest's finishing school in Chelsea perform Henry Purcell's *Dido and Aeneas*, the first English operatic masterpiece.

1730

***Romeo and Juliet*, the first Shakespeare play to be presented in America, is performed in New York.**

1733

***La Serva Padrona* by Giovanni Pergolesi is performed in Naples, heralding the popularity of opera buffa or comic opera.**

1735

Ballet arrives in America, staged by Englishman Henry Holt, for the amusement of the Charleston, South Carolina, elite. John Hippisley's Flora, the first opera performed in America, is also presented in Charleston, South Carolina.

1973
The Christensen Brothers
(Lew, Harold and William)
Rudolf Nureyev

1974
Gerald Arpino
Maurice Béjart
Anthony Tudor

1975
Alvin Ailey
Cynthia Gregory
Arthur Mitchell

1976
Michael Bennett
Suzanne Farrell
E. Virginia Williams

1977
Murray Louis
Natalia Makarova
Peter Martins

1978
Mikhail Baryshnikov
Raoul Gelabert
Bella Lewitzky

1979
Aaron Copland
Jorge Donn
Erick Hawkins

1980
Patricia McBride
Ruth Page
Paul Taylor
Herbert Ross and Nora Kaye

1981
Selma Jeanne Cohen
Sir Anton Dolin
Twyla Tharp
Stanley Williams

1982
Fernando Bujones
Laura Dean
Arnold Spohr
Lee Theodore

1983
Jeannot Cerrone
John Neumeier
Michael Smuin
Martine van Hamel

1984
Alexandra Danilova
Robert Irving
Donald Saddler
Tommy Tune
Dance Masters of America, Inc.

1985
Charles "Honi" Coles
Richard Cragun
Frederic Franklin
Heather Watts
Walter Sorell

1986
No Awards

1987
Merrill Ashley
Trisha Brown
Liz Thompson
David White
Doris Hering

1988
"Dancing for Life"
Moscelyne Larkin and Roman Jasinski
P. W. Manchester
Kyra Nichols

1989
No Awards

1990
Garth Fagan
Eliot Feld
Hanya Holm

Mikhail Baryshnikov

1991
Virginia Johnson
Mark Morris
Jennifer Tipton

1992
Darci Kistler
Meredith Monk
Helgi Tomasson

1993
Bill T. Jones
Pierre Dulaine and Yvonne Marceau
Beatriz Rodriguez

1994
Christine Dakin
Kate Johnson
Jiří Kylián

1751

The first professional theater company in the colonies, the Virginia Company of Comedians, opens a temporary wooden playhouse in Williamsburg, Virginia.

1762

Christoph Willibald von Gluck's *Orfeo ed Euridice* premieres at the Hofburgtheater in Vienna, marking revolutionary changes and reform in opera seria.

1766

The first permanent American theater building, Southwark Theater, is erected in Philadelphia.

1778

Milan's Teatro alla Scala, Italy's leading opera house and one of the world's most renowned, is built.

1781

***Idomeneo,* Mozart's first mature opera seria premieres in Munich.**

1786

Mozart collaborates with Lorenzo da Ponte on *The Marriage of Figaro,* which premieres in Vienna. He completes *Don Giovanni* the following year, and it premieres in Prague.

Capezio Dance Awards

The Capezio Dance Awards, presented annually by the Capezio/Ballet Makers Dance Foundation, Inc., honor with a cash gift the performer, choreographer, critic, teacher, producer or administrator who has made a significant contribution to the art.

1952
Zachary Solov

1953
Lincoln Kirstein

1954
Doris Humphrey

1955
Louis Horst

1956
Genevieve Oswald

1957
Ted Shawn

1958
Alexandra Danilova

1959
Sol Hurok

1960
Martha Graham

1961
Ruth St. Denis

1962
Barbara Karinska

1963
Donald McKayle

1964
José Limón

1965
Maria Tallchief

1966
Agnes de Mille

1967
Paul Taylor

1968
Lucia Chase

1969
John Martin

1970
William Kolodney

1971
Arthur Mitchell

1972
La Meri

Reginald and Gladys Laubin

1973
Isadora Bennett

1974
Robert Joffrey

1975
Robert Irving

1976
Jerome Robbins

1977
Merce Cunningham

1978
Hanya Holm

1979
Alvin Ailey

1980
Walter Terry

1981
Dorothy Alexander

1982
Alwin Nikolais

1983
Harvey Lichtenstein

1984
William Christensen

Harold Christensen

Lew Christensen

1985
Doris Hering

1986
Antony Tudor

Bob Fosse

1987
Fred Astaire

Bob Fosse

Rudolf Nureyev

Jac Venza

1988
Charles "Honi" Coles

1989
Edward Villella

1990
Jacques d'Amboise

1991
John Curry

Katherine Dunham

Darci Kistler

Igor Youskevitch

1992
Frederic Franklin

1993
Dance/USA

1994
Urban Bush Women

1814

The third and most successful version of Ludwig von Beethoven's only opera, *Fidelio* premieres at Vienna's Theater an der Wien.

1816

Gioachino Rossini completes his great musical farce, *Il Barbiere di Siviglia*, which

premieres in Rome. Gaslighting is used for the first time in American theater at Philadelphia's Chesnut Street Theatre.

1859

Charles Gounod's *Faust* premieres at the Théâtre Lyrique in Paris. The French Opera House, the first great opera house in America,

is built in New Orleans.

1871

Giuseppe Verdi's *Aïda* premieres in Cairo, Egypt. The first collaboration of W.S. Gilbert and Sir Arthur Sullivan, *Thespis,* is performed at London's Gaiety Theatre.

1876

The first complete production of Wagner's *Ring* cycle, a titanic cycle of four musical dramas, opens the first Bayreuth Festival.

CONTINUED PAGE 679 ▶

Bessie Awards

The New York Dance and Performance Awards (Bessies), named in honor of renowned dance teacher Bessie Schönberg, honor the creative individuals and organizations that define modern dance.

1984

CHOREOGRAPHERS AND CREATORS
Anne Bogart, *South Pacific*

Timothy Buckley, *Barn Fever*

Yoshiko Chuma and the School of Hard Knocks,
Collective work

Eiko and Koma, *Grain* and *Night Tide*

Julia Heyward, *No Local Stops*

Fred Holland and Ishmael Houston-Jones, *Cowboys, Dreams
and Ladders*

Mark Morris, season

Stephanie Skura, *It's Either Now or Later* and *Art Business*

Nina Wiener, *Wind Devil*

PERFORMERS
Pina Bausch and the Wuppertaler Tanztheatre, *1980*

Rob Besserer

Chuck Greene, *Sweet Saturday Night*

Steven Humphrey

John McLaughlin

Sara Rudner

Valda Setterfield

LIGHTING DESIGNERS
Beverly Emmons, sustained achievement

Carol Mullins, collective work

Jennifer Tipton, sustained achievement

VISUAL DESIGNERS
Power Boothe, *Variety Show* and *Framework*

Judy Pfaff, *Wind Devil*

COMPOSERS
Anthony Davis, *Hemispheres*

Lenny Pickett with Clifford Arnell, *Adrift*

SUSTAINED CREATIVE ACHIEVEMENT
Trisha Brown, *Set and Reset* and sustained achievement

David Gordon, *Framework*, *The Photographer* and sustained
achievement

SPECIAL ACHIEVEMENT CITATION
Studies Project of Movement Research, Inc.: Mary Overlie,
Wendell Beavers and Renee Rockoff

1985

CHOREOGRAPHERS AND CREATORS
Johanna Boyce, *Johanna Boyce With the Calf Women and
Horse Men*

Tom Brazil/Courtesy of Mark Morris Dance Group

Mark Morris Dance Group

John Jesurun, *Chang in a Void Moon*

Robert Longo, *Marble Fog*

Susan Marshall, *Concert*

Judith Ren-Lay, *The Grandfather Tapes*

Susan Rethorst, *Son of Famous Men*

Cydney Wilkes, *16 Falls in Color Searching for Girl*

PERFORMERS
Frederike Bedard, *Businessman in the Process of Becoming
an Angel*

Sean Curran, *Secret Pastures*

Louise LeCavalier, *Businessman in the Process of Becoming
an Angel*

Vicky Shick, sustained achievement

Teri Weksler, sustained achievement

LIGHTING DESIGNERS
Tony Giovannetti, sustained achievement

Carol McDowell, *Be Good to Me*

VISUAL DESIGNERS
Pepon Osorio, *Cocinando*

Renata Petroni

Huck Snyder, *Go West* and *Diary of a Somnambulist*

Liliana Villegas, *Aga*

COMPOSERS
Peter Gordon, *Secret Pastures* and *Falso Movimento*

David Linton, *Simpleton's Guide to the Universe*

Dudu Tucci, *Of a Body in a Moon*

SUSTAINED COLLABORATIVE ACHIEVEMENT
Dana Reitz and Jim Turrell, *Severe Clear*

SUSTAINED CREATIVE ACHIEVEMENT
Meredith Monk

The Wooster Group, sustained achievement

SPECIAL ACHIEVEMENT CITATIONS
Val Bourne and the London Dance Umbrella

Cornelius Conboy and Dennis Gattra for 8BC

Robert Ellis Dunn

Deborah Jowitt

National Endowment for the Arts Dance Program directors: Ruth Mayleas, June Arey, Don Anderson, Joe Krakora, Rhoda Grauer, Suzanne Weil and Nigel Redden

COMPOSERS
David Linton, *Walk-In*

David Van Tieghem, collective work

SUSTAINED COLLABORATIVE ACHIEVEMENT
Trisha Brown, Beverly Emmons, Nancy Graves and Peter Zummo, *Lateral Pass*

Laura Dean and Steve Reich, *Impact* and *Force Field*

SPECIAL ACHIEVEMENT CITATIONS
John Cage and Merce Cunningham

Ellen Robbins

Louise Roberts

1986

CHOREOGRAPHERS AND CREATORS
John Bernd, *Lost and Found* (Scenes From a Life)

David Cale, *The Redthroats*

Molissa Fenley, *Cenotaph*

Bill T. Jones and Arnie Zane, *Freedom of Information*

John Kelly, collective work

Edouard Lock, *Human Sex*

Bebe Miller, *Spending Time Doing Things* and *Gypsy Pie*

Stephen Petronio, *Walk-In*

PERFORMERS
Jeannie Hutchins

Amy Pivar

Guillermo Resto

Mary Shultz

Erin Thompson

LIGHTING DESIGNERS
Blu, sustained achievement

Gary Mintz, *Esperanto*

Phil Sandstrom, *Twain*

VISUAL DESIGNERS
Terry Allen, *Pedal Steal*

Eva Buchmuller, *Dreamland*

Roy Faudree, *Last Resort*

Joe Fyfe, Laurie Hawkinson, Kristin Jones, Andrew Ginzel, Ricardo Scofidio, Elizabeth Diller, Kit-Yin Snyder, Allan Wexler, Elyn Zimmerman and George Palumbo, *Memory Theater of Giulio Camillo*

1987

CHOREOGRAPHERS AND CREATORS
The Adaptors, *The Bed Experiment One*

Anne Teresa de Keersmaeker, *Rosas Danst Rosas*

Ethyl Eichelberger, collective work

Karen Finley, *The Constant State of Desire*

Ralph Lemon and Bebe Miller, *Two*

Steve Paxton, collective work, *Part* and *Goldberg Variations*

Dana Reitz and Jennifer Tipton, *Circumstantial Evidence*

Robert Wilson, David Byrne and Suzushi Hanayagi, *The Knee Plays*

PERFORMERS
Meg Eginton

Donald Fleming, collective work

Lisa Nelson, *Part* and ongoing work

Nicky Paraiso, collective work

Shelley Washington, sustained achievement

LIGHTING DESIGNERS
Remon Fromont, *Rosas Danst Rosas*

Phil Sandstrom, Mark Morris season

VISUAL DESIGNERS
Charles Atlas, Bodymap and Leigh Bowery, *No Fire Escape in Hell*

Pierre Hebert, *The Technology of Tears*

COMPOSER
Edwina Lee Tyler, *Life Dance*

SPECIAL ACHIEVEMENT CITATIONS
Charles Atlas

Ellen Stewart

1879
Henrik Ibsen's, *A Doll's House,* a revolutionary play that centers on the repression of women, deeply offends conservatives and thrills a newly awakened European conscience when it premieres at the Royal Theatre in Copenhagen.

1883
The Metropolitan Opera House in New York opens with Gounod's *Faust.*

1896
Giacomo Puccini's *La Bohème* premieres at the Teatro Reggio in Turin, Italy, conducted by Arturo Toscanini.

1901
Founder of the Moscow Art Theatre, Konstantin Stanislavski formulates the revolutionary Stavislavski Method of acting, which requires actors to see and hear on stage as they do in real life, enabling them to react to theatrical situations in the same way they would in real life.

1902
Claude Debussy introduces impressionism in *Pelléas and Mélisande* at the Opéra Comique in Paris.

1904
Anton Chekhov introduces modern realism at the premiere of *The Cherry Orchard* at the Moscow Art Theatre.

1988

CHOREOGRAPHERS AND CREATORS
Ann Carlson, *Animals*

William Forsythe, *Artifact, Behind the China Dogs* and *Steptext*

Ann Hamilton, *The Earth Never Gets Flat*

Bill Irwin, *Largely* and *New York*

John Kelly, *Find My Way Home*

Tere O'Connor, *Heaven Up North*

Otrabanda Co., *Brain Cafe*

Elizabeth Streb, collective work

Wim Vandekeybus/Maximalist! (Thierry De Mey and Peter Vermeersch), *What the Body Does Not Remember*

PERFORMERS
Lance Gries

Kate Johnson, sustained achievement

Joseph Lennon

Norwood Pennewell

Keith Sabado

Ron Vawter, sustained achievement

LIGHTING DESIGNERS
David Ferri, collective work

Carol Mullins, *Cinderella/Cendrillon*

Stan Pressner, *Find My Way Home*

VISUAL DESIGNER
Janie Geiser, *The Three Lives of Lucie Cabrol*

COMPOSERS
James Baker, *Heaven Up North*

Jeff Halpern, *Cinderella/Cendrillon, Miracolo D'Amore* and *Find My Way Home*

"Blue" Gene Tyranny, sustained achievement

SPECIAL ACHIEVEMENT CITATIONS
ACT-UP

Bessie Schönberg

1989

CHOREOGRAPHERS AND CREATORS
Dancenoise, *All the Rage*

Molissa Fenley, *State of Darkness*

Guillermo Gomez-Pena, *Border Brujo*

Bill T. Jones, *D-Man in the Waters*

John Malpede, Kevin Williams and LAPD, *LAPD Inspects America*

Linda Mancini, concert

Dianne McIntyre, *In Living Color*

John O'Keefe, *Shimmer*

Ralf Ralf, *The Summit*

PERFORMERS
Arthur Aviles

Christopher Batenhorst

Susan Blankensop, collective work

Laurie Carlos, *Thought Music* and *Heat*

Diane Madden

Harry Whittaker Sheppard, *School of Hard Knocks*

LIGHTING DESIGNERS
Dave Feldman, *In Motion*

Mark Lancaster, *Five Stone Wind*

David Moodey, *State of Darkness*

Howard Thies, collective work

VISUAL DESIGNER
Annette Zindel, *Changing Face* and *Fear of Standing Upright*

COMPOSERS
Jacob Burckhardt, collective work

Mieczyslaw Litwinski, *Safe Tradition*

SPECIAL ACHIEVEMENT CITATIONS
Ellie Covan

Lori E. Seid

1990

CHOREOGRAPHERS AND CREATORS
Ulysses Dove, *Episodes*

Eiko and Koma, *Passage*

Garth Fagan, sustained achievement

Karen Finley, *We Keep Our Victims Ready*

Margarita Guergue and Hahn Rowe, *We Were Never There*

Robbie McCauley, *Sally's Rape*

Mark Morris, *Dido and Aeneas*

Pat Oleszko, sustained achievement

Wim Vandekeybus, *Les Porteuses de Mauvaises Nouvelles*

1905

Audiences are offended by Richard Strauss's *Salome* at the Dresden Opera. Isadora Duncan establishes the first school of modern dance in Berlin.

1911

***Der Rosenkavalier*, Richard Strauss's masterpiece, premieres in** Dresden. The Winter Garden Theater opens in New York.

1920

Eugene O'Neill's first full-length play, *Beyond the Horizon*, is produced on Broadway and wins a Pulitzer Prize, marking the beginning of modern American drama. Rising popular interest in African-American literature sparks the beginning of the Harlem Renaissance.

1925

Alban Berg adopts atonal composition and *sprechstimme* or speech-song in his opera *Wozzeck*, which premieres at Berlin's State Opera.

1926

Martha Graham, the American pioneer of the modern-dance revolt, gives her first New York performance, consisting of 18 barefoot, exotically costumed dances.

PERFORMERS
Arthur Armijo
Victoria Finlayson
Penny Hutchinson
Jonathan Riseling, *Tease*
Louise Smith, *Brightness*
Gail Turner, collective work

LIGHTING DESIGNERS
Roma Flowers
Susanne Poulin

VISUAL DESIGNERS
Liz Prince, collective work
Matthew Yokobowsky, *Brightness*

COMPOSERS
Hans Peter Kuhn, *Suspect Terrain*
A. Leroy and Mimi Goese, *Last Forever*
Max Roach, collective work

SPECIAL ACHIEVEMENT CITATIONS
Annabelle Gamson
Beate Gordon
Martha Wilson

1991

CHOREOGRAPHERS AND CREATORS
Richard Elovich, *Someone Else From Queens Is Queer*
Alice Farley, collective work
Dan Froot, *17 Kilos of Garlic*
David Gordon, *The Mysteries and What's So Funny*
David Hammons, *Retrospective* and collective work
James Luna, *Take a Picture of an Indian*
Music and Dance of Sumatra, *Festival of Indonesia*
Lora Nelson, Paul Clay and Cydney Wilkes, *Window on the Nether Sea*
Paul Zaloom, *My Civilization*

PERFORMERS
Kyle DeCamp
Paula Gifford
Chris Komar, sustained achievement
Jeremy Nelson, sustained achievement
David Neumann
Desmond Richardson

VISUAL DESIGNER
Anthony Chase, sustained achievement
Mimi Gross, sustained achievement
Sue Reese, *Running*
Huck Snyder, *Love of a Poet, Maybe It's Cold Outside* and *Last Supper*

COMPOSERS
Tom Cora, *San Andreas*
Julius Hemphill, *Last Supper* and *Long Tongues*
Pauline Oliveros, *Contenders*

SPECIAL ACHIEVEMENT CITATIONS
Nancy Duncan
Carlos Gutierrez-Solana
Yuriko

1992

CHOREOGRAPHERS AND CREATORS
Bernard Djola Branner, Brian Freeman and Eric Gupton (Pomo Afro Homos), *Fierce Love: Stories From Black Gay Life*
Donald Byrd, *The Minstrel Show*
Ping Chong, collective work
Frank Conversano, collective work
Craig Harris and Sekou Sundiata, *Saturday Concert of the Fire Wall Festival*
Linda Montano, *7 Years of Living Art*
Marta Renzi, *Vital Signs*
The Rhythm Technicians and Rock Steady Crew, collective work
Urban Bush Women, collective work

PERFORMERS
Kim Y. Bears, *Philadanco*
Steve Mellor, *7 Blowjobs*
Mark Robison, *Ringside*
Natalie Rogers, *Griot/New York*
Viola Sheely, *Praise House* and *Vanquished by Voodoo*
Scot Willingham

LIGHTING DESIGNER
Michael Mazzola

1927
The Broadway musical links with opera in Jerome Kern's revolutionary *Show Boat*.

1930
Jean Rosenthal, one of the greatest lighting designers in theater history, pioneers the concept of stage lighting.

1931
The Metropolitan Opera House broadcasts *Hänsel und Gretel* as the first of its weekly Saturday matinee radio programs.

1934
George Balanchine opens the School of American Ballet in New York City.

1935
George Gershwin combines black folk idiom and Broadway musical techniques in *Porgy and Bess*.

1948
Long-playing records make complete opera recordings available for the mass market.

1950
Broadway's skyrocketing production costs spur the popularity of Off-Broadway and regional theater. The Broadway Movement prompts the conversion of lofts, cafes and other spaces into theaters.

Merce Cunningham

VISUAL DESIGNERS
Gabriel Berry, *The Minstrel Show* and *Place*

Donna Dennis, *Quintland*

Martin Puryear, *Griot/New York*

COMPOSERS
Leroy Jenkins, *The Mother of Three Sons*

Robert Mirabal, *Land*

Carl Riley, *Praise House*

SPECIAL ACHIEVEMENT CITATIONS
Chuck Davis and Dance Africa

Howard Moody and Judson Memorial Church

Nuyorican Poets Cafe: Miguel Algarin, Willie Correa, Lois Griffith, Bob Holman and Roland Legiardi-Laura

1993

CHOREOGRAPHERS AND CREATORS
Idris Ackamoor and Rhodessa Jones, *Big Butt Girls, Hard-Headed Women*

Maureen Angelos, Babs Davy, Dominique Dibbell, Peg Healey and Lisa Kron (The Five Lesbian Brothers), Collective work

Beverly Blossom, sustained achievement

David Cale and Roy Nathanson, *Deep in a Dream of You*

Laurie Carlos, *White Chocolate*

Merce Cunningham, *Enter*

Yvonne Meier, *The Shining*

Alyson Pou, *To Us at Twilight*

Sally Silvers, *Small Room*

Mary Ellen Strom, *Witness*

PERFORMERS
Nikki Castro, sustained achievement

Niles Ford, *Historias*

Mimi Goese, *Every Day Newt Burman* (The Trilogy of Cyclic Existence)

Everett Quinton, *Brother Truckers*

Eileen Thomas, sustained achievement

Sam Weber, sustained achievement

LIGHTING DESIGNER
Robert Wierzel, sustained achievement

VISUAL DESIGNERS
Bloolips, Ivan, Gretal Feather and David Kavanagh, *Get Hur*

Kyle Chepulis, *Land of Fog and Whistles*

Bill Morrison, *Every Day Newt Burman* (The Trilogy of Cyclic Existence)

COMPOSERS
Tan Dun, *Jo Ha Kyu*

Christopher Hyams-Hart, *Momentary Order*

James Lo, *Furnished/Unfurnished*

Arthur Russell, sustained achievement

SPECIAL ACHIEVEMENT CITATIONS
Joan Duddy

Donna Ann McAdams

1994

No awards were given this year due to insufficient funding.

Major U. S. Dance Companies

David Turner/Courtesy of Lar Lubovitch Dance Company

Lar Lubovitch Dance Company

Alvin Ailey American Dance Theatre
211 W. 61st St., 3rd Floor
New York, NY 10023
(212) 767-0940

American Ballet Theatre
890 Broadway
New York, NY 10003
(212) 477-3030

Ballet Hispanica of New York
167 W. 89th St.
New York, NY 10024
(212) 362-6710

Ballet West
50 W. 200th S.
Salt Lake City, UT 84101
(801) 524-8300

Boston Ballet
19 Clarendon St.
Boston, MA 02116
(617) 695-6950

Trisha Brown Co.
225 Lafayette St., Suite 807
New York, NY 10012
(212) 334-9374

Lucinda Childs Dance Co.
541 Broadway
New York, NY 10012
(212) 431-7599

Cunningham Dance Foundation
55 Bethune St.
New York, NY 10014
(212) 255-8240

Dance Theatre of Harlem
466 W. 152nd St.
New York, NY 10031
(212) 690-2800

Garth Fagan Dance
50 Chesnut St.
Rochester, NY 14604
(716) 454-3260

Feld Ballets/NY
890 Broadway, 8th Floor
New York, NY 10003
(212) 777-7710

Martha Graham Dance Co.
360 E. 63rd St.
New York, NY 10021
(212) 832-9166

Erick Hawkins Dance Co.
375 W. Broadway, 5th Floor
New York, NY 10012
(212) 226-5363

Houston Ballet
1921 W. Bell
P.O. Box 130487
Houston, TX 77019-0487
(713) 523-6300

Hubbard Street Dance Chicago
218 S. Wabash Ave., 3rd Floor
Chicago, IL 60604
(312) 663-0853

Jazz Dance
276 Riverside Drive
New York, NY 10025
(212) 662-7256

Joffrey Ballet
130 W. 56th St., 8th Floor
New York, NY 10019
(212) 265-7300

Bill T. Jones Dance Co.
853 Broadway, Suite 1706
New York, NY 10003
(212) 477-1850

Paula Josa-Jones
185 Green St.
Cambridge, MA 02139
(617) 864-3191

Liz Lerman Dance Exchange
1664 Columbia Road N.W., Suite 21
Washington D.C. 20009
(202) 232-0833

Lewitsky Dance Co.
1055 Wilshire Blvd., Suite 1140
Los Angeles, CA 90017
(213) 580-6338

José Limón Dance Foundation
611 Broadway, 9th Floor
New York, NY 10012
(212) 777-3353

Nikolais Louis Dance Theatre
375 W. Broadway, 5th Floor
New York, NY 10012
(212) 226-7700

Lar Lubovitch Dance Co.
15 W. 18th St., 7th Floor
New York, NY 10011-4604
(212) 242-0633

Miami City Ballet
905 Lincoln Road
Miami Beach, FL 33139
(305) 532-4880

Momix Dance Co.
P.O. Box 1035
Washington, CT 06793
(203) 868-7454

Elisa Monte Dance Co.
9 Great Jones St., #3
New York, NY 10012
(212) 533-2226

Mark Morris Dance Co.
225 Lafayette St., Suite 504
New York, NY 10012
(212) 219-3660

Jennifer Muller
131 W. 24th St., 4th Floor
New York, NY 10011
(212) 691-3803

New York City Ballet
20 Lincoln Center
New York, NY 10023
(212) 870-5656

Ohio Ballet
354 E. Market St.
Akron, OH 44325
(216) 972-7900

Pacific Northwest Ballet
301 Mercer St.
Seattle, WA 98109
(206) 441-9411

The Parsons Dance Co.
130 W. 56th St.
New York, NY 10019
(212) 247-3203

Pennsylvania Ballet
1101 S. Broad St.
Philadelphia, PA 19147
(215) 551-7000

Philadanco
9 N. Preston St.
Philadelphia, PA 19104
(215) 387-8200

Pilobolus Dance Theatre
P.O. Box 388
Washington Depot, CT 06794
(203) 868-0538

Pittsburgh Ballet Theater
2900 Liberty Ave.
Pittsburgh, PA 15201-1500
(412) 281-0360

San Francisco Ballet
455 Franklin St.
San Francisco, CA 94102
(415) 861-5600

Paul Taylor Dance Co.
552 Broadway
New York, NY 10012
(212) 431-5562

Twyla Tharp Dance Co.
336 Central Park W.
New York, NY 10025
(212) 932-3000

Washington Ballet
3515 Wisconson Ave., N.W.
Washington D.C. 20016
(202) 362-3606

White Oak Dance Project
1830 Rittenhouse Square
Philadelphia, PA 19103
(215) 731-0722

Major U.S. Opera Companies

Arizona Opera
3501 N. Mountain Ave.
P.O. Box 42828
Tucson, AZ 85733
(602) 293-4336

Baltimore Opera Co.
1202 Maryland Ave.
Baltimore, MD 21201
(410) 625-1600

Central City Opera
621 17th St., Suite 1601
Denver, CO 80293
(303) 292-6500

Cincinnati Opera Associates
1241 Elm St.
Cincinnati, OH 45210
(513) 621-1919

Cleveland Opera
1422 Euclid Ave., Suite 1052
Cleveland, OH 44115
(216) 575-0900

The Dallas Opera
3102 Oaklawn Ave., Suite 480
Dallas, TX 75219
(214) 443-1043

Florentine Opera Company
735 N. Water St., Suite 1315
Milwaukee, WI 53202-4106
(414) 291-5700

Florida Grand Opera Associates
1200 Coral Way
Miami, FL 33145
(305) 854-1643

Houston Grand Opera Association
510 Preston
Houston, TX 77002-1594
(713) 546-0200

Kentucky Opera
101 S. Eighth St.
Louisville, KY 40202
(502) 584-4500

Los Angeles Music Center Opera
135 N. Grand Ave.
Los Angeles, CA 90012
(213) 972-7211

Lyric Opera of Chicago
20 N. Wacker Drive
Chicago, IL 60606
(312) 332-2244

Lyric Opera of Kansas City
1029 Central St.
Kansas City, MO 64105
(816) 471-4933

Metropolitan Opera Association
Lincoln Center
New York, NY 10023
(212) 799-3100

Michigan Opera Theatre
Lothrop Landing
104 Lothrop
Detroit, MI 48202
(313) 874-7850

The Minnesota Opera
620 N. First St.
Minneapolis, MN 55401
(612) 333-2700

New York City Opera
20 Lincoln Center
New York, NY 10023
(212) 870-5500

The Ohio Light Opera
The College of Wooster
Wooster, OH 44691
(216) 263-2090

Opera Colorado
695 S. Colorado Blvd., Suite 20
Denver, CO 80222
(303) 778-1500

Opera Company of Philadelphia
510 Walnut St., Suite 1600
Philadelphia, PA 19106
(215) 928-2100

Opera Pacific
9 Executive Circle, Suite 190
Irvine, CA 92714
(714) 474-4488

Opera Theatre of St. Louis
539 Garden Ave.
St. Louis, MO 63119
(314) 961-0171

Pittsburgh Opera, Inc.
711 Penn Ave., 8th Floor
Pittsburgh, PA 15222
(412) 281-0912

Portland Opera Association
1515 S.W. Morrison
Portland, OR 97205
(503) 241-1401

San Diego Opera
1200 Third Ave., Suite 1824
San Diego, CA 92101
(619) 232-7636

San Francisco Opera
301 Van Ness Ave.
San Francisco, CA 94102
(415) 861-4008

Seattle Opera Association
1020 John St.
P.O. Box 9248
Seattle, WA 98109-0248
(206) 389-7600

Virginia Opera
160 Virginia Beach Blvd.
Norfolk, VA 23510
(804) 627-9545

Utah Opera Company
50 W. 200th S.
Salt Lake City, UT 84111
(801) 323-6868

The Washington Opera
Kennedy Center
Washington D.C. 20566-0012
(202) 416-7890

Performing Arts Magazines and Journals

THEATER

American Theatre
355 Lexington Ave.
New York, NY 10017
(212) 697-5230

Backstage
1515 Broadway
New York, NY 10036-8986
(212) 764-7300

BCA News
Business Committee for the Arts, Inc.
1775 Broadway, Suite 510
New York, NY 10019-1942
(212) 664-0600

Ford Foundation Report
Office of Communications
320 E. 43rd St.
New York, NY 10017
(212) 573-5000

Lighting Dimensions
32 W. 18th St.
New York, NY 10011
(212) 229-2965

TCI
32 W. 18th St.
New York, NY 10011-4612
(212) 229-2965

Theater Week
28 W. 25th St., 4th Floor
New York, NY 10010
(212) 627-2120

Theatre Design and Technology
10 W. 19th St., Suite 5A
New York, NY 10011
(212) 924-9088

Variety
249 W. 17th St.
New York, NY 10016
(212) 645-0067

DANCE

Dance Chronicle
Marcel Dekker, Inc.
270 Madison Ave.
New York, NY 10016
(212) 696-9000

Dance Ink
145 Central Park W.
New York, NY 10023
(212) 826-9607

Dance Magazine
33 W. 60th St., 10th Floor
New York, NY 10023
(212) 245-9050

Dance Research Journal
Congress on Research in Dance
SUNY — Brockport
Department of Dance
350 New Campus Drive
Brockport, NY 14420-2939
(716) 395-2590

Dance/USA Journal
1156 15th St. N.W., Suite 820
Washington D.C. 20005
(202) 833-1717

Danceview
P.O. Box 34435
Martin Luther King Station
Washington D.C. 20043
(202) 554-5818

OPERA

Opera Fanatic Bel Canto Society
11 Riverside Drive
New York, NY 10023-2504
(212) 877-1595

Opera News
Metropolitan Opera Guild
70 Lincoln Center Plaza
New York, NY 10023-6593
(212) 769-7080

Performing Arts Glossary

act A unit of theatrical action composed of several scenes.

adagio 1. A ballet movement that is performed slowly. **2.** The first part of the traditional pas de deux, which requires skill in balancing, lifting and turning.

antagonist The character who opposes the action and motivations of the leading character.

apron The area of a stage extending beyond the proscenium.

aria An accompanied solo vocal performance, usually found in opera or oratorio.

Luciano Pavarotti performs an aria

arabesque The ballet position in which the dancer extends one leg to the rear while holding up one or both arms.

aside 1. A form of address that is directed at the audience outside the dialogue on stage. **2.** A line a character speaks without other characters hearing.

assemblé A jump from one foot while the other leg is raised.

backing The flat used to block the view of the area beyond doors and windows in a theater.

balletomane A ballet enthusiast.

barn door The four-doored device that fits around a lighting instrument, shaping the light beam and keeping it in place.

bas The dance term that refers to the arms being held down, close to the body.

batterie The crisscrossing movement of the legs during a jump.

beat 1. The smallest unit of drama and the primary building block of a scene. **2.** A moment that builds conflict and reveals motivation.

bel canto Operatic singing in the Italian manner, characterized by legato, rich tone, evenness and agility in passagework. It is usually found in works from the 17th and 18th centuries.

blocking The director's plan for the actors' movements.

border 1. The material hung above the stage that prevents audiences from seeing into the fly space. **2.** The lighting hung above the stage.

bourées Small dance steps taken together, en pointe.

box set The standard form of an interior set that shows three walls of a room.

ciseaux A jump in which the legs open wide.

climax The apex of the action and conflict in a drama.

closed positions The first, third and fifth ballet positions in which the feet are together.

conflict The opposition between characters or within one character that motivates dramatic action.

corps de ballet The dancers in a ballet company who perform as a group.

counterweight The sand bag or iron weight that balances the weight of scenery suspended from lines.

cue A word, musical entry or action that spurs a response from an actor or signals a task for the crew.

curtain raiser A short performance offered before the main presentation.

cyclorama The curved drop that when illuminated simulates the sky or creates an abstract background. Also called **cyc.**

dégagé A sliding motion of the foot outward from one of the five ballet positions.

denouement The resolution of action and conflict occurring after the climax.

dimmer The electronic device that controls the brightness of a lighting instrument.

downstage The area of the stage closest to the audience.

drop A large piece of fabric painted and used as scenery.

échappé The jump taken from the fifth position that is completed in the second or fourth position.

en pointe The ballet position in which a dancer performs on his or her toes.

entrechat The crossing of the legs at the thigh or calf while in the air.

flat A flat piece of painted scenery, generally made from wood and fabric.

fly The area over the stage that contains lighting instruments, scenery and equipment to raise and lower scenery.

follow spot A bright spotlight used to track an actor's movements on the stage.

footlights The strip of lights near the apron on the stage floor.

fourth wall The imaginary wall that exists between the stage and the audience.

gelatin The colored plastic sheets placed in front of lighting instruments. Also called **gel.**

glissade A gliding step in ballet that enables a dancer to easily move in any direction.

green room The room backstage where actors and crew wait for their call or cue.

grid The metal framework above the stage to which blocks and pulleys for scenery and lighting instruments are attached.

grip A stagehand who helps in moving scenery.

house 1. A theater or auditorium that provides entertainment. **2.** The audience or patrons of such an establishment.

house manager The theater employee who deals with issues related to the audience or theater.

jeté The jump in which a dancer leaps on one leg and lands on the other.

libretto The text of an opera, oratorio or other musical drama.

jeté

lift The movement when one dancer lifts another.

light plot A scale drawing that shows each lighting instrument and its location.

minuet The French court dance of the 17th century performed in 3/4 time.

off book The term that refers to the point in the rehearsal process when the actors have memorized their lines so they no longer need to carry scripts.

open position The second and fourth ballet positions in which the feet do not touch.

pas de deux A ballet dance for two.

pirouette The rotation of the body on one leg, with the toe of one leg touching the knee of the other.

places The call given by the stage manager before the curtain rises.

plié A ballet move in which the hips, legs and feet turn outward, the heels touch and the knees bend.

pointe A principal element of classical dance in which the dancer appears to rest his or her weight on the toe.

port de bras The arm positions that correspond to the five classical foot positions of ballet.

practical A prop or piece of scenery that is used by or handled by the actors.

prompt To give an actor his or her lines during a rehearsal or performance.

prompt book The stage manager's reference to all cues and blocking.

proscenium The area of a theater located between the curtain and the orchestra.

rake To elevate the stage at an angle.

recitative The speech-like singing style found in opera or oratorio.

relevé To change dance positions to half pointe or full pointe from having the foot flat on the floor.

repertoire Also called **repertory**. The body of plays that a company is prepared to perform.

scrim A material that turns transparent when lit from behind and is opaque when lit from the front. A scrim is used for windows and special lighting effects in theater.

set The scenery that delineates the performing space of a play.

soliloquy A speech in which an actor gives voice to his or her thoughts when alone or unaware that other actors are nearby.

stage manager The supervisor of the stage crew who is responsible for the entire performance of the play.

strike To remove a set or props from the stage.

trap A door in the stage that allows actors to enter and exit.

turnout The dance position that places the legs at a ninety-degree angle from the hips.

upstage 1. The rear of the stage. **2.** To speak while upstage, forcing other actors to turn their backs to the audience.

wings The flats at the sides of the stage and parallel to the front of the stage that hide the backstage area.

Publi

The best way to read musi

Gramophone

october 1996 $6.95 US $7.00 Can

Over 200 reviews
including a new "Tristan
und Isolde" from Daniel
Barenboim Claudio Abbado
conducting Hindemith John
Lill in Rachmaninov
piano works Wolfgang
Holzmair singing Schumann
Lieder A live "Trovatore"
from Salzburg under
Herbert von Karajan

Audio feature
**Options for
High-Density CD**

What next ?
Gramophone's guide
to exploring repertoire

Ton Koopman

CMJ
NEW MUSIC MONTHLY

BEST NEW MUSIC
BEN FOLDS FIVE
ED'S REDEEMING QUALITIES
PORTASTATIC
GERALDINE FIBBERS
YOUNG GODS

URGE OVERKILL

SOUTHERN CULTURE
ON THE SKIDS
CHARLIE HUNTER
JOHN COLTRANE
AND BURNING SPEAR
SUGAR BURNING SPEAR
PAW · X · BEASTIE BOYS

FORTUNE

WARREN BUFFETT'S NEXT SA

**MY LIFE
AS A MOLE
FOR THE
FBI**

"My name is Mark
Whitacre. I am
38 years old.
I was the top
candidate to be
the next president of Archer Daniels
Midland Co. I know because my bosses
told me. And I have it on tape. I have
lot of stuff on tape..

For Whitacre's exclusive stor
as told to Ronald Henkof
turn to page 5

shing

MEMNOCH
THE DEVIL
THE VAMPIRE CHRONICLES

ANNE R

NEW YORK TIMES BESTSELLER

THE
HOT
ZONE

A TERRIFYING TRUE STORY
RICHARD PRESTON

AUTHOR OF THE PRINCE OF TIDES

Beach Music

FIRST FICTION: SOME ◆ Handselling to Inde
NOTABLE FALL DEBUTS ◆ June Sales Figures
◆ Mondadori Tops in

PublishersWeekly

A Cahners/R.R. Bowker Publication THE INTERNATIONAL NEWS MAGAZINE OF BOOK PUBLISHING AND BOOKSELLING August 21, 1995 $3.00

My Fellow Americans

A FAMILY ALBUM

Alice Provensen

HARCOURT BRACE & COMPANY,

The Big Time

■ BY DAVID STREITFELD

David Streitfield covers books and publishing for the *Washington Post*.

A BOOKSTORE USED TO BE A SIMPLE THING with a single function: You went in, browsed for a moment and then left, clutching a volume that would help while away the hours more pleasantly or maybe just help do your income taxes quicker. It's likely that the bookstore was in a mall, and that your purchase was merely a small part of the afternoon's shopping.

Now the neighborhood bookstore is likely to be a destination in itself, and probably a frequent one. On a rainy Sunday afternoon, you browse for a while through the history section, finally plopping down on a convenient couch to make a lengthy perusal of a particular text. On Tuesday night, you go to a reading by an up-and-coming literary novelist. Planning a trip with some friends, you meet them on Saturday morning at the store's cafe. After all, the guidebooks in the travel section are available for easy reference.

BOOKS

The "superstores" are huge outlets that carry at least 100,000 titles and usually come equipped with well-stocked music departments as well as cafes serving up coffee and croissants. They are often free-standing instead of being part of a mall. They represent the hottest, the most encouraging and the most worrisome trend in the book business.

In 1994, according to a poll commissioned by the American Booksellers Association, the number of new and used books bought by Americans hit an estimated one billion for the first time. The fact that the number was up 31 percent since 1991 clearly reflected the growth of the superstores. In the same poll, book buyers said they made 27 percent of their purchases at chain stores of all types, including superstores, up from 22.1 percent three years earlier.

The biggest players in the superstore game are the Borders, Crown, Books-A-Million and Barnes & Noble chains. In 1993, they had a combined 334 superstores; in 1994, 458; by the end of 1995, the total was expected to reach 600. Some of this growth was fed by fresh demand, but, in other cases, market share was taken away from the independently owned stores that had often been part of a community for decades. As a result of the chains' invasion of Chicago, for example, the local Kroch's and Brentano's operation has been reduced from 21 stores to three. In the ABA poll, only 19 percent of the respondents said they made their purchases at independent stores, down sharply from nearly a third in 1991.

If you disregard their predatory aspect, superstores have many amiable features. Their desire to make their stores into community centers, where something is happening every night, means an endless number of writers are trotted by, from the most obscure local poet to former President Carter and former British Prime Minister Thatcher. Writers tend to grumble about these dog-and-pony shows, but don't complain too loudly because they know this is how books get sold.

Usually. The most surprising literary event of the year was the one that didn't happen. Martin Amis, who has occupied for some time both the bad boy and the wunderkind slots among English novelists, generated a massive amount of publicity when he fired his agent (who happened to be the wife of his one-time good friend, fellow novelist Julian Barnes), left his longtime publisher and received a huge sum of money (insiders say between $730,000 and $795,000) for his novel, *The Information*. The titillation factor was sharply increased

The Borders superstore in Chicago

when it was disclosed that Amis wanted the extra money to help pay for a new set of teeth, as well as when novelist A.S. Byatt publicly denounced him for being greedy.

The *New York Times, The New Yorker, New York* magazine and *Vanity Fair,* the four most influential publications in the media universe, all wrote about the Amis affair, sometimes extensively. *The New Yorker,* for instance, printed an excerpt from the novel, ran an article analyzing the implications of the brouhaha and finished with a piece by Amis himself talking about his U.S. book tour. And yet the book never made the *Times*'s bestseller list, ultimately selling at best about 35,000 copies. That was much less than octogenarian novelist Dorothy West's *The Wedding,* a volume that received nowhere near the same amount of exposure and whose author was too infirm to venture away from her Martha's Vineyard home.

Martin Amis

A pessimist would conclude from this that the audience for literary fiction these days is so small that even relentless publicity, a long author tour and favorable reviews can't power a serious novel onto the bestseller lists. But an optimist would conclude on somewhat surer ground that the audience can't be manipulated into buying and reading something it never wanted to begin with.

When people decide they do like a literary novel, a powerful chain reaction can be ignited. The best case in point is

E. Annie Proulx's *The Shipping News,* which started with a tiny hardcover printing and scant attention. Then it won the National Book Award and the Pulitzer Prize. The media wrote about her, celebrating a late-blooming new writer who had a sure command of the language and a compelling way to tell the old story of a man who goes home and finds himself. (Journalists also liked it because it contained a wicked portrait of a small-town newspaper.) Book discussion groups picked it up, and enough of those readers liked it to tell their friends. Within a year, the paperback had more than one million copies in print and it was heading for two.

Proulx started small and became big. Some writers find things are increasingly going the other way. If a publisher thinks its scandalous new book about Michael Jackson is going to be a smash, it prints several hundred thousand copies and sends them out to the stores. But if customers decide they're not interested, what's to be done with all those books? More and more often, the price is suddenly cut in half. Such has been the recent fate of Christopher Anderson's book on Jackson, as well as autobiographical tomes by Marlon Brando, Audrey Meadows and Lauren Bacall, novels by James Michener, Barbara Taylor Bradford, Robert B. Parker, Joseph Heller, Jackie Collins and Larry McMurtry, not to mention Andrew Morton's book on Princess Diana and Dave Barry's *Gift Guide to End All Gift Guides*. With the real turkeys, even a 50-percent-off sale doesn't help. The books are sent back to the publisher and ultimately pulped. It's a high-stakes game.

No wonder publishers were beset by doubt and anxiety. In 1994, Simon & Schuster closed the Atheneum imprint, recently acquired when it bought Macmillan; Houghton Mifflin shuttered the Ticknor and Fields imprint; and, most surprising, Harcourt Brace slashed its list of adult titles and gave many of the employees responsible a pink slip. All three of these imprints had venerable histories, and there was much wailing and gnashing of teeth in the industry about how it was getting increasingly difficult to publish serious books. Perhaps, some suggested, it was time for the traditional publishers to call it quits and let the electronic book take over.

In 1995, there was a recovery of sorts. For one thing, fear of multimedia dwindled as products like CD-ROMs became an unexceptional reality. The current thinking is that high-tech ways of distributing information will revolutionize reference and children's titles, but have a much slower impact on fiction and general nonfiction. Already, however, the cyberworld is nibbling at the edges of the mainstream. The first novel has now been serialized on the Internet. Mainstream novelist Michael Chabon, author of *Wonder Boys,* has published his E-mail address on the book's dustjacket flap. And a store called Cybersmith opened in Cambridge, Massachusetts. It was founded by Marshall Smith, an experienced retailer of books, videos and educational tools. Cybersmith customers can drink coffee, hook up to the Internet, try out CD-ROM demos and yes, buy a few old-fashioned books. If successful, the store is likely to become a prototype for the bookstore of the immediate future.

Meanwhile, new publishing imprints have been springing up: Delacorte announced the rebirth of the Dial Press, another name with a distinguished pedigree, while Delacorte's parent company, Bantam Doubleday Dell, set up an entire fourth division that will start in fall 1996 and eventually publish more than a hundred books a year. Meanwhile Putnam, a house known more for its commercial inclinations than literary aspirations, started a new division, Riverhead, to do worthy material. Most intriguing, a group of Minnesota booksellers connected with the *Hungry Mind Review* has set up the Hungry Mind Press, a small-scale but innovative attempt to show the big publishers how to do it right. This means authors and booksellers will be

Inside a Barnes and Noble superstore

consulted instead of ignored, and that all trendiness will be eschewed. The first title is a symbolic declaration of independence from the Manhattan publishing milieu: *Leaving New York: Writers Look Back.*

Clearly, the future will bring huge bookstores filled with good stuff. It's probable, too, that every one of those books will get an award. Prizes, publishers have discovered, help their books get media coverage, which causes bookstores to feature them, which helps them sell. The Pulitzer and the National Book Award work best in this regard and winning either generally creates a star. Carol Shields was on the ascent even before she won the 1995 Pulitzer Prize for *The Stone Diaries,* but after the news was announced the number of paperback copies in print quickly went from 30,000 to 100,000.

Gary Kopelow/Courtesy of Penguin Books

Carol Shields

At this rate, Shields, too, will need to employ the sort of answering machine message used by Charles Johnson, winner of the 1990 NBA for his novel *Middle Passage:* "If you'd like to send a fax, please dial. . . . If you're calling about the possibility of a speaking engagement, please call my agent in Washington D.C. . . . If your call concerns literature or publishing, please call my agent in New York. . . . If your call concerns screenwriting, please call. . . ."

Pity the poor losers, who are never heard from again. In 1995 and 1994, runners-up for the PEN/Faulkner Award for Fiction refused to attend the ceremony when they found out they were not the winners. The foundation that administers the award promptly passed a measure that said truculence would no longer be considered a good excuse; henceforth, cranky nominees who boycott the ceremony will forfeit their $5,000 prize.

One new prize doesn't need to worry about the losers becoming obnoxious. Everyman Paperbacks, a classics line, has started awarding Booker Prizes for the best title published a century ago. Winner of the 1894 Booker was *Esther Waters* by George Moore, a rather obscure title that beat out *The Prisoner of Zenda* and Kipling's *Jungle Book,* among others. No cash prizes were given, but the complete run of Everyman paperbacks — some 300 volumes — was donated to a school library. This is definitely one of the more worthy awards.

If there was a prize for the most culturally ignorant, many members of Congress would doubtless tie for first place. As part of Advocacy Day for Arts and Culture, an annual lobbying effort that took on special significance in 1995 with the threat to the National Endowment for the Arts, Ross Thomas, Susan Isaacs and Walter Mosley visited 10 Republican congressmen. The mystery writers were joined near the end by Mary Higgins Clark; Elmore Leonard had to back out at the last minute.

Since there's no point in preaching to the converted, the representatives were all hard-liners, firmly against government grants to writers. Thomas says that no opinions were swayed, either. Still, "it was worth the effort on my part, because I got a close look at how determined they were to do nothing for anyone," he said. The writers were chosen because they were popular, yet Thomas says that — save for a congresswoman who was an old friend of Clark's — none of the politicians betrayed the slightest hint they had ever heard of any of them. This was made explicit at the tour's final stop, the office of Rep. Howard P. McKeon (R-Calif.).

"I used to read a lot, but now I work all the time. But I still never heard of you people," McKeon said bluntly. This is the worst way to offend a writer, but Thomas concludes that McKeon and the others are "no better and no worse informed than the general public. I think they reflect their constituents." ∎

1994's Longest-Running Bestsellers

The following books appeared on *Publishers Weekly's* year-end, cumulative bestseller list in the January 2, 1995 issue. Number of weeks on the bestseller list indicates time spent on the 1994 charts. Some of the titles listed below have appeared on bestseller lists for several years.

HARDCOVER

FICTION

THE BRIDGES OF MADISON COUNTY

Author: Robert James Waller
Publisher: Warner ($16.95)
Release: 4/92
Number of weeks on bestseller list: 51

Clint Eastwood directed the 1995 film starring Eastwood and Meryl Streep. Worldly, self-absorbed photographer Robert Kincaid falls madly in love with a middle-aged farm wife, Francesca Johnson, while passing through Madison County, Iowa, on a photo shoot. The pair, taking advantage of Francesca's empty house, spend four passionate days together.

THE CELESTINE PROPHECY

Author: James Redfield
Publisher: Warner ($17.95)
Release: 3/94
Number of weeks on bestseller list: 43

In matters of the spirit, many Americans look south, most notably with Carlos Castañeda's hallucinogen-enhanced Don Juan series. For '90s soul seekers, *The Celestine Prophecy* offers the path to discovering a "completely spiritual culture on Earth." Disillusioned and burned-out, the unnamed narrator journeys to Macchu Picchu, where he finds the Manuscript, an ancient document possessing the nine key insights into human life.

LIKE WATER FOR CHOCOLATE

Author: Laura Esquivel
Publisher: Doubleday ($19.95)
Release: 10/92
Number of weeks on bestseller list: 26

Alfonso Arau, Esquivel's ex-husband, directed the 1992 film starring Lumi Cavazos, Marco Leonardi and Regina Torne.

Tita, a young, upper-class Mexican beauty desperately wants to marry Pedro. Her dictatorial mother prevents the union by arranging the marriage of her oldest daughter and Pedro. Tita substitutes cooking for sex, finding a release in preparing erotic meals. Included throughout the book, which is set during the Mexican Revolution, are recipes for Tita's culinary masterpieces.

THE ALIENIST

Author: Caleb Carr
Publisher: Random House ($22)
Release: 3/94
Number of weeks on bestseller list: 25

Carr's historical thriller provides a portrait of turn-of-the-century New York, revealing corruption in the New York Police Department that leads to the appointment of Theodore Roosevelt as police commissioner. Dr. Lazlo Kreizler, the "alienist," enlists the help of two reformist detectives, a *New York Times* reporter, Roosevelt and his secretary to capture a deranged serial killer who preys on young male prostitutes.

POLITICALLY CORRECT BEDTIME STORIES

Author: James Finn Garner
Publisher: Macmillan ($8.95)
Release: 4/94
Number of weeks on bestseller list: 24

Garner puts a humorous spin on classic stories including *Little Red Riding Hood, The Three Little Pigs, Snow White* and *Cinderella*. He rewrites the tales in politically and environmentally correct prose, eliminating the discriminatory and insensitive language often found in classic tales.

SLOW WALTZ IN CEDAR BEND
Author: Robert James Waller
Publisher: Warner ($16.95)
Release: 11/93
Number of weeks on bestseller list: 21
Waller, trying to duplicate the huge commercial success of *The Bridges of Madison County*, centers the plot of this bestseller around a middle-aged couple involved in an ardent affair. Michael Tillman, a renegade economics professor, falls in love with the wife of one of his colleagues, Jellie. In the midst of their fiery affair, Jellie runs away to India, and, predictably, Michael darts off in pursuit of her and learns of Jellie's past and complex personality.

DISCLOSURE
Author: Michael Crichton
Publisher: Knopf ($24)
Release: 1/94
Number of weeks on bestseller list: 20
Barry Levinson directed the 1994 movie starring Demi Moore and Michael Douglas.
Tom Sanders, a rising executive at a high-tech computer company, quickly falls from the corporate ladder when his new boss, who is also his former girlfriend, accuses him of sexual harassment. He risks everything to prove he is the victim of sexual harassment, not the perpetrator.

THE CHAMBER
Author: John Grisham
Publisher: Doubleday ($24.95)
Release: 7/94
Number of weeks on bestseller list: 19
Straying from Grisham's characteristic legal-suspense genre, *The Chamber* explores family relationships and a man's troubled past rather than following an explosive courtroom battle. After years of appeal, Sam Cayhall, convicted of bombing the office of a civil-rights lawyer and killing the lawyer's two sons, awaits "the chamber" in a Mississippi state penitentiary. Cayhall's grandson, recently admitted to the bar, stages a last-ditch effort to save Cayhall from the gas.

DEBT OF HONOR
Author: Tom Clancy
Publisher: Putnam ($25.95)
Release: 8/94
Number of weeks on bestseller list: 17
Since the Cold War is no longer a viable topic, Clancy has decided to focus on other international issues, but judging by *Debt of Honor*, he has not yet found his niche. Jack Ryan returns as Clancy's protagonist, but he disappears in the whirlwind of subplots that include a U.S.-Japanese trade war followed by a shooting war, rape charges against the vice president, the capture of two C.I.A. operatives by a Mideast drug terrorist, a stock-market crash and a crusade against defective automobile gas tanks.

ACCIDENT
Author: Danielle Steel
Publisher: Delacorte ($23.95)
Release: 3/94
Number of weeks on bestseller list: 15
Page Clarke's perfect life crumbles around her when her daughter, Allyson, is left brain-damaged in a coma after a car accident, and her husband reveals a secret that destroys their marriage. True to classic Steel form, another man arrives to comfort Page during the crises and help her find new love.

NONFICTION

MEN ARE FROM MARS, WOMEN ARE FROM VENUS
Author: John Gray
Publisher: HarperCollins ($23)
Release: 6/92
Number of weeks on bestseller list: 51
In what has been labeled the relationship book of the '90s, Gray suggests that in order to improve relationships between men and women, people should focus on the differences between the sexes, not analyze why the differences exist.

THE BOOK OF VIRTUES
Author: William J. Bennett
Publisher: Simon & Schuster ($20)
Release: 6/92
Number of weeks on bestseller list: 48
The former secretary of education and director of drug control under presidents Reagan and Bush, Bennett draws upon nearly 30 centuries of writing to elucidate his views on self-discipline, friendship, compassion, courage, perseverance, honesty, loyalty and faith. Coupling the writings of, for example, Paul Revere, Aesop and Plato, with his own ideology, Bennett aims to influence the moral education of the young.

EMBRACED BY THE LIGHT

Author: Betty J. Eadie
Publisher: Gold Leaf Press ($16.95)
Release: 12/92
Number of weeks on bestseller list: 39
Of all the near-death-experience books currently on the market, Eadie's account of heaven and its inhabitants stands out for its originality. Eadie, a mother of seven, "died" on a hospital bed just prior to a partial hysterectomy when she was 31 years old. Instead of a celestial paradise, she found a heaven resembling the not-so-perfect earth.

MIDNIGHT IN THE GARDEN OF GOOD AND EVIL

Author: John Berendt
Publisher: Random House ($24)
Release: 1/94
Number of weeks on bestseller list: 36

Berendt, *Esquire* columnist and former editor of *New York* magazine, spent eight years in Savannah, Georgia, compiling anecdotes and meeting its inhabitants. The personalities he encountered could easily pass for the main characters in a best-selling novel: a black drag queen, an inventor with enough poison to contaminate Savannah's water supply and a voodoo priestess. Looming over Savannah is the murder trial of antiques dealer Jim Williams, who is charged with murdering his companion.

IN THE KITCHEN WITH ROSIE

Author: Rosie Daley
Publisher: Knopf ($14.95)
Release: 4/94
Number of weeks on bestseller list: 35

Oprah Winfrey's personal chef, Daley, helped the talk-show maven finally overcome the diet roller coaster by serving up delicious, low-fat and low-calorie meals. Winfrey's favorites include the Unfried Fried Chicken, Unfried French Fries and low-fat cheesecake. Mmm mmm.

MAGIC EYE

Author: Thomas Baccei
Publisher: Andrews & McMeel ($12.95)
Release: 11/93
Number of weeks on bestseller list: 32
Stare into a colorful page of the *Magic Eye,* and an engaging three-dimensional image appears. It takes some patience as the figure does not always jump right off the page. A computer and an image-rendering system, the "Salitsky Dot," generate the seemingly random splashes of color.

MAGIC EYE II

Author: Thomas Baccei
Publisher: Andrews & McMeel ($12.95)
Release: 4/94
Number of weeks on bestseller list: 22
A follow-up to the immensely popular *Magic Eye, Magic Eye II* uses the same image-rendering system to create colorful pages that contain three-dimensional images.

SOUL MATES

Author: Thomas Moore
Publisher: HarperCollins ($25)
Release: 2/94
Number of weeks on bestseller list: 21
A former student of theology, Moore draws upon mythology, religion and literature to explain the underlying patterns of human relationships, exploring relations in terms of the soul's needs.

AGELESS BODY, TIMELESS MIND

Author: Deepak Chopra, M.D.
Publisher: Harmony ($23)
Release: 7/93
Number of weeks on bestseller list: 17

Ageless Body, Timeless Mind, another New Age spiritual self-help book, professes to have the answer to living a longer, healthier life. Chopra, a follower of Maharishi Mahesh Yogi, founder of the transcendental meditation movement, offers suggestions to aid the human mind in controlling or reversing the aging process.

STOP THE INSANITY

Author: Susan Powter
Publisher: Simon & Schuster ($22)
Release: 10/93
Number of weeks on bestseller list: 12
The buzz-cut, blond infomercial queen maintains her drill-sergeant presence in print, urging readers to outwit the fitness and diet industries by taking control of their lives and not falling prey to misleading packaging. Powter empowers readers to control their weight by making educated food and exercise choices.

COUPLEHOOD

Author: Paul Reiser
Publisher: Bantam Books ($19.95)
Release: 10/94
Number of weeks on bestseller list: 16

Reiser, the star of NBC's *Mad About You,* offers his take on being part of a couple, lightheartedly highlighting the good and bad associated with relationships.

HAVING OUR SAY: THE DELANY'S SISTERS FIRST 100 YEARS

Authors: Sarah and A. Elizabeth Delany with Amy Hearth
Publisher: Kodansha ($20)
Release: 9/94
Number of weeks on bestseller list: 15

Made into a Broadway play in 1995, which starred Gloria Foster and Mary Alice

The Delany sisters tell the story of their lives in a memoir that is both a historical chronicle and an entertaining look at two women who have spent more than 100 years together. Raised in a middle-class North Carolina family, both led successful lives in New York overcoming obstacles as black women — Bessie as one of the first black woman dentists and Sadie as a high school home economics teacher and a subtle integration activist.

BARBARA BUSH: A MEMOIR

Author: Barbara Bush
Publisher: Scribner ($25)
Release: 9/94
Number of weeks on bestseller list: 15

Writing a memoir is an undertaking we've come to expect from former first ladies. In hers, Barbara Bush employs the candor that endeared her to many to focus on the twin pillars of her life, politics and family.

PAPERBACK

MASS MARKET

THE CLIENT

Author: John Grisham
Publisher: Dell ($6.99)
Release: 3/94
Number of weeks on bestseller list: 31

Joel Schumacher directed the 1994 film starring Susan Sarandon, Tommy Lee Jones and Brad Renfro. Immediately before committing suicide, a mob lawyer reveals a secret to a young boy. A district attorney and the Mafia pursue the boy in an attempt to learn the man's last words. The clever child obtains the services of a headstrong attorney, and together they struggle to protect the boy and his family.

1994 NATIONAL BOOK AWARDS

Fiction
A Frolic of His Own, William Gaddis (Knopf)

Nonfiction
How We Die: Reflections on Life's Final Chapter, Sherwin B. Nuland (Knopf)

Poetry
Worshipful Company of Fletchers, James Tate (Ecco Press)

1995 PEN LITERARY AWARD WINNERS

The 1995 PEN Literary Awards were presented in New York City on March 31, 1995. The Hemingway Prize was awarded in Boston on April 2, 1995.

Ernest Hemingway Award for First Fiction ($7,500)
Susan Power, *The Grass Dancer* (Putnam)

PEN/Book of the Month Club Translation Prize
Burton Watson, *Selected Poems by Su Tung-p'o* (Copper Canyon)

PEN/Spielvogel-Diamonstein Award for Best Essay ($5,000)
John Brinckerhoff Jackson, *A Sense of Place, A Sense of Time* (Yale)

PEN/Martha Albrand Award for First Nonfiction ($1,000)
Louise Gluck, *Proofs & Theories: Essays on Poetry* (Ecco Press)

Emerging Writer Prize — Children's Fiction
Angela Johnson

Emerging Writer Prize — Nonfiction
Kim Barnes

1995 BOLLINGEN PRIZE IN POETRY

The Bollingen Prize, administered by Yale University and the Bollingen Foundation, is awarded every two years to one or more living American poet or poets for lifetime achievement in poetry, or for the best collection published during the previous two years.

Kenneth Koch

1994 Nobel Prize for Literature

Kenzaburo Oe, Japan

1995 Pulitzer Prizes in Letters

Fiction
The Stone Diaries, Carol Shields (Viking)

General Nonfiction
The Beak of the Finch: A Story of Evolution in Our Time, Jonathan Weiner (Knopf)

History of the United States
No Ordinary Time: Franklin and Eleanor Roosevelt: The Home Front in World War II, Doris Kearns Goodwin (Simon & Schuster)

Biography or Autobiography
Harriet Beecher Stowe: A Life, Joan D. Hedrick (Oxford University Press)

Poetry
Simple Truth, Philip Levine (Knopf)

Drama
The Young Man From Atlanta, Horton Foote

1994 National Book Critics Circle Awards

Fiction
The Stone Diaries, Carol Shields (Viking)

General Nonfiction
The Rape of Europa: The Fate of Europe's Treasures in the Third Reich and the Second World War (Knopf)

Biography or Autobiography
Shot in the Heart, Mikal Gilmore (Doubleday)

Poetry
Rider, Mark Rudman (Wesleyan University Press)

Criticism
The Culture of Bruising: Essays on Prizefighting, Literature and Modern American Culture, Gerald Early (Ecco Press)

Without Remorse
Author: Tom Clancy
Publisher: Berkley ($6.99)
Release: 7/94
Number of weeks on bestseller list: 24
Clancy's regular hero, the soldier John Kelly, mourning the death of his pregnant wife shortly after he returned from Vietnam, befriends a young prostitute trying to clean up her act. When the woman is brutally murdered by Asian drug dealers, Kelly seeks revenge. Conveniently, the Pentagon sends him on a mission in Southeast Asia, where he can take care of official and unofficial business.

Smilla's Sense of Snow
Author: Peter Hoeg
Publisher: Dell ($6.50)
Release: 9/94
Number of weeks on bestseller list: 18

A woman's crusade to determine why her six-year-old neighbor plunged from an apartment building to his death leads her to the Arctic, where she risks her life to uncover a secret lying miles beneath the frozen sea.

A Case of Need
Author: Michael Crichton
Publisher: Signet ($6.99)
Release: 7/94
Number of weeks on bestseller list: 16
Originally published more than a quarter of a century ago under the pseudonym Jeffery Hudson, the medical thriller A Case of Need made its way to the bestseller list following Michael Crichton's success with Jurassic Park and Disclosure. A doctor in a Boston medical center weaves his way through a labyrinth of medical data and secrets to determine if a patient was the victim of malpractice, murder or botched surgery.

Degree of Guilt
Author: Richard N. Patterson
Publisher: Ballantine ($6.99)
Release: 1/94
Number of weeks on bestseller list: 15
Christopher Paget, a hotshot lawyer, has not argued a murder case in years, and he is not enthusiastic about defending his former lover Mary Carelli, a famous television interviewer accused of murdering her literary agent. He begrudgingly accepts the case only to protect his and Carelli's son.

FORREST GUMP

Author: Winston Groom
Publisher: Pocket Books ($5.99)
Release: 7/94
Number of weeks on bestseller list: 15

Robert Zemeckis directed the 1994 film starring Tom Hanks, Gary Sinise, Robin Wright and Sally Field, which won six Oscars including Best Picture, Best Director and Best Actor.

Forrest Gump, a simple man with an IQ of 75, overcomes many obstacles, including his mental challenge, and finds history-making success in virtually everything he does from football, to Vietnam, to dabbling in business.

I'LL BE SEEING YOU

Author: Mary Higgins Clark
Publisher: Pocket Books ($6.50)
Release: 5/94
Number of weeks on bestseller list: 15

Meghan Collins, a New York City television reporter, finds herself entangled in a mishmash of complicated mysteries and problems involving herself and her family. Multi-best-selling author Clark manages to transform insurance scams, in-vitro fertilization, a stalker and unrequited love into another credible, page-turning novel.

LIKE WATER FOR CHOCOLATE

Author: Laura Esquivel
Publisher: Doubleday/Anchor ($5.99)
Release: 9/94
Number of weeks on bestseller list: 15
See page 694

DISCLOSURE

Author: Michael Crichton
Publisher: Ballantine ($6.99)
Release: 10/94
Number of weeks on bestseller list: 25
See page 695

TRADE

THE ROAD LESS TRAVELED

Author: M. Scott Peck, M.D.
Publisher: Simon & Schuster/Touchstone ($12)
Release: 1980
Number of weeks on bestseller list: 51

A perennial top seller that has enjoyed more than 360 weeks on the bestseller list since it was first published in 1980, psychiatrist Peck's pioneering combination of spiritual and psychiatric insight has made this penetrating book a classic, must-have aid to self-discovery. Peck's lasting influence is seen in the abundance of New Age spiritual books on bookshelves today.

SEVEN HABITS OF HIGHLY EFFECTIVE PEOPLE

Author: Stephen R. Covey
Publisher: Simon & Schuster/Fireside ($12)
Release: 8/90
Number of weeks on bestseller list: 51

Though indulging in the free-to-be-synergy language of self-help, *7 Habits of Highly Effective People* effectively addresses the ills of life and work. In his runaway bestseller, management consultant Covey brings a sensible, soulful approach to professional and personal empowerment.

CARE OF THE SOUL

Author: Thomas Moore
Publisher: HarperPerennial ($13)
Release: 2/94
Number of weeks on bestseller list: 50

Care of the Soul explores human spiritual needs and offers sound, reassuring advice on using everyday life as a guide to personal depth. Moore, a Jung-inspired therapist, lived in a Catholic seminary for 12 years before he began his writing career.

WHAT TO EXPECT WHEN YOU'RE EXPECTING

Authors: A. Eisenberg, H. Murkoff and S. Hathway
Publisher: Workman ($10.95)
Release: 5/91
Number of weeks on bestseller list: 45

The bible for pregnant women, *What to Expect When You're Expecting* outlines the month-by-month physical and emotional changes a mother experiences and the attendant growth and changes in her baby.

WHERE ANGELS WALK

Author: Joan W. Anderson
Publisher: Ballantine ($12)
Release: 8/93
Number of weeks on bestseller list: 36

In these miraculous stories told to the author, angels appear as voices, lights, thoughts and in human form at crucial moments and perform amazing feats of rescue, saving potential victims from gang attacks, car accidents and other calamities.

THE SHIPPING NEWS

Author: E. Annie Proulx
Publisher: Simon & Schuster/Touchstone ($12)
Release: 5/94
Number of weeks on bestseller list: 30

Deserted by his wife and left with two small daughters, hapless journalist Quoyle returns to his family's original home in Newfoundland. As eccentric as the locals, he enters village life and discovers that his ancestors were wilder than he had ever imagined.

T-FACTOR FAT-GRAM COUNTER

Authors: Jamie Pope-Cordle and Martin Katahn
Publisher: W. W. Norton ($5.95)
Release: 10/89
Number of weeks on bestseller list: 27

This pocket-size nutrition book teaches readers how to monitor saturated fat intake, the real culprit in weight gain. No longer is it necessary to count every calorie in order to lose weight. The fat-gram counter lists the fat content of hundreds of foods.

ALL THE PRETTY HORSES

Author: Cormac McCarthy
Publisher: Vintage ($12)
Release: 7/93
Number of weeks on bestseller list: 23

Three teenage boys, seeing no future in post-World War II Texas, embark on a journey to Mexico, where they expect to find hope and opportunity in the ancient lands. Instead, the boys encounter unexpected challenges. *All the Pretty Horses* is the first book in McCarthy's *Border Trilogy*.

SCHINDLER'S LIST

Author: Thomas Keneally
Publisher: Simon & Schuster/Touchstone ($12)
Release: 12/93
Number of weeks on bestseller list: 23

Steven Spielberg directed the 1993 film starring Liam Neeson, Ben Kingsley and Ralph Fiennes which won seven Oscars including Best Picture and Best Director. Oskar Schindler, the real-life entrepreneur who prospered by complying with the Nazis, ultimately lost his fortune saving the lives of more than 1,000 Polish Jews. Instead of sending the workers to death camps, Schindler employed them in his factory offering them hope for survival.

CHICKEN SOUP FOR THE SOUL

Editors: Jack Canfield and Mark Hansen
Publisher: Health Communications ($12.95)
Release: 5/93
Number of weeks on bestseller list: 22

Taking the advice of their audiences, motivational speakers Canfield and Hansen compiled their inspirational stories and published them. Also included are stories from Art Buchwald, Gloria Steinem and Bennett Cerf.

MAMA MAKES UP HER MIND

Author: Bailey White
Publisher: Vintage ($10)
Release: 5/94
Number of weeks on bestseller list: 20

White, a first-grade teacher in Georgia and regular contributor to National Public Radio's *All Things Considered*, writes about the eccentricities of southern living. In this collection of essays, she invites the reader into her unique world highlighted by her truly strange, but endearing family.

PIGS IN HEAVEN

Author: Barbara Kingsolver
Publisher: HarperPerennial ($13)
Release: 3/94
Number of weeks on bestseller list: 19

Taylor Greer adopts a six-year-old Cherokee girl she found abandoned in a car. The two bond as though they are natural mother and daughter. Their relationship is threatened when Cherokee attorney Annawake Fourkiller gets wind of the adoption. Fourkiller believes that Cherokee children should be raised by Cherokee parents to preserve the identity of the dying tribe, and in this case, she has legal ground to separate the mother and daughter. Greer feels her only option is to flee, and the two go on a road trip with little money but a lot of love.

LISTENING TO PROZAC

Author: Peter Kramer, M.D.
Publisher: Penguin ($12.95)
Release: 6/94
Number of weeks on bestseller list: 18

Prozac, the wonder anti-depressant drug that makes the shy become social and can make the clumsy dexterous, has been prescribed to more than 5 million Americans. Kramer explores the drug and its effect on people and delves into philosophical issues: Is the drug used for cosmetic rather than medicinal purposes? Can and should science really alter the human psyche?

A HISTORY OF GOD

Author: Karen Armstrong
Publisher: Ballantine ($14)
Release: 9/94
Number of weeks on bestseller list: 17

Armstrong, one of England's most respected writers on religion, traces the evolution of Christianity, Judaism and Islam from the time of Abraham to present, along the way discussing how people have perceived and experienced God.

REENGINEERING THE CORPORATION

Authors: Michael Hammer and James Champy
Publisher: HarperBusiness ($13)
Release: 4/94
Number of weeks on bestseller list: 16

This self-help book for corporations provides the basics for redesigning a company's organization, structure and culture to ensure radical improvements in performance, profits and customer satisfaction. The authors use Hallmark, Taco Bell, Capital Holdings and Bell Atlantic as models for their successful business plan.

INTRODUCING...

DO IT YOURSELF

Analysts predict that by the year 2000, for the first time in U.S. history, more money will be spent on home renovations than on new home construction. Magazine publishers have responded by creating publications that specialize in renovation tips. In 1995, Time Publishing Ventures introduced *This Old House*, a magazine based on the PBS series; Meredith Magazines put *Traditional Home Renovation* and *Country Home Sourcebook: Products for Vintage Homes* on the newsstands; and in 1996, Hearst Magazines plans to publish *Country Living Renovation*.

1995 CALDECOTT MEDAL

The Caldecott Medal is awarded annually by the American Library Association for the most distinguished American picture book for children.

Caldecott Medal for Best Picture Book
 Smoky Night, illustrated by David Diaz, written by Eve Bunting (Harcourt Brace)

Caldecott Honor Books
 Swamp Angel, illustrated by Paul O. Zelinsky, written by Anne Isaacs (Dutton's Children's Books)

 John Henry, illustrated by Jerry Pinckey, written by Julius Lester (Dial Books for Young Readers)

 Time Flies, written and illustrated by Eric Rohmann (Crown)

1995 JOHN NEWBERY MEDAL

The Newbery Medal is awarded annually by the American Library Association for the most distinguished contribution to American literature for children.

Newbery Medal for Best Book
 Walk Two Moons, Sharon Creech (HarperCollins)

Newbery Honor Books
 Catherine, Called Birdy, Karen Cushman (Clarion Books)

 The Ear, the Eye and the Arm, Nancy Farmer (Richard Jackson/Orchard Books)

THE 1994 BOOKER PRIZE

The Booker Prize, Britain's foremost literary prize awarded for a full-length novel, was presented in October 1994.

How Late It Was, How Late, James Kelman (Norton)

1995 Bestsellers

The Entertainment Almanac's bestseller list for the first half of 1995 includes books that appeared regularly or for long stretches on the *Publishers Weekly*, the *New York Times* and the *Wall Street Journal* lists. Some of the titles listed below were released over the summer and got off to a great start. We included them because we anticipate they will continue to do well for the remainder of the year.

HARDCOVER

FICTION

1. THE RAINMAKER
Author: John Grisham
Publisher: Doubleday
($25.95)
Release: 5/95

Grisham's sixth legal/courtroom thriller, though filled with slimy ambulance chasers, has a scrupulous young lawyer at its center. Rudy Baylor, fresh out of Memphis State law school and after much pavement pounding goes to work for Bruiser Stone, whose practice is as questionable as his name. In his first case, a typical David versus Goliath situation, Baylor represents a leukemia victim who is dying because his insurance company refuses to pay for a bone marrow transplant. Grisham adds extra spice to the tale with a love story, a will and underworld types.

2. THE CELESTINE PROPHECY
Author: James Redfield
Publisher: Warner Books ($17.95)
Release: 3/94
See page 694

3. POLITICALLY CORRECT BEDTIME STORIES
Author: James Finn Garner
Publisher: Macmillan ($8.95)
Release: 4/94
See page 694

4. ROSE MADDER
Author: Stephen King
Publisher: Viking ($22.95)
Release: 6/95
Rosie Daniels, after 14 years of sexual and physical abuse, wakes up one morning and summons the courage to leave her savage husband Norman. When Norman discovers his wife has fled, his already frail sanity is shattered, and he embarks on a murderous journey in pursuit of his wife. King's 29th novel is ripe with feminist

themes from the sense of sorority Rosie feels at Daughters and Sisters, a women's shelter, to the mystical and revengeful powers she finds in a bewitching painting.

5. ORIGINAL SIN: AN ADAM DALGLIESH MYSTERY
Author: P. D. James
Publisher: Knopf ($24)
Release: 2/95
James gave Scotland Yard's bard-commander Adam Dalgliesh his own subtitle in her latest thriller/mystery, and he earns it in this murder case set in a London publishing house. Trouble begins when a veteran employee of Peverell Press commits suicide in the office shortly after she was let go. Dalgliesh enters the scene when a prankster tampers with page proofs and threatens Peverell's authors. Then a director of the company is murdered, also in the office. Dalgliesh soon discovers that nearly every employee of Peverell had motive to kill the man.

6. BEACH MUSIC
Author: Pat Conroy
Publisher: Doubleday/Talese ($27.50)
Release: 6/95
Haunted by his wife's suicide, Jack McCall moves to Rome with his daughter. McCall's escape is shortlived as his sister-in-law begs him to return home and two old friends seek his help in tracking down another who disappeared years ago when protesting the Vietman war. Back in his native South Carolina, McCall must come to terms with his troubled past and tackle his own personal conflicts.

7. THE BRIDGES OF MADISON COUNTRY
Author: Robert James Waller
Publisher: Warner Books ($16.95)
Release: 4/92
See page 694

8. Moo

Author: Jane Smiley
Publisher: Knopf ($24)
Release: 4/95

Smiley attacks the country's education system, the 1980s, politics and bureaucracy in this satire set in a fictional Iowa university, Moo U. Her characters are professors, students and administrators, but none of them seem to care much about education. Each has his or her own agenda that thrives in the university environment.

9. Ladder of Years

Author: Anne Tyler
Publisher: Knopf ($24)
Release: 5/95

While feminist pioneers such as Gloria Steinem, Erica Jong and Susan Faludi were breaking new ground for women, Delia Grinstead was rearing children as the perfect surburban housewife. After 20 years of marriage, Grinstead begins to question her life and the choices she made along the way. She abandons her family while on vacation and tries to start a new life, but then takes a job as a nanny/housekeeper. Grinstead finds herself at a crossroads, unable to decide if she's too fickle to follow through with her new life or if she really did enjoy taking care of her family.

10. Memnoch the Devil

Author: Anne Rice
Publisher: Knopf ($25)
Release: 7/95

Rice has announced that this is the last installment in her *Vampire Chronicles* series, and it's too bad she ended it on a down note. Unlike the other novels, *Memnoch the Devil* seems to be a platform for Rice to vent her feelings on religion and God. But there is a story here: Lestat, pursuing his latest victim, a murderous drug dealer, is being pursued by a force he thinks is Satan. His assumption is correct, and Satan asks Lestat to help him battle God. Lestat must decide whom to serve.

NONFICTION

1. Men Are From Mars, Women Are From Venus

Author: John Gray
Publisher: HarperCollins ($23)
Release: 6/92
See page 695

2. The Hot Zone

Author: Richard Preston
Publisher: Random House ($23)
Release: 9/94

This is probably not the book for the queasy or chronic worriers. Journalist Preston describes in excruciating detail the symptoms and terrible death caused by the Ebola virus. He visited a cave in Kenya where scientists think the virus originated, and then traveled to Reston, Virginia, where, in 1989, a group of lab monkeys contracted a form of the virus. Perhaps more distressing than his gory descriptions is Preston's warning that we are not safe from other deadly viruses that could be easily brought to the United States through animals and humans.

3. The Seven Spiritual Laws of Success

Author: Deepak Chopra
Publisher: New World Library ($14)
Release: 1/95

Multi-best-selling author Chopra breaks down into seven principles his self-help philosophy that if followed will promise success in every aspect of one's life. He teaches readers how to become in tune with their true nature and natural law, which results in fulfilled relationships, a sense of well being, energy and material abundance.

4. The Death of Common Sense

Author: Philip K. Howard
Publisher: Random House ($18)
Release: 1/95

New York attorney Howard believes there are too many rules and regulations in the United States, which complicate even the simplest project and offend common sense. He uses several anecdotes, one involving Mother Teresa, to prove his point and to attack nearly every form of regulation: fire safety codes, environmental laws, OSHA rules and bureaucratic guidelines. Though he does have a point, Howard seems to be yearning for the good old days when there weren't as many regulations but there were many more accidents.

5. Dave Barry's Complete Guide to Guys: A Fairly Short Book
Author: Dave Barry
Publisher: Random House ($21)
Release: 5/95

Don't be confused: this is not a book about men, it's a book about guys. There's a big difference there. Men understand their innermost feelings; guys don't have any. Men value the beauty of a free-flowing river; guys see who can pee farthest into one. Barry's latest offers humor that is best appreciated in small doses.

6. In the Kitchen With Rosie
Author: Rosie Daley
Publisher: Knopf ($14.95)
Release: 4/94
See page 696

7. Sisters
Authors: Carol Saline and Sharon Wohlmuth
Publisher: Running Press ($27.50)
Release: 10/94

Journalist Saline and photojournalist Wohlmuth explore relationships between female siblings, highlighting with essays and black-and-white photos 36 famous and not-so-famous sets of sisters. The Turlington sisters talk about their supermodel sister Christy; Coretta Scott King and her sister Edythe correspond about Martin Luther King, Jr.; and Janice Coffey discusses her sister Elizabeth, who used to be her brother.

8. How to Argue and Win Every Time
Author: Gerry Spence
Publisher: St. Martin's Press ($22.95)
Release: 3/95

Successful trial lawyer Spence provides readers the tools necessary to achieve positive results in everyday arguments, whether they be with a spouse, co-worker, child or teacher. Claiming that argument is both an art and a technique, Spence recommends that people argue out of the "heart zone," use fear as an ally, let their emotions run free and know when and when not to argue.

9. Spontaneous Healing
Author: Andrew Weil, M.D.
Publisher: Knopf ($23)
Release: 5/95

Weil advocates alternative medicine and treatments for most ailments, from simple aches and pains to life-threatening conditions. In *Spontaneous Healing*, he outlines the treatments available — acupuncture, biofeedback, guided imagery and herbal medicines — and provides information on how to keep the body in good health by optimizing food, exercise, environmental factors and vitamins. He offers case histories as evidence of the success of alternative medicine.

10. Midnight in the Garden of Good and Evil
Author: John Berendt
Publisher: Random House ($24)
Release: 1/94
See page 696

Paperback

Mass Market

1. The Chamber
Author: John Grisham
Publisher: Dell ($7.50)
Release: 4/95
See page 695

2. The Alienist
Author: Caleb Carr
Publisher: Bantam ($6.99)
Release: 7/95
See page 694

3. Debt of Honor
Author: Tom Clancy
Publisher: Berkley ($7.50)
Release: 8/95
See page 695

4. Tom Clancy's Op-Center
Author: Tom Clancy
Publisher: Berkley ($6.99)
Release: 2/95

Based on the NBC miniseries starring Harry Hamlin, Lindsay Frost, Kim Cattrall, Wilford Brimley and Rod Steiger
The day that Paul Hood steps in as director of the National Crisis Management Center, a government agency that keeps an eye on international hot spots, rebel KGB guards steal three nuclear warheads from the Ukraine. Hood's problems at home are just as troubling, and the president he serves would rather be in bed with a reporter/spy than in the Oval Office.

5. CIRCLE OF FRIENDS

Author: Maeve Binchy
Publisher: Dell ($6.50)
Release: 11/91

Pat O'Connor directed the 1995 film starring Minnie Driver, Chris O'Donnell and Geraldine O'Rawe.

Eve, who grew up in an orphanage, and Benny, who came from a middle-class background, continue their childhood friendship as they attend the same university in Dublin. The girls come of age while studying in the city, and the plump, homely Benny wins the heart of the school's heart-throb, Jack.

6. THE DAY AFTER TOMORROW

Author: Allan Folsom
Publisher: Warner Vision ($6.99)
Release: 4/94

There was much publicity surrounding the deal made for *The Day After Tomorrow*, Folsom's first novel, which earned him an unprecedented $5.3 million in book and movie rights. His advance, the largest ever for a first novel was $750,000. The story: Paul Osborn sitting in a Paris cafe spots the man who killed his father 28 years earlier. The man gets away, but Osborn begins an obsessive quest to find the man, ask him why he committed the murder and then kill him. The high-tech thriller zooms between Paris, New York, London, Los Angeles and Switzerland.

7. CONGO

Author: Michael Crichton
Publisher: Ballantine ($6.99)
Release: 1/93

Frank Marshall directed the 1995 film starring Dylan Walsh, Laura Linney, Ernie Hudson, Joe Don Baker, Tim Curry and Taylor Nichols.

Amy, a gorilla with a 620-word sign-language vocabulary, has knowledge of the Congo that is dear to explorers in pursuit of treasures in King Solomon's mines. A professor who has been studying Amy takes her back to the jungle, and the fortune hunters join the pair hoping to capitalize on Amy's familiarity with the Congo.

8. THE ROBBER BRIDE

Author: Margaret Atwood
Publisher: Bantam ($6.50)
Release: 3/95

In this mystical, surreal tale spanning three decades, Zenia, a selfish, deceitful woman, uses three other women (Tony, Charis and Roz) to get what she wants, including their men. Each of the women do battle with Zenia and the demon gets her just desserts.

9. REMEMBER ME

Author: Mary Higgins Clark
Publisher: Pocket Books ($6.99)
Release: 5/95

A young couple, Menley and Adam Nichols, take an 18th-century house a sea captain built for his bride as a summer rental. Their romantic coastal retreat suddenly becomes ominous when a murder and other equally disturbing events shake the quaint shore town.

10. EMBRACED BY THE LIGHT

Author: Betty J. Eadie
Publisher: Bantam ($5.99)
Release: 10/94
See page 696

TRADE

1. CHICKEN SOUP FOR THE SOUL

Editors: Jack Canfield and Mark Hansen
Publisher: Health Communications ($12.95)
Release: 5/93
See page 700

2. SEVEN HABITS OF HIGHLY EFFECTIVE PEOPLE

Author: Stephen R. Covey
Publisher: Simon & Schuster/Fireside ($12)
Release: 8/90
See page 699

3. THE STONE DIARIES

Author: Carol Shields
Publisher: Penguin ($10)
Release: 4/95

Canadian novelist Shields won a Pulitzer and National Book Award for *The Stone Diaries*, which is the fictional autobiography of Daisy Stone Goodwill. Goodwill, an octogenarian, looks back on her life, beginning when her mother died in childbirth, and later as a wife and mother, stating matter-of-factly her sorrows, regrets and what she missed in life. Adding to the autobiographical feel of the novel, Shields used pictures of her children to depict Goodwill's descendants.

4. The Shipping News
Author: E. Annie Proulx
Publisher: Simon & Schuster/Touchstone ($12)
Release: 5/94
See page 700

5. The Celestine Prophecy: Experiential Guide
Author: James Redfield and Carol Adrienne
Publisher: Warner Books ($8.99)
Release: 9/95
This is meant to be a companion to the *Celestine Prophecy* as it helps the reader expand and intensify the nine insights detailed in the original book and use them to improve his or her own life and the lives of family and partners.

6. Ten Stupid Things Women Do to Mess up Their Lives
Author: Laura Schlessinger
Publisher: HarperPerennial ($10)
Release: 1/95
Schlessinger uses examples from her psychotherapy practice and her nationally syndicated radio show to dispense advice to women on how to take control of their lives. She recommends that women involved in unhappy relationships dump the "jerks" and seek "nice guys." She also suggests that women could realize their potential if they were willing to take risks.

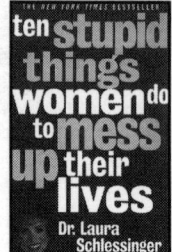

7. Reviving Ophelia
Author: Mary Pipher
Publisher: Ballantine ($12.50)
Release: 3/95
Pipher, a clinical psychologist who has worked with adolescent girls for more than 20 years, lets young girls tell their own personal and painful stories of living in a "girl-poisoned culture," one that stifles girls' creativity and intelligence and dictates that females should be skinny and beautiful. Pipher, urging parents to confront these issues, provides strategies to battle growing sexism and violence against women.

8. Care of the Soul
Author: Thomas Moore
Publisher: HarperPerennial ($13)
Release: 12/93
See page 699

9. The Artist's Way
Authors: Judith Cameron with Mark Bryan
Publisher: Jeremy Tarcher ($13.95)
Release: 7/92

For aspiring and established artists, *The Artist's Way* includes a comprehensive 12-week program to enhance and improve creativity by overcoming and eliminating such stumbling blocks as fear, jealousy, guilt and self-sabotage and replacing them with confidence and productivity.

10. What to Expect When You're Expecting
Authors: A. Eisenberg, H. Murkoff and S. Hathaway
Publisher: Workman ($10.95)
Release: 5/91
See page 699

 # Introducing...

Cyber Primer

As Internet and World Wide Web use rapidly grows — reaching older users who are not as computer savvy as the younger generation — so does the number of books about the Internet. In 1994, sales of reference books and guides to the Internet totaled more than $40 million, and that number is expected to grow significantly in 1995. Viacom's Macmillan Computer Publishing created the imprint Sams.net, which hopes to publish 30 books in 1995. I.D.G. Books publishes a line of "Dummy" books to help introduce newbies to the Net and computer programs. Other publishers of Internet books include: Sybex, Osborne/McGraw Hill and O'Reilly and Associates.

1994's New and Dead Magazines

The Magazine Publishers of America compiled lists of magazines that debuted and folded in 1994.

NEW MAGAZINES

1. **AIDS Digest**
   Publisher NA

2. **Airport Business**
   Johnson Hill Press

3. **Adoptive Families**
   Adoptive Families of America

4. **American How To**
   North American Outdoor Group, Inc.

5. **American Rider**
   T.L. Enterprises

6. **ARTnewz**
   Artnews

7. **Association Publishing**
   Society of National Association Publications

8. **Babybug**
   The Cricket Magazine Group

9. **Baltimore Made Easy**
   ESS Ventures, Inc.

10. **Barney**
    Welsh Publishing Group

11. **Beckett Racing Monthly**
    Beckett Publications

12. **Better Homes & Gardens Craft & Wear**
    Meredith Corporation

13. **Better Homes & Gardens Floral & Nature Crafts**
    Meredith Corporation

14. **BIZ**
    American City Business Journals and Dow Jones & Co.

15. **Blast**
    Creative Technology Ltd.

16. **Bloomberg Personal**
    Bloomberg L.P.

17. **Byte Middle East**
    McGraw-Hill Inc./Arabian Communications & Publishing

18. **Camiones**
    Newport Communications

19. **Can Technology International**
    Trend Publishing, Inc.

20. **Carolina Style**
    Carolina Style, Inc.

21. **CashSaver**
    LFP, Inc.

22. **Casino Games**
    International Inc.

23. **Central Virginia Gardening Guide**
    Eden Communications

24. **CFW: Competitor for Women**
    Babbitt & Lois Schwartz

25. **Chicago Bride**
    Chicago Bride

26. **Cinescape**
    Sendai Media Group

27. **City Family**
    Arthur Schiff

28. **CityScope**
    New York Times Co.

29. **Civilization**
    Management Corp.

30. **Clarity**
    NavPress

31. **Coffee Talk**
    Coffee Talk, Inc.

32. **Computer Life**
    Consumer Media Group

33. **Cosmopolitan Russia**
    Magazines/Independent Media

34. **Country Home Folk Crafts**
    Meredith Corporation

35. **Country Weekly**
    Enquirer/Star Group

36. **Crayola Kids**
    Meredith Corporation

37. **Creative Retirement**
    Vacation Publications

38. **D Magazine**
    Publisher NA

39. **Destinations West**
    Hands on Communications

40. **Destination: Vietnam**
    Global Directions, Inc.

41. **Drug Prices**
    Edmund Publications

42. **Drum Business**
    Drummer Publications, Inc.

43. **EcoTraveler**
    Skies America

44. **Electric Car**
    Argus Publishers Corp.

45. **Electronic Entertainment**
    Infotainment World (IDG)

46. **Elle Top Model**
    Hachette-Filipacchi

47. **ESPN2/Dirt**
    Lang Communications

48. **Eternelle**
    Eternelle Magazine Co.

49. **European Service Industry**
    The Association of Service Management International

50. **Executive Directions**
    Peterson's Guide Publications

51. **Family PC**
    Walt Disney Co. and Ziff Davis Publishing

52. **Family Times Magazine**
    Active Times Publications Inc.

The Rites of Spring

Dead Magazines

Top 200 Consumer Magazines by Paid Circulation for the Last Half of 1994

RANK	MAGAZINE	CIRCULATION	RANK	MAGAZINE	CIRCULATION
1.	*Modern Maturity*	21,716,727	40.	*Popular Mechanics*	1,636,210
2.	*Reader's Digest*	15,126,664	41.	*Life*	1,596,862
3.	*TV Guide*	14,037,062	42.	*Outdoor Life*	1,503,257
4.	*National Geographic*	9,203,079	43.	*Sunset*	1,498,417
5.	*Better Homes & Gardens*	7,613,661	44.	*Golf Digest*	1,465,494
6.	*Good Housekeeping*	5,223,935	45.	*Soap Opera Digest*	1,422,958
7.	*Ladies' Home Journal*	5,048,081	46.	*Penthouse*	1,304,719
8.	*Family Circle*	5,005,301	47.	*Mademoiselle*	1,304,059
9.	*Woman's Day*	4,724,500	48.	*New Woman*	1,301,859
10.	*McCall's*	4,611,848	49.	*'Teen*	1,280,148
11.	*The Cable Guide*	4,256,486	50.	*Gold Magazine*	1,269,642
12.	*Time*	4,063,146	51.	*Men's Health*	1,258,493
13.	*Prevention*	3,427,803	52.	*Cooking Light*	1,248,939
14.	*AAA World*	3,425,655	53.	*Boys' Life*	1,242,594
15.	*People*	3,424,858	54.	*First for Women*	1,236,019
16.	*Redbook*	3,401,775	55.	*Rolling Stone*	1,221,417
17.	*Playboy*	3,401,264	56.	*Consumers Digest*	1,208,643
18.	*Sports Illustrated*	3,252,641	57.	*Self*	1,201,395
19.	*Newsweek*	3,158,617	58.	*Bon Appetit*	1,187,437
20.	*National Enquirer*	3,066,032	59.	*Vogue*	1,181,313
21.	*The American Legion Magazine*	2,945,123	60.	*Us*	1,177,395
22.	*Star*	2,752,280	61.	*Woman's World*	1,167,314
23.	*Cosmopolitan*	2,527,928	62.	*Vanity Fair*	1,130,993
24.	*Southern Living*	2,472,649	63.	*Car & Driver*	1,125,119
25.	*U.S. News & World Report*	2,240,710	64.	*Sesame Street Magazine*	1,116,756
26.	*Smithsonian*	2,214,509	65.	*Entertainment Weekly*	1,115,024
27.	*Motorland*	2,194,221	66.	*Kiplinger's Personal Finance*	1,095,652
28.	*Glamour*	2,181,316	67.	*PC Magazine*	1,051,381
29.	*Home & Away*	2,146,295	68.	*The Family Handyman*	1,041,098
30.	*NEA Today*	2,115,968	69.	*Scouting*	1,037,291
31.	*V.F.W. Magazine*	2,038,216	70.	*Weight Watchers Magazine*	1,031,177
32.	*Field & Stream*	2,004,087	71.	*House Beautiful*	1,023,697
33.	*Money*	1,982,123	72.	*Globe*	1,021,929
34.	*Seventeen*	1,978,155	73.	*Country Home*	1,018,362
35.	*Ebony*	1,937,095	74.	*Home Mechanix*	1,009,347
36.	*YM*	1,933,775	75.	*Discover*	1,008,916
37.	*Country Living*	1,932,840	76.	*Home*	1,005,751
38.	*Parents*	1,852,517	77.	*Country America*	1,001,089
39.	*Popular Science*	1,808,140	78.	*Endless Vacation*	975,869

RANK	MAGAZINE	CIRCULATION
79.	Disney Adventures	961,992
80.	AAA Going Places	953,194
81.	PC World	951,849
82.	Motor Trend	951,650
83.	Essence	950,634
84.	Martha Stewart Living	948,838
85.	Jet	948,254
86.	Travel & Leisure	927,790
87.	Health	916,952
88.	Gourmet	912,342
89.	Condé Nast Traveler	909,092
90.	Victoria	907,034
91.	Elle	905,498
92.	PC/Computing	900,165
93.	Sports Illustrated for Kids	894,040
94.	Architectural Digest	881,232
95.	Business Week	880,357
96.	Nation's Business	861,620
97.	Parenting Magazine	856,019
98.	Midwest Living	852,704
99.	The New Yorker	830,307
100.	Working Mother	828,729
101.	American Health	827,643
102.	Shape	817,629
103.	American Legion Auxiliary National News	816,071
104.	Hot Rod	804,851
105.	Tennis	804,687
106.	Organic Gardening	803,535
107.	Sassy	800,592
108.	Working Woman	783,006
109.	Forbes	777,353
110.	True Story	774,948
111.	Traditional Home	771,552
112.	Food & Wine	757,188
113.	Esquire	756,030
114.	Harper's Bazaar	752,711
115.	Fortune	750,971
116.	Sport	750,418
117.	Road & Track	728,456
118.	Omni	725,816
119.	American Homestyle	707,403
120.	Traveler	704,254
121.	Yankee	700,265
122.	Workbench	679,278
123.	Flower & Garden	676,198

1995 NATIONAL MAGAZINE AWARDS

The National Magazine Awards, sponsored by the American Society of Magazine Editors and administered by the Columbia University Graduate School of Journalism, were presented April 12, 1995 at New York's Waldorf-Astoria Hotel.

General Excellence
Entertainment Weekly
The New Yorker
Men's Journal
I.D. Magazine

Personal Service
Smart Money

Special Interest
GQ

Reporting
The Atlantic Monthly

Feature Writing
GQ

Public Interest
The New Republic

Design
Martha Stewart Living

Photography
Rolling Stone

Fiction
Story

Essays and Criticism
Harper's Magazine

Single-Topic Issue
Discover

Source: Advertising Age

1994's Top 100 Magazines by Revenue

RANK	MAGAZINE	TOTAL REVENUE (IN THOUSANDS)*
1.	TV Guide	$1,036,903
2.	People	762,714
3.	Sports Illustrated	653,789
4.	Time	638,616
5.	Reader's Digest	477,817
6.	Parade	447,650
7.	Newsweek	427,730
8.	Better Homes and Gardens	353,462
9.	PC Magazine	325,701
10.	Good Housekeeping	315,259
11.	U.S. News and World Report	315,023
12.	Business Week	279,241
13.	Family Circle	260,980
14.	Woman's Day	245,187
15.	Ladies' Home Journal	242,484
16.	Forbes	235,901
17.	National Enquirer	221,197
18.	Cosmopolitan	220,404
19.	USA Weekend	218,095
20.	National Geographic	212,605
21.	Fortune	208,885
22.	PC Week	194,609
23.	Star Magazine	188,984
24.	McCall's	188,815
25.	Money	178,611
26.	Playboy	169,984
27.	Southern Living	166,294
28.	Redbook	158,561
29.	Vogue	149,384
30.	Glamour	147,230
31.	Entertainment Weekly	132,055
32.	Computerworld	128,346
33.	Golf Digest	126,349
34.	Rolling Stone	124,944
35.	PC World	123,109
36.	Cable Guide	119,777
37.	InfoWorld	114,383
38.	Computer Reseller News	113,216
39.	New York Times Magazine	110,656
40.	Country Living	110,099
41.	Consumer Reports	108,714
42.	The New Yorker	107,778
43.	Car and Driver	107,351
44.	Modern Maturity	105,370
45.	Prevention	103,753
46.	PC Computing	102,865
47.	Parents	100,135
48.	Computer Shopper	98,564
49.	Penthouse	98,169
50.	Soap Opera Digest	96,043
51.	Seventeen	88,475
52.	Elle	86,732
53.	Smithsonian	86,353
54.	Golf Magazine	82,975
55.	Life	82,929
56.	Sunset	82,347
57.	Woman's World	80,255
58.	Bride's & Your New Home	78,581
59.	Vanity Fair	78,172
60.	Travel and Leisure	78,171
61.	Travel Weekly	77,952
62.	Self	75,968
63.	Architectural Digest	75,865
64.	Ebony	73,820
65.	Harper's Bazaar	72,066
66.	Byte	71,901
67.	The Economist	71,409
68.	Windows	71,362
69.	Inc.	71,351
70.	Road and Track	71,253
71.	New York	70,029
72.	Endless Vacation	69,834
73.	House Beautiful	68,933
74.	Barron's	67,783
75.	Macworld	67,493
76.	GQ	67,459
77.	Field and Stream	67,386
78.	CommunicationsWeek	66,307
79.	Globe	65,966
80.	Popular Mechanics	64,771
81.	Mademoiselle	64,671
82.	Travel Agent	63,701
83.	Modern Bride	62,666
84.	Gourmet	61,034

85.	*Highlights for Children*	60,716
86.	*YM*	59,579
87.	*Home*	59,328
88.	*MacUser*	59,259
89.	*Electronic Engineering Times*	59,253
90.	*Sporting News*	58,875
91.	*Parenting*	58,531
92.	*Motor Trend*	58,530
93.	*Popular Science*	58,439

94.	*Jet*	56,414
95.	*InformationWeek*	55,948
96.	*New Woman*	55,718
97.	*Network World*	55,477
98.	*Us*	55,444
99.	*Conde Nast Traveler*	54,818
100.	*Tennis Magazine*	52,910

Source: Advertising Age. *Figures are based on advertising rate cards and undiscounted newsstand and subscription prices.*

Taking a Swing

WITH SO MANY MAGAZINES GOING ONLINE, SO MANY OTHERS burgeoning exclusively in electronic form and with the increased price of paper, one wonders why anyone would *want* to create a print periodical.

Twentysomething David Lauren, son of super-designer Ralph Lauren, made that choice with his slick monthly *Swing*, which launched in November 1994, and has not second-guessed his decision.

"I think people generally want something they can hold onto and take with them to the beach or on the subway," Lauren said. "I would consider taking *Swing* online. But a magazine online is inaccessible to the masses. Not everyone has the technology or wants the technology." Ironically, *Swing* is targeted to anti-slackers who don't buy into the Gen-X philosophy and are sick of being associated with the lazy, McJob crowd — just the group that is undoubtedly wired.

Lauren, who has ruminated the on-line route, has serious concerns about the option. "If and when we do go online, I'd like to have a discussion group to see what people like and what they would like to see included in an on-line magazine," he said. "I wouldn't want the [print] magazine and an electronic magazine to be exactly the same. Consumers wouldn't want that either. You have to be more creative to go online. There would have to be longer articles and more articles."

The on-line quandary remains an issue for the future, however. The new magazine keeps Lauren busy enough, worrying about content and sales. "I think a lot of people who buy this magazine sit on the floor in the back of a bookstore or magazine store, read a bit of the magazine and then buy it. They bring it home, read a few stories and then pick it up the next day and read it again and tear pages out for friends," he explained. "I've heard a lot about pass-along readership. You just can't get that with an electronic magazine."

Lauren started the magazine because he was frustrated with what was offered at the newsstand. As an ambitious twentysomething guy, he wanted to enjoy a publication that was an alternative to the Gen-X, celebrity and image mags that are targeted to his generation. "There was no magazine out there for me to read. I tried to fill a void. There were a lot of hip and trendy magazines out there but nothing of substance," he said. "I wanted to create something different from all the others."

And that he did. "*Swing* is a general-interest magazine and I'm hoping to attract all twentysomethings. I took the concept of *Time* and made it accessible to a younger generation. It is not urban-centered, it's not downtown or trendy. It's mainstream," Lauren said. Mainstream for Lauren means focusing on his peers, people like the ones he sat next to in class at Duke University, doing exceptional things in their careers and personal life. "Most magazine publishers trying to appeal to a wide audience slap celebrities on the cover. We profile young successful people in their 20s and hope to give readers something to aspire to. I think most people are interested in the stories of their peers."

Time will tell if Lauren takes *Swing* to another dimension. For now, readers can E-mail Lauren and his staff via America Online at Swingmag@aol.com ∎

For Adults Only: The New Comic Books

■ BY MARIA REIDELBACH

I T'S A FUNNY TIME IN THE HISTORY OF COMIC BOOKS. SERIOUSLY. SINCE THEIR INVENTION IN 1935 they've been maligned, made scapegoats and demonized as vulgar, illiterate and corrupting. But recently the medium has seen its first Pulitzer Prize (for Art Speigelman's *Maus*), and original artwork from comic books has begun to command respectable prices at preeminent New York art auction houses. The industry can't even agree on what to call the media. Forget "funny books" — nobody's used that term for years. Try "graphic novels," "sequential art" or just plain "commix" instead.

The industry itself is split: on one side are the behemoth, old-time publishers, mainly D.C. Comics and Marvel Comics, both of which have been around

COMICS

since the 1930s. D.C. is owned by Time Warner and publishes *Superman* and *Batman* comics, among others. Marvel Comics, owned by Revlon cosmetics magnate Ron Perelman, is the house behind *Spiderman*, *The X-Men* and the *Fantastic Four*. D.C. and Marvel both survived the great comic book censorship wars of the 1950s with lines of cleaned-up, watered-down, child-safe superhero comics. Although these publishers sell quite a few comic books, they generate their real money in Hollywood movies and related licensing.

The other branch of the comic book family tree is where the dirty laundry hangs — the alternative and underground comics. The forerunner of these, in the 1950s, was *MAD* magazine. In the 1960s, underground comics, like *MAD,* began as black-and-white, advertisement-free, Comics-Code-Authority-scorning publications. By the late 1970s, underground comics had transformed into what was dubbed alternative comics. These were published by a flourishing number of small presses for an adult, or nearly adult, audience. By the 1980s, the popularity of such alternative comics as *Teenage Mutant Ninja Turtles*, *Raw* and others led even D.C. and Marvel to develop their own alternative imprints "for adults only." The independent comic book scene was also the industry leader in a change in the policy regarding ownership of work — artists (though not necessarily writers) now own their work and earn royalties.

The influence of all these developments on the creative talents behind comic books vary. Some artists/writers are producing pretentious, arty, autobiographical offerings. Others turn their backs on the culture that rejected them, preferring to wallow in a grungy mire of gratuitous sex and violence. There's no denying that both the effete and the vulgar have their fascinations, but the most interesting work is being created by the artists who are using contemporary culture as well as the history of comics as a vast resource to create works that are personal expressions of an ambitious range of subjects and ideas. The best of these efforts combine stylish graphic art with captivating storytelling and vivid dialogue.

T ake, for example, *Love and Rockets*, a dramatically black-and-white comic with ongoing stories by the brothers Jaime and Gilbert Hernandez. Jaime's work often depicts the day-to-day lives and adventures of Hopey, a twentyish Mexican-American woman, her family, friends and co-workers. On the surface, his style resembles *Archie* comics, with crisp lines and square mouths, but the variety of characters is enormous — men are young and handsome, and also young and plump, getting older but still good looking, alcoholic, you name it. Yet the women — the variety of women blows television and the movies out of the water — have body types, body shapes and postures that are as unique as a voice. You can tell that Jaime is enthralled with women, and men, too. Gilbert's stories more often take place in Mexico, and slip in and out of the allegorical and magical. Gilbert's graphic style is less realistic as well, with characters becoming caricatured and regularly violating the laws of science and nature. In one recent tale, several village women produce and star in a celebrity exercise show in the States, while back in the village a marriage deteriorates and a girl who brandishes her dismembered right arm in her left gets lost while stalking a crow. Gilbert thoughtfully supplies footnote translations of the many Spanish terms that season his work.

Another narrative comic book, *Bug House*, is today's version of a funny animal comic. Steve Lafler's insectoid characters populate a comique noir of the nightclub world in post-war New York City. Lafler intends the comic to be an investigation of the creative spirit as manifested in be-bop music. Its graphics are also evocative of period, humorous illustration: fast, supple, shaded lines and lots of patterning and texture. Jimmy Watts is an up-and-coming sax player with his own band and a growing bug-juice habit. He and Julie, his slinky lover (and it's amazing how slinky a praying mantis can be) survive addiction, sleazy managers and more each issue.

Meat Cake, by Dame Darcy, has a period look as well, but here it's Edward Gorey meets Yellow Kid Victorian, adorned with dense accumulations of swags and curleyques. Her characters lead fairy-tale lives: vegetables sing and play zithers, young women meet cruel early deaths, Siamese twins and living Pez dispensers take a helicopter ride to Hawaii to visit the mermaids. Darcy includes as a regular feature a comic that can be read upside-down as well as rightside up.

A contemporary master of the narrative comic whose illustrations frequently appear in the mainstream press is Charles Burns. He manages to combine a bold, abstracted, high-contrast graphic style with cinematic pacing and framing to depict stories of teenage lust and fear. *Black Hole* includes some of Burns's favorite themes: disfiguring disease, murder, vivid dream sequences. Burns carefully controls every millimeter of each page, and the look is iconic and nearly religious.

In complete contrast, Roberta Gregory has cultivated an expressive line with which she can quickly depict and animate her heroine, *Bitchy Bitch*. Bitchy is fast approaching middle-age, has to work a job that she can barely tolerate with people she disdains. She's got no love in her life and her family tortures her via her answering machine. Bitchy overreacts to everything, her teeth-gritting expression swinging crazily from bug-eyed exasperation to slavish obsequiousness, but she slogs it out, day after day, and manages to have her moments of fun and adventure despite herself.

Autobiography is another rich narrative field for contemporary comic artists. Many (maybe too many) focus on adolescent angst, but the teenage years seem especially appropriate for the medium. Recent efforts include Peter Kuper's *Wild Life*, where an urbane, pipe-smoking Kuper flies back in time to visit himself in the 1970s. The stories, depicted in a scratch-board technique (in which lighter values are revealed by scratching through a dark surface), tell of shy, young Peter's escapades with sex, drugs and rock and roll. Kuper's illustrations for the color covers are wonderful mixed-media and found object interpretations of his comics.

Ritchie Kill'd My Toads is an especially lyrical look by Scott Getchell at his coming of age. Getchell, also a musician, tells of that confusing time when we began to realize that there's plenty of competition to simply exist, and that there was something between our legs that could cause "weird feelings in the pit of my gut." *Ritchie* also contains some of the most revealing boy stories I've read. Getchell's drawings are notable for facial expression, page layout, and a Japanese sumi-painting-like abstraction.

Juliee Doucet's comics are a real clutter-fest: they're the kind you can read over and over and still notice new details. Her recent comics are tales of her college years: reading them makes one realize how the stories of young women are underrepresented in the media. Doucet, a Canadian, creates detailed portraits of the romances and her attempts to lose her virginity during her years as an art student.

Of course, the patron saints of autobiographical comics are Robert Crumb and Aline Kominsky Crumb whose current vehicle is *Self-Loathing Comics*. The Crumbs are masters of the comic form, and *Self-Loathing Comics* tells of the family's recent move to a village in the south of France. As always, through a combination of outrageous candor and impeccable draftsmanship, Robert makes the mundane details of everyday life fascinating. While Robert's technical mastery provides a slick package for his sometimes shocking domestic tales, Aline's ruthless deprecation rendered in a faux-naive style provides only the haven of humor. But she's very funny.

Since the success of Art Speigelman's *Maus*, many more artists have turned their attention to nonfiction comics. In the series *Palestine*, Joe Sacco assumes the life of a foreign (comic book) correspondent. Although the world of Palestinian women remains mysterious and mostly inaccessible to him, he spends many hours roaming the streets and drinking tea and coffee with the locals. And while he watches them, he watches himself watching, scrutinizing his motives and learning just as much about his own world view as he does about theirs.

And just for fun, there's always *Sex Kinks of the Rich and Famous* to keep you warm on a breezy beach. The premiere issue features the intimate habits of Art Linkletter, trash filmmaker Ed Wood, Jr., Andy Warhol and anarchist Emma Goldman, depicted by a variety of artists.

One of the best nonfiction comics recently published is *Introducing Kafka* written by David Zane Mairowitz and illustrated by Robert Crumb. Perhaps because both are creative artists themselves (Mairowitz is a playwright), they have created a strikingly original overview of Kafka's life and works, including some of the best work by Crumb seen anywhere. This is a labor of love that stretches the possibilities of the media, gracefully incorporating printed text with hand lettering, and including illustrated excerpts of many of Kafka's short stories.

Also deliciously good is Donna Barr's long-running series, *The Desert Peach*, a fictionalized story featuring Field Marshall Erwin Rommel's homosexual younger brother, Pfirsich. The younger Rommel is the out-of-the-closet commander of a German battalion of misfits in the African desert. The outrageous story line of the comic is impeccably researched, bilingual and beautifully drawn. Barr just can't seem to keep her pen from further elaborating expressive character and narrative drawings — even the page numbers are illustrated with exuberant marginalia.

Many of these publications have small press runs, aren't carried in bookstores and some are hard to find even in comic-book shops. Many comic-book publishers offer mail order catalogs with other goodies besides comics themselves. Here are addresses for some publishers along with other titles worth checking out:

Buzzard
Bug House
Cat-Head Comics
P.O. Box 576
Hudson, MA 01749

Grendel Tales
Madman Comics
Dark Horse Comics
10956 S.E. Main St.
Milwaukie, OR 99722

Purty Plotte
Drawn & Quarterly
5550 Jeanne-Mance St., Apt 16
Montreal, Quebec, Canada

Sex Kinks of the Rich and Famous
Rip Off Press
P.O. Box 4686
Auburn, CA 95604

Yet another interesting historical comic is *Dropsie Avenue: The Neighborhood*, by one of the original masters of the comic media, Will Eisner, creator of the legendary *Spirit*. This ambitious work tells the story of a fictional, though archetypal, street in the Bronx, from the days of the Dutch settlers in the 18th century to the present. It's obvious that Eisner is a lover of the Bronx, and also that he spent a great deal of time studying the ebbs and flows of immigration in that part of the city. Yet the strength of Dropsie Avenue is that he has populated it with a cast of very believable people, people who are absorbed with problems that are peculiar to their time, yet universal as well. The characters include a social-climbing Irish family whose daughter becomes a prostitute, a World War I hero whose job planning the routes of the elevated trains makes him one of the most influential men in the neighborhood and a young Jewish lawyer who becomes a city councilman.

A roundup of good comics wouldn't be complete without featuring the books that include a variety of subjects in a wild variety of forms, the comics that are the most direct heirs of the undergrounds of the 1960s. There are plenty of good ones. One of my current favorites is *Eightball* by Daniel Clowes. He's got a graphic style  that is one part Bernard Krigstein (an avant-garde comic artist in the 1950s), one part Bob Clark (from *MAD*) and the rest a combination of photocopied office cartoons and images culled from the dregs of popular culture. The stories aren't bad, but it's the images that are marvelous.

Jim, by Jim Woodring, is another terrifically original comic. Many of the tales feature funny animals and are at once mundane and macabre, dreamlike and violent, silly and painful. Woodring's use of color is luminescent and he beautifully combines line drawings with more photographically

rendered characters. One story tells of a group of children, a dying grandmother and Pulque, a stinking, drunken, brilliantly hued frog-like creature who instantly hits it off with Grandma.

The Acme Novelty Library emulates the look of period publications while containing charmingly rendered comics. Issue three is an impeccable take on an early 20th-century "little magazine" including small-type advertisements in the back and an etching of "our facilities." Inside, a little spud of a protagonist cavorts and careens with other, well-known characters like Dick Tracy and Nancy. It's a hilarious pastiche of 20th-century print media. For an interesting variety of (mostly male) artists, check out *Buzzard*. Editor and writer Stephen Beaupre has catholic tastes and almost always chooses work that's funny, innovative and amusing.

One of the nicer aspects of all these comics is their lack of advertising. It's a welcome relief from the relentless hucksterism of television, mainstream magazines and all the other advertising that resides in virtually every form of media these days. Because these books are published for readers, rather than advertisers, the content is dramatically affected. They're more individualistic, idiosyncratic and eccentric, and they're not written to appeal to the broadest possible audience. This means that when you're browsing comic books, you'll find that the vast majority of them don't appeal to you. But when you find the ones that do, it's a special, private pleasure, and you're likely to feel that the comic was created just for you. And in a way, it was. ■

....

Maria Reidelbach is the author of Completely MAD: A History of the Comic Book and Magazine *(Little Brown) and* Miniature Golf *(Abbeville Press)*

Hate!
Idiotland
Jim
Love and Rockets
Meatcake
Naughty Bits
Palestine
Self-Loathing Comics
Wild Life
Fantagraphics Books
7563 Lake City Way N.E.
Seattle, WA 98115

Black Hole
The Crow
Dropsie Avenue: The Neighborhood
Illegal Alien
Introducing Kafka
Steven and Bunny
Kitchen Sink Press
320 Riverside Drive
Northampton, MA 01060

The Desert Peach
MU/AEON
5014-D Roosevelt Way NE
Seattle, WA 98105

The Big Book of Death
The Big Book of Weirdos
The Big Book of Urban Legends
Paradox Press
D.C. Comics
1325 Avenue of the Americas
New York, NY 10019

Ritchie Kill'd My Toads
Skidmark Press
83 Pleasant St. #2
Cambridge, MA 02139

An overwhelming number of comic books and related paraphernalia can be found at

Bud Plant Comic Art
P.O. Box 1689
Grass Valley, CA 95945

The National Book Awards

The National Book Awards, administered annually by the National Book Foundation, are considered one of the most prestigious literary honors, rivaled only by the Pulitzer Prizes. The awards include $10,000 a prize.

1950

FICTION
The Man With the Golden Arm, Nelson Algren

NONFICTION
Ralph Waldo Emerson, Ralph L. Rusk

POETRY
Paterson: Book III and Selected Poems, William Carlos
    Williams

1951

FICTION
*The Collected Stories of
    William Faulkner,*
    William Faulkner

NONFICTION
Herman Melville,
    Newton Arvin

POETRY
The Auroras of Autumn,
    Wallace Stevens

William Faulkner

1952

FICTION
From Here to Eternity,
    James Jones

NONFICTION
The Sea Around Us, Rachel Carson

POETRY
Collected Poems, Marianne Moore

1953

FICTION
The Invisible Man, Ralph Ellison

NONFICTION
The Course of an Empire, Bernard A. De Voto

POETRY
Collected Poems, 1917–1952, Archibald MacLeish

1954

FICTION
The Adventures of Augie March, Saul Bellow

NONFICTION
A Stillness at Appomattox, Bruce Catton

POETRY
Collected Poems, Conrad Aiken

1955

FICTION
A Fable, William Faulkner

NONFICTION
The Measure of Man, Joseph Wood Krutch

POETRY
The Collected Poems of Wallace Stevens, Wallace Stevens

SPECIAL CITATION
Poems, 1923–1954, e. e. cummings

1956

FICTION
Ten North Frederick, John O'Hara

NONFICTION
An American in Italy, Herbert Kubly

POETRY
The Shield of Achilles, W. H. Auden

1957

FICTION
The Field of Vision, Wright Morris

NONFICTION
Russia Leaves the War, George F. Kennan

POETRY
Things of This World, Richard Wilbur

1958

FICTION
The Wapshot Chronicle,
    John Cheever

NONFICTION
The Lion and the Throne,
    Catherine Drinker
    Bowen

POETRY
*Promises: Poems,
    1954–1956,* Robert
    Penn Warren

John Cheever

1959

FICTION
The Magic Barrel, Bernard Malamud

NONFICTION
Mistress to an Age: A Life of Madame de Stael,
    J. Christopher Herold

POETRY
Words for the Wind, Theodore Roethke

1960

FICTION
Goodbye, Columbus, Philip Roth

NONFICTION
James Joyce, Richard Ellmann

POETRY
Life Studies, Robert Lowell

1961

FICTION
The Waters of Kronos, Conrad Richter

NONFICTION
The Rise and Fall of the Third Reich, William L. Shirer

POETRY
The Woman at the Washington Zoo, Randall Jarrell

1962

FICTION
The Moviegoer, Walker Percy

NONFICTION
The City in History: Its Origins, Its Transformations and Its Prospects, Lewis Mumford

POETRY
Poems, Alan Dugan

1963

FICTION
Morte D'Urban, J. F. Powers

NONFICTION
Henry James, Vol. II: The Conquest of London and *Henry James, Vol. III: The Middle Years,* Leon Edel

POETRY
Traveling Through the Dark, William Stafford

1964

ARTS AND LETTERS
John Keats: The Making of a Poet, Aileen Ward

FICTION
The Centaur, John Updike

HISTORY AND BIOGRAPHY
The Rise of the West: A History of the Human Community, William H. McNeill

POETRY
Selected Poems, John Crowe Ransom

SCIENCE, PHILOSOPHY AND RELIGION
Man-Made America, Christopher Tunnard and Boris Pushkarev

1965

ARTS AND LETTERS
Oysters of Locmariaquer, Eleanor Clark

FICTION
Herzog, Saul Bellow

HISTORY AND BIOGRAPHY
The Life of Lenin, Louis Fischer

POETRY
The Far Field, Theodore Roethke

SCIENCE, PHILOSOPHY AND RELIGION
God and Golem, Inc.: A Comment on Certain Points Where Cybernetics Impinges on Religion, Norbert Wiener

1966

ARTS AND LETTERS
Paris Journal, 1944–65, Janet Flanner

FICTION
The Collected Stories of Katherine Anne Porter, Katherine Anne Porter

HISTORY AND BIOGRAPHY
A Thousand Days, Arthur M. Schlesinger, Jr.

POETRY
Buckdancer's Choice: Poems, James Dickey

Katherine Anne Porter

SCIENCE, PHILOSOPHY AND RELIGION
No award

1967

ARTS AND LETTERS
Mr. Clemens and Mark Twain: A Biography, Justin Kaplan

FICTION
The Fixer, Bernard Malamud

HISTORY AND BIOGRAPHY
The Enlightenment, Vol. I: An Interpretation: The Rise of Modern Paganism, Peter Gay

POETRY
Nights and Days, James Merrill

SCIENCE, PHILOSOPHY AND RELIGION
La Vida, Oscar Lewis

TRANSLATION
Julio Cortazar's Hopscotch, Gregory Rabassa
Casanova's History of My Life, Willard Trask

1968

ARTS AND LETTERS
Selected Essays, William Troy

FICTION
The Eighth Day, Thornton Wilder

HISTORY AND BIOGRAPHY
Memoirs: 1925–1950, George F. Kennan

POETRY
The Light Around the Body, Robert Bly

SCIENCE, PHILOSOPHY AND RELIGION
Death at an Early Age, Jonathan Kozol

TRANSLATION
Soren Kierkegaard's Journals and Papers, Howard and Edna Hong

1969

ARTS AND LETTERS
The Armies of the Night: History as a Novel, the Novel as History, Norman Mailer

CHILDREN'S LITERATURE
Journey From Peppermint Street, Meindert DeJong

FICTION
Steps, Jerzy Kosinski

HISTORY AND BIOGRAPHY
White Over Black: American Attitudes Toward the Negro, 1550–1812, Winthrop D. Jordan

POETRY
His Toy, His Dream, His Rest, John Berryman

THE SCIENCES
Death in Life: Survivors of Hiroshima, Robert J. Lifton

TRANSLATION
Calvino's Cosmicomics, William Weaver

1970

ARTS AND LETTERS
An Unfinished Woman: A Memoir, Lillian Hellman

CHILDREN'S BOOKS
A Day of Pleasure: Stories of a Boy Growing Up in Warsaw, Isaac Bashevis Singer

FICTION
Them, Joyce Carol Oates

HISTORY AND BIOGRAPHY
Huey Long, T. Harry Williams

Lillian Hellman

PHILOSOPHY AND RELIGION
Gandhi's Truth: On the Origins of Militant Nonviolence, Erik H. Erikson

POETRY
The Complete Poems, Elizabeth Bishop

TRANSLATION
Celine's Castle to Castle, Ralph Manheim

1971

ARTS AND LETTERS
Cocteau: A Biography, Francis Steegmuller

CHILDREN'S BOOKS
The Marvelous Misadventures of Sebastian, Lloyd Alexander

FICTION
Mr. Sammler's Planet, Saul Bellow

HISTORY AND BIOGRAPHY
Roosevelt: The Soldier of Freedom, James MacGregor Burns

POETRY
To See, To Take, Mona Van Duyn

THE SCIENCES
Science in the British Colonies of America, Raymond Phineas Sterns

TRANSLATION
Brecht's Saint Joan of the Stockyards, Frank Jones
Yasunari Kawabata's The Sound of the Mountain, Edward G. Seidensticker

1972

ARTS AND LETTERS
The Classical Style: Haydn, Mozart, Beethoven, Charles Rosen

BIOGRAPHY
Eleanor and Franklin: The Story of Their Relationship, Based on Eleanor Roosevelt's Private Papers, Joseph P. Lash

CHILDREN'S BOOKS
The Slightly Irregular Fire Engine or the Hithering Thithering Djinn, Donald Barthelme

CONTEMPORARY AFFAIRS
The Last Whole Earth Catalog, Stewart Brand, editor

FICTION
The Complete Stories of Flannery O'Connor, Flannery O'Connor

HISTORY
Ordeal of the Union, vols. VII and VIII: The Organized War, 1863–1864 and *The Organized War to Victory,* Allan Nevins

PHILOSOPHY AND RELIGION
Righteous Empire: The Protestant Experience in America, Martin E. Marty

POETRY
Selected Poems, Howard Moss
The Collected Poems of Frank O'Hara, Frank O'Hara

THE SCIENCES
The Blue Whale, George L. Small

TRANSLATION
Jacques Monod's Chance and Necessity, Austryn Wainhouse

1973

ARTS AND LETTERS
Diderot, Arthur M. Wilson

BIOGRAPHY
George Washington, Vol. IV: Anguish and Farewell, 1793–1799, James Thomas Flexner

CHILDREN'S BOOKS
The Farthest Shore, Ursula K. LeGuin

CONTEMPORARY AFFAIRS
Fire in the Lake: The Vietnamese and the Americans in Vietnam, Frances FitzGerald

FICTION
Chimera, John Barth
Augustus, John Williams

HISTORY
The Children of Pride, Robert Manson Myers
Judenrat, Isaiah Trunk

PHILOSOPHY AND RELIGION
A Religious History of the American People, S. E. Ahlstrom

POETRY
Collected Poems, 1951–1971, A. R. Ammons

THE SCIENCES
The Serengeti Lion: A Study of Predator-Prey Relations, George B. Schaller

TRANSLATION
The Aeneid of Virgil, Allen Mandelbaum

1974

ARTS AND LETTERS
Deeper Into the Movies, Pauline Kael

BIOGRAPHY
Macaulay: The Shaping of the Historian, John Clive

Malcolm Lowry: A Biography, Douglas Day

CHILDREN'S BOOKS
The Court of the Stone Children, Eleanor Cameron

CONTEMPORARY AFFAIRS
The Briar Patch, Murray Kempton

FICTION
Gravity's Rainbow,
Thomas Pynchon

A Crown of Feathers and Other Stories, Isaac Bashevis Singer

HISTORY
Macaulay: The Shaping of the Historian, John Clive

PHILOSOPHY AND RELIGION
Edmund Husserl: Philosopher of Infinite Tasks, Maurice Natanson

Allen Ginsberg

POETRY
The Fall of America: Poems of These States, Allen Ginsberg

Diving Into the Wreck: Poems 1971–1972, Adrienne Rich

THE SCIENCES
Life: The Unfinished Experiment, S. E. Luria

TRANSLATION
The Confessions of Lady Nijo, Karen Brazell

Octavio Paz' Alternating Current, Helen R. Lane

Paul Valery's Monsieur Teste, Jackson Mathews

1975

ARTS AND LETTERS
Marcel Proust, Roger Shattuck

The Lives of a Cell: Notes of a Biology Watcher, Lewis Thomas

BIOGRAPHY
The Life of Emily Dickinson, Richard B. Sewall

CHILDREN'S BOOKS
M. C. Higgins the Great, Virginia Hamilton

CONTEMPORARY AFFAIRS
All God's Dangers: The Life of Nate Shaw, Theodore Rosengarten

FICTION
Dog Soldiers, Robert Stone

The Hair of Harold Roux, Thomas Williams

HISTORY
The Ordeal of Thomas Hutchinson, Bernard Bailyn

PHILOSOPHY AND RELIGION
Anarchy, State and Utopia, Robert Nozick

POETRY
Presentation Piece, Marilyn Hacker

THE SCIENCES
Interpretation of Schizophrenia, Silvano Arieti

The Lives of a Cell: Notes of a Biology Watcher, Lewis Thomas

TRANSLATION
Miguel D. Unamuno's The Agony of Christianity and Essays on Faith, Anthony Kerrigan

1976

ARTS AND LETTERS
The Great War and Modern Memory, Paul Fussell

CHILDREN'S LITERATURE
Bert Breen's Barn, Walter D. Edmonds

CONTEMPORARY AFFAIRS
Passage to Ararat, Michael J. Arlen

FICTION
Jr, William Gaddis

HISTORY AND BIOGRAPHY
The Problem of Slavery in the Age of Revolution, 1770–1823, David Brion Davis

POETRY
Self-Portrait in a Convex Mirror, John Ashbery

1977

BIOGRAPHY AND AUTOBIOGRAPHY
Norman Thomas: The Last Idealist, W. A. Swanberg

CHILDREN'S LITERATURE
The Master Puppeteer, Katherine Paterson

CONTEMPORARY THOUGHT
The Uses of Enchantment: The Meaning and Importance of Fairy Tales, Bruno Bettelheim

FICTION
The Spectator Bird, Wallace Stegner

HISTORY
World of Our Fathers, Irving Howe

JUDGES' STATEMENT:
Because Alex Haley's *Roots* does not accommodate itself to the category of History, but transcends that and other categories, members of the History panel were unable to name it as one of the nominees in History. They are at one, however, that its distinguished literary quality jusitifies according it a special citation of merit.

Alex Haley

POETRY
Collected Poems, 1930–1976, Richard Eberhart

TRANSLATION
Master Tung's Western Chamber Romance, Li-Li Ch'en

1978

BIOGRAPHY AND AUTOBIOGRAPHY
Samuel Johnson, W. Jackson Bate

CHILDREN'S LITERATURE
The View From the Oak, Judith Kohl and Herbert Kohl

CONTEMPORARY THOUGHT
Winners and Losers, Gloria Emerson

FICTION
Blood Ties, Mary Lee Settle

HISTORY
The Path Between the Seas: The Creation of the Panama Canal 1870–1914, David McCullough

POETRY
The Collected Poems of Howard Nemerov, Howard Nemerov

TRANSLATION
Uwe George's In the Deserts of This Earth, Richard Winston and Clara Winston

1979
BIOGRAPHY AND AUTOBIOGRAPHY
Robert Kennedy and His Times, Arthur M. Schlesinger, Jr.

CHILDREN'S LITERATURE
The Great Gilly Hopkins, Katherine Paterson

CONTEMPORARY THOUGHT
The Snow Leopard, Peter Matthiessen

FICTION
Going After Cacciato, Tim O'Brien

HISTORY
Intellectual Life in the Colonial South, 1585–1763, Richard Beale Davis

POETRY
Mirabell: Book of Numbers, James Merrill

TRANSLATION
Cesar Vallejo's The Complete Posthumous Poetry, Clayton Eshleman and José Rubia Barcia

1980
AUTOBIOGRAPHY
HARDCOVER
Lauren Bacall by Myself, Lauren Bacall
PAPERBACK
And I Worked at the Writer's Trade: Chapters of Literary History 1918–1978, Malcolm Cowley

BIOGRAPHY
HARDCOVER
The Rise of Theodore Roosevelt, Edmund Morris
PAPERBACK
Max Perkins: Editor of Genius, A. Scott Berg

CHILDREN'S BOOKS
HARDCOVER
A Gathering of Days: A New England Girl's Journal, Joan W. Blos
PAPERBACK
A Swiftly Tilting Planet, Madeleine L'Engle

CURRENT INTEREST
HARDCOVER
Julia Child and More Company, Julia Child
PAPERBACK
The Culture of Narcissism, Christopher Lasch

FICTION
HARDCOVER
Sophie's Choice, William Styron
PAPERBACK
The World According to Garp, John Irving

FIRST NOVEL
Birdy, William Wharton

GENERAL NONFICTION
HARDCOVER
The Right Stuff, Tom Wolfe
PAPERBACK
The Snow Leopard, Peter Matthiessen

GENERAL REFERENCE BOOKS
HARDCOVER
Congressional Quarterly's Guide to the U.S. Supreme Court, Elder Witt, editor

Tom Wolfe

PAPERBACK
The Complete Directory of Prime Time Network TV Shows: 1946–Present, Tim Brooks and Earle Marsh

HISTORY
HARDCOVER
The White House Years, Henry A. Kissinger
PAPERBACK
A Distant Mirror: The Calamitous 14th Century, Barbara W. Tuchman

MYSTERY
HARDCOVER
The Green Ripper, John D. MacDonald
PAPERBACK
Stained Glass, William F. Buckley, Jr.

POETRY
Ashes, Philip Levine

RELIGION/INSPIRATION
HARDCOVER
The Gnostic Gospels, Elaine Pagels
PAPERBACK
A Severe Mercy, Sheldon Vanauken

SCIENCE
HARDCOVER
Godel, Escher, Bach: An Eternal Golden Braid, Douglas Hofstadter
PAPERBACK
The Dancing Wu Li Masters: An Overview of the New Physics, Gary Zukav

SCIENCE FICTION
HARDCOVER
Jem, Frederik Pohl
PAPERBACK
The Book of the Dun Cow, Walter Wangerin, Jr.

TRANSLATION
Cesare Pavese's Hard Labor, William Arrowsmith

Osip E. Mandelstam's Complete Critical Prose and Letters, Jane Garry Harris and Constance Link

WESTERN
Bendigo Shafter, Louis L'Amour

1981
AUTOBIOGRAPHY/BIOGRAPHY
HARDCOVER
Walt Whitman, Justin Kaplan
PAPERBACK
Samuel Beckett, Deirdre Bair

CHILDREN'S BOOKS, FICTION
HARDCOVER
The Night Swimmers, Betsy Byars
PAPERBACK
Ramona and Her Mother, Beverly Cleary

CHILDREN'S BOOKS, NONFICTION
HARDCOVER
Oh, Boy! Babies, Alison Cragin Herzig and Jane Lawrence Mali

FICTION
HARDCOVER
Plains Song, Wright Morris
PAPERBACK
The Stories of John Cheever, John Cheever

FIRST NOVEL
Sister Wolf, Ann Arensberg

GENERAL NONFICTION
HARDCOVER
China Men, Maxine Hong Kingston
PAPERBACK
The Last Cowboy, Jane Kramer

HISTORY
HARDCOVER
Christianity, Social Tolerance and Homosexuality, John Boswell
PAPERBACK
Been in the Storm So Long: The Aftermath of Slavery, Leon F. Litwak

POETRY
The Need to Hold Still, Lisel Mueller

SCIENCE
HARDCOVER
The Panda's Thumb: More Reflections in Natural History, Stephen Jay Gould
PAPERBACK
The Medusa and the Snail, Lewis Thomas

TRANSLATION
The Letters of Gustave Flaubert, Francis Steegmuller
Arno Schmidt's Evening Edged in Gold, John E. Woods

1982
AUTOBIOGRAPHY/BIOGRAPHY
HARDCOVER
Mornings on Horseback, David McCullough
PAPERBACK
Walter Lippmann and the American Century, Ronald Steel

CHILDREN'S BOOKS, FICTION
HARDCOVER
Westmark, Lloyd Alexander
PAPERBACK
Words by Heart, Ouida Sebestyen

CHILDREN'S BOOKS, NONFICTION
HARDCOVER
A Penguin Year, Susan Bonners

CHILDREN'S BOOKS, PICTURE BOOKS
HARDCOVER
Outside Over There, Maurice Sendak
PAPERBACK
Noah's Ark, Peter Spier

FICTION
HARDCOVER
Rabbit Is Rich, John Updike
PAPERBACK
So Long, See You Tomorrow, William Maxwell

FIRST NOVEL
Dale Loves Sophie to Death, Robb Forman Dew

GENERAL
NONFICTION
HARDCOVER
The Soul of a New Machine, Tracy Kidder
PAPERBACK
Naming Names, Victor S. Navasky

John Updike

HISTORY
HARDCOVER
People of the Sacred Mountain: A History of the Northern Cheyenne Chiefs and Warrior Societies, 1830–1879, Father Peter John Powell
PAPERBACK
The Generation of 1914, Robert Wohl

POETRY
Life Supports: New and Collected Poems, William Bronk

SCIENCE
HARDCOVER
Lucy: The Beginnings of Humankind, Donald C. Johanson and Maitland A. Edey
PAPERBACK
Taking the Quantum Leap: The New Physics for Nonscientists, Fred Alan Wolf

TRANSLATION
Higuchi Ichiyo's In the Shade of Spring Leaves, Robert Lyons Danly
The Ten Thousand Leaves: A Translation of the Man'Yoshu, Japan's Premier Anthology of Classical Poetry, Ian Hideo Levy

1983
AUTOBIOGRAPHY/BIOGRAPHY
HARDCOVER
Isak Dinesen: The Life of a Storyteller, Judith Thurman
PAPERBACK
Nathaniel Hawthorne in His Time, James R. Mellow

CHILDREN'S FICTION
HARDCOVER
Homesick: My Own Story, Jean Fritz
PAPERBACK
A Place Apart, Paula Fox
Marked by Fire, Joyce Carol Thomas

CHILDREN'S BOOKS, NONFICTION
Chimney Sweeps, James Cross Giblin

CHILDREN'S PICTURE BOOKS
HARDCOVER
Miss Rumphius, Barbara Cooney
Doctor De Soto, William Steig

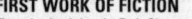
PAPERBACK
A House Is a House for Me, Mary Ann Hoberman; Betty Fraser,
    illustrator

FICTION
HARDCOVER
The Color Purple, Alice
    Walker
PAPERBACK
*Collected Stories of
    Eudora Welty,*
    Eudora Welty

FIRST NOVEL
*The Women of
    Brewster Place,*
    Gloria Naylor

**GENERAL
NONFICTION**
*China: Alive in the Bitter
    Sea,* Fox
    Butterfield

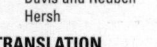

Alice Walker

PAPERBACK
National Defense, James Fallows

HISTORY
HARDCOVER
*Voices of Protest: Huey Long, Father Coughlin and the Great
    Depression,* Alan Brinkley
PAPERBACK
Utopian Thought in the Western World, Frank E. Manuel and
    Fritzie P. Manuel

ORIGINAL PAPERBACK
The Red Magician, Lisa Goldstein

POETRY
Selected Poems, Galway
    Kinnell
*Country Music: Selected
    Early Poems,* Charles
    Wright

SCIENCE
HARDCOVER
*"Subtle Is the Lord . . .":
    The Science and Life
    of Albert Einstein,*
    Abraham Pais
PAPERBACK
*The Mathematical
    Experience,* Philip J.
    Davis and Reuben
    Hersh

Galway Kinnell

TRANSLATION
Charles Baudelaire's Les Fleurs du Mal, Richard Howard

1984
FICTION
Victory Over Japan: A Book of Stories, Ellen Gilchrist

FIRST WORK OF FICTION
Stones for Ibarra, Harriet Doerr

NONFICTION
*Andrew Jackson and the Course of American Democracy,
    1833–1845,* Robert V. Remini

1985
FICTION
White Noise, Don DeLillo

FIRST WORK OF FICTION
Easy in the Islands, Bob Shacochis

NONFICTION
*Common Ground: A Turbulent Decade in the Lives of Three
    American Families,* J. Anthony Lukas

1986
FICTION
World's Fair, E. L. Doctorow

NONFICTION
Arctic Dreams, Barry Lopez

1987
FICTION
Paco's Story, Larry Heinemann

NONFICTION
The Making of the Atom Bomb, Richard Rhodes

1988
FICTION
Paris Trout, Pete Dexter

NONFICTION
A Bright Shining Lie: John Paul Vann and America in Vietnam,
    Neil Sheehan

1989
FICTION
Spartina, John Casey

NONFICTION
From Beirut to Jerusalem, Thomas L. Friedman

1990
FICTION
Middle Passage, Charles Johnson

NONFICTION
*The House of Morgan: An American Banking Dynasty and the
    Rise of Modern Finance,* Ron Chernow

1991
FICTION
Mating, Norman Rush

NONFICTION
Freedom, Orlando Patterson

POETRY
What Work Is, Philip Levine

1992
FICTION
All the Pretty Horses, Cormac McCarthy

NONFICTION
Becoming a Man: Half a Life Story, Paul Monette

POETRY
New and Selected Poems, Mary Oliver

1993
FICTION
The Shipping News, E. Annie Proulx

NONFICTION
United States: Essays 1952–1992, Gore Vidal

POETRY
Garbage, A. R. Ammons

Pulitzer Prizes in Letters

The Pulitzer Prizes, established and endowed by Joseph Pulitzer (1847–1911), honor accomplishment in American literature, journalism, drama and music. The prizes, administered by Columbia University, bestow on winners both literary prestige and a cash prize.

Fiction

1918
His Family, Ernest Poole
1919
The Magnificent Ambersons, Booth Tarkington
1920
No award
1921
The Age of Innocence, Edith Wharton
1922
Alice Adams, Booth Tarkington
1923
One of Ours, Willa Cather
1924
The Able McLaughlins, Margaret Wilson
1925
So Big, Edna Ferber
1926
Arrowsmith, Sinclair Lewis
1927
Early Autumn, Louis Bromfield
1928
The Bridge of San Luis Rey, Thornton Wilder
1929
Scarlet Sister Mary, Julia Peterkin
1930
Laughing Boy, Oliver La Farge
1931
Years of Grace, Margaret Ayer Barnes
1932
The Good Earth, Pearl S. Buck
1933
The Store, T. S. Stribling
1934
Lamb in His Bosom, Caroline Miller
1935
Now in November, Josephine Winslow Johnson
1936
Honey in the Horn, Harold L. Davis
1937
Gone With the Wind, Margaret Mitchell
1938
The Late George Apley, John Phillips Marquand

Edith Wharton

1939
The Yearling, Marjorie Kinnan Rawlings
1940
The Grapes of Wrath, John Steinbeck
1941
No award
1942
In This Our Life, Ellen Glasgow
1943
Dragon's Teeth, Upton Sinclair
1944
Journey in the Dark, Martin Flavin
1945
A Bell for Adano, John Hersey
1946
No award
1947
All the King's Men, Robert Penn Warren
1948
Tales of the South Pacific, James A. Michener
1949
Guard of Honor, James Gould Cozzens
1950
The Way West, A. B. Guthrie, Jr.
1951
The Town, Conrad Richter
1952
The Caine Mutiny, Herman Wouk
1953
The Old Man and the Sea, Ernest Hemingway
1954
No award

1955
A Fable, William Faulkner
1956
Andersonville, MacKinlay Kantor
1957
No award
1958
A Death in the Family, James Agee
1959
The Travels of Jaimie McPheeters, Robert Lewis Taylor
1960
Advise and Consent, Allen Drury
1961
To Kill a Mockingbird, Harper Lee
1962
The Edge of Sadness, Edwin O'Connor
1963
The Reivers, William Faulkner
1964
No award
1965
The Keepers of the House, Shirley Ann Grau
1966
Collected Stories of Katherine Anne Porter, Katherine Anne Porter
1967
The Fixer, Bernard Malamud
1968
The Confessions of Nat Turner, William Styron
1969
House Made of Dawn, N. Scott Momaday

Ernest Hemingway

Toni Morrison

1970
Collected Stories, Jean Stafford
1971
No award
1972
Angle of Repose, Wallace Stegner
1973
The Optimist's Daughter, Eudora Welty
1974
No award
1975
The Killer Angels, Michael Shaara
1976
Humboldt's Gift, Saul Bellow
1977
No award
1978
Elbow Room, James Alan McPherson
1979
The Stories of John Cheever, John
   Cheever
1980
The Executioner's Song, Norman Mailer
1981
A Confederacy of Dunces, John
   Kennedy Toole
1982
Rabbit Is Rich, John Updike
1983
The Color Purple, Alice Walker
1984
Ironweed, William Kennedy
1985
Foreign Affairs, Alison Lurie
1986
Lonesome Dove, Larry McMurtry
1987
A Summons to Memphis, Peter Taylor
1988
Beloved, Toni Morrison
1989
Breathing Lessons, Anne Tyler

1990
The Mambo Kings Play Songs of Love,
   Oscar Hijeulos
1991
Rabbit at Rest, John Updike
1992
A Thousand Acres, Jane Smiley
1993
*A Good Scent From a Strange
   Mountain,* Robert Olen Butler
1994
The Shipping News, E. Annie Proulx

General Nonfiction

1962
The Making of the President, 1960,
   Theodore H. White
1963
The Guns of August, Barbara W.
   Tuchman
1964
Anti-Intellectualism in American Life,
   Richard Hofstadter
1965
O Strange New World, Howard
   Mumford Jones
1966
Wandering Through Winter, Edwin Way
   Teale
1967
*The Problem of Slavery in Western
   Culture,* David Brion Davis
1968
Rousseau and Revolution, Will and Ariel
   Durant
1969
So Human an Animal, Rene Jules Dubos
   and *The Armies of the Night,*
   Norman Mailer
1970
Gandhi's Truth, Erik H. Erikson
1971
The Rising Sun, John Toland
1972
*Stilwell and the American Experience in
   China, 1911–1945,* Barbara W.
   Tuchman
1973
*Fire in the Lake: The Vietnamese and
   the Americans in Vietnam,* Frances
   FitzGerald
Children of Crisis (vols.1 and 2), Robert
   M. Coles
1974
The Denial of Death, Ernest Becker
1975
Pilgrim at Tinker Creek, Annie Dillard

1976
Why Survive? Being Old in America,
   Robert N. Butler
1977
*Beautiful Swimmers: Watermen, Crabs
   and the Chesapeake Bay,*
   William W. Warner
1978
The Dragons of Eden, Carl Sagan
1979
On Human Nature, Edward O. Wilson
1980
*Gödel, Escher, Bach: An Eternal Golden
   Braid,* Douglas R. Hofstadter
1981
*Fin-de-Siecle Vienna: Politics and
   Culture,* Carl E. Schorske
1982
The Soul of a New Machine, Tracy
   Kidder
1983
Is There No Place on Earth for Me?,
   Susan Sheehan
1984
*Social Transformation of American
   Medicine,* Paul Starr
1985
*The Good War: An Oral History of World
   War II,* Studs Terkel
1986
*Move Your Shadow: South Africa, Black
   and White,* Joseph Lelyveld
*Common Ground: A Turbulent Decade
   in the Lives of Three American
   Families,* J. Anthony Lukas
1987
*Arab and Jew: Wounded Spirits in a
   Promised Land,* David K. Shipler
1988
The Making of the Atomic Bomb,
   Richard Rhodes
1989
A Bright Shining Lie, Neil Sheehan
1990
And Their Children After Them, Dale
   Maharidge and Michael
   Williamson
1991
The Ants, Bert Holldobler and Edward
   O. Wilson
1992
*The Prize: The Epic Quest for Oil, Money
   and Power,* Daniel Yergin
1993
*Lincoln at Gettysburg: The Words That
   Remade America,* Garry Wills
1994
*Lenin's Tomb: The Last Days of the
   Soviet Empire,* David Remick

Poetry

1918
Love Songs, Sara Teasdale
1919
Old Road to Paradise, Margaret
Widdemer and *Corn Huskers,* Carl
Sandburg
1922
Collected Poems, Edwin Arlington
Robinson
1923
*The Ballad of the Harp-Weaver; A Few
Figs From Thistles;* eight sonnets in
*American Poetry, 1922, A
Miscellany,* Edna St. Vincent Millay
1924
*New Hampshire: A Poem With Notes
and Grace Notes,* Robert Frost
1925
The Man Who Died Twice, Edwin
Arlington Robinson

Robert Lowell

1926
What's O'Clock, Amy Lowell
1927
Fiddler's Farewell, Leonora Speyer
1928
Tristram, Edwin Arlington Robinson
1929
John Brown's Body, Stephen Vincent
Benét
1930
Selected Poems, Conrad Aiken
1931
Collected Poems, Robert Frost
1932
The Flowering Stone, George Dillon
1933
Conquistador, Archibald MacLeish
1934
Collected Verse, Robert Hillyer
1935
Bright Ambush, Audrey Wurdemann

1936
Strange Holiness, Robert P. T. Coffin
1937
A Further Range, Robert Frost
1938
Cold Morning Sky, Marya Zaturenska
1939
Selected Poems, John Gould Fletcher
1940
Collected Poems, Mark Van Doren
1941
Sunderland Capture, Leonard Bacon
1942
The Dust Which Is God, William Rose
Benét
1943
A Witness Tree, Robert Frost
1944
Western Star, Stephen Vincent Benét
1945
V-Letter and Other Poems, Karl Shapiro
1946
No award
1947
Lord Weary's Castle, Robert Lowell
1948
The Age of Anxiety, W. H. Auden
1949
Terror and Decorum, Peter Viereck
1950
Annie Allen, Gwendolyn Brooks
1951
Complete Poems, Carl Sandburg
1952
Collected Poems, Marianne Moore
1953
Collected Poems, 1917–1952, Archibald
MacLeish
1954
The Waking, Theodore Roethke
1955
Collected Poems, Wallace Stevens
1956
Poems — North & South, Elizabeth
Bishop
1957
Things of This World, Richard Wilbur
1958
Promises: Poems, 1954–1956, Robert
Penn Warren
1959
Selected Poems, 1928–1958, Stanley
Kunitz
1960
Heart's Needle, William Snodgrass
1961
*Times Three: Selected Verse From
Three Decades,* Phyllis McGinley
1962
Poems, Alan Dugan
1963
Pictures From Breughel, William Carlos
Williams

Robert Frost

1964
At the End of the Open Road, Louis
Simpson
1965
77 Dream Songs, John Berryman
1966
Selected Poems, Richard Eberhart
1967
Live or Die, Anne Sexton
1968
The Hard Hours, Anthony Hecht
1969
Of Being Numerous, George Oppen
1970
Untitled Subjects, Richard Howard
1971
The Carrier of Ladders, William S.
Merwin
1972
Collected Poems, James Wright
1973
Up Country, Maxine Winokur Kumin
1974
The Dolphin, Robert Lowell
1975
Turtle Island, Gary Snyder
1976
Self-Portrait in a Convex Mirror, John
Ashbery
1977
Divine Comedies, James Merrill
1978
Collected Poems, Howard Nemerov
1979
Now and Then: Poems, 1976–1978,
Robert Penn Warren
1980
Selected Poems, Donald Rodney
Justice
1981
The Morning of the Poem, James
Schuyler
1982
The Collected Poems, Sylvia Plath

1983
Selected Poems, Galway Kinnell

1984
American Primitive, Mary Oliver

1985
Yin, Carolyn Kizer

1986
The Flying Change, Henry Taylor

1987
Thomas and Beulah, Rita Dove

1988
Partial Accounts: New and Selected Poems, William Meredith

1989
New and Collected Poems, Richard Wilbur

1990
The World Doesn't End, Charles Simic

1991
Near Changes, Mona Van Duyn

1992
Selected Poems, James Tate

1993
The Wild Iris, Louise Gluck

1994
Neon Vernacular, Yusef Komunyakaa

Biography or Autobiography

1917
Julia Ward Howe, Laura E. Richards and Maude Howe Elliott, assisted by Florence Howe Hall

1918
Benjamin Franklin, Self-Revealed, William Cabell Bruce

1919
The Education of Henry Adams, Henry Adams

1920
The Life of John Marshall, Albert J. Beveridge

1921
The Americanization of Edward Bok, Edward Bok

1922
A Daughter of the Middle Border, Hamlin Garland

1923
The Life and Letters of Walter H. Page, Burton J. Hendrick

1924
From Immigrant to Inventor, Michael Idvorsky Pupin

1925
Barrett Wendell and His Letters, M. A. DeWolfe Howe

1926
The Life of Sir William Osler, Harvey Cushing

John Kennedy

1927
Whitman, Emory Holloway

1928
The American Orchestra and Theodore Thomas, Charles Edward Russell

1929
The Training of an American: The Earlier Life and Letters of Walter H. Page, Burton J. Hendrick

1930
The Raven, Marquis James

1931
Charles W. Eliot, Henry James

1932
Theodore Roosevelt, Henry F. Pringle

1933
Grover Cleveland, Allan Nevins

1934
John Hay, Tyler Dennett

1935
R. E. Lee, Douglas S. Freeman

1936
The Thought and Character of William James, Ralph Barton Perry

1937
Hamilton Fish, Allan Nevins

1938
Pedlar's Progress, Odell Shepard
Andrew Jackson, Marquis James

1939
Benjamin Franklin, Carl Van Doren

1940
Woodrow Wilson. Life and Letters, vols. *VII* and *VIII,* Ray Stannard Baker

1941
Jonathan Edwards, Ola E. Winslow

1942
Crusader in Crinoline, Forrest Wilson

1943
Admiral of the Ocean Sea, Samuel Eliot Morison

1944
The American Leonardo: The Life of Samuel F. B. Morse, Carleton Mabee

1945
George Bancroft: Brahmin Rebel, Russel Blaine Nye

1946
Son of the Wilderness, Linnie Marsh Wolfe

1947
The Autobiography of William Allen White

1948
Forgotten First Citizen: John Bigelow, Margaret Clapp

1949
Roosevelt and Hopkins, Robert E. Sherwood

1950
John Quincy Adams and the Foundations of American Foreign Policy, Samuel Flagg Bemis

1951
John C. Calhoun: American Portrait, Margaret Louise Coit

1952
Charles Evans Hughes, Merlo J. Pusey

1953
Edmund Pendleton, 1721–1803, David J. Mays

1954
The Spirit of St. Louis, Charles A. Lindbergh

1955
The Taft Story, William S. White

1956
Benjamin Henry Latrobe, Talbot F. Hamlin

1957
Profiles in Courage, John F. Kennedy

1958
George Washington, Douglas Southall Freeman (vols. 1–6) and John Alexander Carroll and Mary Wells Ashworth (Vol. 7)

1959
Woodrow Wilson, American Prophet, Arthur Walworth

1960
John Paul Jones, Samuel Eliot Morison

1961
Charles Sumner and the Coming of the Civil War, David Donald

1962
No award

1963
Henry James: Vol. II, The Conquest of London, 1870–1881; Vol. III, The Middle Years, 1881–1895, Leon Edel

1964
John Keats, Walter Jackson Bate

1965
Henry Adams (3 Vols.), Ernest Samuels

1966
A Thousand Days, Arthur M. Schlesinger, Jr.

1967
Mr. Clemens and Mark Twain, Justin Kaplan

1968
Memoirs, 1925–1950, George F. Kennan
1969
The Man From New York, B. L. Reid
1970
Huey Long, T. Harry Williams
1971
Robert Frost: The Years of Triumph, 1915–1938, Lawrence Thompson
1972
Eleanor and Franklin: The Story of Their Relationship Based on Eleanor Roosevelt's Private Papers, Joseph P. Lash
1973
Luce and His Empire, W. A. Swanberg
1974
O'Neill, Son and Artist, Louis Sheaffer
1975
The Power Broker: Robert Moses and the Fall of New York, Robert A. Caro
1976
Edith Wharton: A Biography, Richard W. B. Lewis
1977
A Prince of Our Disorder, John E. Mack
1978
Samuel Johnson, Walter Jackson Bate
1979
Days of Sorrow and Pain: Leo Baeck and the Berlin Jews, Leonard Baker
1980
The Rise of Theodore Roosevelt, Edmund Morris
1981
Peter the Great, Robert K. Massie
1982
Grant: A Biography, William S. McFeely
1983
Growing Up, Russell Baker
1984
Booker T. Washington, Louis R. Harlan
1985
The Life and Times of Cotton Mather, Kenneth Silverman
1986
Louise Bogan: A Portrait, Elizabeth Frank
1987
Bearing the Cross: Martin Luther King, Jr. and the Southern Christian Leadership Conference, David J. Garrow
1988
Look Homeward: A Life of Thomas Wolfe, David Herbert Donald
1989
Oscar Wilde, Richard Ellmann
1990
Machiavelli in Hell, Sebastian de Grazia
1991
Jackson Pollock: An American Saga, Steven Naifeh and Gregory White Smith

Russell Baker

1992
Fortunate Son: The Healing of a Vietnam Vet, Lewis B. Puller, Jr.
1993
Truman, David McCullough
1994
W.E.B. DuBois: Biography of a Race, 1868–1919, David Levering Lewis

History of the United States

1917
With Americans of Past and Present Days, J. J. Jusserand, Ambassador of France to United States
1918
A History of the Civil War, 1861–1865, James Ford Rhodes
1919
No award
1920
The War With Mexico, Justin H. Smith
1921
The Victory at Sea, William Sowden Sims in collaboration with Burton J. Hendrick
1922
The Founding of New England, James Truslow Adams
1923
The Supreme Court in United States History, Charles Warren
1924
The American Revolution — A Constitutional Interpretation, Charles Howard McIlwain

1925
A History of the American Frontier, Frederic L. Paxson
1926
The History of the United States, Edward Channing
1927
Pinckney's Treaty, Samuel Flagg Bemis
1928
Main Currents in American Thought, Vernon Louis Parrington
1929
The Organization and Administration of the Union Army, 1861–1865, Fred Albert Shannon
1930
The War of Independence, Claude H. Van Tyne
1931
The Coming of the War: 1914, Bernadotte E. Schmitt
1932
My Experiences in the World War, John J. Pershing
1933
The Significance of Sections in American History, Frederick J. Turner
1934
The People's Choice, Herbert Agar
1935
The Colonial Period of American History, Charles McLean Andrews
1936
The Constitutional History of the United States, Andrew C. McLaughlin
1937
The Flowering of New England, Van Wyck Brooks
1938
The Road to Reunion, 1865–1900, Paul Herman Buck
1939
A History of American Magazines, Frank Luther Mott
1940
Abraham Lincoln: The War Years, Carl Sandburg
1941
The Atlantic Migration, 1607–1860, Marcus Lee Hansen
1942
Reveille in Washington, Margaret Leech
1943
Paul Revere and the World He Lived In, Esther Forbes
1944
The Growth of American Thought, Merle Curti
1945
Unfinished Business, Stephen Bonsal
1946
The Age of Jackson, Arthur M. Schlesinger, Jr.
1947
Scientists Against Time, James Phinney Baxter, 3rd

Carl Sandburg

1948
Across the Wide Missouri, Bernard DeVoto
1949
The Disruption of American Democracy, Roy Franklin Nichols
1950
Art and Life in America, Oliver W. Larkin
1951
The Old Northwest, Pioneer Period 1815–1840, R. Carlyle Buley
1952
The Uprooted, Oscar Handlin
1953
The Era of Good Feelings, George Dangerfield
1954
A Stillness at Appomattox, Bruce Catton
1955
Great River: The Rio Grande in North American History, Paul Horgan
1956
The Age of Reform, Richard Hofstadter
1957
Russia Leaves the War: Soviet-American Relations, 1917–1920, George F. Kennan
1958
Banks and Politics in America: From the Revolution to the Civil War, Bray Hammond
1959
The Republican Era: 1869–1901, Leonard D. White, assisted by Jean Schneider
1960
In the Days of McKinley, Margaret Leech
1961
Between War and Peace: The Potsdam Conference, Herbert Feis
1962
The Triumphant Empire, Thunder-Clouds Gather in the West, Lawrence H. Gipson
1963
Washington, Village and Capital, 1800–1878, Constance McLaughlin Green

1964
Puritan Village: The Formation of a New England Town, Sumner Chilton Powell
1965
The Greenback Era, Irwin Unger
1966
Life of the Mind in America, Perry Miller
1967
Exploration and Empire: The Explorer and Scientist in the Winning of the American West, William H. Goetzmann
1968
The Ideological Origins of the American Revolution, Bernard Bailyn
1969
Origins of the Fifth Amendment, Leonard W. Levy
1970
Present at the Creation: My Years in the State Department, Dean Acheson
1971
Roosevelt: The Soldier of Freedom, James McGregor Burns
1972
Neither Black Nor White, Slavery and Race Relations in Brazil and the United States, Carl N. Degler
1973
People of Paradox: An Inquiry Concerning the Origin of American Civilization, Michael Kammen
1974
The Americans: The Democratic Experience, Vol. 3, Daniel J. Boorstin
1975
Jefferson and His Time, Dumas Malone
1976
Lamy of Santa Fe, Paul Horgan
1977
The Impending Crisis: 1841–1861, David M. Potter (posthumous)
1978
The Invisible Hand: The Managerial Revolution in American Business, Alfred D. Chandler, Jr.

George Kennan

1979
The Dred Scott Case: Its Significance in Law and Politics, Don E. Fehrenbacher
1980
Been in the Storm So Long, Leon F. Litwack
1981
American Education: The National Experience; 1783–1876, Lawrence A. Cremin
1982
Mary Chestnut's Civil War, C. Vann Woodward, editor
1983
The Transformation of Virginia, 1740–1790, Rhys L. Isaac
1984
No award
1985
The Prophets of Regulation, Thomas K. McCraw
1986
. . . the Heavens and the Earth: A Political History of the Space Age, Walter A. McDougall
1987
Voyagers to the West: A Passage in the Peopling of America on the Eve of the Revolution, Bernard Bailyn
1988
The Launching of Modern American Science 1846–1876, Robert V. Bruce
1989
Parting the Waters, Taylor Branch
Battle Cry of Freedom, James M. McPherson
1990
In Our Image: America's Empire in the Philippines, Stanley Karnow
1991
A Midwife's Tale: The Life of Martha Ballard, Based on Her Diary 1785–1812, Laurel Thatcher Ulrich
1992
The Fate of Liberty: Abraham Lincoln and Civil Liberties, Mark E. Neely, Jr.
1993
The Radicalism of the American Revolution, Gordon S. Wood
1994
The Disruption of American Democracy, Roy Franklin Nichols

Drama

1918
Why Marry?, Jesse Lynch Williams
1919
No award
1920
Beyond the Horizon, Eugene O'Neill
1921
Miss Lulu Bett, Zona Gale

1922
Anna Christie, Eugene O'Neill

1923
Icebound, Owen Davis

1924
Hell-Bent fer Heaven, Hatcher Hughes

1925
They Knew What They Wanted, Sidney Howard

1926
Craig's Wife, George Kelly

1927
In Abraham's Bosom, Paul Green

1928
Strange Interlude, Eugene O'Neill

1929
Street Scene, Elmer L. Rice

1930
The Green Pastures, Marc Connelly

1931
Alison's House, Susan Glaspell

1932
Of Thee I Sing, George S. Kaufman, Morrie Ryskind and Ira Gershwin

1933
Both Your Houses, Maxwell Anderson

1934
Men in White, Sidney Kingsley

1935
The Old Maid, Zoe Akins

1936
Idiot's Delight, Robert E. Sherwood

1937
You Can't Take It With You, Moss Hart and George S. Kaufman

1938
Our Town, Thornton Wilder

1939
Abe Lincoln in Illinois, Robert E. Sherwood

1940
The Time of Your Life, William Saroyan

1941
There Shall Be No Night, Robert E. Sherwood

1942
No award

1943
The Skin of Our Teeth, Thornton Wilder

1944
No award

1945
Harvey, Mary Chase

1946
State of the Union, Russel Crouse and Howard Lindsay

1947
No award

1948
A Streetcar Named Desire, Tennessee Williams

1949
Death of a Salesman, Arthur Miller

1950
South Pacific, Richard Rodgers, Oscar Hammerstein II and Joshua Logan

1951
No award

1952
The Shrike, Joseph Kramm

1953
Picnic, William Inge

1954
The Teahouse of the August Moon, John Patrick

1955
Cat on a Hot Tin Roof, Tennessee Williams

1956
The Diary of Anne Frank, Frances Goodrich and Albert Hackett

1957
Long Day's Journey Into Night, Eugene O'Neill

1958
Look Homeward, Angel, Ketti Frings

1959
J.B., Archibald MacLeish

1960
Fiorello!, George Abbott, Jerome Weidman, Jerry Bock and Sheldon Harnick

1961
All the Way Home, Tad Mosel

1962
How to Succeed in Business Without Really Trying, Frank Loesser and Abe Burrows

1963
No award

1964
No award

1965
The Subject Was Roses, Frank D. Gilroy

1967
A Delicate Balance, Edward Albee

1968
No award

1969
The Great White Hope, Howard Sackler

1970
No Place to Be Somebody, Charles Gordone

1971
The Effect of Gamma Rays on Man-in-the-Moon Marigolds, Paul Zindel

1972
No award

1973
That Championship Season, Jason Miller

1974
No award

1975
Seascape, Edward Albee

1976
A Chorus Line, conceived by Michael Bennett

Eugene O'Neill

1977
The Shadow Box, Michael Cristofer

1978
The Gin Game, Donald L. Coburn

1979
Buried Child, Sam Shepard

1980
Talley's Folly, Lanford Wilson

1981
Crimes of the Heart, Beth Henley

1982
A Soldier's Play, Charles Fuller

1983
Night, Mother, Marsha Norman

1984
Glengarry Glen Ross, David Mamet

1985
Sunday in the Park With George, Stephen Sondheim and James Lapine

1986
No award

1987
Fences, August Wilson

1988
Driving Miss Daisy, Alfred Uhry

1989
The Heidi Chronicles, Wendy Wasserstein

1990
The Piano Lesson, August Wilson

1991
Lost in Yonkers, Neil Simon

1992
The Kentucky Cycle, Robert Schenkkan

1993
Angels in America: Millennium Approaches, Tony Kushner

1994
Three Tall Women, Edward Albee

Nobel Prize for Literature

The Nobel Prize for Literature, one of the six international awards administered by the Nobel Foundation, honors outstanding achievement in letters. The estate of Alfred Bernhard Nobel (1833–1896), the Swedish inventor of dynamite, funds the awards.

W. B. Yeats

1901
René F. A. Sully Prudhomme, France

1902
Theodor Mommsen, Germany

1903
Björnstjerne Björnson, Norway

1904
Frédéric Mistral, France and José Echegaray, Spain

1905
Henryk Sienkiewicz, Poland

1906
Giosuè Carducci, Italy

1907
Rudyard Kipling, England

1908
Rudolf Eucken, Germany

1909
Selma Lagerlöf, Sweden

1910
Paul von Heyse, Germany

1911
Maurice Maeterlinck, Belgium

1912
Gerhart Hauptmann, Germany

1913
Rabindranath Tagore, India

1914
No award

1915
Romain Rolland, France

1916
Verner von Heidenstam, Sweden

1917
Karl Gjellerup, Denmark and Henrik Pontoppidan, Denmark

1918
No award

1919
Carl Spitteler, Switzerland

1920
Knut Hamsun, Norway

1921
Anatole France, France

1922
Jacinto Benavente, Spain

1923
William B. Yeats, Ireland

1924
Wladyslaw Reymont, Poland

1925
George Bernard Shaw, Ireland

1926
Grazia Deledda, Italy

1927
Henri Bergson, France

1928
Sigrid Undset, Norway

1929
Thomas Mann, Germany

1930
Sinclair Lewis, United States

1931
Erik A. Karlfeldt, Sweden

1932
John Galsworthy, England

1933
Ivan G. Bunin, Russia

1934
Luigi Pirandello, Italy

1935
No award

G. B. Shaw

PUBLISHING TIME LINE

808
The world's oldest known printed book, *The Diamond Sutra*, a seven-page scroll printed with wood blocks on paper, is produced in China.

11th century
The Chinese and Koreans continue to experiment with movable type, using clay, wood, bronze and iron. The complexity of Chinese and Korean symbols create a major stumbling block in the process.

1440
German Johann Gutenberg invents movable type by developing foundry-cast metal characters and a wooden printing press.

1455
Gutenberg prints his first book, a Latin Bible.

1475
Englishman William Caxton produces the first book printed in English, *The Recuyell of the Historyes of Troye*.

1663
Erbauliche Monaths-Unterredungen ("Edifying Monthly Discussions"), considered the world's first magazine, is published in Germany.

1936
Eugene O'Neill, United States

1937
Roger Martin du Gard, France

1938
Pearl S. Buck, United States

1939
Frans Eemil Sillanpää, Finland

1940
No award

1941
No award

1942
No award

1943
No award

1944
Johannes V. Jensen, Denmark

1945
Gabriela Mistral, Chile

1946
Hermann Hesse, Switzerland

1947
André Gide, France

1948
Thomas Stearns Eliot, England

1949
William Faulkner, United States

1950
Bertrand Russell, England

1951
Pär Lagerkvist, Sweden

1952
François Mauriac, France

1953
Sir Winston Churchill, England

1954
Ernest Hemingway, United States

1955
Halldór Kiljan Laxness, Iceland

1956
Juan Ramón Jiménez, Spain

1957
Albert Camus, France

Saul Bellow

1958
Boris Pasternak, U.S.S.R. (declined)

1959
Salvatore Quasimodo, Italy

1960
St-John Perse (Alexis St.-Léger Léger), France

1961
Ivo Andric, Yugoslavia

1962
John Steinbeck, United States

1963
Giorgios Seferis (Seferiades), Greece

1964
Jean-Paul Sartre, France (declined)

1965
Mikhail Sholokhov, U.S.S.R.

1966
Shmuel Yosef Agnon, Israel and Nelly Sachs, Sweden

1967
Miguel Angel Asturias, Guatemala

1968
Yasunari Kawabata, Japan

1969
Samuel Beckett, Ireland

1970
Aleksandr Solzhenitsyn, U.S.S.R.

1971
Pablo Neruda, Chile

1972
Heinrich Böll, Germany

1973
Patrick White, Australia

1974
Eyvind Johnson, Sweden and Harry Martinson, Sweden

1975
Eugenio Montale, Italy

1976
Saul Bellow, United States

1977
Vicente Aleixandre, Spain

1978
Isaac Bashevis Singer, United States

1979
Odysseus Elytis, Greece

1980
Czeslaw Milosz, United States

1981
Elias Canetti, Bulgaria

1982
Gabriel García Márquez, Colombia

1983
William Golding, England

1984
Jaroslav Seifert, Czechoslovakia

1985
Claude Simon, France

1986
Wole Soyinka, Nigeria

1987
Joseph Brodsky, United States

1988
Naguib Mahfouz, Egypt

1989
Camilo José Cela, Spain

1990
Octavio Paz, Mexico

1991
Nadine Gordimer, South Africa

1992
Derek Walcott, Trinidad

1993
Toni Morrison, United States

1690

America's first newspaper, *Publick Occurrences Both Forreign and Domestick*, is printed in Boston, Massachusetts, and subsequently suspended for operating without a royal license.

1741

Benjamin Franklin plans to publish America's first magazine, *General Magazine*, but is beaten to the punch when *American Magazine* comes out three days before Franklin's.

1764

Pierre Fournier of France develops the
point system to measure type sizes. His system is further refined by Francois Didot, establishing consistency in type measure throughout the world.

1771

Encyclopaedia Brittanica, the first English-language encyclopedia, is published in Edinburgh, Scotland.

1793

The Pennsylvania Evening Post becomes America's first daily newspaper.

1796

German Alois Senefelder develops lithography, a method of image transfer that produces high quality printed images.

Major U.S. Trade Publishing Houses

Abbeville Press
488 Madison Ave.
New York, NY 10022
(212) 888-1969
Includes: Artabras, Canopy Books and
Cross River

Harry N. Abrams Inc.
Subsidiary of the Times Mirror Company
100 Fifth Ave.
New York, NY 10011
(212) 206-7715
Includes: Abradale

Addison-Wesley Publishing Co. Inc.
Subsidiary of Pearsons PLC
1 Jacob Way
Reading, MA 01867
(617) 944-3700

**Bantam Doubleday Dell Publishing
Group Inc.**
Affiliate of Bertelsmann AG
1540 Broadway
New York, NY 10036
(212) 354-6500
Bantam includes: Bantam Classics,
Bantam Doubleday Dell Books for Young
Readers, Golden Apple, New Age
Books, New Fiction, New Sciences,
Peacock Press, Perigord Press, Spectra
and Sweet Dreams

Doubleday includes: Anchor Books,
Currency, Dolphin Books, Double D
Western, Foundation Books, Galilee
Books, Image Books, Loveswept, Made
Simple Books, Main Street/Back List,
Nan A. Talese Books, Perfect Crime and
Spy Books

Dell includes: Delacorte Press, Dell
Books, Dell Hardcovers, Delta Books,
Dial Press, DTP Trade Paperbacks,
Island Books and Laurel Books

Chronicle Books
Subsidiary of the Hearst Group
275 Fifth St.
San Francisco, CA 94103
(415) 777-7240

Dorling Kindersley
95 Madison Ave., 10th Floor
New York, NY 10016
(212) 213-4800

Farrar, Straus & Giroux Inc.
Subsidiary of the Holtzbrinck Group
19 Union Square W.
New York, NY 10003
(212) 741-6900
Includes: Noonday Press, North Point
Press and Sunburst Books

Grove-Atlantic
841 Broadway, 4th Floor
New York, NY 10003
(212) 614-7850
Includes: Grove Press and Atlantic
Monthly Press

Harcourt Brace and Co.
Division of Harcourt General
15 E. 26th St.
New York, NY 10010
(212) 592-1000
Includes: Brown Deer Press, Gulliver
Books, Gulliver Green, Harvest Books,
Red Wagon Books, Kurt and Helen
Wolff Books and Jane Yolen Books

HarperCollins Publishers
Subsidiary of News Corp.
10 E. 53rd St.
New York, NY 10022
(212) 207-7000
Includes: Basic Books, Collins San
Francisco, Harper Business,
HarperCollins Children's Books,
HarperCollins Trade, Harper Perennial,
Harper Reference and Harper San
Francisco

Henry Holt and Co., Inc.
Subsidiary of the Holtzbrinck Group
115 W. 18th St.
New York, NY 10011
(212) 886-9200
Includes: Books for Young Readers,
Henry Holt Books, Henry Holt
Reference, Metropolitan Books, Owl
Books and 21st Century Books

Houghton Mifflin Co.
222 Berkeley St.
Boston, MA 02116
(617) 351-5000
Includes: Clarion Books

Hyperion
Division of Disney Book Publishing Inc.
114 Fifth Ave.
New York, NY 10011
(212) 633-4400
Includes: Hyperion Paperbacks for
Children and Miramax Books

Little, Brown and Co.
Subsidiary of Time Warner Inc.
1271 Ave. of the Americas
New York, NY 10020
(212) 522-8700
Includes: Bullfinch Press and Back Bay
Books

William Morrow & Company Inc.
Subsidiary of the Hearst Group
1350 Ave. of the Americas
New York, NY 10019
(212) 261-6500
Includes: Avon; Green Willow Books,
Hearst Books, Mulberry, Beachtree
Books, Lothrop, Lee and Shepard,
William Morrow Books, Morrow Junior
Books, Quill Books and Tamborine
Books

W. W. Norton & Company Inc.
500 Fifth Ave.
New York, NY 10110
(212) 354-5500

---

ca. 1800

**The Third Earl of
Stanhope manufactures
an all-metal printing
press.**

1822

**American-born William
Church invents the first
mechanical typesetting
device.**

1828

**Noah Webster, often
referred to as the
"father of his country's
language," publishes
the *American Dictionary
of the English Language,*
in an attempt to encour-
age American indepen-
dence in both written
and spoken English.**

1829

***Encyclopaedia
Americana,* America's
first encyclopedia, is
published in
Philadelphia.**

1841

**Horace Greeley estab-
lishes the New York
Tribune. Unlike other
publishers at the time,
Greeley feels that**

including advertise-
ments and police
reports in the newspa-
per is a disgrace.

1842

***Illustrated London
News* uses woodcuts
and engravings for the
first time, prompting the
growth of illustrated
journals throughout the
end of the century.**

CONTINUED ON PAGE 738 ▶

Penguin U.S.A.
375 Hudson St.
New York, NY 10014
(212) 366-2000
Includes: Dutton, Penguin, Penguin
Classics, Plume, Puffin, Signet, Signet
Classics, Viking and Viking Studio

The Putnam Berkley Group Inc.
Subsidiary of MCA Inc.
200 Madision Ave.
New York, NY 10016
(212) 951-8400
Includes: Ace, Berkley Prime Crime,
Coward-McCann, Diamond, Grosset &
Dunlap, Grosset Books, HP Books, Jove,
Perigee Books, Philomel, Platt & Munk,
Price Stern Sloan, G.P. Putnam's Sons,
Riverhead Books, Sandcastle,
Serendipity, Jeremy P. Tarcher, Wee
Sing and Wonder Books

Random House Inc.
Subsidiary of Advance Publications
201 E. 50th St.
New York, NY 10022
(212) 751-2600
Includes: Ballantine, Crown, Fawcett,
Fodor's, Ivy, Alfred A. Knopf, Modern
Library, Pantheon, Clarkson Potter
Publishers, Random House Adult Books,
Schocken, Times Books, Villard and
Vintage

Simon & Schuster
Division of Viacom Inc.
1230 Ave. of the Americas
New York, NY 10020
(212) 698-7000
Includes: Baseball America, H&R Block,
Collier Books, Lisa Drew Books,
Fireside, Hudson River Editions,
Macmillan Publishing USA, MTV Books,
Pocket Books, Prentice Hall, Rawson
Associates, Scribner, Charles Scribner's
Sons, Thorndike Press, Touchstone and
Twayne Publishers

St. Martin's Press Inc.
Subsidiary of Macmillan Publishers Ltd.
(England)
175 Fifth Ave.
New York, NY 10010
(212) 674-5151
Includes: Bedford Books, Forge, Orb,
Picador, Tor Books and A. Wyatt Books

Warner Books
Division of Time Warner Inc.
1271 Ave. of the Americas
New York, NY 10020
(212) 522-7200

Workman Publishing Co.
708 Broadway
New York, NY 10003
(212) 254-5900
Includes: Algonquin Books and Artisan
Books

Magazine and Book Publications

American Book Review
Publications Center
Campus Box 4226
University of Colorado
Boulder, CO 80309
(303) 492-8938

American Bookseller
American Booksellers Association
828 S. Broadway
Tarrytown, NY 10591
(914) 591-2665

Book World
The Washington Post Co.
1150 15th St., NW
Washington D.C. 20071
(202) 334-6000

Boston Book Review
30 Brattle St., 4th Floor
Cambridge, MA 02138
(617) 497-0344

Editor and Publisher
11 W. 19th St.
New York, NY 10011
(212) 675-4380

Entertainment Weekly
1675 Broadway
New York, NY 10019
(212) 522-5600

Firsts: Collecting Modern First Editions
Lucerne Group
575 N. Lucerne Blvd.
Los Angeles, CA 91104-4805
(213) 469-9189

Horn Book Magazine
11 Beacon St., Suite 1000
Boston, MA 02108
(617) 227-1555

New York Review of Books
251 W. 56th St., Suite 1321
New York, NY 10107
(212) 757-8070

New York Times Book Review
229 W. 43rd St.
New York, NY 10036
(212) 556-1234

Publishers Weekly
Cahners Publishing Co.
249 W. 17th St.
New York, NY 10011
(212) 645-0067

Small Press
Moyer Bell Ltd.
Kymbolde Way
Wakefield, RI 02879
(401) 789-0074

Women's Review of Books
Wellesley College
Center for Research on Women
Wellesley, MA 02181
(617) 283-2555

The Writer
120 Boylston St.
Boston, MA 02116
(617) 423-3157

Writer's Digest
F&W Publications
1507 Dana Ave.
Cincinnati, OH 45209
(800) 333-0133

Publishing Glossary

AA (author's alteration) A change to the proof requested by the author rather than the editor.

ABA (American Booksellers Association) The trade group that represents book retailers and wholesalers and organizes the largest book convention in the United States.

acquisition editor The book editor who works with agents and authors to bring book projects to a publisher.

advance 1. The fee paid to the author before publication which is recouped by the publisher from royalties. **2.** The number of books ordered by book sellers before publication.

ALA (American Library Association) A professional organization for librarians that also administers the Caldecott and Newbery medals.

auction The offer of a book for publication to several publishers simultaneously with publishing rights going to the highest bidder.

backlist A list comprised of perennial sellers, which a publisher always keeps in print. Book salesmen also refer to recently published titles that are still available as backlist.

binding The creation of a book or magazine by gathering the printed signatures, securing them with glue, sewing or stapling and attaching the cover.

blad A sample of a book used for sales that contains a small selection of representative pages.

bleed also **full bleed** An image that extends to the edge of the paper.

blues Proofs made from printer's film before platemaking. Reading blues is generally the last stage of proofreading. Also called **salts**.

boards The cardboard inside the cloth of a hardcover binding.

bound galley Pages of a book — in its early stage — that are bound and used for sales and reviews.

bulk The thickness of a book.

case binding The hardcover binding of a book.

coated paper Paper used for magazines and books that has a glossy appearance and is used primarily for printed material that contains photos and illustrations.

colophon The publisher's name and mark or logo generally found on the title page.

color separation To prepare material for color printing by separating it into different color images on printer's film from which printing plates are then made.

copy editing To prepare a manuscript for publication by reading it for sense, grammar and spelling. The work is done by a manuscript editor or copy editor.

cover The protective outside covering of a book or magazine. The cover of a book can be either paper or hardcover; a magazine cover is generally heavy, and often coated, paper stock.

crop To use only the desired portion of a photograph's full frame.

dingbat Typographical ornaments used to highlight items on page or as decorative elements.

dummy A bound sample containing few, if any, printed pages but using proposed paper stock to demonstrate a book's bulk.

dust jacket The paper wrapping around a hardcover book. The dust jacket is different from the cover (see above).

editing The process of acquiring material and preparing it for publication, corresponding with authors, copy editing, proofreading and rewriting.

edition A specific version of a book. Over time a book's text may change due to an update or a format change (paper, hardcover, mass market paper, etc.).

endpapers Decorative pages, often of different paper stock, at the beginning and end of a book.

F and Gs The folded and gathered signatures produced prior to be being bound. Sometimes read by reviewers.

first serialization Publication of a book, or portion of a book, in installments by a periodical prior to publication of the book. Publication by a periodical after publication of the book is called **second serialization**.

flaps The part of the dust jacket that wraps around the cover. Publishers use them for promotional copy and authors' photos.

folio The page number.

font Within a given typeface, the various ways in which a character can be formatted, for example, in bold, or in italics.

foreign rights The right to publish a work overseas, generally administered by the subsidiary rights office at a publisher or by the agent for the work's author.

1851
Selling for a penny a copy, the *New York Times* begins publication.

1861
The Chicago *Times* publicizes its motto: "It is a newspaper's duty to print the news, and raise hell."

1895
In its first issue, American magazine *The Bookman* includes a list of "Books in Demand," which predates the bestseller list, later developed by Frank Mott.

1902
McClure's Magazine prints the article "Tweed Days in St.Louis" by C.H. Wetmore and Lincoln Steffens. The article introduces the muckraking era.

1936
Allen Lane's Penguin Press, an English publishing house, introduces the paperback book.

1985
With the availability of relatively inexpensive laser printers and computers, desktop publishing becomes accessible and popular.

form A unit of pages created by folding and trimming the press sheet prior to gathering and binding.

frontispiece A decorative page at the front of a book that carries a photo or an illustration.

front matter The pages before the main text of a book usually consisting of a copyright page, title page, dedications, an introduction and a table of contents.

gathering The process of assembling the folded press sheets into signatures.

gutter The area at the center of a book and at the bind in a magazine.

half title page The abbreviated title page, not containing the publisher's colophon, that precedes the title page. Also called **bastard title.**

headband The striped or colored ribbon at the top of the binding on a hardcover book. A **footband** appears at the bottom of the binding.

imposition The arrangement of pages into a press sheet so when the sheet is folded and trimmed the pages will be in correct sequence.

imprint A publisher who publishes books through a larger company and is identified on the title page of the book.

ISBN (International Standard Book Number) The 10-digit number assigned to and printed on every book for identification. The digits indicate country of origin, publisher, book number and a check digit to identify errors in the preceding digits.

justified type A form of typography in which the lines are of equal width throughout.

leading The space between lines of type.

list A publisher's offerings for a particular selling season.

literary agent The author's representative who sells book projects to editors and negotiates the contract on behalf of the author.

lower case The small letters in a character set.

managing editor The editor who is responsible for work flow and scheduling. At a publishing house, the managing editor also usually manages the manuscript editors.

mass market paperback A paperback book that is sold at volume through non-book outlets in addition to book retailers. A paperback is usually smaller in size than a hardcover or trade book.

offset printing A printing process in which an impression is made on paper by a rubber blanket that has had the image of the page created on it by a photosensitive printer's plate. **Web offset printing** indicates that the paper for the printing press is supplied by a roll rather than sheet by sheet.

OP (Out of print) Out of print books are no longer available.

OS (Out of stock) The time when a book is temporarily unavailable prior to a reprint.

packager A publishing entity that supplies the editorial, design and production process for books that are subsequently manufactured and marketed by a publisher.

paperback A book with a paper cover.

PE (Printer's error) An error in text caused by the printer or production staff.

perfect binding A square binding that is made by gluing folded signatures onto a cover.

plate The surface from which the rubber blanket receives the page image in offset printing.

point The unit of measure for size of a typeface.

pulping The rendering of unsalable books back into the paper pulp from whence they came.

recto The right-hand page of a book.

remainder A publishers' overstocked books that are sold at discount prices.

returns Unsold books that are sent back to the publisher from the retailer or wholesaler.

review copy A book that is sent to book reviewers at magazines and newspapers.

rough front The pages left untrimmed at the outside edge. **Rough foot** pages are left untrimmed at the bottom.

royalty An author's take from book sales, usually as a percentage of retail or wholesale sales.

running heads Headings at the top of pages that indicate the name of the book or the chapter title.

stitching Binding with a staple, which is known as saddle wire, through the spine.

sheet-fed The use of a printing press that is fed paper in sheets rather than rolls.

short run The printing of a few copies of a magazine or book.

signature The unit created by folding the press sheets to create a group of pages for binding. This group is made up of units of eight pages, generally 16-page units, but possibly eight-, 32- or 64-page signatures.

smyth sewn A very durable binding made by sewing together signatures prior to binding.

special sales A unit in the sales division of a publishing company that concentrates on selling books outside the normal book retailing channels, such as in gift shops or hardware stores.

spine The edge of a book where the binding is located.

subsidiary rights The granting of permission to use the content of a book or magazine after its publication, including movie rights, book-club editions, translations or serializations.

title page The page found at the beginning of the book where the book's title and the publisher's name and colophon can be found.

trade books Books published for the general consumer market and sold through book retailers.

trade paperbacks Paperback books intended to be sold in traditional book retailers. Generally larger in format and more expensive than mass market paperbacks.

traveler The term for book sales representative who goes on the road to sell to book stores.

trim The outside dimensions of a book or magazine.

typeface The design of a character set in various sizes, weights and shapes.

uppercase The capital letters in a character set.

vanity press A publishing company that will print and bind a manuscript for a fee paid by the author.

verso The left-hand page of a book.

Lana Turner

Eva Gabor

Date

Seiji Ozawa
conducting the
Boston
Symphony
Orchestra

Ginger
Rogers

Raul Julia

Peter
Cook

OOOK

Brian De Palma helming
Mission: Impossible

Gone but Not Forgotten

Here is a list of loved and respected figures from the arts and entertainment world who died between October 1, 1994 and September 1, 1995.

George Abbott *Mr. Broadway* — A playwright, actor, director and producer whose career paralleled and influenced the development of modern theater. He was involved in more than 120 productions in a  career that extended from 1912 to the late 1980s. His Pulitzer, Tony and other awards would be too numerous to list, as would be the stars he discovered or the plays in which he was involved. His autobiography is *Mr. Abbott.* (1887–1995)

Reza Abdoh *theater artist* (1963–1995)

Lindsay Anderson *British director* — director of *O Lucky Man!, If. . .* and *This Sporting Life* (1923–1995)

Danny Apolinar *composer* — wrote *Your Own Thing*, which is considered the first rock musical (1934–1995)

Danny Arnold *writer and producer* — created the TV series *Barney Miller* (1925–1995)

Rick Aviles *comedian, actor* — Aviles's last role was in *Waterworld*. On television, he was host of *Showtime at the Apollo*, HBO's *One Night Stand* and the miniseries *The Stand*. His films include *Cannonball Run, Mystery Train, Ghost, The Godfather Part III, Green Card, Carlito's Way* and *Joe's Apartment.* (1954–1995)

Rachid Baba-Ahmed *producer of Algerian rai records* — murdered by Islamic fundamentalists (1948–1995)

Tony Azito *stage and TV actor* — Tony winner for his role in *Pirates of Penzance* (1949–1995)

Ian Ballantine *publisher* — Ballantine was the founder of Penguin, U.S.A., Bantam Books and Ballantine Books. He also popularized paperbacks. (1916–1995)

Joy Barlowe *film actress* — Barlowe appeared in *Destination Tokyo, Thank Your Lucky Stars, Hollywood Canteen* and *The Big Sleep.* (1924–1995)

Irwin Bazelon *composer* (1922–1995)

Talley Beatty *dancer* — Beatty danced with Katherine Dunham and choreographed works that depicted the struggle of African Americans. (ca.1920–1995)

Courtney Benson *actor* (1915–1995)

David Begelman *agent, head of Columbia Pictures* — Begelman was in charge of Columbia for a string of hits including *Close Encounters of the Third Kind* and *Kramer vs. Kramer* but was brought down by a bizarre check-forging scandal. (1922–1995)

Julius Berger *pianist, composer* (1897–1995)

Julian Blaustein *film producer* — produced *The Day the Earth Stood Still* (1913–1995)

Robert Bolt *screenwriter* (1925–1995)

Phillip Borsos *film director* — Borsos's work included *Far From Home: The Adventures of Yellow Dog*, the Oscar-nominated documentary *Nails* and *The Grey Fox.* (1954–1995)

Tommy Boyce *songwriter, singer* — Boyce was best known for the songs he penned for The Monkees with Bobby Hart. He also wrote "Pretty Little Angel Eyes" and "Come a Little Bit Closer," a 1964 hit for Jay and the Americans. (1940–1995)

Bill Boyd *executive director of the Academy of Country Music* (1931–1995)

John Boylan *actor* (1912–1994)

Rossano Brazzi *film actor* — Brazzi was a handsome, suave leading man of the 1950s and 1960s. He first appeared in Hollywood in *Little Women* (1949), subse-  quently wooing audiences and leading ladies in *Three Coins in the Fountain, The Barefoot Contessa, Summertime, Interlude, South Pacific, A Certain Smile* and many others. (1916–1994)

Robert Paul Breslo *screenwriter* (1958–1995)

Don Brockett *actor, musician* — He was loved by American children for his portrayal of Chef Brockett on *Mister Rogers' Neighborhood*. (19?–1995)

Phyllis Brooks *actress* — Discovered by Hollywood in the 1930s as "The Ipana Girl," Brooks appeared in Charlie Chan movies before moving to Broadway success. Brooks was married to Cary Grant and U.S. Representative Torbert MacDonald of Massachusetts. (1915–1995)

Brigid Brophy *writer, critic* — Brophy was a novelist, playwright and acerbic critic as well as a fiery crusader for innumerable causes. (1929–1995)

Philip Burton *stage director, actor* — foster father of Richard Burton (1905–1995)

Rita Cadillac *striptease artist* — helped win international celebrity for the Crazy Horse Saloon nightclub in Paris in the early 1960s (1939–1995)

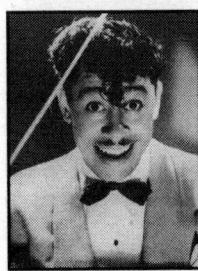

Cab Calloway *singer* — Known around the world as the "hi-de-ho" man, Calloway was a zoot-suited, scat-singing favorite of audiences from his first Cotton Club broadcasts in 1931 until his death. His band was among the most successful of the big-band era. He appeared on Broadway as Sportin' Life in *Porgy and Bess* and in *Hello, Dolly!* and was featured in numerous movies. (1907–1994)

Mifflin James (Miff) Campbell *singer* — one of the original members of the Ink Spots (19?–1995)

Christopher Chadman *dancer* — choreographed the recent revival of *Guys and Dolls* (1948–1995)

Jack Clayton *British film director* (1922–1995)

David Cole *record producer* — one half of C&C Music Factory (1963–1995)

Earl Coleman *jazz balladeer* — recorded with Charlie Parker (1926–1995)

David Connell *TV producer* — created *Sesame Street* (1931–1995)

Elisha Cook, Jr. *film actor* — Cook appeared in character roles in more than 100 movies, including *Shane* and *The Maltese Falcon*. (1907–1995)

Peter Cook *satirist, writer, performer* — Cook was one of Britain's best-loved comedic talents, rising to fame as a member of Beyond the Fringe in the early 1960s. He went on to team with Dudley Moore in a long-running revue, and later appeared in movies, TV and on recordings. (1938–1995)

Denny Cordell *record producer* — produced Tom Petty, Procol Harum, Moody Blues, Joe Cocker and Melissa Etheridge (1944–1995)

Howard Cosell *sportscaster* — Cosell was best known for boxing coverage and his caustic commentary on *ABC's Monday Night Football*. He became controversial far beyond the realm of sports coverage. (1918–1995)

John Costello *author* — wrote books on the Cold War, code-making, code-breaking and counterintelligence (195?–1995)

Nathan Daniel *guitar maker* — creator of Danelectro guitars (1912–1994)

Severn Darden *actor* — appeared in *Planet of the Apes* (1930–1995)

Sonja Davis *stuntwoman* (1963–1995)

Reuel Denny *poet* — author of works analyzing American popular culture (1913–1995)

William Dillard *trumpeter* — played in big-band era bands and was a mentor to Dizzy Gillespie (1912–1995)

Norma Donaldson *singer, actress* (1926–1994)

Gerald Durrell *British writer and zoologist, his brother was author Lawrence Durrell* — Durrell's best-sellers were full of witty depictions of the animal kingdom. He may be best remembered for pioneering animal conservation though he wrote the million-copy bestseller *My Family and Other Animals* and *The Overloaded Ark*. Durrell also brought success to the BBC's Natural History Unit. (1925–1995)

Eazy-E (Eric Wright) *rapper, producer* — popularized gangsta rap as a member of N.W.A. and as a solo performer (1964–1995)

George Eels *biographer of entertainment figures* (1923–1995)

Alfred Eisenstaedt *photographer* — Eisenstaedt's work helped shape and define 20th-century American photojournalism. He started working for *Life* magazine in 1936 as one of its original four photographers and maintained an  office at the magazine until his death. Eisenstaedt is perhaps most famous for his photograph of a uniformed American sailor kissing a nurse in Times Square on V-J Day. (1898–1995)

Les Elgart — *trumpeter and band leader* (1918-1995)

Stanley Elkin *writer* — wrote lyrically descriptive novels and short stories (1930–1995)

John M. Elton *composer, arranger, pianist* (1922–1995)

Cy Endfield *film director* (1914–1995)

Ted Estabrook *TV director, producer* (1919–1995)

Tom Ewell *actor* — Ewell was best known for his wry performance in *The Seven Year Itch.* (1909–1995)

Leonard Feather *critic, writer, musician* — Feather was the winner of the first Grammy for criticism. He produced a series of concerts and books that created new audiences for jazz. (1914–1995)

Annie Fisher *pianist* — noted for Mozart interpretations (1914–1995)

Ed Flanders *actor* — best known for his role as Dr. Westphall on *St. Elsewhere;* also appeared in several movies and TV specials (1935–1995)

Art Fleming *actor* — original host of TV's *Jeopardy* (1925–1995)

Canray Fontenot — *Creole singer and fiddle player* (1923 –1995)

Melvin Franklin *singer* — member of the Temptations (1943–1995)

Gottlob Frick *singer* — bass; prominent for his Wagnerian roles (1906–1994)

Otto Friedrich *author, journalist* (1929–1995)

Eva Gabor *actress* — loved by millions for her role in TV's *Green Acres* (1922–1995)

Rory Gallagher *musician* — bluesy rock guitarist (1948–1995)

Jerry Garcia *musician* — Garcia's 30-year career as guitarist and vocalist for the Grateful Dead earned him the love of millions of devoted fans worldwide. What started as a San Francisco jug band grew into a traveling road show that played arenas yet maintained the communal feeling  of a family. Garcia's music built on the American idioms of country and bluegrass with his own signature psychedelic excursions. Known early on as Captain Trips for his LSD experimentation, Garcia embodied for many the most appealing aspects of the 1960s counterculture. (1942–1995)

J. S. Garon *literary agent, former actor* — In 1987, Garon received three chapters of a mystery/thriller novel from a Mississippi lawyer and liked them enough to call the author, John Grisham. The two would go on to make publishing and movie history, negotiating multimillion-dollar book and movie deals. (192?–1995)

Michael Gazzo *actor, playwright* — wrote *Hatful of Rain*; appeared in *The Godfather Part II* (1924–1995)

Carl Giles *British cartoonist* 1916–1995

John Gilmore *tenor saxophonist* — pioneer in avant-garde jazz (193?–1995)

Dwayne Goettel *musician* — keyboard player for the Canadian rock band Skinny Puppy (1963–1995)

Gale Gordon *radio, TV actor* — Gordon was the sputtering comic foil to Lucille Ball. (1906–1995)

Harry Guardino *actor* — Guardino appeared in numerous films, stage productions and television shows. (1926–1995)

Alexander Godunov *ballet dancer, film actor* (1950–1995)

Albert Hackett *playwright, screenwriter* — Pulitzer Prize winner for *The Diary of Anne Frank*, also scripted *The Thin Man, Father of the Bride* (1950) and *Seven Brides for Seven Brothers* (1900–1995)

Anthony Hamilton *TV actor* (1953–1995)

Wilbert Harrison *rhythm and blues performer* — best known for his 1959 hit "Kansas City" (1929–1994)

Ted Hawkins *musician* — known for his soulful voice and poignant songs (1937–1995)

Julie Haydon *Broadway and film actress* — Haydon played Laura Wingfield in the original production of Tennessee Williams's *The Glass Menagerie*, and was credited with supplying Fay Wray's scream in *King Kong*. She was married to Broadway critic George Jean Nathan. (1910–1994)

Thomas Hayward *singer* — leading tenor at The Metropolitan Opera in the 1940s (1918–1995)

Joseph Hazen *studio executive, lawyer* — Hazen drew up the contract for *The Jazz Singer* and was the partner of Hal Wallis. (1898–1994)

Julius Hemphill *alto saxophonist, founder of Black Artists Group* — considered a leader of the jazz avant garde in last quarter century (1938–1995)

Robert Hershman *CBS News producer* (1954–1995)

Patricia Highsmith *mystery novelist* — Highsmith's most acclaimed work was her first novel, *Strangers on a Train*. She authored a series of books featuring the character Tom Ripley, a charming psychopath, as her hero. (1921–1995)

Sir Michael Hordern *British film and stage actor* — appeared in *Cleopatra* and *The Taming of the Shrew* (1912–1995)

John Howard *actor* — appeared in *Lost Horizon* and *Philadelphia Story* (1913–1995)

Hugh Hurd *actor, civil-rights activist* (1925–1995)

Phyllis Hyman *jazz singer* (1950–1995)

Burl Ives *folk singer, stage, TV and film actor* — Known for many popular folk recordings, Ives was immortalized as Big Daddy in the stage and film versions of Tennessee Williams's *Cat on a Hot Tin Roof*. Ives appeared in *East of Eden, Desire Under the Elms, The Big Country* and *Ensign Pulver*. On TV, he played the title role in *O.K. Crackerby* and a lawyer in *The Lawyers*. Ives was a top recording artist with more than 70 albums that popularized the folk song. (1910–1995)

Edward James *TV writer* — developed *Father Knows Best* (1908–1995)

George Richard James *saxophonist* — performed with Louis Armstrong, Fats Waller and others (1907–1995)

Antonio Carlos Jobim *Brazilian composer* — Jobim sparked the craze for Latin-tinged pop and jazz in the 1960s. His most famous compositions were "The Girl From Ipanema" and "Desafinado." (1927–1994)

Helene Johnson *Harlem Renaissance poet* (1906–1995)

Romain Johnston *TV production designer* (1930–1995)

Raul Julia *actor* — Julia was a romantic lead with a distinguished career in film and on stage beginning with Shakespearean roles for the New York Shakespeare Festival. He earned renown for roles in movies such as *The Addams Family* and *Kiss of the Spider Woman*. (1940–1994)

Connie Kay *musician* — Kay was the drummer for the Modern Jazz Quartet and house drummer at Atlantic Records for some of the greatest rock records of all time. (1928–1995)

Ulysses Kay *composer* (1917–1995)

Kevin Kelly *critic* — the *Boston Globe*'s chief theater critic for 32 years (1930–1994)

Sidney Kingsley *playwright* — Kingsley's realistic dramas broke new ground for Broadway and inspired Hollywood's *Dead End Kids, Detective Story* and TV police and medical dramas. Kingsley won the Pulitzer Prize for his 1933 play *Men in White* about doctors and their private lives. (1907–1995)

Helen Hedrick Knopf *poet, writer* — widow of publisher Alfred A. Knopf (1903–1995)

Howard Koch *screenwriter* — Koch's diverse career included penning scripts for the radio drama *War of the Worlds* and movies *Casablanca* and *Sergeant York*. (1902–1995)

Sylvia Koscina *film actress* — her best known films include Federico Fellini's *Juliet of the Spirits* and *A Lovely Way to Die* opposite Kirk Douglas (1934–1995)

Irwin Kostal *orchestrator, conductor* — Kostal worked on such films as *West Side Story, Mary Poppins* and *The Sound of Music*. (191?–1994)

Savely Kramerov *Russian actor, comedian* (1935–1995)

Henry Kraus *Chronicler of labor movements* (1906–1995)

Burt Lancaster *film actor* — Noted for his athleticism and rugged appeal, the unpredictable Lancaster had a long and varied career, including being one of the first actors to form his own production company. His major

roles include *The Killers, Sweet Smell of Success, Criss Cross, From Here to Eternity, Elmer Gantry, The Leopard, The Birdman of Alcatraz, Atlantic City* and *Local Hero.* (1913–1994)

Priscilla Lane *film actress of the 1930s* (1919–1995)

Robert Lansing *film, TV actor* — known to TV audiences as Frank Savage on *12 O'Clock High* (1928–1994)

Lawrence Lamm *pioneer in book packaging* 1896–1995

Phil Lathrop *cinematographer* (1912–1995)

Leo Lerman *editor, writer* — Lerman was an editor at Condé Nast and often wrote on opera and the arts. (191?–1994)

Jerry Lester *comedian, first talk show host* — His *Broadway Open House* TV show began in May 1950 and launched the careers of Steve Allen, Jack Parr and Johnny Carson. (1910–1995)

Will Lieberson *playwright, theater director* (1916–1995)

Samuel Lipman *critic, publisher, pianist* — the founding publisher of *The New Criterion* (1934–1994)

John Lotas *theater producer* 192?–1995

Giovanni "Nanni" Loy *Italian film and television director* — Loy directed films about the Italian Resistance, tragicomedies and television shows. 192?–1995

Ida Lupino *film actress, director, producer* — Lupino was a Hollywood pioneer for women: an actress who became a writer, director and producer. After a few British films, Lupino went to Warners in the 1940s playing gun molls and tough broads in such films as *They Drive by Night, High Sierra* and *Road House.* By the 1950s, Lupino turned most of her attention to directing and producing for film and TV, including the features *Outrage* and *The Bigamist.* She will be remembered most for her insinuating gaze and husky-voiced screen presence. (1918–1995)

Adele Marcus *pianist* — teacher to many piano greats (1906–1995)

Donald March *TV producer* (1942–1995)

Carmen McRae *jazz singer* — known for her lyrical interpretations (1920–1994)

Floyd McDaniel — *rhythm and blues guitarist* (1915–1995)

Keith McDaniel *dancer* — principal dancer with the Alvin Ailey troupe, featured on Broadway and in the movies (1957–1995)

Ray McKinley *drummer* — played with the Dorsey Brothers and Glenn Miller bands (1911–1995)

Howard Meighan *CBS executive* — pioneered the use of videotape (1906–1995)

Lewis Meltzer *screenwriter* — wrote *Golden Boy* and *The Man With the Golden Arm* (1911–1995)

James Merrill *poet* — Winner of the Pulitzer Prize, Bollingen Award, National Book Award and many others, Merrill turned moments and places from his life into memorable lyricism. (1926–1995)

Arturo Benedetti Michaelangeli *pianist* (1920–1995)

Jimmy Miller *record producer* — produced such bands as Traffic and Steve Winwood, but his finest work may be found with the classic The Rolling Stones records *Let It Bleed, Sticky Fingers* and *Exile on Main Street* (1942–1994)

Patsy Ruth Miller *silent film star, author* — appeared with Valentino, was married to director Tay Garnett and once known as "the most engaged girl in Hollywood" for her active romantic life (1904–1995)

Francisco Moncion *dancer* — charter member of New York City Ballet (1919–1995)

Julius Monk *maestro* — Monk was a celebrated host of satirical revues and cabarets from the 1940s through the 1960s. (1912–1995)

Paul Monette *writer* — Monette's *Becoming A Man: Half a Life Story*, a memoir of homosexuality, won the 1992 National Book Award. (1945–1995)

Jean-Louis Morin *dancer, choreographer* (1953–1995)

H. Sterling Morrison *musician* — Morrison was a founding member of the seminal 1960s rock group, Velvet Underground. (1942–1995)

Gilbert Moses *stage director* (1943–1995)

Harriet Nelson *actress* — surrogate mother for Americans in *The Adventures of Ozzie and Harriet* on radio and TV (1914–1995)

Esther Muir *actress* — Muir toured with the Marx Brothers and was once married to Busby Berkeley. (1920–1995)

Ernest Nukanen *documentary filmmaker* — was cameraman for the surrealist film *Dreams That Money Can Buy* (1920–1995)

Eileen O'Casey *actress, author* — wife of playwright Sean O'Casey (1900–1995)

Gordon Oliver *actor and producer* (1911–1995)

John Osborne *playwright* — Known as the angry young man who introduced a cold blast of realism into theater with his "kitchen sink" dramas, Osborne earned his first and lasting renown for *Look Back in Anger*. Osborne also wrote *The Entertainer*, *Inadmissable Evidence* and *A Patriot for Me*. (1929–1994)

Tessie O'Shea *musical performer on stage and TV* (1913–1995)

Martin Paich *arranger, orchestrator* (1925–1995)

Clarence Paul *songwriter, producer* — influential in Stevie Wonder's career (1928–1995)

Wyman Pendleton *stage, film TV actor* (1916–1995)

Frank Perry *movie director* — directed *Mommie Dearest, David and Lisa* and *Diary of a Mad Housewife* (1930–1995)

Lydia Peterkoch *film actress* (1965–1994)

Donald Pleasence *British character actor and movie villain* — Pleasence appeared in *The Great Escape , You Only Live Twice* and several *Halloween* films. In his prolific career, Pleasence won a number of stage awards as well as an Order of the British Empire medal and played a number of Shakespearean stage roles. "He was one of the finest character actors Britain has ever produced," film director Michael Winner said. (1920–1995)

Eric Porter *actor* — appeared in *The Forsyte Saga* (1928–1995)

Don Pullen *jazz pianist* (1942–1995)

Ezra Rachlin *conductor, pianist* — music director of the Austin Symphony Orchestra (1916–1995)

Bob Randall *TV producer, writer* (1938–1995)

Jimmy Raney *jazz guitarist* (1928–1995)

Martha Raye *singer, actress* — appeared in *Monsieur Verdoux*, many musical comedies and entertained troops in World War II (1916–1994)

Lawrence Reddick *historian, biographer* (1910–1995)

Charlie Rich *singer* — Known as the "Silver Fox," Rich had a smooth style that crossed over from country to pop. (1932–1995)

Ron Richardson *actor, singer* — won a Tony Award for *Big River* (1952–1995)

Ginger Rogers *actress, dancer* — Rogers will be forever teamed in movie history with Fred Astaire in a series of the most memorable movie musicals ever produced. Best known for her grace and elegance in those roles, Rogers was also effective in non-dancing roles in movies such as her Oscar-winning *Kitty Foyle*. (1912–1995)

Henry Rogers *legendary Hollywood press agent* (1913–1995)

Tony Romeo *songwriter* — wrote first Partridge Family hit, "I Think I Love You" (1939–1995)

Norman Rosten *poet, playwright, novelist* (1914–1995)

Paul Rothchild *record producer* — Rothchild's most notable recordings were the first six Doors albums and with the West Coast rock group Love. He produced more than 150 records and the soundtracks for *The Rose* and Oliver Stone's *The Doors* (193?–1995)

Miklos Rosza *film composer* — The Academy Award-winning composer of some of Hollywood's most meticulously researched scores. His work included the music for *Quo Vadis, The Four Feathers, Double Indemnity, The Naked City* and *Eye of the Needle*. He also composed for the concert hall. (1907–1995)

Max Rudolf *former conductor of The Metropolitan Opera* — Rudolf's book *The Grammar of Conducting* was regarded as the standard text for conductors. He also led the Cincinnati Orchestra for 12 years. (1902–1995)

Matthew Rushton *film, TV producer* (1952–1995)

May Sarton *poet and novelist* — Sarton was best known for her poetry about solitude, love and feminist consciousness (1912–1995)

Norman Schwartz *jazz record producer* (1928–1995)

Allan Scott *screenwriter* — collaborated on many Astaire/Rogers musicals (1907–1995)

Sylvia Seaman *writer, women's suffragist* (1901–1995)

Selena (Quintanilla Perez) *singer* — Selena was considered the queen of *tejano*. She won a 1993 Grammy in the Mexican-American album category. (1972–1995)

Irving Shulman *novelist and screenwriter* — wrote *The Amboy Dukes* and the treatment for *Rebel Without a Cause* (1914–1995)

Jim Simon *former Mutual Broadcasting System president* — regarded by some as "father of talk radio" (1934–1995)

Sidney Slon *radio scriptwriter* — wrote for *The Shadow* and *Dick Tracy* radio serials (1911–1995)

John Smith *movie, TV actor* (1922–1995)

Warren Sonbert *filmmaker* (1948–1995)

Sir Stephen Spender *British poet* — ushered in an era of socially conscious poetry (1909–1995)

Viola Spolin *actor, teacher* — Spolin was known as the mother of improvisational theater. Her book *Improvisations for the Theater* became the standard text on the subject. (190?–1995)

Kathleen Squire *theater, film, TV actress* (1903–1995)

Jess Stacy *musician* — key figure in the swing era as pianist for Benny Goodman's orchestra (1905–1995)

Lionel Stander *film actor* — Blacklisted in the 1950s in the middle of a long career in movies, Stander was first widely known as a member of Preston Sturges's stock company. He was later known as Max, the butler, on TV's *Hart to Hart*. His Hollywood career

began with the original *A Star is Born* (1937), and his other films include *Mr. Deeds Goes to Town*, *Guadalcanal Diary*, *Cul de Sac* and *New York, New York.* (1908–1994)

Vivian Stanshall *musician* — member of Bonzo Dog Band (19?–1995)

Alfred Steinberg *historical biographer* (1918–1995)

Bob Stinson *musician* — guitarist with The Replacements (1960–1995)

Woody Strode *character actor* — Strode appeared in *Spartacus*, *The Man Who Shot Liberty Valance*, *The Ten Commandments* and *The Quick and the Dead.* (1915–1995)

Otis Stuart *dance critic, biographer* (1952–1995)

Jule Styne *composer* — A giant of the musical, the Tony- and Oscar-winning Styne penned music and songs for shows including *High Button Shoes*, *Gentlemen Prefer Blondes*, *Bells Are Ringing*, *Gypsy*, *Funny Girl* and *The Red Shoes.* (1906–1994)

Joseph Sugar *film executive* — developed reserved-seat, road show concept (1922–1995)

Sunnyland Slim *blues pianist* — member of Muddy Waters bands (1908–1995)

John Cameron Swayze *newscaster* — One of the first TV newscasters, Swayze became as well known as the TV spokesperson for Timex watches. (1906–1995)

Ferrucio Tagliavini *singer* — lyric tenor of the 1940s and 1950s most noted for Puccini roles (1914–1995)

S. Mark Taper *philanthropist* — the Mark Taper Forum in downtown Los Angeles bears his name (1903–1995)

Art Taylor *drummer* — Renowned jazz drummer of the 1950s, playing with the greats of be-bop, Taylor was a major influence in the course of jazz drumming. His most important work can be heard on recordings such as John Coltrane's *Giant Steps*, Miles Davis's *Miles Ahead* and the Town Hall sessions of Thelonious Monk. (1930–1995)

Rachel Thomas *Welsh film actress* (1905–1995)

Jeff Tornberg *film producer* (1952–1995)

Genevieve Tobin *actress* — Tobin appeared in *One Hour With You*, *Dark Hazard* and *The Petrified Forest* among others. She was married to director William Keighley. (1902–1995)

Lana Turner *screen goddess —* Hollywood's Sweater Girl, Turner began her career, after being discovered in a Hollywood drugstore, in gun moll roles, later moving to melodramas such as *Imitation of Life*. Her personal life matched her on-screen melodramas, culminating in the notorious murder of her lover, gangster Johnny Stompanato, by her daughter. Her best roles, including *The Postman Always Rings Twice*, employed her sultry sexuality. (1920–1995)

Kathleen Tynan *novelist, journalist and editor —* perhaps best known for biography of husband, critic Kenneth Tynan (1938–1995)

Tommy Valando *Backer of many notable Broadway musicals* (1923–1995)

Tom Villard *actor* (1954–1994)

Gian Maria Volonte *film actor —* best remembered for his appearances in spaghetti Westerns (1933–1994)

Janet Ward *stage and TV actress* (1925–1995)

Jack Warner, Jr. *filmmaker and son of the legendary Warner Bros. studio boss —* He produced the 1949 movie, *The Hasty Heart* starring Ronald Reagan and *The Man Who Cheated Himself*, and was in charge of television production for the studio. In 1982, he wrote *Bijou Dream*, a novel about a movie family similar to his own. (1916–1995)

David Warrilow *British movie and stage actor —* Warrilow was best known for his roles in Samuel Beckett plays. Beckett wrote *A Piece of Monologue* for Warrilow, which went on to be one of the actor's signature performances. Though British, Warrilow was most often found on U.S. and French stages. He also appeared in the films *Barton Fink* and *Radio Days*. (1934–1995)

Willard Waterman *actor —* Waterman appeared on stage, radio, screen and TV as the star of *The Great Gildersleeve*. (1915–1995)

Frank Waters *writer* (1903–1995)

David Wayne *actor —* Wayne appeared on stage, screen and television, earning the first Tony Award for supporting actor (1947) for *Finian's Rainbow*. He may be best remembered for film roles in movies such as *How to Marry a Millionaire*, *Adam's Rib* and *The Three Faces of Eve*. (1914–1995)

Ronny White *musician —* White, Smokey Robinson, Bobby Rogers, Peter Moore and Claudette Rogers formed the Motown group the Miracles. He co-wrote the songs "My Girl" and "My Guy." (193?–1995)

Isabel Wilder *novelist —* sister of Thornton Wilder (1900–1995)

Frances Williams *actress —* founder of first black theater company in Los Angeles (1906–1995)

Calder Willingham *writer, screenwriter —* Willigham wrote some of Hollywood's best-known films, including the Oscar-nominated *The Graduate*. Other pictures he scripted include *Paths of Glory*, *The Vikings*, *One-Eyed Jacks*, *Little Big Man* and *Thieves Like Us*. He adapted *Rambling Rose* from his 1972 novel and collaborated with director David Lean on the script for *Bridge on the River Kwai*. (1923–1995)

Wolfman Jack *disk jockey —* Wolfman Jack was one of the pioneers of border radio, and was linked ever after with the golden era of rock. He reached a wider audience with a movie role in *American Graffiti*. (1938–1995)

Evelyn Wood *pioneer of speed reading techniques —* Wood developed a speed reading course that taught students to read between 1,500 and 6,000 words a minute. Presidents Kennedy and Nixon sent members of their staff to her courses. (1909–1995)

George Woodcock *Canadian writer —* founder of first journal of Canadian literature (1913–1995)

Pedro Zamora *actor, activist —* Zamora came to the nation's attention on the MTV series, *The Real World*, as the first openly gay cast member, and then through his public struggle with AIDS and his activism. He died one day after the last episode of his series aired. (1972–1994) ∎

Datebook

Here is a calendar of upcoming events and openings we're looking forward to.

OCTOBER 1995

Country Music Awards
October 4

Fool Moon opening on Broadway on October 29 at the Ambassador Theatre

Hello, Dolly opening on Broadway on October 19 at the Neil Simon Theatre

Patti Lupone on Broadway opening on October 12 at the Walter Kerr Theatre

The Queen of Spades opening at The Metropolitan Opera (new production)

Victor/Victoria opening on Broadway on October 25 at the Marquis Theatre

Alice, a new collaboration between theater artist Robert Wilson and musician Tom Waits premieres October 6 at the Next Wave Festival in New York

Paul Taylor debuts his *Offenbach Overtures* October 10 at New York's City Center

The San Francisco Ballet visits New York's City Center October 31–November 5

Three Plays in Rep, an evening directed by Andre Serban, opening October 11 at La Mama

Geri Allen visits the Village Vanguard in New York October 10–15

NOVEMBER 1995

Busker Alley opening on Broadway on November 2 at the St. James Theatre

Arvo Part's *Te Deum* will be performed at New York's Alice Tully Hall on November 2

Martha Argerich and Gidon Kremer debut a duo recital November 1 at New York's Carnegie Hall

Master Class by Terence McNally and starring Zoe Caldwell opening on Broadway on November 5 at the John Golden Theatre

Streets of Laredo, **Larry McMurtry's follw-up to** *Lonesome Dove,* premieres on CBS

Eiko and Koma 20th anniversary celebration runs November 16–18 at the Japan Society in New York

DECEMBER 1995

Down Beat **Readers Poll** will appear in the December issue

Alvin Ailey American Dance Theater premieres a new production, *Rainbow Round My Shoulder*, December 22 at New York's City Center

Mark Morris Dance Group presents eight New York premieres December 9–17 at the Next Wave Festival

We'll Take Manhattan, a celebration of Duke Ellington compositions, will be performed on December 16 at New York's Alice Tully Hall

Strindberg's *The Father* **starring Frank Langella** premieres December 13 at New York's Roundabout Theatre

The Civil Wars, Rome Section, by Robert Wilson and Philip Glass will be heard in a concert setting on December 3 with Dennis Russell Davies conducting at New York's Carnegie Hall

Robert Redford

JANUARY 1996

Big, the musical adaptation of the motion picture opening on Broadway at the Shubert Theatre

Blue Window, directed by Joe Mantello, the director of *Love! Valour! Compassion!,* opening January 16 at the Manhattan Theatre Club

The Makropoulas Case opening at The Metropolitan Opera (new production)

Oscar ballots mailed January 12

Sundance Film Festival January 18–20

Brian Friel's *Molly Sweeny* opens with Catherine Byrne in the title role January 3 at the Roundabout Theatre

Television and radio journalist John Hockenberry debuts a one-man show, *Spoke Man,* January 24 at the American Place Theatre

Pride and Prejudice, a new production by the BBC, will debut January 14 on the A&E network

FEBRUARY 1996

Andrea Chenier opening at The Metropolitan Opera (new production)

Cosi fan Tutte opening at The Metropolitan Opera (new production)

La Forza del Destino opening at the Metropolitan Opera (new production)

Oscar nomination polls close at 5 P.M. February 1

Oscar nominees announced February 13

Caldecott and Newbery medals awarded early February

Steve Reich and Musicians debut three new works February 10 at New York's Alice Tully Hall

Emauel Ax, Yo Yo Ma and Friends perform February 14 at New York's Alice Tully Hall

1996 Movie Releases

The following movies should be released in early 1996.

Before and After, director: Barbet Schroeder; cast: Meryl Streep and Liam Neeson

Birds of a Feather, director: Mike Nichols; cast: Robin Williams, Nathan Lane, Gene Hackman and Dianne Wiest (United Artists)

Boys aka The Girl in His Room, director: Stacy Cochran; cast: Winona Ryder and Lukas Haas (Touchstone)

City Hall, director: Harold Becker; cast: Al Pacino and John Cusack

Courage Under Fire, director: Ed Zwick; cast: Denzel Washington (Fox 2000)

The Craft, director: Andrew Fleming; cast: Robin Tunney, Fairuza Balk, Neve Campbell and Rachel True (Columbia)

The Crucible, director: Nicholas Hytner; cast: Daniel Day-Lewis, Winona Ryder and Paul Scofield (Twentieth Century-Fox)

Dead Drop, director: Andrew Davis; cast: Keanu Reeves and Morgan Freeman (Twentieth Century-Fox)

Diabolique, cast: Sharon Stone, Chazz Palminteri and Isabelle Adjani

Down Periscope, director: David Ward; cast: Kelsey Grammer, Lauren Holley, William H. Macy, Harry Dean Stanton, Bruce Dern and Rip Torn (Twentieth Century-Fox)

Executive Decision, director: Stuart Baird; cast: Kurt Russell, Halle Berry, Steven Seagal and John Leguizamo (Warner Bros.)

An Eye for an Eye, director: John Schlesinger; cast: Sally Field, Ed Harris, Kiefer Sutherland, Beverly D'Angelo and Joe Mantegna (Paramount)

A Family Thing, director: Richard Pearce; cast: Robert Duvall, James Earl Jones, Michael Beach and Regina Taylor (United Artists)

CONTINUED ON NEXT PAGE ▶

CONTINUED FROM PREVIOUS PAGE

Father Goose (Working title), **director:** Carroll Ballard; **cast:** Anna Paquin and Jeff Daniels (Columbia)

Fierce Creatures, **director:** Robert Young; **cast:** John Cleese, Jamie Lee Curtis, Kevin Kline, Michael Palin and Robert Lindsay (Universal)

Flipper, **director:** Alan Shapiro; **cast:** Paul Hogan, Elijah Wood and Chelsea Field (Universal)

Frighteners, **director:** Peter Jackson; **cast:** Michael J. Fox, Trini Alvarado and Jeffrey Combs (Universal)

Girl 6, **director:** Spike Lee; cast: Theresa Randle and Spike Lee

The Great White Hype, **director:** Reginald Hudlin; **cast:** Samuel L. Jackson, Jeff Goldblum, Peter Berg, Damon Wayans, Jon Lovitz, John Rhys-Davies, Corbin Bernsen and Cheech Martin (Twentieth Century-Fox)

Homeward Bound II, **director:** David R. Ellis; **cast:** Robert Hays, Kim Griest and Michael J. Fox (Walt Disney)

Independence Day (Working title), **director:** Roland Emmerich; **cast:** Bill Pullman, Will Smith, Jeff Goldblum, Mary McDonnell, Judd Hirsch and Randy Quaid (Twentieth Century-Fox)

Last Dance, **director:** Constanin Costa-Gavras; **cast:** Rob Morrow and Sharon Stone (Touchstone)

Matilda, **director:** Danny DeVito; **cast:** Mara Wilson, Danny DeVito and Rhea Perlman (TriStar)

Michael Collins, **director:** Neil Jordan; **cast:** Liam Neeson, Julia Roberts, Stephen Rea and Aidan Quinn

Mighty Ducks 3, **director:** Rob Lieberman; **cast:** Emilio Estevez, Joshua Jackson and Matt Doherty (Walt Disney)

Mission: Impossible, **director:** Brian De Palma; **cast:** Tom Cruise, Emmanuelle Beart, Jon Voight, Ving Rhames and Henry Czerny (Paramount)

Anthony Hopkins and Emma Thompson

MARCH 1996

Academy Awards
March 25

Grammy Awards
early March

Independent Spirit Awards
March 23

National Book Awards
late March

South by Southwest Music Festival
March 13–17

Maurizio Pollini concludes his seasonlong review of the Beethoven Piano Sonatas March 23 at New York's Carnegie Hall

Horton Foote's hit *The Young Man From Atlanta* bows on Broadway with Ralph Waite in the cast March 29 at a theater to be announced

New Orleans Jazz and Heritage Festival
last weekend in April through first weekend in
May

National Magazine Awards
mid-April

Pulitzer Prizes
April

Anne Sofie Von Otter, mezzo-soprano, debuts
in New York on April 21

The New York City Opera debuts *The Dreyfus
Affair* on April 2

The Shawl by Cynthia Ozick, directed by
Sidney Lumet and starring Dianne Wiest, runs
April 13–May 5 at the Jewish Repertory Theater
in New York

*A Funny Thing Happened On the Way to The
Forum* makes a Broadway comeback at a theater to be announced

The Bebe Miller Dance Company visits The
Joyce Theater April 16–21

**Rodgers and Hammerstein's Cinderella, a CBS
miniseries,** is slated for the spring

**Gulliver's Travels an ambitious miniseries
from NBC** is scheduled for the spring

Al Pacino

Moll Flanders, **director:** Pen Densham; **cast:**
Robin Wright, Morgan Freeman, John Lynch,
Stockard Channing, Aisling Corcoran and
Geraldine James (MGM)

Mrs. Winterbourne, **director:** Richard
Benjamin; **cast:** Shirley MacLaine, Ricki Lake
and Brendan Fraser (TriStar)
Mulholland Falls, **director:** Lee Tamahori;
cast: Nick Nolte, Melanie Griffith, Chazz
Palminteri, Michael Madsen, Chris Penn and
Treat Williams (MGM)

The Nutty Professor, **director:** Tom Shadyac;
cast: Eddie Murphy, Jada Pinkett and John Ales
(Universal)

Primal Fear, **director:** Greg Hoblit; **cast:**
Richard Gere, Laura Linney, John Mahoney,
Alfre Woodard and Frances McDormand
(Paramount)

Race the Sun, **director:** Charlie Kanganis; **cast:**
Jim Belushi, Halle Berry, Casey Affleck and
Eliza Dushku (TriStar)

Sgt. Bilko, **director:** Johnathan Lynn; **cast:**
Steve Martin, Phil Hartman and Dan Aykroyd
(Universal)

The Shadow Conspiracy, **director:** George
Cosmatos; **cast:** Charlie Sheen, Linda Hamilton,
Donald Sutherland and Stephen Lang
(Columbia)

Stretch Armstrong, **director:** Jay Dubin (Walt
Disney/Caravan Pictures)

Tales From the Crypt, **director:** Gilbert Adler;
cast: Dennis Miller, Erika Eleniak and Angie
Everhart (Universal)

Twister, **director:** Jan De Bont; **cast:** Helen
Hunt, Bill Paxton, Cary Elwes and Jami Gertz
(Warner Bros.)

Two Days in the Valley, **director:** John
Herzfeld; **cast:** Danny Aiello, Jeff Daniels, Teri
Hatcher, Glenne Headley and Peter Horton
(MGM)

Unforgettable (Working title), **director:** John
Dahl; **cast:** Ray Liotta, Linda Fiorentino, Peter
Coyote and Christopher McDonald (MGM)

Up Close and Personal, **director:** Jon Avnet;
cast: Robert Redford and Michelle Pfeiffer
(Touchstone) ■

New Music Releases

We've been told to keep our ears open for new releases from the following artists and labels late in 1995 and in the first half of 1996.

Alice in Chains (Columbia)

Bardo Pond (Matador)

Beach Boys, *Smile* (Capitol boxed set)

Tony Bennett, *Here's to the Ladies* (Columbia)

Mariah Carey, *Daydream* (Columbia)

Tracy Chapman, *New Beginning* (Elektra)

John Coltrane: The Atlantic Records Box Set (Rhino)

Combustible Edison (Sub Pop)

Damon and Naomi, *The Wondrous World of Damon and Naomi* (Sub Pop)

Thornetta Davis (Sub Pop)

Guided by Voices (Matador)

Billy Joel (Columbia)

Marsalis on Music, Wynton Marsalis's four-part introduction to the principles of music, which aired on PBS in October, will be available from Sony Video for $19.95 per program and in a four-tape box for $80.

The Monkees, *Missing Links 3* (Rhino)

Carl Reiner and Mel Brooks, *2000 Years With Carl Reiner and Mel Brooks* (Rhino)

Silkworm, *Firewater* (Matador; double album)

Smashing Pumpkins, *Mellon Collie and the Infinite Sadness* (Virgin)

Soundtrack, *Ben-Hur* (Rhino)

Soundtrack, *Korngold at Warner Bros.* (Rhino)

Sonic Youth, *Washing Machine* (Geffen)

Spinanes (Sub Pop)

Teen Angels (Sub Pop)

Velocity Girl (Sub Pop)

David Pirner and Winona Ryder

May 1996

Cannes Film Festival
May 9–29

Obie Awards
late May

Pavarotti Plus! opens May 1 at Avery Fisher Hall in New York

Robert Shaw conducts Rachmaninoff's *Vespers* May 2 at New York's Carnegie Hall

The St. Louis Symphony visits Powell Symphony Hall May 19 with Leonard Slatkin conducting for the final time with this orchestra

JUNE 1996

American Dance Festival
first week of June through the first week in July

Brevard Music Festival
third weekend in June

Chicago Blues Festival
early June

Fan Fair Music Festival
June 10–16

Glimmerglass Opera Festival
early July

Jacob's Pillow Dance Festival
last week of June

JVC Jazz Festival
last weekend in June through the first weekend in July

Tanglewood Festival
last weekend in June

Tony Awards
early June

The Bang on a Can Marathon of New Music on June 2 at New York's Alice Tully Hall

The Bill T. Jones/Arnie Zane Dance Company visits The Joyce Theater June 11–23

JULY 1996

Central City Opera Summer Series
second week in July

Lake George Opera Festival
end of July

Lollapalooza
kicks off July 4th weekend

Serious Fun! Dance Festival
early July; usually opens July 4th weekend

AUGUST 1996

Ben & Jerry's Newport Folk Festival
first weekend in August

Down Beat Critics Poll
will appear in the August issue

Everyone has an opinion when it comes to movies, music, TV and the other subjects included in this book. We want to hear yours. Did we miss anything? Anything you would like to see more of? Less of? Please write or E-mail us with your favorite movie, recording, on-line site, computer game, television series or book that was released between September 1995 and September 1996, and we will report back to you next year. You can visit us online at http://www.wmedia.com/IPEAhome.html or E-mail us at IPEA@aol.com. You can also write us at:

The Entertainment Almanac
Working Media
18 Shawmut Street
Boston, MA 02116